Italy

Trento &
the Dolomites
(p303)

Friuli
Venezia Giulia
(p407)

Turin,
Piedmont & the
Italian Riviera
(p161)

Milan &
the Lakes
(p238)

Venice &
the Veneto
(p335)

Emilia-Romagna
& San Marino
(p434)

Florence &
Tuscany
(p479)

Umbria &
Le Marche
(p576)

Rome &
Lazio
(p62)

Abruzzo &
Molise
(p633)

Sardinia
(p840)

Naples &
Campania
(p650)

Puglia, Basilicata
& Calabria
(p714)

Sicily
(p774)

THIS EDITION WRITTEN AND RESEARCHED BY

Cristian Bonetto,

Abigail Blasi, Kerry Christiani, Gregor Clark,

Belinda Dixon, Duncan Garwood, Paula Hardy,

Brendan Sainsbury, Donna Wheeler, Nicola Williams

Contents

POMPEII, P686

CINQUE TERRE, P181

Contents

ON THE ROAD

ANDREAS STRAUSS/GETTY IMAGES ©

ST PETER'S BASILICA, P94

Contents

UNDERSTAND

SURVIVAL GUIDE

SPECIAL FEATURES

Welcome to Italy

Italy is an extraordinary feast of heart-thumping, soul-stirring art, food and landscapes rivalled by few and coveted by millions.

Cultural Riches

Epicentre of the Roman Empire and birthplace of the Renaissance, Italy groans under the weight of its cultural cachet: it's here that you'll stand in the presence of Michelangelo's *David* and Sistine Chapel frescoes, Botticelli's *Birth of Venus* and *Primavera* and da Vinci's *The Last Supper.* In fact, Italy has more Unesco World Heritage Sites than any other country on Earth. Should you walk in the footsteps of saints and emperors in Rome, revel in Ravenna's glittering Byzantine treasures or get breathless over Giotto's revolutionary frescoes in Padua? It's a cultural conundrum as thrilling as it is overwhelming.

Bella Vita

In few places do art and life intermingle so effortlessly. This may be the land of Dante, Titian and Verdi, but it's also the home of Prada, Gualtiero Marchesi and Renzo Piano. Beauty, style and flair furnish every aspect of daily life, from those immaculately knotted ties and perfect espressos, to the flirtatious smiles of striking strangers. The root of Italian psychology is a dedication to living life well and, effortless as it may seem, driving that dedication is a reverence for the finer things. So slow down, take note and indulge in a little *bella vita*.

Buon Appetito

It might look like a boot, but food-obsessed Italy feels more like a decadently stuffed Christmas stocking. From delicate *tagliatelle al ragù* to velvety *cannoli,* every bite feels like a revelation. The secret: superlative ingredients and strictly seasonal produce. And while Italy's culinary soul might be earthy and rustic, it's equally ingenious and sophisticated. Expect some of the world's top fine-dining destinations, from San Pellegrino 'World's Best 50' hotspots to Michelin-starred musts. So whether you're on a degustation odyssey in Modena, truffle hunting in Piedmont or swilling powerhouse reds in the Valpolicella wine region, prepare to swoon.

Luscious Landscapes

Italy's fortes extend beyond its galleries, plates and wardrobes. The country is one of Mother Nature's masterpieces, its geography offering extraordinary natural diversity. From the north's icy Alps and glacial lakes to the south's volcanic craters and turquoise grottoes, this is a place for doing as well as seeing. One day you're tearing down Courmayeur's powdery slopes, the next you could be riding cowboy-style across the marshes of the Maremma, or diving in coral-studded Campanian waters.

Why I Love Italy

By Cristian Bonetto, Author

Italy's 20 regions feel more like 20 independent states, each with its own dialects, traditions, architecture and glorious food. From nibbling on *knödel* in an Alto Adige chalet to exploring souk-like market streets in Sicily, the choices are as diverse as they are seductive. Then there's the country's incomparable artistic treasures, which amount to more than the rest of the world's put together. It's hard not to feel a little envious sometimes, but it's even harder not to fall madly in love.

For more about our authors, see page 976

Above: Geisler Gruppe, Alto Adige (Südtirol; p317)

Italy

ELEVATION

| 2500m |
| 2000m |
| 1500m |
| 1000m |
| 500m |
| 300m |
| 100m |
| 0 |

Gran Paradiso
Hike across high-altitude passes (p235)

Lago di Como
Cruise Lombardy's VIP Alpine lake (p268)

Dolomites
Scale Italy's most awesome granite peaks (p303)

Venice
Count millions of mosaic tesserae at San Marco (p338)

Emilia-Romagna
Tuck into Italy's culinary epicentre (p435)

Piedmont
Indulge in a gourmand's Valhalla (p196)

Italian Riviera
Village-hop along the Cinque Terre (p181)

SWITZERLAND

AUSTRIA

HUNGARY

SLOVENIA

CROATIA

SERBIA

BOSNIA & HERCEGOVINA

MONTENEGRO

BERN

VADUZ

LJUBLJANA

ZAGREB

SARAJEVO

PODGORICA

Zürich

Geneva

Innsbruck

Graz

Pécs

Osijek

Banja Luka

Dubrovnik

Courmayeur

Valtournenche

Varallo

Aosta

Parco Nazionale del Gran Paradiso

Milky Way

Briançon

Modane

Turin

PIEDMONT

Tanaro

Nice

LIGURIA

Riviera di Ponente

Gulf of Genoa

Genoa

Riviera di Levante

Milan

Bergamo

Brescia

Cremona

Mantua

Lago di Como

Parco Nazionale dello Stelvio

Valtellina

Alpe di Siusi

Bolzano

Merano

Trento

Rovereto

Lago di Garda

Verona

Vicenza

Padua

VENETO

Venice

Po Delta

Dolomites

CARNIA

Tolmezzo

Tarvisio

Udine

Gorizia

Grado

Lignano

Palmanova

Pordenone

Trieste

Rijeka

Adriatic Sea

EMILIA-ROMAGNA

Parco Nazionale delle Cinque Terre

Garfagnana

Lucca

Pisa

Livorno

Volterra

Massa Marittima

Elba

Pianosa

Capraia

Gorgona

Bologna

Ravenna

SAN MARINO

Florence

CHIANTI

Siena

TUSCANY

Arezzo

Perugia

Gubbio

Assisi

UMBRIA

Todi

Orvieto

Spoleto

Sarnano

Norcia

Urbino

Pesaro

Ancona

Parco Del Conero

Macerata

Ascoli Piceno

Pescara

Chieti

LAZIO

Danube

Po

Ticino

Arno

Isole

43°N

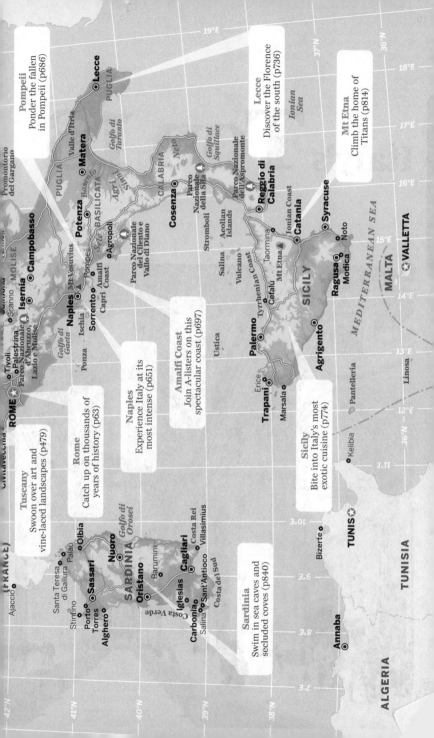

Pompeii
Ponder the fallen
in Pompeii (p686)

Lecce
Discover the Florence
of the south (p736)

Mt Etna
Climb the home of
Titans (p814)

Tuscany
Swoon over art and
vine-laced landscapes (p479)

Rome
Catch up on thousands of
years of history (p63)

Naples
Experience Italy at its
most intense (p651)

Amalfi Coast
Join A-listers on this
spectacular coast (p697)

Sicily
Bite into Italy's most
exotic cuisine (p774)

Sardinia
Swim in sea caves and
secluded coves (p840)

Italy's Top 18

Eternal Rome

1 Once *caput mundi* (capital of the world), Rome was legendarily spawned by a wolf-suckled boy, grew to be Western Europe's first superpower, became the spiritual centrepiece of the Christian world and is now the repository of over two millennia of European art and architecture. From the Pantheon and the Colosseum to Michelangelo's Sistine Chapel and countless works by Caravaggio, there's simply too much to see in one visit. So, do as countless others have done before you: toss a coin into the Trevi Fountain and promise to return. St Peter's Basilica (p94)

Virtuoso Venice

2 Step through the portals of Basilica di San Marco (p339) and try to imagine what it might have been like for a humble medieval labourer glimpsing those glittering gold mosaic domes for the first time. It's not such a stretch – seeing the millions of tiny gilt tesserae (hand-cut glazed tiles) fuse into a singular heavenly vision can make every leap of human imagination since the 12th century seem comparatively minor. Indeed, one visit is never enough; the basilica's sheer scale, exquisite detailing and ever-shifting light promising endless revelations. Basilica di San Marco

ANDREAS STRAUSS/LOOK-FOTO/GETTY IMAGES ©

H & D ZIELSKE/LOOK-FOTO/GETTY IMAGES ©

Tackling the Dolomites

3 Scour the globe and you'll find plenty of taller, bigger and more geologically volatile mountains, but few can match the romance of the pink-hued, granite Dolomites (p303). Maybe it's their harsh, jagged summits, the vibrant skirts of spring wildflowers or the rich cache of Ladin legends. Then again, it could just be the magnetic draw of money, style and glamour at Italy's most fabled ski resort, Cortina d'Ampezzo. Whatever the reason, this tiny pocket of northern Italy takes seductiveness to dizzying heights.

Amalfi Coast

4 Italy's most celebrated coastline blends superlative beauty and gripping geology: coastal mountains plunge into blue sea in a scene of precipitous crags, sun-bleached villages and lush forests. Between sea and sky, mountain-top hiking trails deliver Tyrrhenian panoramas fit for a god. While some may argue that the peninsula's most beautiful coast is Liguria's Cinque Terre or Calabria's Costa Viola, it was the Amalfi Coast (p697) that American writer John Steinbeck described as a 'dream place that isn't quite real when you are there and...beckoningly real after you have gone'. Positano, Amalfi Coast

Touring Tuscany

5 Italy's most romanticised region, Tuscany (p479) was tailor made for fastidious aesthetes. From Brunelleschi's Duomo to Masaccio's Cappella Brancacci frescoes, Florence (p498), according to Unesco, contains 'the greatest concentration of universally renowned works of art in the world'. Beyond its blockbuster museums, jewel-box churches and flawless Renaissance streetscapes is an undulating world of regional masterpieces, from the Gothic majesty of Siena, the Manhattan-esque skyline of medieval San Gimignano, to the vine-laced hills of Italy's most famous wine region, Chianti. Ponte Vecchio, Florence

Piedmont on a Plate

6 Piedmont (p196) is Italy's gastronomic powerhouse, a knee-weakening Promised Land of culinary highs. At it best in the autumn, this is the place to search through woods for prestigious fungi, to savour decadent cocoa concoctions in gilded cafes, not to mention sip cult-status reds in Slow-Food villages. Stock the larder at Turin's food emporium Eataly, savour rare white truffles in Alba, and compare the nuances of vintage Barolo and Barbaresco wines on the vine-graced slopes of the Langhe Hills. Truffles at the market in Alba (p216)

Mighty Masterpieces

7 A browse through any art history book will highlight seminal movements in Western art, from classical, Renaissance and baroque to futurist. All were forged in Italy by a roll call of artists including Giotto, da Vinci, Michelangelo, Botticelli, Bernini, Caravaggio, the Carracci brothers, Boccioni, Balla and de Chirico. Find the best of them in Rome's Museo e Galleria Borghese and Vatican Museums, Florence's Uffizi, Venice's Gallerie dell'Accademia, Milan's Museo del Novecento, and Naples' Palazzo Reale di Capodimonte. Galleria degli Uffizi (p49.

Ghostly Pompeii

8 Frozen in its death throes, the sprawling, time-warped ruins of Pompeii (p686) hurtle you 2000 years into the past. Wander through chariot-grooved Roman streets, lavishly frescoed villas and bathhouses, food stores and markets, theatres, even an ancient brothel. Then with your eye on ominous Mt Vesuvius, ponder Pliny the Younger's terrifying account of the town's final hours: 'Darkness came on again, again ashes, thick and heavy. We got up repeatedly to shake these off; otherwise we would have been buried and crushed by the weight'. Statue at the Casa dei Vettii (p691), Pompeii

Neapolitan Street Life

9 Nowhere else in Italy are people as conscious of their role in the theatre of everyday life as in Naples (p651). And in no other Italian city does daily life radiate such drama and intensity. Naples' ancient streets are a stage, cast with boisterous matriarchs, bellowing *baristi* (bartenders) and tongue-knotted lovers. To savour the flavour, dive into the city's rough-and-tumble Porta Nolana market, a loud, lavish opera of hawking fruit vendors, wriggling seafood and the irresistible aroma of just-baked *sfogliatelle* (sweetened ricotta pastries).

Murals & Mosaics

10 Often regarded as just plain 'dark', the Italian Middle Ages had an artistic brilliance that's hard to ignore. Perhaps it was the sparkling hand-cut mosaics of Ravenna's Byzantine basilicas (p469) that provided the guiding light, but something inspired Giotto di Bondone to leap out of the shadows with his daring naturalistic frescoes in Padua's Cappella degli Scrovegni and the Basilica di San Francesco in Assisi. These gave the world a new artistic language, and from there it was just a short step to Masaccio's Trinity and the dawning light of the Renaissance. Mosaics at Basilica di Sant'Apollinare Nuovo (p469), Ravenna

Sardinian Shores

11 The English language fails to accurately describe the varied blue, green and, in the deepest shadows, purple hues of the sea in Sardinia (p840). While models, ministers and perma-tanned celebrities wine, dine and sail along the glossy Costa Smeralda, much of Sardinia remains a wild, raw playground. Slather on that sunscreen and explore the island's rugged coastal beauty, from the tumbledown boulders of Santa Teresa di Gallura and the wind-chiselled cliff face of the Golfo di Orosei, to the windswept beauty of the Costa Verde's dune-backed beaches. Cala Goloritzè (p882)

Living Luxe on Lake Como

12 If it's good enough for George Clooney, it's good enough for mere mortals. Nestled in the shadow of the Rhaetian Alps, dazzling Lake Como (p268) is the most spectacular of the Lombard lakes, its Liberty-style villas home to movie moguls, fashion royalty and Arab sheikhs. Surrounded on all sides by lush greenery, the lake's siren calls include the gardens of Villa Melzi d'Eril, Villa Carlotta and Villa Balbianello, which blush pink with camellias, azaleas and rhododendrons in April and May. Bellagio (p273)

Hiking the Italian Riviera

13 For the sinful inhabitants of the Cinque Terre's (p181) five sherbert-coloured villages – Monterosso, Vernazza, Corniglia, Manarola and Riomaggiore – penance involved a lengthy and arduous hike up the vertiginous cliffside to the local village sanctuary to appeal for forgiveness. Scale the same trails today, through terraced vineyards and hillsides smothered in *macchia* (shrubbery). As the heavenly views unfurl, it's hard to think of a more benign punishment. Hiking near Corniglia (p185), Cinque Terre

Scaling Mount Etna

14 Known to the Greeks as the 'column that holds up the sky', Mt Etna (p814) is not only Europe's largest volcano, it's one of the world's most active. The ancients believed the giant Tifone (Typhoon) lived in its crater and lit the sky with spectacular pyrotechnics. At 3329m, it literally towers above Sicily's Ionian Coast. Whether you tackle it on foot or on a guided 4WD tour, scaling this time bomb rewards with towering views and the secret thrill of having come cheek-to-cheek with a towering threat.

Savouring Sicily

15 Sour, spicy and sweet, the flavours of Sicily (p774) reflect millennia of cross-cultural influences. Tuck into golden *panelle* (chickpea fritters) in Palermo, fragrant couscous in Trapani and chilli-spiked chocolate in Modica. From Palermo's Mercato di Ballarò to Catania's Pescheria, market stalls burst with local delicacies: Bronte pistachios, briny olives, glistening swordfish and nutty Canestrato cheese. Just leave room for a slice of sweet Sicilian *cassata* (sponge cake, cream, marzipan, chocolate and candied fruit). Traditional *cassata*

Devouring Emilia Romagna

16 They don't call Bologna 'la Grassa' (the fat one) for nothing. Many of Italy's belt-busting classics originated here, from *mortadella* and tortellini to its trademark *tagliatelle al ragù* (pasta with meat sauce). Shop the deli-packed Quadrilatero, and side-trip to the city of Modena for world-famous aged balsamic vinegar. Just leave room for a trip to Parma, hometown of *parmigiano reggiano* cheese and the incomparable *prosciutto di Parma*. Then toast with a glass of the region's (p435) renowned Lambrusco or sauvignon blanc.

display of *prosciutto* and other cured Italian meats

Baroque Lecce

17 There's baroque, and then there's *barocco leccese* (Lecce baroque), the hyper-extravagant spin-off defining many a Puglian town. It's all down to the local stone, so impossibly soft it led art historian Cesare Brandi to claim it could be carved with a pen-knife. Craftspeople vied for heights of creativity, crowding facades with swirling vegetal designs, gargoyles and strange zoomorphic figures. Queen of the architectural crop is Lecce's Basilica di Santa Croce (p736), so insanely detailed the Marchese Grimaldi said it made him think a lunatic was having a nightmare.
Basilica di Santa Croce

Escaping to Paradiso

18 If you're pining for a retreat, wear down your hiking boots on the 724km of marked trails traversing 'Grand Paradise'. Part of the Graian Alps and the very first of Italy's national parks, Gran Paradiso's (p235) pure, pristine spread encompasses 57 glaciers and Alpine pastures awash with wild pansies, gentians and Alpenroses, not to mention a healthy population of Alpine ibex for whose protection the park was originally established. The eponymous Gran Paradiso mountain (4061m) is the park's only peak, accessed from tranquil Cogne.

Need to Know

For more information, see Survival Guide (p937)

Currency
Euro (€)

Language
Italian

Visas
Generally not required for stays of up to 90 days (or at all for EU nationals); some nationalities need a Schengen visa.

Money
ATMs at every airport, most train stations and widely available in towns and cities. Credit cards accepted in most hotels and restaurants.

Mobile Phones
Local SIM cards can be used in European, Australian and some unlocked US phones. Other phones must be set to roaming.

Time
Central European Time (GMT/UTC plus one hour)

Room Tax
Visitors may be charged an extra €1 to €7 per night 'room occupancy tax'.

When to Go

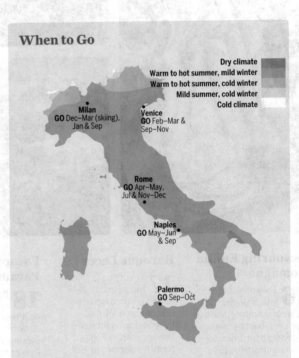

Dry climate
Warm to hot summer, mild winter
Warm to hot summer, cold winter
Mild summer, cold winter
Cold climate

Milan
GO Dec–Mar (skiing), Jan & Sep

Venice
GO Feb–Mar & Sep–Nov

Rome
GO Apr–May, Jul & Nov–Dec

Naples
GO May–Jun & Sep

Palermo
GO Sep–Oct

High Season (Jul–Aug)

➡ Queues at big sights and on the road, especially in August.

➡ Prices also rocket for Christmas, New Year and Easter.

➡ Late December to March is high season in the Alps and Dolomites.

Shoulder (Apr–Jun & Sep–Oct)

➡ Good deals on accommodation, especially in the south.

➡ Spring is best for festivals, flowers and local produce.

➡ Autumn provides warm weather and the grape harvest.

Low Season (Nov–Mar)

➡ Prices up to 30% less than in high season.

➡ Many sights and hotels closed in coastal and mountainous areas.

➡ A good period for cultural events in large cities.

Websites

Lonely Planet (www.lonely planet.com/italy) Destination information, hotel bookings, traveller forum and more.

Trenitalia (www.trenitalia.com) Italian railways website.

Agriturismi (www.agri turismi.it) Guide to farm accommodation.

Enit Italia (www.italia.it) Official Italian-government tourism website.

The Local (www.thelocal.it) English-language news from Italy, including travel-related stories.

Important Numbers

From outside Italy, dial your international access code, Italy's country code (39) then the number (including the '0').

Italy country code	☑39
International access code	☑00
Ambulance	☑118
Police	☑113
Fire	☑115

Exchange Rates

Australia	A$1	€0.62
Canada	C$1	€0.67
Japan	¥100	€0.73
NZ	NZ$1	€0.56
Switzerland	Sfr1	€0.91
UK	UK£1	€1.36
US	US$1	€0.88

For current exchange rates see www.xe.com.

Daily Costs

Budget: Less than €100

➡ Dorm bed: €15–30

➡ Double room in a budget hotel: €50–110

➡ Pizza or pasta: €6–12

Midrange: €100–250

➡ Double room in a hotel: €110–200

➡ Local restaurant dinner: €25–50

➡ Admission to museum: €4–15

Top End: More than €250

➡ Double room in a four- or five-star hotel: €200–450

➡ Top restaurant dinner: €50–150

➡ Opera ticket: €40–200

Opening Hours

Opening hours vary throughout the year. We've provided high-season opening hours; hours will generally decrease in the shoulder and low seasons. 'Summer' times generally refer to the period from April to September or October, while 'winter' times generally run from October or November to March.

Banks 8.30am-1.30pm & 2.45-3.45 or 4.30pm Monday to Friday

Restaurants noon–2.30pm & 7.30–11pm or midnight

Cafes 7.30am–8pm

Bars and clubs 10pm–4am or 5am

Shops 9am–1pm & 4–8pm Monday to Saturday, some also open Sunday

Arriving in Italy

The following local transport options will get you from the airport to the city centre.

Fiumicino airport, Rome (p146)

➡ **Express train** €14; every 30 minutes, 6.23am to 11.23pm

➡ **Bus** €5 to €7; four daily plus night services at 1.15am, 2.15am and 3.30am

➡ **Taxi** €48 set fare; 45 mins

Malpensa airport, Milan (p256)

➡ **Express train** €12; every 30 minutes, 6.53am to 9.53pm

➡ **Bus** €10; every 20 minutes, 5am to 10.30pm, then hourly through the night

➡ **Taxi** €90 set fare; 50 mins

Marco Polo airport, Venice (p381)

➡ **Ferry** €15; every 30 to 60 minutes, 6.15am to 1.15am

➡ **Bus** €6; every 30 minutes, 8am to midnight

➡ **Water taxi** €110; 30 mins

Capodichino airport, Naples (p673)

➡ **Shuttle bus** €3 to €4; every 20 minutes, 6.30am to 11.40pm

➡ **Taxi** €19 set fare; 30 mins

Getting Around

Train Reasonably priced, with extensive coverage and frequent departures. High-speed trains connect major cities.

Car Handy for visiting regions with minimal public transport. Not a good idea for travelling within major urban areas.

Bus Cheaper and slower than trains. Useful for more remote villages not serviced by trains.

For much more on **getting around**, see p953

First Time Italy

For more information, see Survival Guide (p937)

Checklist

➡ Ensure your passport is valid for at least six months past your arrival date

➡ Check airline baggage restrictions

➡ Organise travel insurance

➡ Make bookings (for popular museums, entertainment and accommodation)

➡ Inform your credit- or debit-card company of your travels

➡ Check you can use your mobile (cell) phone

➡ Check requirements for hiring a car

What to Pack

➡ Good walking shoes for those cobblestones

➡ Hat, sunglasses, sunscreen

➡ Electrical adapter and phone charger

➡ A detailed driving map for Italy's rural backroads

➡ A smart outfit and shoes

➡ Patience: for coping with inefficiency

➡ Phrasebook: for ordering and charming

Top Tips for Your Trip

➡ Visit in spring and autumn – good weather and thinner crowds.

➡ If you're driving, head off the main roads: some of Italy's most stunning scenery is best on secondary or tertiary roads.

➡ Speak at least a few Italian words. A little can go a long way.

➡ Queue-jumping is common in Italy: be polite but assertive.

➡ Avoid restaurants with touts and the mediocre *menu turistico* (tourist menu).

What to Wear

Appearances matter in Italy. Milan, Italy's fashion capital, is rigidly chic. Rome and Florence are marginally less formal, but with big fashion houses in town, sloppy attire just won't do. In the cities, suitable wear for men is generally trousers and shirts or polo shirts, and for women skirts, trousers or dresses. Shorts, T-shirts and sandals are fine in summer and at the beach, but long sleeves are required for dining out. For evening wear, smart casual is the norm. A light sweater or waterproof jacket is useful in spring and autumn, and sturdy shoes are good when visiting archaeological sites.

Sleeping

Book ahead for the high season, especially in popular areas, or if visiting cities during major events.

➡ **Hotels** All prices and levels of quality, from cheap-and-charmless to sleek-and-exclusive boutique.

➡ **Farm stays** Perfect for families and for relaxation, *agriturismi* range from rustic farmhouses to luxe country estates.

➡ **B&Bs** Often great value, can range from rooms in family houses to self-catering studio apartments.

➡ **Pensions** Similar to hotels, though *pensioni* are generally of one- to three-star quality and family run.

➡ **Hostels** You'll find both official HI-affiliated and privately run *ostelli*, many also offering private rooms with bathroom.

Money

Credit and debit cards can be used almost everywhere with the exception of some rural towns and villages.

Visa and MasterCard are widely recognised. American Express is only accepted by some major chains and big hotels, and few places take Diners Club.

ATMs are everywhere, but be aware of transaction fees. Some ATMs in Italy reject foreign cards. If this happens, try a few before assuming your card is the problem.

For more information, see p945.

Bargaining

Gentle haggling is common in markets. Haggling in stores is generally unacceptable, though good-humoured bargaining at smaller artisan or craft shops in southern Italy is not unusual if making multiple purchases.

Tipping

Tipping is customary in restaurants, but optional elsewhere.

➡ **Taxis** Optional, but most people round up to the nearest euro.

➡ **Hotels** Tip porters about €4 at high-end hotels.

➡ **Restaurants** Service (*servizio*) is generally included in restaurants – if it's not, a euro or two is fine in pizzerias, 10% in restaurants.

➡ **Bars** Optional, though many Italians leave small change on the bar when ordering coffee. If drinks are brought to your table, a small tip is generally appreciated.

Language

You can get by with English, but you'll improve your experience no end by mastering a few basic words and expressions. This is particularly true in restaurants where menus don't always have English translations and some places rely on waiters to explain what's on. For more on language, see p278.

1 **What's the local speciality?**
Qual'è la specialità di questa regione?
kwa·*le* la spe·cha·lee·*ta* dee *kwes*·ta re·jo·ne

A bit like the rivalry between medieval Italian city-states, these days the country's regions compete in speciality foods and wines.

2 **Which combined tickets do you have?**
Quali biglietti cumulativi avete?
kwa·lee bee·*lye*·tee koo·moo·la·*tee*·vee a·ve·te

Make the most of your euro by getting combined tickets to various sights; they are available in all major Italian cities.

3 **Where can I buy discount designer items?**
C'è un outlet in zona? che oon owt·let in zo·na

Discount fashion outlets are big business in major cities – get bargain-priced seconds, samples and cast-offs for *la bella figura*.

4 **Let's meet at 6pm for pre-dinner drinks.**
Ci vediamo alle sei per un aperitivo.
chee ve·dya·mo a·le say per oon a·pe·ree·tee·vo

At dusk, watch the main piazza get crowded with people sipping colourful cocktails and snacking the evening away: join your new friends for this authentic Italian ritual!

Etiquette

Italy is a surprisingly formal society; the following tips will help avoid awkward moments.

➡ **Greetings** Shake hands and say *buongiorno* (good day) or *buona sera* (good evening) to strangers; kiss both cheeks and say *come stai* (how are you) to friends. Use *lei* (you) in polite company; use *tu* (you) with friends and children. Only use first names if invited.

➡ **Asking for help** Say *mi scusi* (excuse me) to attract attention; and use *permesso* (permission) when you want to pass someone in a crowded space.

➡ **Religion** Dress modestly (cover shoulders, torsos and thighs) and show respect when visiting religious sites.

What's New

Farm-to-Table Deli Dining, Florence

Slow Food comes naturally in agricultural Tuscany, but a new take on the concept has been spawned with the arrival of urban deli dining spots like Mercato Centrale (p508), Eataly (p514) and Michelin-starred La Bottega del Buon Caffè (p507). Counter hop at the market or deli, then grab a table and watch your lunch being freshly prepared. Produce is seasonal, local and invariably organic. Beyond Florence, try Local Food Market in Lucca (p568).

Museo Egizio, Turin

A major renovation of the city's world-renowned Egyptian Museum delivers dramatic new spaces and almost twice as many objects on display. (p201)

Hidden Secrets Walking Tours, Milan

Milan is more than catwalks, couture and cash. Just ask Città Nascosta Milano, an outfit that runs cultural tours that dig deeper into the city, revealing lesser-known angles and cognoscenti secrets. (p249)

Accademia Carrara, Bergamo

After a seven-year facelift, one of northern Italy's most respected art galleries has re-opened, its enviable collection of Italian masters including works by A-listers Botticelli, Raphael and Titian. (p293)

Ghetto restorations, Venice

In honour of its 500th anniversary in 2016, Venice's Ghetto quarter is shining brighter after the restoration of its Museo Ebraico (p355) and synagogues Schola Italiana, Schola Tedesca and Schola Canton (p355).

New Moon Walking Tour, Volterra

Twilight fans are skulking around ancient alleyways in the Tuscan town of Volterra, the setting of Stephanie Meyer's *New Moon* novel and proud possessor of a new vampire-themed walking tour. (p539)

Barberini Gardens, Castel Gandolfo

Once off limits, the immaculate gardens of the pope's summer residence are now yours to explore on a 90-minute guided tour. Explore everything from on-site ancient ruins to labyrinthine hedges. (p157)

New metro stations, Naples

Naples' metro Line 1 is wowing commuters with its latest showpiece stations: Duomo, designed by Massimiliano Fuksas, and Municipio, designed by Àlvaro Siza and Eduardo Souto de Moura. The latter features unearthed ancient ruins and a video painting by Israeli artist Michal Rovner.

Urban renewal, Matera

Matera is sprucing up for its upcoming role as European Capital of Culture in 2019. The top new sight is Casa Noha, a multimedia exhibit documenting the town's social history and extraordinary cave dwellings. (p752)

Sublime Sleeps, Sicily

Sicily is bidding *sogni d'oro* (sweet dreams) with a string of fetching new slumber spots. Among our favourites are waterfront Henry's House (p820) in Ortygia (Syracuse) and Ostello degli Elefanti in Catania (p811).

> For more recommendations and reviews, see lonelyplanet.com/italy

If You Like...

Masterpieces

Sistine Chapel More than just Michelangelo's show-stealing ceiling fresco, this world-famous chapel in Rome also features work by Botticelli, Ghirlandaio and Perugino. (p100)

Galleria degli Uffizi Cimabue, Botticelli, da Vinci, Raphael, Titian: Florence's blockbuster art museum delivers a who's who of artistic deities. (p492)

Museo e Galleria Borghese A perfectly sized serve of Renaissance and baroque masterpieces in an elegant villa in Rome. (p112)

Giotto See just how Giotto revolutionised art with his masterly works in the **Cappella degli Scrovegni** (p384) and **Basilica di San Francesco** (p594).

Ravenna Take in some of Italy's finest early-Christian mosaics at the **Basilica di San Vitale** (p469) and the **Basilica di Sant'Apollinare Nuovo** (p469), two of eight World Heritage sites in town.

Museo del Novecento Modigliani, de Chirico, Kandinsky, Picasso, Fontana: a first-class 20th-century art museum in modernist Milan. (p244)

Pompeii The Dionysiac frieze in the dining room of the Villa dei Misteri is one of the world's largest ancient frescoes. (p691)

Palazzo Grassi The exceptional contemporary collection of French billionaire François Pinault is showcased against Tadao Ando interior sets in Venice. (p346)

Museion Bolzano's contemporary collection highlights the ongoing dialogue between the Südtirol, Austria and Germany. (p318)

Pinturicchio Perugia and Spello showcase the work of Umbria's home-grown Renaissance talent, Pinturicchio. (p581)

Fabulous Food

Bologna Nicknamed *la grassa* (literally 'the fat one'), Bologna straddles Italian food lines between the butter-led north and the tomato-based cuisine of the south. (p444)

Truffles Sniff around Piedmont, Tuscany and Umbria for the world's most coveted fungi.

Osteria Francescana Rave about Massimo Bottura's ingenious flavour combinations at the world's second-hottest restaurant. (p452)

Seafood So fresh you can eat it raw in Venice, Sardinia, Sicily and Puglia. In Campania, order a plate of *spaghetti alle vongole* (spaghetti with clams).

Pizza Italy's most famous export, but who makes the best: Naples or Rome?

Parmigiano Reggiano Parma's cheese is the most famous. Just leave room for Lombardy's Taleggio, Campania's buffalo mozzarella, *burrata* (cheese made from mozzarella and cream) from Puglia. (p461)

Eataly Eat, drink and stock larder and cellar at this giant emporium of top-notch Italian food and drink, with locations including **Rome** (p135), **Turin** (p211), **Genoa** and **Florence** (p514).

Tuscan T-bone Carnivores drool over Florence's iconic *bistecca alla fiorentina* (T-bone steak), hailing from Tuscany's prized Val di Chiana. (p527)

Sicily Buxom eggplants (aubergines), juicy raisins, fragrant couscous, and velvety marzipan – cross-cultural Sicily puts the fusion in Italian cuisine. (p774)

Medieval Hill Towns

Asolo This cosy, elegant hilltop town in Veneto is home to one of the region's best-loved antiques markets. (p156)

Umbria and Le Marche Medieval hill towns galore: start with Spello and Spoleto, and end with Todi and Urbino. (p576)

Montalcino A pocket-sized Tuscan jewel lined with wine bars pouring the area's celebrated Brunello wines. (p541)

Erice Splendid coastal views from the hilltop Norman castle make this western Sicily's most photogenic village. (p838)

San Gimignano A medieval Tuscan Manhattan, studded with skyscraping towers from centuries past. (p533)

Ravello Lording over the Amalfi Coast, Campania's cultured jewel has wowed the best of them, from Wagner to Capote. (p703)

Maratea A 13th-century *borgo* (medieval town) with pint-sized piazzas, winding alleys and startling views across the Gulf of Policastro. (p758)

Puglia From the Valle d'Itria to the sierras of the Salento, Puglia is dotted with biscuit-coloured hilltop villages. (p715)

Wine Tasting

From Etna's elegant whites to Barolo's complex reds, Italian wines are as varied as the country's terrain. Sample them in cellars, over long, lazy lunches or dedicate yourself to a full-blown tour.

Tuscan wine routes Discover why Chianti isn't just a cheap table wine left over from the 1970s. (p526)

Festa dell'Uva e del Vino In early October the wine town of Bardolino is taken over by wine and food stalls. (p290)

Vinitaly Sample exceptional, rarely exported blends at Italy's largest annual wine expo. (p30)

Museo del Vino a Barolo Explore the history of vino through art and film at Barolo's wine museum. (p221)

Top: Antiques market, Arezzo (p572)
Bottom: Villa Rufolo (p704), Ravello

Colli Orientali and Il Carso International oenophiles revere these two wine-growing areas in Friuli Venezia Giulia for their Friuliano and blended 'super-whites'. Stop at an *osmize* (rustic pop-up) for a taste. (p417)

Valpolicella and Soave Wine tastings in these two Veneto regions include blockbuster drops both white and red. (p401)

Alto Adige's Weinstraße A valley trail where native grapes Lagrein, Vernatsch and Gewürztraminer thrive alongside well-adapted imports pinot blanc, sauvignon, merlot and cabernet. (p324)

Cantine Aperte Private wine cellars throughout the country open their doors to the public on the last Sunday in May.

Villas & Palaces

Reggia di Caserta As seen in *Star Wars;* the Italian baroque's spectacular epilogue. (p674)

Rome Don't miss **Galleria Doria Pamphilj** (p86), **Palazzo Farnese** (p84) and **Palazzo Barberini** (p91).

Palazzo Ducale The doge's Venetian palace comes with a golden staircase and interrogation rooms. (p342)

Villa Maser Andrea Palladio and Paolo Veronese conspired to create the Veneto's finest country mansion. (p393)

Reggia di Venaria Reale Piedmont's sprawling Savoy palace inspired French rival Versailles. (p204)

Palazzi dei Rolli A collection of 42 Unesco-protected lodging palaces in Genoa. (p167)

Villa Romana del Casale See where the home decor obsession began with this Roman villa's 3500-sq-metre mosaic floor. (p827)

Il Vittoriale degli Italiani Gabriele d'Annunzio's estate would put a Roman emperor to shame. (p284)

Palazzo Ducale A crenellated, 500-room palace lavished with frescoes in Mantua. (p297)

Markets

Porta Nolana Elbow your way past singsong fishing folk, fragrant bakeries and bootleg CD stalls for a slice of Neapolitan street theatre. (p657)

Rialto Market Shop for lagoon specialities at Venice's centuries-old produce market. (p373)

Mercato di Ballarò Fruit, fish, meat and veg stalls packed under striped awnings down cobbled alleys: Palermo's market is more African bazaar than Italian *mercato*. (p779)

Porta Portese A modern *commedia dell'arte* takes place every Sunday between vendors and bargain hunters at Rome's mile-long flea market. (p144)

Arezzo On the first weekend of every month, Arezzo hosts Italy's oldest and biggest antiques market. (p572)

Luino Straddling the eastern shore of Lake Maggiore, Luino is home to one of northern Italy's largest flea markets, held weekly on Wednesdays. (p264)

Porta Palazzo Turin's outdoor food market is the continent's largest. (p209)

Islands & Beaches

Counting all its offshore islands and squiggly indentations, Italy's coastline stretches 7375km from the sheer cliffs of the Cinque Terre, down through Rimini's brash resorts to the bijou islands in the Bay of Naples and Puglia's sandy shores.

Puglia Italy's best sandy beaches, including the gorgeous Baia dei Turchi near Otranto and the cliff-backed beaches of the Gargano. (p715)

Aeolian Islands Sicily's seven volcanic islands sport hillsides of silver-grey pumice, black lava beaches and lush green vineyards. (p792)

Borromean Islands Graced with villas, gardens and wandering peacocks, Lake Maggiore's trio of islands are impossibly refined. (p263)

Sardinia Take your pick of our favourite beaches, including the Aga Khan's personal fave, Spiaggia del Principe. (p840)

Procida Pretty, pastel-hued Procida has seduced many a cinematographer. (p683)

Rimini Swap high culture for thumping beats and raves on the beach in Rimini. (p473)

Elba This island sits at the heart of the Parco Nazionale Arcipelago Toscano, Europe's largest marine park. (p554)

Gardens

Italy's penchant for the 'outdoor room' has been going strong since Roman emperors landscaped their holiday villas. Renaissance princes refined the practice, but it was 19th-century aristocrats who really went to town.

Reggia di Venaria Reale Take a botanical, cultural or gastronomic tour to explore the 10 hectares of the Venaria's gardens. (p204)

The Italian Lakes Fringed with fabulous gardens such as those

Cala Goloritzè (p882), Sardinia

at **Isola Madre** (p264), **Villa Balbianello** (p275) and **Villa Taranto** (p265).

Villa d'Este Tivoli's superlative High Renaissance garden dotted with fantastical fountains and cypress-lined avenues. (p151)

Ravello View the Amalfi Coast from the Belvedere of Infinity and listen to classical-music concerts in romantic 19th-century gardens. (p704)

La Mortella A tropical paradise inspired by the gardens of Granada's Alhambra. (p681)

Giardini Pubblici Venice's first green space and the home of the celebrated Biennale with its avant-garde pavilions. (p359)

Unspoilt Wilderness

Parco Nazionale del Gran Paradiso Spectacular hiking trails, Alpine ibex and a refreshing lack of ski resorts await at Valle d'Aosta's mountain-studded wonderland. (p235)

Parco del Conero Lace up those hiking boots and hit this protected pocket of Le Marche, laced with fragrant forest, gleaming white cliffs and pristine bays. (p621)

Selvaggio Blu Sardinia's toughest hiking trek doesn't shortchange on rugged beauty – from cliffs and caves to spectacular coastal scenery. (p872)

Parco Nazionale dei Monti Sibillini Head for the border between Umbria and Le Marche for forests and subalpine meadows dotted with peregrine falcons, wolves and wildcats. (p631)

Northern Lagoon, Venice Take a boat tour of Venice's World Heritage–listed lagoon; it's Europe's largest coastal wetland and home to a bounty of migrating birds from September to January. (p364)

Riserva Naturale dello Zingaro Dip in and out of picturesque coves along the wild coastline of Sicily's oldest nature reserve. (p839)

Month by Month

January

Following hot on the heels of New Year is Epiphany. In the Alps and Dolomites it's ski season, while in the Mediterranean south winters are mild and crowd-free, although many resort towns are firmly shut.

Regata della Befana

Witches in Venice don't ride brooms: they row boats. Venice celebrates Epiphany on 6 January with the Regatta of the Witches, complete with a fleet of brawny men dressed in their finest *befana* (witch) drag.

Ski Italia

Italy's top ski resorts are in the northern Alps and the Dolomites, but you'll also find resorts in Friuli, the Apennines, Le Marche and even Sicily. The best months of the season are January and February.

February

'Short' and 'accursed', is how Italians describe February. In the mountains the ski season hits its peak in line with school holidays. Further south it's chilly, but almond trees blossom and herald the carnival season.

Carnevale

In the period leading up to Ash Wednesday, many Italian towns stage pre-Lenten carnivals, with whimsical costumes, confetti and special festive treats. Venice's Carnevale (www.carnevale.venezia.it) is the most famous, while Viareggio's version (viareggio.ilcarnevale.com) is well known for its giant papier-mâché floats.

Sa Sartiglia

Masqueraded horse riders and fearless equestrian acrobatics define this historic event (www.sartiglia.info), held in the Sardinian town of Oristano on the last Sunday before Lent and on Shrove Tuesday.

Mostra Mercato del Tartufo Nero

An early-spring taste of truffles from the gastronomic Umbrian town of Norcia. Thousands of visitors sift through booths tasting all things truffle alongside other speciality produce.

March

The weather in March is capricious: sunny, rainy and windy all at once. The official start of spring is 21 March, but the holiday season starts during Easter.

Taste

For three days in March, gourmands flock to Florence for Taste (www.pittimmagine.com), a bustling food fair held inside industrial-sleek Stazione Leopolda. The program includes culinary-themed talks, cooking demonstrations and the chance to sample food, coffee and liquor from more than 300 Italian artisan producers.

✿✿ Settimana Santa

On Good Friday, the Pope leads a candlelit procession to the Colosseum and on Easter Sunday he gives his blessing in St Peter's Square, while in Florence, a cartful of fireworks explodes in Piazza del Duomo. Other notable processions take place in Procida and Sorrento (Campania), Taranto (Puglia) and Trapani (Sicily).

April

Spring has sprung and April sees the Italian peninsula bloom. The gardens of northern Italy show off their tulips and early camellias, and as April edges towards May, the mountains of Sicily and Calabria begin to fill with wildflowers.

◉ Salone Internazionale del Mobile

Held annually in Milan, the world's most prestigious furniture fair (salonemilano.it) is joined in alternate years by lighting, accessories, office, kitchen and bathroom shows too.

☆ Maggio Musicale Fiorentino

Established in 1933, Italy's oldest art festival (www. operadifirenze.it) brings world-class performances of theatre, classical music, jazz and dance to Florence's sparkling new opera house and other venues across the city. Events run from late April to June.

◉ Settimana del Tulipano

Tulips erupt in spectacular bloom during the Week of the Tulip, held at Lake Maggiore's Villa Taranto; the dahlia path and dogwood are also in bloom in what is considered one of Europe's finest botanical gardens.

🍷 Vinitaly

Sandwiched between the Valpolicella and Soave wine regions, Verona hosts one of the world's largest and most prestigious wine fairs, Vinitaly (www.vinitaly. com), with over 4000 international exhibitors. Events include wine tastings, lectures and seminars.

May

The month of roses, early summer produce and cultural festivals makes May a perfect time to travel. The weather is warm but not too hot and prices throughout Italy are good value. An especially good month for walkers.

✿✿ Maggio dei Monumenti

As the weather warms up, Naples rolls out a mammoth, month-long program of art exhibitions, concerts, performances and tours around the city. Many historical and architectural treasures usually off-limits to the public are open and free to visit.

☆ Ciclo di Rappresentazioni Classiche

Classical intrigue in an evocative Sicilian setting, the Festival of Greek Theatre (www.indafondazione. org), held from mid-May to mid-June, brings Syracuse's 5th-century-BC amphitheatre to life.

🍷 Wine & The City

A two-week celebration of regional vino in Naples (www.wineandthecity.it), with free wine degustations, *aperitivo* sessions, theatre, music and exhibitions. Venues span museums, castles and galleries to restaurants and yachts.

June

The summer season kicks off in June. The temperature cranks up quickly, beach lidos start to open in earnest and some of the big summer festivals commence. Republic Day, on 2 June, is a national holiday.

✿✿ Napoli Teatro Festival Italia

For three weeks in June, Naples celebrates all things performative with the Napoli Teatro Festival Italia (www.napoliteatrofestival. it). Using both conventional and unconventional venues, the program ranges from classic works to specially commissioned pieces from both local and international acts.

✿✿ La Biennale di Venezia

Held in odd-numbered years, the Venice Biennale (www.labiennale.org) is one of the art world's most prestigious events. Exhibitions are held in venues around the city from June to October.

☆ Estate Romana

Between June and October Rome puts on a summer calendar of events that turn the city into an outdoor stage. Dubbed Estate Romana (www.romeguide.it/estate_romana), the program encompasses music, dance, literature and film, with events staged in some of Rome's most evocative venues.

✨ Ravello Festival

Perched high above the Amalfi Coast, Ravello draws world-renowned artists during its summer-long Ravello Festival (www.ravellofestival.com). Covering everything from music and dance to film and art exhibitions, several events take place in the exquisite Villa Rufolo gardens from late June to early September.

✨ Giostra del Saracino

A grandiose affair deep-rooted in neighbourhood rivalry, this medieval jousting tournament sees the four *quartieri* (quarters) of Arezzo put forward a team of knights to battle on one of Tuscany's most beautiful and unusual city squares, Piazza Grande; third Saturday in June and first Sunday in September.

✨ Spoleto Festival dei Due Mondi

Held in the Umbrian hill town of Spoleto from late June to mid-July, the Spoleto Festival (www.festivaldispoleto.it) is a world-renowned arts event, featuring international theatre, dance, music and art.

July

School is out and Italians everywhere are heading away from the cities and to mountains or beaches for their summer holidays. Prices and temperatures rise. While the beach is in full swing, many cities host summer art festivals.

✨ Sagra della Madonna della Bruna

A colourful procession escorts the Madonna della Bruna in a papier-mâché-adorned chariot around Matera on 2 July. The Madonna is carried into the Duomo and her chariot is left to be torn to pieces by the crowd, taking home the scraps as souvenirs. Fireworks add to the frenzy.

✨ Il Palio di Siena

Daredevils in tights thrill the crowds with this chaotic bareback horse race around the piazza in Siena. Preceding the race is a dashing medieval-costume parade. Held on 2 July and 16 August.

☆ Taormina Arte

Ancient ruins and languid summer nights set a seductive scene for Taormina Arte (www.taormina-arte.com), a major arts festival held through July and September. Events include film screenings, theatre, opera and concerts.

☆ Giffoni Film Festival

Europe's biggest children's film festival (www.giffonifilmfestival.it) livens up the town of Giffoni Valle Piana, east of Salerno, Campania. The 10-day event includes screenings, workshops, seminars and big-name guests such as Mark Ruffalo and Robert De Niro.

✨ Festa di Sant'Anna

The Campanian island of Ischia celebrates the feast day of Sant'Anna to spectacular effect on July 26. Local municipalities build competing floats to sail in a flotilla, with spectacular fireworks and a symbolic 'burning' of Ischia Ponte's medieval Castello Aragonese.

August

August in Italy is hot, expensive and crowded. Everyone is on holiday and, while not everything is shut, many businesses and restaurants do close for part of the month.

✨ Ferragosto

After Christmas and Easter, Ferragosto, on 15 August, is Italy's biggest holiday. It marks the Feast of the Assumption, but even before Christianity the Romans honoured their gods on Feriae Augusti. Naples celebrates with particular fervour.

✨ Mostra Internazionale d'Arte Cinematografica

The Venice International Film Festival (www.labiennale.org/en/cinema) is one of the world's most prestigious silver-screen events. Held at the Lido from late August to early September, it draws the international film glitterati with its red-carpet premieres and paparazzi glamour.

September

This is a glorious month to travel in Italy. Summer waxes into autumn and the start of the harvest season sees lots of local *sagre* (food festivals) spring up. September is also the start of the grape harvest.

�֍ Regata Storica

On the first Sunday in September, gondoliers in period dress work those biceps in Venice's Historic Regatta. Period boats are followed by gondola and other boat races along the Grand Canal.

🍷 Chianti Classico Wine Fair

There is no finer opportunity to taste Tuscany's Chianti Classico than at Greve in Chianti's annual Chianti Classico Expo (www.expochianticlassico.com), the second weekend in September. Festivities begin the preceding Thursday. Buy a glass and swirl, sniff, sip and spit your way round.

✕ Festival delle Sagre

On the second Sunday in September more than 40 communes in the province of Asti put their wines and local gastronomic products on display at this appetite-piquing, waist-expanding culinary fest (www.festivaldellesagre.it).

✕ Couscous Fest

The Sicilian town of St Vito celebrates multiculturalism and its famous fish couscous at this 10-day event in late September (www.couscousfest.it). Highlights include an international couscous cook-off, tastings and live world-music gigs.

October

October is a fabulous time to visit the south, when the days still radiate with late-summer warmth and the *lidi* (beaches) are emptying out. Further north the temperature starts to drop and festival season comes to an end.

☆ Romaeuropa Festival

From late September to early December, top international artists take to the stage for Rome's premier festival of theatre, opera and dance (romaeuropa.net).

✕ Salone Internazionale del Gusto

Hosted by the home-grown Slow Food Movement, this biennial food expo (www.salonedelgusto.it) takes place in Turin in even-numbered years. Held over five days, appetite-piquing events include workshops, presentations and tastings of food, wine and beer from Italy and beyond.

November

The advent of winter creeps down the peninsula in November, but there's plenty going on. For gastronomes, this is truffle season. It's also the time for the chestnut harvest, mushroom picking and All Saints' Day.

✖✕ Ognissanti

Celebrated all over Italy as a national holiday, All Saints' Day on 1 November commemorates the Saint Martyrs, while All Souls' Day, on 2 November, honours the deceased.

✕ Truffle Season

From the Piedmontese towns of Alba (www.fieradeltartufo.org) and Asti, to Tuscany's San Miniato and Le Marche's Acqualagna, November is prime truffle time, with local truffle fairs, events and music.

☆ Opera Season

Italy is home to four of the world's great opera houses: La Scala in Milan, La Fenice in Venice, Teatro San Carlo in Naples and Teatro Massimo in Palermo. The season traditionally runs from mid-October to March, although La Scala opens later on St Ambrose Day, 7 December.

December

The days of alfresco living are firmly at an end. December is cold and Alpine resorts start to open for the early ski season, although looming Christmas festivities keep life warm and bright.

✖✕ Natale

The weeks preceding Christmas are studded with religious events. Many churches set up nativity scenes known as *presepi*. Naples is especially famous for these. On Christmas Eve the Pope serves midnight mass in St Peter's Square.

Itineraries

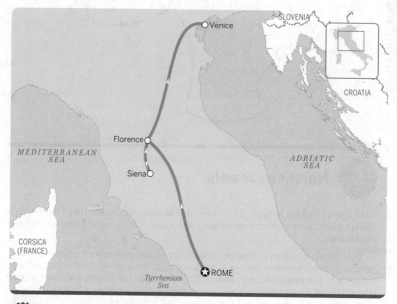

9 DAYS Italian Highlights

A perfect introduction to Italy, this easy tour ticks off some of the country's most seductive sights, including Roman ruins, Renaissance masterpieces and the world's most beautiful lagoon city.

Start with three days in mighty **Rome**, punctuating blockbuster sights like the Colosseum, Palatine and Sistine Chapel with market grazing in the Campo de' Fiori and late-night revelry in Trastevere.

On day four, head to Renaissance **Florence**. Drop in on Michelangelo's *David* at the Galleria dell'Accademia and pick your favourite Botticelli at the Uffizi Gallery. For a change of pace, escape to the Tuscan countryside on day six for a day trip to Gothic **Siena**.

The following day, continue north for three unforgettable days in **Venice**. Check off musts like the mosaic-encrusted Basilica di San Marco, art-slung Gallerie dell'Accademia and secret passageways of the Palazzo Ducale, then live like a true Venetian, noshing on the city's famous *cicheti* (Venetian tapas), and toasting with a Veneto *prosecco* (sparkling wine).

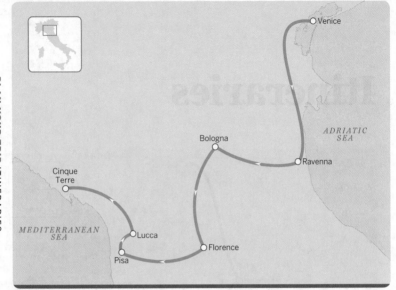

2 WEEKS Northern Jewels

Like a jewel-studded necklace, this route takes in some of northern Italy's most extraordinary assets, from cultural powerhouse cities to one of Italy's most arresting stretches of coastline.

Begin with three days in **Venice**, its trading port pedigree echoed in the Near East accents of its architecture and the synagogues of its 500-year-old Ghetto. On day four, continue to **Ravenna**, former capital of the Western Roman Empire and home to eight Unesco World Heritage-listed Sites. Among these are the basilicas of San Vitale and Sant'Apollinare Nuovo, adorned with extraordinary Byzantine mosaics.

Spend days six and seven in erudite **Bologna**, home to the world's fifth-largest church and its oldest university. The university district is the location of the Pinacoteca Nazionale, its powerhouse art collection including works by regional master Parmigianino. One of Bologna's fortes is gastronomy, a fact not lost on its deli-packed Quadrilatero district.

Dedicate the next three days to **Florence**. It's here that you'll find many of Western art's most revered works. The city's Renaissance credentials extend to its architecture, which includes Filippo Brunelleschi's show-stopping Duomo dome. Even the city's gardens are manicured masterpieces, exemplified by the supremely elegant Giardino di Boboli.

On day 11, pit-stop in **Pisa** to eye-up the architectural ensemble that makes up the Piazza dei Miracoli, then continue to nearby Renaissance show pony **Lucca**. Spend the following day exploring Lucca's elegant streets, picnicking on its centuries-old ramparts and meditating on Tintoretto's soul-stirring *Last Supper* in the Cattedrale di San Martino. Human ingenuity merges with natural beauty on days 13 and 14, where your sojourn ends among colourful fishing villages and weathered vines of Liguria's fabled **Cinque Terre**.

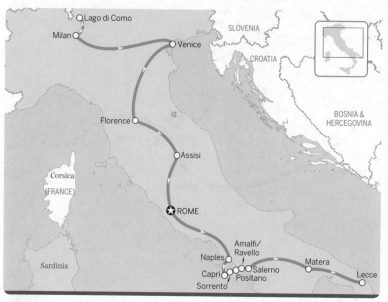

The Grand Tour

From salubrious northern cities and lakes to bewitching southern seas and dwellings, this grand tour encapsulates Italy's incredible natural and cultural diversity.

Start in style with two days in **Milan**. Shop its coveted boutiques, dine its hotspot restaurants and demand an encore at its gilded La Scala. Come day three, continue to **Lago di Como** (Lake Como), basing yourself in Como or Bellagio and spending two romantic days among its sublime waterside villas and villages. If you haven't been wooed by Hollywood royalty, continue to **Venice** on day five, where the following trio of days burst with Titians and Tintorettos, artisan studios and convivial *bacari* (Venetian-style bars). On day eight, shoot southwest to **Florence**, allowing three days to tackle its blockbuster art and sink your teeth into its legendary *bistecca alla fiorentina* (T-bone steak). Gluttonous acts are forgiven on day 11 as you travel to the pilgrimage city of **Assisi**, its Gothic basilica lavished with Giotto frescoes. Head southwest to **Rome** on day 13 and spend three full days exploring its two-millennia-worth of temples, churches, piazzas and artistic marvels.

On day 17, slip south to **Naples** and its explosion of baroque architecture and subterranean ruins. Day-trip it to the ruins of Pompeii on day 19, then sail to **Capri** on day 20 for three seductive days of boating, bucolic hikes and piazza-side posing. If it's high season, catch a ferry directly to laidback **Sorrento** on day 23, spending a night in town before hitting the hairpin turns of the glorious Amalfi Coast. Allow two days in chi-chi **Positano**, where you can hike the heavenly Sentiero degli Dei (Walk of the Gods). Spend day 26 in deeply historic **Amalfi** before continuing to sky-high **Ravello**, long-time haunt of composers and Hollywood stars. Stay the night to soak up its understated elegance, and spend the following morning soaking up its uber-romantic gardens. After an evening of bar hopping in upbeat **Salerno**, shoot inland to **Matera** on day 28 to experience its World Heritage-listed *sassi* (former cave dwellings) and dramatic Matera Gravina gorge. Come day 30, continue through to architecturally astounding **Lecce**, the 'Florence of the South' and your final cross-country stop.

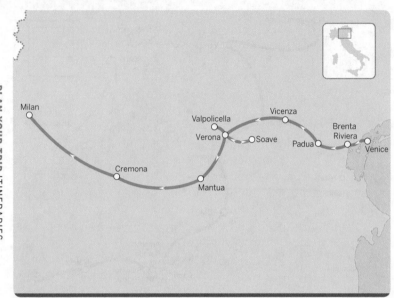

2 WEEKS Venice to Milan

Aristocratic villas, renegade frescoes, star-struck lovers and cult-status wines; this easy two-week journey serves up a feast of northern highlights.

In the 16th century the Venetian summer began early in June, when every household loaded onto barges for a summer sojourn along the **Brenta Riviera**. You too can make like a Venetian on a boat trip along the Riviera after spending a few days in **Venice**. Marvel at the Tiepolo frescoes of Villa Pisani Nazionale, drop in to the Shoemakers' Museum at Villa Foscarini Rossi and stop in at Palladio's Villa Foscari.

Boat trips along the Brenta Riviera end in **Padua** where you can overnight overlooking the Basilica di Sant'Antonio. With advance booking, you can see Padua's crowning glory, Giotto's frescoed Scrovegni Chapel.

On day six hop on the train to **Vicenza**. Spend the afternoon watching sunlight ripple across the soaring facades of Palladio's *palazzi* (mansions) and illuminate the Villa Valmarana 'ai Nani', covered floor-to-ceiling with frescoes by Giambattista and Giandomenico Tiepolo, then head on to **Verona** for three or four days.

Here you can view Mantegnas at Basilica di San Zeno Maggiore, and explore modern art at the Galleria d'Arte Moderna Achille Forte. Then listen to opera in the Roman Arena and wander Verona's balconied backstreets where Romeo wooed Juliet. From Verona, consider a day trip northwest to **Valpolicella** to sip highly prized Amarone (red wine) by appointment at Giuseppe Quintarelli, or back east to **Soave** for a sampling of its namesake DOC white wine at Azienda Agricola Coffele.

On day 11 dip southwest to regal **Mantua** for an impressive display of dynastic power and patronage at the Gonzagas' fortified family pad, the Palazzo Ducale. Finish up with a two-day stop in **Cremona** where you can chat with artisans in one of the 100 violin-making shops around Piazza del Comune before hearing them in action at the Teatro Amilcare Ponchielli and then heading on to end your tour in **Milan**.

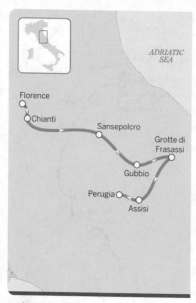

10 DAYS Central Italian Escape

Revered vineyards, medieval hilltop towns and Unesco-lauded artwork: this trip takes in evocative landscapes, from well-trodden Tuscany to lesser-known Umbria and Le Marche.

Begin with two cultured days in **Florence**, then enjoy two decadent days in **Chianti**, toasting to the area's vino and indulging in lazy lunches and countryside cycling. On day five, head east, stopping in tiny **Sansepolcro** to meditate on Pietro della Francesca's trio of masterpieces and calling it a night in the Umbrian hilltop town of **Gubbio**. Spend the following day exploring the town's Gothic streets, then drive into Le Marche on day seven for a guided tour of the incredible **Grotte di Frasassi** cave system. The same day, head back into Umbria to **Assisi**, one of Italy's most beautiful medieval towns. Stay two nights, taking in the frescoes of the Basilica di San Francesco and finding peace on the hiking trails flanking Monte Subasio. Come day nine, make your way to the lively university city of **Perugia**, where your adventure ends with arresting Gothic architecture and world-famous Baci chocolates.

2 WEEKS Northeastern Interlude

Discover a lesser-known corner of the country laced with cross-cultural influences, hot-list wines, cult-status charcuterie and stunning Alpine landscapes.

After three days in **Venice**, head east to Trieste via the Roman ruins of **Aquileia** and the medieval heart of **Grado**. Take two days for **Trieste's** gilded cafes, literary heritage and central European air, then catch a ferry to **Muggia**, the only Italian settlement on the Istrian peninsula. On day seven, head inland for celebrated whites in the **Collio** wine region, slumbering among the vines at Terra & Vini. Spend two days in **Udine**, dropping in on the Museum of Modern and Contemporary Art and sidestepping to **Cividale dei Friuli**, home to Europe's only surviving example of Lombard architecture and artwork. On day 10, pit-stop in **San Daniele del Friuli** for Italy's best prosciutto before hitting breathtaking mountain scenery on your way to ski town **Cortina d'Ampezzo**. Allow two days to ski in winter or hike in summer. Either way, head south on day 14, stopping for afternoon bubbles in the *prosecco* heartland of **Conegliano** before wrapping things up in Venice.

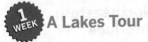

A Lakes Tour

Tickling the snow-capped Alps, Italy's glacial lakes have lured romantics for centuries. Live the dream, if only for a week.

A short drive northwest of Malpensa airport, **Milan**, and you're on the edge of serene Lago Maggiore. Start with three nights in belle époque **Stresa** and visit the lavish **Borromean Islands**: Isola Madre for its romantic gardens and wisteria-clad Staircase of the Dead; and Isola Bella for its priceless art collection, vast ballrooms and shell-encrusted grotto. Take the funicular up to **Monte Mottarone** and day trip to **Lago d'Orta** and bijou **Isola San Giulio**. On day four head north from Stresa to **Verbania**, picnicking amid the tulips of Villa Taranto before gliding east across the lake to **Laveno** and straight on to celebrity haunt **Como**. Amble the flower-laden lakeside to view art exhibits at Villa Olmo before finding a sun lounge at the Lido di Villa Olmo. You could spend days in Como, hiring out boats or hiking the mountainous Triangolo Lariano. If you're ambitious you can walk to chic **Bellagio**. Otherwise, take the lake road and lunch on perch in **Lezzeno** before one last romantic night lakeside.

Southern Coastal Route

Graeco-Roman ruins, a Bourbon palace and some of Italy's most dramatic coastline: crank up the romance on this journey through the sun-baked south.

Rev things up with three days in exhilarating **Naples**, day-tripping it to **Caserta** to explore Italy's largest royal palace. On day four, head south to the Amalfi Coast, allowing for two nights in **Positano**, followed by a day in **Amalfi** and **Ravello** on your way to **Salerno**. Come day seven, continue to the World Heritage–listed temples of **Paestum**, then through the **Parco Nazionale del Cilento e Vallo di Diano** to cognoscenti coastal jewel **Maratea**. Spend two nights in town, followed by lunch in **Tropea** (one of Calabria's most beautiful coastal towns) on your way to **Villa San Giovanni**. Catch the ferry across to Sicily and treat yourself to three nights in fashionable **Taormina**, Sicily's former Byzantine capital and home to the world's most spectacularly located Greek amphitheatre. Sun-kissed and relaxed, continue to **Catania** on day 13, taking two days to soak up the city's ancient sites, extraordinary baroque architecture and vibrant market life.

Vegetable stall, Florence

Plan Your Trip
Eat & Drink Like a Local

Gastronomy is one of Italy's raisons d'être. In fact, the country feels like one gargantuan kitchen, jam-packed with superlative produce, irresistible bites and finely tuned culinary know-how. Locals are fiercely proud of their regions' specialities, and devouring them is an essential part of any Italian sojourn.

The Year in Food

While *sagre* (local food festivals) go into overdrive in autumn, there's never a bad time to raise your fork in Italy.

Spring (Mar–May)

Asparagus, artichokes and Easter specialities, plus a handful of festivals like Turin's Cioccolatò and Ascoli Piceno's Fritto Misto all'Italiana.

Summer (Jun–Aug)

Aubergines, peppers and berries. Tuck into tuna at Carloforte's Girotonno tuna catch in June and beat the heat with gelato and Sicilian *granita*.

Autumn (Sep–Nov)

Food festivals, chestnuts, mushrooms and game. Truffle hunters head to Piedmont, Tuscany and Umbria, while wine connoisseurs hit Elba's wine harvest and Merano's wine festival.

Winter (Dec–Feb)

Christmas and Carnevale treats. Fishers serve up sea urchins and mussels on Sardinia's Poetto beach, while Umbria celebrates black truffles with the Mostra Mercato del Tartufo Nero.

➡ **Dal Pescatore**, **Mantua** (p300) The first female Italian chef to hold three Michelin stars, Nadia Santini is a self-taught culinary virtuoso.

➡ **Il Frantoio**, **Puglia** (p732) Legendary 10-course Sunday lunch at an olive-grove-fringed *masseria* (working farm).

Cheap Treats

➡ **Pizza al taglio** 'Pizza by the slice' is the perfect piazza-side nibble.

➡ **Arancini** Deep-fried rice balls stuffed with *ragù* (meat sauce), tomato and vegetables.

➡ **Porchetta rolls** Warm sliced pork (roasted whole with fennel, garlic and pepper) in a crispy roll.

➡ **Pane e panelle** Palermo chickpea fritters on a sesame roll.

➡ **Gelato** The best Italian gelato uses seasonal ingredients and natural colours.

Dare to Try

➡ **Pajata** A creamy Roman pasta dish made with calves' entrails still containing the mothers' congealed milk.

➡ **Missoltini** Como's sun-dried fish cured in salt and bay leaves.

➡ **Lampredotto** Cow's stomach boiled, sliced, seasoned and bunged between bread in Florence.

➡ **Pani ca meusa** A Palermo sandwich of beef spleen and lungs dipped in boiling lard.

➡ **Zurrette** Sardinian black pudding made of sheep's blood, cooked in a sheep's stomach with herbs and fennel.

Food Experiences

So much produce, so many specialities, so little time! Fine-tune your culinary radar with the following edible musts.

Meals of a Lifetime

➡ **Osteria Francescana**, **Modena** (p452) Bold reinterpretations underline the world's second-best restaurant, as voted in the 2015 San Pellegrino World's Best 50 Restaurants.

➡ **President**, **Pompeii** (p692) One of Italy's best-priced Michelin-starred restaurants, serving whimsical re-interpretations of Campanian cuisine.

➡ **La Leggenda dei Frati**, **Florence** (p510) Superlative, seasonal Tuscan cuisine from the highly regarded Sporito brothers.

Local Specialities

The Italian term for 'pride of place' is *campanilismo,* but a more accurate word would be *formaggismo:* loyalty to the local cheese. Clashes among medieval city-states involving castle sieges and boiling oil have been replaced by competition in producing speciality foods and wines.

Piedmont

Birthplace of the Slow Food Movement. Guzzle Lavazza coffee and vermouth in Turin, also famed for its nougat and buzzing *aperitivo* scene (predinner drinks with snacks). Devour *gianduja* (a chocolate hazelnut spread) and sip a *bicerin* (a chocolate, coffee and cream libation). Alba treats taste buds to white truffles, hazelnuts, and pedigreed Barolo and Barbaresco reds, while Cherasco is celebrated for its *lumache* (snails).

Lombardy

Lombardy is all about *burro* (butter), risotto and gorgonzola cheese. Milan delivers *risotto alla milanese* (saffron and bone-marrow risotto), *panettone* (a yeast-risen sweet bread), uberfashionable restaurants and food emporium Peck. Renaissance Mantua remains addicted to *tortellini di zucca* (pumpkin-stuffed pasta), wild fowl and its *mostarda mantovana* (apple relish). The Valtenesi area is home to some of Italy's finest emerging olive oils, including Comincioli's award-winning Numero Uno.

Venice & the Veneto

Not all bubbly *prosecco* (local sparkling wine) and fiery grappa, Italy's northeast peddles *risotto alle seppie* (cuttlefish-ink risotto), *polenta con le quaglie* (polenta with quails), as well as the odd foreign spice – think *sarde in saor* (grilled sardines in a sweet-and-sour sauce). Sail into Venice for *cicheti* (Venetian bar snacks) at local *bacari* (bars) and to scour Rialto Market produce such as lagoon seafood (look for tags reading *nostrano,* meaning 'ours'). The prime wine region of Valpollicella is celebrated for Amarone, Ripasso, Valpollicella Superiore, Recioto, and inspired renegade *Indicazione geografica*

Beef carpaccio salad

tipica (IGT) red blends from winemakers like Giuseppe Quintarelli and Zýmē.

Emilia-Romagna

Emilia-Romagna claims some of Italy's most famous exports. Bologna piques appetites with *mortadella* (pork cold cut), *stinco di maiale al forno con porcini* (roasted pork shanks with porcini mushrooms) and *tagliatelle al ragù* (pasta with white wine, tomato, oregano, beef and pork belly). It's also famous for soothing *tortellini in brodo* (pasta stuffed with ground meats in a meat broth). While Parma is world-famous for *parmigiano reggiano* cheese (Parmesan) and *prosciutto di Parma* (cured ham), lesser-known classics include *pesto di cavallo* (raw minced horse meat with herbs and parmesan).

Tuscany

In Florence, feast on *bistecca alla fiorentina* (T-bone steak), made with Chianina beef from the Val di Chiana. The valley is also famous for *ravaggiolo* (sheep's-milk cheese wrapped in fern fronds). Head to Castelnuovo di Garfagnana for autumnal porcini and chestnuts, and to San

---

TABLE MANNERS

While Italian diners will usually forgive any foreign faux pas, the following few tips should make things go smoothly.

➡ Make eye contact when toasting.

➡ Eat spaghetti with a fork, not a spoon.

➡ Don't eat bread with your pasta; using it to wipe any remaining sauce from your plate (called *fare la scarpetta*) is fine.

➡ Whoever invites usually pays. Splitting *il conto* (the bill) is common enough, itemising it is not.

Traditional Neapolitan pizza margher

Miniato for white truffles (from October to December). These prized fungi are celebrated at San Miniato's white-truffle fair (Sagra del Tartufo), held over three weekends in November. Savour *cinta senese* (indigenous Tuscan pig), *pecorino* (sheep's-milk cheese) and prized extra-virgin olive oils in Montalcino, a place also known for its Brunello and Rosso di Montalcino reds. Montepulciano is the home of Vino Nobile red, its equally quaffable second-string Rosso di Montepulciano, and Terre di Siena extra-virgin olive oil. Just leave time for Chianti's world-famous vineyards.

Umbria

Uncork a bottle of Sagrantino di Montefalco red and grate a black truffle from Norcia over fresh *tagliatelle* (ribbon pasta) or *strozzapreti* (an elongated pasta literally meaning 'priest-strangler'). Black truffles aside, Norcia is Italy's capital of pork. Another popular meat is wild boar. In Lago Trasimeno, freshwater fish flavours dishes like *regina alla porchetta* (roasted carp stuffed with garlic, fennel and herbs) and *tegemacchio* (fish stew made with garlic, onions, tomatoes and a medley of under-water critters). Meanwhile, on the Strada dei Vini del Cantico wine trail, the town of Torgiano celebrates wine and olives with two dedicated museums.

Rome & Lazio

Carb-up with *spaghetti alla carbonara*, *bucatini all'amatriciana* (with bacon, tomato, chilli and *pecorino* cheese) and *spaghetti cacio e pepe* (with *pecorino* cheese and black pepper). Head to Rome's Testaccio neighbourhood for nose-to-tail staples like *trippa alla romana* (tripe cooked with potatoes, tomato, mint and *pecorino* cheese), and to the Ghetto for kosher deep-fried *carciofi* (artichokes). Southeast of the city in Frascati, tour the vineyards and swill the area's delicate white vino.

Naples & Campania

Procida lemons get cheeky in *limoncello* (lemon liqueur) while the region's vines create intense red Taurasi and the dry white Fiano di Avellino. Naples is home to superlative street food, including *pizza fritta* (fried pizza dough stuffed with salami, dried lard cubes, smoked provolone cheese, ricotta and tomato). The town of

Taralli biscuits

caciocavallo cheese), and feast on *pasta con le sarde* (pasta with sardines, pine nuts, raisins and wild fennel) and *involtini di pesce spada* (thinly sliced swordfish fillets rolled up and filled with breadcrumbs, capers, tomatoes and olives). In Catania, tackle *pasta alla Norma* (pasta with basil, aubergine, ricotta and tomato). Further south, taste-test Modica's spiced chocolate.

Sardinia

Sardinia's waters provide *ricci di mare* (sea urchins) and *bottarga* (salted, pressed and dried mullet roe), while its interior delivers *porceddu* (roast suckling pig, often served on a bed of myrtle leaves). Pasta classics include *culurgiones* (pasta pockets stuffed with potato and *casu de fitta* cheese), *fregola* (granular pasta similar to couscous) and *malloreddus* (a gnocchi-pasta hybrid), while its cheeses include top-notch *pecorino*. A lesser-known *formaggio* (cheese) is *casumarzu* (rotten maggoty cheese), though this can be hard to find unless you know a farmer with a stash in the Nuoro region.

Gragnano produces prized pasta, perfect for *spaghetti alle vongole* (spaghetti with clam sauce). Leave room for a *sfogliatella* (sweetened ricotta pastry) and *babà* (rum-soaked sponge cake). Both Caserta and the Cilento produce prime *mozzarella di bufala* (buffalo mozzarella).

Puglia

Head southeast for peppery olive oil and honest *cucina povera* (peasant cooking). Breadcrumbs lace everything from *strascinati con la mollica* (pasta with breadcrumbs and anchovies) to *tiella di verdure* (baked vegetable casserole), while snacks include *puccia* (bread with olives) and ring-shaped *taralli* (pretzel-like biscuits). In Salento, linger over lunch at a *masseria* and make a toast with hearty reds like Salice Salentino and Primitivo di Manduria.

Sicily

Channel ancient Arab influences with fish couscous and spectacular sweets like *cannoli* (pastry shells filled with sweet ricotta). In Palermo, snack on *sfincione* (spongy, oily pizza topped with onions and

WHAT TO BOOK

Avoid disappointment with the following tips:

➡ Book high-end and popular restaurants, especially for Friday and Saturday evenings and Sunday lunch. In tourist hot spots, always book restaurants in summer and during Easter and Christmas.

➡ Book cooking courses like Bologna's La Vecchia Scuola Bolognese (p442), Venice's Cook in Venice (p371), Florence's Cucina Lorenzo de' Medici (p502) and Desinare (p502), Rome's Roman Kitchen (p116) and Lecce's Awaiting Table (p739).

➡ Book multi-destination culinary tours, such as those run by **Italian Food Artisans** (www.foodartisans. com/workshops), **Culinary Adventures** (www.peggymarkel.com) and **Tasting Places** (www.tasting places.com), as well as wine-tasting courses, such as Rome's Vino Roma (p117).

Aperitivo

➡ **Enoteca** A wine bar often serving snacks to accompany your tipple.

➡ **Agriturismo** A working farmhouse offering food made with farm-grown produce.

➡ **Pizzeria** Cheap grub, cold beer and a convivial vibe. The best pizzerias are often crowded: be patient.

➡ **Tavola calda** Cafeteria-style spots serving cheap premade food such as pasta.

Menu Decoder

➡ **Menù a la carte** Choose whatever you like from the menu.

➡ **Menù di degustazione** Degustation menu, usually consisting of six to eight 'tasting size' courses.

➡ **Menù turistico** The 'tourist menu' usually signals mediocre fare – steer clear!

➡ **Piatto del giorno** Dish of the day.

➡ **Antipasto** A hot or cold appetiser. For a tasting plate of different appetisers, request an *antipasto misto* (mixed antipasto).

➡ **Primo** First course, usually a substantial pasta, rice or *zuppa* (soup) dish.

➡ **Secondo** Second course, often *carne* (meat) or *pesce* (fish).

➡ **Contorno** Side dish, usually *verdura* (vegetable).

➡ **Dolce** Dessert; including *torta* (cake).

➡ **Frutta** Fruit; usually the epilogue to a meal.

➡ **Nostra produzione** Made in-house.

➡ **Surgelato** Frozen; usually used to denote fish or seafood not freshly caught.

How to Eat & Drink

When to Eat

➡ **Colazione (breakfast)** Often little more than an espresso and a *cornetto* (Italian croissant) or brioche.

➡ **Pranzo (lunch)** Traditionally the main meal of the day. Standard restaurant times are noon to 2.30pm, though most locals don't lunch before 1pm.

➡ **Aperitivo** Post-work drinks usually take place between 5pm and 8pm, when the price of your drink includes a buffet of tasty morsels.

➡ **Cena (dinner)** Traditionally lighter than lunch, though still a main meal. Standard restaurant times are 7.30pm to around 11pm.

Where to Eat

➡ **Ristorante (restaurant)** Formal service and refined dishes.

➡ **Trattoria** Cheaper than a restaurant, with more-relaxed service and regional classics.

➡ **Osteria** Historically a tavern focused on wine, the modern version is often an intimate trattoria or wine bar offering a handful of dishes.

CAFFÈ, ITALIAN STYLE

➡ Caffè latte and cappuccino are considered morning drinks, with espresso and macchiato the preferred post-lunch options.

➡ Baristas may offer a glass of water, either *liscia* (still) or *frizzante* (sparkling), with your espresso. Many (especially southern Italians) drink it before their coffee.

➡ Take the edge off with a *caffè corretto*, a shot of espresso spiked with liqueur (usually grappa).

➡ Coffee with dessert is fine, but ordering one with your main meal is a travesty.

3 WEEKS Italian Food Odyssey

Kick off your cross-country feast with two days in **Milan**, famed for its hearty *risotto alla milanese*, *panettone* and gourmet deli Peck. Hit hotspot restaurants like La Brisa and tuck into Lombard classics at Trattoria Milanese. Spend two days in **Turin**, shopping at Eataly, sipping at 18th-century Al Bicerin and indulging in high-end *aperitivi* at Bar Cavour. Annual events in town include Slow Food expo Salone Internazionale del Gusto (October) and chocolate festival Cioccolatò (November).

Next, base yourself in **Alba** for three days, a town famed for its exquisite white truffles. Include day trips to the wine-growing towns of Barolo and Barbaresco, then continue east to **Parma** for *prosciutto di Parma* (cured ham) and *parmigiano reggiano* at Trattoria del Tribunale. On day nine, shop for *aceto balsamico* (balsamic vinegar) in **Modena**, and dine at Massimo Bottaga's world-famous Osteria Francescana (book months ahead). Following this, dedicate two days to food-obsessed **Bologna**. Bag fresh produce at the Mercato delle Erbe, deli-hop in the Quadrilatero district and take a pasta-making course at La Vecchia Scuola Bolognese.

Spend days 12 and 13 in appetite-piquing **Florence**, hunting down prized olive oils at Mercato Centrale, tucking into succulent *bistecca alla fiorentina* (T-bone steak) at Trattoria Mario and noshing at farm-to-table Culinaria Bistrot. With bellies full, slow down the pace with two days of vineyard hopping and cycling in Tuscany's **Chianti** wine region.

Come day 16, shoot east to **Perugia** to tour (or take a chocolate-making course) at Casa del Cioccolato Perugina before pushing on to **Norcia** the following day, a town renowned for its black truffles and *norcinerie* (butcher shops).

Days 18 and 19 see you in **Rome**, sampling Jewish-Roman cuisine in the Ghetto and dining nose-to-tail in the Testaccio district. End with two gut-rumbling days in **Naples**, chowing down Italy's best pizza at Pizzeria Starita and its best buffalo mozzarella at Muu Muzzarella Lounge. Conclude with one final feast at Eccellenze Campane, a sprawling showcase for Campanian gastronomy.

Outdoor Experiences

Blessed with mountains, lakes and 7600km of coastline, Italy is like one giant, pulse-racing playground. Whether you're after adrenalin-piqued skiing in the Alps, hard-core hiking in the Dolomites, coastal climbs in Sardinia, white-water rafting in Calabria or low-key cycling through Piedmont – Madre Natura (Mother Nature) has you covered.

Best Experiences

Hiking The Dolomites, Piedmont's Gran Paradiso, Trentino's Stelvio and Calabria's Pollino parks, Umbria's Piano Grande and the coastal tracks of the Cinque Terre, the Amalfi Coast, Sicily and Sardinia.

Cycling The Po Delta and Bolzano offer good networks, as do the wine regions of Franciacorta, Barolo, Barbaresco and Chianti. Urban options include Rome's Via Appia Antica, Ferrara, Lucca, Bologna and Lecce.

Skiing Cross-border skiing into Slovenia at Sella Nevea; skiing and snowboarding in Courmayeur; downhill and cross-country in Cortina d'Ampezzo, the Valle d'Aosta and Sella Ronda.

Diving The best spots are off the Cinque Terre, the Gargano Promontory, Elba, the Sorrento Peninsula, the Aeolian Islands, Ustica and Sardinia.

Best Times to Go

April to June Walk among wildflowers.

July & September Water sports and warm-water diving without the August crowds.

December, February & March The best ski months for atmosphere, snow and value respectively.

On Land

From skyscraping Alps to the soft undulations of the Tuscan hills, Italy's diverse geography provides a plethora of land-locked diversions. The Alps are alive with the sound of skiing, snowboarding and mountain biking, while the vine-laced landscapes of Tuscany and Piedmont put the romance into cycling, with gentle inclines and mile after glorious mile of country routes. Further south, the precipitous peaks of the Amalfi Coast harbour an ancient network of shepherds' paths, making for heavenly hikes.

Hiking & Walking

Italy is laced with thousands of kilometres of *sentieri* (marked trails). Most local and regional tourist office websites have information about walking in their area. **Italian Parks** (www.parks.it) lists walking trails through each of the country's 24 national parks, as well as providing updates on Italy's marine parks and other protected areas. Another useful website is that of Italy's major walking club, the **Club Alpino Italiano** (www.cai.it) – follow the *rifugi* (mountain huts) link for information about trail routes and accommodation.

Bear in mind that most Italians take their summer holidays in August, so this is when the trails are at their most crowded and the *rifugi* are often jam-packed – you'll need to book weeks, if not months, in advance. On lower terrain, August's intense heat can be oppressive. Sidestep this month if you can. Also note that back-country or wild camping is not permitted in Italy; if you want to pitch a tent, you'll have to do so at a private campsite.

For detailed information on hiking routes in specific regions, check out the reliable **Cicerone** (www.cicerone.co.uk) series of walking guides.

The Alps & Dolomites

Italy's wild, lushly wooded Alps stretch from France in the west, via the southern borders of Austria and Switzerland, to Slovenia in the east. For hikers, they offer heady mountain vistas, swooping forested valleys and views over large glacial lakes such as Garda, Como and Maggiore.

In the far west, dropping into Piedmont and Liguria, are the Graian, Maritime and Ligurian Alps, which take in the full sweep of the Valle d'Aosta, the vast Gran Paradiso park and the lesser-known Parco Naturale delle Alpi Marittime, before making a sharp and dramatic descent to the Cinque Terre and Portofino park on the Ligurian coastline.

To the east in Friuli Venezia Giulia you'll find the Giulie and Carnic Alps, where you can hike in pursuit of lynx, marmots and eagles amid supercute Tyrolean villages. Heading west, the white ridges pass through Trento's Parco Nazionale dello Stelvio, northern Italy's (and the Alps') largest national park, spilling into Lombardy. Lombardy's great lakes – encompassing Garda, Como, Iseo, Maggiore and Orta – are prime hiking territory mixing mountain and lake vistas. Particularly scenic is the crumpled ridge of mountains in Como's Triangolo Lariano and Garda's Monte Baldo.

Soaring across the borders of the Veneto, Trentino and Alto Adige, the enormous limestone fangs of the Dolomites have the edge when it comes to wild beauty. The Unesco World Heritage–listed mountain range offers some of Italy's most dramatic and vertiginous hiking trails. The multi-day, hut-to-hut *alte vie* (high routes) that slice through the heart of the range are

Hikers in Val D'Aosta (p227)

among the most stunning in Europe. To up the ante somewhat, the region is laced with *vie ferrate*, fixed routes that snake and ladder up the peaks and allow would-be mountaineers to flirt with rock climbing with the security of a cable to hook onto.

Accommodation in the mountains is in *rifugi* or chalets, which should be booked ahead in high season (see p945). For serious hiking you'll need to bring appropriate equipment and get detailed trail maps. Tourist offices and visitor centres provide some information, resources and basic maps for easier tourist routes.

Top Trails

➡ **Alpe di Siusi, Alto Adige** (p329) Europe's largest plateau ends dramatically at the base of the Sciliar Mountains. Average stamina will get you to Rifugio Bolzano, one of the Alps' oldest mountain huts. The more challenging peaks of the Catinaccio group and the Sassolungo are nearby.

➡ **Val Pusteria, Alto Adige** (p333) This narrow Tyrolean valley runs from Bressanone to San Candido. At the far end of the valley are the Sesto Dolomites, criss-crossed with spectacular

ITALY'S BEST PARKS & RESERVES

PARK	FEATURES	ACTIVITIES	BEST TIME TO VISIT
Abruzzo, Lazio e Molise	granite peaks, beech woods, bears, wolves	hiking, horse riding	May–Oct
Appennino Tosco-Emiliano	mountains, forests, lakes	skiing, cycling, hiking, horse riding	Feb–Oct
Arcipelago di La Maddalena	rocky islets, beaches, translucent sea	sailing, diving, snorkelling	Jun–Sep
Asinara	albino donkeys, former prison	cycling, boat tours, snorkelling	Jun–Sep
Aspromonte	coniferous forests, high plains, vertiginous villages	hiking	May–Oct
Basilicata	mountains, beech forests, meadows, pastures	hiking, Roman ruins at Grumentum	Apr–Oct
Cilento e Vallo di Diano	Greek temples, dramatic coastline, caves	hiking, swimming, birdwatching	May–Oct
Cinque Terre	Unesco World Heritage Site, colourful fishing villages, terraced hillsides	hiking, diving	Apr–Oct
Delta del Po	marshes, wetlands	cycling, birdwatching	May–Oct
Dolomiti Bellunesi	Unesco World Heritage Site, rock spires, highland meadows, chamois	skiing, hiking, mountain biking	Dec–Oct
Dolomiti di Sesto	jagged mountains, Tre Cime di Lavaredo (Three Peaks)	hiking, mountain biking, rock climbing	Jun–Sep
Etna	active volcano, black lava fields, forests	hiking, horse riding	May–Oct
Gargano	ancient forests, limestone cliffs, grottoes	diving, hiking, cycling, snorkelling	Jun–Sep

walking trails, including moderate trails around the iconic Tre Cime di Lavaredo (Three Peaks).

➜ **Val Gardena, Alto Adige** (p328) One of only five valleys where Italy's Ladin heritage is still preserved. Located amid the peaks of the Gruppo del Sella and Sassolungo, there are challenging *alte vie* (high-altitude) trails and easier nature walks such as the Naturonda at Passo di Sella (2244m).

➜ **Brenta Dolomites, Trentino** (p311) The Brenta group is famed for its sheer cliffs and tricky ascents, which are home to some of Italy's most famous *vie ferrate* including the Via Ferrata delle Bocchette.

➜ **Parco Nazionale delle Dolomiti Bellunesi, Veneto** (p404) A Unesco World Heritage park offering trails amid wildflowers. This park also harbours the high-altitude Alte Vie delle Dolomiti trails, accessible between June and September.

Central Italy

Abruzzo's national parks are among Italy's least explored. Here, you can climb Corno Grande, the Apennines' highest peak at 2912m, and explore vast, silent valleys. A top hike here is the three- to four-day trek through the Majella mountains, which follows an old POW escape route from Sulmona to Casoli.

In neighbouring Umbria, the glacier-carved valleys, beech forests and rugged mountains of Monti Sibillini and the Piano Grande, a 1270m-high plain flanked by the peaks of the Apennines, are well off the trodden path and beg to be discovered on foot. Both are spattered with a painter's palette of vibrant wildflowers in spring and early summer.

Tuscany's only significant park with good walking trails is in the southern Maremma, where you can sign up for

PARK	FEATURES	ACTIVITIES	BEST TIME TO VISIT
Golfo di Orosei e del Gennargentu	sheer cliffs, granite peaks, prehistoric ruins	hiking, sailing, rock climbing, canyoning	May–Sep
Gran Paradiso	Alpine villages, mountains, meadows, ibex	skiing, snowboarding, hiking, climbing, mountain biking	Dec–Oct
Gran Sasso e Monti della Laga	ragged peaks, birds of prey, wolves	skiing, hiking, climbing	Dec–Mar
Madonie	Sicily's highest peaks, wooded slopes, wolves, wildflowers	hiking, horse riding	May–Jun, Sep–Oct
Majella	mountains, deep gorges, bears	hiking, cycling	Jun–Sep
Maremma	reclaimed marshes, beaches	hiking, horse riding, birdwatching	May–Oct
Monti Sibillini	ancient hamlets, mountains, eagles	hiking, mountain biking, paragliding	May–Oct
Parco Nazionale Val Grande	Alpine woodlands, chamois, wolves, birdlife	hiking, birdwatching	May–Sep
Pollino	mountains, canyons, forest, Larico pines, rare orchids	rafting, canyoning, hiking	Jun–Sep
Prigionette	forest paths, albino donkeys, Giara horses, wild boar	hiking, cycling	May–Oct
Sciliar-Catinaccio	pasture lands, valleys, storybook alpine villages	hiking, cycling	Jun–Sep
Sila	wooded hills, lakes, remote villages, mushrooms	skiing, hiking, canyoning, horse riding	Dec–Mar, May–Oct
Stelvio	Alpine peaks, glaciers, forests	year-round skiing, hiking, cycling, mountain biking	Dec–Sep

walks of medium difficulty. The tower-topped medieval town of San Gimignano is also a fine base for guided nature walks into the hills. The Apuane Alps and the stunning Garfagnana valleys are for serious hikers, with hundreds of trails encompassing everything from half-day hikes to long-distance treks. For most people though, an easy amble through the picturesque vineyards of Chianti suits just fine – with a little wine tasting thrown in for good measure, naturally. Autumn, when the wine and olive harvests start, has a particularly mellow appeal.

Edging northwest, Cinque Terre is postcard stuff, with its collection of five rainbow-bright villages pasted precariously to the clifftops, which look as though the slightest puff of wind would make them topple into the Ligurian Sea any second. The area is honeycombed with terrific

trails that teeter through the vines and along the precipitous coastline. The star trek is undoubtedly the serpentine Sentiero Azzuro ('blue trail') linking all five villages, while the Sentiero Rosso ('red trail') presents a highly scenic alternative.

The South

For spectacular sea views hit the Amalfi Coast and Sorrento Peninsula, where age-old paths such as the Sentiero degli Dei (Path of the Gods) disappear into wooded mountains and ancient lemon groves. Across the water, Capri subverts its playboy image with a series of bucolic walking trails far from the crowds.

Crossing the border between Calabria and Basilicata is the Parco Nazionale del Pollino, Italy's largest national park. Claiming the richest repository of flora and fauna in the south, its varied landscapes range from deep river canyons to alpine meadows. Calabria's other national parks – the Sila and Aspromonte – offer similarly dramatic hiking, particularly the area around Sersale in the Sila, studded with waterfalls and the possibility of trekking through the Valli Cupe canyon.

Close to the heel of the stiletto in the sun-baked region of Puglia, the Parco della Murgia Materana, part of Matera's Unesco World Heritage Site, is full of fascinating cave churches and great for birdwatching.

Sicily & Sardinia

With their unique topographies, Sicily and Sardinia provide unforgettable walking opportunities. Take your pick of volcano hikes in Sicily: the mother of them all is Mt Etna, but there's a whole host of lesser volcanoes on the Aeolian Islands from the slumbering Vulcano, where you can descend to the crater floor, to a three-hour climb to the summit of Stromboli to see it exploding against the night sky. On Salina, you can clamber up extinct volcano Monte Fossa delle Felci for staggering views of symmetrically aligned volcanic peaks. From Etna you can also trek across into the Madonie park, or, on Sicily's northwest coast, you can track the shoreline in the Riserva Naturale dello Zingaro.

Hiking Sardinia's granite peaks is more challenging. The Golfo di Orosei e del Gennargentu park offers a network of old shepherd tracks on the Supramonte plateau and incorporates the prehistoric site of Tiscali and the Gola Su Gorropu canyon, which requires a guide and a little rock climbing. Arguably the toughest trek in Italy, the island's seven-day Selvaggio Blu is not for the faint-hearted. Stretching 45km along the Golfo di Orosei, the trek traverses wooded ravines, gorges and cliffs and a string of stunning coves. It's not well signposted (a deliberate decision to keep it natural), there's no water en route and some climbing and abseiling is involved.

Rock Climbing & Mountaineering

The huge rock walls of the Dolomites set testing challenges for rock climbers of all levels, with everything from simple, single-pitch routes to long, multi-pitch ascents, many of which are easily accessible by road. To combine rock climbing with high-level hiking, clip into the *vie ferrate* in the Brenta Dolomites.

Climbs of all grades are found in the Trentino town of Arco, home to the world-famous **Rock Master Festival** (www.rockmasterfestival.com), from short, single-pitch sport routes to lengthier, Dolomite-style climbs. Hard-core mountaineers can pit themselves against Western Europe's highest peaks in the Valle d'Aosta. Courmayeur and Cogne, a renowned ice-climbing centre, make good bases. To the south, the Gran Sasso massif is a favourite. Of its three peaks, Corno Grande (2912m) is the highest and Corno Piccolo (2655m) the easiest to get to. Other hot spots include Monte Pellegrino outside Palermo in Sicily, and Domusnovas, Ogliatra and the Supramonte in Sardinia.

The best source of climbing information is the Club Alpino Italiano. Another good information source is the website **Climb Europe** (www.climb-europe.com), which sells rock-climbing guidebooks for Italy.

Skiing & Snowboarding

Most of Italy's top ski resorts are in the northern Alps, where names like Sestriere, Cortina d'Ampezzo, Madonna di Campiglio and Courmayeur are well known to serious skiers. Travel down the peninsula and you'll find smaller resorts dotted throughout the Apennines, in Lazio, Le Marche and Abruzzo. The Apeninnes often receive mega snowfalls and fewer crowds (so shorter lift queues), and historic villages such as Scanno and Pescocostanzo are far more charming than some of the bigger resorts found elsewhere. Even Sicily's Mt Etna is skiable in winter.

Two snowboarding hot spots are Trentino's Madonna di Campiglio and Valle d'Aosta's Breuil-Cervinia. Madonna's facilities are among the best in the country and

---

FLIGHT OF ANGELS

How do angels fly? At the speed of light, apparently. Il Volo dell'Angelo (p757) in Basilicata is one of the world's longest (1452m) and fastest (120kmh) ziplines, racing you between two villages: Castelmezzano and Pietrapertosa. If you want to amp up the adventure, this is the ultimate high-wire thrill.

TOP SKI RESORTS

Friuli Venezia Giulia

➡ **Tarvisio** 60km of cross-country tracks and great freeriding.

➡ **Forni di Sopra** Family friendly, offering skiing, ice skating and tobogganing.

Valle d'Aosta

➡ **Courmayeur** Dominated by spectacular Mont Blanc, Courmayeur allows access to legendary runs such as the Vallée Blanche.

➡ **Breuil-Cervinia** In the shadow of the Matterhorn and within skiing distance of Zermatt; good for late-season snow and family facilities.

➡ **Monte Rosa** Comprised of three valleys – Val d'Ayas, Val d'Gressoney and Alagna Valsesia – Monte Rosa is characterised by Walser villages and white-knuckle off-piste skiing and heli-skiing.

Piedmont

➡ **Via Lattea** 400km of pistes linking five ski resorts, including one of Europe's most glamorous, Sestriere.

➡ **Limone Piemonte** 80km of runs, including some for Nordic skiing.

Trento & the Dolomites

➡ **Sella Ronda** This 40km circumnavigation of the Gruppo di Sella range (3151m, at Piz Boé) is one of the Alps' iconic ski routes.

➡ **Alta Badia** 130km of slopes including the legendary Gran Risa.

➡ **Madonna di Campiglio** Numerous ski runs and a snowboarding park in the heart of the Dolomites.

Veneto

➡ **Cortina d'Ampezzo** Downhill and cross-country skiing with runs ranging from bunny slopes to the legendary Staunies black mogul run.

---

include a snowboard park with descents for all levels and a dedicated boarder-cross zone. Breuil-Cervinia, situated at 2050m in the shadow of the Matterhorn, is better suited to intermediate and advanced levels.

Facilities at the bigger centres are generally world-class, with pistes ranging from nursery slopes to tough black runs. As well as *sci alpino* (downhill skiing), resorts might offer *sci di fondo* (cross-country skiing) and *sci alpinismo* (ski mountaineering). The ski season runs from December to late March, although there is year-round skiing in Trentino-Alto Adige and on Mont Blanc (Monte Bianco) and the Matterhorn in the Valle d'Aosta. Generally, January and February are the best, busiest and priciest months. For better value, consider Friuli's expanding Sella Nevea runs or Tarvisio, one of the coldest spots in the Alps, where the season is often extended into April.

The best bargain of the ski year is the *settimana bianca* (literally 'white week'), a term used by resorts that generally refers to an all-inclusive ski package that covers accommodation, food and ski passes.

Online, **J2Ski** (www.j2ski.com), **Iglu Ski** (www.igluski.com), **On the Snow** (www.onthesnow.co.uk) and **If You Ski** (www.ifyouski.com) have detailed information about Italy's ski resorts, including facilities, accommodation, updated snow reports, webcams and special offers.

Cycling

Whether you're after a gentle ride between trattorias, a 100km road race or a teeth-rattling mountain descent, you'll find a route to suit. Tourist offices can usually provide details on trails and guided rides, and bike hire is available in most cities and key activity spots.

Tuscany's rolling countryside has enduring appeal for cyclists, with gentle rides

BIKE TOURS

➡ **I Bike Tuscany** (www.ibiketuscany.com) Year-round one-day bike tours for riders of every skill level. Transport to Chianti and a support vehicle are provided. They also offer electric bike tours. Multi-day tours are available through US-based **We Bike Tuscany** (www.webiketuscany.com).

➡ **Iseobike** (www.iseobike.com) Tours around the Franciacorta wine region, with wine tastings.

➡ **Bicisì** (bicisi.wix.com/bicisi) Bike rental and themed foodie tours. Will deliver to accommodation in the Valtenesi.

➡ **Kayak Cardedu** (www.cardedu-kayak.com) Organises scenic road half-day mountain bike excursions and downhill rides on old mule tracks in Ogliastra, Sardinia.

➡ **Colpo di Pedale** (www.colpodipedale.it) Trips for all levels on racers, mountain bikes and city bikes around Piedmont's Langhe wine region.

➡ **Ciclovagando** (www.ciclovagando.com) Organises full-day tours of 20km, departing from various Puglian towns including Ostuni and Brindisi.

between achingly pretty villages, vines and olive groves. The wine-producing Chianti area south of Florence is a particular favourite. In Umbria, the Valnerina and Piano Grande at Monte Vettore have beautiful trails and quiet country roads to explore. Further north, the flatlands of Emilia-Romagna and the terraced vineyards of Barolo, Barbaresco and Franciacorta are also ideally suited to bike touring. Cycling meets architecture on the Veneto's Brenta Riviera, which offers 150km of bike routes past glorious Venetian villas. In the south, Puglia's flat rolling countryside and coastal paths are also satisfying.

In summer, many Alpine ski resorts offer wonderful cycling. Mountain bikers are in their element whizzing among the peaks around Lago di Garda, Lake Maggiore and the Dolomites in Trentino-Alto Adige. Another challenging area is the granite landscape of the Supramonte in eastern Sardinia. A useful first port of call for two-wheel adventures is the website http://italy-cycling-guide.info, which gives the lowdown on major national and international routes in Italy, as well as route options (including maps and GPS files) for a number of regions.

On Water

On the coast, sport goes beyond posing on packed beaches. Sardinia's cobalt waters and Sicily's Aeolian Islands claim some of Italy's best diving. Windsurfers flock to Sardinia, Sicily and the northern lakes, while adrenalin junkies ride rapids from Piedmont to Calabria.

Diving

Diving is one of Italy's most popular summer pursuits, and there are hundreds of schools offering courses, dives for all levels and equipment hire. Most diving schools open seasonally, typically from about June to October. If possible, avoid August, when the Italian coast is besieged by holidaymakers and peak-season prices.

Information is available from local tourist offices and online in Italian at **Dive Italy** (www.diveitaly.com).

Top Dive Sites

➡ **Aeolian Islands, Sicily** A volcanic ridge with warm waters encompassing the islands of Vulcano, Lipari, Salina, Panarea, Stromboli, Alicudi and Filicudi. Dive in sea grottoes around the remains of old volcanoes.

➡ **Capri, Ischia & Procida, Campania** These three islands in the Bay of Naples offer exceptional diving amid sun-struck sea caves.

➡ **Cinque Terre Marine Reserve, Liguria** One of the few places to dive in the north of the country. Dives head out of Riomaggiore and Santa Margherita.

➡ **Capo Caccia, Sardinia** The dive site for Sardinia's coral divers, Capo Caccia also features the largest underwater grotto in the Mediterranean.

→ **Isole Tremiti, Puglia** These wind-eroded islands off Puglia's Gargano Promontory are pock-marked with huge sea caves.

→ **Parco Nazionale dell'Arcipelago di La Maddalena** The Maddalena marine park boasts translucent waters and diving around 60 islets.

→ **Parco Nazionale Arcipelago Toscano, Tuscany** Europe's largest marine park encompasses the Tuscan archipelago and the island of Elba.

→ **Punta Campanella Marine Reserve, Campania** Vivid marine life flourishing among underwater grottoes and ancient ruins. Dives head out from Marina del Cantone.

→ **Ustica, Sicily** Italy's first marine reserve, this volcanic island is rich with underwater flora and fauna.

Sailing

Italy has a proud maritime tradition and it's easy to hire a paddle boat or sleek sailing yacht. Sailors of all levels are catered for: experienced skippers can island-hop around Sicily and Sardinia, or along the Amalfi, Tuscan, Ligurian or Triestino coasts on chartered yachts; weekend boaters can explore hidden coves in rented dinghies around Puglia, in the Tuscan archipelago and around the Sorrento Peninsula; and speed freaks can take to the Lombard lakes in sexy speedboats.

Down south, on the Amalfi Coast, prime swimming spots are often only accessible by boat. It's a similar story on the islands of Capri, Ischia, Procida and Elba.

In Sicily, the Aeolian Islands are perfect for idle island-hopping. Across in Sardinia, the Golfo di Orosei, Santa Teresa di Gallura, the Arcipelago di La Maddalena and the Costa Smeralda are all top sailing spots. Sardinia's main sailing portal is www.sailingsardinia.it.

Italy's most prestigious sailing regattas are Lago di Garda's September **Centomiglia** (www.centomiglia.it), which sails just south of Gargnano, and the Barcolana (p412) held in Trieste in October. The latter is the Med's largest regatta. Reputable yacht charter companies include **Bareboat Sailing Holidays** (www.bareboat sailingholidays.com).

White-Water Rafting & Kayaking

A mecca for water rats, the Sesia river in northern Piedmont is Italy's top white-water destination. At its best between April and September, it runs from the slopes of Monte Rosa down through the spectacular scenery of the Valsesia. Operators in Varallo offer various solutions to the rapids: there's canoeing, kayaking, white-water rafting, canyoning, hydrospeed and tubing.

In Alto Adige, the Val di Sole is another white-water destination, as is Lake Ledro in Trentino, where you can canyon beneath invigorating waterfalls. Further south, Monti Sibillini in Umbria is another good choice for white-water adventures.

On the southwest coast, Kayak Napoli offers great tours of the Neapolitan coastline for all levels, ticking off often-inaccessible ruins, neoclassical villas, gardens and grottoes from the water.

At the southern end of the peninsula, the Lao river rapids in Calabria's Parco Nazionale del Pollino provide exhilarating rafting, as well as canoeing and canyoning. Trips can be arranged in Scalea.

The compelling red granite coastline of Ogliastra in Sardinia is best seen on a relaxed paddle with Kayak Cardedu.

Windsurfing

Considered one of Europe's prime windsurfing spots, Lago di Garda enjoys excellent wind conditions: the northerly *peler* blows in early on sunny mornings, while the southerly *ora* sweeps down in the early afternoon as regular as clockwork. The two main centres are Torbole, home of the World Windsurf Championship, and Malcesine, 15km south.

For windsurfing on the sea, head to Sardinia. In the north, Porto Pollo, also known as Portu Puddu, is good for beginners and experts – the bay provides protected waters for learners, while experts can enjoy the high winds as they funnel through the channel between Sardinia and Corsica. To the northeast, there's good windsurfing on the island of Elba, off the Tuscan coast. Competitions such as the Chia Classic are held off the southwest coast in June.

An excellent guidebook to windsurfing and kitesurfing spots across Italy and the rest of Europe is Stoked Publications' *The Kite and Windsurfing Guide: Europe.* Equipment hire is available at all the places mentioned here.

Travel with Children

Be it the kid-friendly capital, smouldering volcano or beach-laced coast, Italy spoils families with its rich mix of historical and cultural sights, staggering portfolio of outdoor activities and stunning natural landscapes.

Best Regions for Kids

Rome & Lazio

Ancient Roman ruins and world-class museums make Rome interesting for older children.

Naples & Campania

Gold for every age: subterranean ruins in Naples, gladiator battlefields in Pompeii and Herculaneum, volcanoes, thermal pools and coastal caves.

Puglia, Basilicata & Calabria

Beautiful seaside views and towns, islands loaded with swashbuckling adventure and a simple, unembellished cuisine that most kids love.

Sicily

Volcano climbing for sporty teens, beachside fun for sand-loving tots and traditional 18th-century puppet theatre to entertain all ages.

Sardinia

Alfresco paradise overflowing with dazzling beaches, water-sports action, horseriding and scenic hikes suitable for all ages and abilities.

Trento & the Dolomites

Ski or snowboard in some of Italy's best family-friendly winter ski resorts. Summer ushers in mountain hiking and biking for all ages.

Italy for Kids

Italian family travels divide into two camps: urban and rural. Cities in Italy are second-to-none in extraordinary sights and experiences, and savvy parents can find kid-appeal in almost every museum and monument.

Away from urban areas the pace slows. Sandcastles, sea swimming and easy beachside ambles are natural elements of coastal travel (beach-rich Puglia, the Amalfi Coast, Sardinia and Sicily sizzle with family fun on and off the sand), while mountains and lakes inland demand immediate outdoor action from kids aged five and over – the older the child, the more daredevil and adrenalin-pumping the activity gets.

Museums & Monuments

When it comes to learning about art and history, Italy's wealth of museums beat school textbooks hands-down. Few organise specific tours and workshops for children (there are dazzling exceptions in Florence), but an increasing number cater to younger-generation minds with multimedia displays, touchscreen gadgets and audioguides.

Discounted admission for children is available at most attractions. State-run museums and archaeological sites usually offer free entry to EU citizens under the age of 18. Otherwise, museums offer a reduced admission fee (generally half the adult price) for children, usually from the ages of 6 to 18. Some offer money-saving family tickets for two adults and two or more children.

Planning a family visit to museum-laden cities such as Rome and Florence on the first weekend of the month cuts costs dramatically: since July 2014, admission to state-run museums and monuments countrywide is free for everyone on the first Sunday of each month.

Dining Out

Children are welcomed in most eateries, especially in casual trattorias and *osterie* – often family-owned with overwhelmingly friendly, indulgent waiting staff and a menu featuring simple pasta dishes as well as more elaborate items. A *menù bambini* (children's menu) is fairly common. It's also acceptable to order a *mezzo piatto* (half-portion) or a simple plate of pasta with butter or olive oil and Parmesan.

Italian families eat late. Few restaurants open their doors before 7.30pm or 8pm, making pizzerias – many open early – more appealing for families with younger children. High chairs are only occasionally available; if your toddler absolutely needs to be strapped in, bring your own portable cloth seat.

Pizza al taglio (pizza by the slice), *panini* from delicatessens and gelato are tasty, on-the-run snacks. Markets everywhere burst with salami, cheese, olives, bread, fruit and other inspiring picnic supplies.

Baby requirements are easily met; pharmacies and supermarkets sell baby formula, nappies (diapers), ready-made baby food and sterilising solutions. Fresh cow's milk is sold in cartons in supermarkets and in bars with a *'Latteria'* sign.

Children's Highlights

History Trips

➡ **Colosseum** (p66) Throw yourself into Ancient Rome with tales of brave gladiators and wild beasts in the Roman Empire's mightiest stadium.

➡ **Pompeii** (p687) & **Herculaneum** (p684) Evocative ruins with ancient shops and houses, chariot-grooved streets, swimming pools and a gladiator battlefield.

➡ **Palazzo del Podestà, Bergamo** (p291) High-tech gadgetry, animated maps and interactive gizmos bring Bergamo's Venetian age vividly to life.

➡ **Palazzo Comunale & Torre Grossa, San Gimignano** (p535) Slip on augmented-reality glasses to learn about frescoes and this Tuscan town's medieval past.

Best Museums

➡ **Museo Nazionale della Scienza e della Tecnologia** in Milan (p247) Italy's best science

---

PLANNING

Travelling in Italy with children involves little extra pre-departure planning. Your most important decisions will be about which seaside resort to pick (Cala Gonone, Stintino and Santa Teresa di Gallura are Sardinian favourites; on Sicily consider Cefalù, Taormina, and the Aeolian or Egadi Islands) and when to visit – perhaps timing your Italian caper with one of the country's vibrant kid-appealing festivals such as Siena's famous Palio (p523), carnival in Venice (p365) or Viareggio (p569), or Florence's Easter-time Scoppio del Carro (p503). Beware July and August when prices soar and the country broils, even more so in the sizzling hot south.

Accommodation is a key driver. *Agriturismi* (rural farm stays) are family-perfect, often with self-catering facilities, mountains of green space to play around in and stacks of outdoor activities (swimming, tennis, horse-riding and mountain biking) alongside traditional rural pastimes such as olive picking, feeding the pigs, making bread in ancient stone ovens and cultivating saffron. In southern Italy, kids enjoy accommodation in circular, whitewashed *trulli* and quiet, often luxurious, *masserias* (fortified farmhouses, such as family-friendly Masseria Torre Coccaro (p732) near Alberobello).

and technology museum makes budding inventors go gaga.

➡ **Museo Nazionale del Cinema, Turin** (p202) Multimedia displays and movie memorabilia make this museum a winner for kids and adults alike.

➡ **Explora, Rome** (p120) Hands-on exhibitions span bio-science, society and media at Rome's Children's Museum (c3 to 12 years).

➡ **MAV, Herculaneum** (p686) Multimedia installations at Ercolano's virtual archaeological museum bring famous ancient ruins back to life.

➡ **Palazzo Vecchio, Florence** (p488) Theatrical tours for children and families through secret staircases and hidden rooms, led by historical figures.

Outdoor Fun

➡ **Sardinia** (p840) Albino donkey spotting, horseriding, water sports on some of Italy's top beaches (including excellent bubblemaker diving courses for kids), rock climbing and caving adventures.

➡ **Aeolian Islands** (p792) Seven tiny volcanic islands off Sicily with everything from spewing lava to black-sand beaches.

➡ **The Dolomites** (p303) Hit Alto Adige's Alpe di Siusi and Kronplatz for abundant blue and red ski runs, or cycle through orchards and farmland on a Dolomiti di Brenta bike tour.

➡ **Venice** (p335) Glide across Venetian waters on a customised sailing or kayaking tour, or learn to row standing up like an authentic gondolier.

Cool Climbs

➡ **St Peter's Basilica, Rome** (p94) Climbing up inside the dome of Italy's largest, most spectacular church is undeniably cool. Repeat the experience in Florence with Brunelleschi's dome (children over 5 years).

➡ **Catacombe dei Cappuccini, Palermo** (p782) Climb down to the creepy catacombs, packed with mummies in their Sunday best. Find more catacombs beneath Via Appia Antica in Rome and Naples (children over 12 years).

➡ **Napoli Sotterranea, Naples** (p665) A secret trap door, war-time hideouts, sacred catacombs and ghoulish cemeteries make for a gripping subterranean tour (children over 8 years).

➡ **Leaning Tower, Pisa** (p558) The bare interior of Pisa's pearly-white icon is accessible to children from ages 8 and up; otherwise snap your kids propping up the tower.

➡ **Torre dell'Orologio, Venice** (p343) Climb inside the world's first digital clock to examine its Renaissance mechanisms and the two bronze Moors hammering out the hour (children over 6 years).

➡ **Stromboli, Sicily** (p802) A guided ascent to the firework-spitting crater of Sicily's volcano is a total thrill for active teenagers.

Culinary Adventures

➡ **Pasta** Challenge your child to taste different shapes and colours of pasta while in Italy: *strozzapreti* ('priest strangler' pasta) is an Umbrian highlight, while in southern Italy Puglia's *orecchiette con le cima di rape* (ear-shaped pasta with turnip greens) is the perfect way of ensuring your kids eat some vegetables.

➡ **Pizza in Naples** Hands-down the best in Italy. Favourite addresses include Starita (p669) and Pizzeria Gino Sorbillo (p667).

➡ **Gelato Museum Carpigiani** (p446) Gelato-themed tours with lots of tasting, or make your own with masters from the neighbouring Gelato University; 30 minutes from Bologna in Anzola. In Florence, **Curious Appetite** (www.curiousappetitetravel.com) arranges gelato-making workshops for kids.

➡ **Cook in Venice** (p371) Kid-friendly food tours and cooking classes by Venetian *mamma* of two, Monica Cesarato.

➡ **Casa del Cioccolato Perugina** (p582) Wonka-esque chocolate-making workshops and tours at the Baci Perugina chocolate factory in Perugia.

Regions at a Glance

Rome & Lazio

History
Art
Scenery

Ancient Glories

Rome's ancient centre is history in 3D. Romulus killed Remus on the Palatino (Palatine Hill), Christians were fed to lions in the Colosseum and emperors soaked at the Terme di Caracalla. Ponder the remains of the great and the good in the catacombs along Via Appia Antica.

Museums & Galleries

The breadth of cultural treasures housed in Rome's museums and galleries is, quite frankly, embarrassing. If you plan on hitting several of them, consider one of the various discount cards available.

Unexpected Treasures

Often upstaged by Rome's urban must-sees, the Lazio region harbours lesser-known delights, from the classic Mediterranean beauty of the Isole Pontine to the extraordinary stone village of Civita Bagnoregio.

p62

Turin, Piedmont & the Italian Riviera

Activities
Villages
Food & Wine

Hiking & Skiing

From the slopes of Piedmont's Milky Way and the Valle d'Aosta to wild coastal hikes along the Cinque Terre, this northwest corner of the country is a pulse-raising paradise.

Unspoilt Villages

With chic medieval fishing villages along the Cinque Terre, quaint wine-growing villages on Langhe hilltops and secret villages in the Valle d'Aosta, it's not hard finding your ideal storybook refuge.

Gourmet Paradise

Home to the Slow Food movement, Piedmont has an embarrassment of culinary riches, from the truffles of Alba to the *vini* of the Langhe region.

p161

Milan & the Lakes

Shopping
Gardens
Food & Wine

Fashion Capital

Every fashion addict knows that Milan takes fashion and design as seriously as others take biotech or engineering. Top-notch discount outlets mean that everyone can make a *bella figura* (good impression) here.

Villas & Gardens

Framed by gazebos, blushing bushes of camellias, artfully tumbling terraces and world-class statuary, Lombardy's lakeside villas knock the socks off the 'luxury getaway' concept.

Culture & Cuisine

Bergamo, Brescia, Cremona and Mantua, the cultured cities of the Po Plain, combine wonderful art and architecture with a slew of sophisticated, regional restaurants.

p238

Trento & the Dolomites

Activities
Wellness
Food & Wine

Adrenalin Rush

Ski, hike, ice-climb, sledge-ride or Nordic walk in the Sella Ronda and the remote Parco Nazionale dello Stelvio. Real adrenalin junkies will want to scale the WWI-era *vie ferrate* (trails with permanent cables and ladders).

Thermal Spas

Attend to your wellness in the thermal baths at Terme Merano, then stock up on tisanes and cosmetics infused with Alpine herbs, grapes, apples and mountain pine.

Austrian Accents

Bolzano beer halls, strudels, Sachertorte, sourdough breads and buckwheat cakes are just some of the region's Austro-Italian specialities. Combine with regional wines such as Gewürz traminer and riesling.

p303

Venice & the Veneto

Art
Architecture
Wine

Moving Pictures

Action-packed canvases by Titian and Veronese, stirring frescoes by Tintoretto and Tiepolo, all illuminating the path to the contemporary artworks at the Venice Biennale.

Reflected Glories

Formidable castles, gracious country villas and an entire city of palaces on the water, the Veneto's architectural landmarks admire their own reflections in snaking canals.

Inspired Wine Pairings

One of Italy's winegrowing heavyweights, home to Valpolicella's cult-status Amarone, Soave's mineral whites and Conegliano's *prosecco* (sparkling wine), not to mention dozens of innovative blends.

p335

Friuli Venezia Giulia

Culture
Wine
Activities

Bordertown Mystique

The geographic proximity of *Mitteleuropa* (Central Europe) is echoed in earthy Slavic flavours, Austrian cakes, minority languages and the cosmopolitan other-worldliness of Trieste.

Wild Wines

Italy's northeast corner is home to an ever-growing number of small, innovative and often natural wine producers, swilled by locals well known for their love of fine libations.

Natural Thrills

Dramatic, unspoilt Alpine wilderness sets an enticing scene for laidback winter skiing, sublime summertime hikes and no shortage of wildlife sightings, from lynx to deer.

p407

Emilia-Romagna & San Marino

Food & Wine
Architecture
Activities

Famous Flavours

Indulge in Modena's aged balsamic, Parma's ham and cheese, Ferrara's *cappellacci di zucca* (pumpkin pasta dumplings), not to mention Bologna's *ragù* (meat-and-tomato sauce).

Holy Architecture

Tour the churches for a quick art history lesson, from Ravenna's dazzling Byzantine mosaics and Modena's Romanesque cathedral to Bologna's Gothic-Renaissance Basilica di San Petronio.

Urban Cycling

Parma is a pedestrianised role model and Bologna's cobbled streets recall a continental Oxford. Best of all are the 9km of old city walls in cycle-friendly Ferrara.

p434

Florence & Tuscany

Art
Food & Wine
Scenery

Enlightening Frescoes

Read the story of the evolving Renaissance within the vibrant frescoes in Florence, Siena, Arezzo and San Gimignano. Notable names include Giot to, Masaccio and Ghirlandaio.

The Tuscan Table

Succulent *bistecche* (steaks) and white truffles – few regions whet the appetite so lasciviously. Add a glass of Montepulciano's Vino Nobile or Montalcino's world-famous Brunello, and rediscover bliss.

Masterpiece Landscapes

Cypress-lined gardens in Florence, terraced hills in Chianti, the Unesco-lauded beauty of the Val d'Orcia and Val di Chiana: Tuscany's landscapes seem sketched by its artistic greats.

p479

Umbria & Le Marche

Villages
Scenery
Food & Wine

Medieval Towns

Perched snugly on their peaks like so many storks on chimneys, Umbria's hill towns – Perugia, Assisi, Gubbio, Urbino, Spoleto, Todi – are the postcard-pretty protectors of local traditions.

Spectacular Views

Mountainous and wild, views come at you from all angles. Shoot up the *funivia* (cable car) in Gubbio or strike out into the snowcapped ranges of Monti Sibillini and the wildflower-flecked Piano Grande.

Forest Fare

Richly forested and deeply rural, the Umbrian larder is stocked with robust flavours, from wild boar and pigeon, to Norcia's *cinta senese* (Tuscan pig) salami and black truffles.

p576

Abruzzo & Molise

Scenery
Activities
Wilderness

Roads Less Taken

Old-school Italy lives on in the isolated mountain villages of Pescocostanzo, Scanno, Chie ti and Sulmona. En route from Sulmona to Scanno, the untamed scenery of the Gole di Sagittario gorge will bewitch you.

Mighty Mountains

From Corno Grande (2912m) to Monte Amaro (2793m), Abruzzo's parks offer free-from-the-crowds hiking and skiing. The best-loved route: the ascent of Corno Grande.

Captivating Wildlife

These regions excel in outstanding natural beauty. Laced with walking trails, the ancient forests of three national parks still rustle with bears, chamois and wolves.

p633

Naples & Campania

Scenery
History
Food & Wine

Cliffs & Coves

From Ischia's tropical gardens and Capri's dramatic cliffs, to the citrus-fringed panoramas of the Amalfi Coast, the views from this sun-drenched coastline are as famous as the stars who holiday here.

Haunting Ruins

Sitting beneath Mt Vesuvius, the Neapolitans abide by the motto carpe diem. And why not? All around them – at Pompeii, Herculaneum, Cuma and the Phlegraean Fields – are vivid reminders that life is short.

Pizza & Pasta

Campania produces powerhouse coffee, pizzas, tomato pasta, *sfogliatelle* (sweetened ricotta pastries) and an incredible panoply of seafood, eaten every which way you can.

p650

Puglia, Basilicata & Calabria

Beaches
Wilderness
Food & Wine

Seaside Savvy

Lounge beneath white cliffs in the Gargano, gaze on violet sunsets in Tropea and soak up summer on the golden beaches of Otranto and Gallipoli.

Wild Places

A crush of spiky mountains, Basilicata and Calabria are where the wild things are. Burst through the clouds in mountain-top Pietrapertosa, pick bergamot in the Aspromonte and swap pleasantries with curious locals.

Peasant Food

Puglia has turned its poverty into a culinary art: sample vibrant, vegetable-based pasta dishes like *orecchiette con le cima di rape* (pasta with turnip greens) and wash it down with a Salento red from Italy's heel.

p714

Sicily

Food & Wine
History
Activities

Seafood & Sweets

Sicilian cuisine seduces seafood lovers and sets sweet teeth on edge. Tuna, sardines, swordfish and shellfish come grilled, fried or seasoned with mint or wild fennel. Desserts are lavished with citrus, ricotta, almonds and pistachios.

Cultural Hybrid

A Mediterranean crossroads for centuries, Sicily spoils history buffs with Greek temples, Roman and Byzantine mosaics, Phoenician statues, Norman-Romanesque castles and flouncy art-nouveau villas.

Volcanoes & Islands

Outdoor enthusiasts can swim and dive in Ustica's pristine waters, hike the Aeolian Islands' dramatic coastlines or watch the thrilling fireworks of Stromboli and Etna.

p774

Sardinia

Beaches
Activities
History

Sun, Sand & Surf

Famous for its fjord-like coves, crystalline waters and windswept sand dunes, surfers, kitesurfers, sailors and divers flock to the Costa Smeralda, Porto Pollo, the Golfo di Orosei and the Archipelago di La Maddalena.

Moving Mountains

Sardinia's awe-inspiring mountains thrill hikers and free climbers. Climbs deliver stunning sea views, while Supramonte hikes traverse old shepherd routes.

Prehistoric Rocks

With its landscape of grey granite rocks, the island is littered with strange prehistoric dolmens, menhirs, wells and *nuraghi* (huge, mysterious stone towers built by the island's earliest inhabitants).

p840

On the
Road

Rome & Lazio

Best Places to Eat

➡ Glass Hostaria (p133)

➡ Casa Coppelle (p126)

➡ Flavio al Velavevodetto (p135)

➡ L'Asino d'Oro (p131)

➡ Colline Emiliane (p128)

Best Places to Stay

➡ Palm Gallery Hotel (p124)

➡ Residenza Maritti (p119)

➡ Arco del Lauro (p124)

➡ Villa Spalletti Trivelli (p123)

➡ Beehive (p123)

Why Go?

Ever since its glory days as an ancient superpower, Rome has been astonishing visitors. Its historic cityscape, piled high with haunting ruins and iconic monuments, is achingly beautiful, and its museums and basilicas showcase some of Europe's most celebrated masterpieces. But no list of sights and must-sees can capture the sheer elation of experiencing Rome's operatic streets and baroque piazzas, of turning a corner and stumbling across a world-famous fountain or a colourful neighbourhood market. Its streetside cafes are made for idling and elegant Renaissance *palazzi* provide the perfect backdrop for romantic alfresco dining.

But for all its appeal, Rome can be exhausting and when it starts to wear you down, change gear and head out of town. The surrounding Lazio region boasts natural beauty and cultural riches, offering everything from sandy beaches and volcanic lakes to Roman ruins, Etruscan tombs and remote hilltop monasteries.

When to Go
Rome

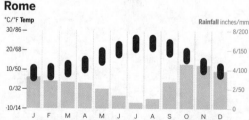

Apr Sunshine, Easter celebrations, Rome's birthday and azaleas on the Spanish Steps.

May–Jul Rome's festival calendar gets into full swing as summer temperatures soar.

Sep & Oct Still warm but the crowds die down and the Roma Europa festival rolls into town.

ROME

POP 2.86 MILLION

History

According to myth, Rome was founded on the Palatino (Palatine Hill) by Romulus, the twin brother of Remus. Historians proffer a more prosaic version of events, claiming that Romulus became the first king of Rome on 21 April 753 BC and the city comprised Etruscan, Latin and Sabine settlements on the Palatino, Esquilino and Quirinale hills.

Rise and Fall of the Roman Empire

The Roman Republic was founded in 509 BC after the fall of Tarquin the Proud, the last of Rome's seven Etruscan kings. From modest beginnings, it grew to become the dominant Western superpower until internal rivalries led to civil war. Julius Caesar, the last of the Republic's consuls, was assassinated in 44 BC, leaving Mark Antony and Octavian to fight for the top job. Octavian prevailed and, with the blessing of the Senate, became Augustus, the first Roman emperor.

Augustus ruled well, and the city enjoyed a period of political stability and unparalleled artistic achievement – a golden age for which the Romans yearned as they later endured the depravities of Augustus' successors Tiberius, Caligula and Nero. A huge fire reduced Rome to tatters in AD 64 but the city bounced back, and by AD 100 it had a population of 1.5 million and was the undisputed *caput mundi* (capital of the world). It couldn't last, though, and when Constantine moved his power base to Byzantium in 330, Rome's glory days were numbered. In 455 it was routed by the Vandals and in 476 the last emperor of the Western Roman Empire, Romulus Augustulus, was deposed.

The Middle Ages

By the 6th century, Rome was in a bad way and in desperate need of a leader. Into the breach stepped the Church. Christianity had been spreading since the 1st century AD thanks to the underground efforts of apostles Peter and Paul, and under Constantine it received official recognition. In the late 6th century Pope Gregory I did much to strengthen the Church's grip over the city, laying the foundations for its later role as capital of the Catholic world.

The medieval period was a dark age, marked by continuous fighting. The city was reduced to a semi-deserted battlefield as the powerful Colonna and Orsini families battled for supremacy, and the bedraggled population trembled in the face of plague, famine and flooding (the Tiber regularly broke its banks).

ROME IN...

Two Days

Start early at the **Colosseum** (p66), before moving onto the **Palatino (Palatine Hill)** (p67) and **Roman Forum** (p71). Spend the afternoon and evening in the *centro storico* (historic centre), exploring the atmospheric lanes around **Piazza Navona** (p83) and the **Pantheon** (p77). On day two, hit the **Vatican Museums** (p96) and **St Peter's Basilica** (p94). Afterwards, head over the river to check out the **Spanish Steps** (p86) and throw a coin into the **Trevi Fountain** (p87). Round the day off in the **Campo de' Fiori** (p84) area.

Four Days

Spend day three investigating **Villa Borghese** (p112) – making sure to book for the **Museo e Galleria Borghese** (p112) – and the streets around **Piazza del Popolo** (p87). End the day with dinner and drinks in **Trastevere**. Next day, marvel at classical art at the **Capitoline Museums** (p75) or the **Museo Nazionale Romano: Palazzo Massimo alle Terme** (p105) before checking out the mighty basilicas on the **Esquilino**. See the evening out in boho **Monti**.

One Week

Venture out to **Via Appia Antica** (p115), home of the catacombs, and take a day trip, choosing between **Ostia Antica** (p148), **Tivoli** (p150) or the Etruscan treasures of **Cerveteri** (p151).

Rome & Lazio Highlights

1 Getting your first spine-tingling glimpse of the **Colosseum** (p66).

2 Marvelling at Michelangelo's masterpieces in the **Sistine Chapel** (p96).

3 Gazing heavenwards in the **Pantheon** (p77).

4 Being blown away by the super-sized opulence of **St Peter's Basilica** (p94).

5 Admiring baroque sculpture at the **Museo e Galleria Borghese** (p112).

6 Exploring haunting ruins on the **Palatino** (p67).

Map labels

1 km
0.5 miles

Tivoli (30km)

TIBURTINO

Cimitero di Campo Verano

Via Tiburtina

Via del Ramni

Nomentana

Viale XXI Aprile

Via Nomentana

Bologna

Villa Torlonia

Castro Pretorio

Stazione Termini

Termini

Museo Nazionale Romano: Palazzo Massimo alle Terme

TRIESTE

Via del Foro Italico

Via Salaria

Villa Ada

Viale Regina Margherita

SALARIO

Repubblica

ESQUILINO

MONTI

PARIOLI

Museo e Galleria Borghese

See Villa Borghese Map (p113)

Barberini

Giardino del Quirinale

TREVI

Villa Borghese

Spagna

Auditorium Parco della Musica

Euclide

FLAMINIO

Flaminio

Pantheon

Stadio Flaminio

Via Cassia

Viale Tiziano

Via Flaminia

Cerveteri (35km); Civitavecchia (80km); Tarquinia (90km)

Museo Nazionale delle Arti del XXI Secolo (MAXXI)

Tiber River

Viale Mazzini

Stadio Olimpico

FORO ITALICO

Via del Foro Italico

Parco della Vittoria

Lgt Maresciallo Cadorna

PRATI

Lepanto

Ottaviano-San Pietro

Viale Giuseppe Mazzini

TRIONFALE

Cipro-Musei Vaticani

VATICAN CITY

St Peter's Basilica

Sistine Chapel

See Vatican City, Borgo & Prati Map (p92)

Stazione

7 Checking out ancient mosaics at the **Museo Nazionale Romano: Palazzo Massimo alle Terme** (p105).

8 Delving into frescoed Etruscan tombs in **Tarquinia** (p152).

9 Poking around the preserved port town of **Ostia Antica** (p148).

BEST VIEWPOINTS

Enjoy fabulous views from:

➡ **Il Vittoriano** (p77) A colossal monument commanding vast 360-degree views.

➡ **Palatino** (p67) Get grandstand views of the Roman Forum.

➡ Dome of **St Peter's Basilica** (p94) Spy on pilgrims in St Peter's Square, 120m below.

➡ **Priorato dei Cavalieri di Malta** (p111) See St Peter's Dome perfectly framed through a keyhole.

➡ **Gianicolo** (p106) Survey Rome's rooftops from this leafy hilltop.

Historic Makeovers

But out of the ruins of the Middle Ages grew Renaissance Rome. At the behest of the city's great papal dynasties – the Barberini, Farnese and Pamphilj – the leading artists of the 15th and 16th centuries were summoned to work on projects such as the Sistine Chapel and St Peter's Basilica. But the enemy was never far away, and in 1527 the Spanish forces of Holy Roman Emperor Charles V ransacked Rome.

Another rebuild was in order, and it was to the 17th-century baroque masters Bernini and Borromini that Rome's patrons turned. Exuberant churches, fountains and *palazzi* (mansions) sprouted all over the city, as the two rivals competed to produce ever-more virtuosic masterpieces.

The next makeover followed the unification of Italy and the declaration of Rome as its capital. Mussolini, believing himself a modern-day Augustus, also left an indelible stamp, bulldozing new imperial roads and commissioning ambitious building projects such as the monumental suburb of EUR.

Modern Styling

Post-fascism, the 1950s and '60s saw the glittering era of *la dolce vita* and hasty urban expansion, resulting in Rome's sometimes wretched suburbs. A clean-up in 2000 had the city in its best shape for decades, and in recent years some dramatic modernist building projects have given the Eternal City some edge, such as Renzo Piano's Auditorium Parco della Musica and Massimiliano Fuksas' ongoing Nuvola building in EUR.

Sights

◉ Ancient Rome

★**Colosseum** RUIN
(Colosseo; Map p68; ☏ 06 3996 7700; www.coop culture.it; Piazza del Colosseo; adult/reduced incl Roman Forum & Palatino €12/7.50; ◷ 8.30am-1hr before sunset; Ⓜ Colosseo) Rome's great gladiatorial arena is the most thrilling of the city's ancient sights. Inaugurated in AD 80, the 50,000-seat Colosseum, originally known as the Flavian Amphitheatre, was clad in travertine and covered by a huge canvas awning held aloft by 240 masts. Inside, tiered seating encircled the arena, itself built over an underground complex (the hypogeum) where animals were caged and stage sets prepared. Games involved gladiators fighting wild animals or each other.

The emperor Vespasian (r AD 69–79) originally commissioned the amphitheatre in AD 72 in the grounds of Nero's vast Domus Aurea complex. But he never lived to see it finished and it was completed by his son and successor Titus (r 79–81) a year after his death. To mark its inauguration, Titus held games that lasted 100 days and nights, during which some 5000 animals were slaughtered. Trajan (r 98–117) later topped this, holding a marathon 117-day killing spree involving 9000 gladiators and 10,000 animals.

The arena was originally named after Vespasian's family (Flavian), and although it was Rome's most fearsome arena, it wasn't the biggest – the Circo Massimo could hold up to 250,000 people. The name Colosseum, when introduced in medieval times, was not a reference to its size but to the Colosso di Nerone, a giant statue of Nero that stood nearby.

The outer walls have three levels of arches, framed by decorative columns topped by capitals of the Ionic (at the bottom), Doric and Corinthian (at the top) orders. They were originally covered in travertine and marble statues filled the niches on the second and third storeys. The upper level, punctuated with windows and slender Corinthian pilasters, had supports for the masts that held the awning over the arena, shielding the spectators from sun and rain. The 80 entrance arches, known as vomitoria, allowed the spectators to enter and be seated in a matter of minutes.

The Colosseum's interior was divided into three parts: the arena, *cavea* and podium.

The arena had a wooden floor covered in sand to prevent the combatants from slipping and to soak up the blood. Trapdoors led down to the underground chambers and passageways beneath the arena floor – the hypogeum. Animals in cages and sets for the various battles were hoisted up to the arena by a complicated system of pulleys. The cavea, for spectator seating, was divided into three tiers: magistrates and senior officials sat in the lowest tier, wealthy citizens in the middle and the plebs in the highest tier. Women (except for Vestal Virgins) were relegated to the cheapest sections at the top. The podium, a broad terrace in front of the tiers of seats, was reserved for emperors, senators and VIPs.

With the fall of the Roman Empire in the 5th century, the Colosseum was abandoned. In the Middle Ages it became a fortress occupied by two of the city's warrior families: the Frangipani and the Annibaldi. Later, it was plundered of its precious travertine, and marble stripped from it was used to make huge palaces such as Palazzo Venezia, Palazzo Barberini and Palazzo Cancelleria.

Pollution and vibrations caused by traffic and the metro have also taken their toll. The Colosseum is currently undergoing a €25-million clean-up, and until restoration is finished in 2016 you may well find parts of the outer wall covered in scaffolding.

The top tier and hypogeum are open to the public by guided tour only. Visits, which cost €9 on top of the normal Colosseum ticket, require advance booking.

Arco di Costantino   MONUMENT

(Map p68; M Colosseo) On the western side of the Colosseum, this monumental triple arch was built in AD 315 to celebrate the emperor Constantine's victory over his rival Maxentius at the Battle of the Milvian Bridge (AD 312). Rising to a height of 25m, it's the largest of Rome's surviving triumphal arches.

★ Palatino   ARCHAEOLOGICAL SITE

(Palatine Hill; Map p68; ☑ 06 3996 7700; www.coopculture.it; Via di San Gregorio 30 & Via Sacra; adult/reduced incl Colosseum & Roman Forum €12/7.50; ☉ 8.30am–1hr before sunset; M Colosseo) Sandwiched between the Roman Forum and the Circo Massimo, the Palatino (Palatine Hill) is an atmospheric area of towering pine trees, majestic ruins and memorable views. It was here that Romulus supposedly founded the city in 753 BC and Rome's em-

❶ COLOSSEUM TIPS

....

Some useful tips to beat the Colosseum queues:

➡ Buy your ticket from the Palatino entrance (about 250m away at Via di San Gregorio 30).

➡ Book your ticket online at www.coopculture.it (plus booking fee of €2).

➡ Get the Roma Pass.

➡ Join an official English-language tour – €5 on top of the regular Colosseum ticket price.

➡ Visit in the late afternoon rather than mid-morning.

perors lived in unabashed luxury. Look out for the **stadio** (stadium) (Map p68) , the ruins of the **Domus Flavia** (imperial palace) (Map p68) , and grandstand views over the Roman Forum from the **Orti Farnesiani** (Map p68).

Roman myth holds that Romulus established Rome on the Palatino after he'd killed his twin brother Remus in a fit of anger. Archaeological evidence clearly can't prove this, but it has dated human habitation here to the 8th century BC.

As the most central of Rome's seven hills, and because it was close to the Roman Forum, the Palatino was the ancient city's most exclusive neighbourhood. The emperor Augustus lived here all his life and successive emperors built increasingly opulent palaces. But after Rome's decline it fell into disrepair, and in the Middle Ages churches and castles were built over the ruins. During the Renaissance, members of wealthy families established gardens on the hill.

Most of the Palatino as it appears today is covered by the ruins of Emperor Domitian's vast complex, which served as the main imperial palace for 300 years. Divided into the Domus Flavia, Domus Augustana, and a *stadio*, it was built in the 1st century AD.

On entering the complex from Via di San Gregorio, head uphill until you come to the first recognisable construction, the **stadio**. This sunken area, which was part of the main imperial palace, was probably used by the emperors for private games and events. To the southeast of the stadium are the remains of a complex built by Septimius Severus, comprising baths (the **Terme di Settimio Severo** (Map p68)) and a palace (the **Domus Severiana** (Map p68)) where,

Ancient Rome

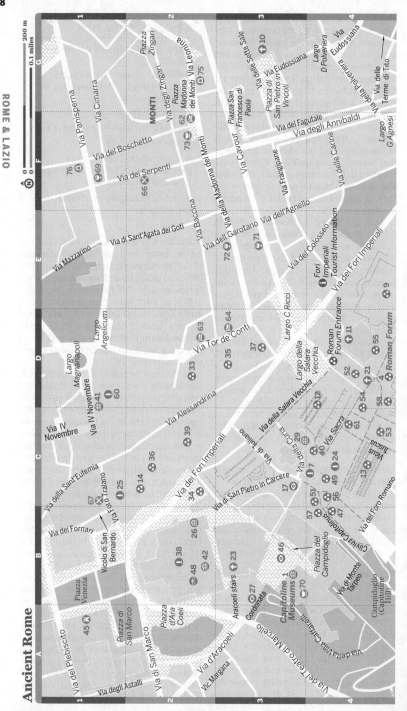

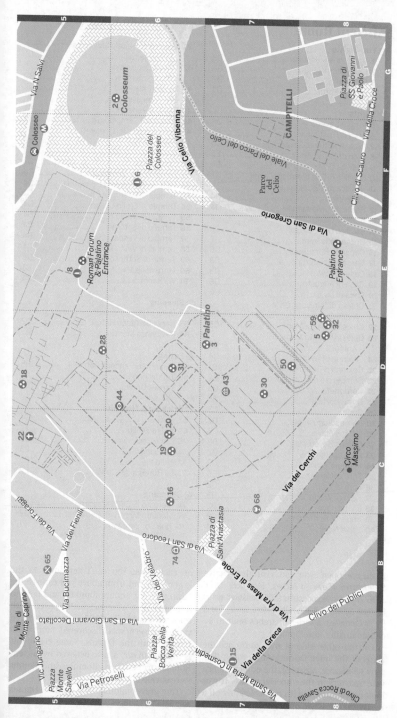

Ancient Rome

if they're open, you can visit the **Arcate Severiane** (Severian Arches; Map p68; ☎06 3996 7700; www.coopculture.it; admission incl in Palatino ticket; ☺8.30am-1hr before sunset Tue & Fri; Ⓜ Colosseo), a series of arches built to facilitate further development.

On the other side of the *stadio* are the ruins of the huge **Domus Augustana** (Emperor's Residence; Map p68), the emperor's private quarters in the imperial palace. It was built on two levels, with rooms leading off a *peristilio* (peristyle or porticoed courtyard)

on each floor. You can't get down to the lower level, but from above you can see the basin of a big, square fountain and beyond it rooms that were originally paved with coloured marble. In 2007 a mosaic-covered vaulted cavern was discovered more than 15m beneath the Domus. Some claim this is the *Lupercale*, a cave believed by ancient Romans to be where Romulus and Remus were suckled by a wolf.

The grey building next to the Domus Augustana houses the **Museo Palatino**

(Map p68; admission incl in Palatino ticket; ⊙ 8.30am-1hr before sunset; Ⓜ Colosseo), a small museum dedicated to the history of the area. Archaeological artefacts on show include a beautiful 1st-century bronze, the *Erma di Canefora*, and a celebrated 3rd-century graffito depicting a man with a donkey's head on the cross.

North of the museum is the **Domus Flavia**, the public part of the palace complex. This was centred on a grand columned peristyle – the grassy area you see with the base of an octagonal fountain – off which the main hall led. To the north was the emperor's throne room; to the west, a second big hall that the emperor used to meet his advisers; and to the south, a large banqueting hall, the *triclinium*.

Near the Domus, the **Casa di Augusto** (Map p68; ☑ 06 3996 7700; www.coopculture.it; incl Casa di Livia €4; ⊙ guided tour 1pm daily, pre-booking necessary; Ⓜ Colosseo), Augustus' private residence, features some superb frescoes in vivid reds, yellows and blues. Further illustrations adorn the **Casa di Livia** (Map p68; ☑ 06 3996 7700; www.coopculture.it; incl Casa di Augusto €4; ⊙ guided tour 1pm daily, pre-booking necessary; Ⓜ Colosseo), the separate home of Augustus' wife Livia. Built around an atrium leading onto what were once reception rooms, the Casa is frescoed with depictions of mythological scenes, landscapes, fruits and flowers.

Behind the Casa di Augusto are the **Capanne Romulee** (Romulean Huts; Map p68), where it's thought Romulus and Remus were brought up by a local shepherd called Faustulus.

Northeast of the Casa di Livia lies the **criptoportico** (Map p68), a 128m tunnel where Caligula was thought to have been murdered, and which Nero later used to connect his Domus Aurea with the Palatino. Lit by a series of windows, it's now used to stage temporary exhibitions.

The area west of this was once Tiberius' palace, the Domus Tiberiana, but is now the site of the 16th-century **Orti Farnesiani**, one of Europe's earliest botanical gardens. A viewing balcony at the northern end of the garden commands breathtaking views over the Roman Forum.

★ **Roman Forum** ARCHAEOLOGICAL SITE (Foro Romano; Map p68; ☑ 06 3996 7700; www.coopculture.it; Largo della Salara Vecchia & Via Sacra; adult/reduced incl Colosseo & Palatino €12/7.50; ⊙ 8.30am-1hr before sunset; ▣ Via dei

ⓘ POSING CENTURIONS

Outside the Colosseum, Roman Forum and Vittoriano, you might find yourself being hailed by costumed centurions offering to pose for a photo with you. They're not doing this for love and will expect payment. There's no set rate but coins are sufficient, certainly no more than €5 – and that's €5 in total, not per person.

Fori Imperiali) An impressive – if rather confusing – sprawl of ruins, the Roman Forum was ancient Rome's showpiece centre, a grandiose district of temples, basilicas and vibrant public spaces. The site, which was originally an Etruscan burial ground, was first developed in the 7th century BC, growing over time to become the social, political and commercial hub of the Roman empire. Landmark sights include the Arco di Settimio Severo, the Curia, and the Casa delle Vestali.

Like many of Rome's great urban developments, the Forum fell into disrepair after the fall of the Roman Empire until eventually it was used as pasture land. In the Middle Ages it was known as the Campo Vaccino ('Cow Field') and extensively plundered for its stone and marble. The area was systematically excavated in the 18th and 19th centuries, and excavations continue to this day.

Entering from Largo della Salara Vecchia – you can also enter directly from the Palatino or via an entrance near the Arco di Tito – you'll see the **Tempio di Antonino e Faustina** (Map p68) ahead to your left. Erected in AD 141, this was transformed into a church in the 8th century, the **Chiesa di San Lorenzo in Miranda** (Map p68). To your right the 179 BC **Basilica Fulvia Aemilia** (Map p68) was a 100m-long public hall with a two-storey porticoed facade.

At the end of the path, you'll come to **Via Sacra** (Map p68), the Forum's main thoroughfare, and the **Tempio di Giulio Cesare** (Tempio del Divo Giulio; Map p68) (also known as the Tempio del Divo Giulio). Built by Augustus in 29 BC, this marks the spot where Julius Caesar was cremated.

Heading right up Via Sacra brings you to the **Curia** (Map p68), the original seat of the Roman Senate. This barn-like construction was rebuilt on various occasions before being converted into a church in the Middle

Roman Forum

In ancient times, a forum was a market place, civic centre and religious complex all rolled into one, and the greatest of all was the Roman Forum (Foro Romano). Situated between the Palatino (Palatine Hill), ancient Rome's most exclusive neighbourhood, and the Campidoglio (Capitoline Hill), it was the city's busy, bustling centre. On any given day it teemed with activity. Senators debated affairs of state in the **Curia** ❶, shoppers thronged the squares and traffic-free streets, crowds gathered under the **Colonna di Foca** ❷ to listen to politicians holding forth from the **Rostrum** ❷. Elsewhere, lawyers worked the courts in basilicas including the **Basilica di Massenzio** ❸, while the Vestal Virgins quietly went about their business in the **Casa delle Vestali** ❹.

Special occasions were also celebrated in the Forum: religious holidays were marked with ceremonies at temples such as **Tempio di Saturno** ❺ and **Tempio di Castore e Polluce** ❻, and military victories were honoured with dramatic processions up Via Sacra and the building of monumental arches like **Arco di Settimio Severo** ❼ and **Arco di Tito** ❽.

The ruins you see today are impressive but they can be confusing without a clear picture of what the Forum once looked like. This spread shows the Forum in its heyday, complete with temples, civic buildings and towering monuments to heroes of the Roman Empire.

TOP TIPS

» Get grandstand views of the Forum from the Palatino and Campidoglio.

» Visit first thing in the morning or late afternoon; crowds are worst between 11am and 2pm.

» In summer it gets hot in the Forum and there's little shade, so take a hat and plenty of water.

Colonna di Foca & Rostrum

The free-standing, 13.5m-high Column of Phocus is the Forum's youngest monument, dating to AD 608. Behind it, the Rostrum provided a suitably grandiose platform for pontificating public speakers.

Campidoglio (Capitoline Hill

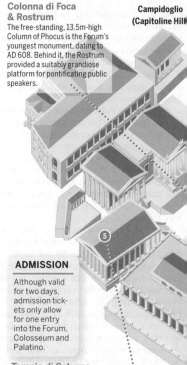

ADMISSION

Although valid for two days, admission tickets only allow for one entry into the Forum, Colosseum and Palatino.

Tempio di Saturno

Ancient Rome's Fort Knox, the Temple of Saturn was the city treasury. In Caesar's day it housed 13 tonnes of gold, 114 tonnes of silver and 30 million sestertii worth of silver coins.

JONATHAN SMITH/GETTY IMAGES©

LONELY PLANET/GETTY IMAGES ©

Tempio di Castore e Polluce

Only three columns of the Temple of Castor and Pollux remain. The temple was dedicated to the Heavenly Twins after they supposedly led the Romans to victory over the Latin League in 496 BC.

Arco di Settimio Severo
One of the Forum's signature monuments, this imposing triumphal arch commemorates the military victories of Septimius Severus. Relief panels depict his campaigns against the Parthians.

Curia
This big barn-like building was the official seat of the Roman Senate. Most of what you see is a reconstruction, but the interior marble floor dates to the 3rd-century reign of Diocletian.

THE JPEN/GETTY IMAGES ©

Basilica di Massenzio
Marvel at the scale of this vast 4th-century basilica. In its original form the central hall was divided into enormous naves; now only part of the northern nave survives.

JULIUS CAESAR
Julius Caesar was cremated on the site where the Tempio di Giulio Cesare now stands.

Via Sacra

Tempio di Giulio Cesare

Arco di Tito
Said to be the inspiration for the Arc de Triomphe in Paris, the well-preserved Arch of Titus was built by the emperor Domitian to honour his elder brother Titus.

Casa delle Vestali
White statues line the grassy atrium of what was once the luxurious 50-room home of the Vestal Virgins. The virgins played an important role in Roman religion, serving the goddess Vesta.

MANANIN/GETTY IMAGES ©

TOP FIVE FILM LOCATIONS

➡ **Piazza Navona** (p83) Jep Gambardella walks a beautiful blonde through the dark, deserted piazza in *The Great Beauty*.

➡ **Trevi Fountain** (p87) Scene of Anita Ekberg's sensual dip in *La Dolce Vita*.

➡ **Bocca della Verità** (p77) Gregory Peck goofs around with Audrey Hepburn in *Roman Holiday*.

➡ **Piazza di Spagna** (p86) Drama over drinks at the foot of the Spanish Steps in *The Talented Mr Ripley*.

➡ **Pantheon** (p77) Tom Hanks checks out Raphael's tomb in *Angels and Demons*.

Other films set in Rome include: *Three Coins in a Fountain*; *Yesterday, Today and Tomorrow*; *Bicycle Thieves*; *Rome, Open City*; *Eat, Pray, Love*; *To Rome with Love*; and *Spectre*, the latest James Bond outing.

Ages. What you see today is a 1937 reconstruction of how it looked in the reign of Diocletian (r 284–305).

In front of the Curia, and hidden by scaffolding, is the **Lapis Niger** (Map p68), a large piece of black marble that's said to cover the tomb of Romulus.

At the end of Via Sacra, the 23m-high **Arco di Settimio Severo** (Arch of Septimius Severus; Map p68) is dedicated to the eponymous emperor and his two sons, Caracalla and Geta. It was built in AD 203 to commemorate the Roman victory over the Parthians.

In front of the arch are the remains of the **Rostrum** (Map p68), an elaborate podium where Shakespeare had Mark Antony make his famous 'Friends, Romans, countrymen...' speech. Facing this, the **Colonna di Foca** (Column of Phocus; Map p68) rises above what was once the Forum's main square, Piazza del Foro.

The eight granite columns that rise behind the Colonna are all that remain of the **Tempio di Saturno** (Temple of Saturn; Map p68), an important temple that doubled as the state treasury. Behind it are (from north to south): the ruins of the **Tempio della Concordia** (Temple of Concord; Map p68), **Tempio di Vespasiano** (Temple of Vespasian and Titus; Map p68), and the **Portico degli Dei Consenti** (Map p68).

From the path that runs parallel to Via Sacra, you'll pass the stubby ruins of the **Basilica Giulia** (Map p68), which was begun by Julius Caesar and finished by Augustus. At the end of the basilica, three columns remain from the 5th-century BC **Tempio di Castore e Polluce** (Temple of Castor and Pollux; Map p68). Nearby, the 6th-century **Chiesa di**

Santa Maria Antiqua (Map p68), is the oldest Christian church in the Forum.

Back towards Via Sacra is the **Casa delle Vestali** (House of the Vestal Virgins; Map p68) (currently off-limits), home of the virgins who tended the sacred flame in the adjoining **Tempio di Vesta** (Map p68). The six virgin priestesses were selected from patrician families when aged between six and 10 to serve in the temple for 30 years. If the flame in the temple went out the priestess responsible would be flogged, and if she lost her virginity she would be buried alive. The offending man would be flogged to death.

Continuing up Via Sacra, past the **Tempio di Romolo** (Temple of Romulus; Map p68), you'll come to the **Basilica di Massenzio** (Basilica di Costantino; Map p68), the largest building on the forum. Started by the Emperor Maxentius and finished by Constantine in 315, it originally measured approximately 100m by 65m. Its currently out of bounds due to construction work on a new metro line.

Beyond the basilica, the **Arco di Tito** (Arch of Titus; Map p68) was built in AD 81 to celebrate Vespasian and Titus' victories against rebels in Jerusalem.

asilica di SS Cosma e Damiano BASILICA

(Map p68; Via dei Fori Imperiali 1; presepio donation €1; ⊙ 9am-1pm & 3-7pm, presepio 10am-1pm & 3-6pm Fri-Sun Sep-Jul; 🚇 Via dei Fori Imperiali) Backing onto the Roman Forum, this 6th-century basilica incorporates parts of the **Foro di Vespasiano** and **Tempio di Romolo**, visible at the end of the nave. The real reason to visit, though, is to admire the church's vibrant 6th-century apse mosaics, depicting Peter and Paul presenting saints Cosma, Damian, Theodorus and Pope Felix IV to Christ.

Also worth a look is the 18th-century Neapolitan **presepio** (nativity scene) in a room off the 17th-century cloister.

Carcere Mamertino   HISTORIC SITE
(Mamertine Prison; Map p68; ☑ 06 69 89 61; Clivo Argentario 1; with/without tour €5/3; ☻ 9.30am-7pm summer, to 5pm winter; 🚇 Via dei Fori Imperiali) At the foot of the Campidoglio, the Mamertine Prison was ancient Rome's maximum-security jail. St Peter did time here and while imprisoned supposedly created a miraculous stream of water to baptise his jailers. On the bare stone walls you can just make out early Christian frescoes depicting Jesus and Saints Peter and Paul.

If you just want to nip in and have a look, get the €3 ticket, otherwise guided multimedia tours take about half an hour.

Imperial Forums   ARCHAEOLOGICAL SITE
(Fori Imperiali; Map p68; Via dei Fori Imperiali; 🚇 Via dei Fori Imperiali) The forums of Trajan, Augustus, Nerva and Caesar are known collectively as the Imperial Forums. These were largely buried when Mussolini bulldozed Via dei Fori Imperiali through the area in 1933, but excavations have since unearthed much of them. The standout sights are the **Mercati di Traiano** (Trajan's Markets), accessible through the Museo dei Fori Imperiali (p75), and the landmark **Colonna di Traiano** (Trajan's Column; Map p68; 🚇 Via dei Fori Imperiali).

Little recognisable remains of the **Foro di Traiano** (Trajan's Forum; Map p68), except for some pillars from the **Basilica Ulpia** (Map p68) and the Colonna di Traiano, whose minutely detailed reliefs celebrate Trajan's military victories over the Dacians (from modern-day Romania).

To the southeast, three temple columns arise from the ruins of the **Foro di Augusto** (Augustus' Forum; Map p68), now mostly under Via dei Fori Imperiali. The 30m-high wall behind the forum was built to protect it from the fires that frequently swept down from the nearby Suburra slums.

The **Foro di Nerva** (Nerva's Forum; Map p68) was also buried by Mussolini's road-building, although part of a temple dedicated to Minerva still stands. Originally, it would have connected the Foro di Augusto to the 1st-century **Foro di Vespasiano** (Vespasian's Forum; Map p68), also known as the Forum of Peace. On the other side of the road, three columns on a raised platform are the most visible remains of the **Foro di Cesare** (Caesar's Forum; Map p68).

Mercati di Traiano Museo dei Fori Imperiali   MUSEUM
(Map p68; ☑ 06 06 08; www.mercatiditraiano.it; Via IV Novembre 94; adult/reduced €11.50/9.50; ☻ 9.30am-7.30pm, last admission 6.30pm; 🚇 Via IV Novembre) This striking museum brings to life the **Mercati di Traiano**, emperor Trajan's great 2nd-century market complex, while also providing a fascinating introduction to the **Imperial Forums** with multimedia displays, explanatory panels and a smattering of archaeological artefacts.

Sculptures, friezes and the occasional bust are set out in rooms opening onto what was once the market's Great Hall. But more than the exhibits, the real highlight here is the chance to explore the echoing ruins of the vast complex. The three-storey hemicycle that housed the markets is in remarkably good shape and it doesn't take a huge leap of imagination to picture it full of traders selling everything from oil and vegetables to flowers, silks and spices.

Rising above the markets is the **Torre delle Milizie** (Militia Tower; Map p68), a 13th-century red-brick tower.

Piazza del Campidoglio   PIAZZA
(Map p68; 🚇 Piazza Venezia) This hilltop piazza, designed by Michelangelo in 1538, is one of Rome's most beautiful squares. You can reach it from the Roman Forum, but the most dramatic approach is via the graceful **Cordonata** (Map p68) staircase up from Piazza d'Ara Coeli.

The piazza is flanked by **Palazzo Nuovo** and **Palazzo dei Conservatori**, together home to the Capitoline Museums, and **Palazzo Senatorio**, seat of Rome city council. In the centre is a copy of an **equestrian statue** of Marcus Aurelius.

The original, which dates to the 2nd century AD, is in the Capitoline Museums.

★ Capitoline Museums   MUSEUM
(Musei Capitolini; Map p68; ☑ 06 06 08; www.museicapitolini.org; Piazza del Campidoglio 1; adult/reduced €11.50/9.50; ☻ 9.30am-7.30pm, last admission 6.30pm; 🚇 Piazza Venezia) Dating to 1471, the Capitoline Museums are the world's oldest public museums. Their collection of classical sculpture is one of Italy's finest, including crowd-pleasers such as the iconic *Lupa capitolina* (Capitoline Wolf), a sculpture of Romulus and Remus under a wolf, and the *Galata morente* (Dying Gaul), a moving depiction of a dying Gaul warrior. There's also a formidable picture gallery

ROME & LAZIO ROME

with masterpieces by the likes of Titian, Tintoretto, Rubens and Caravaggio.

Note that ticket prices go up when there's a temporary exhibition on.

The museums' entrance is in **Palazzo dei Conservatori**, where you'll find the original core of the sculptural collection on the first floor and the Pinacoteca (picture gallery) on the second floor.

Before you head upstairs, take a moment to admire the ancient masonry littered around the ground-floor **courtyard**, most notably a mammoth head, hand and foot. These all come from a 12m-high statue of Constantine that originally stood in the Basilica di Massenzio in the Roman Forum.

Of the sculpture on the first floor, the Etruscan *Lupa capitolina* is the most famous. Donated to the Roman people by Pope Sixtus IV, the 5th-century-BC bronze wolf stands over her suckling wards, who were added in 1471. Other highlights include the *Spinario,* a delicate 1st-century-BC bronze of a boy removing a thorn from his foot, and Gian Lorenzo Bernini's *Medusa*. Also on this floor, in the modern **Esedra di Marco Aurelio**, is the original of the equestrian statue that stands outside in Piazza del Campidoglio.

Upstairs, the museums' picture collection is on show in the **Pinacoteca**. Each room harbours masterpieces, but two stand out: the **Sala Pietro da Cortona**, which features Pietro da Cortona's famous depiction of the *Ratto delle sabine* (Rape of the Sabine Women), and the **Sala Santa Petronella**, named after Guercino's huge canvas *Seppellimento di Santa Petronilla* (The Burial of St Petronilla). This airy hall also boasts two important works by Caravaggio: *La buona ventura* (The Fortune Teller; 1595), which shows a gypsy pretending to read a young man's hand but actually stealing his ring; and *San Giovanni Battista* (St John the Baptist; 1602), a sensual and unusual depiction of the New Testament saint.

A tunnel links Palazzo dei Conservatori to **Palazzo Nuovo** on the other side of the square via the **Tabularium**, ancient Rome's central archive, beneath **Palazzo Senatorio**.

Palazzo Nuovo contains some real show-stoppers. Chief among them is the *Galata morente,* a Roman copy of a 3rd-century-BC Greek original that touchingly depicts the anguish of a dying Gaul warrior. Another superb figurative piece is the *Venere capitolina* (Capitoline Venus), a sensual yet demure portrayal of the nude goddess.

Chiesa di Santa Maria in Aracoeli CHURCH
(Map p68; Piazza Santa Maria in Aracoeli; ⌚9am-6.30pm summer, to 5.30pm winter; 🚌Piazza Venezia) Atop the steep 14th-century Aracoeli staircase, this 6th-century Romanesque church marks the highest point of the Campidoglio. Its rich interior boasts several treasures including a wooden gilt ceiling, an impressive Cosmati floor and a series of 15th-century Pinturicchio frescoes illustrating the life of St Bernadine of Siena. Its main claim to fame, though, is a wooden baby Jesus that's thought to have healing powers.

ROME'S OPTICAL ILLUSIONS

Aptly for such a theatrical city, Rome contains some magical visual tricks:

Palazzo Spada (Map p78; ☎06 683 24 09; http://galleriaspada.beniculturali.it; Piazza Capo di Ferro 13; adult/reduced €5/2.50; ⌚8.30am-7.30pm Wed-Mon; 🚌Corso Vittorio Emanuele II) This grand Mannerist *palazzo* is home to a celebrated illusion known as Borromini's *Prospettiva* (Perspective). What appears to be a 25m-long corridor lined with columns leading to a hedge and life-sized statue is, in fact, only 10m long. The sculpture, which was a later addition, is actually hip-height and the columns diminish in size not because of distance but because they actually get shorter. And look closer at that perfect-looking hedge – Borromini didn't trust the gardeners to clip a real hedge precisely enough so he made one of stone.

Chiesa di Sant'Ignazio di Loyola (Map p78; Piazza di Sant'Ignazio; ⌚7.30am-7pm Mon-Sat, 9am-7pm Sun; 🚌Via del Corso) This Jesuit church boasts two celebrated trompe l'œil frescoes by Andrea Pozzo. One cleverly depicts a fake dome, whilst the other shows St Ignatius Loyola being welcomed into paradise by Christ and the Madonna. For the best views, stand on the small yellow spot on the nave floor and look up.

In fact, the Jesus doll is a copy. The original, which was supposedly made of wood from the garden of Gethsemane, was pinched in 1994 and has never been recovered.

The church sits on the site of the Roman temple to Juno Moneta and has long had an association with the nativity. According to legend, it was here that the Tiburtine Sybil told Augustus of the coming birth of Christ.

Il Vittoriano MONUMENT
(Map p68; Piazza Venezia; ⊙9.30am-5.30pm summer, to 4.30pm winter; ◻Piazza Venezia) **FREE** Love it or loathe it, as most locals do, you can't ignore Il Vittoriano (aka the Altare della Patria; Altar of the Fatherland), the massive mountain of white marble that towers over Piazza Venezia. Begun in 1885 to honour Italy's first king, Victor Emmanuel II, it incorporates the **Museo Centrale del Risorgimento** (Map p68; www.risorgimento.it; Il Vittoriano, Piazza Venezia; adult/reduced €5/2.50; ⊙9.30am-6.30pm, closed 1st Mon of month; ◻Piazza Venezia), a small museum documenting Italian unification, and the **Tomb of the Unknown Soldier**.

For Rome's best 360-degree views, take the **Roma dal Cielo** (Map p68; Il Vittoriano , Piazza Venezia; adult/reduced €7/3.50; ⊙9.30am-6.30pm Mon-Thu, to 7.30pm Fri-Sun; ◻Piazza Venezia) lift to the top.

Housed in the monument's eastern wing is the **Complesso del Vittoriano** (Map p68; ✆06 678 06 64; Via di San Pietro in Carcere; ⊙variable; ◻Via dei Fori Imperiali), a gallery space that regularly hosts major art exhibitions.

Palazzo Venezia PALACE
(Map p68; Piazza Venezia; ◻Piazza Venezia) Built between 1455 and 1464, this was the first of Rome's great Renaissance palaces. For centuries it served as the embassy of the Venetian Republic, but it's most readily associated with Mussolini, who installed his office here in 1929, and famously made speeches from the balcony. Nowadays, it's home to the tranquil **Museo Nazionale del Palazzo Venezia** (Map p78; ✆06 678 01 31; http://museopalazzovenezia.beniculturali.it; Via del Plebiscito 118; adult/reduced €5/2.50; ⊙8.30am-7.30pm Tue-Sun; ◻Piazza Venezia) and its eclectic collection of Byzantine and early Renaissance paintings, furniture, ceramics, bronze figures, weaponry and armour.

ⓘ EXHIBITION SUPPLEMENTS

Note that many of Rome's museums and monuments regularly host temporary exhibitions. When these are on, ticket prices are increased, typically by about €3.

Basilica di San Marco BASILICA
(Map p78; Piazza di San Marco 48; ⊙9am-12.30pm & 4-6pm Tue-Sat, 10am-1pm & 4-8pm Sun; ◻Piazza Venezia) The early-4th-century Basilica di San Marco stands over the house where St Mark the Evangelist is said to have stayed while in Rome. Its main attraction is the golden 9th-century apse mosaic showing Christ flanked by several saints and Pope Gregory IV.

Bocca della Verità MONUMENT
(Mouth of Truth; Map p68; Piazza Bocca della Verità 18; donation €0.50; ⊙9.30am-5.50pm summer, to 4.50pm winter; ◻Piazza Bocca della Verità) A bearded face carved into a giant marble disc, the *Bocca della Verità* is one of Rome's most popular curiosities. Legend has it that if you put your hand in the mouth and tell a lie, the Bocca will slam shut and bite your hand off.

The mouth, which was originally part of a fountain, or possibly an ancient manhole cover, now lives in the portico of the **Chiesa di Santa Maria in Cosmedin**, a handsome medieval church.

Originally built in the 8th century, the church was given a major revamp in the 12th century, when the seven-storey bell tower and portico were added and an inlaid Cosmati floor was laid.

⊙ Centro Storico

★Pantheon CHURCH
(Map p78; Piazza della Rotonda; ⊙8.30am-7.30pm Mon-Sat, 9am-6pm Sun; ◻Largo di Torre Argentina) **FREE** A striking 2000-year-old temple, now a church, the Pantheon is the best-preserved of Rome's ancient monuments and one of the most influential buildings in the Western world. Built by Hadrian over Marcus Agrippa's earlier 27 BC temple, it has stood since around AD 125, and although its greying, pockmarked exterior looks its age, it's still a unique and exhilarating experience to pass through its vast bronze doors and gaze up at the largest unreinforced concrete dome ever built.

Centro Storico

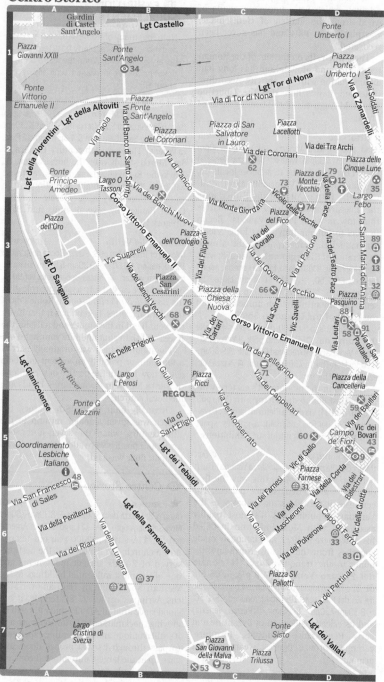

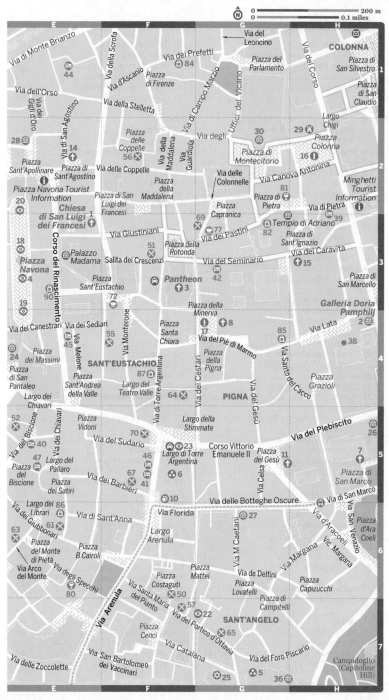

Centro Storico

For centuries the inscription under the pediment – 'M:AGRIPPA.L.F.COS.TERTIVM. FECIT' or 'Marcus Agrippa, son of Lucius, consul for the third time built this' – led scholars to think that the current building was Agrippa's original temple. However, 19th-century excavations revealed traces of an earlier temple and historians realised that Hadrian had simply kept Agrippa's original inscription.

Hadrian's temple was dedicated to the classical gods – hence the name Pantheon, a derivation of the Greek words *pan* (all) and *theos* (god) – but in AD 608 it was consecrated as a Christian church and it's now officially known as the Basilica di Santa Maria ad Martyres.

Thanks to this consecration, it was spared the worst of the medieval plundering that reduced many of Rome's ancient buildings to near dereliction. But it didn't escape entirely unscathed – its gilded-bronze roof tiles were removed and bronze from the portico was used by Bernini for his baldachin at St Peter's Basilica. These days the exterior is somewhat the worse for wear, but it's still an imposing sight with 16 Corinthian columns supporting a triangular pediment. Rivets and holes in the brickwork indicate where the original marble-veneer panels were removed.

During the Renaissance, the building was much studied – Brunelleschi used it as inspiration for his cupola in Florence – and it became an important burial chamber. In the cavernous marble-clad interior, you'll find the tomb of the artist Raphael alongside those of kings Vittorio Emanuele II and Umberto I.

The real fascination of the Pantheon, however, lies in its massive dimensions and awe-inspiring dome. Considered the ancient Romans' greatest architectural achievement, it was the largest cupola in the world until the 15th century and is still the largest unreinforced concrete dome in existence. Its harmonious appearance is due to a precisely calibrated symmetry – its diameter is exactly equal to the Pantheon's interior height of 43.3m. At its centre, the 8.7m-diameter oculus, which symbolically connected the temple with the gods, plays a vital structural role by absorbing and redistributing the dome's huge tensile forces. Rainwater enters but drains away through 22 almost-invisible holes in the sloping marble floor.

Elefantino
MONUMENT

(Map p78; Piazza della Minerva; 🚌 Largo di Torre Argentina) Just south of the Pantheon, the Elefantino is a curious and much-loved statue of a puzzled-looking elephant carrying a 6th-century-BC Egyptian obelisk. Completed in 1667 in honour of Pope Alexander VII, the elephant, symbolising strength and wisdom, was sculpted by Ercole Ferrata to a design by Bernini. The obelisk was taken from the nearby Basilica di Santa Maria Sopra Minerva.

Basilica di Santa Maria Sopra Minerva
BASILICA

(Map p78; www.santamariasopraminerva.it; Piazza della Minerva 42; ⊘ 6.45am-7pm Mon-Fri, 6.45am-12.30pm & 3.30-7pm Sat, 8am-12.30pm & 3.30-7pm Sun; 🚌 Largo di Torre Argentina) Built on the site of three pagan temples, including one to the goddess Minerva, the Dominican Basilica di Santa Maria Sopra Minerva is Rome's only Gothic church. However, little remains of the original 13th-century structure and these days the main drawcard is a minor Michelangelo sculpture and the colourful, art-rich interior.

Inside, to the right of the altar in the Cappella Carafa (also called the Cappella della Annunciazione), you'll find two superb 15th-century frescoes by Filippino Lippi and the majestic tomb of Pope Paul IV.

Left of the high altar is one of Michelangelo's lesser-known sculptures, *Cristo Risorto* (Christ Bearing the Cross; 1520), depicting Jesus carrying a cross while wearing some jarring bronze drapery. This wasn't part of the original composition and was added after the Council of Trent to preserve Christ's modesty.

An altarpiece of the *Madonna and Child* in the second chapel in the northern transept is attributed to Fra' Angelico, the Dominican friar and painter, who is also buried in the church.

The body of St Catherine of Siena, minus her head (which is in Siena), lies under the high altar, and the tombs of two Medici popes, Leo X and Clement VII, are in the apse.

★ Chiesa di San Luigi dei Francesi
CHURCH

(Map p78; Piazza di San Luigi dei Francesi 5; ⊘ 10am-12.30pm & 3-7pm, closed Thu afternoon; 🚌 Corso del Rinascimento) Church to Rome's French community since 1589, this opulent baroque *chiesa* is home to a celebrated trio

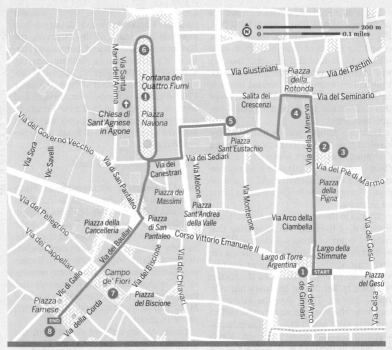

🏃 City Walk
Centro Storico

START LARGO DI TORRE ARGENTINA
END PALAZZO FARNESE
LENGTH 1.5KM; THREE HOURS

Follow this tour through Rome's tightly packed historical centre and even without trying you'll come across some of the city's best-known sights.

Start in ❶ **Largo di Torre Argentina** (p84), a busy square set around the ruins of four Republic-era temples and the site of Julius Caesar's assassination in 44 BC. From here it's a short walk up Via dei Cestari, past Bernini's much-loved ❷ **Elefantino** (p81), to the 13th-century ❸ **Basilica di Santa Maria Sopra Minerva** (p81), Rome's only Gothic church. Continue past the church to the ❹ **Pantheon** (p77), ancient Rome's best-preserved monument. Built in 27 BC, modified by Hadrian in the 2nd century AD and consecrated as a Christian church in AD 608, it's an architectural masterpiece capped by the largest unreinforced concrete dome ever built.

From the Pantheon, follow signs towards Piazza Navona, stopping en route for a coffee at ❺ **Caffè Sant'Eustachio** (p136), reckoned by many to serve the capital's best caffeine hit. A short hop away, ❻ **Piazza Navona** (p83) is central Rome's showpiece square, where you can compare the two giants of Roman baroque: Bernini, creator of the Fontana dei Quattro Fiumi, and Borromini, author of the Chiesa di Sant'Agnese in Agone.

On the other side of Corso Vittorio Emanuele II, the busy road that bisects the *centro storico* (historic centre), life centres on ❼ **Campo de' Fiori** (p84). By day this noisy square stages a colourful market but at night it transforms into a rowdy open-air pub, beloved of foreign students and lusty Romans. Just beyond it, Piazza Farnese is overlooked by the Renaissance ❽ **Palazzo Farnese** (p84), home to some superb frescoes that are said to rival those of the Sistine Chapel's. To see them, though, you'll need to book well in advance.

of Caravaggio paintings: the *Vocazione di San Matteo* (The Calling of Saint Matthew), the *Martirio di San Matteo* (The Martyrdom of Saint Matthew) and *San Matteo e l'angelo* (Saint Matthew and the Angel), known collectively as the St Matthew cycle.

These are among the earliest of Caravaggio's religious works, painted between 1600 and 1602, but they are inescapably his, featuring a down-to-earth realism and the stunning use of chiaroscuro (the bold contrast of light and dark).

Before you leave the church, take a moment to enjoy Domenichino's faded 17th-century frescoes of St Cecilia in the second chapel on the right. St Cecilia is also depicted in the altarpiece by Guido Reni, which is a copy of a work by Raphael.

Chiesa di Sant'Agostino   CHURCH

(Map p78; Piazza di Sant'Agostino 80; ⊙7.45am-noon & 4-7.30pm; ◻Corso del Rinascimento) The plain white facade of this early Renaissance church, built in the 15th century and renovated in the late 1700s, gives no indication of the impressive art inside. The most famous work is Caravaggio's *Madonna dei Pellegrini* (Madonna of the Pilgrims) but you'll also find a fresco by Raphael and a much-venerated sculpture by Jacopo Sansovino.

Museo Nazionale Romano:
Palazzo Altemps   MUSEUM

(Map p78; ✆06 3996 7700; www.coopculture.it; Piazza Sant'Apollinare 44; adult/reduced €7/3.50; ⊙9am-7.45pm Tue-Sun; ◻Corso del Rinascimento) Just north of Piazza Navona, Palazzo Altemps is a beautiful late-15th-century *palazzo*, housing the best of the Museo Nazionale Romano's formidable collection of classical sculpture. Many pieces come from the celebrated Ludovisi collection, amassed by Cardinal Ludovico Ludovisi in the 17th century.

Prize exhibits include the beautiful 5th-century *Trono Ludovisi* (Ludovisi Throne), a carved marble block whose central relief depicts a naked Venus (Aphrodite) being modestly plucked from the sea. In the neighbouring room, the *Ares Ludovisi*, a 2nd-century-BC representation of a young, clean-shaven Mars, owes its right foot to a Gian Lorenzo Bernini restoration in 1622.

Another affecting work is the sculptural group *Galata Suicida* (Gaul's Suicide), a melodramatic depiction of a Gaul knifing himself to death over a dead woman.

The building's baroque frescoes provide an exquisite decorative backdrop. The walls of the Sala delle Prospettive Dipinte are decorated with landscapes and hunting scenes seen through trompe l'oeil windows. These frescoes were painted for Cardinal Altemps, the rich nephew of Pope Pius IV (r 1560–65) who bought the *palazzo* in the late 16th century.

The museum also houses the Museo Nazionale Romano's Egyptian collection.

★ Piazza Navona   PIAZZA

(Map p78; ◻Corso del Rinascimento) With its ornate fountains, baroque *palazzi* (mansions) and colourful cast of street artists, hawkers and tourists, Piazza Navona is central Rome's elegant showcase square. Built over the 1st-century Stadio di Domiziano (Domitian's Stadium; Map p78; ✆06 4568 6100; www.stadiodomiziano.com; Via di Tor Sanguigna 3; adult/reduced €8/6; ⊙10am-7pm Sun-Fri, to 8pm Sat; ◻Corso del Rinascimento), it was paved over in the 15th century and for almost 300 years hosted the city's main market. Its grand centrepiece is Bernini's Fontana dei Quattro Fiumi (Fountain of the Four Rivers; Map p78; Piazza Navona; ◻Corso del Rinascimento), an ornate, showy fountain featuring personifications of the rivers Nile, Ganges, Danube and Plate.

Legend has it that the Nile figure is shielding his eyes from the nearby Chiesa di Sant'Agnese in Agone (Map p78; www.santagneseinagone.org; Piazza Navona; concerts €13; ⊙9.30am-12.30pm & 3.30-7pm Mon-Sat, 10am-1pm & 4-8pm Sun; ◻Corso del Rinascimento) designed by Bernini's hated rival, Francesco Borromini. In truth, Bernini completed his fountain two years before his contemporary started work on the church's facade and the gesture simply indicated that the source of the Nile was unknown at the time.

The Fontana del Moro (Map p78; Piazza Navona; ◻Corso del Rinascimento) at the southern end of the square was designed by Giacomo della Porta in 1576. Bernini added the Moor holding a dolphin in the mid-17th century, but the surrounding Tritons are 19th-century copies. At the northern end of the piazza, the 19th-century Fontana del Nettuno (Map p78; Piazza Navona; ◻Corso del Rinascimento) depicts Neptune fighting with a sea monster, surrounded by sea nymphs.

The piazza's largest building is the 17th-century Palazzo Pamphilj (Map p78; Piazza Navona; ◻Corso del Rinascimento), built for Pope Innocent X and now home to the Brazilian Embassy.

ROME & LAZIO ROME

Museo di Roma
MUSEUM

(Map p78; ☑06 06 08; www.museodiroma.it; Piazza di San Pantaleo 10 & Piazza Navona 2; adult/reduced €9.50/7.50; ⊗10am-7pm Tue-Sun; ☐Corso Vittorio Emanuele II) The baroque Palazzo Braschi houses the Museo di Roma's eclectic collection of paintings, photographs, etchings, clothes and furniture, charting the history of Rome from the Middle Ages to the early 20th century. But as striking as the collection is the 17th-century *palazzo* itself, with its courtyard, monumental baroque staircase, and frescoed halls.

Chiesa di Santa Maria della Pace & Chiostro del Bramante
CHURCH, GALLERY

(Map p78; www.chiostrodelbramante.it; Via Arco della Pace 5; exhibitions adult/reduced €13/11; ⊗church 9am-11.50pm Mon, Wed & Sat, cloister 10am-8pm; ☐Corso del Rinascimento) Tucked away in the back streets behind Piazza Navona, this small church boasts a columned semi-circular facade by Pietro da Cortona and a celebrated Raphael fresco, *Sibille* (Sibyls; c 1515). Next door, the Chiostro del Bramante (Bramante Cloister) is a masterpiece of High Renaissance architectural styling that is now used to stage art exhibitions and cultural events.

Campo de' Fiori
PIAZZA

(Map p78; ☐Corso Vittorio Emanuele II) Noisy, colourful 'Il Campo' is a major focus of Roman life: by day it hosts one of Rome's best-known markets, while at night it morphs into a raucous open-air pub. For centuries the square was the site of public executions, and it was here that the philosopher Giordano Bruno was burned at the stake for heresy in 1600. The spot is marked by a sinister statue of the hooded monk, created by Ettore Ferrari and unveiled in 1889.

Palazzo Farnese
HISTORIC BUILDING

(Map p78; www.inventerrome.com; Piazza Farnese; admission €5; ⊗guided tours 3pm, 4pm & 5pm Mon, Wed & Fri; ☐Corso Vittorio Emanuele II) Now home of the French Embassy, this formidable Renaissance *palazzo,* one of Rome's finest, was started in 1514 by Antonio da Sangallo the Younger, continued by Michelangelo and finished by Giacomo della Porta. Inside, it boasts a series of frescoes by Annibale Carracci that are said by some to rival Michelangelo's in the Sistine Chapel. The highlight, painted between 1597 and 1608, is the monumental ceiling fresco *Amori degli Dei* (The Loves of the Gods) in the recently restored Galleria dei Carracci.

Visits to the *palazzo* are by 45-minute guided tour only, for which you'll need to book at least a week in advance – see the website for details. Photo ID is required for entry and children under 10 are not admitted.

The twin fountains in the square outside are enormous granite baths taken from the Terme di Caracalla.

Largo di Torre Argentina
PIAZZA

(Map p78; ☐Largo di Torre Argentina) A busy transport hub, the Largo di Torre Argentina is set around the sunken Area Sacra (Map p78; Largo di Torre Argentina; ☐Largo di Torre Argentina) and the remains of four Republican-era temples, all built between the 2nd and 4th centuries BC. These ruins, which are among the oldest in the city, are out of bounds to humans but home to a thriving population of around 250 stray cats and a volunteer-run cat sanctuary (Map p78; www.romancats.com; Largo di Torre Argentina; ⊗noon-6pm daily; ☐Largo di Torre Argentina).

On the piazza's western flank, Teatro Argentina, Rome's premier theatre, stands near the spot where Julius Caesar was assassinated in 44 BC.

Chiesa del Gesù
CHURCH

(Map p78; www.chiesadelgesu.org; Piazza del Gesù; ⊗7am-12.30pm & 4-7.45pm, St Ignatius rooms 4-6pm Mon-Sat, 10am-noon Sun; ☐Largo di Torre Argentina) An imposing example of Counter-Reformation architecture, Rome's most important Jesuit church is a treasure trove of baroque art. Headline works include a swirling vault fresco by Giovanni Battista Gaulli (aka Il Baciccia), and Andrea del Pozzo's opulent tomb for Jesuit founder Ignatius Loyola. The Spanish saint lived in the church from 1544 until his death in 1556 and you can visit his private rooms to the right of the main building.

The church, which was consecrated in 1584, is fronted by an impressive and much-copied facade by Giacomo della Porta. But more than the masonry, the real draw here is the church's lavish interior. The cupola frescoes and stucco decoration were designed by Baciccia, who also painted the hynotic ceiling fresco, the *Trionfo del Nome di Gesù* (Triumph of the Name of Jesus).

In the northern transept, the Cappella di Sant'Ignazio houses the tomb of Ignatius Loyola, the Spanish soldier and saint who founded the Jesuits in 1540. The altar-tomb, designed by baroque maestro Andrea Pozzo,

MUSEUM DISCOUNT CARDS

Serious museum-goers should consider:

→ **Classic Roma Pass** (€36; valid for three days) Provides free admission to two museums or sites, as well as reduced entry to extra sites, unlimited city transport and discounted entry to other exhibitions and events.

→ **48-hour Roma Pass** (€28; valid for 48 hours) Gives free admission to one museum or site and then as per the classic pass.

→ **Archaeologia Card** (adult/reduced €27.50/17.50; valid for seven days) Covers the Colosseum, Palatino, Roman Forum, Terme di Caracalla, Palazzo Altemps, Palazzo Massimo alle Terme, Terme di Diocleziano, Crypta Balbi, Mausoleo di Cecilia Metella and Villa dei Quintili.

These are all available at participating museums or online at www.coopculture.it. You can also get the Roma Pass at tourist information points.

is an opulent marble-and-bronze affair with lapis lazuli–encrusted columns, and, on top, a lapis lazuli globe representing the Trinity. On either side are sculptures whose titles neatly encapsulate the Jesuit ethos: to the left, *Fede che vince l'Idolatria* (Faith Defeats Idolatry); and on the right, *Religione che flagella l'Eresia* (Religion Lashing Heresy).

Museo Nazionale Romano: Crypta Balbi
MUSEUM

(Map p78; ☑06 3996 7700; www.coopculture.it; Via delle Botteghe Oscure 31; adult/reduced €7/3.50; ☯9am-7.45pm Tue-Sun; ☐Via delle Botteghe Oscure) The least known of the Museo Nazionale Romano's four museums, the Crypta Balbi sits over the ruins of several medieval buildings, themselves set atop the Teatro di Balbo (13 BC). Archaeological finds illustrate the urban development of the surrounding area, while the museum's underground excavations, visitable by guided tour, provide an interesting insight into Rome's multi-layered past.

Jewish Ghetto
NEIGHBOURHOOD

(Map p78; ☐Lungotevere de' Cenci) Centred on lively Via Portico d'Ottavia, the Jewish Ghetto is a wonderfully atmospheric area studded with artisans' studios, vintage clothes shops, kosher bakeries and popular trattorias.

Rome's Jewish community dates back to the 2nd century BC, making it one of the oldest in Europe. At one point there were as many as 13 synagogues in the city but Titus's defeat of Jewish rebels in Jerusalem in AD 70 changed the status of Rome's Jews from citizen to slave. Confinement to the Ghetto came in 1555 when Pope Paul IV ushered in

a period of official intolerance that lasted, on and off, until the 20th century. Ironically, though, confinement meant that Jewish cultural and religious identity survived intact.

Museo Ebraico di Roma
SYNAGOGUE, MUSEUM

(Jewish Museum of Rome; Map p78; ☑06 6840 0661; www.museoebraico.roma.it; Via Catalana; adult/reduced €11/8; ☯10am-6.15pm Sun-Thu, 9am-3.15pm Fri summer, 10am-4.15pm Sun-Thu, 9am-1.15pm Fri winter; ☐Lungotevere de' Cenci) The historical, cultural and artistic heritage of Rome's Jewish community is chronicled in this small but engrossing museum. Housed in the city's early-20th-century synagogue, Europe's second largest, it displays parchments, precious fabrics, marble carvings, and a collection of 17th- and 18th-century silverware. Documents and photos attest to life in the Ghetto and the hardships suffered by the city's Jewry during WWII.

Area Archeologica del Teatro di Marcello e del Portico d'Ottavia
ARCHAEOLOGICAL SITE

(Map p78; entrances Via del Teatro di Marcello 44 & Via Portico d'Ottavia 29; ☯9am-7pm summer, 9am-6pm winter; ☐Via del Teatro di Marcello) **FREE** To the east of the Jewish Ghetto, the **Teatro di Marcello** (Theatre of Marcellus; Map p78; Via del Teatro di Marcello) is the star turn of this dusty archaeological area. This 20,000-seat mini-Colosseum was planned by Julius Caesar and completed in 11 BC by Augustus, who named it after a favourite nephew, Marcellus. In the 16th century, a *palazzo*, which now contains several exclusive apartments, was built on top of the original structure.

Beyond the theatre, the **Portico d'Ottavia**, currently covered in scaffolding, is the oldest *quadriporto* (four-sided porch) in Rome. The dilapidated columns and fragmented pediment once formed part of a vast rectangular portico, supported by 300 columns, that measured 132m by 119m. Erected by a builder called Octavius in 146 BC, it was rebuilt in 23 BC by Augustus, who kept the name in honour of his sister Octavia. From the Middle Ages until the late 19th century, the portico housed Rome's fish market.

◎ Tridente, Trevi & the Quirinale

★ Piazza di Spagna & the Spanish Steps
PIAZZA

(Map p88; M Spagna) A magnet for visitors since the 18th century, the Spanish Steps (Scalinata della Trinità dei Monti) provide a perfect people-watching perch and you'll almost certainly find yourself taking stock here at some point.

Piazza di Spagna was named after the Spanish Embassy to the Holy See, although the staircase, designed by the Italian Francesco de Sanctis and built in 1725 with a legacy from the French, leads to the French Chiesa della Trinità dei Monti. This landmark church, which was commissioned by King Louis XII of France and consecrated in 1585, commands memorable views and boasts some wonderful frescoes by Daniele da Volterra, including a masterful Deposizione (Deposition). At the foot of the steps, the Barcaccia (the 'sinking boat' fountain) is believed to be by Pietro Bernini, father of the more famous Gian Lorenzo. In 2015 the fountain was damaged by Dutch football fans, and the Dutch subsequently offered to repair it. To the southeast of the piazza, adjacent Piazza Mignanelli is dominated by the Colonna dell'Immacolata, built in 1857 to celebrate Pope Pius IX's declaration of the Immaculate Conception.

Keats–Shelley House
MUSEUM

(Map p88; ☑06 678 42 35; www.keats-shelley-house.org; Piazza di Spagna 26; adult/reduced €5/4, ticket gives discount for Casa di Goethe; ☺10am-1pm & 2-6pm Mon-Fri, 11am-2pm & 3-6pm Sat; M Spagna) The Keats–Shelley House is where Romantic poet John Keats died of tuberculosis at the age of 25, in February 1821. A year later, fellow poet Percy Bysshe Shelley drowned off the coast of Tuscany. The small apartment evokes the impoverished lives of the poets, and is now a small museum crammed with memorabilia, from faded letters to death masks.

Villa Medici
PALACE

(Map p88; ☑06 6 76 11; www.villamedici.it; Viale Trinità dei Monti 1; gardens adult/reduced €12/6; ☺tours Tue-Sun in Italian, French & English, check website for current times; cafe 11am-6pm Tue-Sun; M Spagna) This sumptuous Renaissance palace was built for Cardinal Ricci da Montepulciano in 1540 and it remained in Medici hands until 1801, when Napoleon acquired it for the French Academy. Take a tour to see the wonderful landscaped gardens, the cardinal's painted apartments, and incredible views over Rome. The villa's most famous resident was Galileo, who was imprisoned here between 1630 and 1633 during his trial for heresy, though Keith Richards and Anita Pallenberg stayed here in the 1960s. There are up to 19 resident French-speaking artists and musicians, with exhibitions and performances at the end of February and June. There's a lovely, high-ceilinged cafe that sells reasonably priced panini and light lunches (€3 to €12), plus *prosecco* (sparkling

---

ART & POLITICS ON VIA DEL CORSO

On Via del Corso, the arrow-straight road that links Piazza Venezia to Piazza del Popolo, you'll find one of Rome's finest private art galleries. The **Galleria Doria Pamphilj** (Map p78; www.dopart.it; Via del Corso 305; adult/reduced €11/7.50; ☺ 9am-7pm, last admission 6pm ◻ Via del Corso) houses an extraordinary collection of works by the likes of Raphael, Tintoretto, Brueghel, Titian, Caravaggio, Bernini and Velázquez. Masterpieces abound but the undisputed star is Velázquez' portrait of Pope Innocent X, who grumbled that the depiction was 'too real'.

A short walk to the north of the gallery, the 30m-high **Colonna di Marco Aurelio** (Map p78; Piazza Colonna; ◻ Via del Corso) heralds the presence of **Palazzo Chigi** (Map p78; www.governo.it; Piazza Colonna 370; ☺ guided visits 9am-1pm Sat Oct-May, bookings required; ◻ Via del Corso) **FREE**, the official residence of the Italian prime minister. Next door, on Piazza di Montecitorio, the Bernini-designed **Palazzo di Montecitorio** (Map p78; ☑800 012955; www.camera.it; Piazza di Montecitorio; ☺ guided visits noon-2.30pm 1st Sun of month; ◻ Via del Corso) **FREE** is home to Italy's Chamber of Deputies.

wine; €4). You can also stay at the villa, for a price: see the website.

★ **Piazza del Popolo** PIAZZA

(Map p88; MFlaminio) This dazzling piazza was laid out in 1538 to provide a grandiose entrance to what was then Rome's main northern gateway. It has since been remodelled several times, most recently by Giuseppe Valadier in 1823.

Guarding its southern approach are Carlo Rainaldi's twin 17th-century churches, **Chiesa di Santa Maria dei Miracoli** (Map p88; MFlaminio) and **Chiesa di Santa Maria in Montesanto** (Map p88; MFlaminio). In the centre, the 36m-high obelisk (Map p88; MFlaminio) was brought by Augustus from ancient Egypt and first stood in Circo Massimo.

On the northern flank, the **Porta del Popolo** (Map p88; MFlaminio) was created by Bernini in 1655 to celebrate Queen Christina of Sweden's defection to Catholicism, while rising to the east is the viewpoint of the **Pincio Hill Gardens** (Map p88; MFlaminio).

Chiesa di Santa Maria del Popolo CHURCH

(Map p88; Piazza del Popolo; ⊘7am-noon & 4-7pm Mon-Sat, 7.30am-1.30pm & 4.30-7.30pm Sun; MFlaminio) A magnificent repository of art, this is one of Rome's earliest and richest Renaissance churches. Of the numerous works of art on display, it is the two Caravaggio masterpieces that draw the most onlookers – the *Conversion of Saul* and the *Crucifixion of St Peter* – but it contains other fine works, including several by Pinturicchio and Bernini. The first chapel was built here in 1099 to exorcise the ghost of Nero, who was secretly buried on this spot and whose ghost was thought to haunt the area. It had since been overhauled, but the church's most important makeover came when Bramante renovated the presbytery and choir in the early 16th century and Pinturicchio added a series of frescoes. Bernini further reworked the church in the 17th century.

Look out for Raphael's **Cappella Chigi**, which was completed by Bernini some 100 years later.

Museo dell'Ara Pacis MUSEUM

(Map p88; ☑06 06 08; http://en.arapacis.it; Lungotevere in Auga; adult/reduced €10.50/8.50, audioguide €4; ⊘9am-7pm, last admission 6pm; MFlaminio) The first modern construction in Rome's historic centre since WWII, Richard Meier's controversial and widely detested glass-and-marble pavilion houses the *Ara Pacis Augustae* (Altar of Peace), Augustus' great monument to peace. One of the most important works of ancient Roman sculpture, the vast marble altar – measuring 11.6m by 10.6m by 3.6m – was completed in 13 BC. The altar was originally positioned near Piazza San Lorenzo in Lucina, slightly to the southeast of its current site. The location was calculated so that on Augustus' birthday the shadow of a huge sundial on Campus Martius would fall directly on it. Over the centuries the altar fell victim to Rome's avid art collectors, and panels ended up in the Medici collection (see the garlanded reliefs embedded in the walls of the Villa Medici), the Vatican and the Louvre. However, in 1936 Mussolini unearthed the remaining parts and decided to reassemble them in the present location.

Of the reliefs, the most important depicts Augustus at the head of a procession, followed by priests, the general Marcus Agrippa and the entire imperial family.

Mausoleo di Augusto MONUMENT

(Map p88; Piazza Augo Imperatore; ☐Piazza Augusto Imperatore) This mausoleum was built in 28 BC and is the last resting place of Augustus, who was buried here in AD 14, and his favourite nephew and heir Marcellus. Mussolini had it restored in 1936 with an eye to being buried here himself. Once one of Ancient Rome's most imposing monuments, it's now an unkempt mound of earth, smelly and surrounded by unsightly fences. Work is allegedly ongoing, but there hasn't been much discernible development at the site.

★ **Trevi Fountain** FOUNTAIN

(Fontana di Trevi; Map p88; Piazza di Trevi; MBarberini) The Fontana di Trevi, scene of Anita Ekberg's dip in *La Dolce Vita,* is a flamboyant baroque ensemble of mythical figures and wild horses. It takes up the entire side

---

THE TREVI COINS

On an average day around €3000 are thrown into the Trevi Fountain. This is collected daily and handed over to the Catholic charity Caritas. The fountain's yield has increased noticeably since 2012 when city authorities clamped down on thieves helping themselves and introduced legislation making it illegal to remove coins from the water.

Tridente & Trevi

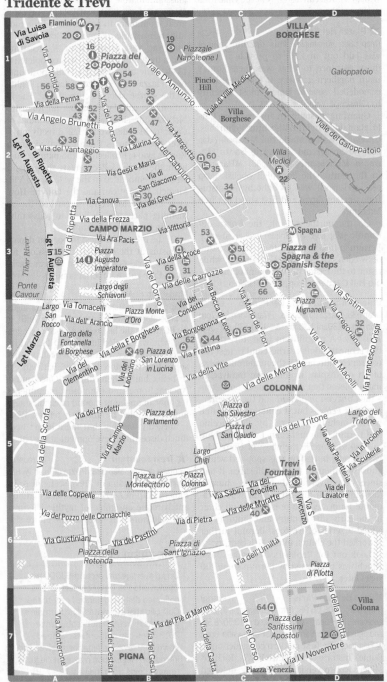

of the 17th-century Palazzo Poli. A Fendi-sponsored restoration was completed in 2015, and the fountain now gleams brighter than it has for years.

The tradition is to toss a coin into the water, thus ensuring that you'll return to Rome.

On average about €3000 is thrown in every day. The fountain's design, the work of Nicola Salvi in 1732, depicts Neptune's chariot being led by Tritons with seahorses – one wild, one docile – representing the moods of the sea. In the niche to the left of Neptune a statue represents Abundance; to the right is Salubrity. The water comes from the *aqua virgo*, a 1st-century-BC underground aqueduct, and the name Trevi refers to the *tre vie* (three roads) that converge at the fountain.

The fountain gets very busy during the day, so it's worth trying to visit later in the evening when you can appreciate its foaming majesty without such great hordes.

Galleria Colonna   GALLERY
(Map p88; ☏ 06 678 43 50; www.galleriacolonna.it; Via della Pilotta 17; adult/reduced €12/10; ⊗ 9am-1.15pm Sat, closed Aug; ⌷ Via IV Novembre) The only part of Palazzo Colonna open to the public, this opulent 17th-century gallery houses the Colonna family's private art collection. It's not the capital's largest collection but with works by Salvatore Rosa, Guido Reni, Guercino and Annibale Carracci, it's well worth the ticket price

The gallery's six rooms are crowned by glorious ceiling frescoes, all dedicated to Marcantonio Colonna, the family's greatest ancestor, who defeated the Turks at the naval Battle of Lepanto in 1571. Works by Giovanni Coli and Filippo Gherardi in the Great Hall, Sebastiano Ricci in the Landscapes Room and Giuseppe Bartolomeo Chiari in the Throne Room commemorate his efforts. Of the paintings on display, Annibale Carracci's *Mangiafagioli* (The Bean Eater) is generally considered the outstanding masterpiece. Note also the cannonball lodged in the gallery's marble stairs, a vivid reminder of the 1849 siege of Rome. A wing opened more recently to the public includes the sumptuous Chapel Hall and the rich 17th-century Artemisia tapestries collection. From May to October a terrace cafe is open.

Palazzo del Quirinale   PALACE
(Map p88; ☏ 06 4 69 91; www.quirinale.it; Piazza del Quirinale; admission €10, ½hr tour €1.50, 2½hr tour €10; ⊗ 9.30am-4pm Tue, Wed & Fri-Sun, closed

Tridente & Trevi

Aug; MBarberini) Overlooking Piazza del Quirinale, this immense palace is the official residence of Italy's head of state, the Presidente della Repubblica. For almost three centuries it was the pope's summer residence, but in 1870 Pope Pius IX begrudgingly handed the keys over to Italy's new king. Later, in 1948, it was given to the Italian state.

You can visit by booking at least five days ahead; the shorter tour visits the sumptuous reception rooms, while the longer tour includes the interiors as well as the gardens and the carriages. On the other side of the piazza, the palace's former stables, the **Scuderie Papali al Quir-**inale (Map p88; ☏06 3996 7500; www.scuderiequirinale.it; Via XXIV Maggio 16; tickets around €12), host excellent art exhibitions.

Chiesa di Sant'Andrea al Quirinale
CHURCH
(Map p88; Via del Quirinale 29; ⊘8.30am-noon & 2.30-6pm winter, 9am-noon & 3-6pm summer; ☐Via Nazionale) It's said that in his old age Bernini liked to come and enjoy the peace of this late-17th-century church, regarded by many as one of his greatest. Faced with severe space limitations, he managed to produce a sense of grandeur by designing an elliptical floor plan with a series of chapels opening onto the central area.

Chiesa di San Carlo alle Quattro Fontane
CHURCH

(Map p88; Via del Quirinale 23; ⊙10am-1pm & 3-6pm Mon-Fri, 10am-1pm Sat, noon-1pm Sun; ▣Via Nazionale) This tiny church is a masterpiece of Roman baroque. It was Borromini's first church, and the play of convex and concave surfaces and the dome illuminated by hidden windows cleverly transform the small space into a place of light and beauty.

The church, completed in 1641, stands at the intersection known as the Quattro Fontane, after the late-16th-century fountains on its four corners, representing Fidelity, Strength and the rivers Arno and Tiber. A clean-up job was completed in 2015, and they look better than they have for years – just watch out for traffic as you admire them.

★Galleria Nazionale d'Arte Antica: Palazzo Barberini
GALLERY

(Map p88; ☑06 3 28 10; www.galleriabarberini. beniculturali.it; Via delle Quattro Fontane 13; adult/reduced €7/3.50, incl Palazzo Corsini, valid 3 days €9/4.50; ⊙8.30am-7pm Tue-Sun; Ⓜ Barberini) Commissioned to celebrate the Barberini family's rise to papal power, Palazzo Barberini is a sumptuous baroque palace that impresses even before you go inside and start on the breathtaking art. Many high-profile architects worked on it, including rivals Bernini and Borromini: the former contributed a large squared staircase, the latter a helicoidal one.

Amid the masterpieces, don't miss Pietro da Cortona's *Il Trionfo della Divina Provvidenza* (Triumph of Divine Providence; 1632–39), the most spectacular of the palazzo's ceiling frescoes in the 1st-floor main salon. Other must-sees include Hans Holbein's famous portrait of a pugnacious Henry VIII (c 1540), Filippo Lippi's luminous *Annunciazione e due devoti* (Annunciation with two Kneeling Donors) and Raphael's *La fornarina* (The Baker's Girl), a portrait of his mistress who worked in a bakery in Trastevere. Works by Caravaggio include *San Francesco d'Assisi in meditazione* (St Francis in Meditation), *Narciso* (Narcissus; 1571–1610) and the mesmerisingly horrific *Giuditta e Oloferne* (Judith Beheading Holophernes; c 1597–1600).

Piazza Barberini
PIAZZA

(Map p88; Ⓜ Barberini) More a traffic thoroughfare than a place to linger, this noisy square is named after the Barberini family, one of Rome's great dynastic clans. In the centre, the Bernini-designed Fontana del Tritone (Fountain of the Triton; Map p88) depicts the sea-god Triton blowing a stream of water from a conch while seated in a large scallop shell supported by four dolphins. Bernini also crafted the Fontana delle Api (Fountain of the Bees; Map p88) in the northeastern corner, again for the Barberini family, whose crest featured three bees in flight.

Convento dei Cappuccini
MUSEUM

(Map p88; ☑06 487 11 85; Via Vittorio Veneto 27; adult/reduced €8/6, audioguide €4; ⊙9am-7pm; Ⓜ Barberini) This church and convent complex has turned its extraordinary Capuchin cemetery into cash by adding a flashy museum and bumping up the entrance fee. However, it's still worth visiting what is possibly Rome's strangest sight: crypt chapels where everything from the picture frames to the light fittings is made of human bones. The multimedia museum tells the story of the Capuchin order of monks, including a work attributed to Caravaggio: *St Francis in Meditation*.

Between 1528 and 1870 the resident Capuchin monks used the bones of 4000 of their departed brothers to create this mesmerising, macabre memento mori (reminder of death). There's an arch crafted from hundreds of skulls, vertebrae used as fleurs-de-lis and light fixtures made of femurs. Happy holidays!

◉ Vatican City, Borgo & Prati

The Vatican, the world's smallest sovereign state (a mere 0.44 sq km), sits atop the low-lying Vatican hill just a few hundred metres west of the Tiber. Centred on the domed bulk of St Peter's Basilica, it is the capital of the Catholic world and jealous guardian of one of the world's greatest artistic patrimonies.

The state, established under the terms of the 1929 Lateran Treaty, is the modern vestige of the Papal States, the papal fiefdom that ruled Rome and much of central Italy until Italian unification in 1861. As part of the agreement, signed by Mussolini and Pope Pius XI, the Holy See was also given extraterritorial authority over a further 28 sites in and around Rome, including the basilicas of San Giovanni in Laterano, Santa Maria Maggiore and San Paolo Fuori le Mura.

Vatican City, Borgo & Prati

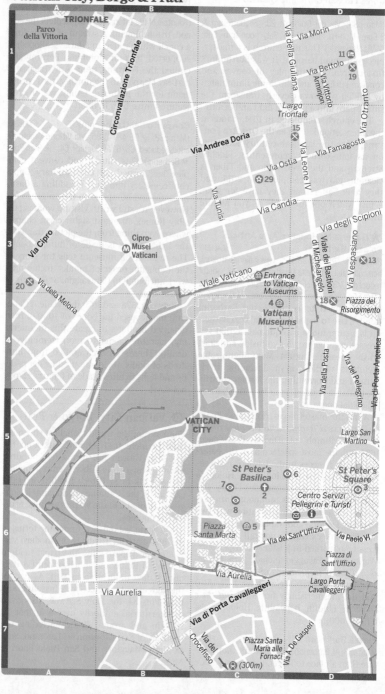

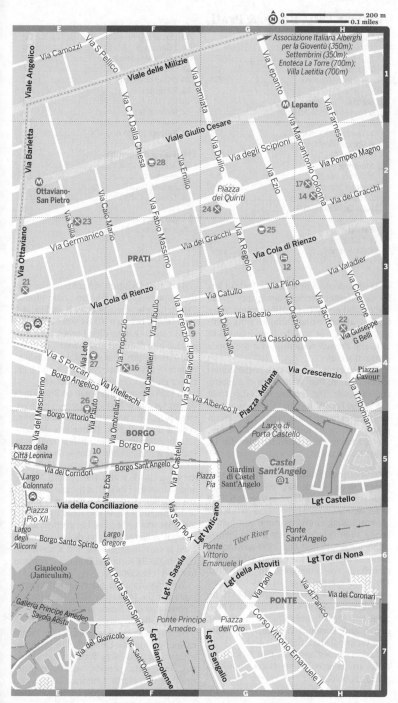

Associazione Italiana Alberghi
per la Gioventù (350m);
Settembrini (350m);
Enoteca La Torre (700m);
Villa Laetitia (700m)

0   200 m
0   0.1 miles

Via Camozzi
Viale Angelico
Via S Pellico
Viale delle Milizie
Via Damiata
Via Leparito

Ⓜ Lepanto

Via Farnese

Via C A Dalla Chiesa
Viale Giulio Cesare
Via Duilio
Via degli Scipioni
Via Marcantonio Colonna
Via Pompeo Magno

Via Barletta

Ⓜ Ottaviano-San Pietro
Via Caio Mario
Via Germanico
Via Emilio
Piazza dei Quiriti
Via Ezio
17 ✕
14 ✕
Via dei Gracchi

🍴 28

🍴 23

Via Silla
Via Fabio Massimo
24 ✕
Via dei Gracchi
Via A Regolo
🍴 25
Via Cola di Rienzo

PRATI

Via Ottaviano
Via Cola di Rienzo
Via Catullo
Via Plinio
🏨 12
Via Valadier
Via Cicerone

🍴 21

Via Tibullo
Via Terenzio
Via Boezio
Via Orazio
Via Tacito
22 ✕
Via Guiseppe G Belli

🍴 9
Via Della Valle
Via Cassiodoro

🏠 🏠
Via Leto
Via S Porcari
27 ✕
Via Properzio
Via Cancellieri
Via S Pallavicini
Via Crescenzio
Piazza Cavour

Borgo Angelico
Via Vitelleschi
16 ✕
Via Alberico II
Piazza Adriana
Via Triboniano

Via del Mascherino
Borgo Vittorio
26 🏠
Via Plauto
Via Ombrellari
BORGO
Borgo Pio
Largo di Porta Castello

Piazza della Città Leonina
🏨 10
Borgo Sant'Angelo
Via P Castello
Castel Sant'Angelo
🏛 1

Largo Colonnato
Via dei Corridori
Via Erba
Piazza Pia
Giardini di Castel Sant'Angelo
Lgt Castello

Piazza Pio XII
Via della Conciliazione

Largo degli Alicorni
Borgo Santo Spirito
Largo I Gregore
Via San Pio X
Lgt Vaticano
Tiber River
Ponte Sant'Angelo
Lgt Tor di Nona

Gianicolo (Janiculum)
Via di Porta Santo Spirito
Lgt in Sassia
Ponte Vittorio Emanuele II
Lgt della Altoviti
Via Paola
PONTE
Via di Panico
Via dei Coronari

Galleria Principe Amedeo Savoia Aosta
Ponte Principe Amedeo
Piazza dell'Oro
Corso Vittorio Emanuele II

Via del Gianicolo
Vic Sant'Onofrio
Lgt Gianicolense
Lgt D Sangallo

Vatican City, Borgo & Prati

As an independent state, the Vatican has its own postal service, newspaper, radio station and army. The nattily dressed Swiss Guards, all practising Catholics from Switzerland, were first used by Pope Julius II in 1506 and are still responsible for the pope's personal security.

The Vatican's current look is the culmination of more than 1000 years of chipping and chopping. The Leonine walls date from 846 when Leo IV had them put up after a series of Saracen raids, while the Vatican palace, now home to the Vatican Museums, was originally constructed by Eugenius III in the 12th century.

★ **St Peter's Basilica** BASILICA
(Basilica di San Pietro; Map p92; www.vatican.va; St Peter's Sq; ⊙ 7am-7pm summer, to 6.30pm winter; Ⓜ Ottaviano-San Pietro) FREE In this city of outstanding churches, none can hold a candle to St Peter's (Basilica di San Pietro), Italy's largest, richest and most spectacular basilica. Built atop an earlier 4th-century church, it was completed in 1626 after 120 years' construction. Its lavish interior contains many spectacular works of art, including three of Italy's most celebrated masterpieces: Michelangelo's *Pietà*, his soaring dome, and Bernini's 29m-high baldachin over the papal altar.

Expect queues and note that strict dress codes are enforced, so no shorts, miniskirts or bare shoulders.

The original church was commissioned by the emperor Constantine and built around 349 on the site where St Peter is said to have been buried between AD 64 and 67. But like many churches in medieval times, it eventually fell into disrepair and it wasn't until the mid-15th century that efforts were made to restore it, first by Pope Nicholas V and then, rather more successfully, by Julius II.

In 1506 construction began on Bramante's design for a new basilica based on a Greek-cross plan, with four equal arms and a huge central dome. But on Bramante's death in 1514, building ground to a halt as architects, including Raphael and Antonio da Sangallo, tried to modify his original plans. Little progress was made and it wasn't until Michelangelo took over in 1547 at the age of 72 that the situation changed. Michelangelo simplified Bramante's plans and drew up designs for what was to become his greatest architectural achievement, the dome. He never lived to see it built, though, and it was left to Giacomo della Porta and Domenico Fontana to finish it in 1590.

With the dome in place, Carlo Maderno inherited the project in 1605. He designed the monumental facade and lengthened the nave towards the piazza.

Free English-language tours of the basilica are run from the Centro Servizi Pellegrini e Turisti at 9am every Tuesday and Thursday. In certain periods, volunteers from the Pontifical North American College also lead tours. The timetable for these varies, but they typically start at 2.15pm Monday through Friday.

➡ Facade

Built between 1608 and 1612, Carlo Maderno's immense facade is 48m high and 118.6m wide. Eight 27m-high columns support the upper attic on which 13 statues stand representing Christ the Redeemer, St John the Baptist and the 11 apostles. The central balcony is known as the Loggia della Benedizione, and it's from here that the pope delivers his *Urbi et Orbi* blessing at Christmas and Easter.

➡ Interior

The cavernous 187m-long interior covers more than 15,000 sq m and contains many artistic masterpieces, including Michelangelo's hauntingly beautiful *Pietà* at the head of the right nave. Sculpted when he was only 25, it is the only work he ever signed – his signature is etched into the sash across the Madonna's breast.

Nearby, a red floor disk marks the spot where Charlemagne and later Holy Roman Emperors were crowned by the pope.

Dominating the centre of the basilica is Bernini's famous baldachin. Supported by four spiral columns and made with bronze taken from the Pantheon, it stands over the high altar, which itself sits on the site of St Peter's grave. The pope is the only priest permitted to serve at the altar.

Above, Michelangelo's dome soars to a height of 119m. Based on Brunelleschi's design for the Duomo in Florence, the towering cupola is supported by four stone piers named after the saints whose statues adorn the Bernini-designed niches – Longinus, Helena, Veronica and Andrew.

At the base of the Pier of St Longinus is Arnolfo di Cambio's much-loved 13th-century bronze **statue of St Peter**, whose right foot has been worn down by centuries of caresses.

➡ Dome

From the dome (Map p92; with/without lift €7/5; ⊙ 8am-5.45pm summer, to 4.45pm winter; Ⓜ Ottaviano-San Pietro) entrance on the right of the basilica's main portico, you can walk the 551 steps to the top or take a small lift halfway and then follow on foot for the last 320 steps. Either way, it's a long, steep climb. But make it to the top, and you're rewarded with stunning rooftop views.

PAPAL AUDIENCES
....

At 11am every Wednesday, the pope addresses his flock at the Vatican (in July and August in Castel Gandolfo near Rome). For details of how to apply for free tickets, see the **Vatican website** (www.vatican.va/various/prefettura/index_en.html).

When he's in Rome, the pope blesses the crowd in St Peter's Square on Sunday at noon. No tickets are required.

➡ Museo Storico Artistico

Accessed from the left nave, the **Museo Storico Artistico** (Tesoro; Map p92; adult/reduced €7/5; ⊙ 9am-6.15pm summer, to 5.15pm winter; Ⓜ Ottaviano-San Pietro) sparkles with sacred relics, including a tabernacle by Donatello and the 6th-century *Crux Vaticana*, a jewel-studded cross that was a gift of the emperor Justinian II.

➡ Vatican Grottoes

Extending beneath the basilica, the **Vatican Grottoes** (Map p92; ⊙ 9am-6pm summer, to 5pm winter; Ⓜ Ottaviano-San Pietro) **FREE** contain the tombs and sarcophagi of numerous popes, as well as several huge columns from the original 4th-century basilica. The entrance is in the Pier of St Andrew.

➡ Tomb of St Peter

Excavations beneath the basilica have uncovered part of the original church and what archaeologists believe is the **Tomb of St Peter** (Map p92; 06 6988 5318; admission €13, over 15s only; Ⓜ Ottaviano-San Pietro). In 1942 the bones of an elderly, strongly built man were found in a box hidden behind a wall covered by pilgrims' graffiti. And while the Vatican has never definitively claimed that the bones belong to St Peter, in 1968 Pope Paul VI said that they had been identified in a way that the Vatican considered 'convincing'.

The excavations can only be visited by guided tour. To book a spot, email the Ufficio Scavi (scavi@fsp.va) as far in advance as possible.

★ St Peter's Square   PIAZZA

(Piazza San Pietro; Map p92; Ⓜ Ottaviano-San Pietro) Overlooked by St Peter's Basilica, the Vatican's central square was laid out between 1656 and 1667 to a design by Gian Lorenzo Bernini. Seen from above, it resembles a giant keyhole with two semicircular colonnades, each consisting of four rows of Doric columns, encircling a giant ellipse that straightens out to funnel believers into the basilica. The effect was deliberate – Bernini described the colonnades as representing 'the motherly arms of the church'.

The scale of the piazza is dazzling: at its largest it measures 340m by 240m. There are 284 columns and, atop the colonnades, 140 saints. The 25m obelisk in the centre was brought to Rome by Caligula from Heliopolis in Egypt and later used by Nero as a turning post for the chariot races in his circus.

Leading off the piazza, the monumental approach road, Via della Conciliazione, was commissioned by Mussolini and built between 1936 and 1950.

★Vatican Museums   MUSEUM
(Musei Vaticani; Map p92; ☏ 06 6988 4676; http://mv.vatican.va; Viale Vaticano; adult/reduced €16/8, last Sun of month free; ☉ 9am-4pm Mon-Sat, 9am-12.30pm last Sun of month; Ⓜ Ottaviano-San Pietro) Founded by Pope Julius II in the early 16th century and enlarged by successive pontiffs, the Vatican Museums boast one of the world's greatest art collections. Exhibits, which are displayed along about 7km of halls and corridors, range from Egyptian mummies and Etruscan bronzes to ancient busts, old masters and modern paintings. Highlights include the spectacular collection of classical statuary in the Museo Pio-Clementino, a suite of rooms frescoed by Raphael, and the Michelangelo-painted Sistine Chapel.

Housing the museums are the lavishly decorated halls and galleries of the Palazzo Apostolico Vaticano. This vast 5.5-hectare complex consists of two palaces – the Vatican palace (nearer to St Peter's) and the Belvedere Palace – joined by two long galleries. On the inside are three courtyards: the Cortile della Pigna, the Cortile della Biblioteca and, to the south, the Cortile del Belvedere. You'll never cover it all in one day, so it pays to be selective.

On the whole, exhibits are not well labelled, so consider hiring an audioguide (€7) or buying the Guide to the Vatican Museums and City (€14).

The museums are well equipped for visitors with disabilities, with suggested itineraries, lifts and specially fitted toilets. Wheelchairs are available free of charge from the Special Permits desk in the entrance hall,

🏃 Museum Tour
Vatican Museums

LENGTH THREE HOURS
SEE VATICAN MUSEUMS

Follow this tour to see the museums' greatest hits, culminating in the Sistine Chapel.

From the entrance complex, head up the modern spiral ramp (or escalator) to the **1 Cortile delle Corazze**, the starting point for all routes through the museums. Take a moment to nip out to the terrace for views over St Peter's dome and the Vatican Gardens. Re-enter and follow through to the **2 Cortile della Pigna**, named after the huge Augustan-era bronze pine cone in the monumental niche. Cross the courtyard and enter the long corridor that is the **3 Museo Chiaramonti**. Don't stop here, but continue left, up the stairs, to the Museo Pio-Clementino, home of the Vatican's finest classical statuary. Follow the flow of people through to the **4 Cortile Ottagono** (Octagonal Courtyard), where you'll find the mythical masterpieces, the Laocoön and Apollo Belvedere.

Continue through a series of rooms – the **5 Sala degli Animali** (Animal Room), the **6 Sala delle Muse** (Room of the Muses), home of the famous Torso Belvedere, and the **7 Sala Rotonda** (Round Room), centred on a vast red basin. From the neighbouring **8 Sala Croce Greca** (Greek Cross Room), the Simonetti staircase leads up to the **9 Galleria dei Candelabri** (Gallery of the Candelabra), the first of three galleries along a lengthy corridor. It gets very crowded up here as you're funnelled through the **10 Galleria degli Arazzi** (Tapestry Gallery) and onto the **11 Galleria delle Carte Geografiche** (Map Gallery), a 120m long hall hung with huge topographical maps.

At the end of the corridor, carry on through the **12 Sala Sobieski** to the **13 Sala di Costantino**, the first of the four Stanze di Raffaello (Raphael Rooms) – the others are the **14 Stanza d'Eliodoro**, the **15 Stanza della Segnatura**, featuring Raphael's superlative La Scuola di Atene, and the **16 Stanza dell'Incendio di Borgo**. Anywhere else these magnificent frescoed chambers would be the star attraction, but here they serve as the warm-up for the grand finale, the **17 Sistine Chapel**.

VATICAN MUSEUMS

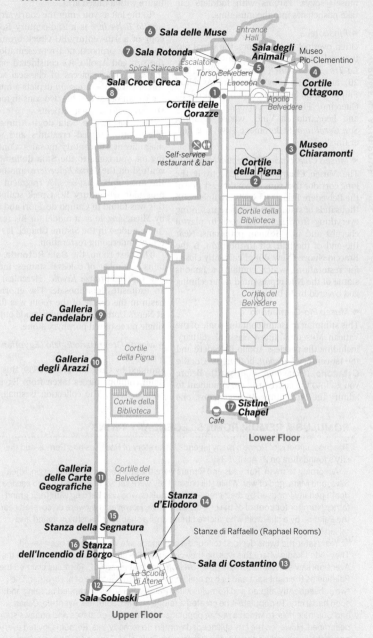

6 **Sala delle Muse**

Entrance Hall

7 **Sala Rotonda**

Sala degli Animali **5**

Museo Pio-Clementino

Spiral Staircase *Escalator*

Torso Belvedere **4**

Sala Croce Greca

8

Laocoön

Cortile Ottagono

1

Cortile delle Corazze

Apollo Belvedere

Museo Chiaramonti **3**

Self-service restaurant & bar

Cortile della Pigna

2

Cortile della Biblioteca

Cortile del Belvedere

Galleria dei Candelabri **9**

Cortile della Pigna

Galleria degli Arazzi **10**

Cortile della Biblioteca

Sistine Chapel **17**

Cafe

Lower Floor

Galleria delle Carte Geografiche **11**

Cortile del Belvedere

Stanza d'Eliodoro **14**

15

Stanza della Segnatura

Stanze di Raffaello (Raphael Rooms)

16 **Stanza dell'Incendio di Borgo**

Sala di Costantino **13**

La Scuola di Atene

12

Sala Sobieski

Upper Floor

and can be reserved by emailing accoglienza. musei@scv.va. Parents with toddlers can take pushchairs into the museums.

➡ *Pinacoteca*

Often overlooked by visitors, the papal picture gallery contains Raphael's last work, *La Trasfigurazione* (Transfiguration; 1517–20), and paintings by Giotto, Fra' Angelico, Filippo Lippi, Perugino, Titian, Guido Reni, Guercino, Pietro da Cortona, Caravaggio and Leonardo da Vinci, whose haunting *San Gerolamo* (St Jerome; c 1480) was never finished.

➡ *Museo Chiaramonti & Braccio Nuovo*

The Museo Chiaramonti is effectively the long corridor that runs down the east side of the Belvedere Palace. Its walls are lined with thousands of statues and busts representing everything from immortal gods to playful cherubs and ugly Roman patricians. Near the end of the hall, off to the right, is the Braccio Nuovo (New Wing; currently closed for restoration), which contains a famous statue of the Nile represented as a reclining god covered by 16 babies.

➡ *Museo Pio-Clementino*

This stunning museum contains some of the Vatican Museums' finest classical statuary, including the peerless Apollo Belvedere and the 1st-century *Laocoön*, both in the **Cortile Ottagono** (Octagonal Courtyard). Before you go into the courtyard take a moment to admire the 1st-century *Apoxyomenos,* one of the earliest known sculptures to depict a figure with a raised arm.

To the left as you enter the courtyard, the *Apollo Belvedere* is a 2nd-century Roman copy of a 4th-century-BC Greek bronze. A beautifully proportioned representation of the sun god Apollo, it's considered one of the great masterpieces of classical sculpture. Nearby, the *Laocoön* depicts a muscular Trojan priest and his two sons in mortal struggle with two sea serpents.

Back inside, the **Sala degli Animali** is filled with sculpted creatures and some magnificent 4th-century mosaics. Continuing on, you come to the **Sala delle Muse**, centred on the *Torso Belvedere,* another of the museum's must-sees. A fragment of a muscular 1st-century BC Greek sculpture, this was found in Campo de' Fiori and used by Michelangelo as a model for his *ignudi* (male nudes) in the Sistine Chapel. It's currently undergoing restoration.

The next room, the **Sala Rotonda**, contains a number of colossal statues, including a gilded-bronze *Ercole* (Hercules) and an exquisite floor mosaic. The enormous basin in the centre of the room was found at Nero's Domus Aurea and is made out of a single piece of red porphyry stone.

➡ *Museo Gregoriano Egizio (Egyptian Museum)*

Founded by Gregory XVI in 1839, this museum contains pieces taken from Egypt in Roman times. The collection is small, but

---

ROMULUS & REMUS, ROME'S LEGENDARY TWINS

The most famous of Rome's many legends is the story of Romulus and Remus and the city's foundation on 21 April 753 BC.

According to myth, Romulus and Remus were the children of the vestal virgin, Rhea Silva, and Mars, god of war. While still babies they were set adrift on the Tiber to escape a death penalty imposed by their great-uncle Amulius, who was battling with their grandfather Numitor for control of the city of Alba Longa. However, they were discovered near the Palatino by a she-wolf, who suckled them until a shepherd, Faustulus, found and raised them.

Years later the twins decided to found a city on the site where they'd been saved. They didn't know where this was, so they consulted the omens. Remus, standing on the Aventino, saw six vultures; his brother over on the Palatino saw 12. Romulus claimed the Palatino as the right spot and began building, much to the outrage of his brother. The two subsequently argued and Romulus killed Remus. Romulus continued building and soon had a city. To populate it he created a refuge on the Capitoline, Aventino, Celian and Quirinale hills, to which a ragtag population of criminals, ex-slaves and outlaws soon decamped. However, the city still needed women. To remedy this, Romulus invited everyone in the surrounding country to celebrate the Festival of Consus (21 August). As the spectators watched the festival games, Romulus and his men pounced and abducted all the women, an act that went down in history as the Rape of the Sabine Women.

there are fascinating exhibits including the *Trono di Ramses II* (part of a statue of the seated king), vividly painted sarcophagi dating from around 1000 BC, and some macabre mummies.

➡ Museo Gregoriano Etrusco

At the top of the 18th-century Simonetti staircase, the Museo Gregoriano Etrusco contains artefacts unearthed in the Etruscan tombs of northern Lazio, as well as a superb collection of vases and Roman antiquities. Of particular interest is the *Marte di Todi* (Mars of Todi), a black bronze of a warrior dating to the late 5th century BC.

➡ Galleria delle Carte Geografiche (Map Gallery)

The last of three galleries – the other two are the **Galleria dei Candelabri** (Gallery of the Candelabra) and the **Galleria degli Arazzi** (Tapestry Gallery) – this 120m-long corridor is hung with 40 16th-century topographical maps of Italy.

➡ Stanze di Raffaello (Raphael Rooms)

These four frescoed chambers, currently undergoing partial restoration, were part of Pope Julius II's private apartments. Raphael himself painted the Stanza della Segnatura (1508–11) and the Stanza d'Eliodoro (1512–14), while the Stanza dell'Incendio (1514–17) and the Sala di Costantino (1517–24) were decorated by students following his designs.

The first room you come to is the **Sala di Costantino**, which features a huge fresco depicting Constantine's defeat of Maxentius at the battle of Milvian Bridge.

The **Stanza d'Eliodoro**, which was used for private audiences, takes its name from the *Cacciata d'Eliodoro* (Expulsion of Heliodorus from the Temple), an allegorical work reflecting Pope Julius II's policy of forcing foreign powers off Church lands. To its right, the *Messa di Bolsena* (Mass of Bolsena) shows Julius paying homage to the relic of a 13th-century miracle at the lakeside town of Bolsena. Next is the *Incontro di Leone Magno con Attila* (Encounter of Leo the Great with Attila) by Raphael and his school, and, on the fourth wall, the *Liberazione di San Pietro* (Liberation of St Peter), a brilliant work demonstrating Raphael's masterful ability to depict light.

The **Stanza della Segnatura**, Julius' study and library, was the first room that Raphael painted, and it's here that you'll find his great masterpiece, *La Scuola di Atene* (The School of Athens), featuring

---

❶ QUEUE JUMPING AT THE VATICAN MUSEUMS

Avoiding the queues is largely a matter of luck but there are some things you can do to reduce waiting time:

➡ Book tickets online (http://biglietteriamusei.vatican.va/musei/tickets/do; €4 booking fee). On payment, you'll receive email confirmation, which you should print and present, along with valid ID, at the museum entrance. You can also book guided tours (adult/reduced €32/24) online.

➡ Time your visit: Tuesdays and Thursdays are quietest; Wednesday mornings are good as everyone is at the pope's weekly audience; afternoon is better than the morning; and avoid Mondays when many other museums are shut.

➡ Book a tour with a reputable guide.

---

philosophers and scholars gathered around Plato and Aristotle. The seated figure in front of the steps is believed to be Michelangelo, while the figure of Plato is said to be a portrait of Leonardo da Vinci, and Euclide (the bald man bending over) is Bramante. Raphael also included a self-portrait in the lower right corner – he's the second figure from the right.

The most famous work in the **Stanza dell'Incendio di Borgo** is the *Incendio di Borgo* (Fire in the Borgo), which depicts Pope Leo IV extinguishing a fire by making the sign of the cross. The ceiling was painted by Raphael's master, Perugino.

➡ Sistine Chapel (Capella Sistina)

The jewel in the Vatican crown, and home to two of the world's most famous works of art – Michelangelo's ceiling frescoes (1508–1512) and his *Giudizio Universale* (Last Judgment; 1535–1541) – the Sistine Chapel is the one place everyone wants to see, and on a busy day you could find yourself sharing it with up to 2000 people.

The Sistine Chapel provided the greatest challenge of Michelangelo's career, pushing him to the limits of his genius and spurring him to produce what many regard as the greatest feat of painting ever accomplished by a single artist.

SISTINE CHAPEL CEILING

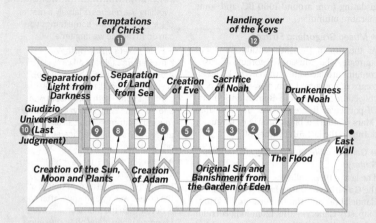

Temptations of Christ ⓫

Handing over of the Keys ⓬

Separation of Light from Darkness

Separation of Land from Sea

Creation of Eve

Sacrifice of Noah

Drunkenness of Noah

Giudizio Universale ⓾ **(Last Judgment)**

⑨ ⑧ ⑦ ⑥ ⑤ ④ ③ ② ①

East Wall

The Flood

Creation of the Sun, Moon and Plants

Creation of Adam

Original Sin and Banishment from the Garden of Eden

🚶 Museum Tour
Sistine Chapel

LENGTH 30 MINUTES

On entering the chapel head over to the main entrance in the far (east) wall for the best views of the ceiling.

Michelangelo's ceiling design – which took him four years to complete – covers the entire 800-sq-metre surface. With painted architectural features and a colourful cast of biblical figures, it centres on nine central panels depicting the Creation, Adam and Eve, the Fall, and the plight of Noah.

As you look up from the east wall, the first panel is the ❶ **Drunkenness of Noah**, followed by ❷ **The Flood**, and the ❸ **Sacrifice of Noah**. Next, ❹ **Original Sin and Banishment from the Garden of Eden** famously depicts Adam and Eve being sent packing after accepting the forbidden fruit from Satan, represented by a snake with the body of a woman coiled around a tree. The ❺ **Creation of Eve** is naturally followed by the ❻ **Creation of Adam**. This, one of the

most famous images in Western art, shows a bearded God pointing his finger at Adam, thus bringing him to life. Completing the sequence are the ❼ **Separation of Land from Sea**, the ❽ **Creation of the Sun, Moon and Plants** and the ❾ **Separation of Light from Darkness**, featuring a fearsome God reaching out to touch the sun.

Straight ahead of you on the west wall is Michelangelo's mesmeric ❿ **Giudizio Universale** (Last Judgment), showing Christ (in the centre near the top) passing sentence over the souls of the dead as they are torn from their graves to face him. The saved get to stay up in heaven (in the upper right), the damned are sent down to face the demons in hell (in the bottom right).

The chapel's side walls also feature stunning Renaissance frescoes, representing the lives of Moses (to your left) and Christ (to the right). Look out for Botticelli's ⓫ **Temptations of Christ** and Perugino's ⓬ **Handing over of the Keys**.

The chapel was originally built in 1483 for Pope Sixtus IV, after whom it is named. But apart from the wall frescoes and floor, little remains of the original decor, which was sacrificed to make way for Michelangelo's two masterpieces. The first, the ceiling, was commissioned by Pope Julius II and painted between 1508 and 1512; the second, the *Giudizio Universale* (Last Judgment), was completed almost 30 years later in 1541.

Both were controversial works influenced by the political ambitions of the popes who commissioned them. The ceiling came as part of Julius II's drive to transform Rome into the Church's showcase capital, while Pope Paul III intended the *Giudizio Universale* to serve as a warning to Catholics to toe the line during the Reformation in Europe.

When Pope Julius II first approached Michelangelo about the 800-sq-metre ceiling – some say on the advice of his architect, Bramante, who was keen for Michelangelo to fail – the artist was reluctant to accept. He regarded himself as a sculptor and had had little experience of painting frescoes. But Julius persisted and in 1508 he commissioned Michelangelo for a fee of 3000 ducats (approximately €1.5 to €2 million).

Originally, Julius had envisaged a design based on the 12 apostles, but Michelangelo rejected this and came up with a much more complex plan centred on stories from the book of Genesis. It's this design that you see today.

Michelangelo's second stint in the chapel resulted in the *Giudizio Universale*, his highly charged depiction of Christ's second coming on the 200-sq-metre west wall.

The project, commissioned by Pope Clement VII and encouraged by his successor Paul III, was controversial from the start. Critics were outraged when Michelangelo destroyed two Perugino frescoes when preparing the wall, and when it was unveiled in 1541, its swirling mass of 391 predominantly naked bodies provoked scandal. Pope Pius IV later had Daniele da Volterra cover 41 nudes, earning the artist the nickname *il braghettone* (the breeches maker).

Near the bottom, on the right, you'll see a man with donkey ears and a snake wrapped around him. This is Biagio de Cesena, the papal master of ceremonies, who was a fierce critic of Michelangelo's composition. Another famous figure is St Bartholomew, just beneath Christ, holding his own flayed skin. The face in the skin is said to be a self-portrait of Michelangelo, its anguished look reflecting the artist's tormented faith.

As well as providing a showcase for priceless art, the Sistine Chapel also serves an important religious function as the place where the conclave meets to elect a new pope.

★**Castel Sant'Angelo**　　MUSEUM, CASTLE
(Map p92; ☎06 681 91 11; http://castelsantangelo.beniculturali.it; Lungotevere Castello 50; adult/reduced €7/3.50; ⊙9am-7.30pm Tue-Sun; 🚊Piazza Pia) With its chunky round keep, this castle is an instantly recognisable landmark. Built as a mausoleum for the emperor Hadrian, it was converted into a papal fortress in the 6th century and named after an angelic vision that Pope Gregory the Great had in 590. Nowadays, it houses the **Museo Nazionale di Castel Sant'Angelo** and its eclectic collection of paintings, sculpture, military memorabilia and medieval firearms.

Many of these weapons were used by soldiers fighting to protect the castle, which, thanks to a secret 13th-century passageway to the Vatican (the Passetto di Borgo), provided sanctuary to many popes in times of danger. Most famously, Pope Clemente VI holed up here during the 1527 sack of Rome.

The castle's upper floors are filled with lavishly decorated Renaissance interiors, including the beautifully frescoed **Sala Paolina**. Two storeys up, the **terrace**, immortalised by Puccini in his opera *Tosca*, offers unforgettable views over Rome.

Note that ticket prices may increase during temporary exhibitions.

Ponte Sant'Angelo　　BRIDGE
(Map p78; 🚊Piazza Pia) The emperor Hadrian built the Ponte Sant'Angelo in 136 to provide an approach to his mausoleum, but it was Bernini who brought it to life, designing the angel sculptures in 1668. The three central arches of the bridge are part of the original structure; the end arches were restored and enlarged in 1892–94 during the construction of the Lungotevere embankments.

⊙ Monti, Esquilino & San Lorenzo

★**Basilica di Santa Maria Maggiore**　　BASILICA
(Map p102; Piazza Santa Maria Maggiore; basilica/museum/loggia/archaeological site free/€3/5/5; ⊙7am-7pm, museum & loggia 9am-5.30pm; 🚊Piazza Santa Maria Maggiore) One of Rome's

Monti, Esquilino & San Lorenzo

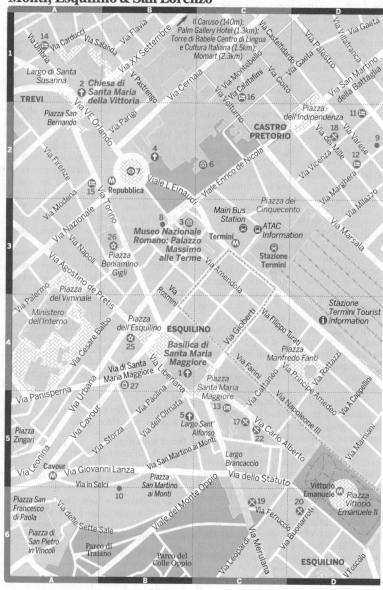

four patriarchal basilicas, this monumental 5th-century church stands on the summit of the Esquiline Hill, on the spot where snow is said to have miraculously fallen in the summer of AD 358. Much altered over the centuries, it's something of an architectural hybrid with a 14th-century Romanesque belfry, an 18th-century baroque facade, a largely baroque interior, and a series of glorious 5th-century mosaics.

Outside, the exterior is decorated with glimmering 13th-century mosaics, protected by Ferdinand Fuga's 1741 baroque loggia. Rising behind, the belfry, Rome's tallest, tops out at 75m.

The vast interior retains its original structure, despite the basilica's many overhauls. Particularly spectacular are the 5th-century mosaics in the triumphal arch and nave, depicting Old Testament scenes. The central image in the apse, signed by Jacopo Torriti,

Monti, Esquilino & San Lorenzo

dates from the 13th century and represents the coronation of the Virgin Mary. Beneath your feet, the nave floor is a fine example of 12th-century Cosmati paving.

The baldachin over the high altar is heavy with gilt cherubs; the altar itself is a porphyry sarcophagus, which is said to contain the relics of St Matthew and other martyrs. A plaque embedded in the floor to the right of the altar marks the spot where Gian Lorenzo Bernini and his father Pietro are buried. Steps lead down to the *confessio* (a crypt in which relics are placed), where a statue of Pope Pius IX kneels before a reliquary containing a fragment of Jesus' manger.

The sumptuously decorated Cappella Sistina, last on the right, was built by Domenico Fontana in the 16th century and contains the tombs of Popes Sixtus V and Pius V.

Through the souvenir shop on the right-hand side of the church is a museum with a glittering collection of religious artefacts. Most interesting, however, is the upper loggia, where you'll get a close look at the facade's iridescent 13th-century mosaics, as well as Bernini's spiral staircase.

Chiesa di Santa Prassede   CHURCH
(Map p102; Via Santa Prassede 9a; ⊙7.30am-noon & 4-6.30pm; 🚇Piazza Santa Maria Maggiore) Famous for its brilliant mosaics, this

9th-century church is dedicated to St Praxedes, an early Christian heroine who hid Christians fleeing persecution and buried those she couldn't save in a well. The position of the well is now marked by a marble disc on the floor of the nave.

The mosaics, produced by artists whom Pope Paschal I had brought in specially from Byzantium, bear all the hallmarks of their eastern creators, with bold gold backgrounds and a marked Christian symbolism. The apse mosaics depict Christ flanked by Sts Peter, Pudentiana and Zeno on the right, and Paul, Praxedes and Pope Paschal on the left. All the figures have golden halos except for Paschal, whose head is shadowed by a blue nimbus to indicate that he was still alive at the time. Further treasures await in the heavily mosaiced **Cappella di San Zenone**, including a piece of the column to which Christ was tied when he was flogged, brought back from Jerusalem – it's in the glass case on the right.

Basilica di San Pietro in Vincoli   BASILICA
(Map p68; Piazza di San Pietro in Vincoli 4a; ⊙8am-12.20pm & 3-7pm summer, to 6pm winter; 🅜Cavour) Pilgrims and art lovers flock to this 5th-century basilica for two reasons: to marvel at Michelangelo's colossal *Moses* (1505) sculpture and to see the chains that supposedly bound St Peter when he was

imprisoned in the Carcere Mamertino (near the Roman Forum).

Access to the church is via a flight of steps through a low arch that leads up from Via Cavour.

The church was built specially to house the shackles of St Peter, which had been sent to Constantinople after the saint's death, but were later returned as relics. They arrived in two pieces and legend has it that when they were reunited they miraculously joined together. They are now displayed under the altar.

To the right of the altar, Michelangelo's *Moses* forms the centrepiece of his unfinished tomb for Pope Julius II. The prophet strikes a muscular pose with well-defined biceps, a magnificent waist-length beard and two small horns sticking out of his head. These were inspired by a mistranslation of a biblical passage: where the original said that rays of light issued from Moses' face, the translator wrote 'horns'. Michelangelo was aware of the mistake, but gave Moses horns anyway. Flanking Moses are statues of Leah and Rachel, probably completed by Michelangelo's students.

The tomb, despite its imposing scale, was never finished – Michelangelo originally envisaged 40 statues, but got sidetracked by the Sistine Chapel – and Pope Julius II was buried in St Peter's Basilica.

Domus Aurea   ARCHAEOLOGICAL SITE
(Golden House; Map p110; ☑ 06 3996 7700; www.coopculture.it; Viale della Domus Aurea; admission/with online booking fee €10/12; ⊙ guided tours Sat & Sun; ⓂColosseo) Nero had his Domus Aurea constructed after the fire of AD 64 (which it's rumoured he had started to clear the area). Named after the gold that lined its facade and interiors, it was a huge complex covering up to a third of the city. The excavated part of the site has been repeatedly closed due to flooding, but opened for weekend guided tours from late 2014; check the website for current opening status.

Piazza della Repubblica   PIAZZA
(Map p102; ⓂRepubblica) Flanked by grand 19th-century neoclassical colonnades, this landmark piazza was laid out as part of Rome's post-unification makeover. It follows the lines of the semicircular *exedra* (benched portico) of Diocletian's baths complex and was originally known as Piazza Esedra.

★Museo Nazionale Romano: Palazzo Massimo alle Terme   MUSEUM
(Map p102; ☑ 06 3996 7700; www.coopculture.it; Largo di Villa Peretti 1; adult/reduced €7/3.50; ⊙9am-7.45pm Tue-Sun; ⓂTermini) One of Rome's great unheralded museums, this is a fabulous treasure trove of classical art. The ground and first floors are devoted to sculpture with some breathtaking pieces – check out the *Pugile* (Boxer), a 2nd-century-BC Greek bronze; the graceful *Ermafrodite dormiente* (Sleeping Hermaphrodite) from the 2nd-century-BC; and the idealised *Il discobolo* (Discus Thrower). The magnificent and vibrantly coloured frescoes on the second floor are the undisputed highlight.

The second-floor fresco panels illustrate a range of natural, mythological, domestic and erotic themes, according to the rooms they were originally placed in. There are intimate *cubicula* (bedroom) frescoes, which feature religious, erotic and theatre subjects; and delicate landscape paintings from the dark-painted winter triclinium (dining room). Particularly breathtaking are the frescoes (dating from 30 BC to 20 BC) from Villa Livia, one of the homes of Augustus' wife Livia Drusilla. These cover an entire room and depict a paradisiacal garden full of a wild tangle of roses, pomegranates, irises and camomile under a deep-blue sky. They once decorated a summer triclinium, a large living and dining area built half underground to provide protection from the heat.

The second floor also features some exquisitely fine mosaics and rare inlay work.

In the basement, the unexciting-sounding coin collection is far more absorbing than you might expect, tracing the Roman Empire's propaganda offensive through its coins. There's also jewellery dating back several millennia, and the disturbing remains of a mummified eight-year-old girl, the only known example of mummification dating from the Roman Empire.

Note that the museum is one of four that collectively make up the Museo Nazionale Romano. The ticket, which is valid for three days, also gives admission to the other three sites: the Terme di Diocleziano, Palazzo Altemps and the Crypta Balbi.

Museo Nazionale Romano: Terme di Diocleziano   MUSEUM
(Map p102; ☑ 06 3996 7700; www.coopculture.it; Viale Enrico de Nicola 78; adult/reduced €7/3.50; ⊙9am-7.30pm Tue-Sun; ⓂTermini) The Terme di Diocleziano was ancient Rome's largest

ISOLA TIBERINA

One of the world's smallest inhabited islands, the boat-shaped Isola Tiberina (Tiber Island), has been associated with healing since the 3rd century BC, when the Romans built a temple to Aesculapius, the Graeco-Roman god of medicine, here. These days patients make for the Ospedale Fatebenefratelli, whilst churchgoers head to the 10th-century **Chiesa di San Bartolomeo** (Map p108; Piazza di San Bartolomeo all'Isola 22; ⊙ 9.30am-1.30pm & 3.30-5.30pm Mon-Sat, 9.30am-1pm Sun; ⊜ Lungotevere dei Pierleoni) on the site where the temple once stood. Inside the church, a marble well head is said to stand over the spring that provided the temple's healing waters.

The island is connected to the mainland by two bridges: the 62 BC Ponte Fabricio, Rome's oldest standing bridge, which links with the Jewish Ghetto, and Ponte Cestio, which runs over to Trastevere. Visible to the south are the remains of Ponte Rotto (Broken Bridge), ancient Rome's first stone bridge, which was all but swept away in a 1598 flood.

bath complex, covering about 13 hectares and with a capacity for 3000 people. Today its ruins constitute part of the impressive Museo Nazionale Romano. This branch of the National Roman Museum supplies a fascinating insight into Roman life through memorial inscriptions and other artefacts. Outside, the vast, elegant cloister was constructed from drawings by Michelangelo.

It's lined with classical sarcophagi, headless statues and huge sculptured animal heads, thought to have come from the Foro di Traiano.

Elsewhere in the museum, look out for exhibits relating to cults and the early development of Christianity and Judaism. There's a particularly interesting section about amulets and spells, which were cast on neighbours and acquaintances to bring them bad luck and worse. Upstairs exhibits tomb objects dating from the 11th to 9th centuries BC, including jewellery and amphora.

As you wander the museum, you'll see glimpses of the original complex, which was completed in the early 4th century as a state-of-the-art combination of baths, libraries, concert halls and gardens – the Aula Ottagona and Basilica di Santa Maria degli Angeli buildings were also once part of this enormous endeavour. It fell into disrepair after the aqueduct that fed the baths was destroyed by invaders in about AD 536.

Basilica di Santa Maria degli Angeli
BASILICA

(Map p102; www.santamariadegliangeliroma. it; Piazza della Repubblica; ⊜ Repubblica) This hulking basilica occupies what was once the central hall of Diocletian's baths complex. It was originally designed by Michelangelo,

but only the great vaulted ceiling remains from his plans.

★ Chiesa di Santa Maria della Vittoria
CHURCH

(Map p102; Via XX Settembre 17; ⊙ 8.30am-noon & 3.30-6pm; ⊜ Repubblica) This modest church is an unlikely setting for an extraordinary work of art – Bernini's extravagant and sexually charged *Santa Teresa trafitta dall'amore di Dio* (Ecstasy of St Teresa). This daring sculpture depicts Teresa, engulfed in the folds of a flowing cloak, floating in ecstasy on a cloud while a teasing angel pierces her repeatedly with a golden arrow.

⊙ Trastevere & Gianicolo

Over the river from the *centro storico* – hence its name, a derivation of the Latin *trans Tiberim* or across the Tiber – Trastevere is one of Rome's prettiest and most vibrant neighbourhoods, an atmospheric warren of cobbled lanes, colourful *palazzi* and art-laden churches.

Behind it, the Gianicolo (Janiculum) Hill rises serenely above the maelstrom offering incredible views.

Piazza Santa Maria in Trastevere
PIAZZA

(Map p108; ⊜ Viale di Trastevere, ⊜ Viale di Trastevere) Trastevere's focal square is a prime people-watching spot. By day it's full of mums with strollers, chatting locals and guidebook-toting tourists; by night it's the domain of foreign students, young Romans and out-of-towners, all out for a good time. The fountain in the centre of the square is of Roman origin and was restored by Carlo Fontana in 1692.

★ Basilica di Santa Maria in Trastevere
BASILICA

(Map p108; Piazza Santa Maria in Trastevere; ⊙7.30am-9pm; ☒Viale di Trastevere, ☒Viale di Trastevere) Nestled in a quiet corner of Trastevere's focal square, this is said to be the oldest church dedicated to the Virgin Mary in Rome. In its original form it dates to the early 3rd century, but a major 12th-century makeover saw the addition of a Romanesque bell tower and glittering facade. The portico came later, added by Carlo Fontana in 1702.

Inside, the 12th-century mosaics are the headline feature. In the apse, look out for Christ and his mother flanked by various saints and, on the far left, Pope Innocent II holding a model of the church. Beneath this are six mosaics by Pietro Cavallini illustrating the life of the Virgin (c 1291).

According to legend, the church stands on the spot where a fountain of oil miraculously sprang from the ground. It incorporates 21 ancient Roman columns, some plundered from the Terme di Caracalla, and boasts a 17th-century wooden ceiling.

Villa Farnesina
HISTORIC BUILDING

(Map p78; ☒06 6802 7268; www.villafarnesina.it; Via della Lungara 230; adult/reduced €6/5; ⊙9am-2pm daily, to 5pm 2nd Sun of month; ☒Lgt della Farnesina, ☒Viale di Trastevere) This gorgeous 16th-century villa's interior is fantastically frescoed from top to bottom. Several paintings in the Loggia of Cupid and Psyche and the Loggia of Galatea, on the ground floor, are attributed to Raphael. On the first floor, Peruzzi's dazzling frescoes in the Salone delle Prospettive are a superb illusionary perspective of a colonnade and panorama of 16th-century Rome.

Galleria Nazionale d'Arte Antica di Palazzo Corsini
GALLERY

(Map p78; ☒06 6880 2323; www.galleriacorsini.beniculturali.it; Via della Lungara 10; adult/reduced €5/2.50, incl Palazzo Barberini €9/4.50; ⊙8.30am-7.30pm Wed-Mon; ☒Lgt della Farnesina, ☒Viale di Trastevere) Once home to Queen Christina of Sweden, whose richly frescoed bedroom witnessed a stready stream of male and female lovers, 16th-century Palazzo Corsini was designed by Ferdinando Fuga, in grand Versailles style, and houses part of Italy's national art collection. The highlights include Caravaggio's mesmerising *San Giovanni Battista* (St John the Baptist), Guido Reni's unnerving *Salome con la testa di San Giovanni Battista* (Salome with the Head of John the Baptist), and Fra' Angelico's Corsini Triptych, plus works by Rubens, Poussin and Van Dyck.

Tempietto di Bramante & Chiesa di San Pietro in Montorio
CHURCH

(Map p108; www.sanpietroinmontorio.it; Piazza San Pietro in Montorio 2; ⊙Chiesa 8.30am-noon & 3-4pm Mon-Fri, Tempietto 9.30am-12.30pm & 2-4.30pm Tue-Fri, 9am-3pm Sat; ☒Via Garibaldi) Considered the first great building of the High Renaissance, Bramante's sublime Tempietto (Little Temple; 1508) is a perfect surprise, squeezed into the courtyard of the Chiesa di San Pietro in Montorio, on the spot where St Peter is said to have been crucified. It's small, but perfectly formed; its classically inspired design and ideal proportions epitomise the Renaissance zeitgeist.

It has a circular interior surrounded by 16 columns and topped by a classical frieze, elegant balustrade and dome. More than a century later, in 1628, Bernini added a staircase. Bernini also contributed a chapel to the adjacent church, the last resting place of Beatrice Cenci, an Italian noblewoman

---

BEST LESSER-KNOWN HITS

Away from Rome's headline sights, there's a whole host of lesser-known hits to savour. Here are some of our favourites:

➡ **Chiesa di Santa Prassede** (p104) An easy-to-miss church with spectacular Byzantine mosaics.

➡ **Cimitero Acattolico per gli Stranieri** (p112) Final resting place of the poets Keats and Shelley.

➡ **Priorato dei Cavalieri di Malta** (p111) Boasts a magical keyhole view of St Peter's dome.

Trastevere & Gianicolo

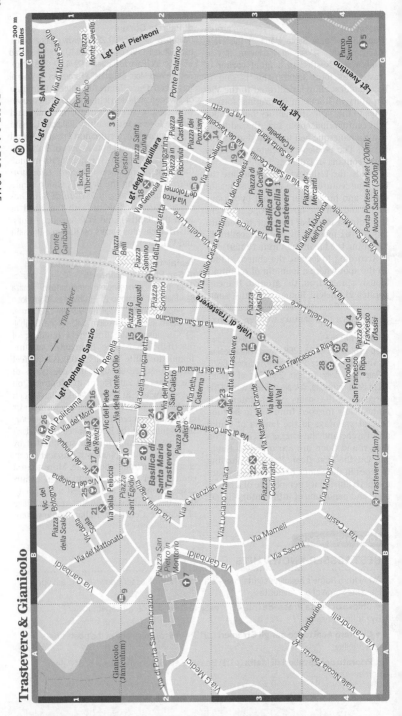

Trastevere & Gianicolo

ROME & LAZIO ROME

who helped murder her abusive father in the the 16th century, and subsequently was tried and beheaded on Ponte Sant'Angelo. It's quite a climb uphill, but you're rewarded by the views. To cheat, take bus 870 from Via Paola just off Corso Vittorio Emanuele II near the Tiber.

★ Basilica di Santa Cecilia in Trastevere
BASILICA

(Map p108; Piazza di Santa Cecilia; fresco & crypt each €2.50; ⊙basilica & crypt 9.30am-1pm & 4-7.15pm, fresco 10am-2.30pm Mon-Sat; ☐Viale di Trastevere, ☐Viale di Trastevere) The last resting place of the patron saint of music features Pietro Cavallini's stunning 13th-century fresco in the nuns' choir. Inside the church itself, Stefano Maderno's mysterious sculpture depicts St Cecilia's miraculously preserved body, unearthed in the Catacombs of San Callisto in 1599. You can also visit the excavations of Roman houses, one of which was possibly that of Cecilia.

Chiesa di San Francesco d'Assisi a Ripa
CHURCH

(Map p108; Piazza di San Francesco d'Assisi 88; ⊙7.30am-noon & 2-7.30pm; ☐Viale di Trastevere, ☐Viale di Trastevere) St Francis is said to have stayed here in the 13th century, and you can still see the rock that he used as a pillow and his crucifix in his cell. Rebuilt several times, the church's current incarnation dates from the 1680s. It contains one of Bernini's most daring works, the *Beata Ludovica Albertoni* (Blessed Ludovica Albertoni; 1674), a work of highly charged sexual ambiguity.

◎ San Giovanni & Celio

★ Basilica di San Giovanni in Laterano
BASILICA

(Map p110; Piazza di San Giovanni in Laterano 4; basilica/cloister free/€5; ⊙7am-6.30pm, cloister 9am-6pm; Ⓜ San Giovanni) For a thousand years this monumental cathedral was the most important church in Christendom. Commissioned by Constantine and consecrated in AD 324, it was the first Christian basilica built in the city and, until the late 14th century, was the pope's main place of worship. It's still Rome's official cathedral and the pope's seat as the bishop of Rome.

The basilica has been revamped several times, most notably by Borromini in the 17th century, and by Alessandro Galilei, who added the immense white facade in 1735.

Surmounted by 15 7m-high statues – Christ with St John the Baptist, John the Evangelist and the 12 Apostles – Galilei's facade is an imposing example of late-baroque classicism. The central bronze doors were moved here from the Curia in the Roman Forum, while, on the far right, the Holy Door is only opened in Jubilee years.

The interior owes much of its present look to Francesco Borromini, who redecorated it for the 1650 Jubilee. It's a breathtaking sight

ROME & LAZIO ROME

San Giovanni & Celio

San Giovanni & Celio

with a golden gilt ceiling, a 15th-century mosaic floor, and a wide central nave lined with 4.6m-high sculptures of the apostles.

At the head of the nave, the pointed Gothic baldachin over the papal altar is said to contain the relics of the heads of Sts Peter and Paul. In front, a double staircase leads down to the confessio and the Renaissance tomb of Pope Martin V.

Behind the altar, the massive apse is decorated with sparkling mosaics. Parts of these date to the 4th century, but most were added in the 19th century.

At the other end of the basilica, on the first pilaster in the right-hand nave is an in-

complete Giotto fresco. While admiring this, cock your ear towards the next pillar, where a monument to Pope Sylvester II (r 999–1003) is said to sweat and creak when the death of a pope is imminent. To the left of the altar, the beautiful 13th-century cloister is a lovely, peaceful place with graceful twisted columns set around a central garden.

Palazzo Laterano   HISTORIC BUILDING
(Map p110; Piazza di San Giovanni in Laterano; Ⓜ San Giovanni) Adjacent to the Basilica di San Giovanni in Laterano, Palazzo Laterano was the official papal residence until the pope moved to the Vatican in 1377. It's still technically Vatican property and today hous-

es offices of the Vicariate of Rome. Much altered over the centuries, it owes its current form to a 16th-century facelift by Domenico Fontana. Overlooking the *palazzo* is Rome's oldest and tallest obelisk (Map p110).

Battistero
CHAPEL

(Map p110; Piazza di San Giovanni in Laterano; ☺9am-12.30pm & 4-6.30pm; Ⓜ San Giovanni) Built by Constantine in the 4th century, this octagonal baptistry served as the prototype for later Christian churches and bell towers. The chief interest, apart from the architecture, is the decorative mosaics, some of which date to the 5th century.

Santuario della Scala Santa & Sancta Sanctorum
CHAPEL

(Map p110; www.scala-santa.it; Piazza di San Giovanni in Laterano 14; admission Scala free, Sancta with/without audioguide €5/3.50; ☺Scala 6am-1pm & 3-7pm summer, to 6.30pm winter, Sancta Sanctorum 9.30am-12.40pm & 3-5.10pm Mon-Sat; Ⓜ San Giovanni) The Scala Sancta, said to be the staircase that Jesus walked up in Pontius Pilate's Jerusalem palace, was brought to Rome by St Helena in the 4th century. Pilgrims consider it sacred and climb it on their knees, saying a prayer on each of the 28 steps. At the top, the richly frescoed Sancta Sanctorum (Holy of Holies) was formerly the pope's private chapel.

★ Basilica di San Clemente
BASILICA

(Map p110; www.basilicasanclemente.com; Via di San Giovanni in Laterano; excavations adult/reduced €10/5; ☺9am-12.30pm & 3-6pm Mon-Sat, 12.15-6pm Sun; ☐Via Labicana) Nowhere better illustrates the various stages of Rome's turbulent past than this fascinating multi-layered church. The ground-level 12th-century basilica sitson top of a 4th-century church, which, in turn, stands over a 2nd-century pagan temple and a 1st-century Roman house. Beneath everything are foundations dating from the Roman Republic.

The medieval church features a marvellous 12th-century apse mosaic depicting the *Trionfo della Croce* (Triumph of the Cross) and some wonderful Renaissance frescoes in the Chapel of St Catherine.

Steps lead down to the 4th-century *basilica inferiore,* mostly destroyed by Norman invaders in 1084, but with some faded 11th-century frescoes illustrating the life of San Clement. Follow the steps down another level and you'll come to a 1st-century Roman house and a dark, 2nd-century temple to

VIEWS ON THE AVENTINO

Head up to the Aventino Hill for one of Rome's most celebrated views. Flanking the Piazza dei Cavalieri di Malta, the **Priorato dei Cavalieri di Malta** (Map p134; Piazza dei Cavalieri di Malta; ☺closed to the public; ☐Lungotevere Aventino) is the Roman headquarters of the *Cavalieri di Malta* (Knights of Malta). The building is closed to the public, but look through its keyhole and you'll see the dome of St Peter's Basilica perfectly aligned at the end of a hedge-lined avenue.

Just down from the piazza, there are more gorgeous views to be had at **Parco Savello** (Map p108; Via di Santa Sabina; ☺7am-6pm Oct-Feb, to 8pm Mar & Sep, to 9pm Apr-Aug; ☐Lungotevere Aventino).

Mithras, with an altar showing the god slaying a bull. Beneath it all, you can hear the eerie sound of a subterranean river flowing through a Republic-era drain.

◉ Aventino & Testaccio

★ Terme di Caracalla
ARCHAEOLOGICAL SITE

(☑06 3996 7700; www.coopculture.it; Viale delle Terme di Caracalla 52; adult/reduced €6/3; ☺9am-1hr before sunset Tue-Sun, 9am-2pm Mon; ☐Viale delle Terme di Caracalla) The remains of the emperor Caracalla's vast baths complex are among Rome's most awe-inspiring ruins. Inaugurated in 216, the original 10-hectare site, which comprised baths, gyms, libraries, shops and gardens, was used by up to 8000 people daily.

Most of the ruins are what's left of the central bath house. This was a huge rectangular edifice bookended by two palestre (gyms) and centred on a frigidarium (cold room), where bathers would stop after spells in the warmer tepidarium and a dome-capped caldaria (hot room).

But while the customers enjoyed the luxurious facilities, below ground hundreds of slaves sweated in a 9.5km tunnel network, tending to the complex plumbing systems.

The baths remained in continuous use until 537, when the Visigoths cut off Rome's water supply. Excavations in the 16th and 17th centuries unearthed important sculptures, many of which found their way into the Farnese family's art collection.

In summer the ruins are used to stage spectacular opera and ballet performances.

Cimitero Acattolico per gli Stranieri
CEMETERY

(Map p134; www.cemeteryrome.it; Via Caio Cestio 5; voluntary donation €3; ⊙9am-5pm Mon-Sat, to 1pm Sun; ⓂPiramide) Despite the roads that surround it, Rome's 'non-Catholic' Cemetery is a verdant oasis of peace. An air of Grand Tour romance hangs over the site where up 4000 people lie buried, including poets Keats and Shelley, and Italian political thinker Antonio Gramsci.

Among the gravestones and cypress trees look out for the *Angelo del Dolore* (Angel of Grief), a much-replicated 1894 sculpture that US artist William Wetmore Story created for his wife's grave.

⊙ Villa Borghese & Northern Rome

★Museo e Galleria Borghese
MUSEUM

(Map p113; 📞06 3 28 10; www.galleriaborghese. it; Piazzale del Museo Borghese 5; adult/reduced €11/6.50; ⊙9am-7pm Tue-Sun; 🚌Via Pinciana) If you only have the time (or inclination) for one art gallery in Rome, make it this one. Housing what's often referred to as the 'queen of all private art collections', it boasts paintings by Caravaggio, Raphael and Titian, as well as some sensational sculptures by Bernini. Highlights abound, but look out for Bernini's *Ratto di Proserpina* (Rape of Proserpina) and Canova's *Venere vincitrice* (Venus Victrix).

To limit numbers, visitors are admitted at two-hourly intervals, so you'll need to pre-book your ticket and get an entry time.

The museum's collection was formed by Cardinal Scipione Borghese (1579–1633), the most knowledgeable and ruthless art collector of his day. It was originally housed in the cardinal's residence near St Peter's but in the 1620s he had it transferred to his new villa just outside Porta Pinciana. And it's here, in the villa's central building, the Casino Borghese, that you'll see it today.

Over the centuries the villa has undergone several overhauls, most notably in the late 1700s when Prince Marcantonio Borghese added much of the lavish neoclassical decor.

The museum is divided into two parts: the ground-floor gallery, with its superb sculptures, intricate Roman floor mosaics and over-the-top frescoes, and the upstairs picture gallery.

Things get off to a cracking start in the entrance hall, decorated with 4th-century floor mosaics of fighting gladiators and a 2nd-century *Satiro combattente* (Fighting Satyr). High on the wall is a gravity-defying bas-relief of a horse and rider falling into the void (*Marco Curzio a cavallo*) by Pietro Bernini (Gian Lorenzo's father).

Sala I is centred on Antonio Canova's daring depiction of Napoleon's sister, Paolina Bonaparte Borghese, reclining topless as *Venere vincitrice* (1805–08). But it's Gian Lorenzo Bernini's spectacular sculptures – flamboyant depictions of pagan myths – that really steal the show. Just look at Daphne's hands morphing into leaves in the swirling *Apollo e Dafne* (1622–25) in Sala III, or Pluto's hand pressing into the seemingly soft flesh of Persephone's thigh in the *Ratto di Proserpina* (1621–22) in Sala IV.

Caravaggio dominates Sala VIII. There's a dissipated-looking *Bacchino malato* (Young Sick Bacchus; 1592–95), the strangely beautiful *La Madonna dei Palafenieri* (Madonna with Serpent; 1605–06), and *San Giovanni Battista* (St John the Baptist; 1609–10), probably Caravaggio's last work. There's also the much-loved *Ragazzo col canestro di frutta* (Boy with a Basket of Fruit; 1593–95), and the dramatic *Davide con la Testa di Golia* (David with the Head of Goliath; 1609–10) – Goliath's severed head is said to be a self-portrait.

Upstairs, the pinacoteca offers a wonderful snapshot of Renaissance art. Don't miss Raphael's extraordinary *La Deposizione di Cristo* (The Deposition; 1507) in Sala IX, and his *Dama con liocorno* (Lady with a Unicorn; 1506). In the same room is Fra Bartolomeo's superb *Adorazione del Bambino* (Adoration of the Christ Child; 1495) and Perugino's *Madonna con Bambino* (Madonna and Child; first quarter of the 16th century).

Other highlights include Correggio's erotic *Danae* (1530–31) in Sala X, Bernini's self-portraits in Sala XIV, and Titian's early masterpiece, *Amor Sacro e Amor Profano* (Sacred and Profane Love; 1514) in Sala XX.

Villa Borghese
PARK

(Map p113; entrances at Piazzale San Paolo del Brasile, Piazzale Flaminio, Via Pinciana, Via Raimondo, Largo Pablo Picasso; ⊙dawn-dusk; 🚌Porta Pinciana) Locals, lovers, tourists, joggers – no one can resist the lure of Rome's most celebrated

Villa Borghese

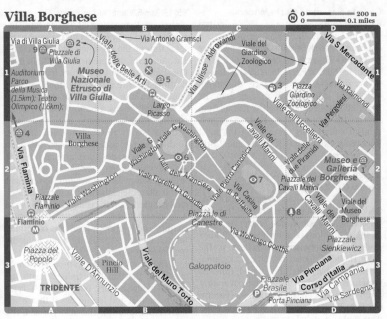

Villa Borghese

◎ Top Sights

◎ Sights

⊗ Eating

park. Originally the 17th-century estate of Cardinal Scipione Borghese, it covers about 80 hectares of wooded glades, gardens and grassy banks. Among its attractions are several excellent museums, the landscaped **Giardino del Lago** (Map p113; boat hire per person €3 for 20 minutes; ⊗7am-9pm), and **Piazza di Siena** (Map p113; ⊜Porta Pinciana), a dusty arena used for Rome's top equestrian event in May.

★**Museo Nazionale Etrusco di Villa Giulia**   MUSEUM
(Map p113; www.villagiulia.beniculturali.it; Piazzale di Villa Giulia; adult/reduced €8/4; ⊗8.30am-7.30pm Tue-Sun; ⊜Via delle Belle Arti) Pope Julius III's 16th-century villa provides the charming setting for Italy's finest collection of Etruscan and pre-Roman treasures. Exhibits, many of which came from burial tombs in the surrounding Lazio region, range from bronze figurines and black *bucchero* tableware to temple decorations, terracotta vases and a dazzling display of sophisticated jewellery.

Must-sees include a polychrome terracotta statue of Apollo, the 6th-century-BC *Sarcofago degli sposi* (Sarcophagus of the Betrothed), and the *Euphronios krater*, a celebrated Greek vase.

Further finds relating to the Umbri and Latin peoples are on show in the nearby **Villa Poniatowski** (Map p113; ☎06 321 96 98; www.villagiulia.beniculturali.it; Piazzale di Villa Giulia; incl Museo Nazional Etrusco di Villa Giulia adult/reduced €8/4; ⊗9am-1.30pm Tue-Sat, booking necessary; ⊜Via delle Belle Arti) You'll need to book to enter here, with Sunday visits restricted to guided tours run by the Coop Arteingioco. Call ☎06 4423 9949 for details.

ROME & LAZIO ROME

Galleria Nazionale d'Arte Moderna e Contemporanea
GALLERY

(Map p113; ☑ 06 3229 8221; www.gnam.beni culturali.it; Viale delle Belle Arti 131, disabled entrance Via Gramsci 73; adult/reduced €8/4; ⊙ 8.30am-7.30pm Tue-Sun; ⓠ Piazza Thorvaldsen) Housed in a vast belle époque palace, this often-overlooked gallery is an unsung gem. Its superlative collection runs the gamut from neoclassical sculpture to abstract expressionism with works by many of the most important exponents of 19th- and 20th-century art.

Museo Nazionale delle Arti del XXI Secolo (MAXXI)
GALLERY

(☑ 06 320 19 54; www.fondazionemaxxi.it; Via Guido Reni 4a; adult/reduced €11/8; ⊙ 11am-7pm Tue-Sun, to 10pm Sat; ⓠ Viale Tiziano) As much as the exhibitions, the highlight of Rome's leading contemporary art gallery is the Zaha Hadid–designed building it occupies. Formerly a barracks, the curved concrete structure is striking inside and out with a multilayered geometric facade and a cavernous light-filled interior full of snaking walkways and suspended staircases.

The gallery has a small permanent collection but more interesting are the temporary exhibitions. In recent times these have included installations by avant-garde Chinese sculptor Hang Yong Ping and an exhibition of contemporary Iranian art.

☉ Southern Rome

Capitoline Museums at Centrale Montemartini
MUSEUM

(☑ 06 06 08; www.centralemontemartini.org; Via Ostiense 106; adult/reduced €7.50/6.50, incl Capitoline Museums €16/14, valid 7 days; ⊙ 9am-7pm Tue-Sun; ⓠ Via Ostiense) Housed in a former power station, this fabulous outpost of the Capitoline Museums (Musei Capitolini) boldly juxtaposes classical sculpture against diesel engines and giant furnaces. The collection's highlights are in the Sala Caldaia, where ancient statuary strike poses around the giant furnace. Beautiful pieces include the *Fanciulla seduta* (Seated Girl) and the *Musa Polimnia* (Muse Polyhymnia), and there are also some exquisite Roman mosaics, depicting favourite subjects such as hunting scenes and foodstuffs.

Basilica di San Paolo Fuori le Mura
BASILICA

(www.abbaziasanpaolo.net; Via Ostiense 190; cloisters €4, archaeological walk €4, audioguide

€5; ⊙ 7am-6.30pm; ⓜ San Paolo) The largest church in Rome after St Peter's (and the world's third-largest), this magnificent basilica stands on the site where St Paul was buried after being decapitated in AD 67. Built by Constantine in the 4th century, it was largely destroyed by fire in 1823 and much of what you see is a 19th-century reconstruction.

However, many treasures survived, including the 5th-century triumphal arch, with its heavily restored mosaics, and the Gothic marble tabernacle over the high altar. This was designed around 1285 by Arnolfo di Cambio together with another artist, possibly Pietro Cavallini. To the right of the altar, the elaborate Romanesque Paschal candlestick was fashioned by Nicolò di Angelo and Pietro Vassalletto in the 12th century and features a grim cast of animal-headed creatures. St Paul's tomb is in the nearby confessio.

Looking upwards, doom-mongers should check out the papal portraits beneath the nave windows. Every pope since St Peter is represented and legend has it that when there is no room for the next portrait, the world will fall.

Also well worth a look is the stunning 13th-century Cosmati mosaic work that decorates the columns of the cloisters of the adjacent Benedictine abbey.

ⓘ APPIA ANTICA TIPS

The Appia Antica Regional Park Information Point (☑ 06 513 53 16; www. parcoappiaantica.it; Via Appia Antica 58-60; ⊙ 9.30am-1pm & 2-5.30pm Mon-Sat, to 5pm winter, 9.30am-6.30pm Sun, to 5pm winter; ⓠ Via Appia Antica) sells maps of the park and hires bikes (per hour/day €3/15). In spring and summer, it organises tours of the area – see the website for the latest program.

➡ The first 1km stretch of the road from Porta San Sebastiano isn't a pleasant walk, even on supposedly 'traffic free' Sundays. Much better is the genuinely traffic-free section near the Basilica di San Sebastiano.

➡ To get to Via Appia Antica, catch bus 218 from Piazza di San Giovanni in Laterano, bus 660 from Colli Albani metro station (line A), or bus 118 from the Piramide metro station (line B).

Appia Antica

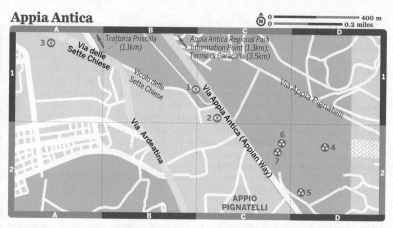

Appia Antica

★ Via Appia Antica   HISTORIC SITE

(Appian Way; ☎ 06 513 53 16; www.parcoappia
antica.it; bike hire hr/day €3/15; ⊗ Info Point
9.30am-1pm & 2-5.30pm Mon-Fri, 9.30am-6.30pm
Sat & Sun, to 5pm winter; ☐ Via Appia Antica)
Named after consul Appius Claudius Cae-
cus who laid the first 90km section in 312
BC, ancient Rome's *regina viarum* (queen
of roads) was extended in 190 BC to reach
Brindisi on Italy's southern Adriatic coast.
Via Appia Antica has long been one of
Rome's most exclusive addresses, a beautiful cobbled thoroughfare flanked by grassy
fields, Roman structures and towering pine
trees. Most splendid of the ancient houses
was **Villa dei Quintili**, so desirable that emperor Commodus murdered its owners and
took it for himself.

The Appian Way has a dark history, however – it was here that Spartacus and 6000
of his slave rebels were crucified in 71 BC,
and it was here that the early Christians
buried their dead in 300km of underground
catacombs. You can't visit all 300km, but
three major catacombs (San Callisto, San Sebastiano and Santa Domitilla) are open for
guided exploration.

Catacombe di San Sebastiano   CATACOMB

(Map p115; ☎ 06 785 03 50; www.catacombe.org;
Via Appia Antica 136; adult/reduced €8/5; ⊗ 10am-
5pm Mon-Sat, closed Dec; ☐ Via Appia Antica) The
Catacombe di San Sebastiano were the first
burial chambers to be called catacombs, the
name deriving from the Greek *kata* (near)
and *kymbas* (cavity), because they were
located near a cave. During the persecutory
reign of Vespasian, they provided a safe hav-
en for the remains of Saints Peter and Paul.

The 1st level is now almost completely
destroyed, but frescoes, stucco work and epigraphs can be seen on the 2nd level. There
are also three perfectly preserved mausol-
eums and a plastered wall with hundreds of
invocations to Peter and Paul, engraved by
worshippers in the 3rd and 4th centuries.

Above the catacombs, the **Basilica di San
Sebastiano**, a much-altered 4th-century
church, preserves one of the arrows allegedly used to kill St Sebastian, and the column
to which he was tied.

Catacombe di San Callisto   CATACOMB

(Map p115; ☎ 06 513 01 51; www.catacombe.roma.
it; Via Appia Antica 110 & 126; adult/reduced €8/5;
⊗ 9am-noon & 2-5pm, closed Wed & Feb; ☐ Via Appia Antica) These are the largest and busiest
of Rome's catacombs. Founded at the end of
the 2nd century and named after Pope Ca-
lixtus I, they became the official cemetery of
the newly established Roman Church. In the
20km of tunnels explored to date, archaeologists have found the tombs of 500,000
people and seven popes who were martyred
in the 3rd century.

The patron saint of music, St Cecilia, was
also buried here, though her body was later

THE CATACOMBS

Built as communal burial grounds, the catacombs were the early Christians' solution to the problem of what to do with their dead. Belief in the Resurrection meant that they couldn't cremate their corpses, as was the custom at the time, and Roman law forbade burial within the city walls. Furthermore, as a persecuted minority they didn't have their own cemeteries. So, in the 2nd century they began to dig beneath Via Appia Antica, where a number of Christians already had family tombs.

Over time, as Christianity became more popular, competition for burial space became fierce and a cut-throat trade in tomb real estate developed. However, by the late 4th century, Christianity had been legalised and the Christians had begun to bury their dead near the basilicas that were springing up within the city walls. By the Middle Ages the catacombs had been all but abandoned.

More than 30 catacombs have been uncovered in the Rome area since scholars started researching them in the 19th century.

removed to the Basilica di Santa Cecilia in Trastevere. When her body was exhumed in 1599, more than a thousand years after her death, it was apparently perfectly preserved, as depicted in Stefano Maderno's softly contoured sculpture, a replica of which is here.

Catacombe di Santa Domitilla   CATACOMB
(Map p115; ☑06 511 03 42; www.domitilla.info; Via delle Sette Chiese 283; adult/reduced €8/5; ⊙9am-noon & 2-5pm Wed-Mon, closed Jan; ☐Via Appia Antica) Among Rome's largest and oldest, these wonderful catacombs stretch for about 18km. They were established on the private burial ground of Flavia Domitilla, niece of the emperor Domitian and a member of the wealthy Flavian family. They contain Christian wall paintings and the haunting underground **Chiesa di SS Nereus e Achilleus**, a 4th-century church dedicated to two Roman soldiers martyred by Diocletian.

Villa di Massenzio   RUINS
(Map p115; ☑06 780 13 24; www.villadimassenzio. it; Via Appia Antica 153; ⊙9am-1pm Tue-Sat; ☐Via Appia Antica) The outstanding feature of Maxentius' enormous 4th-century palace complex is the **Circo di Massenzio** (Map p115; Via Appia Antica 153; ☐Via Appia Antica), Rome's best-preserved ancient racetrack – you can still make out the starting stalls used for chariot races. The 10,000-seat arena was built by Maxentius around 309, but he died before ever seeing a race here.

Above the arena are the ruins of Maxentius' imperial residence. Near the racetrack, the **Mausoleo di Romolo** (Tombo di Romolo; Map p115; Via Appia Antica 153; ☐Via Appia Antica) was built by Maxentius for his 17-year-old son Romulus. The huge mausoleum was

originally crowned with a large dome and surrounded by an imposing colonnade, in part still visible. The Torlonia family extended the tomb, turning it into a country house.

Mausoleo di Cecilia Metella   RUIN
(Map p115; ☑06 3996 7700; www.coopculture.it; Via Appia Antica 161; adult/reduced incl Terme di Caracalla & Villa dei Quintili €7/4; ⊙9am-1hr before sunset Tue-Sun; ☐Via Appia Antica) Dating to the 1st century BC, this great drum of a mausoleum encloses a burial chamber, now roofless. In the 14th century it was converted into a fort by the Caetani family, who were related to Pope Boniface VIII, and who frightened passing travellers into paying a toll.

EUR   AREA
(Ⓜ EUR Palasport) This Orwellian quarter of wide boulevards and linear buildings was built for an international exhibition in 1942, and although war intervened and the exhibition never took place, the name stuck – Esposizione Universale di Roma (Roman Universal Exhibition) or EUR.

The area's main interest lies in its rationalist architecture, which finds perfect form in the **Palazzo della Civiltà del Lavoro**, aka the Square Colosseum.

Courses

Cooking & Wine Tasting

Roman Kitchen   COOKING
(Map p78; ☑06 678 57 59; www.italiangourmet. com; per day €200) Cookery writer Diane Seed (*The Top One Hundred Pasta Sauces*) runs cooking courses from her kitchen in Palazzo Doria Pamphilj. There are one-day, two-day, three-day and week-long courses costing €200 per day and €1000 per week.

Vino Roma WINE COURSE
(Map p102; ☑ 328 4874497; www.vinoroma.com; Via in Selci 84/G; 2hr tastings per person €50) With beautifully appointed 1000-year-old cellars and a chic tasting studio, Vino Roma guides novices and experts in tasting wine, under the knowledgeable stewardship of sommelier Hande Leimer and his expert team. Tastings are in English, but German, Japanese, Italian and Turkish sessions are available on special request. It also offers a wine-and-cheese dinner (€60), with snacks, cheeses and cold cuts to accompany the wines, and bespoke three-hour food tours. Book online.

Language

There are hundreds of schools offering language courses. Costs vary enormously, but bank on €380 to €440 for a two-week group course or €35 to €45 for individual lessons. Some schools also offer accommodation packages.

**Divulgazione Lingua
Italiana** LANGUAGE COURSE
(Map p102; ☑ 06 446 25 93; www.dilit.it; Via Marghera 22) School offering a range of language and cultural courses.

**Torre di Babele Centro di Lingua
e Cultura Italiana** LANGUAGE COURSE
(☑ 06 4425 2578; www.torredibabele.com; Via Cosenza 7) As well as language lessons, offers courses on cooking, art, architecture and several other subjects.

Arts & Crafts

If the sight of so much art in the Vatican has inspired you, head to the **Art Studio Café** (Map p92; ☑ 06 3260 9104; www.artstudiocafe. it; Via dei Gracchi 187a; ☺ 7.30am-9pm Mon-Sat; Ⓜ Lepanto), a bright cafe that doubles as a mosaic and craft school. There are various courses on offer, including a two-hour introduction to mosaic-making (€50 or €35 for children), an eight-lesson course in ceramics (€300), and a six-lesson course in drawing and painting (€180).

☞ Tours

A Friend in Rome TOUR
(☑ 340 5019201; www.afriendinrome.it) Silvia Prosperi organises private tailor-made tours (on foot, by bike or scooter) to suit your interests. She covers the Vatican and main historic centre as well as areas outside the capital. Rates are €50 per hour, with a minimum of three hours for most tours. She

can also arrange kid-friendly tours, cooking classes, vintage-car tours and more.

Roman Guy TOUR
(http://theromanguy.com) A professional setup that organises a wide range of group and private tours. Packages, led by English-speaking experts, include early-bird visits to the Vatican Museums (US$84), foodie tours of Trastevere and the Jewish Ghetto (US$84), and a bar hop through the historic centre's cocktail bars.

Eating Italy Food Tours FOOD TOUR
(www.eatingitalyfoodtours.com; €75; ☺ daily) This cheery food tour company is run by American ex-pat Kenny Dunn, and offers informative four-hour tours around the Testaccio (the heartland of traditional Roman cooking), or Trastevere, with chances to taste 12 delicacies on the way. There are a maximum of 12 people to a tour.

Top Bike Rental & Tours BICYCLE TOUR
(Map p110; ☑ 06 488 28 93; www.topbikerental. com; Via Labicana 49; ☺ 10am-7pm) Offers a series of bike tours throughout the city, including a four-hour 16km exploration of the city centre (€45) and an all-day 30km ride through Via Appia Antica and environs (€79). Out-of-town tours take in Castel Gandolfo, Civita di Bagnoregio and Orvieto.

Open Bus Cristiana BUS TOUR
(www.operaromanapellegrinaggi.org; single tour €15, 24/48hr ticket €20/48; ☺ 9am-6pm) The Vatican-sponsored Opera Romana Pellegrinaggi runs a hop-on, hop-off bus departing from Via della Conciliazione and Termini. Stops are situated near to main sights including St Peter's Basilica, Piazza Navona, the Trevi Fountain and the Colosseum. Tickets are available on board or at the meeting point just off St Peter's Sq.

☆ Festivals & Events

Carnevale Romano CARNIVAL
(www.carnevaleroma.com; ☺ Feb) Rome goes to town for carnival with leaping horse shows on Piazza del Popolo, costumed parades down Via del Corso, street performers on Piazza Navona and crowds of kids in fancy dress.

Easter RELIGIOUS
(☺ Mar/Apr) On Good Friday, the pope leads a candlelit procession around the Colosseum. At noon on Easter Sunday he blesses the crowds in St Peter's Square.

Mostra delle Azalee CULTURAL
From mid-April to early May, the Spanish Steps are decorated with 600 vases of blooming azaleas in the Exhibition of Azaleas.

Natale di Roma CULTURAL
Rome celebrates its birthday on 21 April with music, historical re-enactments and fireworks. Action is centred on Via dei Fori Imperiali and the city's ancient sites.

Primo Maggio MUSIC
Rome's May Day rock concert attracts huge crowds and big-name Italian performers to Piazza di San Giovanni in Laterano.

Estate Romana CULTURAL
(www.estateromana.comune.roma.it) From June to October Rome's big summer festival includes hundreds of cultural events and activities across the capital.

Lungo il Tevere ARTS
(www.lungoiltevereroma.it) Summer-long festival, with comedy acts, jazz, film, craft stalls and bars, clustered around the banks of Tiberina island.

Festa dei Santi Pietro e Paolo RELIGIOUS
Romans celebrate the feast of patron saints Peter and Paul on 29 June. Festivities are centred on St Peter's Basilica and Via Ostiense.

Festa de'Noantri CULTURAL
Trastevere's annual party, held in the third week of July, involves plenty of food, wine, prayer and dancing.

RomaEuropa PERFORMING ARTS
(http://romaeuropa.net) From September to November, top international artists take to the stage for Rome's autumn festival of theatre, opera and dance.

Festa del Cinema di Roma FILM
(www.romacinemafest.it) Held at the Auditorium Parco della Musica in late October, Rome's film festival rolls out the red carpet for big-screen big shots.

🛌 Sleeping

While there's plenty of choice, accommodation in Rome is expensive. The most atmospheric place to stay is the *centro storico*, where you'll have everything on your doorstep. Midrange choices abound, but there's only a smattering of good budget options. Near the Vatican, Prati is a good bet with a decent range of options, excellent restaurants and convenient metro stations (line A). Trastevere is drop-dead gorgeous and a great place to spend summer evenings, but it can be noisy.

The cheapest places are around Stazione Termini. This area, though not as bad as it's sometimes made out to be, is not Rome's most beautiful, and some of the streets to the west of the station, particularly Via Giolitti, can be dodgy at night. Women in particular should be careful. That said, it's convenient and most sights are only a metro ride away.

Rome doesn't have a low season as such but rates are at their lowest from November to March (excluding Christmas and New Year) and from mid-July through August. Expect to pay top whack in spring (April to June) and autumn (September and October) and over the main holiday periods (Christmas, New Year and Easter). Always try to book ahead.

You'll find a full list of accommodation options at www.060608.it.

Accommodation Options
The bulk of accommodation in Rome is made up of *alberghi* (hotels) and *pensioni* (small hotels often in converted apartments). Most central hotels tend to be three-star and up.

Alongside traditional family-run B&Bs, Rome has a large number of boutique-style B&Bs and guesthouses offering chic, designer accommodation at midrange to top-end prices. The following agencies both offer online booking services: **Bed & Breakfast Association of Rome** (www.b-b.rm.it), which lists B&Bs and short-term apartment rentals, and **Bed & Breakfast Italia** (www.bbitalia.it), Rome's longest-established B&B network.

Rome's hostels cater to everyone from backpackers to budget-minded families. Many offer traditional dorms as well as hotel-style rooms with private bathrooms.

Many of Rome's religious institutions offer budget accommodation. These often impose strict curfews and are fairly short on frills. For a list of institutions, check out www.santasusanna.org/comingToRome/convents.html.

For longer stays, renting an apartment will generally work out cheaper than an extended hotel sojourn. Bank on about €900 per month for a studio apartment or one-bedroom flat. Useful resources include **Rome As You Feel** (www.romeasyoufeel.

com), which offers apartment rentals, from cheap studio flats to luxury apartments, and **Sleep in Italy** (www.sleepinitaly.com), a reliable rental operator.

🛏 Ancient Rome

★ **Residenza Maritti** GUESTHOUSE €€
(Map p68; ☑06 678 82 33; www.residenzamaritti.com; Via Tor de' Conti 17; s €50-120, d €80-170, tr €100-190; ❄ 🗢; Ⓜ Cavour) Boasting stunning views over the forums, this gem has rooms spread over several floors. Some are bright and modern, others are more cosy in feel with antiques and family furniture. There's no breakfast but you can use a fully equipped kitchen.

Nerva Boutique Hotel BOUTIQUE HOTEL €€
(Map p68; ☑06 678 18 35; www.hotelnerva.com; Via Tor de' Conti 3; s €70-180, d €90-300; ❄ 🗢; Ⓜ Cavour) Fresh from a recent makeover, this friendly hotel is tucked away behind the Imperial Forums. Its snug rooms display a contemporary look in shades of cream, grey and black, with padded leather bedsteads, hanging lamps, and the occasional art tome.

🛏 Centro Storico

Hotel Pensione Barrett PENSION €
(Map p78; ☑06 686 84 81; www.pensionebarrett.com; Largo di Torre Argentina 47; s €115, d €125, tr €150; ❄ 🗢; 🖳 Largo di Torre Argentina) This charming pension boasts a convenient central location and an exuberant decor that marries leafy pot plants with statues, busts and vibrant stucco. Rooms are cosy and come with thoughtful extras like foot spas and fully stocked fridges.

Albergo del Sole HOTEL €
(Map p78; ☑06 687 94 46; www.soledelbiscione.it; Via del Biscione 76; s €70-100, d €100-145, tr €120-180; ❄ 🗢; 🖳 Corso Vittorio Emanuele II) This simple, no-frills place is supposedly the oldest hotel in Rome, dating to 1462. There's nothing special about the functional rooms, but each floor has its own outdoor terrace, and the location near Campo de' Fiori is excellent. No breakfast.

Albergo Cesàri HISTORIC HOTEL €€
(Map p78; ☑06 674 97 01; www.albergocesari.it; Via di Pietra 89/A; s €70-150, d €110-250; ❄ 🗢; 🖳 Via del Corso) This friendly three-star has been welcoming guests since 1787 and both Stendhal and Mazzini are said to have slept here. Modern visitors can expect tradition-

al rooms, a stunning rooftop terrace, and a wonderful central location.

Hotel Due Torri HOTEL €€
(Map p78; ☑06 6880 6956; www.hotelduetorriroma.com; Vicolo del Leonetto 23; s €70-140, d €110-220, tr €140-240; ❄ 🗢; 🖳 Via di Monte Brianzo) If the rooms at this refined hotel could talk, they'd have some stories to tell. The Due Torre might now be a classically attired three-star with period furniture and 26 cosy rooms, but in centuries past it has housed a cardinals' residence and a brothel.

Argentina Residenza BOUTIQUE HOTEL €€
(Map p78; ☑06 6819 3267; www.argentinaresidenza.com; Via di Torre Argentina 47; r €120-200; ❄ 🗢; 🖳 Largo di Torre Argentina) Escape the hustle and relax in the comfort of this quiet boutique hotel on Largo di Torre Argentina. Its six decently sized rooms sport a low-key contemporary look with design touches and elegant furnishings.

Hotel Navona HOTEL €€
(Map p78; ☑06 6821 1392; www.hotelnavona.com; Via dei Sediari 8; s €60-170, d €60-260; ❄ 🗢; 🖳 Corso del Rinascimento) This small hotel offers a range of handsome, modern rooms in a 15th-century *palazzo* near Piazza Navona. They come in various shapes and looks but the most striking feature a showy silver-and-grey design. Breakfast costs €10 extra.

Hotel Teatro di Pompeo HOTEL €€
(Map p78; ☑06 6830 0170; www.hotelteatrodipompeo.it; Largo del Pallaro 8; s €90-165, d €110-220; ❄ @ 🗢; 🖳 Corso Vittorio Emanuele II) Tucked away behind Campo de' Fiori, this charming hotel sits atop the 1st-century-BC Theatre of Pompey – the basement breakfast

---

HOTEL TAX

Everyone overnighting in Rome has to pay a room-occupancy tax on top of their regular accommodation bill. This amounts to:

➡ €3 per person per night in one- and two-star hotels

➡ €3.50 in B&Bs and room rentals

➡ €4/6/7 in three-/four-/five-star hotels

The tax is applicable for a maximum of 10 consecutive nights. Prices quoted in this section don't include the tax.

room is actually in the theatre's ruins. Rooms are attractive with classic wooden furniture, terracotta floor tiles, and, in some, sloping wood-beamed ceilings.

Dimora degli Dei
BOUTIQUE HOTEL €€

(Map p78; ☑06 6819 3267; www.pantheondimoradeglidei.com; Via del Seminario 87; r €80-200; ❄️ 🗣️; ⬜Largo di Torre Argentina) Location and discreet style are the selling points of this elegant bolthole near the Pantheon. On the 1st floor of a centuries-old *palazzo*, it has six high-ceilinged tastefully furnished rooms. Breakfast (€10) is optional.

★Hotel Campo de' Fiori
BOUTIQUE HOTEL €€€

(Map p78; ☑06 687 48 86; www.hotelcampodefiori.com; Via del Biscione 6; r €90-400, apt €80-350; ❄️ @ 🗣️; ⬜Corso Vittorio Emanuele II) This rakish four-star has got the lot – baroque boudoir decor, an enviable location, professional staff and a fabulous panoramic roof terrace. The interior feels delightfully decadent with its boldly coloured walls, low wooden ceil-

ings, gilt mirrors and restored bric-a-brac. Also available are 13 apartments.

🛏️ Tridente, Trevi & the Quirinale

La Controra
HOSTEL €

(Map p102; ☑06 9893 7366; Via Umbria 7; dm €20-40, d €80-110; ❄️ @ 🗣️; Ⓜ️Barberini, Ⓜ️Repubblica) Quality budget accommodation is thin on the ground in the upmarket area north of Piazza Repubblica, but this great little hostel is a top choice. It has a friendly laid-back vibe, cool staff, double rooms and bright, airy mixed dorms (for three and four people), with parquet floors, air-con and private bathrooms.

Hotel Panda
PENSION €

(Map p88; ☑06 678 01 79; www.hotelpanda.it; Via della Croce 35; s €65-90, d €85-130, tr €120-150, q €160-190; ❄️ 🗣️; Ⓜ️Spagna) Near the Spanish Steps, in an area where a bargain is a Bulgari watch bought at the sales, the Panda

---

ROME FOR CHILDREN

Romans love children and even if there are few child-specific sights in town, your little ones will be welcome just about everywhere.

Practicalities

➡ Cobbled streets and badly parked cars make getting around with a pram or pushchair difficult.

➡ Restaurants are generally laid-back when it comes to accommodating children and will happily serve a *mezza porzione* (child's portion) and provide a *seggiolone* (high chair). Some hotels can supply a *culla* (cot) on request.

➡ Buy baby formula and sterilising solutions at pharmacies. Disposable nappies/diapers (*pannolini* in Italian) are available from supermarkets and pharmacies.

➡ Children under 10 travel free on public transport.

Sights

Rome's museums and galleries are not ideal for rampaging toddlers, but many of the bigger ones now offer educational services and children's workshops.

Suggested sights for kids include the **Colosseum** (p66) and **Villa Borghese** (p112), home to Rome's zoo, the **Bioparco** (Map p113; ☑06 360 82 11; www.bioparco.it; Viale del Giardino Zoologico 1; adult/reduced €15/12; ⊙9.30am-6pm summer, to 5pm winter; ⬜Bioparco). They might also enjoy putting their hands in the **Bocca della Verità** (p77) and throwing coins into the **Trevi Fountain** (p87). The catacombs on **Via Appia Antica** (p115) are best for children over about 12.

Explora (Map p113; ☑06 361 37 76; www.mdbr.it; Via Flaminia 82; adult/reduced €8/5; ⊙entrance 10am, noon, 3pm & 5pm Tue-Sun; Ⓜ️Flaminio) is a hands-on, feet-on museum dedicated to kids under 12. Bookings are advised and essential on weekends. Outside there's a free play park open to all.

Out of town in **Tivoli**, the gardens at **Villa D'Este** (p151) are fun to explore and the extensive ruins of **Villa Adriana** (p150) provide ample opportunity for playing hide-and-seek.

flies the flag for budget accommodation. It's a friendly place with high-ceilinged rooms and simple, tasteful decor. Air-con is free in summer, but €6 in other periods.

La Piccola Maison
B&B €€

(Map p88; ☑ 06 4201 6331; www.lapiccolamaison. com; Via dei Cappuccini 30; s €50-180, d €70-270; ❄ ☎; Ⓜ Barberini) The excellent Piccola Maison is housed in a 19th-century building in a great location close to Piazza Barberini, and has pleasingly plain, neutrally decorated rooms and thoughtful staff. It's a great deal.

Daphne Inn
BOUTIQUE HOTEL €€

(Map p88; ☑ 06 8745 0086; www.daphne-rome. com; Via di San Basilio 55; s €115-180, d €130-240, ste €190-290, without bathroom s €70-130, d €90-160; ❄ ☎; Ⓜ Barberini) Run by an American-Italian couple, the Daphne has helpful staff who speak English, and chic, comfortable rooms. They come in various shapes and sizes, but the overall look is smart contemporary. There's a second branch, Daphne Trevi, offering more of the same at Via degli Avignonesi 20.

Hotel Suisse
PENSION €€

(Map p88; ☑ 06 678 36 49; www.hotelsuisserome. com; Via Gregoriana 54; s €80-100, d €135-170, tr €180-200; @ ☎; Ⓜ Spagna, Ⓜ Barberini) An air of old-school elegance pervades this delightful family-run pension. Attractive antique furniture and creaking, polished parquet floors set the tone for the 12 tasteful, modestly decorated rooms.

Gregoriana
HOTEL €€

(Map p88; ☑ 06 679 42 69; www.hotelgregoriana. it; Via Gregoriana 18; s €120-168, d €150-288; ❄; Ⓜ Spagna) This low-key, polished art-deco hotel is fantastically set behind the Spanish Steps. Beds have beautiful, circular maplewood headboards, snow-white linen and lots of gleaming rosewood. Staff are friendly and unpretentious.

Margutta Glamour Studios
APARTMENT €€

(Map p88; ☑ 333 7982702; www.marguttaglamour studios.com; Via Margutta 54-55; apartment €150-180; Ⓜ Spagna) Four charming apartments on one of Rome's prettiest streets, which has a village feel despite being in the thick of Tridente. All are decorated with flair, and the two larger apartments, in former artists' studios, are spectacular, with double height ceilings; the smaller two are charming, with pretty outlooks.

Hotel Mozart
HOTEL €€

(Map p88; ☑ 06 3600 1915; www.hotelmozart.com; Via dei Greci 23b; r €140-200; ❄ @ ☎; Ⓜ Spagna) The Mozart has classic, immaculate rooms, decorated in dove greys, eggshell blues, golden yellows and rosy pinks, with comfortable beds, gleaming linen and polished wooden furniture; deluxe rooms have jacuzzis and small terraces.

Hotel Barocco
HOTEL €€

(Map p88; ☑ 06 487 20 01; www.hotelbarocco.com; Piazza Barberini 9; d €160-290; ❄ @ ☎; Ⓜ Barberini) Very central, this well-run, welcoming 41-room hotel overlooking Piazza Barberini (the pricier rooms have views) has a classic feel, with rooms featuring oil paintings, spotless linen, gentle colour schemes and fabric-covered walls. Breakfast is ample and served in a wood-panelled room.

Hotel Modigliani
HOTEL €€

(Map p88; ☑ 06 4281 5226; www.hotelmodigliani. com; Via della Purificazione 42; s €100-160, d €100-270; ❄ ☎; Ⓜ Barberini) Run by an artistic couple, the Modigliani is all about attention to detail and customer service. The 23 dove-grey rooms are spacious and light, and the best ones have views and balconies, either outside or over the quiet internal courtyard garden.

★ Babuino 181
BOUTIQUE HOTEL €€€

(Map p88; ☑ 06 3229 5295; www.romeluxurysuites. com/babuino; Via del Babuino 181; r €240-715; ❄ ☎; Ⓜ Flaminio) A beautifully renovated old *palazzo*, Babuino offers discreet luxury with great attention to detail, a sleek roof terrace and modern, chic rooms with touches such as a Nespresso machine and fluffy bathrobes. A new annexe across the street has added more suites and rooms that continue the theme of understated elegance. The same company runs the similarly impressive **Margutta 54** (Map p88; ☑ 06 322 95 295; www. romeluxurysuites.com/margutta/default-en.html; Via Margutta 54; d from €250; Ⓜ Spagna) and Mario de' Fiori 37.

Casa Fabbrini
B&B €€€

(Map p88; ☑ 06 324 3706; www.casafabbrini.it; Vicolo delle Orsoline 13; r €280; Ⓜ Spagna) A beautifully styled boutique B&B that could have sprung from the pages of *Elle Decoration*, with weathered antique doors as bedheads, coloured glass lamps, and painted furniture.

🛏 Vatican City, Borgo & Prati

Hotel San Pietrino
HOTEL €

(Map p92; ☑06 370 01 32; www.sanpietrino.
it; Via Bettolo 43; s €45-75, d €55-112; ❄@🖥;
ⓜOttaviano–San-Pietro) Within easy walking distance of St Peter's, family-run San
Pietrino is an excellent budget choice. Its
11 cosy rooms are characterful and prettily decorated with terracotta-tiled floors
and the occasional statue. No breakfast.

Colors Hotel
HOTEL €

(Map p92; ☑06 687 40 30; www.colorshotel.
com; Via Boezio 31; s €30-90, d €45-122; ❄🖥;
🚇Via Cola di Rienzo) Popular with young
travellers, this welcoming hotel impresses
with its fresh, artful design and vibrantly
coloured rooms. These come in various
shapes and sizes, including some cheaper ones with shared bathrooms and, from
June to August, dorms for guests under
38. Breakfast on request costs €6.50.

Le Stanze di Orazio
B&B €€

(Map p92; ☑06 3265 2474; www.lestanzedi
orazio.com; Via Orazio 3; r €85-135; ❄@🖥;
ⓜLepanto) This small boutique B&B is excellent value for money. It has five bright,
playfully decorated rooms – think shimmering rainbow wallpaper, lilac accents,
and designer bathrooms – and a small
breakfast area.

Hotel Bramante
HISTORIC HOTEL €€

(Map p92; ☑06 6880 6426; www.hotelbram
ante.com; Vicolo delle Palline 24-25; s €100-
160, d €140-240, tr €175-260, q €190-300;
❄🖥; 🚇Borgo Sant'Angelo) Nestled under
the Vatican walls, the Bramante exudes
country-house charm with its cosy internal courtyard, wood-beamed ceilings
and antique furniture. It's housed in the
16th-century building where architect Domenico Fontana once lived.

★ Villa Laetitia
BOUTIQUE HOTEL €€€

(☑06 322 67 76; www.villalaetitia.com; Lungotevere delle Armi 22; r €200-280, ste €500; ❄🖥;

GAY & LESBIAN ROME

Rome has a thriving, if low-key, gay scene. And while tolerance is widespread, discretion
is still wise.

The highlights of the city's LGBT calendar are **Roma Pride** (www.romapride.it), a colourful annual parade held in mid-June, and **Gay Village**, which hosts a summer season
of gigs and club nights, usually in EUR.

There are relatively few queer-only venues, but close to the Colosseum, **Via di San
Giovanni in Laterano** is a favourite hang-out with a cluster of popular bars. There's
also a gay beach, **Settimo Cielo**, outside town at Capocotta, accessible via bus 61 from
Ostia Lido or bus 70 from EUR.

For local information, pick up the monthly magazine *AUT* published by **Circolo
Mario Mieli** (☑800 110611; www.mariomieli.org; Via Efeso 2a), Rome's main gay cultural
organisation. There's also info at **AZ Gay** (www.azgay.it). Lesbians can find out about
the local scene at **Coordinamento Lesbiche Italiano** (Map p78; www.clrbp.it; Via San
Francesco di Sales 1b).

Many gay venues require an **Arcigay** (☑06 6450 1102; www.arcigayroma.it; Via Nicola
Zabaglia 14) membership card. These cost €15/8 per year/three months and are available
from any venue that requires one.

La Foresteria Orsa Maggiore (Map p78; ☑06 689 37 53; www.casainternazionaledelle-
donne.org; 2nd fl, Via San Francesco di Sales 1a; dm €26, s/d €75/110, without bathroom s/d
€52/72; @🖥; 🚇Piazza Trilussa) A women-only guesthouse (boys aged 12 or younger are
welcome) run by the Casa Internazionale delle Donne (International Women's House) in
a quiet corner of Trastevere.

Coming Out (Map p110; www.comingout.it; Via di San Giovanni in Laterano 8; ⏰7am-2am;
🚇Via Labicana) An easygoing bar in the shadow of the Colosseum, recognisable by its
rainbow sign and the convivial crowds that spill out onto the street.

L'Alibi (Map p134; Via di Monte Testaccio 44; ⏰11.30pm-5am Thu-Sun; 🚇Via Galvani) Sultry,
cavernous gay club that puts on kitsch shows, and house, techno and dance music. Saturday's Tommy Night is the hot date right now.

⌨Lungotevere delle Armi) Villa Laetitia is a stunning boutique hotel in a riverside art-nouveau villa. Its 20 rooms, each individually designed by Anna Venturini Fendi of the famous fashion house, marry modern design touches with vintage pieces and rare finds, such as an original Picasso in the Garden Room.

Monti, Esquilino & San Lorenzo

★ Beehive   HOSTEL €

(Map p102; ☑ 06 4470 4553; www.the-beehive. com; Via Marghera 8; dm €25-35, s €50-80, d €90-100, without bathroom s €60-70, d €70-80, tr €95-105; ✳ 🛜; M Termini) 🏖 More boutique chic than backpacker dive, the Beehive is Rome's best hostel; book well ahead. There's a spotless, eight-person mixed dorm or six private double rooms, some with air-con. Original artworks and funky modular furniture add colour, plus there's a cafe. Some bright, well-cared-for off-site rooms, sharing communal bathrooms and kitchen, are another bargain (single €40 to €50, double €60 to €80).

Blue Hostel   HOSTEL €

(Map p102; ☑ 340 9258503; www.bluehostel.it; Via Carlo Alberto 13, 3rd fl; d €60-150, apt €100-180; ✳ 🛜; M Vittorio Emanuele) A hostel in name only, this pearl offers small, hotel-standard rooms, each with its own en suite bathroom, and decorated in tasteful low-key style – beamed ceilings, wooden floors, French windows, black-and-white framed photos. There's also an apartment, with kitchen, that sleeps up to four. No lift and no breakfast.

Welrome Hotel   HOTEL €

(Map p102; ☑ 06 4782 4343; www.welrome.it; Via Calatafimi 15-19; d/tr/q €110/148/187; ✳ 🛜 ♿; M Termini) A small, spotless hotel in a quiet backstreet not far from Termini. Owners Mary and Carlo take great pride in looking after their guests and will enthusiastically advise you on where to eat, what to do and where to avoid. Their seven simply decorated rooms are clean and comfortable. No breakfast but kettles and fridges are provided, and there are plenty of nearby bars for a *cornetto* (croissant) and coffee.

Alessandro Palace Hostel   HOSTEL €

(Map p102; ☑ 06 446 19 58; www.hostelsalessan dro.com; Via Vicenza 42; dm €19-35, d €70-110, tr €85-120; ✳ @ 🛜; M Castro Pretorio) This long-standing, well-kept favourite offers spick-and-span, terracotta-floored doubles and triples, as well as dorms sleeping from four to eight, all with cheery bedspreads. Every room has its own bathroom with hairdryer. There's a basement bar, and it runs local tours.

Hotel Artorius   HOTEL €€

(Map p88; ☑ 06 482 11 96; www.hotelartorius rome.com; Via del Boschetto 13; d €86-140; ✳ @ 🛜; M Cavour) The art-deco lobby looks promising, and the rest delivers too in this 10-room Monti hotel with a family-run feel. Rooms are simple and plain – not large, but perfectly comfortable – and one (room 109) has a terrace. Book well ahead.

Residenza Cellini   GUESTHOUSE €€

(Map p102; ☑ 06 4782 5204; www.residenzacellini. it; Via Modena 5; s €100-135, d €115-150; ✳ @ 🛜; M Repubblica) With grown-up furnishings featuring potted palms, polished wood, pale-yellow walls, oil paintings and a hint of chintz, this charming, family-run place on a quiet road parallel to Via Nazionale offers spacious, elegant rooms, all with satellite TV and jacuzzi or hydro-massage shower. There's a sunny flower-surrounded terrace for summer breakfasts.

Duca d'Alba   HOTEL €€

(Map p68; ☑ 06 48 44 71; www.hotelducadalba. com; Via Leonina 14; r €115-380; ✳ 🛜; M Cavour) This appealing four-star hotel in the Monti district has small but charming rooms: most have fabric-covered or handpainted walls, wood-beamed ceilings, big flat-screen TVs and sleek button-studded headboards.

★ Villa Spalletti Trivelli   HOTEL €€€

(Map p88; ☑ 06 4890 7934; www.villaspalletti.it; Via Piacenza 4; r €450-620; ✳ @ 🛜; M Spagna) With 12 rooms in a glorious mansion in central Rome, Villa Spalletti Trivelli was built by Gabriella Rasponi, widow of Italian senator Count Venceslao Spalletti Triveli and the niece of Carolina Bonaparte (Napoleon's sister). It offers a soujourn in a stately home: rooms are soberly and elegantly decorated, and the sitting rooms are hung with 16th-century tapestries or lined by antique books. There's a basement spa.

Trastevere & Gianicolo

Maria-Rosa Guesthouse   B&B €

(Map p108; ☑ 338 7700067; www.maria-rosa.it; Via dei Vascellari 55; s €45-65, d €65-80, tr €80-120; @ 🛜; ⌨ Viale di Trastevere, ⌨ Viale di Trastevere) This is a delightful B&B on the 3rd floor of a Trastevere townhouse. It's a simple affair with two guest rooms sharing a single bathroom and a small living room, but the homey decor, pot plants and books create a lovely, warm atmosphere. The owner, Sylvie, also has a further three rooms on the floor above at **La Casa di Kaia** (Map p108; ☑338 7700067; www.kaia-trastevere.it; Via dei Vascellari 55; with shared bathroom s €45-55, d €65-75; ❀; ☐Viale di Trastevere, ☐Viale di Trastevere). No lift.

★ Arco del Lauro   B&B €€

(Map p108; ☑346 2443212, 9am-2pm 06 9784 0350; www.arcodellauro.it; Via Arco de' Tolomei 27; s €72-132, d €132-145; ❀❀; ☐Viale di Trastevere, ☐Viale di Trastevere) A real find, this fab six-room B&B occupies a centuries-old *palazzo* on a narrow cobbled street. Its gleaming white rooms combine rustic charm with a modern low-key look and comfortable beds. The owners extend a warm welcome and are always ready to help.

Relais Le Clarisse   HOTEL €€

(Map p108; ☑06 5833 4437; www.leclarisse. com; Via Cardinale Merry del Val 20; r €80-230; ❀❀; ☐Viale di Trastevere, ☐Viale di Trastevere) Set hacienda-style around a pretty internal courtyard with an olive tree and a smattering of cast-iron tables, this is a delightful oasis in Trastevere's bustling core. In contrast to the urban mayhem outside, the hotel is a picture of farmhouse charm with rooms, each named after a plant, decorated in rustic style with wrought-iron bedsteads and wood-beamed ceilings.

Hotel Santa Maria   HOTEL €€

(Map p108; ☑06 589 46 26; www.hotelsanta maria.info; Vicolo del Piede 2; s €90-225, d €100-290, tr €130-330 ; ❀@❀; ☐Viale di Trastevere, ☐Viale di Trastevere) Walk along the ivy-lined approach and you'll enter a tranquil haven. Surrounding a spacious modern cloister (a former convent site), shaded by orange trees, rooms are cool and comfortable, decorated in sunny colours, and with terracotta floors. There are some larger family rooms. Staff are helpful and professional, and there's access for people with a disability. There are deals offered for longer stays in summer.

★ Donna Camilla Savelli   HOTEL €€€

(Map p108; ☑06 58 88 61; www.hoteldonna camillasavelli.com; Via Garibaldi 27; d €165-250; ❀@❀; ☐Viale di Trastevere, ☐Viale di Trastevere) It's seldom you have such an exquisite opportunity as to stay in a converted convent that was designed by baroque genius Borromini. It's been beautifully updated; muted colours complement the serene concave and convex curves of the architecture, and service is excellent. The pricier of the 78 rooms overlook the lovely cloister garden or have views of Rome, and are decorated with antiques – it's worth forking out that bit extra.

🛏 San Giovanni & Celio

Hotel Lancelot   HOTEL €€

(Map p110; ☑06 7045 0615; www.lancelothotel. com; Via Capo d'Africa 47; s €100-128, d €130-196; ❀❀; ☐Via di San Giovanni in Laterano) A great location near the Colosseum, striking views, and super-helpful English-speaking staff – the family-run Lancelot scores across the board. The lobby and communal areas gleam with marble and crystal while the spacious rooms exhibit a more modest classic style.

🛏 Aventino & Testaccio

★ Althea Inn   B&B €

(☑339 4353717, 06 9893 2666; www.altheainn. com; Via dei Conciatori 9; d €70-125; Ⓜ Piramide) In a workaday apartment block, this friendly B&B offers superb value for money and easy access to Testaccio's bars, clubs and restaurants. Its spacious, light-filled rooms sport a modish look with white walls and tasteful modern furniture. Each also has a small terrace.

★ Hotel Sant'Anselmo   HOTEL €€€

(Map p134; ☑06 57 00 57; www.aventinohotels. com; Piazza Sant'Anselmo 2; s €90-265, d €99-290; ❀❀; ☐Via Marmorata) A ravishing romantic hideaway in the elegant Aventino district. Its rooms are not the biggest but they are stylish, juxtaposing four-poster beds, Liberty-style furniture and marble bathrooms with modern touches and contemporary colours.

🛏 Villa Borghese & Northern Rome

★ Palm Gallery Hotel   HOTEL €€

(☑06 6478 1859; www.palmgalleryhotel.com; Via delle Alpi 15d; s €100-120, d €100-210; ❀❀; ☐Via Nomentana, ☐Viale Regina Margherita) Housed in an early-20th-century villa, this gorgeous hotel sports an eclectic look that

TOP 10 GELATERIE

Eating gelato is as much a part of Roman life as traffic jams and dodgy politicians, and the city has some superb *gelaterie artigianale* (artisanal ice-cream shops). To gauge the quality of a place, check out the pistachio flavour: if it's a grey–olive green it's good; if it's bright green, go elsewhere.

Here's our road-tested guide to Rome's top 10 gelaterie:

Fatamorgana (Map p88; Via Laurina 10; ⊗noon-11pm; Ⓜ Flaminio) Rome's finest artisanal flavours. Also has branches in Prati, Monti and Trastevere.

Il Gelato (Viale Aventino 59; gelato €2-4.50; ⊗10am-midnight summer, 11am-9pm winter; Ⓡ Viale Aventino) Creative, and sometimes bizarre, flavours from Rome's gelato king Claudio Torcè.

Gelateria del Teatro (Map p78; Via dei Coronari 65; gelato from €2.50; ⊗11.30am-midnight; Ⓡ Corso del Rinascimento) Has around 40 choices of gelato, all made on site.

Il Caruso (Via Collina 15; ⊗noon-9pm; Ⓜ Repubblica) A small but perfect selection of creamy flavours.

Gelarmony (Map p92; Via Marcantonio Colonna 34; gelato €1.50-3; ⊗10am-late; Ⓜ Lepanto) A Sicilian gelateria specialising in island flavours such as pistachio or *cassata*.

Dei Gracchi (Map p88; Via di Ripetta 261; gelato from €2; ⊗11.30am-10pm, to midnight Jun-Sep; Ⓜ Flaminio) A taste of heaven in several locations across Rome.

Fior di Luna (Map p108; ☑06 6456 1314; Via della Lungaretta 96; gelato from €1.70; ⊗noon-12.30am Tue-Sun; Ⓡ Viale di Trastevere, Ⓡ Viale di Trastevere) Great artisanal ice cream in Trastevere.

Old Bridge (Map p92; www.gelateriaoldbridge.com; Viale dei Bastioni di Michelangelo 5; gelato €2-5; ⊗9am-2am Mon-Sat, 2.30pm-2am Sun; Ⓡ Piazza del Risorgimento, Ⓡ Piazza del Risorgimento) Makes for a refreshing pit stop after visiting the Vatican Museums. Has a second branch in Trastevere.

Venchi (Map p78; Via degli Orfani 87; gelato from €2.50; ⊗10.30am-10pm Sun-Thu, to 11pm Fri & Sat; Ⓡ Via del Corso) Specialises in all things chocolatey. Has a second branch near the Spanish Steps.

Vice (Map p78; www.viceitalia.it; Corso Vittorio Emanuele II 96; gelato from €2.50; ⊗11am-1am; Ⓡ Largo di Torre Argentina) A contemporary outfit serving traditional and modern flavours.

As an alternative to ice cream, Romans like to cool down with a *grattachecca* (crushed ice drowned in fruit syrup) by the river. There are several riverside stands around Rome's central bridges.

effortlessly blends African and Middle Eastern art with original art-deco furniture, exposed brickwork and hand-painted tiles. Rooms are individually decorated, with the best offering views over the wisteria and thick greenery in the surrounding streets.

 Eating

Rome teems with trattorias, *ristoranti*, pizzerias, *enoteche* (wine bars serving food) and gelaterie. Excellent places dot the *centro storico*, Trastevere, Prati, Testaccio and San Lorenzo. The area around Termini has quite a few substandard res-

taurants, as does the Vatican, which is packed with tourist traps.

✕ Ancient Rome

★ **Terre e Domus**   LAZIO CUISINE €€
(Map p68; ☑06 6994 0273; Via Foro Traiano 82-4; meals €30; ⊗7.30am-12.30am Mon-Sat; Ⓡ Via dei Fori Imperiali) This modern white-and-glass restaurant is the best option in the touristy Forum area. Overlooking the Colonna di Traiano, it serves a menu of traditional staples, all made with ingredients sourced from the surrounding Lazio region, and a thoughtful selection of regional wines. Lunchtime can be busy but it quietens down in the evening.

PICNIC PROVISIONS

Trawling through Ancient Rome's ruins can be hungry work. But rather than stop off for an overpriced bite in a touristy restaurant, search out **Alimentari Pannella Carmela** (Map p68; Via dei Fienili 61; panini €2-3.50; ☺8.30am-2.30pm Mon-Sat & 5-8pm Mon-Fri; ⃞Via Petroselli) for a fresh, cheap *panino*. A small, workaday food store concealed behind a curtain of creeping ivy, it's a lunchtime favourite, supplying many local workers with sliced pizza, take away salads, and hearty ham-and-cheese sandwiches.

✖ Centro Storico

★ Supplizio   FAST FOOD €

(Map p78; Via dei Banchi Vecchi 143; supplì €3-5; ☺noon-4pm Mon-Sat plus 5.30-10pm Mon-Thu, to 11pm Fri & Sat; ⃞Corso Vittorio Emanuele II) Rome's favourite snack, the *supplì* (a fried croquette filled with rice, tomato sauce and mozzarella), gets a gourmet makeover at this elegant new streetfood joint. Sit back on the vintage leather sofa and dig into the classic article or throw the boat out and try something different, maybe a mildly spicy fish *supplì* stuffed with anchovies, tuna, parsley, and just a hint of orange.

Forno Roscioli   PIZZA, BAKERY €

(Map p78; Via dei Chiavari 34; pizza slices from €2, snacks from €1.50; ☺7am-7.30pm Mon-Sat; ⃞Via Arenula) This is one of Rome's top bakeries, much loved by lunching locals who crowd here for luscious sliced pizza, prize pastries and hunger-sating *supplì*. There's also a counter serving hot pastas and vegetable side dishes.

Forno di Campo de' Fiori   PIZZA, BAKERY €

(Map p78; Campo de' Fiori 22; pizza slices from €3; ☺7.30am-2.30pm & 4.45-8pm Mon-Sat; ⃞Corso Vittorio Emanuele II) This buzzing bakery on Campo de' Fiori does a roaring trade in *panini* and delicious fresh-from-the-oven *pizza al taglio* (by the slice). Aficionados swear by the *pizza bianca* ('white' pizza with olive oil, rosemary and salt), but the *panini* and *pizza rossa* ('red' pizza, with olive oil, tomato and oregano) taste plenty good, too.

I Dolci di Nonna Vincenza   PASTICCERIA, CAFE €

(Map p78; www.dolcinonnavincenza.it; Via Arco del Monte 98a; pastries from €2.50; ☺8am-9pm Sun-Thu, to midnight Fri & Sat; ⃞Via Arenula) Bringing the flavours of Sicily to Rome, this pastry shop is hard to resist. Browse the traditional cakes and tempting *dolci* (sweets) in the old wooden dressers, before adjourning to the adjacent bar to tear into the heavenly selection of creamy, flaky, puffy pastries.

Alfredo e Ada   TRATTORIA €

(Map p78; ☏06 687 88 42; Via dei Banchi Nuovi 14; meals €25; ☺noon-3pm & 7-10pm Tue-Sat; ⃞Corso Vittorio Emanuele II) For an authentic trattoria meal, search out this much-loved local eatery. It's distinctly no-frills with spindly, marble-topped tables and homey clutter, but there's a warm, friendly atmosphere and the traditional Roman food is filling and flavoursome.

Chiostro del Bramante Caffè   CAFE €

(Map p78; www.chiostrodelbramante.it; Via Arco della Pace 5; meals €15-20; ☺10am-8pm Mon-Fri, to 9pm Sat & Sun; ☏; ⃞Corso del Rinascimento) Many of Rome's galleries and museums have in-house cafes but few are as beautifully located as the Chiostro del Bramante Caffè on the 1st floor of Bramante's elegant Renaissance cloister. With outdoor tables overlooking the central courtyard and an all-day menu offering everything from cakes and coffee to baguettes, light lunches and aperitifs, it's a great spot for a break.

★ Casa Coppelle   RISTORANTE €€

(Map p78; ☏06 6889 1707; www.casacoppelle.it; Piazza delle Coppelle 49; meals €35-40; ☺12-3.30pm & 6.30-11.30pm; ⃞Corso del Rinascimento) Exposed brick walls, flowers and subdued lighting set the stage for creative Italian- and French-inspired food at this intimate, romantic restaurant. There's a full range of starters and pastas, but the real tour de force are the deliciously tender steaks and rich meat dishes. Service is attentive and the setting, on a small piazza near the Pantheon, memorable. Book ahead.

★ **La Ciambella** ITALIAN €€
(Map p78; www.laciambellaroma.com; Via dell'Arco della Ciambella 20; fixed-price lunch menus €10-25, meals €30; ⊙7.30am-midnight; ▣Largo di Torre Argentina) From breakfast pastries and lunchtime pastas to afternoon tea, Neapolitan pizzas and aperitif cocktails, this all-day eatery is a top find. Central but as yet undiscovered by the tourist hordes, it's a spacious, light-filled spot set over the ruins of the Terme di Agrippa, visible through transparent floor panels. The mostly traditional food is spot on, and the atmosphere laid back and friendly.

Armando al Pantheon TRATTORIA €€
(Map p78; ☑06 6880 3034; www.armandoalpantheon.it; Salita dei Crescenzi 31; meals €40; ⊙12.30-3pm & 7-11pm Mon-Fri, 12.30-3pm Sat; ▣Largo di Torre Argentina) An institution in these parts, Armando al Pantheon is a rare find – a genuine family-run trattoria in the touristy Pantheon area. It's been on the go for more than 50 years and has served its fair share of celebs, but it hasn't let fame go to its head and remains one of the best bets for earthy Roman cuisine. Reservations essential.

Renato e Luisa TRATTORIA €€
(Map p78; ☑06 686 96 60; www.renatoeluisa.it; Via dei Barbieri 25; meals €45; ⊙8pm-midnight Tue-Sun; ▣Largo di Torre Argentina) Highly rated locally, this small backstreet trattoria is always packed. Chef Renato takes a creative approach to classic Roman cooking, resulting in dishes that are modern and seasonal yet undeniably local, such as

his signature *cacio e pepe e fiori di zucca* (pasta with pecorino cheese, black pepper and zucchini flowers). Bookings recommended.

Matricianella TRATTORIA €€
(Map p88; ☑06 683 21 00; www.matricianella.it; Via del Leone 2/4; meals €40; ⊙12.30-3pm & 7.30-11pm Mon-Sat; ▣Via del Corso) With its gingham tablecloths, chintzy murals and fading prints, Matricianella is an archetypal trattoria, much loved for its traditional Roman cuisine. Its loyal clientele go crazy for ever-green crowd-pleasers like battered vegetables, artichoke *alla giudia* (fried, Jewish style), and *saltimbocca* (veal cutlet with ham and sage). Booking is essential.

Cul de Sac WINE BAR, TRATTORIA €€
(Map p78; ☑06 6880 1094; www.enoteca culdesacroma.it; Piazza Pasquino 73; meals €30; ⊙noon-12.30am; ▣Corso Vittorio Emanuele II) A perennially popular wine bar just off Piazza Navona, with an always-busy terrace and narrow, bottle-lined interior. Choose your tipple first – the encyclopaedic wine list boasts about 1500 labels – and then pick what to go with it from the ample menu of no-nonsense Roman staples, Gallic-inspired cold cuts, pâtés, and cheeses. Book ahead for the evening to ensure you're not disappointed .

Ditirambo ITALIAN €€
(Map p78; ☑06 687 16 26; www.ristorantediti rambo.it; Piazza della Cancelleria 72; meals €40; ⊙1-3pm & 7.20-10.30pm, closed Mon lunch; ▣Corso Vittorio Emanuele II) Since opening

ROME & LAZIO ROME

KOSHER ROME

If you want to eat kosher in Rome head to Via del Portico d'Ottavia, the main strip through the Jewish Ghetto. Lined with trattorias and restaurants specialising in Roman-Jewish cuisine, it's a lively hang-out, especially on hot summer nights when diners crowd the many footpath tables.

For a taste of typical Ghetto cooking, try **Nonna Betta** (Map p78; ☑06 6880 6263; www.nonnabetta.it; Via del Portico d'Ottavia 16; meals €30-35; ⊙ noon-4pm & 6-11pm, closed Fri dinner & Sat lunch; ▣ Via Arenula), a small tunnel of a trattoria serving local staples such as *carciofi alla giudia* (crisp fried artichokes). Further down the road, the unmarked **Cremeria Romana** (Map p78; Via del Portico d'Ottavia 1b; gelato €2-5; ⊙ 8am-11pm Sun-Thu, to 4pm Fri, 6pm-midnight Sat; ▣ Via Arenula) at No 1b has a small selection of tasty kosher gelato. For simple, sliced pizza head to **Antico Forno Urbani** (Map p78; Piazza Costaguti 31; pizza slices from €1.50; ⊙ 7.40am-2.30pm & 5-8.45pm Mon-Fri, 9am-1.30pm Sat & Sun; ▣ Via Arenula).

FAST-FOOD PASTA

For most of the day, **Pastificio** (Map p88; Via della Croce 8; pasta, wine & water €4; ⊙lunch 1-3pm Mon-Sat; ⓂSpagna) goes about its business as a fresh pasta shop, but at lunchtime it turns itself into the Tridente neighbourhood's budget diner. Locals pile in to fill up on the daily pasta dishes (there's a choice of two) eaten out of plastic bowls wherever there's room.

in 1996, Ditirambo has won an army of fans with its informal trattoria vibe and seasonal, organic cuisine. Dishes cover many bases, ranging from old-school favourites to thoughtful vegetarian offerings and more exotic fare such as pasta with Sicilian prawns, basil and lime. Book ahead.

Casa Bleve   RISTORANTE, WINE BAR €€€
(Map p78; ☎06 686 59 70; www.casableve.it; Via del Teatro Valle 48-49; meals €50-65; ⊙12.30-3pm & 7.30-10.30pm Mon-Sat; 🚇Largo di Torre Argentina) Ideal for a special-occasion dinner, this palatial restaurant–wine bar dazzles with its column-lined dining hall and stained-glass roof. Its wine list, one of the best in town, accompanies a small but considered menu of hard-to-find cheeses, cold cuts, seasonal pastas and refined main courses.

✖ Tridente, Trevi & the Quirinale

Pompi   DESSERTS €
(Map p88; Via della Croce 82; tiramisu €4; ⊙10.30am-9.30pm; ⓂSpagna) Rome's most famous vendor of tiramisu (which literally means 'pick me up') sells takeaway cartons of the deliciously yolky yet light-as-air dessert. As well as classic, it comes in pistachio and strawberry flavours.

Buccone   RISTORANTE, WINE BAR €
(Map p88; ☎06 361 21 54; Via di Ripetta 19; meals €20; ⊙12.30-2.30pm & 7.30-10.30pm Mon-Sat; ⓂFlaminio) Step in under the faded gilt-and-mirrored sign and you'll feel as though you've gone back in time. Once a coach house, then a tavern, this building became Buccone in the 1960s, furnished with 19th-century antiques and lined with around a thousand Italian wines. It serves simple food such as mixed plates of cured

meat and cheese, but on Saturday offers a proper hot *cena* (dinner).

Pizza Ré   PIZZA €
(Map p88; ☎06 321 14 68; Via di Ripetta 14; pizzas €7-10; ⊙noon-midnight; ⓂFlaminio) Part of a chain, but a good one, this popular pizzeria offers Neapolitan-style pizzas, with thick doughy bases and diverse toppings. The salads are fresh and the antipasti is great – try the fried things or the *mozzarella fresca di bufala e prosciutto San Daniele* (buffalo mozzarella with San Daniele dry-cured ham). It's a good choice with kids.

★ **Colline Emiliane**   ITALIAN €€
(Map p88; ☎06 481 75 38; Via degli Avignonesi 22; meals €50; ⊙12.45-2.45pm Tue-Sun & 7.30-10.45pm Tue-Sat, closed Aug; ⓂBarberini) This welcoming, tucked-away restaurant just off Piazza Barberini flies the flag for Emilia-Romagna, the well-fed Italian province that has blessed the world with Parmesan, balsamic vinegar, bolognese sauce and Parma ham. This is a consistently excellent place to eat; there are delicious meats, homemade pasta and rich *ragù*. Try to save room for dessert, too.

Al Gran Sasso   TRATTORIA €€
(Map p88; ☎06 321 48 83; www.algransasso. com; Via di Ripetta 32; meals €35; ⊙12.30-2.30pm & 7.30-11.30pm Sun-Fri; ⓂFlaminio) A top lunchtime spot, this is a classic, dyed-in-the-wool trattoria specialising in old-school country cooking. It's a relaxed place with a welcoming vibe, garish murals on the walls (strangely, often a good sign) and tasty, value-for-money food. The fried dishes are excellent, or try one of the daily specials, chalked up on the board outside.

Il Margutta RistorArte   VEGETARIAN €€
(Map p88; ☎06 678 60 33; www.ilmargutta.it; Via Margutta 118; meals €40; ⊙12.30-3pm & 7-11.30pm; ✗; ⓂSpagna, Flaminio) Vegetarian restaurants in Rome are rarer than parking spaces, and this airy art gallery–restaurant is an unusually chic way to eat your greens. Dishes are excellent and most produce is organic, with offerings such as artichoke hearts with potato cubes and smoked provolone cheese. Best value is the weekday (€15 to €18) and weekend (€25) buffet brunch. There's a vegan menu and live music weekends.

Baccano
BRASSERIE €€

(Map p88; www.baccanoroma.com; Via delle Muratte 23; meals €45; ⊗8.30am-2am; 🚇Via del Corso) Offering all-day dining in elegant, laid-back surroundings (it's nailed the Balthazar look: polished wood, potted palms, high ceilings, cosy booths). However, if you're in the mood: dinner, burgers, club sandwiches, cocktails, *aperitivi* – you name it, they've got it covered.

Il Chianti
TUSCAN €€

(Map p88; 📞06 678 75 50; Via del Lavatore 81-82; meals €45, pizza €8-12; ⊗12.30-3.30pm & 7-11.30pm; 🚇Via del Tritone) This pretty ivy-clad wine bar is bottle-lined and wood-beamed inside, with watch-the-world-go-by streetside seating, backed by a picturesque cascade of ivy, in summer. Cuisine is Tuscan, so the beef is particularly good, but it also serves up imaginative salads and pizza (for lunch or dinner).

★Enoteca Regionale Palatium
RISTORANTE, WINE BAR €€€

(Map p88; 📞06 692 02 132; Via Frattina 94; meals €55; ⊗11am-11pm Mon-Sat, closed Aug; 🚇Via del Corso) A rich showcase of regional bounty, run by the Lazio Regional Food Authority, this sleek wine bar serves excellent local specialities, such as *porchetta* (pork roasted with herbs) or *gnocchi alla Romana con crema da zucca* (potato dumplings Roman-style with cream of pumpkin), as well as an impressive array of Lazio wines (try lesser-known drops such as Aleatico). *Aperitivo* is a good bet, too.

Babette
ITALIAN €€€

(Map p88; 📞06 321 15 59; Via Margutta 1; meals €45-55; ⊗1-3pm Tue-Sun, 7-10.45pm daily, closed Jan & Aug; 🖉; 🚇Spagna, Flaminio) Babette is run by two sisters who used to produce a fashion magazine, which accounts for its effortlessly chic interior of exposed brick walls and vintage painted signs. You're in for a feast too, as the cooking is delicious, with a sophisticated, creative French twist (think *tortiglioni* with zucchini-and-pistachio pesto). The *torta Babette* is the food of the gods, a light-as-air lemon cheesecake.

All'Oro
ITALIAN €€€

(Map p88; Via del Vantaggio 14; tasting menu €98, meals €90; 🚇Flaminio) A Michelin-starred fine-dining restaurant, All'Oro established itself under chef Riccardo Di Giacinto in the upmarket suburb of Parioli. It's now trans-ferred to the contemporary art–styled First Luxury Art Hotel, with white surroundings and sophisticated dishes such as ravioli filled with mascarpone, duck ragout and red-wine reduction, and roasted suckling pig with potatoes and black truffle sauce.

✕ Vatican City, Borgo & Prati

★Pizzarium
PIZZA €

(Map p92; Via della Meloria 43; pizza slices from €3; ⊗11am-10pm; 🚇Cipro–Musei Vaticani) Pizzarium, or 'Bonci pizza rustica #pizzarium', as it has recently re-branded itself, serves some of Rome's best sliced pizza. Scissor-cut squares of meticulously crafted dough are topped with original combinations of seasonal ingredients and served on paper trays for immediate consumption. There's also a daily selection of freshly fried *supplì* (crunchy rice croquettes).

Fa-Bìo
SANDWICHES €

(Map p92; 📞06 6452 5810; www.fa-bio.com; Via Germanico 43; sandwiches €5; ⊗10am-5.30pm Mon-Fri, to 4pm Sat) 🖉 Sandwiches, salads and smoothies are all prepared with speed, skill and fresh organic ingredients at this tiny takeaway. Locals and in-the-know visitors come to grab a quick lunchtime bite, and if you can squeeze in the door you'd do well to follow suit.

Mondo Arancina
FAST FOOD €

(Map p92; Via Marcantonio Colonna 38; arancini from €2.50; ⊗10am-midnight; 🚇Lepanto) All sunny yellow ceramics, cheerful crowds and tantalising deep-fried snacks, this bustling takeaway brings a little corner of Sicily to Rome. Star of the show are the classic fist-sized *arancini*, fried rice balls stuffed with fillers ranging from classic *ragù* to more exotic fare such as truffle risotto and quail's eggs.

Romeo
PIZZA, RISTORANTE €€

(Map p92; 📞06 3211 0120; www.romeo.roma. it; Via Silla 26a; pizza slices €2.50, meals €45; ⊗9am-midnight; 🚇Ottaviano–San Pietro) This chic, contemporary outfit is part bakery, part deli, part takeaway, and part restaurant. For a quick bite, there's delicious sliced pizza or you can have a *panino* made up at the deli counter; for a full restaurant meal, the à la carte menu offers a mix of traditional Italian dishes and forward-looking international creations.

Velavevodetto Ai Quiriti   LAZIO CUISINE €€

(Map p92; ☑ 06 3600 0009; www.ristorante velavevodetto.it; Piazza dei Quiriti 5; meals €35; ⊗ 12.30-2.30pm & 7.30-11.30pm; Ⓜ Lepanto) This welcoming restaurant continues to win diners over with its unpretentious, earthy food and honest prices. The menu reads like a directory of Roman staples, and while it's all pretty good, standout choices include *fettuccine con asparagi, guanciale e pecorino* (pasta ribbons with asparagus, guanciale and pecorino cheese) and *polpette di bollito* (fried meat balls).

Il Sorpasso   ITALIAN €€

(Map p92; www.sorpasso.info; Via Properzio 31-33; meals €20-35; ⊗ 7am-1am Mon-Fri, 9am-1am Sat; ⬛ Piazza del Risorgimento) A bar-restaurant hybrid sporting a vintage cool look – vaulted stone ceilings, hanging hams, white bare-brick walls – Il Sorpasso is a hot ticket right now. Open throughout the day, it caters to a fashionable neighbourhood crowd, serving everything from pasta specials to aperitifs, *trapizzini* (pyramids of stuffed pizza), and a full dinner menu.

Hostaria Dino e Tony   TRATTORIA €€

(Map p92; ☑ 06 3973 3284; Via Leone IV 60; meals €25-30; ⊗ 12.30-3pm & 7-11pm, closed Sun & Aug; Ⓜ Ottaviano-San Pietro) An authentic old-school trattoria, Dino e Tony offers simple, no-frills Roman cooking. Kick off with the monumental antipasto, a minor meal in its own right, before plunging into the trattoria's signature *rigatoni all'amatriciana* (pasta tubes with bacon-like *guanciale*, chilli and tomato sauce). No credit cards.

Osteria dell'Angelo   TRATTORIA €€

(Map p92; ☑ 06 372 94 70; Via Bettolo 24; fixed-price menu €25-35; ⊗ 12.30-2.30pm Tue-Fri, 8.30-11pm Mon-Sat; Ⓜ Ottaviano-San Pietro) With rugby paraphernalia on the walls and basic wooden tables, this laid-back neighbourhood trattoria is a popular spot for genuine local cuisine. The fixed-price menu features a mixed antipasti, a robust Roman-style pasta and a choice of hearty mains with a side dish. To finish off, spiced biscuits are served with sweet dessert wine. Reservations recommended.

Pizzeria Amalfi   PIZZA €€

(Map p92; ☑ 06 3973 3165; Via dei Gracchi 12; pizzas €6.50-9.50, meals €25-30; ⊗ noon-3pm & 7pm-12.30am; Ⓜ Ottaviano-San Pietro) This brassy, brightly coloured pizzeria-cum-restaurant flies the flag for Neapolitan cuisine with its buffalo mozzarella starters, soft, doughy pizzas and calzones. If pizza doesn't appeal, you can choose from a lengthy list of grilled meats, pastas, salads and fish dishes. Note that there's a second branch across the road at Via dei Gracchi 5.

Enoteca La Torre   RISTORANTE €€€

(☑ 06 4566 8304; www.enotecalatorreroma.com; Villa Laetitia, Lungotevere delle Armi 22; fixed-price lunch menu €55, meals €110; ⊗ 12.30-2.30pm Tue-Sat, 7.30-10pm Mon-Sat; ⬛ Lungotevere delle Armi) The art-nouveau Villa Laetitia provides the romantic setting for this refined Michelin-starred restaurant. A relative newcomer to the capital's fine-dining scene, chef Danilo Ciavattino has quickly established himself with his original culinary style and love of authentic country flavours.

Ristorante L'Arcangelo   RISTORANTE €€€

(Map p92; ☑ 06 321 09 92; www.larcangelo.com; Via Belli 59-61; tasting menus lunch/dinner €25/55, meals €60; ⊗ 12.30-2.30pm Mon-Fri, 8-11pm Mon-Sat; ⬛ Piazza Cavour) Styled as an informal bistro with wood-panelling, leather banquettes and casual table settings, L'Arcangelo enjoys a stellar local reputation. The highlight for many are the classic Roman staples such as carbonara and *amatriciana*, but there's also a limited selection of more innovative modern dishes. The wine list is a further plus, boasting some interesting Italian labels.

Settembrini   RISTORANTE €€€

(☑ 06 323 26 17; www.viasettembrini.it; Via Settembrini 25; menus lunch €28-38, dinner €48-65; ⊗ 12.30-3pm Mon-Fri, 8-11pm Mon-Sat; ⬛ Piazza Giuseppe Mazzini) All labels, suits and media gossip, this fashionable restaurant is part of the ever-growing Settembrini empire. Next door is a stylish all-day cafe, while over the way, Libri & Cucina is a laid-back bookshop eatery, and L'Officina an upscale food store. At the casually chic main restaurant expect contemporary Italian cuisine and quality wine to match.

🍴 Monti, Esquilino & San Lorenzo

Panella l'Arte del Pane   BAKERY, CAFE €

(Map p102; ☑ 06 487 24 35; Via Merulana 54; snacks €3.50; ⊗ 8am-11pm Mon-Thu, to midnight Fri & Sat, 8.30am-4pm Sun; Ⓜ Vittorio Emanuele) With a magnificent array of *pizza al taglio, arancini*, focaccia, fried croquettes and pastries, this smart bakery-cum-cafe is good any time of the day. The outside tables are ideal for a leisurely breakfast or chilled evening drink, or you can perch on a high stool and lunch on something from the sumptuous counter display.

Roscioli
PIZZA, BAKERY €

(Map p102; Via Buonarroti 48; pizza slices €3.50; ⊗7am-8pm Mon-Sat; ⓂVittorio Emanuele) Off-the-track branch of this splendid deli-bakery-pizzeria, with delish *pizza al taglio*, pasta dishes and other goodies that make it ideal for a swift lunch or picnic stock-up. It's on a road leading off Piazza Vittorio Emanuele II.

Gainn
KOREAN €

(Map p102; ☑06 4436 0160; Via dei Mille 18; meals around €25; ⊗lunch & dinner Mon-Sat; ⓂTermini) A serene choice close to Rome's main train station, where you'll get a warm, friendly welcome, and dishes come with an array of enticing little salads and pickles, known as kimchi. The diners here are mainly Korean and Chinese, and the good food makes for a refreshing change if you're hankering after something non-Italian.

★L'Asino d'Oro
ITALIAN €€

(Map p88; ☑06 4891 3832; Via del Boschetto 73; meals €45; ⊗12.30-2.30pm Sat, 7.30-11pm Tue-Sat; ⓂCavour) This fabulous restaurant was transplanted from Orvieto and its Umbrian origins resonate in Lucio Sforza's delicious, exceptional cooking. It's unfussy yet innovative, with dishes featuring lots of flavourful contrasts, such as lamb meatballs with pear and blue cheese. Save room for the amazing desserts. For such excellent food, this intimate, informal yet classy place is one of Rome's best deals. Hours are changeable so call ahead.

★Necci
CAFE €€

(☑06 9760 1552; www.necci1924.com; Via Fanfulla da Lodi 68; dinner around €45, lunch mains around €8; ⊗8am-2am; 🐾; 🚃Via Prenestina) Iconic Necci opened as gelataria in 1924 and later became a favourite of director Pier Paolo Pasolini. Good for a drink or a meal, it serves up sophisticated Italian cooking to an eclectic crowd of all ages, with a lovely, leafy garden terrace (ideal for families).

Temakinho
SUSHI €€

(Map p68; www.temakinho.com; Via dei Serpenti 16; meals €40; ⊗12.30-3.30pm & 7pm-midnight; ⓂCavour) In a city where food is still mostly resolutely (though deliciously) Italian, this Brazilian–Japanese hybrid serves up sushi and ceviche, and makes for a refreshing, sensational change. As well as delicious, strong *caipirinhas*, which combine Brazilian *cachaça*, sugar, lime and fresh fruit, there are '*sakehinhas*' made with sake. It's very popular; book ahead.

Trattoria Monti
RISTORANTE €€

(Map p102; ☑06 446 65 73; Via di San Vito 13a; meals €45; ⊗12.45-2.45pm Tue-Sun, 7.45-11pm Tue-Sat, closed Aug; ⓂVittorio Emanuele) The Camerucci family runs this elegant brick-arched place, proffering top-notch traditional cooking from Le Marche region. There are wonderful *fritti* (fried things), delicate pastas and ingredients such as *pecorino di fossa* (sheep's cheese aged in caves), goose, swordfish and truffles. Try the egg-yolk *tortelli* pasta. Desserts are delectable, including apple pie with *zabaglione*. Word has spread, so book ahead.

Tram Tram
OSTERIA €€

(Map p102; ☑06 49 04 16; www.tramtram.it; Via dei Reti 44; meals around €45; ⊗12.30-3.30pm & 7.30-11.30pm Tue-Sun; 🚃Via Tiburtina) This trendy yet old-style lace-curtained trattoria takes its name from the trams that rattle past outside. It's a family-run concern whose menu is an unusual mix of Roman and Pugliese (southern Italian) dishes, featuring taste sensations such as *tiella riso, patata* and *cozze* (baked rice dish with rice, potatoes and mussels). Book ahead.

★Open Colonna
ITALIAN €€€

(Map p88; ☑06 4782 2641; www.antonellocolonna.it; Via Milano 9a; meals €20-80; ⊗12.30-3.30pm Tue-Sun, 8-11.30pm Tue-Sat; 🚃Via Nazionale) Spectacularly set at the back of Palazzo delle Esposizioni, superchef Antonello Colonna's superb restaurant is tucked onto a mezzanine floor under an extraordinary glass roof. The cuisine is new Roman: innovative takes on traditional dishes, cooked with wit and flair. The best thing? There's a more basic but still delectable fixed two-course lunch for €16, and Saturday and Sunday brunch is €30, served in the dramatic, glass-ceilinged hall, with a terrace for sunny days.

Agata e Romeo
ITALIAN €€€

(Map p102; ☑06 446 61 15; Via Carlo Alberto 45; meals €120; ⊗12.30-2.30pm & 7.30-11.30pm Mon-Fri; ⓂVittorio Emanuele) This elegant, restrained place was one of Rome's gastronomic pioneers and still holds its own as one of the city's most gourmet takes on Roman cuisine. Chef Agata Parisella prepares

ROME & LAZIO ROME

the menus and runs the kitchen, offering creative uses of Roman traditions; husband Romeo curates the wine cellar; and daughter Maria Antonietta chooses the cheeses. Bookings essential.

✕ Trastevere & Gianicolo

Pianostrada Laboratorio di Cucina
ITALIAN €

(Map p108; Vicolo del Cedro; meals €25; ⊗1-4pm & 7.30-11.30pm Tue-Sun; ☐ Piazza Trilussa) A diminutive, tucked-away place, this all-female-run foodie stop has been attracting attention with its delicious meals such as parmigiana with aubergine and pumpkin, meatballs, burgers, pasta with swordfish and wild fennel, and gourmet sandwiches. It's all exquisitely made and conceived, so squeeze in along the bar or take one of the tiny tables with barstools.

Bir & Fud
PIZZA €

(Map p78; Via Benedetta 23; meals €25; ⊗7.30pm-midnight, to 2am Fri & Sat; ☐ Piazza Trilussa) This orange-and-terracotta, vaulted, yet contemporary-styled pizzeria wins plaudits for its organic take on pizzas, crostini and fried things (potato, pumpkin etc) and has a microbrewery on site, so serves seasonable tipples such as Birrificio Troll Palanfrina (winter only, made from chestnuts).

Da Augusto
TRATTORIA €

(Map p108; ☑06 580 37 98; Piazza de' Renzi 15; meals €25; ⊗12.30-3pm & 8-11pm; ☐ Viale di Trastevere, ☐ Viale di Trastevere) For a Trastevere feast, plonk yourself at one of Augusto's rickety tables, either inside or out on the small piazza, and prepare to enjoy some mamma-style cooking. The gruff waiters dish out hearty platefuls of *rigatoni all'amatriciana* and *stracciatella* (clear broth with egg and Parmesan) among a host of Roman classics. Be prepared to queue. Cash only.

Pizzeria Ivo
PIZZA €

(Map p108; ☑06 581 70 82; Via di San Francesco a Ripa 158; pizzas from €7; ⊗7pm-midnight Wed-Mon; ☐ Viale di Trastevere, ☐ Viale di Trastevere) One of Trastevere's most famous pizzerias, Ivo's has been slinging pizzas for some 40 years, and still the hungry come. With the TV on in the corner and the tables full (a few outside on the cobbled street), Ivo is a noisy and vibrant place, and the waiters fit the gruff-and-fast stereotype.

Forno la Renella
BAKERY €

(Map p108; ☑06 581 72 65; Via del Moro 15-16; pizza slices from €2.50; ⊗7am-2am Tue-Sat, to 10pm Sun & Mon; ☐ Piazza Trilussa) The wood-fired ovens at this historical Trastevere bakery have been going for decades, producing a delicious daily batch of pizza, bread and biscuits. Piled-high toppings (and fillings) vary seasonally. It's popular with everyone from skinheads with big dogs to elderly ladies with little dogs.

★La Gensola
SICILIAN €€

(Map p108; ☑06 581 63 12; Piazza della Gensola 15; meals €45; ⊗12.30-3pm & 7.30-11.30pm, closed Sun mid-Jun–mid-Sep; ☐ Viale di Trastevere,

---

ROME'S TOP FOOD MARKETS

Rome's produce markets are a fabulous feature of the city's foodscape, and most neighbourhoods have their own daily market, operating from around 7am to 1.30pm, Monday to Saturday. There are also some excellent farmers markets, mostly taking place on weekends.

Campo de' Fiori (Map p78; ⊗6am-2pm Mon-Sat; ☐ Corso Vittorio Emanuele II) Famous market on one of the historic centre's focal piazzas.

Mercato di Circo Massimo (Map p68; www.mercatocircomassimo.it; Via di San Teodoro 74; ⊗9am-6pm Sat, to 4pm Sun, closed Sun Jul & all Aug; ☐ Via dei Cerchi) Popular farmers market showcasing seasonal produce.

Nuovo Mercato Esquilino (Map p102; Via Lamarmora; ⊗5am-3pm Mon-Sat; Ⓜ Vittorio Emanuele) Cheap, colourful market; the best place for exotic herbs and spices.

Piazza San Cosimato (Map p108; ⊗7am-2pm Mon-Sat; ☐ Viale di Trastevere, ☐ Viale di Trastevere) Trastevere's neighbourhood market, still the business for fresh food.

Nuovo Mercato di Testaccio (Map p134; entrances Via Galvani, Via Beniamino Franklin; ⊗6am-3pm Mon-Sat; ☐ Via Marmorata) Historic Testaccio market on a modern, purpose-built site.

Viale di Trastevere) This tranquil, classy yet unpretentious trattoria thrills foodies with delicious food that has a Sicilian slant and emphasis on seafood, including an excellent tuna tartare, linguine with fresh anchovies and divine *zuccherini* (tiny fish) with fresh mint.

Le Mani in Pasta
RISTORANTE €€

(Map p108; ☎06 581 60 17; Via dei Genovesi 37; meals €35; ☺12.30-3pm & 7.30-11pm Tue-Sun; Viale di Trastevere, Viale di Trastevere) Popular and lively, this rustic, snug place has arched ceilings and an open kitchen that serves up delicious fresh pasta dishes such as *fettucine con ricotta e pancetta*. The grilled meats are great, too.

Da Teo
TRATTORIA €€

(Map p108; ☎06 581 83 85; Piazza dei Ponziani 7; meals around €30; ☺12.30-3pm & 7.30-11.30pm Mon-Sat; Viale di Trastevere) Tucked away on the quieter side of Trastevere, Da Teo gets packed out with locals dining on its steaming platefuls of Roman standards, such as *cacio e pepe* or fried lambchops. It's great to eat out on the small piazza when the weather suits. Book ahead.

★ Glass Hostaria
ITALIAN €€€

(Map p108; ☎06 5833 5903; Vicolo del Cinque 58; meals €90; ☺7.30-11.30pm Tue-Sun; Piazza Trilussa) Trastevere's foremost foodie address, the Glass is a modernist-styled, sophisticated setting decorated in warm wood and contemporary gold, with fabulous cooking to match. Chef Cristina Bowerman creates inventive, delicate dishes that combine fresh ingredients and traditional elements to delight and surprise the palate. There are tasting menus at €75, €80 and €100.

Paris
RISTORANTE €€€

(Map p108; ☎06 581 53 78; www.ristoranteparis. it; Piazza San Calisto 7a; meals €45-55; ☺7.30-11pm Mon, 12.30-3pm & 7.30-11pm Tue-Sun; Viale di Trastevere, Viale di Trastevere) An old-school restaurant set in a 17th-century building with tables on a small piazza, Paris – named for its founder, not the French capital – is the best place outside the Ghetto to sample Roman-Jewish cuisine. Signature dishes include *gran fritto vegetale con baccalà* (deep-fried vegetables with salt cod) and *carciofi alla giudia* (fried artichoke).

MENU DECODER

The hallmark of an authentic Roman menu is the presence of offal. The Roman love of nose-to-tail eating arose in Testaccio around the city abattoir, and many of the neighbourhood's trattorias still serve traditional offal-based dishes. So whether you want to avoid it or try it, look out for *pajata* (veal's intestines), *trippa* (tripe), *coda alla vaccinara* (oxtail), *coratella* (heart, lung and liver), *animelle* (sweetbreads), *testarella* (head), *lingua* (tongue) and *zampone* (trotters).

✖ San Giovanni & Celio

★ Cafè Cafè
BISTRO €

(Map p110; ☎06 700 87 43; www.cafecafebistrot. it; Via dei Santissimi Quattro Coronati 44; meals €15-20; ☺9.30am-11pm; Via di San Giovanni in Laterano) Cosy, relaxed and welcoming, this cafe-bistro is a far cry from the usual impersonal eateries in the Colosseum area. With its rustic wooden tables, butternut walls and wine bottles, it's a charming spot to recharge your batteries over tea and homemade cake, a light lunch or laid-back dinner. There's also brunch on Sundays.

Li Rioni
PIZZA €

(Map p110; ☎06 7045 0605; Via dei Santissimi Quattro Coronati 24; meals €15-20; ☺7pm-midnight Thu-Tue, closed Aug; Via di San Giovanni in Laterano) Locals swear by Li Rioni, arriving for the second sitting around 9pm after the tourists have left. A classic neighbourhood pizzeria, it buzzes most nights as diners squeeze into the kitschy interior – set up as a Roman street scene – and tuck into wood-fired thin-crust pizzas and crispy fried starters.

✖ Aventino & Testaccio

Pizzeria Da Remo
PIZZA €

(Map p134; ☎06 574 62 70; Piazza Santa Maria Liberatrice 44; pizzas from €5.50; ☺7pm-1am Mon-Sat; Via Marmorata) For an authentic Roman experience, join the noisy crowds at this, one of the city's best-known and most popular pizzerias. It's a spartan-looking place, but the thin-crust Roman pizzas are the business, and there's a cheerful, boisterous vibe. Expect to queue after 8.30pm.

Aventino & Testaccio

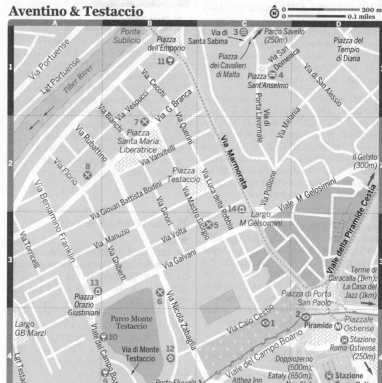

Aventino & Testaccio

Trapizzino   FAST FOOD €
(Map p134; www.trapizzino.it; Via Branca 88;
trapizzini from €3.50; ⊙noon-1am Tue-Sun;
📵Via Marmorata) This pocket-size joint is
the birthplace of the *trapizzino*, a kind of

hybrid sandwich made by stuffing a small
cone of doughy bread with fillers like *polpette al sugo* (meatballs in tomato sauce)
or *pollo alla cacciatore* (stewed chicken).
They're messy to eat but quite delicious.

★**Flavio al Velavevodetto** TRATTORIA €€
(Map p134; ☑06 574 41 94; www.ristorante velavevodetto.it; Via di Monte Testaccio 97-99; meals €30-35; ☺12.30-3pm & 7.45-11pm; ☑Via Galvani) Housed in a rustic Pompeian-red villa, this welcoming eatery specialises in earthy, no-nonsense *cucina romana* (Roman cuisine). Expect *antipasti* of cheeses and cured meats, huge helpings of homemade pastas, and uncomplicated meat dishes.

Da Felice LAZIO CUISINE €€
(Map p134; ☑06 574 68 00; www.feliceatestaccio. it; Via Mastro Giorgio 29; meals €35-40; ☺12.30-3pm & 7.30-10.30pm; ☑Via Marmorata) Foodies swear by this historic stalwart, famous for its unwavering dedication to local culinary traditions. In contrast to the light-touch modern decor, the menu is pure old-school with a classic weekly timetable: *pasta e fagioli* (pasta and beans) on Tuesdays, *bollito di manzo* (boiled beef) on Thursdays, seafood on Fridays. Reservations essential.

✗ Southern Rome

Eataly ITALIAN €
(☑06 9027 9201; www.eataly.net/it_en; Air Terminal Ostiense, Piazzale XII Ottobre 1492; ☺shop 10am-midnight, restaurants noon-11.30pm; Ⓜ Piramide) Eataly is an enormous, mall-like complex, a glittering, gleaming, somewhat confusing department store, entirely devoted to Italian food. As well as foodstuffs from all over the country, books, and cookery implements, the store is also home to 19 cafes and restaurants, including excellent pizzas, pasta dishes, ice cream and more.

Trattoria Priscilla TRATTORIA €€
(☑06 513 63 79; Via Appia Antica 68; meals €€; ☺1-3pm daily, 8-11pm Mon-Sat; ☑Via Appia Antica) Set in a 16th-century former stable, this intimate family-run trattoria has been feeding hungry travellers along the Appian Way for more than a hundred years, serving up traditional *cucina Romana,* so think carbonara, *amatriciana* and *cacio e pepe.* The tiramisu wins plaudits.

✗ Villa Borghese & Northern Rome

Caffè delle Arti CAFE, RISTORANTE €€
(Map p113; ☑06 3265 1236; www.caffedellearti roma.com; Via Gramsci 73; meal €45; ☺12.30-3.30pm daily & 7.30-11pm Tue-Sun; ☑Piazza Thor-valdsen) The cafe-restaurant of the Galleria Nazionale d'Arte Moderna (p114) sits in neo classical splendour in a tranquil corner of Villa Borghese. An elegant venue, it's at its best on sultry summer evenings when you can sit on the terrace and revel in the romantic atmosphere over coffee, cocktails or an alfresco dinner of classic Italian cuisine.

🍷 Drinking & Nightlife

Rome has plenty of drinking venues, ranging from traditional *enoteche* (wine bars) and streetside cafes to cool cocktail bars, pubs and counterculture hang-outs. During the day people usually head to bars for a quick coffee, while early evening sees the city's hipsters turn out for the evening *aperitivo* (aperitif).

Much of the action is in the *centro storico* – Campo de' Fiori fills with young, rowdy drinkers, while the lanes around Piazza Navona host a calmer, dressier scene. Over the river, Trastevere is another popular spot with dozens of bars and pubs, while to the east of Termini, the bars of San Lorenzo and Pigneto attract students and an arty alternative crowd.

Rome's clubs cater to most tastes, with DJs spinning everything from lounge and jazz to house, dancehall and hip hop. The scene is centred on Testaccio (mainstream clubs) and Ostiense (industrial, warehouse vibe for serious clubbers), although you'll also find places in Trastevere and the *centro storico*. Out from the centre, San Lorenzo and Pigneto are happening areas.

You'll need to dress the part for the big clubs, which can be tricky to get into, especially for groups of men. Events are often listed for 10pm but don't kick off until around 11pm, while clubs rarely hot up until well after 1am. Drinks are expensive, typically €10 to €16. Note also that many clubs shut between mid-June and mid-September.

🍷 Ancient Rome

0,75 BAR
(Map p68; www.075roma.com; Via dei Cerchi 65; ☺11am-2am; 🛜; ☑Via dei Cerchi) This welcoming bar on the Circo Massimo is good for a lingering drink, an *aperitivo* (6.30pm onwards) or a light meal (mains €6 to €13.50, salads €5.50 to €7.50). It's a friendly place with a laid-back vibe, an attractive exposed-brick look and cool tunes.

Caffè Capitolino
CAFE

(Map p68; Piazzale Caffarelli 4; ⊙9am-7.30pm Tue-Sun; 🚇Piazza Venezia) The Capitoline Museums' charming terrace cafe is a good place to relax over a drink or light snack (*panini*, salads and pizza) and enjoy wonderful views across the city's rooftops. Although part of the museum complex, you don't need a ticket to come here as it's accessible via an independent entrance on Piazzale Caffarelli.

Cavour 313
WINE BAR

(Map p68; ✆06 678 54 96; www.cavour313.it; Via Cavour 313; ⊙12.30-2.45pm & 7.30pm-12.30am, closed Sun summer; Ⓜ Cavour) Close to the Forum, wood-panelled Cavour 313 attracts everyone from tourists to actors and politicians. It serves a daily food menu and a selection of salads, cold cuts and cheeses (€8 to €12), but the headline act is the wine. And with more than 1200 labels to choose from you're sure to find something to tickle your palate.

 ## Centro Storico

★Barnum Cafe
CAFE

(Map p78; www.barnumcafe.com; Via del Pellegrino 87; ⊙9am-10pm Mon, 8.30am-2am Tue-Sat; 🛜; 🚇Corso Vittorio Emanuele II) A relaxed, friendly spot to check your email over a freshly squeezed orange juice or spend a pleasant hour reading a newspaper on one of the tatty old armchairs in the white bare-brick interior. Come evenings and the scene is cocktails, smooth tunes and coolly dressed-down locals.

Caffè Sant'Eustachio
CAFE

(Map p78; www.santeustachioilcaffe.it; Piazza Sant'Eustachio 82; ⊙8.30am-1am Sun-Thu, to 1.30am Fri, to 2am Sat; 🚇Corso del Rinascimento) This small, unassuming cafe, generally three deep at the bar, is reckoned by many to serve

---

APERITIVO ROME STYLE

Originally a northern Italian custom, the *aperitivo* is now an established part of Rome's social scene and many bars serve lavish buffets between 6pm and 9pm. To partake, order a drink – there's usually a standard charge of around €8 to €10 – and dig in.

Top spots include **Freni e Frizioni** (p139), **Doppiozeroo** (p139) and **Momart** (p139).

---

the best coffee in town. Created by beating the first drops of espresso and several teaspoons of sugar into a frothy paste, then adding the rest of the coffee, it's superbly smooth and guaranteed to put some zing into your sightseeing.

La Casa del Caffè Tazza d'Oro
CAFE

(Map p78; www.tazzadorocoffeeshop.com; Via degli Orfani 84-86; ⊙7am-8pm Mon-Sat, 10.30am-7.30pm Sun; 🚇Via del Corso) A busy, stand-up cafe with burnished 1940s fittings, this is one of Rome's best coffee houses. Its espresso hits the mark nicely and there's a range of delicious coffee concoctions, including a cooling *granita di caffè*, a crushed-ice coffee drink served with whipped cream. There's also a small shop and, outside, a coffee *bancomat* (ATM) for those out-of-hours caffeine emergencies.

Etablì
BAR, RISTORANTE

(Map p78; ✆06 9761 6694; www.etabli.it; Vicolo delle Vacche 9a; ⊙11am-2am, closed Mon in winter, Sun in summer; 🛜; 🚇Corso del Rinascimento) Housed in a lofty 16th-century *palazzo*, Etablì is a rustic-chic lounge-bar-restaurant where you can drop by for a morning coffee, have a light lunch or chat over an *aperitivo*. It's laid-back and good-looking, with original French-inspired country decor – think leather armchairs, rough wooden tables, and a crackling fireplace. It also serves weekend brunch, full restaurant dinners (€45), and the occasional jam session.

Open Baladin
BAR

(Map p78; www.openbaladinroma.it; Via degli Specchi 6; ⊙noon-2am; 🛜; 🚇Via Arenula) A hip, shabby-chic lounge bar near Campo de' Fiori, Open Baladin is a leading light in Rome's craft-beer scene, with more than 40 beers on tap and up to 100 bottled brews, many from Italian artisanal microbreweries. There's also a decent food menu with *panini,* gourmet burgers and daily specials.

No.Au
BAR

(Map p78; Piazza Montevecchio 16; ⊙6pm-1am Tue-Thu, noon-1am Fri-Sun; 🚇Corso del Rinascimento) Opening onto a charming *centro storico* piazza, No.Au – pronounced Know How – is a cool bistrot-bar set-up. Like many fashionable bars, it's big on beer and offers a knowledgeable list of artisanal craft brews, as well as local wines and a small but select food menu.

Il Goccetto WINE BAR
(Map p78; Via dei Banchi Vecchi 14; ⊙11.30am-2pm Tue & Sat, 6.30pm-midnight Mon-Sat, closed Aug; ⍰Corso Vittorio Emanuele II) This old-school *vino e olio* (wine and oil) shop has everything you could want in a neighbourhood wine bar – a colourful cast of regulars, a cosy, bottle-lined interior, a selection of cheeses and cold cuts, and a serious, 800-strong wine list.

Jerry Thomas Project COCKTAIL BAR
(Map p78; ☑06 9684 5937; www.thejerrythomasproject.it; Vicolo Cellini 30; ⊙10pm-4am; ⍰Corso Vittorio Emanuele II) A self-styled speakeasy with a 1920s look and a password to get in – check the website and call to book – this hidden bar is setting the standards for the cocktail trend currently sweeping Rome. Its hipster mixologists know their stuff and the retro decor lends the place a real Prohibition-era feel.

Circus BAR
(Map p78; www.circusroma.it; Via della Vetrina 15; ⊙10.30am-2am; ⍰; ⍰Corso del Rinascimento) A great little bar, tucked around the corner from Piazza Navona. It's a relaxed place popular with out-of-town students who come here to catch up on the news – wi-fi is free and there are international newspapers to read – and hang out over a drink. The atmosphere hots up in the evening when cocktails and shots take over from tea and cappuccino.

Salotto 42 BAR
(Map p78; www.salotto42.it; Piazza di Pietra 42; ⊙10.30am-2am Tue-Sun; ⍰Via del Corso) On a picturesque piazza, facing the columns of the Temple of Hadrian, this is a glamorous lounge bar, complete with subdued lighting, vintage 1950s armchairs, Murano lamps and a collection of heavyweight design books. Come for the daily lunch buffet or to hang out with the 'see and be-seen' crowd over an evening cocktail.

Tridente, Trevi & the Quirinale

La Scena BAR
(Map p88; Via della Penna 22; ⊙7am-1am; Ⓜ Flaminio) Part of the art-deco Hotel Locarno, this bar has a faded Agatha Christie–era feel, and a greenery-shaded outdoor terrace bedecked in wrought-iron furniture. Cocktails cost €13 to €15, or you can partake of after-

noon tea from 3pm to 6pm and *aperitivo* from 7pm to 10pm.

Stravinskij Bar – Hotel de Russie BAR
(Map p88; ☑06 328 88 70; Via del Babuino 9; ⊙9am-1am; Ⓜ Flaminio) Can't afford to stay at the celeb-magnet Hotel de Russie? Then splash out on a drink at its swish bar. There are sofas inside, but best is a drink in the sunny courtyard, with sunshaded tables overlooked by terraced gardens. Impossibly romantic in the best *dolce vita* style, it's perfect for a cocktail (from €20) or beer (€13) and some posh snacks.

Micca Club CLUB
(Map p88; ☑393 3236244; www.miccaclub.com; Via degli Avignonesi; Ⓜ Barberini) No longer in its brick-arched cellar in southern Rome, but now close to Piazza Barberini, Micca Club now has a less arresting interior but still retains its vintage, quirky vibe. This is Rome's burlesque club, where you can sip cocktails while watching shimmying acts upping the kitsch factor. Reserving a table by phone is advised.

Rosati CAFE
(Map p88; ☑06 322 58 59; Piazza del Popolo 5; ⊙7.30am-11.30pm; Ⓜ Flaminio) Rosati, overlooking the vast disc of Piazza del Popolo, was once the hang-out of the left-wing chattering classes. Authors Italo Calvino and Alberto Moravia used to drink here while their right-wing counterparts went to the **Canova** (Map p88; ☑06 361 22 31; Piazza del Popolo 16; ⊙8am-midnight; Ⓜ Flaminio) across the square. Today tourists are the main clientele, and the views are as good as ever.

Vatican City, Borgo & Prati

★**Sciascia Caffè** CAFE
(Map p92; Via Fabio Massimo 80/A; ⊙7.30am-6.30pm Mon-Sat; Ⓜ Ottaviano–San Pietro) The timeless elegance of this polished cafe is perfectly suited to the exquisite coffee it makes. There are various options but nothing can beat the *caffè eccellente,* a velvety smooth espresso served in a delicate cup that has been lined with melted chocolate. The result is nothing short of magnificent.

Makasar WINE BAR, TEAHOUSE
(Map p92; www.makasar.it; Via Plauto 33; ⊙noon-midnight Tue-Thu, to 2am Fri & Sat, 5.30-11.30pm Sun; ⍰Piazza del Risorgimento) Recharge your batteries with a quiet drink at this oasis of bookish tranquillity. Pick your

tipple from the nine-page tea menu or opt for an Italian wine and sit back in the casually stylish, softly lit interior. For something to eat, there's a small menu of salads, bruschette, baguettes and healthy hot dishes.

Passaguai WINE BAR
(Map p92; ✆ 06 8745 1358; www.passaguai.it; Via Leto 1; ⏱10am-2am Mon-Fri, 6pm-2am Sat & Sun; 🛜; 🚇 Piazza del Risorgimento) A cosy basement bar with tables in a vaulted interior and on a quiet sidestreet, Passaguai feels pleasingly off-the-radar. It's a great spot for a beer or glass of wine – there's an excellent choice of both – accompanied by cheese and cold cuts, or even a full meal from the limited menu. Free wi-fi.

🍷 Monti, Esquilino & San Lorenzo

⭐ **Il Tiaso** BAR
(✆ 06 4547 4625; www.iltiaso.com; Via Perugia 20; 🛜; 🚇 Circonvallazione Casilina) Think living room with zebra-print chairs, walls of indie art, Lou Reed biographies shelved between wine bottles, and 30-something owner Gabriele playing his latest New York Dolls album to neo-beatnik chicks, corduroy professors and the odd neighbourhood dog. Well-priced wine, an intimate chilled vibe, and regular live music.

Ai Tre Scalini WINE BAR
(Map p68; Via Panisperna 251; ⏱12.30pm-1am; 🚇 Cavour) The 'Three Steps' is always packed, with crowds spilling out into the street. Apart from a tasty choice of wines, it sells the damn fine Menabrea beer, brewed in northern Italy. You can also tuck into a heart-warming array of cheeses, salami and dishes such as *polpette al sugo* (meatballs with sauce; €7.50).

Fafiuché WINE BAR
(Map p68; ✆ 06 699 09 68; www.fafiuche.it; Via della Madonna dei Monti 28; ⏱5.30pm-1am Mon-Sat; 🚇 Cavour) Fafiuché means 'light-hearted fun' in the Piedmontese dialect, and this place lives up to its name. The narrow, bottle-lined warm-orange space exudes charm: come here to enjoy wine and artisanal beers, eat delicious dishes originating from Puglia to Piedmont, or buy delectable foodstuffs. *Aperitivo* is from 6.30pm to 9pm.

La Bottega del Caffè CAFE
(Map p68; Piazza Madonna dei Monti 5; ⏱8am-2am; 🚇 Cavour) Ideal for frittering away any balmy section of the day, this appealing cafe-bar, named after a comedy by Carlo Goldoni, has greenery-screened tables out on the pretty Piazza Madonna dei Monti. As well as drinks, it serves snacks, from simple pizzas to cheeses and salamis.

La Barrique WINE BAR
(Map p88; Via del Boschetto 41b; ⏱12.30-3.30pm & 5.30pm-1am Mon-Sat; 🚇 Cavour) This appealing *enoteca*, with wooden furniture and whitewashed walls, is a classy yet informal place to hang out and sample excellent French, Italian and German wines; a choice of perfectly cooked, delicious main courses provide a great accompaniment, or you can stick to artisanal cheeses and cold cuts.

Co.So BAR
(Via Braccio da Montone 80; cocktails €10; ⏱7pm-3am Mon-Sat; 🚇 Via Prenestina) The chicest bar in the Pigneto district, this tiny place, opened by Massimo d'Addezio, former master mixologist at Hotel de Russie, is buzzing and is hipster to the hilt, with its Carbonara Sour cocktail (with vodka infused with pork fat), bubblewrap coasters, and popcorn and M&M bar snacks.

Locanda Atlantide CLUB, LIVE MUSIC
(Map p102; ✆ 06 4470 4540; Via dei Lucani 22b; admission free or €3-5; ⏱9pm-2am Oct-Jun; 🚇 Via Tiburtina, 🚇 Scalo San Lorenzo) Come, tickle Rome's grungy underbelly. Descend through a door in a graffiti-covered wall into this cavernous basement dive, packed to the rafters with studenty, alternative crowds and featuring everything from prog-folk to DJ-spun electro music. It's good to know that punk is not dead.

Gente di San Lorenzo BAR
(Map p102; ✆ 06 445 44 25; Via degli Aurunci 42; ⏱7am-2am; 🚇 Via dei Reti) On the corner of San Lorenzo's Piazza dell'Immacolata, which gets thronged with students on balmy nights, this is a relaxed place for a drink and snack or meal. The interior is airy, with warm wooden floors and brick arches, and there are some outdoor tables as well as regular DJs and occasional live music.

🍷 Trastevere & Gianicolo

Ma Che Siete Venuti a Fà PUB
(Map p78; www.football-pub.com; Via Benedetta 25; ⏱11am-2am; 🚇 Piazza Trilussa) Named after a football chant, which translates politely as 'What did you come here for?', this pint-sized

Trastevere pub is a beer-buff's paradise, packing in at least 13 international craft beers on tap and even more by the bottle.

Bar San Calisto
CAFE

(Map p108; ☑ 06 589 56 78; Piazza San Calisto 3-5; ⊙ 6am-1.45am Mon-Sat; ⬚ Viale di Trastevere, ⬚ Viale di Trastevere) Those in the know head to the down-at-heel 'Sanca' for its basic, stuck-in-time atmosphere and cheap prices (beer €1.50). It attracts everyone from intellectuals to keeping-it-real Romans, alcoholics and American students. It's famous for its chocolate – hot with cream in winter, with ice cream in summer. Try the *Sambuca con la mosca* ('with flies' – raw coffee beans). Expect occasional late-night jam sessions.

Freni e Frizioni
BAR

(Map p108; ☑ 06 4549 7499; www.freniefrizioni. com; Via del Politeama 4-6; ⊙ 6.30pm-2am; ⬚ Piazza Trilussa) This perennially cool Trastevere bar is housed in a former mechanic's workshop – hence its name ('brakes and clutches'). It draws a young *spritz*-loving crowd that swells onto the small piazza outside to sip well-priced cocktails (from €7) and to snack on the daily *aperitivo* (€6 to €10, 7pm to 10pm).

Da Biagio
WINE BAR

(Map p108; www.dabiagio.it; Via della Scala 64; ⊙ 10am-1.30pm & 5pm-midnight; ⬚ Piazza Sonnino) With the sign 'Vini & Olio' scrawled above the door, this is a hole-in-the-wall Trastevere institution, lined by bottles of grappa and wine-for-sale, but also offering wine and spirits by the glass, shots and beer on tap. The owner is a funny guy, and has been serving up tipples since 1972. In the evening, drinkers spill out on the cobbled Trastevere street.

🍸 Aventino & Testaccio

Rec 23
BAR

(Map p134; ☑ 06 8746 2147; www.rec23.com; Piazza dell'Emporio 2; ⊙ 6.30pm-2am daily & 12.30-3.30pm Sat & Sun; ⬚ Via Marmorata) All plate glass and exposed brick, this popular, NY-inspired venue caters to all moods, serving aperitifs, restaurant meals, and a weekend brunch. Arrive thirsty to take on the Testaccio Mule, one of a long list of cocktails, or get to grips with the selection of Scottish whiskies and Latin American rums. It also hosts regular live gigs.

Big Bang
CLUB

(Map p134; www.bigbangroma.org; Via di Monte Testaccio 22; ⊙ 10pm-4.30am Fri & Sat; ⬚ Via Galvani) For one of the capital's best reggae parties, head to the Bababoomtime Friday-night session at Big Bang. The club, housed in Rome's graffiti-sprayed former slaughterhouse, draws a casual, music-loving crowd who know their reggae, dancehall, dub and techno.

🍸 Villa Borghese & Northern Rome

Momart
BAR

(www.momartcafe.it; Viale XXI Aprile 19; ⊙ noon-2am Mon-Fri, 6pm-2am Sat & Sun; ⬚ Via XXI Aprile) A spacious modern bar in the university district near Via Nomentana, Momart serves one of Rome's most popular aperitifs. A mixed crowd of students and local professionals flocks here to fill up on the pizza-led buffet and kick back over cocktails on the pavement terrace.

🍸 Southern Rome

Doppiozeroo
BAR

(☑ 06 5730 1961; www.doppiozeroo.com; Via Ostiense 68; ⊙ 7am-2am Mon-Sat; Ⓜ Piramide) This easygoing bar was once a bakery, hence the name ('double zero' is a type of flour). But today the sleek, modern interior attracts hungry, trendy Romans like bees to honey, especially for the cheap lunches (*primo/secondo* €4.50/6.50) and famously lavish, dinnertastic *aperitivo* between 6pm and 9pm.

Porto Fluviale
BAR

(☑ 06 574 31 99; www.portofluviale.com; Via del Porto Fluviale 22; ⊙ 10.30am-2am; Ⓜ Piramide) A large bar in a converted factory, this has an

> ### SUMMER NIGHTS IN ROME
>
> From mid-June to mid-September, many of the city's clubs and music joints close, with some moving to Fregene or Ostia for a summer of beachfront dancing. However, the **Estate Romana** (p118) festival supplies ample after-dark entertainment. Concerts, exhibitions, theatrical performances and open-air cinema are staged across town, while the city's nightlife goes alfresco for the summer-long **Lungo il Tevere** (p118) festival.

ROME & LAZIO ROME

ex-industrial look – dark-green walls and a brickwork floor – and is a relaxing, appealing place for morning coffee, *aperitivo* or an evening drink to a soundtrack of plinky jazz. In line with Rome's current love of artisanal brews, it serves its own Porto Fluviale craft beer (medium €5.50).

Goa
CLUB

(⌚ 06 574 82 77; www.goaclub.com; Via Libetta 13; ⊗ 11.30pm-4.30am Thu-Sat; Ⓜ Garbatella) Goa is Rome's serious super-club, with international names, ethnic-styling, a fashion-forward crowd, podium dancers and a heavies on the door.

Neo Club
CLUB

(Via degli Argonauti 18; ⊗ 11pm-4am Fri & Sat; Ⓜ Garbatella) This small, dark two-level club has an underground feel and is one of the funkiest choices in the zone, featuring a dance-tastic mish-mash of breakbeat, techno and old-skool house.

☆ Entertainment

Entertainment in Rome can be simply parking yourself at a streetside table and watching the world go by, but the city has a thriving cultural scene with a year-round calendar of concerts, performances and festivals. In summer, cultural events are staged across town, many in atmospheric parks, piazzas, ruins and churches. Autumn is another good time, with festivals dedicated to dance, drama and jazz.

A useful listings guide is *Trova Roma*, a free insert with *La Repubblica* newspaper every Thursday. Upcoming events are also listed on www.turismoroma.it, www.060608.it, www.inromenow.com and www.romamusica.it.

Hotels can often reserve tickets for guests. Otherwise you can try Orbis (Map p102; ⌚ 06 482 79 15; Piazza dell'Esquilino 37), which accepts cash payment only, or the online agency Hellò Ticket (⌚ 892 234; www.helloticket.it).

Classical Music

The city's musical hub is the Auditorium Parco della Musica, but free concerts are often held in churches, especially at Easter, Christmas and New Year.

Auditorium Parco della Musica
CONCERT VENUE

(⌚ 06 8024 1281; www.auditorium.com; Viale Pietro de Coubertin 30; ⊡ Viale Tiziano) The hub of Rome's thriving cultural scene, the Auditorium is the capital's premier concert venue and

one of Europe's most popular arts centres. Its three concert halls offer superb acoustics, and, together with a 3000-seat open-air arena, stage everything from classical-music concerts to jazz gigs, public lectures, and film screenings.

The Auditorium is also home to Rome's world-class Orchestra dell' Accademia Nazionale di Santa Cecilia (www.santacecilia.it).

Teatro Olimpico
THEATRE

(⌚ 06 326 59 91; www.teatroolimpico.it; Piazza Gentile da Fabriano 17; ⊡ Piazza Mancini, ⊡ Piazza Mancini) The Teatro Olimpico is home to the Accademia Filarmonica Romana (www.filarmonicaromana.org), a classical-music organisation whose past members have included Rossini, Donizetti and Verdi. The theatre offers a varied program of classical and chamber music, opera, ballet, one-man shows and comedies.

Opera

Opera is staged in the city's main opera house and, in summer, amidst the spectacular ruins of the Terme di Caracalla.

Teatro dell'Opera di Roma
OPERA

(Map p102; ⌚ 06 481 70 03; www.operaroma.it; Piazza Beniamino Gigli; ballet €12-80, opera €17-150; ⊗ 9am-5pm Tue-Sat, to 1.30pm Sun; Ⓜ Repubblica) Rome's premier opera house boasts a plush-and-gilt interior, a Fascist 1920s exterior and an impressive history: it premiered Puccini's *Tosca*, and Maria Callas once sang here. Opera and ballet performances are staged between September and June.

Jazz, Blues, Indie & Rock

Alexanderplatz
JAZZ

(Map p92; ⌚ 06 3972 1867; www.alexanderplatzjazzclub.com; Via Ostia 9; ⊗ 8.30pm-2am, concerts 9.45pm; Ⓜ Ottaviano-San Pietro) Small, intimate and underground, Rome's most celebrated jazz club draws top Italian and international performers and a respectful cosmopolitan crowd. Book a table for the best stage views or if you want to dine to the tunes. Check the website for upcoming gigs.

La Casa del Jazz
JAZZ

(⌚ 06 70 47 31; www.casajazz.it; Viale di Porta Ardeatina 55; admission varies; ⊗ gigs start 8-9pm; Ⓜ Piramide) In the middle of a 2500-sq-metre park in the southern suburbs, the Casa del Jazz is housed in a three-storey 1920s villa that once belonged to a Mafia boss. When he was caught, the Comune di Roma (Rome

Council) converted it into a jazz-fuelled complex, with a 150-seat auditorium, rehearsal rooms, a cafe and a restaurant. Some events are free.

Big Mama
BLUES

(Map p108; ☑ 06 581 25 51; www.bigmama.it; Vicolo di San Francesco a Ripa 18; ◷ 9pm-1.30am, shows 10.30pm, closed Jun-Sep; ⊠ Viale di Trastevere, ⊠ Viale di Trastevere) Head to this cramped Trastevere basement for a mellow night of Eternal City blues. A long-standing venue, it also stages jazz, funk, soul and R&B, as well as popular Italian cover bands.

ConteStaccio
LIVE MUSIC

(Map p134; www.contestaccio.com; Via di Monte Testaccio 65b; ◷ 7pm-4am Tue-Sun; ⊠ Via Galvani) With an under-the-stars terrace and cool, arched interior, ConteStaccio is one of the top venues on the Testaccio clubbing strip. It's something of a multi-purpose outfit with a cocktail bar, a pizzeria and a restaurant but is best known for its daily concerts. Gigs by emerging groups set the tone, spanning indie, rock, acoustic, funk and electronic.

Lettere Caffè Gallery
LIVE MUSIC

(Map p108; ☑ 06 9727 0991; www.letterecaffe.org; Vicolo di San Francesco a Ripa 100/101; ◷ 7pm-2am, closed mid-Aug–mid-Sep; ⊠ Viale di Trastevere, ⊠ Viale di Trastevere) Like books? Poetry? Blues and jazz? Then you'll love this place – a clutter of barstools and books, where there are regular live gigs, poetry slams, comedy and gay nights, plus DJ sets playing indie and new wave.

Cinemas

Of Rome's 80-odd cinemas, only a handful show films in the original language (marked VO or *versione originale* in listings). Expect to pay around €8, with many cinemas offering discounts on Wednesdays.

In Trastevere, try the **Alcazar Cinema** (Map p108; ☑ 06 588 00 99; Via Merry del Val 14; ⊠ Viale di Trastevere, ⊠ Viale di Trastevere) or **Nuovo Sacher** (☑ 06 581 81 16; www.sacherfilm.eu; Largo Ascianghi 1; ⊠ Viale di Trastevere, ⊠ Viale di Trastevere), owned by cult Roman filmmaker Nanni Moretti.

Sport

Watching a game of football at the **Stadio Olimpico** (☑ 06 3685 7520; Viale dei Gladiatori 2, Foro Italico) is an unforgettable experience, although you'll have to keep your wits about you as crowd trouble is not unheard of.

Throughout the season (September to May), there's a game most Sundays involving one of Rome's two teams: **AS Roma**, known as the *giallorossi* (yellow and reds; www.asroma.it), or **Lazio**, the *biancazzuri* (white and blues; www.sslazio.it, in Italian). Ticket prices start at €16 and can be bought at Lottomatica outfits (lottery centres), the stadium, ticket agencies, www.listicket.it, or one of the several Roma or Lazio stores around town.

The stadium also hosts Italy's 6 Nations rugby matches between February and March.

To get to the stadium take metro line A to Ottaviano and then bus 32.

🔒 Shopping

Rome boasts the usual cast of flagship chain stores and glitzy designer outlets, but what makes shopping here fun is its legion of small, independent shops – historic, family-owned delis, small-label fashion boutiques, artists' studios and neighbourhood markets.

For designer clothes head to Via dei Condotti, Rome's top shopping strip, and the grid of streets around Piazza di Spagna. For something more left field, check out the vintage shops and boutiques on Via del Governo Vecchio, around Campo de' Fiori, and in the Monti neighbourhood.

If you're after antiques or arty gifts, try Via dei Coronari, Via dei Banchi Vecchi or Via Margutta.

For the best bargains, come for the *saldi* (sales). Winter sales run from early January to mid-February and summer sales from July to early September.

🔒 Centro Storico

★ **Confetteria Moriondo & Gariglio** FOOD

(Map p78; Via del Piè di Marmo 21-22; ◷ 9am-7.30pm Mon-Sat; ⊠ Via del Corso) Roman poet Trilussa was so smitten with this historic chocolate shop – established by the Torinese confectioners to the royal house of Savoy – that he dedicated several sonnets to it. And we agree, it's a gem. Many of the bonbons and handmade chocolates laid out in ceremonial splendour in the glass cabinets are still prepared according to original 19th-century recipes.

★ **Ibiz – Artigianato in Cuoio** ACCESSORIES

(Map p78; Via dei Chiavari 39; ◷ 9.30am-7.30pm Mon-Sat; ⊠ Corso Vittorio Emanuele II) In their diminutive workshop, Elisa Nepi and her

HELP FIGHT THE MAFIA

To look at it there's nothing special about **Pio La Torre** (Map p78; www.libera terra.it; Via dei Prefetti 23; ☺10.30am-7.30pm Tue-Sat, 10.30am-2.30pm Sun, 3.30-7.30pm Mon ; ⓓ Via del Corso), a small, unpretentious food store near Piazza del Parlamento. But shop here and you're making a small but concrete contribution to the fight against the Mafia. All the gastro goodies on sale, including organic olive oil, pasta, flour, honey and wine, have been produced on land confiscated from organised crime outfits in Calabria and Sicily. The shop is one of several across the country set up by Libera Terra, a grassroots movement of agricultural cooperatives working on terrain that was once owned by the Mob.

father craft exquisite, well-priced leather goods, including wallets, bags, belts and sandals, in simple but classy designs and myriad colours. You can pick up a belt for about €35, while for a bag you should bank on at least €110.

SBU
FASHION

(Map p78; www.sbu.it; Via di San Pantaleo 68-69; ☺10am-7.30pm Mon-Sat; ⓓ Corso Vittorio Emanuele II) The flagship store of hip fashion label SBU, aka Strategic Business Unit, occupies a 19th-century workshop near Piazza Navona, complete with cast-iron columns and wooden racks. Pride of place goes to the jeans, superbly cut from top-end Japanese denim, but you can also pick up shirts, jackets, hats, sweaters and T-shirts.

Officina Profumo Farmaceutica di Santa Maria Novella
BEAUTY

(Map p78; www.smnovella.it; Corso del Rinascimento 47; ☺10am-7.30pm Mon-Sat; ⓓ Corso del Rinascimento) This, the Roman branch of one of Italy's oldest pharmacies, stocks natural perfumes and cosmetics as well as herbal infusions, teas and pot pourri, all shelved in wooden, glass-fronted cabinets under a Murano chandelier. The original pharmacy was founded in Florence in 1612 by the Dominican monks of Santa Maria Novella, and many of its cosmetics are based on 17th-century herbal recipes.

Le Artigiane
CLOTHING, HANDICRAFTS

(Map p78; www.leartigiane.it; Via di Torre Argentina 72; ☺10am-7.30pm; ⓓ Largo di Torre Argentina) A space for local artisans to showcase their wares, this eclectic shop is the result of an ongoing project to sustain and promote Italy's artisanal traditions. It's a browser's dream with an eclectic range of handmade clothes, costume jewellery, ceramics, design objects and lamps.

Luna & L'Altra
FASHION

(Map p78; Piazza Pasquino 76; ☺10am-2pm Tue-Sat, 3.30-7.30pm Mon-Sat; ⓓ Corso Vittorio Emanuele II) An address for fashionistas with their fingers on the pulse, this is one of a number of independent boutiques on and around Via del Governo Vecchio. In its austere, gallery-like interior, clothes by Comme des Garçons, Issey Miyake, Yohji Yamamoto and others are exhibited in reverential style.

Nardecchia
ARTS

(Map p78; Piazza Navona 25; ☺10am-1pm Tue-Sat, 4.30-7.30pm Mon-Sat; ⓓ Corso del Rinascimento) Famed for its antique prints, this historic Piazza Navona shop sells everything from 18th-century etchings by Giovanni Battista Piranesi to more affordable 19th-century panoramas. Bank on paying at least €150 for a small framed print.

Borini
SHOES

(Map p78; Via dei Pettinari 86-87; ☺9am-1pm Tue-Sat, 3.30-7.30pm Mon-Sat; ⓓ Via Arenula) Don't be fooled by the discount, workaday look – those in the know head to this seemingly down-at-heel shop for the latest footwear fashions. Women's styles, ranging from ballet flats to heeled boots, are displayed in the functional glass cabinets, alongside a small selection of men's leather shoes.

Bartolucci
TOYS

(Map p78; www.bartolucci.com; Via dei Pastini 98; ☺10am-10pm; ⓓ Via del Corso) It's difficult to resist going into this magical toy shop where everything is carved out of wood. It's guarded by a cycling Pinocchio and a full-sized motorbike, and within are all manner of ticking clocks, rocking horses, planes and more Pinocchios than you'll have ever seen in your life.

🔒 Tridente, Trevi & the Quirinale

Bottega di Marmoraro   ARTS
(Map p88; Via Margutta 53b; ⊘8am-7.30pm Mon-Sat; Ⓜ Flaminio) A particularly charismatic hole-in-the-wall shop lined with marble carvings, where you can get marble tablets engraved with any inscription you like (€15). Peer inside at lunchtime and you might see the cheerfully quizzical *marmoraro*, Enrico Fiorentini, cooking pasta for his lunch next to the open log fire.

Danielle   SHOES
(Map p88; ☑06 679 24 67; Via Frattina 85a; ⊘10.30am-7.30pm; Ⓜ Spagna) If you're female and in need of an Italian shoe fix, this is an essential stop on your itinerary. It sells both classic and fashionable styles – foxy heels, boots and ballet pumps – at extremely reasonable prices. Shoes are of soft leather and come in myriad colours.

Pelletteria Nives   ACCESSORIES
(Map p88; ☑333 3370831; Via delle Carrozze 16; ⊘9am-1pm & 4-8pm Mon-Sat; Ⓜ Spagna) Take the rickety lift to this workshop, choose from the softest leathers, and you will shortly be the proud owner of a handmade, designer-style bag, wallet, belt or briefcase – take a design with you. Bags cost €200 to €350 and take around a week to make.

Vertecchi Art   ARTS
(Map p88; Via della Croce 70; ⊘3.30-7.30pm Mon, 10am-7.30pm Tue-Sat; Ⓜ Spagna) Ideal for last-minute gift buying, this large paperware and art shop has beautiful printed paper, cards and envelopes that will inspire you to bring back the art of letter writing, plus an amazing choice of notebooks, art stuff and trinkets.

Lucia Odescalchi   JEWELLERY
(Map p88; ☑06 6992 5506; Palazzo Odescalchi, Piazza dei Santissimi Apostoli 81; ⊘9.30am-2pm Mon-Fri; Ⓜ Spagna) If you're looking for a unique piece of statement jewellery that will make an outfit, this is the place to head. Housed in the evocative archives of the family *palazzo*, the avant-garde pieces often have an almost medieval beauty, and run from incredible polished steel and chain mail to pieces created out of pearls and fossils. Beautiful. Prices start at around €140.

C.U.C.I.N.A.   HOMEWARES
(Map p88; ☑06 679 12 75; Via Mario de' Fiori 65; ⊘3.30-7.30pm Mon, 10am-7.30pm Tue-Fri, 10.30am-7.30pm Sat; Ⓜ Spagna) If you need a foodie gadget, C.U.C.I.N.A. is the place. Make your own *cucina* (kitchen) look the part with the designerware from this famous shop, with myriad devices you'll decide you simply must have, from jelly moulds to garlic presses.

Sermoneta   ACCESSORIES
(Map p88; ☑06 679 19 60; www.sermonetagloves.com; Piazza di Spagna 61; ⊘9.30am-8pm Mon-Sat, 10am-7pm Sun; Ⓜ Spagna) Buying leather gloves in Rome is a rite of passage for some, and its most famous glove-seller is the place to do it. Choose from a kaleidoscopic range of quality leather and suede gloves lined with silk and cashmere. An expert assistant will size up your hand in a glance – just don't expect them to crack a smile.

Fausto Santini   SHOES
(Map p88; ☑06 678 41 14; Via Frattina 120; ⊘11am-7.30pm Mon, 10am-7.30pm Tue-Sat, 11am-2pm & 3-7pm Sun; Ⓜ Spagna) Rome's best-known shoe designer, Fausto Santini is famous for his beguilingly simple, architectural shoe designs, with beautiful boots and shoes made from butter-soft leather. Colours are beautiful, the quality impeccable. Seek out the end-of-line **discount shop** (Map p102; ☑06 488 09 34; Via Cavour 106; ⊘3.30-7.30pm Mon, 10am-1pm & 3.30-7.30pm Tue-Sat; Ⓜ Cavour) if this looks out of your price range.

🔒 Monti, Esquilino & San Lorenzo

Mercato Monti Urban Market   MARKET
(Map p68; www.mercatomonti.com; Via Leonina 46; ⊘10am-8pm Sat & Sun; Ⓜ Cavour) Vintage clothes, accessories, one-off pieces by local designers, this market in the hip hood of Monti is well worth a rummage.

Tina Sondergaard   CLOTHING
(Map p68; ☑334 3850799; Via del Boschetto 1d; ⊘3-7.30pm Mon, 10.30am-7.30pm Tue-Sat, closed Aug; Ⓜ Cavour) Sublimely cut and whimsically retro-esque, these handmade threads are a hit with female fashion cognoscenti, including Italian rock star Carmen Consoli and the city's theatre and TV crowd. You can have adjustments made (included in the price), and dresses cost around €140.

ⓘ WATCH YOUR VALUABLES

Rome is a safe city, but petty crime is rife. Pickpockets follow the tourists, so watch out around the Colosseum, Piazza di Spagna, St Peter's Square and Stazione Termini. Be particularly vigilant around the bus stops on Via Marsala, where thieves prey on travellers fresh in from Ciampino Airport. Crowded public transport is another hot spot – the 64 Vatican bus is notorious. If travelling on the metro, try to use the end carriages, which are usually less crowded.

🏠 Trastevere & Gianicolo

Porta Portese Market   MARKET

(Piazza Porta Portese; ⊙ 6am-2pm Sun; 🚋 Viale di Trastevere, 🚋 Viale di Trastevere) To see another side of Rome, head to this mammoth flea market. With thousands of stalls selling everything from rare books and fell-off-a-lorry bikes to Peruvian shawls and MP3 players, it's crazily busy and a lot of fun. Keep your valuables safe and wear your haggling hat.

🏠 Aventino & Testaccio

Volpetti   FOOD & DRINK

(Map p134; www.volpetti.com; Via Marmorata 47; ⊙ 8am-2pm & 5-8.15pm Mon-Sat; 🚋 Via Marmorata) This superstocked deli, considered by many the best in town, is a treasure trove of gourmet delicacies. Helpful staff will guide you through the extensive selection of smelly cheeses, homemade pastas, olive oils, vinegars, cured meats, veggie pies, wines and grappas. It also serves excellent sliced pizza.

ⓘ Orientation

Rome is a sprawling city but the centre is relatively compact and most sights are concentrated in the area between Stazione Termini, the city's main transport hub, and the Vatican to the west. Halfway between the two, the Pantheon and Piazza Navona lie at the heart of the *centro storico*, while to the south, the Colosseum lords it over the city's great ancient ruins: the Roman Forum and Palatino. On the west bank of the Tiber, St Peter's Basilica trumpets the presence of the Vatican.

Distances are not great so walking is often the best way to get around.

ⓘ Information

EMERGENCY

Ambulance	🎵 118
Fire	🎵 115
Police	🎵 112, 113

INTERNET ACCESS

➡ Free wi-fi is now widely available in hostels, B&Bs and hotels. Some places also provide laptops/computers for guests' use.

➡ Free public wi-fi is available in hot spots around town, but to use it you'll have to register with the provider – the **Provincia di Roma** (www.provincia.roma.it), **Roma Wireless** (www. romawireless.com) or **Wimove** (www.wimove.it) – using an Italian mobile number. Much easier is to head to one of the many cafes or bars offering free wi-fi.

➡ There are a number of internet cafes in the area around Stazione Termini.

MEDIA

The following are available in English:

Osservatore Romano (www.osservatore romano.va) The online edition of the Vatican's official daily newspaper.

Wanted in Rome (www.wantedinrome.com) Expat magazine with news, classified ads, listings and reviews.

MEDICAL SERVICES

For problems that don't require hospital treatment, call the **Guardia Medica** (🎵 06 884 01 13; Via Mantova 44; ⊙ 24 hr).

More convenient, if you have insurance and can afford to pay up front, is to call a doctor for a home visit. Try the **International Medical Centre** (🎵 06 488 23 71; Via Firenze 47; GP call-out & treatment fee €140, 8pm-9am & weekends €200; ⊙ 24hr).

Pharmacists will serve prescriptions and can provide basic medical advice. Night pharmacies are listed in daily newspapers and in pharmacy windows.

Farmacia Vaticana (🎵 06 6988 9806; Palazzo Belvedere, Via di Porta Angelica; ⊙ 8.30am-6pm Mon-Fri Sep-Jun, 8.30am-3pm Mon-Fri Jul & Aug, plus 8.30am-1pm Sat year-round) In the Vatican, the **Farmacia Vaticana** sells certain drugs that are not available in Italian pharmacies, and will fill foreign prescriptions (something local pharmacies can't do).

Pharmacy (🎵 06 488 00 19; Piazza dei Cinquecento 51; ⊙ 7am-11.30pm Mon-Fri, 8am-11.30pm Sat & Sun) There's also a pharmacy in Stazione Termini, next to platform 1, open 7.30am to 10pm daily.

Policlinico Umberto I (☑06 4 99 71; www.policlinicoumberto1.it; Viale del Policlinico 155) Near Stazione Termini.

MONEY

ATMs are liberally scattered around the city.

There are money-exchange booths at Stazione Termini and Fiumicino and Ciampino airports. In the centre, there are numerous bureaux de change, including the **American Express** (☑06 6 76 41; Piazza di Spagna 38; ☺9am-5.30pm Mon-Fri, 9am-12.30pm Sat) office.

POST

Main Post Office (Map p78; ☑06 6973 7205; Piazza di San Silvestro 19; ☺8.20am-7.05pm Mon-Fri, 8.20am-12.35pm Sat)

Vatican Post Office (Map p92; ☑06 6989 0400; St Peter's Sq; ☺8.30am-6.45pm Mon-Fri, 8.30am-2pm Sat) Letters can be posted in blue Vatican post boxes only if they carry Vatican stamps.

TOURIST INFORMATION

For phone enquiries, the Comune di Roma runs a free multilingual **tourist information line** (☑06 06 08; ☺9am-9pm).

There are tourist information points at Rome's two international airports – **Fiumicino** (Terminal 3, International Arrivals; ☺8am-7.30pm) and **Ciampino** (International Arrivals, baggage claim area; ☺9am-6.30pm) – and at locations across the city. These include:

Piazza delle Cinque Lune (Map p78; ☺9.30am-7.15pm) Near Piazza Navona.

Stazione Termini (Map p102; ☺8am-7.45pm) In the hall that runs parallel to platform 24.

Fori Imperiali (Map p68; Via dei Fori Imperiali; ☺9.30am-7pm)

Via Marco Minghetti (Map p78; Via Marco Minghetti; ☺9.30am-7.15pm) Near the Trevi Fountain.

Via Nazionale (Map p88; Via Nazionale; ☺9.30am-7.15pm)

For information about the Vatican, contact the **Centro Servizi Pellegrini e Turisti** (Map p92; ☑06 6988 1662; St Peter's Sq; ☺8.30am-6pm Mon-Sat).

USEFUL WEBSITES

060608 (www.060608.it) Provides information on sites, accommodation, shows, transport.

Coop Culture (www.coopculture.it) Information and ticketing for Rome's monuments, museums and galleries.

In Rome Now (www.inromenow.com) Savvy internet magazine compiled by two American expats.

Turismo Roma (www.turismoroma.it) Rome's official tourist website. Lists accommodation options, upcoming events and more.

Vatican (www.vatican.va) The Vatican's official website.

🛈 Getting There & Away

AIR

Rome's main international airport, Leonardo da Vinci (p146), better known as Fiumicino, is on the coast 30km west of the city.

The much smaller **Ciampino Airport** (☑06 6 59 51; www.adr.it/ciampino), 15km southeast of the city centre, is the hub for European low-cost carrier Ryanair (p953).

BOAT

The nearest port to Rome is at Civitavecchia, about 80km north of the city. Ferries sail here from Spain and Tunisia, as well as Sicily and

TRAIN SERVICES TO MAJOR CITIES

From Stazione Termini you can catch direct trains to the following cities and many others. All fares quoted are 2nd class.

TO	SERVICE TYPE	FARE (€)	DURATION (HR)
Florence	fast	39-54	1½
	slow	20.65	3¾
Milan	fast	79-116	3-3½
Naples	fast	39-43	1¼
	slow	11.80	2¾
Palermo	day	77.50	11½
	overnight	59-69	12-12½
Venice	fast	69-80	3¾
	overnight	48	6¾

Sardinia. Check www.traghettiweb.it for route details, prices and to book.

Bookings can also be made at the Termini-based **Agenzia 365** (☑ 06 488 16 78; www.agenzie365.it; ⊙7am-9pm), at travel agents or directly at the port.

Half-hourly trains run to Civitavecchia from Termini (€5 to €15, 40 minutes to 1¼ hours). On arrival, it's about 700m to the port – go right as you exit the station.

BUS

Long-distance national and international buses use the **Autostazione Tiburtina** (Piazzale Tiburtina; Ⓜ Tiburtina) near Stazione Tiburtina, east of the city centre. Take metro line B from Stazione Termini.

You can get tickets at the bus station or at travel agencies.

Bus operators include:

Interbus (☑ 091 34 25 25; www.interbus.it) To/from Sicily.

Marozzi (☑ 080 579 01 11; www.marozzivt.it) To/from Sorrento, Bari and Puglia.

SENA (☑ 0861 199 19 00; www.sena.it) To/from Siena, Bologna and Milan.

Sulga (☑ 800 099661; www.sulga.it) To/from Perugia, Assisi and Ravenna.

For destinations in the Lazio region, Cotral (p156) buses depart from points across the city. The company is linked with Rome's public transport system, so you can buy tickets that cover city buses, trams, metro and train lines, as well as regional buses and trains.

CAR & MOTORCYCLE

Driving into central Rome is a challenge, involving traffic restrictions, one-way systems, a shortage of street parking and aggressive drivers.

Rome is circled by the *Grande Raccordo Anulare* (GRA) to which all autostradas (motorways) connect, including the main A1 north–south artery (the Autostrada del Sole) and the A12, which runs to Civitavecchia and Fiumicino Airport.

Car Hire

Rental cars are available at the airport and Stazione Termini.

Avis (☑ 199 100 133; www.avisautonoleggio.it)
Europcar (☑ 199 30 70 30; www.europcar.it)
Hertz (☑ 02 6943 0019; www.hertz.it)
Maggiore National (☑ 199 151 120; www.maggiore.it)

TRAIN

Almost all trains serve **Stazione Termini** (Piazza dei Cinquecento; Ⓜ Termini), Rome's main train station and principal transport hub. There are regular connections to other European coun-

BUSES FROM TERMINI

From Piazza dei Cinquecento outside Stazione Termini buses run to all corners of the city.

DESTINATION	BUS NO
Campo de' Fiori	40/64
Colosseum	75
Pantheon	40/64
Piazza Navona	40/64
Piazza Venezia	40/64
St Peter's Square	40/64
Terme di Caracalla	714
Trastevere	H
Villa Borghese	910

tries, all major Italian cities and many smaller towns.

Train information is available from the customer service area on the main concourse. Alternatively, check www.trenitalia.com or phone ☑ 892021.

Left luggage (Stazione Termini; 1st 5hr €6, 6-12hr per hour €0.90, 13hr & over per hour €0.40; ⊙ 6am-11pm) is available on the lower-ground floor under platform 24.

Rome's other principal train stations are Tiburtina, Ostiense and Trastevere.

ⓘ Getting Around

TO/FROM THE AIRPORT

Fiumicino

The easiest way to get to/from Fiumicino is by train, but there are also buses and private shuttle services.

Leonardo Express (one way €14) Runs trains to/from Stazione Termini. Departures from the airport every 30 minutes between 6.23am and 11.23pm; from Termini between 5.35am and 10.35pm. Journey time is 30 minutes.

FL1 (one way €8) Trains connect to Trastevere, Ostiense and Tiburtina stations, but not Termini. Departures from the airport every 15 minutes (half-hourly on Sundays and public holidays) between 5.57am and 10.42pm; from Tiburtina every 15 minutes between 5.46am and 7.31pm, then half-hourly to 10.02pm.

Airport Shuttle (www.airportshuttle.it) Transfers to/from your hotel for €25 for one person, then €6 for each additional passenger up to a maximum of eight.

Cotral (www.cotralspa.it; one way €5, if bought on the bus €7) Runs buses to/from Fiumicino from Stazione Tiburtina via Termini. Eight daily departures including night services from the

ℹ TICKETS

Public-transport tickets are valid on all Rome's bus, tram and metro lines, except for routes to Fiumicino airport. They come in various forms:

BIT (*biglietto integrato a tempo*; €1.50) A single ticket valid for 100 minutes and one metro ride.

Roma 24h (€7) Valid for 24 hours.

Roma 48h (€12.50) Valid for 48 hours.

Roma 72h (€18) Valid for 72 hours.

CIS (*carta integrata settimanale*; €24) A weekly ticket.

Abbonamento mensile (restricted to a single user €35; used by anyone €53) A monthly pass.

Children under 10 travel free.

Buy tickets at *tabacchi*, newsstands and from vending machines at main bus stops and metro stations. They must be purchased before you start your journey and validated in the machines on buses, at the entrance gates to the metro or at train stations. Passengers without a ticket risk an on-the-spot €50 fine.

The Roma Pass (p85; two/three days €28/36) comes with a two-/three-day travel pass valid within the city boundaries.

airport at 1.15am, 2.15am, 3.30am and 5am, and from Tiburtina at 12.30am, 1.15am, 2.30am and 3.45am. Journey time is one hour.

Taxi The set fare to/from the city centre is €48, which is valid for up to four passengers with luggage. Note that taxis registered in Fiumicino charge more, so make sure you catch a Comune di Roma taxi – they are white with the words *Roma Capitale* on the side, along with the driver's ID number.

Ciampino

To get into town, the best bet is to take one of the dedicated bus services. You can also take a bus to Ciampino station and pick up a train to Stazione Termini.

Terravision (www.terravision.eu; one way €6, online €4) Twice hourly bus departures to/from Via Marsala outside Stazione Termini. From the airport services are between 8.15am and 12.15am; from Via Marsala between 4.30am and 9.20pm. Buy tickets at Terracafè in front of the Via Marsala bus stop. Journey time is 40 minutes.

SIT (☑ 06 591 68 26; www.sitbusshuttle.com; from/to airport €4/6) Regular bus departures from the airport to Via Marsala outside Stazione Termini between 7.45am and 11.15pm; from Termini between 4.30am and 9.30pm. Get tickets on the bus. Journey time is 45 minutes.

Atral (www.atral-lazio.com) Runs buses to/from Anagnina metro station (€1.20) and Ciampino train station (€1.20), where you can get a train to Termini (€1.30).

Taxi The set fare is €30.

CAR & MOTORCYCLE

Access & Parking

➡ Most of the historic centre is closed to unauthorised traffic from 6.30am to 6pm Monday to Friday, from 2pm to 6pm (10am to 7pm in some places) Saturday, and from 11pm to 3am Friday and Saturday. Evening restrictions also apply in Trastevere, San Lorenzo, Monti and Testaccio, typically from 9.30pm or 11pm to 3am on Fridays and Saturdays.

➡ All streets accessing the 'Limited Traffic Zone' (ZTL) are monitored by electronic-access detection devices. If you're staying in this zone, contact your hotel. For further information, check www.agenziamobilita.roma.it.

➡ Blue lines denote pay-and-display parking – get tickets from meters (coins only) and *tabacchi*.

➡ Expect to pay up to €1.20 per hour between 8am and 8pm (11pm in some places). After 8pm (or 11pm) parking is free until 8am the next morning.

➡ Traffic wardens are vigilant and fines are not uncommon. If your car gets towed away, call ☑ 06 6769 2303.

➡ There's a comprehensive list of car parks at www.060608.it – click on the transport tab and car parks.

Scooter Hire

Daily prices for scooter hire range from about €30 to €120. Reliable operators include:

Bici e Baci (Map p102; ☑ 06 482 84 43; www.bicibaci.com; Via del Viminale 5; ⊘ 8am-7pm)

Eco Move Rent (☑ 06 4470 4518; www.eco moverent.com; Via Varese 48-50; ⊗8.30am-7.30pm)

PUBLIC TRANSPORT

Rome's public transport system includes buses, trams, metro and a suburban train network.

Metro

➡ Rome has two main metro lines, A (orange) and B (blue), which cross at Termini. A branch line, 'B1', serves the northern suburbs, and a line C runs through the southeastern outskirts, but you're unlikely to need these.

➡ Trains run between 5.30am and 11.30pm (to 1.30am on Fridays and Saturdays).

➡ All stations on line B have wheelchair access except Circo Massimo, Colosseo and Cavour. On line A, Ottaviano–San Pietro and Termini are equipped with lifts.

➡ Take line A for the Trevi Fountain (Barberini), Spanish Steps (Spagna) and St Peter's (Ottaviano–San Pietro).

➡ Take line B for the Colosseum (Colosseo).

Bus & Tram

➡ Rome's buses and trams are run by **ATAC** (☑ 06 5 70 03; www.atac.roma.it).

➡ The main bus station is in front of Stazione Termini on Piazza dei Cinquecento, where there's an **information booth** (Map p102; ⊗7.30am-8pm).

➡ Other important hubs are at Largo di Torre Argentina and Piazza Venezia.

➡ Buses generally run from about 5.30am until midnight, with limited services throughout the night.

➡ Rome's night bus service comprises more than 25 lines, many of which pass Termini and/ or Piazza Venezia. Buses are marked with an 'n' before the number and bus stops have a blue owl symbol. Departures are usually every 15 to 30 minutes between about 1am and 5am, but can be much less frequent.

Overground Rail Network

Rome's overground rail network is useful only if you are heading out of town to the Castelli Romani, the beaches at Lido di Ostia or the ruins at Ostia Antica.

TAXI

➡ Official licensed taxis are white with an ID number and *Roma Capitale* on the sides.

➡ Always go with the metered fare, never an arranged price (the set fares to/from the airports are exceptions).

➡ In town (within the ring road) flag fall is €3 between 6am and 10pm on weekdays and Saturdays, €4.50 on Sundays and holidays, and €6.50 between 10pm and 6am. Then it's €1.10

per kilometre. Official rates are posted in taxis and on www.agenziamobilita.roma.it.

➡ You can hail a taxi, but it's often easier to wait at a rank or phone for one. There are taxi ranks at the airports, Stazione Termini, Piazza della Repubblica, Piazza Barberini, Piazza di Spagna, the Pantheon, the Colosseum, Largo di Torre Argentina, Piazza Belli, Piazza Pio XII and Piazza del Risorgimento.

➡ You can book a taxi by phoning the Comune di Roma's automated taxi line on ☑ 06 06 09 or by calling a taxi company direct.

➡ Note that when you call for a cab, the meter is switched on straight away and you pay for the cost of the journey from wherever the driver receives the call.

La Capitale (☑ 06 49 94)

Pronto Taxi (☑ 06 66 45)

Radio 3570 (☑ 06 35 70; www.3570.it)

Samarcanda (☑ 06 55 51; www.samarcanda.it)

Tevere (☑ 06 41 57)

LAZIO

With a capital like Rome, it's unsurprising that the rest of Lazio gets overlooked. But venture out of the city and you'll discover a region that's not only beautiful – verdant and hilly in the north, parched and rugged in the south – but also littered with historical and cultural gems.

Ostia Antica

One of Lazio's prize sights, the ruins of ancient Ostia are wonderfully complete, like a smaller version of Pompeii.

Founded in the 4th century BC, Ostia (the name means the mouth or *ostium* of the Tiber) grew to become a great port and commercial centre with a population of around 50,000.

Decline set in after the fall of the Roman Empire, and by the 9th century the city had largely been abandoned, its citizens driven off by barbarian raids and outbreaks of malaria. Over subsequent centuries, it was plundered for marble and building materials and its ruins were gradually buried in river silt, hence their survival.

◉ Sights

★Scavi Archeologici di
Ostia Antica   ARCHAEOLOGICAL SITE
(☑ 06 5635 0215; www.ostiaantica.beniculturali. it; Viale dei Romagnoli 717; adult/reduced €10/6;

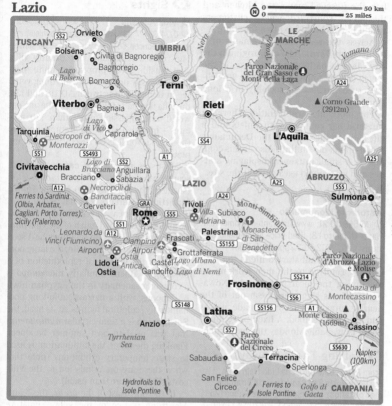

Lazio

0 ——— 50 km
0 ——— 25 miles

TUSCANY SS2 Orvieto
Bolsena Civita di Bagnoregio
Lago Bagnoregio
di Bolsena Bomarzo
Terni

UMBRIA

LE MARCHE

Parco Nazionale del Gran Sasso e Monti della Laga

A24

Viterbo Bagnaia Rieti ▲ Corno Grande (2912m)

Lago di Vico Capranola
Tarquinia *Necropoli di Monterozzi* SS4 L'Aquila

SS1 SS493 *Lago di Bracciano* SS2 A1
Civitavecchia Bracciano Anguillara LAZIO A25 ABRUZZO
A12 Sabazia *Monti Simbruini* SS5 Sulmona
Ferries to Sardinia *Necropoli di Banditaccia* A24
(Olbia, Arbatax, Cerveteri GRA Tivoli Subiaco
Cagliari, Porto Torres); Rome SS5 *Villa Adriana* *Monastero di San Benedetto*
Sicily (Palermo) SS1 Palestrina Parco Nazionale d'Abruzzo Lazio e Molise
Leonardo da A12 Ciampino Frascati SS155
Vinci (Fiumicino) Airport Grottaferrata *Abbazia di Montecassino*
Airport Ostia *Castel* *Lago Albano* SS214
Lido di *Antica* Gandolfo *Lago di Nemi* Frosinone SS6
Ostia Monte Cassino A1
SS148 Latina SS156 (1669m) Cassino
Anzio SS7 SS630 Naples (100km)
Tyrrhenian Parco Nazionale del Circeo
Sea Sabaudia Terracina CAMPANIA
San Felice Sperlonga
Circeo Golfo di
Hydrofoils to Ferries to Gaeta
Isole Pontine Isole Pontine

⊙ 8.30am-6.15pm Tue-Sun summer, earlier closing winter) An easy train ride from Rome, Ostia Antica is one of Italy's most underappreciated archaeological sites. The ruins of ancient Rome's main seaport are spread out and you'll need a few hours to do them justice. Highlights include the **Terme di Nettuno** (Baths of Neptune), a steeply stacked amphitheatre, and an ancient cafe, complete with bar and traces of the original menu frescoed on the wall.

Note that the site gets busy at weekends, but is much quieter on weekdays.

Near the entrance, **Porta Romana** gives onto the **Decumanus Maximus**, the site's central strip, which runs over 1km to **Porta Marina**, the city's original sea-facing gate.

On the Decumanus, the Terme di Nettuno is a must-see. This baths complex, one of 20 that originally stood in town, dates to the 2nd century and boasts some superb mosaics, including one of Neptune driving his sea-horse chariot. In the centre of the complex are the remains of an arcaded **Palestra** (gym).

Next to the Terme is the **Teatro**, an amphitheatre built by Agrippa and later enlarged to hold 4000 people.

The grassy area behind the amphitheatre is the **Piazzale delle Corporazioni** (Forum of the Corporations), home to the offices of Ostia's merchant guilds. The mosaics that line the perimeter – ships, dolphins, a lighthouse, an elephant – are thought to represent the businesses housed on the square: ships and dolphins indicated shipping agencies, whilst the elephant probably referred to a business involved in the ivory trade.

The **Forum**, Ostia's main square, is overlooked by what remains of the **Capitolium**, a temple built by Hadrian and dedicated to Jupiter, Juno and Minerva.

Nearby is another highlight: the **Thermopolium**, an ancient cafe. Check out the bar, the frescoed menu, the kitchen and the small courtyard where customers would have relaxed next to a fountain.

Across the road are the remains of a 2nd-century **Terme del Foro**, originally the city's largest baths complex. Here, in the *forica* (public toilet), you can see 20 well-preserved latrines set sociably in a long stone bench.

For more modern facilities, there's a cafeteria/bar complex with toilets and a gift shop to the north of the Decumanus (head up Via dei Mulini). Also at this complex is a small **museum** displaying statues and sarcophagi excavated at the site.

Eating

Ristorante Monumento   RISTORANTE **€€**
(☑06 565 00 21; www.ristorantemonumento.it; Piazza Umberto I 8; fixed-price lunch menu €14, meals €30; ☺12.30-3.30pm & 8-11pm) This historic restaurant started life in the 19th century, catering to the men working on reclaiming the local marshlands. Nowadays, it feeds sightseers fresh out of the nearby ruins, serving homemade pastas and excellent seafood. A fixed-price lunch menu is available Monday through Friday.

❶ Getting There & Away

From Rome, take the Ostia Lido train from Stazione Porta San Paolo (next to Piramide metro station), getting off at Ostia Antica (25 minutes, every 15 minutes). The trip is covered by a standard Rome public-transport ticket.

By car, take Via del Mare, which runs parallel to Via Ostiense, and follow signs for the *scavi* (excavations).

Tivoli

POP 56,460 / ELEV 235M

A summer retreat for ancient Romans and the Renaissance rich, the hilltop town of Tivoli is home to two Unesco World Heritage Sites: Villa Adriana, the sprawling estate of Emperor Hadrian, and the 16th-century Villa d'Este, a Renaissance villa famous for its landscaped gardens and lavish fountains.

Information is available from the **tourist information point** (☑0774 31 35 36; Piazzale delle Nazione Unite; ☺9.30am-5.30pm Tue-Sun) near where the bus arrives.

◉ Sights

★ **Villa Adriana**   ARCHAEOLOGICAL SITE
(☑0774 38 27 33; www.villaadriana.beniculturali.it; adult/reduced €8/4; ☺9am-1hr before sunset) The ruins of Hadrian's vast country villa, 5km outside Tivoli proper, are quite magnificent, easily on a par with anything you'll see in Rome. Built between AD 118 and 138, the villa was one of the largest in the ancient world, encompassing more than 120 hectares – of which about 40 are now open to the public. You'll need several hours to explore it.

Must-sees include the **canopo**, a landscaped canal overlooked by a *nymphaeum* (shrine to the water nymph), and the **Teatro Marittimo**, Hadrian's personal refuge.

Hadrian, a great traveller and enthusiastic architect, designed much of the villa himself, basing his ideas on buildings he'd seen around the world. The **pecile**, the large pool area near the walls, is a reproduction of a building in Athens. Similarly, the *canopo* is a copy of a sanctuary in the Egyptian town of Canopus, with a narrow 120m-long pool flanked by sculptural figures. At its head, the **Serapaeum** is a semi-circular *nymphaeum* that was used to host summer banquets. Flanking the water, the antiquarium is used to stage temporary exhibitions (note that when these are on, admission to the Villa costs slightly more than usual).

To the northeast of the *pecile*, the Teatro Marittimo is one of the villa's signature buildings, a mini-villa built on an island in an artificial pool. Originally accessible only by swing bridges, it's currently off-limits due to ongoing restoration.

To the east, **Piazza d'Oro** makes for a memorable picture, particularly in spring when its grassy centre is cloaked in wild yellow flowers.

❶ TIVOLI IN A DAY

Tivoli makes an excellent day trip from Rome but to cover its two main sites you'll have to start early. The best way to see both is to visit Villa d'Este first, then have lunch up in the centre, before heading down to Villa Adriana. To get to the villa from the centre, take local CAT bus 4 or 4X (€1, 10 minutes, half-hourly) from Largo Garibaldi. After you've visited Villa Adriana, pick up the Cotral bus back to Rome.

There are also several bath complexes, temples and barracks. Parking (€3) is available at the site.

Villa d'Este
HISTORIC BUILDING, GARDENS

(📞0774 31 20 70; www.villadestetivoli.info; Piazza Trento; adult/reduced €8/4; ☺8.30am-1hr before sunset Tue-Sun) In Tivoli's hilltop centre, the steeply terraced grounds of Villa d'Este are a superlative example of a Renaissance garden, complete with monumental fountains, elegant tree-lined avenues and landscaped grottoes. The villa, originally a Benedictine convent, was converted into a luxury retreat by Lucrezia Borgia's son, Cardinal Ippolito d'Este, in the late 16th century. It later provided inspiration for composer Franz Liszt who stayed here between 1865 and 1886 and immortalised it in his 1877 piano composition *The Fountains of the Villa d'Este*.

The manicured gardens feature water-spouting gargoyles and shady lanes flanked by lofty cypresses and extravagant fountains, all powered by gravity alone. Look out for the Bernini-designed **Fountain of the Organ**, which uses water pressure to play music through a concealed organ, and the 130m-long **Avenue of the Hundred Fountains**.

Eating

Trattoria del Falcone
TRATTORIA €€

(📞0774 31 23 58; Via del Trevio 34; meals €30; ☺noon-4pm & 6.30-11pm) Near Villa d'Este, this cheerful, family-run trattoria has been serving pizzas, classic pastas, meat and seafood since 1918. Boasting exposed stone decor and a small internal courtyard, it's popular with both tourists and locals.

Sibilla
RISTORANTE €€€

(📞0774 33 52 81; Via della Sibilla 50; meals €50; ☺12.30-3pm & 7.30-10.30pm) With tables set out by two ancient Roman temples and water cascading down the green river gorge below, the Sibilla's outdoor terrace sets a romantic stage for seasonally driven food and superlative wine.

❶ Getting There & Around

Tivoli, 30km east of Rome, is accessible by Cotral bus (€2.20, 50 minutes, every 15 to 20 minutes) from Ponte Mammolo metro station.

By car you can either take Via Tiburtina or the quicker Rome–L'Aquila autostrada (A24).

Trains run from Rome's Stazione Tiburtina to Tivoli (€2.60, one hour, at least hourly).

LAZIO'S NORTHERN LAKES

North of Rome, Lazio's verdant landscape is pitted with volcanic lakes. The closest to the capital is **Lago di Bracciano**, a beautiful blue expanse surrounded by picturesque medieval towns. There's a popular lakeside beach at **Anguillara Sabazia** and you can visit a 15th-century castle, **Castello Odescalchi** (📞06 9980 4348; www.odescalchi.it; Via Gregorio VII 368; adult/reduced €8.50/6; ☺10am-noon & 2-5pm Tue-Fri, 10am-6pm Sat & Sun summer, shorter hours winter), at **Bracciano**.

Both towns are accessible by half-hourly trains from Roma Ostiense (Anguillara €2.60, 55 minutes; Bracciano €3, one hour).

In the north of the region, **Lago di Bolsena** is one of Europe's largest volcanic lakes. Its main town is **Bolsena**, a charming place with a hilltop medieval centre and a famous 13th-century miracle story.

Hourly Cotral buses serve Bolsena from Viterbo (€2.20, 50 minutes).

Cerveteri

POP 37,230 / ELEV 81M

A quiet provincial town 35km northwest of Rome, Cerveteri is home to one of Italy's great Etruscan treasures – the Necropoli di Banditaccia. This ancient burial complex, now a Unesco World Heritage Site, is all that remains of the formidable Etruscan city that once stood here.

Founded in the 9th century BC, the city that the Etruscans knew as Kysry and Latin-speakers called Caere was a powerful member of the Etruscan League and, for a period between the 7th and 5th centuries, one of the Mediterranean's most important commercial centres. It eventually came into conflict with Rome and, in 358 BC, was annexed into the Roman Republic.

◎ Sights

★ Necropoli di Banditaccia
ARCHAEOLOGICAL SITE

(📞06 994 06 51; www.tarquinia-cerveteri.it; Via della Necropoli 43/45 ; adult/reduced €8/5, incl museum €10/6; ☺8.30am-1hr before sunset) This haunting 12-hectare necropolis is a veritable city of the dead, with streets, squares and terraces of *tumuli* (circular tombs cut into the earth and capped by turf). Some tombs, including the 6th-century-BC **Tomba dei Rilievi**, retain traces of painted reliefs, many of which illustrate endearingly domestic household items, as well as figures from the underworld.

Another interesting tomb is the 7th-century BC **Tumulo Mengarelli**, whose plain interior shows how the tombs were originally structured.

To bone up on the site's history, you can watch short films in the **Sala Mengarelli** at half past every hour. You can also take a tour that features 3D installations reconstructing the tombs' frescoes and funerary items.

Museo Nazionale Cerite   MUSEUM
(☑ 06 994 13 54; www.tarquinia-cerveteri.it; Piazza Santa Maria 4; adult/reduced €8/5, incl necropolis €10/6; ⊙ 8.30am-7.30pm Tue-Sun) Housed in a medieval fortress on what was once ancient Caere's acropolis, this splendid museum charts the history of the Etruscan city, housing archaeological treasures unearthed at the necropolis.

On the ground floor, a multimedia display illustrates the stories behind some of the collection's prize exhibits.

✗ Eating

Antica Locanda le Ginestre   REGIONAL ITALIAN €€
(☑ 06 994 33 65; www.anticalocandaleginestre.com; Piazza Santa Maria 5; fixed-price menus €20-30, meals €40-45; ⊙ 12.30-2.30pm & 7.30-10.30pm Tue-Sun) On a delightful *centro storico* piazza, this family-run restaurant is a top choice for quality regional food. Dishes such as risotto with asparagus tips and saffron are prepared with seasonal local produce and served in an elegant dining room and flower-filled courtyard. Book ahead.

ⓘ Information

Tourist Information Point (☑ 06 9955 2637; Piazza Aldo Moro; ⊙ 9.30am-12.30pm Mon-Sat, 10am-1pm Sun winter, 9.30am-12.30pm & 4-6pm spring, 9.30am-12.30pm & 5.30-7.30pm summer) A kiosk by the entrance to the historic centre.

ⓘ Getting There & Around

Cerveteri is easily accessible from Rome by Cotral bus (€2.80, 55 minutes, half-hourly) from the Cornelia metro station (line A).

To get to the necropolis from the town centre, take bus G from the main square (€1.10, five minutes, approximately hourly).

By car, take either Via Aurelia (SS1) or the Civitavecchia autostrada (A12) and exit at Cerveteri–Ladispoli.

Tarquinia

POP 16,480 / ELEV 169M

Some 90km northwest of Rome, Tarquinia is the pick of Lazio's Etruscan towns. The highlight is the magnificent Unesco-listed necropolis and its extraordinary frescoed tombs, but there's also a fantastic Etruscan museum (the best outside of Rome) and an atmospheric medieval centre.

Legend holds that Tarquinia was founded towards the end of the Bronze Age in the 12th century BC. It was later home to the Tarquin kings of Rome, reaching its peak in the 4th century BC, before a century of struggle ended with surrender to Rome in 204 BC.

◉ Sights

★ **Necropoli di Monterozzi**   ARCHAEOLOGICAL SITE
(☑ 0766 84 00 00; www.tarquinia-cerveteri.it; Via Ripagretta; adult/reduced €6/3, incl museum €8/4; ⊙ 8.30am-7.30pm Tue-Sun summer, to 1hr before sunset winter) This remarkable 7th-century BC necropolis is one of Italy's most important Etruscan sites. At first sight, it doesn't look like much – a green field littered with corrugated huts – but once you start ducking into the tombs and seeing the vivid frescoes, you'll realise what all the fuss is about.

Some 6000 tombs have been excavated in this area since digs started in 1489, of which 140 are painted and 16 are currently open to the public.

For the best frescoes search out the **Tomba della Leonessa**, the **Tomba della Caccia e della Pesca**, which boasts some wonderful hunting and fishing scenes, the **Tomba dei Leopardi**, and the **Tomba della Fustigazione**, which is named after a scratchy scene of an S&M threesome.

To get to the necropolis, which is about 1.5km from the centre, take the free shuttle bus B from near the tourist office. You can also take bus D (€1) or walk – head up Corso Vittorio Emanuele, turn right into Via Porta Tarquinia and follow straight into Via Ripagretta; the walk takes about 20 minutes.

Museo Archeologico Nazionale
Tarquiniense MUSEUM
(☑0766 85 00 80; www.tarquinia-cerveteri.it; Via Cavour 1; adult/reduced €6/3, incl necropoli €8/4; ⊙8.30am-7.30pm Tue-Sun) This charming museum, beautifully housed in the 15th-century Palazzo Vitelleschi, is a treasure trove of locally found Etruscan artefacts. Highlights include a series of stone sarcophagi, a terracotta frieze of winged horses (the *Cavalli alati*), a room full of painted friezes, and several vibrantly frescoed tombs.

🍽 Sleeping & Eating

Camere Del Re HOTEL €
(☑0766 85 58 31; www.cameredelre.com; Via San Pancrazio 41; s €55-70, d €69-120, q €99-129; ✳🢰) Just off the historic centre's main strip, this quiet hotel has 10 spacious rooms decorated in simple, monastic style with vaulted ceilings, wrought-iron bedsteads and the occasional fresco.

Il Cavatappi ITALIAN €€
(☑0766 84 23 03; www.cavatappirestaurant.it; Via dei Granari 2; meals €30; ⊙7.30-9.45pm Wed-Mon, 12.30-2pm Fri-Sun, longer hours summer) Tarquinia has several decent eateries, including this family-run restaurant in the *centro storico*. It specialises in traditional regional dishes, so expect cheese and local salamis, flavoursome grilled meats and *acquacotta*, a soup thickened with bread and vegetables.

ℹ Information

Tourist Office (☑0766 84 92 82; www.tarquiniaturismo.it; Barriera San Giusto; ⊙9am-12.30pm & 4-7pm) In the town's medieval gate (Barriera San Giusto).

ℹ Getting There & Away

The best way to reach Tarquinia from Rome is to take the Pisa train from Termini (€6.90, one hour and 20 minutes, hourly). From Tarquinia station, catch bus BC (€1) to the historic centre.

By car, take the autostrada for Civitavecchia and then Via Aurelia (SS1).

Viterbo

POP 66,560 / ELEV 327M

The largest town in northern Lazio, Viterbo is a much overlooked gem with a handsome medieval centre and a relaxed, provincial atmosphere.

Founded by the Etruscans and later taken over by the Romans, it developed into an important medieval centre, and in the 13th century became the seat of the popes. It was bombed heavily in WWII, but much of its historic core survived and is today in remarkably good nick. This, together with its good bus connections, makes it a pleasant base for exploring Lazio's rugged north.

◉ Sights

⭐**Palazzo dei Priori** HISTORIC BUILDING
(entrance Via Ascenzi 1 Mon-Fri, Piazza del Plebiscito 14 Sat & Sun; ⊙9am-1pm & 3-6.30pm Mon-Fri, 9am-noon & 4-7pm Sat, 9am-noon Sun) **FREE** Viterbo's 15th-century city hall dominates Piazza del Plebiscito, the elegant Renaissance square that has long been the city's political and social hub. It's not all open to the public but you can visit a series of impressively decorated halls whose 16th-century frescoes colourfully depict Viterbo's ancient origins.

Outside, the elegant courtyard and fountain were added two centuries after the *palazzo* was completed in the late 1400s.

Cattedrale di San Lorenzo CATHEDRAL
(Piazza San Lorenzo; ⊙10am-1pm & 3-7pm Tue-Sun, to 6pm winter) With its landmark black-and-white bell tower, Viterbo's 12th-century *duomo* looms over Piazza San Lorenzo, the religious nerve centre of the medieval city. Originally built to a simple Romanesque design, it owes its current Gothic look to a 14th-century makeover and a partial post-WWII reconstruction.

Many of its treasures are today housed in the adjacent **Museo Colle del Duomo** (☑320 7911328; www.museocolledelduomo.com; Piazza San Lorenzo 8; admission €3, incl guided visit to cathedral & Palazzo dei Papi €9; ⊙10am-1pm & 3-7pm Tue-Sun, to 6pm winter), including a reliquary said to contain St John the Baptist's chin.

⭐**Palazzo dei Papi** HISTORIC BUILDING
(☑320 7911328; www.museocolledelduomo.com; Piazza San Lorenzo; incl cathedral & Museo Colle del

Viterbo

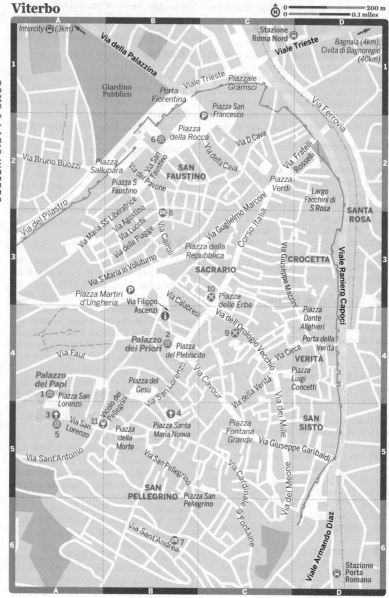

Duomo €9; ⊙ guided tours only) **FREE** Flanking Piazza San Lorenzo, this handsome Gothic *palazzo* was built for the popes who lived in Viterbo from 1257 to 1281. To go inside you'll have to sign up for a tour at the Museo Colle del Duomo, but you can sometimes pop up the stairs to the **loggia** (colonnade) and peer into the **Sala del Conclave**, scene of the first and longest ever papal conclave.

The story goes that in 1271, three years after the death of Clemente IV, the college of cardinals still hadn't elected a successor.

Viterbo

To encourage them in their deliberations, the Viterbesi locked the dithering priests in the turreted *sala* and fed them nothing but bread and water until they eventually elected Pope Gregory X.

Chiesa di Santa Maria Nuova   CHURCH
(Piazza Santa Maria Nuova; ◎ church 7am-7pm, cloisters 10am-noon & 4-7pm) This 11th-century Romanesque church, the oldest in Viterbo, was restored to its original form after sustaining bomb damage in WWII. Traces of 13th-century frescoes line the solemn, grey interior, whilst outside you can see a stone pulpit where St Thomas Aquinas preached in 1266. Also of note is the church's cloister, the so-called **Chiostro Longobardo**.

Museo Nazionale Etrusco   MUSEUM
(☑ 0761 32 59 29; Piazza della Rocca; adult/reduced €6/3; ◎ 8.30am-7.30pm Tue-Sun) Housed in the Albornaz fortress, this modest museum is the place for a shot of ancient culture. Reconstructions and locally found artefacts illustrate the Etruscan lifestyle, while a series of life-sized statues hark back to the city's Roman past.

🛏 Sleeping

★ **Medieval House**   B&B €
(☑ 393 4501586; www.bbmedievalhouse.com; Via Sant'Andrea 78; s €40-60, d €60-110; ❋ 🛜) Run by the gregarious Matteo, this welcoming B&B near the medieval walls makes for a wonderful base – it's within easy walking

distance of all the main sights but is far enough out to offer a quiet night's sleep. The look is exposed brick and homey furniture, and breakfast is a feast of *cornetti* (croissants) and cured meats.

Tuscia Hotel   HOTEL €
(☑ 0761 34 44 00; www.tusciahotel.com; Via Cairoli 41; s €40-64, d €62-82; ❋ 🛜) The best of the city's central hotels, this business-like three-star has large and light rooms in a convenient and easy-to-find location. There's also a sunny roof terrace and parking (€8). Note that not all rooms have air-con.

🍴 Eating & Drinking

★ **Al Vecchio Orologio**   OSTERIA, PIZZA €€
(☑ 335 337754; www.alvecchioorologio.it; Via dell'Orologio Vecchio 25; meals €30, pizzas €6.50-8; ◎ 7.30-10.30pm daily & 12.30-2.30pm Sat & Sun) This much-lauded eatery hits the bullseye with its charming location – in a vaulted *centro storico palazzo* – and excellent local cuisine. There's a full range of pizzas but to get the best out of the kitchen, opt for the main menu and dishes like ricotta and asparagus *tortelloni* with saffron, speck and radicchio, and lamb glazed with balsamic vinegar.

Ristorante Tre Re   TRATTORIA €€
(☑ 0761 30 46 19; Via Gattesco 3; meals €30; ◎ 12.30-2.30pm & 7.30-10pm Fri-Wed) Viterbo's oldest trattoria is a cosy spot for steaming plates of seasonally driven dishes and earthy specialities such as *pollo alla viterbese*, roast chicken with spiced potato and olives.

Magnamagna   WINE BAR
(Vicolo dei Pellegrini 2; ◎ 12.30-3pm & 6.30pm-1am, closed Mon & Tue lunch) Join the 30-something crowd for a glass of wine in the atmospheric setting of Piazza della Morte. The bar, which also serves craft beers and local foodie specialities, is standing room only, but there's seating outside in the piazza and in a vaulted hall known as the Winter Garden, where you can kick back to jazz gigs and DJ sets.

ℹ Information

Tourist Office (☑ 0761 32 59 92; Via Filippo Ascenzi 4; ◎ 9am-1pm & 2.30-3pm Mon, 10am-1pm & 3-7pm Tue-Sun)

AROUND VITERBO

Largely overlooked by travellers, the lush, emerald-green countryside around Viterbo hides some wonderful treasures. Chief among them is **Palazzo Farnese** (📞 0761 64 60 52; Piazza Farnese 1, Caprarola; adult/reduced €5/2.50; ⊘8.30am-6.45pm Tue-Sun, garden entry 10am, 11am, noon, 3pm & 4pm Tue-Fri winter, plus 5pm summer), 20km southeast of Viterbo in Caprarola. A 16th-century Renaissance *palazzo*, it features a distinct pentagonal design and, inside, an internal circular courtyard and extraordinary columned staircase. Visits take in the richly frescoed rooms and, on weekdays, the beautiful hillside gardens.

For more horticultural splendours, head to Bagnaia and **Villa Lante** (📞 0761 28 80 08; Via Jacopo Barozzi 71 ; adult/reduced €5/2.50; ⊘8.30am-1hr before sunset Tue-Sun), whose 16th-century mannerist gardens feature monumental fountains and an ingenious water cascade.

Some 30km north of Viterbo, Bagnoregio is home to one of Lazio's most dramatic apparitions, the **Civita di Bagnoregio**, aka *il paese che muore* (the dying town). This medieval village, accessible by footbridge only, sits atop a huge stack of slowly crumbling rock in a dramatic deep-cut valley.

The best way to get around the area is by car, although you can also get to all the places listed here by **Cotral** (📞 800 174471; www.cotralspa.it) bus from Viterbo.

❶ Getting There & Away

From Rome, Cotral buses (€4.50, 1½ hours, half-hourly) depart from Saxa Rubra station – get to Saxa Rubra by Ferrovia Roma-Nord train from Piazzale Flaminio.

In Viterbo, make sure you get off at Porta Romana, not the intercity bus station at Riello, which is a few kilometres northwest of town.

By car, Viterbo is about a 1½-hour drive up Via Cassia (SS2). Once in town, the best bet for parking is either Piazza Martiri d'Ungheria or Piazza della Rocca.

Trains from Rome's Ostiense station depart hourly from Monday to Saturday and every two hours on Sunday to Viterbo Porta Romana (€5 one way, nearly two hours).

Castelli Romani

A pretty pocket of verdant hills and volcanic lakes 20km southeast of Rome, the Colli Albani (Alban Hills) and their 13 towns are collectively known as the Castelli Romani. Since early Roman days they've provided a green refuge from the city and still today Romans flock to the area on hot summer weekends.

❶ Getting There & Around

The best way to get to Frascati is by train from Stazione Termini (€2.10, 30 minutes, hourly Monday to Saturday, every two hours Sunday). Likewise there are regular trains to Castel Gandolfo from Termini (€2.10, 45 minutes).

To travel between the Castelli towns you'll need to take the bus. From Frascati's Piazza Marconi, **Cotral** (www.cotralspa.it) buses connect with Grottaferrata (€1.10, 10 minutes, twice hourly) and Castel Gandolfo (€1.10, 30 minutes).

If travelling by car, exit Rome on Via Tuscolana (SS215) for Frascati and Grottaferrata or Via Appia (SS7) for Castel Gandolfo and Lago Albano.

Frascati

An easy train ride from Rome, the famous wine town of Frascati makes for a refreshing day trip with its compact historic centre and delicious food and drink.

◉ Sights

Scuderie Aldobrandini MUSEUM
(📞 06 941 71 95; Piazza Marconi 6; adult/reduced €5.50/3; ⊘10am-6pm Tue-Fri, 10am-7pm Sat & Sun) The former stables of Villa Aldobrandini, restored by architect Massimiliano Fuksas, house Frascati's single museum of note, the **Museo Tuscolano**. Dedicated to local history, its collection includes ancient Roman artefacts and several interesting models of local villas.

Villa Aldobrandini Gardens GARDENS
(Via Cardinal Massai 18; ⊘9am-5.30pm Mon-Fri) **FREE** Looming over Frascati's main square, Villa Aldobrandini is a haughty 16th-century villa designed by Giacomo della Porta and built by Carlo Maderno. It's closed to the public, but you can visit its impressive baroque gardens during the week.

SUBIACO

Set amidst wooded hills in Lazio's remote eastern reaches, Subiaco is one of the region's hidden pearls. Nero had a villa here but it was St Benedict who put the town on the map when he spent three years meditating in a local cave. This grotto is now incorporated into the **Monastero di San Benedetto** (www.benedettini-subiaco.org; ⊙9.30am-12.15pm & 3.30-6.15pm), a spectacularly sited hilltop monastery that boasts a series of rich 13th- to 15th-century frescoes.

At the foot of the same hill, the **Monastero di Santa Scolastica** (☑0774 8 55 69; www.benedettini-subiaco.org; ⊙9.30am-12.15pm & 3.30-6.15pm) offers spartan accommodation (per person B&B €37) and fixed-price meals (€23).

To get to Subiaco from Rome, there's a Cotral bus (€3.90, 1¼ hours, twice hourly, less frequently at weekends) from Ponte Mammolo metro station. This stops some way from the Monastero di Santa Scolastica, to which it's a 3km uphill walk.

🍴 Eating & Drinking

The real reason many come to Frascati is to eat and drink. There are plenty of good restaurants but for a more down-to-earth bite, pick up a *panino con porchetta* (sandwich filled with herb-roasted pork) from a stand on Piazza del Mercato, or head to a traditional *cantina* (cellar-cum-trattoria).

Cantina Simonetti OSTERIA € (www.cantinasimonetti.com; Piazza San Rocco 4; meals €20; ⊙7.45-midnight Wed-Sun & 1-4pm Sat & Sun, longer hours summer) For an authentic dining experience, search out this traditional *cantina* and sit down to a casual meal of *porchetta*, cold cuts and cheese, accompanied by local white wine. In keeping with the food, the decor is rough-and-ready rustic with plain wooden tables and paper tablecloths.

Cacciani RISTORANTE €€€ (☑06 942 03 78; www.cacciani.it; Via Armando Diaz 13; fixed-price lunch menu €25, meals from €45; ⊙12.15-3pm & 7-11pm Tue-Sat, 12.15-3pm Sun) Frascati's most renowned restaurant offers fine food and twinkling terrace views over Rome. The menu lists various modern creative dishes, but it's the classics like *cannelloni con ragù* (cannelloni with meat sauce) that really stand out. There's also a weighty wine list and a couple of fixed-price menus, including a €25 weekday lunch option.

ⓘ Information

Frascati Point Tourist Office (☑06 9401 5378; Piazza Marconi 5; ⊙8am-8pm Mon-Fri, 10am-8pm Sat & Sun) As well as town information, can provide details about tours of local vineyards.

Grottaferrata

The well-heeled town of Grottaferrata merits a quick stop for its fortified abbey, the last remaining example of the Byzantine-Greek abbeys that once dotted medieval Italy.

◉ Sights

Monastero Esarchico di Santa Maria di Grottaferrata CHURCH (www.abbaziagreca.it; Viale San Nilo; ⊙9am-noon & 4-7pm Mon-Sat) Better known as the Abbazia Greca di San Nilo, this fortified monastery was founded in 1004. The walls and battlements were added 400 years later to provide a protective perimeter to the Chiesa di Santa Maria di Grottaferrata. This bejewelled, icon-laden church features a series of 17th-century frescoes by Domenichino and a revered Byzantine image of Santa Maria.

Castel Gandolfo

One of the Castelli's prettiest towns, Castel Gandolfo is a refined hilltop *borgo* (medieval town). There are no must-see sights but **Piazza della Libertà** is a lovely spot for an ice cream, and the views over Lago Albano are gorgeous. Facing onto the piazza is the pope's 17th-century summer residence, the **Palazzo Pontificio** (closed to the public), where the current pope still holds his regular weekly audiences in July and August.

◉ Sights

Barberini Gardens GARDENS (http://biglietteriamusei.vatican.va/musei/tickets/do; guided tours €26; ⊙by reservation Mon-Sat) Castel Gandolfo's Palazzo Pontificio might be off-limits, but you can explore its gardens on a guided visit. The 90-minute tours, which

MONTECASSINO'S MOUNTAIN-TOP MONASTERY

Abbazia di Montecassino (☎ 0776 31 15 29; www.abbaziamontecassino.org; ☺ 8.30am-7pm summer, 9am-12.30pm & 3.30-5pm winter) Dramatically perched on a mountain top near the regional border with Campania, the Abbazia di Montecassino was one of the most important Christian centres in the medieval world. St Benedict founded it in 529 AD, supposedly after three ravens led him to the spot, and lived there until his death in 547.

Throughout its history it has been destroyed and rebuilt several times, most recently after WWII. During the war it was at the centre of heavy fighting as the Germans sought to stop the Allied push north. After almost six months of bloody deadlock, the Allies bombed it to rubble in May 1944 in a desperate bid to break through German defences.

To reach the abbey from Rome, take one of the half-hourly trains from Stazione Termini to Cassino (€8.20, two hours) and then one of the infrequent local buses up from the station.

must be booked online, take in Roman ruins and sweeping views as they navigate the garden's immaculately manicured lanes.

 Eating

Antico Ristorante Pagnanelli RISTORANTE €€€
(☑ 06 936 00 04; www.pagnanelli.it; Via Antonio Gramsci 4, Castel Gandolfo; meals €60-70; ☺ noon-3.30pm & 6.30-11.45pm) Housed in a wisteria-clad villa, this celebrated restaurant is a great place for a romantic meal. It's no casual trattoria, erring on the formal and touristy side, but the seasonally driven food is excellent, there's a colossal wine list and the views over Lago Albano are unforgettable.

Lago Albano

The largest and most developed of the Castelli's two volcanic lakes – the other is Lago di Nemi – Lago Albano is set in a steeply banked wooded crater. It's a popular hangout, particularly in spring and summer, when Romans flock here to top up their tans and eat in the many lakeside eateries.

Palestrina

Archaeology buffs should make a beeline for Palestrina and its charming hilltop museum. In ancient times, Palestrina, then known as Praeneste, was home to a spectacular temple, the Santuario della Fortuna Primigenia, which covered much of what is now the *centro storico*. This has long since been built over but you can see a model in the **Museo Archeologico Nazionale di Palestrina** (☑ 06 953 81 00; Piazza della Cortina; admission incl sanctuary €5; ☺ 9am-8pm, sanctuary 9am-

1hr before sunset) alongside an interesting collection of ancient sculpture and Roman mosaics. The crowning glory, though, is the breathtaking *Mosaico nilotico*, a brilliant 2nd-century BC mosaic depicting the flooding of the Nile and everyday life in ancient Egypt.

For a bite to eat, try the highly regarded **Zi' Rico** (☑ 06 8308 2532; www.zirico.it; Via Enrico Toti 2; meals €35-40; ☺ 12.30-3pm & 8-11.30pm, closed Sun dinner & Mon) near the cathedral.

Cotral buses run to Palestrina from Rome's Ponte Mammolo metro station (€2.20, one hour, hourly). By car, follow Via Prenestina (SS155) for approximately 40km.

South Coast

Lazio's southern coast boasts the region's best beaches and tracts of beautiful, unspoilt countryside around Monte Circeo, a rocky promontory that rises to a height of 541m as it juts into the sea.

Anzio

Anzio, 40km south of Rome, was at the centre of ferocious WWII fighting in the wake of a major Allied landing on 22 January 1944. Nowadays, it's a likeable port popular with day-trippers who come to eat at its seafood restaurants and hang out on its sandy beaches.

For lunch, head down to the port where you'll find a string of popular fish restaurants, including **La Nostra Paranza** (☑ 338 2303844; Via Porto Innocenziano 23; set menu €20; ☺ noon-3pm & 7-11pm, closed Wed & Sun dinner), a bustling trattoria whose set menu is exceptional value for money.

Trains serve Anzio from Termini (€3.60, 70 minutes) every hour (every two hours on Sundays).

Sabaudia

The modern, rather uninspiring town of Sabaudia makes a convenient base for the beach and the Parco Nazionale del Circeo.

For information, accommodation lists and bike hire (€8 per day), ask at the tourist office (⊠0773 51 50 46; www.prolocosabaudia.it; Piazza del Comune 18; ⊗9.15am-12.30pm & 4-7.45pm Mon-Sat, 9.05am-12.45pm Sun).

◉ Sights

Parco Nazionale del Circeo PARK
(www.parcocirceo.it) Encompassing around 85 sq km of sand dunes, rocky coastline, forest and wetlands, the Circeo National Park offers a range of activities including hiking, fishing, birdwatching and cycling. Further information is available at the visitor centre (⊠0773 51 13 85; Via Carlo Alberto 188; ⊗information office 9am-1pm & 2.30-5pm) in Sabaudia.

⌂ Sleeping & Eating

Agriturismo I Quattro Laghi AGRITURISMO €€
(⊠0773 59 31 35; www.quattrolaghi.it; Strada Sacramento 32, Sabaudia; half-board per person €52-77; ☀☎⚐) This friendly year-round *agriturismo* (farm stay accommodation) sits in green farmland about 800m from the beach. It's a rustic set-up with homey guest rooms and a large restaurant serving filling farmhouse fare. Meals, open to all, cost €25 to €30. No credit cards.

❶ Getting There & Away

From Rome, hourly Cotral buses cover the 90km to Sabaudia (€5, two hours) from Laurentina metro station. Alternatively, get a train from Termini to Priverno-Fossanova (€5, one hour, hourly) and then a connecting Cotral bus.

Sperlonga

The pick of Lazio's southern coastal towns, Sperlonga is a fashionable summer spot with a steeply stacked medieval centre and two sandy beaches either side of a rocky promontory.

◉ Sights

Museo Archeologico di Sperlonga e Villa di Tiberio MUSEUM
(⊠0771 54 80 28; Via Flacca, km1.6; adult/reduced €5/2.50; ⊗8.30am-7.30pm) Other than the beach – and the great views from the historic centre – Sperlonga's main attraction is this archaeological museum. Here you can admire ancient sculptures and poke around the ruins of Villa Tiberio, emperor Tiberius' seafront villa set around a gaping sea cave, the Grotta di Tiberio.

⌂ Sleeping & Eating

Hotel Mayor HOTEL €€
(⊠0771 54 92 45; www.hotelmayor.it; Via 1 Romita 4; s €60-110, d €75-140; ⊗Mar-Oct; ☀☎) Near the northern entrance to the historic centre, Hotel Mayor offers simple, sunny rooms, some with balconies, and its own patch of private beach. Note that there's a three-night minimum stay in summer.

Gli Archi SEAFOOD €€
(⊠0771 54 83 00; www.gliarchi.com; Via Ottaviano 17; meals €40; ⊗12.30-3pm & 7-11pm Thu-Tue) One of several eateries in the medieval centre, Gli Archi provides a lovely setting for fresh-from-the-boat seafood. Signature dishes include mussel soup, and pasta with squid, asparagus and tomatoes.

❶ Getting There & Away

To get to Sperlonga, take the train from Termini to Fondi-Sperlonga (€6.90, 1¼ hours, hourly) and then a connecting Piazzoli bus to Sperlonga (€1.50, 10 minutes, at least six daily).

By car, Sperlonga is 120km from Rome. Take Via Pontina (SS148) and follow signs to Terracina and then Sperlonga.

Isole Pontine

Off the southern Lazio coast, this group of volcanic islands serves as an Italian Hamptons. Between mid-June and the end of August, Ponza and Ventotene – the only two inhabited islands – buzz with holidaymakers and weekenders who descend in droves to eat shellfish at terrace restaurants, swim in emerald coves and cruise around the craggy coast. Outside of summer, the islands are very quiet, and, although expensive, a joy to explore. Action centres on colourful Ponza town where you'll find the usual array of souvenir shops, cafes and restaurants, as well as a small sandy beach.

◉ Sights & Activities

Cooperativa Barcaioli   BOATING
(☑ 0771 80 99 29; www.barcaioliponza.it; Sotto il Tunnel di S Antonio; ⊙ 9am-midnight) Cooperativa Barcaioli is one of several outfits in Ponza offering trips around the island (€27.50 including lunch) and boats to the beach at Frontone (€5 return).

🛏 Sleeping & Eating

Villa Ersilia   B&B, RENTAL HOUSE €€
(☑ 328 7749461; www.villaersilia.it; Via Scotti 2; d €80-200; 🛜) Housed in a homey villa a short but steep walk up from the harbour (follow the signs), this friendly place wins you over with its simple sunny rooms, flowery terrace and soothing sea views.

Tutti Noi   SEAFOOD €€
(☑ 0771 82 00 44; Via Dante 5; meals €30; ⊙ 11am-3pm & 6pm-midnight daily Jun-Aug, closed Sun dinner Sep-May) A modest trattoria opposite Ponza's beach. The menu depends on the morning catch, but you can depend on excellent seafood pasta and simply cooked fish as a main course.

❶ Information

Tourist Office (☑ 0771 8 00 31; www.proloco diponza.it; Via Molo Musco; ⊙ 9.30am-12.30pm daily, shorter hours winter) Has island maps and accommodation lists.

❶ Getting There & Around

Ponza and Ventotene are accessible from Anzio, Terracina, Naples and Formia. Some services run year-round, including daily ferries from Terracina, but most operate from June to September.

Autolinee Ponza (☑ 0771 83 16 45) operates buses on Ponza and runs regular panoramic tours of the island (€3).

The major ferry companies:

Laziomar (☑ 0771 70 07 10; www.laziomar.it) Ferries from Terracina to Ponza (€10 one way, 2½ hours). Also ferries (€15 one way, 2½ hours) and fast ferries (€22.50 one way, 1½ hours) from Formia.

Navigazione Libera del Golfo (NLG; ☑ 081 552 07 63; www.navlib.it) Hydrofoils from Terracina to Ponza (€39.50 to €45.50 return, 50 minutes) and Ventotene (€50, 1¾ hours).

Vetor (☑ 06 984 50 83; www.vetor.it) Hydrofoils from Anzio to Ponza (€39 one way, 70 minutes).

Turin, Piedmont & the Italian Riviera

Why Go?

The beauty of northwestern Italy is its diversity. Piedmont's capital, Turin, is an elegant, easy city of baroque palaces, cutting-edge galleries and fittingly fabulous dining. The region might be an economic powerhouse, but has managed to retain deep links to the soil. Such is the lure of its famous red wines and Slow Food credentials that it's often touted as the 'new Tuscany'.

Just a couple of hours south, Liguria's slim, often vertical, sliver is home to Italy's Riviera, the fabled port city of Genoa and the beguiling villages of the Cinque Terre. Here dramatic coastal topography, beautifully preserved architecture and one of Italy's most memorable cuisines make for one impossibly romantic destination.

Head north and you'll soon hit the Alps and the semi-autonomous region of Aosta, where you can ski or hike beneath Europe's highest mountains while discovering its delightful French-tinged traditions along the way.

Best Places to Eat

➡ La Piola (p220)

➡ Banco vini e alimenti (p208)

➡ 4 Ciance (p215)

➡ Il Marin (p173)

➡ Scannabue (p208)

Best Places to Stay

➡ Villa Rosmarino (p177)

➡ Via Stampatori (p206)

➡ DuParc Contemporary Suites (p207)

➡ Brandini (p222)

➡ Uve Rooms & Wine Bar (p222)

When to Go
Turin

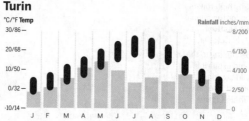

| Jan–Mar Most reliable snow cover for skiing in the Alps. | Apr Fewer crowds and fine days on the Ligurian coast | Sep & Oct Autumn food festivals in Turin and the Langhe. |

Piedmont, Liguria & the Italian Riviera Highlights

1 Exploring the largest collection of Egyptian history outside Cairo at the refurbished **Museo Egizio** (p201) in Turin.

2 Discovering the art and architecture of a once-great maritime empire in Genoa's amazing **Palazzi dei Rolli** (p167).

3 Discussing terroir, tannins and tenacity with the winemakers of the **Barolo region** (p220).

4 Hiking the blue trail, the red trail, the sanctuary trails – in fact, any trail on the stunning cliffsides of **Cinque Terre** (p181).

5 Jumping the border aboard the state-of-the-art Monte Bianco **cable car** (p233) in Valle d'Aosta.

6 Braving the crowds of truffle-snorting high rollers in Alba for the annual **Truffle Festival** (p217) in October.

7 Swimming in the Med and exploring the wild Ligurian hinterland from low-key **Finale Ligure** (p192).

Liguria

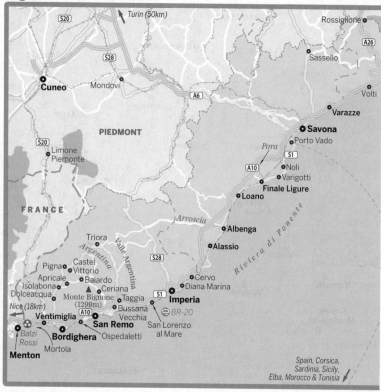

LIGURIA

POP 1.57 MILLION

Liguria, where the Alps and the Apennines cascade into the Mediterranean, is defined by its sinuous, giddy landscapes, with a topography so demanding it has shaped almost every facet of daily life. Farming is carried out on ingeniously terraced cliff faces, and impossibly sited fishing villages have long plundered the sea.

Anchored beside the region's best natural harbour is noble Genoa. Known as La Superba (the Superb One) to biased locals, it's a city that ruled over one of the finest maritime empires in medieval Europe. Fanning out on either side is the Riviera (western 'Ponente', eastern 'Levante'), including the Portofino peninsula, along with legendary Cinque Terre. Surprisingly, given its lack of obvious agricultural land, Liguria is renowned for its food: fat anchovies, fragrant lemons, olive oil-rich focaccia bread and a viridian sauce called pesto.

Genoa

POP 583,500

While Henry James described Genoa as 'the most winding and incoherent of cities', his French counterpart Gustav Flaubert declared it had 'a beauty that tears the soul'. Italy's largest sea port is indefatigably contradictory, full at once of grandeur, squalor, sparkling light and deep shade. Although it's a gateway to the Riviera for travellers today, a weighty architectural heritage speaks of its former glory. The Most Serene Republic of Genoa ruled over the Mediterranean waves during the 12th and 13th centuries and its emblematic flag, the red cross of St George, was greedily hijacked by the upstart English.

History feels alive in Genoa, and no more so in its extensive old city, a tightly twisting

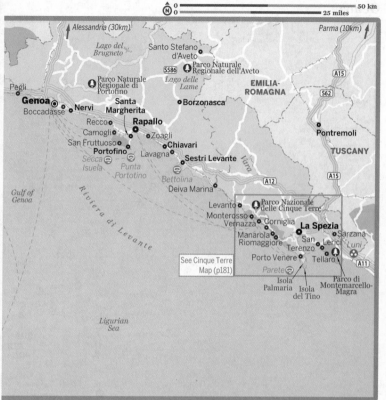

maze of narrow *caruggi* (laneways), largely intact and a compelling, if often confronting, reminder of pre-modern life. Emerge blinking from its dank heart to Via Garibaldi and the splendid Enlightment-era gold-leaf halls of the Unesco-annointed Palazzi dei Rolli.

Since hosting Expo 1992 and as a 2004 European City of Culture, Genoa has undergone some radical makeovers, with its once-tatty port area now hosting Europe's largest aquarium, one of its best maritime museums and a host of eating and drinking options. Its old town, too, has had its own far more organic revitalisation, with a bright new crop of fashionable shops, restaurants and bars lighting the way.

History

Genoa's name is thought to come from the Latin *ianua,* meaning 'door'. Founded in the 4th century BC, Genoa was an impor-

tant Roman port and was later occupied by Franks, Saracens and the Milanese. The first ring of Genoa's defensive walls was constructed in the 12th century. (The only remaining section of these walls, Porta Soprana, was built in 1155, although what you see today is a restored version.)

A victory over Venice in 1298 led to a period of growth, but bickering between the Grimaldis, Dorias, Spinolas and other dynasties caused internal chaos. The Grimaldis headed west, establishing the principality of Monaco, hence the similarity of Monaco's language, Monegasque, to the Genoese dialect.

In the 16th century, under the rule of Imperial Admiral Andrea Doria, Genoa benefited from financing Spanish exploration. Its coffers swelled further in the 17th century, which saw an outer ring of walls added as the city expanded, and its newly built palaces filled with art, attracting masters such

Genoa

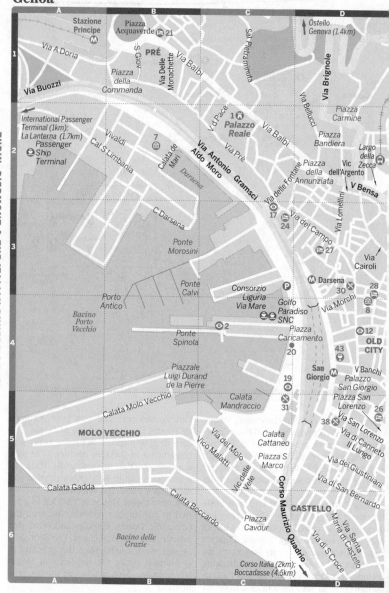

as Rubens. Celebrated architect Galeazzo Alessi (1512–72) designed many of the city's splendid buildings.

The end of the Age of Exploration came as a blow and, as the Mediterranean's mercantile importance declined, so did Genoa's.

Genoa was the first northern city to rise against Nazi occupation and the Italian Fascists during WWII, liberating itself before Allied troops arrived. After the war the city developed rapidly, with southern Italian immigrants manning its docks and factories,

a decaying backwater into a showpiece for the city. Renzo Piano orchestrated the overhaul, adding a number of striking permanent attractions; just over a decade later, in 2004, Genoa was named a European City of Culture.

◉ Sights

Aside from the Ligurian cuisine, Genoa's tour de force is its Palazzi dei Rolli. Fortytwo of these lodging palaces – built between 1576 and 1664 to host visiting European gentry – were placed on the Unesco World Heritage list in 2006. They are mostly on or around Via Garibaldi and Via Balbi.

★ Palazzo Reale   PALACE, MUSEUM

(www.palazzorealegenova.beniculturali.it; Via Balbi 10; adult/reduced €4/2; ⊙9am-7pm Tue-Sat, 1.30pm-7pm Sun) If you only get the chance to visit one of the Palazzi dei Rolli (a group of palaces belonging to the city's most eminent families), make it this one. A former residence of the Savoy dynasty, it has terraced gardens, exquisite furnishings, a fine collection of 17th-century art and a gilded Hall of Mirrors that is worth the entry fee alone.

Musei di Strada Nuova   MUSEUM

(www.museidigenova.it; Via Garibaldi; combined ticket adult/reduced €9/7; ⊙9am-7pm Tue-Fri, to 9pm Thu, 9.30am-7pm Sat & Sun) Skirting the northern edge of what was once the city limits, pedestrianised Via Garibaldi (formerly called the Strada Nuova) was planned by Galeazzo Alessi in the 16th century. It quickly became the city's most sought-after quarter, lined with the palaces of Genoa's wealthiest citizens. Three of these *palazzi* – Rosso, Bianco and Doria-Tursi – today comprise the Musei di Strada Nuova. Between them, they hold the city's finest collection of old masters.

Buy tickets at the bookshop inside Palazzo Doria-Tursi (Via Garibaldi 9). This palace's highlight is the Sala Paganiniana, which showcases a small but absorbing collection of legendary violinist Niccolò Paganini's personal effects. Pride of place goes to his Canone violin, made in Cremona in 1743. One lucky musician gets to play the maestro's violin during October's Paganiniana festival. Elsewhere the collections are centred on ceramics and coins.

Lavishly frescoed rooms in Palazzo Rosso (Via Garibaldi 18) provide the backdrop for several Van Dyck portraits of the local Brignole-Sale family. Other standouts

although by the 1970s, decline had set in as industries folded.

Christopher Columbus is Genoa's most famous son. In 1992 the 500th anniversary of his seminal voyage to America transformed Genoa's ancient harbour from

Genoa

include Guido Reni's *San Sebastiano* and Guercino's *La Morte di Cleopatra* (The Death of Cleopatra), as well as works by Veronese, Dürer and Bernardo Strozzi.

Flemish, Spanish and Italian artists feature at **Palazzo Bianco** (Via Garibaldi 11). Rubens' *Venere e Marte* (Venus and Mars) and Van Dyck's *Vertumna e Pomona* are among the highlights, which also include works by Hans Memling, Filippino Lippi and Spanish masters Murillo and Zurbarán.

Franco Albini Apartment   ARCHITECTURE
(Palazzo Rosso; www.museidigenova.it) One of Italy's best loved 20th-century architects, Franco Albini was a key figure in the restoration of Genova's *palazzi* in the post war period. The third floor of the Palazzo Rosso hides an Italian mid-century gem – an apartment Albini designed for the museum's director, now open to the public. Its mix of signature Albini furniture, clean modern lines and Genovese excess, will delight design fans (the city views aren't bad either).

Cattedrale di San Lorenzo   CATHEDRAL
(Piazza San Lorenzo; ⊙8am-noon & 3-7pm) Genoa's zebra-striped Gothic-Romanesque cathedral owes its continued existence to the poor quality of a British WWII bomb that failed to ignite here in 1941; it still sits on the right side of the nave like an innocuous museum piece.

The cathedral, fronted by three arched portals, twisting columns and crouching lions, was first consecrated in 1118. The two bell towers and cupola were added later in the 16th century.

Inside, above the central doorway, there's a great lunette with a painting of the *Last Judgment*, the work of an anonymous Byzantine painter of the early 14th century. In the sacristy, the **Museo del Tesoro** (Piazza San Lorenzo; adult/child €6/4.50; ⊙9am-noon & 3-6pm Mon-Sat) preserves various dubious holy relics, including the medieval *Sacro Catino*, a glass vessel once thought to be the Holy Grail. Other artefacts include the polished quartz platter upon which Salome is said to have received John the Baptist's head, and a fragment of the True Cross.

Palazzo Ducale MUSEUM
(www.palazzoducale.genova.it; Piazza Giacomo Matteotti 9; admission depends on exhibition; ⊘varies) Once the seat of the independent republic, this grand palace was built in the mannerist style in the 1590s and largely refurbished after a fire in the 1770s. Today it hosts high-profile temporary art exhibitions, several smaller galleries and occasional markets in its lofty atrium. The *palazzo* also has a bookshop and cafe.

Chiesa del Gesù CHURCH
(Piazza Giacomo Matteotti; ⊘4.30-7pm) Half-hidden behind the cathedral but emulating it in its ecclesial brilliance, this former Jesuit church dating from 1597 has an intricate and lavish interior. The wonderfully frescoed walls and ceiling are anchored by two works by the great Dutch artist Rubens. *Circoncisione* (Circumcision) hangs over the main altar, and *Miracoli di San Ignazio* is displayed in a side chapel.

Piazza de Ferrari PIAZZA
Genova's fountain-embellished main piazza is ringed by magnificent buildings that includes the art nouveau **Palazzo della Borsa**, which was once the country's stock exchange, and the hybrid neoclassical-modernist Teatro Carlo Felice (p174), bombed in WWII and not fully rebuilt until 1991.

Old City NEIGHBOURHOOD
The heart of medieval Genoa – bounded by ancient city gates **Porta dei Vacca** and **Porta Soprana**, and the streets of Via Cairoli, Via Garibaldi and Via XXV Aprile – is famed for its *caruggi* (narrow lanes). Looking up at the washing pegged on lines everywhere, it becomes obvious that these dark, cave-like laneways and blind alleys are still largely residential, although the number of fashionable bars, shops and cafes continues to grow.

Parts of the *caruggi* can feel somewhat unnerving, especially after dark. Although it's not particularly dangerous, take care in the zone west of Via San Luca and south to Piazza Banchi, where most street prostitution and accompanying vice concentrates. East of the piazza is Via Orefici, where you'll find market stalls.

Museo d'Arte Orientale MUSEUM
(www.museidigenova.it; Piazzale Mazzini 1; adult/reduced €5/3; ⊘9am-7pm Tue-Sun summer, to 6pm winter) Just east of Via Garibaldi, a path from Piazza Corvetto twists through terraced gardens to one of Europe's largest collections of Japanese art, bringing together some 20,000 items, including porcelain, bronzes, costumes and musical instruments.

Casa della Famiglia Colombo MUSEUM
(Piazza Dante; admission €6; ⊘9am-noon & 2-6pm Sat & Sun) Not the only house claiming to be the birthplace of the navigator Christopher Columbus (Calvi in Corsica is another contender), this one probably has the most merit, as various documents inside testify. Curiously, it stands just outside the old city walls in the shadow of the Porta Soprana gate (built in 1155).

Galleria Nazionale ART GALLERY
(www.palazzospinola.beniculturali.it; Piazza Superiore di Pellicceria 1; adult/reduced €4/2; ⊘8.30am-7.30pm Tue-Sat, from 1.30pm Sun) This gallery's paintings are wonderfully displayed over four floors of the 16th-century **Palazzo Spinola**, once owned by the Spinola family, one of Genoa's most formidable dynasties. The main focus is Italian and Flemish Renaissance art of the so-called Ligurian School (look out for Van Dyck, Rubens and Strozzi), but it's also worth visiting to gape at the decorative architecture.

Porto Antico NEIGHBOURHOOD
(www.portoantico.it) The port that once controlled a small empire is now one of the best places to enjoy a *passeggiata* (evening stroll). Super yacht–fanciers are particularly well catered for and those with kids will love the aquarium, the futuristic Bigo (lookout), the small public swimming pool and the pirate ship.

Acquario AQUARIUM
(www.acquariodigenova.it; Ponte Spinola; adult/reduced €24/15; ⊘9.30am-8pm, to midnight Aug; ☂) Genoa's much-vaunted aquarium is one of the largest in Europe, with more than 5000 sea creatures, including sharks. Moored at the end of a walkway is the ship Nave Blu, a unique floating display, specialising in exhibits of coral reefs. The aquarium's 'cetaceans pavilion' may concern some visitors: while the dolphins here do not perform tricks and the aquarium fulfils its international legal requirements, including rehousing abused dolphins, animal welfare groups

TURIN, PIEDMONT & THE ITALIAN RIVIERA GENOA

> **ⓘ MAKING THE MOST OF YOUR EURO**
>
> Keen museum-goers should pick up the **Card Musei** (24/48hr €12/16). The card gives free admission to 21 of Genoa's museums and discounted access to several more. You can buy it at various museums, information booths and tourist offices.

claim keeping dolphins in enclosed tanks is harmful for these complex creatures.

Buy tickets online to avoid long, hot queues (and harassment from street traders) in summer; a combination ticket (adult €48) gives you access to other port attractions including the Galata Museo del Mare.

Galata Museo del Mare　　　　　　MUSEUM
(www.galatamuseodelmare.it; Calata de Mari 1; admission €11; ⊙10am-7.30pm, closed Mon Nov-Feb) Rivalled only by Barcelona and Venice as a medieval and Renaissance maritime power, Genoa's 'museum of the sea' is, not surprisingly, one of its most relevant and interesting. High-tech exhibits trace the history of seafaring, from Genoa's reign as Europe's greatest dockyard to the ages of sail and steam.

A section on the ground floor is dedicated to native son Christopher Columbus. Alongside is a scale reconstruction of a 17th-century galley ship, given extra drama by added sound effects and snippets of film. The 2nd floor guards a valuable collection of old maps and globes, while the 3rd floor has a more recent documenation of Italian emigration by sea. The top-floor mirador has one of Genoa's best cityscape views. Bring a camera.

La Lanterna　　　　　　　　　LIGHTHOUSE
(Via alla Lanterna; adult/reduced €5/4; ⊙2-6.30pm Sat & Sun) The port may have changed radically since its '90s rebirth, but its emblematic sentinel hasn't moved an inch since 1543. Genoa's lighthouse is one of the world's oldest and tallest – and it still works, beaming its light over 50km to warn ships and tankers. Visitors can climb 172 steps and ponder exhibits in an adjacent museum of lamps, lenses and related history.

La Lanterna is best accessed via a special 800m walking trail that starts at the ferry terminal. It's surrounded by a pleasant park.

Tours

Information and tickets for boat trips around the port and to destinations further afield are available from the **ticket booths** (Ponte Spinola; ⊙9.30am-6.30pm Sep-Jun, 9am-8pm Jul & Aug) beside the aquarium at Porto Antico. The tourist office has information on walking tours, including guided walks of the historic centre, including one exploring its traditional shops.

Whale Watch Liguria　　　WHALE WATCHING
(www.whalewatchliguria.it; tickets €33; ⊙1.30pm Sat Apr-Oct) These five-hour spring and summer tours are run in consultation with the World Wildlife Fund and include fascinating background on the world's largest mammals provided by an on-board biologist.

Genova City Sightseeing　　　　BUS TOUR
(www.genova.city-sightseeing.it; 2-day ticket €15) Hop-on, hop-off open-topped bus tours, with headphone commentary in five languages. Tickets are sold on the bus and stops are located in Piazza de Ferrari and Via XX Settembre. Runs March through November.

Festivals & Events

Slow Fish　　　　　　　　　　　FOOD
(slowfish.slowfood.it) Every odd-numbered year in early May, this festival celebrates seafood with a fish market and tastings. Affiliated with the Slow Food Movement, it also runs free workshops focusing on water pollution, good fishing practices and aquaculture.

Premio Paganini　　　　　　　　MUSIC
(www.premiopaganini.it) In homage to Genoese violinist Niccolò Paganini (1782–1849), this is an international violin competition held in September. Performances are held in the Teatro Carlo Felice (p174).

Sleeping

Dozens of hotels are spread round town. The greatest concentrationis near Stazione Principe, but these are the most mediocre in terms of quality.

★ **Palazzo Cambiaso**　　　　APARTMENT €
(My Place; ☑010 856 61 88; www.palazzocambiaso. it; Via al Ponte Calvi 6; d €110, apt €140-170) A real attention to design is evident in these rooms and apartments, set on the upper floor of a stately palazzo. The larger ones (sleeping up to six) come with full marble kitchens, long dining tables and laundries, but even the

cheapest double is spacious, soothing and has the signature Frette linen.

Hotel Cristoforo Colombo
HOTEL €

(☑ 010 251 36 43; www.hotelcolombo.it; Via di Porta Soprana 27; s/d €80/100; 🛜) A totally charming family-run hotel ideally situated near Cattedrale di San Lorenzo, Cristoforo Colombo has 18 colour-accented rooms with eclectic furnishings. Breakfast is served on an inviting 6th-floor rooftop terrace.

La Superba
B&B €

(☑ 010 869 85 89; la-superba.com; Via del Campo 12; s/d €80/90; 🕸🛜) A lovingly cared-for, well-equipped place at a bargain price, with rooms spread over the two top floors of an old *palazzo*. Top-floor rooms have pretty mansard ceilings and one has a tiny terrace with spectacular port and city views (along with the Genovese soundtrack of crosstown traffic). There's also generous lounge and breakfast areas.

Hotel Meuble Suisse
HOTEL €

(☑ 010 54 11 76; www.meublesuisse.com; 3rd fl, Via XX Settembre 21; s/d €55/70; 🛜) Clean, uncluttered rooms, service with a smile and your own personal chandelier. What more could you want? Climb the stairs to the 3rd floor of this strapping Genoa building near Stazione Brignole for a bit of faded fin-de-siècle magic.

Ostello Genova
HOSTEL €

(☑ 010 242 24 57; www.ostellogenova.it; Via Costanzi 120; dm €15, s/d €28/52, without bathroom €23/46; 🅿🛜) A steep 2km north of the centre, Genoa's only hostel has rules that won't endear it to free-spirited backpackers: its eight-bed dorms are single-sex, there's a lockout from 9am to 3.30pm, a 1am curfew, and Hostelling International (HI) cards are mandatory. Catch bus 40 from Stazione Brignole to the end of the line. Has access for guests with disabilities. Reception is open 24 hours.

Le Nuvole
BOUTIQUE HOTEL €€

(☑ 010 251 00 18; www.hotellenuvole.it; Piazza delle Vigne 6; d €130; 🕸@🛜) A bright newcomer full of smart modern furniture and slick bathrooms makes the most of the original architecture of an ancient *palazzo*, with lofty ceilings, lovingly restored plaster moldings and beautiful tilework. Owners are hands-on and helpful.

Quarto Piano
B&B €€

(☑ 348 7426779; www.quarto-piano.it; Piazza Pellicceria 2/4; d/ste €130/165; 🕸🛜) Four elegant, cosy modern rooms share the fourth floor here, complete with a terrace for breakfast or a hot tub dip.

Locanda di Palazzo Cicala
BOUTIQUE HOTEL €€

(☑ 010 251 88 24; www.palazzocicala.it; Piazza San Lorenzo 16; d/ste €125/170; 🕸@🛜) In stark contrast to its grand 18th-century stucco exterior, the six minimalist rooms include pieces by Jasper Morrison and Philippe Starck. Great stuff, but don't expect any TLC and do make sure you get a firm confirmation of where exactly you'll sleep, as guests are often palmed out to adequate but far less appealing apartments in the surrounding streets.

Hotel Bristol Palace
HOTEL €€

(☑ 010 59 25 41; www.hotelbristolpalace.com; Via XX Settembre 35; s €120/150; 🅿🕸@🛜) Under the huge portals of Via XX Settembre lies Genoa's belle époque masterpiece. Atmospheric, airy rooms with plush curtains, parquetry and original antiques are fabulously, unironically old school.

Grand Hotel Savoia
HOTEL €€

(☑ 010 2 77 21; www.grandhotelsavoiagenova.it; Via Arsenale di Terra 5; s/d €130/159; 🕸@🛜) The sprawling Grand Savoia has done a recent refurb that adds modern murals to its elegant old rooms. It's next to Stazione Porta Principe – not the city's most fetching locale, but the views are spectacular. On-site parking is available for €25 per day.

✗ Eating

It would be criminal to come to Genoa and not try *pesto genovese*. The city's famous pasta sauce really does taste, and look, better here than anywhere else, a result of the basil that's used (young plants are plucked daily from hothouses on city hillsides), as well as techniques honed through generations. Ubiquitous local specialities focaccia and *farinata* (flat bread made from chickpea flour) make cheap takeaway snacks. *Torta pasqualina* (spinach, artichoke ricotta and egg tart), *polpettone* (a potato gratin and egg slice, rather than meatballs), *pansotti* (a filled pasta of wild, wilted greens with a creamy walnut sauce) and freshly caught seafood are also unmissable.

Trattoria Da Maria
TRATTORIA €

(☑ 010 58 10 80; Vico Testadoro 14r; meals €15; ☉ 11.45am-3pm Mon-Sat, 7-9.30pm Thu & Fri) Brace yourself for lunchtime mayhem. This is a totally authentic, if well tourista, workers' trattoria and there's much squeezing into tiny tables, shouted orders and a fast and furious succession of plates plonked on tables. A daily hand-scrawled menu is a roll call of elemental favourites that keep all-comers full and happy, along with the jugs of ridiculously cheap wine.

Cross your fingers you're there on a *minestrone alla genovese,* pesto lasgne or donkey *ragù* day – pure Ligurian bliss.

Le Dolcezze Salate Di Angelo
BAKERY €

(Via XXV Aprile 22; focaccia from €1.50; ☉ 8am-3.30pm Tue-Sun) Every Genovese has a favourite focaccia spot, but this one gets recommended more than most. Pungent with Ligurian olive oil and spiked with flecks of sea salt, the basic model is morish to a fault. To-go lunch options include the onion-topped or straccino-cheese-stuffed version or an earthy spinach pie.

Pasticceria Profumo
PASTRIES €

(www.villa1827.it; Via del Portello 2; ☉ 9am-1pm & 3.30-7.30pm Tue-Sat) A traditional *pasticceria* and chocolate shop that follows the seasons – chocolate, chestnuts and cream dominate in winter, fresh stone fruit and berries in summer – this is also one of Genova's most pretty, with bright, stylish packaging that makes for fantastic take-home gifts.

Gelateria Profumo
GELATERIA €

(www.villa1827.it; Vico Superiore del Ferro 14; cones from €2; ☉ noon-7.30pm Tue-Sat) A wonderfully old-fashioned place, with fragrant scoops appearing from under metal-topped vats The *panera* (a Genovese coffee-and-cream blend), creamy Sorento lemon and bitter orange flavours are standouts.

Gelateria San Luca
GELATERIA €

(Via San Luca 88; cones from €2; ☉ noon-7pm) A selection of beautiful traditional gelato flavours are complemented by a creative menu of semi-freddo cups, icecream sandwiches and chocolate-coated popsicles. If you have a gelato emergency out of hours, the sweet owner has been known to dish out a mercy cone if you knock and ask nicely.

Trattoria Rosmarino
TRATTORIA €€

(☑ 010 251 04 75; www.trattoriarosmarino.it; Salita del Fondaco 30; meals €30; ☉ noon-3pm & 7-11pm Mon-Sat) Rosmarino cooks up the standard local specialities, yes, but the straightforwardly priced menu has an elegance and vibrancy that set it apart. With two nightly sittings, there's always a nice buzz (though there's also enough nooks and crannies that a romantic night for two isn't out of the question). Call ahead for an evening table.

Officina 34
MODERN ITALIAN €€

(☑ 010 302 71 84; www.officina34.it; Via di Ravecca 34; meals €30) Genova is a long way from Berlin or Brooklyn, but that urban aesthetic is in full force at Officina 34. Subway tile jokes aside, it's a beautifully fitted-out space in a pretty location, and has a simple, gently innovative menu that shows the kitchen cares about quality ingredients. A young, good-looking crowd comes for raw plates and *apertivo* and often ends up staying late.

La Berlocca
TRATTORIA €€

(☑ 010 796 33 33; www.laberlocca.com; Via Soziglia 45r; meals €30; ☉ 12.30-3pm & 7.30-11pm Tue-Sun) On one of the old city's nicest streets, this one-time *farinata* shop has a handwritten menu of Ligurian standards – tripe, stockfish with pine nuts and potatoes – as well as fresh and inventive dishes like smoked gnocchi. Lunch deals here start at €10 and top at €18 for an all-in feast that includes a quarter litre of wine.

Trattoria della Raibetta
TRATTORIA €€

(☑ 010 246 88 77; www.trattoriadellaraibetta.it; Vico Caprettari 10-12; meals €35; ☉ noon-2.30pm & 7.30-11pm Tue-Sun) Totally *typica* Genoese food can be found in the family-run joints hidden in the warren of streets near the cathedral. This, a snug trattoria with a low brick-vaulted ceiling, serves regional classics

LOCAL KNOWLEDGE

BREAKING FOCACCIA

Spend a week frequenting the bars and bakeries of the Ligurian coast and you'll quickly ascertain that no two focaccias are alike. The classic focaccia, called *alla genovese*, is a simple oven-baked flat-bread made with flour, yeast, water, salt and olive oil, and topped with salt, oil and sometimes rosemary. But various regional variations crop up only a short train ride away. To the east, the *galletta di Camogli* is a crisp focaccia that's more akin to a biscuit and was supposedly invented for the town's sailors to take on long voyages. In nearby Recco, the delicious *focaccia col formaggio* spreads mild creamy cheese (usually *crescenza*) between two thin slices of bread made without yeast. It traces its roots back to the Saracen invasions of the Early Middle Ages. San Remo, on the Riviera di Ponente, has concocted *sardenara*, a pizza-like focaccia topped with tomatoes, onions, capers and – as the name implies – sardines. And, yes, you've seen right: Ligurians think nothing of dipping a slice of *alla genovese* into their morning coffee.

such as *trofiette al pesto* or octopus salad alongside excellent fresh fish.

Ombre Rosse
TRADITIONAL ITALIAN €€

(☑010 275 76 08; Vico Indoratori 20; meals €35; ⊗12.30-10pm Mon-Fri, 7.45-10.30pm Sat) Encased in one of the oldest medieval houses in the city, dating from the early 13th century, Ombre Rosse has a dark but romantic interior, full of books, posters and interesting nooks. There's also alfresco seating in a delightful small park opposite (one of the few in Genoa's dense urban grid) not to mention good Ligurian dishes and thoughtful service.

★ Il Marin
SEAFOOD €€€

(Eataly Genova; ☑010 869 87 22; www.eataly. net; Porto Antico; meals €50; ⊗noon-3pm & 7-10.30pm) Eating by the water often means a compromise in quality, but Eataly's 3rd-floor fine-dining space delivers both panoramic port views and Genoa's most innovative seafood menu. Rustic wooden tables, Renzo Piano–blessed furniture and an open kitchen make for an easy, relaxed glamour, while dishes use unusual Mediterranean-sourced produce and look gorgeous on the plate.

This is the destination restaurant the city has long needed. Book ahead.

🍷 Drinking & Nightlife

The revamped Porto Antico has an early night-time scene, but never underestimate the lure of the *caruggi* (narrow lanes) later on. You'll find a number of new drinking spots intermingled with old-time favourites throughout the city, particularly in the streets just northwest of Piazza de Ferrari. Piazza delle Erbe pulls the *ragazzi* for cheap and cheerful *aperitivi* and occasionally gets rowdy well into the night.

★ Les Rouges
COCKTAIL BAR

(☑010 246 49 56; www.lesrouges.it; Piazza Campetto 8a, 1st floor; ⊗5.30-11pm Tue-Thu & Sun, to 12.30am Fri & Sat) One of Genova's surfeit of crumbling *palazzi* is being put to excellent use in this atmospheric cocktail bar. Three bearded, vest-wearing, red-headed brothers – the 'rouges' of the name – man the floor and shake up the city's only new-wave cocktails, using top-shelf ingredients and herbal or floral flavours like camomile and kaffir lime.

There's a small menu if all the staring at those distant frescoed ceilings makes you hungry – pesto, ricotta and lemon-scented tagliatelle, rabbit kebab or slow-roasted beef are suitably hipster-does-trad.

Cambi Cafe
BAR

(www.cambicafe.com; Via Falamonica 9; ⊗10am-11pm) Admire the exquisite 17th-century frescoes of Bernardo Strozzi while sipping on your morning cappuccino or your afternoon *aperitivo* in this spectacular bar-cafe (it also serves lunch and dinner) encased in an old Doria palace. For somewhere so elegantly storied, staff are friendly and welcoming.

Enoteca Pesce
WINE BAR

(Via Sottoripa; ⊗8.30am-7.30pm Mon-Sat) Tiny wine bars dot Genoa's old city, although this one, under the arches by the port, is particularly characteristic, full of colourful locals and serious about its product. Glasses hover around the €2 mark, so it's a good place to get to know Liguria's unusual grapes. Grab a cone of fried sardines from the nameless neighbouring *friggitoria* (fry shop) and make an afternoon of it.

Fratelli Klainguti
CAFE

(Via di Soziglia; ⊙8am-8pm) Pre-dating cappuccinos, Klainguti opened in 1828 and its Mittel European charms, and presumably its strudel and pastries, had Verdi and Garibaldi coming back for more. Waiters in bow ties toil under an impressive chandelier and the decor is a fabulous, if tatty, mid-century historical pastiche.

Café degli Specchi
CAFE

(Via Salita Pollaiuoli 43r; ⊙7am-9pm Mon-Sat) A bit of Turin disconnected and relocated 150km to the south, this tiled art deco showpiece was (and is) a favourite hang-out of Genova's intellectuals. You can sink your espresso at street level or disappear upstairs amid the velvet seats and mirrors for coffee, cake and an *aperitivo* buffet.

Bar Berto
BAR, RESTAURANT

(Piazza delle Erbe 6; ⊙10.30am-1am Sun-Thu, to 2am Fri & Sat) Piazza delle Erbe's sliver of bars is *the* place for Genoa's youth to enjoy an alfresco drink. The tables of various bars merge in the cobbled square, but Bar Berto's interior wins if you feel the need to head indoors.

☆ Entertainment

At the western end of the Porto Antico, the Magazzini del Cotone (one-time cotton warehouses) have been converted into an entertainment area with a multiplex cinema, games arcade and shops.

Teatro Carlo Felice
THEATRE

(☑010 538 12 24; www.carlofelice.it; Passo Eugenio Montale 4) Genoa's stunning four-stage opera house.

Teatro della Tosse
THEATRE

(www.teatrodellatosse.it; Piazza Renato Negri 4) Casanova trod the boards of the city's oldest theatre, which dates from 1702.

🛍 Shopping

Heading southwest, elegant Via Roma, adjacent to the glass-covered **Galleria Mazzini**, is Genoa's designer shopping street. It links Piazza Corvetto with Piazza de Ferrari. The old city's lanes are full of all kinds of traditional shops and vintage boutiques.

★ Via Garibaldi 12
HOMEWARES, DESIGN

(☑010 253 03 65; www.viagaribaldi12.com; Via Garibaldi 12; ⊙10am-2pm & 3.30-7pm Tue-Sat) Even if you're not in the market for designer homewares, it's worth trotting up the noble stairs here just to be reminded how splendid a city Genoa can be. There's an incredibly canny collection of contemporary furniture and objects on display, but it's the shop's original architecture – an aesthetic onslaught of columns, arched windows and baroque painted ceilings – that will make your jaw drop.

Butteghetta Magica di Tinello Daniela
HOMEWARES, NATIVITY SCENES

(☑010 247 42 25; Via della Maddalena 2; ⊙3-7pm Mon, 10am-1pm & 3-7pm Tue-Sat) Stock your kitchen from a selection of brightly glazed traditional ceramics and beautiful contemporary kitchenware. This is also the place to buy a *corzetti*, a carved wooden stamp that is used to make a local pasta speciality of the same name. If you're here during the Christmas season, the 'magica' of the title comes into play with spectacular nativity scenes to admire.

Pietro Romanengo fu Stefano
CHOCOLATES

(www.romanengo.com; Via Soziglia 74r; ⊙3.30-7.30pm Mon, 9am-1pm & 3.15-7.15pm Tue-Sat) An intriguing historic chocolate shop that specialises in candied flowers and floral waters.

🛈 Information

Main Post Office (Via Dante 4; ⊙8am-6.30pm Mon-Sat)

Ospedale San Martino (☑010 55 51; Largo Rosanna Benci 10)

Police Station (☑010 5 36 61; Via Armando Diaz 2)

Tourist Office (☑010 557 29 03; www.visit genoa.it; Via Garibaldi 12r; ⊙9am-5.30pm, to 8pm in summer)

🛈 Getting There & Away

AIR

Cristoforo Colombo Airport (☑010 6 01 51; www.airport.genova.it) Regular domestic and international services, including Ryanair flights to/from London Stansted, use Cristoforo Colombo Airport, 6km west of the city, in Sestri Ponente.

BOAT

From June to September, **Golfo Paradiso SNC** (www.golfoparadiso.it) operates boats from Porto Antico to Camogli (one way/return €10/16), Portofino (€12/20) and Porto Venere (€20/35).

Consorzio Liguria Via Mare (www.liguriaviamare.it) runs a range of seasonal trips to Camogli, San Fruttuoso and Portofino; Monterosso in the Cinque Terre; and Porto Venere.

Only cruise ships use the 1930s Ponte dei Mille terminal while ferries sailing to Spain, Sicily, Sardinia, Corsica, Morocco and Tunisia use the neighbouring international passenger terminals.

Fares listed here are for one-way, deck-class tickets. Ferry operators include the following:

Grandi Navi Veloci (GNV; ☎ 010 209 45 91; www.gnv.it) Ferries to Sardinia (Porto Torres, €52) and Sicily (Palermo, €88). Also to Barcelona (Spain), Tunis (Tunisia) and Tangier (Morocco).

Moby Lines (☎ 199 303040; www.mobylines. it) Ferries year-round to Corsica (Bastia, €28) and Sardinia (Olbia, €47).

BUS

Buses to international cities depart from Piazza della Vittoria, as do buses to/from Milan's Malpensa airport (€19, two hours, 6am and 3pm) and other interregional services. Tickets are sold at **Geotravels** (Piazza della Vittoria 57; ⊘ 9am-12.30pm & 3-7pm Mon-Fri, 9am-noon Sat).

TRAIN

Genoa's Stazione Principe and Stazione Brignole are linked by train to the following destinations.

TO	FARE (€)	DURATION (HR)	FREQUENCY
Milan	13	1½	up to 22 daily
Pisa	19	2	up to 28 daily
Rome	60.50	5	up to 12 daily
Turin	22.20	1¾	up to 21 daily

Stazione Principe tends to have more trains, particularly going west to San Remo (€11.40, two hours, five daily) and Ventimiglia (€13.20, 2¼ hours, six daily).

❶ Getting Around

TO/FROM THE AIRPORT

AMT (www.amt.genova.it) line 100 runs between Stazione Principe and the airport at least every hour from 5.30am to 11pm (€6, 30 minutes), with a stop also in Piazza de Ferrari. Tickets can be bought from the driver.

A taxi to or from the airport will cost around €20.

PUBLIC TRANSPORT

AMT operates buses throughout the city and there is an **AMT information office** (Via d'Annunzio 8; ⊘ 7.15am-6pm Mon-Fri, 7am-7pm Sat & Sun) at the bus terminal. Bus line 383 links Stazione Brignole with Piazza de Ferrari and Stazione Principe. A ticket valid for 90 minutes costs €1.50. Tickets can be used on main-line trains within the city limits, as well as on the **metro** (www.genovametro.com).

Around Genoa

Nervi

A former fishing village engulfed by Genoa's urban sprawl, modern Nervi serves as Genoa's summer playground with a string of resort-style beach clubs and seasonal bars along the waterfront. Its bounty of museums and galleries, and the 2km cliffside promenade, the Passeggiata Anita Garibaldi, make for a pleasant day trip, whatever the season.

◉ Sights

All four of Nervi's museums and galleries can be accessed in a combined ticket (€10) or on the Genoa Museum Card.

Galleria d'Arte Moderna ART GALLERY
(Via Capolungo 3; adult/reduced €6/5; ⊘ 11am-6pm Tue-Fri, noon-7pm Sat & Sun summer, 11am-5pm Tue-Sun winter) This museum, set in the 16th-century Villa Saluzzo, displays the former Prince Odone di Savoia's collection, mostly works by 19th- and early-20th-century artists such as futurist Fortunato Depero, semi-official fascist sculptor Arturo Martini and the lyrical eccentric Filippo De Pisis.

Wolfsoniana MUSEUM
(www.wolfsoniana.it; Via Serra Gropallo 4; adult/reduced €5/4; ⊘ 11am-6pm Tue-Fri, noon-7pm Sat & Sun summer, 11am-5pm Tue-Sun winter) Some 18,000 items from the period 1880–1945 are displayed in the Wolfson Collection, including paintings, sculptures, furniture, decorative arts, propaganda, everyday objects and industrial design. Absolute eye-candy for design and interiors fans, they also form an incredibly rich, and sometimes troubling, document of post-Risorgimento Italy's cultural complexity.

Raccolte Frugone ART GALLERY
(Via Capolungo 9; adult/reduced €4/2.80; ⊘ 9am-7pm Tue-Fri, 10am-7pm Sat & Sun) The 19th- and early-20th-century Italian collection here includes Edoardo Rubino's sensual marble nude *Il Risveglio* (the Awakening) is displayed in the Ligurian-to-the-max Villa Grimaldi Fassio, overlooking the leafy, squirrel-filled Parchi di Nervi.

Museo Giannettino Luxoro MUSEUM
(Via Mafalda di Savoia 3; adult/reduced €5/3; ⊘ 9am-2pm Tue-Sat) This early-20th-century villa has a huge collection of decorative

objects: 18th-century clocks, silverware, ceramics and furniture. Don't expect modern lines – the cliff-side former holiday home was built in a historicist style specifically to house the collection.

✕ Eating

Bagni Blue Marlin SEAFOOD €
(☎349 6413692; Passeggiata Anita Garibaldi 25; snacks €8-15, meals €18-30; ☺9am-11pm Apr-Sep) Part natural rock formation, part whitewashed concrete, this little place juts right out into the Med, making for a magical place to spritz a sunset away or snaffle up snap-fried anchovies in a paper cone. It morphs from daytime bathing spot into a restaurant and laid-back beach bar later in the evening.

❶ Getting There & Away

Nervi is 7km east of Genoa and is best reached by frequent trains from Stazione Brignole and Stazione Principe (€1.80, 15 to 25 minutes).

Pegli

Just 9km west of Genoa's centre, flower-filled parks make Pegli a peaceful spot to retreat from the urban tumult. Like Nervi, this former seafront village now lies within the city boundaries of Genoa and, again like Nervi, it has yet more museums. A combined ticket for all of the following sights, including bus transport, will cost you €10.

◉ Sights

Museo di Archeologia Ligure MUSEUM
(www.museidigenova.it; Villa Pallavicini, Via Pallavicini 11; admission €5; ☺9am-7pm Tue-Fri, 10am-7pm Sat & Sun) This museum in the striking Villa Pallavicini holds displays of locally excavated artefacts from prehistoric times through the Roman period, as well as a collection of Egyptian antiquities.

Museo Navale MUSEUM
(www.museidigenova.it; Villa Doria, Piazza Bonavino 7; admission €5; ☺9am-1pm Tue-Fri, 10am-6pm Sat, to 1pm Sun) Maritime matters are covered in a former residence of the Doria clan, with an exhibition of models, photographs and other reminders of the days when Genoa sported a significant sea force, which lasted from the 15th to the 19th centuries.

❶ Getting There & Away

Frequent trains from Genoa's Stazione Brignole and Stazione Principe (€1.70, 20 to 25 minutes) travel to Pegli.

Riviera di Levante

Beyond Genoa's claustrophobic eastern sprawl, this narrow strip of coast between the deep blue waters of the Mediterranean and the ruggedly moutainous Ligurian hinterland are home to some of Italy's most elite resorts, including jet-set favourite Portofino, the gently faded Santa Margherita and poetic Lerici. Anything but off the beaten track, this glittering stretch of coast is hugely popular, but retains pockets of extreme natural beauty.

Camogli

POP 5580
Camogli, 25km east of Genoa, is famous for its sheer number of *trompe l'œil* villas and its photogenic terraced streets winding down to a perfect cove of pebble beach amid a backdrop of umbrella pines and olive groves. Pretty as it is, the town remains a working fishing hub – the town's name means 'house of wives', hailing from the days when the womenfolk ran the show while the husbands were away at sea. Come the second weekend in May, the town celebrates its maritime heritage with the **Sagra del Pesce** (Fish Festival) and a huge fish fry – hundreds are cooked in 3m-wide pans along the waterfront.

Delve down the lanes away from the water for the town's best focaccia and some nice dining options.

◉ Sights & Activities

San Rocco Trail WALKING
A trail from the train station leads along Via Nicolò Cuneo and up countless steps to the church of San Rocco di Camogli: follow the two red dots. From here the path continues 3km to the clifftop battery, a WWII German anti-aircraft gun emplacement.

Punta Chiappa SWIMMING
(www.golfoparadiso.it; one way/return €6/10, hourly in summer, 3-7 times per day rest of year) From the main esplanade, Via Garibaldi, boats sail to the Punta Chiappa, a rocky outcrop on the Portofino promontory where you can swim and sunbathe like an Italian. By sea it's a

five-minute trip; otherwise it's an easy 3km walk along the trail that begins at the end of Via San Bartolomeo.

🛏 Sleeping

★ Villa Rosmarino   B&B €€

(📞 0185 77 15 80; www.villarosmarino.com; Via Figari 38; d €140-280; 🅿❄🛜🌊) Villa Rosmarino's motto is 'you don't stay, you live' and it's apt. Simply taking in the views here is life affirming. This elegant pink 1907 villa is a typical Ligurian beauty on the outside, a calming oasis of modernity on the inside.

Mario and Fulvio's collection of 20th-century furniture and contemporary art works are scattered throughout the lounge, library and light-filled rooms. Despite the design credentials, there's a sensual warmth to it all. Even breakfasts – taken around the dining table – pop with colour and texture. The setting is sublimely tranquil but Camogli's bustle is just a 15-minute walk down a picturesque lane.

Hotel Cenobio dei Dogi   HOTEL €€€

(📞 0185 72 41; www.cenobio.com; Via Cuneo 34; s/d €130/220; 🅿❄🛜🌊) The Cenobio's name means 'gathering place of the doges', and yes, the Genovese dukes used to holiday here eons ago. A private beach and saltwater swimming pool signal you're in the Riviera, as do the 105 refined, if old-fashioned, rooms.

🍴 Eating & Drinking

Da Paolo   SEAFOOD, LIGURIAN €€

(📞 0185 77 35 95; www.ristorantedapaolocamogli.com; Via San Fortunato 14; meals €35-50; ⊙ noon-2.30pm Wed-Sun, 7.30-10.30pm Tue-Sun) Up a back lane from the waterfront, stylish Da Paolo has the town's best fish, all fresh off the boats and done in a variety of simple local styles. Pastas include a fabulous fish ravioli.

The wine list is primarily white to match the seafood menu; it includes some great small Ligurian producers as well as a careful selection from Piemonte, Tuscany, Friuli and Alto Adige.

La Mancina   BAR

(Via al Porto Camogli; ⊙ 5pm-2am Thu-Tue) A couple of stools outside will give you a sea view, but the real action here is inside, where books line the walls and locals chat with the welcoming owner over *spritzes* or local wines.

ℹ Information

Tourist Office (www.camogliturismo.it; Via XX Settembre 33; ⊙ 9am-noon & 3.30-6.30pm Mon-Sat, from 10am Sun) Has a list of diving schools and boat-rental operators.

ℹ Getting There & Away

Camogli is on the Genoa–La Spezia train line, with regular connections to Santa Margherita (€2.10, five minutes) and Rapallo (€2.10, 10 minutes).

The **Golfo Paradiso SNC** (www.golfoparadiso.it) runs boats year-round to Punta Chiappa (one-way/return €6/10) and San Fruttuoso (€9/13). Between June and September there are services to Genoa's Porto Antico (€10/16), Portofino (€11/18) and the Cinque Terre (€19/29).

San Fruttuoso

San Fruttuoso is a slice of ancient tranquillity preserved amid some of Italy's busiest coastal resorts. There are no roads here – thank heavens! Several good seafood places ring the pretty beach, but if you're on a budget consider bringing a picnic.

◎ Sights

Abbazia di San Fruttuoso di Capodimonte   CHURCH

(www.visitfai.it/sanfruttuoso; adult/reduced €6/3; ⊙ 10am-5.45pm summer, to 3.45pm winter) The hamlet's sensitively restored Benedictine abbey was built as a final resting place for Bishop St Fructuosus of Tarragona, martyred in Spain in AD 259. It was rebuilt in the mid-13th century with the assistance of the Doria family. The abbey fell into decay with the decline of the religious community; by the 19th century it was divided into small living quarters.

There's one apartment for overnight stays within the compound; for details get in touch with the FAI. In 1954 a bronze statue of Christ was lowered 15m to the seabed, offshore from the abbey, to bless the waters. Either dive to see it or, if the waters are calm, take a boat tour run by the Golfo Paradiso SNC. Replicas were lowered in St George's harbour in Grenada in 1961, and off Key Largo in Florida in 1966.

ℹ Getting There & Away

San Fruttuoso's blissful isolation means you have only two transport options: foot or sea. Walk in from Camogli (a tricky, rocky hike with metal hand supports) or Portofino, a steep but easier 5km cliffside walk. Both hikes take about 2½ hours one way. Alternatively, you can catch a boat from Camogli (one way/return €9/13), Punta Chiappa (€6/10) and, in summer, Genoa (€12/20).

Portofino

POP 495

Even the trees are handsome in Portofino, a small but perfectly coiffured coastal village that sits on its own peninsula, seemingly upping the exclusivity factor by mere geography. Hotels here are hushed and headily priced, but a drink by Portofino's yacht-filled harbour or a stroll around its designer shops can be easily enjoyed on a day trip from Genoa.

◉ Sights

Castello Brown　　　　　　　　　　　CASTLE
(www.castellobrown.com; Via alla Penisola 13a; admission €5; ☺10am-7pm summer, 10am-5pm Sat & Sun winter) A flight of stairs signposted 'Salita San Giorgio' leads from the harbour and past the **Chiesa di San Giorgio** to Portofino's unusual castle, a 10-minute walk (do confirm with the tourist office that it's open before setting out, as the castle often closes for private events). The Genoese-built castle saw action against the Venetians, Savoyards, Sardinians and Austrians, and later fell to Napoleon.

In 1867 it was transformed by the British diplomat Montague Yeats Brown into a private mansion. The fabulous tiled staircase is one of the showpieces of the neo-Gothic interior, while there are great views from the garden. For a better outlook, continue for another 400m or so along the same track to the lighthouse.

🏃 Activities

Boat-taxi operators around the harbour host snorkelling and sightseeing trips (from €25).

Parco Naturale Regionale di Portofino　　　　　　　　　　　HIKING
(www.parks.it/parco.portofino) The Portofino peninsula's 60km of narrow trails are a world away from the sinuous sports-car-lined road from Santa Margherita. Many of them are absolutely remote and all of them are free of charge. The tourist office has maps.

A good but tough day hike (there are exposed sections) is the 18km coastal route from Camogli to Santa Margherita via San Fruttuoso and Portofino. There are handy train connections at both ends.

🛏 Sleeping

Eight Hotels Paraggi　　　　　　　HOTEL €€€
(☎0185 28 99 61; paraggi.eighthotels.it; Via Paraggi a Mare 8; d €580; ❋ 🛜) This low-key hotel has simple, luxurious rooms, but its real appeal is the location. Right on the perfect crescent of Paraggi beach, there's a sense of calm here that can be elusive around the cove in Portofino proper. Such beauty doesn't come cheap, however: rooms with balconies start at €690 per night.

Domina Home Picolo　　　BOUTIQUE HOTEL €€€
(☎0185 26 90 15; www.dominahomepiccolo.com; Via Duca degli Abruzzi 31; d €230; ❋ 🛜) Another just-out-of-town place, Domina does the luxe minimalist look in an old villa on its own rocky beach in between Portofino and Paraggi.

Eden　　　　　　　　　　BOUTIQUE HOTEL €€€
(☎0185 26 90 91; www.hoteledenportofino.com; Vico Dritto 18; s/d €140/210; 🅿❋) Pretty and unpretentious Eden feels like it slipped out of an EM Forster novel. Its floral wallpaper and residence-hotel appeal is coupled with a great location, 100m up a quiet cobbled side street from the harbourfront.

🍴 Eating & Drinking

Pizzeria Il Portico　　　　　　　　PIZZA €
(Via Roma 21; meals €25; ☺noon-10pm Wed-Mon) Wander a block from the harbour and pizza margheritas can be procured for €6. You can also enjoy dishes such as octopus salad, *vongole* (clams) and Genovese specials on chequered tablecloths outside.

Ristorante Puny　　　　　　　　LIGURIAN €€
(☎0185 26 90 37; Piazza Martiri dell'Olivetta; meals €40; ☺noon-3pm & 7-11pm Wed-Fri) Puny's harbourside location is the one you've come to Portofino for and the owners treat everyone like they're a visiting celeb. The food sticks loyally to Ligurian specialities, especially seafood.

❶ Information

Tourist Office (Via Roma 35; ☺10am-1pm & 2-4.30pm Tue-Sun) Has free trail maps for the Parco Naturale Regionale di Portofino and information on mountain-bike rental, as well as seasonal sail- and motorboat rental.

ℹ Getting There & Around

ATP (www.atp-spa.it) bus 882 runs to Portofino from outside the tourist office in Santa Margherita (€1.50, every 30 minutes), but by far the best way is to walk. A designated path tracks the gorgeous coastline for 3km.

From April to October, **Servizio Marittimo del Tigullio** (www.traghettiportofino.it) runs daily ferries from Portofino to/from San Fruttuoso (€8.50/12), Rapallo (€8/11.50) and Santa Margherita (€6.50/9.50).

Motorists must park at the village entrance, with obligatory parking fees starting from €6 per hour (cash only).

Santa Margherita

POP 10,035

Santa Margherita materialises like a calm Impressionist painting. You wouldn't want to change a single detail of its picture-perfect seaside promenade, where elegant hotels with Liberty facades overlook yachts in this fishing-village-turned-retirement-spot. It's decidly less bling than Portofino, with affordable hotel options and a surpisingly workaday town behind the waterfront.

◉ Sights & Activities

An idyllic position on a sheltered bay on the turquoise Golfo di Tigullio makes the town a good base for sailing, water-skiing and scuba diving. Those feeling less active can simply stretch out on its popular beach.

Villa Durazzo   VILLA, GARDEN
(www.villadurazzo.it; Piazzale San Giacomo 3; ⊙9am-1pm & 2.30-6.30pm) FREE This exquisitely turned-out mansion and gardens, part of a 16th-century castle complex, overlooks the sea. You can take an aromatic stroll among lemon trees, hydrangea and camellia hedges, and other flora typical of the town's mild climate in the lavish Italian gardens, or wander among its recently restored collection of 17th-century painting.

A cafe is open year-round and sometimes serves free canapés and wine on its lovely terrace.

Santuario di Nostra Signora della Rosa   CHURCH
(Piazza Caprera) You'll gasp audibly when entering Santa Margherita's small yet lavish baroque church, not just at the truly dazzling array of gold leaf, frescoes, chandeliers and stained glass, but also at the sheer serendipity of it being here at all.

🛌 Sleeping

Lido Palace Hotel   HOTEL €€
(☑0185 28 58 21; www.lidopalacehotel.com; Via Doria 3; d €180; P❄🛜) Right on the waterfront, this endearingly fussy Liberty-style grande dame offers the quintessential Santa Margherita experience. Rooms are generously proportioned and the breakfast buffet is bountiful.

Bludite House   BOUTIQUE HOTEL €€€
(☑0185 28 71 87; www.bludite.com; Via Favale 30; d €250; P❄🛜) Once a rambling old Ligurian villa, the Bludite has 20 clean-lined rooms. Colours echo the Ligurian landscape and they are funished with mid-century-design pieces. A rooftop terrace overlooks a baroque church and treetops to the blue of the gulf.

★**Grand Hotel Miramare**   HISTORIC HOTEL €€€
(☑0185 28 70 13; www.grandhotelmiramare.it; Via Milite Ignoto 30; s/d €300/400; P❄🛜🏊) The Miramare, which looks back over to the town across the Gulf of Tigullio, feels like it's from another time, the antithesis of vulgarity. Staff are gracious, public spaces are elegant, facilities are plentiful and rooms are soothing. While it's much in the grand European tradition, it also has a friendly, relaxed vibe and a surprisingly youthful clientele, including families.

🍴 Eating & Drinking

L'Altro Eden   SEAFOOD €€
(☑0185 29 30 56; www.laltro.ristoranteeden.com; Calata San Porto 11; meals €35-55; ⊙noon-midnight Mon-Fri, noon-2.30pm & 7-10pm Sat & Sun) A seafood place right on the docks, yes, but this grey-and-white streamlined vaulted space is a maritime kitsch-free zone. Romantic and cosy on colder evenings; its outside tables are right by the boats in summer. Fish is done by weight and to order, but they are best known for crudo and risotto with fresh prawns or, in season, squid ink.

ℹ Information

Parco Naturale Regionale di Portofino (www.parks.it/parco.portofino; Viale Rainusso 1; ⊙9am-1pm Mon-Fri) Maps and information on hiking.

Tourist Office (www.apttigullio.liguria.it; Piazza Vittorio Veneto; ⊙9.30am-noon & 2.30-5.30pm Mon-Sat) Has a raft of information about water sports along the gulf.

❶ Getting There & Around

ATP Tigullio Trasporti (www.tigulliotrasporti. it) runs buses to/from Portofino (every 20 minutes) and Camogli (every 30 minutes).

By train, there are hourly services to/from Genoa (€4.60, 35 minutes) and La Spezia (€7.80, 1½ hours).

Servizio Marittimo del Tigullio (www.traghetti portofino.it; Via Palestro 8/1b) runs seasonal ferries to/from Cinque Terre (one way/return €18/26), Porto Venere (€22.50/34), San Fruttuoso (€10.50/15.50), Portofino (€6.50/9.50) and Rapallo (€4.50/5.50).

Rapallo

POP 30,575

WB Yeats, Max Beerbohm and Ezra Pound all garnered inspiration in Rapallo and it's not difficult to see why. With its bright-blue changing cabins, palm-fringed beach and diminutive 16th-century castle perched above the sea, the town has a poetic and nostalgic air. It's at its busiest on Thursdays, when market stalls fill central Piazza Cile.

◉ Sights

Rapallo's seafront promenade, Lungomare Vittorio Veneto, hosts a daily parade of locals and visitors. It's worth checking inside the picturesque, impossible-to-miss castle, where temporary exhibitions are sometimes held.

Cable Car   CABLE CAR

(Piazzale Solari 2; one way/return €5.50/8; ⊙9am-12.30pm & 2-5pm) When you've had your fill of the promenade poseurs, rise above them in a 1934-vintage cable car up to **Santuario Basilica di Montallegro** (612m), built on the spot where, in 1557, the Virgin Mary was reportedly sighted. Walkers and mountain bikers can follow an old mule track (5km, 1½ hours) to the hilltop site.

🍽 Sleeping & Eating

Behind the rows of parked scooters, the waterfront has plenty of places to eat, drink and snack.

Europa Hotel Design Spa 1877   HOTEL €€

(☑0185 66 95 21; www.gruppoplinio.it/europa hotel; Via Milite Ignoto 2; s/d €110/160; 🅿 ❄ 🕱) Close to the beach and with its own spa facilities – a thermal bath and steam room – this recently refurbished place is super relaxing. Whitewashed rooms are pretty but modern, while public areas do the shiny Italian glam thing.

Bansin   TRATTORIA €

(☑0185 23 11 19; www.trattoriabansin.it; Via Venezia 105; meals €20; ⊙noon-2pm & 7.15-10.30pm, closed Sun lunch summer & Mon lunch winter) Ligurian comfort food – salt cod fritters, chickpea soup, spinach-stuffed pasta with walnut sauce, mussels gratin – gets served up here with a minimum of fuss and not just a little bit of love. Lunch menus are €10 and there's a garden courtyard in summer.

Vecchia Rapallo   SEAFOOD €€

(☑0185 5 00 53; www.vecchiarapallo.com; Via Cairoli 20/24; meals €30; ⊙noon-2.30pm & 6-11pm daily summer, shorter hr winter) Seafood is again the star here, and it's done well with the occasional creative touch. House-made stuffed pastas have particular appeal – snapper ravioli comes with beetroot and prawn sauce, while a chard-filled variety is shaved with truffles. There's a cocktail and wine bar if you're just after a drink too.

Ristorante Eden   SEAFOOD €€€

(☑0185 5 05 53; www.ristoranteeden.com; Via Diaz 5; meals €45; ⊙noon-2.30pm & 7-10pm Thu-Tue) Eden serves whatever the market's offering on any given day. Rest assured your octopus, calamari, clams or anchovies will be cooked skilfully and complemented, if you wish, by fine homemade pasta.

❶ Information

Tourist Office (www.apttigullio.liguria.it; Lungo Vittorio Veneto 7; ⊙9.30am-12.30pm & 2.30-5.30pm Mon-Sat) Details of walks in the area, plus maps.

❶ Getting There & Away

Trains run along the coast to Genoa (€3.40, 40 minutes) and La Spezia (€6.30, one hour).

Servizio Marittimo del Tigullio (www. traghettiportofino.it) runs boats to/from Santa Margherita (one way/return €4.50/5.50), Portofino (€8/12), San Fruttuoso (€11/16.50), Genoa (€14.50/20.50), the Cinque Terre (€22.50/34) and Porto Venere (€22.50/34). Not all operate daily, and many are seasonal – the website posts updated schedules.

Cinque Terre

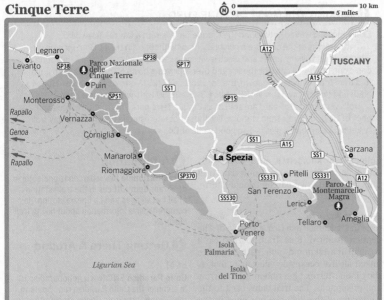

Cinque Terre

Set amid some of the most dramatic coastal scenery on the planet, these five ingeniously constructed fishing villages can bolster the most jaded of spirits. A Unesco World Heritage Site since 1997, Cinque Terre isn't the undiscovered Eden it once was, but, frankly, who cares? Sinuous paths traverse seemingly impregnable cliffsides, while a 19th-century railway line, cut through a series of coastal tunnels, ferries the footsore from village to village. Thankfully, cars were banned over a decade ago.

Rooted in antiquity, Cinque Terre's five villages date from the early medieval period. Monterosso, the oldest, was founded in AD 643, when beleaguered hill dwellers moved down to the coast to escape from invading barbarians. Riomaggiore came next, purportedly established in the 8th century by Greek settlers fleeing persecution in Byzantium. The others are Vernazza, Corniglia and Manarola. Much of what remains in the villages today dates from the late High Middle Ages, including several castles and a quintet of illustrious parish churches.

Fetching vernacular architecture aside, Cinque Terre's unique historical feature are the steeply terraced cliffs bisected by a complicated system of fields and gardens that have been hacked, chiselled, shaped and layered over the course of nearly two millennia. So marked are these artificial contours that some scholars have compared the extensive *muretti* (low stone walls) to the Great Wall of China in their grandeur and scope.

In October 2011 flash floods along the Ligurian coast wreaked havoc in Vernazza and Monterosso, burying historic streets and houses under metres of mud and killing half-a-dozen people. The villages, in resilient Ligurian style, recovered swiftly, but some of the walking trails remain fragile and closed to visitors.

🏃 Activities

Walking

Since the 2011 floods, many of Cinque Terre's walking paths have been in a delicate state and prone to periodic or permanent closure. At the time of writing only half of the iconic Sentiero Azzurro was open. However, Cinque Terre has a whole network of spectacular trails and you can still plan a decent village-to-village hike by choosing from any of 30 numbered paths, although bear in mind that this can add

> ### ℹ MAKING THE MOST OF YOUR EURO
>
> Easily the best way to get around the Cinque Terre is with a Cinque Terre card.
>
> Two versions of the card are available: with or without train travel. Both include unlimited use of walking paths and electric village buses, as well as cultural exhibitions. The basic one-/two-day card for those aged over four years costs €7.50/14.50. With unlimited train trips between the town, the card costs €12/23. A one-day family card for two adult and two children (under 12) costs €31.50/19.60 with/without train travel.
>
> Both versions of the card are sold at all Cinque Terre park information offices and each of Cinque Terre's train stations. For those not interested in hiking, an all-day train ticket between the villages is also good value at €4.

quite a few kilometres onto your walk. Check ahead for the most up-to-date trail information at www.parconazionale5terre.it/sentieri_parco.asp.

Sentiero Azzurro   WALKING

(Blue Trail; admission with Cinque Terre Card) The Sentiero Azzurro (Blue Trail; marked No 2 on maps), a 12km old mule path that once linked all five oceanside villages by foot, is the Cinque Terre's blue-ribbon hike, narrow and precipitous. The trail dates back to the early days of the Republic of Genoa in the 12th and 13th centuries and, until the opening of the railway line in 1874, it was the only practical means of getting from village to village.

At the time of writing, the path between Riomagiorre (the famed via dell'Amore) and Manarola and that between Manarola and Corniglia were closed and will possibly remain so until at least 2017. Only very experienced and well-equipped hikers should attempt the current alternative route from Manarola to Corniglia via Volastra.

Sentiero Rosso   HIKING

Just a few kilometres shy of a full-blown marathon, the 38km Sentiero Rosso (Red trail; marked No 1 on maps), which runs from Porto Venere to Levanto, dangles a tempting challenge to experienced walkers who aim to complete it in nine to 12 hours.

For every 100 people you see on the Sentiero Azzurro, there are less than a dozen up here plying their way along a route that is mainly flat, tree-covered and punctuated with plenty of shortcuts. An early start is assured by an efficient train and bus connection to Porto Venere (via La Spezia), while refreshments en route are possible in a liberal smattering of welcoming bars and restaurants.

ℹ Information

Parco Nazionale (www.parconazionale5terre.it; ⊘7am-8pm) Offices in the train stations of all five villages and La Spezia station; has comprehensive information about hiking trail closures.

ℹ Getting There & Around

BOAT

Golfo Paradiso SNC (www.golfoparadiso.it) In summer the Golfo Paradiso runs boats to the Cinque Terre from Genoa (one way/return €18/33).

Servizio Marittimo del Tigullio (www.traghettiportofino.it) Seasonal boat services to/from Santa Margherita (one way/return €18/26).

Consorzio Marittimo Turistico Cinque Terre Golfo dei Poeti (www.navigazionegolfodeipoeti.it) From late March to October, La Spezia–based Consorzio Marittimo Turistico Cinque Terre Golfo dei Poeti runs daily shuttle boats between all of the Cinque Terre villages (except Corniglia), costing €9 one way, including all stops, or €20 for an all-day ticket.

CAR & MOTORCYCLE

Private vehicles are not allowed beyond village entrances. If you're arriving by car or motorcycle, you'll need to pay to park in designated car parks (€12 to €25 per day). In some villages, minibus shuttles depart from the car parks (one way/return €1.50/2.50) – park offices have seasonal schedules.

TRAIN

Between 6.30am and 10pm, one to three trains an hour trundle along the coast between Genoa and La Spezia, stopping at each of the Cinque Terre's villages. Unlimited 2nd-class rail travel between Levanto and La Spezia is covered by the Cinque Terre card, or you can buy a €4 all day ticket that allows unlimited travel between the five villages. The IC train from La Spezia is €8 one way; the slower regional is €2.70.

THE SANCTUARY WALKS

Each of Cinque Terre's villages is associated with a sanctuary perched high on the cliff-sides above the azure Mediterranean. Reaching these religious retreats used to be part of a hefty Catholic penance, but these days the walks through terraced vineyards and across view-splayed cliffs are a heavenly reward in themselves.

Monterosso to Santuario della Madonna di Soviore From Via Roma in the village, follow trail 9 up through forest and past the ruins of an old hexagonal chapel to an ancient paved mule path that leads to Soviore, Liguria's oldest sanctuary dating from the 11th century. Here you'll find a bar, a restaurant and views as far as Corsica on a clear day.

Vernazza to Santuario della Madonna di Reggio From underneath Vernazza's railway bridge, follow trail 8 up numerous flights of steps and past 14 sculpted Stations of the Cross to this 11th-century chapel with a Romanesque facade.

Corniglia to Santuario della Madonna delle Grazie This sanctuary can be approached from either Corniglia (on trail 7b) or Vernazza (trail 7), though the latter is better. Branch off the Sentiero Azzurro and ascend the spectacular Sella Comeneco to the village of San Bernardino, where you'll find the church with its adored image of Madonna and child above the altar.

Manarola to Santuario della Madonna delle Salute The pick of all the sanctuary walks is this breathtaking traverse (trail 6) through Cinque Terre's finest vineyards to a diminutive Romanesque-meets-Gothic chapel in the tiny village of Volastra.

Riomaggiore to Santuario della Madonna di Montenero Trail 3 ascends from the top of the village, up steps and past walled gardens to a restored 18th-century chapel which has a frescoed ceiling and sits atop an astounding lookout next to the park's new cycling centre.

TURIN, PIEDMONT & THE ITALIAN RIVIERA CINQUE TERRE

Monterosso

POP 1527

The most accessible village by car and the only Cinque Terre settlement to sport a proper beach, Monterosso is the furthest west and least quintessential of the quintet. The village, known for its lemon trees and anchovies, is split in two, its new and old halves linked by an underground tunnel burrowed beneath the blustery San Cristoforo promontory. Monterosso was badly hit by the 2011 floods, but recovered remarkably quickly.

◎ Sights

Convento dei Cappuccini CHURCH

Monterosso's most interesting church and convent complex is set on the hill that divides the old town from the newer Fegina quarter. The striped church, the **Chiesa di San Francesco**, dates from 1623 and has a painting attributed to Van Dyck (*Crocifissione*) to the left of the altar.

Nearby, the ruins of an old castle have been converted into a cemetery.

🛏 Sleeping

Unlike the other four towns, Monterosso has quite a few hotels to choose from.

★ Hotel Pasquale HOTEL €€

(☎0187 81 74 77; www.hotelpasquale.it; Via Fegina 4; s €80-160, d €140-220, tr €170-300; ☽Mar–mid-Nov; ❋☎) Offering soothing views and 15 unusually stylish, modern guest rooms, this friendly seafront hotel is built into Monterosso's medieval sea walls. To find it, exit the train station and go left through the tunnel towards the *centro storico*.

Hotel La Spiaggia HOTEL €€

(☎0187 81 75 67; www.laspiaggiahotel.com; Via Lungomare 98; d €185; ❋☎) Book early (up to six months in advance); welcoming La Spiaggia is right on Monterosso's *spiaggia* (beach) and its 20 large-ish rooms are popular. If you miss out on the fabulous views of a sea-facing room, console yourself with a back room with a terrace instead. The first floor rooms have been recently refurbished.

La Poesia
B&B €€

(☎0187 81 72 83; www.lapoesia-cinqueterre. com; Via Genova 4; d €120; ✳🤙) Shoehorned up a backstreet in the older part of town, La Poesia's three rooms occupy an early-17th-century house, where breakfast is served on a terrace surrounded by lemon trees. Remains open over the winter.

Eating

Along the seafront, restaurants dish up local anchovies straight out of the sea.

Trattoria da Oscar
LIGURIAN €€

(Via Vittorio Emanuele 67; meals €33; ⊙noon-2pm & 7-10pm) Behind Piazza Matteoti, in the heart of the old town, this vaulted dining room is run by a young, friendly team. The town's famed anchovies dominate the menu; whether you go for the standard fried-with-lemon, with a white wine sauce or deep fried, they are all good. No credit cards.

Miky
SEAFOOD €€€

(☎0187 81 76 08; www.ristorantemiky.it; Lungomare Fegina 104; meals €45-60; ⊙noon-2.30pm & 7-10pm Wed-Mon summer) If you're looking for something a litte more elegant than a seafront fry-up, Miky does a seasonal fish menu in a moody, modern dining room. Booking ahead is advised; if you miss out on a table, they also have casual beach-side tables at their *cantina* (wine bar); ask for directions.

Vernazza
POP 865

Vernazza's small harbour – the only secure landing point on the Cinque Terre coast – guards what is perhaps the quaintest of the five villages. Lined with little cafes, a main cobbled street, Via Roma, links seaside Piazza Marconi with the train station. Side streets lead to the village's trademark Genoa-style *caruggi* (narrow lanes), where sea views pop at every turn.

Sights & Activities

Piazza Matteotti and the harbour are a delight. There's a tiny sandy beach here and swimming is possible.

Chiesa di Santa Margherita d'Antiochia
CHURCH

(Piazza Matteotti) The waterfront is framed by a small Gothic-Ligurian church, built in 1318 after a murky legend about the bones of St Margaret being found in a wooden box on a nearby beach. It is notable for its 40m-tall octagonal tower.

Castello Doria
CASTLE

(admission €1.50; ⊙10am-7pm summer, to 6pm winter) This castle, the oldest surviving fortification in the Cinque Terre, commands superb views. Dating to around 1000, it's now largely a ruin except for the circular tower in the centre of the esplanade. To get there, head up the steep, narrow staircase by the harbour.

Vernazza Winexperience
WINE TASTING

(Deck Giani Franzi; ☎331 3433801; www.cinque terrewinetasting.com; Via San Giovanni Battista 41; ⊙5-9pm May-Oct) Sommelier Alessandro Villa's family have lived in Vernazza for over six generations. Let him take you through the rare, small-yield wines that come from the vineyards that tumble down the surrounding hills. While the wine and stupendous sunset view will be pleasure enough, knowing you're also helping keep a unique landscape and culture alive feels good.

Sleeping

★ La Mala
BOUTIQUE HOTEL €€

(☎334 2875718; www.lamala.it; Via San Giovanni Battista 29; d €140-220; ✳🤙) These four rooms are some of the Cinque Terre's nicest. Up in the cliffside heights of the village, they are in a typical Ligurian house that's run by the grandson of the original owner. The fit out is a clean-lined contemporary one, providing both comfort and a place to soak in some fabulous sea views, either from bed or a sunny terrace.

Gianni Franzi Rooms
B&B €€

(☎0187 82 10 03; www.giannifranzi.it; Via San Giovanni Battista 41; d €130; 🤙) Spread over two locations, one above the attached restaurant, the other up the hill, rooms here are an atmospheric mix of antique furniture and super simple traditional architecture, all kept with care. Breakfast on the deck delivers not just *cornetti* and cappucino, but sublime sea-drenched views; there's a small garden under the Doria castle for guest use.

Eating & Drinking

Batti Batti
SNACKS €

(Via Visconti 3; focaccia €3-5, seafood €8-12) Batti Batti knocks out the best foccacia slices in the village (some would say in the whole Cinque Terre), along with bountifully topped pizza. Their *friggitoria*, a few shops down, turns out *fritto misto* (fried seafood) to take away in paper cones.

Gianni Franzi
SEAFOOD €€

(☎0187 82 10 03; www.giannifranzi.it; Piazza Matteotti 5; meals €22-30; ⊙mid-Mar–early Jan) Traditional Cinque Terre seafood (mussels, seafood, ravioli and lemon anchovies) has been served up in this harbourside trattoria since the 1960s. When it comes to seafood this fresh, if it's not broken, don't fix it.

Gambero Rosso
SEAFOOD €€

(www.ristorantegamberorosso.net; Piazza Marconi 7; mains €30-35; ⊙noon-3pm & 7-10.30pm Fri-Wed) If you've been subsisting on focaccia, Gambero's house specials – *tegame di Vernazza* (anchovies with baked potatoes and tomatoes), skewered baby octopus or stuffed mussels – will really hit the spot. Bookings recommended.

Gelateria Vernazza
GELATERIA €

(Via Roma 13; gelato €2-3.50) Slick gelateria with natural, authentic flavours, desert cups and vegan specials.

Burgus Bar
WINE BAR

(Piazza Marconi 4; ⊙7am-1am) A charming little hole in the wall, with only a couple of ringside benches looking over the piazza to the little beach, this neighbourhood bar serves up glasses of the Cinque Terre DOC, a fragrant, ethereal mix of local Albarola, Bosco and Vermentino grapes, breakfast pastries, sandwiches and *aperitvo*. They also stock a range of local produce to take away.

Corniglia

POP 545

Corniglia is the 'quiet' middle village that sits atop a 100m-high rocky promontory surrounded by vineyards. It is the only Cinque Terre settlement with no direct sea access, although steep steps lead down to a rocky cove. Narrow alleys and colourfully painted four-storey houses characterise the ancient core, a timeless streetscape that was namechecked in Boccaccio's *Decameron*. To reach the village proper from the railway station you must first tackle the **Lardarina**, a 377-step brick stairway or jump on a shuttle bus (one way €2.50).

◉ Sights

Corniglia, by virtue of its elevation and central position, is the only place where you can see all five settlements in the same panorama.

La Torre
LOOKOUT

This medieval lookout is reached by a stairway that leads up from the diminutive main square, Piazza Taragio.

Belvedere di Santa Maria
LOOKOUT

Enjoy dazzling 180-degree sea views at this heart-stopping lookout in hilltop Corniglia. To find it, follow Via Fieschi through the village until you eventually reach the clifftop balcony.

Guvano Beach
BEACH

This hard-to-find, clothing-optional beach is situated between Corniga and Vernazza. Getting there involves walking through an abandoned railway tunnel – ask a local for directions.

🛏 Sleeping & Eating

As elsewhere in the Cinque Terre, fish is the mainstay of Corniglia's restaurants – you can't go wrong by asking for whatever's fresh.

Ostello di Corniglia
HOSTEL €

(☎0187 81 25 59; www.ostellocorniglia.com; Via alla Stazione 3; dm/d €24/60; 🛜) One of only two hostels in Cinque Terre, Ostello di Corniglia is perched at the top of the village and has two eight-bed dorms and four doubles (with private bathroom). Prices are negotiable. There's a lockout from 1pm to 3pm. No breakfast.

Case di Corniglia
APARTMENT €

(☎0187 81 23 42; www.casedicorniglia.eu; Via alla Stazione 19; price varies; 🅿🛜) These rent-a-rooms are spread over two buildings in the village's main street. All have kitchens; they're good for families or groups.

🍷 Drinking

★ La Scuna
BAR

(☎347 7997527; Via Fieschi 185; ⊙9am-1am late-March–Nov) Vinyl, beer and a panoramic terrace? This bastion of hipsterdom comes as a surprise in this most traditional of regions but Andrea's welcome is warm and the beers on tap are both cold and a cut way above bottled Peroni.

ANDREW PEACOCK/GETTY IMAGES ©

1. Hiking past vineyards between Manarola and Corniglia
2. Colourful houses in Manarola (p188) 3. Harbour at Vernazza
(p184) 4. Fishing boats at Riomaggiore (p188)

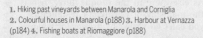

CHRISTOPHER GROENHOUT/GETTY IMAGES ©

Cinque Terre

Climb above the crowds on Cinque Terre's terraced cliffs and you might have to pinch yourself to check that you're still in the 21st century. Rooted in antiquity and bereft of modern interferences, these five historic fishing villages have embellished the Ligurian coastline with subtle human beauty and a fascinating medieval heritage.

Terraced Fields

Cinque Terre's cleverly cultivated cliff terraces are so old no one truly knows who built them. Held in place by hundreds of kilometres of dry stone walls, they add a strange human beauty to a stunning natural landscape.

Manarola

Grapes grow abundantly on Cinque Terre's terraced plots, especially around the village of Manarola. The area's signature wine is the sweet white Sciacchetrà, a blend of Bosco, Albarola and Vermentino grapes best sampled with cheese or sweet desserts.

Riomaggiore

The unofficial capital's pleasantly peeling medieval houses are tucked into a steep ravine. Jump on a boat to best experience one of the Cinque Terre's most iconic views: the warm pastel glow of Riomaggiore's pastel facades as the sun sets.

Vernazza

Sporting the best natural harbour of the five towns, Vernazza rises tightly from its central square. Its tightly clustered streets and lanes are a labyrinth of steep, switchback stairs rewarding the strong of thigh with stunning sea views from a cluster of handkerchief-sized terraces.

Manarola

POP 840

Bequeathed with more grapevines than any other Cinque Terre village, Manarola is famous for its sweet Sciacchetrà wine. It's also awash with priceless medieval relics, supporting claims that it is the oldest of the five. The spirited locals here speak an esoteric local dialect known as Manarolese. Due to its proximity to Riomaggiore (852m away), the village is heavily trafficked, especially by Italian school parties.

⊙ Sights

Piazzale Papa Innocenzo IV PIAZZA

At the northern end of Via Discovolo, you'll come upon this small piazza dominated by a bell tower that was once used as a defensive lookout. Opposite, the **Chiesa di San Lorenzo** dates from 1338 and houses a 15th-century polyptych.

If you're geared up for a steep walk, from nearby Via Rollandi you can follow a path that leads through vineyards to the top of the mountain.

Punta Bonfiglio LOOKOUT

Manarola's prized viewpoint is on a rocky promontory on the path out of town towards Corniglia where walkers stop for classic photos of the village. A rest area, including a kid's playground, has been constructed here and there's also a bar just below. Nearby are the ruins of an old chapel once used as a shelter by local farmers.

🛏 Sleeping & Eating

Ostello 5 Terre HOSTEL €

(☑0187 92 00 39; www.hostel5terre.com; Via Riccobaldi 21; dm/d/f €25/70/108; ⊙closed mid-Jan–mid-Feb; @ 🛜) Manarola's hostel sits at the top of the village next to the Chiesa di San Lorenzo. It has single-sex, six-bed dorms, each with their own bathroom and great views, and several double and family rooms.

Hotel Marina Piccola BOUTIQUE HOTEL €€

(☑0187 92 07 70; www.hotelmarinapiccola.com; Via Birolli 120; s/d €110/140; 🕸🛜) This recently refurbished hotel has 12 big, comfortable, contemporary rooms, with a few looking over the sea. The lovely lobby and lounge area, which sports a surprisingly on-trend interior, is a welcome respite from the busy daytime streets. A real find

at this price, although there is a minimum two-day stay in summer.

★La Torretta Charme & Relax BOUTIQUE HOTEL €€€

(☑0187 92 03 27; www.torrettas.com; Vico Volto 20; s/d/ste €170/200/300; 🕸🛜) A recent makeover has taken this already outstanding small luxury hotel into the extraordinary. Sitting high up above the village, a collection of both private and public terraces commands spectacular views. Decor differs in each of the rooms, with a seductive Italian maximalist mash of contemporary pieces, mosaic tiles, murals and unexpected surprises like a dedicated toilet TV. Service here is a priority, with twice-daily room servicing, breakfast in bed if you want it, and they'll arrange luggage transfers from the station or parking area.

Da Aristide SEAFOOD €

(☑0187 92 00 00; www.aristidemanarola.it; Via Discovolo 290; meals €25; ⊙11am-11pm Fri-Wed) Up the hill, not far from the train station, Aristide has tables in an old village house and in a bright, modern marquee terrace on the square. Order a few of the heaped plates of stuffed anchovies or lemon-doused grilled octopus to share or keep one of their fish ravioli or homemade papparedelle wtih mussels and aubergine for yourself.

Marina Piccola SEAFOOD €€

(☑0187 76 20 65; www.hotelmarinapiccola.com; Via Lo Scalo 16; meals €30; ⊙noon-10.30pm Wed-Mon; 🛜) A shoal of fish dishes, including some tasty antipasti like *soppressata di polpo* (sliced boiled octopus) are served up here along with right-by-the-sea-views.

Riomaggiore

POP 1695

Cinque Terre's easternmost village, Riomaggiore is the largest of the five and acts as its unofficial HQ (the main park office is based here). Its peeling pastel buildings march down a steep ravine to a tiny harbour – the region's favourite postcard view – and glow romantically at sunset.

⊙ Sights & Activities

Outside the train station near the water's edge, murals depict the back-breaking work of Cinque Terre farmers, who, over the centuries, built the Cinque Terre with their bare hands. The village also has a couple of small churches and a ruined castle on a headland overlooking the settlement.

Via dell'Amore
WALKING

This beautiful coastal path that links Riomaggiore to Manarola in a leisurely 20-minute stroll was, until rock slides caused its closure in 2012, the Cinque Terre's most popular. The name is a nod to the number of marriages the opening of the path engendered between villagers of the once geographically divided hamlets.

The first 200m of the path, from Manarola's train station to Bar Via dell'Amore, reopened in spring 2015. It's uncertain when the rest will be completed, with 2017 a mooted date, much to the consternation of locals; the path is not just a thoroughfare for them, but an integral part of village social life.

Torre Guardiola
NATURE RESERVE

(admission €1.50; ◷9am-1pm & 4-7pm Feb-Jul, Sep & Oct, 9am-1pm Aug) 🌿 Birdlife and local flora can be seen from a nature observation and bird-watching centre on a promontory of land just east of Riomaggiore. The building was a former naval installation in WWII, known as La Batteria Racchia. It's reachable via a trail that starts just west of Fossola Beach.

Fossola Beach
BEACH

This small pebbly beach is immediately southeast of Riomaggiore marina. It's rugged but secluded. Swimmers should be wary of rocks and currents.

Cooperative Sub 5 Terre
DIVING

(☑0187 92 00 11; www.5terrediving.it; Via San Giacomo; ◷seasonal) 🌿 To dive or snorkel in the translucent waters of the protected marine park, contact this outfit in the subway at the bottom of Via Colombo. It also rents out canoes and kayaks.

🛏 Sleeping

B&Bs and a handful of hotels are situated in the village, along with several room- and apartment-rental agencies.

La Casa di Venere
RENTAL ACCOMMODATION €€

(☑338 3297153; www.lacasadivenere.com; Via Colombo 194; s/d/t/q €60/120/ €150/180) This agency offers some of the cheapest harbourside rooms. All are clean, bright and modern, and some have to-die-for views.

Hotel Zorza
HOTEL €€

(www.hotelzorza.com; Via Colombo 231; d €130; ⏏) Basic but well-kept rooms are spread across the sinuous 17th-century house of a former winegrower.

Eating

Dau Cila
MODERN ITALIAN €€

(☑0187 76 00 32; www.ristorantedaucila.com; Via San Giacomo 65; meals €40; ◷8am-2am Mar-Oct) Perched within pebble-lobbing distance of Riomaggiore's wee harbour, Dau Cila is a smart, kitsch-free zone, and specialises in classic seafood and local wines. Pair the best Cinque Terre whites with cold plates such as smoked tuna with apples and lemon, or lemon-marinated anchovies.

La Lampara
MODERN ITALIAN €€

(Via Malborghetto 2; meals €25; ◷7am-midnight) There are always lots of tourists here, but you won't feel like one as the service is so genuinely personable. Fish dishes predominate, though the pizza and pasta *al pesto* are also made with care.

Around Cinque Terre

La Spezia
POP 95.641

It's an understandable oversight. Situated minutes to the east of Cinque Terre by train, the hard-working port town of La Spezia is routinely overlooked. But it's an affordable place to overnight if you're heading to the Cinque Terre, and worthy of a once-over. It's home to Italy's largest naval base, the winding streets of the old town are atmospheric and there are plenty of cosy trattorias showcasing the Ligurian table at its best.

La Spezia's bustle peaks on 19 March, the **feast day** of the city's patron saint, San Giuseppe (St Joseph). Celebrations see a giant market fill the port and surrounding streets, and the naval base (off-limits the rest of the year) opens to the public.

◉ Sights

Museo Amedeo Lia
MUSEUM

(http://museolia.spezianet.it; Via Prione 234; adult/reduced €7/4.50; ◷10am-6pm Tue-Sun) This fine-arts museum in a restored 17th-century friary is La Spezia's star cultural attraction. The collection spans the 13th to 18th centuries and includes paintings by masters such as Tintoretto, Montagna, Titian and Pietro

Lorenzetti. Also on show are Roman bronzes and ecclesiastical treasures, such as Limoges crucifixes and illuminated musical manuscripts.

Castello di San Giorgio CASTLE
(http://museodelcastello.spezianet.it; Via XXVII Marzo; adult/reduced €5.50/4; ☉ 9.30am-12.30pm Wed-Mon, 2-5pm Wed-Sun, 5-8pm in summer) An assortment of local archaeological artefacts from prehistoric to medieval times are displayed at the city's hilltop fortifications.

🛏 Sleeping

There are plenty of cheap hotels around the train station, but the city's B&Bs are a better deal.

Alta Marea GUESTHOUSE €
(☏ 377 5448365; www.affittacamerealtamarea.it; Via Torino 70; d €70-100; 🅿 🛜) Friendly Andrea will be there to great you at this small B&B and can be counted on for his local knowledge and restaurant tips. Rooms are spotless, airy and bright and the location is handy for making an early morning train to the Cinque Terre.

Albergo Birillo HOTEL €
(☏ 0187 73 26 66; www.albergobirillo.it; Via Dei Mille 11/13; s/d €65/100; 🛜) This haven has rather tight-fitting rooms, which are more than made up for by the ultrafriendly owners. A few blocks from Via Prione and near plenty of good places to eat.

🍴 Eating & Drinking

Vicolo Intherno MODERN ITALIAN €€
(www.vicolointherno.it; Via della Canonica 20; meals €30; ☉ noon-3pm & 7-midnight Tue-Sat) 🍴 Take a seat around chunky wooden tables beneath beamed ceilings at this buzzing Slow Food–affiliated restaurant and wash down the *torte di verdure* (Ligurian vegetable pie), stockfish or roast beef with local vintages.

Odioilvino WINE BAR
(☏ 392 2141825; Via Daniele Manin; ☉ noon-3.30pm & 6-11.30pm) A dark, bohemian, elegantly disheveled wine bar on a pretty street in the pedestrian centre, Odioilvino is a fine place to relax with locals over a local or French wine. Small plates such as a fish tartare or octopus salad are on offer, too.

ℹ Information

Cinque Terre Park Office (☏ 0187 74 35 00; ☉ 7am-8pm) Inside La Spezia's train station.

Tourist Office (www.myspezia.it; Viale Italia 5; ☉ 9am-5pm Mon-Sat, to 1pm Sun)

ℹ Getting There & Away

Buses run by **Azienda Trasporti Consortile** (ATC; www.atclaspezia.it) are the only way to reach Porto Venere (€1.50, approximately every 30 minutes) and Lerici (€1.50, approximately every 15 minutes). Catch buses on Via Domenico Chiodo close to the intersection with Via del Prione.

La Spezia is on the Genoa–Rome railway line and is also connected to Milan (€26.50, three hours, four daily), Turin (€27.50, 3½ hours, several daily) and Pisa (€5.20, 50 minutes, almost hourly). The Cinque Terre and other coastal towns are easily accessible by train and boat.

Porto Venere
POP 3942

If Cinque Terre were ever to pick up an honorary sixth member, Porto Venere would surely be it. Perched on the dreamy Gulf of Poets' western promontory, the village's sinuous seven- and eight-storey harbourfront houses form an almost impregnable citadel around the muscular Castello Doria. The Romans built Portus Veneris as a base en route from Gaul to Spain, and in later years the Byzantines, Lombards, Genovese and Napoleon all passed through here. Cinque Terre's marathon-length Sentiero Rosso (Red Trail) to Levanto starts here, just behind the castle.

◉ Sights

Outside the hectic summer season, Porto Venere is something of a ghost town – and all the more alluring for it.

Chiesa di San Pietro CHURCH
This stunning wind- and wave-lashed church, built in 1198 in Gothic style, stands on the ruins of a 5th-century palaeo-Christian church. Before that it was a Roman temple dedicated to the goddess Venus, born from the foam of the sea, from whom Porto Venere takes its name.

Castello Doria CASTLE
(admission €3; ☉ 10.30am-1.30pm & 2.30-6pm) No one knows when the original castle was built, though the current structure – a formidable example of Genoese military architecture – dates from the 16th century. A highly strategic citadel in its time, it once stood on the front line with Genoa's maritime feud with Pisa. There are magnificent views from its ornate terraced gardens.

Grotta Arpaia
CAVE

At the end of the quay, a Cinque Terre panorama unfolds from the rocky terraces of Grotta Arpaia, a former haunt of Lord Byron, who once swam across the gulf from Porto Venere to Lerici to visit his mate Shelley. Traces of a pagan temple have been uncovered on the quay, inside the black-and-white-marble **Chiesa di San Pietro**, which was built in 1277.

Just off the promontory lie the tiny islands of **Palmaria**, **Tino** and **Tinetto**.

🛏 Sleeping & Eating

A half-dozen or so restaurants line Calata Doria, by the sea. A block inland, Porto Venere's main old-town street, Via Cappellini, has several tasty choices.

La Lanterna
B&B €

(☎ 0187 79 22 91; www.lalanterna-portovenere.it; Via Capellini 109; d €75-100; ▣) Down by Porto Venere's picturesque harbourfront, this little guesthouse has just two homey rooms (there's also an option of a four-person apartment on request).

Anciua
SNACKS €

(☎ 331 7719605; Via Cappellini 40; snacks from €5; ⊙ 10am-7pm) A perfect spot to pick up something to snack on while dangling your feet off the nearby port, this is Ligurian street food made with love. Grab a panini stuffed with anchovies or cod and olive paste, or pick up a whole spinach pie for a picnic. The sweet, fragrant rice pudding cake is also highly recommended.

ℹ Information

Tourist Office (Piazza Bastreri 7; ⊙ 10am-noon & 3-8pm Jun-Aug, to 6pm Thu-Tue Sep-May) Sells a couple of useful maps and walking guides in English.

ℹ Getting There & Away

Porto Venere is served by daily buses from La Spezia.

From late March to October, **Consorzio Marittimo Turistico Cinque Terre Golfo dei Poeti** (☎ 0187 73 29 87; www.navigazionegolfodeipoeti.it) sails from Porto Venere to/from Cinque Terre villages (all day, all stops €25, one way €20, afternoon only ticket €20) and runs boat excursions to the islands of Palmaria, Tino and Tinetto (€12).

Lerici & Around
POP 10,150

Magnolia, yew and cedar trees grow in the 1930s public gardens at Lerici, an exclusive retreat of terraced villas clinging to the cliffs along its beach. The seafront is lined with places to eat and drink and is a favoured *passeggiata* spot; in another age Byron and Shelley sought inspiration here.

◉ Sights & Activities

From Lerici, a scenic 3km coastal stroll leads northwest to **San Terenzo**, a seaside village with a sandy beach and Genoese castle. The Shelleys stayed at the waterfront Villa Magni (closed to visitors) in the early 1820s and Percy drowned here when his boat sank off the coast in 1822 on a return trip from Livorno.

Another coastal stroll, 4km southeast, takes you past magnificent little bays to **Tellaro**, a fishing hamlet with pink-and-orange houses cluttered about narrow lanes and tiny squares. Sit on the rocks at the **Chiesa San Giorgio** and imagine an octopus ringing the church bells – which, according to legend, it did to warn the villagers of a Saracen attack.

🛏 Sleeping & Eating

Locanda Miranda
INN €€

(☎ 0187 96 40 12; Via Fiascherina 92; d €120, set menus €40-60; ▣) Tellaro, a few kilometres around the bay from Lerici proper, is home to this gourmet hideaway, a traditional seven-room inn with art- and antiques-decorated rooms, and a Michelin-starred restaurant specialising exclusively in seafood. Half-board packages can be arranged.

Eco Del Mare
RESORT €€€

(☎ 0187 96 86 09; www.ecodelmare.it; Via Fiascherino 4; d €280; ⊙ May-Sep) One of the Riviera's loveliest beaches is home to this exclusive, remote-seeming hotel and beach club. An insouciant glamour pervades here; rooms are deeply romantic, filled with an idiosyncratic mix of decor, and the restaurant, despite the prices, gives off beach shack vibes. Day guests pay €60 to €100 for two people, depending on the month, which includes sun loungers and umbrellas.

ⓘ Information

Tourist Office (Via Biaggini 6; ⊙9am-1pm & 3-5.30pm Mon-Sat, to 1pm Sun) Can advise on walking and cycling in the area, as well as accommodation.

Riviera di Ponente

Curving west from Genoa to the French border, the Ponente stretch of the Ligurian coast is more down-to-earth than the flashy Rivieria di Levante. As a result, it shelters some relatively well-priced escape hatches, particularly along the stretch of coast from Noli to Finale Ligure.

Savona

POP 62,500

Behind Savona's sprawling port facilities, the city's unexpectedly graceful medieval centre is well worth a stop. Among the old-town treasures to survive destruction by Genoese forces in the 16th century are the baroque **Cattedrale di Nostra Signora Assunta** (Piazza Cattedrale) and the lumbering **Fortezza del Priamàr** (Piazza Priamar).

◉ Sights & Activities

Civico Museo Storico Archeologico   MUSEUM
(www.comune.savona.it; Piazza Priamàr; admission €4; ⊙10.30am-3pm Wed-Mon, reduced hr winter) Part of the imposing Fortezza del Priamàr, this museum has a small but interesting collection of local archaeological finds

Pinacoteca Civica Savona   GALLERY
(www.comune.savona.it; Piazza Chabrol 1/2; admission €6; ⊙10am-1.30pm daily, 3.30-6.30pm Thu-Sat) The city pinacoteca has an important collection of religious painting dating from the 14th to 15th centuries, including a Madonna and child by Taddeo di Bartolo, along with two Picassos.

Whale Watching Trips   WHALE WATCHING
(www.whalewatchliguria.it; tickets €35) Six- to seven-hour whale-watching trips depart Savona at 10am from July to September.

🛏 Sleeping & Eating

The tourist office can help book accommodation, both in the city and the coastal towns to the west.

Villa de' Franceschini   HOSTEL €
(☑019 26 32 22; www.ostello-de-franceschini.com; Via alla Strà 'Conca Verde' 29; dm/s/d €16/22/38; ⊙mid-Mar–Oct; ℗ @) Savona has one of Liguria's few hostels, a big place set in a sprawling park, 3km from the train station.

Mare Hotel   HOTEL €€
(☑019 26 32 77; www.marehotel.it; Via Nizza 41; d €160; ❄@🛜🏊) The four-star seafront Mare Hotel with its infinty pool, private beach and candle-lit open-air restaurant is Italian beach bling in action. New rooms adopt a Milanese nightclub aesthetic, while older rooms (around €100) are comfortable, if a little frumpy. It's 2km west along the beach from the station – regular buses run there.

Vino e Farinata   TRADITIONAL ITALIAN €
(Via Pia 15; meals €20; ⊙11am-10pm Tue-Sat) To enter this place in the cobbled centre, you'll have to walk past the two ancient chefs: one shovelling fish into a wood-fired oven and the other mixing up batter in a barrel-sized whisking machine. The result: Ligurian *farinata* (flat bread made from chickpea flour), the menu staple in this very local restaurant that also pours some excellent local wines.

ⓘ Information

Tourist Office (Via Paleocapa 76r; ⊙9am-12.30pm & 3-6pm Mon-Sat, to 1pm Sun) A short stroll from Savona's sandy beach.

ⓘ Getting There & Around

SAR (☑0182 2 15 44) and **ACTS** (www.tpllinea. it) buses, departing from Piazza del Popolo and the train station, are the best options for reaching points inland.

Trains run along the coast to Genoa's Stazione Brignole (€4.70, 45 minutes, almost hourly) and San Remo (€8, 1¾ hours, eight daily).

Corsica Ferries (www.corsica-ferries.fr) runs up to three boats daily between Savona's Porto Vado and Corsica.

Finale Ligure

POP 11,650

Set amid lush Mediterranean vegetation, this township comprises several districts. **Finale Ligure** has a wide, fine-sand beach. The walled medieval centre, known as **Finalborgo**, is a knot of twisting alleys set 1km back from the coast on the Pora river. **Finale Marina** sits on the waterfront, the more residential **Finale Pia** runs along the

Sciusa river and the Finalese rises up into the hinterland.

🛏️ Sleeping & Eating

The promenade along Via San Pietro and Via Concezione is crammed with eateries.

★ Val Ponce AGRITURISMO €
(🕿329 3154169; www.valleponci.it; Val Ponci 22, Localita Verzi; d/apt €80/160) Only 4km from the beach, Val Ponce feels deliciously wild, tucked away in a rugged Ligurian valley. Horses graze, grapevines bud and the restaurant turns out fresh Ligurian dishes, with vegetables and herbs from a kitchen garden. On weekend evenings and Sunday lunch, there's live music or classic vinyl. Rooms are simple but show the keen eye of the Milanese-escapee owners.

There are some wonderful hiking and moutain-biking paths around here: ask the knowledgeable Giorgio for a map and tips of the historical and archaeological sites to look out for.

Hotel Florenz HOTEL €
(🕿019 69 56 67; www.hotelflorenz.it; Via Celesia 1; s/d €70/110; ⊗closed Nov & Feb; 🅿@🏊👪) This rambling 18th-century former convent just outside Finalborgo's village walls (800m from the sea) is simple and homey but one of the area's most atmospheric spots to sleep.

Osteria ai Cuattru Canti OSTERIA €
(Via Torcelli 22; set menus €20; ⊗noon-2pm & 8-10pm Tue-Sun) Simple and good Ligurian specialities are cooked up at this rustic place in Finalborgo's historic centre.

ℹ️ Information

Tourist Office (Via San Pietro 14; ⊗9am-12.30pm & 3-6pm Mon-Sat year-round, 9am-noon Sun Jul & Aug) From the train station on Piazza Vittorio Veneto, at Finale Marina's western end, walk down Via Saccone to the sea and this office.

ℹ️ Getting There & Away

TPL (🕿0182 2 15 44; www.tpllinea.it) buses yo-yo every 30 minutes to/from Finale Ligure and Savona (€2.30, 50 minutes), stopping en route in Finalborgo (€1.20, five minutes) and Noli (€1.50, 20 minutes).

San Remo

POP 57,000

Fifty kilometres east of Europe's premier gambling capital lies San Remo, Italy's own Monte Carlo, a sun-dappled Mediterranean resort with a casino, a clutch of ostentatious villas and lashings of Riviera-style grandeur. Known colloquially as the City of Flowers for its colourful summer blooms, San Remo also stages an annual music festival (the supposed inspiration for the Eurovision Song Contest) and the world's longest professional one-day cycling race, the 298km Milan–San Remo classic.

During the mid-19th century the city became a magnet for regal European exiles, such as Empress Elisabeth of Austria and Tsar Nicola of Russia, who favoured the town's balmy winters. Swedish inventor Alfred Nobel maintained a villa here, and an onion-domed Russian Orthodox church reminiscent of Moscow's St Basil's Cathedral still turns heads down by the seafront.

Beyond the manicured lawns and belle époque hotels, San Remo hides a little-visited old town, a labyrinth of twisting lanes that cascade down the Ligurian hillside. Curling around the base is a 25km bike and walking path that tracks the coast as far as Imperia, following the course of a former railway line and passing through the town's two character-filled harbours.

◉ Sights

Chiesa Russa Ortodossa CHURCH
(Via Nuvoloni 2; admission €1; ⊗9.30am-noon & 3-6pm) Built for the Russian community that followed Tsarina Maria to San Remo in 1906, the Russian Orthodox church – with its onion domes and heavenly pale-blue interior – was designed by Alexei Shchusev, who later planned Lenin's mausoleum in Moscow. These days it's used as an exhibition space for Russian icons.

Il Casinò Municipale CASINO
(www.casinosanremo.it; Corso degli Inglesi) San Remo's belle époque casino, one of only four in Italy, was dealing cards when Vegas was still a waterhole in the desert. The building dates from 1905 and was designed by Parisian architect Eugenio Ferret. Slot machines (over 400 of them) open at 10am; other games (roulette, blackjack, poker etc) kick off at 2.30pm. Dress smart-casual and be sure to bring ID.

Museo Civico MUSEUM
(Palazzo Borea d'Olmo; Corso Matteotti 143; adult/reduced €3/2; ⊗9am-noon & 2-7pm Tue-Sat) FREE Housed in a 15th-century *palazzo*, several rooms in this museum, some with fine

San Remo

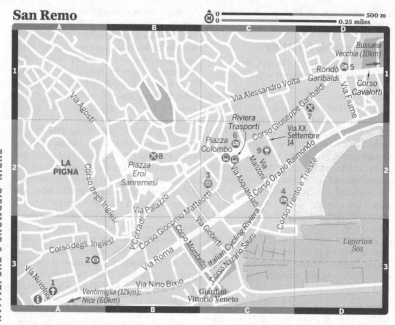

San Remo

◉ Sights
1 Chiesa Russa Ortodossa	A3
2 Il Casinò Municipale	A3
3 Museo Civico	C2

⬤ Sleeping
4 B&B San Remo	C2
5 Hotel Liberty	D1
6 Pisolo Resort	C2

✖ Eating
7 Cuvèa	D1
8 Ristorante Urbicia Vivas	B2

◉ Drinking & Nightlife
9 Pietro	C2

frescoed ceilings, display local prehistoric and Roman archaeological finds, paintings and temporary exhibitions. Highlights include Maurizio Carrega's 1808 homage, *Gloria di San Napoleone*, and bronze statues by Franco Bargiggia.

Bussana Vecchia HISTORIC SITE
Ten kilometres northeast of San Remo lies an intriguing artists' colony. On Ash Wednesday 1887, an earthquake destroyed the village of Bussana Vecchia. It remained a ghost town until the 1960s, when artists and counterculture devotees moved in and began rebuilding the ruins using the original stones from the rubble. A thriving community of international artists remains in residence today. To get there, take a bus to Bussana, 5km east of San Remo, and walk up (30 minutes).

🏃 Activities

Parco Costiero della Riviera dei Fiori CYCLING
As befits a city that hosts professional cycling's greatest Spring Classic, San Remo has a 25km *pista ciclabile* (cycling path) through what is known as the Parco Costiero della Riviera dei Fiori. The path, which runs along the route of a former railway line, connects Ospedaletti to San Lorenzo al Mare via San Remo and eight other seaside towns.

Bike-hire outlets and refreshment/rest stops are set up along the route, including at San Remo's old train station, Stazione Vecchia.

🎊 Festivals & Events

Corso Fiorito CULTURAL
Held over the last weekend in January, this colourful parade kicks off the town's annual festivities.

Festival di San Remo   MUSIC
(www.festivaldisanremo.com) Celebrating Italian popular music, this festival has been going strong since 1951, and attracts top Italian and international talent each March.

Rally Storico   CAR RALLY
(www.acisanremo.it/rallysanremo) In April, San Remo's famous car rally revs up for cars made between 1931 and 1981.

🛏 Sleeping

San Remo has no shortage of hotels, although summer and festival times can be busy and a few places shut from September until just before Christmas.

B&B San Remo   B&B €
(☑ 320 4253218; www.bbsanremo.it; Corso Nazario Sauro 59; d/t €60/90) A delightful mother-daughter team, Piera and Alice, run this comfortable apartment stay like a traditional B&B, with breakfast and freshly made coffee ready for you at an appointed time, but otherwise there's absolute privacy. There's a second bedroom available if you're travelling with a family, and Alice is happy to help organise places to eat and explore.

Pisolo Resort   B&B €
(☑ 340 8748323; www.pisoloresort.it; Piazza Colombo 29; s/d €70/90; ❄ ☎) Hard to find despite being in San Remo's main square, Pisolo offers five modern rooms. There's no reception but you'll get a basket of breakfast snacks and a coffee machine, and staff are on call.

Hotel Liberty   HOTEL €
(☑ 0184 50 99 52; www.hotellibertysanremo.com; Rondò Garibaldi 2; s/d €45/85; P ❄) A 10-room hotel is set in a Liberty-style villa off a small traffic circle about 100m from the train station. It's quiet, clean and run by helpful young owners.

🍴 Eating & Drinking

Cheap trattorias fill the old-town alleys around Piazza Eroi Sanremesi and open-air snack bars stud the length of Corso Nazario Sauro, the promenade overlooking the old port.

Cuvèa   TRADITIONAL ITALIAN €
(Corso Giuseppe Garibaldi 110; meals €20; ☺ noon-2.30pm & 7-10pm) This cosy, brightly lit place lined with wine bottles overflows with locals tucking into homemade traditional dishes such as pesto-doused pasta; the most genial host in town.

Ristorante Urbica Vivas   LIGURIAN €€
(☑ 0184 57 55 66; Piazza Dolori 5; meals €30; ☺ 10.30am-midnight) Basking in a quiet medieval square in San Remo's remarkable old town, Urbicia is slavishly faithful to old Ligurian recipes with a strong bias towards seafood. There's a €12 lunch deal and Friday night is risotto night.

Pietro   WINE BAR
(☑ 0184 50 72 11; www.dapietrosanremo.it; Via XX Settembre 14) A lively if sophisticated bar once you've had enough seaside fun for the day. Friendly staff, excellent wines and great *aperitivo* snacks draw the locals.

ℹ Information

Tourist Office (www.visitrivieradeifiori.it; Largo Nuvoloni 1; ☺ 9am-7pm Mon-Sat, 9am-1pm Sun; 🛗)

ℹ Getting There & Away

Riviera Trasporti (Piazza Colombo 42) buses leave regularly from the bus station for the French border, and destinations east along the coast and inland.

From San Remo's underground train station there are trains to/from Genoa (€9.80, 2½ hours, hourly), Ventimiglia (€2.70, 15 minutes, hourly) and stations in between.

Ventimiglia

POP 25,693

Bordertown Ventimiglia once harboured a stoic Roman town known as Albintimulium, which survived until the 5th century AD, when it was besieged by the Goths. These days it's besieged by a weekly horde of French bargain hunters who cross the border each market day.

◎ Sights

On a hill on the western bank of the Roia river, Ventimiglia's medieval town is crowned with a 12th-century **cathedral** (Via del Capo). The town itself is largely residential.

Area Archeologica   ARCHAEOLOGICAL SITE
(☺ 3-5.30pm Sat & Sun) FREE Sandwiched between the road and the railway line on the eastern edge of town, these Roman ruins bear testimony to Ventimiglia's Roman romance and include the remains of an amphitheatre and baths dating from the 2nd and 3rd centuries AD.

DOLCEAQUA AFTERNOON

Up a narrow, dead-end valley lies Dolceaqua, a serene medieval town that once inspired Monet. Its original, steeply sited heart is watched over by a recently restored castle, while its new town, a typical 19th-century affair, sits across a fast-flowing river, joined by an ancient humpback stone bridge. It's a lovely place to simply wander the *carrugi* (laneways) and have a leisurely lunch away from the mayhem of the coast.

Join the fashionably dressed French-border hoppers at **Casa e Bottega** (340 5665339; www.ristocasaebottega.it; Piazza Garibaldi 2; meals €25; noon-3pm daily, 6-10pm Fri-Sun) a stylishly bucolic, all-day restaurant, cafe, homewares shop and general village epicentre. Lunch and dinnner dishes are fresh, bold reworkings of local dishes, and almost have a new world sensibility. Perfect fare for alfresco dining with a jug of wine.

Market
MARKET

(8am-3pm Fri) Ventimiglia is best known for its huge Friday market when hundreds of stalls sell food, clothes, homewares, baskets and everything else under the sun. The market is concentrated on Piazza della Libertà, near the river.

Giardini Botanici Hanbury
GARDENS

(www.giardinihanbury.com; Corso Montecarlo 43; adult/reduced €7.50/4.50; 9.30am-6pm) Established in 1867 by English businessman Sir Thomas Hanbury, the 18-hectare Villa Hanbury estate is planted with 5800 botanical species from five continents, including cacti, palm groves and citrus orchards. Today it's a protected area, under the care of the University of Genoa.

Take bus 1a from Via Cavour in Ventimiglia; the bus continues on to the Ponte San Lodovico frontier post, from where you can walk down to the Balzi Rossi caves and beach on the French border.

Eating

Cheap and cheerful eateries congregate around Via Cavour.

Pasta & Basta
LIGURIAN €

(0184 23 08 78; Via Marconi 20; meals €20; noon-3pm & 7-10pm Tue-Sun, lunch only Mon) Duck into the underpass near the seafront on the border side of town to the perpetually redeveloping port area. Various house-made fresh pasta can be mixed and matched with a large menu of sauces, including a good pesto or *salsa di noci* (walnut puree), and washed down with a carafe of their pale and refreshing Pigato, a local white.

Information

Tourist Office (Lungo Roja Rossi; 9am-12.30pm & 3.30-7pm Mon-Sat Jul & Aug, 9am-12.30pm & 3-6.30pm Mon-Sat Sep-Jun) Just steps from the train station.

Getting There & Away

From the **train station** (Via della Stazione), Corso della Repubblica leads to the beach. Trains connect Ventimiglia with Genoa (€13.20, two to 3½ hours, hourly), Nice (50 minutes, hourly) and other destinations in France.

PIEDMONT

POP 4.36 MILLION

Italy's second-largest region is arguably its most elegant: a purveyor of Slow Food and fine wine, regal *palazzi* and an atmosphere that is superficially more *français* than *italiano*. But dig deeper and you'll discover that Piedmont has 'Made in Italy' stamped all over it. Emerging from the chaos of the Austrian wars, the unification movement first exploded here in the 1850s, when the noble House of Savoy provided the nascent nation with its first prime minister and its dynastic royal family.

Most Piedmont journeys start in the stately Turin, famous for football and Fiats. Beyond the car factories, Piedmont is also notable for its food – everything from rice to white truffles – and pretty pastoral landscapes not unlike nearby Tuscany.

The region's smaller towns were once feuding fiefdoms that bickered over trade and religion. Today the biggest skirmishes are more likely to be over recipes and vintages as they vie for the gourmet traveller euro.

Turin

POP 911,800 / ELEV 240M

There's a whiff of Paris in Turin's elegant tree-lined boulevards and echoes of Vienna in its stately art nouveau cafes, but make no mistake – this elegant, Alp-fringed city is utterly self-possessed. The innovative Torinese gave the world its first saleable hard chocolate, perpetuated one of its greatest mysteries (the Holy Shroud), popularised a best-selling car (the Fiat) and inspired the black-and-white stripes of one of the planet's most iconic football teams (Juventus).

Turin also gave the world Italy as we now know it: Piedmont, with its wily Torinese president, the Count of Cavour, was the engine room of the Risorgimento (literally 'the Resurgence', referring to Italian unification). Turin also briefly served as Italy's first capital and donated its monarchy – the venerable, possibly past it, House of Savoy – to the newly unified Italian nation in 1861.

The 2006 Winter Olympics shook the city from a deep post-industrial malaise, and sparked an urban revival, with a cultural knock-on effect that has seen a contemporary art, architecture and design scene blossom in the city.

History

The ancient Celtic-Ligurian city of Taurisia was destroyed by Hannibal in 218 BC and the Roman colony of Augusta Taurinorum, established here almost two centuries later, saw succeeding invasions of Goths, Lombards and Franks. In 1563 the Savoys abandoned their old capital of Chambéry (now in France) to set up court in Turin, which shared the dynasty's fortunes thereafter. The Savoys annexed Sardinia in 1720, but Napoleon put an end to their power when he occupied Turin in 1798. Turin was then controlled by Austria and Russia before Vittorio Emanuele I restored the House of Savoy and re-entered Turin in 1814. Nevertheless, Austria remained the true power throughout northern Italy until the Risorgimento in 1861, when Turin became the nation's inaugural capital. Its capital status lasted only

TURIN IN...

One Day

Begin your day with a coffee at one of Piazza San Carlo's spelendid cafes, then hit the **Museo Egizio** (p201) before the crowds. Then take in the Savoy splendour of beautiful Piazza Castello before heading to **Consorzio** (p208) for lunch. Stock up on Piedmont's gourmet produce at the city branch of **Eataly** (p207), then take in the views form the **Mole Antonelliana** (p202). An *apertivo* at **Bar Cavour** (p210) may morph into dinner or grab a few small plates at **Banco vini e alimenti** (p208).

Two Days

After a heart-starting chocolate coffee bomb at **Al Bicerin** (p209), jump on the metro to Lingotto and **Pinacoteca Agnelli** (p205) to see a few modern masterpieces and for a lap of the iconic Fiat rooftop track. Head to **Eataly** (p211) next door for a browse and lunch, then make your way over to the **Museo Nazionale dell'Automobile** (p205) followed by a boat back down the Po for a drink at one of the riverside bars or a quick jog up to the **Basilica di Superga** (p205) for sunset views.

Four Days

Contemporary art lovers can devote a whole day to galleries, with morning visits to **GAM** (p203), **Fondazione Sandretto Re Rebaudengo** (p204) and **Fondazione Merz** (p204), then an afternoon trip to Castello di Rivoli's **Museo d'Arte Contemporanea** (p203). Or visit the **Museo della Sindone** (p202), for the history of the Holy Shroud, and the **Museo Nazionale del Risorgimento Italiano** (p202). Snack on waffles at **Gofri Piemontéisa** (p207) before strolling the shopping strips of Via Lagrange or Garibaldi, or try the heaving **Porta Palazzo** (p209) market, with a gelato from **Grom** (p208). Next morning pick up picnic supplies at **Sapori di Tassinari** (p211) and take a final leisurely day to explore the **Reggia di Venaria Reale** (p204). Back in town, it's time for an alfresco *aperitivo* on Piazza Emanuel Filiberto and evening bar-hopping at the Quadrilatero Romano.

Piedmont

0 50 km
0 25 miles

SWITZERLAND

FRANCE

LOMBARDY

VALLE
D'AOSTA

Chamonix

Mont Blanc
(4810m)

Courmayeur

Allein

Aosta

Pila

Cogne

Val Soana

Val Grande

Parco Nazionale
del Gran Paradiso

Valle Orco

Val di Ala

Orco

Dora Baltea

Lessolo

Caselle
Airport

A5

Ivrea

Biella

A4

A5

Matterhorn
(Monte Cervino)
(4478m)

Monte Rosa
(4633m)

Punta Indren
(3260m)

Macugnaga

Parco Naturale
Alta Valle Sesia

Alagna
Valsesia

Balmuccia

Rassa

Valsesia

Sacro Monte
di Varallo

Varallo

Borgosesia

Vercelli

River Sesia

A26

Lago
d'Orta

Omegna

Monte
Mottarone
(1491m)

Borgomanero

Novara

A4

Verbania

Parco
della Val
Grande

Cannobio

Stresa

Arona

Lago
Maggiore

Borromeau
Islands

Malpensa
Airport

A7

Domodossola

Locarno

Bellinzona

Lugano

Varese

Como

Milan

Pavia

Vigevano

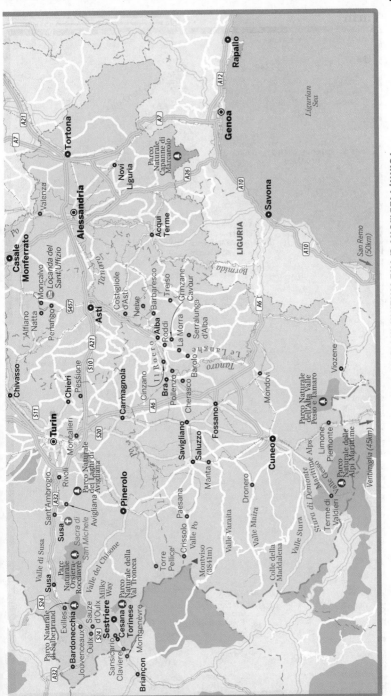

Turin

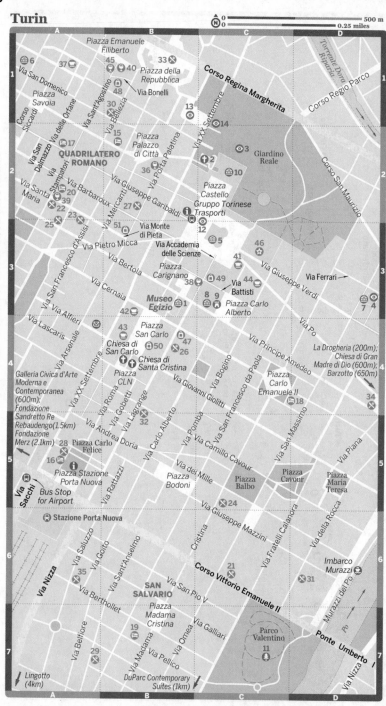

Turin

until 1864, and the parliament had already moved to Florence by the time full-sized chambers were completed.

Turin adapted quickly to its loss of political significance, becoming a centre for industrial production during the early 20th century. Giants such as Fiat lured hundreds of thousands of impoverished southern Italians to Turin and housed them in vast company-built and -owned suburbs. Fiat's owners, the Agnelli family (who also happen to own the Juventus football club, Turin's local newspaper and a large chunk of the national daily *Corriere della Sera*), remain one of Italy's most powerful establishment forces. Fiat's fortunes declined later in the 20th century, however, and only revived around a decade ago.

The highly successful 2006 Winter Olympics were a turning point for the city. The Olympics not only ushered in a building boom, including a brand-new metro system, but also transformed Turin from a staid industrial centre into a vibrant metropolis. Turin was European Capital of Design in 2008, hosting conferences and exhibitions, and the national focus of celebrations of the 150th anniversary of the Risorgimento in 2011.

◎ Sights

Got a week? You might need it to see all the sights Turin has to offer. The time-poor can concentrate on a trio of highlights: the Museo Egizio, the Mole Antonelliana and the Museo Nazionale dell'Automobile.

★ Museo Egizio   MUSEUM
(Egyptian Museum; Map p200; www.museoegizio. it; Via Accademia delle Scienze 6; adult/reduced €13/9; ⏲ 8.30am-7.30pm Tue-Sun, 9am-2pm Mon) Opened in 1824 and housed in the austere Palazzo dell'Accademia delle Scienze, this Turin institution houses the most important collection of Egyptian treasure outside Cairo. Among its many highlights are a statue of Ramses II (one of the world's most important pieces of Egyptian art), the world's largest papyrus collection and over 500 funerary and domestic items found in 1906 in

ℹ PIEDMONT DISCOUNT CARD

Serious sightseers will save a bundle with a Torino+Piemonte Card (1/2/3/5 days €23/35/42/51). It covers admission to 190 of the region's monuments and museums, and offers reductions on various forms of public transport, including Turin's Sassi–Superga tram, GTT boats on the Po river and the Turismo Bus Torino. It also offers discounts on some guided tours and theatres. You can buy the card at Turin's tourist office.

the tomb of royal architect Kha and his wife Merit (from 1400 BC).

A major renovation was completed in 2015 and, although the old museum's rambling rooms had their dusty charm, the new minimalist spaces almost double the amount of the collection available for public display. Modern museological techniques – splicing in documentary photographs and films about the early-20th-century digs, dramatic lighting and a well-articulated chronological narrative – make for an absorbing experience.

Mole Antonelliana   LANDMARK

(Map p200; Via Montebello 20; panoramic lift adult/reduced €7/5, incl Museo €14/11; ⏱ lift 10am-8pm Tue-Fri & Sun, to 11pm Sat) The symbol of Turin, this 167m tower with its distinctive aluminium spire appears on the Italian two-cent coin. It was originally intended as a synagogue when construction began in 1862, but was never used as a place of worship, and nowadays houses the **Museo Nazionale del Cinema** (Map p200; www.museocinema.it; ⏱ 9am-8pm Tue-Fri & Sun, to 11pm Sat). For dazzling 360-degree views, take the **Panoramic Lift** up to the 85m-high outdoor viewing deck.

Museo Nazionale del Risorgimento Italiano   MUSEUM

(Map p200; www.museorisorgimentotorino.it; Via Accademia delle Scienze 5; adult/reduced €10/8; ⏱ 10am-6pm Tue-Sun) After extensive renovations, this signigicant museum reopened in 2011 to coincide with the centenary of the *risorgimento* (unification). An astounding 30-room trajectory illustrates the creation of the modern Italian state in the very building – the baroque **Palazzo Carignano** (Map p200) – where many of the key events hap-

pened. Not only was this the birthplace of Carlo Alberto and Vittorio Emanuele II, but it was also the seat of united Italy's first parliament from 1861 to 1864.

It's a history lesson and a half, but one that's accomplished with flair and drama, along with an incredible collection of portraiture and documentary objects.

Museo della Sindone   MUSEUM

(Map p200; www.sindone.org; Via San Domenico 28; adult/reduced €6/5; ⏱ 9am-noon & 3-7pm) Encased in the crypt of Santo Sudario church, this fascinating museum documents one of the most studied objects in human history: the Holy Shroud. Despite the shroud's dubious authenticity, its story unfolds like a gripping suspense mystery, with countless plots, subplots and revelations.

Duomo di San Giovanni   CATHEDRAL

(Map p200; Piazza San Giovanni; ⏱ 8am-7pm Mon-Sat) Turin's cathedral was built between 1491 and 1498 on the site of three 14th-century basilicas and, before that, a Roman theatre. Plain interior aside, as home to the famous **Shroud of Turin** (alleged to be the burial cloth in which Jesus' body was wrapped) this is a highly trafficked church. A copy of the cloth is on permanent display to the left of the cathedral altar.

The separate Romanesque-style bell tower looks older than it really is; it was designed by Juvarra and built in 1723. Just to the north lie the remains of a 1st-century **Roman amphitheatre**, while a little further to the northwest lies **Porta Palatina** the red-brick remains of a Roman-era gate.

Piazza Castello   PIAZZA

(Map p200) Turin's central square is lined with museums, theatres and cafes. The city's Savoy heart, although laid out from the mid-1300s, was mostly constructed from the 16th to 18th centuries. Dominating it is the part-medieval, part-baroque **Palazzo Madama**, the original seat of the Italian parliament. To the north, is the exquisite facade of the **Palazzo Reale**, the royal palace built for Carlo Emanuele II in the mid-1600s.

Museo Civico d'Arte Antica   MUSEUM

(Palazzo Madama; Map p200; www.palazzomadamatorino.it; Piazza Castello; adult/reduced €10/8; ⏱ 10am-6pm Tue-Sat, to 7pm Sun) A part-medieval, part-baroque castle built in the 13th century on the site of the old Roman gate, this *palazzo* is named after Madama Reale Maria Cristina, the widow of Vittorio

WORTH A TRIP

RIVOLI'S CUTTING-EDGE CASTELLO

Around 14km west of Turin's centre, just as the city's suburban sprawl begins to thin, Rivoli's Savoy castle is the spectacular home to what is arguably Italy's most prestigious contemporary art museum. Fittingly, it also hosts an internationally acclaimed gastronomic restaurant that for over a decade has been pushing boundaries of its own.

The establishment of the Castello di Rivoli Museum of Contemporary Art **Castello di Rivoli** (Map p205; Museo d'Arte Contemporanea; www.castellodirivoli.org; Piazza Mafalda di Savoia; adult/reduced €6.50/4.50; ⊙10am-5pm Tue-Fri, to 7pm Sat & Sun) in 1984 came about as the canny Torinese realised contemporary art could help build a new identity for the city. Its ambition and reach, not to mention healthy regional funding, has since been the envy of Milan, Venice and Rome's art worlds. Temporary exhibitions have included international heavyweights such as Sophie Calle, Gilbert & George and Jospeh Kosuth, spliced with some hard-hitting Italian mid-careerists.

The permanent collection has a sizeable number of Arte Povera works, along with pieces from the Transavanguardia, Minimal, Body and Land Art and other movements. This includes an impressive selection of video work from artists such as Nam June Paik, Bill Viola and Vanessa Beecroft.

While there's definitely an academic seriousness to the place, its impressive mix of contemporary and baroque architecture, amazing views, and highly engaging, often provocative, shows are never dull.

Take the metro to Paradiso station and then bus 36 to Rivoli bus station. Journey time is around 45 minutes. Otherwise, take the metro to the Fermi stop, from where there's a free daily shuttle – see the website for shuttle schedules. From March to October, the city sightseeing bus also stops here. **Radio Taxis** (p213) offers a flat fare of €30 from the city centre if you mention the Castello di Rivoli concession when booking.

At **Combal Zero** (☑011 956 52 25; www.combal.org; Piazza Mafalda di Savoia; 5-course tasting menu from €130; ⊙8-11pm Tue-Sat), Davide Scabin's tasting menus are theatrical, visual, visceral and mischeveous, but despite such experimentation are still deeply rooted in Piemontese culinary traditions.

Amedeo I (Duke of Savoy, 1630–37). Today, much of the building houses this expansive museum, which contains four floors of mostly decorative arts from medieval times to the post-unification period, along with temporary exhibitions of contemporary art.

Palazzo Reale
MUSEUM
(Map p200; www.ilpalazzorealeditorino.it; Piazza Castello; adult/reduced €12/6; ⊙8.30am-7.30pm Tue-Sun, free first Sun of month) Statues of the mythical twins Castor and Pollux guard the entrance to this eye-catching palace and, according to local hearsay, also watch over the magical border between the sacred and diabolical halves of the city. Built for Carlo Emanuele II around 1646, its lavishly decorated rooms house an assortment of furnishings, porcelain and other decorative objects. The **Giardino Reale** (Royal Garden; Map p200; ⊙9am-1hr before sunset) FREE, north and east of the palace, was designed in 1697 by An-

dré le Nôtre, who also created the gardens at Versailles.

The Palazzo Reale ticket allows you to view the **Galleria Sabauda**, the personal art collection of the Savoy monarchy, which was amassed over 400 years and includes gems by Van Dyck, Rubens and Lippi. Since 2012, the collection has been housed in the Manica Nuova, the newer wing of the Palazzo Reale.

Galleria Civica d'Arte Moderna e Contemporanea
ART GALLERY
(GAM; www.gamtorino.it; Via Magenta 31; adult/reduced €10/8; ⊙10am-6pm Tue-Sun) GAM was one of Italy's first modern art musueums and has an astounding 45,000 works in its vaults dedicated to 19th- and 20th-century European artists, including De Chirico, Otto Dix and Klee. It's a great place to expand your knowledge of Italy's postwar period: Paolini, Boetti, Anselmo, Penone and Pistoletto are all represented.

DON'T MISS

ITALY'S VERSAILLES

OK, it may not enjoy the weighty publicity of its French counterpart, but **Reggia di Venaria Reale** (Map p205; 011 499 23 33; www.lavenaria.it; Piazza della Repubblica; admission €25, Reggia & gardens only €16, gardens only €5; 9am-5pm Tue-Fri, to 7pm Sat & Sun) is one of the largest royal residences in the world, rescued from ruin by a €235 million 10-year-long restoration project. Humungous, ostentatious, regal, yet strangely under-publicised, this Unesco-listed baroque palace complex was built as a glorified hunting lodge in 1675 by the frivolous Duke of Savoy, Carlo Emanuele II.

Among the jewels bequeathed by its erstwhile royal rulers are a vast garden complex, a glittering stag fountain (with water shows), a conspicuous-consumption-style Grand Gallery, plus the attached Capella di Sant'Uberto and Juvarra stables. The last three were all designed by the great Sicilian architect Filippo Juvarra in the 1720s.

To enjoy the permanent exhibition alone, you'll need to walk 2km through the aptly named Theatre of History and Magnificence, a museum journey that relates the 1000-year history of the Savoy clan set in their former royal residential quarters, with a Brian Eno soundtrack and film installations care of Peter Greenaway.

On top of this are numerous temporary exhibitions, regular live concerts, an on-site cafe and restaurant, and an adjacent *borgo* (old village), that's now engulfed by Turin's suburbs, and full of cosy places to eat and drink. Take note of the scale and allow the best part of a day to visit. You can reach the palace complex (10km northwest of the city centre) via the Venaria Express shuttle, one of the tourist office's summer sightseeing buses or bus 11 or 72 from Porta Nuova station.

Fondazione Sandretto re Rebaudengo ART MUSEUM

(FSRR; 011 2799 7600; www.fsrr.org; Via Modane 16; adult/reduced €5/3, free after 8pm Thu; noon-7pm Fri-Sun, to 11pm Thu) This classic white-cube contemporary gallery space was created with Italian super curator Francesco Bonami and runs a great exhibition program, with big-name Italians like Maurizio Cattelan often making an appearance, along with provocative thematic shows that bring mid-career Europeans together with their younger peers.

Fondazione Merz ART MUSEUM

(011 1971 9437; fondazionemerz.org; Via Limone 24; adult/reduced €5/3; 11am-7pm Tue-Sun) The Arte Povera powerhouse, Mario Merz, was born in Milan but spent most of his artistic life in Turin. This foundation space, an evocative reworking of the former Lancia heating plant, holds regular exhibitions of his work, as well as an astute program of Italian contemporary art and emerging artist prizes.

Parco Valentino PARK

(Map p200;) Opened in 1856, this 550,000-sq-metre French-style park kisses the banks of the Po and and is filled with joggers, promenaders and lovers night and day. Walking southwest along the river brings you to **Castello del Valentino** (open for events only), a gorgeous mock chateau built in the 17th century.

Chiesa di Gran Madre di Dio CHURCH

Providing a grand backdrop to the Piazza Vittorio Veneto across the Po , this church was built in the style of a mini-Pantheon from 1818 to 1831 to commemorate the return of Vittorio Emanuele I from exile. It's small and rounded inside; some claim it's yet another secret repository for the Holy Grail.

In 1969 the church was memorably featured in the film *The Italian Job* when Michael Caine and his gang drove their Mini Coopers down the front staircase.

Lingotto Fiere LANDMARK

(www.lingottofiere.it; Via Nizza 294; Lingotto) Turin's former Fiat factory, one of Italy's most praised examples of early-20th-century industrial architecture, is 5km south of the city centre. It was redesigned by architect Renzo Piano in the 1980s to house an exhibition centre, a university campus and hotels. While still starkly beautiful, the shopping mall that occupies much of its accessible space is less than inspiring.

Lingotto is on the M1 metro line and easily accessible from the city centre.

Pinacoteca Giovanni e Marella Agnelli
ART GALLERY

(Lingotto; www.pinacoteca-agnelli.it; Via Nizza 230; adult/reduced €4/2.50; ⏰10.30am-7pm Tue-Sun; Ⓜ Lingotto) On the rooftop of the Lingotto Fiere, this intimate gallery houses the personal collection of late Fiat head Gianni Agnelli, with masterpieces by Canaletto, Renoir, Manet, Matisse and Picasso, among others. Apart from the paintings, your ticket grants you access to the Lingotto's famous rooftop test track.

It also has an attached (and free) bookshop, full of wonderful art and design titles. It's around 3km south of the centre and accessible by both metro and bus.

★ Museo Nazionale dell' Automobile
MUSEUM

(Map p205; 📞011 67 76 66; www.museoauto.it; Corso Unità d'Italia 40; adult/reduced €8/6; ⏰10am-7pm Wed, Thu & Sun, to 9pm Fri & Sat, to 2pm Mon, 2-7pm Tue; Ⓜ Lingotto) As the historic birthplace of one of the world's leading car manufacturers – the 'T' in Fiat stands for Torino – Turin is the obvious place for a car museum. And this dashing modern museum, located roughly 5km south of the city centre, doesn't disappoint with its precious collection of over 200 automobiles – everything from an 1892 Peugeot to a 1980 Ferrari 308 (in red, of course).

The museum – rather than leaving you to gawp helplessly at boring engines – takes you on a roller-coaster journey spread over three floors; the first part a car chronology, the second a more technical look at car design, and the third a self-critical assessment of issues such as pollution and congestion.

Basilica di Superga
BASILICA

(Map p205; www.basilicadisuperga.com; Strada della Basilica di Superga 73) 🆓 Vittorio Amedeo II's 1706 promise, to build a basilica to honour the Virgin Mary if Turin was saved from besieging French and Spanish armies, resulted in this wedding cake edifice, built on a hill across the Po river.

Architect Filippo Juvarra's Basilica di Superga became the final resting place of the Savoy family, whose lavish tombs make for interesting viewing, as does the dome. In 1949 the basilica gained less welcome reknown when a plane carrying the entire Turin football team crashed into the church in thick fog, killing all on board. Their tomb rests at the rear of the church.

Around Turin

0 — 5 km
0 — 2.5 miles

To get here take tram 15 from Piazza Vittorio Veneto to the Sassi–Superga stop on Corso Casale, then walk 20m to **Stazione Sassi** (Strada Comunale di Superga 4), from where an original 1934 **tram** (one way €4-6, return €6-9; ⏰hr vary) rattles the 3.1km up the hillside in 18 minutes, every day except Tuesday.

Courses

Eataly
COOKING

(www.eataly.net; courses free-€75) 🍴 Food sampling, tasting, sommelier secrets and cookery workshops take place at Turin's famous Slow Food supermarket; mostly in Italian.

👉 Tours

Turismo Bus Torino
BUS

(www.gtt.to.it; 1-day ticket adult/child €20/10, Line C €10/5, 2-day ticket €25/12, all three lines €30/15; ⏰10am-6pm) This hop-on, hop-off bus service with audioguides in English has a central stop on Piazza Castello at the corner of Via Po. Line A serves over a dozen different points around central Turin, Line B takes in Lingotto and other southern attractions and Line C covers Reggia di Venaria Reale, Rivoli and the Juventus stadium.

Navigazione sul Po
BOAT

(return €4-9) Grupo Torinese Transporti operates boat trips on the Po. Boats to the Borgo Medievale in Parco Valentino and on to Museo Nazionale dell'Automobile depart from **Imbarco Murazzi** (Map p200; Murazzi del Po 65) four to nine times daily in summer and on weekends in winter.

Somewhere
WALKING TOUR

(www.somewhere.it) Turin's alleged 'black and white magic' is illuminated on a quirky walking tour, Torino Magica (€22), and its underbelly is examined during Underground Turin (€28). You can opt for more traditional food or royal palace tours if the dark arts aren't your cup of chocolate. Confirm departure points when booking.

Festivals & Events

The tourist office has details of these and other events.

Salone Internazionale del Libro di Torino
BOOK FAIR

(http://en.salonelibro.it) Held every May, Turin's book fair is one of the most important in Europe.

Salone Internazionale del Gusto
FOOD

(www.salonedelgusto.it) Every October in even-numbered years, food-lovers roll into town for this Slow Food talk-and-taste fest, with traditional producers from around the world showcasing their wares at Lingotto Fiere. Day passes cost around €20.

Torino Film Festival
FILM

(www.torinofilmfest.org) Well-respected international festival with main screenings at the Mole Antonella during the last weeks of November.

Cioccolatò
FOOD

(www.cioccola-to.it) Turin celebrates chocolate and its status as a world chocolate capital in late November.

Sleeping

★ Via Stampatori
B&B €

(Map p200; 339 2581330; www.viastampatori.com; Via Stampatori 4; s/d €70/110;) This utterly lovely B&B occupies the top floor of a frescoed Renaissance building. Six bright, stylish and uniquely furnished rooms overlook either a sunny terrace or a leafy inner courtyard. The owner's personal collection of 20th-century design is used through-out the rooms and several serene common areas. It's central but blissfully quiet.

San Giors
BOUTIQUE HOTEL €

(011 521 63 57; www.hotelsangiors.it; Via Borgo Dora 3; s/d €75/99;) If you're not perturbed by a still-gentrifying neighbourhood, this small, welcoming family-run place offers rooms that are basic but elegantly furnished with beautiful vintage design pieces and a witty, bohemian eye. Its restaurant comes highly recommended, and come Saturday, you're in the thick of the Balon, one of Italy's best flea markets. Breakfast is €8 extra.

Hotel Roma e Rocca Cavour
HOTEL €

(Map p200; 011 561 27 72; www.romarocca.it; Piazza Carlo Felice 60; s/d €65/95;) Hallways are wide, ceilings are high and rooms are generously proportioned at this hotel that's been in the same family since 1854. 'Tourist' class rooms are good value, but consider paying extra for an economy or comfort room – their floor boards and antiques add a lot of charm. Opposite the Porta Nuova train station.

Tomato Backpackers Hotel
HOSTEL €

(Map p200; 011 020 94 00; www.tomato.to.it; Via Pellico 11; dm €25, s €38, d €56, tr €72;) This ecofriendly hostel in the happening San Salvario area is one of the few central places that caters to budget travellers. And it does so with style and soul, offering pristine dorms, smart private rooms, a kitchen and communal lounge. There's a relaxed, inclusive vibe and a long list of extras including laundry facilities and left luggage.

Hotel Dogana Vecchia
HOTEL €

(Map p200; 011 436 67 52; www.hoteldoganavecchia.com; Via Corte d'Appello 4; s/d €80/95;) Mozart, Verdi and Napoleon are among those who have stayed at this historic three-star inn. Renovations have fortunately preserved much of its old-world charm, and while it's unrepentantly dowdy, its location in the Quadrilatero Romano is hard to beat.

Ostello Torino
HOSTEL €

(011 660 29 39; www.ostellotorino.it; Via Giordano Bruno 191; dm/s/tw with shared bathroom €17/25/42; mid-Jan–mid-Dec;) Turin's neat 76-bed HI hostel, 1.8km from Stazione Porta Nuova, is around 10 minutes' walk from Lingotto station or can be reached by bus 52. Facilities include free breakfast, computer use and wi-fi; towels and AIG/HI membership are extra.

★ DuParc Contemporary Suites
DESIGN HOTEL €€

(☑ 011 650 83 83; www.duparcsuites.com; Corso Massimo D'Azeglio 21; d/ste €135/145; P ☀ 🗢) A business-friendly location doesn't mean this isn't a great choice for all travellers. Staff are young and friendly, and the building's stark modern lines are softened with a fantastic contemporary art collection, bold colour and tactile furnishings. Best of all, even the cheapest rooms here are sumptuously large, with king beds, ample cupboard space, huge baths and floor-to-ceiling windows.

Le Due Matote
B&B €€

(Map p200; Via Garibaldi 31; s/d €100/130; ☀ 🗢) Perched above Turin's favourite *passeggiata* parade, this elegant B&B is a bastion of calm, with three classically decorated rooms with features that are rare at this price: Nespresso machines in all rooms, marble-topped baths in the two larger ones and a lushly planted terrace with the largest of them all.

NH Piazza Carlina
DESIGN HOTEL €€€

(Map p200; ☑ 848 390230; www.nh-hotels.com; Piazza Carlo Emanuele II; s/d €180/220) Situated on one of Turin's most beautiful squares, this sprawling property occupies a 17th-century building, once the *Albergo di Virtù*, a Savoy charitable institution; it also once housed the political theorist Antonio Gramsci. The decor is cutting edge, highly atmospheric and deeply luxurious. Guests have access to roof-top terraces, and breakfast is served in a stately courtyard.

NH Lingotto Tech
BUSINESS HOTEL €€€

(☑ 011 664 20 00; www.nh-hotels.com; Via Nizza 262; d €200; P ☀ 🗢) This old Fiat factory hotel comes with a unique perk: the 1km running track on the roof is Fiat's former testing track and featured in the film *The Italian Job*. Its 20th-century industrial bones also mean rooms are huge and bright; the fit out is slick, high-naughties industrial too. As a corporate favourite, it's facilities are comprehensive and include a 24-hour gym.

✗ Eating

Turin is blessed with a hinterland fabulously rich in produce and tradition along with an increasing number of young and innovative restauranteurs and chefs. Specialities include *risotto alla piemontese* (risotto with butter and cheese), *vitello tonnato* (veal with tuna sauce) and panna cotta as well as

tajarin (a thin tagliatelle). Sushi and sushi hybrids are also Torinese favourites.

While you won't go hungry in the centre, the youthful San Salvario neighbourhood, in the southeastern part of the city, has a new crop of highly respected restaurants with a host of multicultural places, particularly around Piazza Madama Cristina, as well as some of the city's best pizzerias, bars and pubs.

Eataly Incontra
PIEDMONT, SUPERMARKET €

(Map p200; ☑ 011 037 32 21; www.eataly.net; Via Lagrange 3; €18-25; ☺ noon-10.30pm, cafe from 8am, shop from 10am) Perfect for a casual lunch or dinner, this mini-Eataly has shaded tables on the lovely pedestrian stretch of Lagrange. Food is fresh, simple and quick – think octopus and potato salad, *cruda* (raw minced steak) or linguine with pistachio pesto and stracciatella cheese – and the drinks list includes sulphur-free wines and artisan beers.

The cafe is a **Caffè Vergnano 1882** concession and makes one of the city's best capuccinos.

È Cucina
MODERN ITALIAN €

(Map p200; www.cesaremarretti.com; Via Bertola 27a; meals €25; ☺ noon-2pm & 7-10pm) Northern Italians are fond of a 'concept' and Bolognese chef Cesare Marretti's concept here is *sorpesa* (surprise). Beyond the choice of meat, fish or vegetables and the number of courses you want, it's up to the kitchen. What is certain is the innovative cooking and excellent produce that will arrive. Local's tip: don't be tempted to over order.

Perino Vesco
BAKERY €

(Map p200; ☑ 011 068 60 56; www.perinovesco.it; Via Cavour 10; snacks from €5; ☺ 7.30am-7.30pm Mon-Sat) 🍴 Cult Slow Food baker Andrea Perino turns out the city's best *grissini* (bread sticks) along with dense, fragrant *torta langarola* (hazelnut cake), naturallly yeasted *panettone* and focaccia that draws sighs from homesick Ligurians. Join the queues for takeaway pizza and focaccia slices or head out the back and nab a seat for sandwiches, pizza slices, savoury tarts and coffee.

Gofri Piemontéisa
SNACKS €

(Map p200; www.gofriemiassepiemontesi.it; Via San Tommaso 4a; €4.40-5; ☺ 11.30am-7.30pm Mon-Sat) 🍴 *Gofri* (thin waffles snap cooked in hot irons) are a traditional dish from the mountainous regions of northern Piedmont and have been reinvented here by a local chef as tasty fast food. Try the house *gofre*

LOCAL KNOWLEDGE

APERICENAS

Who needs *cena* (dinner) when you've got bar snacks the size of...well...dinners? Turin's answer to the aperitif is the *apericena*, where bar-side buffets resemble full-blown meals. Turin's most groaning, if not always the best quality, *apericenas* can be had along Via Po and in Piazza Vittorio Veneto. Here, places such as **La Drogheria** (p211) serve up brimming bowls of pasta, artichoke pies and risotto along with meats, cheese and bread. The Quadrilatero quarter is another buffet wonderland – **Pastis** (p211) and **Boka** (p210) on Piazza Fili berto do a full carb-heavy spread, or keep it classy with just cheese at **I Tre Galli** (Map p200; www.3galli.com; Via Sant'Agostino 25; ⊘12.30-2.30pm & 6.30pm-midnight Mon-Wed, to 2am Thu-Sat). Expect to pay between €6 to €12 for an *apericena*-hour drink; the small surcharge applies to subsequent drinks too.

with ham, *toma* (alpine cheese) and artichokes or one of the equally delicious *miasse*, a corn-based variation, also adapted from ancient recipes.

Grom   GELATERIA €

(Map p200; www.grom.it; Piazza Pietro Paleocapa 1d; cones & cups from €2.50; ⊘11am-11pm Sun-Thu, to midnight Fri & Sat winter, to 1am Fri & Sat summer) 🦶 At the vanguard of the gourmet gelato trend, the Grom chain founded its first store here in 2003, eschewing syrups and embracing sustainably sourced fresh ingredients. You can now lick a Grom cone in Paris or New York, but it's sweeter grabbing one in its home town. Look out for original Piedmontese flavours like *gianduja* (hazelnut chocolate) and lemon-scented cream.

Alberto Marchetti   ICE CREAM €

(Map p200; ☎011 839 08 79; www.albertomarchet ti.it; Corso Vittorio Emanuele II 24; ⊘noon-midnight Tue-Sat, 1-11pm Sun) 🦶 Riding in the slipstream of the Grom ice-cream phenomenon, Alberto Marchetti is a master of quality, managing every part of his ice-cream making process, from fruit selection to the type of milk used. Better than Grom? You decide.

★ **Banco vini e alimenti**   PIEDMONTESE €€

(Map p200; ☎011 764 02 39; www.bancovinie alimenti.it; Via dei Mercanti 13f; €25-28) A new breed hybrid restaurant-bar-deli, this smartly designed but low-key place does clever small-dish dining for lunch and dinner. While it might vibe causual wine bar, with young staff in T-shirts and boyfriend jeans, don't underestimate the food: this is serious Piedmontese cooking. It's open all day, so you can grab a single-origin pour-over here in the morning, or a herbal house *spritz* late afternoon.

Consorzio   PIEDMONTESE €€

(Map p200; ☎011 276 76 61; http://ristorante consorzio.com; Via Monte Pietà 23; mains €30-40, set menus €32; ⊘12.30-2.30pm Mon-Fri, 7.30-11pm Mon-Sat) It can be almost impossible to secure a table at this Quadrilatero Romano institution. Do book ahead, don't expect flash decor and pay the not-always-accomodating staff no mind. Everyone is here for the pristinely sourced, spot-on Piedmontese cooking that's so traditional it's innovative. The wine list, too, is thoughtful and occasionally provocative, and much of it is sourced from a family vineyard near Asti.

Scannabue   PIEDMONTESE €€

(Map p200; ☎011 669 66 93; www.scannabue.it; Largo Saluzzo 25h; meals €35; ⊘12.30-2.30pm & 7.30-10.30pm) Scannabue, housed in a former corner garage, is a retro-fitted bistro that has a touch of Paris in its cast-iron doors and tiled floors. There's a casual feel, but the cooking is some of Turin's most lauded.

Staples like *baccalà* (cod) are freshly matched with Jerusalem artichoke puree and crisped leeks, a starter reworks the French *tarte Tatin* into thoroughly modern onion pie, and there's a club sandwich on offer if you miss service.

L'Acino   PIEDMONTESE €€

(Map p200; ☎011 521 70 77; Via San Domenico 2a; meals €35-40; ⊘7.30-11.30pm Mon-Sat) Half a dozen tables and a legion of enamoured followers mean this inviting restaurant is hard to get into. Book ahead or arrive at the stroke of 7.30pm for snails, tripe and *ragù* (meat stew) cooked in Roero wine, or classic Piedmontese pasta staples such as *plin* (ravioli). The *bonet* (chocolate pudding) is considered one of the city's best.

Contesto Alimentare   MODERN PIEDMONTESE €€

(Map p200; ☎011 817 86 98; www.contestoalimen tare.it; Via Accademia Albertina 21; meals €30-40;

⊙12.30-2.30pm & 7.30-10.30pm Tue-Sun) This small dining room is run by a friendly young couple and makes a nice change from historic, moody Turin. A simple, architecturally astute fit-out makes the most of a vaulted old shop front, and dishes that may sound conceptual on the menu are far from fussy on the plate. Desserts like bergamot panna cotta unabashedly depart from the traditional and are a highlight.

The wine list is pan-Italian, and notable for its focus on natural wines; bottles can be bought to take away.

Porto di Savona
TRATTORIA €€

(Map p200; Piazza Vittorio Veneto 2; meals €28; ⊙12.30-2.30pm & 7.30-10.30pm) An unpretentious trattoria that dates to Turin's capital days (ie the 1860s), it has a deserved reputation for superb *agnolotti al sugo arrosto* (Piedmontese ravioli in a meat gravy), and *gnocchi di patate al gorgonzola*. The mains, including *bollito misto alla piemontese* (boiled meat and vegetable stew), are equally memorable.

La Sartoria
MODERN PIEDMONTESE €€

(Map p200; ☎011 046 16 83; www.ristorante lasartoria.com; Via Sant'Anselmo 27a; meals €28) A forward-thinking chef runs this diminutive San Salvario place with much attention to detail and plenty of whimsical touches, both in his cooking and in the sweetly evocative tailor-shop decor. The pace is leisurely, the wine list good and dishes can be had as starters or mains. The menu, mostly creative takes on the Piedmont kitchen, makes occasional strides into the international (fish and chips! green curry!).

Oinos
SUSHI, FUSION €€

(Map p200; ☎011 83 50 84; www.oinosristorante.it; Via della Rocca 39g; dishes €10-15; ⊙12.30-3pm & 8pm-midnight Mon-Sat) Turin's sushi obsession runs possibly only second to Milan's. Yes, like many of its counterparts, Oinos offers top-quality traditional Japanese raw plates, but also has a 'susciliano' menu that fuses Japanese technique with the ingredients of Italy's Mediterranean ports, especially those of Sicily. Raw fish teamed with citrus oils and capers, basil powder and almonds or spicy caponata? Genius.

Self-Catering

Porto Palazzo
MARKET €

(Map p200; http://scopriportapalazzo.com; Piazza della Repubblica; ⊙7am-1pm Mon-Fri, to 7pm Sat) Europe's largest food market has hundreds of stalls, including a large open-air market with a separate local and organic produce area, and a large covered fish and meat area. It's frantic, fabulously multicultural and fun.

Drinking & Nightlife

Aperitivi and more substantial *apericenas* are a Turin institution – this is the home of vermouth, after all. As in Milan, if you're on a tight budget, you can fill up on a generous buffet of bar snacks for the cost of a drink. Nightlife concentrates in the riverside area around Piazza Vittoria Veneto, the Quadrilatero Romano district and increasingly the southern neighbourhoods of San Salvarino and Vanchiglia.

Turin's historical cafes have their rivals – Trieste and Rome to name but two – but these are evocative places indeed, full of literary legend, architectural bling, aromatic coffee and the city's best idlers. Then there's hot chocolate, another of the Torinese's best-in-Italy claims.

The city's main clubbing action centres on Murazzi del Po (also called Lungo Po Murazzi), the arcaded riverside area stretching between Ponte Vittorio Emanuele I and Ponte Umberto I, although the more cutting-edge places are either in Dora or south of the city.

Al Bicerin
CAFE, CHOCOLATE

(Map p200; www.bicerin.it; Piazza della Consolata 5; ⊙8.30am-7.30pm Thu-Tue, closed Aug) Founded in 1763, with an exquisitely simple boiserie interior dating to the early 1800s, this one-room cafe takes its name from its signature drink, a potent combination of chocolate, coffee and cream. It fuelled the likes of Dumas, Puccini, Nietzsche and Calvino, along with Savoy royalty and Turin's workers – the price didn't rise for a century to ensure no one missed out.

Zabaione, an eggy, boozy concoction, is also a speciality, plus there's either cake or cocktails for afternoon sustenence.

Caffè Mulassano
CAFE

(Map p200; Piazza Castello 15; ⊙7.30am-10.30pm) Elbow your way to the bar or hope for a seat at one of the five wee tables at this art nouveau gem, where regulars sink espresso *in piedi* (standing) while discussing Juventus' current form with the bow-tied baristas.

DON'T MISS

FOOTBALL PILGRIMS

If paying your respects to the Holy Shroud has little appeal, you might prefer to tap into Italy's other religion: *calcio* (football). Its cathedral is the **Juventus Stadium**, inaugurated in 2011 as the home ground to the legendary *bianconeri*, Italy's most successful football club. The state-of-the-art ground has a **Juventus Museum** (www.juventus.com; Strada Comunale di Altessano 131; admission €10, incl stadium vist €18; ☉10.30am-6.30pm Mon & Wed-Fri, to 7.30pm Sat & Sun) that will blind you with its silverware (28 league titles – and the rest!) and proudly recount how it was all amassed.

On the other side of town, the **Stadio Olimpico** (which hosted the 2006 Winter Olympics) is home to Turin's other team, Torino FC. Until 2011, Torino shared their ground with Juventus, but now they've got the place to themselves except when they play the *bianconeri* in the hotly fought Derby della Mole. The Stadio Olimpico also offers a stadium tour and hosts a more general sports museum, the **Museo dello Sport** (www. olympicstadiumturin.com; Corso Agnelli; admission €10, incl stadium €14; ☉10am-6pm).

To get to the Juventus Stadium from the city centre, catch bus 72 from the corner of Via XX Settembre and Via Bertola. To get to the Stadio Olimpico, take tram 4 from Porta Nuova train station and get off after eight stops.

Caffè San Carlo
CAFE

(Map p200; Piazza San Carlo 156; ☉8am-midnight Tue-Fri, to 1am Sat, to 9pm Mon) Perhaps the most gilded of the gilded, this glittery cafe dates from 1822. You'll get neckache admiring the weighty chandelier and pay for the priviledge (€4 and upwards for coffee), but the service is the most genial of the old-school cafe clique.

Caffè Torino
CAFE

(Map p200; Piazza San Carlo 204; ☉7.30am-1am) This chandelier-lit showpiece opened in 1903. A brass plaque of the city's emblem, a bull (*torino* means 'little bull'), is embedded in the pavement out front; rub your shoe across it for good luck.

Fiorio
CAFE

(Map p200; Via Po 8; ☉8.30am-1am Tue-Sun) Garner literary inspiration in Mark Twain's old window seat as you contemplate the gilded interior of a cafe where 19th-century students once plotted revolutions and the Count of Cavour deftly played whist. The bittersweet hot chocolate remains inspirational.

Bar Cavour
COCKTAIL BAR

(Del Cambio; Map p200; ☎011 54 66 90; http://delcambio.it; Piazza Carignano 2; 7pm-1.30am Tue-Sat) Named for its most famous barfly, the ubiquitous Count of Cavour, this beautiful room combines a magical, mirrored historical setting with a great collection of contemporary art and design savvy. Upstairs from Del Cambio, a Michelin-starred restaurant, the *aperitivo* here doesn't come cheap but is an elegant respite from pizza slices. There's a bar menu until midnight too (it can be hard to tear yourself away from such extreme luxury).

Caffè-Vini Emilio Ranzini
WINE BAR

(Map p200; ☎011 765 04 77; Via Porta Palatina 9g; ☉9.30am-8.30pm Mon-Fri, 10.30am-5pm Sat) Location scouts looking for a neighbourhood bar from Turin's mid-century glory days would jump on this little place. A crew of local shopkeepers, creatives and students frequently prop up its dark wooden bar and loll about the summer courtyard with wines by the glass, €1 boiled eggs and small plates.

Boka
COCKTAIL BAR, WINE BAR

(Map p200; Piazza Emanuele Filiberto 7c; ☉5pm-1am) A welcome newcomer to the Piazza Filiberto scene, Boka may have a moody, high-style Torinese interior, but it also gives off a nice international feel with good cocktails, switched-on bar staff and interesting DJs as the night wears on.

Bazaaar
BAR, CAFE

(Map p200; www.bazaaar.it; Via Stampatori; ☉7am-2am) This big, bright corner space offers up everything from breakfast espressos to gelato to cocktails, all day, everyday. A relaxing place to while away a few hours, you can also stay busy here with a calendar of musical acts on Saturday nights, and weekly events, including themed 'cook & roll' music and cooking nights.

Barzotto COCKTAIL BAR
(Corso Moncalieri 5; ⊘6pm-3am Tue-Sun) This side of the river attracts an older crowd who escape the Po-side madness and come for expertly made cocktails. Enjoy the outside tables in summer with beautiful river and city views.

Pastis WINE BAR
(Map p200; Piazza Emanuele Filiberto 9; ⊘9am-3.30pm & 6pm-2am) A cute take on Paris in the '60s, this day-night bar has a loyal local following. Young Torinese come for big weekend brunches, a nightly *aperitivo* spread or a late night *amaro* or three.

La Drogheria BAR
(www.la-drogheria.it; Piazza Vittorio Veneto 18; ⊘10am-2am) Occupying an old pharmacy, La Drogheria's vintage sofas are coveted by a laid-back, studenty crowd who enjoy drinks and a groaning, and unusually healthy, *aperitivi* buffet before hitting the clubs down by the Po.

Hiroshima Mon Amour CLUB
(www.hiroshimamonamour.org; Via Bossoli 83; admission free-€15; ⊘hr vary) This legendary dance club features everything from folk and punk to tango and techno. Check the website for specific opening hour and details on the weekend night bus.

☆ Entertainment

Most live music venues are also out of the centre.

Teatro Regio Torino THEATRE
(Map p200; ✆ 011 881 52 41; www.teatroregio.torino.it; Piazza Castello 215; ⊘ticket office 10.30am-6pm Tue-Fri, to 4pm Sat & 1hr before performances) Sold-out performances can sometimes be watched free on live TV in the adjoining Teatro Piccolo Regio, where Puccini premiered *La Bohème* in 1896. Sadly, much of Carlo Molino's visionary mid-century fit-out did not survive subsequent renovations, but it's still worth a peek. Ticket prices start at €55.

Spazio 211 LIVE MUSIC
(✆011 1970 5919; www.spazio211.com; Via Cigna 21) This long-established live music venue, a 10-minute taxi ride north of the city centre, is the city's main venue for international indie acts, interesting theme nights, as well as big Italian names like Guida. Book tickets on the website.

ⓘ BIKE-SHARE

[To]Bike (www.tobike.it; half-day/day passes €8/13), Turin's ever-expanding bike-sharing scheme, is one of the largest in Italy. To use a fetching bright-yellow *bicicletta*, buy your tourist pass at the Piazza Castello or Carlo Felice tourist offices. For longer subscriptions, see the website.

🛍 Shopping

Via Roma's arcaded walkways shelter the city's big-label boutiques, while the cheap and cheerful line up along pedestrianised Via Garibaldi. Via Po has some great secondhand dealers, while upmarket vintage and young designer's keep shop in the Quadrilatero Romano.

Eataly Torino Lingotto CAFE, SUPERMARKET
(www.eataly.net; Via Nizza 230; ⊘10am-10.30pm) 🖉 The global Slow Food phenomena began here in Lingotto. Set in a vast converted factory, the Eataly mothership houses a staggering array of sustainable food and drink, along with kitchenware and cookbooks. Specialist counters that correspond to their produce area – bread and pizza, cheese, pasta, seafood, Piedmontese beef – serve lunch from 12.30pm to 2.30pm. Food lovers heaven!

Guido Gobino CHOCOLATE
(Map p200; www.guidogobino.it; Via Lagrange 1; ⊘10am-8pm Tue-Sun, 3-8pm Mon) 🖉 Relative newcomer Guido Gobino's extreme attention to detail, flair and innovation have made him Turin's favourite chocolatier. Have a box of his tiny tile-like ganache chocolates made to order: highly evocative flavours include vermouth, Barolo and lemon and clove, or grab a bag of his classic *gianduiotto* (triangular chocolates made from gianduja – Turin's hazelnut paste).

There's also a slim back cafe where you can order hot chocolates and a chocolate tasting plate.

Sapori di Tassinari FOOD & DRINK
(Map p200; ✆011 53 03 47; Via San Tommaso 12; ⊘Tue-Sat 9am-7.30pm) This neighbourhood pasta shop and *rosticceria* (delicatessan) has been run with love by Maurizio and Iva for 30 years. Choose from the brimming window of prepared dishes sold by

weight that include roast salmon, meatballs, Russian salad and gratin of leeks or artichokes: perfect perfect picnic or hotel room fare.

If you're busting to try their splendid array of house-made fresh pastas – from traditional *tajarin* to Sardinian pockets filled with ricotta and mint – but can't self-cater, they'll cook and plate you up your choice, with either a butter or tomato sauce (from €6) to be eaten at one of their counter-side tables or taken away. There are vegan and vegetarian options too.

Laboratorio Zanzara CRAFTS
(Map p200; ☑011 026 88 53; www.laboratorio zanzara.it; Via Bonelli 3a; ◷10am-12.30pm & 2-4pm Mon-Fri, 10am-12.30pm & 3.30-7pm Sat) A delightfully eccentric collection of handmade objects, light fittings, posters and calendars fill this bright shop, which is run as a nonprofit cooperative, employing people with intellectual disabilities. It's a noble enterprise, yes, but its wares are the model of Torinese cool, with the co-op's director, Gianluca Cannizzo, also one of the city's most celebrated creatives.

Balon MARKET
(www.balon.it; Via Borgo Dora; ◷7am-7pm Sat) This sprawling flea market has brought street merchants to the north of Porta Palazzo for over 150 years. It's both fascinating and overwhelming, but can turn up some spendid vintage finds for the persistant and sharp of eye. The pace settles down come midafternoon and there are plenty of artfully dishevelled cafes and bars to grab a coffee or *spritz*.

The Gran Balon, with more specialised antique and vintage dealers, happens on the second Sunday of the month, from 8am.

Libreria Luxemburg BOOKS
(Map p200; Via Battisti 7; ◷9am-7.30pm Mon-Sat, 10am-1pm, 3-7pm Sun) This dark, rambling Anglophone bookshop is well stocked with literary fiction, light reading, international magazines and a full stash of travel guides, including Lonely Planet guidebooks. They also carry UK newspapers.

San Carlo dal 1973 FASHION
(San Carlo 1; Map p200; ☑011 511 41 11; www.san carlodal1973.com; Piazza San Carlo 201; ◷3-7pm Mon, 10.30am-7pm Tue-Sat) This Torinese fashion institution – the city's first 'concept store' – stocks a tightly curated selection of Italian and European high fashion, along with a selection of perfumes and candles. It's Turin at its most elegant and worth a wander for the architecture and people-watching alone.

ℹ Information

A bank, ATM and exchange booth can all be found within Stazione Porta Nuova; others are dotted throughout the city.

Farmacia Boniscontro (☑011 53 82 71; Corso Vittorio Emanuele II 66; ◷9am-12.30pm & 3.30-9.30pm)

Ospedale Mauriziano Umberto I (☑011 5 08 01; Largo Turati 62) Hospital.

Piazza Carlo Felice Tourist Office (Map p200; ☑011 53 51 81; Piazza Carlo Felice; ◷9am-7pm) On the piazza in front of Stazione Porta Nuova.

Piazza Castello Tourist Office (Map p200; ☑011 53 51 81; www.turismotorino.org; Piazza Castello; ◷9am-7pm) Central and multilingual.

Police Station (☑011 5 58 81; Corso Vinzaglio 10; 🖪)

Post Office (Map p200; Via Alfieri 10; ◷8.30am-7pm Mon-Fri, to 1pm Sat)

ℹ Getting There & Away

AIR

Turin Airport (Caselle; www.turin-airport.com; Strada Aeroporto 12) Turin's airport, 16km northwest of the city centre in Caselle, has connections to national and European destinations. Budget airline Ryanair operates flights to London Stansted, Barcelona, Berlin and Ibiza.

BUS

Most international, national and regional buses terminate at the **bus station** (Corso Castelfidardo), 1km west from Stazione Porta Nuova along Corso Vittorio Emanuele II, including services to Milan's Malpensa airport.

TRAIN

Regular daily trains connect Turin's **Stazione Porta Nuova** (Piazza Carlo Felice) to the following destinations.

TO	FARE (€)	DURATION (HR)	FREQUENCY
Aosta	9.45	2	21
Genoa	12.20	2	16
Milan	12.25	1¾	28
Rome	61	7	11
Venice	55.55	4½	17

Some international trains also depart from the **Stazione Porta Susa** (Corso Inghilterra) terminal.

ℹ️ Getting Around

TO/FROM THE AIRPORT

Sadem (www.sadem.it) runs buses to the airport from Stazione Porta Nuova (one way/return €7.50/12, 40 minutes), also stopping at Stazione Porta Susa (30 minutes). Buses depart every 30 minutes between 5.15am and 10.30pm and run from 6.10am to midnight from the airport.

A taxi between the airport and the city centre will cost around €40 to €50.

PUBLIC TRANSPORT

The city boasts a dense network of buses, trams, a cable car and a small metro system, all run by the **Gruppo Torinese Trasporti** (GTT; Map p200; www.gtt.to.it/en; Piazza Castello; ⏲️10am-6pm), which has an **information office** (⏲️7am-9pm) at Stazione Porta Nuova. Buses and trams run from 6am to midnight and tickets cost €1 (€13.50 for a 15-ticket *carnet* and €3.50 for a one-day pass).

Turin's single-line metro runs from Fermi to Lingotto. It first opened for the Winter Olympics in February 2006 and reached Lingotto in 2011. The line will extend south to Piazza Bengazi, two stations south of Lingotto (ETA 2017). Tickets cost €1.50 and allow 90minute connections with bus and tram networks.

TAXI

Radio Taxi (☎ 011 57 30; www.radiotaxi.it) Flagfall €3.50, night fee €2.50.

CAR & MOTORCYCLE

Major car-rental agencies have offices at Stazione Porta Nuova and the airport.

The Milky Way

Neither a chocolate bar nor a galaxy of stars, Piedmont's Milky Way (Via Lattea) consists of two parallel valleys just west of Turin that offer top-notch skiing facilities. The more northern of the two, **Valle di Susa**, meanders past a moody abbey, the old Celtic town of Susa and pretty mountain villages. Its southern counterpart, the **Valle di Chisone**, is pure and simple ski-resort territory. The valleys hosted many events at the 2006 Winter Olympics, and the facilities and infrastructure remain state of the art.

◎ Sights

Sacra di San Michele ABBEY
(www.sacradisanmichele.com; admission €5; ⏲️9.30am-12.30pm & 2.30-6pm, closed Mon Oct-May, reduced hr winter) This Gothic-Romanesque abbey, brooding above the road 14km from Turin, has kept sentry atop Monte Pirchiriano (962m) since the 10th century. It housed a powerful, bustling community of Benedictine monks for over 600 years and was a staging point for high-society pilgrims. Look out for the whimsical 'Zodiac Door', a 12th-century doorway sculpted with *putti* (cherubs) pulling each other's hair.

To get to the abbey by public transport, there's a 90-minute steep hike from Sant'Ambrogio station. Alternatively, there's a special bus from Avigliana train station six times a day from May to September.

Roman Ruins RUINS
(Susa) These Roman ruins make for an interesting stop on the way to the western ski resorts. In addition to the remains of a Roman aqueduct, a still-used amphitheatre and the triumphal Arco d'Augusto (dating from 9 BC), a druid well remains as testimony to its Celtic origins before it fell under the Roman Empire's sway.

🏃 Activities

The tourist offices have mountains of information on every conceivable summer and winter sport, including heli-skiing, bobsledding, golfing on Europe's highest golf course, walking, free-climbing and mountain biking.

Skiing

The **Via Lattea** (www.vialattea.it) ski domain embraces 400km of pistes and five interlinked ski resorts: Sestriere (2035m), Sauze d'Oulx (1509m), Sansicario (1700m), Cesana Torinese (1350m) and Claviere (1760m) in Italy; and Montgenèvre (1850m) in neighbouring France. Its enormous range of slopes and generally reliable snow conditions provide for skiers and boarders of all abilities. A single daily ski pass costing €36 covers the entire Milky Way; or a €47 pass includes the French slopes.

Built in the 1930s by the Agnelli clan of Fiat fame, **Sestriere** (population 885) ranks among Europe's most glamorous ski resorts due to its enviable location in the eastern realms of the vast Milky Way ski area.

Cross-country skiing in the area is centred on **Bardonecchia** (population 3084, elevation 1312m), the last stop in Italy before the Fréjus Tunnel.

Hiking & Biking

Avigliana's tourist office has route maps and information on summertime walking and mountain biking, including the protected lakes and marshlands in the **Parco Naturale dei Laghi di Avigliana** (www. parks.it/parco.laghi.avigliana) on the town's western fringe. From Avigliana, experienced walkers can tackle a strenuous climb or take a 30km circular bike trail to the Sacra di San Michele abbey.

🛏 Sleeping & Eating

Hotel choice here does not match that of Italy's other alpine resorts and many only offer weekly rates during peak season. Note that most are closed outside winter and high summer. The area's tourist offices can make hotel reservations and source apartments. Sestriere's central square, Piazza Fraiteve, is loaded with places to eat and drink.

Casa Cesana HOTEL €
(☑0122 8 94 62; www.hotelcasacesana.com; Viale Bouvier, Cesana Torinese; s/d €60/90, weekly only in high season; P❄) Right across from Cesana Torinese's ski lift, this timber chalet was built for the 2006 Olympics. Its rooms are light-filled and spotless, there's a bustling restaurant open to non-guests (set menus from €20) and its bar is one of the area's liveliest.

Hotel Susa Stazione HOTEL €
(☑0122 62 22 26; www.hotelsusa.it; Corso Stati Uniti 4/6, Susa; s/d €55/80; P) A handy all-round base for the area and located directly opposite Susa's train station, this cycle-friendly hotel has 12 pleasantly old-school rooms, plus a restaurant with a good local menu (meals from €20-28). Staff hand out maps and itinerary proposals. A free ski shuttle bus stop is outside the door.

ⓘ Information

Tourist Office (☑0122 85 80 09; Viale Genevris 7, Sauze d'Oulx; ☺9am-noon & 3-6pm)

Tourist Office (☑0122 8 92 02; Piazza Vittorio Amedeo 3, Cesana Torinese; ☺9am-1pm & 2-6pm Wed-Sun)

Tourist Office (☑0122 75 54 44; Via Louset, Sestriere; ☺9am-1pm & 2-6pm)

ⓘ Getting There & Away

The main Italy–France motorway and railway line roar along the Valle di Susa, making the area easily accessible by both public transport and car.

Turin-based Sadem (p213) buses link Susa with Avigliana (€3.80, 35 minutes), Oulx (€4.15, 45 minutes), Turin (€5.25, 1¼ hours) and the Milky Way resorts. From Sestriere, buses serve Cesana Torinese (€1.90, 25 minutes), Oulx (€2.70, 45 minutes) and Turin (€6.35, two to three hours) up to five times daily.

Southern & Eastern Piedmont

Gourmets get ready to indulge: the rolling hills, valleys and townships of southern and eastern Piedmont are northern Italy's specialist pantry, weighed down with sweet hazelnuts, rare white truffles, Arborio rice, delicate veal, precious cheeses and Nebbiolo grapes that metamorphose into the magical Barolo and Barbaresco wines. Out here in the damp Po river basin, the food is earthy but sublime, steeped in traditions as old as the towns that foster them. There's Alba, the region's vibrant, pretty capital; Pollenzo, host to the University of Gastronomic Sciences; Bra, home of the Slow Food Movement; workaday Asti, the sparkling wine hub and a number of charming villages.

Many trace the gourmet routes in a car, but there are also excellent walking and cycling opportunities among spectacular countryside.

South of Cuneo, and forgotten by most, are the Maritime Alps, a one-time hunting ground for Savoy kings that's now open to hikers.

Cuneo & Around

POP 55,310 / ELEV 543M

There is a raft of reasons why you should drop by stately Cuneo, not least being the food, the bike friendliness, the hiking possibilities nearby, and, last but certainly not least, the city's signature rum-filled chocolates.

Sitting on a promontory of land between two rivers, Cuneo enjoys excellent Alpine views framed by the high pyramid-shaped peak of Monte Viso (3841m) in the Cottian Alps.

◎ Sights

The city's Napoleonic avenues give the city a stately air; make sure to wander the small, atmospheric streets of the historic centre north of the Piazza Galimberti.

HIKING IN THE MARITIME ALPS

Northern Italy, crowded? Not if you bring your hiking boots. Shoehorned between the rice-growing plains of Piedmont and the sparkling coastline of Liguria lie the brooding Maritime Alps – a small pocket of dramatically sculpted mountains that rise like stony-faced border guards along the frontier of Italy and France. Smaller yet no less majestic than their Alpine cousins to the north, the Maritimes are speckled with mirror-like lakes, foraging ibexes and a hybrid cultural heritage that is as much southern French as northern Italian.

Despite their diminutive size, there's a palpable wilderness feel to be found among these glowering peaks. Get out of the populated valleys and onto the imposing central massif and you'll quickly be projected into a high-altitude Shangri-La. Whistling marmots scurry under rocky crags doused in mist above a well-marked network of mountain trails where the sight of another hiker – even in peak season – is about as rare as an empty piazza in Rome. This is Italy at its most serene and serendipitous.

The main trailheads lie to the south of the city of Cuneo in a couple of ruggedly attractive regional parks: the **Parco Naturale delle Alpi Marittime** and the **Parco Naturale dell'Alta Valle Pesio e Tamaro**. The Lago di Valscura Circuit (21km) starts in the airy spa of **Terme di Valdieri** and follows an old military road via the Piano del Valasco to an icy lake near the French border. It loops back past the Rifugio Questa before descending via the same route. For a two-day hike try the Marguareis Circuit (35km), which begins in the small ski centre of Limone Piemonte and tracks up across passes and ridges to the **Rifugio Garelli** (☏ 0171 73 80 78; dm €17, with half-board €40; ⊙ mid-Jun–mid-Sep). Day two involves looping back through a small segment of France to your starting point in Limone. For more information on both hikes check out Lonely Planet's *Hiking in Italy* guide or consult the APT offices in either Terme or Limone.

Piazza Galimberti   PIAZZA

Arriving in Cuneo's gargantuan main piazza, you'd think you had just touched down in a capital city. Finished in 1884, it sits aside an older portico-embellished town founded in 1198.

Museo Civico di Cuneo   MUSEUM

(Via Santa María 10; admission €3; ⊙ 3.30-6.30pm, Tue-Sun) Cuneo has some wonderfully dark and mysterious churches. The oldest is the deconsecrated San Francisco convent and church, which today hosts this museum tracking the history of the town and province.

🏃 Activities

To the southwest lie the Maritime Alps, a rugged outdoor adventure playground where French and Italian influences mix.

Limone Piemonte   SKIING

(www.limonepiemonte.it) Limone Piemonte, 20km south of Cuneo and reachable by regular trains (€3.55, 40 minutes), has been a ski station since 1907 and maintains 15 lifts and 80km of runs, including some put aside for Nordic skiing. The town (population 1600) has numerous hotels and ski-hire shops.

Sleeping

Hotel Royal Superga   HOTEL €

(☏ 0171 69 32 23; www.hotelroyalsuperga.com; Via Pascal 3; s/d €70/95; P ❄ @ 🛜) This appealing old-fashioned hotel hidden off a corner of Piazza Galimberti mixes some regal touches with friendly, professional staff that go way beyond the call of duty. The delicious breakfast spread is all made from organic produce.

Hotel Ligure   HOTEL €

(☏ 0171 63 45 45; www.ligurehotel.com; Via Savigliano 11; s/d €60/75; P ❄ 🛜) In the heart of the old town, this two-star hotel is run by a charming, elegant family and has simple but spotless rooms and self-catering apartments for longer stays.

🍴 Eating & Drinking

Cuneo is an under-the-radar culinary powerhouse and has some standout places to wine and dine.

★ 4 Ciance   PIEDMONT €

(☏ 0171 48 90 27; www.4cianceristorante.it; Via Dronero 8C; meals €25, degustation €32; ⊙ 7.45-10pm Mon, noon-2pm & 7.45-10pm Tue-Sat) A warm, unpretentious place that makes everything from scratch, including the bread. Local specialities (beef cheek in Nebbiolo wine) are requisitely earthy but plated with an unexpected elegance for such a well-priced restaurant.

Bove's
STEAK, PIEDMONT €

(☑0171 69 26 24; www.boves1929.it; Via Dronero 2; meals €24; ☺noon-3pm & 6.30-midnight Thu-Tue) This dark corner bar may seem like a Brooklyn transplant with its tiles and high stools, but it's the real deal, serving up high quality Piedmontese *cruda* (raw minced beef) and steaks since 1929. These days they've added an ever-so-slightly international burger menu: the smoked beef with crunchy pancetta (€11.50) comes highly recommended.

Arione
CHOCOLATE, CAFE €

(www.arione-cuneo.com; Piazza Galimberti 14; ☺8am-8pm Tue-Sat, 8am-1pm & 3.30-8pm Sun) This 1920s-vintage chocolatier invented the *Cuneesi al Rhum*, a large, rum-laced praline wrapped in cellophane. The chocolates came to the attention of Hemingway, who made a detour from Milan en route to Nice in 1954 to try them and there's a photograph of his visit in the window. We're with Hemingway: buy a bag.

Osteria della Chiocciola
GASTRONOMIC €€

(☑0171 6 62 77; Via Fossano 1; meals €30, degustation €38; ☺12.30-11pm Mon-Sat) 🍝 Slow Food–affiliated Chiocciola's upstairs dining room is the colour of buttercups and makes for a soothing setting to linger over expertly crafted local, seasonal dishes. Their lunch menu (€15-23) is a fabulous deal, or if you are on the fly, you can still stop by on the ground floor, for a glass of wine with cheese.

ℹ Information

Tourist Office (www.comune.cuneo.it; Via Roma 28; ☺8.30am-10pm & 2.30-6pm Mon-Fri, 10am-1pm & 2-5pm Sat)

ℹ Getting There & Away

Regular trains run from Cuneo's central train station, at Piazzale Libertà, to Turin (€5.90, 1¼ hours, up to eight daily), San Remo (€8, 2¼ hours, three daily) and Ventimiglia (€7, two hours, around four daily), as well as Nice (€15, 2¾ hours, at least six daily) in France. A second train station for the Cuneo–Gesso line serves the small town of Mondovì, from where there are connections to Savona and Genoa.

Alba
POP 31,620 / ELEV 172M

A once-powerful city-state – its centre sported over 100 towers – Alba is considered the capital of the Langhe and has a big city confidence and energy while retaining all the grace and warmth of a small rural town. Alba's considerable gastronomic reputation comes courtesy of its white truffles, dark chocolate and wine. Its annual autumn truffle fair draws huge crowds and the odd truffle-mad celebrity. The *vendemmia* (grape harvest) remains refreshingly local and low key, if ecstatic in its own way.

The vine-striped Langhe Hills radiate out from the town like a giant undulating vegetable garden, replete with grapes, hazelnut groves and wineries. Exploring Alba's fertile larder on foot or with two wheels is a delicious pleasure.

◉ Sights

Alba is one of those towns where sights seem but a distraction from lunch, dinner or wine tasting.

Cattedrale di San Lorenzo
CATHEDRAL

(Piazza Duomo) There's been a cathedral here since the 12th century, though the current terracotta-brick affair is mostly a result of an almost complete neo-Gothic 19th-century makeover. The intricate choir stalls date from 1512.

Centro Culturale San Giuseppe
CULTURAL CENTRE

(☑0173 29 61 63; www.centroculturalesangiuseppe.it; Piazza Vernazza 6) A converted church turned cultural center, this is a lovely place to catch a choral or chamber music performance, or undertake a bracing hike up 134 steps to the 36m belltower (€1). In the basement, 2nd-century archaeological remains from the vanquished Roman Empire have been uncovered and they also host temporary art exhibitions.

☞ Tours

Consorzio Turistico Langhe Monferrato Roero
TOURS

(☑0173 36 25 62; www.booking-experience.tartufoevino.it; Piazza Risorgimento 2) The Alba-based consortium organises a wide variety of tours and classes unique to the Alba region. Truffle hunting can be arranged seasonally for white truffles (September to December) or black truffles (May to September) for €80 per person. Year-round, you can tour a hazelnut farm for €30 or take part in a four-hour cooking course for €130.

There are various wine-themed excursions, including a guided tour of a Barolo winery (€15), as well as the ostensibly non-foodie horseriding and donkey trekking. All tours can be booked up to a day in advance at Alba's tourist office.

Festivals & Events

Fiera del Tartufo   FOOD
(Truffle Festival; www.fieradeltartufo.org) 🍴 October's precious white truffle crop is bought, sold and celebrated at this annual festival, held every weekend from mid-October to mid-November. Come and watch princely sums being exchanged and sample autumn's bounty. Book accommodation well ahead.

🛏 Sleeping

Hotel Langhe   HOTEL €
(☑0173 36 69 33; www.hotellanghe.it; Strada Profonda 21; s/d €80/110; [P][❄][🛜]) Two kilometres from the city centre, Hotel Langhe sits on the edge of vineyards that push up against Alba's not entirely unpleasant suburban sprawl. Staff are friendly and the pace is relaxed, with a wine conservatory, a bright breakfast area and downstairs rooms with French windows that open onto a sunny forecourt.

L'Orto delle Rose   B&B €
(☑333 2614143; http://ortodellerose.weebly.com; Via Cuneo 5; s/d €85/100; [P][❄][🛜]) High ceilings and beautiful original bones make this one-room family-run B&B a real find. Bonus points for the fact that it puts you in the historic centre but has a small garden and a car space.

Casa Bona   B&B, APARTMENT €
(☑0173 29 05 35; Corso Nino Bixio 22; r €85; [P][🛜]) Disregard the unremarkable building. This collection of several apartments with modern bedrooms and bathrooms are thoughtfully equipped (you get your own stovetop espresso-maker), along wtih an owner who will drop by with home-made cakes. No credit cards.

Casa Dellatorre   B&B €€
(☑0173 44 12 04; www.casadellatorre.net; Via Elvio Pertinace 20; s/d €110/140; [❄]) Three sisters run this central, upmarket B&B, once their family home, with love. Three

CHERASCO'S SNAIL TRAIL

Within the Langhe's lush wine country, Cherasco, 23km west of Alba, is best known for *lumache* (snails). The town is home to the **Istituto Internazionale di Elicicoltura** (International Institute for Heliciculture; ☑0172 48 92 18; www.lumache-elici.com; Via Vittorio Emanuele 55), which provides technical advice for snail breeders (heliciculture is edible-snail breeding). Snails in this neck of the woods are dished up *nudo* (shell-less) and are pan-fried, roasted, dressed in an artichoke sauce or minced inside ravioli. The snail-mad should time their visit for late September for the annual snail festival.

classically decorated, antique-filled rooms share a flowery internal courtyard, where breakfast is served in the summer; in winter it's in the sisters' pretty cafe.

🍴 Eating

Alba's fantastic cuisine comes in the Michelin-starred variety, but also represents the best of quotidian pleasure in its word-of-mouth, no-menu osteria.

Golosi di Salute   PASTRIES €
(☑0173 44 29 83; www.golosidisalute.it; Place Rossetti 6; ⊗8am-12.30pm & 3.30-7.30pm) Pastry chef Luca Montersino is known throughout northern Italy for his biscuits, cakes, tarts and spreads that variously avoid gluten, dairy or sugar; these days his produce is available as far afield as New York. He is an Alba local (with a killer gluten-free *torta di nocciole* to prove it) and this, his flagship, carries a large range.

Osteria dei Sognatori   OSTERIA €
(Via Macrino 8b; meals €12-20; ⊗noon-2pm & 7-11pm Thu-Tue) Menu? What menu? You get whatever's in the pot at this dimly lit place. Munch on the theatrically large breadsticks while you wait for an array of antipasti to arrive, then try and keep up as the dishes mount up. Walls are bedecked with football memorabilia and B&W snaps of bearded wartime partisans look over rowdy tables of locals. Bookings advised.

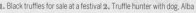

1. Black truffles for sale at a festival 2. Truffle hunter with dog, Alba
3. Digging up truffles 4. Black truffle appetiser

CHRISTOPHER PILLITZ/GETTY IMAGES ©

Truffles: Food of the Gods

One of the world's most mystical, revered foodstuffs, truffles are Italy's gastronomic gold. Roman emperor Nero called them the 'food of the gods', while composer Rossini hailed them as the 'mushrooms of Mozart'.

Hunting them out is a specialist activity. Truffles – subterranean edible fungi, similar to mushrooms, that colonise the roots of certain tree species – are notoriously hard to find. The most prized variety is the white truffle from the Alba region in Piedmont. Other slightly less aromatic white truffles are found in Tuscany, while black truffles are most prevalent in Umbria and Le Marche. White truffles are harvested from early October to December; black truffles are available from November to March.

Italy's biggest truffle festival is held in Alba every weekend for a month from mid-October to mid-November, while other notable events are the Tuscan towns of San Miniato and San Giovanni d'Asso, near Siena, during the second half of November. The season is crowned in a boisterous celebration of the black truffle in the Umbrian town of Norcia during late February and early March.

JOINING A TRUFFLE HUNT

Alba Tourist Office (www.langheroero. it) Organises truffle hunts and lists local restaurants offering truffle menus.

Tartufo e Vino (www.tartufoevino.it) From Alba, hit the woods with an expert *trifulau* for white truffles in autumn and winter, black in spring and summer.

Assotartufi San Giovanni (www.asso tartufi.it) Organises hunts year-round in San Giovanni d'Asso, southern Tuscany.

Barbialla Nuova (www.barbiallanuova. it) An organic truffle farm *agriturismo* known for its hunts near the town of San Miniato in Tuscany.

Love Umbria (www.love-umbria. com) Agency offering culinary tours of Umbria, including truffle-hunting weekends around Norcia.

★ La Piola
MODERN PIEDMONTESE €€

(📞0173 44 28 00; www.lapiola-alba.it; Piazza Risorgimento 4; meals €25-45; ◷noon-2.30pm & 7-10pm Mon-Sat, closed Mon in summer) Part of the Ceretto family's small empire, La Piola offers a faithful menu of traditional Piedmontese dishes but at the same time manages to be stylish, modern and relaxed (let's put it down to *sprezzatura* – the Italian art of studied nonchalance). With a kitchen run by one of Italy's most respected chefs, Enrico Crippa from gastronomic Piazza Duomo upstairs, expect wonderful produce and technique, along with a sense-grabbing flair. Engaged young staff and great contemporary artwork (including specially commissioned plates) make the experience a special one. Check the website for details of their monthly dinners that celebrate Piedmontese classics often too difficult to do for single diners.

Piazza Duomo
GASTRONOMIC €€€

(📞0173 44 28 00; www.piazzaduomoalba.it; Piazza Risorgimento 4; meals €130, set menus €180-220; ◷12.30-2pm & 7.30-10pm Tue-Sat) Enrico Crippa's Michelin-starred restaurant is now in its second decade and considered one of Italy's best. Dreamlike frescos by Francesco Clemente fill the fleshy pink dining room, which is otherwise a bastion of calm restraint. On the plate, expect the high concept play beloved of Italian fine-dining chefs, along with spectacular produce (this is truffle country), including vegetables from the restaurant's own garden.

Four elegant rooms are available for restaurant guests who just want to fall in a heap after a long night of degustation dining (from €240 a night).

Drinking & Nightlife

Pensavo Peggio
BREWERY, BAR

(Corso Langhe 59; ◷8am-10.30pm Tue-Sat) A 15-minute walk from the old town, this *microbirrificio e ristoro* (brewery and restaurant), is also one of the city's liveliest places to drink. Join Alba's younger set here for excellent microbrews and interesting wines, including Nascetta, a local white. The kitchen dishes up hearty belly liners like tortellini or roast beef with your choice of sides.

Vincafé
WINE BAR

(www.vincafe.com; Via Vittorio Emanuele II 12; ◷7am-midnight) Squeeze through the door and sift through a list of over 350 varieties or, if in doubt, have a Barolo. Downstairs, in a vaulted stone cellar, the restaurant serves up huge healthy salads and pasta.

I LOVE BA
WINE BAR

(📞327 3276081; Via Alberione 1; ◷8am-9pm) BA here stands for Barbaresco and this bright and welcoming little enoteca is a relaxed *aperitivo* favourite, with a good range of local wines and knowledgeable staff. Located on the historic centre's perimeter road, it's also convenient for grabbing supplies for a picnic or last minute gourmet gifts on the way out of town.

Bistrot dei Sognatori
BAR

(Piazza San Giovanni 5; ◷8am-1am Tue-Sun, from 2pm Mon) This nondescript corner bar packs in the *ragazzi* (guys) every night: perfect if you're done with fine dining and upmarket enoteca. Wine choices are still excellent, as are the *spritz*, cocktails and late night sound track.

❶ Information

Tourist Office (www.langheroero.it; Piazza Risorgimento 2; ◷9am-6pm Mon-Fri, from 9.30am Sat & Sun) In the town's historic centre, this office sells walking maps and can advise on a huge range of food and wine tours.

❶ Getting There & Around

From the **bus station** (Corso Matteotti 10) there are frequent buses to/from Turin (€4.50, 1½ hours, up to 10 daily) and infrequent buses to/from Barolo (€2.20, 25 minutes, two daily) and other surrounding villages.

From Alba's **train station** (Piazza Trento e Trieste) regular trains run to/from Turin (€4.85 via Bra/Asti, 1½ hours, hourly).

The irregularity of buses makes touring the Langhe better by car or bike. For bike hire (from €20 a day) book through the tourist office. Car hire goes from about €35 per day or the tourist office can hook you up with a driver (prices vary).

Barolo Region

This tiny, 1800-hectare parcel of undulating land immediately southwest of Alba knocks out what is arguably the finest *vino* in Italy. Yes, it's Barolo (after the eponymous village where it is produced), long hailed as the 'wine of kings' and currently the next big thing with Anglophone collectors.

BAROLO

POP 690

A viticulturally inclined village for at least four centuries, Barolo is far too deeply rooted in the soil and the seasons to have wine-snob attitude. The hilltop village is delightful enough itself to warrant a stroll; being able to taste its precious, aromatic wines in a relaxed and welcoming tasting room makes visiting a sublime experience indeed.

Sights & Activities

Castello Comunale Falletti di Barolo
WINE TASTING, CASTLE

(www.baroloworld.it; Piazza Falletti; ⊘ enoteca 10am-12.30pm & 3-6.30pm Fri-Wed) Barolo village is lorded over by a castle once owned by the powerful Falletti banking family. Its origins lie in the 10th century, though most of the current structure dates from the 1600s. The castle hosts the Museo del Vino a Barolo (p221) and, in its cellars, the **Enoteca Regionale del Barolo**, organised and run by the region's 11 wine-growing communities.

The *enoteca* (wine bar) has a number of Barolo wines available for tasting, costing from €3 for one.

Museo del Vino a Barolo
MUSEUM

(www.wimubarolo.it; Castello Comunale Falletti di Barolo; adult/reduced €8/6; ⊘ 10.30am-7pm, closed Jan & Feb) A capricious jaunt through the history of viticulture via light, film and installations, care of the wild imagination of Swiss designer François Confino (who also designed Turin's cinema museum). It's set over three floors of the village's stunning medieval castle and best braved after a tasting session, when it all will seem to make sense.

Gianni Gagliardo
WINE TASTING, SHOP

(☎ 0173 5 08 29; www.gagliardo.it; Via Roma 35; ⊘ 11am-7pm) Gianni Gagliardo is known as the 'father of Favorita', the man responsible for bringing that native white grape back from obscurity in the 1970s. Favorita forays aside, this shop and tasting room is yet another temple to the Nebbiolo grape. There's some extreme vintages represented, along with 'collectors' prices to match. You can also buy Nebbiolo and Favorita seedlings (€10) here to DIY at home.

Sleeping

Casa Svizzera
AGRITURISMO €

(☎ 0173 56 64 08; www.casasvizzera.com; Via Roma 65; d €100; P ☎) Five minutes from the Germano's family's vines, these three pretty, balconied rooms sit above their central *enotecta* and former bottling plant. It's quiet and ridiculously atmospheric, but also puts you in toddling distance of all the village's tasting rooms and restaurants. Kindly staff will happily make local recommendations and reservations for you.

Hotel Barolo
HOTEL €€

(☎ 0173 5 63 54; www.hotelbarolo.it; Via Lomondo 2; s/d €80/120; P @ ☎) Overlooked by the famous *enoteca*-castle, Hotel Barolo is a fabulously old-school place; sit back on the terrace with a glass of you-know-what, contemplating the 18th-century Piedmontese architecture that guards its shimmering swimming pool. Follow up with a meal at the in-house restaurant (they've been serving up truffles and the like for four generations). The family has been making wine since 1885.

Eating & Drinking

La Cantinetta
PIEDMONT €€

(☎ 0173 5 61 98; Via Roma 33; meals €25-35) A sunny outside terrace is the big draw here, although you'll be far from unhappy with the menu of local dishes: Ligurian rolled rabbit, risotto with radicchio, veal tongue with salsa verde. Don't miss the antipasto dish of egg in pasta (€7), one of those culinary experiences that's better than the sum of its parts.

Barolo Friends
PIEDMONT, WINE BAR €€

(☎ 0173 56 05 42; www.barolofriends.it; Piazza Castello 3; meals €20-30; ⊘ 11am-11pm Thu-Tue) An easy, contemporary place that does Piedmontese staples but doesn't keep to rigid restaurant hours or menu formats. Need a quick *vitello tonnato* (cold sliced veal with tuna sauce) or soup? Fancy a late afternoon glass of something special as the sun dips over the vines? Here's your place.

La Vita Turchese
WINE BAR

(☎ 366 4556744; www.laviteturchese.com; Via Alba 5; ⊘ 11am-9.30pm Wed-Sat, to 7.30pm Mon) This super friendly *enoteca* is run by passionate young staff who will talk you through their good stock of local wines, and also branch out to some other great Italians and internationals. Daily cheese and *salumi* choices are sourced with love and it's a local favourite for *aperitivo*.

WINE-TREKKING

The three main villages of the diminutive Barbaresco wine region – Barbaresco, Neive and Treiso – lie several kilometres east, northeast and southeast (respectively) of Alba; however, by combining a short bus ride with a little leg work, you can make a wine-tasting tour of all three without ever having to get behind the wheel of a car.

Start by catching the hourly Asti-bound bus from outside Alba train station. The bus stops in Neive, one of Piedmont's prettiest villages, studded with baroque palaces and criss-crossed by a web of footpaths. The village proper lies a little uphill from the bus station and is accessed by passing beneath the arch of San Rocco. Despite its obvious Barbaresco bias, Neive is known as the village of 'four wines', meaning there's a quadruple-whammy of tasting opportunities to enjoy. Line up the Barbaresco, Dolcetto, Barbera and Moscato bottles in the **Bottega dei Quattro Vini** (p223).

If you walk south from Neive for 6km on the **Sentiero delle Rocche dei Sette Fratelli**, you'll end up in Treiso, the region's highest village, which is known for its lighter-bodied Barbaresco. Imbibe the flavours at the **Bottega dei Grandi Vini di Treiso** (Piazza Baracco; ☺10am-1pm & 2-7pm Thu-Mon). Equally enticing is the shorter 5km trek northwest from Neive over gentle vine-striped hills on the **Sentiero dei Barbaresco** to Barbaresco village.

Producing 45% of the region's wine, tiny Barbaresco has over a dozen *cantine* (wine cellars) and two *enoteche* (wine bars/shops). Stay for the afternoon and you'll find ample opportunity to taste, pair, discuss and get mildly inebriated on the local plonk, though you might want to save enough energy to retrace your footsteps to Neive afterwards. Alternatively, you can trek directly back to Alba (approximately 5km) along a path that roughly tracks the Tanaro river. Helpful walking maps of the area can be purchased from the tourist office in Alba.

LA MORRA

POP 2670

Atop a hill surrounded by vines with the Alps as a backdrop, La Morra is bigger and quieter than Barolo, though no less beguiling. The village's *cantina comunale* provides lists of places to do tastings.

🛏 Sleeping & Eating

★ Brandini
AGRITURISMO €€

(www.agricolabrandini.it; Borgo Brandini 16; s/d/ste €85/120/190; 🅿️ ❋ 🛜 🛝) 🍴 A five-minute drive below La Morra, this vineyard restaurant and cellar has five cosy, modern rooms. Each is named for a writer and graced with appropriate quotes and reading material, along with equally inspiring views of the Alps. All fittings, from paint to wood to bedding, are made from sustainable, non-toxic materials in line with their organic agricultural practices.

Cooking classes that explore the specialities of the Langhe can be organised for groups or individuals in English or Italian.

Uve Rooms & Wine Bar
BOUTIQUE HOTEL €€

(☎ 333 7137892; www.uve.info; Via Umberto I 13; s/d €180/200; ❋ 🛜) 🍴 A stylish newcomer to La Morra, eight rooms and a couple of suites sport smart, often recyled furniture and design-savvy bathrooms. Set around a beautifully rustic, white-washed courtyard in a former monastery, there's rest and contemplation on offer here, or you can worship the grape downstairs at their own *enoteca*. Guest bikes or bespoke tours will get you out into the countryside.

Villa Carita B&B
B&B €€

(☎ 0173 50 96 33; www.villacarita.it; Via Roma 105; d €130; 🅿️) La Morra has some of the best views in the Langhe and those across sun-dappled vineyards by day and twinkling village lights after dark at this B&B are pinch-yourself perfect. Tucked below the main building, one room and one suite, each with a kitchen, are hidden in the hillside with their own private terraces.

Fontanazza
PIEDMONT €

(☎ 01 735 07 18; www.locandafontanazza.it; Strada Fontanazza 4; meals €25; ☺7.30pm-10pm Fri-Wed, noon-2.30pm Tue, Wed, Fri-Sun) You can take the sun on the terrace in summer or warm up by the open fire on chilly days and enjoy simple, traditional dishes like *tajarin al ragù di arrosto di vitello* (pasta with veal stew) along with a number of vegetable-focused options and whimsical deserts.

Barbaresco Region

Only a few kilometres separate Barolo from Barbaresco, the home of the renowned wine of the same name. A rainier microclimate, nutrient-rich soil and fewer ageing requirements have made the latter into a softer, more etheral red that plays 'queen' to Barolo's 'king'.

BARBARESCO
POP 650

The village of Barbaresco is surrounded by vineyards and characterised by its 30m-high, 11th-century tower, visible from miles around. There are over 40 wineries and two *enoteches* (wine bars) in the area.

 Activities

★ **Le Rocche dei Barbari**   WINE TASTING
(📞0173 63 51 38; Via Torino 62; ☺8am-6pm)
An historic winery, with a moody tasting room and cellar, this is a Langhe highlight. You're greeted by the family dog, generous complimentary tastings are conducted by the owner, cheese is offered on pewter platters and the stories of each vintage are enchanting.

Enoteca Regionale del Barbaresco   WINE TASTING
(Piazza del Municipio 7; ☺9.30am-6pm Thu-Tue)
Fittingly for a wine that conjures such reverence, this intimate *enoteca* is housed inside a deconsecrated church, with wines lined up where the altar once stood. It costs €2 per tasting glass; six Barbaresco wines are available to try each day.

Sentiero dei Barbaresco   HIKING
Various trails surround the village, including this 13km loop through the undulating vineyards. The Enoteca Regionale has maps.

🛏 Sleeping & Eating

The village has four fine restaurants, one of which – Antinè – has a Michelin star.

Casa Boffa   PENSION €
(📞0173 63 51 74; www.boffacarlo.it; Via Torino 9a; s/d/tr €70/85/105; 📶) In a lovely house in the centre of the village, Boffa offers four modern rooms and one suite above a stunning terrace with limitless Langhe valley views. Boffa's cellars are open for tasting daily except Wednesday.

Ristorante Rabayà   TRADITIONAL ITALIAN €€
(📞0173 63 52 23; Via Rabayà 9; set menus €30-45; ☺noon-2pm & 7-10pm Tue-Sun) 🍴 Rabayà, on the fringe of the village, has the ambience of dining at a private home. The signature rabbit in Barbaresco works better in its antique-furnished dining room in front of a roaring fire, but its terrace is set high above the vineyards is perfect for a summer evening plate of cheese. A snail menu also makes the occasional appearance.

NEIVE
POP 2930

Ping-ponged between Alba and Asti during the Middle Ages, Neive is a quieter proposition these days, its hilltop medieval layout earning it a rating as one of Italy's *borghi più belli* (most beautiful towns). Come here to taste the village's four legendary wines – Dolcetto d'Alba, Barbaresco, Moscato and Barbera d'Alba – amid sun-dappled squares and purple wisteria.

🏃 Activities

The tourist office has a list of six different local day hikes, ranging from 12.5km to 20km in distance.

Bottega dei Quattro Vini   WINE TASTING
(www.bottegadei4vini.com; Piazza Italia 2; ☺10am-6pm) 🍴 This two-room shop was set up by the local community to showcase the four DOC wines produced on Neive's hills. Inside you can sample wines by the glass (€1.80 to €4.50), accompanied by cold local specialities (€3.50 to €10).

🛏 Sleeping

La Contea   PENSION €
(📞0173 6 71 26; www.la-contea.it; Piazza Cocito 8; s/d €70/100; 📶) The family-run La Contea has been part of Neive's fabric for eons. The rooms are traditional, stuffy even, but comfortable, and there is an *enoteca*, shop and restaurant.

Borgo Vecchio   APARTMENT €€
(📞377 4911705; www.borgovecchioneive.it; Via Borgese 10; ste €180; 🌀📶) These large, slickly furnished apartment-style suites can sleep three to four adults and have espresso machines, terraces and, in the largest, a jacuzzi. No breakfast.

SLOW FOOD

Slow Food was the 1980s brainchild of a group of disenchanted Italian journalists from the Piemontese town of Bra. United by their taste buds, they ignited a global crusade against the fast-food juggernaut threatening to engulf Italy's centuries-old gastronomic heritage. Their mantra was pleasure over speed and taste over convenience in a manifesto that promoted sustainability, local production and the protection of long-standing epicurean traditions. Paradoxically, Slow Food grew quickly after its 1987 inauguration and by the early 2000s it was sponsoring more restaurants in Piedmont than McDonald's. In 2004 its founder, Carlo Petrini, set up a University of Gastronomic Sciences in Pollenzo as a way of passing the baton on to future generations. The mindset worked. Today Slow Food counts 100,000 members in 150 countries and has attracted big-name affiliates, such as Turin-founded supermarket company Eataly and popular ice-cream manufacturer Grom, as well as dozens of characterful and refreshingly slow restaurants – all of them simultaneously tradition-bound and forward looking.

Eating & Drinking

I LOVE BA Osteria OSTERIA €€
(Via Borgese 10; noon-2.30pm & 7-10pm Fri-Wed) Yes, the Langhe does hipster and this innitmate upstairs dining room is it. Never fear, there's no quinoa on the menu, just careful renditions of *plin* (meat ravioli), veal *ragù* and Piedmontese beef steaks. If you've been pining for salad, you can order a leafy side here. Staff are friendly and happy to match wines by the glass.

Al Nido Della Cinciallegra WINE BAR
(0173 6 73 67; www.alnidodellacinciallegra.com; Piazza Cocito 8; 8am-10pm) Join Neive's winemakers and restaurateurs here for a wine and a generous *aperitivo* plate; if the weather's warm, you'll all boisterously spill out onto the pretty square. This is the Langhe at its unpretentious best: on one side of the shop buy a brilliant Barolo, on the other, batteries or a ballpoint pen. It's both *enoteca* and village cornershop.

Getting There & Away

Hourly buses from Alba (€2.10) depart from Piazzale Dogliotti.

Bra & Pollenzo

POP 29,850

Bra seems like a small, unassuming Piedmontese town, but as the place the Slow Food Movement first took root in 1986, it's also something of a gastronomic pilgrimage site. There are no supermarkets in the historic centre, where small, family-run shops are replete with organic sausages, handcrafted chocolates and fresh local farm produce. Naturally, shops shut religiously for a 'slowdown' twice a week.

Sights

Università di Scienze Gastronomiche UNIVERSITY
(University of Gastronomic Sciences; www.unisg.it; Piazza Vittorio Emanuele 9) Another creation of Carlo Petrini, founder of the Slow Food Movement, this university, established in the village of Pollenzo (4km southeast of Bra) in 2004, occupies a former royal palace and offers three-year courses in gastronomy and food management. Its **Banca del Vino** (www.bancadelvino.it; Piazza Vittorio Emanuele II 13), a wine cellar-library of Italian wines, conducts free guided tastings by appointment.

Chiesa di San Andrea CHURCH
(Piazza Caduti) The sloping main square in Bra contains some stately baroque architecture best exemplified in the **Chiesa di San Andrea**, designed by Bernini.

Sleeping & Eating

Albergo Cantine Ascheri DESIGN HOTEL €€
(0172 43 03 12; www.ascherihotel.it; Via Piumati 25, Bra; s/d €115/150; P ❄ @) Built around the Ascheri family's winery (established in 1880), this ultra-contemporary hotel incorporating wood, steel mesh and glass, includes a mezzanine library, 27 sun-drenched rooms and a vine-lined terrace overlooking the rooftops. From the lobby you can see straight down to the vats in the cellar (guests get a free tour). It's just one block south of Bra's train station.

Albergo Dell'Agenzia HOTEL €€
(☑ 0172 45 86 00; www.albergoagenzia.it; Via Fossano 21, Pollenzo; s/d €110/160; P ❄ ☎ ☎) Part of the same sprawling complex that houses Pollenzo's Università di Scienze Gastronomiche, the rooms are spacious and elegantly furnished, with huge beds, walk-in wardrobes, marble bathrooms and the occasional roof terrace that looks over village rooftops. With a restaurant run by people who really know their business, a well-stocked wine cellar and a park, its ever-so-slight corporate edge soon melts away.

Osteria del Boccondivino OSTERIA €€
(☑ 0172 42 56 74; www.boccondivinoslow.it; Via Mendicità Istruita 14, Bra; meals €25-32; ☺ noon-2.30pm & 7-10pm Tue-Sat) 🍴 On the 1st floor of the Slow Food Movement's courtyard headquarters, this bottle-lined dining room was the first to be opened by the emerging organisation back in the 1980s. Service can be rather humourless, but the menu, which changes daily, is, as you'd expect, a picture of precise providence and seasonality, and dishes are beautifully prepared.

ℹ Information

Tourist Office (☑ 0172 43 01 85; www.turismoinbra.it; Piazza Caduti della Liberta 20, Bra; ☺ 8.30am-12.30pm & 3-6pm Mon-Fri, 9am-noon Sat & Sun) Has information on both towns and the region.

ℹ Getting There & Away

From the train station on Piazza Roma, trains link Bra with Turin (€4.60, 45 minutes), via Carmagnola, while buses connect Bra with Pollenzo (€1.10, 15 minutes).

Asti

POP 75,800 / ELEV 123M

Just 30km apart, Asti and Alba were fierce rivals in medieval times, when they faced off against each other as feisty, independent strongholds ruled over by feuding royal families. These days the two towns maintain a friendly rivalry – workaday Asti sniffs at Alba's bourgeoning glamour – but are united by viticulture. Asti produces the sparkling white Asti Spumante wine made from white muscat grapes.

◉ Sights & Activities

Torre Troyana o Dell'Orologio LANDMARK
(Piazza Medici; ☺ 10am-1pm & 4-7pm Apr-Sep, 10am-1pm & 3-6pm Sat & Sun Oct) **FREE** During the late 13th century the region became one of Italy's wealthiest, with 150-odd towers springing up in Asti alone. Of the 12 that remain, only this one can be climbed. Troyana is a 38m-tall tower that dates from the 12th century. The clock was added in 1420.

Cattedrale di Santa Maria Assunta CATHEDRAL
(Piazza Cattedrale) Rising above Asti's historic core is the enormous belfry of this 13th-century Romanesque-Gothic cathedral. Its grandly painted interior merits a peek.

Enoteca Boero di Boero Mario WINE TASTING
(Piazza Astesano 17; ☺ 9am-noon & 3-8pm Tue-Sun, 3-8pm Mon) Roll up your sleeves and get down to Asti's most pleasurable activity – wine tasting. This small, unassuming *enoteca* lines up the glasses morning and afternoon. It's all good, but you're here for the Barbera d'Asti and the sparkling Moscato.

🎊 Festivals & Events

Palio d'Asti HORSE RACING
Held on the third Sunday of September, this bareback horse race commemorates a victorious battle against Alba during the Middle Ages and draws over a quarter of a million spectators from surrounding villages. Cheeky Alba answers with a donkey race on the first Sunday in October.

Douja d'Or FOOD
🍷 This 10-day festival (a *douja* is a terracotta wine jug unique to Asti), held in early September, is complemented by the **Delle Sagre** food festival on the second Sunday of September.

🛏 Sleeping & Eating

Outside the town centre, there are some lovely spots to sleep in the nearby Monferrato vineyards – ask Asti's tourist offices for a list of properties.

⭐ **Villa Pattono** BOUTIQUE HOTEL €€
(☑ 0141 96 20 21; www.villapattono.com; Strada Drotte, Costiglione d'Asti; d €120/160; ☺ late-Mar–Dec; P ❄ ☎ ☎) Around a 20-minute drive south of Asti, surrounded by vineyards and rolling hills, Villa Pattono is a painstakingly restored 18th-century country mansion with frescoed ceilings, dark wood floors and marble bathrooms. There are just nine plush rooms located in the main house, a couple more in the annexed farm buildings and a

magnificent three-floor suite in a neo-medieval tower.

The hotel is part of the Renatto Ratto winery, where guided tastings and visits to the cellar can be arranged on request.

Hotel Palio HOTEL €€
(☎0141 3 43 71; www.hotelpalio.com; Via Cavour 106; s/d €90/120; P✳@☎) Wedged between the train station and the old town, the Palio's utilitarian exterior belies comfortable facilities inside. The owners also run the Ristorante Falcon Vecchia, one of Asti's oldest, which opened in 1607.

Osteria La Vecchia Carrozza OSTERIA €
(Via Caducci 41; meals €18-25; ☉noon-2pm & 7-10pm Tue-Sat) You could be sharing the room with a quartet of nuns or a birthday party of celebrating college graduates at this local spot. Bedecked with white tablecloths, your truffle-scented pasta comes with much down-to-earth Piedmontese cheer.

CasaMàr SEAFOOD €€
(☎0141 35 11 00; casamar.it; Vicolo GB Giuliani 3; meals €35; ☉12.30-2pm & 7.30-11.30pm Tue-Fri, lunch only Sat & Sun) A fabulous surprise: a bright, modern seafood place in the heart of tradition-bound, landlocked Piedmont. Some of the international leaning dishes can be a little ambitious but locals, who obviously need the occasional break from the deep earthy Langhe flavours, come for the tasty seafood pastas and citrus-spritzed fish tartares.

❶ Information

Tourist Office (www.astiturismo.it; Piazza Alfieri 29; ☉9am-1pm & 2.30-6.30pm Mon-Sat) Has details of September's flurry of wine festivals.

❶ Getting There & Away

Asti is on the Turin–Genoa railway line and is served by hourly trains in both directions. Journey time is 30 to 55 minutes to/from Turin (€4.35), and 1¾ hours to/from Genoa (€7.60). To get to Alba you must take a bus.

Monferrato Region

Vineyards fan out around Asti, interspersed with castles and celebrated restaurants. Buses run from Asti to many of the villages; Asti's tourist offices can provide schedules.

A land of literary giants (contemporary academic and novelist Umberto Eco and 18th-century dramatist Vittorio Alfieri hail from here) and yet another classic wine (the intense Barbera del Monferrato), the Monferrato area occupies a fertile triangle of terrain between Asti, Alessandria and its historical capital, **Casale Monferrato** (population 38,500).

◉ Sights

The tiny hamlet of **Moncalvo** (population 3320), 15km north of Asti along the S457, makes a perfect photo stop, with a lookout above its castle.

Many producers conduct cellar tours; the **Consorzio Operatori Turistici Asti e Monferrato** (www.terredasti.it; Piazza Alfieri 29) in Asti has a detailed list of tours and can provide directions.

🛏 Sleeping & Eating

Cascina Rosa AGRITURISMO €
(☎0141 92 52 35; www.cascinarosa33.it; Viale Pininfarina 33; s/d €50/80; P✳☎≋) A great find in not-always-budget-friendly Piedmont, this farmhouse B&B stands on a hilltop and enjoys a 360° panorama of the lush Monferrato countryside. Switched-on owners really want you to unwind and enjoy the region and besides providing simple, stylish and suitably rustic rooms, offer up a host of ideas for rides, walks and other leisurely persuits.

Locanda del Sant'Uffizio LUXURY HOTEL €€
(☎0141 91 62 92; www.relaissantuffizio.com; Strada Sant'Uffizio 1; d/ste €140/190; P✳@≋) This knockout, restored 17th-century convent (and sleek wellness centre) is set in 4 hectares of vineyards. Many of the convent's rooms, some with original frescoes, reflect the colour of the flowers after which they are named. Bike rental is free, and a pick-up service from Asti can be arranged.

Sant'Uffizio has a small, elegant **restaurant**, which is open to non-guests, though you'll need to book ahead. The *locanda* (inn) is 3.3km south of Moncalvo.

Varallo & the Valsesia

Situated 66km northwest of Vercelli in northern Piedmont, Varallo guards the **Sacro Monte di Varallo** (www.sacromonte divarallo.it; ☉8am-noon & 2-5.30pm) **FREE**, the oldest of Italy's nine Sacri Monti (Sacred Mountains), all a Unesco World Heritage Site from 2003. The complex consists of an astounding 45 chapels, with 800 statues depicting the Passion of Christ set on a rocky buttress on the slopes of Monte Tre Croci. A Franciscan friar created the site in 1491, hoping to reproduce an alpine simulacrum of Jerusalem for locals who couldn't make the pilgrimage to the real deal. The complex is anchored by a basilica dating from 1614, and the subsequent chapels follow the course of Christ's life told through frescoes and life-size terracotta statues. The scenes are sometimes macabre. The Monte is accessed via a winding walking path from Piazza Ferrari in town.

Beyond Varallo, the Sesia river heads spectacularly north to the foot of the Monte Rosa massif. Alpine slopes climb sharply, offering numerous walking, cycling and white-water-rafting possibilities. The valley's last village, **Alagna Valsesia**, is an ancient Swiss-Walser settlement-turned-ski-resort, which is part of the Monte Rosa Ski Area (p228). It is well known for its off-piste runs. From the town a cable car climbs to Punta Indren (3260m), from where fit walkers or climbers can strike out for the highest

rifugio (mountain chalet) in Europe, the **Capanna Regina Margherita** (☑0163 9 10 39; www.rifugimonterosa.it; dm €45, with half-board €75), perched atop Punta Gnifetti on the Swiss–Italian border at an astounding 4554m. The ascent requires glacier travel, but non-experts can hire a guide through **Corpo Guide Alagna** (www.guidealagna. com; Piazza Grober 1). Costs are €300 for a four-person group for the five-day excursion (June to September).

VALLE D'AOSTA

POP 128,500

While its Dolomite cousins tend to the Tyrolean, Aosta's nuances are French. The result is a hybrid culture known as Valdostan, a long-ago mingling of the French Provençal and northern Italian that is notable in the local architecture, the dining table and in the survival of an esoteric local language, Franco-Provençal or Valdôtain, which is still used by approximately 55% of the population.

Comprising one large glacial valley running east–west, bisected by several smaller valleys, the semi-autonomous Val d'Aosta is overlooked by some of Europe's highest peaks, including Mont Blanc (4810m), the Matterhorn (Monte Cervino; 4478m), Monte

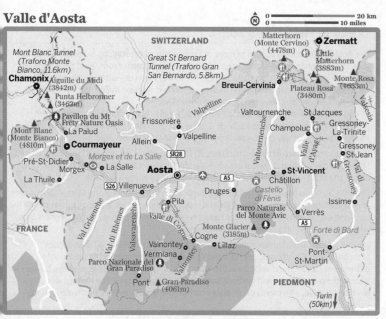

Valle d'Aosta

Rosa (4633m) and Gran Paradiso (4061m). Not surprisingly, the region offers some of the best snow facilities on the continent, with opportunities for skiers to descend hair-raisingly into France and Switzerland over lofty glaciers or traverse them in equally spectacular cable cars.

When the snow melts, the hiking is just as extraordinary, with access to the 165km Tour du Mont Blanc, Parco Nazionale del Gran Paradiso, and Aosta's two blue-riband, high-altitude trails: the Alte Vie 1 and 2.

Aosta's roots are Roman – the eponymous town guards some significant ruins – while annexation by the House of Savoy in the 11th century led to the building of numerous medieval castles. In the 12th and 13th centuries, German-speaking Walsers from Switzerland migrated into the Val di Gressoney, and a handful of villages still preserve this language and vernacular architecture.

Aosta

POP 34,800 / ELEV 565M

Jagged Alpine peaks rise like marble cathedrals above the regional capital Aosta, a once-important Roman settlement that retains a charming historic centre, while also sprawling rather untidily across the valley floor. Bounced around between Burgundy (France) and Savoy (Italy) in the Middle Ages, the modern town remains bilingual, with a Valdostan culture that can be heard in its musical local dialect and simple but hearty cuisine.

◉ Sights

Roman Ruins   ARCHAEOLOGICAL SITE

FREE Aosta's 2000-year-old centre is awash with Roman ruins. The grand triumphal arch, **Arco di Augusto** (Piazza Arco di Augusto), has been strung with a crucifix in its centre since medieval times. From the arch, head east across the Buthier river bridge to view the cobbled **Roman bridge** – in use since the 1st century AD.

Backtracking west 300m along Via Sant'Anselmo brings you to **Porta Praetoria**, the main gate to the Roman city. Heading north along Via di Bailliage and down a dust track brings you to Aosta's **Roman theatre** (Via Porta Praetoria; ⊙9am-7pm Sep-Jun, to 8pm Jul & Aug). Part of its 22m-high facade is still intact. In summer, performances are held in the better-preserved lower section. Further north, the forbidding 12th-century **Torre dei Balivi**, a former prison, marks one corner of the Roman wall and peers down on the smaller **Torre dei Fromage** – named after a family rather than a cheese. It's

---

SKIING IN THE VALLE D'AOSTA

The Aosta Valley allows access to three of Europe's most prestigious ski areas – Courmayeur, Breuil-Cervinia and Monte Rosa – plus numerous smaller runs. A lift pass covering the entire Valle d'Aosta costs €133.50/293 for three/seven days; seven day pass holders can choose an international option that gives you two ski days in Zermatt for €346. For up-to-date prices and pass variations see www.skivallee.it.

The best of the smaller resorts is **Pila** (p230), easily accessible by cable car from Aosta town, while the pristine **Valle di Cogne**, in Parco Nazionale del Gran Paradiso, is an idyllic place to enjoy cross-country skiing in relative solitude.

Courmayeur (www.courmayeurmontblanc.it) Courmayeur is dominated by spectacular Mont Blanc vistas and allows access to legendary runs such as the Vallée Blanche. Down below, the pretty Alpine town hosts a chilled, non-glitzy après-ski scene.

Breuil-Cervinia (www.cervinia.it) Breuil-Cervinia, in the shadow of the Matterhorn, is set at a high altitude and has more reliable late-season snow. There are good intermediate runs and kids' facilities here, but the resort is rather tacky in places. On the brighter side, you can ski across into Zermatt in Switzerland.

Monte Rosa Ski Area (www.monterosa-ski.com) The Monte Rosa ski area consists of three valleys. Champoluc anchors the Valle d'Ayas, Gressoney lights up the Val d'Gressoney and Alagna Valsesia is the focal point in the Valsesia. These valleys have a less manic resort scene and harbour some quiet Walser villages. The skiing, however, is white-knuckle, with plenty of off-piste and heli-skiing possibilities, particularly in the Valsesia.

Aosta

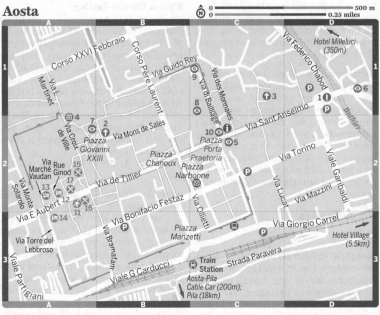

Aosta

closed to the public except during temporary art exhibitions; the tourist office has a program. All that remains of the **Roman forum**, another couple of blocks west, beneath Piazza Giovanni XXIII, is a colonnaded underground walkway known as Criptoportico.

Chiesa di Sant'Orso　　　　CHURCH
(Via Sant'Orso; ⊘9am-7pm) This intriguing church is part of a still-operating monastery. The church dates back to the 10th century but was altered on several occasions, notably in the 15th century, when Giorgio di Challant of the ruling family ordered the original frescoes to be painted over and a new, lower roof installed.

All was not lost: the renovations left the upper levels of the frescoes intact above the new roofline. You can ask the warden to unlock the door, letting you clamber up a narrow flight of wooden steps into the cavity between the original and the 15th-century ceilings to view the well-preserved remnants.

Museo Archeologico Regionale　　MUSEUM
(Piazza Roncas 12; ⊘10am-1pm & 2-6pm Tue-Sun) **FREE** Aosta's little city museum does an excellent job of detailing the city's

Roman history with a scale model of Aosta's Roman layout plus various antediluvian remains and some fascinating finds from a necropolis discovered at the gates of the Roman city.

Cattedrale Santa Maria Assunta CATHEDRAL
(Piazza Giovanni XXIII; ⏱6.30am-noon & 3-7pm) The neoclassical facade of Aosta's cathedral belies the impressive Gothic interior. Inside, the carved 15th-century walnut-wood choir stalls are particularly beautiful. Two mosaics on the floor, dating from the 12th to the 13th centuries, are also notable, as are the treasures displayed in the lovingly attended **Museo del Tesoro**.

🏃 Activities

Skiing

Pila SKIING
(www.pila.it; half-/full-day pass €28/37; ⏱mid-Dec–mid-Apr) The 1800m-high resort of Pila, accessible by the Aosta–Pila cable car from town or a zigzagging 18km drive south. Its 70km of runs, served by 13 lifts, form one of the valley's largest ski areas. Its highest slope, in the shadow of Gran Paradiso, reaches 2700m and sports an ace snow park with a half-pipe, jump and slide, and freestyle area for boarders and freestyle skiers.

The ski station is a village of sorts, but services such as tourist information and medical services are handled from Aosta.

Hiking & Mountain Biking

The lower slopes leading down from Pila into the Dora Baltea valley provide picturesque walks and rides. Mountain bikes can be transported for free on the **Aosta–Pila cable car** (one way/return €3/5; ⏱8am-12.15pm & 2-5pm Jun-early Sep) and mountain bikers can buy a combination pass (€13) for the cable car and chairlifts. The tourist office gives advice on mountain-biking itineraries and walking trails and has lists of Alpine guides and mountain accommodation.

Meinardi Sport OUTDOOR EQUIPMENT
(www.meinardisport.com; Via E Aubert 14; ⏱9.30am-12.30pm & 3-7.30pm Tue-Sat, 3-7.30pm Mon) A well-stocked sports shop with walking supplies and maps.

Wine & Cheese Tasting

Morgex et de La Salle WINE TASTING
(www.caveduvinblanc.com; Chemin des Iles 31) 🍷 The Valle d'Aosta is home to vineyards producing sought-after wines that are rarely available outside the region, including those from Europe's highest vineyard, named after the two villages that are strung together by its vines. Aosta's tourist office has a free, comprehensive booklet in English with information on cellars you can tour and taste. The vineyard is 25km west of Aosta.

Take the A5 before branching off onto SS26.

Valpelline Visitors' Centre CHEESE TASTING
(www.fontinacoop.it; Frissonière; ⏱8.30am-12.30pm & 2.30-6.30pm Mon-Fri, 9am-noon & 3-6pm Sat & Sun) FREE Aosta's signature *fontina* cheese is made from the full-cream, unpasteurised milk of Valdostan cows that have grazed on pastures up to 2700m above sea level, before being matured for three months in underground rock tunnels. You can learn more about the history, terroir (the land) and production of *fontina* and other Aostan cheeses at this museum-cum-visitors centre.

You'll need a car to get here from Aosta. Follow the SR28 for 7km north to Valpelline, turn east towards Ollomont and after 1.5km turn west along a mountain road to Frissonière.

🎉 Festivals & Events

Fiera di Sant'Orso ART
For over 1000 years the annual winter wood fair has been held on 30 and 31 January around Porta Praetoria, in honour of the town's patron saint, who made wooden shoes for the poor (hence the many wooden shoes you'll see in craft shops around town).

Woodcarvers from all over the valley gather to display their works and present an item to the saint at the Chiesa di Sant'Orso.

🛏 Sleeping

Aosta's hotel offerings are like the city itself: small, pretty and very low key. If you've got your own transport, there are a number of fantastic farm stays – the tourist office has a list.

INTO THE VALLEYS

While the rest of the Valle d'Aosta leans culturally towards France, the three valleys of Ayas, Gressoney and Sesia (the latter in Piedmont) are home to an 800-year-old Walser tradition. The German-descended Walsers migrated from Switzerland's Valais region in the 13th century, and their community has survived intact; many of the people who live in this rugged region still speak German (and Tich dialect) as a mother tongue and inhabit traditional Walser wood-slatted houses built on short stilts.

The main nexus in the **Valsesia** is Alagna Valsesia (1191m), a small ski resort at the valley head. Buses run from Turin or Aosta to Varallo, where you can connect to Alagna Valsesia.

To the west the **Valle d'Ayas** harbours its own ski resort, Champoluc (1560m), a storybook spot saved from tourism overload by the difficult road twisting from the A5 exit at Verrès around some tortuous hairpin bends. Verrès is on the main Turin–Aosta train line and is the dropping-off point for the Ayas. From here regular buses ply the road to Champoluc (€3.50, one hour, nine daily).

The main villages in the **Val di Gressoney** are pretty lakeside Gressoney-St-Jean (1385m), and **Gressoney-La-Trinité** (1637m), a few kilometres north – both Walser strongholds.

Hotel Village   HOTEL €

(☑0165 77 49 11; www.hotelvillageaosta.it; Torrent de Maillod 1; d/cabin €80/115) Don't let the proximity to the highway and suburban surrounds put you off, the Village has got so much else going for it. Cabins are set among tall trees and have a contemporary dark-hued style with lots of space and rustic balconies, while rooms in the main building are pure Scando cool.

The hotel also boasts the region's only Swedish restaurant and it's both beautifully designed and a beacon for those who can't face another plate of polenta. A good pick if you're driving and want to make early starts for the mountains.

Maison Colombot   GUESTHOUSE €

(☑0165 23 57 23; www.aostacamere.com; Via Torre del Lebbroso 3; s/d €55/90) This sweetly old-fashioned place has six rooms with rustic furniture and beamed ceilings overlooking the pretty main pedestrian street or a rustic courtyard. Breakfast here is delivered to your door on a tray – so cosy.

Coeur de Ville   APARTMENT €

(☑0165 23 06 79; www.coeurdeville.it; Rue Ginod 6; studio/1-bed apt €80/130) These good-sized modern apartments (they can sleep up to four people) are spread over four floors and have full kitchens, comfortable furniture and just enough decorative flair; ask for a place on an upper floor as the two ground-level studios are set slightly below street level and can be noisy.

★ Le Rêve Charmant   GUESTHOUSE €€

(☑0165 23 88 55; www.lerevecharmant.com; Via Marché Vaudan 6; d €130; P❄☎) Tucked away in a quiet historic laneway, this 12-room hotel is full of traditional Aostan furniture and decoration but keeps it simple and rather stylish. A warm, welcoming lounge leads to surprisingly spacious rooms that have beautiful modern bathrooms and high ceilings. The young owners are charming and service is top rate.

Hotel Milleluci   HOTEL €€€

(☑0165 4 42 74; www.hotelmilleluci.com; Loc Porossan 15; d €180-270; P❄@☎) Old wooden skis, traditionally carved wooden shoes, claw-foot baths, indoor and outdoor pools, a jacuzzi, sauna and gym, and sumptuous skiers' breakfasts make this large, family-run converted farmhouse seem more like a luxury resort. Set on a hillside above town, its balconied rooms look out to the eponymous 'thousand lights' twinkling from Aosta below.

✖ Eating & Drinking

Traditional dishes include *seupa valpellinentze* (a thick soup of cabbage, bread, beef broth and *fontina*) and *carbonada con polenta* (soup traditionally made with chamois, though these days usually beef). Open-air cafe terraces spring up on Piazza Chanoux in summer.

Croix de Ville
MODERN ITALIAN, WINE BAR €

(☑0165 23 07 38; www.la-dolce-vite.com; Via Croix de Ville 25; dishes €15-18; ☺10.30am-3.30pm & 5.30-10pm) Croix de Ville's smart, bustling dining room serves up contemporary Italian favourites such as tartares, beef *tagliata* (rare slices) with rocket and parmesan, and Mediterranan-tinged pastas, dispensing with the strict first- and second-course format. Similarly, the wine list takes it pan-Italian and international, though there's no reason to stray from the beautiful Aostan drops on offer.

Osteria dell'Oca
VALDOSTAN €€

(☑0165 23 14 19; www.ristoranteosteriadelloca. com; Via E Aubert 15; meals €25-32, pizza €4-9; ☺12.30-2.30pm & 7.30-10.30pm Tue-Sun) *Oca* means 'goose' and there are plenty, both on the menu and reproduced in hilariously kitsch china forms around the room. This quaint perch under an archway off Via E Aubert is Valdostan food heaven: dig into one-plate wonders like veal stew spooned over polenta or sausages covered in *fontina*.

Trattoria degli Artisti
TRATTORIA €€

(Via Maillet 5-7; meals €22-30; ☺12.30-2.30pm & 7-10pm Tue-Sat) Fabulous Valdostan cuisine is dished up at this dark and cosy trattoria, tucked down an alleyway off Via E Aubert. Antipasti such as puff pastry filled with Valdostan fondue, cured ham and regional salami are followed by dishes such as roe venison with polenta, and beef braised in Morgex et de La Salle white wine.

Vecchia Aosta
TRADITIONAL ITALIAN €€

(☑0165 36 11 86; Piazza Porta Praetoria 4; set menus €30-35; ☺noon-2.30pm & 7.30-10.30pm) Grafted onto a section of the old Roman wall, the Vecchia's setting is highly atmospheric. No post-piste boozer, this is a formal place with knowledgeable, sometimes capricious, staff and a traditional menu that includes *crespella alla Valdostana* (*fontina*-and-ham filled crepes) and beef braised in red wine.

In Bottiglieria
WINE BAR

(☑0165 4 08 85; www.inbottiglieria.com; Via E Aubert 15; ☺10.30am-10pm Tue-Sat) Hidden down a laneway, a young, well-dressed local crowd fill this stone-vaulted cellar for *aperitivo* and later on weekends. The wine selection is great and they also are known for their huge list of champagne and Italian sparklings.

ℹ Information

Aosta Tourist Office (www.lovevda.it; Piazza Porta Praetoria 3; ☺9am-7pm; 🐾) Housed in the old Roman gateway to the city, this helpful office has good maps, lists of wine and cheese producers in the region as well as extensive listings of farm stays and B&Bs.

Farmacia Centrale (☑0165 26 22 05; Piazza Chanoux 35; ☺8.30am-12.30pm & 3.30-7.30pm Mon-Fri)

Hospital (Ospedale Regionale; ☑0165 30 41; Viale Ginevra 3)

Police Station (☑0165 26 21 69; Corso Battaglione Aosta 169) West of the town centre.

Post Office (Piazza Narbonne; ☺8.15am-6pm Mon-Fri, to 1pm Sat)

ℹ Getting There & Away

Buses operated by **Savda** (www.savda.it) run to Milan (€17, 1½ to 3½ hours, two daily), Turin (€9, two hours, up to 10 daily) and Courmayeur (€3.50, one hour, up to eight daily), as well as to French destinations, including Chamonix. Services leave from Aosta's **bus station** (Via Giorgio Carrel), almost opposite the train station. To get to Breuil-Cervinia, take a Turin-bound bus to Châtillon (€1.50, 30 minutes, eight daily), then a connecting bus (€2.90, one hour, seven daily) to the resort.

Aosta's train station, on Piazza Manzetti, is served by trains from most parts of Italy. All trains to Turin (€9.45, two to 2½ hours, more than 10 daily) change at Ivrea.

Aosta is on the A5, which connects Turin with the Mont Blanc tunnel and France. Another exit road north of the city leads to the Great St Bernard tunnel and on to Switzerland.

Courmayeur

POP 2950 / ELEV 1224M

Flush up against France and linked by a dramatic cable-car ride to its cross-border cousin in Chamonix, Courmayeur is an activity-oriented Aosta village that has grafted upmarket ski facilities onto an ancient Roman balwark. Its *pièce de résistance* is lofty Mont Blanc, Western Europe's highest mountain – 4810m of solid rock and ice that rises like an impregnable wall above the narrow valleys of northwestern Italy, igniting awe in all who pass.

In winter Courmayeur is a fashion parade of skiers bound for the high slopes above town that glisten with plenty of late-season snow. In summer it wears a distinctly different hat: the Società delle Guide Alpine di Courmayeur is bivouacked

Activities

Courmayeur is heaven for outdoorsy types.

Società delle Guide Alpine di Courmayeur
MOUNTAINEERING

(☑0165 84 20 64; www.guidecourmayeur.com; Strada del Villair) Founded in 1859, this is Italy's oldest guiding association. In winter, guides lead adventure seekers off-piste, up frozen waterfalls and on heli-skiing expeditions. In summer, rock climbing, canyoning, canoeing, kayaking and hiking are among its many outdoor activities.

Terme di Pré-Saint-Didier
SPA

(☑0165 86 72 72; www.termedipre.it; Allée des Thermes; admission €35-50; ⊙9.30am-9pm Mon-Thu, 8.30am-11pm Fri & Sat, to 9pm Sun) Bubbling up a natural 37°C from the mountains' depths, the thermal water at Pré-Saint-Didier, a 10-minute drive south of Courmayeur, has been a source of therapeutic treatments since the bath-loving Romans marched into the valley. A spa opened here in 1838, with the newest addition dating to the 1920s. Admission includes use of a bathrobe, towel and slippers, plus water and herbal teas.

In addition to saunas, whirlpools and toning waterfalls, there's an indoor-outdoor thermal pool. It's lit by candles and torches at night, and is spectacular amid the snow and stars in wintertime. The older of the two spa buildings, accessed by a tunnel, has stunning high ceilings and fabulous views from its relaxation areas. Historical bonus: there's a little Roman bridge arcing over a trout-filled river, 50-odd metres beyond the car park in the opposite direction to the village.

Skiing

Courmayeur offers some extraordinary skiing in the spectacular shadow of Mont Blanc. The two main ski areas – the Plan Checrouit and Pré de Pascal – are interlinked by various runs (100km worth) and a network of chairlifts. Three lifts leave from the valley floor: one from Courmayeur itself, one from the village of Dolonne and one from nearby Val Veny. They are run by Funivie Courmayeur Mont Blanc (www.courmayeur-montblanc.com; Strada Regionale 47). Daily ski passes (€46) give you access to Courmayeur and Mont Blanc, 3-day passes and above include all of Aosta's resorts (3-/7-day pass €128/265). Queues are rarely an issue.

---

here and the town is an important staging post on three iconic long-distance hiking trails: the Tour du Mont Blanc (TMB), Alta Via 1 and Alta Via 2.

⊙ Sights

★ Funivie Monte Bianco
CABLE CAR

(Skyway; www.montebianco.com; return €45, Pavillon du Mt Fréty return €25; ⊙8.30am-12.40pm & 2-4.30pm) The Mont Blanc cable car might not be the world's highest, but it's surely the most spectacular. This astounding piece of engineering reaches three-quarters of the way up Western Europe's highest mountain before heading across multiple glaciers into France. New stations, with glass surfaces and futuristic cantilevers, opened in summer 2015, along with the introduction of state-of-the-art the 360° rotating cabins. It departs every 20 minutes from the village of La Palud, 15 minutes from Courmayeur's main square by free bus.

First stop is the 2173m-high midstation Pavillon du Mt Fréty, while at the top of the ridge is Punta Helbronner (3462m). All three stations have restaurants and other facilities; there's a sparkling wine cellar at the Pavillion and, in summer, the Giardino Botanico Alpino Saussurea (www.saussurea.net; admission €3, free with cable-car ticket in high summer; ⊙9.30am-6pm Jul-Sep) and a crystal room at Helbronner. Take ample warm clothes and sunglasses for the blinding snow, and head up early in the morning to avoid the heavy weather that often descends in the early afternoon.

From Punta Helbronner another cable car (from late May to late September, depending on weather conditions, €33.50) takes you on a breathtaking 5km transglacial ride across the Italian border into France to the Aiguille du Midi (3842m), from where the world's highest cable car transports you down to Chamonix (€77). The return trip from Chamonix to Courmayeur by bus is €15. An expensive day out, but a spectacular one.

Pavillon du Mt Fréty Nature Oasis
NATURE RESERVE

A protected zone of 1200 hectares tucked between glaciers, this nature oasis is accessible from the Pavillon du Mt Fréty. Enjoy numerous trails, including the Sentiero Francesco e Giuditta Gatti, where you have a good chance of spotting ibexes, marmots and deer.

Vallée Blanche SKIING

This is an exhilarating off-piste descent from Punta Helbronner across the Mer de Glace glacier into Chamonix, France. The route itself is not difficult – anyone of intermediate ability can do it – but an experienced guide is essential to steer you safely round the hidden crevasses.

All up, the 24km Vallée Blanche takes around four to five hours, allowing time to stop and take in the view.

Toula Glacier SKIING

Only highly experienced, hard-core skiers need apply for this terrifying descent, which also takes off from Punta Helbronner and drops for six sheer kilometres to La Palud. A guide is essential; it's usually easy to join a group.

Scuola di Sci Monte Bianco SKIING

(www.scuolascimontebianco.com; Strada Regionale 51) Founded in 1922, this veritable ski school offers instructors for downhill and snowboarding (1hr/day €48/360), along with specialist courses in freeride, telemark and cross-country.

Walking

From June until early September, Courmayeur's cable cars whisk walkers and mountain bikers up into the mountains.

Tour du Mont Blanc WALKING TRAIL

For many walkers (some 30,000 each summer), Courmayeur's trophy hike is the Tour du Mont Blanc (TMB). This 169km trek cuts across Italy, France and Switzerland, stopping at nine villages en route. Snow makes it impassable for much of the year. The average duration is anything from one week to 12 days; smaller sections are also possible.

You can undertake the hike solo, but if you're unfamiliar with the area, hooking up with a local guide is a good idea as the route traverses glacial landscapes. Easy day hikes will take you along the TMB as far as the Rifugio Maison Vieille (one hour 50 minutes) and Rifugio Bertone (two hours). Follow the yellow signposts from the Piazzale Monte Bianco in the centre of Courmayeur.

Swimming

Plan Chécrouit Swimming Pool SWIMMING

(half-day/day lift and pool admission €18/25; ◔10.30am-5pm mid-Jul–Aug) Yes, there's a highest heated swimming pool in Europe, and, at 1700m, this is it. Take the Dolonne cable car for a dip with a view and a laze among lush green surrounds, or hike up from Courmayeur in around an hour.

Mountain Biking

Mountain bikes can be hired for around €15 per day at **Noleggio Sci e Mountain Bike** (✆377 2494096; Stada Regionale 17).

🛏 Sleeping

Ask the tourist office for a list of *rifugi* (mountain huts), usually open from late June to mid-September.

Hotel Svizzero HOTEL €€

(✆0165 84 81 70; www.hotelsvizzero.com; Strada Statale 26/11; d €145; P❉❀) On the road just outside of the town's pedestrian centre, the family-run Svizzero has 27 rustic-contemporary rooms, as well as a chalet that can be rented on a weekly basis. The lovely old recycled wood and stone used throughout make for loads of atmosphere and provide the Alpine essentials of steam room and lift shuttle.

Hotel Bouton d'Or HOTEL €€

(✆0165 84 67 29; www.hotelboutondor.com; Strada Statale 26/10; s €95, d €170; P❉@ ❀🐾) Charmingly folksy Bouton d'Or is in the centre of Courmayeur and not only has incredible views of the imposing hulk of Mont Blanc, but also a sauna, a lounge full of interesting Alpine paraphernalia and, in summer, a peaceful garden.

Hotel Triolet HOTEL €€

(✆0165 84 68 22; www.hoteltriolet.com; Strada Regionale 63; s/d €100/170; P❉❀❉) Triolet is a tad smaller than your average ski digs, with only 20 rooms, allowing service to remain personal as well as affable. Aside from the usual tick-list, there's a pleasant spa (jacuzzi, steam room, sauna), ski lockers and a vista-laden breakfast room.

🍴 Eating

Bars, cafes and restaurants line Via Roma.

La Padella AOSTAN, PIZZA €€

(✆0165 84 19 77; Vicolo Dolonne 7; meals €25) Friendly, cosy and popular, there's a huge menu of polenta and *fontina* cheese dishes – add your topping of mushroom, sausage or various other meats. They also run a takeaway prepared-meal place,

BARD

A moutain gorge flanked by steep peaks has made this narrow pass a strategic prize throughout history: fortifications have existed here since pre-Roman times. Both the fort itself and its tumble of a village below gaze upon a valley that has long inspired both poets and soldiers. It's a day-trip favourite but if you fancy overnighting, there are a number of good restaurant options and a lovely small hotel; the village's intact medieval layout and pristine architecture is an absolute delight.

Forte di Bard (www.fortedibard.it; fort entrance free, Museo delle Alpi adult/reduced €8/6; ⊙10am-6pm Tue-Fri, to 7pm Sat & Sun) Plucky Italian soldiers, outnumbered 100 to one, fought off Napoleon's army for two weeks here in 1800; the French emperor was so piqued he razed the fortress to the ground. The current 1830s Savoy replacement is, rest assured, as imposing as ever, set high up upon a rocky escarpment at the jaws of the Valle d'Aosta. It makes for a great day's diversion from skiing or hiking at around 70 minutes from Aosta by bus.

Ride up a series of super-modern panoramic lifts, where you can admire the inspiring Alpine views and visit the Vallée Culture rooms, which offer interesting nuggets of information on Aosta's history and traditions. The **Museo delle Alpi**, a clever, interactive museum, takes you on a journey across the entire Alps – children love the Flight of the Eagle, a cinematic simulation of a bird's flight over valleys, villages, lakes and snow-capped peaks. The fort's **prisons**, which were still in use right up until the end of WWII, can also be visited (adult/reduced €4/3) and there's an excellent program of big-ticket 20th-century art and photography shows.

Hotel Ad Gallias (☑0125 80 98 78; www.hoteladgallias.com; Via Vittorio Emanuele 5/7; d €130; 🅿❄🕸) Occupying a couple of village houses at the entrance to the village, this stylish hotel has views of the fort and fabulous wellness area built around a Roman wall with hot tub, sauna, steam room and treatments.

Mmmartine, a good option for lazy self-caterers or picnicking.

La Terraza   INTERNATIONAL, PIZZA €€€
(www.ristorantelaterrazza.com; Via Circonvalazione 73; meals €40; ⊙noon-2.30pm & 7-10.30pm) This lively, central bar-restaurant-pizzeria has the full gamut of pizzas, steaks and the usual over-ambitious international-style après-ski nosh. True to the local spirit there are also plenty of Valdostan dishes, including venison with mushrooms.

🛈 Information

For mountain rescue, call ☑800 319 319.
Centro Traumatologico (☑0165 84 46 84; Strada dei Volpi 3) Medical clinic. The nearest hospital is in Aosta.
Tourist Office (☑0165 84 20 60; www. lovecourmayeur.com; Piazzale Monte Bianco 13; ⊙9am-12.30pm & 3-6.30pm)

🛈 Getting There & Away

Three trains a day from Aosta terminate at Pré-St-Didier, with bus connections (20 to 30 minutes, eight to 10 daily) to **Courmayeur bus station** (Piazzale Monte Bianco), outside the tourist office. There are up to eight direct Aosta–Courmayeur buses daily (€3.50, one hour), and long-haul buses serve Milan (€19.50, 4½ hours, three to five daily) and Turin (€10, 3½ to 4½ hours, two to four daily).

Immediately north of Courmayeur, the 11.6km Mont Blanc tunnel leads to Chamonix in France (one way/return €43.50/54.30). At the Italian entrance, a plaque commemorates Pierlucio Tinazzi, a security employee who died while saving at least a dozen lives during the 1999 disaster when a freight truck caught fire in the tunnel.

Parco Nazionale del Gran Paradiso

Italy's oldest national park, the aptly named Gran Paradiso, was created in 1922 after Vittorio Emanuele II gave his hunting reserve to the state, ostensibly to protect the endangered ibex. The park preceded the rise of the modern ski resort; as a result, the area has so far resisted the lucrative lure of the mass tourist trade. Its tangible wilderness feel is rare in Italy.

Gran Paradiso incorporates the valleys around the eponymous 4061m peak (Italy's 7th highest), three of which are in the Valle d'Aosta: the Valsavarenche, Val di Rhêmes and the beautiful Valle di Cogne. On the Piedmont side of the mountain, the park includes the valleys of Soana and Orco.

The main stepping stone into the park is tranquil Cogne (population 1481, elevation 1534m), a refreshing antidote to over-developed Breuil-Cervinia on the opposite side of the Valle d'Aosta. Aside from its plethora of outdoor opportunities, Cogne is known for its lace-making, and you can buy local products at several craft and antique shops.

◉ Sights

Giardino Alpino Paradisia GARDENS
(☑0165 7 53 01; www.pngp.it; adult/reduced €3/1.50; ⏰10am-5.30pm mid-Jun–mid-Sep, to 6.30pm Jul & Aug) The park's amazing biodiversity, including butterflies and Alpine flora, can be seen in summer at this fascinating Alpine botanical garden in the tiny hamlet of Valnontey (1700m), 3km south of Cogne. Guided nature walks are available from July to September.

🏃 Activities

Gran Paradiso is one of Italy's best walking areas, with over 700km of trails linked by a recuperative network of *rifugi* (mountain huts). The tourist office has free winter and summer trail maps for walkers and skiers.

Skiing

Despite its wilderness credentials, there are in fact 9km of downhill slopes here. A one-day ski pass covering the use of Cogne's single cable car, chairlift and drag lift costs €24. But most winter visitors come here for the 80km of well-marked cross-country skiing trails (admission per day €5) that line the unspoilt Valle di Cogne. Try trail 23 up to Valnontey and Vermiana, or head east to Lillaz. Skiing lessons are offered by the Società Guide Alpine di Cogne (☑0165 7 40 50; www.guidealpinecogne.it; Piazza Chanoux 1). They also offer ice-climbing expeditions on the Lillaz waterfall.

Walking

Easy walks around Cogne include the 3km stroll (wheelchair accessible) to the village of Lillaz on trail 23, where there is a geological park and a waterfall that drops 150m in three stages. Trails 22 and 23 will also get you to the village of Valnontey, where you can continue up the valley to the hamlet of Vermiana (1½ hours one way). Trail 8 from Cogne leads to another waterfall (Pila) via the village of Gimillian.

A classic, moderately strenuous hike from Valnontey is to the Rifugio Sella (☑0165 7 43 10; www.rifugiosella.com; dm €22), a former hunting lodge of King Vittorio Emanuele II. From the town bridge, follow the Alta Via 2 uphill for two to 2½ hours. More adventurous hikers can continue along the exhilarating Sella-Herbetet Traverse (15km), a seven-hour loop that will drop you back in Valnontey. You'll need a head for heights and a good map.

Climbing

The main point of departure for the Gran Paradiso peak is Pont in the Valsavarenche. Technically it's no Mont Blanc and can be completed in a day, but you'll need a guide (a two-day ascent for two people starts at €500, less for larger groups). Contact the Società Guide Alpine di Cogne.

Horse Riding

Horse riding and 45-minute horse-and-carriage rides through the mountain meadows are run by Le Traîneau Equestrian Tourism Centre (☑333 3147248; www.letraineau.too.it) in Valnontey.

🛏 Sleeping & Eating

Wilderness camping is forbidden in the park, but there are 11 *rifugi* (mountain huts). The tourist office has a list.

Camping Lo Stambecco CAMPGROUND €
(☑0165 7 41 52; www.campeggiolostambecco.it; Frazione Valnontey 6; camping €24; ⏰May-Sep; ℗) Pitch up under the pine trees in the heart of the park at this well-run and friendly site. Its sister hotel, La Barme, rents bikes to explore the mountains. No tent? Ask if one of their caravans are available (€40 per night).

Hotel Sant'Orso HOTEL €€
(☑0165 7 48 21; www.cognevacanza.com; Via Bourgeois 2; d €160; ⏰spring & autumn closures vary; ℗🏊🐕) Cogne personified (ie tranquil, courteous and understated), the Sant'Orso is nonetheless equipped with plenty of hidden extras, including a new wellness area and huge gardens. Further kudos is

gained by the fact that you can start your cross-country skiing pretty much from the front door. The owners also run the Hotel du Gran Paradis nearby.

★ **Hotel Bellevue** LUXURY HOTEL €€€
(☑0165 7 48 25; www.hotelbellevue.it; Rue Grand Paradis 22; s/d €220/240, 2-person chalets €330; ☺mid-Dec–mid-Oct; P☒) Overlooking meadows, this green-shuttered mountain hideaway evokes its 1920s origins with romantic canopied timber 'cabin beds', weighty cowbells strung from old beams, claw-foot baths and the occasional open fire (it's definitely not for minimalists). Afternoon tea is included in the price, as is use of the health spa, and you can also rent mountain bikes and snowshoes.

Its four restaurants include a Michelin-starred gourmet affair, a wonderful cheese restaurant (goat raclette!) with produce from the family's own cellar, a lunchtime terrace restaurant and a dark, historic brasserie on the village's main square, a few moments' stroll away.

Hotel Ristorante Petit Dahu TRADITIONAL ITALIAN €€
(☑0165 7 41 46; www.hotelpetitdahu.com; Frazone Valnontey 27; meals €35; ☺closed May & Oct) Straddling two traditional stone-and-wood buildings, this friendly, family-run spot has a wonderful restaurant (also open to nonguests; advance bookings essential) preparing rustic mountain cooking using wild Alpine herbs. It also has pretty rooms to stay in (s/d half-board €70/140).

❶ Information

Tourist Office (www.cogne.org; Piazza Chanoux 36; ☺9am-12.30pm & 2.30-5.30pm Mon-Sat) Has detailed information on all aspects of the park and a list of emergency contact numbers.

❶ Getting There & Around

Up to ten buses run daily to/from Cogne and Aosta (€2.90, 50 minutes). Cogne can also be reached by cable car from Pila.

Valley buses (up to 10 daily) link Cogne with Valnontey (€1.10, five minutes) and Lillaz (€1.10, five minutes).

Valtournenche

One of Europe's most dramatic – and deadly – mountains, the Matterhorn (4478m) frames the head of Valtournenche. Byron once stood here and marvelled at 'Europe's noble rock'. Today he'd also get an eyeful of one of the Alps' most architecturally incongruous ski resorts, Breuil-Cervinia. But, ugly or not, Cervinia's ski facilities are second to none; you can hit the snow year-round up here and even swish across into Zermatt, Switzerland.

🏃 Activities

Plateau Rosa (3480m) and the Little Matterhorn (3883m) in the Breuil-Cervinia ski area offer some of Europe's highest skiing, while the Campetto area has introduced the Valle d'Aosta to night skiing. A couple of dozen cable cars, four of which originate in Breuil-Cervinia, serve 200km of downhill pistes. Ski passes covering Breuil-Cervinia and Valtournenche cost €41/115/237 for 1/3/7 days.

Contact Breuil-Cervinia's **Scuola di Sci del Breuil Cervinia** (www.scuolascibreuil. com) or **Scuola Sci del Cervino** (www.scuola cervino.com) for skiing and snowboarding lessons, and its mountain-guide association **Società Guide del Cervino** (www. guidedelcervino.com; Via J Antoine Carrel 20) to make the most of the Matterhorn's wild off-piste opportunities.

Between July and September several cable cars and lifts to Plateau Rosa continue to operate, allowing year-round skiing on the Swiss side of the mountain. A one-day international ski pass costs €57.

❶ Getting There & Away

Savda (p232) operates buses from Breuil-Cervinia to Châtillon (€2.90, one hour, seven daily), from where there are connecting buses to/from Aosta.

Milan & the Lakes

Best Places to Eat

➡ La Brisa (p252)

➡ Un Posto a Milano (p252)

➡ Locanda di Orta (p268)

➡ Gatto Nero (p275)

➡ Dal Pescatore (p300)

Best Places to Stay

➡ Maison Borella (p250)

➡ LaFavia Four Rooms (p250)

➡ Locanda San Vigilio (p290)

➡ Albergo Verbano (p264)

➡ Avenue Hotel (p271)

Why Go?

Wedged between the Alps and the Po valley, the glacial lakes of Lombardy (Lombardia) were formed at the end of the last ice age, and have been a popular holiday spot since Roman times. At the region's heart is Milan, capital of the north and Italy's second-largest metropolis. Home to the nation's stock exchange, one of Europe's biggest trade-fair grounds and an international fashion hub, it is also Italy's economic powerhouse.

Beyond Milan pretty countryside unfolds, dotted with patrician towns including Pavia, Monza, Bergamo, Cremona and Mantua; all are steeped in history, hiding fabulous Unesco monuments and world-class museums. To the north a burst of Mediterranean colour and a balmy microclimate awaits around lakes Orta, Maggiore, Como, Garda and Iseo. Ringed by hot-pink oleanders in luxurious tiered gardens, the lakes are powerfully seductive. No wonder George Clooney is smitten.

When to Go
Milan

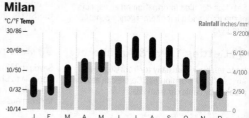

May & Jun Spring flowers, mild weather and concerts in Cremona herald the start of summer.

Sep As many as 350 vessels turn out for the Centomiglia, Lago di Garda's prestigious regatta.

Dec Winter warmers include the Feast of St Ambrogio and opera at La Scala.

MILAN

POP 1.3 MILLION

Milan is Italy's city of the future, a fast-paced metropolis with New World qualities: ambition, aspiration and a highly individualistic streak. In Milan appearances really do matter and materialism requires no apology. The Milanese love beautiful things, luxurious things, and it is for that reason perhaps that Italian fashion and design maintain their esteemed global position.

But like the models that work the catwalks, Milan is considered by many to be vain, distant and dull. And it is true that the city makes little effort to seduce visitors. However, this superficial lack of charm disguises a city of ancient roots and many treasures, which, unlike in the rest of Italy, you'll often get to experience without the queues. So while the Milanese may not always play nice, jump in and join them regardless in their intoxicating round of pursuits, whether that means precision-shopping, browsing edgy contemporary galleries or loading up a plate with local delicacies while downing an expertly mixed negroni cocktail.

History

Celtic tribes settled along the Po in the 7th century BC, and the area encompassing modern-day Milan has remained inhabited since. In AD 313 Emperor Constantine made his momentous edict granting Christians freedom of worship here. The city had already replaced Rome as the capital of the empire in 286, a role it kept until 402.

A *comune* (town council) was formed by all social classes in the 11th century, and, from the mid-13th century, government passed to a succession of dynasties – the Torrianis, Viscontis and, finally, the Sforzas. It fell under Spanish rule in 1525 and Austrian rule in 1713. Milan became part of the nascent Kingdom of Italy in 1860.

Benito Mussolini, one-time editor of the socialist newspaper *Avanti!*, founded the Fascist Party in Milan in 1919. He joined Italy with Germany in WWII in 1940. By early 1945, Allied bombings had destroyed much of central Milan. Mussolini was eventually strung up here by partisans after he sought to escape to Switzerland in 1945.

At the vanguard of two 20th-century economic booms, Milan cemented its role as Italy's financial and industrial capital. Immigrants poured in from the south and were later joined by others from China, Africa, Latin America, India and Eastern Europe, making for one of the most diverse cities in Italy. Culturally, the city was the centre of early Italian film production, and in the 1980s and '90s it ruled the world as the capital of design innovation and production. Milan's self-made big shot and media mogul Silvio Berlusconi made the move into politics in the 1990s and was then elected prime minister three more times – scandal and economic armageddon finally forced him from office in 2011.

Determined not to be consigned to the economic doldrums of the *crisi* (crisis), Milan staged the multibillion euro world Expo in 2015. Although riddled with controversy over corruption and overspending, the Expo has given Milan the gleaming new Porta Nuova district, a rehabilitated dock and canal system, miles of new cycle routes, expanded bike- and car-sharing schemes, a clutch of new museums and a much-needed injection of international interest.

◉ Sights

Milan's runway-flat terrain and monumental buildings are defined by concentric ring roads that trace the path of the city's original defensive walls. Although very little remains of the walls, ancient *porta* (gates) act as clear compass points. Almost everything you want to see, do or buy is contained within these city gates.

★ Duomo
CATHEDRAL

(Map p246; www.duomomilano.it; Piazza del Duomo; roof terraces adult/reduced via stairs €8/4, lift €13/7, Battistero di San Giovanni €4/2; ⊙ duomo 7am-6.40pm, roof terraces 9am-6.30pm, battistero 10am-6pm Tue-Sun; Ⓜ Duomo) A vision in pink Candoglia marble, Milan's extravagant Gothic cathedral, 600 years in the making, aptly reflects the city's creativity and ambition. Its pearly white facade, adorned with 135 spires and 3400 statues rises like the filigree of a fairy-tale tiara, wowing the crowds with its extravagant detail. The interior is no less impressive, punctuated by the largest stained-glass windows in Christendom, while in the crypt saintly Carlo Borromeo is interred in a rock-crystal casket.

Begun by Giangaleazzo Visconti in 1386, the cathedral's design was originally considered unfeasible. Canals had to be dug to transport the vast quantities of marble to the centre of the city and new technologies were invented to cater for the never-before-attempted scale. There was also that

Milan & the Lakes Highlights

1 Pondering the power of Leonardo's **Last Supper** (p247), the world's most famous painting.

2 Climbing to the roof terraces of Milan's marble **cathedral** (p239) for views of spires and flying buttresses.

3 Discovering the modernists who shaped Milan at the **Museo del Novecento** (p244).

4 Coming face to face with Old Masters in Bergamo's newly renovated **Accademia Carrara** (p293).

5 Strolling in Lago Maggiore's most spectacular island garden, **Isola Bella** (p263).

6 Making a tour of Lago di Como James Bond–style in your own **cigarette boat** (p274).

7 Sailing, surfing and kayaking beneath the snowcapped peaks in **Riva del Garda** (p289).

8 Marvelling at sumptuous Renaissance frescoes in Mantua's **Palazzo Ducale** (p297).

9 Discovering your own slice of lake-side bliss in Lago d'Orta's enchanting, historic **Orta San Giulio** (p267).

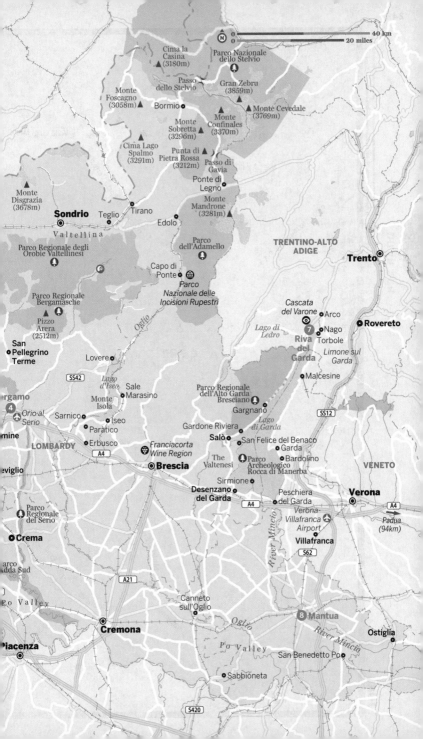

Milan

MILAN & THE LAKES

0 1 km / 0.5 miles

Via Censio
Via Losanna
Via Fauché
Via Mussi
Via Piero della Francesca
Former Expo Site (850m); Fieramilanocity (850m); Malpensa (46km)
Via Fratelli Induno
Via Giulio Cesare Procaccini
Piazza Gerusalemme
Via Giulio Cesare Procaccini
Corso Sempione
Via Canova
Via Mario Pisani

Via Brianza
Viale Brianza
Orio al Serio (48km)
Bus Services
Caiazzo
Stazione Centrale
Tunnel (250m)
Via Tonale
Sondrio
Via Dom Scarlatti
Via Dom Vitruvio
Via Settembrini
Piazza Duca d'Aosta
Torre Pirelli
Centrale FS
Via Fabio Filzi
Via Vittor Pisani
Via Mauro Macchi
Via San Gregorio
Via Felice Casati
Viale Tunisia
Corso Buenos Aires
Lima
Porta Venezia
Via Tadino
Viale Luigi Majno
Viale Piave
Via Poerio
Via Lambro
Via Venezia
Palestro
Giardini Pubblici
Piazza Cavour
Via Senato
Via Fatebenefratelli
Via Brera
Via Pontaccio
Via Panfilo Castaldi
Viale Vittorio Veneto
Bastioni di Porta Venezia
Turati
Repubblica
Corso di Porta Nuova
Via G Galilei
Via Generale Gustavo Fara
Gioia
Monza (12.5km); Bergamo (48km)
Zara
Piazzale Lagosta
Via Borsieri
Via Pollaiuolo
Piazza Fidia
Via Pastrengo
ISOLA
Via Sebenico
Via Isola
Via F Confalonieri
Via Gaetano De Castillia
Via Melchiorre Gioia
Piazza Sigmund Freud
Piazzale XXV Aprile
Viale F Crispi
Via Marsala
Via Castelfidardo
Via Solferino
BRERA
Lanza
Via Legnano
Moscova
Largo La Foppa
Viale Pasubio
Stazione Porta Garibaldi
Garibaldi
Via Tazzoli
Via G Pepe
Piazza Fidia
Piazzale Cimitero Monumentale
Cimitero Monumentale
Via Ceresio
Via Donato Bramante
Viale Montello
Viale Elvezia
Via Paolo Sarpi
Via Luigi Canonica
Parco Sempione
Via Melzi d'Eril
Piazza Sempione
Viale Emilio Alemagna
Viale Gadio

5
7
10
13
19
20
21
25
26
27
30
4

MILAN & THE LAKES

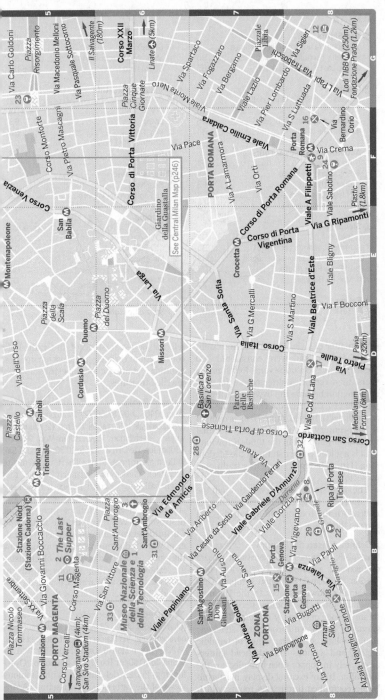

Via Carlo Goldoni
Piazza Risorgimento
Via Macedonio Melloni
Via Pasquale Sottocorno
Il Salvagente (180m)

Corso XXII Marzo
Linate (5km)

23

Piazzale Libia
Via L. Papi
Via Tiraboschi
Via Sigieri
12
Lodi TIBB (250m);
Fondazione Prada (1.2km)

Corso Montorte
Via Pietro Mascagni
Piazza Cinque Giornate

Via Spartaco
Via Fogazzaro
Via Bergamo
Via Lazio
Via Pier Lombardo
Via S. Luttuada

Corso Venezia

Corso di Porta Vittoria

Viale Monte Nero

Viale Emilio Caldara

Via Pace

Porta Romana
16
9
24
Via Bernardino Corio
Via Crema

San Babila Ⓜ

Montenapoleone Ⓜ

Giardino della Guastalla

See Central Milan Map (p246)

PORTA ROMANA

Via A Lamarmora
Via Orti

Corso di Porta Romana

Viale A Filippetti
Viale Sabotino

Piazza della Scala
Piazza del Duomo

Duomo Ⓜ

Via Larga

Crocetta Ⓜ

Corso di Porta Vigentina

Via G Ripamonti
Plastic (1.8km)

Via dell'Orso

Piazza Castello

Cairoli Ⓜ

Cordusio Ⓜ

Missori Ⓜ

Cadorna Triennale Ⓜ

Basilica di San Lorenzo
Parco delle Basiliche

Corso di Porta Ticinese

Via Santa Sofia
Via G Mercalli

Corso Italia
Via S Martino

Viale Beatrice d'Este
Viale Bligny
Via F Bocconi

Viale Col di Lana

Via Pietro Teulié
17

Pavia (32km)
Mediolanum Forum (6km)

Corso San Gottardo

Piazza Nicolò Tommaseo
Via XX Settembre
Via Giovanni Boccaccio

Stazione Nord (Stazione Cadorna) Ⓜ

PORTO MAGENTA
11
2 The Last Supper

Concilazione Ⓜ
Corso Vercelli

Lampugnano (4km);
San Siro Stadium (4km)

Corso Magenta
Via San Vittore
Piazza Sant'Ambrogio

Sant'Ambrogio Ⓜ
1
3
31

Museo Nazionale della Scienza e della Tecnologia
33

Via Edmondo de Amicis

Via Papiniano

Viale Gabriele D'Annunzio

28

Via Arena
Via Ariberto
Via Cesare da Sesto
Via Gaudenzio Ferrari
Viale Gorizia

Ripa di Porta Ticinese

Darsena
14
8
32
29
22

Porta Genova Ⓜ
15
Stazione Porta Genova Ⓜ
18

Via Vigevano
Via Paoli
Via Valenza
Naviglio Grande

Via Andrea Solari

ZONA TORTONA
Via Bergognone
Via Tortona
6
Armani Silos

Via Savona
Via Ausonio
Sant'Agostino
Parco Don Giussani
Viale Papiniano

Porta Genova
Via Bugatti

Alzaia Naviglio Grande

Milan

small matter of style. The Gothic lines went out of fashion and were considered 'too French', so it took on several looks as the years, then centuries, dragged on. Its slow construction became the byword for an impossible task (*'fabrica del Dom'*, in the Milanese dialect). Indeed, much of its ornament is 19th-century neo-Gothic, with the final touches only applied in the 1960s. Crowning it all is a gilded copper statue of the Madonnina (Little Madonna), the city's traditional protector.

The most spectacular view is through the innumerable marble spires and pinnacles that adorn the rooftop. On a clear day you can see the Alps.

Il Grande Museo del Duomo   MUSEUM
(Map p246; www.museo.duomomilano.it; Piazza del Duomo 12; adult/reduced €6/4; ◎10am-6pm Tue-Sun; Ⓜ Duomo) Stepping through Guido Canali's glowing spaces in the Duomo's new museum is like coming upon the sets for an episode of *Game of Thrones*. Tortured gargoyles leer down through the shadows; shafts of light strike the wings of heraldic angels; and a monstrous godhead glitters awesomely in copper once intended for the high altar. It's an exciting display, masterfully choreographed through 26 rooms, which

tell the 600-year story of the cathedral's construction through priceless sculptures, paintings, stained glass, tapestries and bejewelled treasures.

Palazzo Reale   MUSEUM, PALACE
(Map p246; ☑02 87 56 72; www.comune.milano.it/palazzoreale; Piazza del Duomo 12; admission varies; ◎exhibitions 2.30-7.30pm Mon, 9.30am-7.30pm Tue, Wed, Fri & Sun, to 10.30pm Thu & Sat; Ⓜ Duomo) Empress Maria Theresa's favourite architect, Giuseppe Piermarini, gave this town hall and Visconti palace a neoclassical overhaul in the late 18th century. The supremely elegant interiors were all but destroyed by WWII bombs; the Sala delle Cariatidi remains unrenovated as a reminder of war's indiscriminate destruction. Now the once opulent palace hosts blockbuster art exhibits attracting serious crowds to shows as diverse as Warhol, Chagall, da Vinci and Giotto.

★ Museo del Novecento   GALLERY
(Map p246; ☑02 8844 4061; www.museodelnovecento.org; Via Marconi 1; adult/reduced €5/3; ◎2.30-7.30pm Mon, 9.30am-7.30pm Tue, Wed, Fri & Sun, to 10.30pm Thu & Sat; Ⓜ Duomo) Overlooking Piazza del Duomo, with fabulous views of the cathedral, is Mussolini's Aren-

gario, from where he would harangue huge crowds in his heyday. Now it houses Milan's museum of 20th-century art. Built around a futuristic spiral ramp (an ode to the Guggenheim), the lower floors are cramped, but the heady collection, which includes the likes of Umberto Boccioni, Campigli, de Chirico and Marinetti, more than distracts.

Gallerie d'Italia
MUSEUM

(Map p246; www.gallerieditalia.com; Piazza della Scala 6; adult/reduced €10/8; ⊘9.30am-7.30pm Tue-Sun; ⓜDuomo) Housed in three fabulously decorated palaces, the enormous art collection of Fondazione Cariplo and Intesa Sanpaolo bank pays homage to 18th- and 19th-century Lombard painting. From a magnificent sequence of bas-reliefs by Antonio Canova to luminous Romantic masterpieces by Francesco Hayez, the works span 23 rooms and document Milan's significant contribution to the rebirth of Italian sculpture, the patriotic romanticism of the Risorgimento (reunification period) and the birth of futurism at the dawn of the 20th century.

★ Pinacoteca di Brera
GALLERY

(Map p246; ☑02 7226 3264; www.brera.beni culturali.it; Via Brera 28; adult/reduced €10/7; ⊘8.30am-7.15pm Tue-Sun; ⓜLanza, Montenapoleone) Located upstairs from the centuries-old Accademia di Belle Arti (still one of Italy's most prestigious art schools), this gallery houses Milan's impressive collection of Old Masters, much of it 'lifted' from Venice by Napoleon. Rembrandt, Goya and Van Dyck all have a place in the collection, but look for the Italians: Titian, Tintoretto, Veronese, and the Bellini brothers. Much of the work has tremendous emotional clout, most notably Mantegna's brutal *Lamentation over the Dead Christ*.

Museo Poldi Pezzoli
MUSEUM

(Map p246; ☑02 79 48 89; www.museopoldi pezzoli.it; Via Alessandro Manzoni 12; adult/reduced €10/7; ⊘10am-6pm Wed-Mon; ⓜMontenapoleone) Inheriting his fortune at the age of 24, Gian Giacomo Poldi Pezzoli also inherited his mother's love of art. During extensive European travels he was inspired by the 'house museum' that was to become London's V&A and had the idea of transforming his apartments into a series of themed rooms based on the great art periods (the Middle Ages, early Renaissance, baroque etc.). Crammed with big-ticket Renaissance artworks, these

Sala d'Artista are exquisite works of art in their own right.

Villa Necchi Campiglio
MUSEUM

(Map p246; ☑02 7634 0121; www.fondoambi ente.it; Via Mozart 14; adult/child €9/4; ⊘10am-6pm Wed-Sun; ⓜSan Babila) This exquisitely restored 1930s villa was designed by rationalist architect Piero Portaluppi for Pavian heiresses Nedda and Gigina Necchi, and Gigina's husband Angelo Campiglio. The trio were proud owners of one of Milan's only swimming pools, as well as terrarium-faced sunrooms and streamlined electronic shuttering. Portaluppi's commingling of art deco and rationalist styles powerfully evokes Milan's modernist imaginings while at the same time remaining anchored to a past that was rapidly slipping away.

Castello Sforzesco
CASTLE, MUSEUM

(Map p246; ☑02 8846 3703; www.milanocastello .it; Piazza Castello; adult/reduced €5/3; ⊘9am-7.30pm Tue-Sun, to 10.30pm Thu; ⓜCairoli) Originally a Visconti fortress, this iconic red-brick castle was later home to the mighty Sforza dynasty, who ruled Renaissance Milan. The castle's defences were designed by the multitalented da Vinci; Napoleon later drained the moat and removed the drawbridges. Today, it houses seven specialised museums, which gather together intriguing fragments of Milan's cultural and civic history, including Michelangelo's final work, the *Rondanini Pietà*, now housed beautifully in the frescoed hall of the castle's Ospedale Spagnolo (Spanish Hospital).

Of the museums, the most interesting is the **Museum of Ancient Art** (Civiche Raccolta d'Arte Antica), which is displayed in the ducal apartments, some of which are

---

ⓘ DIY TRAM TOURS

Enjoy your own city tour by hopping on **Tram No 1**. This retro orange beauty, complete with wooden seats and original fittings, runs along Via Settembrini before cutting through the historic centre along Via Manzoni, through Piazza Cordusio and back up towards Piazza Cairoli and the Castello Sforzesco. A 75-minute ticket (€1.50), which is also valid for the bus and metro, should be purchased from any tobacconist before boarding. Stamp it in the original *obliteratrice* on the tram.

Central Milan

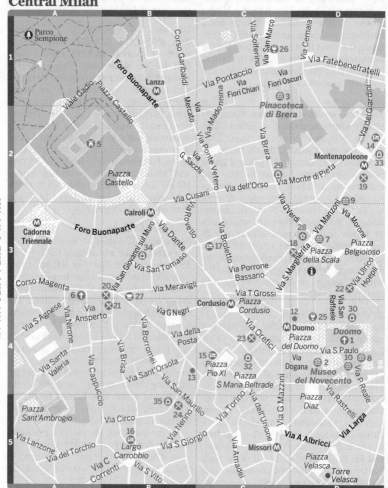

frescoed by Leonardo da Vinci. Included in the collection are early paleo-Christian sculptures, the superb equestrian tomb of Bernarbò Visconti and sculpted reliefs depicting Milan's triumph over Barbarossa. The exhibit eloquently tells the story of the birth of Italy's first city *comune* through murderous dynastic and regional ambitions, which made this one of the most powerful courts in Europe.

On the 1st floor the **Museo dei Mobile** (Furniture Museum) and **Pinacoteca** (Picture Gallery) blend seamlessly, leading you from ducal wardrobes and writing desks through to a collection of Lombard Gothic art. Among the masterpieces are Andrea Mantegna's *Trivulzio Madonna*, Vincenzo Foppa's *St Sebastian* and Bramantino's *Noli me tangere* (Touch me not).

Free entry is offered from 2pm every Tuesday and for the last hour of every day. To tour the castle battlements and underground rooms, consider a tour with Ad Artem (p249).

Triennale di Milano MUSEUM
(Map p242; ☑ 02 72 43 41; www.triennaledesign museum.it; Viale Emilio Alemanga 6; adult/reduced

Piazza Cavour
Giardini Pubblici
Via D. Manin
Via Palestro
Via Borgospesso
Via della Spiga
Via Santa Spirito
Via Gesù Spiga
Via Marina
Via Senato
Via S Primo
Via Monte Napoleone
Via Bigli
4 Quadrilatero d'Oro
Via Sant'Andrea
Via Bagutta
Corso Venezia
Via Mozart
11
Corso G Matteotti
31
Via San Paolo
Piazza San Babila
Corso Monforte
San Babila M
Via Borgogna
Piazza del Liberty
Corso Europa
Via Cerva
Via Durini
Piazza Beccaria
Via Pattari
Via Verziere
Via C Battisti
Via Festa del Perdono
Via Francesco Sforza
Via P. Andreani
Via Carlo Freguglia
Giardino della Guastalla

★**The Last Supper** ARTWORK

(Il Cenacolo; Map p242; ☎02 9280 0360; www.cenacolovinciano.net; Piazza Santa Maria delle Grazie 2; adult/reduced €8/4.75; ⏰8.15am-7pm Tue-Sun; Ⓜ Cadorna) Milan's most famous mural, Leonardo da Vinci's *The Last Supper* (Il Cenacolo) is hidden away on a wall of the refectory adjoining the **Basilica di Santa Maria delle Grazie** (Map p242; www.grazieop.it; Piazza Santa Maria delle Grazie; ⏰7am-noon & 3-7.30pm Mon-Sat, 7.30am-12.30pm & 3.30-9pm Sun; Ⓜ Cadorna, ⛟16). Depicting Christ and his disciples at the dramatic moment when Christ reveals he's aware of his betrayal, it's a masterful psychological study and one of the world's most iconic images. To see it you must book in advance or sign up for a guided city tour.

★**Museo Nazionale della Scienza e della Tecnologia** MUSEUM

(Map p242; ☎02 48 55 51; www.museoscienza.org; Via San Vittore 21; adult/child €10/7, submarine tours €8; ⏰9.30am-5pm Tue-Fri, to 6.30pm Sat & Sun; ♿; Ⓜ Sant'Ambrogio) Kids, would-be inventors and geeks will go goggle-eyed at Milan's impressive museum of science and technology, the largest of its kind in Italy. It is a fitting tribute in a city where arch-inventor Leonardo da Vinci did much of his finest work. The 16th-century monastery where it is housed features a collection of more than 10,000 items, including models based on da Vinci's engineering sketches, and outdoor hangars housing steam trains, planes, full-sized galleons and Italy's first submarine, *Enrico Toti*.

The museum's fabulous **MUST Shop** (Map p242; ☎02 4855 5340; www.mustshop.it; Via Olona 6; ⏰10am-7pm Tue-Sun; ♿; Ⓜ Sant'Ambrogio) is the place for all manner of science-inspired books, design items, gadgets and games. Access it through the museum or from Via Olona.

Chiesa di San Maurizio CHURCH

(Map p246; Corso Magenta 15; ⏰9.30am-5.30pm Tue-Sat, 1.30-5.30pm Sun; Ⓜ Cadorna) The 16th-century royal chapel and convent of San Maurizio is Milan's hidden crown jewel, every inch of it covered in breathtaking frescoes, several of them executed by Bernardino Luini who worked with Leonardo. Many of the frescoes immortalise Ippolita Sforza, Milanese literary maven, and other members of the powerful Sforza clan.

€8/6.50; ⏰10.30am-8.30pm Tue, Wed, Sat & Sun, to 11pm Thu & Fri; Ⓜ Cadorna) Italy's first Triennale took place in 1923 in Monza. It aimed to promote interest in Italian design and applied arts, from 'the spoon to the city', and its success led to the creation of Giovanni Muzio's **Palazzo d'Arte** in Milan in 1933. Since then this exhibition space has championed design in all its forms, although the triennale formula has since been replaced by long annual events, with international exhibits as part of the program.

Central Milan

Basilica di Sant'Ambrogio BASILICA
(Map p242; ☑ 02 8645 0895; www.basilicasant
ambrogio.it; Piazza Sant'Ambrogio 15; ⊙10am-
noon & 2.30-6pm Mon-Sat, 3-5pm Sun; Ⓜ Sant'Ambrogio) St Ambrose, Milan's patron saint and
one-time superstar bishop, is buried in the
crypt of this red-brick cathedral, which he
founded in AD 379. It's a fitting legacy, built
and rebuilt with a purposeful simplicity
that is truly uplifting: the seminal Lombard
Romanesque basilica. Shimmering altar
mosaics and a biographical 835 AD golden
altarpiece, which once served as the cladding for the saint's sarcophagus, light up the
shadowy vaulted interior.

Fondazione Prada GALLERY
(☑ 02 5666 2612; www.fondazioneprada.org; Largo Isarco 2; adult/reduced €10/8; ⊙10am-9pm;
Ⓜ Lodi) Seven years in the making, the new
Fondazione Prada, conceived by author and
architect Miuccia Prada and Rem Koolhaas,
is as innovative and creative as the minds
that gave it shape. Seven renovated buildings and three new structures have transformed a dilapidated former brandy factory
into 19,000 sq metres of exciting, multilevel
exhibition space. The buildings, including
a four-storey Haunted House tower clad in
gold leaf, work seamlessly together, presenting some stunning visual perspectives.

Inside, temporary and permanent
exhibits fill the diverse spaces that finally allow for the display of the foundation's
extensive contemporary collection, which
includes pieces by Anish Kapoor, Louise
Bourgeois, Francesco Vezzoli and Nathalie
Djurberg. Film screenings, performances and events are also part of the cultural
program, with more to come once the nine-
storey tower is finished.

Almost as popular as the exhibits is the
Wes Anderson–designed cafe, Bar Luce,
with its wallpapered walls and ceiling, and
1950s-inspired interior furnished with juke-
box, pinball machines and rows of candy
jars.

Activities

Navigli Lombardi BOAT TOUR
(Map p242; ☑ 02 667 91 31; www.naviglilombardi.
it; Alzaia Naviglio Grande 4; adult €8-12; ⊙Apr-Sep;
Ⓜ Porta Genova, ⚑3) Canals were once the
autostradas of medieval Milan, transporting
timber, marble, salt, oil and wine into town.
The largest of them, the Navigli Grande,
grew from an irrigation ditch to one of
the city's busiest thoroughfares by the 13th
century. Four cruises run from April to September; the most popular, the Conche Trail,

loops round the Naviglio Grande and Naviglio Pavese back through the dock.

QC Terme Milano   SPA
(Map p242; ✆02 5519 9367; www.termemilano.
com; Piazzale Medaglie d'Oro 2; day ticket week-days/weekend €45/50, beauty ticket weekdays/weekend €55/60; ◷9.30am-11pm Mon-Thu & Sun,
8.30-12.30am Fri & Sat; Ⓜ Porta Romana) Pad
down the high hallways of Milan's former
public transport headquarters and make
yourself comfortable in a pine-clad railway
carriage for a bio sauna session. Such is the
ingenuity of this remodelled spa, which has
turned the art deco, industrial building into
a luxurious wellness centre. Outside, the
garden is dotted with jacuzzi pools around
which fatigued Milanese office workers
snooze.

Tours

Ad Artem   CULTURAL TOUR
(Map p242; ✆02 659 77 28; http://adartem.
it; Via Melchiorre Gioia 1; tours €8-17.50; ◷9am-
1pm & 2-4pm; 🚻; Ⓜ Sondrio) Unusual cultural
tours of Milan's museums and monuments
with qualified art historians and actors.
Highlight tours include a walk around the
battlements of Castello Sforzesco; explorations of the castle's subterranean Ghirlanda
passageway; and family-friendly tours of the
Museo del Novecento, where kids are invited
to build and design their own artwork.

Autostradale   GUIDED TOUR
(Map p246; www.autostradale.it; Piazza Castello
1; tickets €65; ◷Tue-Sun) Autostradale's three-
hour city bus tours include admission to *The
Last Supper,* Castello Sforzesco and the Teatro alla Scala (La Scala) museum. Tours depart from the taxi rank on the western side
of Piazza del Duomo at 9.30am.

Bike & the City   BICYCLE TOUR
(Map p242; ✆338 3624475; www.bikeandthecity.
it; day/sunset tours €40/35; ◷tours 10am, 3.30pm
& 6.30pm May-Sep; Ⓜ Porta Venezia) Make
friends while you get the inside scoop on
city sights during these leisurely, four-hour
cycle tours. Tours start from Piazza Oberdan
at the corner of Corso Buenos Aires.

★ Città Nascosta Milano   CULTURAL TOUR
(Map p246; ✆347 3661174; www.cittanascosta
milano.it; Via del Bollo 3; annual membership €5-
35; ◷9.30am-1.30pm Mon-Fri, 2.30-6.30pm Tue &
Thu; Ⓜ Duomo, Missori) Dedicated to showing
you the hidden side of Milan, this nonprofit
outfit runs exciting cultural tours. Previous

offerings have lifted the curtain on Milan's
Liberty tennis club, Casa Valerio and the
emerging neighbourhood of Lambrate.
Other themed programs include Einstein
in Milan and the Interrupted Dream of
Napoleon. It also runs multilingual tours
during the annual Cortili Aperti.

Participation requires a small annual
membership fee, which gives access to the
tours, as well as those of affiliated organisations in Florence and Rome.

Festivals & Events

Milan has two linked trade-fair grounds,
collectively known as **Fiera Milano** (www.
fieramilano.it; Strada Statale del Sempione 28,
Rho; Ⓜ Rho). The older of the two, **Fieramilanocity**, is close to the centre (metro line
2, Lotto Fieramilanocity stop), while the
main grounds, **Fieramilano**, are west of
town in the satellite town of Rho (metro
line 2, Rho Fiera stop). The furniture fair,
fashion shows and most large trade fairs
take place here.

Carnevale Ambrosiano   RELIGIOUS
Lent comes late to Milan, with Carnevale
sensibly held on the Saturday that falls
after everyone else's frantic February Fat
Tuesday.

MiArt   FAIR
(www.miart.it; ◷Apr) Milan's annual modern
and contemporary art fair held in April
may not be Basel but it attracts more than
30,000 art-lovers, more than 200 exhibitors and increasing amounts of international attention.

Salone Internazionale del Mobile   FAIR
(International Furniture Fair; www.salonemilano.it;
◷Apr) The world's most prestigious furniture fair is held annually at Fiera Milano,
with satellite exhibitions in Zona Tortona.
Alongside the Salone runs the **Fuorisalone**
(http://fuorisalone.it) – literally, the outdoor
lounge – which incorporates dozens of
spontaneous design-related events, parties, exhibits and shows that animate the
entire city.

Cortili Aperti   CULTURAL
(www.adsi.it; ◷May) Over the last weekend
in May, the gates to some of the city's most
beautiful private courtyards are flung
open. Print a map and make your own itinerary, or sign up for tours with Città Na-
costa Milano.

Festa di Sant'Ambrogio & Fiera degli Obei Obei
RELIGIOUS

(☉Dec) The feast day of Milan's patron saint is celebrated on 7 December with the opening of the opera season at Teatro alla Scala (La Scala). In conjunction, a large Christmas Fair – Obej! Obej! (pronounced o-bay, o-bay) – sets up in Castello Sforzesco with stalls selling regional foods, sweets, and seasonal handicrafts.

Sleeping

Great-value accommodation is hard to come by in Milan, particularly during the Salone del Mobile furniture fair, the fashion shows and other large fairs, at which time you should book months in advance. The tourist office distributes *Milano Hotels,* which lists more than 350 options.

★ Ostello Bello
HOSTEL €

(Map p246; ☑02 3658 2720; www.ostellobello. com; Via Medici 4; dm €28-35, d €80-98, tr €110-130; ❄ 🤖 👪; 🚇2, 14) A breath of fresh air in Milan's stiffly suited centre, this is best hostel in town. Entrance is through its lively bar-cafe, open to nonguests, where you're welcomed with a smile and a complimentary drink. Beds are in mixed dorms or spotless private rooms, and there's a kitchen, a small terrace, and a basement lounge equipped with guitars, board games and table football.

Weekly events, including jam sessions, cinema forums and a monthly vintage market, offer a great way to meet locals.

Foresteria Cascina Cuccagna
HOSTEL €

(Map p242; ☑02 8342 1007; www.cuccagna.org; Via Cuccagna 2; dm €35, d €70-90; 🚇Porta Romana) Check in to this 'country' guesthouse in downtown Milan. Two six-bed dorm rooms and two doubles offer simply styled accommodation in large rooms with distressed walls and artfully functional furniture and lighting. Bonuses include an on-site bike-hire outlet, access to a convivial shared living room and library, and a sun-trap patio and garden. The adjoining restaurant, Un Posto a Milano (p252), is excellent.

★ LaFavia Four Rooms
B&B €€

(Map p242; ☑347 7842212; http://lafavia 4rooms.com; Via Carlo Farini 4; s €90-105, d €100-125; ❄🤖) Marco and Fabio's four-room bed and breakfast in the former Rabarbaro Zucca factory is a multicultural treat with rooms inspired by their travels through India, Mexico and Europe. Graphic wallpapers by Manuela Canova in zippy greens and oranges are complemented by lush window views onto plant-filled verandahs. Best of all is the rooftop garden where an organic breakfast is served in summer.

★ Maison Borella
BOUTIQUE HOTEL €€

(Map p242; ☑02 5810 9114; www.hotelmaison borella.com; Alzaia Naviglio Grande 8; d €160-280; ❄ @ 🤖; 🚇Porta Genova) With geranium-clad balconies overhanging the Naviglio Grande and its striking black, white and grey decor, this canalside hotel offers a touch of class in a dedicated bohemian neighbourhood. Converted from an old apartment building, the hotel's rooms are arranged around an internal courtyard and mix mid-century and contemporary furnishings with period features such as parquet floors, beamed ceilings and elegant *boiserie* (sculpted panelling).

Palazzo Segreti
DESIGN HOTEL €€

(Map p246; ☑02 4952 9250; www.palazzo segreti.com; Via San Tomaso 8; d €180, ste €250-350; ❄🤖; 🚇Cairoli, Cordusio) This 19th-century palace of secrets hides a shockingly modern interior and 18 subdued rooms with raw concrete finishes, rough antique wooden floorboards and shadowy chiaroscuro lighting effects. It appeals to design buffs who favour its minimal furnishings, open-plan bathrooms and achingly hip bar where folk gather in the evening to gossip over goldfish-bowl-sized wine glasses.

Hotel Gran Duca di York
HOTEL €€

(Map p246; ☑02 87 48 63; www.ducadiyork. com; Via Moneta 1; d €160-270; ❄ 🤖 👪; 🚇Duomo) This lemon-yellow *palazzo,* literally a stone's throw from the Duomo, was once a residence for scholars working in the nearby Ambrosiana library. Now it offers smiling service and 33 small rooms (some with balconies), plump beds and neat, marble bathrooms. Our advice is to skip the rather dull breakfast and opt for five-star pastries at Princi a few blocks away.

Antica Locanda Leonardo
HOTEL €€

(Map p242; ☑02 4801 4197; www.anticalocanda leonardo.com; Corso Magenta 78; s €95-170, d €110-225; ❄ @ 🤖; 🚇Conciliazione) A charmer hidden in a 19th-century residence near Leonardo's *The Last Supper.* Rooms exude homey comfort, from the period furniture and parquet floors to the plush drapes, while breakfast is served in the small, scented garden. Managed by the same family for more than 40 years, this place is a real home away from home.

Armani Hotel Milano
DESIGN HOTEL €€€

(Map p246; ☑ 02 8883 8000; http://milan.armani hotels.com; Via Manzoni 31; d €400-800; ❄ ☎ ☒; Ⓜ Montenapoleone) Armani's new flagship hotel rises above Via Manzoni like a new-age temple, attracting acolytes who slip into its branded lifestyle as easily as into one of his trouser suits. Let your personal Lifestyle Manager escort you to one of the 98 leather-lined rooms, book you a spa session or design you a personal itinerary of the city.

3Rooms
B&B €€€

(Map p242; ☑ 02 62 61 63; www.3rooms-10corso como.com; Corso Como 10; d €270-340; Ⓟ ❄ @ ☎; Ⓜ Garibaldi) Can't drag yourself away from concept shop Corso Como? You don't have to – the villa's three guest rooms (mini-apartments with bedroom, bathroom and sitting room) let you sleep between Eames bedspreads, lounge on Arne Jacobsen chairs and dine off Eero Saarinen's iconic tables. Thrown in are some vintage items and a few eye-catching artworks, just to keep you on your toes.

 ## Eating

Milan's dining scene is much like its fashion scene, with new restaurant openings hotly debated and seats at Michelin-starred tables hard to come by. Whether it's dyed-in-tradition or fusion cuisine you're after, you're sure to eat some of Italy's most sophisticated food here.

Milan's provincial specialities include polenta, *risotto alla milanese* (saffron and bone-marrow risotto), *busecca* (sliced tripe boiled with beans) and *cotoletta alla milanese* (breaded veal). Milan is also the home of *panettone* (yeast-risen sweet bread), now internationally popular at Easter and Christmas. Reservations are essential for top-end establishments.

Mercato Metropolitano
ITALIAN €

(Map p242; www.mercatometropolitano.com; Porta Genova; meals €10-20; ⊙ 11am-midnight Mon-Thu, to 2am Fri, 9-2am Sat, 9am-noon Sun; ⚇; Ⓜ Porta Genova) 'Good Italian food is not a luxury' is the cry of Milan's new food market located in former railway housings near Porta Genova. Choose from small-producer food stalls selling oysters, DOP Franciacorta, and gourmet *panini* made with 24-year-aged San Daniele ham. Plant stalls, artisanal ice-cream carts, craft beer, cocktail purveyors, and even cooking classes and seminars give it a convivial country-fair feel.

FEELING PECKISH?

Peck (Map p246; ☑ 02 802 31 61; www. peck.it; Via Spadari 9; ⊙ 3.30-7.30pm Mon, 9.30am-7.30pm Tue-Sat; Ⓜ Duomo) Milan's historic deli is smaller than its reputation suggests, but what it lacks in space it makes up for in variety. It's home to a mind-boggling selection of *parmigiano reggiano* (Parmesan) and myriad other treasures – chocolates, pralines, pastries, freshly made gelato, seafood, caviar, pâté, fruit and vegetables, truffle products, olive oils and balsamic vinegars.

Peck also runs an all-day restaurant, **Peck Italian Bar** (Map p246; ☑ 02 869 30 17; www.peck.it; Via Cantù 3; meals €35-45; ⊙ 11.30am-9.30pm Mon-Sat; Ⓜ Duomo), which appeals to a banking and business lunch crowd. Like the clientele, the food is traditional and the service efficient.

Gattullo
PASTRIES €

(Map p242; ☑ 02 5831 0497; www.gattullo.it; Piazzale di Porta Lodovico 2; pastries from €1.50; ⊙ 7am-9pm Sep-Jul; ⚇; ⚊ 3, 9) Hailing from that great southern baking town Ruvo di Puglia in 1961, Joseph Gattullo built his small bakery into a pastry empire. It is still located in its 1970s premises, resplendent with sci-fi Murano chandeliers and an elegant veneered wooden bar. Come for breakfast, lunch or *aperitivo*; it's all fantastic.

De Santis
SANDWICHES €

(Map p246; www.paninidesantis.it; Corso Magenta 9; sandwiches €6-8; ⊙ noon-11.30pm; ⚇; Ⓜ Cadorna) Sandwiches here are so damn good you may eschew restaurant dining just to sample that *panini* with proscuitto, spicy goat cheese, pepperoni, aubergine and artichokes. The more than 200 variations on the menu and De Santis' decades of experience explain the queues at this tiny venue. Beer is served on tap to those who find seating.

Luini
FAST FOOD €

(Map p246; www.luini.it; Via Santa Radegonda 16; panzerotti €2.50; ⊙ 10am-3pm Mon, to 8pm Tue-Sat; ⚇; Ⓜ Duomo) This historic joint is the go-to place for *panzerotti*, delicious pizzadough parcels stuffed with a combination of mozzarella, spinach, tomato, ham or spicy salami, and then fried or baked in a wood-fired oven.

⭐ **Un Posto a Milano**   MODERN ITALIAN €€
(Map p242; ✆02 545 77 85; www.unposto
amilano.it; Via Cuccagna 2; meals €10-35; ⊗12.30-
3pm & 7.20-11pm Tue-Sun; ☑🅰; Ⓜ Porta Romana)
A few years ago this country *cascina* (farmhouse) was a derelict ruin, until a collection
of cooperatives and cultural associations
returned it to multifunctional use as restaurant, social hub and hostel. Delicious salads,
homemade foccacia, soups and snacks are
served throughout the day at the bar, while
the restaurant serves simple home cooking
using locally sourced ingredients.

Children are particularly welcome here.
High chairs are provided; there's a childrens'
menu and a lovely garden for postprandial
playing.

Trattoria Milanese   MILANESE €€
(Map p246; ✆02 8645 1991; Via Santa Marta 11;
meals €30-45; ⊗12.30-2.30pm & 7-11.30pm; 🚇2,
14) Like an old friend you haven't seen in
years, this true trattoria welcomes you with
generous goblets of wine, hearty servings of
traditional Milanese fare and convivial banter over the vegetable buffet. Regulars slide
into their favourite spots, barely needing
to order as waiters bring them their usual:
meatballs wrapped in cabbage, minestrone
or the sinfully good *risotto al salto* (refried
risotto).

Corsia del Giardino   MODERN ITALIAN €€
(Map p246; ✆02 7628 0726; www.corsiadel
giardino.it; Via Manzoni 16; meals €20-30; ⊗8am-
8.30pm Mon-Sat, from 9am Sun; Ⓜ Montenapoleone) Named for the gardens that once
lined Via Manzoni, this contemporary cafe-
cum-restaurant occupies a leafy niche off
the main drag. Its sleek interior and elegant
menu match the stylish clientele, workers
from nearby shops in the Quad, who come
here for top-quality salads, meat plates with
18-month aged Parma ham, artisanal ice
cream and sweet fruit tarts.

Dongiò   CALABRESE €€
(Map p242; ✆02 551 13 72; Via Bernardino Corio
3; meals €25-35; ⊗noon-3.30pm & 7pm-midnight
Mon-Fri, 7pm-midnight Sat; Ⓜ Porta Romana)
One of the best value-for-money restaurants in Milan, this big-hearted Calabrese
trattoria serves the spicy flavours of the
south on delicious homemade pasta. Starters include bountiful platters of southern
salami and piquant cheeses. Reservations
recommended.

VINTAGE FINDS

Il Salvagente (✆02 7611 0328; www.
salvagentemilano.it; Via Fratelli Bronzetti 16;
⊗10am-7pm Tue-Sat, 3-7pm Mon; 🚌60, 62
& 92) The grim basement courtyard of Il
Salvagente gives scant indication of the
big brand names inside. Prada, Dolce &
Gabbana, Versace and Alberta Ferretti
are just a few of the names discounted
on the tightly packed racks. Payment is
cash only.

Cavalli e Nastri (Map p246; ✆02 7200
0449; www.cavalliienastri.com; Via Brera 2;
⊗10.30am-7.30pm Tue-Sat, 3.30-7.30pm
Mon; Ⓜ Montenapoleone) This gorgeously
colourful shop is known for its vintage
clothes and accessories. It specialises in
lovingly curated frocks, bags, jewellery
and even shoes, sourced from early and
mid-20th-century Italian fashion houses, and priced accordingly. You'll find
its **menswear store** (Map p242; www.
cavalliienastri.com; Via Mora 3; ⊗10.30am-
7.30pm Tue-Sun; 🚇2, 14) at Via Mora 3.

Café Trussardi   ITALIAN €€
(Map p246; ✆02 806 88 295; www.cafetrussardi
.it; Piazza della Scala 5; meals €25-40; ⊗noon-
12.30pm; Ⓜ Duomo) Whether for a glass of
wine and some root-vegetable crisps at the
bar, or a posh lamb kebab with yoghurt and
mint from the small, changing menu beneath Patrick Blanc's beautiful vertical garden in the courtyard, this is one of Milan's
most stylish, low-key dining options. Upstairs, the **Trussardi alla Scala** (Map p246;
✆02 8068 8201; www.trussardiallascala.com; Piazza della Scala 5; menus from €140; ⊗12.30-2.30pm
& 8-10.30pm Mon-Fri, 8-10.30pm Sat; Ⓜ Duomo)
restaurant serves Michelin-starred fare from
talented chef Luigi Taglienti.

⭐ **La Brisa**   MODERN ITALIAN €€€
(Map p246; ✆02 8645 0521; www.ristorantela
brisa.it; Via Brisa 15; meals €50-70; ⊗12.45-
2.30pm & 7.45-10.30pm Mon-Fri, 7.45-10.30pm Sun;
Ⓜ Cairoli, Cordusio) Discreet, elegant and exquisitely romantic. Push open the screened
door and the maître d' will guide you to a
table beneath centuries-old linden trees
in a secluded courtyard, where ivy climbs
the walls and pink hydrangea's bob in the
breeze. Chef Antonio Facciolo's seasonal
menus are similarly elegant, his signature
dish a mouthwatering roast pork in a myrtle-
berry drizzle.

Basara

SUSHI €€€

(Map p242; ☑02 5811 1649; www.basara milano.it; Via Tortona 12; meals €50-70; ☺8.30am-3.30pm & 7pm-12.30am Mon-Sat; ⓂPorta Genova) Making a name for yourself in Milan's sophisticated sushi scene isn't easy, but chef Hiro's lobster maki roll sings a siren song that packs this place out for two sittings every evening. The raw-fish plates are superb, particularly the pretty block of red Sicilian shrimps served on a black slate slab with a sprinkle of sea salt.

 Drinking & Nightlife

Milanese bars are generally open until 2am or 3am, and virtually all serve *aperitivi*. The Navigli canal district, the cobbled backstreets of Brera, and swish Corso Como are all drinking hot spots. Super-stylish hotel and museum bars include Bar Luce at the Fondazione Prada, Armani Hotel's Bamboo Bar, the Bulgari bar, and the bar at 10 Corso Como.

Clubs are generally open until 3am or 4am from Tuesday to Sunday; cover charges vary from €10 to upwards of €25. Door policies can become formidable as the night wears on.

★ Ceresio 7

BAR

(Map p242; ☑02 3103 9221; www.ceresio7. com; Via Ceresio 7; aperitivo €15, meals €60-80; ☺12.30pm-1am; ☒2, 4) Heady views match the heady price of *aperitivo* at Milan's coolest rooftop bar, sitting atop the former 1930s Enel (electricity company) HQ. Two pools, two bars and a restaurant under the guidance of former Bulgari head chef Elio Sironi make this a hit with Milan's beautiful people. In the summer you can book a whole day by the pool from €110.

Pasticceria Marchesi

CAFE

(Map p246; ☑02 87 67 30; www.pasticceriamarchesi.it; Via Santa Maria alla Porta 11a; ☺7.30am-8pm Tue-Sat, 8.30am-1pm Sun; ⓂCardusio, Cairoli) Coffee that's perfect every shot since 1824, accompanied by a delectable array of sweets, biscuits and pastries.

Mag Café

BAR, CAFE

(Map p242; Ripa di Porta Ticinese 43; cocktails €7-9, brunch €10; ☺7.30-2am Mon-Fri, 9-2am Sat & Sun; ☒2, 9) A Milanese speakeasy with wingback armchairs in whisky-coloured velvet, marble-topped tables, a patchwork of Persian rugs and huge lampshades that look like birds'

nests. Like the decor, the drinks are creatively crafted, utilising interesting herbs and syrups, and served in vintage glassware. Mag also does a popular brunch on weekends.

Nottingham Forest

COCKTAIL BAR

(Map p242; www.nottingham-forest.com; Viale Piave 1; cocktails €10; ☺6.30pm-2am Tue-Sat, 6pm-1am Sun; ☒9, 23) If Michelin awarded stars for bars, Nottingham Forest would have a clutch of them. This eclectically decorated Asian-cum-African tiki bar named after an English football team is the outpost of molecular mixologist Dario Comino, who conjures smoking cocktails packed with dry ice and ingenuity. Unique cocktails include the Elite, a mix of vodka, ground pearls and sake – supposedly an aphrodisiac.

Camparino in Galleria

BAR, CAFE

(Map p246; www.camparino.it; Piazza del Duomo 21; drinks €12-24; ☺7.15am-8.40pm) Open since the inauguration of the Galleria Vittorio Emanuele II shopping arcade in 1867, this perfectly preserved art nouveau bar has served drinks to the likes of Verdi, Toscanini, Dudovich and Carrà. Cast-iron chandeliers, huge mirrored walls trimmed with wall mosaics of birds and flowers set the tone for a classy Campari-based *aperitivo*. Drinks at the bar are cheaper.

N'Ombra de Vin

WINE BAR

(Map p246; ☑02 659 96 50; www.nombradevin. it; Via San Marco 2; ☺10-2am; ⓂLanza, Moscova) This *enoteca* (wine bar) is set in a one-time Augustine refectory. Tastings can be had all day and you can also indulge in food such as *carpaccio di pesce spade agli agrumi* (swordfish carpaccio prepared with citrus) from a limited menu. Check the website for occasional cultural events and DJ nights.

Dry

COCKTAIL BAR

(Map p242; ☑02 6379 3414; www.drymilano.it; Via Solferino 33; cocktails €8-13, meals €20-25; ☺7pm-midnight; ⓂMoscova) The brainchild of Michelin-starred chef Andrea Berton, Dry mixes its cocktails with gourmet pizzas. The inventive cocktail list includes the Corpse Reviver (London Dry gin, cointreau, Cocchi Americano and lemon juice) and the Martinez (Boompjes genever, vermouth, Maraschino liqueur and Boker's bitters), the latter inspired by French gold hunters in Martinez, the birthplace of barman Jerry Thomas.

BEHIND THE SCENES AT LA SCALA

To glimpse the inner workings of La Scala, visit the **Ansaldo Workshops** (Map p242; ☑02 4335 3521; www.teatroalla scala.org; Via Bergognone 34; per person €5, groups €100-120; ☺individuals 3pm, groups 9am-noon & 2-4pm Tue & Thu; ⓂPorto Genova) where the stage sets are crafted and painted, and where some 800 to 1000 new costumes are handmade each season. Tours must be booked in advance and are guided by the heads of each creative department.

Living
BAR

(Map p242; ☑02 3310 0824; www.livingmilano. com; Piazza Sempione 2; cocktails €8-10; ☺8am-2am; ⓂMoscova) Living has one of the city's prettiest settings, with a corner position and floor-to-ceiling windows overlooking the Arco della Pace. The bounteous *aperitivo* spread and expertly mixed cocktails draw crowds of smart-casual 20- and 30-somethings. Its sister bar, **Refeel** (Map p242; ☑02 5832 4227; www.refeel.it; Viale Sabotino 20; ☺7am-2am Mon-Sat, noon-4pm Sun; ⓂPorta Romana), in Porta Romana is also worth a trip.

Plastic
CLUB

(Via Gargano 15; ☺11pm-5am Fri-Sat, to 3am Sun; ☐24) A legendary club still going strong after 30 years. Madonna, Amy Winehouse, Blur and a whole host of other big names have performed here alongside more transgressive acts, attracting a mixed crowd of creatives and Milan's coolest kids. You'll find it just south of the Lodi metro stop just off Viale Brenta. No door charge.

Tunnel
CLUB

(www.tunnel-milano.it; Via Sammartini 30; admission €15-25; ☺11pm-5am Wed-Sat; ⓂCentrale) A landmark of Milan's alternative scene, Tunnel takes its moniker as top underground club seriously and is literally housed in a tunnel beneath the rail tracks of the Stazione Centrale. Friday night's Le Cannibale features indie acts and eletronic, while Saturday evenings attract top DJs from the techno scene, such as Ellen Alien, Nina Kraviz, Nicolaar Jaar and Ame & Dixon.

☆ Entertainment

Most big events and names that play Milan do so at major venues outside the city centre, which run shuttle buses for concerts. They include **Mediolanum Forum** (☑02 48 85 71; www.mediolanumforum.it; Via Giuseppe di Vittorio 6; ⓂAssago Milanofiori) and the San Siro Stadium.

★ Teatro alla Scala
OPERA

(La Scala; Map p246; ☑02 8 87 91; www.teatroalla scala.org; Piazza della Scala; ⓂDuomo) One of the most famous opera stages in the world, La Scala's season runs from early December through July. You can also see theatre, ballet and concerts here year-round (except August). Buy tickets online or by phone up to two months before the performance, and then from the central **box office** (☑02 72 00 37 44; www.teatroallascala.org; Galleria Vittorio Emanuele II; ☺noon-6pm; ⓂDuomo).

When rehearsals are not in session, you can get a glimpse of the gilt-encrusted interior, or visit the **museum** (La Scala Museum; Map p246; Largo Ghiringhelli 1; admission €7; ☺9am-12.30pm & 1.30-5.30pm; ⓂDuomo) next door. On performance days, 140 tickets for the gallery are sold two hours before the show (one ticket per customer). Queue early.

Blue Note
JAZZ

(Map p242; ☑02 6901 6888; www.bluenote milano.com; Via Borsieri 37; tickets €22-40; ☺7.30pm-midnight Tue-Sun Sep-Jun, brunch noon Sun Oct-Mar; ⓂIsola, Zara) Top-class jazz acts from around the world perform here at the only European outpost for New York's Blue Note jazz club. If you haven't prebooked you can buy tickets at the door from 7.30pm. It also does a popular easy-listening Sunday brunch (€35 per adult, or €70 for two adults and two children under 12).

La Fabbrica del Vapore
PERFORMING ARTS

(Map p242; www.fabbricadelvapore.org; Via Procaccini 4; ♿; ☐7, 12, 14) This industrial site once housed a factory for electric trams; now it lends its vast warehouses to a centre of the arts particularly aimed at developing the creative skills of young people. Dance, photography, theatre, cinema and concerts fill the factory's program year-round.

San Siro Stadium
FOOTBALL

(Stadio Giuseppe Meazza; www.sansiro.net; Piazzale Angelo Moratti, museum & tours gate 14; tickets from €20; ⓂSan Siro) San Siro Stadium wasn't designed to hold the entire population of Milan, but on a Sunday afternoon amid 85,000 football-mad citizens it can certainly feel like it. The city's two clubs, AC Milan and FC

Internazionale Milano (aka Inter), play on alternate weeks from October to May.

Guided tours of the 1920s-built stadium take you behind the scenes to the players' locker rooms and include a visit to the **Museo Inter e Milan** (☑02 404 24 32; www.sansiro.net; Via Piccolomini 5, Gate 21; museum & tour adult/reduced €17/12; ⊙9.30am-6pm; ⓐ; ⓂLotto, ⓔ16, shuttle from Piazzale Lotto to stadium), a shrine of memorabilia and film footage. You can buy tickets for games on the clubs' websites (www.acmilan.com and www.inter.it).

Take tram 24, bus 95 or 161, or the metro to the San Siro stop.

 Shopping

Beyond the hallowed streets of the Quadrilatero d'Oro, designer outlets and chains can be found along Corso Buenos Aires and Corso Vercelli; younger, hipper labels live along Via Brera and Corso Magenta; while Corso di Porta Ticinese and Navigli are home of the Milan street scene and subculture shops.

★ **Spazio Rossana Orlandi**   HOMEWARES
(Map p242; ☑02 46 74 47; www.rossanaorlandi .com; Via Matteo Bandello 14; ⊙3-7pm Mon, 10am-7pm Tue-Sat; ⓂSant'Ambrogio) Installed in a former tie factory in the Magenta district, this iconic interior design studio is a challenge to find. Once inside, though, it's hard to leave this treasure trove stacked with vintage and contemporary limited-edition pieces from upcoming artists.

Monica Castiglioni   JEWELLERY
(Map p242; ☑02 8723 7979; www.monicacastiglioni.com; Via Pastrengo 4; ⊙11am-8pm Thu-Sat; ⓂGaribaldi) Daughter of famous industrial designer Achille Castiglioni, Monica Castiglioni has a deep understanding of materials and proportions. To this she adds her own unique vision, turning out organic, industrial-style jewellery in bronze, silver and gold using an ancient lost-wax casting technique.

Moroni Gomma   HOMEWARES, ACCESSORIES
(Map p246; ☑02 79 62 20; www.moronigomma. it; Corso Matteotti 14; ⊙3-7pm Mon, 10am-7pm Tue-Sun; ⓂSan Babila) Stocked with irresistible gadgets and great accessories for the bathroom, kitchen and office, this family-owned design store is a one-stop shop for funky souvenirs and Milanese keepsakes. Who but the strongest willed will be able to resist the cuckoo clock shaped like the Duomo, a retro telephone in pastel colours or classic Italian moccasins in nonslip rubber?

Pellini   JEWELLERY, ACCESSORIES
(Map p246; ☑02 7600 8084; www.pellini.it; Via Manzoni 20; ⊙3.30-7.30pm Mon, 9.30am-7.30pm Tue-Sat Sep-Jul; ⓂMontenapoleone) For unique, one-off costume jewellery pieces, bags and hair pieces, look no further than the boutique of Donatella Pellini, granddaughter of famous costume designer Emma Pellini. The Pellini women have been making their trademark resin jewellery for three generations, and their fanciful creations incorporating flowers, sand and fabric are surprisingly affordable.

Wait and See   FASHION
(Map p246; ☑02 7208 0195; www.waitandsee.it; Via Santa Marta 14; ⊙3.30-7.30pm Mon, 10.30am-7.30pm Tue-Sat; ⓂDuomo, Missori) With collaborations with international brands and designers such as Missoni, Etro and Anna Molinari under her belt, Uberta Zambeletti launched her own collection in 2010. Quirky Wait and See indulges her eclectic tastes and showcases unfamiliar brands alongside items exclusively designed for the store, including super-fun Clodomiro T-shirts and Sartorio Vico knitted necklaces.

Risi   FASHION
(Map p246; ☑02 8909 2185; www.risimilano. com; Via San Giovanni sul Muro 21; ⊙3-7.30pm Mon, 10am-2.30pm & 3-7.30pm Tue-Sat; ⓂCairoli) Head to Risi for a dose of effortless Milanese chic. Here you can stock up on soft grey and white linen shirts and trousers, honeycomb

---

NAVIGLI MARKETS

Nuovo Mercato Ticinese (Map p242; Piazza XXIV Maggio; ⊙8.30am-1pm & 4-8pm Tue-Sat; ⓂPorta Genova, ⓔ3) Overlooking the revitalised Darsena, where boats once docked in medieval Milan, the city's main food market now has a swish new glass-and-steel enclosure. Inside, a myriad stalls sell meat, cheese, fresh fruit and veg.

Mercatone dell'Antiquariato (Map p242; www.navigliogrande.mi.it; Alzaia Naviglio Grande; ⊙9am-6pm last Sun of month; ⓂPorta Genova) This antiques market is the city's most scenic market, and sets up along a 2km stretch of the Naviglio Grande. With more than 400 well-vetted antique and secondhand traders, it provides hours of treasure-hunting pleasure.

DON'T MISS

QUADRILATERO D'ORO

Quadrilatero d'Oro (Golden Quad; Map p246; M Monte Napoleone) A stroll around the Quadrilatero d'Oro, the world's most famous shopping district, is a must. This quaintly cobbled quadrangle of streets – bounded by Via Monte Napoleone, Via Sant'Andrea, Via della Spiga and Via Alessandro Manzoni – has always been synonymous with elegance and money (Via Monte Napoleone was where Napoleon's government managed loans). Even if you don't have the slightest urge to sling a swag of glossy carriers, the window displays and people-watching are priceless.

polo shirts in sober colours and comfortable beachwear in classic pinstripes. Season-appropriate weights and an absence of logos mean you'll blend in with the natives.

La Rinascente   DEPARTMENT STORE
(Map p246; ☑02 8 85 21; www.rinascente.it; Piazza del Duomo; ☺8.30am-midnight Mon-Sat, 10am-midnight Sun; M Duomo) Italy's most prestigious department store doesn't let the fashion capital down – come for Italian diffusion lines, French lovelies and LA upstarts. The basement also hides a 'Made in Italy' design supermarket and chic hairdresser Aldo Coppola is on the top floor. Take away edible souvenirs from the 7th-floor food market (and peer across to the Duomo while you're at it).

10 Corso Como   FASHION
(Map p242; ☑02 2900 2674; www.10corso como.com; Corso Como 10; ☺10.30am-7.30pm Tue & Fri-Sun, to 9pm Wed & Thu, 3.30-7.30pm Mon; M Garibaldi) This might be the world's most hyped 'concept shop', but Carla Sozzani's selection of desirable things (Lanvin ballet flats, Alexander Girard wooden dolls, a demicouture frock by a designer you've not read about *yet*) makes 10 Corso Como a fun window-shopping experience. There's a bookshop upstairs with art and design titles, and a hyper-stylish bar and restaurant in the main atrium and picture-perfect courtyard.

Bargain hunters take note: the **outlet store** (Map p242; ☑02 2900 2674; www .10corsocomo.com; Via Tazzoli 3; ☺1-7pm Fri,

11am-7pm Sat & Sun; M Garibaldi, ☐3, 4) nearby sells last season's stock at a discount.

ℹ Information

EMERGENCY

Police Station (Questura; ☑02 6 22 61; Via Fatebenefratelli 11; ☺8am-2pm & 3-8pm Mon-Fri, 8am-2pm Sat; M Turati) Milan's main police station.

MEDICAL SERVICES

24-Hour Pharmacy (☑02 669 07 35; Galleria delle Partenze, Stazione Centrale; ☺7.30am-8.30pm; M Centrale FS) Located on the 1st floor of the central station.

Ospedale Maggiore Policlinico (☑02 5503 6672; www.policlinico.mi.it; Via Francesco Sforza 35; M Crocetta) Milan's main hospital; offers an outpatient service.

American International Medical Centre (AIMC; ☑02 5831 9808; www.aimclinic.it; Via Mercalli 11; M Crocetta) Private, international health clinic with English-speaking staff.

TOURIST INFORMATION

Milan Tourist Office (Map p246; ☑02 8845 6555; www.turismo.milano.it; Galleria Vittorio Emanuele II 11-12; ☺9am-7pm Mon-Fri, to 6pm Sat, 10am-6pm Sun; M Duomo) Centrally located with helpful English-speaking staff and tons of maps and brochures.

ℹ Getting There & Away

AIR

In addition to its own airports, Milan has direct transport links to Bergamo's Orio al Serio (p295) airport.

Linate Airport (LIN; ☑02 23 23 23; www. milanolinate-airport.com) Located 7km east of Milan city centre; domestic and European flights only.

Malpensa Airport (MXP; ☑02 23 23 23; www. milanomalpensa-airport.com) About 50km northwest of Milan city; northern Italy's main international airport.

BUS

Lampugnano Bus Terminal (Via Giulia Natta) Milan's main bus station is west of the city centre next to the Lampugnano metro station. Most national services are run by Autostradale (p249).

CAR & MOTORCYCLE

The A1, A4, A7 and A8 converge from all directions on Milan.

TRAIN

International high-speed trains from France, Switzerland and Germany arrive in Milan's **Stazi-**

one **Centrale** (Piazza Duca d'Aosta). The ticketing office and left luggage are located on the ground floor. For regional trips, skip the queue and buy your tickets from the multilingual, touch-screen vending machines, which accept both cash and credit card. Daily international and long-distance destinations include the following:

TO	FARE (€)	DURATION (HR)	FREQUENCY
Florence	35-60	1½-3½	hourly
Geneva	79	4	3 daily
Munich	90-130	7½-8½	7 daily
Rome	85-130	3	half-hourly
Venice	19-47	2½-3½	half-hourly
Vienna	40-70	11-14	2 daily

ⓘ Getting Around

TO/FROM THE AIRPORT

Bus

Starfly (Map p242; ☎02 5858 7237; www.airportbusexpress.it; one way/return €5/9) Departs from Milan's Stazione Centrale for Linate airport every half-hour between 7.45am and 10.45pm, and between 5.30am and 10pm in the other direction. Tickets are sold on board.

Orio al Serio Bus Express (Map p242; ☎02 7200 13 04; www.autostradale.it; 1 Piazza Castello; one way/return €5/9) This Autostradale service departs Piazza Luigi di Savoia at Stazione Centrale approximately every half hour between 2.45am to 11.15pm, and from Orio al Serio airport between 7.45am and 11.15am. The journey takes one hour.

Malpensa Shuttle (Map p242; www.malpensashuttle.it; one way/return €10/16) This Malpensa airport shuttle runs every 20 minutes between 5am and 10.30pm from Stazione Centrale, and hourly throughout the rest of the night. It stops at both terminals and the journey time is 50 minutes.

Taxi

There is a flat fee of €90 to and from Malpensa Airport to central Milan. The drive should take 50 minutes outside peak traffic times. For travellers to Terminal 2, this might prove the quickest option. The taxi fare to Linate Airport costs between €20 and €30.

Train

Malpensa Express (☎02 7249 4949; www.malpensaexpress.it; one way €12) From 6.53am to 9.53pm trains run every 30 minutes between Malpensa airport Terminal 1, Cadorna Stazione Nord (35 minutes) and Stazione Centrale (45 minutes). Passengers for Terminal

ⓘ MAPS & PASSES

Bus and tram route maps are available at ATM Info points. Otherwise download the IATM app. There are several good money-saving passes available for public transport:

One-day ticket (€4.50) Valid 24 hours.

Three-day ticket (€8.25) Valid 72 hours.

Carnet of 10 tickets (€13.80) Valid for 90 minutes each.

2 need to take the free shuttle bus to/from Terminal 1.

BICYCLE

BikeMi (www.bikemi.it) Register to use Milan's bike-sharing scheme by using your mobile phone and credit card (no debit cards), and you'll have use of a bike for €0.50 per hour for a maximum of two hours. Exceed the time limit and a €2 penalty is charged. Bike stations are plentiful across the city.

CAR & MOTORCYCLE

It simply isn't worth having a car in Milan. Many streets have restricted access and parking is a nightmare. In the centre, street parking costs €2 per hour. To pay, buy a SostaMilano card from a tobacconist, scratch off the date and hour, and display it on your dashboard. Only park in the blue spaces; those marked in yellow are reserved for residents. Underground car parks charge between €25 and €40 for 24 hours. Check out www.tuttocitta.it/parcheggi/milano to find one near you.

PUBLIC TRANSPORT

ATM (Azienda Trasporti Milano; ☎02 4860 7607; www.atm.it) Runs the metro, buses and trams. The metro is the most convenient way to get around and consists of four underground lines (red M1, green M2, yellow M3 and lilac M5) and a suburban rail network, the blue Passante Ferroviario. Services run from 6am to 12.30am. A ticket costs €1.50 and is valid for one metro ride or up to 90 minutes' travel on buses and trams.

TAXI

Taxis are only available at designated taxi ranks; you cannot flag them down. Alternatively, call ☎02 40 40, ☎02 69 69 or ☎02 85 85. The average short city ride costs €10. Be aware that when you call for a cab, the meter runs from receipt of call, not pick up.

Fashion

Northern Italian artisans and designers have been dressing and adorning Europe's affluent classes since the early Middle Ages. At that time Venetian merchants imported dyes from the East and Leonardo da Vinci helped design Milan's canal system, connecting the wool merchants and silk weavers of the lakes to the city's market places. Further south, Florence's wool guild grew so rich they were able to fund a Renaissance.

Global Powerhouses

In the 1950s Florence's fashion houses, which once produced only made-to-measure designs, began to present seasonal collections to a select public. But Milan literally stole the show in 1958, hosting Italy's first Fashion Week. With its ready factories, cosmopolitan workforce and long-established media presence, Milan created ready-to-wear fashion for global markets.

Recognising the enormous potential of mass markets, designers such as Armani, Missoni and Versace began creating and following trends, selling their 'image' through advertising and promotion. In the 1980s Armani's power suits gave rise to new unisex fashions, Dolce & Gabbana became a byword for Italian sex appeal and Miuccia Prada transformed her father's ailing luxury luggage business by introducing democratic, durable totes and backpacks made out of radical new fabrics (like waterproof Pocono, silk faille and parachute nylon).

Fashion Mecca Milan

Milan's rise to global fashion prominence was far from random. No other Italian

1. Prada store in Galleria Vittorio Emanuele II, Milan
2. Fashion show
3. Milan street style

city, not even Rome, was so well suited to take on this mantle. First, thanks to its geographic position, the city had historically strong links with European markets. It was also Italy's capital of finance, advertising, television and publishing, with both *Vogue* and *Amica* magazines based there. What's more, Milan always had a fashion industry based around the historic textile and silk production of upper Lombardy. And, with the city's postwar focus on trade fairs and special events, it provided a natural marketplace for the exchange of goods and ideas.

As a result, by 2011 Milan emerged as Italy's top (and the world's fourth-biggest) fashion exporter. The Quadrilatero d'Oro, that 'Golden Quad', is now dominated by more than 500 fashion outlets in an area barely 6000 sq metres. Such is the level of display, tourists now travel to Milan to 'see' the fashion. Helping them do just that, in 2015 King Giorgio opened Armani Silos, a museum dedicated to over 40 years of Armani success showcasing 600 couture outfits and 200 accessories.

FASHION WEEKS

The winter shows are held in January (men) and February (women) and the spring/summer events are in June (men) and September (women). You'll enjoy the full carnival effect as more than 100,000 models, critics, buyers and producers descend on the city to see 350-plus shows.

For a full timetable check out www. cameramoda.it or http://milanfashion weeklive.com.

Around Milan

Pavia

POP 71,300

Founded by the Romans as a military garrison, Pavia has long been a strategic city. It sits at the centre of an agricultural plain, is an important provincial player with strong Lega Nord leanings, and its university (founded in the 14th century) is one of the best in Italy. Aside from its buzzy, student atmosphere, Pavia has a lovely historic centre and is the location of the extraordinary Carthusian monastery, the Certosa di Pavia.

◎ Sights

Certosa di Pavia　　　　　MONASTERY

(☑ 0382 92 56 13; www.certosadipavia.com; Viale Monumento; entry by donation; ⊙ 9-11.30am & 2.30-5.30pm Tue-Sun) **FREE** One of the Italian Renaissance's most notable buildings is the splendid Certosa di Pavia. Giangaleazzo Visconti of Milan founded the monastery, 10km north of Pavia, in 1396 as a private chapel and mausoleum for the Visconti family. Originally intended as an architectural companion piece to Milan's Duomo, the same architects worked on its design; the final result, however, completed more than a century later, is a unique hybrid between late-Gothic and Renaissance styles.

The church is fronted by a spacious courtyard and flanked by a small cloister, which itself leads onto a much grander, second cloister, under whose arches are 24 cells, each a self-contained living area for one monk. Several cells are open to the public, but you need to join one of the guided tours (Italian only) to access these. In the former sacristy is a giant sculpture, dating from 1409 and made from hippopotamus teeth, including 66 small bas-reliefs and 94 statuettes. In the chapels you'll find frescoes by, among others, Bernardino Luini and the Umbrian master Il Perugino.

❶ Getting There & Away

Sila (☑ 199 153155; www.sila.it) bus 175 (Pavia–Binasco–Milano) links Pavia bus station and Certosa di Pavia (€1.10, 15 minutes, every 30 minutes). Trains to Certosa di Pavia from Milan (€3.60, 40 minutes) involve a change in Rogoredo. You can also cycle to Certosa di Pavia from Milan along the Pavese canal. For the route check out www.piste-ciclabili.com.

Monza

POP 123,150

Known to many as the home of a classic European Formula One track (where high-speed races have been held annually in September since 1950), historic Monza is sadly overlooked by visitors to Milan.

◎ Sights & Activities

Duomo　　　　　CATHEDRAL

(☑ 039 38 94 20; www.duomomonza.it; Piazza del Duomo; Corona Ferrea adult/reduced €4/3; ⊙ 9am-6pm Tue-Sun, 3-6pm Mon) The Gothic *duomo*, with its white-and-green-banded facade, contains a key early-medieval treasure, the **Corona Ferrea** (Iron Crown), fashioned according to legend with one of the nails from the Crucifixion. Charlemagne, King of the Franks and the first Holy Roman Emperor, saw it as a symbol of empire, and he was not alone. Various other Holy Roman Emperors, including Frederick I (Barbarossa), and Napoleon had themselves crowned with it. It's on show in the chapel (from Tuesday to Sunday) dedicated to the Lombard queen Theodolinda.

Museo e Tesoro del Duomo　　　　　MUSEUM

(☑ 039 32 63 83; www.museoduomomonza.it; Piazza del Duomo; adult/reduced €7/5, incl Corona Ferrea €10/8; ⊙ 9am-6pm Tue-Sun, 3-6pm Mon) Monza's cathedral museum contains one of the best collections of religious art in Europe. It's split into two parts: the first section of the display incorporates treasures from the original Palatine Chapel founded by Lombard queen Theodolinda; the second contains masterpieces intended for the 'new' cathedral. Highlights include a unique collection of Barbarian and Carolingian art (from the 4th to the 9th centuries) and a priceless collection of Lombard gold work. Admission includes viewing the Corona Ferrea (Iron Crown) in the *duomo*'s chapel.

Villa Reale　　　　　PALACE, GALLERY

(☑ 199 15 11 40; www.villarealedimonza.it; Piazza della Repubblica 30; ⊙ hours vary) Built between 1777 and 1780 as a viceregal residence for Archduke Ferdinand of Austria, Giuseppe Piermarini's vast Villa Reale was modelled on Vienna's Schönbrunn Palace. It served as the summer home for Italian royalty, but was abandoned following the murder of Umberto I. Two years of restoration have now revived its 3500-sq-metre frescoed, tuccooed and gilded interior for use as an xhibition and events centre.

Parco di Monza PARK
www.reggiadimonza.it; Porta Monza, Viale Cavriga; ⏲7am-7pm) This enormous park is the green ung of the city; it's also one of the largest enlosed parks in Europe, with some 295 hectares of *bello bosco* (charming woodland). t sits on the Lambro river and incorpoates the Autodromo di Monza racecourse, a horse-racing track, a golf course, tennis ourts, a 50m Olympic **swimming pool** Porta Santa Maria delle Selve, Via Vedano; adult/reduced €8/3; ⏲10am-7pm Jun-Aug) and miles of ycle paths. You can hire bikes at the Porta li Monza entrance (€3 per hour).

Autodromo di Monza CAR RACING
☑039 248 2212; www.monzanet.it; Via Vedano 5, Parco di Monza) Monza's racetrack with its ong straights, tricky chicane and sweeping Curva Parabolica is one of the most famous racetracks in the world. In addition to glitzy ace days, the track hosts year-round events ncluding cycle races, bike fests and even narathons. In winter, you can roll up in your own vehicle and tool around the infamous chicane; or go all out and take a spin in a Ferrari (www.puresport.it; from €256).

ⓘ Getting There & Away

Frequent trains connect Milan's Porta Garibaldi station with Monza (€2.20, 15 to 20 minutes), 23km to the north, making this an easy half-day trip.

THE LAKES

Writers from Goethe and Stendhal to DH Lawrence and Hemingway have lavished praise on the Italian Lakes, a dramatic region of vivid-blue waters ringed by snow-powdered peaks. Curling Lago Maggiore is home to the bewitching Borromean Islands and offers a blast of the belle époque. Mountain-fringed Lago di Como delivers extravagant villas and film-star glamour. Families find fun in the southern amusement parks of Lago di Garda while adrenalin junkies are drawn to the spectacular mountains in the north. Little Lago d'Iseo serves up soaring slopes while the villages and islands of diminutive, often bypassed Lago d'Orta are laced with laid-back charm.

Lago Maggiore

Even in this region of breathtaking beauty, Lake Maggiore shines. Its wide waters reflect mountains that are often snow-topped; its shores are lined with rich architectural reminders of a grand 19th-century past. And it boasts the beguiling palace-dotted Borromean Islands, which, like a fleet of fine vessels, lie at anchor in the Borromean Gulf.

ⓘ Information

The website www.illagomaggiore.com features lake-wide information.

ⓘ Getting There & Around

BOAT
Navigazione Lago Maggiore (☑800 551801; www.navigazionelaghi.it) Operates passenger ferries and hydrofoils around the lake; its ticket booths are next to embarkation quays. Services include those connecting Stresa with Arona (€6.20, 40 minutes), Angera (€6.20, 35 minutes) and Verbania Pallanza (often just called Pallanza; €5, 35 minutes). Day passes include a ticket linking Stresa with Isola Superiore, Isola Bella and Isola Madre (€16.90). Services are drastically reduced in autumn and winter.
The only car ferry connecting the western and eastern shores sails between Verbania Intra (often just called Intra) and Laveno. Ferries run every 20 to 30 minutes; one-way transport costs from €8 to €13 for a car and driver; €5 for a bicycle and cyclist.

BUS
SAF (☑0323 55 21 72; www.safduemila.com) operates the daily Verbania Intra to Milan service, linking Stresa with Arona (€2.70, 20 minutes), Verbania Pallanza (€2.70, 20 minutes), Verbania Intra (€2.70, 25 minutes) and Milan (€9.20, 1½ hours).

SAF also runs **Alibus**, a prebooked shuttle bus connecting the same towns with Malpensa airport (€15).

TRAIN
Stresa is on the Domodossola–Milan train line. Domodossola, 30 minutes northwest of Stresa, is on the Swiss border – from there trains continue to Brig and Geneva.

Stresa

POP 5000
Stresa's easy accessibility from Milan has long made it a favourite among writers and artists, and today its sunny lake-front promenades are backed by architectural reminders

of its heyday. Among the high-profile visitors to Stresa was author Ernest Hemingway. In 1918 he recovered from a war wound here, and set some pivotal scenes of *A Farewell to Arms* at the Grand Hôtel des Iles Borromées – which remains the most palatial of the hotels garlanding the lake.

Sights & Activities

Parco della Villa Pallavicino — ZOO

(☑ 0323 31 5 33; www.parcozoopallavicino.it; adult/reduced €9.50/6.50; ⊙ 9am-7pm mid-Mar–Oct) Barely 1km southeast of central Stresa along the SS33 main road, exotic birds and animals roam relatively freely in the woods and meadows of this child-friendly 20 hectare park. Some 40 species of animals, including llamas, Sardinian donkeys, zebras, flamingos and toucans, keep everyone amused.

Giardino Botanico Alpinia — GARDENS

(☑ 0323 3 02 95; adult/reduced €3/2.50; ⊙ 9.30am-6pm Apr-Oct) More than 1000 Alpine and sub-Alpine species flourish in this 4 hectare botanical garden set part-way up Monte Mottarone. It was founded in 1934 and profiles trees and shrubs from as far away as China and Japan against a backdrop of fine lake views. Access is via the Stresa–Mottarone cable car; get off at the Alpino midstation (803m).

Funivia Stresa–Mottarone — CABLE CAR

(☑ 0323 3 02 95; www.stresa-mottarone.it; Piazzale della Funivia; return adult/reduced €13.50/8.50, to Alpino station €8/5.50; ⊙ 9.30am-5.30pm Apr-Oct, 8.10am-5.30pm Nov-Mar) Captivating lake views unfold during a 20-minute cable-car journey to the top of 1491m-high Monte Mottarone. On a clear day you can see Lago Maggiore, Lago d'Orta and Monte Rosa on the Swiss border. At the **Alpino** midstation a profusion of Alpine plants flourish in the Giardino Botanico Alpinia. The mountain itself offers good hiking and biking trails. At time of writing the cable car was closed for repairs; a re-opening date had not yet been set.

Bicicò — MOUNTAIN BIKING

(☑ 340 3572189; www.bicico.it; Piazzale della Funivia; half-/full-day rental €25/30; ⊙ 9.30am-12.30pm & 1.30-5.30pm) Bicicò rents mountain bikes from its base at the foot of the Stresa–Monte Mottarone cable-car. Rates include a helmet and road book detailing an easy 25km, three-hour panoramic descent from the mountain top back to Stresa. Also runs

guided trips (half/full day €80/150) and advises on other mountain- and road-bike routes. Book trips and hire two days in advance.

Sleeping

There are some 40 campgrounds along Maggiore's western shore; the tourist office has a list. Seasonal closings (including hotels) are generally from November to February, but this can vary; check ahead.

Hotel Saini Meublè — HOTEL

(☑ 0323 93 45 19; www.hotelsaini.it; Via Garibaldi 10; s €70-94, d €72-112) With their warm tones and wooden cabinets and floors, the rooms in Hotel Saini have a timeless feel – fitting for a house that's some 400 years old. Spacious bedrooms, a swirling spiral staircase and a location in the heart of the old town add to the appeal.

Hotel Elena — HOTEL

(☑ 0323 3 10 43; www.hotelelena.com; Piazza Cadorna 15; s/d/tr/q €60/85/110/130; P) Adjoining a cafe, the old-fashioned Elena is slap-bang on Stresa's central pedestrian square. Comfortable rooms feature parquet floors and balconies, many overlooking the piazza. Wheelchair access is possible.

Casa Kinka — B&B

(☑ 0323 3 00 47; www.casakinka.it; Strada Comunale Lombartino 21, Magognino; d €160; ⊙ Mar-Oct; P @) It's hard to imagine a more appealing midrange hilltop hideaway: wood-framed mirrors, stately furniture and artfully arranged antiques define cosy bedrooms; birdsong and flowers fill the garden; most of the windows feature bewitching lake views. It's just over 1km southeast of Stresa, off the A26.

Villa e Palazzo Aminta — HOTEL €€€

(☑ 0323 93 38 18; www.villa-aminta.it; Via Sempione Nord 123; d €235-500, ste €640-1125; P ❀ ⊛ ☎) Luxuriate in turn-of-the-century style at Villa Aminta, which offers picture-perfect views of an island-studded lake. Rooms decked out with Murano chandeliers, silk curtains, and acres of velvet and gilt echo the opulence of Stresa's belle époque. The hotel also has its own private beach, heated pool and fitness centre.

Eating & Drinking

Taverna del Pappagallo — TRATTORIA €

(☑ 0323 3 04 11; www.tavernapappagallo.com; Via Principessa Margherita 46; meals €20-25; ⊙ 6.30

1pm Thu-Tue) It's not fancy and it's not superserious but this welcoming backstreet trattoria is where you'll find Stresa's families tucking into tasty regional dishes ranging from pizzas cooked in an old wood-fired oven to risotto with lake fish.

The clams with homemade pasta are positively steeped in garlic and white wine.

★ Piemontese
PIEDMONTESE €€

(☑ 0323 3 02 35; www.ristorantepiemontese.com; Via Mazzini 25; meals €35-45; ☉ 12.30-2pm & 6.30-9.30pm) The name gives a huge clue as to the focus of this refined *ristorante*. Regional delights include gnocchi with gorgonzola and hazelnuts; cold veal with tuna sauce; and risotto made using Piedmont's own Barolo wine. The Lake Menu (€34) features carp, trout, perch and pike, while the set lunch menu is a steal (two/three courses €23/28).

Ristorante Il Vicoletto
RISTORANTE €€

(☑ 0323 93 21 02; www.ristorantevicoletto.com; Vicolo del Pocivo 3; meals €30-45; ☉ noon-2pm & 6.30-10pm Fri-Wed) Located a short, uphill walk from the centre of Stresa, Il Vicoletto has a commendable regional menu including lake trout, wild asparagus, and traditional risotto with radicchio and taleggio cheese. The dining room is modestly elegant with bottle-lined dressers and linen-covered tables, while the local clientele speaks volumes in this tourist town.

La Botte
TRATTORIA €€

(☑ 0323 3 04 62; Via Mazzini 6; meals €25-30; ☉ noon-2.30pm & 7-11pm Fri-Wed) Regional dishes are at the heart of this tiny trattoria's business, so expect grilled lake fish, tasty veal and plenty of polenta (the version with blue cheese and pears is superb). The decor is old-style *osteria* (casual tavern or eatery presided over by a host) with dark timber furniture and decades of accumulated knick-knacks.

Grand Hotel des Iles Borromées
COCKTAIL BAR

(☑ 0323 93 89 38; www.borromees.it; Corso Umberto I 67; ☉ 6pm-late) Following his WWI stint on the Italian front, Ernest Hemingway checked in here to nurse his battle scars, and to write *A Farewell to Arms*. The passionate antiwar novel featured this sumptuous hotel. You might baulk at room prices (guests have included Princess Margaret and the Vanderbilts) but you can still slug back a Manhattan on the terraces with cinematic views.

❶ LAGO MAGGIORE EXPRESS

Lago Maggiore Express (www.lago maggioreexpress.com; adult/child 1-day tour €34/17, 2-day tour €44/22) The Lago Maggiore Express is a picturesque day trip you can do under your own steam. It includes train travel from Arona or Stresa to Domodossola, from where you get the charming Centovalli (Hundred Valleys) train to Locarno in Switzerland, before hopping on a ferry back to Stresa. Tickets are available from the **Navigazione Lago Maggiore** (p261) ticket booths at each port.

❶ Information

Stresa Tourist Office (☑ 0323 3 13 08; www.stresaturismo.it; Piazza Marconi 16; ☉ 10am-12.30pm & 3-6.30pm summer, reduced hours winter)

Borromean Islands

The Borromean Gulf forms Lago Maggiore's most beautiful corner, sheltering as it does the palaces and gardens of the Borromean Islands. These can be reached from various points around the lake, but Stresa and the village of Baveno (3km to the north) offer the best access.

ISOLA BELLA

Isola Bella was named after Isabella, wife of Carlo Borromeo III, when the island's centrepiece Palazzo Borromeo was built for the aristocratic family in the 17th century. Both villa and gardens were designed to lend the whole island the appearance of a ship, with the villa at the prow and the gardens dripping down terraces at the rear.

◉ Sights

★ Palazzo Borromeo
PALACE

(☑ 0323 3 05 56; www.isol0eborromee.it; Isola Bella; adult/child €15/8.50, incl Palazzo Madre €21/10; ☉ 9am-5.30pm mid-Mar–mid-Oct) Presiding over 10 tiers of ornate terraced gardens roamed by peacocks, this baroque palace is arguably Lago Maggiore's finest building. Wandering the grounds and 1st floors reveals guest rooms, studies and reception halls. Particularly striking rooms include the Sala di Napoleone, where the emperor Napoleon stayed with his wife in 1797; the grand Sala da Ballo (Ballroom); the ornate

LUINO MARKET

The otherwise sleepy town of Luino becomes a consumer madhouse on market day each week at the **Luino market** (⊘8.30am-4.30pm Wed). The market was first held in 1535 and today some 370 stands fill the old town centre, selling everything from local cheese to vintage threads. Unless you can arrive very early, don't even try to drive here; catch one of the extra ferries, or the bus or train.

Sala del Trono (Throne Room); and the Sala delle Regine (Queen's Room). Paintings from a 130-strong Borromeo collection hang all around.

Highlights of the artworks are pieces by several old masters, including Rubens, Titian, Paolo Veronese, Andrea Mantegna, Van Dyck and José Ribera (Spagnoletto). You'll also find Flemish tapestries, sculptures by Antonio Canova and – in the Salone Grande – a 200-year-old wooden model of the palace and island.

Below the ground floor, a 3000-year-old fossilised boat is displayed in the cool palace grottoes, which are studded with pink marble, lava stone and pebbles from the lake bed. White peacocks, whose fanned feathers resemble bridal gowns, strut about the gardens, which are considered one of the finest examples of baroque Italian landscaping.

In summer, the family that owns Palazzo Borromeo moves in and occupies the 2nd and 3rd floors (off-limits to visitors), totalling a mere 50-odd rooms.

A combined ticket also covers admission to Palazzo Madre on nearby Isola Madre.

✗ Eating

Elvezia　　　　　　　　　　ITALIAN €€

(☑0323 3 00 43; Via Vittorio Emanuele 18; meals €30-35; ⊘noon-2pm & 6.30-9pm Tue-Sun Mar-Oct, Fri-Sun only Nov-Feb) With its rambling rooms, fish-themed portico and upstairs pergola and balcony dining area, this is the best spot on Isola Bella for home cooking. Dishes include ricotta-stuffed ravioli, various risottos and lake fish such as *coregone alle mandorle* (lake whitefish in almonds).

ISOLA MADRE

⭐**Palazzo Madre**　　　　　　PALACE

(☑0323 3 05 56; www.isoleborromee.it; adult/child €12/6.50, incl Palazzo Borromeo €21/10; ⊘9am-5.30pm mid-Mar–mid-Oct) The 16th- to 18th-century Palazzo Madre is a wonderfully decadent structure crammed full of all manner of antique furnishings and adornments. Highlights include Countess Borromeo's doll collection, a neoclassical puppet theatre designed by a scenographer from Milan's La Scala, and a 'horror' theatre with a cast of devilish marionettes. Outside, its gardens blaze with colourful azaleas, rhododendrons, camellias and hibiscus.

ISOLA SUPERIORE (PESCATORI)

Although it lacks any specific sights, tiny Fishermen's Island retains much of its original village atmosphere. A huddle of streets shelters the **Chiesa di San Vittore**, which has an 11th-century apse and a 16th-century fresco, but the real reasons to visit are the island's restaurants, which specialise in grilled fish.

🛏 Sleeping & Eating

⭐**Albergo Verbano**　　　　　HOTEL €€

(☑0323 3 04 08; www.hotelverbano.it; Via Ugo Ara 2; s €70-170, d €80-230; ⊘Mar-Dec; 🖻) Set at the southern tip of enchanting Isola Superiore, Albergo Verbano has been putting up guests in this idyllic spot since 1895. Dishes from a fish-focused menu are served on the tree-shaded waterside terrace, and bedrooms are a study in unstuffy elegance – choose one looking out towards Isola Bella or Isola Madre; the views are exquisite either way.

Albergo Ristorante Belvedere　HOTEL €€

(☑0323 3 22 92; www.belvedere-isolapescatori.it; Isola Superiore; d €99-170; ⊘Apr-Oct) Perfectly located towards the quieter northern end of Isola Superiore, this cheerful little hotel-restaurant has eight simply styled bedrooms, most with a balcony or terrace giving superb views of the lake, Isola Madre and the mountains beyond.

The gardens of the restaurant (open from noon to 2pm and 7pm to 9pm) are shaded by vines; if you book for supper you can be collected from Stresa by boat.

⭐**Casabella**　　　　　　　RISTORANTE €€€

(☑0323 3 34 71; www.isola-pescatori.it; Via del Marinaio 1; meals €30-50, five-course tasting menu €55; ⊘noon-2pm & 6-8.30pm Feb-Nov) The set-

...ing is bewitching – right by the shore – and the food is acclaimed. The admirably short menu might feature home-smoked beef with spinach, blanched squid with ricotta or perfectly cooked lake fish. Leave room for dessert; the pear cake with chocolate fondant is faultless.

If you don't want to leave after dinner (likely) there are two snug bedrooms on site.

Verbania
POP 31,100

Sprawling Verbania is split into three districts. Of these, Verbania Pallanza is the most interesting, with a tight web of lanes in its old centre. Verbania Intra has a pleasant waterfront backed by elegant houses, and provides handy car ferries to Laveno on the eastern shore.

○ Sights

Villa Taranto   GARDENS
(📞 0323 55 66 67; www.villataranto.it; Via Vittorio Veneto 111, Verbania Pallanza; adult/reduced €10/5.50; ⊙ 8.30am-6.30pm mid-Mar–Sep, 9am-4pm Oct) The grounds of this late-19th-century villa are one of Lago Maggiore's highlights. Scot, Neil McEacharn, bought the Normandy-style villa from the Savoy family in 1931 after spotting an ad in the *Times*. He planted some 20,000 plant species over 30 years, and today it's considered one of Europe's finest botanic gardens. Even the main entrance path is a grand affair, bordered by lawns and a cornucopia of colourful flowers. It's a short walk from the Villa Taranto ferry stop.

🛏 Sleeping

Aquadolce   HOTEL €
(📞 0323 50 54 18; www.hotelaquadolce.it; Via Cietti 1, Verbania Pallanza; s €70, d €95-105; ❇ 🔊) Ask for a room at the front of this bijou waterfront address and your window will be filled with a glittering lake backed by the mountains rearing up behind. Inside it's a beautifully lit, genteel affair, with all the quiet assurance of a well-run hotel.

Hotel Pallanza   HOTEL €
(📞 0323 50 32 02; www.pallanzahotels.com; Viale Magnolie 8, Verbania Pallanza; s €97, d €105-120, tr €130; ❇ 🔊) A tall, balcony-dotted facade in subtle olive and terracotta tones signals what to expect inside: an elegant art nouveau waterfront hotel with sweeping lake views.

🍴 Eating

★ Osteria Castello   OSTERIA €€
(📞 0323 51 65 79; www.osteriacastello.com; Piazza Castello 9, Verbania Intra; meals €25; ⊙ 11am-3pm & 6pm-midnight, closed Sun) Its 100-plus years of history run like a rich seam through this enchanting *osteria*, where archive photos and bottles line the walls. Order a glass of wine from the vast selection; sample some ham; or tuck into the pasta or lake fish.

Osteria dell'Angolo   PIEDMONTESE €€
(📞 0323 55 63 62; Piazza Garibaldi 35, Verbania Pallanza; meals €30-35; ⊙ noon-2.30pm & 7-9.30pm Tue-Sun) Greenery drapes a terrace dotted with only eight tables at this *osteria* and well-presented dishes showcase creative Piedmontese cuisine. The lake fish is particularly fine while the well-chosen wine list means it could turn into a very long lunch.

★ Ristorante Milano   MODERN ITALIAN €€€
(📞 0323 55 68 16; www.ristorantemilanolago maggiore.it; Corso Zanitello 2, Verbania Pallanza; meals €50-70; ⊙ noon-2pm & 7-9pm Wed-Sun, noon-2pm Mon) The setting really is hard to beat: Milano directly overlooks Pallanza's minuscule horseshoe-shaped harbour (200m south of the ferry jetty); a scattering of tables sits on lakeside lawns amid the trees. It's an idyllic spot to enjoy lake fish, local lamb and some innovative Italian cuisine, such as *risotto ai petali di rosa* (risotto with rose petals).

❶ Information

Verbania Tourist Office (📞 0323 50 32 49; www.verbania-turismo.it; Corso Zanitello 6, Verbania Pallanza; ⊙ 9am-1pm Mon-Fri)

Cannobio
POP 5140

Sheltered by a high mountain at the foot of the Val Cannobino, the medieval hamlet of Cannobio, just 5km from the Swiss border, is a dreamy place with some of the best restaurants and hotels on Lake Maggiore.

🏃 Activities

Tomaso Surf & Sail   WATER SPORTS
(📞 333 7000291; www.tomaso.com; Via Nazionale 7) Offers lessons in windsurfing (per hour €75), sailing (per hour €105) and waterskiing (per half-hour €85). Experienced watersports enthusiasts can also rent equipment (windsurf board and rig per one/four hours

VAL CANNOBINO

To explore the wildly beautiful valley that winds northwest out of Cannobio, take the scenic SP75. It snakes for 28km beside a waterway via heavily wooded hills to Malesco in Valle Vigezzo. Just 2.5km along the valley, in Sant'Anna, the powerful Torrente Cannobino forces its way through a narrow gorge known as the **Orrido di Sant'Anna**, crossed at its narrowest part by a Romanesque bridge. A further 7km on, a steep 3km side road leads, via switchbacks and hairpin bends, up to the central valley's main town, **Falmenta**. Hire mountain bikes in Cannobio from **Cicli Prezan** (☎ 0323 7 12 30; www.cicliprezan.it; Viale Vittorio Veneto 9; per hr/day €10/20; ⊗ 8.30am-noon & 3-7pm Mon-Sat, 8.30pm-noon Sun).

€22/70; sailing dinghy per one/two hours €35/55).

🛏 Sleeping & Eating

★ **Hotel Pironi**   HOTEL €€
(☎ 0323 7 06 24; www.pironihotel.it; Via Marconi 35; s €120, d €150-195, tr €185-230; P 🕸 ❄) Set in a 15th-century mini-monastery (later home of the noble Pironi family) high in Cannobio's cobbled maze, Hotel Pironi is a charming choice. Thick-set stone walls shelter interiors evocative of another era; it's full of antiques, frescoed vaults, exposed timber beams and stairs climbing off in odd directions.

Lo Scalo   MODERN ITALIAN €€
(☎ 0323 7 14 80; www.loscalo.com; Piazza Vittorio Emanuele III 32; meals €35-45; ⊗ noon-2.30pm & 6-9pm Wed-Sun, 6-9pm Tue) The pick of the restaurants along the main promenade, elegant Lo Scalo serves cuisine that is sophisticated and precise, featuring dishes such as an inky-black ravioli with squid and a pea and bergamot sauce. The set two-course lunch (€25) and five-course *menù degustazione* (€50) are both great-value treats.

ℹ Information

Tourist Office (☎ 0323 7 12 12; www.pro cannobio.it; Via Giovanola 25; ⊗ 9am-noon & 4-7pm Mon-Sat, 9am-noon Sun)

Santa Caterina del Sasso

★ **Santa Caterina del Sasso**   MONASTERY
(www.santacaterinadelsasso.com; Via Santa Caterina 13; ⊗ 9am-noon & 2-6pm Apr-Sep, to 5pm Mar & Oct, closed weekdays Nov-Feb) **FREE** One of northern Italy's most spectacularly sited monasteries, Santa Caterina del Sasso clings to the high rocky face of Lago Maggiore's southeast shore. The buildings span the 13th and 14th centuries; the porticoes and chapels are packed with frescoes; and the views from the tiny courtyards are superb. The monastery is reached either by climbing up 80 steps from the Santa Caterina ferry quay or by clattering down a 268-step staircase from the car park (there is a lift, too).

Arona

POP 14,300

Work-a-day Arona, southern Lake Maggiore's biggest town, has one must-see sight: the Sacro Monte di San Carlo. It honours San Carlo Borromeo, the locally born son of the Count of Arona and Margherita de' Medici.

◎ Sights

Sacro Monte di San Carlo   LANDMARK
(☎ 0322 24 96 69; Piazza San Carlo; admission €7; ⊗ 9am-12.30pm & 2.30-6pm Apr-Oct, to 4.30pm Sat & Sun Nov-Mar) When Milan's superstar bishop San Carlo Borromeo (1538–84) was declared a saint in 1610 his cousin, Federico, ordered the creation of a *sacro monte* in his memory, featuring 15 chapels lining a path to a church. The church and three of those chapels were built, along with a special extra: a hollow 35m bronze-and-copper statue of the saint. Commonly known as the Sancarlone (Big St Charles) you can climb up inside it to discover spectacular views through the giant's eyes.

🍴 Eating

Taverna del Pittore   RISTORANTE €€€
(☎ 0322 24 33 66; www.ristorantetavernadel pittore.it; Piazza del Popolo 39; meals €60-80; ⊗ noon-2.30pm & 7.30-10pm Fri-Wed) What is possibly Largo Maggiore's most romantic restaurant has a waterside terrace and views of the illuminated Rocca di Angera fortress at night. The refined food is no less fabulous, with squid, duck and octopus transformed into exquisitely arranged dishes featuring ravioli, broth, risotto and gnocchi.

Lago d'Orta

Shrouded by thick, dark-green woodlands and backed by Monte Mottarone, little Lago d'Orta is just 13.4km long and 2.5km wide. The key points of the lake are the medieval village of Orta San Giulio and the Isola San Giulio, which sits just offshore.

⊙ Sights

Orta San Giulio Old Town   AREA

The medieval village of Orta San Giulio (population just 1150), often referred to simply as Orta, is the focal point of Lago d'Orta and is the lake's main village. At its heart the central square, Piazza Motta, is framed by cream-coloured houses and roofed with thick slate tiles. It's overlooked by the Palazotto, a frescoed 16th-century building borne up by stilts above a small loggia.

Basilica di San Giulio   CHURCH

⊙9.30am-6pm Tue-Sun, 2-5pm Mon Apr-Sep, 9.30am-noon & 2-5pm Tue-Sun, 2-5pm Mon Oct-Mar) Isola San Giulio is dominated at its south end by the 12th-century Basilica di San Giulio, which is full of vibrant frescoes that alone make a trip to the island worthwhile. The church, island and mainland town are named after a Greek evangelist, Giulio, who's said to have rid the island of snakes, dragons and assorted monsters in the late 4th century. Regular ferries (p268) shuttle between the island and Orta San Giulio.

Sacro Monte di San Francesco CHAPEL, PARK

Beyond the lush gardens and residences that mark the hill rising behind Orta is a kind of parallel 'town' – the *sacro monte*, where 20 small chapels dedicated to St Francis of Assisi dot the hillside. The views down the lake are captivating, and meandering from chapel to chapel is a wonderfully tranquil way to pass a few hours.

⊨ Sleeping

★ Locanda di Orta   BOUTIQUE HOTEL €

(☑ 0322 90 51 88; www.locandaorta.com; Via Olina 18, Orta San Giulio; s €65-70, d €85-90, ste €150-160; ☎) Teaming white leather and bold pink beside medieval grey stone walls is a bold design choice – but it works. Because of the age and size of the building, the cheaper rooms are tiny, but still delightful. Suites are roomier; each features a jacuzzi and a pocket-sized balcony overlooking the cobbled lane.

Piccolo Hotel Olina   HOTEL €

(☑ 0322 90 56 56; www.ortainfo.com; Via Olina 40, Orta San Giulio; s/d/tr/q €75/95/110/125; ☀) Jauntily decorated with contemporary prints, bright colours and light-wood furniture, this ecofriendly hotel places modern design right in Orta San Giulio's medieval heart.

Leon d'Oro   HOTEL €€

(☑ 0322 9 02 54; www.albergoleondoro.it; Piazza Motta 42, Orta San Giulio; s €100, d €110-180, ste €200-300) At this grand 200-year-old hotel a red carpet leads you through the front door, stately rooms feature silky furnishings and the waterfront terrace offers gorgeous Isola San Giulio views.

✗ Eating

Enoteca Al Boeuc   PIEDMONTESE €

(☑ 339 5840039; http://alboeuc.beepworld. it; Via Bersani 28, Orta San Giulio; meals €15-20; ⊙11.30am-3pm & 6.30pm-midnight Wed-Mon) This candlelit stone cavern has been around since the 16th century. These days it offers glasses of fine wines (try the velvety Barolo for €8) and snacks including mixed bruschette with truffles and mushrooms, meat and cheese platters, and that Piedmontese favourite: *bagna caüda* (a hot dip of butter, olive oil, garlic and anchovies in which you bathe vegetables).

Cucchiaio di Legno   AGRITURISMO €

(☑ 339 5775385; www.ilcucchiaiodilegno.com; Via Prisciola 10, Orta San Giulio; set menu €24; ⊙6-9pm Thu-Sun, noon-2.30pm Sat & Sun; ℗☎) Delicious home cooking emerges from the kitchen of this honest-to-goodness *agriturismo* (farm stay accommodation); expect fish fresh from the lake, and salami and cheese from the surrounding valleys. When eating alfresco on the vine-draped patio it feels rather like you're dining at the house of a friend. Bookings required.

There's a clutch of bright, snazzy rooms too (doubles €80). It's 800m from the Orta–Miasino train station.

Venus   TRATTORIA €€

(☑ 0322 9 03 62; www.venusorta.it; Piazza Motta 50, Orta San Giulio; meals €20-30; ⊙noon-3pm & 6-10pm Tue-Sun) The place with the best views is also one of the best places to eat in town. The menu of rich local dishes might feature a creamy risotto flavoured with cheese,

ALESSI OUTLET STORE

Lake Orta's Alessi has been transforming modern kitchens with humorous, ultra-cool utensils since 1921, thanks to designers including Achille Castiglioni, Philippe Starck, Massimiliano Fuksas and Zaha Hadid. At their huge factory **outlet** (☑ 0323 86 86 48; www.alessi.com; Via Privata Alessi 6, Omegna; ⊙ 9.30am-6pm Mon-Sat, 2.30-6pm Sun) the whole range sits alongside special offers and end-of-line deals.

venison and blueberries, or polenta with cheese, cabbage and pistachios.

★ **Locanda di Orta**　　MODERN ITALIAN €€€
(☑ 0322 90 51 88; www.locandaorta.com; Via Olina 18, Orta San Giulio; meals €50; ⊙ noon-2.30pm & 7.30-9pm) Tiny Orta can now boast its very own Michelin star – in the wisteria-draped Locanda di Orta, squeezed into the heart of the old town. It's a supremely stylish, intimate affair (it only seats around 17 people) where culinary alchemy converts traditional Lago d'Orta ingredients into works of foodie art.

The 250-strong wine list is also impressive.

ℹ Information

Main Tourist Office (☑ 0322 90 51 63; www.distrettolaghi.it; Via Panoramica, Orta San Giulio; ⊙ 10am-12.30pm & 2.30-5.30pm Mon-Thu, 11am-1pm & 2.30-6.30pm Fri-Sun) Can provide information on the whole of Lago d'Orta.

Pro Loco (☑ 0322 9 01 55; Via Bossi 11, Orta San Giulio; ⊙ 11am-1pm & 2-4pm Mon, Tue & Thu, 10am-1pm & 2-4pm Fri-Sun) In the town hall.

ℹ Getting There & Around

BOAT

Navigazione Lago d'Orta (☑ 345 5170005; www.navigazionelagodorta.it) Operates ferries from its landing stage on Piazza Motta to places including Isola San Giulio (one way/ return €2/3), Omegna, Pella and Ronco. A day ticket for unlimited travel anywhere on the lake costs €8.

BUS

From June to September buses run three times daily from Orta to Stresa (€4).

TRAIN

Orta Miasino train station is 3km from the centr of Orta San Giulio. From Milan there are frequer trains from Stazione Centrale (change at Novara; €8.50, two hours).

Lago di Como

Set in the shadow of the snow-covered Rhae tian Alps and hemmed in by steep, woode hills, Lago di Como (also known as Lag di Lario) is the most spectacular of the re gion's three main lakes. Shaped like an up side-down letter Y, its winding shoreline i dotted with ancient villages and exquisit villas.

The lake's main town, Como, sits wher the southern and western shores converge.

★ Festivals

Lake Como Festival　　MUSI
(www.lakecomofestival.com; ⊙ May & Jun) Musi cal concerts are held at some of Lago di Co mo's finest villas.

ℹ Information

The website www.lakecomo.it features information covering the whole lake.

ℹ Getting There & Around

BOAT

Navigazione Lago di Como (☑ 800 551801; www.navigazionelaghi.it) Operates year-round lake-wide ferries and hydrofoils, which in Como depart from the jetties beside Piazza Cavour. Single fares range between €2.50 (to Cernobbio) and €12.60 (to Lecco). Return fares cost double. The faster hydrofoil services cost €1.40 to €4.90 extra. Car ferries link Menaggio on the west shore of Lago di Como with Varenna on the east and Bellagio to the south.

Ferries operate year-round, but services are reduced in winter. Zonal passes (per day €6.90 to €28; per six days €10.40 to €84) allow unlimited journeys and can work out cheaper than buying single or return tickets.

BUS

ASF Autolinee (☑ 031 24 72 47; www.sptlinea. it) Operates regular buses around Lago di Como, which in Como depart from the bus station on Piazza Matteotti. Key routes include Como to Colico (€6, two hours, three to five daily), via all the villages on the western shore, and Como to Bellagio (€3.40, 70 minutes, hourly).

CAR

From Milan, take the A9 motorway, turning off at Monte Olimpino for Como. The SS36 leads east to Lecco while the SS233 heads west to Varese. The roads around the lake are superbly scenic, but also windy, narrow and busy in summer.

TRAIN

Como's main train station (Como San Giovanni) is served from Milan's Stazione Centrale and Porta Garibaldi stations (€4.80 to €13, 30 minutes to one hour, hourly); some trains continue on to Switzerland. Trains from Milan's Stazione Nord Cadorna (€4.10, one hour) use Como's lakeside Como Nord Lago (Stazione FNM). Trains from Milan to Lecco continue north along the eastern shore. When heading for Bellagio, it's best to continue on the train to Varenna and make the short ferry crossing from there.

Como

POP 84,900

With its lively historic centre, 12th-century city walls and a self-confident air, Como is an elegant and prosperous town. Built on the wealth of the silk industry, its pedestrianised core is chock-full of bars, restaurants and places to sleep, making the town an ideal southern Lago di Como base.

◉ Sights

Passeggiata Lino Gelpi   WATERFRONT
One of Como's most charming walks is the lakeside stroll west from Piazza Cavour. Passeggiata Lino Gelpi leads past the **Monumento ai Caduti** (Memorial; Viale Puecher 9), a 1931 memorial to Italy's WWI dead and a classic example of Fascist-era architecture. Next you'll pass a series of mansions and villas, including **Villa Saporiti** and **Villa Gallia**, both now owned by the provincial government and closed to the public, before arriving at the garden-ringed Villa Olmo.

Villa Olmo   HISTORIC BUILDING
(☑031 25 23 52; Via Cantoni 1; gardens free, villa entry varies by exhibition; ⏰villa during exhibitions 9am-12.30pm & 2-5pm Mon-Sat, gardens 7.30am-11pm summer, to 7pm winter) Set facing the lake, the grand creamy facade of neoclassical Villa Olmo is one of Como's biggest landmarks. The extravagant structure was built in 1728 by the Odescalchi family, related to Pope Innocent XI. If there's an art exhibition showing, you'll get to admire the sumptuous Liberty-style interiors. Otherwise, you can enjoy the Italianate and English gardens.

MOTORBIKE TOURS

Lake Como Motorbike (☑349 4277542; www.lakecomomotorbike.com) If travelling by motorbike through Lago di Como's cinematic scenery sounds irresistible, try this operator, which offers guided day trips (€180) and bike hire for experienced riders (per day €115 to €180). Helmet, jacket and gloves are provided. If you've not driven a bike before, don't worry – you can ride pillion on the back of the guide's bike (€150).

★**Duomo**   CATHEDRAL
(Piazza del Duomo; ⏰7.30am-7.30pm Mon-Sat, to 9.30pm Sun) Although largely Gothic in style, elements of Romanesque, Renaissance and baroque can also be seen in Como's imposing, marble-clad *duomo*. The cathedral was built between the 14th and 18th centuries, and is crowned by a high octagonal dome.

Basilica di Sant'Abbondio   BASILICA
(Via Regina; ⏰8am-6pm summer, to 4pm winter) About 500m south of the city walls is the remarkable 11th-century Romanesque Basilica di Sant'Abbondio. Aside from its proud, high structure and impressive apse decorated with a beautiful geometric relief around the outside windows, the highlights are the extraordinary frescoes inside the apse.

Depicting scenes from the life of Christ, from the Annunciation to his burial, the frescoes were restored to their former glory in the 1990s. A university occupies what was once the cloister. To get a closer glimpse of the apse exterior, stroll into its grounds.

★**Basilica di San Fedele**   BASILICA
(Piazza San Fedele; ⏰8am-noon & 3.30-7pm) With three naves and three apses, this evocative basilica is often likened to a clover leaf. Parts of it date from the 6th century while the facade is the result of a 1914 revamp. The 16th-century rose window and 16th- and 17th-century frescoes enhance the appeal. The apses are centuries-old and feature some eye-catching sculpture on the right.

Museo della Seta   MUSEUM
(Silk Museum; ☑031 30 31 80; www.museoseta como.com; Via Castelnuovo 9; adult/reduced €10/7; ⏰10am-6pm Tue-Fri, to 1pm Sat) Lago di Como's aspiring silk makers still learn their trade in the 1970s-built Istituto Tecnico Industriale di Setificio textile technical school. It's also

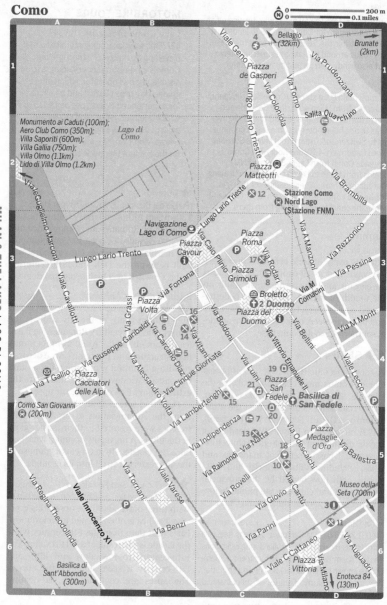

home to the Museo della Seta, which draws together the threads of the town's silk history. Early dyeing and printing equipment features amid displays that chart the entire fabric production process.

Activities

★ **Lido di Villa Olmo**   SWIMMING

(☏ 031 57 08 71; www.lidovillaolmo.it; Via Cernobbio 2; adult/reduced €7/3.50; ⏰ 9am-7pm mid-May–Sep) What a delight: a compact *lido* (beach) where you can plunge into open-air

Como

MILAN & THE LAKES LAGO DI COMO

pools, sunbathe beside the lake, rent boats, sip cocktails at the waterfront bar and soak up mountain views. Bliss.

★**Aero Club Como** SCENIC FLIGHTS
(☑031 57 44 95; www.aeroclubcomo.com; Viale Masia 44; 30 min flight from €140) For a true touch of glamour, take one of these seaplane tours and buzz about the skies high above Como. The often-bumpy take-off and landing on the lake itself is thrilling, as are the views down onto the miniature villas and villages dotted far below. Flights are popular; in summer book three or four days ahead.

Funicolare Como–Brunate CABLE CAR
(☑031 30 36 08; www.funicolarecomo.it; Piazza de Gasperi 4; adult one way/return €3/5.50, reduced €2/3.20; ☉half-hourly departures 8am-midnight summer, to 10.30pm winter) Prepare for some spectacular views. The Como–Brunate cable car (built in 1894) takes seven minutes to trundle up to the quiet hilltop village of **Brunate** (720m), revealing a memorable panorama of mountains and lakes. From there a steep 30-minute walk along a stony mule track leads to **San Maurizio** (907m), where 143 steps climb to the top of a lighthouse.

🛏 Sleeping

★**Quarcino** HOTEL €
(☑031 30 39 34; www.hotelquarcino.it; Salita Quarchino 4; s/d/tr/q €57/80/115/130; P❋🐾) You'll struggle to find a more appealing, central budget hotel in Como. The modern decor is simple but stylish, the bathrooms are

pristine and there are lake glimpses from many of the front rooms.

Le Stanze del Lago APARTMENT €
(☑031 30 11 82; www.lestanzedellago.com; Via Rodari 6; 2-/4-person apt €110/140; ❋) For a touch of loft living Como-style, check into one of these five serviced apartments, where sloping wooden ceilings and rough stone walls meet bright furnishings. If you're staying for longer than five days you can use the kitchen; that and a location in the heart of Como make these a great deal.

★**Avenue Hotel** BOUTIQUE HOTEL €€
(☑031 27 21 86; www.avenuehotel.it; Piazzolo Terragni 6; d €170-240, ste from €340; P❋🐾) An assured sense of style at this delightful hotel sees ultramodern, minimalist rooms team crisp white walls with shots of purple or fuchsia-pink. Breakfast is served in a chic courtyard, service is warm but discreet and you can borrow a bike for free.

Albergo del Duca HOTEL €€
(☑031 26 48 59; www.albergodelduca.it; Piazza Mazzini 12; s €60-75, d €100-130) The setting is an attractive one (on the edge of a pedestrianised square); the atmosphere is all friendliness; and the rooms are as neat as a pin, with polished wooden floors.

Albergo Firenze HOTEL €€
(☑031 30 01 01; www.hotelfirenzecomo.it; Piazza Volta 16; s €98, d €130-160, tr €160-195; ❋🐾) Tucked above a women's fashion boutique on Piazza Volta, this smart hotel has bright, spotless rooms. Don't be put off by the somewhat gloomy reception area, but do consider paying extra for a superior room with a

piazza view, as those rooms out the back can be a little dark.

Eating & Drinking

Como's **food market** (⊙8.30am-1pm Tue & Thu, to 7pm Sat) is held outside **Porta Torre**.

★ Natta Café
CAFE €

(☑031 26 91 23; www.nattacafe.com; Via Natta 16; meals €15-20; ⊙12.30-3pm & 6.30-midnight Tue-Sat, 12.30-3pm & 7.30-11.30pm Sun; ☎) It's almost as if this is an *osteria* for the next generation. Yes, there's a proud focus on superb local ingredients and classic wines, but this laid-back cafe also has a beatnik atmosphere. So you get Chianti on the wine list, risotto with lake perch on the menu and Edith Piaf on the soundtrack. One cool vibe.

Castiglioni
TRATTORIA €

(☑031 26 33 88; www.castiglionistore.com; Via Cantù 9; meals €20; ⊙8am-2.30pm & 4-7pm Mon-Fri, 8am-7.30pm Sun) Going strong since 1958, Castiglioni's wonderful deli has evolved to include a wine bar and now a restaurant. Sample dozens of local vintages with plates of sweet prosciutto, or take lunch on the pleasant outdoor patio. The menu, which includes all manner of charcuterie plates, lake fish and mountain meat dishes, is surprisingly refined and great value.

Gelateria Ceccato
GELATERIA €

(☑031 2 33 91; Lungo Lario Trieste 16; gelato €2-4; ⊙noon-midnight summer, hours vary winter) For generations *comaschi* (people from Como) have turned to Ceccato for their Sunday-afternoon gelato and then embarked on a ritual *passeggiata* (stroll) with their dripping cones along the lakeshore. You can do no better than imitate them: order a creamy *stracciatella* (chocolate chip) or perhaps a mix of fresh fruit flavours and head off for a relaxed promenade.

Enoteca 84
ITALIAN €

(☑031 27 04 82; Via Milano 84; meals €20-25; ⊙10am-2.30pm & 7-10pm) It has the feel of a neighbourhood eatery – and that's because it is. Set outside Como's pedestrianised core, this snug spot serves a handful of traditional dishes on its menu, which might include *lavarello* (white fish) in butter and sage, polenta with beef and mushrooms or *pappardelle alla lepre* (ribbon pasta with hare).

★ Osteria del Gallo
ITALIAN €€

(☑031 27 25 91; www.osteriadelgallo-como.it; Via Vitani 16; meals €25-30; ⊙12.30-3pm Mon, to 9pm Tue-Sat) An ageless *osteria* that looks exactly the part. In the wood-lined dining room, wine bottles and other goodies fill the shelves, and diners sit at small timber tables to tuck into traditional local food. The menu is chalked up daily and might include a first course of *zuppa di ceci* (chickpea soup), followed by lightly fried lake fish.

Pane e Tulipani
CAFE €€

(☑031 26 42 42; www.pane-e-tulipani.com; Via Lambertenghi 3; meals €30; ⊙noon-3pm & 6-11pm Tue-Sun) With its vast number of grappa bottles, shabby-chic furniture and huge vases of flowers, this sweet eatery – which is part-cafe, part-bistro and part–flower shop – has a bohemian air. This means you get to sample creative twists on Italian standards (don't expect big portions) or tuck into elaborate pastries surrounded by a profusion of blooms.

COMO SILK

Como's silk makers are legendary. By the 18th and 19th centuries Como was the world's third-largest producer of silk (after China and Japan) and silk was Italy's single most important export, comprising a third of all export goods.

The industry survived an epidemic in 1855, which wiped out the Italian silk-moth species, and it was only after the 1929 economic crash and the advent of new synthetic fabrics that it spiralled into decline.

Today Como remains Europe's most important producer of silk products, but these days raw silk is imported from China and only the finishing, dyeing and printing work is carried out locally. Out of hundreds of silk houses only three big firms remain: **Seteria Ratti** (www.ratti.it), **Mantero** (www.mantero.com) and **Canepa** (www.canepa.it). These still employ nearly one third of the Como population, while Como's Istituto Tecnico Industriale di Setificio, founded in 1869, continues to turn out world-class designers, printers and chemical-dyeing experts. The result? You can buy scarves and ties here for a fraction of usual costs.

Ristorante Sociale
ITALIAN €€

☑031 26 40 42; www.ristorantesociale.it; Via
Odari 6; meals €25-30; ⊙noon-2pm & 7-10.30pm
Wed-Mon) A work-a-day street round the
back of the *duomo* is an unlikely spot for
such a bewitching restaurant. The menu is
packed with local meat and lake produce,
and might feature perch and porcini mushrooms. Tuck in under the red-brick barrel
ceiling, or in the charming courtyard.

Ristorante da Rino
TUSCAN €€

☑031 27 30 28; www.ristoranterino.com; Via Vi-
ani 3; meals €30; ⊙12.30-2pm & 7.30-10pm Tue-
Sat, 12.30-1.45pm Sun) When the (acclaimed)
specialities of the house all involve truffles,
you tend to be onto a good thing. There's
a stellar range of *primi* and *secondi,* and
you'll find truffles with *tagliolini* (thin ribbon pasta), risotto and eggs. The pick is a
tender beef fillet steeped in truffles and red
wine.

Enoteca Castiglioni
WINE BAR

☑031 26 18 60; www.castiglionistore.com; Via
Rovelli 17; ⊙10am-8pm Mon-Fri, to 9pm Sun) If
you're lucky you'll bag one of the clutch of
tiny tables beside the ranks of wine-bottle
lined shelves. It's a smart, modern setting
in which to sample top-quality deli produce
along with first-rate vintages.

🛍 Shopping

A weekly **craft and antiques market** (Piazza San Fedele; ⊙9am-7pm Sat) fills the piazza
beside the Basilica di San Fedele.

Enoteca da Gigi
WINE

☑031 26 31 86; www.enotecagigi.com; Via Luini
8; ⊙11am-1.30pm & 2.30-8pm Mon, 9am-8pm
Tue-Fri, to 9pm Sat) Wines, vintage whiskies
and grappas, along with olive oils and balsamic vinegars, line the walls of this sociable wine shop and bar. Drop by in the
evening for a glass of *prosecco* (sparkling
wine) or a sauvignon blanc (from around
€2.50) and enjoy the free, freshly prepared
bruschetta.

Picci
GIFTS

☑031 26 13 69; Via Vittorio Emanuele II 54;
⊙3-7.30pm Mon, 9am-12.30pm & 3-7.30pm Tue-
Sat) First opened in 1919, this is the last
remaining silk shop in town dedicated to
selling Como-designed-and-made silk ties,
scarves, throws and sarongs. Products are
grouped in price category (starting at €10
for a tie), reflecting the skill and workmanship involved.

ℹ Information

Main Tourist Office (☑031 26 97 12; www.
comotourism.it; Piazza Cavour 17; ⊙9am-1pm
& 2-5pm Mon-Sat) Como's main tourist office.

Tourist Office (☑031 26 42 15; www.como
tourism.it; Via Comacini; ⊙10.30am-5.30pm
Mon-Fri, 10am-6pm Sat & Sun) Beside the
duomo.

Tourist Office (☑ 031 449 95 39; www.
comotourism.it; Como San Giovanni, Piazzale
San Gottardo; ⊙9am-5pm summer, 9.30pm-
4.30pm Wed-Mon winter) Inside the San
Giovanni train station.

Bellagio
POP 3090

Bellagio's waterfront of bobbing boats, its
maze of steep stone staircases and its gardens filled with rhododendrons are a true
joy. Inevitably these draw the summer
crowds – stay overnight for a more authentic
feel and the full magical effect.

👁 Sights

★ Villa Serbelloni
GARDENS

(☑031 95 15 55; Piazza della Chiesa 14; adult/child
€9/5; ⊙tours 11.30am & 2.30pm Tue-Sun mid-
Mar–Oct) The lavish gardens of Villa Serbello-
ni cover much of the promontory on which
Bellagio sits. The villa has been a magnet for
Europe's great and good, including Austria's
emperor Maximilian I, Ludovico il Moro and
Queen Victoria. The interior is closed to the
public, but you can explore the terraced park
and gardens by guided tour only. Numbers
are limited; tickets are sold at the Promo-
Bellagio (p275) information office near the
church.

Villa Melzi d'Eril
GARDENS

(☑339 4573838; www.giardinidivillamelzi.it; Lungo
Lario Manzoni; adult/reduced €6.50/4; ⊙9.30am-
6.30pm Apr-Oct) The grounds of neoclassical
Villa Melzi d'Eril are a highlight among Lago
di Como's (many) delightful parks. The villa
was built in 1808 for one of Napoleon's asso-
ciates and is coloured by flowering azaleas
and rhododendrons in spring. The statue-
studded gardens was the first English-
style park on the lake.

🏃 Activities

Lido
SWIMMING

(☑031 95 11 95; www.lidodibellagio.com; Via Car-
cano 1; per half/full day €8/12; ⊙10.30am-6.30pm
Tue-Sun May, Jun & Sep, daily to 7.30pm Jul &
Aug) With its sand-covered decking, diving

platforms and gazebos, Bellagio's *lido* is a prime place to laze on a sun lounger or plunge into the lake.

Bellagio Water Sports   KAYAKING
(☑ 340 3949375; www.bellagiowatersports.com; Pescallo Harbour; rental per 2/4hr €18/30, tours €35) Sit-on-top kayak rental and two-hour tours taking in some of Como's most photogenic sites are possible from this experienced outfit in Pescallo, on the east side of the Bellagio headland.

Barindelli's   BOAT TOUR
(☑ 338 2110337; www.barindellitaxiboats.it; Piazza Mazzini; tours per hr €140) For a touch of film-star glamour, take a tour in one of Barindelli's chic mahogany cigarette boats. The group offers hour-long sunset tours around the Bellagio headland and can also tailor-make outings around the lake.

Courses

Bellagio Cooking Classes   COOKING COURSE
(☑ 333 7860090; www.gustoitalianobellagio.com; Salita Plinio 5; per person €65-80) A wonderful way to really get to know Bellagio, these cooking classes have a personal touch – they take you to the village shops to buy the food and then local home cooks lead the sessions. Classes are small (a minimum of two, maximum of five).

Sleeping

Locanda Barchetta   B&B €
(☑ 031 95 10 30; www.ristorantebarchetta.com; Via Centrale 13; d €95; 🕤) A great-value, central hideaway tucked into Bellagio's maze of cobbled streets. Barchetta provides small, unfussy but spruce rooms and a fabulous breakfast.

Residence La Limonera   APARTMENT €
(☑ 031 95 21 24; www.residencelalimonera.com; Via Bellosio 2; studio €85-110, 4-person apt €90-180; ❄@🕤🐾) It's a steep but supremely picturesque hike up cobbled lanes to this elegant villa, set high up in the town in an old lemon grove. Once there you'll discover 11 spacious and thoughtfully furnished self-catering apartments for two to four people.

★ Hotel Silvio   HOTEL €€
(☑ 031 95 03 22; www.bellagiosilvio.com; Via Carcano 10; d from €135-185, meals €30-40; P❄🕤🐾) Located above the fishing hamlet of Loppia a short walk from the village, this family-run hotel is one of Bellagio's best. Here you can wake up in a contemporary Zen-like room and gaze out over the gardens of some of Lago di Como's most prestigious villas. The spend the morning at Bellagio's *lido;* it's free for hotel guests.

Il Borgo   APARTMENT €
(☑ 031 95 24 97; www.borgoresidence.it; Salita Plinio 4; 1-bed apt €100-125, 2-bed apt €115-125 ❄🕤) With their blond-wood beams and sleek lines, these stylish apartments make it easy to imagine living in Bellagio full time. Especially as you're just a minute's walk down a picturesque lane to the lake and are surrounded by countless eateries and bars.

Eating & Drinking

★ Ittiturismo da Abate   SEAFOOD €
(☑ 031 91 49 86; www.ittiturismodabate.it; Frazione Villa 4, Lezzeno; meals €25-35; ⏰ 7-10.30pm Tue-Sun, noon-2.30pm Sun; P🐾) Most dishes at Slow Food–focused Da Abate feature fish that's been caught that day in the lake (the restaurant will only open if they've caught enough), so you can sample *lavarello* in balsamic vinegar, linguine with perch and black olives, and the robust *missoltino* (fish dried in salt and bay leaves). Da Abate is 8km south of Bellagio. Bookings advised.

Terrazza Barchetta   ITALIAN €
(☑ 031 95 13 89; www.ristorantebarchetta.com; Salita Mella 13; pizza €10, meals €40-45; ⏰ noon-2.30pm & 7-10.30pm) The intimate terrace just above a crossroads of laneways in Bellagio's old town is a fine place for a meal. The restaurant has been around since 1887, which is plenty of time to perfect dishes such as deboned white lake fish in a pistachio crust or guinea fowl with whisky and mushroom sauce.

Bar Rossi   CAFE, BAR
(☑ 031 95 01 96; Piazza Mazzini 22; snacks €3-8; ⏰ 7.30am-midnight Apr-Sep, to 10.30pm Oct-Mar) All gleaming walnut wood, glinting mirrors and regiments of bottles, the art nouveau Bar Rossi is one cafe not to miss. Revel in the elegant interior or take a seat outside under the arches and watch the ferries come and go.

Shopping

Caligari Alimentaria   FOOD
(Via Bellosio 1; ⏰ 8.15am-1pm & 4-7pm Tue-Sat) The smells wafting out from this deli will surely tempt you to step inside. Among the piled-high Larian goodies are dried porcini

mushrooms (€7.50 per 50g), DOP Laghi Lombardi-Lario olive oil and *missoltini*.

ℹ️ Information

PromoBellagio (☑031 95 15 55; www.bellagio lakecomo.com; Piazza della Chiesa 14; ☺9.30am-1pm Mon, 9-11am & 1.30-3.30pm Tue-Sun Apr-Oct) A consortium of local businesses that provides useful information.

Tourist Office (☑031 95 02 04; prombell@ tin.it; Piazza Mazzini; ☺9am-12.30pm & 1-6pm Mon-Sat, 10am-2pm Sun summer, reduced hours winter) The official tourist office, next to the boat landing stage. Can provide information on water sports, mountain biking and other activities.

Cernobbio to Lenno

The sunny, western lake-front stretch from Cernobbio to Lenno is one of Lago di Como's most glamorous. The big draws here are the blockbuster villas; some are open to the public (such as the bewitching Villa Balbianello); some are most definitely closed (including George Clooney's place, Villa Oleandra, in Laglio).

👁️ Sights

⭐ **Villa Balbianello** VILLA, GARDENS
(☑0344 5 61 10; www.fondoambiente.it; Via Comoedia 5, Località Balbianello; villa & gardens adult/reduced €15/7 gardens only €8/3; ☺gardens 10am-6pm Tue & Thu-Sun mid-Mar–mid-Nov) A 1km walk along the lake shore from Lenno's main square, Villa Balbianello has cinematic pedigree: this was where scenes from *Star Wars Episode II* and the 2006 James Bond remake of *Casino Royale* were shot. The reason? It is one of the most dramatic locations anywhere on Lago di Como, providing a genuinely stunning marriage of architecture and lake views.

Built by Cardinal Angelo Durini in 1787, Villa Balbianello was used for a while by Allied commanders at the tail end of WWII. The sculpted gardens, which seem to drip off the high promontory like sauce off a melting gelato cone, are the perfect place for hopelessly romantic elopers to spend a day. Visitors are only allowed to walk the 1km path (amid vegetation so florid as to seem Southeast Asian) from the Lenno landing stage to the estate on Tuesdays and at weekends. On other days, you have to take a **taxi boat** (☑349 2290952; www. taxiboatlecco.com; return €7) from Lenno. If you want to see inside the villa, you must join a guided tour (generally conducted in Italian) by 4.15pm.

🛏️ Sleeping

Villa d'Este HISTORIC HOTEL €€€
(☑031 34 81; www.villadeste.it; Via Regina 40, Cernobbio; d €970-1140, ste €1530-1780; P❄️@☎️🏊) Much of Lago di Como draws the rich and glamorous; this hotel draws the richest and most glamorous of the lot. The 16th-century palace is beyond luxury: rich brocades drape beside marble bathrooms; balconies are bigger than some hotel rooms; fountains burble beside statues gazing onto exquisite lake views. George Clooney has been known to drop by for dinner, too.

Relais Regina Teodolinda LUXURY HOTEL €€€
(☑031 40 00 31; www.villareginateodolinda. com; Via Vecchia Regina 58, Laglio; r €200-550; ☺Mar-Oct; P❄️@☎️🏊) For a taste of the A-lister lifestyle, head for this sumptuous villa, slightly north of the village of Laglio (sometime residence of one Mr and Mrs Clooney). Elegant and deliciously tasteful rooms, many with lake views, emit refined sophistication; the welcome is discretion itself. Approach by the lake road or by boat via the private landing stage; you'll pass through delightful gardens either way.

🍴 Eating & Drinking

⭐ **Gatto Nero** MODERN ITALIAN €€€
(☑031 51 20 42; www.ristorantegattonero.com; Via Monte Santo 69, Cernobbio; meals €42-75; ☺noon-2pm & 7.30-10pm Wed-Sun, 7.30-10pm Tue) The jet set loves this eatery high above Cernobbio, and for good reason. Book a front-row table and you'll have unobstructed views of the lake stretching out far below. Inside, dark-tile floors, plenty of timber and low lighting continue the romantic theme. The food meanwhile is strictly modern Italian, well presented and packed with flavour.

Harry's Bar BAR
(Piazza Risorgimento 2; ☺10am-midnight) The real appeal of this lively bar in the centre of Cernobbio is the lake view from the verandah and the possibility that some of Como's Hollywood crowd might drop in for a drink (they often do, apparently).

GARDEL BERTRAND/HEMIS.FR/GETTY IMAGES ©

1. Lago di Garda (p281)
The largest of the Italian lakes, Garda is fringed with villages, mountains, vineyards and citrus groves.

2. Villa Carlotta (p278)
This 17th-century waterfront villa and its gardens is a must-see for any visitor to Lago di Como.

3. Varenna (p278)
Pastel-coloured houses rise steeply up the hillside in pretty Varenna on Lago di Como's eastern shore.

4. Lago Maggiore (p261)
Dating from the 13th and 14th centuries, the Santa Caterina del Sasso monastery clings to the rocky lakeshore.

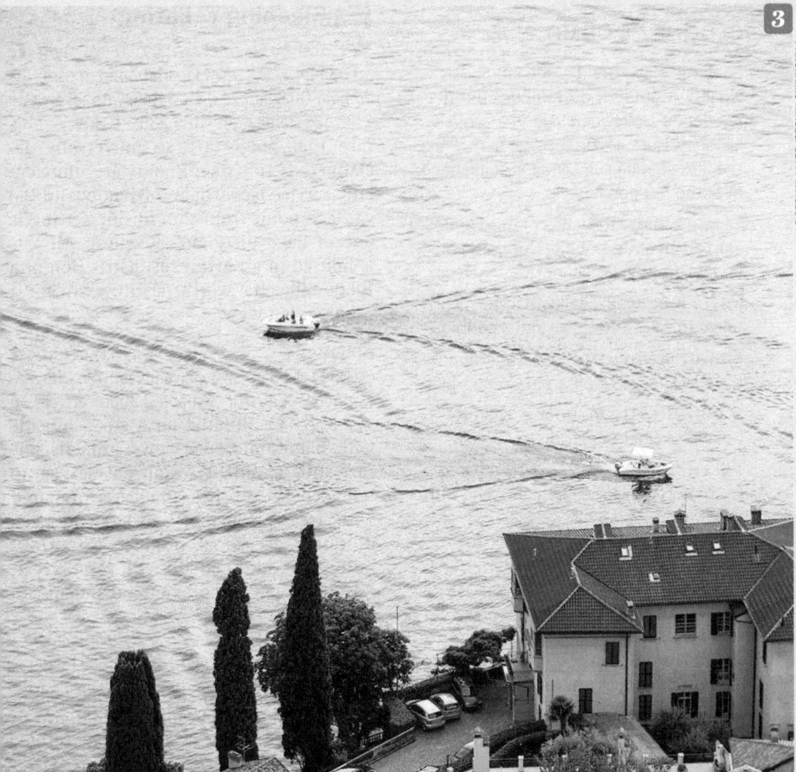

3

PANORAMIC IMAGES/GETTY IMAGES ©

CLOONEY'S COMO

Long the playground of the fabulously wealthy, Como's most famous current resident is Hollywood legend George Clooney. Here are our tips for sampling the film-star lifestyle, and for doing Lago di Como – Clooney-style.

Laglio Wander the lanes of this hamlet, 7km north of Cernobbio; George's pad is waterfront Villa Oleandra.

Harry's Bar (p275) Slug back a cocktail at this A-listers' local in Cernobbio.

Motorbike tours (p269) Get around the way George does, amid Como's hills.

Barindelli's (p274) Book a cigarette boat for a cinematic trip.

Villa d'Este (p275) and **Gatto Nero** (p275) Drop by for dinner, and dine with the stars.

Tremezzo

POP 1240

Tremezzo draws fleets of ferries thanks to its 17th-century Villa Carlotta and spectacular Lago di Como views.

 Sights

Villa Carlotta   VILLA, GARDENS
(☑034 44 04 05; www.villacarlotta.it; Via Regina 2; adult/reduced €9/7; ☉9am-7.30pm Apr–mid-Oct) Waterfront Villa Carlotta sits high on Como's must-visit list. The botanic gardens are filled with colour from orange trees interlaced with pergolas, while some of Europe's finest rhododendrons, azaleas and camellias bloom. The 17th-century villa, strung with paintings, sculptures (some by Antonio Canova) and tapestries, takes its name from the Prussian princess who was given the place in 1847 as a wedding present from her mother.

Upstairs, rooms with period furniture provide an irresistible insight into the royal lifestyle. You too can swan from the Salotto Impero (Empire Room) to Carlotta's bedroom and wonder just what it must have been like to hit the hay after a hard day at the lake. Villa Carlotta is a short walk southwest of the Cadenabbia car ferry stop.

Sleeping & Eating

★ **Hotel La Perla**   HOTEL €€
(☑0344 4 17 07; www.laperlatremezzo.com; Via Romolo Quaglino 7; d €125-145, with lake views €140-165, family ste €185-235; P❈❤❄) It's rare that hotels are so universally acclaimed as this one. Rooms are immaculate, service is warm and friendly and the vantage point from the hillside setting is one of Lago di Como's loveliest. All this is housed in an artful reconstruction of a 1960s villa. It's worth paying extra for a room with a view.

Al Veluu   RISTORANTE €€€
(☑0344 4 05 10; www.alveluu.com; Via Rogaro 11; meals €40-70; ☉noon-2.30pm & 7-10pm Wed-Mon; ☝) Situated on a steep hillside with panoramic lake views from its terrace, this excellent restaurant serves up home-cooked dishes that are prepared with great pride. They also reflect Lago di Como's seasonal produce, so expect butter-soft, milk-fed kid with rosemary at Easter or wild asparagus and polenta in spring.

ⓘ Information

Tremezzo Tourist Office (☑0344 4 04 93; Via Statale Regina; ☉9am-noon & 3.30-6.30pm Wed-Mon Apr-Oct) By the boat jetty.

Varenna

Varenna clings to Lago di Como's shadier, wilder eastern shore, vying for the title of prettiest village on the lake. Its pastel-coloured houses rise steeply up the hillside; a series of lanes and stairways slither down to the water's edge.

◉ Sights

Villa Cipressi   GARDENS
(☑0341 83 01 13; www.hotelvillacipressi.it; Via IV Novembre 22; adult/child €4/2; ☉10am-6pm Mar-Oct) In Villa Cipressi's gardens, cypress trees, palms, magnolias and camellias fill terraces that descend to the lake. Even getting here is picturesque: from the square next to the boat jetty (Piazzale Martiri della Libertà), follow the narrow lakeside promenade around the shore then bear left (inland) up the steps to central Piazza San Giorgio. The villa is signposted from there.

Villa Monastero
VILLA, GARDENS

(☑0341 29 54 50; www.villamonastero.eu; Via IV Novembre; villa & gardens adult/reduced €8/4, gardens only €5/2; ⊘gardens 9.30am-7pm, villa 9.30am-7pm Fri-Sun Mar-Jul & Sep, daily Aug) At Villa Monastero elegant balustrades and statues sit amid exotic shrubs; spiky yucca trees frame lake and mountain views. The villa itself is a former convent that was turned into a private residence in the 18th century – which explains the giddy opulence of some of the 11 rooms.

Sleeping

Albergo Milano
HOTEL €€

(☑0341 83 02 98; www.varenna.net; Via XX Settembre 35; s €125, d €150-190; ⊘Mar-Oct; ✱◉⊛) In the middle of Varenna on the pedestrian main street (well, lane), hillside Albergo Milano opens onto a terrace with magnificent lake vistas. Most of the 12 rooms have some kind of lake view and balcony – they're also tastefully appointed, with gaily painted iron bedsteads, dark-wood wardrobes and creamy-white linen.

✗ Eating

★ Vecchia Varenna
ITALIAN €€

(☑0341 83 07 93; www.vecchiavarenna.it; Contrada Scoscesa 14; meals €35-45; ⊘12.30-2pm & 7.30-9.30pm Tue-Sun) You can't get more lakeside than these 15 or so tables set on a terrace suspended over the water. Which means you can dine on lake fish, duck breast or little gnocchi cooked in goat 'scheese, cream and truffle oil while gazing over towards Como's western shore.

Ristorante La Vista
ITALIAN €€

(☑0341 83 02 98; www.varenna.net; Via XX Settembre 35; meals €39-46, 3/4 courses €45/48; ⊘7-10pm Wed-Sat & Mon mid-Mar–late Oct) The fabulous views from the terrace high in Varenna's old town are only half the story here. The fresh, inventive food is from a menu that changes with the seasons; service rarely misses a beat.

Cavallino
TRATTORIA €€

(☑0341 81 52 19; www.cavallino-varenna.it; Piazza Martiri della Libertà 5; meals €30-40; ⊘noon-2.30pm & 7-9.30pm Thu-Tue; ☺) Lake fish specialities pack the menu of this Slow Food eatery set on Varenna's quay. Among the highlights are *crostoni* topped with a fish and Calvados pâté; ravioli filled with *lavarello* in a creamy radicchio sauce; and

a risotto of perch, Parmesan, butter and sage.

Osteria Quatro Pass
ITALIAN €€

(☑0341 81 50 91; www.quattropass.com; Via XX Settembre 20; meals €25-40; ⊘noon-2pm & 7-10pm, closed Mon-Wed winter) Places that don't have a lake view in Varenna are at a distinct disadvantage, which is why this place works just that extra bit harder with the food and service. Cured meats, lake fish and other local specialities are perfectly prepared and presented.

☻ Drinking & Nightlife

Il Molo
BAR

(☑0341 83 00 70; www.barilmolo.it; Via Riva Garibaldi 14; ⊘11am-1am Apr-Oct) The tiny terrace of Bar Il Molo is Varenna's most sought-after *aperitivi* spot. It's raised above the water with cracking views north right up the lake.

❶ Information

Tourist Office (☑0341 81 40 09; www.varennaitaly.com; Via Per Esino 3; ⊘9.30am-12.30pm & 2-6.30pm Tue-Sat, 9.30am-12.30pm Sun Jul, shorter hours rest of year) Varenna's tourist office can provide information on the lake's entire eastern shore.

Lago d'Iseo

Cradled in a deep glacial valley and shut in by soaring mountains, little-known Lake Iseo (aka Sebino) is a magnificent sight. The main town, picturesque **Iseo** (population 9180), is tucked into the southwest shore. To the west, the lovely old town of **Sarnico** (population 6640) features Liberty villas, while in the north **Lovere** (population 5390) is a working harbour with a higgledy-piggledy old centre and a wealth of walking trails.

Lago d'Iseo is less than 50km from both Bergamo and Brescia. To its north stretches the **Valle Camonica**, renowned for its prehistoric rock carvings; to the south sits the rolling **Franciacorta** wine region.

⊙ Sights & Activities

Monte Isola
ISLAND

Monte Isola towers from the south end of Lago d'Iseo, making it easily the lake's most striking feature. It's Europe's largest lake island, at 4.28 sq km, and today remains dotted with fishing villages. From Carzano, in

WINE ROADS

South of Lago d'Iseo the **Franciacorta wine region** (www.franciacorta.net) harks back to the Middle Ages, when monks were granted tax privileges ('franchises', or *franchae curtes*) to work the land. The **Iseo tourist office** (p280) can help book winery visits (bookings essential on weekdays).

Pick up the route at **Paràtico** in the northwest of the region, and head south to the quaint villages around **Corte Franca**, which are home to the most prestigious winemakers. Nearby, at **Provaglio d'Iseo**, the 11th-century **Monastero San Pietro in Lamosa** (☑ 030 982 36 17; www.sanpietroinlamosa.org; Provaglio d'Iseo; ⊙ 10am-noon & 3-6pm Sat & Sun Apr-Oct, 10am-noon & 2-5pm Sat & Sun Nov-Mar) sits above a 2-sq-km protected wetland, the **Riserva Naturale Torbiere del Sebino** (☑ 030 982 31 41; www.torbiere.it; Via Europa 5, Provaglio d'Iseo; ⊙ hours vary), formed from 18th-century peat beds.

The route ends at **Rodengo-Saiano** and another impressive monastic complex, the **Abbazia di San Nicola** (☑ 030 61 01 82; www.monteolivetomaggiore.it; Rodengo Saiano; ⊙ hours vary).

---

the northeast – where many ferries land – you can climb rough stairs to the scattered rural settlements and follow a path to the top of the island (599m).

A 15km trail allows you to walk or cycle right around the island.

Accademia Tadini   GALLERY
(☑ 035 96 27 80; www.accademiatadini.it; Via Tadini 40, Lovere; adult/reduced €7/5; ⊙ 3-7pm Tue-Sat, 10am-noon & 3-7pm Sun May-Sep) A considerable art collection with works by Jacopo Bellini, Giambattista Tiepolo and Antonio Canova set in an imposing neoclassical palace on the lake front in Lovere.

Iseobike   CYCLING
(☑ 340 3962095; www.iseobike.com; Via Per Rovato 26, Iseo; bike rental per 2hr/day €4.50/17, helmet €3; ⊙ 9.30am-12.15pm & 2.30-7pm Apr-Sep) Iseobike hires out bikes and can put together tailor-made cycling tours around the lake into the Franciacorta wine region.

🛏 Sleeping & Eating

⭐ **Hotel Milano**   HOTEL €
(☑ 030 98 04 49; www.hotelmilano.info; Lungolargo Marconi 4, Iseo; s/d €47/96; ❄@🛜) One of only two hotels in the centre of Iseo, the two-star, lake-front Milano is an excellent deal. It's definitely worth paying extra (€12) for the appealing lake-view rooms (one-week minimum stay from mid-July to mid-August), so you have a front-row seat for sunset behind the mountains over the lake.

Gös   TRATTORIA €
(☑ 030 982 18 18; Viale Repubblica 6, Iseo; meals €20; ⊙ 6pm-midnight daily, 11.30am-2pm Sat & Sun) Behind Gös' nondescript front sits a gleaming microbrewery where happy locals tuck into meat-rich, homemade pasta dishes – try the beef, butter and cheese *casoncelli* (stuffed pasta). It's all best washed down with a glass or two of Gös' own zesty unfiltered brew.

⭐ **Locanda al Lago**   ITALIAN €€
(☑ 030 988 64 72; www.locandaallago.it; Località Carzano 38, Monte Isola; meals €25-35) The Soardi family has been serving up local dishes since 1948, perfecting deceptively simple treatments of lake fish. It means you can sit on their waterside terrace and feast on trout carpaccio or the day's catch combined with *trenette* (a flat pasta) and lashings of extra virgin Monte Isola olive oil. It's near the quay where ferries from Sale Marasino stop.

La Tana dell'Orso   RISTORANTE €€
(☑ 030 982 16 16; Vicolo Borni 19, Iseo; meals €30-40; ⊙ 7-9.30pm Mon, Tue & Thu, noon-2pm & 7-9.30pm Fri-Sun) For an intimate ambience and fine local fare head to this excellent eatery where a barrel ceiling sits above rough stone walls. It's hidden away down a cobbled *vicolo* (alley) off Piazza Garibaldi. Their three-course set menu (complete with an aperitif) is a snip at €30.

❶ Information

Iseo Tourist Office (☑ 030 986 85 33; www.agenzialagoiseofranciacorta.it; Lungolago Marconi 2, Iseo; ⊙ 10am-12.30pm & 3.30-6.30pm Easter-Sep, shorter hours winter)

❶ Getting There & Around

Iseo Train Station (Via XX Settembre) Links Iseo with Brescia (€6, 30 minutes, one to two hourly), where you can connect to Bergamo.

Navigazione sul Lago d'Iseo (☑ 035 97 14 83; www.navigazionelagoiseo.it) The most frequent ferries start in Iseo town and Tavernola Bergamasca, and call at Monte Isola (one way from €2.20). Ferries also link east-shore Sale Marasino and Sulzano with Carzano and Peschiera (respectively) on Monte Isola (adult/child return €3.60/3.20). Between two and eight services daily link northern Pisogne with Sarnico in the south (two to three hours, €6.70).

SAB (☑ 035 28 90 00; www.arriva.it) Regular buses run between Sarnico and Bergamo (€3.45, 50 minutes).

Lago di Garda

Poets and politicians, divas and dictators, they've all been drawn to Lago di Garda. At 370 sq km it is the largest of the Italian lakes, straddling the border between Lombardy and the Veneto, with soaring mountains to the north and softer hills to the south. Everywhere villages line a string of natural harbours, and vineyards, olive groves and citrus trees range up the slopes.

❶ Information

The website www.visitgarda.com is a good source of lake-wide information.

❶ Getting There & Around

AIR

Verona-Villafranca Airport (☑ 045 809 56 66; www.aeroportoverona.it) Verona-Villafranca is linked to numerous Italian destinations, plus European cities including Barcelona, Frankfurt, London (Gatwick) and Paris. The airport is 12km west of Verona and is linked to the city's train station by ATV Aerobus (€6, 15 minutes, every 20 to 40 minutes from 5.35am to 10.50pm).

BOAT

Navigazione Lago di Garda (☑ 800 551801; www.navigazionelaghi.it) Lago di Garda has an extensive ferry network. One-day, unlimited-travel foot passenger tickets include: lakewide (adult/reduced €34/28), lower lake (€23/19) and upper lake (€20/17). Sample single passenger fares include Sirmione to Salò (adult/reduced €10/8) and Riva del Garda to Gardone Riviera (€12/10). Car ferries link Toscolano-Maderno with Torri del Benaco and (seasonally) Limone with Malcesine.

VALLE CAMONICA

The Valle Camonica, just northeast of Lago d'Iseo, is peppered with Unesco-recognised rock carvings. The main site is the **Parco Nazionale delle Incisioni Rupestri** (☑ 0364 43 34 65; www. arterupestre.it; Via Piana 29, Nadro di Ceto; admission €3; ⊙ 9am-5.30pm Mar-Oct, to 4pm Nov-Feb; 🖫), a 30-hectare open-air museum with prehistoric engravings. Colour-coded paths loop through chestnut woods revealing an intriguing array of stick figures, huntsmen on horseback and fighting warriors, all etched onto rock slabs.

BUS

ATV (☑ 045 805 79 22; www.atv.verona.it) Runs buses up the lake's west side, including regular connections between Desenzano del Garda train station and Riva del Garda (€5.20, two hours, three to six daily), via Salò and Gardone. Also shuttles along the lake's east coast with regular services between Riva del Garda and Verona, via Garda.

SIA (☑ 840 620001; www.arriva.it) Operates regular buses from Brescia up the western side of the lake to Riva del Garda (€9, three hours, two-hourly). It also runs hourly buses linking Brescia with Desenzano, Sirmione, Peschiera and Verona along the southern shore.

Trentino Trasporti (☑ 0461 82 10 00; www. ttesercizio.it) Connects Riva del Garda with Trento (€4, one hour, every two hours).

CAR

Largo di Garda lies north of the A4 Milan–Venice autostrada, and just west of the A22 Modena–Trento route. A single-lane road circles the lake shore and is heavy with traffic in summer. Local tourist offices can advise on car hire.

TRAIN

The Milan–Venice rail route runs through some key towns on Lago di Garda's southern shore, with at least hourly trains between Milan and Desenzano del Garda (€9, 1½ hours) and Peschiera del Garda (€11, 1¾ hours).

Sirmione

POP 8010

Sitting on an impossibly narrow peninsula on the southern shore, Sirmione is often proclaimed Largo di Garda's most picturesque village. Throughout the centuries it has attracted notables from the Roman poet

Catullus to Maria Callas, and today thousands continue to follow in their footsteps.

Sights & Activities

Rocca Scaligera
CASTLE

(Castello Scaligero; ☑ 030 91 64 68; adult/reduced €4/2; ⊙ 8.30am-7pm Tue-Sat, to 1.30pm Sun) Expanding their influence northwards, the Scaligeri of Verona built this enormous square-cut castle right at the entrance to Sirmione. It guards the only footbridge into town, and looms over it with impressive crenellated turrets and towers. There's not a lot inside, but the climb up 146 steps to the top of the tower affords beautiful views over Sirmione's rooftops and the enclosed harbour.

★ Grotte di Catullo
ARCHAEOLOGICAL SITE

(☑ 030 91 61 57; www.grottedicatullo.benicultur ali.it; Piazzale Orti Manara 4; adult/reduced €6/3; ⊙ 8.30am-7.30pm Tue-Sat, 9.30am-6.30pm Sun Apr-Oct, 8.30am-2pm Tue-Sun Nov-Mar) Occupying 2 hectares at Sirmione's northern tip, this ruined 1st-century AD Roman villa is a picturesque complex of teetering stone arches and tumbledown walls, some three storeys high. It's the largest domestic Roman villa in northern Italy and wandering its terraced hillsides offers fantastic views.

★ Aquaria
SPA

(☑ 030 91 60 44; www.termedisirmione.com; Piazza Piatti; pools per hour/day €15/53; treatments from €30; ⊙ pools 10am-10pm Sun-Wed & Fri, to midnight Thu & Sat Mar-Dec, hours vary Jan & Feb) Sirmione is blessed with a series of offshore thermal springs that pump out water at a

natural 37°C. They were discovered in the late 1800s and the town's been tapping into their healing properties ever since. At the Aquaria spa you can wallow in two thermal pools – the outdoor one is set right beside the lake.

Sleeping & Eating

Many of Sirmione's hotels close from the end of October through to March. Four campgrounds lie near the town; the tourist office can advise.

★ Grifone
HOTEL €

(☑ 030 91 60 14; www.gardalakegrifonehotel.eu; Via Gaetano Bocchio 4; s €65-75, d €85-115, tr €125-140) The location is superb: set right beside the shore, Grifone's many bedrooms directly overlook the lake and Sirmione's castle. With this family-run hotel you get five-star views for two-star prices. Inside its all old-school simplicity, but very spic and span.

Hotel Marconi
HOTEL €€

(☑ 030 91 60 07; www.hotelmarconi.net; Via Vittorio Emanuele II 51; s €45-75, d €80-135; [P][❄][🌐]) Blue-and-white-striped umbrellas line the lakeside deck at this stylish, family-run hotel. The quietly elegant light-filled rooms, some with balconies and lake views, sport subtle shades and crisp fabrics, while the breakfasts and homemade pastries are a treat.

La Fiasca
TRATTORIA €€

(☑ 030 990 61 11; www.trattorialafiasca.it; Via Santa Maria Maggiore; meals €30; ⊙ noon-2.30pm & 7-10.30pm Thu-Tue) In this authentic trattoria, tucked away in a backstreet just off the main square, the atmosphere is warm and bustling, and the dishes are packed with traditional Lago di Garda produce. Prepare for some gutsy flavours: *bigoli* (thick spaghetti) with sardines, fillets of perch with asparagus, and duck with cognac and juniper.

Information

Tourist Office (☑ 030 91 61 14; iat.sirmione@ provincia.brescia.it; Viale Marconi 8; ⊙ 9am-12.30pm & 3-6pm, closed Sat afternoon & Sun winter) On the main road into Sirmione, just before the castle.

The Valtenesi

The Valtenesi stretches languidly between Desenzano and Salò, its rolling hills etched with vine trellises and flecked with olive groves. The main lake road bypasses it, which allows for gentle explorations of an array of wineries and small towns, including Manerba del Garda and San Felice del Benaco.

◎ Sights & Activities

★ **Parco Archeologico**
Rocca di Manerba   NATURE RESERVE
(✆0365 55 25 33; www.parcoroccamanerba.net; Via Rocca 20, Manerba del Garda; ⊙10am-8pm Apr-Sep, to 6pm Thu-Sun Oct-Mar) **FREE** Protected by Unesco, the gorgeous 'rock of Minerva' juts out scenically into the lake just north of Moniga del Garda. The park contains the remaining low rubble walls of a medieval castle, a restful nature reserve of evergreen woods, orchid meadows and walking trails, and some of the best beaches on the lake.

Strolling from Pieve Vecchia to Porto del Torchio via Punta del Rio reveals glorious views and idyllic spots for a dip or a paddle. The park takes its name from a long-gone Roman temple dedicated to the goddess Minerva.

Santuario della Madonna del Carmine   MONASTERY
(✆0365 6 20 32; www.santuariodelcarmine-sanfelice.it; Via Fontanamonte 1, San Felice del Benaco; ⊙7am-noon & 3-6pm) The sanctuary of the Madonna del Carmine dates from 1452. Its simple Gothic-Romanesque exterior does little to prepare you for the technicolour frescoes inside, depicting images of Christ and the Virgin and scenes resonant with the Carmelite Order.

Bicisì   BICYCLE RENTAL
(✆335 5335374; http://bicisi.wix.com; hire per day €14) 🚲 Will deliver to your accommodation in the Valtenesi (and sometimes further afield); hire includes helmet. Bicisì also runs a range of themed tours focusing on wine, food and ferries; prices start from €35 for 20km (three hours).

La Basia   HORSE RIDING
(✆0365 55 59 58; www.labasia.it; Via Predefitte 31, Puegnago del Garda; per 1/5hr €25/120) At this rambling vineyard and riding school you can have a formal riding lesson or head out for a trot among the vines, before sampling wines and wild honey on the terrace. Between March and September you can also bed down in one of the family-sized apartments (from €345 to €550 per week).

LAGO DI GARDA FOR KIDS

Lago di Garda features two top theme parks, which offer enough rides and stunt shows to thrill all day long.

Gardaland (✆045 644 97 77; www.gardaland.it; Via Dema 4, Castelnuovo del Garda; adult/reduced €39/32, family €92-150; ⊙10am-11pm mid-Jun–mid-Sep, 10am-6pm Apr–mid-Jun) Expect larger-than-life dinosaurs, pirate ships, roller coasters and a glass tunnel that leads underneath swimming sharks.

CanevaWorld (✆045 696 99 00; www.canevaworld.it; Località Fossalta 58; adult/reduced €31/25; ⊙10am-6pm mid-May–mid-Sep, to 7pm Aug) Two theme parks in one: Aquaparadise overflows with water slides; Movieland features stunt-packed action shows.

🛏 Sleeping & Eating

★ **Campeggio Fornella**   CAMPGROUND €
(✆0365 6 22 94; www.fornella.it; Via Fornella 1, San Felice del Benaco; camping 2 people, car & tent €22-34, 2-/5-person mobile home from €70/130; P❄@🏊♿) This luxury, four-star campground boasts a private beach, lagoon pool, jacuzzi, children's club, boat centre, restaurant, bar and pizzeria. Chose from a scenic pitch, mobile home or five-person safari-style tent (€80 to €120).

La Dispensa   MODERN ITALIAN €€
(✆0365 55 70 23; Piazza Municipio 10, San Felice del Benaco; meals €30-45; ⊙7-11.30pm) A fun and colourful wine bar and restaurant offering a mouthwatering modern Italian menu with a focus on sensational fish and handsome charcuterie platters. Ingredients are top-notch, market fresh and locally sourced – and sometimes come accompanied by live jazz.

Salò
POP 10,600
Wedged between the lake and precipitous mountains, Salò exudes an air of grandeur. Its long waterfront promenade is lined with ornate buildings and palm trees, while the graceful bell tower of its 15th-century cathedral overlooks picturesque lanes.

WORTH A TRIP

ROMAN VILLA

Villa Romana (☑ 030 914 35 47; Via Crocifisso 2, Desenzano del Garda; adult/reduced €2/1; ☉ 8.30am-7pm mid-Mar–mid-Oct, to 4.30pm mid-Oct–mid-Mar, closed Mon) Before the Clooneys and Versaces, wealthy Roman senators and poets had holiday homes on Italy's northern lakes. One survivor is Desenzano's now-ruined Roman villa, which once extended over a hectare of prime lakeside land. Today, wooden walkways snake through the villa above a colourful collage of black, red, olive and orange mosaics, many depicting hunting, fishing and chariot riding, garlanded by fruits and flowers.

◉ Sights

★ **Isola del Garda**　　ISLAND, GARDENS
(☑ 328 6126943; www.isoladelgarda.com; tour incl boat ride €25-30; ☉ Apr-Oct) It's not often you get to explore such a stunning private island, villa and grounds. Anchored just off Salò, this speck of land is crowned with impressive battlements, luxurious formal gardens and a sumptuous neo-Gothic Venetian villa. Boats depart from towns including Salò, San Felice del Benaco, Gardone Riviera and Sirmione, but they only leave each location one or two times a week, so plan ahead.

The island is owned by the aristocratic Cavazza family; you may well see some of them strolling around. The tour price includes a small *aperitivo*.

Republic of Salò　　AREA
In 1943 Salò was named the capital of the Social Republic of Italy as part of Mussolini and Hitler's last efforts to organise Italian Fascism in the face of advancing American forces. This episode, known as the Republic of Salò, saw more than 16 public and private buildings in the town commandeered and turned into Mussolini's ministries and offices. Strolling between the sites is a surreal tour of the dictator's doomed mini-state. Look out for the multilingual plaques scattered around town.

🛏 Sleeping

★ **Aromi**　　BOUTIQUE HOTEL €€
(☑ 0365 2 20 49; www.aromipiccolohotel.com; Via Calsone 34; s €75-100, d €95-120; @ 🛜)

With its ultracool lines, oatmeal-and-cream colour scheme and supersleek bathrooms, the town-centre Aromi is irresistible. It is set beside a main road, but the swish design and breakfasts piled high with pastries and fruit more than compensate. The same outfit runs three smart two-to-four person apartments (€80 to €155) in the pedestrianised old town nearby.

Hotel Laurin　　HISTORIC HOTEL €€
(☑ 0365 2 20 22; www.laurinhotelsalo.com; Viale Landi 9; d €155-300; P ✳ @ 🛜 ⊠) An art nouveau gem with some real history behind it, the Hotel Laurin (formerly the Villa Simonini) was the Foreign Ministry during Mussolini's short-lived Republic. Downstairs salons retain wonderful details: frescoes by Bertolotti, intricate parquet floors, and wood inlay and wrought-iron volutes.

Gambero　　HOTEL €€
(☑ 0365 29 09 41; www.gamberohotel.it; Piazza Carmine 1; s €70, d €120-160; @ 🛜) Ask for a balcony room for partial lake and *duomo* views from this comfortable contemporary hotel. Breakfast is served in the streetside *pasticceria,* where the coffee and pastries are superb.

Gardone Riviera
POP 270

Gardone's glory days were in the late 19th and early 20th centuries, and today the resort's opulent villas and ornate architecture make it one of Lago di Garda's most elegant holiday spots.

About 12km north of Gardone lies Gargnano, a tiny harbour that fills with million-dollar yachts come September when sailing fans gather for the Centomiglia, the lake's most prestigious sailing regatta.

◉ Sights

★ **Il Vittoriale degli Italiani**　　MUSEUM
(☑ 0365 29 65 11; www.vittoriale.it; Piazza Vittoriale; gardens & museums adult/reduced €16/12; ☉ grounds 8.30am-8pm Apr-Sep, to 5pm Oct-Mar, museums 8.30am-6.30pm Tue-Sun Apr-Sep, 9am-1pm & 2-5pm Tue-Sun Oct-Mar) Poet, soldier, hypochondriac and proto-Fascist, Gabriele d'Annunzio (1863–1938) defies easy definition, and so does his estate. Bombastic, extravagant and unsettling, it's home to every architectural and decorative excess imaginable and is full of quirks that help shed light on the man. Visit and you'll take in a dimly lit, highly idiosyncratic villa, a war museum

and tiered gardens complete with full-sized battleship.

By 1914 d'Annunzio was an established poet, but his fame was cemented by a series of daring military adventures in WWI. His most dramatic exploit was an unsanctioned occupation of Fiume, now Rijeka, on the Adriatic. Outraged that it was to be handed over to Yugoslavia, not Italy, at the end of the war, he gathered a mini-army, invaded the port and proclaimed himself the ruler. Despite eventually surrendering he was hailed a national hero. In the 1920s d'Annunzio became a strong supporter of Fascism and Mussolini, while his affairs with wealthy women were legendary.

In his main house, the **Prioria**, stained-glass windows cast an eerie light on gloomy rooms with black velvet drapes (he had an eye condition that made exposure to sunlight painful). The rooms are crammed with classical figurines, leather-bound books, leopard skins, gilded ornaments, lacquer boxes and chinoiserie. Highlights include the bronze tortoise that sits on the guests' dining table (in admonition of gluttony; it was cast from a pet that died of overindulgence); the bright blue bathroom suite with more than 2000 pieces of bric-a-brac; his spare bedroom where he would retire to lie on a coffin-shaped bed and contemplate death; and his study with its low lintel – designed so visitors would have to bow as they entered. Guided visits, in Italian only, tour the house every 15 minutes and last half an hour.

If you aren't already overwhelmed by d'Annunzio's excesses, the estate's **Museo della Guerra** is housed nearby in the art nouveau Casa Schifamondo (Escape from the World). It is full of mementoes, banners and medals of d'Annunzio's wartime exploits, while the gardens offer the chance to wander the deck of the full-sized battleship *Puglia,* which d'Annunzio used in his Fiume exploits.

★ **Giardino Botanico Fondazione André Heller**   GARDENS, SCULPTURE
(☎336 41 08 77; www.hellergarden.com; Via Roma 2; adult/child €10/5; ☉9am-7pm Mar-Oct) Gardone's heyday was due in large part to its mild climate, something which benefits the thousands of exotic blooms that fill artist André Heller's sculpture garden. Laid out in 1912 by Arturo Hrus-

ka, the garden is divided into pocket-sized climate zones, with tiny paths winding from central American plains to African savannah, via swathes of tulips and bamboo.

The playful touches hidden among the greenery include 30 pieces of contemporary sculpture – look out for the jagged red figure by Keith Haring near the entrance, Rudolf Hirt's Gaudi-esque *Ioanes, God of Water,* and Roy Lichtenstein's polka-dot take on the pyramids.

🛏 Sleeping & Eating

★ **Locanda Agli Angeli**   B&B €€
(☎0365 2 09 91; www.agliangeli.biz; Via Dosso 7; s €70, d €135-170; P❄☎) It's a perfect hillside Lago di Garda bolt-hole: a beautifully restored, rustic-chic *locanda* (inn) with a pint-sized pool and a terrace dotted with armchairs. Ask for room 29 for a balcony with grandstand lake and hill views, but even the smaller bedrooms are full of charm.

The restaurant (hours vary) is renowned for classic Lago di Garda dishes, or opt for supper in the inn's new nearby pizzeria, which comes with wide water views.

ⓘ Information

Tourist Office (☎0365 374 87 36; Corso della Repubblica 8; ☉9am-12.30pm & 2.15-6pm Mon-Sat) The tourist office stocks information on activities.

Design

Better living by design: what could be more Italian? From the cup that holds your morning espresso to your bedside light, there's a designer responsible and almost everyone in Milan will know their name. Design here is a way of life.

Modern Italian Design

The roots of Italian design stretch back to early-20th-century Milan, with the development of the Fiera trade fair, the rebuild of the Rinascente department store (Giorgio Armani started there as window dresser), the founding of architectural and design magazines *Domus* and *Casabella* and the opening of the Triennale in 1947. Where elaborate French rococo and ornate Austrian art nouveau had captured the imagination of a genteel prewar Europe, the dynamic deco style of Italian futurism was a perfect partner for the industrial revolution and Fascist philosophies.

Fascist propaganda co-opted the radical, neoclassical streamlining that futurism inspired and Italy implemented these ideas into architecture and design. Modern factories had to aid the war effort and Fascist tendencies towards centralised control boosted Italian manufacturing. Through an inherent eye for purity of line, modern Italian design found beauty in balance and symmetry. This refreshing lack of detail appealed to a fiercely democratising war-torn Europe where minimalism and utility came to represent the very essence of modernity.

1. Alessi design store
2. 1935 Alfa Romeo Spider
3. Vespas

'From the Spoon to the City'

Milan's philosopher-architects and designers – Giò Ponti, Vico Magistretti, Gae Aulenti, Achille Castiglioni, Ettore Sottsass and Piero Fornasetti – saw their postwar mission as not only rebuilding the bombed city but redesigning the urban environment. A defining statement came from Milanese architect Ernesto Rogers, who said he wished to design 'everything, from the spoon to the city'.

Far from being mere intellectual theorists, this cadre of architect-designers benefited from a unique proximity to artisanal businesses located in Brianza province, north of Milan. This industrial district grew from rural society and thus retained many specialist peasant craft skills. While these production houses remained true to the craft aspect of their work, they were able to use modern sales and production techniques via the central marketplace of the Triennale. This direct connection between craftsman, producer and marketplace allowed for a happy symbiosis between creativity and commercialism, ultimately fine-tuning Italian design to achieve the modernist ideal of creating beautiful, *useful* objects.

DESIGN CLASSICS

Alessi Crafted kitchen utensils designed by big-name architect-designers.

Vespa 1946 Piaggio mini-motor scooter that transformed the lives of urbanites.

Cassina 'Masters' collection furniture by Le Corbusier, Frank Lloyd Wright and Giò Ponti.

Alfa Romeo This legendary roadster, launched in 1910, is the most famous product from Milanese petrolheads.

Riva del Garda & Around

POP 16,700

Even though situated on a lake that is blessed with dramatic scenery, Riva del Garda still comes out on top. Encircled by towering rock faces and a looping strip of beach, its appealing centre is a medley of elegant architecture, maze-like streets and wide squares.

Riva is in the Alpine region of Trentino-Alto Adige but for centuries its strategic position saw it fought over by the Republic of Venice, Milan's Viscontis and Verona's Della Scala families, with the town remaining part of Austria until 1919.

○ Sights

★ Cascata del Varone   WATERFALL

(☑ 0464 52 14 21; www.cascata-varone.com; Via Cascata 12; admission €5.50; ☺ 9am-7pm May-Aug, to 6pm Apr & Sep, to 5pm Mar & Oct) Prepare to get wet – this 100m waterfall thunders down sheer limestone cliffs through an immense, dripping gorge. Spray-soaked walkways snake 50m into the mountain beside the crashing torrent, and strolling along them is like walking in a perpetual thunderstorm. You'll find it signposted 3km northwest of Riva's centre.

Museo Alto Garda   MUSEUM

(La Rocca; ☑ 0464 57 38 69; www.museoaltogarda.it; Piazza Cesare Battisti 3; adult/reduced €3/1.50; ☺ 10am-6pm Tue-Sun mid-Mar–May & Oct, daily Jun-Sep) Housed in Riva's compact medieval castle, the civic museum features local archaeology, frescoes from Roman Riva, documents and paintings. In light of Riva's much fought over past, perhaps the most revealing exhibits are the antique maps dating from 1579 and 1667, and a 1774 *Atlas Tyrolensis*, which evocatively convey the area's shifting boundaries.

🛌 Sleeping

★ Hotel Garni Villa Maria   HOTEL €

(☑ 0464 55 22 88; www.garnimaria.com; Viale dei Tigli; s €40-75, d €70-115, apt €100-340; P ✱ 🛜 🐾) Beautifully designed, ubermodern rooms make this small family-run hotel a superb deal. Pristine bedrooms have a Scandinavian vibe, with all-white linens, sleek modern bathrooms and accents of orange and lime green. There's a tiny roof garden, and bedrooms with balconies offer soaring mountain views.

Residence Filanda   APARTMENT €€

(☑ 0464 55 47 34; www.residencefilanda.com; Via Sant'Alessandro 51; d €110-140, q €165-210; P ✱ @ 🛜 🐾 🐾) Located 2km outside Riva this burnt-orange residence situated amid olive groves and vineyards is a haven for families. Rooms and apartments overlook lush grounds that include a heated pool, tennis and volleyball courts and 2 acres of child-friendly gardens.

Lido Palace   HISTORIC HOTEL €€€

(☑ 0464 02 18 99; www.lido-palace.it; Viale Carducci 10; d €290-420, ste €450-755; P ✱ @ 🛜 ≋) If you're going to splash the cash, this is the place to do it. Riva's captivating Lido Palace dates back to 1899. Sensitive renovations mean modern bedrooms with muted colour schemes now sit in the grand Liberty-style villa, offering peerless views over lawns and lake.

✖ Eating

★ Cristallo Caffè   GELATERIA €

(☑ 0464 55 38 44; www.cristallogelateria.com; Piazza Catena 11; cones €2.50; ☺ 7am-1am) More than 60 flavours of artisanal gelato are served up in this lakeside cafe, crafted by the Panciera family, which has been making gelato since 1892. It's also a top spot to sip a *spritz* (cocktail made with Prosecco) while enjoying water and lake views.

★ Restel de Fer   ITALIAN €€

(☑ 0464 55 34 81; www.resteldefer.com; Via Restel de Fer 10; meals €40-60; ☺ noon-2.30pm & 7-11pm daily Jul & Aug, Thu-Tue Sep, Oct & Dec-Jun; P 🛜) Going to the restaurant at this family-run *locanda* feels like dropping by a friend's rustic-chic house: expect worn leather armchairs, copper cooking pots and glinting blue glass. The menu focuses on seasonal, local delicacies such as rabbit wrapped in smoked mountain ham, char with crayfish, and veal with Monte Baldo truffles.

Upstairs, swish farmhouse-style accommodation (single €70, double €90 to €120) is chock-full of old oak dressers and hand-woven rugs. It's 1km east of the centre of Riva.

★ Osteria Le Servite   OSTERIA €€

(☑ 0464 55 74 11; www.leservite.com; Via Passirone 68, Arco; meals €30-45; ☺ 7-10.30pm Tue-Sun Apr-Sep, 7-10.30pm Wed-Sat Oct-Mar; P 🐾) Tucked away in Arco's wine-growing region, this elegant little *osteria* serves dishes that are so seasonal the menu changes weekly. You

ACTIVITIES AROUND RIVA DEL GARDA

The area's triangle of towns – Riva del Garda, Arco and Torbole – offer world-class outdoor activities.

Canyoning

With limestone slopes worn smooth by glacial meltwaters, Riva's mountains offer endless abseils, jumps and slides. **Canyon Adventures** (☑ 334 8698666; www.canyonadv.com; from €68; ☺May-Oct) arranges trips to the Palvico and Rio Nero gorges in the Val di Ledro and the Vione canyon in Tignale.

Climbing

Arco is one of Europe's most popular climbing destinations. Offering hundreds of routes of all grades, climbs are divided between short, bolted, single-pitch sports routes and long Dolomite-style climbs; some extend up to 1400m. **Guide Alpine Arco** (www.guidealpinearco.com) can advise about climbing courses and routes.

Cycling

Carpentari (☑ 046 450 55 00; www.carpentari.com; Via Matteotti 95, Torbole; per day from €45; ☺8.30am-7.30pm Apr-Sep) rents out quality mountain bikes.

Watersports

Surfsegnana (☑ 046 450 59 63; www.surfsegnana.it; Foci del Sarca, Torbole) operates from Lido di Torbole and Porfina Beach in Riva, running lessons in windsurfing (€60), kitesurfing (€120) and sailing (€70). It also hires out windsurfing kits (per half day €40), sail boats (per two hours €50 to €65) and kayaks (per two hours €16).

might be eating mimosa gnocchi, tender *salmerino* (Arctic char) or organic ravioli with *stracchino* cheese.

Each dish comes with a suggested wine. In summer you can sit on the patio and sip small-production DOC Trentino vintages.

 Information

Tourist Office (☑ 0464 55 44 44; www.gardatrentino.it; Largo Medaglie d'Oro; ☺9am-7pm May-Sep, to 6pm Oct-Apr) Can advise on everything from climbing and paragliding to wine tasting and markets.

Malcesine

POP 3740

With the lake lapping right up to the tables of its harbourside restaurants and the vast ridge of Monte Baldo looming behind, Malcesine is a Largo di Garda hot spot. Its maze-like network of cobbled streets is crowned by a chalky-white, late-6th-century fortress.

🏃 Activities

Funivia Malcesine–Monte Baldo CABLE CAR (☑ 045 740 02 06; www.funiviedelbaldo.it; Via Navene Vecchia 12; adult/reduced return €20/15; ☺8am-7pm Apr-Sep, to 5pm Oct-Mar) Jump aboard this cable car and glide 1760m above sea level for spectacular views – rotating cabins reveal the entire lake and surrounding mountains. For the first 400m the slopes are covered in oleanders, and olive and citrus trees – after that, oak and chestnut take over. Mountain-bike trails wind down from the summit.

Xtreme Malcesine BICYCLE RENTAL (☑ 045 740 01 05; www.xtrememalcesine.com; Via Navene Vecchia 10; road/mountain bike per day €15/25; ☺8am-6pm) Rents bikes from its shop at the base of the Monte Baldo cable car.

Consorzio Olivicoltori di Malcesine TASTING (☑ 045 740 12 86; www.oliomalcesine.it; Via Navene 21; ☺9am-12.30pm & 3.30-6.30pm Mon-Sat, 9am-1pm Sun, shorter hours winter) **FREE** Olives harvested around Malcesine are milled into first-rate extra-virgin olive oil by this local consortium. You can sample the product here. Known as 'El nos Oio' (Our Oil), it's a gold-green liquid that's low in acidity and has a light, fruity, slightly sweet taste. Prices of the cold-pressed extra virgin DOP oil range from €13 for 0.5L to €62 for 5L.

✕ Eating

Speck Stube
BARBECUE €

(☎045 740 11 77; www.speckstube.com; Via Navene Vecchia 139; meals €10-25; ☺noon-11pm Mar-Oct; 🅿🚼) Wood-roast chickens, sausages and pork on the bone are the specialities at this family-friendly place 2.5km north of Malcesine. Chow down on hearty portions and mugs of beer at trestle tables beneath the olive trees, while the kids let off steam in the play park.

★ Vecchia Malcesine
GASTRONOMIC €€€

(☎045 740 04 69; www.vecchiamalcesine.com; Via Pisort 6; meals €55-100; ☺noon-2.30pm & 7-10.30pm Thu-Tue) The lake views from the terrace at hillside Vecchia Malcesine do their best to upstage the food. But the Michelin-starred menu wins; its exquisitely presented, creative dishes might include trout with horseradish, smoked caviar and white chocolate, or risotto with lake fish, apple and raspberry.

ℹ Information

Tourist Office (☎045 740 00 44; www.malcesinepiu.it; Via Capitanato 8; ☺9.30am-12.30pm & 3-6pm Mon-Sat, 9.30am-12.30pm Sun summer) Malcesine's seasonal tourist office, near the ferry quay, can advise on water sports, walking and cycling.

Punta San Vigilio

Picturesque Punta San Viglio is a popular destination for beach-goers.

◉ Sights

★ Punta San Vigilio
BEACH

(🚼) The leafy headland of Punta San Vigilio curls out into the lake 3km north of Garda. An avenue of cypress trees leads from the car park towards a gorgeous crescent of bay backed by olive groves. There the **Parco Baia delle Sirene** (☎045 725 58 84; www.parcobaiadellesirene.it; Punta San Viglio; adult/child €12/6, reduced admission after 4.30pm; ☺10am-7pm Apr & May, 9.30am-8pm Jun-Aug) offers sun loungers beneath the trees; there's also a children's play area.

Entry is free at sunset. Alternatively, from the parking place walk north a short distance and head off down the paths that lead to a couple of smaller, quieter public coves.

🛏 Sleeping & Eating

★ Locanda San Vigilio
BOUTIQUE HOTEL €€€

(☎045 725 66 88; www.punta-sanvigilio.it; Punta San Viglio; d €270-375, ste €440-900; 🅿❄@🏊) This enchanting 16th-century *locanda* feels just like a luxurious English manor house: discreet, understated and effortlessly elegant. Dark wood, stone floors and plush furnishings ensure an old-world-meets-new luxury feel. The excellent restaurant (lunch/dinner €40/55) sits right beside the water, offering memorable food and views.

🍷 Drinking & Nightlife

★ Taverna San Vigilio
BAR

(☎045 725 51 90; Punta San Viglio; ☺10am-5.30pm) With an olive-tree-shaded garden and tables strung out along a tiny crab-claw harbour, the Taverna San Vigilio is one of the most atmospheric bars on the lake. Nibbles include lobster, veal and *prosciutto crudo* (cured ham).

Bardolino

More than 70 vineyards and wine cellars (many within DOC and even stricter DOCG requirements) grace the gentle hills rolling east from low-key Bardolino. These produce an impressive array of pink Chiaretto, ruby Classico, dry Superiore and young Novello.

◉ Sights & Activities

Museo del Vino
MUSEUM

(☎045 622 83 31; www.museodelvino.it; Via Costabella 9; ☺9am-1pm & 2.30-7pm mid-Mar–Sep, hours vary Oct–mid-Mar) **FREE** The Museo del Vino is within the Zeni winery and rarely has a museum smelled so good. Rich aromas surround displays of wicker grape baskets, cooper's tools, drying racks and immense wooden presses. Tastings of Zeni's red, white and rosé wines are free, or pay to sample pricier vintages, including barrel-aged Amarone.

Zeni Winery
WINERY

(☎045 721 00 22; www.zeni.it; Via Costabella 9; tours €5) Zeni has been crafting quality wines from Bardolino's morainic hills since 1870. Get an insight into that process with an hour-long winery tour that ends with a mini-tasting in the *cantina* (cellar). Reservations aren't necessary; tours run every Wednesday at 11am, from May to September.

Or book a place on the two-hour Dolceamaro Raisining tour (per two people €100), and taste four dry Valpolicella wines, along with tangy local cheese, mustard and Monte Baldo honey, rounded off with a sweet Recioto dessert wine and some chocolaty *tortellini di Valeggio*.

Sleeping & Eating

Corte San Luca APARTMENT €

(☑ 345 8212906; www.cortesanluca.com; Piazza Porta San Giovanni 15; d €90, 4-person apt per night/week from €200/2100; P✲⊛⊠) Someone with a flair for design has created 11 smart central apartments – expect suspended furniture, moulded chairs and glass-topped tables. With their fully kitted-out kitchens, laundries and 32in TVs the apartments are a particularly smart home away from home. There's a minimum week stay in July and August.

★ **Il Giardino delle Esperidi** OSTERIA €€

(☑ 045 621 04 77; Via Goffredo Mameli 1; meals €35-50; ⊘ 7-10pm Mon, Wed-Fri, noon-2.30pm & 7-10pm Sat & Sun) Bardolino's gourmets head for this intimate little *osteria* where sourcing local delicacies is a labour of love for its sommelier-owner. The intensely flavoured baked truffles with *parmigiano reggiano* (Parmesan) are legendary, and the highly seasonal menu may feature rarities such as goose salami or guinea fowl salad.

🍷 Drinking & Nightlife

La Bottega del Vino WINE BAR

(☑ 348 604 18 00; Piazza Matteotti 46; snacks €5, glass of wine from €2.50; ⊘ 10.30am-2pm & 5-10pm Sun-Thu, to midnight Fri & Sat) To experience some authentic Bardolino atmosphere head to this no-nonsense bar in the centre of town. Inside, a stream of lively banter passes between locals and staff beside walls lined with bottles four deep.

❶ Information

Tourist Office (☑ 045 721 00 78; www.tourism.verona.it; Piazzale Aldo Moro 5; ⊘ 9am-noon & 3-6pm Mon-Sat, 10am-2pm Sun) Operates a hotel booking service and can advise on the surrounding wine region.

THE PO PLAIN

Stretching from the foot of the pre-Alps to low-lying, lake-fringed plains, this is a region that's overlooked by many but is itching to spring a surprise. In the north, edged by mountains and encircled by defensive walls, you'll find Bergamo, an ancient hill town rich in architecture and art. Nearby, Brescia showcases gutsy cuisine and impressive fragments of its Roman past. In unique Cremona, home to Antonio Stradivari, discover a vibrant musical heritage and old-town vibe. And in the far east comes captivating Mantua, surrounded by lakes, enriched by art-packed palaces and ready to delight with the architectural harmony of its interlocking squares.

Bergamo

POP 118,700

Bergamo is one of northern Italy's most attractive, interesting cities, with a walled Città Alta (Upper Town) that incorporates an array of medieval, Renaissance and baroque architecture. Despite sitting at the foot of the pre-Alps, the city was ruled by Venice for 350 years (1428–1797), until Napoleon arrived.

A funicular runs to the Città Alta from the more modern Città Bassa (Lower Town). A different funicular runs from the Città Alta to the quaint quarter of San Vigilio, which offers some stunning views.

◉ Sights

Cafe-clad Piazza Vecchia (Old Square) lies at the heart of the Città Alta's tangle of medieval streets. Lined by elegant architecture it was dubbed by Le Corbusier 'the most beautiful square in Europe'.

★ **Torre del Campanone** TOWER

(☑ 035 24 71 16; Piazza Vecchia; adult/child €3/free; ⊘ 9.30am-6pm Tue-Fri, to 8pm Sat & Sun Apr-Oct, reduced hours winter) Bergamo's colossal, square-based Torre del Campanone soars 52m above the city. It still tolls a bell at 10pm, the legacy of the old curfew. Taking the lift to the top of the tower reveals sweeping views down onto the town, up to the pre-Alps and across to the Lombard plains.

★ **Palazzo del Podestà** MUSEUM

(Museo Storico dell'Età Veneta; ☑ 035 24 71 16; www.palazzodelpodesta.it; Piazza Vecchia; adult/reduced €7/5; ⊘ 9.30am-1pm & 2.30-6pm Tue-Sun) In this superbly imaginative seven-room museum a rich range of audiovisual and interactive displays tell the story of Bergamo's Venetian age. Expect animated maps, high-tech re-creations of printing typefaces and a mock-up shop with drawers full of snakes.

Bergamo

0 0.2 miles

0 400 m

Via Nazario Sauro

Nuovo Ostello di Bergamo (2.3km)

Piazza Carrara

Accademia Carrara 1

10

Via San Giovanni

Via Pignolo

7

Via della Noca

CITTÀ ALTA (UPPER TOWN)

Via San Tomaso

Via Pignolo

Via Giuseppe Verdi

6

Via della Fara

Piazzale della Fara

Via della Porta Dipinta

8

Viale delle Mura

Via Monte Ortigara

Chiesa dei Santi Bartolomeo e Stefano (400m)

Via della Fara

Via Solata

Via della Rocca

Piazza Mercato del Fieno

Piazza Mercato delle Scarpe

Città Alta Funicular Station

Viale Vittorio Emanuele II

Via Antonio Locatelli

Via San Lorenzo

17

Via Gombito

Via Donizetti

Via di San Giacomo

Città Bassa Funicular Station

CITTÀ BASSA (LOWER TOWN)

Via della Boccola

Via Tassis

12

15

13

Piazza Vecchia 14

11

9

Piazza Giuliani

Via del Lupo

18

Via Tre Armi

ATB Infopoint (800m); (1km); (1km); (5km)

Città Bassa Tourist Office (1km); Orio al Serio (5km)

Palazzo del Podestà 2

Torre del Campanone 3

4

5

Piazza del Duomo

Via Arena

Via Vittorio Rosate

Via Tre Armi

Via San Colleoni

16

Via San Salvatore

Viale delle Mura

Citadel

Piazza della Citadella

Piazza Mascheroni

Funicular to San Vigilio

Via Santa Lucia

Bergamo

It's all set in the medieval, fresco-dotted Palazzo del Podestà, the traditional home to Venice's representative in the town.

Palazzo della Ragione HISTORIC BUILDING
(Piazza Vecchia) The imposing arches and columns of the Palazzo della Ragione sit at the southern end of Piazza Vecchia. Built in the 12th century, it bears the lion of St Mark – a reminder of Venice's long reign here. The animal is actually an early 20th-century replica of the 15th-century original, which was torn down when Napoleon took over in 1797. Note the sun clock in the pavement beneath the arches and the curious Romanesque and Gothic animals and busts decorating the pillars.

Duomo CATHEDRAL
(☑ 035 21 02 23; Piazza del Duomo; ⊕ 7.30-11.45am & 3-6.30pm) Roman remains were discovered during renovations of Bergamo's baroque cathedral. A rather squat building, it has a brilliant white facade. Among the relics in a side chapel is the one-time coffin of the beatified Pope John XXII.

Basilica di Santa Maria Maggiore BASILICA
(Piazza del Duomo; ⊕ 9am-12.30pm & 2.30-6pm Apr-Oct, shorter hours Nov-Mar) Begun in 1137, the Basilica di Santa Maria Maggiore is quite

a mishmash of styles. To its whirl of Romanesque apses (on which some external frescoes remain visible), Gothic additions were added. Influences seem to come from afar, with dual-colour banding (black and white, and rose and white) typical of Tuscany and an interesting *trompe l'œil* pattern on part of the facade.

Cappella Colleoni CHAPEL
(Piazza del Duomo; ⊕ 9am-12.30pm & 2-6.30pm Mar-Oct, 9am-12.30pm & 2-4.30pm Tue-Sun Nov-Feb) The Cappella Colleoni was built between 1472 and 1476 as a magnificent mausoleum-cum-chapel for the Bergamese mercenary commander Bartolomeo Colleoni (c 1400–75), who led Venice's armies in campaigns across northern Italy. He lies buried inside in a magnificent tomb.

★ **Accademia Carrara** GALLERY
(☑ 035 23 43 96; www.lacarrara.it; Piazza Carrara 82; adult/reduced €10/8; ⊕ 9am-7pm) Just east of the old city walls is one of Italy's great art repositories. Founded in 1780, it contains an exceptional range of Italian masters. Raphael's *San Sebastiano* is a highlight, and other artists represented include Botticelli, Canaletto, Mantegna and Titian.

The collection was started by local scholar Count Giacomo Carrara (1714–96) and has now swelled to 1800 paintings dating from the 15th to 19th centuries. Reopened after a seven-year renovation, the gallery's displays revolve around 28 rooms. Highlights include the sections on Giovanni Bellini, Florence and the major local artists Lorenzo Lotto and Giovanni Battista Moroni.

Galleria d'Arte Moderna e Contemporanea GALLERY
(GAMeC; ☑ 035 27 02 72; www.gamec.it; Via San Tomaso 53; ⊕ 10am-1pm & 3-7pm Tue-Sun) FREE
The modern works by Italian artists displayed here include pieces by Giacomo Balla, Giorgio Morandi, Giorgio de Chirico and Filippo de Pisis. A contribution from Vassily Kandisky lends an international touch.

🛏 Sleeping

Albergo Il Sole HOTEL €
(☑ 035 21 82 38; www.ilsolebergamo.com; Via Colleoni 1; s/d/tr €65/85/110; ☎) Bright rugs and throws bring bursts of the modern to this traditional, family-run *albergo* (hotel) in the heart of the Città Alta; exposed stone and picture windows add to the quaint feel. The

IN SEARCH OF LORENZO LOTTO

One of the great painters of the late Venetian Renaissance, Lorenzo Lotto worked for 12 years in and around Bergamo from 1513. Many of his stunning masterpieces – depictions of *sacra conversazione* (sacred conversations) between Madonna and saints – remain in situ in Bergamo's churches.

Chiesa dei Santi Bartolomeo e Stefano (Largo Belotti 1; ⊙7.30am-noon & 3.30-6.30pm Mon-Sat, 4-6.30pm Sun) Inside is Lorenzo Lotto's largest altarpiece, the *Pala Martinengo* (c 1513–16), where his Madonna sits in a Bramante-esque temple framed by saints and overlooked by a Mantegna-inspired oculus.

Chiesa del Santo Spirito (Church of the Holy Spirit; Via Tasso 100; ⊙8-11am & 3-6pm Thu-Tue) Look for the Venetian-inspired countryside and colour palette that defines Lorenzo Lotto's *Pala di Santo Spirito* (1521), where the Madonna sits beneath a garland of energetic winged *putti* (cherubs).

Chiesa di San Bernardino (Via Pignolo 59; ⊙9.30-10.30am Sun) Worth a visit for Lorenzo Lotto's stylistically evolved altarpiece, the *Pala di San Bernardino* (1521), which depicts the Madonna beneath a dynamic, foreshortened canopy deep in intense conversation with her saintly companions.

Chiesa di San Michele al Pozzo Bianco (St Michael at the Well; Via Porta Dipinta; ⊙9am-5pm Mon-Fri) This church is home to an entire Lorenzo Lotto fresco-cycle devoted to the *Storie della Vergine* (Stories of the Virgin Mother; 1525).

best room is 107, where the balcony offers mountain glimpses and roof-top views.

Nuovo Ostello di Bergamo HOSTEL € (☑035 36 17 24; www.ostellodibergamo.it; Via Ferraris 1, Monterosso; dm/s/d €20/35/50; P@🛇) Bergamo's state-of-the-art HI hostel is about 4km north of the train station. Its 27 rooms offer views over Bergamo's old town centre. Take bus 6 from Largo Porta Nuova near the train station (get off at Leonardo da Vinci stop) or bus 3 for Ostello from the Città Alta.

★**Hotel Piazza Vecchia** HOTEL €€ (☑035 25 31 79; www.hotelpiazzavecchia.it; Via Colleoni 3; d €100-300; ❄@🛇) The perfect Città Alta bolt-hole, this 13th-century town house oozes atmosphere, from the honey-coloured beams and exposed stone to the tasteful art on the walls. Rooms have parquet floors and bathrooms that gleam with chrome; the deluxe ones have a lounge and a balcony with mountain views.

✗ Eating

The *bergamaschi* (people from Bergamo) like their polenta, and have even named a classic sweet after it: *polenta e osei* are pudding-shaped cakes filled with jam and cream, topped with icing and chocolate birds. Bergamo's other famous dish is *casonsèi*, aka *casoncelli* (a kind of ravioli stuffed with spicy sausage meat).

★**Il Fornaio** PIZZA, BAKERY € (Via Bartolomeo Colleoni 1; pizza slices €1.10-2; ⊙8am-8pm Mon-Sat, 7.30am-8pm Sun) Join the crowds that mill around this local favourite for coffee that packs a punch and pizza slices that drip with ingredients: spinach laced with creamy mozzarella or gorgonzola studded with walnuts. Take it away or compete for a table upstairs.

Polentone ITALIAN € (☑348 804 60 21; Piazza Mercato delle Scarpe 1; meals €12; ⊙11.30am-3.30pm & 6-10pm Mon-Thu, 11.30am-1am Sat, to 10pm Sun) Styling itself as Italy's first polenta takeaway, Polentone serves up steaming bowls of polenta in the sauce of your choice, including wild boar and venison. Choose between *gialla* (simple, corn polenta) or *taragna* (with taleggio cheese and butter).

★**Osteria della Birra** OSTERIA €€ (☑035 24 24 40; www.elavbrewery.com; Piazza Mascheroni 1; meals €25-30; ⊙noon-3pm & 6pm-2am Mon-Fri, noon-2am Sat & Sun) Being the official *osteria* of craft brewers, this convivial eatery ensures there's a top selection on tap; the tangy Indie Ale tastes particularly fine. So squeeze in at a tiny table or lounge in the courtyard and chow down on platters piled high with local meats, or polenta with beef simmered in Elav's own-brewed beer.

Ristorante a Modo
MODERN ITALIAN €€

(☑ 035 21 02 95; www.ristoranteamodo.com; Viale Vittorio Emanuele II 19; meals €40; ⊘ 12.15-2.15pm & 7.30-10.30pm Tue-Sat, 7.30-10.30pm Mon) Inventive takes on modern Italian cooking make this our pick of the Città Bassa restaurants. Try the gnocchi with basil and clams or the thyme-scented sea bass carpaccio. Ultramodern decor blends black-and-white prints with quirky twists, such as the giant pink snail on the patio.

★ Colleoni & Dell'Angelo
ITALIAN €€€

(☑ 035 23 25 96; www.colleonidellangelo.com; Piazza Vecchia 7; meals €50-60; ⊘ noon-2.30pm & 7-10.30pm Tue-Sun) Grand Piazza Vecchia provides the ideal backdrop to savour truly top-class creative cuisine. Sit at an outside table in summer or opt for the noble 15th-century interior; either way expect to encounter dishes such as black risotto with ricotta and grilled cuttlefish, or venison medallions with chestnut purée and redcurrant jam.

ℹ Information

Airport Tourist Office (☑ 035 32 04 02; www.visitbergamo.net; arrivals hall; ⊘ 8am-9pm)
Città Alta Tourist Office (☑ 035 24 22 26; www.visitbergamo.net; Via Gombito 13; ⊘ 9am-5.30pm) In the heart of the Upper Town.
Città Bassa Tourist Office (☑ 035 21 02 04; www.visitbergamo.net; Viale Papa Giovanni XXIII 57; ⊘ 9am-12.30pm & 2-5.30pm) Near the train and bus stations, in the Lower Town.

ℹ Getting There & Away

AIR
Orio al Serio (Aeroporto Il Caravaggio; ☑ 035 32 63 23; www.sacbo.it) Low-cost carriers link Bergamo airport with a wide range of European cities. It has direct transport links to Milan.

BUS
Bus Station (☑ 800 139392; www.bergamo trasporti.it) Located just off Piazza Marconi.
SAB (☑ 035 28 90 00; www.arriva.it) Part of the Arriva group, operates regular services to Brescia, Mantua and the lakes.

TRAIN
Train Station (☑ 035 24 79 50; Piazza Marconi) Services to Milan (€5, one hour), Lecco (€3.80, 40 minutes) and Brescia (€4.30, one hour, with connections for Lake Garda and Venice).

ℹ Getting Around

TO/FROM THE AIRPORT
ATB (☑ 035 23 60 26; www.atb.bergamo.it) Buses run to/from the airport every 20 minutes from Bergamo bus and train stations (€2.20, 15 minutes). Regular, direct buses also connect the airport with Milan (adult/reduced €5/4, one hour).

ATB also offers unlimited travel passes that cover Bergamo's funicular and bus network, including services to the airport (per 24/72 hours €5/7).

PUBLIC TRANSPORT
Bus 1a (run by ATB) connects the train station with the funicular to Città Alta and with Largo Colle Aperto in the Città Alta. Going the other way not all buses continue to the train station; instead they stop at the more northerly Porta Nuova.
Funicular (☑ 035 23 60 26; www.atb.bergamo. it; ⊘ 7.30am-11.45pm) A hillside tramway links the Città Bassa (Lower Town) with the Città Alta (Upper Town). Single tickets (€2.20) are valid for 90 minutes on the entire bus and funicular network.

Brescia
POP 193,600

Urban sprawl, a seedy bus and train station, and the odd 1960s skyscraper don't hint at Brescia's fascinating old town, which serves as a reminder of its substantial history. Its narrow streets are home to some of the most important Roman ruins in Lombardy and an extraordinary circular Romanesque church.

◉ Sights

★ Santa Giulia
MUSEUM, MONASTERY

(Museo della Città; ☑ 030 297 78 34; www.brescia musei.com; Via dei Musei 81; adult/reduced €10/5.50; ⊘ 10.30am-7pm Tue-Sun mid-Jun–Sep, shorter hours winter) The jumbled Monastero di Santa Giulia and Basilica di San Salvatore is Brescia's single-most intriguing sight. Inside this rambling church and convent complex, the Museo della Città houses collections that run the gamut from prehistory to the age of Venetian dominance. Highlights include Roman mosaics and medieval jewels.

The building of the monastery, which started as early as the 8th century, absorbed two *domus* (Roman houses), which were left standing in what would become the monk's garden (Ortaglia) near the north cloister.

The remains have become known as the **Domus dell'Ortaglia**. Raised walkways allow you to wander round the **Domus di Dioniso** (so called because of a mosaic of Dionysius, god of wine) and the **Domus delle Fontane** (named after two marble fountains). The beautiful floor mosaics and colourful frescoes in these two *domus* rank among the highlights of the monastery-museum.

The other star piece of the monastery collections is the 8th-century **Croce di Desiderio**, an extraordinary Lombard cross encrusted with hundreds of jewels.

Tempio Capitolino   RUIN
(www.bresciamusei.com; Via dei Musei; adult/reduced €4/3; ⊙10am-5pm Tue-Sun Mar-Sep, Fri-Sun Oct-Feb) Brescia's most impressive Roman relic is this temple built by Emperor Vespasian in AD 73. Today, six Corinthian columns stand before a series of cells. Guided tours (50 minutes, hourly) reveal authentic decorations, including original coloured marble floors, altars and religious statues.

Tickets also secure admission to Brescia's nearby Roman Theatre.

Roman Theatre   RUIN
(off Via dei Musei; adult/reduced €4/3; ⊙10am-5pm Fri-Sun) At the height of the Roman era, the theatre of Brescia (then Brixia) could seat 15,000 spectators. The surviving ruins are now somewhat overgrown; find them at the end of cobbled Vicolo del Fontanon.

Duomo Vecchio   CHURCH
(Old Cathedral; Piazza Paolo VI; ⊙9am-noon & 3-6pm Wed-Sat, 9-10.45am & 3-6pm Sun) The most compelling of all Brescia's religious monuments is the 11th-century Duomo Vecchio, a rare example of a circular-plan Romanesque basilica, built over a 6th-century church. The inside is surmounted by a dome borne by eight sturdy vaults resting on thick pillars.

Interesting features include fragmentary floor mosaics (perhaps from a thermal bath that might have stood here in the 1st century BC) and the elaborate 14th-century sarcophagus of Bishop Berado Maggi.

Duomo Nuovo   CATHEDRAL
(New Cathedral; Piazza Paolo VI; ⊙7.30am-noon & 4-7pm Mon-Sat, 8am-1pm & 4-7pm Sun) The Duomo Nuovo was begun in 1604 but wasn't finished until 1825. Repeated alterations over the centuries make it a bit of a mishmash; the lower part of the facade is baroque; the

upper part showcases the classical flourishes of the later 1700s.

Museo Mille Miglia   MUSEUM
(⊘030 336 56 31; www.museomillemiglia.it; Viale della Rimembranza 3; adult/reduced €7/5; ⊙10am-6pm) The original Mille Miglia (Thousand Miles) ran between 1927 and 1957 and was one of Italy's most legendary endurance car races – it started in Brescia and took some 16 hours to complete. The race's colourful museum is loaded with some of the greatest cars to cross the finish line, as well as old-style petrol pumps and archive race footage.

🍴 Sleeping & Eating

Risotto, beef dishes and *lumache alla Bresciana* (snails cooked with Parmesan cheese and fresh spinach) are common in Brescia.

⭐**Albergo Orologio**   HOTEL €
(⊘030 375 54 11; www.albergoorologio.it; Via Beccaria 17; s €64-85, d €84-94; ❄@📶) Just opposite from its namesake clock tower and just steps away from central Piazza Paolo VI, the medieval Albergo Orologio boasts fragrant rooms dotted with antiques. Bedrooms feature terracotta floors, soft gold, brown and olive furnishings, and snazzy modern bathrooms.

⭐**Osteria al Bianchi**   OSTERIA €€
(⊘030 29 23 28; www.osteriaalbianchi.it; Via Gasparo da Salò 32; meals €25; ⊙9am-2pm & 4.30pm-midnight Thu-Mon) Squeeze inside this classic bar, in business since 1880, or grab a pavement table and be tempted by the *pappardelle al taleggio e zucca* (broad ribbon pasta with taleggio cheese and pumpkin), followed by anything from *brasato d'asino* (braised donkey) to *pestöm* (minced pork served with polenta).

🍷 Drinking & Nightlife

Il Bottega   WINE BAR
(⊘030 240 00 59; Via dei Musei 21; ⊙6pm-midnight Tue-Sun, to 1am Fri & Sat, noon-2pm Sat & Sun) A cool crowd crams into this buzzing bar to sip on classy wines and sample piled-high platters of meats and cheese (€4 to €7).

ℹ Information

Main Tourist Office (⊘030 240 03 57; www.turismobrescia.it; Via Trieste 1; ⊙9.30am-1pm & 1.30-5pm, to 6pm summer) Brescia's main tourist office, on the edge of Piazza Paolo VI, can advise on exploring the city's churches and Roman sites.

There's another, smaller tourist office at the **train station** (☑ 030 837 85 59; www.turismo brescia.it; Piazzale Stazione).

❶ Getting There & Around

Bus Station (☑ 030 4 49 15; Via Solferino) Near the main train station.

SAIA Trasporti (☑ 030 288 99 11; www.arriva. it) Buses serve destinations throughout the province including Desenzano del Garda and Mantua. Some services leave from another station off Via della Stazione.

Metro (per 90min €1.40) A smart new metro links the train station with Piazza della Vittoria (one stop) in the heart of the old town.

Train Station (☑ 030 4 41 08; Viale della Stazione 7) Brescia is on the Milan–Venice line, with regular services to Milan (€7.30 to €20, 45 minutes to 1¼ hours) and Verona (€6.75, 40 minutes). There are also secondary lines to Cremona (€5.50, one hour), Bergamo (€4.80, one hour) and Parma (€7.65, two hours).

Mantua

POP 48,600

As serene as the three lakes it sits beside, Mantua is home to sumptuous ducal palaces and a string of atmospheric, cobbled squares. The city's heritage is rich: Latin poet Virgil was born here, Shakespeare had Romeo hear of Juliet's death here and Verdi set his tragic opera *Rigoletto* in these fog-bound streets. In 1328 the city fell to the fast-living, art-loving Gonzaga dynasty – their legacy lingers in the city today.

◉ Sights

The tight-knit centre of Mantua is like an alfresco medieval and Renaissance architectural museum, comprising from north to south: Piazza Sordello, Piazza Broletto, Piazza delle Erbe and Piazza Mantegna.

★ Palazzo Ducale   PALACE
(☑ 041 241 18 97; www.ducalemantova.org; Piazza Sordello 40; adult/reduced €13/8; ◷ 8.15am-7.15pm Tue-Sun) For more than 300 years the enormous Palazzo Ducale was the seat of the Gonzaga – a family of wealthy horse breeders who rose to power in the 14th century to become one of Italy's leading Renaissance families. Their 500-room palace is vast; a visit today winds through 40 of the finest chambers. Along with works by Morone and Rubens, the highlight is the witty mid-15th-century fresco by Mantegna in the **Camera degli Sposi** (Bridal Chamber).

Executed between 1465 and 1474, the room, which is entirely painted, shows the marquis, Lodovico, going about his courtly business with family and courtiers in tow. Painted naturalistically and with great attention to perspective, the arched walls appear like windows on the courtly world – looking up at the Duke's wife Barbara, you can even see the underside of her dress as if she's seated above you. Most playful of all though is the *trompe l'œil* oculus featuring bare-bottomed *putti* (cherubs) balancing precariously on a painted balcony, while smirking courtly pranksters appear ready to drop a large potted plant on gawping tourists below. Other palace highlights are Domenico Morone's *Expulsion of the Bonacolsi* (1494), in room 1, depicting the Gonzaga coup d'état of 1328, and Rubens' vast *Adoration of the Magi* in the **Sala degli Arcieri** (Room of Archers), which Napoleonic troops brutally dismembered in 1797. In room 2, the **Sala del Pisanello**, fragments and preliminary sketches of Pisanello's frescoes of Arthurian knights remain, while the cream-and-gold **Galleria degli Specchi** (Gallery of Mirrors) is actually a complete 17th-century Austrian reworking – under the Gonzaga the gallery housed prized paintings, including Caravaggio's radical *Death of the Virgin* (which is now in the Louvre).

The palace's finest remaining features are its frescoed and gilt ceilings including, in room 2, a labyrinth, predicting the capricious nature of good fortune. As if in illustration, are two portraits of Eleanor Gonzaga (1630–86), who rose to marry a Habsburg emperor, and Vicenzo II (1594–1627), who lost the entire family fortune and one of Europe's most enviable art collections.

Rooms 34 to 36 house the **Stanze degli Arazzi**, some of the only original artworks commissioned by the family: nine 16th-century Flemish tapestries reproduced from Raphael's original designs for the Sistine Chapel. Woven in Brussels using the finest English wool, Indian silk and Cypriot gold and silver thread, they represent the cosmopolitan sophistication of the Gonzaga court.

Rotonda di San Lorenzo   CHURCH
(☑ 0376 32 22 97; Piazza delle Erbe; ◷ 10am-1pm & 3-6pm Mon-Fri, 10am-6pm Sat & Sun) The weather-worn 11th-century Rotonda di San Lorenzo is sunk below the level of the square, its red-brick walls still decorated with the shadowy remains of 12th- and 13th-century frescoes.

Mantua

200 m
0.1 miles

Lago di
Mezzo

Lago
Inferiore

Lago
Superiore

Boats to San Benedetto Po & Venice

Boats to San Benedetto Po, Venice & Mincio

Via Legnago

Parco della Scienza

Lungolago del Gonzaga

Boats to San Benedetto Po, Venice & Mincio

Porta San Giorgio

Piazza Castello

Palazzo Ducale

Piazza Santa Barbara

Piazza 10
Arche

La Rigola (330m)

Palazzo Ducale Entrance

Teatro Bibiena

Piazza 1
Sordello

Cattedrale

Piazza del Accademia

Via Ardigò

Torre della Gabbia

Via dell Broletto

Piazza Broletto

Piazza delle Erbe

Via G Bertani

Vicolo Nazione

Via Roma

Via Cavour

Piazza Mantegna

Salumeria (100m)

Vicolo Albergo

Corso del Sogliari

Corso Umberto I

Palazzo Te (1.1km)

Via Ippolito Nievo

Via Giovanni Arrivabene

Via Domenico Fernelli

Piazza San Giovanni

Via Concezione

Via Finzi

Via Due Catene

Via Dario Tassoni

Via Fratelli Cairoli

Piazza Virgiliana

Bike Trail

Viale Mincio

Viale Mincio

Peschiera del Garda (36km); Verona (60km)

Porta Mulini

Via Trento

Via Porto

Via Cappuccine

Via XXV Aprile

Piazza d'Arco

Via A Scarsellini

Via Bandiera

Via Marangoni

Via Solferino e San Martino

Corso Vittorio Emanuele II

Piazza Cavallotti

Sottoriva

Via Alberto Pitentino

Boat tours of Lago Superiore

Motonavi Andes Boats to Lake Superiore

Bike Trail

Navi Andes Boats to Lago Superiore (500m)

APAM

Piazza Don Leoni

Train Station

Dal Pescatore (38km); Cremona (75km); Brescia (100km)

Mantua

Basilica di Sant'Andrea　　　BASILICA
(☎ 0376 32 85 04; Piazza Mantegna; ⊙ 8am-noon & 3-7pm) This towering basilica safeguards the golden vessels said to hold earth soaked by the blood of Christ. Longinus, the Roman soldier who speared Christ on the cross, is said to have scooped up the earth and buried it in Mantua after leaving Palestine. Today, these containers rest beneath a marble octagon in front of the altar and are paraded around Mantua in a grand procession on Good Friday.

★ Teatro Bibiena　　　THEATRE
(Teatro Scientifico; ☎ 0376 32 76 53; www.societadellamusica.it; Via dell'Accademia 47; adult/reduced €2/1.20; ⊙ 10am-1pm & 3-4pm Tue-Fri, 10am-6pm Sat & Sun) If ever a theatre were set to upstage the actors, it's the 18th-century Teatro Bibiena. Dimly lit and festooned with plush velvet, its highly unusual, intimate bell-shaped design sees four storeys of ornate, stucco balconies arranged around curving walls. It was specifically intended to allow its patrons to be seen – balconies even fill the wall behind the stage.

Palazzo Te　　　PALACE
(☎ 0376 32 32 66; www.palazzote.it; Viale Te 13; adult/reduced €12/9; ⊙ 1-6pm Mon, 9am-6pm Tue-Sun) Palazzo Te was where Frederico II Gonzaga escaped for love trysts with his mistress Isabella Boschetti, and it's decorated in play-boy style with stunning frescoes, playful motifs and encoded symbols. A Renaissance pleasure-dome, it is the finest work of star architect Giulio Romano, whose sumptuous Mannerist scheme fills the palace with fanciful flights of imagination.

Having escaped a Roman prison sentence for designing pornographic prints, Romano, Raphael's most gifted student, was the perfect choice for the Palazzo Te commission. Using the *trompe l'œil* technique, he eschewed the cool classicism of the past in favour of wildly distorted perspectives, a pastel colour palette and esoteric symbols.

The second room, the **Camera delle Imprese** (Room of the Devices), sets the scene with a number of key symbols: the salamander, the symbol of Federico; the four eagles of the Gonzaga standard; and Mt Olympus, the symbol of Charles V, Holy Roman Emperor, from whom the Gonzaga received their titles and in whose name they ruled Mantua. The purpose of Renaissance devices was to encode messages, mottos and virtues so that visitors to the palace could 'read' where loyalties lay and navigate political power structures. Federico's device, the salamander, is accompanied by the quote: *'Quod hic deest, me torquet'* (What you lack, torments me), alluding to his notoriously passionate nature when compared to the cold-blooded salamander.

The culmination of the symbolic narrative, however, comes together masterfully in the **Camera dei Giganti** (Chamber of the Giants), a domed room where frescoes cover every inch of wall with towering figures of the rebellious giants (disloyal subjects) clawing their way up Mt Olympus (symbol of Charles V) only to be laid low by Jupiter's (Charles') thunderbolt. As the viewer you are in the centre of the scene, the worried faces of Olympian gods staring down at you.

⚡ Activities

La Rigola　　　CYCLING
(☎ 0376 36 66 77; Via Trieste 5; per day from €10; ⊙ 9.30am-12.30pm & 2.30-7pm) Rents bikes by the day.

☞ Tours

Boat Tours　　　BOAT TOUR
Short one- to two-hour tours on the lakes that surround Mantua are offered by two competitor companies, **Motonavi Andes** (☎ 0376 32 28 75; www.motonaviandes.it; Via San Giorgio 2) and **Navi Andes** (☎ 0376 32 45 06;

WORTH A TRIP

DAL PESCATORE RESTAURANT

Petals of egg pasta frame slices of guinea fowl caramelized in honey saffron while silky tortellini are stuffed to bursting with pumpkin, nutmeg, cinnamon and candied *mostarda* (fruit in a sweet mustard sauce). You can practically eat the Mantuan countryside in Nadia Santini's internationally acclaimed restaurant Dal Pescatore (✆ 0376 72 30 01; www.dalpescatore.com; Località Runate, Canneto sull'Oglio; meals €160-260; ⊙ noon-4pm & 7.30pm-late Thu-Sun, 7.30pm-late Wed; P), where quietly brilliant food focuses on balancing simplicity with the very finest natural produce.

The restaurant is 40km west of Mantua. Nearby, 9 Muse B&B (✆ 335 800 76 01; www.9muse.it; Via Giordano Bruno 42a, Canneto sull'Oglio; s €45-55, d €73-90; P ❄ @ ⭑) provides elegant accommodation.

www.naviandes.com; Piazza Sordello 48), between April and October. Trips start at around €9 and skirt lotus flowers, reed beds and heron roosts, providing panoramic city views. Both companies also occasionally offer longer trips to Venice (one way €81) and San Benedetto Po (adult/child €15.50/14.50) through Parco del Mincio. These trips leave from jetties either on Viale Mincio or Lungolago dei Gonzaga.

★ **Visit Mantua**   WALKING TOUR
(✆ 347 4022020; www.visitmantua.it; tours per 2 people 90min/5hr €100/300) Get the insider view of Renaissance dukes and duchesses – what they ate for breakfast, how they conspired at court and the wardrobe crises of the day – with Lorenzo Bonoldi's fascinating conversational tours of Mantua's palaces.

🛏 Sleeping

Casa Margherita   B&B €
(✆ 349 7506117; www.lacasadimargherita.it; Via Broletto 44; s €60-65, d €80-100; ❄) For a budget sleep, it's hard to top this elegant town house, set in the heart of historic Mantua. Artfully lit bedrooms combine soft tones with subtle furnishings; bathrooms team mod-cons with retro designs. Some rooms have views onto Piazza Broletto.

★ **C'a delle Erbe**   B&B €€
(✆ 0376 22 61 61; www.cadelleerbe.it; Via Broletto 24; d €120-140; ❄ 🗢) In this exquisite 16th-century town house historic features have had a minimalist makeover: exposed stone walls surround paired-down furniture; white-painted beams coexist with lavish bathrooms and modern art. The pick of the bedrooms? The one with the balcony overlooking the iconic Piazza delle Erbe.

Palazzo Arrivabene   B&B €€
(✆ 0376 32 86 85; www.palazzoarrivabene.net; Via Bandiera 20; s €100-120, d €120-140; ❄ 🗢) You may well feel like a duke or duchess, lounging around this 15th-century *palazzo*, delighting in the frescoed ceilings, vast marble fireplaces and cherub-framed doors. The grand style continues into the bedroom, where polished wooden floors meet rich rugs and patterned prints. Come mid-week if you can; the higher prices are charged at weekends.

🍴 Eating & Drinking

Mantua's most famous dish is melt-in-your-mouth *tortelli di zucca* (pumpkin-stuffed pasta). Look out too for *salumi* (salt pork), *prosciutto crudo* (salt-cured ham) and the sweet mustards *mostarda di mele* and *mantovana* (made with apples or pears).

Osteria delle Quattro Tette   OSTERIA €
(✆ 0376 32 94 78; Vicolo Nazione 4; meals €10-15; ⊙ 12.30-2.30pm Mon-Sat) Take a pew at rough-hewn wooden tables beneath barrel-vaulted ceilings and order up pumpkin pancakes, pike in sweet salsa or *risotto alla pilota* (risotto with spiced sausage). It's spartan, rustic and extremely well priced, which is why half of Mantua is in here at lunchtime.

Salumeria   DELI €
(Via Orefici 16; ⊙ 7.30am-1pm & 4-7pm, closed Mon afternoons) Step into this traditional deli and feel the clock turning right back. Hanging hams and salami, stacks of pungent local cheese and see-through vats of Mantua's speciality *mostarda* ensure prime picnic shopping. There are wines to wash it all down with, too.

Fragoletta   MANTUAN €€
(✆ 0376 32 33 00; www.fragoletta.it; Piazza Arche 5; meals €30; ⊙ noon-3pm & 8-11pm Tue-Sun; ⭑) Wooden chairs scrape against the tiled floor as diners eagerly tuck into Slow Food-accredited *culatello di Zibello* (lard) at this friendly local trattoria. Other Mantuan spe-

cialities feature, such as *risotto alla pilota* (rice studded with sausage meat) and pumpkin ravioli with melted butter and sage.

⭐ **Il Cigno**   MODERN ITALIAN €€€
(☑0376 32 71 01; www.ristoranteilcignomantova. com; Piazza d'Arco 1; meals €55-65; ◎12.30-2.30pm & 7-11pm Wed-Sun, closed part of Aug) The building is as beautiful as the food: a lemon-yellow facade dotted with faded olive-green shutters. Inside, Mantua's gourmets graze on delicately steamed risotto with spring greens, poached cod with polenta or gamey guinea fowl with spicy *mostarda*.

Bar Caravatti   CAFE, BAR
(☑0376 32 78 26; Portici Broletto 16; ◎7am-8.30pm) All of Mantua passes through Caravatti at some point during the day for coffee, *spritz* or Signor Caravatti's 19th-century *aperitivo* of aromatic bitters and wine.

ℹ️ Information

Tourist Office (☑0376 43 24 32; www. turismo.mantova.it; Piazza Mantegna 6; ◎9am-1.30pm & 2.30-6pm Tue-Fri, to 5pm Mon, 9am-6pm Sat & Sun)

ℹ️ Getting There & Around

Bus Station (Piazza Don Leoni; ◎ticket office 7.30am-5.45pm Mon-Fri, to 12.45pm Sat)

APAM (☑0376 23 03 46; www.apam.it). Runs buses to Sabbioneta, San Benedetto Po and Brescia. Most leave from Piazza Don Leoni, near the train station, but some leave from Viale Risorgimento.

Train Station (Piazza Don Leoni) Regular services include those to Cremona (€6.10, 40 to 60 minutes), Milan (€11.50, two hours) and Verona (€3.75, 50 minutes).

Cremona

POP 71,200

A wealthy, independent city-state for centuries, Cremona boasts some fine medieval architecture, but is best known internationally for making the world's best violins.

◎ Sights

Piazza del Comune   PIAZZA
This beautiful, pedestrian-only piazza is considered one of the best-preserved medieval squares in all Italy. To maintain divisions between Church and state, Church buildings were erected on the eastern side and those for secular affairs were built on the west.

Duomo   CATHEDRAL
(Piazza del Comune; ◎8am-noon & 2.30-6pm Mon-Sat, noon-12.30pm & 3.30-6pm Sun) Cremona's cathedral started out as a Romanesque basilica, but the simplicity of that style later gave way to an extravagance of designs. The interior frescoes are utterly overwhelming, with the *Storie di Cristo* (Stories of Christ) by Pordenone perhaps the highlights. One of the chapels contains what is said to be a thorn from Jesus' crown of thorns.

Torrazzo   TOWER
(Piazza del Comune; adult/reduced €5/4; ◎10am-1pm & 2.30-6pm, closed Mon winter) Cremona's 111m-tall *torrazzo* (bell tower, although '*torazzo*' translates literally as 'great, fat tower') soars above the city's central square. A total of 502 steps wind up to marvelous views across the city.

Chiesa di Sant'Agostino   CHURCH
(Piazza Sant'Agostino; ◎8am-noon & 2.30-6pm Mon-Sat, noon-12.30pm & 3.30-6pm Sun) Once inside the Chiesa di Sant'Agostino, head for the third chapel on the right, the **Cappella Cavalcabò**, which features a stunning late-Gothic fresco cycle by Bonifacio Bembo and his assistants. One of the altars is graced with a 1494 painting by Pietro Perugino, *Madonna in trono e santi* (The Madonna Enthroned with Saints).

🎉 Festivals & Events

Festival di Cremona Claudio Monteverdi   MUSIC
(www.teatroponchielli.it; ◎May) A month-long series of concerts centred on Monteverdi and other baroque-era composers, held in the Teatro Amilcare Ponchielli.

CREMONA'S VIOLINS

It was in Cremona, in the 17th century, that master craftsman Antonio Stradivari lovingly put together his first violins. His legacy continues today, in the 100 violin-making workshops clustered around Piazza del Comune. The Stradivarius violin is typically made from spruce (the top of the violin), willow (the internal blocks and linings) and maple (the back, ribs and neck), and is prized for its unique sound.

Cremona's state-of-the-art **Museo del Violino** (☑0372 08 08 09; www.museodelviolino.org; Piazza Marconi 5; adult/reduced €10/7; ☉10am-6pm Tue-Sun) brings together the city's historic violin collections, presenting them alongside the tools of the trade. It also houses a special room containing the drawings, moulds and tools Stradivari used in his workshop. To hear Cremona's violins in action, head to the 19th-century **Teatro Amilcare Ponchielli** (☑0372 02 20 01; www.teatroponchielli.it; Corso Vittorio Emanuele II 52); its season runs from October to June.

Stradivari Festival MUSIC
(www.museodelviolino.org; ☉mid-Sep–mid-Oct) Focusing on music for string instruments. Held between mid-September and mid-October, it's organised by the Museo del Violino.

Festa del Torrone FOOD
(www.festadeltorronecremona.it; ☉Nov) A weekend full of exhibitions, performances and tastings dedicated to that Cremona-made Christmas sweet, *torrone* (nougat).

Sleeping

Albergo Duomo HOTEL €
(☑0372 3 52 42; www.hotelduomocremona.com; Via Gonfalonieri 13; s/d/tr €60/80/100; P🏵🕸) Despite being embedded in the heart of the old town, this is a sleek modern affair, with chocolate-brown and cream decor, smart bathrooms, music-themed prints and views over a jumble of historic roofs.

L'Archetto HOSTEL €
(☑0372 80 77 55; www.ostellocremona.com; Via Brescia 9; dm/s/d €27/30/58; 🏵@🕸) Cost-conscious musicians love this central,

positively luxurious hostel where cheerful, modern bedrooms and three-bed dorms are pristine and thoughtfully furnished. Sadly, the limited reception hours (8am to 10am and 5pm to 9pm) – and no option to leave luggage – might be inconvenient.

Delliarti Design Hotel DESIGN HOTEL €€
(☑0372 2 31 31; www.hoteldellearti.com; Via Bonomelli 8; s/d from €100/130; 🏵🕸) A firm favourite with visiting fashionistas, Cremona's hippest hotel is a high-tech vision of glass, concrete and steel. Stylish bedrooms feature clean lines, bold colours and artistic lighting. There are also some fun flourishes: undulating gold, corrugated corridors, and a bowl of Liquorice Allsorts on the front desk.

Eating

★**Hosteria '700** CREMONESE €€
(☑0372 3 61 75; www.hosteria700.it; Piazza Gallina 1; meals €30-35; ☉noon-3pm Wed-Mon, 7.30-10pm Wed-Sun) Behind the dilapidated facade lurks a sparkling gem. Some of the vaulted rooms come with ceiling frescoes and the hearty Lombard cuisine comes at a refreshingly competitive cost.

La Sosta OSTERIA €€
(☑0372 45 66 56; www.osterialasosta.it; Via Sicardo 9; meals €35-40; ☉12.15-2pm Tue-Sun, 7.15-10pm Tue-Sat) La Sosta is surrounded by violin-makers' workshops and is a suitably harmonious place to feast on regional delicacies such as *tortelli di zucca* (pumpkin pasta parcels) and baked snails.

Centrale CREMONESE €€
(☑0372 2 87 01; www.ristorantecentralecremona.it; Via Pertusio 4; meals €30; ☉noon-2pm & 7-9.30pm Fri-Wed) Centrale's been feeding happy diners since 1960, and the place has an appealingly old-fashioned feel. You'll often find locals playing cards in the bar and staff rolling pasta in the corner of the dining room. Treats include pork-shank stew with polenta and a decadent chocolate tart.

ℹ Information

Tourist Office (☑0372 40 63 91; www.turismocremona.it; Piazza del Comune 5; ☉9.30am-1pm & 2-5pm)

ℹ Getting There & Away

Train Station (Via Dante) Trains to Brescia (€5.50, one hour), Mantua (€6.10, 40 to 60 minutes), Milan (€8, two hours) and Piacenza (€5, one hour) run roughly hourly.

Trento & the Dolomites

Best Places to Eat

→ Scrigno del Duomo (p309)

→ Zur Kaiserkron (p321)

→ Paradeis (p324)

→ Restaurant Ladinia (p333)

Best Places to Stay

→ Ottmanngut (p324)

→ Gasthof Grüner Baum (p326)

→ Park Hotel Azalea (p316)

→ Chalet Fogajard (p314)

Why Go?

While they're not Italy's tallest mountains, the Dolomites' red-hued pinnacles are the country's most spectacular, drawing a faithful fan club of hikers, skiers, poets and fresh-air fanciers for at least the last few centuries.

Protected by seven natural parks, the two semi-autonomous provinces of Trentino and Alto Adige offer up a number of stunning wilderness areas, where adventure and comfort can be found in equal measure. Wooden farmhouses dot vine- and orchard-covered valleys and the region's cities – the southerly enclave of Trento, the Austro-Italian Bolzano and the very Viennese Merano – are easy to navigate, cultured and fun. From five-star spa resorts to the humblest mountain hut, multi-generational hoteliers combine genuine warmth with extreme professionalism.

Nowhere are the oft-muddled borders of Italy's extreme north reflected more strongly than on the plate: don't miss out on tasting one of Europe's most fascinating cultural juxtapositions.

When to Go
Bolzano

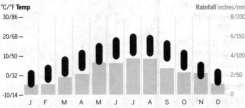

Jan Grab a bargain on the slopes after the Christmas high.

Jul Hit the high-altitude trails and mountain huts of the Alta Vie.

Dec Get festive at Tyrolean Christmas markets in Bolzano, Merano and Bressanone.

Trento & the Dolomites Highlights

1 Working up a high-altitude appetite on the slopes, then hitting the fine-dining hot spot of **Alta Badia** (p332).

2 Being enchanted by the endless green pastures of the **Alpe di Siusi** (p329).

3 Testing your mettle on a vertiginous **via ferrata** (p313) in the Brenta Dolomites.

4 Sipping a Veneziana *spritz* on a frescoed piazza in **Trento** (p309).

5 Floating away beneath palm trees and snowy peaks at **Terme Merano** (p324).

6 Uncovering the excellent modern and contemporary art collections in Rovereto's **MART** (p311).

7 Discovering Italy's most elegant white wines along the **Weinstrasse** (p324).

8 Getting high above Bolzano's pretty streets on one of its three **cable cars** (p318).

9 Feasting your way through schnitzel and *spätzle*, strudel and *knödel* in the **Val Pusteria** (p333).

10 Mountain biking the apple-clad hills of the **Val di Sole** (p315).

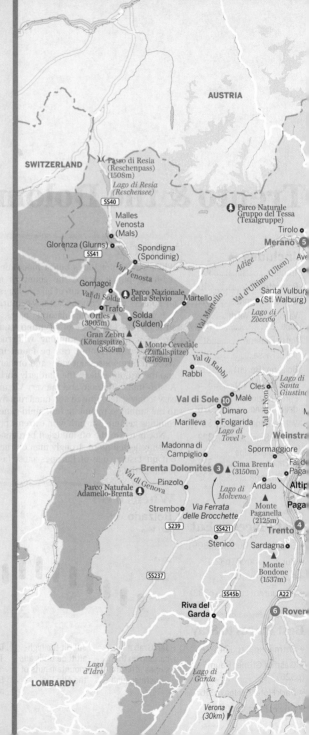

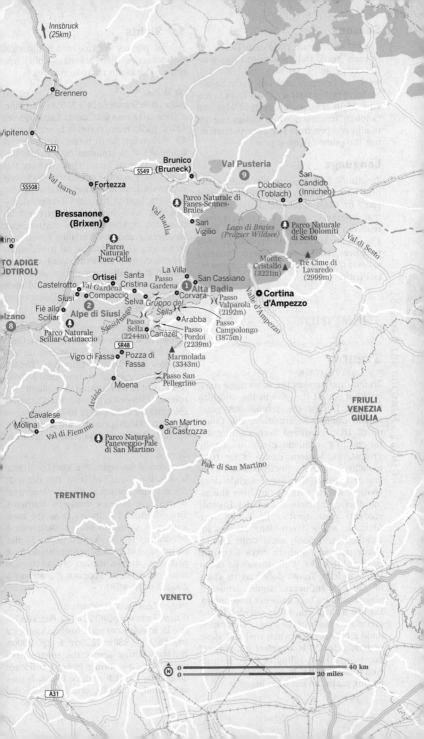

Seasons

The ski season runs from early December to early April, and high season hits mid-December to 6 January, the last two weeks of February and any early Easter. Summer rates plummet, apart from in August. Many resorts shut in April/May and October/November, while *rifugi* (mountain huts) open from late June to September, the prime hiking season.

Language

Trentino's first language is Italian but head north to Alto Adige (Südtirol) and you'll find 75% of the population are German speakers, a legacy of the region's relatively recent absorption into Italy. The Ladin language is spoken in both provinces, across five eastern Dolomiti valleys; it's a direct descendant of provincial Latin.

TRENTINO

Trento

POP 117,300 / ELEV 194M

Trento rarely makes the news these days, but that wasn't the case in the mid-16th century. During the tumultuous years of the Counter-Reformation, the Council of Trent convened here, dishing out far-reaching condemnations to uppity Protestants. Modern Trento is far from preachy; instead it's quietly confident, liberal and easy to like. Bicycles glide along spotless streets fanning out from the atmospheric, intimate Piazza del Duomo, students clink *spritzes* by Renaissance fountains and a dozen historical eras intermingle seamlessly amid stone castles, shady porticoes and the city's signature medieval frescoes. While there's no doubt you're in Italy, Trento does have its share of Austrian influence: apple strudel is ubiquitous and beer halls not uncommon. Set in a wide glacial valley guarded by the crenulated peaks of the Brenta Dolomites, amid a patchwork of vineyards and apple orchards, Trento is a perfect jumping-off point for hiking, skiing or wine tasting. And road cycling is huge: 400km of paved cycling paths fan out from here.

◉ Sights

Helpful plaques indicate which historical era various buildings belong to – often several at once in this many-layered city.

★ MUSE
MUSEUM

(Museo della Scienze; ☑ 0461 27 03 11; www.muse.it; Corso del Lavoro e della Scienza 3; adult/reduced €10/8, guided tours (in English by appointment) €3; ◷ 10am-6pm Tue-Fri, to 9pm Wed, to 7pm Sat & Sun; 🔄) ✦ A stunning new architectural work, care of Renzo Piano, houses this 21st-century science museum and cleverly echoes the local landscape. Curatorially, the museum typifies the city's brainy inquisitiveness, with highly interactive exhibitions that explore the Alpine environment, biodiversity and sustainability, society and technology. Highlights are an truely amazing collection of taxidermy, much of it suspended in a multistorey atrium, along with a fabulous experiential kids area and open working **laboratories** (◷ visits 11.30am-noon, 3-3.30pm Wed-Fri).

Castello del Buonconsiglio
MUSEUM

(☑ 0461 23 37 70; www.buonconsiglio.it; Via Clesio 5; adult/reduced €8/5; ◷ 9.30am-5pm Tue-Sun) Guarded by hulking fortifications, Trento's bishop-princes holed up here until Napoleon's arrival in 1801. Behind the walls are the original 13th-century castle, the Castelvecchio, and the Renaissance residence **Magno Palazzo**, which provides an atmospheric backdrop for a varied collection of artefacts.

Duomo
CATHEDRAL

(Cattedrale di San Vigilio; ◷ 6.30am-6pm) Once host to the Council of Trent, this dimly lit Romanesque cathedral displays fragments of medieval frescoes inside its transepts. Two colonnaded stairways flank the nave, leading, it seems, to heaven. Built over a 6th-century temple devoted to San Vigilio, patron saint of Trento, the foundations form part of a palaeo-Christian **archaeological area** (incl with Museo Diocesano; ◷ 10am-noon & 2.30-5.30pm Mon-Sat).

Museo Diocesano Tridentino
MUSEUM

(Palazzo Pretorio; ☑ 0461 23 44 19; Piazza del Duomo 18; adult/reduced incl Duomo's archaeological area €5/3; ◷ 9.30am-12.30pm & 2.30-5.30pm Wed-Mon) Sitting across the square from the *duomo*, this former bishop's residence dates from the 11th century. It now houses one of Italy's most important ecclesiastical

Trento

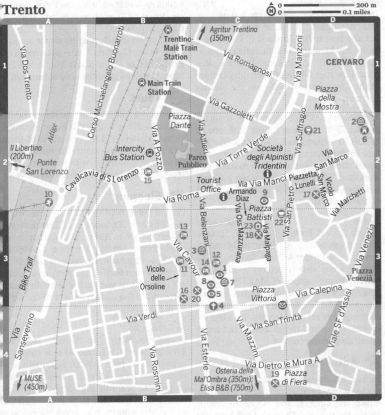

Trento

◎ Sights
1 Casa Cazuffi-Rella	C3
2 Castello del Buonconsiglio	D2
3 Civica	C3
4 Duomo	C4
5 Fontana di Nettuno	C3
6 Magno Palazzo	D2
7 Museo Diocesano Tridentino	C3
8 Piazza del Duomo	C3
9 Tridentum La Città Sotterranea	C2

☺ Activities, Courses & Tours
10 Funivia Trento-Sardagna	A2

🛏 Sleeping
11 Al Cavour 34	B3
12 Al Palazzo Malfatti	C3
13 Albergo Accademia	B3
14 Hotel Venezia	C3
15 Ostello Giovane Europa	B2

✗ Eating
16 Al Vicoli	B3
17 Il Cappello	D2
18 Moki	C3
19 Pedavena	C4
20 Scrigno del Duomo	C3

♬ Drinking & Nightlife
21 Cafe de la Paix	D2
22 Casa del Caffe	C3

🛍 Shopping
23 Raccolta Differenziata	C3

collections with enormous documentary paintings of the Council of Trent, along with Flemish tapestries, exquisite illustrated manuscripts, vestments and some particularly opulent reliquaries.

Piazza del Duomo
PIAZZA

Trento's heart is this busy yet intimate piazza, dominated, of course, by the *duomo*, but also host to the Fontana di Nettuno, a flashy late-baroque fountain rather whimsically dedicated to Neptune. Intricate, allegorical frescoes fill the 16th-century facades of the Casa Cazuffi-Rella, on the piazza's northern side.

Tridentum La Città Sotterranea
ROMAN SITE

(☑0461 23 01 71; Piazza Battisti; adult/reduced €2.50/1.50; ⊗9am-1pm & 2-5.30pm, to 6pm Jun-Sep) Explore Roman Tridentum's city walls, paved streets, tower, domestic mosaics and workshop. The site was discovered less than two decades ago, during restoration works on the nearby theatre.

Civica
ART GALLERY

(Galleria Civica di Trento; ☑0461 98 55 11; www.mart.tn.it/galleriacivica; Via Belenzani 44; admission €2; ⊗10am-1pm & 2-6pm Tue-Sun) FREE This new city gallery project space is the current Trento campus of MART (Museo di Arte Moderna e Contemporanea di Trento e Rovereto) and focusses on 20th-century and contemporary art of the region. It's a beautiful little space and there's a small but interesting shop in the entrace.

Activities

For suggested walking itineraries, and information on *vie ferrate* (trails with permanent cables and ladders) and *rifugi* (mountain huts), visit the local Società degli Alpinisti Tridentini (SAT; ☑0461 98 28 04; www.sat.tn.it; Palazzo Saracini Cresseri, Via Manci 57; ⊗9am-noon & 3-7pm Mon-Fri, afternoons only in winter), staffed by friendly mountaineers.

Funivia Trento-Sardagna
CABLE CAR

(☑0461 23 21 54; Via Montegrappa 1; one way/return €3/5; ⊗7am-10pm) A brief but spectacular cable-car ride from Trento's valley floor delivers you to the pretty village of Sardagna – admire the vista over a grappa or two.

Vaneze di Monte & Monte Bondone
SKIING

(www.montebondone.it; ski pass 1/3/7 days €33/85/153) The small ski station of Vaneze di Monte (1350m) is a 17km winding drive from Trento and is connected by cable car to its higher counterpart, Vasòn, and the gentle slopes of Monte Bondone (1537m), crisscrossed by 37km of cross-country ski trails and nine downhill runs in winter. On weekends between December and March, Skibus Monte Bondone, run by Trentino Trasporti, wends its way from Trento to Vason and Viote (free with TrentoRovereto card, one way €3, 7-day pass €15).

Monte Bondone's pristine slopes are also home to the Giardino Alpine Botanico, with a collection of Alpine plants from across Europe, as well as an indigenous nature trail.

☞ Tours

The tourist office runs two-hour multilingual walking tours (€6) every Saturday, visiting Castello del Buonconsiglio at 10am or around the town centre at 3pm. The afternoon slot finishes with a Trento DOC sparkling tasting at the Palazzo Roccabruno.

🛏 Sleeping

Central hotels book out in early June, when the Festival Economia (2012.festivaleconomia.eu) comes to town, and during other conferences. Agritur Trentino (☑0461 23 53 23; www.agriturismotrentino.com; Via Aconcio 13; ⊗9am-noon Mon-Fri) can put you in touch with rural B&Bs and *agriturismi* (farm stay accommodation), often only a short drive from the centre.

Al Cavour 34
B&B €

(www.alcavour34.it; Via Cavour 34; s/d €70/100; ❄🤏) This little B&B is run by a young couple, both five-star hospitality veterans, who infuse all with a wonderful mix of genuine warmth and absolute professionalism. Rooms are large and decorated in a contemporary style; breakfast is taken around a large table with daily surprises from the local baker or home-baked treats like cookies or apple crumble.

Al Palazzo Malfatti
B&B €

(☑0461 92 21 33; www.bbpalazzomalfatti.it; Via Belenzani 47; s/d €70/100; ❄🤏) Perched on a rooftop, this beautifully designed B&B is a calm and airy retreat that's smack bang in the centre. Upstairs rooms are super private but it retains the feeling of a welcoming home with an elegant living area to relax in and a terrace when it's warm. The charming host dispenses organic breakfasts, along with invaluable local tips.

Elisa B&B
B&B €

(☑0461 92 21 33; www.bbelisa.com; Viale Rovereto 17; s/d €60/90; ❄🤏) This is a true B&B in an architect's beautiful family home, with two private, stylish rooms and breakfasts that are a feast of home-baked cakes, freshly squeezed juice and artisanal cheese. It's located in a smart residential neighbourhood, a pleasant stroll from the city centre, with lots of eating, shopping and drinking options along the way.

Hotel Venezia
HOTEL €

(☑ 0461 23 41 14; www.hotelveneziatn.it; Piazza del Duomo 45; s/d €59/82, without bathroom €46/€62; ☎) Rooms in this friendly place overlook the Piazza del Duomo, pretty Via Belanzani or a quiet inner courtyard. The hotel has been recently remodelled, including flash bathrooms, while prices remain the same.

Ostello Giovane Europa
HOSTEL €

(☑ 0461 26 34 84; www.gayaproject.org; Via Torre Vanga 9; dm/s/d €17/28/45, single night stays €2 extra; ⊙ reception closed 10am-2pm; ☎) Squeaky-clean rooms are comfortable and upper floors have mountain views; the mansard-roofed family room on the top floor is particularly spacious. While it's conveniently located, it can get noisy.

Albergo Accademia
HOTEL €€

(☑ 0461 23 36 00; www.accademiahotel.it; Vicolo Colico 4/6; s/d €89/120; P ❋ @) Elegant small hotel in a historic medieval house with rooms that are modern and airy (if a little on the staid side). Suites are luxuriously spacious, including one with a large private terrace and sauna.

Eating & Drinking

Trento's table is a hearty one and draws many of its ingredients – beef, game, cheese, mushrooms – from its fertile hinterland. There's a lot of cross-cultural traffic too: *cotoletta* (schnitzel) and *canederli* (dumplings) are decidedly Tyrolean, polenta and asparagus evoke the Veneto, and Garda's olive oil conjures the Mediterranean. Bakeries brim with apple strudel, but don't overlook the local carrot cake. Wines to look out for include Trento DOC, a sparkling wine made from chardonnay grapes, the white Nosiola and the extremely drinkable red, Teroldego Rotaliano DOC. Trentino's smartly bottled Surgiva mineral water is considered one of Italy's best, for taste and purity.

Moki
MODERN ITALIAN €

(☑ 347 0431426; www.moki-trento.it; Via Malpaga 20; meals €23; ⊙ 9am-8pm Mon, 9am-10pm Tue-Sat) A warren of bright white rooms, welcoming staff, new ideas and a stack of great magazines make Moki a perfect choice for breakfast, lunch or an *aperitivo* (if there's

a bottle of the pink Revi Trento DOC open, don't say no). Dinners on Friday and Saturday nights begin with 'tapas' style platters and the fresh, tasty mains always include a vegetarian option.

Pedavena
BREWERY €

(☑ 0461 98 62 55; Piazza di Fiera 13; meals €20-30; ⊙ Wed-Mon 9am-midnight, Fri & Sat to 1am) Proudly crowd-pleasing and perennially popular, this sprawling 1920s beer hall (complete with fermenting brew in the corner) serves up the comfort food you'd expect: bratwurst, schnitzel and steaming plates of polenta with mushroom stew and slabs of melty white *tosella* cheese.

★ Scrigno del Duomo
GASTRONOMIC €€

(☑ 0461 22 00 30; www.scrignodelduomo.com; Piazza del Duomo 29; meals €35, degustation from €55; ⊙ wine bar 11am-2.30pm & 6-11pm, dining room 12.30-2.30pm & 7.30-10pm Tue-Sun, dinner only Sat) Trento's culinary and social epicentre is discreetly housed in a building dating back to the 1200s. For degustation dining take the stairs down to the formal restaurant, with its glassed-in Roman-era cellar. Or stay upstairs underneath the beautiful painted wooden ceiling, where there's simple, stylishly done local specialities.

Think lamb with camomile and cauliflower, asparagus lasagne with *puzzone* cheese from Moena, or just grab a bar stool, wine and generous helpings of Scrigno's baton-like *grissini* (Turin-style breadstick), Parmesan chunks and olives.

Al Vicoli
SEAFOOD, WINE BAR €€

(☑ 0461 26 06 73; www.aivicoli.it; Piazza Verzeri 1; meals €30-35; ⊙ noon-2pm & 7-10.30pm Mon-Sat) This dark, industrial back lane space could be a nightclub and yes, its wine bar kicks on until midnight. But it's the mezzanine restuarant that has the locals talking: its excellent seafood menu, including a sublime fish raviolio in sage and butter, is unusual in Trento. The noteworthy wine here is mostly local, but there are also some great Abruzzese drops.

Il Cappello
TRENTINO €€

(☑ 0461 23 58 50; www.osteriailcappello.it; Piazzetta Lunelli 5; meals €35; ⊙ noon-2.30pm & 7-10pm Tue-Sat, noon-3pm Sun) This intimate dining room has an unexpectedly rustic feel, with wooden beams and a terrace set in a quiet courtyard. The menu is Trentino to the core, and simple presentation makes the most of

TRENTOROVERETO CARD

Available from the tourist office and some museums, this card (adult plus one child €20, 48 hours) gets you free entry to all city and regional museums, the Botanical Alpine Gardens as well as wine tastings and walking tours, bike hire and free public transport – including the Trento–Sardagna cable car and regional trains and buses. Register online and the card lasts a further three months, free transport aside.

beautiful artisan produce. Wines too are local and rather special.

Il Libertino
TRENTINO €€

(☑ 0461 26 00 85; www.ristoranteillibertino.com; Piazza Piedicastello 4-6; meals €26-30; ⊙noon-2.30pm & 6.30-10.30pm Wed-Mon) Stroll the bridge over the fast-flowing Adige to this woody, hushed restaurant for carefully prepared traditional dishes. Think venison, chestnuts, radicchio, boar sausage and river trout, along with an encyclopediac wine list of Trentino DOCs. Best of all, it's open for Sunday lunch.

Casa del Caffe
CAFE

(Via San Pietro 38; ⊙7.30am-12.30pm & 3-7.30pm Mon-Sat) Follow your nose to this coffee bar and chocolate shop for Trento's best espresso. Beans are roasted on the premises and the crowded shelves feature some of the country's best boutique products.

Osteria della Mal'Ombra
BAR

(www.osteriadellamalombra.com; Corso III Novembre 43; ⊙8.30am-2.30pm & 3.30pm-midnight Mon-Fri, 4pm-1am Sat) Join the university set for good wine and grappa, possibly some spirited political debate, and music on Tuesdays.

Cafe de la Paix
BAR

(www.cafedelapaix.org; Passaggio Teatro Osele; ⊙10am-midnight Mon-Sat, 5.30pm-midnight Sun) With its vintage aesthetic and laidback staff, this hideaway bar, off Via Suffragio, is a departure from Trento's conservative norm. Students start the day here with toast (€2), and the party gets going later with an international menu of snacks, well-priced *spritzes* and a rock-and-roll soundtrack.

Shopping

Raccolta Differenziata
FASHION

(☑ 0461 26 12 92; Via Malpaga 16-18; ⊙3pm-7pm Mon, 11am-7pm Tue-Sat) Luigi Andreis has long been Trento's super stylist and it's worth seeking out his shop, tucked away in a quiet courtyard of an ancient *palazzo* from the 1400s, to experience his fascinating eye and treat yourself to one of the beautiful pieces from mostly Italian designers.

Information

Hospital (☑ 0461 90 31 11; Largo Medaglie d'Oro 9)

Police Station (☑ 0461 89 95 11; Piazza della Mostra 3)

Post Office (Piazza Vittoria; ⊙8am-6.30pm Mon-Fri, to 12.30pm Sat)

Tourist Office (☑ 0461 21 60 00; www.apt.trento.it; Via Manci 2; ⊙9am-7pm)

Getting There & Away

Trento is well connected. Regular trains leave from the main train station (Piazza Dante) for the following destinations:

Bologna (€15.10, 3¼ hours, every two hours)

Bolzano (€6.40, 30 minutes, three per hour)

Venice (€14.65, 2½ hours, hourly)

Verona (€7.70, one hour, every 30 minutes)

Next door to the main station, the Trento–Malè–Marilleva train line connects the city with Cles in the Val di Non.

From the **InterCity bus station** (Via Andrea Pozzo), local bus company **Trentino Trasporti** (☑ 0461 82 10 00; www.ttesercizio.it) runs buses to and from Madonna di Campiglio, San Martino di Castrozza, Molveno, Canazei and Rovereto.

Rovereto

POP 37,550

In the winter of 1769, Leopold Mozart and his soon-to-be-famous musical son visited Rovereto and found it to be 'rich in diligent people engaged in viticulture and the weaving of silk'. The area is no longer known for silk, but still produces some outstanding wines, including the inky, cherry-scented Marzemino (the wine's scene-stealing appearance in *Don Giovanni* suggests it may have been a Mozart family favourite). Those on a musical pilgrimage come for the annual **Mozart Festival** (www.festivalmozartrovereto.it; ⊙Jul) in August. The town that Mozart knew still has its haunting, tightly coiled streets, but it's the shock of the new that now lures most: Rovereto is home to one of Italy's best contemporary and 20th-century art museums.

◎ Sights

★ Museo di Arte Moderna e Contemporanea Rovereto ART GALLERY
(MART; ☑ 0464 43 88 87; english.mart.trento.it; Corso Bettini 43; adult/reduced €11/7, incl Casa del Depero €13/9; ⊙ 10am-6pm Tue-Thu, Sat & Sun, to 9pm Fri) The four-floor, 12,000-sq-metre steel, glass and marble behemoth, care of the Ticinese architect Mario Botta, is both imposing and human in scale, with mountain light gently filling a central atrium from a soaring cupola. It's home to some huge 20th-century works, including Warhol's *Four Marilyns* (1962), several Picassos and a clutch of contemporary art stars, including Bill Viola, Kara Walker, Arnuf Rainer and a whopping-great Anslem Keifer.

Italian work is, naturally, also well represented, with excellent pieces from Giacomo Balla, Giorgio Morandi, Giorgio de Chirico, Lucio Fontana and Piero Manzoni. Temporary exhibitions cast a broad net, from easygoing shows of Monet or Modigliani to cutting-edge contemporary surveys.

Casa del Depero MUSEUM
(☑ 0424 60 04 35; Via Portici 38; adult/reduced €7/4, incl MART admission €13/9; ⊙ 10am-6pm Tue-Sun) Those Futurists were never afraid of a spot of self-aggrandisement and local lad Fortunato Depero was no exception. This self-designed museum was first launched shortly before his death in 1960, and was then restored and reopened by MART in recent years. The obsessions of early-20th-century Italy mix nostalgically, somewhat unnervingly, with a historic past – bold tapestries and machine-age-meets-troubadour-era furniture decorate a made-over medieval town house.

Church of San Marco CHURCH
(Piazza San Marco; ⊙ 8.30am-noon & 2-7pm) It was here that the 13-year-old Wolfgang Mozart wowed the Roveretini.

✗ Eating & Drinking

Osteria del Pettirosso WINE BAR
(www.osteriadelpettirosso.com; Corso Bettini 24; ⊙ 10am-11pm Mon-Sat) There's a moody downstairs dining room but most people come here for the blackboard menu of wines by the glass, many from small producers, a plate of cheese (€8) or a couple of *crostone all lardo* (toasts with cured pork fat).

ⓘ Information

Tourist Office (☑ 0464 43 03 63; www.visitrovereto.it; Piazza Rosmini 16; ⊙ 9am-1pm & 2-6pm Mon-Sat, 10am-4pm Sun) The tourist office has lots of information on Rovereto, town maps and details of cycling trails.

ⓘ Getting There & Away

Rovereto is around 15 minutes by train from Trento on the Bologna–Brennero line (€6), or a pleasantly rural bus ride (€3.15, 45 minutes).

Brenta Dolomites

The Brenta group lies like a rocky island to the west of the main Dolomite range. Protected by the Parco Naturale Adamello-Brenta, these sharp, majestic peaks are well known among mountaineers for their sheer cliffs and tricky ascents. They are home to some of the world's most famous *vie ferrate* routes, including the Via Ferrata delle Bocchette, pioneered by trailblazing British climber Francis Fox Tuckett in the 1860s.

On the eastern side of the Brenta group is the Altipiano della Paganella, a high plateau offering some skiing and a range of outdoor adventures. On the densely forested western side is the popular resort of Madonna di Campiglio. The wiggly S421, S237 and S239 linking the two make for some scenic driving. Regular bus connections with Trento are plentiful in the high seasons.

The **Superskirama pass** (www.skirama.it; 1/3/7 days €49/142/290) covers the entire Brenta.

Altipiano Della Paganella
POP 5000 / ELEV 2098M

Less than an hour's drive northwest of Trento, this dress-circle plateau looks out onto the towering Brenta Dolomites. The Altipiano incorporates five small villages: ski resort **Fai della Paganella**, touristy **Andalo**, lakeside **Molveno** and little **Cavedago** and **Spormaggiore**.

◎ Sights & Activities

Parco Naturale Adamello Brenta PARK
(www.pnab.it) FREE Parco Naturale Adamello Brenta is a wild and beautiful park encompassing more than 80 lakes and the vast Adamello glacier which was once home to

the Alps' only brown bears. Although this became a protected area in 1967, by then bear numbers had dwindled to just three. Beginning in 1999, park authorities set about reintroducing Alpine brown bears from Slovenia. The first cubs were born in the park in 2002 and more are born every winter.

Bears aside, the 620-sq-km park – Trentino's largest protected area – is home to ibexes, red deer, marmots, chamois and 82 bird species, along with 1200 different mountain flowers, including two (*Nigritella luschmannie* and *Eryshimum auranthiacum*) that are unique to the area. This wildlife thrives around the banks of Lago di Tovel, set deep in a forest some 30km north of Spormaggiore in the park's heart. An easy one-hour walking trail encircles the once red lake. The lakeside visitors centre has extensive information on other walks.

Casa dell'orso Spormaggiore　ANIMAL RESERVE
(☑ 0461 65 36 22; Via Alt Spaur 6; ⊙ 9am-12.30pm & 2-6pm Tue-Sun Jun-Sep, book for other periods) **FREE** This is the top place to see the Parco Naturale Adamello Brenta's 20-odd population of brown bears. There are cute displays for kids, and you can book to see the bears in winter dormancy via infrared camera. It's 15km northeast of Molveno.

Paganella Ski Area　SKIING
The Paganella ski area is accessible from Andalo by cable car and Fai della Paganella by chairlift. It has two cross-country skiing trails and 50km of downhill ski slopes, ranging from beginner-friendly green runs to the heart-pounding black.

Gruppo Guide Alpine Dolomiti di Brenta　GUIDE
(☑ 0461 58 53 53; www.mountainfriends.it) Organises rock climbing and guided walks in summer, and ski-mountaineering, ice climbing and snowshoeing excursions in winter.

🛏 Sleeping & Eating

The plateau's five villages have a huge stock of hotels; alternatively, check with the tourist offices for details of the equally numerous farm stays and self-catering apartments.

Agriturismo Florandonole　FARMSTAY €
(☑ 0461 58 10 39; www.florandonole.it; Via ai Dossi 22, Fai della Paganella; d €85; P 🛜 🐕) 🍃 This modern farmhouse may look like every other from the outside. Inside, however, smart local wood furniture and crisp goosedown duvets give this place a luxury feel. If the views over fields towards the Brenta Dolomites or Paganella ranges beckon, grab a complimentary mountain bike. This is also a working honey farm, with hives, production facilities and a shop to explore.

Camping Spiaggia　CAMPGROUND €
(☑ 0461 58 69 78; www.campingmolveno.it; Via Lungolago 25, Molveno; camping €37, bungalow €60-150; ⊙ reception 9am-noon & 2-7pm year-round; P @ 🌊) These pleasant sites on the shores of Lago di Molveno come with free use of the neighbouring outdoor pool, tennis court and table tennis. It's an easy stroll into Molveno's bustling village centre, and entertainment and water sports are on tap in high summer.

Al Penny　TRENTINO, PIZZA €€
(☑ 0461 58 52 51; Viale Trento 23, Andalo; meals €28; ⊙ 11am-2.30pm & 5pm-midnight) First impressions may clock the decor as a little too Alpine-for-dummies, but this is a genuinely cosy spot. A glass of warming Marzemino sets the scene, then out come authentic and tasty Trentino specialities – venison *ragù* (meat and tomato sauce) with pine nuts, *taiadele smalzade* (pan-fried fat noodles) or mushroom *canederli*, all served with home-made bread. The pizza also rates.

ℹ Information

All these tourist offices share a website (www. visitdolomitipaganella.it).

Andalo Tourist Office (☑ 0461 58 58 36; Piazza Dolomiti 1; ⊙ 9am-12.30pm & 3-6.30pm Mon-Sat, 9.30am-12.30pm Sun) The main office with good information for both winter and summer activities.

Fai della Paganella Tourist Office (☑ 0461 58 31 30; Via Villa; ⊙ 9am-12.30pm & 3-6.30pm Mon-Tue & Thu-Sat)

Guardia Medica Notturna (☑ 0461 58 56 37; Piazza Centrale 1, Andalo; ⊙ 8pm-8am) After-hours medical call-out service.

Molveno Tourist Office (☑ 0461 58 69 24; Piazza Marconi 5; ⊙ 9am-12.30pm & 3-6.30pm Mon-Sat)

ℹ Getting There & Around

Free ski buses serve the area in winter.

Trentino Trasporti (☑ 0461 82 10 00; www. ttesercizio.it) Runs buses between all five villages and Trento (€3.30 to €4.70, 1–2½ hours, up to nine daily) and services to Madonna di Campiglio (€5.70) and Riva del Garda (€6.50) on Lago di Garda; tourist offices have timetables.

Madonna Di Campiglio & Pinzolo

POP 700 / ELEV 1522M

Welcome to the Dolomites' bling belt, where ankle-length furs are standard après-ski wear and the formidable downhill runs often a secondary concern to the social whirl and Michelin-starred dining. Austrian royalty set the tone in the 19th century, in particular Franz Joseph and wife Elisabeth (Sissi). This early celeb patronage is commemorated in late February, when fireworks blaze and costumed pageants waltz through town for the annual **Habsburg Carnival**. Despite the traffic jams and mall-like hotel complexes, the town is overlooked by a pretty stone church and the jutting battlements of the Brenta Dolomites beyond. In summer this is an ideal base for hikers and *via ferrata* enthusiasts.

Pinzolo (population 2000, elevation 800m), in a lovely valley 16km south, misses out on the most spectacular views but has a lively historic centre and quite a few less tickets on itself.

Sights & Activities

Chiesa di San Vigilio   CHURCH
Pinzolo's beautifully sited 16th-century Chiesa di San Vigilio merits a visit for its *danza macabra* (dance of death) decor.

Val di Genova   VALLEY
North of Pinzolo is the entrance to the Val di Genova, often described as one of the Alps' most beautiful valleys. It's great walking country, lined with a series of spectacular waterfalls. Four mountain huts strung out along the valley floor make overnight stays an option – Pinzolo's tourist office has details.

Funivie Madonna di Campiglio   CABLE CAR
(☎0465 44 77 44; www.funiviecampiglio.it; round-trip summer €8.30-12.60) A network of cable cars take skiers and boarders from Madonna to its numerous ski runs and a snowboarding park in winter and to walking and mountain-biking trails in summer. In **Campo Carlo Magno**, 2km north of Madonna, the Cabinovia Grostè takes walkers to the Passo Grostè (2440m). Brenta's most famous *via ferrata*, the **Via Bocchetta di Tuckett** (trail No 305), leaves from the cable-car station.

Funivia Pinzolo   CABLE CAR
(☎0465 50 12 56; www.doss.to; Via Nepomuceno Bolognini 84; one way/return summer €6/9; ⊙8.30am-12.30pm & 2-6pm mid-Dec–Apr & Jun–mid-Sep) This cable car climbs to the 2100m-high **Doss del Sabion**, stopping at midstation **Pra Rodont** en route. Mountain bike hire is available.

Sleeping

Budget beds in Madonna are nonexistent in winter, and most midrange hotels insist on at least half-board and minimum stays during high season. Commuting to the ski fields from the Val di Sole is a doable alternative, and Pinzolo has a few more affordable options.

IRON WAYS

During WWI, the Italian army was engaged in a lengthy conflict against their Austrian foes on a vertiginous battlefront that sliced across the Dolomites, and the scars of this brutal campaign are still etched indelibly over the Alpine landscape.

In order to maximise ease of movement up in the rugged, perilous peaks, the two armies attached ropes and ladders across seemingly impregnable crags in a series of fixed-protection climbing paths known as *vie ferrate* (iron ways). Renovated with steel rungs, bridges and heavy-duty wires after the war, the *vie ferrate* evolved into a cross between standard hiking and full-blown rock climbing, allowing non-mountaineers, with the right equipment, to experience such challenging terrain.

Madonna di Campiglio and Cortina d'Ampezzo are the gateways to the most spectacular routes, but *vie ferrate* exist all over the Dolomites.

From mid-June to mid-September, a network of mountain huts offering food and accommodation line the route – **Tourism Südtirol** (www.trekking.suedtirol.info) maintains a comprehensive list. Tourist offices can provide maps and details of skill level required, and descriptions of each route can be found at www.dolomiti-altevie.it.

Camping Parco Adamello CAMPGROUND €
(2 0465 50 17 93; www.campingparcoadamello.it; Località Magnabò, Pinzolo; camping €40, apt s/d €45/90; ⊙year-round; P) Beautifully situated within the national park 1km north of Pinzolo, this campground is a natural starting point for outdoor adventures such as skiing, snowshoeing, walking and biking. There are also weekly apartment rentals.

Chalet Fogajard AGRITURISMO €€
(www.chaletfogajard.it; Località Fogajard 36, Madonna di Campiglio; d half-board €190; ☎) ✦ If you're looking for a mountain retreat, this six-room Alpine idyl will fit the bill. Its remote location, down a steep dirt track way south of Madonna's resort row, is stupefyingly beautiful and blissfully silent. Rooms have a craft ethos that seems from another era and an atmospheric dining room delivers hearty, wholesome locally sourced meals.

With uninterrupted views of a deep, wooded valley and the jagged Brenta peaks beyond, balcony rooms are worth the extra euros.

Hotel Chalet Del Brenta HOTEL €€
(2 0465 44 31 59; www.hotelchaletdelbrenta.com; Via Castelletto Inferiore 4, Madonna di Campiglio; s/d €95/130; P ✳ ☎ ☂ ☖) This large place offers smart, comfortable rooms, all with balconies and the full-range of resort services, including a kids' club. It's in one of Madonna's most picturesque streets, close to the village but quiet; there's a speedy shuttle service to the lifts.

DV Chalet DESIGN HOTEL €€€
(2 0465 44 31 91; www.dvchalet.it; Via Castelletto Inferiore 10, Madonna di Campiglio; d €300; P ✳ ☎ ☂) This is the latest entry in the Madonna ultraluxe hotel stakes, with friendly staff and a quiet, wooded setting. The bar keeps the Milanese fashion set happy come *aperitivo* hour, there's a worthy Michelin-starred restaurant, Dolomieu, and upstairs guests are cocooned in beautiful, earthy rooms.

✗ Eating & Drinking

Le Roi TRENTINO €
(2 0465 44 30 75; www.ristoranteleroicampiglio. com; Via Cima Tosa 40, Madonna di Campiglio; meals €25, pizza €5-11; ⊙noon-3pm & 6-11pm) Touristy, tick, loud and raucous, tick. Yes, this is a typical ski town restaurant, but it's fun, friendly, and affordable. The polenta, mushrooms and fried cheese platter won't

win any prizes for presentation but it is an unbeatable post-piste belly warmer.

Dolomiti PUB
(2 0465 44 06 13; Via degli Sfulmini 21; ⊙8am-2am) This is a fabulously down-to-earth 'local' with big matches on the TV, *panini* well into the night and staff that keep the beers flowing with a smile.

ℹ Information

Madonna Tourist Office (2 0465 44 75 01; www.campigliodolomiti.it; Via Pradalago 4; ⊙9am-12.30pm & 3-7pm Mon-Sat, 10am-noon Sun) Madonna's tourist office teams up with the Parco Naturale Adamello-Brenta in high summer to run guided thematic walks.
Pinzolo Tourist Office (2 0465 50 10 07; www.campigliodolomiti.it; Piazzale Ciciamimo; ⊙9am-1pm & 2-6pm Wed-Mon)
Tourist Medical Service (2 0465 44 08 81; Centro Rainalter, Madonna; ⊙8am-8pm early Dec–Easter)

ℹ Getting There & Away

Madonna di Campiglio and Pinzolo are accessible by bus from Trento (€6.80, 1½ hours, five daily), Brescia (€13, 1½ hours) and Milan (€24, 3¾ hours, one daily). A private transfer service also operates year-round; see the tourist office website for details.
Flyski (2 0461 39 11 11; www.flyskishuttle.com; one way/return €25/39) From mid-December to mid-April, the Flyski shuttle runs weekly services to Madonna and Pinzolo from Verona, Bergamo, Treviso and Venice airports.

Val di Non & Val di Sole

Sandwiched between the Brenta group and Parco Nazionale dello Stelvio, these Italian-speaking farming valleys are an easy train ride from Trento.

Val di Non

The first thing you notice about Val di Non is the apple trees – their gnarly, trellised branches stretch for miles, and in spring their fragrant blossoms scent the air. Craggy castles dot the surrounding rises, including the stunning Castel Thun (2 0461 49 28 29; www.castelthun.com; adult/reduced €6/4; ⊙10am-5pm Tue-Sun). The valley is centred on Cles, whose tourist office (2 0463 42 28 83; Corso Dante 30, Cles; ⊙9am-12.30pm & 3-6pm Mon-Sat, 9am-noon Sun Jul & Aug) is just off the main road through town.

Italy's apple giant, Melinda, is a valley girl. A couple of villages on from Cles, near Mollaro, **Melinda Mondo** (☑ 0463 46 92 99; www.melinda.it; Via della Cooperazione 21; ⊙ 8.30am-12.30pm & 3-7pm Mon-Sat, guided visits Oct-Jun) conducts tours of the orchards and processing plants and has a cheery shop selling apples and all sorts of apple-related products. Look out also for the big cheese next door, the home of **Trentingrana**, Trentino's sweet, subtle 'Parmesan-style' Grana.

Val di Sole

Leaving Cles in the rearview mirror, the apple orchards draw you west into the aptly named Val di Sole (Valley of the Sun) tracing the course of the foaming river Noce, with its charming main town of **Malè**. This valley is renowned for the full complement of outdoor pursuits and is popular with young *trentini*. The Noce offers great rafting and fishing.

In winter, the valley can provide good alternative accommodation to the Brenta resorts.

🏃 Activities

Centro Rafting Val di Sole   RAFTING
(☑ 0463 97 32 78; www.raftingcenter.it; Via Gole 105, Dimaro; ⊙ Jun-Sep) Runs rafting trips (from €39), as well as kayaking, canyoning, Nordic walking and other adventures.

Cicli Andreis   CYCLING
(☑ 0463 90 28 22; www.andreissnc.com; Via Conci 19, Malè; ⊙ 8.30am-noon & 3-7pm Mon-Sat) Offering a huge range of bikes for hire, and friendly, knowledgeable service, Cicli Andreis is handily located just off Malè's main street. Daily/weekly mountain bike rental costs from €20/55.

Dolomiti di Brenta Bike   BICYCLE TRAIL
(www.dolomitibrentabike.it; per bike €2) Sole guards a flattish 35km section of the Brenta Dolomite Bike Loop and there is a special bike train June to September, allowing cyclists to step on and alight when they wish.

🛏 Sleeping

Agritur il Tempo delle Mele   AGRITURISMO €
(☑ 0463 90 13 89; www.agriturdellemele.it; Via Strada Provinciale 65, Caldes; s/d €80/110; 🅿🛜👪) 🍽 This family-owned farm offers both bright, comfortable, modern rooms and easy access to the Folgarida-Marilleva

and Pejo 3000 ski areas, from where you can ski on to Madonna di Campiglio.

Dolomiti Camping Village   CAMPGROUND €
(☑ 0463 97 43 32; www.campingdolomiti.com; Via Gole 105, Dimaro; camping €45, d apt €80; ⊙ mid-May–mid-Oct & Dec-Easter; 🅿@🐕👪) Riverside and adjacent to the rafting centre, the well-kept campsites and bungalows come with access to a wellness centre, indoor and outdoor pools, volleyball courts and trampolines.

❶ Information

Malè Tourist Office (☑ 0463 90 12 80; www.valdisole.net; Piazza Regina Elena 19; ⊙ 3-7pm Mon-Sat) Has good information on the entire valley and can advise you on ski facilities and walking trails in nearby Stelvio.

Val di Fiemme

In a region where few valleys speak the same dialect, let alone agree on the same cheese recipe, the Val di Fiemme's proud individualism is above and beyond. In the 12th century, independently minded local noblemen even set up their own quasi-republic here, the Magnificent Community of Fiemme, and the ethos and spirit of the founders lives on.

From Cavalese, skiers can take a cable car up to the **Cermis ski area** (2229m), part of the extensive Dolomiti Superski region. There is a Fiemme-Obereggen pass (1/3/7 days €41/113/214), or Dolomiti Superski passes can be used. Cavalese's tourist office acts as a contact point for local alpine guide groups who organise, among other things, mountaineering ascents on Pale di San Martino, Cima della Madonna and Sass Maor, a 120km-long high-altitude skiing excursion.

◉ Sights

Palazzo Vescovile   PALACE
(Piazza Battisti) The modern day Magnificent Community of Fiemme is headquartered in the wonderfully frescoed Palazzo Vescovile in Val di Fiemme's main town of Cavalese. The building is worthy of an admiring look.

🛏 Sleeping & Eating

Agritur la Regina dei Prati   AGRITURISMO €
(www.lareginadeiprati.it; Via Margherita Dellafiore 17, Masi di Cavalese; s/d €55/88; 🅿✳🛜👪) Across the river in a village 'suburb' of Cavalese, this is a relaxed, family-run place with spacious contemporary rooms with nice

extras like heated floors and balconies. The rustic setting is magnificent and is ski-in during winter.

⭐ **Park Hotel Azalea**   SPA HOTEL €€
(☑0462 34 01 09; www.parkhotelazalea.it; Via delle Cesure 1; half-board d €90-180; [P][🛜][♿])
🖋 This hotel combines impeccable eco-credentials, super stylish interiors and a warm, welcoming vibe. Rooms are individually decorated and make use of soothing, relaxing colours; some have mountain views, others look across the village's pretty vegetable gardens.

Children's facilities eschew plastic and tat for wood and natural textiles, and there are little daily extras like a groaning afternoon tea spread (all organic, of course). Vegetarians and vegans are welcomed and well catered for.

El Molin   GASTRONOMIC €€€
(☑0462 34 00 74; www.elmolin.info; Piazza Battisti 11, Cavalese; meals €40, degustations €70-110; ☉Wed-Mon noon-2.30pm & 7-11pm) A legend in the valley, this Michelin-starred old mill sits at the historic heart of Cavalese. Downstairs, next to the old waterwheels, you will find playful gastronomic dishes featuring local, seasonal ingredients. Streetside, the wine bar does baked-to-order eggs with Trentingrana or truffles, burgers, hearty mains and creative desserts from €12.

❶ Information

Val di Fiemme Tourist Office (☑0462 24 11 11; www.visitfiemme.it; Via Bronzetti 60; ☉9am-noon & 3.30-7pm Mon-Sat)

Val di Fassa

Val di Fassa is Trentino's only Ladin-speaking valley, framed by the stirring peaks of the **Gruppo del Sella** to the north, the **Catinaccio** to the west and the **Marmolada** (3342m) to the southeast. The valley has two hubs: **Canazei** (popu-

lation 1866, elevation 1465m), beautifully sited but verging on over development, and the pretty riverside village of **Moena** (population 2690, elevation 1114m), more down to earth and increasingly environmentally conscious. Fassa is the nexus of Italy's cross-country skiing scene. Italian cross-country champ Christian Zorzi hails from Moena and the town also plays host to the sport's most illustrious mass-participation race, the annual **Marcialonga** (www.marcialonga.it).

Dolomiti Superski passes are valid; alternatively there are separate passes for either the Val di Fassa/Carezza or the Tre Valli (1/3/7 days €42/125/230) covering the Moena area and San Pellegrino valley.

◎ Sights & Activities

Variety is the spice of life for skiers here, with 120km of downhill and cross-country runs, as well as challenging Alpine tours and the Sella Ronda ski circuit. In summer, you can ski down the Marmolada glacier.

The Gruppo del Sella is approached from **Passo Pordoi**, where a cable car travels to almost 3000m. The best approach to the Catinaccio group is from **Vigo di Fassa**, 11km southwest of Canazei near Pozza di Fassa; a cable car climbs to an elevation of 2000m, dropping you off near the cheerful mountain hut Baita Checco.

For gentler summertime rambles, ask at the tourist office for the brochure *Low-level Walks in the Fassa Valley*, which outlines 29 walks (1.5km to 8km long), including visits to historic Ladin landmarks.

🛏 Sleeping

Garnì Ladin   B&B €
(☑0462 76 44 93; www.ladin.it; Strada de la Piazedela 9, Vigo di Fassa; s/d €70/100; [P][🛜]) Right in the middle of villagey Vigo di Fassa, midway between Moena and Canazei, the rooms here are full of sweetly kitsch Ladinalia but have ultramodern bathrooms.

Villa Kofler   DESIGN HOTEL €€
(☑0462 75 04 44; www.villakofler.it; Via Dolomiti 63, Campitello di Fassa; d €180-220; [P][🛜]) 🖋 An intimate hotel in a valley of giants, just outside of the Canazei bustle; choose from rooms that range across various current design trends and tastes. There's a little gym, a library and, bliss, in-room infrared saunas.

ALPINE RESOURCES

➡ Find a mountain guide at www.bergfuehrer-suedtirol.it.

➡ Lonely Planet's *Hiking in Italy* details five classic Dolomites hikes.

➡ Cicerone (www.cicerone.co.uk) publishes specialist route guides.

WINTER WONDERLAND

The jagged peaks of the Dolomites, or Dolomiti, span the provinces of Trentino and Alto Adige, jutting into neighbouring Veneto. Europeans flock here in winter for highly hospitable resorts, sublime natural settings and extensive, well-coordinated ski networks. Come for downhill, cross-country and snowboarding or get ready for *sci alpinismo*, an adrenalin-spiking mix of skiing and mountaineering, freeride and a range of other winter adventure sports.

The Sella Ronda, a 40km circumnavigation of the Gruppo di Sella range (3151m, at Piz Boé) – linked by various cable cars and chairlifts – is one of the Alps' iconic ski routes. The tour takes in four passes and their surrounding valleys; Alto Adige's Val Gardena, Val Badia, Arabba (in the Veneto) and Trentino's Val di Fassa. Experienced skiers can complete the clockwise (orange) or anticlockwise (green) route in a day.

The region's two flexible passes are Dolomiti Superski (www.dolomitisuperski.com; high season 3/6 days €144/254), covering the east, with access to 450 lifts and some 1200km of ski runs, spread over 12 resorts, and Superskirama (www.skirama.it; 1/3/7 days €47/136/277), covering the western Brenta Dolomites, with 150 lifts, 380km of slopes and eight resorts.

✕ Eating & Drinking

Sausage Stand FAST FOOD €
(Piazza Marconi, Canazei; sausages €4; ⊙ 11am-7pm Sep-Jun, 10am-10pm Jul & Aug) The fork-wielding Ladin-sausage cooks are a Canazei institution, with this roadside stall just by the bus stop, drawing queues of ravenous skiers all winter long and keeping hikers happy into the night in summer.

El Paél TRENTINO €€
(☑ 0462 60 14 33; www.elpael.com; Via Roma 58, Canazei; meals €30; ⊙ noon-2.30pm & 6.30-10pm Tue-Sun) This *osteria tipica trentina* was known for its traditional Ladin specialities of the valley, but now mixes this up with a contemporary Italian slickness. Luckily for the old fans this works: dishes are carefully prepared and always tasty.

Kusk La Locanda BAR
(Via dei Colli 7, Moena; ⊙ 8am-2am Wed-Mon) Legendary throughout the Val di Fassa for après-ski, this four-way split between a pizzeria, American bar, trash disco and Italian restaurant still manages to maintain a Ladin cosiness.

❶ Information

Canazei Tourist Office (☑ 0462 60 96 00; www.fassa.com; Piazza Marconi 5; ⊙ 8.30-12.30pm & 3-7pm daily Jul-Mar, 8.30am-12.30pm & 2.30-6.30pm Mon-Sat Apr-Jun)
Moena Tourist Office (☑ 0462 60 97 70; www.fassa.com; Piazza del Navalge 4; ⊙ 8.30-12.30pm & 3-7pm daily Jul-Mar, 8.30am-12.30pm & 2.30-6.30pm Mon-Sat Apr-Jun)

❶ Getting There & Away

Free ski buses also serve the region in winter.
Trentino Trasporti (☑ 0461 82 10 00; www.ttesercizio.it) Runs buses to the Val di Fassa from Trento year-round (€6.80, 1½ to 2½ hours).
SAD (www.sad.it) Buses from Bolzano (€6, 1½ hours) and the Val Gardena (€5, 2½ hours) from June to mid-September.

ALTO ADIGE (SÜDTIROL)

Bolzano (Bozen)

POP 103,500 / ELEV 265M

The provincial capital of Alto Adige (Südtirol, or South Tyrol) is anything but provincial. Its quality of life – one of the highest in Italy – is reflected in its openness, youthful energy and an all-pervading greenness. A stage-set-pretty backdrop of rotund green hills sets off rows of pastel-painted town houses. Bicycles ply riverside paths and wooden market stalls are laid out with Alpine cheese, speck (cured ham) and dark, seeded loaves. German may be the first language of 95% of the region, but Bolzano is an anomaly. Today its Italian-speaking majority – a legacy of Mussolini's brutal Italianisation program of the 1920s and the more recent siren call of education and employment opportunities – looks both north and south for inspiration.

◉ Sights

★ Museo Archeologico dell'Alto Adige
MUSEUM

(✆0471 32 01 00; www.iceman.it; Via Museo 43; adult/reduced €9/7; ⊙10am-6pm Tue-Sun) The star of the Museo Archeologico dell'Alto Adige is Ötzi, the Iceman, with almost the entire museum being given over to the Copper Age mummy. Kept in a temperature-controlled 'igloo' room, he can be viewed through a small window (peer closely enough and you can make out faintly visible tattoos on his legs). Ötzi's clothing – a wonderful get-up of patchwork leggings, rush-matting cloak and fur cap – and other belongings are also displayed.

Various exhibitions explore his discovery, the world he lived in and his untimely death.

Messner Mountain Museum
MUSEUM

(MMM Firmian; ✆0471 63 31 45; www.messner-mountain-museum.it; Via Castel Firmiano 53; adult/reduced €10/8; ⊙10am-6pm Fri-Wed Mar-Nov) The imposing Castel Firmiano, dating back to AD 945, is the centrepiece of mountaineer Reinhold Messner's five museums. Based around humankind's relationship with the mountains across all cultures, the architecture itself suggests the experience of shifting altitudes, and requires visitors to traverse hundreds of stairs and mesh walkways. The collection is idiosyncratic, but when it works, it's heady stuff. Messner's other museums are scattered across the region, including Ortles.

There's a shuttle from Piazza Walther in summer, or you can catch a taxi or take the suburban train to Ponte Adige/Sigmundskron (beware there is then a long walk up a truck-laden road).

Museion
ART GALLERY

(✆0471 22 34 13; www.museion.it; Via Dante 2; adult/reduced €7/3.50, Thu from 6pm free; ⊙10am-6pm Tue-Sun, to 10pm Thu) The city's contemporary art space is housed in a huge multifaceted glass cube, a brave architectural surprise that beautifully vignettes the old-town rooftops and surrounding mountains from within. There's an impressive permanent collection of international artwork; temporary shows are a testament to the local art scene's vibrancy, or often highlight an ongoing dialogue with artists and institutions from Austria and Germany. The river-facing cafe has a terrace perfect for a post-viewing *spritz*.

BZ '18-'45
MUSEUM

(✆324 5810106; www.monumenttovictory.com; Piazza Vittoria; ⊙11am-1pm & 2pm-5pm Tue & Wed, Fri-Sun, 3-9pm Thu summer, 10.30am-12.30pm & 2.30-4.30pm Tue-Sun winter) FREE This dense but visually seductive new museum explores Bolzano's turbulent interwar years via the history of the Fascist Monument to Victory, where it is sited. It's a thoughtful and overdue examination of a highly complex time in the city's past and covers the city's post-WWI handover to Italy and the later Nazi occupation. The displays about the radical urban transformation of the 1920s – part of Mussolini's 'Italianisation' project – are particularly fascinating.

Castel Roncolo
CASTLE

(Schloss Runkelstein; ✆0471 32 98 08; www.runkelstein.info; Via San Antonio 15; adult/child €8/5.50; ⊙10am-6pm Tue-Sun) This stunningly located castle was built in 1237 but is renowned for its 14th-century frescoes. These are particularly rare, with themes that are drawn from secular literature, including the tale of Tristan and Isolde, as well as depictions of day-to-day courtly life. In summer a free shuttle runs from Piazza Walter (ask at the tourist office for the schedule) or catch suburban bus 12 or 14.

Chiesa dei Domenicani
CHURCH

(Piazza Domenicani; ⊙9.30am-6pm Mon-Sat) The cloisters and chapel here feature touching, vibrant 14th-century frescoes by the Giotto school.

Cathedral
CATHEDRAL

(Piazza Parrocchia; ⊙9.30am-5.30pm Mon-Sat) This splendid Gothic cathedral is Bolzano's most emblematic building, its imposing spires backed by the equally Gothic peaks of the not-so-distant Dolomites.

Chiesa di Francescani
BUILDING

(Via dei Francescani) The 14th-century Chiesa di Francescani features beautiful cloisters and a magnificent Gothic altarpiece, carved in 1500 by Hans Klocker, in the Cappella della Beata Vergine (Chapel of the Blessed Virgin).

🏃 Activities

Bolzano's trio of cable cars whisk you up out of the city, affording spectacular views over the city and valley floor, then of terraced vineyards, tiny farms, ancient mountain chapels and towering peaks beyond. The respective villages are delightful destinations

Bolzano

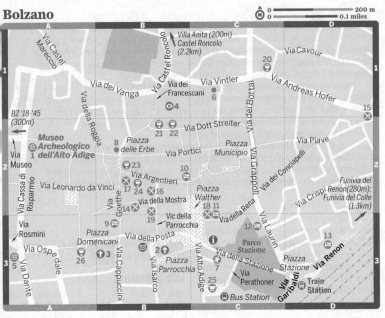

Bolzano

Top Sights

Sights

Activities, Courses & Tours

Sleeping

Eating

Drinking & Nightlife

in themselves or jumping off points for rambles or serious hikes. Walks can also be done from the city centre – ask at the tourist office for the map marked with the routes to Santa Maddalena and San Osvaldo.

Funivia del Renon   CABLE CAR
(Via Renon; one way/return €6/10) The journey over the Renon (Ritten) plateau to Soprabolzano (Oberbozen) runs along the world's longest single track, stretching for 4.56km, passing over eerie red earth pyramids.

Funivia del Colle   CABLE CAR
(Via Campegno 4; one way/return €4/6) This is the world's oldest cable car, dreamt up by a canny inn-keeper in 1908, with a pristine village awaiting at the top.

THE ICEMAN COMETH

When Austrian hikers stumbled upon a human corpse wedged into a melting glacier on Hauslabjoch Pass in 1991, they assumed they'd found the remains of an unfortunate mountaineer caught in a winter storm. But when the mummified body was removed and taken to a morgue, it was discovered to be over 5300 years old.

The male corpse – subsequently nicknamed Ötzi, or the Iceman – is the oldest mummified remains ever found in Europe, dating from an ancient Copper Age civilisation that lived in the Dolomites around the same time as ancient Egypt's founding. What Ötzi was actually doing 3200m up a glaciated mountainside, 52 centuries before alpinism became a serious sport, is still a matter of some debate.

Though initially claimed by the Austrian government, it was later ascertained that Ötzi had been unearthed 100m inside the Italian border on the Schnalstal glacier. After a brief diplomatic impasse and stabilisation work in Innsbruck, the mummy was returned to Italy, where it has been on display in Bolzano's Museo Archeologico dell'Alto Adige since 1998.

Funivia San Genesio CABLE CAR
(Via Sarentino; one way/return €3/5) An ultra-steep ascent takes you to the beautiful terraced village of San Genesio (Jenesien), where there are roof-of-the-world views and forest trails to follow.

Salewa Cube ROCK CLIMBING
(0471 188 68 67; www.salewa-cube.com; Via Waltraud-Gebert-Deeg, Bolzano Sud; adult/reduced €12/10; 9am-11pm) Part of the outdoor clothing empire's HQ, this is Italy's largest indoor climbing centre. There are over 2000m of climbing surface and 180 different routes. In good weather the enormous entrance is open, so climbing has an outdoor feel. Take bus 10A/B from the centre or ask at the tourist office for details of the summer shuttle.

Bike Rental CYCLING
(0471 99 75 78; Via della Stazione 2; 7.30am-7.45pm Easter-Oct) Bicycles can be picked up at the open-air bike rental stall near the train station. Rental is free, but bikes must be returned overnight and you'll need cash for a deposit and ID.

Tours

The tourist office organises free city tours in English and seasonal guided walks and gentle treks in Italian and German. For serious hiking information, contact one of the local walking associations.

Club Alpino Italiano WALKING
(0471 97 81 72; Piazza delle Erbe 46; 11am-1pm & 5-7pm Wed, 1-5pm Tue, Thu & Fri)

Alpine Information Office WALKING
(Alpenverein Südtirol; 0471 81 41 55; www.alpenverein.it; Galleria Vintler 16)

Sleeping

Villa Anita GUESTHOUSE €
(Via Castel Roncolo 16; d/family €68/75 shared bathroom; P) Although it's just a short walk from the historic centre, the surrounding gardens make this beautiful 1905 villa seem like you're already out in the countryside. Rooms are spacious and light, the shared bathrooms are modern and spotlessly maintained and the owner is gracious and kind. You can pay a little extra for a room with a balcony or for a self-catering apartment.

Goethe Guesthouse GUESTHOUSE €
(335 8258599, 070 58 38 346; www.bookingbolzano.com; Via Goethe 28; d €95, no breakfast) If you don't mind hopping down the stairs for breakfast to a *pasticceria* or the market for breakfast and don't need front desk or other hotel facilities, Ivan and Marco's historic town house rooms are super stylish. Contemporary furnishings are minimal but comfortable, while floorboards, subtle lighting and dramatic exposed stone adds atmosphere.

Youth Hostel Bolzano HOSTEL €
(Jugendherberge Bozen; 0471 30 08 65; bozen.jugendherberge.it; Via Renon 23; dm/s €24.50/32;) The three- and four-bed dorms in this airy and friendly hostel are well designed and configured for privacy. Single rooms can squeeze in a foldout if needed. Rooms at the back have balconies, but sadly no longer any view.

Hotel Figl   HOTEL €€
(☑0471 97 84 12; www.figl.net; Piazza del Grano 9; s/d €95/135; ❄@) Affable staff and a busy downstairs bar lend this place a home-away-from-home feel. Mod-Euro rooms are fabulously cosy and look out over a pretty square or town rooftops. Business travellers and long-stay guests can negotiate discounts.

Hotel Greif   DESIGN HOTEL €€
(☑0471 31 80 00; www.greif.it; Piazza Walther; s/d €140/190; ❄🕾) Tumbling golden text courtesy of the troubled poet Ezra Pound greets you in the stairwell (this was, it seems, an 'art hotel' long before its modern makeover). Rooms here are generously proportioned, full of light and richly draped; all include a bath. Guests can use the lush gardens at parent **Parkhotel Laurin**, just down the lane, for cocktails or a swim.

★ Parkhotel Laurin   HOTEL €€€
(☑0471 31 10 00; www.laurin.it; Via Laurin 4; s €95-125, d €130-250; P❄🕾🏊) Set in its own lush gardens in the centre of town, this five-star hotel has large rooms endowed with a weighty, old-fashioned opulence and staff that mesh haute-professionalism with relaxed Alpine charm. There's a distinct individual style and contemporary sensibility throughout though, with an idiosyncratic mix of original artworks, Tyrolean antiques and 1980s Memphis pieces.

The splendid ground floor is home to what's considered one of Bolzano's best restaurants and a dark baronial bar that bustles from early morning to late at night.

✕ Eating

Redolent of rural mountain life one minute, Habsburg splendour the next, Bolzano's restaurants – often in the guise of a traditional wood-panelled dining room called a *stube* – are a profound reminder of just how far north you've come. Goat or rabbit is roasted, bone-warming broths hide *canederli* (dumplings), venison finds its way into gulasch, and speck (the region's IGP cured ham, cold-smoked and juniper- and pepper-scented) turns up in everything bar dessert. Window displays in the city's many *konditorei* (pastry shops) brim with Sachertorte, cheese strudels, *krapfen* (doughnuts) and earthy buckwheat-and-berry cakes. Bakers ply dark, dense seed-studded breads, including *schüttelbrot*, a crispy spiced-rye flat bread. Pick up produce from the daily street market on Piazza delle Erbe.

Vögele   SÜDTIROLEAN €
(☑0471 97 39 38; Via Goethe 3; meals €25; ☺noon-4pm & 6-11pm) Dating back to 1277 and owned by the same family since 1840, this multi-level, antique-stuffed restaurant is well loved for its schnitzels and steaks along with local favourites risotto with rabbit *ragù* and rosemary, or jugged venison with polenta. There's some good vegetarian options and much of the produce is organic. The attached bar (☺9am-1am) is pleasantly rowdy too.

Trattoria da Silvio   TRATTORIA €
(☑0471 32 40 82; Vicolo della Parrocchia 2a; meals €25; ☺10am-3pm & 6pm-midnight) Locals pack out this quirky, cosy place for traditional Italian fare. The menu may eschew the Tyrolean, but brims with equally satisfying regional dishes, including a killer risotto done with whatever is in season.

Gasthaus Fink   SÜDTIROLEAN €
(☑0471 97 50 47; Via della Mostra 9; meals €22; ☺noon-2pm & 7-9.30pm Thu-Mon, noon-2pm Wed) Fink's dining room is a calm, contemporary take on *stube* style where you can fill up on local comfort food that's cooked with care, including a €14 nightly special. A great lunch choice, with pasta and *canederli* under €10.

★ Zur Kaiserkron   MODERN SÜDTIROLEAN €€
(☑0471 98 02 14; www.kaiserkron.bz; Piazza della Mostra 2; meals €45; ☺noon-2.30pm & 7-9.30pm Mon-Sat) Refined but unfussy takes on regional favourites fill the menu at this calm and elegant dining room, and excellent produce is allowed to shine. It's tempting to just choose a selection from their interesting starters – say spelt ravioli with fresh curd cheese or mountain lentil soup with speck chips – but meaty mains are particularly well executed.

Sweetly efficient staff are happy to guide you, as well as providing excellent advice on the hyperlocal labels on the wine list.

Löwengrube   MODERN SÜDTIROLEAN €€
(☑0471 98 00 32; www.loewengrube.it; Piazza Dogana 3; meals €45; ☺10am-midnight Mon-Sat) A glorious 16th-century *stube* is the surprise design element in an otherwise supermodern, glamorous fit out. The menu ranges across local and Mediterranean dishes, and its combinations and presentation push boundaries, as well as borders.

The wine list is extensive and very well priced, but don't miss a peek at the cellar

ⓘ BOLZANO BOZEN CARD

The **Bolzano Bozen card** (adult/child €28/16) grants you entry to most city and regional museums. Transport on local buses, regional trains and Bolzano's three cable cars is included, as well as bike hire, city tours and national park excursions. It's available from the tourist office. It also covers a summer shuttle to some of the city's outlying sites and cable cars.

If you're travelling beyond Bolzano, consider the **Südtirol Museumobil Card** (3-/7-day adult €28/32, child €16/14), which gives you all the above as well as admission to over 80 musuems across the region.

(dating back to 1280). It holds a vast collection that honours international name vineyards as well as local micro-producers (drink in with a modest corkage of €10).

Walthers' · · · · · · · · · · · · · · · · · MODERN ITALIAN €€
(📞0471 98 25 48; www.walthers.it; Piazza Walther 6; meals €35, pizza €5-11; ⏰8am-1am Mon-Sat, to 7pm Sun) Take your *spritz* out onto the piazza terrace, then head inside to the low-lit back room to dine on bold-flavoured, appetite-appeasing dishes that roam from Sicily to Bolzano's backyard. A lively crowd and the management's penchant for Prince and Blondie can see a quick meal turn into a big night out. There's also a pizza menu and they do gluten-free bases.

🍷 Drinking & Nightlife

Bolzano after dark may come as a surprise. The pristine city centre is often hushed at 8pm, but it's a different story around midnight. Follow the locals heading for Piazza delle Erbe's bar strip or the beer halls – including local Forst and the Bavarian Paulaner – along Via Argentieri and Via Goethe.

★ Enovit · WINE BAR
(Via Dott Streiter 30; ⏰10am-1pm & 3.30-8.30pm Mon-Fri, 10am-1pm Sat) An older, well-dressed lot frequents this warm, woody corner bar and shop for expertly recommended, generously poured local wines by the glass. If there's a crowd – and on Fridays there *always* is – it kicks on past closing.

Temple Bar · IRISH PUB
(Piazza Domenicani 20; ⏰10.30am-1am Tue-Sat, 3pm-1am Sun & Mon) Tanya and Stephen's little slice of Dublin was recently awared a coveted 'best Irish pub outside Ireland' title. While it's Irish to the core with welcoming staff, pints and big matches on the big screen, it's also quintisentially Bolzanino, with great *spritzes*, wine and a gang of hiking-, skiing- and sports-mad locals ready to offer up tips and advice.

Il Baccaro · WINE BAR
(Via Argentieri 17; ⏰8am-2pm Mon-Sat, 7-9pm Mon-Fri) Scurry down the cobbled passageway and poke your nose into this wonderful wine burrow, with a good blackboard selection of regional or Friulian wines and delightful hosts. *Stuzzichini* (snacks) are a euro or two and made to order.

Hopfen & Co · · · · · · · · · · · · · SÜDTIROLEAN, PUB
(📞0471 30 07 88; Piazza delle Erbe 17; ⏰9.30am-1am Mon-Sat) The dark bar is the perfect stage for sampling the cloudy, unfiltered beer that's brewed on the premises. This venerable 800-year-old inn also serves up hearty portions of traditional dishes like sauerkraut and sausages cooked in ale (meals €16-22).

Fischbänke · WINE BAR
(Via Dott Streiter 26; ⏰noon-sunset Mon-Fri) Local wines and bruschetta (from €6) care of bon vivant Cobo at the old outdoor fish market; pull up a stool at one of the original marble-slab counters.

Batzen-bräu · PUB
(📞0471 05 09 50; www.batzen.it; Via Andreas Hofer 30; ⏰10am-midnight) A mash of traditional and contemporary architecture makes for many different moods as you elbow your way from one end to the next. A beer garden is welcome during flash Bolzano heatwaves and a basement theatre space turns into a nightclub on weekends.

Pur Südtirol · · · · · · · · · · · · · · · · · · CAFE, SHOP
(www.pursuedtirol.com; Via Perathoner 9; ⏰7.30am-7.30pm Mon-Fri, 9.30am-6pm Sat) Merano's Slow Food–driven produce shop, cafe and wine bar concept has been rolled out to big city Bolzano. Window seats are a great place for morning pastries and coffee or afternoon *aperitivo* and you can pick up some beautiful deli goods for picnics.

ℹ Information

Hospital (☎0471 90 81 11; Via Böhler) Out of the centre of Bolzano towards Merano.

Police Station (☎0471 94 76 80, 0471 94 76 11; Via Marconi 33)

Tourist Office (☎0471 30 70 00; www.bolzano-bozen.it; Piazza Walther 8; ⊙9am-7pm Mon-Fri, 9.30am-6pm Sat)

ℹ Getting There & Around

AIR

Bolzano Airport (Aeroporto di Bolzano; ☎0471 25 52 55; www.abd-airport.it) Bolzano's wee airport is served by twice-daily flights from Rome on Etihad Regional and, seasonally, from Olbia.

BUS

SAD (☎0471 45 01 11; www.sad.it) Local SAD buses leave from the **bus station** (☎840 000471; Via Perathoner) for destinations throughout the province, including hourly routes to Val Gardena, Brunico and Merano. SAD buses also head for resorts outside the province, including Cortina d'Ampezzo.

TRAIN

Train Station (Piazza Stazione) Bolzano's train station is connected by hourly trains with Merano (€5.60, 40 minutes), Trento (€6.40, 30 minutes) and Verona (€12.20, 2½ hours), with less-frequent connections to Bressanone (€6.85, 25 minutes) and Brunico (€12.10, 1½ hours) in the Val Pusteria. Deutsche Bahn trains run to Innsbruck and Munich via Brennero.

Merano (Meran)

POP 38,200 / ELEV 325M

With its leafy boulevards, birdsong, oleanders and cacti, Merano feels like you've stumbled into a valley Shangri-La. Long lauded for its sunny microclimate, this pretty town (and one-time Tyrolean capital) was a Habsburg-era spa and the hot destination of its day. The Jugendstil (art nouveau) villas, recuperative walks and the grand riverside Kurhaus fan out from its intact medieval core. The city's therapeutic traditions have served it well in the new millennium, with spa hotels drawing a new generation of health-conscious visitors and a booming organics movement in the surrounding valleys. German is spoken widely here, sausage and beer stalls dot the streets and an annual open-air play celebrates Napoleonic-era Tyrolean freedom fighter Andreas Hofer. Despite the palm trees, you're far closer to Vienna than Rome.

DON'T MISS

SÜDTIROL'S TRADITIONAL CHRISTMAS MARKETS

Bolzano, Merano, Brixen, Brunico and Vipiteno's annual Christmas markets draw the crowds for their winter wonderland Mittel charm, traditional Alpine crafts, contemporary green values and spectacular food and wine. Good train connections and modest distances mean all can be experienced in a weekend, along with the magical, ultra-authentic village markets of Renon and Chiusa. Held the last weekend of November until either Christmas Eve or Epiphany on January 6, but be sure to book accomodation and restaurants well ahead as the secret is definitely out. See www.suedtirol.info for seasonal dates and details.

◉ Sights

★**Castel Trauttmansdorff** GARDENS
(www.trauttmansdorff.it; Via San Valentino 51a; garden & museum adult/reduced €12/10; ⊙9am-6pm Apr-Nov, to 11pm Fri summer) You could give an entire day to these beautiful botanical gardens a little outside Merano. Exotic cacti and palms, fruit trees and vines, beds of lilies, irises and tulips all cascade down the hillside surrounding a mid-19th-century castle where Sissi – Empress Elisabeth – spent the odd summer. Inside, **Touriseum** charts two centuries of travel in the region, exploring the changing nature of our yearning for the mountains. There's a restaurant and a cafe by the lily pond.

Kunst Meran ART GALLERY
(☎0473 21 26 43; www.kunstmeranoarte.org; Via Portici 16; adult/reduced €6/5; ⊙10am-6pm Tue-Sun, 11am-7pm summer) Shows of high-profile international and regional artists are installed in this contemporary gallery, a thoughtful refiguring of a skinny medieval town house. Ask about their monthly talks over *aperitivo*.

Castel Tirolo MUSEUM
(Schlosstirol; ☎0473 22 02 21; www.schlosstirol.it; admission €7; ⊙10am-5pm Tue-Sun mid-Mar–Dec, to 6pm Aug) The ancestral seat of the counts of Tyrol is home to a dynamically curated museum of Tyrolean history, including, in the keep, the turbulent years of the 20th century. The castle can be reached by taking

WINE TASTING TRAIL

Follow Alto Adige's Weinstraße (wine road) far enough south from Bolzano and you'll hit **Paradeis** (Alois Lageder; ☑ 0471 80 95 80; www.aloislageder.eu/paradeis; Piazza Geltrude 5, Magrè; meals €40-65; ☺ 10am-8pm, dining room noon-4pm Mon-Sat, to 11pm Thu). Take a seat at the long communal table, crafted from the wood of a 250-year-old oak tree, at fourth-generation winemaker Alois Lageder's biodynamic *weinschenke/vineria* (winery), and start tasting. Book for lunch in the stunning dining room or linger over a bottle and plate of cheese in the pretty courtyard. Whites – highly finessed, Germanic in style, but shot through with the warmth and verve of an Italian summer – are the money here; over 70% of production is devoted to pinot grigio, chardonnay and Gewürztraminer. Even so, Lageder's pinot noir and local Lagrein are highly regarded.

If you're up for more tasting, or just a pleasant day's cycle, the Weinstraße begins northwest of Bolzano in Nals, meanders past Terlano (Terlan) through Upper Adige (Überetsch) and Lower Adige (Unterland) until it reaches Salorno (Salurn). Native grape varieties line the route: Lagrein, Vernatsch and local varietal Gewürztraminer, along with well-adapted imports pinot blanc, sauvignon, merlot and cabernet. For details of cellar doors, accommodation and bike trails, see www.weinstrasse.com.

the chairlift from Merano to Tirolo (Dorf Tirol). Book ahead for tours in English.

🏃 Activities

Some 6km east of town, a **cable car** (Via Val di Nova; one way/return €13.50/18.50) carries winter-sports enthusiasts up to **Piffing** in **Merano 2000** (www.hafling-meran2000.eu), with 30km of mostly beginner slopes. Bus 1B links Merano with the valley station. The tourist offices have details of the many other cable cars and lifts that ring the town, including the Falzeben gondola from Avelengo (Hafling) to Piffing (one way/return €10/15) and the chairlift (one way/return €4/5.50) from Merano to the village of Tirolo (Dorf Tirol). In summer, you can buy a 4-day Funicard (adult €48) for unlimited cable car and chairlift access.

★ **Terme Merano**   THERMAL BATHS
(☑ 0473 25 20 00; www.thermemeran.it; Piazza Terme 1; bathing pass 2hr/all day €12.50/18; ☺ 9am-10pm) Bolzano-born Matteo Thun's dream commission – a modern redevelopment of the town's thermal baths – was reopened in 2005. It houses 13 indoor pools and various saunas within a massive glass cube; there's another 12 outdoor pools open in summer. Swim through the sluice and be met by a vision of palm-studded gardens and snow-topped mountains beyond.

Don't forget to bring or rent a towel. The front desk can give first-timers a rundown on the potentially baffling change-room routine; see the website for details of the excellent wellness treatments available upstairs.

Promenades   WALKING
The promenade or *passeggiata* (evening stroll) has long been a Merano institution. Fin-de-siècle-era walks trace the river, traverse pretty parks and skirt Monte Benedetto (514m). A winter and summer pair follow opposing sides of the river, one shady, one sunny. The **Gilfpromenade** follows 24 poems carved on wooden benches (also handy for a breather). The lovley **Tappeiner** meanders above the town for 4km.

The tourist office offers guides in summer, or can give you a detailed map; all routes have helpful signage.

🛏 Sleeping

Youth Hostel Merano   HOSTEL €
(☑ 0473 20 14 75; meran.jugendherberge.it; Via Carducci 77; dm/s €25.50/28; ▣@🛜🛏) A five-minute stroll from both the train station and the riverside promenade, this hostel is bright and modern, with a sunny terrace and other down-time extras. It has 59 beds, either singles or en suite dorms.

★ **Ottmanngut**   BOUTIQUE HOTEL €€
(☑ 0473 44 96 56; www.ottmanngut.it; Via Verdi 18; s/d €110/160; 🛜) 🍃 This boutique hotel encapsulates Merano's beguiling mix of stately sophistication, natural beauty and gently bohemian back story. The remodelled town house has nine rooms scattered over three floors, and is set among terraced vineyards a scant five-minute walk from the centre. Individually furnished, antique-strewn rooms evoke different moods, each highlighting

the different landscape glimpsed from the window.

Multicourse breakfasts are a highlight, both because of the beautiful conservatory where they are served but also because of the care and attention with which they are prepared.

Hotel Aurora
HOTEL €€

(☑ 0473 21 18 00; www.hotelaurora.bz; Passeggiata lungo Passirio 38; s/d €120/180; P ✳ 🛜) A traditional family hotel, just across the river from the Terme, is working some fresh ideas. 'New' rooms are Italian designed, bright and slick, but the parquetry-floored '60s originals have their own vintage charm, along with river-facing balconies. The corridors too are littered with original but pristine mid-century pieces.

★ Miramonti
BOUTIQUE HOTEL €€€

(☑ 0473 27 93 35; www.hotel-miramonti.com; Via Santa Caterina 14, Avelengo; d €190-240; P ✳ 🛉 🐾) 🍃 This extraordinary small hotel, 15 minutes' drive from town, nestles on the side of a mountain at 1230m. Rooms are vast, cosy and have awe-inspiring views – with such a potent mix, it's hard not to retreat entirely. But you'll be coaxed downstairs by the spa facilities, a sun terrace with lambskins and blankets, or a spot of 'forest therapy' in the nearby woods.

The glass-walled Panorama restaurant welcomes nonguests, and serves adventurous, beautifully presented dishes using local produce. The entire young team exemplify Südtirolean hospitality, relaxed but attentive to every detail.

🍴 Eating & Drinking

As befits a town dedicated to bodily pleasure, Merano has an excellent fine-dining scene, including the Michelin-starred Sissi and Castel Fragsburg. Via Portici brims with speck-dealing delis, *konditorei* line Corso della Libertà, and there are more late-night imbibing options, often squirreled down lanes, than you'd imagine.

★ Pur Südtirol
DELI, WINE BAR €

(www.pursuedtirol.com; Corso della Libertà 35; plates from €9; ⊙ 9am-7.30pm Mon-Fri, to 2pm Sat; 🛉) This stylish regional showcase has an amazing selection of farm produce: wine, cider, some 80 varieties of cheese, speck and sausage, pastries and breads, tisanes and body care. Everything is hyperlocal (take An-

ton Oberhöller's chocolate, flavoured with apple, lemon balm or dark bread crisps).

Specially commissioned wood, glass and textiles fill one corner of the shop. Stay for a coffee, glass of wine or the *bretteljause* – a plate of cured meat – at one of the communal tables.

Forsterbräu
BREWERY €€

(☑ 0473 23 65 35; Corso della Libertà 90; meals €32; ⊙ 10.30am-midnight Tue-Sun, 7-11pm Mon) This brewery restaurant has a huge beer garden and a number of beautifully designed and cosy dining rooms. Come for a pint or heaped plates of trout, roast boar or calf's head with pickled onions, cabbage and potatoes. Or really bring it home with the Forst plate: pork leg, spare ribs, sausage, *knödel* (dumplings) and sauerkraut.

Trattoria Da Santoni
TRATTORIA €€

(☑ 0473 23 37 64; Via Mainardo 9; meals €30; ⊙ noon-2pm & 7-10pm Wed-Sun, noon-2pm Mon) Possibly not the cuisine or atmosphere that you've come to Merano for, but this is a happy Roman-style place that serves up crowd-pleasing, well-prepared traditional Italian cooking and is known for it's weekend fish dishes.

Sissi
GASTRONOMIC €€€

(☑ 0473 23 10 62; www.sissi.andreafenoglio.com; Via Galilei 44; meals €60, degustation €60-90) Andrea Fenoglio is one of the region's best-loved chefs and his big personality fills this small early-20th-century room. The food here is inventive, for sure, but the experience is warm and almost casual. Even the most experimental dish retains a connection to the traditional, or what Fenoglio calls 'memory food'.

Up to 20 wines are available by the glass, a pleasure if you're dining solo or just have a wide-roaming palette.

Café Kunsthaus
BAR

(Via Portici 16; ⊙ 8.30am-8pm Mon-Thu, to 1am Fri & Sat, 10am-6pm Sun) You can while away the hours in this relaxed gallery cafe, then find yourself still here when the DJs begin and the beer and pizzas are doing the rounds. Note, evening access is from the back lane off Via Risparmio.

ℹ Information

Ospedale Merano (☑ 0473 26 33 33; Via Rossini 5) For medical emergencies.

Tourist Office (☑ 0473 23 52 23; www.meran info.it; Corso Libertà 35; ⊙ 9am-6pm Mon-Fri, to 4pm Sat, 10am-12.30pm Sun summer, 9am-12.30pm & 2-5pm Mon-Fri, 9.30am-12.30pm Sat winter)

❶ Getting There & Around

SAD buses leave Merano **bus station** (Piazza Stazione) for villages in the Gruppo del Tessa, Silandro and the valleys leading into the Parco Nazionale dello Stelvio and Ortles range.

Bolzano (€5.40, almost hourly) is an easy 40-minute trip from Merano **train station** (Piazza Stazione), while the Venosta/Vinschgau line heads west to Malles, from where you can catch buses to Switzerland or Austria.

Hire a bike and helmet next door to the train station; the **bikemobil card** (www.suedtirolbike.it; 1/3/7 days €24/30/34, children half price; ⊙ Apr-Nov) includes both rental and unlimited regional train travel, or there's free city bikes for €5 per day, opposite the bikemobil shed or on Via Piave near the Terme Merano (Mon-Sat). Bike trails track the 65km route between Bolzano, Merano and Malles.

Val Venosta (Vinschgau)

This northwestern valley is prettily pastoral, dotted with orchards, farms and small-scale, often creative, industries including marble quarries and workshops.

◉ Sights

Glorenza   VILLAGE
(Glurns) A walled medieval town, Glorenza was once a kingpin in the region's salt trade. Its pristine burgher houses, colonnaded shops, town gates, fortifications and ramparts were faithfully restored in the 1970s, and while it's certainly picturesque, it retains a comforting normalcy, with the road to Switzerland passing through its very centre.

Marienberg   MONASTERY
(www.marienberg.it; Malles; museum adult/reduced €5/2.50; ⊙ 10am-5pm Mon-Sat, closed Jan, Feb & Nov) The beautiful Benedictine monastery of Marienberg, perched up some 1340m above Malles, has a museum dedicated to its eight centuries of monastic life, though the view and architecture are worth the drive up alone.

Lago di Resia   LAKE
Just before the Passo di Resia and Austrian border is the deep blue Lago do Resia, a result of 1950s dam projects. The drowned Romanesque church tower in the lake here

might be the region's de rigueur roadside photo op, but is still oddly affecting.

Besides the view, it's a popular destination for sailing and kiteboarding in summer, ice-fishing and snowkiting in winter, and is also a gateway to the Skiparadies Reschenpass area.

🛏 Sleeping

Gasthof Grüner Baum   BOUTIQUE HOTEL €€
(☎ 0473 83 12 06; www.gasthofgruenerbaum.it; Piazza della Città 7, Glorenza; d €120; P ✱ 🛜) Gracious Gasthof Grüner Baum combines arresting contemporary architecture, authentic charm and quiet luxury – freestanding baths, antiques and handcrafted furniture are standard issue in the rooms.

❶ Getting There & Away

Val Venosta is serviced by the SüdtirolBahn Venosta line, from Merano; from Malles, Swiss Post buses run to Zernez across the border and SAD bus 273 runs to Nauders in Austria. Südtirol Express runs coaches to Zürich.

Part of the ancient Via Claudia Augusta forms an easy, and intriguing, 80km bicycle trail from Merano to Malles.

Parco Nazionale dello Stelvio

It's not quite Yellowstone, but 1346-sq-km **Parco Nazionale dello Stelvio** (☎ 0473 83 04 30; www.parks.it/parco.nazionale.stelvio) FREE is the Alps' largest national park, spilling into the next-door region of Lombardy and bordering Switzerland's Parco Nazionale Svizzero. It's primarily the preserve of walkers who come for the extensive network of well-organised mountain huts and marked trails that, while often challenging, don't require the mountaineering skills necessary elsewhere in the Dolomites. Stelvio's central massif is guarded over by **Monte Cevedale** (3769m) and **Ortles** (3905m), protecting glaciers, forests and numerous wildlife species, not to mention many mountain traditions and histories.

Ski facilities are rare, but Stelvio has a couple of well-serviced runs at **Solda** and the **Passo dello Stelvio** (2757m), both of which offer the novelty of year-round skiing. The latter is the second-highest pass in the Alps and is approached from the north from the hamlet of **Trafoi** (1543m) on one of Europe's most spectacular roads, a series of tight switchbacks covering 15km, with some

TRENTO & THE DOLOMITES VAL VENOSTA (VINSCHGAU)

REINHOLD MESSNER

The man invariably venerated as the greatest mountaineer of them all, Reinhold Messner is an Italian (albeit a German-speaking one) from the Alto Adige town of Bressanone (Brixen).

Messner grew up surrounded by the sharp, seductive peaks of the Dolomites. Scaling his first Alpine summit at the age of five, by his early 20s he was recognised as a rising star in the tough world of mountaineering. Derisive of the siege tactics employed by traditional Himalayan expeditions in the 1960s, Messner advocated a simpler Alpine-style approach to climbing that emphasised fast ascents with minimal equipment. By the '70s he had set his sights on Everest, confidently announcing his ambition to climb the mountain 'by fair means' – that is, without supplementary oxygen.

The prophecy was heroically fulfilled in 1978 when Messner and Austrian Peter Habeler became the first men to summit the world's tallest peak without oxygen tanks, a feat that was considered physically impossible, if not suicidal, at the time. Unsatisfied with his team effort, Messner returned two years later and hacked his way up the mountain's north face to the summit, alone – a superhuman achievement.

The iron-willed Messner logged another record in 1986 when, at 42, he became the first person to scale all eight-thousanders (the 14 mountains in the world over 8000m). Shunning a well-earned retirement, he also took part in the first unassisted crossing of Antarctica.

These days Messner treks at a gentler pace, mainly in his home Dolomites. A retired Euro MP for the Italian Green Party, he now also tends to his collection of mountain museums (www.messner-mountain-museum.it), including ones in **Bolzano** (p318), **Ortles**, and a new one in **Kronplatz** (Corones).

very steep gradients. The road is also famous among cyclists, who train all winter to prepare for its gut-wrenching ascent, and often features in the Giro d'Italia. The hair-raising high pass is only open from June to September, and is subject to closures dependent on early or late snowfall.

Val di Solda & Val d'Ultimo

The village of **Solda** (Sulden; 1906m), reached by winding your way up the deep, dark valley of the same name, is surrounded by 14 peaks over 3000m high. This low-key ski resort becomes a busy base for walkers and climbers in summer. Located – literally – inside a hill, the **Messner Mountain Museum – Ortles** (MMM Ortles; ☑ 0473 61 32 66; www.messner-mountain-museum.it; adult/reduced €7/6; ⊙ 1-7pm Wed-Mon summer, 2-6pm Wed-Mon winter, closed May & mid-Oct–Nov) articulates the theme of 'eternal ice'. Messner's **Yak & Yeti** (☑ 0473 61 35 77; Località Solda 55) restaurant, in a 17th-century farmhouse, is at the entrance. The narrow **Val d'Ultimo** is home to a string of picturesque traditional villages where you can partake in winter or summer sports (including great fishing) or just soak up the beautiful silence. The Schwienbacher's **Eggwirt** (☑ 0473 79 53 19; www.eggwirt.

it; Frazione Santa Valburga 112; halfboard d €129; ℗ ❄ ☎) has gorgeously designed contemporary rooms with dreamlike valley views, a free sauna and a wonderful historic stuben dining room. SAD buses connect Merano with Solda (via Spondigna) and Val d'Ultimo (via Lana).

Val Gardena (Gröden/ Gherdëina)

Despite its proximity to Bolzano, Val Gardena's historical isolation amid the turrets of Gruppo del Sella and Sassolungo has ensured the survival of many pre–mass-tourism traditions. Ladin is a majority tongue and this linguistic heritage is carefully maintained. The pretty and bustling villages are full of reminders of this distinct culture too, with folksy vernacular architecture and a profusion of woodcarving shops.

In recent times, the valley, part of Dolomiti Superski, has become an 'everyman' ski area, with the emphasis firmly on classic runs and fine powder. The valley's main trilingual towns, **Ortisei** (St Ulrich; population 6000, elevation 1236m), **Santa Cristina** (population 1900, elevation 1428m) and **Selva** (Wolkenstein; population 2580, elevation 1563m) all have good facilities.

◉ Sights

Museum de Gherdëina MUSEUM
(☑0471 79 75 54; www.museumgherdeina.
it; Via Rezia 83, Ortisei; adult/reduced €7/5.50;
⊙10am-noon & 2-6pm Mon-Fri, closed Mon in
winter) Ortisei's fabulously folky Museum de
Gherdëina has a particularly exquisite collection of wooden toys and sculptures.

⼈ Activities

In addition to its own good runs, the valley
forms part of the Sella Ronda and the Dolomiti Superski area. **Vallunga**, near Selva, is one of the region's best spots for cross-country skiing. There are stunning trails around Forcella Pordoi and Val Lasties in the Gruppo del Sella, and on the Sassolungo.

This is also a walkers' paradise with endless possibilities, from the challenging **Alte Vie** of the Gruppo del Sella and the magnificent **Parco Naturale Puez-Odle**, to picturesque strolls including the **Naturonda**, a signposted nature-and-geology trail beginning at **Passo di Sella** (2244m).

In summer, cable cars operate from all three towns. From Ortisei you can ascend to **Seceda**, which, at 2518m, offers an unforgettable view of the Gruppo di Odle, a cathedral-like series of mountain spires. From Seceda, trail No 2A passes through green, sloping pastures dotted with wooden *malghe* (shepherds' huts).

Both the Sella and Sassolungo walking trails can be reached from Val Gardena resorts, or Canazei, by bus to **Passo di Sella** or **Passo di Pordoi** – steel yourself for some hairpin bends. From Passo di Pordoi (2239m), a cable car takes you to Sasso Pordoi (2950m).

🛏 Sleeping & Eating

If you spend a week or more in the mountains, hotels offer weekly half-board deals that are more affordable than those in Alta Badia or Val di Fassa. Hotel restaurants here are often very good too.

Saslong Smart Hotel HOTEL €
(☑0471 77 44 44; www.saslong.eu; Strada Palua,
Santa Christina; d €100; 🖥) Rooms are small but comfortable and slick (Antonio Citterio had a hand in the design), staff are friendly and the restaurant's great. The 'smart' concept keeps rates low by making daily cleaning and breakfast optional, plus the longer you stay the cheaper the rate.

Charme Hotel Uridl HOTEL €€
(☑0471 79 32 15; www.uridl.it; Via Chemun 43, Santa Christina; s/d €100/180; 🅿 ❄ @) Nestled behind the church in the original 'high' village, this is a friendly, character-filled hotel with bright, simple rooms, a heritage *stube* and beautiful views back over the valley from its sunny garden. They provide daily free transport to the Sellaronda lifts in winter.

Chalet Gerard HOTEL €€€
(☑0471 79 52 74; www.chalet-gerard.com; Plan de Gralba; half-board s/d €160/290; 🖥🅿) Stunning modern chalet with panoramic views, 10 minutes' drive from Selva proper. There are lots of cosy spots for lolling by the fire, a steam room and the option to ski in, plus super cute rooms. The restaurant is relaxingly homey and romantic and highly regarded.

ⓘ Information

Ortisei Tourist Office (☑0471 77 76 00; www.valgardena.it; Via Rezia 1; ⊙8.30am-12.30pm & 2.30-6.30pm Mon-Sat, 9am-noon & 4-6.30pm Sun, reduced hours Apr, May, Oct & Nov)

Santa Cristina Tourist Office (☑0471 77 78 00; www.valgardena.it; Via Chemun 9; ⊙8.30am-noon & 3-6.30pm Mon-Sat, 9am-noon Sun, reduced hours Apr & May, Oct & Nov)

Scuola di Alpinismo Catores (☑0471 79 82 23; www.catores.com; Piazza Stettenect 1;

LADIN LANDS

According to one Val Gardena local in her 20s, to be Ladin is 'just a way of feeling...I've grown up speaking the language; I don't feel Italian, or South Tyrolean, I feel Ladin.' She is but one of 20,000 first-language Ladin speakers; almost half are the Val Gardena, the others spread across valleys in the neighbouring Val Badia and Val di Fassa as well as Arabba and Ampezzo near Cortina in the Veneto.

Children in these valleys are taught in Ladin, alongside German and Italian, and the Ladin cultural and linguistic identity is enshrined in EU law. The culture is underpinned by vibrant poetry as well as legends peopled by the good-natured *salvan* (a Dolomiti cousin of the gnome) and a further pantheon of fairies, giants and heroes.

⊘ 8.30-11.30am & 4.30-6.30pm) Offers botanical walks, climbing courses, glacier excursions and treks.

ⓘ Getting There & Around

The Val Gardena is accessible from Bolzano and Bressonone by SAD buses year-round, and the neighbouring valleys in summer.

Regular buses connect the towns along the valley throughout the year, including a weekend night bus (single/evening €2/4). In winter the Val Gardena Ski Express shuttles between villages and the lifts (included with the free Val Gardena mobilcard for all hotel guests, or 1/7 days €3/10). Timetables are available at tourist offices.

In summer, the Sella Ronda can be navigated by bus, with services to Passo Gardena, Passo Campolongo, Passo Sella and Passo Pordoi. The summer Val Gardena card gets you unlimited regional transport, along wtih summer lifts (3/6 days €60/79).

Alpe di Siusi & Parco Naturale Sciliar-Catinaccio

There are few more jarring or beautiful juxtapositions than the undulating green pastures of the Alpe di Siusi – Europe's largest plateau – ending dramatically at the base of the towering Sciliar Mountains. To the southeast lies the jagged Catinaccio range, its German name 'Rosengarten' an apt description of the eerie pink hue given off by the mountains' dolomite rock at sunset. The two areas are protected in the Parco Naturale Sciliar-Catinaccio. Signposted by their onion-domed churches, the villages that dot the gentle valleys – including **Castelrotto** (Kastelruth), **Fiè allo Sciliar** (Völs am Schlern) and **Siusi** – are lovingly maintained and unexpectedly sophisticated.

🏃 Activities

The region is part of the Dolomiti Superski network, with downhill skiing, ski-mountaineering, cross-country skiing and snowshoe trails all possible. Riding stables are also found throughout the area.

The gentle slopes of the Alpe di Siusi are perfect hiking terrain for families with kids; average stamina will get you to the **Rifugio Bolzano** (☑0471 61 20 24; www.schlernhaus. it; ⊘Jun-Oct), one of the Alps' oldest mountain huts, which rests at 2457m, just under **Monte Pez** (2564m), the Sciliar's summit.

Take the **Panorama chairlift** (one way/return €3.50/5) from Compaccio to the Alpenhotel, followed by paths S, No 5 and No 1 to the *rifugio;* from here it's a 3-hour walk. The more jagged peaks of the Catinaccio group and the Sassolungo are nearby. These mountains are revered among climbers worldwide, and harbour several *vie ferrate* and loads of good bike trails. They're usually accessed from Vigo in Val di Fiemme.

The Seiser Alm **cableway** (www.seiser almbahn.it; one way/return €10/15; ⊘8am-6pm mid-Dec–Mar & mid-May–Oct, to 7pm summer) is a dizzying 15-minute, 4300m trip (800m ascent) from Siusi to Compaccio. The road linking the two is closed to normal traffic when the cableway is open.

🛏 Sleeping

Martina Breakfast Lodge HOTEL **€**
(☑0471 70 63 61; www.martina-lodge.com; Via Panider 19, Castelrotto; d €105; P 🛜 ♨ 🐾) On the road just outside Castelrotto's historic centre, this newly renovated hotel has bright, modern rooms. Opt for one with a balcony and view over Sciliar and Bullaccia. Welcome extras include kitchens in the larger apartments, complimentary laundry facilities and a sauna.

★**Hotel Heubad** SPA HOTEL **€€**
(☑0471 72 50 20; www.hotelheubad.com; Via Sciliar 12, Fiè; s/d €112/190; P ✳ @ ♨ 🐾) As if the views, pretty garden and lounge are as here weren't relaxing enough, the spa is known for its typically Tyrolean hay baths, which have been on offer since 1903 and give the hotel its name. Delightful service is courtesy of the founder's great- and great-great-grandchildren, while rooms are modern, light and spacious.

ⓘ Information

Castelrotto Tourist Office (☑0471 70 63 33; www.alpedisiusi.info; Piazza Kraus 1; ⊘9am-noon & 2-6pm Mon-Fri, 10am-noon Sat)
Fiè allo Sciliar Tourist Office (☑0471 72 50 27; www.alpedisiusi.info; Via Bolzano 4; ⊘9am-noon & 2-6pm Mon-Fri, 10am-noon Sat)

ⓘ Getting There & Away

SAD (www.sad.it) Runs buses to the Alpe di Siusi from Bolzano, the Val Gardena and Bressanone.
Silbernagl (☑0471 70 74 00; www.silbernagl. it) Runs regular buses throughout the area and connects Castelrotto and Siusi.

TRENTO & THE DOLOMITES ALPE DI SIUSI & PARCO NATURALE SCILIAR - CATINACCIO

FRANK FELL/GETTY IMAGES ©

BRUCE YUANYUE BI/GETTY IMAGES ©

GLENN VAN DER KNIJFF/GETTY IMAGES ©

1. Alpe di Siusi (p329)

Cows graze in an Alpine meadow, against a backdrop of the Dolomites.

2. Cortina d'Ampezzo (p405)

This glamorous town offers top-notch skiing in winter and is a stunning base for hiking and biking in summer.

3. Bolzano (p317)

The provincial capital of Alto Adige boasts daily street markets bursting with local produce.

4. Alto Adige (Südtirol) (p317)

Some of Italy's most dramatic and vertiginous hiking trails wind through the wild beauty of the Alto Adige (Südtirol) Dolomites.

Val Badia & Alpe di Fanes

The Badia valley and the adjoining high plains of Fanes are often touted as one of the most evocative places in the Dolomites. Since 1980 they have been protected as part of the Parco Naturale di Fanes-Sennes-Braies. Villages in the valley – Colfosco (1645m), Pedraces (1324m), La Villa (1433m), San Cassiano (St Kassian; 1537m) and Corvara (1568m) – form the Alta Badia ski area. While undoubtedly upmarket, they remain relatively low key and brim with character.

Activities

The Alta Badia is located on the Sella Ronda, with the best access from Corvara, and forms part of the Dolomiti Superski network. Alta Badia passes for 1/3/7 days cost from €43/128/239. Of the Alta Badia's 130km of slopes, the Gran Risa, 4.5km north of Corvara in La Villa, is undoubtedly the most legendary. In summer a cable car ascends into the Parco Naturale di Fanes-Sennes-Braies from the Passo Falzarego (2105m). Alternatively, pick up trail No 12, near La Villa, or trail No 11, which joins Alta Via No 1 at the Capanna Alpina, a few kilometres off the main road between Passo Valparola and San Cassiano. Either trail takes you up to the Alpe di Fanes and the two *rifugi,* Lavarella and Fanes.

Tours

Alta Badia Guides GUIDES
(☑0471 83 68 98; www.altabadiaguides.com; Via Col Alt 94, Corvara; ⊙office 5-7pm) Freeride, ski circuits and ice-climbing courses and tours, as well as snowshoe walks in winter. In summer they organise climbs, including *vie ferrate*, trekking and excursions to the natural parks and WWI sites.

Sleeping & Eating

These resorts are known for their discreet, luxurious hotels. Budget options are scarce, though shoulder season prices do drop dramatically. Residence apartments and mountain huts can be a good deal if booked well in advance. Alta Badia ups the Alpine ante with a disproportionate number of Michelin-starred restaurants and hosts the gastronomic Chef's Cup Food Festival (www.chefscup.it) in January; from July to September organic farmers markets take over village squares.

Garni Ciasa Urban HOTEL
(www.garniurban.it; Via Pantansarè 35, Badia; €85, 4-bed apt €130; [P][⊡]) A simple, welcoming, family-run place, set in a blissfully peaceful spot right at the top of the village. The uncluttered, spacious rooms have spectacular views of Santa Croce and home-cooked dinners can be arranged. Note, the Urban of the name is the house saint, not style or attitude!

★ **Berghotel Ladinia** BOUTIQUE HOTEL €€
(☑0471 83 60 10; berghotelladinia.it; Pedecorvar 10, Corvara; d €140, 4-day minimum stay; [P][⊡][⊡] Hotel La Perla's family owners have taken over this traditional small hotel just above their luxurious place. Rooms are exquisitely simple and the location is sublime. Room rates usually include a food credit (€40 per person, per day) to be used at either the hotel restaurant or at one of La Perla's.

Dolomit B&B B&B €€
(☑0471 84 71 20; www.dolomit.it; Via Colz 9, La Villa; d €140; [P][⊡][@][⊡][⊡]) Rooms here are very prettily decorated, as well as surprisingly spacious (baths! walk-in wardrobes!). You might be right in the middle of town, but the mountain views are still something to behold. The attached La Tor restaurant does Ladin dishes and pizza; its popularity with locals makes it a fun spot year round.

Hotel Rezia HOTEL €€
(☑0471 84 71 55; www.hotelrezia.com; Via Cianins 3, La Villa; half-board s/d €97/180; [P][⊡][⊡]) This hotel is in a lovely bucolic position, just outside of the village on the road to San Cassiano. It's big and there's a recently added ultra-modern wing, but the place retains a very individual, very local feel.

Lagacio Mountain Residence APARTHOTEL €€€
(☑0471 84 95 03; www.lagacio.com; Strada Micurà de Rü 48, San Cassiano; apt €320; [P][⊡][⊡][⊡]) A stylish residence hotel with young, happy staff and casual vibe. Pared-back apartments are decorated with wood, wool and leather; all have heated floors, big baths and balconies. Attention to detail is keen: kitchens come with WMF gear, Nespresso machines and filtered mountain water. There are good spa facilites as well as a guest-only bar.

Delizius DELI €
(☑0471 84 01 55; www.delizius.it; Micurà de Rü 51, San Cassiano; ⊙8am-noon & 3-7pm Mon-Sat)

Specialist cheese and speck counters, well-priced local wine and grappa, plus an excellent selection of prepared meals – *canederli*, gulasch, lasagne – perfect for self-caterers.

Restaurant Ladinia SÜDTIROLEAN €€
(☑0471 83 60 10; www.berghotelladinia.it; meals €28, 4-course menu €40; ⊙noon-2pm & 7-9pm) The Berghotel Ladinia's dining room is appealingly cosy, or you can soak up the sun on a protected terrace on warmer days. Mountain-style food is done in a fresh but unpretentious way: trout carpaccio with chicory, *paccheri* (pasta) with freshwater crayfish, salmon with mashed purple carrots and artichokes, and a yoghurt mousse dessert will wake up stew-and-dumpling–dulled palettes.

St Hubertus GASTRONOMIC €€€
(Hotel Rosa Alpina; ☑0471 84 95 00; www.rosalpina.it; Micurá de Rü 20, San Cassiano; degustation €110-180; ⊙7-10pm Wed-Mon) Part of the luxurious Rosa Alpina Hotel & Spa, this two-Michelin-starred restaurant is quietly elegant. The mountain beef cooked in salt and hay is a menu stalwart, as is suckling pig, though many of Norbert Niederkofler's dishes also take a whimsical turn.

❶ Information

Full ski-pass prices, lift information and the location of ski-pass sales points can be found online (www.altabadia.org) or at tourist offices.
Corvara Tourist Office (☑0471 83 61 76; Via Col Alt 36; ⊙9am-noon & 3-6pm)
La Villa Tourist Office (☑0471 84 70 37; Via Colz 75; ⊙9am-noon & 3-6pm Mon-Sat)
San Cassiano Tourist Office (☑0471 84 94 22; Strada Micurá de Rü 24; ⊙8.30am-noon & 3-6.30pm Mon-Sat, 10am-noon & 4-6pm Sun)

❶ Getting There & Away

SAD (☑800 84 60 47; www.sad.it) buses link the villages with Bolzano (2½ hours) and Brunico (1¼ hours) roughly hourly. Summer services link Corvara with the Val Gardena, Passo di Sella and Passo di Pordoi, Canazei and the Passo Falzarego.

Val Pusteria (Pustertal)

Running from the junction of the Valle Isarco at **Bressanone** (Brixen) to **San Candido** (Innichen) in the far east, the narrow, verdant Val Pusteria is profoundly Tyrolean and almost entirely German speaking.

Dobbiaco (Toblach), where Gustav Mahler once holed up and wrote his troubled but ultimately life-affirming *Ninth Symphony*, is the gateway to the ethereal **Parco Naturale delle Dolomiti di Sesto**, home of the much-photographed **Tre Cime di Lavaredo** ('Three Peaks' or, in German, Drei Zinnen). Down yet another deeply forested valley twist, the jewel-like **Lago di Braies** (Pragser Wildsee) is just the spot for a peaceful lakeside stroll. Serious walkers tackle part of the Alta Via No 1 from here.

The **Plan de Corones** (Kronplaz) ski area – covered by Dolomiti Superski – is 4km to the south of bustling **Brunico** and can be reached by cable car. Ample green and blue runs are spectacularly set — a treat for beginners.

Bumping the Austrian and Veneto borders in the far northeast is a vast, wild territory, the **Sesto Dolomiti**. The Valle Campo di Dentro and Val Fiscalina are criss-crossed with spectacular walking and cross-country ski trails; most around the Tre Cime are easy enough for inexperienced walkers and families. From the Val Fiscalina it's a long but gentle walk along trail No 102 to Rifugio Locatelli (2405m), from where you can see the Tre Cime di Lavaredo in all its glory.

Bressanone (Brixen)

Alto Adige's oldest city, dating to 901, might be the picture of small town calm, but has a grand ecclesiastical past and a lively, cultured side today. Stunning baroque architecture is set against a beguiling Alpine backdrop, a stately piazza leads into a tight medieval core and pretty paths trace the fast-moving Isarco river. Stay, eat, drink or shop by all means, but also come for excellent hiking in summer, or the spectacular views and beautiful 11km ski run at town mountain **Plose** in winter. Hotels usually offer guests the Brixencard, giving you free local transport and museum entries.

◉ Sights

Museo Diocesano MUSEUM
(☑0472 83 05 05; www.hofburg.it; Piazza Palazzo Vescovile 2; adult €7; ⊙10am-5pm Tue-Sun summer & Dec–early Jan) This museum is far more interesting than most of its ilk, its magnificent *palazzo* home testament to the town's once-important religious standing. It has a rather bonkers, 'crib' collection – nativity figures and dioramas.

🛏 Sleeping

★ Hotel Elephant
HISTORIC HOTEL **€€**

(☑ 0472 83 27 50; www.hotelelephant.com; Via Rio Bianco 4; s/d €100/180; P✳🛜❄) This 15th-century inn, as the name suggests, once gave shelter to an Indian elephant, a gift on its way to Archduke Maximilian of Austria. Nowadays there's extremely comfortable rooms and serenely professional service, exquisite historic *stufas* (tiled stoves) in the dining room and museum-worthy paintings lining the stairs.

Hotel Pupp
BOUTIQUE HOTEL **€€**

(☑ 0472 26 83 55; www.small-luxury.it; Via Mercato Vecchio 36; d €180; P✳🛜) Things take a totally contemporary turn at this small and fun hotel, even if its hospitality lineage reaches way back (the owners have branched out from the veritable bakery opposite). Fabulously designed rooms are suite-sized and come with Nespresso machines and wine-stocked fridges; some include a terrace with hot tub.

🍴 Eating & Drinking

Oste Scuro
SÜDTIROLEAN **€€**

(Restaurant Finsterwirt; ☑ 0472 83 53 43; www. ostescuro.com; Vicolo del Duomo 3; meals €45; ⊙ 11.45am-2.15pm & 6.45-9.15pm Tue-Sat, noon-3pm Sun) This place is worth a visit for the decor alone – a wonderful series of dark-wooded rooms strewn with Alpine curios – but the food here is very good if seriously rich. Tips: lunch menus are a steal at €16/20, and don't pass up the post-prandial nut-infused digestives.

Pupp Konditorei Cafe
CAFE

(www.pupp.it; Via Mercato Vecchio 37; ⊙ 7am-7pm Tue-Sat, 7am-noon Sun) In the Pupp family for almost 100 years, this is a Bressanone favourite. The cosy velvet booths of this oh-so-'80s cafe are perpetually filled with locals scoffing great coffee and cake. The poppy-seed or walnut *potize* (stuffed brioche) are known throughout the valley.

La Habana
WINE BAR

(Via Portici Maggiore 14; ⊙ 8am-1pm & 2pm-midnight Mon-Sat) Smart hole-in-the-wall bar that caters equally well to workers sipping morning espresso, ladies who *spritz* mid-morning and students nursing a *hugo* (elderflower and sparkling wine) late into the night.

Peter's Weinbistro
WINE BAR

(Vinus; www.vinothekvinus.it; Via Mercato Vecchio 6; ⊙ 10am-1pm & 4-10pm Mon-Fri, to midnight Wed, 10am-6pm Sat) A classy, dark, low ceilinged space with an extensive wine-by-the-glass list. Peter – yes, that's him – offers a *tavola calda* (a limited hot menu; mains €20) on Wednesdays, Fridays and Saturdays, and sometimes keeps pouring local drops until midnight.

ℹ Getting There & Away

Bressanone is on the main Bolzano–Innsbruck line (IC train, 25 minutes, €8). Regional Val Pusteria trains connect to this line at Fortezza (Franzensfeste), and run down the valley as far as San Candido.

Brunico (Bruneck)

POP 13,700 / ELEV 835M

Brunico gets a bad rap by those who've only driven through its unremarkable main drag. The quintessentially Tyrolean historic centre is, however, a delightful detour.

🍴 Eating & Drinking

Acherer Patisserie & Blumen
PASTRIES **€**

(☑ 0474 41 00 30; www.acherer.com; Via Centrale; ⊙ 8am-7pm Mon-Fri, 8am-5pm Sat & Sun) Right by the town gate, Acherer Patisserie & Blumen sells strudel and Sachertorte that may just be the region's best; the young owner reopened his grandfather's former bakery after apprenticing in Vienna. His inventive cakes and chocolates and seasonal preserves now grace many of the region's five-starred pillows and breakfast buffets.

Wörtz Bäck
BAR

(Via Centrale 12; ⊙ 8am-late Wed-Fri, 8am-7pm Mon, Tue & Sat) A friendly historic-centre bar where locals gather for coffee, jugs of beer and wine, often all at once.

🛍 Shopping

Moessmer
FASHION

(Via Vogelweide; ⊙ 9am-12.30pm & 2.30-6pm Mon-Fri, 9am-2.30pm Sat) Visit local wool manufacturer Moessmer for cashmere and Tyrolean tweeds from its outlet shop on the town's outskirts, or just for an interesting slice of early-20th-century industrial architecture.

ℹ Getting There & Away

SAD buses connect Brunico (45 minutes, hourly) and Cortina (one hour, four daily) to San Candido. Buses run directly between Brunico and Bressanone (€5.45, 1 hour, hourly) or by train via Fortezza (€4.80, 1 hour, half-hourly) and on to Bolzano (€6.20, 1.5 hours, hourly).

Venice & the Veneto

Best Places to Eat

➡ All'Arco (p375)

➡ Trattoria e Bacaro da Fiore (p371)

➡ Osteria Trefanti (p372)

➡ Locanda 4 Cuochi (p397)

➡ Belle Parti (p387)

Best Places to Stay

➡ Hotel Palazzo Barbarigo (p369)

➡ Hotel Flora (p367)

➡ B&B Corte Vecchia (p368)

➡ Corte delle Pigne (p396)

➡ Agriturismo San Mattia (p401)

Why Go?

Venice really needs no introduction. This incomparable union of art, architecture and life has been a fabled destination for centuries. No matter how many photographs, films or paintings you've seen, the reality is more surprising and romantic than you could ever imagine. Most of the world's most famous writers and artists have visited to admire the mosaics of San Marco, the Old Masters in the Accademia and the city's maze of *calle* (lanes) and canals. They've written and painted Venice into the world's imagination, so it is no wonder that tourists outnumber locals by two to one on summer days.

Beyond Venice, the Veneto region is often overlooked, but is no less enticing. Giotto's spectacular frescoes in Padua, Palladio's elegant architecture in Vicenza, Verona's romantic riverside location and the Unesco-designated landscapes of the Dolomites would be unmissable anywhere else. So take our advice: love Venice then leave her. You won't regret it.

When to Go

Venice

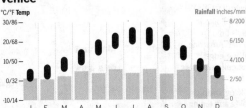

Jan & Feb Snow-covered gondolas, skiers in the Dolomites and Carnevale parties in Venice.

Apr–Jun Canal-side dining, VinItaly toasts and Biennale openings (skip pricey Easter).

Sep–Nov Venice International Film Festival, wild duck pasta and palatial accommodation for less.

Venice & the Veneto Highlights

1 Gazing at the golden mosaic domes of Venice's **Basilica di San Marco** (p339).

2 Comparing Titian's radiant reds and Tintoretto's lightning-strike brush strokes at Venice's **I Frari** (p353) and **Scuola Grande di San Rocco** (p352).

3 Exploring the lagoon with **Row Venice** (p364), **Venice Kayak** (p364) and **Terra e Acqua** (p364).

4 Indulging in art and Palladian architecture in elegant **Vicenza** (p388), one of Italy's most underrated cities.

5 Villa-hopping by barge along the **Brenta Riviera** (p382).

6 Shouting 'Brava!' for opera diva encores at Verona's outdoor **Roman Arena** (p394).

7 Seeing the Renaissance coming in Giotto's moving frescoes at Padua's **Cappella degli Scrovegni** (p384).

8 Sampling one of Italy's boldest red wines, Amarone, at cutting-edge **Valpolicella wineries** (p401).

9 Skiing, hiking, climbing and dining on mountain-fresh fare amid the awesome snow-capped peaks of the **Cinque Torri** (p405).

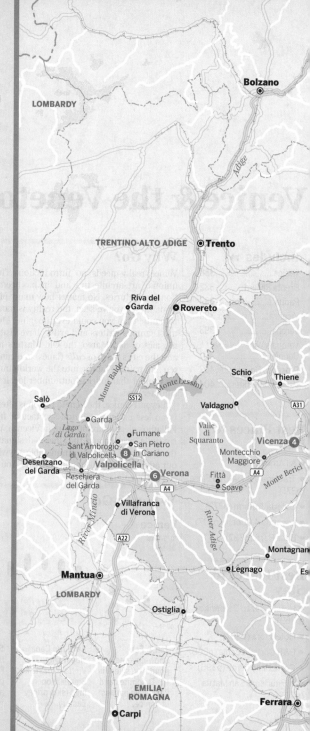

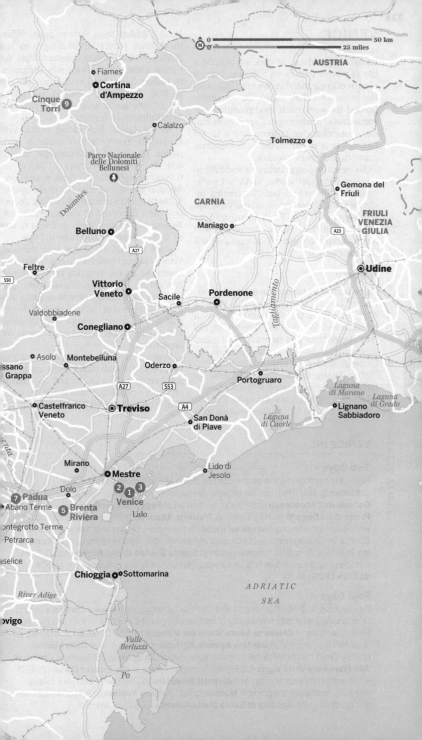

AUSTRIA

Fiames

Cortina
d'Ampezzo

Cinque
Torri ⑨

Calalzo

Tolmezzo

Parco Nazionale
delle Dolomiti
Bellunesi

CARNIA

Gemona del
Friuli

Maniago

FRIULI
VENEZIA
GIULIA

Belluno

A23

Dolomites

Feltre

A27

Udine

S50

Vittorio
Veneto

Sacile

Pordenone

Valdobbiadene

Conegliano

Tagliamento

Asolo

Montebelluna

Oderzo

Portogruaro

Bassano
Grappa

A27

S53

Laguna
di Marano

Laguna
di Grado

Castelfranco
Veneto

A4

Treviso

San Donà
di Piave

Laguna
di Caorle

Lignano
Sabbiadoro

Mirano

Lido di
Jesolo

Dolo

Mestre

⑦ Padua

② ① ③

Abano Terme

Venice

⑤ Brenta
Riviera

Lido

ontegrotto Terme

Petrarca

selice

ovigo

Chioggia ○ Sottomarina

ADRIATIC

SEA

River Adige

Valle
Berluzzi

Po

VENICE

POP 59,000

Imagine the audacity of deciding to build a city of marble palaces on a lagoon. Instead of surrendering to the *acque alte* (high tide) like reasonable folk might do, Venetians flooded the world with vivid paintings, baroque music, modern opera, spice-route cuisine, bohemian-chic fashions and a Grand Canal's worth of *spritz,* the city's signature *prosecco* and Aperol cocktail.

Today cutting-edge architects and billionaire benefactors are spicing up the art scene, musicians are rocking out 18th-century instruments and backstreet *osterie* (taverns) are winning a Slow Food following. Your timing couldn't be better: the people who made walking on water look easy are well into their next act.

History

When barbarian hordes threatened to overwhelm Roman towns along the Veneto's Adriatic coast in the 5th century, Venetian refugees fled to safety on Torcello. In 726 they elected their first doge and established themselves around his ducal palace on the higher ground of the Rivoalto (Rialto).

Next Venice shored up its business interests. The city accepted a Frankish commission of 84,000 silver marks to join the Crusades, even as it continued trading with Muslim leaders from Syria to Spain. When the balance wasn't forthcoming from the Franks, Venice claimed Constantinople 'for Christendom'. After Venice was decimated by plague, Genoa tried to take over the city in 1380. But Venice prevailed, controlling the Adriatic and a backyard that stretched from Dalmatia to Bergamo.

As the Age of Exploration began, Venice lost its monopoly over seafaring trade routes. The fall of Constantinople in 1453 and the Venetian territory of Morea (in Greece) in 1499 gave the Turks control over Adriatic Sea access. The Genovese opened transatlantic trade routes following Columbus' 1492 discovery of the Americas, and Portuguese explorer Vasco da Gama rounded Africa's Cape of Good Hope in 1498.

Once it could no longer rule the seas, Venice changed tack and began conquering Europe by charm. Venetian art was incredibly daring, bringing sensuous colour and sly social commentary even to religious subjects. By the end of the 16th century, Venice was known across Europe for its painting, catchy music and 12,000 registered prostitutes.

Venetian reputations did nothing to prevent Napoleon from claiming the city in 1797 and looting it of its art. By 1817 one-quarter of Venice's population was destitute. When Venice rallied to resist the Austrian occupa-

---

VENICE IN...

Two Days

Rise early to catch the sun on the Basilica di San Marco's mosaics with coffee at **Florian** (p377). Then choose between Renaissance masterpieces at the **Gallerie dell'Accademia** (p347) and modern art at **Peggy Guggenheim** (p348) and the **Punta della Dogana** (p349). Lunch at **Trattoria Altanella** (p375) on Giudecca and then while away the afternoon **kayaking** (p364) in the lagoon. On day two, follow espresso in Campo Santa Margherita with glimpses of heaven in the Tiepolo ceilings at **Ca' Rezzonico** (p348) or Tintoretto's masterpieces at **Scuola Grande di San Rocco** (p352). Then window shop through San Polo and across the Ponte di Rialto to happy hour at **DOK dall'Ava LP26** (p371).

Four Days

Devote a day to divine Cannaregio and Castello, beginning with **Museo Ebraico's** (p355) Ghetto synagogue tour, followed by Grand Canal views at **Ca' d'Oro** (p356) and the marble masterpiece of **Chiesa di Santa Maria dei Miracoli** (p355). Lunch on hearty plates of *cicheti* (bar snacks) at **Cantina Aziende Agricole** (p375) or dine at **Dalla Marisa** (p373). Cross canals to Castello's many-splendoured **Zanipolo** (p356), serene **Chiesa di San Francesco della Vigna** (p359) and sunset cocktails at **Bar Terazza Danieli** (p378) – but don't miss your concert at **Interpreti Veneziani** (p378). Island-hop your fourth day away, with glass shopping in **Murano** (p361), lunch at **Venissa** (p361) on Mazzorbo and mosaics in the **Basilica di Santa Maria Assunta** (p364) on Torcello.

ion in 1848–49, a blockade left it wracked by cholera and short on food. Venetian rebels lost the fight but not the war: they became early martyrs to the cause of Italian independence, and in 1866 Venice joined the independent kingdom of Italy.

In the early 19th century, Venice took on an industrious workaday aspect, with factories springing up on Giudecca and a roadway from the mainland built by Mussolini. Italian partisans joined Allied troops to wrest the Veneto from Fascist control, but the tragedy of war and mass deportation of Venice's Jewish population in 1942–44 shook Venice to its moorings. Postwar, many Venetians left for Milan and other centres of industry.

Like a cat with nine lives, Venice has miraculously survived over 1200 years of war, plague and invasion, but it now faces its greatest threat: rising sea levels. On 4 November 1966 unprecedented floods struck the city, inundating 16,000 Venetian homes. But Venice's cosmopolitan charm was a saving grace: assistance from admirers poured in (from Mexico to Australia, from millionaires to pensioners) and Unesco coordinated some 27 international charities to redress the ravages of the flood.

However, this threat still remains the single biggest challenge facing the lagoon city, with global sea-level rises predicted between 14cm and 80cm by 2100. The 2011 Unesco report *From Global to Regional: Local Sea Level Rise Scenarios*, states 'The question is not if this will happen, but only when it will happen'. At 80cm, Venice will flood twice a day with the tidal oscillation and even the controversial MoSE barriers – currently being built at the mouths of the lagoon to protect the city from high waters – will be ineffectual.

◉ Sights

◉ Piazza San Marco & Around

⭐ **Basilica di San Marco** BASILICA
(St Mark's Basilica; Map p344; ☎041 270 83 11; www.basilicasanmarco.it; Piazza San Marco; ⊙9.45am-5pm Mon-Sat, 2-5pm Sun summer, to 4pm Sun winter; ⑤San Marco) FREE With its Byzantine domes and 8500 sq metres of luminous mosaics, Venice's basilica is an unforgettable sight. It dates to the 9th century when, according to legend, two merchants smuggled the corpse of St Mark out of Egypt

in a barrel of pork fat. When the original burnt down in 932, Venice rebuilt the basilica in its own cosmopolitan image, with Byzantine domes, a Greek-cross layout and walls clad in marbles from Syria, Egypt and Palestine.

The front of the basilica ripples and crests like a wave, its five niched portals capped with shimmering mosaics and frothy stonework arches. In the far-left portal, lunette mosaics dating from 1270 show St Mark's stolen body arriving at the basilica. Grand entrances are made through the central portal, under an ornate triple arch with Egyptian purple porphyry columns and 13th- to 14th-century reliefs of vines, virtues and astrological signs.

Blinking is natural upon your first glimpse of the basilica's glittering mosaics, many made with 24-carat gold leaf fused onto the back of the glass to represent divine light. Just inside the vestibule are the basilica's oldest mosaics: *Apostles with the Madonna,* standing sentry by the main door for more than 950 years. Mystical transfusions occur in the **Dome of the Holy Spirit**, where a dove's blood streams onto the heads of saints. In the central 13th-century **Cupola of the Ascension**, angels swirl overhead while dreamy-eyed St Mark rests on the pendentive. Scenes from St Mark's life unfold over the main altar, in vaults flanking the **Dome of the Prophets**.

The latter is best seen from the **Pala d'Oro**, a gold altarpiece studded with 2000 emeralds, amethysts, sapphires, rubies, pearls and other gemstones. It houses the sarcophagus of St Mark's and is guarded by

Venice

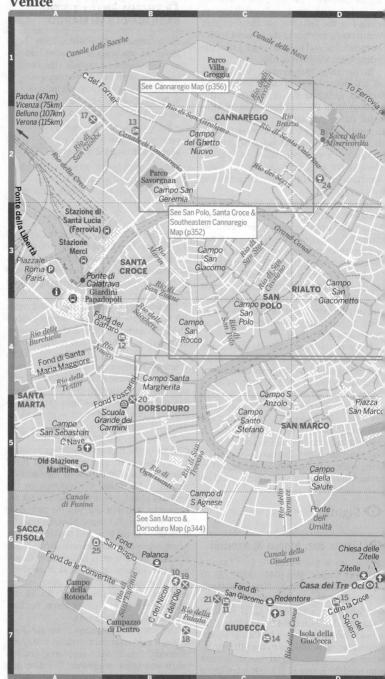

Canale delle Sacche

Canale delle Navi

Parco Villa Groggia

C. del Forner

See Cannaregio Map (p356)

Rio di San Girolamo

Rio degli Zecchini

CANNAREGIO

Rio Brazzo

To Ferrovia

Padua (47km)
Vicenza (75km)
Belluno (107km)
Verona (115km)

17

13

Canale di Cannaregio

Campo del Ghetto Nuovo

Rio di San Giobbe

Rio della Crea

Rio dei Servi

8

Sacca della Misericordia

Parco Savorgnan
Campo San Geremia

24

Ponte della Libertà

Stazione di Santa Lucia (Ferrovia)

See San Polo, Santa Croce & Southeastern Cannaregio Map (p352)

Stazione Merci

Piazzale Roma Parisi

Ponte di Calatrava

SANTA CROCE

Rio Marin

Rio di San Stae

Grand Canal

Campo San Giacomo

Rio di San Cassiano

RIALTO

Campo San Giacometto

Giardini Papadopoli

Rio di San Zuane

SAN POLO

Campo San Polo

Campo San Rocco

Rio delle Sacchere

Rio di San Polo

Fond del Gaffaro

12

Rio delle Burchielle

Fond di Santa Maria Maggiore

Rio Novo

Rio delle Tentor

Fond Foscarini

Campo Santa Margherita

20

DORSODURO

Campo S Anzolo

Piazza San Marco

SANTA MARTA

Scuola Grande dei Carmini

Campo Santo Stefano

SAN MARCO

Campo San Sebastian C Nave

5

Rio di San Trovaso

Old Stazione Marittima

Rio di Ognissanti

Campo della Salute

Canale di Fusina

Campo di S Agnese

See San Marco & Dorsoduro Map (p344)

Rio della Fornace

Ponte dell' Umiltà

SACCA FISOLA

Fond San Biagio

Palanca

Chiesa delle Zitelle

25

Fond de le Convertite

Rio Sant'Eufemia

10 19

C dei Nicoli

C dell'Olio

Canale della Giudecca

Fond di San Giacomo

Redentore

Zitelle

Casa dei Tre Oci

1

Campo della Rotonda

21

11

3

15

C drio la Croce

Campazzo di Dentro

Rio della Palada

18

GIUDECCA

14

Isola della Giudecca

Rio della Croce

C del Squero

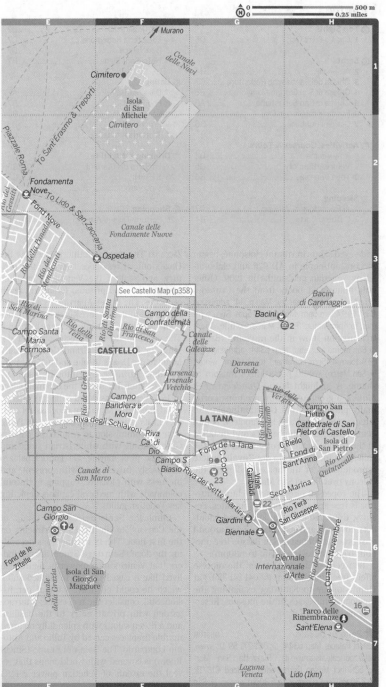

Venice

wide-eyed saints in vibrant cloisonné, begun in Constantinople in AD 976 and elaborated by Venetian goldsmiths in 1209. Other holy bones and booty from the Crusades fill the **Tesoro** (Treasury; Map p344; admission €3; ⊙9.45am-5pm Mon-Sat, 2-5pm Sun summer, to 4pm winter; ⬤San Marco); while ducal treasures on show in the **museum** (Basilica di San Marco Museum; Map p344; admission €5; ⊙9.45am-4.45pm summer, to 3.45pm winter; ⬤San Marco) would put a king's ransom to shame. A highlight is the *Quadriga of St Mark's*, a group of four bronze horses originally plundered from Constantinople and later carted off to Paris by Napoleon before being returned to the basilica and installed in the 1st-floor gallery. Portals lead from the gallery on to the **Loggia dei Cavalli**, where reproductions of the horses gallop off the balcony over Piazza San Marco.

The roped-off circuit of the church interior is free and takes about 15 minutes. For entry, dress modestly (ie knees and shoulders covered) and leave large bags around the corner at Ateneo di San Basso's free one-hour baggage storage (10am to 4.30pm).

Between April and October, the diocese offers free guided tours (☎041 241 38 17) at 11am Monday to Saturday, explaining the theological messages in the mosaics. Reservations are essential.

★ **Palazzo Ducale**   MUSEUM
(Ducal Palace; Map p344; ☎041 271 59 11; www.palazzoducale.visitmuve.it; Piazzetta San Marco 52; incl Museo Correr adult/reduced €18/11; ⊙8.30am-7pm summer, to 5.30pm winter; ⬤San

Zaccaria) This grand Gothic palace was the Doge's official residence from the 9th century, and seat of the Venetian Republic's government (and prisons) for nearly seven centuries. The Doge's Apartments are on the 1st floor, but it's the lavishly decorated 2nd-floor chambers that are the real highlight. These culminate in the echoing **Sala del Maggior Consiglio** (Grand Council Hall), home to the Doge's throne and a 22m-by-7m painting, *Paradise*, by Tintoretto's son Domenico. After fire gutted the original palace in 1577, Venice considered Palladio's offer to build one of his signature neoclassical temples in its place. Instead, Antonio da Ponte won the commission to restore the palace's Gothic facade with white Istrian stone and Veronese pink marble. Da Ponte's palazzo effortlessly mixes past with present and business with pleasure, capping a graceful colonnade with medieval capitals depicting key Venetian guilds.

Climb the **Scala dei Censori** (Stairs of the Censors) to the Doge's Apartments on the first floor. The 18 roaring lions decorating the doge's **Sala degli Stucci** are reminders that Venice's most powerful figurehead lived like a caged lion in his gilded suite, which he could not leave without permission. Still, consider the real estate: a terrace garden with private entry to the basilica, and a dozen salons with splendidly restored marble fireplaces carved by Tullio and Antonio Lombardo. The **Sala del Scudo** (Shield Room) is covered with world maps that reveal the extents of Venetian power c 1483 and 1762.

Ascend Sansovino's 24-carat gilt stucco-work Scala d'Oro (Golden Staircase) and emerge into second-floor rooms covered with gorgeous propaganda. In the Palladio-designed Sala delle Quattro Porte (Hall of the Four Doors), ambassadors awaited ducal audiences under a lavish display of Venice's virtues by Giovanni Cambi, Titian and Tiepolo.

Few were granted an audience in the Palladio-designed Collegio (Council Room), where Veronese's 1575–78 *Virtues of the Republic* ceiling shows Venice as a bewitching blonde waving her sceptre like a wand over Justice and Peace. Father-son team Jacopo and Domenico Tintoretto attempt similar flattery, showing Venice keeping company with Apollo, Mars and Mercury in their *Triumph of Venice* ceiling for the Sala del Senato (Senate Hall).

Government cover-ups were never so appealing as in the Sala Consiglio dei Dieci (Trial Chambers of the Council of Ten), where Venice's star chamber plotted under Veronese's *Juno Bestowing Her Gifts on Venice,* a glowing goddess strewing gold ducats. Over the slot where anonymous treason accusations were slipped into the Sala della Bussola (Compass Room) is his *St Mark in Glory* ceiling.

The cavernous 1419 Sala del Maggior Consiglio (Grand Council Hall) provides the setting for Domenico Tintoretto's swirling *Paradise,* a work that's more politically correct than pretty: heaven is crammed with 500 prominent Venetians, including several Tintoretto patrons. Veronese's political posturing is more elegant in his oval *Apotheosis of Venice* ceiling, where gods marvel at Venice's coronation by angels, with foreign dignitaries and Venetian blondes rubber-necking on the balcony below.

Museo Correr　　　　　　　　MUSEUM
(Map p344; ☑ 041 4273 0892; http://correr.visit muve.it/; Piazza San Marco 52; incl Palazzo Ducale adult/reduced €18/11; ⊙10am-7pm summer, to 5pm winter; ☷San Marco) Napoleon filled his royal digs over Piazza San Marco with the riches of the doges, and took some of Venice's finest heirlooms to France as trophies. But the biggest treasure here couldn't be lifted: Jacopo Sansovino's 16th-century Libreria Nazionale Marciana, covered with larger-than-life philosophers by Veronese, Titian and Tintoretto and miniature back-flipping sea creatures.

Venice successfully reclaimed many ancient maps, statues, cameos and weapons, plus four centuries of artistic masterpieces in the Pinacoteca. Not to be missed are Paolo Veneziano's 14th-century sad-eyed saints (room 25); Lo Schiavone's Madonna with a bouncing baby Jesus, wearing a coral good-luck charm; Jacopo di Barbari's minutely detailed woodblock perspective view of Venice; an entire room of bright-eyed, peach-cheeked Bellini saints (room 36); and a wonderful anonymous 1784 portrait of champion rower Maria Boscola, five-time regatta winner (room 47). Temporary shows in the neoclassical ballroom are hit-and-miss, but Antonio Canova's 1777 statues of star-crossed lovers Orpheus and Eurydice are permanent scene-stealers.

Torre dell'Orologio　　　　　LANDMARK
(Clock Tower; Map p344; ☑ 041 4273 0892; www. museicivicineveneziani.it; Piazza San Marco; adult/

STATE SECRETS REVEALED: ITINERARI SEGRETI

Discover state secrets in the Palazzo Ducale attic on Itinerari Segreti (Secret Passages; ☑ 041 4273 0892; adult/reduced €20.50/14.50; ⊙tours in English 9.55am, 10.45am & 11.35am, in Italian 9.30am & 11.10am, in French 10.20am & noon) a fascinating 75-minute tour. Head through a hidden passageway disguised as a filing cabinet in Sala del Consiglio dei Dieci (Chamber of the Council of Ten), festooned with happy cherubim and Veronese's optimistic *Triumph of Virtue over Vice*. Suddenly you're in the cramped, unadorned Council of 10 Secret Headquarters, adjoining a trial chamber lined with top-secret file drawers.

Follow the path of the accused into the windowless interrogation room, used until the 17th century to extract information. Next are the studded cells of the Piombi, Venice's notorious attic prison. In 1756, Casanova was condemned to five years' confinement here for corrupting nuns and spreading Freemasonry, but he escaped through the roof of his cell and walked confidently out through the front door, even pausing for a coffee on Piazza San Marco.

San Marco & Dorsoduro

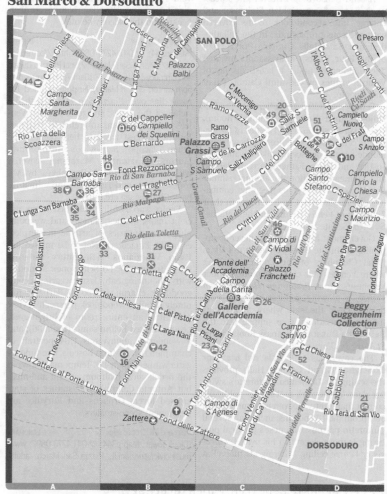

reduced with Museum Pass €12.50/7.50; ⏰ tours in English 10am & 11am Mon-Wed, 2pm & 3pm Thu-Sun, in Italian noon & 4pm daily, in French 2pm & 3pm Mon-Wed, 10am & 11am Thu-Sun; 🚤 San Marco) The two hardest-working men in Venice stand duty on a rooftop around the clock, and wear no pants. No need to file workers' complaints: the 'Do Mori' (Two Moors) exposed to the elements atop the Torre dell'Orologio are made of bronze, and their bell-hammering mechanism runs like, well, clockwork. Below the Moors, Venice's gold-leafed 15th-century timepiece tracks lunar phases.

The clock, designed by Zuan Paolo Rainieri and his son Zuan Carlo in 1493–99, had one hitch: the clockworks required constant upkeep by a live-in clockwatcher and his family until 1998. After a nine-year renovation, the clock's works are in independent working order – 132-stroke chimes keep time in tune, moving barrels indicate minutes and hours on the world's first digital clock face (c 1753), and wooden statues of the three kings and angel emerge from side panels annually on Epiphany and the Feast of the Ascension. Tours climb steep four-storey spiral staircases past the clockworks

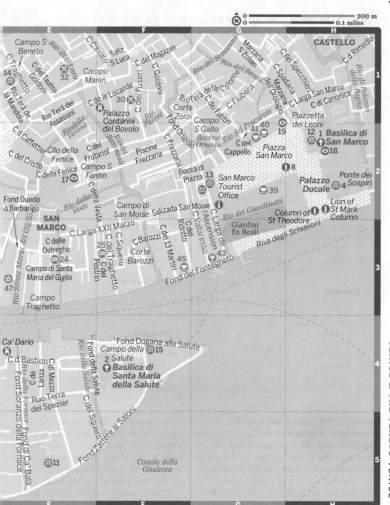

to the roof terrace, for giddy, close-up views of the Moors in action.

Children must be over six years of age to climb the tower and the steep climb is not recommended for pregnant women and those suffering from vertigo or claustrophobia.

Campanile TOWER
(Bell Tower; Map p344; www.basilicasanmarco. it; Piazza San Marco; admission €8; ⊙9am-9pm summer, to 7pm spring & autumn, 9.30am-3.45pm winter; ☒San Marco) The basilica's 99m-tall bell tower has been rebuilt twice since its

initial construction in AD 888. Galileo Galilei tested his telescope here in 1609, but modern-day visitors head to the top for 360-degree lagoon views and close encounters with the Marangona, the booming bronze bell that originally signalled the start and end of the working day for the craftsmen (*marangoni*) at the Arsenale shipyards. Today it rings twice a day: at noon and midnight.

Teatro La Fenice THEATRE
(Map p344; ☑041 78 66 75; www.teatrolafenice. it; Campo San Fantin 1965; theatre visits adult/

San Marco & Dorsoduro

reduced €9/6.50, opera tickets from €66; ⊘tours 9.30am-6pm; 🚤Santa Maria del Giglio) Once its dominion over the high seas ended, Venice discovered the power of high Cs, hiring as San Marco choirmaster Claudio Monteverdi and opening La Fenice ('The Phoenix') in 1792. Rossini and Bellini staged operas here, Verdi premiered *Rigoletto* and *La Traviata*, and international greats Stravinsky, Prokofiev and Britten composed for the house, making La Fenice the envy of Europe. From January to July and September to October, opera season is in full swing. Tours are also possible with advance booking.

Museo Fortuny   MUSEUM
(Map p344; 🕿041 098 81 07; http://fortuny.visit muve.it/; Campo San Beneto 3758; adult/reduced with Museum Pass €13/11; ⊘10am-6pm Wed-Mon; 🚤Sant'Angelo) Find design inspiration at the palatial home-studio of art nouveau designer Mariano Fortuny y Madrazo, whose shockingly uncorseted Delphi goddess frocks set the standard for bohemian chic. First-floor salon walls are eclectic mood boards: Fortuny fashions and Isfahan tapestries, family portraits and the odd dress made of peacock feathers. Art shows in Fortuny's attic warehouse are often overshadowed by the striking architecture and rooftop views.

If these salons inspire design schemes, visit **Fortuny Tessuti Artistici** (Map p340; 🕿041 528 76 97; www.fortuny.com; Fondamenta San Biagio 805; ⊘10am-1pm & 2-6pm Mon-Sat; 🚤Palanca) in Giudecca, where textiles are still hand-printed according to Fortuny's top-secret methods.

★**Palazzo Grassi**   MUSEUM
(Map p344; 🕿box office 199 13 91 39, 041 523 16 80; www.palazzograssi.it; Campo San Samuele 3231; adult/reduced €15/10, 72hr ticket incl Punta della Dogana €20/15; ⊘10am-7pm Wed-Mon mid-Apr-Nov; 🚤San Samuele) Grand Canal gondola riders gasp at first glimpse of massive sculptures by contemporary artists like Thomas Houseago docked in front of Giorgio Masari's 1749 neoclassical palace.

French billionaire François Pinault's provocative art collection overflows Palazzo Grassi, while clever curation and shameless art-star namedropping are the hallmarks of rotating temporary exhibits. Still, despite the artistic glamour, Tadao Ando's creatively repurposed interior architecture steals the show.

Chiesa di Santo Stefano CHURCH
(Map p344; www.chorusvenezia.org; Campo Santo Stefano; admission €3, or with Chorus Pass free; ⊙10am-5pm Mon-Sat; 🚢Accademia) The free-standing bell tower behind it leans disconcertingly, but this brick Gothic church has stood tall since 1325. Credit for ship-shape splendour goes to Bartolomeo Bon for the marble entry portal and to Venetian shipbuilders, who constructed the vast wooden *carena di nave* (ship's keel) ceiling that resembles an upturned Noah's Ark.

Enter the cloisters museum to see Canova's 1808 funerary stelae featuring gorgeous women dabbing their eyes with their cloaks. Also worth looking at are Tullio Lombardo's wide-eyed 1505 saint, and three brooding 1575–80 Tintorettos – *Last Supper*, with a ghostly dog begging for bread; the gathering gloom of *Agony in the Garden*; and the abstract, mostly black *Washing of the Feet*.

⊙ Dorsoduro

★ Gallerie dell'Accademia GALLERY
(Map p344; 🕿041 520 03 45; www.gallerie accademia.org; Campo della Carità 1050; adult/reduced €11/8 plus supplement during special exhibitions, first Sun of the month free; ⊙8.15am-2pm Mon, to 7.15pm Tue-Sun; 🚢Accademia) Venice's historic gallery traces the development of Venetian art from the 14th to 18th centuries, with works by Bellini, Titian, Tintoretto, Veronese and Canaletto among others. The former Santa Maria della Carità convent complex housing the collection maintained its serene composure for centuries until Napoleon installed his haul of Venetian art trophies here in 1807. Since then there's been non-stop visual drama inside its walls.

The grand gallery you enter upstairs features vivid early works that show Venice's precocious flair for colour and drama. Case in point: Jacobello Alberegno's *Apocalypse* (Room 1) shows the whore of Babylon riding a hydra, babbling rivers of blood from her mouth. At the opposite end of the emotional spectrum is Paolo Veneziano's *Coronation of Mary* (Room 1), where Jesus bestows the

---

> ### ❶ OUTSMARTING ACCADEMIA QUEUES
>
> To skip Accademia ticket-booth queues, book ahead by calling 🕿041 520 03 45 (booking fee €1). Otherwise, queues tend to be shorter in the afternoon. But don't wait too long: the last entry to the Accademia is 45 minutes before closing, and proper visits take at least 90 minutes.
>
> Leave any large items at the baggage depot (€1 refundable). Also available at the baggage depot is an audio guide (€6) that is mostly descriptive and largely unnecessary – it's better to avoid the wait and just follow the explanatory wall tags.

---

crown on his mother with a gentle pat on the head to the tune of an angelic orchestra.

UFO arrivals seem imminent in the eerie, glowing skies of Carpaccio's lively *Crucifixion and Glorification of the Ten Thousand Martyrs of Mount Ararat* (Room 2), which offers an intense contrast to Giovanni Bellini's quietly elegant *Madonna and Child between St Catherine and Mary Magdalene* (Room 4). Further along, Room 10 features paintings by Tintoretto and Titian, as well as Paolo Veronese's monumental *Feast in the House of Levi*, originally called *Last Supper*, until Inquisition leaders condemned him for showing dogs, drunkards, dwarves, Muslims and Reformation-minded Germans cavorting with Apostles.

While Rooms 12 to 19 are occasionally used for temporary exhibitions, it's in Room 12 that you'll find Giambattista Piazzetta's saucy, fate-tempting socialite in *Fortune Teller*. Yet even her lure is no match for the glorious works gracing Room 20. Among them is Gentile Bellini's *Procession in St Mark's Square*, which offers an intriguing view of Venice's iconic piazza before its 16th-century makeover. Room 21 is no less captivating, home to Vittore Carpaccio's St Ursula Cycle, a series of nine paintings documenting the saint's ill-fated life.

The original convent chapel (Room 23) is a serene showstopper fronted by a Bellini altarpiece. Sharing the space is Giorgione's highly charged *La Tempesta* (The Storm). Art historians still debate the meaning of the mysterious nursing mother and passing soldier with a bolt of summer lightning: is

ℹ MAKING THE MOST OF YOUR EURO

These passes can help you save on admission costs for Venetian sights. With the exception of the Rolling Venice card, they are all available to purchase online at www.venezia unica.it.

➡ **Civic Museum Pass** (adult/reduced €24.50/18.50) Valid for single entry to 11 civic museums for six months. Purchase online or at participating museums.

➡ **Chorus Pass** (adult/reduced/child €12/8/free) Single entry to 16 Venice churches at any time within six months; on sale online or at church ticket booths.

➡ **Tourist City Pass** (adult/reduced €40/30) Combines the Museum Pass and Chorus Pass as well as reduced entry to the Guggenheim Collection and the Biennale. Purchase online, at tourist offices and at HelloVenezia booths at *vaporetto* (small passenger ferry) stops.

➡ **Rolling Venice** (14-29 years €4) Entitles young visitors to discounted access to monuments and cultural events, plus eligibility for a 72-hour public transport pass for €18 rather than the regular price of €33. Identification is required for purchase at tourism offices or HelloVenezia booths.

this an expulsion from Eden, an allegory for alchemy, or a reference to Venice conquering Padua in the War of Cambria?

Ornamental splendours were reserved for the Scuola della Carita's boardroom, the newly restored Sala dell'Albergo. Board meetings would not have been boring here, under a lavishly carved ceiling and facing Antonio Vivarini's wraparound 1441-50 masterpiece, filled with fluffy-bearded saints keeping a watchful eye on boardroom proceedings.

Titian closes the Accademia with his touching 1534–39 *Presentation of the Virgin*. Here, a young, tiny Madonna trudges up an intimidating staircase while a distinctly Venetian crowd of onlookers point to her example – yet few of the velvet- and pearl-clad merchants offer alms to the destitute mother, or even feed the begging dog.

⭐**Peggy Guggenheim Collection** MUSEUM
(Map p344; ☑041 240 54 11; www.guggen heim-venice.it; Palazzo Venier dei Leoni 704; adult/reduced €15/9; ☺10am-6pm Wed-Mon; ⬚Accademia) After losing her father on the *Titanic,* heiress Peggy Guggenheim became one of the great collectors of the 20th century. Her palatial canalside home, Palazzo Venier dei Leoni, showcases her stockpile of surrealist, futurist and abstract expressionist art with works by up to 200 artists, including her ex-husband Max Ernst, Jackson Pollock (among her many rumoured lovers), Picasso and Salvador Dalí.

⭐**Basilica di Santa Maria della Salute** BASILICA
(La Salute; Map p344; ☑041 241 10 18; www. seminariovenezia.it; Campo della Salute 1b; admission free, sacristy adult/reduced €3/1.50; ☺9am-noon & 3-5.30pm; ⬚Salute) Guarding the entrance to the Grand Canal, this 17th-century domed church was commissioned by Venice's plague survivors as thanks for salvation. Baldassare Longhena's uplifting design is an engineering feat that defies simple logic; in fact, the church is said to have mystical curative properties. Titian eluded the plague until age 94, leaving 12 key paintings in the basilica's art-slung sacristy.

Ca' Rezzonico MUSEUM
(Museum of the 18th Century; Map p344; ☑041 241 01 00; www.visitmuve.it; Fondamenta Rezzonico 3136; adult/reduced €10.50/8, or Museum Pass; ☺10am-6pm Wed-Mon summer, to 5pm winter; ⬚Ca' Rezzonico) Baroque dreams come true at Baldassare Longhena's Grand Canal palace, where a marble staircase leads to gilded ballrooms, frescoed salons and sumptuous boudoirs. Giambattista Tiepolo's Throne Room ceiling is a masterpiece of elegant social climbing, showing gorgeous Merit ascending to the Temple of Glory clutching the Golden Book of Venetian nobles' names – including Tiepolo's patrons, the Rezzonico family.

In the Pietro Longhi Salon, sweeping Grand Canal views are upstaged by the artist's winsome satires of society antics, observed by disapproving lapdogs. **Sala Rosalba Carriera** features Carriera's wry, unvarnished pastel portraits of socialites who aren't conventionally pretty but look like they'd be the life of any party. Giandomenico Tiepolo's swinging court jesters and preening parrots add cheeky humour to the reassembled **Zianigo Villa Frescoes**.

On the top floor, don't miss Emma Ciardi's moody Venice canal views in the Vedutisti Gallery (Gallery Nine), and also an antique pharmacy complete with 183 majolica ceramic jars of 18th-century remedies. Apparently pharmaceutical-grade scorpions don't cure everything: Robert Browning died at Ca' Rezzonico in 1889.

The original entry of Baldassare Longhena's dashingly handsome palace is along the Grand Canal, but the canal-side gate now in use opens onto a courtyard garden where you can picnic (rare in Venice). Also on the ground floor is a cafe and the entry to the mezzanine **Mestrovich Collection**, including notable works by Tintoretto and Bonifacio de' Pitati.

Punta della Dogana
GALLERY

(Map p344; ☑ 041 271 90 39; www.palazzograssi. it; adult/reduced €15/10, incl Palazzo Grassi €20/15; ⊘10am-7pm Wed-Mon; 🚊Salute) Fortuna, the weathervane atop Punta della Dogana, swung Venice's way in 2005, when bureaucratic hassles in Paris convinced art collector François Pinault to showcase his works in Venices's long-abandoned customs warehouses. Built by Giuseppe Benoni in 1677 to ensure no ship entered the Grand Canal without paying duties, the warehouses re-opened in 2009 after a striking reinvention by Tadao Ando. The dramatic space now hosts rotating exhibitions of ambitious, large-scale contemporary artworks from some of the world's most prolific and provocative creative minds.

Chiesa di San Sebastiano
CHURCH

(Map p340; www.chorusvenezia.org; Campo San Sebastiano 1687; admission €3, or with Chorus Pass free; ⊘10am-5pm Mon-Sat; 🚊San Basilio) Antonio Scarpignano's relatively austere 1508-48 facade creates a sense of false modesty at this neighbourhood church in Dorsoduro. Currently undergoing restoration, the interior is adorned with floor-to-ceiling masterpieces by Paolo Veronese,

SQUERO DI SAN TROVASO

The wood cabin along Rio di San Trovaso may look like a stray ski chalet, but it's actually the **Squero di San Trovaso** (Map p344; Campo San Trovaso 1097; 🚊Zattere), one of Venice's three working *squeri* (shipyards), with repainted gondolas drying in the yard. When the door's open, you can peek inside in exchange for a donation left in the can by the door. To avoid startling gondola builders working with sharp tools, no flash photography is allowed.

executed over three decades. According to popular local legend, Veronese found sanctuary at San Sebastiano in 1555 after fleeing murder charges in Verona, and his works in this church deliver lavish thanks to the parish and an especially brilliant poke in the eye of his accusers.

Chiesa dei Gesuati
CHURCH

(Church of Santa Maria del Rosario; Map p344; www.chorusvenezia.org; Fondamenta delle Zattere 918; admission €3, or with Chorus Pass free; ⊘10am-5pm Mon-Sat; 🚊Zattere) That Tiepolo's 1737-39 ceiling frescoes star St Dominic is hardly surprising given that this baroque church – designed by Giorgio Massari and completed in 1735 – was built for the Dominicans. Overwhelming grief grips Mary in Tintoretto's sombre 1565 *Crucifixion*, a painting subsequently restored by Giambattista Piazzetta. Al together lighter is Sebastiano Ricci's 1730-33 *Saints Peter and Thomas with Pope Pius V*, complete with comical cherubs performing tumbling routines.

Magazzini del Sale
ART GALLERY

(Map p344; ☑ 041 522 66 26; www.fondazione vedova.org; Fondamenta delle Zattere 266; adult/reduced €8/6; ⊘during shows 10.30am-6pm Wed-Mon; 🚊Zattere) A retrofit designed by Pritzker Prize–winning architect Renzo Piano transformed Venice's historic **salt warehouses** into **Fondazione Vedova** art galleries, commemorating pioneering Venetian abstract painter Emilio Vedova. Fondazione Vedova shows are often literally moving and rotating: powered by renewable energy sources, 10 robotic arms designed by Vedova and Piano move major modern artworks in and out of storage slots.

VENICE & THE VENETO VENICE

Grand Canal

The 3.5km route of vaporetto (passenger ferry) No 1, which passes some 50 palazzi (mansions), six churches and scene-stealing backdrops featured in four James Bond films, is public transport at its most glamorous.

The Grand Canal starts with controversy: **Ponte di Calatrava** ❶ a luminous glass-and-steel bridge that cost triple the original €4 million estimate. Ahead are castle-like **Fondaco dei Turchi** ❷, the historic Turkish trading-house; Renaissance **Palazzo Vendramin** ❸, housing the city's casino; and double-arcaded **Ca' Pesaro** ❹. Don't miss **Ca' d'Oro** ❺, a 1430 filigree Gothic marvel.

Points of Venetian pride include the **Pescaria** ❻, built in 1907 on the site where fishmongers have been slinging lagoon crab for 600 years, and neighbouring **Rialto Market** ❼ stalls, overflowing with island-grown produce. Cost overruns for 1592 **Ponte di Rialto** ❽ rival Calatrava's, but its marble splendour stands the test of time.

The next two canal bends could cause architectural whiplash, with Sanmicheli-designed Renaissance **Palazzo Grimani** ❾ and Mauro Codussi's **Palazzo Corner-Spinelli** ❿ followed by Giorgio Masari-designed **Palazzo Grassi** ⓫ and Baldassare Longhena's baroque jewel box, **Ca' Rezzonico** ⓬.

Wooden **Ponte dell'Accademia** ⓭ was built in 1930 as a temporary bridge, but the beloved landmark remains. Stone lions flank the **Peggy Guggenheim Collection** ⓮, where the American heiress collected ideas, lovers and art. You can't miss the dramatic dome of Longhena's **Chiesa di Santa Maria della Salute** ⓯ or **Punta della Dogana** ⓰, Venice's triangular customs warehouse reinvented as a contemporary art showcase. The Grand Canal's grand finale is pink Gothic **Palazzo Ducale** ⓱ and its adjoining **Ponte dei Sospiri** ⓲.

Palazzo Grass
French magnate François Pinault scandalised Paris when he relocated his contemporary a collection here, to b displayed in gallerie designed by Gae Au and Tadao Ando.

Ca' Rezzonico
See how Venice lived in baroque splendour at this 18th-century art museum with Tiepolo ceilings, silk-swagged boudoirs and even an in-house pharmacy.

Ponte dell'Accademia

Peggy Guggenheim Collection

Chiesa di Santa M delle Salute

Punta della Dogana
Minimalist architect Tadao Ando creatively repurposed abandoned warehouses as galleries, which now host contemporary art installations from François Pinault's collec

nte di Calatrava
h its starkly streamlined fish-fin shape, the
8 bridge was the first to be built over the
nd Canal in 75 years.

Fondaco dei Turchi
Recognisable by its double colonnade, watchtowers, and dugout canoe parked at the Museo di Storia Naturale's ground-floor loggia.

JEAN-PIERRE LESCOURRET/GETTY IMAGES ©

Ca' d'Oro
Behind the triple Gothic arcades are priceless masterpieces: Titians looted by Napoleon, a rare Mantegna and semiprecious stone mosaic floors.

② ③ **Palazzo Vendramin**

④ ⑤

⑥ **Pescaria**

⑦ **Rialto Market**

Palazzo Grimani

⑩ ⑨

Palazzo Corner-Spinelli

⑧ **Ponte di Rialto**

Ponte dei Sospiri

Palazzo Ducale ⑰ ⑱

Ponte di Rialto
Antonio da Ponte beat out Palladio for the commission of this bridge, but construction costs spiralled to 250,000 Venetian ducats – about €19 million today.

KRZYSZTOF DYDYNSKI/GETTY IMAGES ©

' Pesaro
inally designed by Baldassare Longhena, this
azzo was bequeathed to the city in 1898 to house
Galleria d'Arte Moderna and Museo d'Arte
ntale.

⊙ San Polo & Santa Croce

★ **Scuola Grande di San Rocco**   MUSEUM
(Map p352; ☎ 041 523 48 64; www.scuolagrande
sanrocco.it; Campo San Rocco 3052, San Polo;
adult/reduced €10/8; ⊘9.30am-5.30pm, Tesoro
to 5.15pm; 🚤San Tomà) Everyone wanted the
commission to paint this building dedicated
to the patron saint of the plague-stricken,
so Tintoretto cheated: instead of producing sketches like rival Veronese, he gifted
a splendid ceiling panel of patron St Roch,
knowing it couldn't be refused or matched
by other artists. The artist documents
Mary's life story in the assembly hall, and

both Old and New Testament scenes in the
Sala Grande Superiore upstairs.

In the assembly hall, Mary's life story
starts on the left wall with the Annunciation
and ends on the opposite wall with Tintoretto's dark, cataclysmic Ascension. From
spring to late autumn, the artworks provide
a bewitching backdrop to top-notch concerts of baroque music; ask at the counter or
check the website for details.

Upstairs in the Sala Grande Superiore,
Old Testament scenes painted by Tintoretto between 1575 and 1587 read like a modern graphic novel: you can almost hear the
swoop! overhead as an angel dives to feed

San Polo, Santa Croce & Southeastern Cannaregio

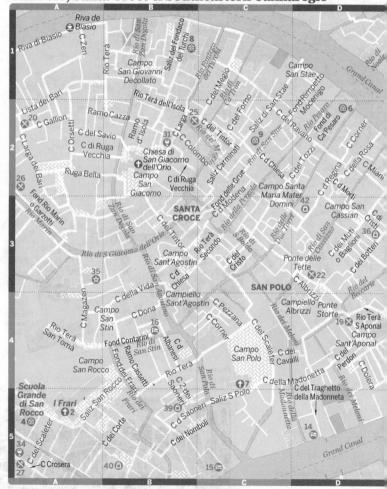

the ailing prophet in *Elijah Fed by an Angel*. Mercy from above is a recurring theme, with Daniel's salvation by angels, the miraculous fall of manna in the desert, and Elisha distributing bread to the hungry. Scenes from Christ's life aren't in chronological order: birth and baptism are followed by resurrection. The drama builds as background characters disappear into increasingly dark canvases, until an X-shaped black void looms at the centre of *Agony in the Garden*.

When Tintoretto painted these works, Venice's outlook was grim indeed: the plague had taken 50,000 Venetians, including the great colourist Titian.

★ I Frari   CHURCH
(Basilica di Santa Maria Gloriosa dei Frari; Map p352; Campo dei Frari, San Polo 3072; adult/reduced €3/1.50; ⊙9am-6pm Mon-Sat, 1-6pm Sun; ⊞; ⊠San Tomà) A soaring Italian-brick Gothic church, I Frari's assets include marquetry choir stalls, Canova's pyramid mausoleum, Bellini's achingly sweet *Madonna with Child* triptych in the sacristy and Longhena's creepy Doge Pesaro funeral monument. Upstaging them all, however, is the small altarpiece. This is Titian's lauded 1518 *Assunta* (Assumption), in which a radiant red-cloaked Madonna reaches heavenward, steps onto a cloud and escapes this mortal

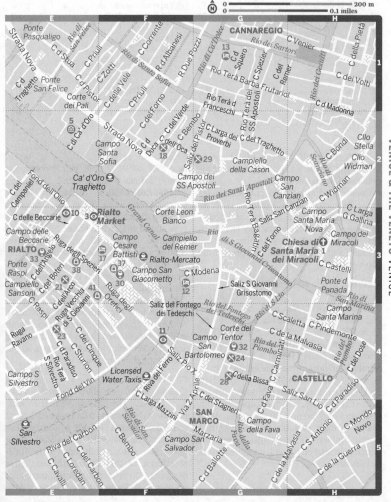

VENICE & THE VENETO VENICE

San Polo, Santa Croce & Southeastern Cannaregio

coil. Titian himself – lost to the plague in 1576 at the age 94 – is buried here near his celebrated masterpiece.

Consecrated in 1492, the current basilica was constructed by the Franciscans to replace a smaller church, built on land donated to the order by Doge Jacopo Tiepolo in 1231. The 12 round pillars running between the nave and aisles are said to represent the apostles.

Museo di Storia Naturale di Venezia   MUSEUM
(Fondaco dei Turchi; Map p352; ☑ 041 275 02 06; www.visitmuve.it; Salizada del Fontego dei Turchi 1730, Santa Croce; adult/reduced €8/5.50; ☺ 10am-6pm Tue-Sun Jun-Oct, 9am-5pm Tue-Fri & 10am-6pm Sat & Sun Nov-May; ☒ San Stae) Never mind the doge: insatiable curiosity rules Venice, and inside the Museo di Storia Naturale (Museum of Natural History) it runs wild. The adventure begins upstairs with dinosaurs and prehistoric crocodiles, then dashes through evolution to Venice's great age of exploration, when adventurers like Marco Polo fetched peculiar specimens from distant lands.

Palazzo Mocenigo   MUSEUM
(Map p352; ☑ 041 72 17 98; http://mocenigo.visit muve.it; Salizada di San Stae 1992, Santa Croce; adult/reduced €8.50/6; ☺ 10am-5pm Tue-Sun summer, to 4pm winter; ☒ San Stae) Venice received a dazzling addition to its property portfolio in 1945 when Count Alvise Nicolò Mocenigo bequeathed his family's 17th-century waterfront *palazzo* to the city. While the ground floor hosts temporary exhibitions, the *piano nobile* is where you'll find a dashing collection of historic fashion, from duchess *andrienne* (hip-extending dresses) to exquisitely embroidered silk waistcoats. Adding to the glamour and intrigue is an exhibition dedicated to the art of fragrance; an ode to Venice's 16th-century status as Europe's capital of perfume.

Ca' Pesaro   MUSEUM
(Galleria Internazionale d'Arte Moderna e Museo d'Arte Orientale; Map p352; ☑ 041 72 11 27; www. visitmuve.it; Fondamenta di Ca' Pesaro 2070, Santa Croce; adult/reduced €10.50/8; ☺ 10am-6pm Tue-Sun summer, to 5pm winter; ☒ San Stae) Like a Carnevale costume built for two, the stately exterior of this Baldassare Longhena–designed 1710 *palazzo* hides two intriguing museums: **Galleria Internazionale d'Arte**

Moderna and **Museo d'Arte Orientale**. While the former includes art showcased at the Venice Biennale, the latter holds treasures from Prince Enrico di Borbone's epic 1887–89 souvenir-shopping spree in Asia.

The Galleria Internazionale d'Arte Moderna spans numerous art movements of the 19th and 20th centuries, including the Macchiaioli, Expressionists and Surrealists. The 1961 De Lisi Bequest added Kandinskys and Morandis to the modernist mix of de Chiricos, Mirós and Moores, plus radical abstracts by postwar Venetian artists Giuseppe Santomaso and Emilio Vedova. Collection highlights include Telemaco Signorini's quietly unsettling *The Room of the Disturbed at the Bonifacio in Florence* (1865), Gustav Klimt's *Judith II (Salome)* from 1909, Marc Chagall's *Rabbi of Vitebsk* (1914–22), and Arturo Martini's anxiety-ridden bronze *The Sprinter* (1935).

Climb the creaky attic stairs of the Museo d'Arte Orientale past samurai warriors guarding a princely collection of Asian travel mementos. Prince Enrico di Borbone reached Japan when Edo art was discounted in favour of modern Meiji, and Edo-era *netsukes*, screens and a lacquerware palanquin are standouts in his collection of 30,000 objets d'art. Around three-quarters of the collection is Japanese, the remaining quarter including a small collection of 12th- to 15th-century Islamic ceramic and an intricately carved Chinese chess set from the 18th century.

Chiesa di San Polo   CHURCH
(Map p352; www.chorusvenezia.org; Campo San Polo 2118, San Polo; admission €3, or with Chorus Pass free; ⊙10am-5pm Mon-Sat; ☒San Tomà) Travellers pass this modest 9th-century Byzantine brick church without guessing that major dramas unfold inside. Under the *carena di nave* ceiling, Tintoretto's *Last Supper* shows apostles alarmed by Jesus' announcement that one of them will betray him. Giandomenico Tiepolo's *Stations of the Cross* sacristy cycle shows onlookers tormenting Jesus, who leaps triumphantly from his tomb in the ceiling panel.

⊙ Cannaregio

Museo Ebraico   MUSEUM
(Map p356; ☎041 715 359; www.museoebraico. it; Campo del Ghetto Nuovo 2902b; adult/reduced €4/3; ⊙10am-7pm Sun-Fri except Jewish holidays Jun-Sep, 10am-5.30pm Sun-Fri Oct-May; ☒Guglie) This museum explores the history of Venice's Jewish community through everyday artefacts, and showcases its pivotal contributions to Venetian, Italian and world history. Opened in 1955, the museum has a small collection of finely worked silverware and other Judaica art objects used in private prayer and to decorate synagogues, as well as early books published in the Ghetto during the Renaissance.

Enquire at the museum for guided synagogue **tours** (adult/reduced €10/8 incl museum; ⊙4 tours daily from 10.30am) lead inside three of the ghetto's seven tiny synagogues: the 1528 **Schola Tedesca** (German Synagogue), with a gilded, elliptical women's gallery modelled after an opera balcony; the 1531 **Schola Canton** (French Synagogue), with eight charming landscapes taken from the biblical parables; and either the simple, darkwood **Schola Italiana** (Italian Synagogue) or the still-active **Schola Spagnola** (Spanish Synagogue), with interiors attributed to Baldassare Longhena. Tours are also possible to the **Antico Cimitero Israelitico** (Old Jewish Cemetery) on the Lido.

★ Chiesa della Madonna dell'Orto   CHURCH
(Map p356; Campo della Madonna dell'Orto 3520; admission €2.50; ⊙10am-5pm Mon-Sat; ☒Madonna dell'Orto) This elegantly spare 1365 brick Gothic cathedral dedicated to the patron saint of travellers remains one of Venice's best kept secrets. It was the parish church of Venetian Renaissance painter Tintoretto, who is buried here in the corner chapel and saved two of his finest works for the apse: *Presentation of the Virgin in the Temple* and his 1546 *Last Judgment*, where lost souls attempt to hold back a teal tidal wave while an angel rescues one last person from the ultimate *acqua alta*.

★ Chiesa di Santa Maria dei Miracoli   CHURCH
(Map p352; Campo dei Miracoli 6074; admission €2.50; ⊙10am-5pm Mon-Sat; ☒Fondamenta Nuove) When Nicolò di Pietro's Madonna icon started miraculously weeping in its outdoor shrine around 1480, crowd control became impossible. With pooled resources and marble scavenged from San Marco slagheaps, neighbours built this chapel (1481–89) to house the painting. Pietro and Tullio Lombardo's miraculous design dropped grandiose Gothic in favour of human-scale harmonies, introducing Renaissance architecture to Venice.

Cannaregio

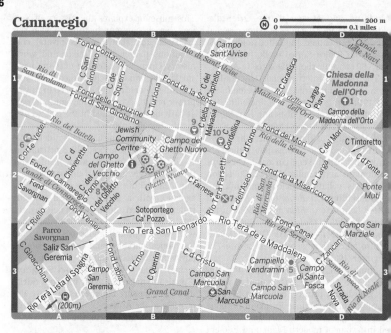

Ca' d'Oro   MUSEUM
(Map p352; ☑ 041 520 03 45; www.cadoro.org;
Calle di Ca' d'Oro 3932; adult/reduced €9.50/6.50;
⊙ 8.15am-2pm Mon, 8.15am-7.15pm Tue-Sun; ☒ Ca'
d'Oro) Along the Grand Canal, you can't miss
15th-century Ca' d'Oro's lacy arcaded Gothic
facade, resplendent even without the original gold-leaf details that gave the palace
its name (Golden House). Baron Franchetti
donated to Venice this treasure-box palace
packed with masterpieces displayed upstairs in **Galleria Franchetti**, alongside Renaissance wonders plundered from Veneto
churches during Napoleon's Italy conquest.

◉ Castello

★**Zanipolo**   BASILICA
(Chiesa dei SS Giovanni e Paolo; Map
p358; ☑ 041 523 59 13; www.basilicasanti
giovanniepaolo.it; Campo Zanipolo; adult/reduced
€2.50/1.25; ⊙ 9am-6pm Mon-Sat, noon-6pm Sun,
tours in English 5.30pm Thu; ☒ Ospedale) When
the Dominicans began building Zanipolo in 1333 to rival the Franciscans' I Frari,
the church stirred passions more common
to Serie A football than architecture. Both
structures feature red-brick facades with
high-contrast detailing in white stone. But
since Zanipolo's facade remains unfinished,
the Frari won a decisive early decision. Over
the centuries, Zanipolo has at least tied the
score with its pantheon of ducal funerary
monuments and the variety of its masterpieces, including works by Bellini, Lorenzetti and Veronese.

THE ORIGINAL GHETTO

The Cannaregio island of **Ghetto Nuovo** once housed Venice's getto (foundry), but its role as Venice's designated Jewish quarter from the 16th to 18th centuries gave the word its current meaning (a usually poor area used to segregate a minority group). In accordance with the 1516 decree, Jewish lenders, doctors and clothing merchants were allowed to attend to Venice's commercial interests by day, while at night and on Christian holidays they were restricted to the island, which was gated and patrolled. Unlike most European cities at the time, pragmatic Venice granted Jewish doctors dispensation for consultations. In fact, Venice's Jewish and Muslim physicians are credited with helping establish the quarantine that spared Venice the worst ravages of plague.

When Jewish merchants fled the Spanish Inquisition for Venice in 1541, there was no place to go in the Ghetto but up. Around **Campo del Ghetto Nuovo**, upper storeys housed new arrivals, synagogues and publishing houses. Despite a 10-year censorship order issued by the church in Rome in 1553, Jewish-Venetian publishers contributed hundreds of titles popularising new Renaissance ideas on religion, humanist philosophy and medicine.

After Napoleon lifted restrictions in 1797, some 1626 Ghetto residents gained standing as Venetian citizens. However, Mussolini's 1938 race laws were throwbacks to the 16th century, and in 1943 most Jewish Venetians were rounded up and sent to concentration camps; only 37 returned.

In 2016, the Ghetto will celebrate its 500th anniversary with a program of educational and artistic activities, including the first ever performance of *The Merchant of Venice* in Venice. To prepare for the year-long celebrations, the Venice Heritage Council is investing in the restoration, maintenance and upgrade of key Ghetto sights such as the museum, the Italian, Canton and German synagogues, and the Spanish and Levantine synagogue gardens. For further information, contact the **Jewish Community Centre** (Map p356; ✆ 041 523 75 65; www.jvenice.org; Ghetto Vecchio; ◷ 9.30am-5pm Mon-Fri).

Built in classic Italian Gothic style, the basilica could accommodate virtually the entire population of 14th-century Castello. And its 33m-high nave provides a fitting setting for 25 doges' tombs. From Pietro Lombardo's three-tier monument celebrating the *Ages of Man* for Pietro Mocenigo (1406–76) to the Gothic tomb of Michele Morosini (1308–82) and Andrea Tirali's bombastic *Tomba dei Valier* (1708), they provide an overview of the stylistic development of Venetian art.

Rarest of all, though, is the surviving 15th-century stained glass in the south transept. Created on Murano, it richly illuminates designs by Bartolomeo Vivarini and Girolamo Mocetto.

★ **Scuola di San Giorgio degli Schiavoni** CHURCH
(Map p358; ✆ 041 522 88 28; Calle dei Furlani 3259a; adult/reduced €5/3; ◷ 2.45-6pm Mon, 9.15am-1pm & 2.45-6pm Tue-Sat, 9.15am-1pm Sun; ⊛ Pietà) Venice's cosmopolitan nature is evident in Castello, where Turkish merchants, Armenian clerics and Balkan and Slavic labourers were considered essential to Venetian commerce and society. This 15th-century religious confraternity headquarters is dedicated to favourite Slavic saints George, Tryphone and Jerome of Dalmatia, whose lives are captured with precision and glowing, early-Renaissance grace by 15th-century master Vittore Carpaccio.

Chiesa di San Giorgio dei Greci CHURCH
(Map p358; www.ortodossia.it; Campiello dei Greci 3412; ◷ 9am-12.30pm & 2.30-4.30pm Mon & Wed-Sat, 9am-1pm Sun; ⊛ Pietà) **FREE** Greek Orthodox refugees who fled to Venice from Turkey with the rise of the Ottoman Empire built a church here in 1536, with the aid of a special dispensation from Venice to collect taxes on incoming Greek ships. Nicknamed 'St George of the Greeks', the little church has an impressive iconostasis, and clouds of fine incense linger over services. The separate, slender bell tower was completed in 1603, though it began to lean right from the start. These days, it seems poised to dive into the canal on which the church sits.

Palazzo Querini Stampalia MUSEUM
(Map p358; ✆ 041 271 14 11; www.querinistampalia.it; Campiello Querini Stampalia 5252; ⊛ San Zaccaria, Rialto) In 1869 Conte Giovanni

Castello

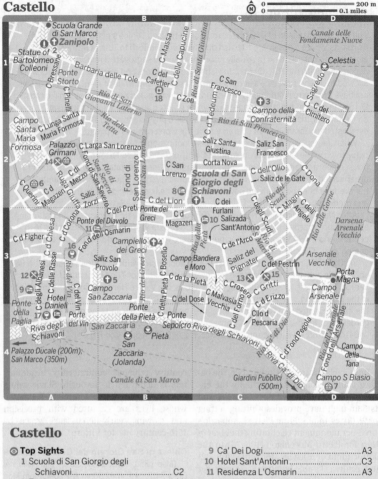

Castello

◎ Top Sights

◎ Sights

🛏 Sleeping

🍴 Eating

🍷 Drinking & Nightlife

🛍 Shopping

Querini Stampalia made a gift of his ancestral *palazzo* to the city on the forward-thinking condition that its 700-year-old library operate late-night openings. Downstairs, savvy

drinkers take their *aperitivi* with a twist of high modernism in the Carlo Scarpa-designed garden, while the *palazzo*'s temporary contemporary shows add an element of the unexpected to the silk-draped salons upstairs.

Enter through the Botta-designed QShop to buy tickets for the **Museo della Fondazione Querini Stampalia** (Map p358; adult/reduced €10/8, Carlo Scarpa garden €8; ☉10am-6pm Tue-Sun; 🚊San Zaccaria). Located in the duke's apartments, the museum reflects the 18th-century tastes and interests of the count: beneath the stuccoed ceilings you'll find rich furnishings and tapestries, Meissen and Sèvres porcelain, marble busts and some 400 paintings. Of these, many are dynastic portraits and conversation pieces, such as Alessandro and Pietro Longhi's genre scenes of masked balls, gambling dens and 18th-century *bon vivants*.

The clear standout in the collection is Giovanni Bellini's arresting *Presentation of Jesus at the Temple*, where the hapless child looks like a toddler mummy, standing up in tightly wrapped swaddling clothes. Other engaging pieces are the 39 winningly naïve *Scenes of Public Life in Venice* by Gabriele Bella (1730–99), which document scenes of the city and its customs during the period. Although rather crude in their realisation, the subject matter – a football game in Sant'Alvise, the frozen lagoon in 1708, the courtesans race on the Rio de la Sensa – is fascinating.

Chiesa di San Francesco della Vigna
CHURCH

(Map p358; Campo San Francesco della Vigna 2786; ☉8.30am-12.30pm & 3-7pm; 🚊Celestia) **FREE** Designed and built by Jacopo Sansovino, with a facade by Palladio, this enchanting Franciscan church is one of Venice's most underappreciated attractions. The Madonna positively glows in Bellini's 1507 *Madonna and Saints* in the **Cappella Santa**, just off the flower-carpeted cloister, while swimming angels and strutting birds steal the scene in the delightful *Virgin Enthroned,* by Antonio da Negroponte (c 1460–70). Bring €0.20 to illuminate them.

Chiesa di San Zaccaria
CHURCH

(Map p358; Campo San Zaccaria 4693; ☉10am-noon & 4-6pm Mon-Sat, 4-6pm Sun; 🚊San Zaccaria) **FREE** When 15th-century Venetian girls showed more interest in sailors than saints, they were sent to the convent adjoining San Zaccaria. The wealth showered on the church by their grateful parents is evident. Masterpieces by Bellini, Titian, Tintoretto and Van Dyck crowd the walls. Bellini's

altarpiece is such a treasure that Napoleon whisked it away to Paris for 20 years when he plundered the city in 1797.

Arsenale
HISTORIC BUILDING

(Map p340; 📞041 274 82 09; http://arsenale.comune.venezia.it; 🚊Celestia) Founded in 1104, the Arsenale soon became the greatest medieval shipyard in Europe, home to 300 shipping companies employing up to 16,000 people. Capable of turning out a new galley in a day, it is considered a forerunner of mass industrial production. Though it's closed to the public most of the year, arty types invade the shipyard during Venice's art and architecture Biennales, when it hosts exhibitions and special events.

Giardini Pubblici
GARDENS

(Map p340; www.labiennale.org; 🚊Giardini, Biennale) Begun under Napoleon as the city's first green space, a large portion of these leafy public gardens serve as the main home of the Biennale, with curators and curiosity-seekers swarming the pavilions, from Carlo Scarpa's daring 1954 raw-concrete-and-glass Venezuelan Pavilion to Denton Corker Marshall's 2015 Australian Pavilion in black Zimbabwean granite. Part of the gardens is open to the public all year round; sometimes during off years you can wander among the pavilions and admire the facades.

Museo Storico Navale
MUSEUM

(Map p358; 📞041 244 13 99; Riva San Biagio 2148; adult/reduced €5/3.50; ☉8.45am-1.30pm Mon-Thu, 8.45am-5.30pm Fri & Sat, 10am-5.30pm Sun; 🚼; 🚊Arsenale) Maritime madness spans 42 rooms at this museum of Venice's seafaring history, featuring scale models of Venetian-built vessels as well as Peggy Guggenheim's not-so-minimalist gondola. On the ground floor, (the barn), you'll find sprawling galleries of fearsome weaponry and 17th-century dioramas of forts and ports. Upstairs you can gawk at a sumptuous model of the *bucintoro*, the doge's gilded ceremonial barge, destroyed by Napoleonic troops in 1798.

🔘 Giudecca

The name Giudecca is probably derived from *zudega* (from *giudicato,* or 'the judged'), the name given to rebellious Venetian nobles banished to Giudecca. The banishments backfired: Giudecca became fashionable and Venetians built weekend garden villas on the island. However, many were abandoned during times of plague and war, and were eventually displaced by 19th-century industry. Today Giudecca is entering its third act, with brick factories converted into artists' lofts and galleries taking over the Fondamenta San Biagio.

★ **Casa dei Tre Oci** CULTURAL CENTRE
(Map p340; ☎041 241 23 32; www.treoci.org; Fondamente de la Croce 43; exhibits €5; ⊗10am-6pm Wed-Mon; ⊠Zitelle) **FREE** Acquired by the Fondazione di Venezia in 2000, this fanciful neo-Gothic house was once the home of early-20th-century artist and photographer Mario de Maria, who conceived its distinctive brick facade with its three arched windows (its namesake 'eyes') in 1910. Now it hosts his photographic archive and fantastic Italian and international exhibitions of contemporary art and photography. The views of San Marco and the Punta della Dogana alone are worth the visit.

Chiesa del Santissimo Redentore CHURCH
(Church of the Redeemer; Map p340; Campo del SS Redentore 194; adult/reduced €3/1.50, or with Chorus Pass free; ⊗10am-5pm Mon-Sat; ⊠Redentore) Built to celebrate the city's deliverance from the Black Death, Palladio's *Il Redentore* was completed under Antonio da Ponte (of Rialto bridge fame) in 1592. Inside there are works by Tintoretto, Veronese and Vivarini, but the most striking is Paolo Piazza's 1619 *Gratitude of Venice for Liberation from the Plague.*

Survival is never taken for granted in this tidal town, and to give thanks during the Festa del Redentore, Venetians have been making the pilgrimage across the canal on a shaky pontoon bridge from the Zattere since 1578.

◉ Isola di San Giorgio Maggiore

Chiesa di San Giorgio Maggiore CHURCH
(Map p340; ☎041 522 78 27; Isola di San Giorgio Maggiore; bell tower adult/reduced €6/4; ⊗9.30am-12.30pm & 2.30-6.30pm Mon-Sat, 2-6.30pm Sun; ⊠San Giorgio Maggiore) Solar eclipses are only marginally more dazzling than Palladio's white Istrian marble facade. Begun in the 1560s, it owes more to ancient Roman temples than the bombastic baroque of Palladio's day. Inside, ceilings billow over a generous nave, with high windows distributing filtered sunshine. Two of Tintoret-

to's masterworks flank the altar, and a lift whisks visitors up the 60m-high bell tower for stirring Ventian panoramas – a great alternative to long lines at San Marco's *campanile.*

Behind the church, a defunct naval academy has been converted into a shipshape gallery by the Fondazione Giorgio Cini (Map p340; ☎041 220 12 15; www.cini.it; Isola di San Giorgio Maggiore; adult/reduced incl guided tour €10/8; ⊗ 10am-5pm Sat & Sun; ⊠San Giorgio Maggiore). After escaping the Dachau internment camp with his son Giorgio, Vittorio Cini returned to Venice on a mission to save San Giorgio Maggiore, which was a ramshackle mess in 1949. Cini's foundation restored the island into a cultural centre. In addition to its permanent collection of Old Masters and modern art, the gallery hosts important contemporary works, from Peter Greenaway to Anish Kapoor.

◉ The Lido

The Lido has been the beach and bastion of Venice for centuries. In the 19th century, it found a new lease on life as a glamorous bathing resort, attracting monied Europeans to its grand Liberty-style hotels. Thomas Mann's novel *Death in Venice* was set here, and you'll spot plenty of ornate villas that date from those decadent days. Walking itineraries around the most extravagant villas are available to download at www2.comune.venezia.it/lidoliberty.

Lido beaches line the southern, seaward side of the island and are easily accessed by *vaporetto* down the Gran Viale. To head further afield, hire a bike from Lido on Bike (☎041 526 80 19; www.lidoonbike.it; Gran Viale 21b; bikes per hour/day €5/9; ⊗9am-7pm; ⊠Lido) and cycle south across the Ponte di Borgo to tiny Malamocco, a miniature version of Venice.

At the southern tip of the island, the Alberoni pine forest slopes down to the Lido's wildest, most scenic beach where marine birds fish in shallow sea pools.

The biggest event on the Lido social calendar is September's Venice Film Festival, when starlets and socialites attempt to blind paparazzi with Italian couture. Major events are held at the 1930s Palazzo del Cinema, which looks like a Fascist airport when stripped of its red carpet.

There are only three 'free' Lido beaches: the **Blue Moon** (Piazzale Bucintoro 1; ⊙10am-6.30pm summer; 🅿; 🚤Lido) complex, the San Nicolò beach to the north and the Alberoni beach at the southern end of the island. The rest of the shoreline is occupied by *stabilimenti*: privately managed sections of beach lined with wooden *capannas* (cabins), a relic of the Lido's 1850s bathing scene. Many of the *capannas* are rented by the same families year in, year out, or reserved for guests of the grand hotels. The *stabilimenti* also offer showers, sun loungers and umbrellas (€13 to €18), and small lockers (€30 to €75). Rates drop a few euros after 2pm.

◉ **Isola di San Michele**

Shuttling between Murano and the Fondamente Nove, *vaporetti* 4.1 and 4.2 stop at Venice's city cemetery, established on Isola di San Michele under Napoleon. Until then, Venetians were buried in parish plots across town – not the most salubrious solution, as Napoleon's inspectors soon realised. Today, goths, hopeless romantics and music lovers pause at the cemetery to pay their respects to Ezra Pound, Sergei Diaghilev and Igor Stravinsky.

◉ **Murano**

Venetians have been working in crystal and glass since the 10th century, but due to fire hazards all glass-blowing was moved to the island of Murano in the 13th century. Woe betide the glass-blower with wanderlust: trade secrets were so jealously guarded that any glass-worker who left the city was accused of treason and subject to assassination. Today, glass artisans ply their trade at workshops along Murano's **Fondamenta dei Vetrai**. To ensure glass you buy is handmade in Murano and not factory-fabricated elsewhere, look for the heart-shaped seal guarantee.

★ **Museo del Vetro**   MUSEUM
(Glass Museum; ☎041 527 47 18; www.museovetro.visitmuve.it; Fondamenta Giustinian 8; adult/reduced €10.50/8; ⊙10am-6pm summer, to 5pm winter; 🚤Museo) Since 1861, Murano's glass-making prowess has been celebrated in Palazzo Giustinian (the seat of the Torcello bishopric from 1659 until its dissolution) and recent renovations finally do justice to the fabulous collection. On entry, a video geeks out on the technical processes innovated on Murano, while upstairs eight rooms walk you through a beautifully curated collection dating back to the 5th century AD.

◉ **Burano**

Venice's lofty Gothic architecture might leave you feeling slightly loopy, but Burano will bring you back to your senses with a reviving shock of colour. The 50-minute ferry from the Fondamente Nove is packed with photographers ready to bound into Burano's backstreets, snapping away at pea-green stockings hung out to dry between hot-pink and royal-blue houses.

Burano is also famed for its handmade lace, which once graced the décolleté of European aristocracy. Some women still maintain the traditions, but few production houses remain. With the exception of **Emilia** (☎041 73 52 99; www.emiliaburano.it; Piazza Galuppi 205; 🚤Burano), most of the lace for sale in local shops is of the imported, machine-made variety.

If you fancy a stroll, hop across the 60m bridge to Burano's even quieter sister island, **Mazzorbo**. Little more than a broad grassy knoll, Mazzorbo is a great place for a picnic or a long, lazy lunch at winery **Venissa** (☎041 527 22 81; www.venissa.it; Fondamenta Santa Caterina 3, Mazzorbo; 4-/5-course tasting menu €100-120; ⊙summer, by reservation only; 🚤Mazzorbo) 🍴.

Museo del Merletto   MUSEUM
(Lace Museum; ☎041 73 00 34; http://museomerletto.visitmuve.it; Piazza Galuppi 187; adult/reduced €5.50/4; ⊙10am-6pm Tue-Sun summer, to 5pm winter; 🚤Burano) Burano's Lace Museum tells the story of a craft that cut across social boundaries, endured for centuries and evoked the epitome of civilisation reached during the Republic's heyday. From the triple-petalled corollas on the fringes of the Madonna's mantle in Torcello's 12th-century mosaics to Queen Margherita's spider-web-fine 20th-century mittens, lace-making was both the creative expression of female sensitivity and a highly lucrative craft.

VENICE & THE VENETO VENICE

Venetian Artistry

Glass

Venetians have been working in crystal and glass since the 10th century, though fire hazards prompted the move of the city's furnaces to Murano in the 13th century. Trade secrets were so closely guarded that any glass-worker who left the city was considered guilty of treason. By the 15th century Murano glassmakers were setting standards that couldn't be equalled anywhere in the world. They monopolised the manufacture of mirrors for centuries, and in the 17th century their skill at producing jewel-bright crystal led to a ban on the production of false gems out of glass. For a short course in Murano's masterly skill, head to the **Museo del Vetro** (p361).

Today, along Murano's Fondamenta dei Vetrai, centuries of tradition are upheld in Cesare Toffolo's winged goblets and Davide Penso's lampworked glass beads, while striking modern glass designs by Nason Moretti at ElleElle, Marina e Susanna Sent and Venini keep the tradition moving forward.

Paper

Embossing and marbling began in the 14th century as part of Venice's burgeoning publishing industry, but these bookbinding techniques and *ebru* (Turkish marbled paper) endpapers have taken on lives of their own. Artisan Rosanna Corrò of Cárte uses bookbinding techniques to create marbled, bookbound handbags and even furniture, while Cartavenezia turns hand-pulped paper into embossed friezes and free-form lamps. Gianni Basso uses 18th-century book symbols to make letter-pressed business cards with old-world flair, and you can watch a Heidelberg press in

1. Detail of a giant glass sculpture, Murano (p361) **2.** Lace-making at Burano (p361) **3.** Hand-printed paper products for sale

action at Veneziastampa, churning out menus and ex-libris (bookplates).

Textiles

Anything that stands still long enough in this city is liable to end up swagged, tasselled and upholstered. Venetian lace was a fashion must for centuries as Burano's **Lace Museum** (p361) attests, and Bevilacqua still weaves luxe tapestries (and donates scraps to nonprofit Banco Lotto 10 to turn into La Fenice costumes and handbags).

But the modern master of Venetian bohemian textiles is Fortuny, whose showroom on Giudecca features hand-stamped wall coverings created in strict accordance with top-secret techniques. But though the methods are secret, Fortuny's inspiration isn't: it covers the walls of his home studio, from Persian

armour to portraits of socialites who tossed aside their corsets for Fortuny's Delphi gowns – now available for modern boho goddesses at Venetia Studium.

> ### TOP FIVE NON-TOURISTY SOUVENIRS
>
> ➡ Customised business cards at **Gianni Basso**.
>
> ➡ Lilac smoking jacket with handprinted scarlet skulls from **Fiorella Gallery**.
>
> ➡ Blown-glass soap-bubble necklaces from **Marina e Susanna Sent** (p379).
>
> ➡ Lux, hand-stamped velvet evening bags in gold and mulberry from **Venetia Studium**.
>
> ➡ Bold, funky, cardboard-and-paper handbags from **Cárte** (p379).

WORTH A TRIP

A NORTHERN LAGOON BOAT TRIP

Whereas other cities sunk their history in foundations, Venice cast out across the lagoon's patchwork of shifting mudflats, so understanding something of the lagoon is integral to understanding Venice. Unesco recognised this by including the 550-sq-km (212-sq-mile) lagoon – the largest coastal wetland in Europe – in its designation of Venice as a World Heritage Site in 1987.

Rich in unique flora and fauna, the tidal *barene* (shoals) and salt marshes are part of the city's psyche. Between September and January more than 130,000 migrating birds nest, dive and dabble in the shallows. Year-round, fishing folk tend their nets and traps, and city-council workers dredge canals and reinforce shifting islands of cord-grass and saltwort so essential to the lagoon's ecology.

Take a boat tour with **Terra e Acqua** (☑ 347 4205004; www.veneziainbarca.it; ⊗ day trips incl lunch 9-12 people €380-460; ⊞) ∅ and dock for wine tasting at the Sant'Erasmo *cantina*, tour the quarantine island of Lazzaretto Nuovo and explore Sant'Andrea, the finest fort in the lagoon. Then return to Venice as a rosy-tinted sunset frames the city's *campaniles* (bell towers).

◉ Torcello

On the pastoral island of Torcello, a three-minute T-line ferry-hop from Burano, sheep outnumber the 14 or so human residents. This bucolic backwater was once a Byzantine metropolis of 20,000, but of its original nine churches and two abbeys, only the brick-built **Chiesa di Santa Fosca** (⊗10am-4.30pm; ☒Torcello) and splendid mosaic-filled Santa Maria Assunta remain.

★ Basilica di Santa Maria Assunta
CHURCH

(☑041 73 01 19; Piazza Torcello; adult/reduced €5/4, incl museum €8/6, incl campanile €9; ⊗10.30am-6pm summer, 10am-5pm winter; ☒Torcello) Life choices are presented in no uncertain terms in the dazzling 12th-century mosaics of Santa Maria Assunta. Look ahead to an afterlife amid saints and a beatific Madonna, or turn your back on her and face the wrath of the devil gloating over lost souls in an extraordinary *Last Judgment* panel. In existence for more than a millennium, the cathedral is the Lagoon's oldest Byzantine-Romanesque monument and after lengthy restorations you can once again enjoy the heavenly views from the Campanile.

🏃 Activities

A **gondola ride** (☑041 528 50 75; www.gondolavenezia.it) gives glimpses into *palazzi* courtyards and hidden canals otherwise unseen on foot. Official daytime rates are €80 for 40 minutes (six passengers maximum), and it's €100 between 7pm and 8am, not including songs (negotiated separately) or tips. Additional time is charged in 20-minute increments (day/night €40/50). Agree on a price, time limit and singing in advance to avoid surcharges. Gondole cluster at *stazi* (stops) along the Grand Canal, and at the train station, the Rialto and near major monuments, but you can also book a pick-up by calling the main number.

Cheaper shared gondola rides are available through **Tu.Ri.Ve** (www.turive.it), either by booking online or through the tourist office.

★ Row Venice
ROWING

(Map p340; ☑347 7250637; rowvenice.org; 90min lessons 1-2 people €80, 4 people €120) The next best thing to walking on water: rowing a traditional *batellina coda di gambero* (shrimp-tailed boat) standing up like gondoliers do. Tours must be booked and commence at the wooden gate of the Sacca Misericordia boat marina at the end of Fondamenta Gasparo Contarini in Cannaregio.

Venice Kayak
KAYAKING

(☑346 4771327; www.venicekayak.com; Isola di Certosa; half/full-day tours 2-6 people €90/120) Of all Venice's watery pursuits, kayaking with René Seindal is probably the best, most affordable fun you can have without a license or the pirouetting skill of a gondolier. His well-planned half- or full-day tours take you into the warren of Venice's canals alongside police boats, fire boats and floating funeral hearses, or out into the broad garden of the lagoon to Burano, Torcello and Sant'Erasmo. Why not do both and you'll come to appreciate how the Lagoon is as much a part of the city's history as the basilica.

Painting In Venice COURSE

(☑340 544 52 27; www.paintinginvenice.com; 3-hour private lesson €90, 2-/4-day workshop €250/580) Sign up for a session with professionally trained and practising artists Caroline, Sebastian and Katrin and you'll strike out into tranquil *campi* in the tradition of classic Venetian *vedutisti* (outdoor artists). Beginners learn the basic concepts of painting 'en plein air', while those with more advanced skills receive tailormade tuition. It's a great way to slow down and really appreciate the colour and composition of each view.

Venice Photo Walk WALKING TOUR

(☑041 963 73 74; www.msecchi.com; 2/3/6 hr walking tour up to 4 people €210/300/600) Throughout San Marco you'll be tripping over iPhone-touting tourists waving selfie sticks. Everyone, it seems, wants to capture the perfect Venetian scene. Getty photojournalist, Marco Secchi, will show you how.

Yoga Venezia YOGA

(Map p340; ☑346 795 59 84; http://yogavenezia.com; Fondament Sant'Eufemia 317; classes €15, tours €30-50; ●; ⛴Palanca) One minute you're admiring Palladio's façade on San Giorgio Maggiore and the next you're striking a warrior pose on *fondamente* as other bemused tourists wonder whether you're the modern art installation. It's all in a day's yoga class for Californian Julia Curtis who leads urban yoga tours around Venice as well as presiding over classes at her Giudecca home and studio. Other classes take place at Venice's most beautiful gym, the palestra on San Giorgio, and at La Serra in Castello.

☞ Tours

From April to October, the tourist office offers a range of guided tours, from the classic gondola circuit (€40 per person) to a penetrating look at Basilica di San Marco (€21 per person) and a four-hour circuit of Murano, Burano and Torcello (€20 per person).

VeniceArtFactory CULTURAL TOUR

(Map p340; ☑349 779 93 85, 328 658 38 71; www.veniceartfactory.org; Via Garibaldi 1794; 2-person tour €180, additional adult/student €40/20; ⛴Arsenale) VeniceArtFactory's Studio Tours allow you to sit down to breakfast or share an aperitif with painters, sculptors and engravers in their studios and homes and ask them what it's like to be an artist in the most artful city in the world.

Walks Inside Venice WALKING TOUR

(☑041 524 17 06; www.walksinsidevenice.com; 2½hr group tours per person €60; ●) A spirited team runs both private tours (maximum six people) and public group tours (maximum eight people) exploring the city's major monuments and hidden backstreets. Group tours include explorations of the San Marco and San Polo, while private tour options include contemporary art and photography, and Venice's lagoon islands.

Venicescapes WALKING TOUR

(☑041 520 63 61; www.venicescapes.org; 4-6hr tour incl book 2 adults US$250-290, additional adult US$60, under 18yr US$30) Intriguing walking tours run by a nonprofit historical society (proceeds support ongoing Venetian historical research) with themes such as 'A City of Nations', exploring multiethnic Venice through the ages, and 'A Most Serene Republic', revealing how Venice kept the peace through politics and espionage.

Venice Day Trips CULTURAL TOURS

(☑049 60 06 72; www.venicedaytrips.com; Via Saetta 18, Padua; semi-private/private tours per person from €165/275) A fantastic selection of off-the-shelf and customised tours run by the ebullient Mario, Rachel and Silvia. Keen to show you the genuine face of the Veneto these bite-sized tours range from cooking classes in Cannaregio to cheese-making on Monte Veronese and tutored wine tastings (Mario and Rachel are qualified sommeliers). Pick-up is from the Isola di Tronchetto *vaporetto* stop in Venice.

🎭 Festivals & Events

Carnevale CARNIVAL

(www.carnevale.venezia.it) Masquerade madness stretches over two weeks in February before Lent. Tickets to masked balls start at €140, but there's a free-flowing wine fountain to commence Carnevale, public costume parties in every *campo* (square) and a Grand Canal flotilla marking the end of festivities.

La Biennale di Venezia CULTURAL

(www.labiennale.org) In odd years the Art Biennale runs from June to October, while in even years the Architecture Biennale runs from September to November. The main venues are Giardini Pubblici pavilions and the Arsenale. Every summer, the Biennale hosts avant-garde dance, theatre, cinema and music programs throughout the city.

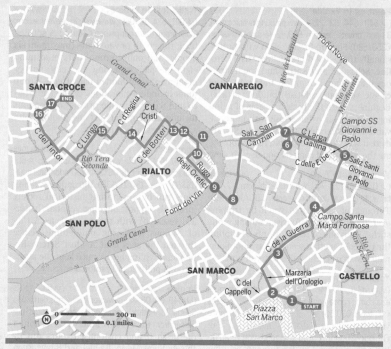

City Walk
Venice Labyrinth

START PIAZZA SAN MARCO
END CAMPO SAN GIACOMO DELL'ORIO
LENGTH 6KM; TWO HOURS

This adventure begins with the obligatory salute to ❶ **Basilica di San Marco** (p339). Duck under the ❷ **Torre dell'Orologio** (p343) and follow the *calle* veering right into ❸ **Campo della Guerra**, where you'll hear Venetian gossip whispered over *spritz*. Pass over the bridge along Calle Casselleria into sunny ❹ **Campo Santa Maria Formosa**. Straight ahead is Calle Santa Maria della Formosa; follow it to the left across two bridges to Salizada Santi Giovanni e Paolo, which leads left to the massive Gothic cathedral, ❺ **Zanipolo** (p356).

Calle Larga Gallina leads over a bridge; after this turn left for a glimpse of heaven at Venice's small wonder, the marble-clad ❻ **Chiesa di Santa Maria dei Miracoli** (p355). Backtrack over the bridge to browse through ❼ **Campo Santa Maria Nova** to Salizada San Canzian, which you'll follow to

skinny ❽ **Chiesa di San Bartolomeo**, lined with souvenir stalls. To the right is ❾ **Ponte di Rialto**; stay on the right as you cross and duck towards happy-hour central, ❿ **Campo Cesare Battisti**. Continue along the ⓫ **Grand Canal** to Venice's tastiest *campi*: produce-piled ⓬ **Campo Rialto Mercato** and the covered seafood market, ⓭ **Pescaria** (p373).

Turning left along Calle dei Botteri and then onto boutique-lined Calle di Cristi, you'll come to ⓮ **Campo San Cassian**, the site of the world's first public opera house. Cross the bridge to Calle della Regina, then head right to cross another bridge to sociable ⓯ **Chiesa di Santa Maria Mater Dominii**, with its cafes and ancient neighbourhood well. Turn left down Calle Lunga and over a bridge until it dead-ends, then jog left to Rio Tera Seconda and right again onto Calle del Tentor. Straight ahead, you'll see the medieval church, ⓰ **San Giacomo dell'Orio**, and your pick of Italy's best natural-process wines at ⓱ **Al Prosecco** (p377). *Cin-cin!*

Festa del Redentore   RELIGIOUS

(Feast of the Redeemer; www.turismovenezia.it)
Walk on water across the Giudecca Canal to
Il Redentore via a wobbly pontoon bridge on
the third Saturday and Sunday in July, then
watch the fireworks from the Zattere.

Venice International Film Festival   FILM

(Mostra del Cinema di Venezia; www.labiennale.
org/en/cinema) The only thing hotter than a
Lido beach in August is the Film Festival's
star-studded red carpet, usually rolled out
from the last weekend in August through
the first week of September.

Regata Storica   CULTURAL

(www.regatastoricavenezia.it) Sixteenth-century
costumes, eight-oared gondolas and ceremonial barques feature in this historical procession (usually held in September), which
re-enacts the arrival of the Queen of Cyprus
and precedes gondola races.

Festa della Madonna della Salute CULTURAL

(www.turismovenezia.it) If you had survived
plague, floods and Austrian invasion, you'd
throw a party too. Every year since the 17th
century, Venetians have crossed a pontoon
bridge across the Grand Canal on 21 November to give thanks at Chiesa di Santa Maria
della Salute and splurge on sweets.

🛏 Sleeping

The website of the **tourist board** (www.turismo
venezia.it) lists hundreds of B&Bs, *affittacamere* (rooms for rent) and apartments to
rent in Venice proper. More can be found at
www.bbplanet.it, www.guestinitaly.com and
www.veniceapartment.com.

The best hotel rates are typically in November, early December, January and the
period between Carnevale and Easter, but
you might swing deals in July and August.

🛏 Piazza San Marco & Around

Albergo San Samuele   HOTEL €

(Map p344; ☑041 852 14 15; www.hotelsan
samuele.com; Salizzada San Samuele 3358; s €30-
50, d €35-80; 🛥 San Samuele) The one-star San
Samuele is one of San Marco's most affordable accommodation options. These neat
digs, wrapped around a central courtyard,
offer 10 simple, en suite rooms furnished
with firm beds and brightened up with
graphic posters from the 1930s. There's no
air con and breakfast isn't served, but you're
steps away from café-fringed Campo San
Stefano. Book at least a month in advance.

Giò & Giò   B&B €

(Map p344; ☑347 3665016; www.giogiovenice.
com; Calle delle Ostreghe 2439; d €90-155; 🕸🛜;
🛥 Santa Maria del Giglio) Restrained baroque
sounds like an oxymoron, but here you have
it: burl-wood bedsteads, pearl-grey silk draperies, polished parquet floors and spotlit
art. Packaged breakfasts are available in the
shared kitchen. Ideally located near Piazza
San Marco, along a side canal; angle for
rooms overlooking the gondola stop, and
wake to choruses of *Volare, oh-oh-ooooh!*

⭐ Hotel Flora   HOTEL €€

(Map p344; ☑041 520 58 44; www.hotelflora.it;
Calle Bergamaschi 2283a; d €105-365; 🕸🛜👪;
🛥 Santa Maria del Giglio) Down a lane from
glitzy Calle Larga XXII Marzo, this ivy-
covered retreat quietly outclasses brash
designer neighbours with its delightful
tearoom, breakfasts around the garden
fountain and gym offering shiatsu massage.
Guest rooms feature antique mirrors, fluffy
duvets atop hand-carved beds, and tiled en
suite baths with apothecary-style amenities.
Damask-clad superior rooms overlook the
garden. Strollers and kids' teatime complimentary; babysitting available.

Bloom & 7 Cielo   B&B €€

(Map p344; ☑340 1498872; www.bloom-venice.
com; Campiello Santo Stefano 3470; d €168-290;
🕸; 🛥 Accademia) Fraternal-twin B&Bs occupy two upper floors of a historic home overlooking Santo Stefano right across the *calle*.
Bloom offers glam-rock rooms in shocking
scarlet, fuchsia and gold damask with leather bedsteads and full-frontal cathedral views.
Downstairs, 7 Cielo (Seventh Heaven) is
artfully romantic, with exposed-brick walls
and Murano glass mosaic bathrooms. Take
breakfast on the sunny top-floor terrace.

⭐ Novecento   BOUTIQUE HOTEL €€€

(Map p344; ☑041 241 37 65; www.novecento.biz;
Calle del Dose 2683/84; d €160-340; 🕸🛜; 🛥 Santa Maria del Giglio) Sporting a boho-chic look,
the Novocento is a real charmer. Its nine
individually designed rooms ooze style with
Turkish kilim pillows, Fortuny draperies and
19th-century carved bedsteads. Outside, its
garden is a lovely spot to linger over breakfast. Want more? You can go for a massage
at sister property Hotel Flora, take a hotel-
organised course in landscape drawing,
or mingle with creative fellow travellers
around the honesty bar.

VENICE & THE VENETO VENICE

🛏 Dorsoduro

★ B&B Corte Vecchia
B&B €

(Map p344; ☑ 041 822 12 33; www.cortevecchia.
net; Rio Terà San Vio 462; s €60-100, d €100-130;
❄ 🛜; 🚤 Accademia) Corte Vecchia is a stylish steal, run by young architects Antonella
and Mauro and a stone's throw from Peggy
Guggenheim, Accademia and Punta della
Dogana. Choose from a snug single with en
suite, or two good-sized doubles: one with
en suite, the other with an external private
bathroom. All are simple yet understatedly
cool, with contemporary and vintage objects, and a tranquil, shared lounge.

Hotel Galleria
INN €

(Map p344; ☑ 041 523 24 89; www.hotelgalleria.it;
Campo della Carità 878a; d €140-240; 🛜 🛗; 🚤 Accademia) Smack on the Grand Canal alongside the Ponte dell'Accademia is this classic
hotel in a converted 18th-century mansion.
Book ahead, especially for rooms 7 and 9,
small doubles overlooking the Grand Canal.
Room 10 sleeps six and comes with an original ceiling fresco. Renovations were under-
way at the time of research to give all rooms
their own private bathroom.

Pensione Accademia Villa Maravege
INN €€

(Map p344; ☑ 041 521 01 88; www.pensione
accademia.it; Fondamenta Bollani 1058; d €145-
340; ❄ 🛜 🛗; 🚤 Accademia) Step through the
ivy-covered gate of this 17th-century garden
villa just off the Grand Canal, and you'll
forget you're a block from the Accademia.
Although some of the 27 guest rooms are
rather small, all are effortlessly elegant,
with parquet floors, antique desks and shiny
bathrooms – one even comes with four-
poster bed, wood-beamed ceilings and
glimpses of the canal.

Locanda San Barnaba
B&B €€

(Map p344; ☑ 041 241 12 33; www.locanda-san
barnaba.com; Calle del Traghetto 2785-6; d €120-
185; ❄ 🛜; 🚤 Ca' Rezzonico) The stage is set for
intrigue at this 16th-century *palazzo* (mansion), with its frescoed grand salon, hidden
courtyard garden and cupboards concealing a secret staircase. Ask for the romantic
wood-beamed Poeta Fanatico room; Campiello, with skylight views of a neighbouring
bell tower; or the superior Il Cavaliere e la
Dama, for 18th-century frescoed ceilings
and balconies dangling over the canal.

Ca' Pisani
DESIGN HOTEL €€€

(Map p344; ☑ 041 240 14 11; www.capisanihotel.
it; Rio Terà Antonio Foscarini 979a; d €210-351;
❄ 🖥 🛜; 🚤 Accademia) Sprawl out in style
right behind the Accademia, and luxuriate
in sleigh beds, jacuzzi tubs and walk-in clos-
ets. Mood lighting and soundproofed walls
make downstairs deco-accented rooms right
for romance, while families appreciate top-
floor rooms with sleeping lofts. Venetian
winters require in-house Turkish steam
baths, while summers mean roof-terrace
sunning and patio breakfasts. A hushed, elegant, antiques-laced retreat.

🛏 San Polo & Santa Croce

Ca' della Corte
B&B €

(Map p340; ☑ 041 715 877; www.cadellacorte.
com; Campo Surian 3560, Santa Croce; d €75-170;
❄ 🛜 🛗; 🚤 Piazzale Roma) Live like a Venetian in this 16th-century family home near
Campo Santa Margherita, yours with a Liberty frescoed salon, adjacent piano room,
self-service bar, top-floor terrace overlooking Gothic palaces, and breakfasts delivered
to your room. Stay in wood-beamed garrets,
chandelier-lit superior rooms or feng-shui
eco-rooms. Sporty types, ask helpful staff to
organise sailing, tennis, and horse-riding on
the Lido; babysitting and shiatsu massage
are also available.

Ca' Angeli
BOUTIQUE HOTEL €€

(Map p352; ☑ 041 523 24 80; www.caangeli.it;
Calle del Traghetto de la Madoneta 1434, San Polo;
d €95-225, ste from €200; ❄ 🛜; 🚤 San Silvestro)
Murano glass chandeliers, a Louis XIV love-
seat and namesake 16th-century angels set a
refined tone at this restored, canalside *palazzo*. Guest rooms are a picture with beamed
ceilings, antique carpets and big bathrooms,
while the dining room looks out onto the
Grand Canal. Breakfast includes organic
products where possible.

Pensione Guerrato
PENSION €€

(Map p352; ☑ 041 528 59 27; www.pensione
guerrato.it; Calle Drio la Scimia 240a, San Polo; d/
tr/q €145/165/185; ❄ 🛜; 🚤 Rialto Mercato) In a
1227 tower that was once a hostel for knights
headed to the Third Crusade, the smart
guest rooms here haven't lost their sense of
history – some have frescoes or glimpses of
the Grand Canal. Sparkling modern bathrooms, a prime Rialto Market location and
helpful owners add to the package. No lift.

The owners also have a couple of apartments (€180 to €240) equipped with kitchens.

★ Oltre il Giardino
BOUTIQUE HOTEL €€€

(Map p352; ☑ 041 275 00 15; www.oltreilgiardino-venezia.com; Fondamenta Contarini, San Polo 2542; d €180-250, ste €200-500; ❉ ⊛; ⊠ San Tomà) Live the dream in this garden villa, the 1920s home of Alma Mahler, the composer's widow. Hidden behind a lush walled garden, its six high-ceilinged guest rooms marry historic charm with modern comfort: marquetry composer's desks, candelabras and 19th-century poker chairs sit alongside flat-screen TVs and designer bathrooms, while outside, pomegranate trees flower in the garden.

★ Hotel Palazzo Barbarigo
DESIGN HOTEL €€€

(Map p352; ☑ 041 740 172; www.palazzobarbarigo.com; Grand Canal 2765, San Polo; d €240-440; ❉ ⊛; ⊠ San Tomà) Brooding, chic and seductive, Barbarigo delivers 18 plush guest rooms combining modern elegance and masquerade intrigue – think dark, contemporary furniture, sumptuous velvets, feathered lamps and the occasional fainting couch. Whether you opt for junior suites overlooking the Grand Canal (get triple-windowed Room 10) or standard rooms overlooking Rio di San Polo, you can indulge in sleek bathrooms, positively royal breakfasts and smart, attentive service.

🛏 Cannaregio

Allo Squero
B&B €

(Map p352; ☑ 041 523 69 73; www.allosquero.it; Corte dello Squero 4692; s €60-80, d €90-120; ⊛ ⶠ; ⊠ Fondamenta Nuove) Dock for the night at this historic gondola *squero* (shipyard), recently converted into a garden retreat. Gondolas passing along two canals are spotted from modern, sunny upstairs guest rooms, with terrazzo marble floors and sleek mosaic-striped en suite baths, some with tubs. Hosts Andrea and Hiroko offer Venice-insider tips over cappuccino and pastry breakfasts in the fragrant, wisteria-filled garden. Cots and cribs available.

Ca' Dogaressa
BOUTIQUE HOTEL €€

(Map p340; ☑ 041 275 9441; www.cadogaressa.com; Fondamenta di Cannaregio 1018; d €50-170, ste €125-300; ❉ @ ⊛; ⊠ Guglie) A splashy canalside inn with Venetian charm – princess beds, gilt mirrors, chandeliers – that won't drain your holiday budget. Roof-terrace

views and designer bathrooms are four-star-worthy, and canalbank breakfasts beat most B&Bs. Your Antenori family hosts offer major hotel-chain perks, including 24-hour reception, laptops for in-room use and laundry service. The annexe is cheaper but smaller, with shared bathrooms.

Domus Orsoni
B&B €€

(Map p356; ☑ 041 275 95 38; www.domusorsoni.it; Corte Vedei 1045; s €80-150, d €100-250; ❉ @; ⊠ Guglie) Surprise: along a tranquil Ghetto lane and behind a rosy, historic facade is Venice's most original artist's retreat. Continental breakfasts are served in the palm-shaded garden near the Orsoni mosaic works, located here since 1885 – hence the custom mosaics glittering across walls, bathrooms and tables. Find artistic bliss in five mosaic-splashed guest rooms, or join Venetian crowds mid-toast just around the corner.

Al Ponte Antico
BOUTIQUE HOTEL €€€

(Map p352; ☑ 041 241 19 44; www.alponteantico.it; Calle dell' Aseo 5768; d €240-430; ⊛; ⊠ Rialto) Like a courtesan's boudoir, the Peruch's 16th century *palazzo* is swathed in damask wall coverings, heavy silk curtains and thick, plush carpets. A smiling host greets you at the padded, golden reception desk and whisks you up to the old-rose salon where guests gossip over coffee and *petit fours* in snug banquettes. Rooms are large and unabashedly lavish with enough gilt to satisfy Louis XIV; and in the evening, romance blossoms on the terrace, framed by views of the Rialto bridge.

🛏 Castello

★ B&B San Marco
B&B €

(Map p358; ☑ 041 522 75 89; www.realvenice.it/smarco; Fondamenta San Giorgio 3385l; d €70-135; ❉ ⶠ; ⊠ Pietà, Arsenale) One of the few genuine B&Bs in Venice. Alice and Marco welcome you warmly to their home overlooking Carpaccio's frescoed Scuola di San Giorgio Schiavoni. The 3rd-floor apartment (there is no elevator), with its parquet floors and large, bright windows, is furnished with family antiques and offers photogenic views over the terracotta rooftops and canals. Marco and Alice live upstairs, so they're always on hand with great recommendations.

★ Hotel Sant'Antonin
BOUTIQUE HOTEL €€

(Map p358; ☑ 041 523 16 21; www.hotelsantantonin.com; Fondamenta dei Furlani 3299; d

€100-280; ✳ 🛜 ♿; 🚤 San Zaccaria) Enjoy the patrician pleasures of a wealthy Greek merchant at this 16th-century *palazzo* perched on a canal near the Greek church. Grand proportions make for light, spacious rooms with cool terrazzo floors, geranium-draped balconies, frescoed ceilings and impressive Baroque furnishings. Come breakfast and you can trip down the stone staircase and out into one of the largest private gardens in Venice, complete with a pretty stone pergola and gurgling fountain. A perfect option for families.

Ca' Dei Dogi   BOUTIQUE HOTEL €€

(Map p358; ☎ 041 241 37 51; www.cadeidogi.it; Corte Santa Scolastica 4242; s €75-95, d €110-250; ✳ @; 🚤 San Zaccaria) Even the nearby Bridge of Sighs can't dampen the high spirits of the sunny yellow Ca' Dei Dogi, with guest-room windows sneaking peeks into the convent cloisters next door. Streamlined, modern rooms look like ships' cabins, with tilted wood-beamed ceilings, dressers that look like steamer trunks, and compact mosaic-covered bathrooms – ask for the one with the terrace and acuzzi.

Friendly staff can arrange concert tickets, free trips to Murano and sunset gondola rides. Book well ahead.

Residenza L'Osmarin   B&B €€

(Map p358; ☎ 347 4501440; www.residenzade losmarin.com; Calle Rota 4960; d €109-180; ✳ 🛜 ♿; 🚤 San Zaccaria) This three-bedroom B&B is extraordinary good value considering it is barely 300m from Piazza San Marco. Rooms – one with a roof terrace and another with a courtyard-facing terrace – are quaintly decorated with quilted bedspreads, painted wardrobes and period furnishings. Hosts Elisabetta and Rodolfo make guests feel warmly welcome with slap-up breakfasts of homemade cakes, brioche and platters of ham and cheese.

Hotel Sant'Elena   HOTEL €€

(Map p340; ☎ 041 271 78 11; www.hotelsant elena.com; Calle Buccari 10; d €105-225; ✳ 🛜 ♿; 🚤 Sant'Elena) Retreat to this once holy convent that was later appropriated by the navy as a holiday resort for admirals. Clever them. Its quiet location, spacious halls, grassy cloister and ample, window-lined rooms are unusual for Venice. Inside a minimalist, modern style complements the 1930s Brutalist makeover while providing a high level of comfort and facilities. Families are particularly well catered for here with cribs,

kids menus, Nintendo and babysitting on tap. The hotel is also well located near the Parco delle Rimembranze and is a one-stop hop to the Lido.

🏠 Giudecca

Gen Venice   HOSTEL €

(Map p340; ☎ 041 877 82 88; www.generato hostels.com; Fondamenta delle Zitelle 86; dm €16-50, d €45-95; ⏱ check-in 3.30-10pm; ✳ @ 🛜 🚤 Zitelle) Giudecca's Generator hostel rocks a sharp, contemporary interior including a fabulous bar-restaurant. Arrive promptly at 3.30pm to claim that perfect bunk by the window. Sheets, a blanket, and a pillow are provided; breakfast is an additional €4.50.

Foresteria Redentore   HOSTEL €

(Map p340; ☎ 041 522 53 96; www.camplusliving.it; Calle de le Cape 194; d €45; 🛜; 🚤 Redentore) The rigorous monastic lives of the Redentore's Capuchin monks was surely eased by the view from their cells over the cypress-lined garden. A recent revamp now gives access to the 48 simple, en suite rooms with kitchen and laundry facilities to boot.

Al Redentore di Venezia   APARTMENTS €€

(Map p340; ☎ 041 522 94 02; www.alredentore divenezia.com; Fondamenta Ponte Longo 234a, Giudecca; 2-person apt €160-280; ✳ 🛜 ♿; 🚤 Redentore) Within the shadow of Il Redentore, these fully serviced apartments offer divine views across the water to San Marco. From the travertine-marble lobby, up the ash-clad staircase to the anallergic pillows and high-end, courtesy bath products, Al Redentore has thought of it all.

🍴 Eating

Venice's cosmopolitan outlook makes local cuisine anything but predictable. Don't be surprised if some Venetian dishes taste vaguely Turkish or Greek rather than strictly Italian, reflecting Venice's preferred trading partners for over a millennium. Spice-route flavours from the Mediterranean and beyond can be savoured in signature Venetian recipes such as *sarde in saor*, traditionally made with sardines in a tangy onion marinade with pine nuts and sultanas.

🍴 Piazza San Marco & Around

Rosticceria Gislon   VENETIAN, DELI €

(Map p352; ☎ 0415 22 35 69; Calle de la Bissa 5424; meals €15-25; ⏱ 9am-9.30pm Tue-Sun,

EATING & DRINKING LIKE A VENETIAN

Why drink alone? **Venice Urban Adventures** (Map p356; 📞 348 980 85 66; www.venice urbanadventures.com; cicheti tour €77; ☺ tours 11.30am & 5.30pm Mon-Sat) offers intimate tours of happy-hour hot spots led by knowledgeable, enthusiastic, English-speaking local foodies. Tours (€77 per person; up to 12 participants), covering *ombre* (wine by the glass) and *cicheti (bar snacks)* in five (yes, five) *bacari* and a tipsy Rialto gondola ride (weather permitting). Tours depart from Campo della Maddalena in Cannaregio and end at Ponte di Rialto (Rialto Bridge).

If you want to learn to cook like an Italian mama or eat like a Venetian gondolieri look no further than **Cook in Venice** (www.cookinvenice.com; tours €35-60, courses €140-225), Monica and Arianna's wonderful cookery classes and food tours. These two Venetian cooks are a tour de force: warmly welcoming, engaging teachers and passionate connoisseurs of Venetian food and wine. Whipping up polpette or zabaione in Arianna's country home is a truly memorable experience, while Monica's food tours have earned high praise from Katie Caldesi, Alex Polizzi and numerous well-fed chefs!

9am-3.30pm Mon; 🚤 Rialto) Serving San Marco workers since the 1930s, this no-frills *rotic-ceria* has an ultramarine canteen counter downstairs and a small eat-in restaurant upstairs. Hot to trot you'll find *arancini* (rice balls), deep fried mozzarella balls, croquettes and fish fry-ups. No one said it was going to be healthy! Those with more time might indulge in surprisingly good seafood risottos, grilled cuttlefish and, of course, the perennially popular roast chicken.

DOK Dall'Ava LP26 ITALIAN €€
(Map p344; 📞 041 296 07 64; www.dallava.com; Campo San Luca 3989; meals €18-30; ☺ 10am-3.30pm & 5.30pm-1am; 🚤 Sant'Angelo) The new kid on the block is a trendy *proscuitteria* with the muscle (and the 24-month-aged proscuitto) of one of San Daniele's biggest proscuitto houses behind it. It's been an instant hit, not least because it combines a coffee bar, an open-plan restaurant overlooking a canal and an enviable roof terrace bar, with live music on summer evenings. Aside from the hard-to-turn-down proscuitto, you can order stone-ground pizzas with Gragnano tomatoes or succulent Chianina burgers.

Ai Mercanti OSTERIA €€
(Map p344; 📞 041 523 82 69; www.aimercanti.com; Corte Coppo 4346/A; meals €40-45; ☺ noon-3pm & 7-11pm Tue-Sat, 7-11pm Mon; 🚤 Rialto) With its pumpkin-coloured walls, gleaming golden fixtures and jet black tables and chairs, Ai Mercanti effortlessly conjures up a romantic mood. No wonder dates whisper over glasses of DOC Veneto wines from the 300 plus bottles in the wine cellar before ordering contemporary dishes of risotto with mullet

and Nori seaweed. If you fancy something simpler, opt instead for the superb 'smokey' burger and a glass of Barolo.

★ Trattoria e Bacaro Da Fiore VENETIAN, CICHETI €€€
(Map p344; 📞 041 523 53 10; www.dafiore.it; Calle delle Botteghe 3461; meals €45-80, cicheti €10-15; ☺ 12.30-2.30pm & 7.30-10.30pm Tue-Sat; 🚤 San Samuele) Possibly the best bang for your buck in San Marco, this elegant trattoria with its rustic-chic decor serves superlative Venetian dishes composed of carefully selected seasonal ingredients from small Veneto producers. Maurizio Martin is justly famous for his seafood dishes such as seabass with balsamic vinegar, although during the Feast of the Redeemer you shouldn't pass up the *castradino* (a sort of Irish stew).

Next door, the *cicheti* (bar snacks) counter serves excellent *cicheti* at more democratic prices. Hurrah! Here, you can fill a plate with *baccala mantecato* (creamed cod), octopus-fennel salad, *arancini* (risotto balls), and Venetian *trippa* (tripe) to enjoy on a stool at the bar or in the *calle*.

✗ Dorsoduro

Bar alla Toletta SANDWICHES €
(Map p344; 📞 041 520 01 96; Calle la Toletta 1192; sandwiches €1.60-5; ☺ 7am-8pm; 📶 📷; 🚤 Ca' Rezzonico) Midway through museum crawls from Accademia to Ca' Rezzonico, Bar Toletta satisfies starving artists with scrumptious, grilled-to-order *panini*, including *prosciutto crudo* (cured ham), rocket and mozzarella, and daily vegetarian options. *Tramezzini* (triangular stacked sandwiches) are tasty,

too – Bar Toletta goes easy on mayonnaise in favour of more flavourful toppings like olive tapenade. Get yours to go, or grab a seat for around a €1 more.

Pizza Al Volo
PIZZA €

(Map p340; ☑ 041 522 54 30; Campo Santa Margherita 2944; pizza slices €2, small pizzas €4-7; ☺ 11am-2am; ☎; ☲ Ca' Rezzonico) Peckish night owls run out of options fast in Venice once restaurants close their kitchens around 10.30pm – but slices here are cheap and tasty, with a thin yet sturdy crust that won't collapse on your bar-hopping outfit.

Pasticceria Tonolo
PASTRIES €

(Map p352; ☑ 041 532 72 09; Calle dei Preti 3764; pastries €1-4; ☺ 7.45am-8pm Tue-Sat, 8am-1pm Sun, closed Sun Jul; ☲ Ca' Rezzonico) Long, skinny Tonolo is the stuff of local legend, a fact confirmed by the never-ending queue of customers. Ditch packaged B&B croissants for flaky *apfelstrudel* (apple pastry), velvety *bignè al zabaione* (marsala cream pastry) and oozing *pain au chocolat* (chocolate croissants). Devour one at the bar with a bracing espresso, then bag another for the road.

★ Ristorante La Bitta
RISTORANTE €€

(Map p344; ☑ 041 523 05 31; Calle Lunga San Barnaba 2753a; meals €35-40; ☺ 6.45-10.45pm Mon-Sat; ☲ Ca' Rezzonico) Recalling a cosy, woody bistro, La Bitta keeps punters purring with hearty rustic fare made using the freshest ingredients – the fact that the kitchen has no freezer ensures this. Scan the daily menu for mouthwatering, seasonal options like tagliatelle with artichoke thistle and gorgonzola or juicy pork *salsiccette* (small sausages) served with *verze* (local cabbage) and warming polenta. Reservations essential. Cash only.

Ristoteca Oniga
VENETIAN €€

(Map p344; ☑ 041 522 44 10; www.oniga.it; Campo San Barnaba 2852; meals €19-35; ☺ noon-2.30pm & 7-10.30pm Wed-Mon; ☎; ☲ Ca' Rezzonico) 🍴 Its menu peppered with organic ingredients, Oniga serves exemplary *sarde in saor* (sardines in tangy onion marinade), seasonal pastas, and the odd Hungarian classic like goulash (a nod to former chef Annika Major). Oenophiles will appreciate the selection of 100-plus wines, handy for toasting to the €19 set lunch menu. Grab a sunny spot in the *campo,* or get cosy in a wood-panelled corner.

Enoteca Ai Artisti
ITALIAN €€€

(Map p344; ☑ 041 523 89 44; www.enotecaartisti com; Fondamenta della Toletta 1169a; meals €45 ☺ noon-3pm & 7-10pm Mon-Sat; ☲ Ca' Rezzonico Indulgent cheeses, exceptional *nero di seppia* (cuttlefish ink) pasta, and tender *tagliata* (sliced steak) drizzled with aged balsamic vinegar atop arugula are paired with exceptional wines by the glass by your gracious oenophile hosts. Sidewalk tables for two make for great people-watching, but book ahead for indoor tables for groups; space is limited. Note: only turf (no surf) dishes on Mondays.

✖ San Polo & Santa Croce

Al Ponte Storto
VENETIAN, CICHETI €

(Map p352; ☑ 041 528 21 44; www.alpontestorto com; Calle del Ponte Storto 1278, San Polo; cicheti from €1, meals €33; ☺ 10.30am-3pm & 6-10pm Tue-Sun; ☎; ☲ San Silvestro) Once an anarchist clubhouse, intimate, art-slung 'At The Crooked Bridge' serves up scrumptious *cicheti*, whether it's radicchio, pancetta and brie quiche or the osteria's famed *polpette* (meatballs). For a more substantial feed plonk yourself down at a table and tuck into house favourites like *pappardelle con scampi e radicchio* (pasta with prawns and chicory). In the warmer months, request one of the two canalside tables.

★ Antiche Carampane
VENETIAN €€

(Map p352; ☑ 041 524 01 65; www.antichecarampane.com; Rio Terà delle Carampane 1911, San Polo; meals €30-45; ☺ 12.45-2.30pm & 7.30-10.30pm Tue-Sat; ☲ San Stae) Hidden in the once-shady lanes behind Ponte delle Tette, this culinary indulgence is a trick to find. Once you do, say goodbye to soggy lasagne and hello to a market-driven menu of silky *crudi* (raw fish or seafood), surprisingly light *fritto misto* (fried seafood) and prawn salad with seasonal vegetables. Never short of a smart, convivial crowd, it's a good idea to book ahead.

★ Osteria Trefanti
VENETIAN €€

(Map p352; ☑ 041 520 17 89; www.osteriatrefanti. it; Fondamenta Garzotti 888, Santa Croce; meals €40; ☺ noon-2.30pm & 7-10.30pm Tue-Sat, noon-2.45pm Sun; ☎; ☲ Riva de Biasio) 🍴 La Serenissima's spice trade lives on at simple, elegant Trefanti, where a vibrant dish of marinated prawns, hazelnuts, berries and caramel might get an intriguing kick from garam masala. Furnished with old pews and

GOURMET CENTRAL: RIALTO DISTRICT

Rialto Market (Map p352; ☑ 041 296 06 58; ☉ 7am-2pm, Pescaria closed Mon; 🚤 Rialto-Mercato) offers superb local produce next to the legendary **Pescaria** (Fish Market; Map p352; Rialto; ☉ 7am-2pm Tue-Sun; 🚤 Rialto), Venice's 600-year-old fish market. Nearby backstreets are lined with bakeries, *bacari* (bars) and three notable gourmet shops:

Casa del Parmigiano (Map p352; ☑ 041 520 65 25; www.aliani-casadelparmigiano.it; Campo Cesare Battisti 214; ☉ 8am-1.30pm Mon-Wed, to 7.30pm Thu-Sat; 🚤 Rialto) Set suitably beside the appetite-piquing Rialto Market , cheery Casa del Parmigiano heaves with coveted cheeses like potent *parmigiano reggiano* that has aged for three years, to rare, local Asiago Stravecchio di Malga. All are kept good company by fragrant cured meats, *baccalà* (cod) and trays of marinated Sicilian olives. Drooling?

Drogheria Mascari (Map p352; ☑ 041 522 97 62; www.imascari.com; Ruga degli Spezieri 381, San Polo; ☉ 8am-1pm & 4-7.30pm Mon, Tue & Thu-Sat, 8am-1pm Wed; 🚤 Rialto) Ziggurats of cayenne, leaning towers of star anise and chorus lines of olive oils draw awestruck foodies to Drogheria Mascari's windows. Indoors, chefs clutch truffle jars like holy relics, kids ogle candy in copper-lidded jars and dazed gourmands confront 50 different aromatic honeys. For small-production Italian vino – including Veneto cult producers like Giuseppe Quintarelli – don't miss the backroom *cantina*, home to around 1000 wines.

Rialto Biocenter (Map p352; ☑ 041 523 95 15; www.rialtobiocenter.it; Calle della Regina, Santa Croce 2264; ☉ 8.30am-8pm Mon-Sat; 🚤 San Stae) For organic edibles, from baby food to biscuits, plus sustainably produced wines, pop into Rialto Biocenter, an easy walk to the west of Rialto Market.

recycled copper lamps, it's the domain of the young and competent Sam Metcalfe and Umberto Slongo, whose passion for quality extends to a small, beautifully curated selection of local and organic wines.

Osteria La Zucca MODERN ITALIAN €€
(Map p352; ☑ 041 524 15 70; www.lazucca.it; Calle del Tentor 1762, Santa Croce; meals €35; ☉ 12.30-2.30pm & 7-10.30pm Mon-Sat; 🚤 San Stae) With its menu of seasonal vegetarian creations and classic meat dishes, this cosy, woody restaurant consistently hits the mark. Herbs and spices are used to great effect in dishes such as cinnamon-tinged pumpkin flan and lamb with dill and pecorino. The small interior can get toasty, so reserve canalside seats in summer.

✕ Cannaregio

Panificio Volpe Giovanni BAKERY €
(Map p356; ☑ 041 71 51 78; Ghetto Vecchio 1143; pastries €1.50-3; ☉ 7am-7.30pm Sun-Fri; 🚤 Guglie) Aside from unleavened pumpkin and radicchio bread, you can try unusual treats such as crumbly almond *impade* (sweet pastry sticks flavoured with ground almonds) and *orecchiette di Amman* (little ears of Amman), ear-shaped pastries stuffed with chocolate.

★ **Dalla Marisa** VENETIAN €€
(Map p340; ☑ 041 72 02 11; Fondamenta di San Giobbe 652b, Cannaregio; set menus lunch/dinner €15/35; ☉ noon-3pm daily & 7-11pm Tue & Thu-Sat; 🚤 Crea) At this Cannaregio institution, you'll be seated where there's room and get no menu – you'll have whatever Marisa's cooking. And you'll like it. Lunches are a bargain at €15 for a first, main, side, wine, water and coffee – pace yourself through prawn risotto to finish steak and grilled zucchini, or Marisa will jokingly scold you over coffee.

Trattoria da Bepi Già "54" VENETIAN €€
(Map p352; ☑ 041 528 50 31; www.dabepi.it; Campo SS Apostoli 4550; meals €30-40; ☉ noon-2.30pm & 7-10pm Fri-Wed; 🚤 Ca' d'Oro) Da Bepi is a traditional trattoria in the very best sense. The interior is a warm, wood-panelled cocoon, the service is efficient and friendly, and host Loris has been welcoming loyal locals and curious culinary travellers for years. Take their advice on the classic Venetian menu and order sweet, steamed spider crabs, briny razor clams, grilled turbot with artichokes and, for once, a tiramisu that doesn't disappoint.

Ai Promessi Sposi VENETIAN €€
(Map p352; ☑ 041 241 27 47; Calle d'Oca 4367; meals €25-35; ☉ 11.30am-3pm & 6.30-11.30pm Thu-Sun & Tue, 6.30-11.30pm Mon & Wed; 🚤 Ca' d'Oro)

Bantering Venetians thronging the bar are the only permanent fixtures at this neighbourhood *osteria*, where handwritten menus created daily feature fresh Venetian seafood and Veneto meats at excellent prices. Seasonal standouts include *seppie in umido* (cuttlefish in rich tomato sauce) and housemade tagliatelle with *anatra* (wild duck), but pace yourself for cloudlike tiramisu and elegant chocolate torte.

✕ Castello

★ Osteria Ruga di Jaffa   OSTERIA €
(Map p358; Ruga Giuffa 4864; meals €20-25; ⊙8am-11pm) Hiding in plain sight on the busy Ruga Giuffa is this excellent *osteria* (casual tavern). You should be able to spot it by the *gondolieri* packing out the tables at lunch time. They may not appreciate the vase of blooming hydrangeas on the bar or the artsy Murano wall lamps, but they thoroughly approve of the select menu of housemade pastas and succulent over-roast pork soaked in its own savoury juices.

Alla Basilica   ITALIAN €
(Map p358; ☑ 041 522 05 24; www.allabasilicavenezia.it; Calle degli Albanesi 4255; meals €14-20; ⊙noon-3pm Tue-Sun; 🚊 San Zaccaria) Continuing the long tradition of welcoming travellers to Venice, the Diocese of Venice lays on a hearty €14 lunch menu in this canteen-style restaurant. Never mind the glaring lighting and the lack of homely decor, the food is home-cooked and surprisingly good. When we visited there was grilled blue shark and lamb *quadrelli* (square-shaped pasta) scattered with fresh herbs.

CoVino   VENETIAN €€
(Map p358; ☑ 041 241 27 05; www.covinovenezia.com; Calle del Pestrin 3829a; 3-course menu €36; ⊙noon-2.30pm & 7-11pm Thu-Sun, 7-11pm Mon) Tiny CoVino has only 14 covers but demonstrates bags of ambition in its inventive, seasonal menu inspired by the Venetian terroir. Speciality products, such as Bronte pistachios and Bra sausages are selected from Slow Food Presidio producers, and wines focus on natural and biodynamic varieties. Chef Dimitri works like an origami artist in the tiniest of kitchens, while host Andrea choreographs the convivial atmosphere in the restaurant like a pro.

★ Trattoria Corte Sconta   MODERN VENETIAN €€€
(Map p358; ☑ 041 522 70 24; Calle del Pestrin 3886; meals €50-65; ⊙12.30-2.30pm & 7-9.30pm Tue-Sat, closed Jan & Aug; 🚊 Arsenale) Well-informed visitors and celebrating locals seek out this vine-covered *corte sconta* (hidden courtyard) for its trademark seafood antipasti and imaginative house-made pasta. Inventive flavour pairings transform the classics: clams zing with the hot, citrus-like taste of ginger; prawn and zucchini linguine is recast with an earthy dash of saffron; and

---

VENICE'S TOP GELATERIE

Alaska Gelateria (Map p352; ☑ 041 71 52 11; Calle Larga dei Bari 1159, Santa Croce; gelato from €1.50; ⊙11am-10pm; 🚼; 🚊 Riva de Biasio) Outlandish organic artisanal gelato. Enjoy a Slow Food scoop of house-roasted local pistachio, or two of the tangy Sicilian lemon with vaguely minty Sant'Erasmo *carciofi*. Or perhaps you're more a star anise, cardamom or green tea kind of gelatista? Even vegans are spoiled for choice of flavours, including watermelon and rose.

Gelateria Suso (Map p352; ☑ 348 564 65 45; www.gelatovenezia.it; Calle della Bissa 5453, Cannaregio; gelati €2-5; ⊙10am-8pm; 🚼; 🚊 Rialto) Indulge in gelato as rich as a doge, in original seasonal flavours like marscapone cream with fig sauce and walnuts. All Suso's gelati are locally made and free of artificial colours, and even the gluten-free flavours are extra creamy. A waffle cone with hazelnut and extra-dark chocolate passes as dinner.

Grom (Map p344; ☑ 041 099 17 51; www.grom.it; Campo San Barnaba 2461; gelati €2.50-5.50; ⊙10.30am-11pm Sun-Thu, 10am-12.30am Fri & Sat, shorter hours winter; 🚊 Ca' Rezzonico) Slow Food shivers at Grom, where gorgeous, fresh gelato is made using top-notch ingredients like Amalfi Coast lemons and Piedmontese hazelnuts. Seasonal flavours range from chestnut cream to apricot sorbet, with liquid treats, including luscious hot chocolate. You'll find other branches in San Polo (Campo dei Frari 3006), Cannaregio (Strada Nova 3844) and at Stazione di Santa Lucia (train station).

CICHETI: VENICE'S BEST MEAL DEALS

Even in unpretentious Venetian *osterie* (casual taverns), most dishes cost a couple of euros more than elsewhere in Italy. But *cicheti* (Venetian bar snacks) are some of the best foodie finds in the country, served at the bar in Venetian *osterie* at lunch and from about 6pm to 8pm. *Cicheti* range from basic €1 to €2 bar snacks to wildly inventive small plates for €2 to €5. You'll find the best at the following places:

All'Arco (Map p352; ☑ 041 520 56 66; Calle dell'Ochialer 436, San Polo; cicheti from €1.50; ⊘ 8am-8pm Wed-Fri, to 3pm Mon, Tue & Sat ; 🚊 Rialto-Mercato) Search out this authentic neighbourhood *osteria* for some of the best *cicheti* (bar snacks) in town. Armed with ingredients from the nearby Rialto market, father-son team Francesco and Matteo serve miniature masterpieces such as *cannocchia* (mantis shrimp) with pumpkin and roe, and *otrega* (butterfish) *crudo* with mint-and-olive-oil marinade.

Cantina Aziende Agricole (Map p356; Rio Tera Farsetti; meals €15-25, cicheti €1-3; ⊘ 9am-1.30pm & 5-10pm Mon-Sat; 🚊 San Marcuola) For 35 years Roberto di Berti and his sister Sabrina have been running this *bacaro* (bar/eatery), serving an impressive array of local wine to a loyal group of customers who treat the place much like a social club. Join them for a glass of chilled red Raboso and heaped platters of lardo, Fossa cheese drizzled with honey and delicious deep-fried pumpkin.

Dai Zemei (Map p352; ☑ 041 520 85 46; www.ostariadaizemei.it; Ruga Vecchia San Giovanni 1045, San Polo; cicheti from €1.50; ⊘ 8.30am-8.30pm Mon-Sat, to 7pm Sun; 🚊 San Silvestro) Running this closet-sized *cicheti* counter are *zemei* (twins) Franco and Giovanni, who serve loyal regulars small meals with outsized imagination: gorgonzola lavished with *peperoncino* (chilli) marmalade, duck breast drizzled with truffle oil, or chicory paired with leek and marinated anchovies. A gourmet bargain for inspired bites and impeccable wines – try a crisp Nosiola or invigorating Prosecco Brut.

---

the roast eel loops like the Brenta River in a drizzle of balsamic reduction.

The evolving wine list now features a notable selection of organic and biodynamic wines.

🍴 Giudecca

Food + Art   VENETIAN €
(Map p340; ☑ 393 559 76 26; Campo Junghans 487; meals €8-15; ⊘ 11am-3pm Mon-Fri) This popular, self-service *mensa* (canteen) was previously located in Giudecca's boatyards. Now it's moved to the more upmarket *campo* near Teatro Junghens, but the formula is still the same – self-service food at reasonable prices in a creative environment. Students can get a three-course meal for €8, otherwise you'll pay the princely sum of €12 to €15.

La Palanca   VENETIAN €€
(Map p340; ☑ 041 528 77 19; Fondamenta al Ponte Piccolo 448; meals €20-30; ⊘ 8am-8.30pm Mon-Sat; 🚊 Palanca) Lunchtime competition for canalside tables is stiff, but the views of the Zattere make *tagliolini ai calamaretti* (narrow ribbon pasta with tiny calamari) and swordfish carpaccio with orange zest. At €7

to €9 for plates of pasta, you'll be forking over half what diners pay along the waterfront in San Marco. Dinner is not served, but you can get *cicheti* (bar snacks) right up to closing time.

★ Trattoria Altanella   VENETIAN €€€
(Map p340; ☑ 041 522 77 80; Calle delle Erbe 268; meals €35-45; ⊘ noon-2.30pm & 7-10.30pm Tue-Sat; 🚊 Palanca) In 1920, fisherman Nane Stradella and his wife, Irma, opened a trattoria overlooking the Rio di Ponte Longo. Their fine Venetian cooking was so successful he soon gave up fishing and the restaurant now sustains a fourth generation of family cooks. Inside, the vintage interior is hung with artworks, reflecting the restaurant's popularity with artists, poets and writers, while outside a flower-fringed balcony hangs over the canal. Eat Irma's potato gnocchi with cuttlefish or Nane's enduringly good John Dory fillet.

🍴 The Lido

★ Al Ponte di Borgo   VENETIAN €€
(☑ 041 77 00 90; Calle delle Mercerie 27, Malamocco; meals €25-35; ⊘ 12.30-2.30pm & 7-10pm

Apr-Oct; ⟨Lido⟩ If you make it this far, you deserve to be rewarded with Mauretto's slap-up plates of sweet, briny crab served in its shell, garlicky bowls of *vongole* (clams) and pasta *alla malamocchina* (with mussels, tomatoes, oregano and smoked cheese). At weekends the shaded patio is crammed with locals and in the evening the bar serves typical *cicheti* with slugs of *prosecco*. Check lunch hours in low season, as it isn't always open.

La Favorita
SEAFOOD €€

(✆ 041 526 16 26; Via Francesco Duodo 33; meals €35-45; ⌚ 12.30-2.30pm & 7-10.30pm Fri-Sun, 7-10.30pm Tue-Thu; ⟨Lido⟩) For long, lazy lunches, bottles of fine wine and impeccable service, look no further than La Favorita. The menu is as elegant as the surroundings, giant *rhombo* (turbot) simmered with capers and olives, spider-crab *gnochetti* (minignocchi) and classic fish risotto. Book ahead for the wisteria-filled garden and well ahead during the film festival, when songbirds are practically out-sung by the ringtones of movie moguls.

Drinking

The usual rules don't seem to apply to drinking in Venice. Don't mix spirits and wine? Venice's classic cocktails suggest otherwise; try a *spritz*, made with *prosecco*, soda water and bittersweet Aperol or bitter Campari. No girly drinks? Tell that to burly boat-builders enjoying frothy *prosecco*.

Piazza San Marco & Around

Bacarando
BAR

(Map p352; ✆ 041 523 82 80; Corte dell'Orso 5495; ⌚ 9.30am-midnight; ⟨⟩) If you've managed to find this warm, wood-pannelled bar in the warren of streets off San Bartolomeo, toast yourself with a radical rum cocktail (this place has over 150 different labels) and order a huge burger or a plate of heaped *cicheti*. Thanks to its clubby vibe and a lively programme of cultural events and live music, it's popular with a hip young crowd.

L'Ombra del Leoni
CAFE, BAR

(Map p344; ✆ 041 521 87 11; www.labiennale.org; Calle Ridotto 1364a; drinks €3-6; ⌚ 9am-midnight summer, 9am-9pm winter; ⟨San Marco⟩) Lucky Biennale folk have Grand Canal views from their upstairs offices in Ca' Giustinian, but you too can enjoy the peerless waterside position of the *palazzo* in the downstairs cafe-

restaurant, which is open to the public. In keeping with the democratic spirit of the institution, drink prices are a bargain, especially if you manage to nab a seat on the outdoor terrace. At lunch there are simple sandwiches and salads.

Harry's Bar
BAR

(Map p344; ✆ 041 528 57 77; Calle Vallaresso 1323; cocktails €12-22; ⌚ 10.30am-11pm; ⟨San Marco⟩) Aspiring auteurs hold court at bistro tables well scuffed by Ernest Hemingway, Charlie Chaplin, Truman Capote and Orson Welles, enjoying the signature €16.50 bellini (Giuseppe Cipriani's original 1948 recipe: white-peach juice and *prosecco*) with a side of reflected glory. Upstairs is one of Italy's most unaccountably expensive restaurants – stick to the bar to save financing for your breakthrough film.

Dorsoduro

Cantinone Già Schiavi
BAR

(Map p344; ✆ 041 523 95 77; Fondamenta Nani 992; ⌚ 8.15am-8.30pm Mon-Sat; ⟨Zattere⟩) Regulars gamely pass along orders to timid newcomers, who might otherwise miss out on smoked swordfish *cicheti* (bar snacks) with top-notch house soave, or *pallottoline* (mini bottles of beer) with generous *sopressa* (soft salami) *panini*. Chaos cheerfully prevails at this legendary canalside spot, where Accademia art historians rub shoulders with San Trovaso gondola builders without spilling a drop.

★ Estro
WINE BAR

(Map p352; www.estrovenezia.com; Dorsoduro 3778; ⌚ 11am-midnight Wed-Mon, kitchen closes 10pm) New-entry Estro is anything you want it to be: wine and charcuterie bar, *aperitivo* pitstop, or sit-down degustation restaurant. The 500 *vini* (wines) – many of them natural-process wines – are chosen by young-gun sibling owners Alberto and Dario, whose passion for quality extends to the grub, from *cicheti* topped with house-made *porchetta* (roast pork), to a succulent burger made with Asiago cheese and house-made ketchup and mayonnaise.

Ai Pugni
BAR

(Map p344; ✆ 041 523 98 31; Ponte dei Pugni 2859; ⌚ 7am-10.30pm; ⟨Ca' Rezzonico⟩) Centuries ago, brawls on the bridge out the front once inevitably ended in the canal, but now Venetians settle differences with one of over 50 wines by the glass at this ever-packed bar, pimped with recycled magnum-bottle lamps and wine-crate tables. The latest drops are listed on the blackboard, with *aperitivo*-friendly nibbles including *polpette* (meatballs) and cured local meats on bread.

Cash only for bills under €25.

Il Caffè Rosso
CAFE

(Map p344; ☑ 041 528 79 98; Campo Santa Margherita 2963; ⊙ 7am-1am Mon-Sat; 🛜; 🚤 Ca' Rezzonico) Affectionately known as *'il rosso'*, this red-fronted cafe has been at the centre of the bar scene on Campo Santa Margherita since the late 1800s. It's at its best in the early evening, when locals snap up the sunny piazza seating to sip on an inexpensive *spritz*.

🍷 San Polo & Santa Croce

⭐ Al Prosecco
WINE BAR

(Map p352; ☑ 041 524 02 22; www.alprosecco.com; Campo San Giacomo dell'Orio, Santa Croce 1503; ⊙ 10am-8pm; 🚤 San Stae) 🌿 The urge to toast sunsets in Venice's loveliest *campo* is only natural – and so is the wine at Al Prosecco. This forward-thinking bar specialises in *vini naturi* (natural-process wines) – organic, biodynamic, wild yeast fermented – from enlightened Italian winemakers like Cinque Campi and Azienda Agricola Barichel. So order a glass of unfiltered 'cloudy' *prosecco* and toast to the good things in life

Al Mercà
WINE BAR

(Map p352; Campo Cesare Battisti 213, San Polo; ⊙ 10am-2.30pm & 6-9pm Mon-Thu, to 9.30pm Fri & Sat; 🚤 Rialto) Discerning drinkers throng to this cupboard-sized counter on a Rialto market square to sip on top-notch *prosecco* and DOC wines by the glass (from €2). Edibles usually include meatballs and mini *panini*

(from €1), proudly made using super-fresh ingredients.

Cantina Do Spade
BAR

(Map p352; ☑ 041 521 05 83; www.cantinadospade.com; Calle do Spade 860, San Polo; ⊙ 10am-3pm & 6-10pm; 🛜; 🚤 Rialto) Famously mentioned in Casanova's memoirs, cosy, brick-lined 'Two Spades' continues to keep Venice in good spirits with its bargain Tri-Veneto wines and young, laid-back management. Come early for market-fresh *fritture* (batter-fried seafood) or linger longer with satisfying, sit-down dishes like *bigoli in salsa* (pasta in anchovy and onion sauce).

🍷 Cannaregio

⭐ Al Timon
WINE BAR

(Map p356; ☑ 041 524 60 66; Fondamenta degli Ormesini 2754; ⊙ 11am-1am Thu-Tue & 6pm-1am Wed; 🚤 San Marcuola) Find a spot on the boat moored out front along the canal and watch the motley parade of drinkers and dreamers arrive for seafood *crostini* (open-face sandwiches) and quality organic and DOC wines by the *ombra* (half-glass of wine) or carafe. Folk singers play sets canalside when the weather obliges; when it's cold, regulars scoot over to make room for newcomers at indoor tables.

Vino Vero
WINE BAR

(Map p340; ☑ 041 275 00 44; Fondamenta della Misericordia 2497; ⊙ 6pm-midnight Mon, 11am-midnight Tue-Sun; 🚤 Ca' d'Oro) Lining the exposed brick walls of Matteo Bartoli's superior local wine bar are interesting small production wines, including a great selection of natural and biodynamic labels. The *cicheti*, too, are deliciously varied: wild boar sausage with aubergine, gorgonzola drizzled

VENICE & THE VENETO VENICE

HISTORIC CAFES

In prime tourist zones, the price of coffee at a table seems more like rent, so take your coffee standing or splash out for architecturally splendid cafes in the Museo Correr, Palazzo Querini Stampalia or Piazza San Marco.

Historic baroque cafes around Piazza San Marco, such as **Caffè Florian** (Map p344; ☑ 041 520 56 41; www.caffeflorian.com; Piazza San Marco 56/59; drinks €10-25; ⊙ 9am-midnight; 🚤 San Marco) and **Caffè Quadri** (Map p344; ☑ 041 522 21 05; www.alajmo.it; Piazza San Marco 120; drinks €6-25; ⊙ 9am-11.30pm; 🚤 San Marco), serve coffee and hot chocolate with live orchestras – though your heart might beat a different rhythm once you get the bill, with orchestra surcharge. Hint: **Caffè Lavena** (Map p344; ☑ 041 522 40 70; www.lavena.it; Piazza San Marco 133/4; drinks €1-12; ⊙ 9.30am-11pm; 🚤 San Marco) offers a €1 espresso at the counter. But this is Venice, and decadence is always in order – might as well order *caffe correto* (*espresso* 'corrected' with liquor), and tango with a stranger.

with honey or creamy *baba ganoush* topped with prosciutto.

Agli Ormesini
PUB

(Da Aldo; Map p356; ☑ 041 71 58 34; Fondamenta degli Ormesini 2710; ⊙8pm-1am Mon-Sat; ⓢMadonna dell'Orto) While the rest of Venice is awash in wine, Ormesini offers more than 100 brews, including reasonably priced bottles of speciality craft ales and local Birra Venezia. The cheery, beery scene often spills into the street – but keep it down, or the neighbours will get testy.

🍷 Castello

★ La Serra dei Giardini
CAFE

(Map p340; ☑ 041 296 03 60; www.serradeigiardini. org; Viale Giuseppe Garibaldi 1254; snacks €4-15; ⊙10am-9.30pm summer, 11am-8pm Mon-Thu & 10am-9pm Fri & Sat winter; 🛜🚻; ⓢGiardini) Order a herbal tisane or the signature pear bellini and sit back amid the hothouse flowers in Napoleon's fabulous greenhouse. Cathedral-like windows look out onto the tranquil greenery of the public gardens, while upstairs workshops in painting and gardening are hosted on the suspended mezzanine. Light snacks and homemade cakes are also available alongside unique micro-brews and Lurisia sodas flavoured with Slow Food Presidia products.

STRANI
BAR

(Map p340; ☑ 041 099 14 34; www.straninvenice. it; Via Garibaldi 1582; cicheti & sandwiches €1.80-€4; ⊙7.30am-1am; ⓢArsenale) There's always a party on at Strani thanks to its excellent selection of beers on tap, well-priced glasses of DOC Veneto wines and platters of sopressa (soft salami) and salami that deserve to be tasted for their flavoursome quality. Fragrant flatbreads, heaped bruschetta of *porchetta* and radicchio and a plethora of *cicheti* keep drinkers fuelled for late-night jam sessions with the locals.

Bacaro Risorto
BAR

(Map p358; Campo San Provolo 4700; cicheti €1.50-4; ⊙9am-9pm Mon-Sat; ⓢSan Zaccaria) Just a footbridge from San Marco, this shoebox of a corner bar overflowing with happy drinkers offers quality wines and abundant *cicheti,* including *crostini* heaped with *sarde in saòr,* soft cheeses and melon tightly swaddled in prosciutto. Note that opening times are 'flexible'.

Bar Terazza Danieli
BAR

(Map p358; ☑ 041 522 64 80; www.starwoodhotels. com; Riva degli Schiavoni 4196; cocktails €18-22; ⊙3-6.30pm mid-Apr–Oct; ⓢSan Zaccaria) Gondolas glide in to dock along the quay, while across the lagoon the white-marble edifice of Palladio's San Giorgio Maggiore turns from gold to pink in the waters of the canal: the late-afternoon scene from the Hotel Danieli's top-floor balcony bar definitely calls for a toast. Linger over a *spritz* (€10) or cocktail – preferably the sunset-tinted signature Danieli cocktail of gin, apricot and orange juices, and a splash of grenadine.

☆ Entertainment

To find out what's on the calendar in Venice during your visit, check listings in free mags distributed citywide and online at Venezia da Vivere (www.veneziadavivere.com) and 2Venice (www.2venice.it).

Teatro La Fenice
OPERA

(Map p344; ☑ 041 78 65 11, theatre tours 041 78 66 75; www.teatrolafenice.it; Campo San Fantin 1965; theatre visits adult/reduced €9/6, concert/opera tickets from €15/45; ⊙tours 9.30am-6pm; ⓢSanta Maria del Giglio) La Fenice, one of Italy's top opera houses, hosts a rich program of opera, ballet and classical music. With advance booking you can tour the theatre, but the best way to see it is with the *loggionisti* – opera buffs in the cheap top-tier seats. Get tickets at the theatre, online or through HelloVenezia (☑041 24 24; Piazzale Roma; ⊙transport tickets 7am-8pm, events tickets 8.30am-6.30pm; ⓢPiazzale Roma).

★ Palazzetto Bru Zane
CLASSICAL MUSIC

(Centre du Musique Romantique Française; Map p352; ☑ 041 521 10 05; www.bru-zane.com; Palazetto Bru Zane 2368, San Polo; adult/reduced €15/5; ⊙box office 2.30-5.30pm Mon-Fri, closed late Jul–mid-Aug; ⓢSan Tomà) Pleasure palaces don't get more romantic than Palazzetto Bru Zane on concert nights, when exquisite harmonies tickle Sebastiano Ricci angels tumbling across stucco-frosted ceilings. Multi-year restorations returned the 1695-97 Casino Zane's 100-seat music room to its original function, attracting world-class musicians to enjoy its acoustics from late September to mid-May.

Interpreti Veneziani
CLASSICAL MUSIC

(Map p344; ☑ 041 277 05 61; www.interpreti veneziani.com; Chiesa San Vidal, Campo di San Vidal 2862; adult/reduced €27/22; ⊙doors open

8.30pm; ⊜Accademia) Everything you've heard of Vivaldi from weddings and mobile ring tones is proved fantastically wrong by Interpreti Veneziani, which plays Vivaldi on 18th-century instruments as a soundtrack for living in this city of intrigue – you'll never listen to *The Four Seasons* again without hearing summer storms erupting over the lagoon, or snow-muffled footsteps hurrying over footbridges in winter's-night intrigues.

Musica a Palazzo OPERA
(Map p344; ☑340 971 72 72; www.musicapalazzo. com; Palazzo Barbarigo-Minotto, Fondamenta Barbarigo o Duodo 2504; tickets incl beverage €75; ⊙doors open 8pm; ⊜Santa Maria del Giglio) Hang onto your *prosecco* and brace for impact: in palace salons, the soprano's high notes imperil glassware, and thundering baritones reverberate through inlaid floors. During 1½ hours of selected arias from Verdi or Rossini, the drama progresses from receiving-room overtures to parlour duets overlooking the Grand Canal, followed by second acts in the Tiepolo-ceilinged dining room and bedroom grand finales.

🔒 Shopping

Venice's ultimate shopping triumphs are unique finds at surprisingly reasonable prices, handmade by artisans in Murano and backstreet studios.

★**Cárte** HANDICRAFTS
(Map p352; ☑320 0248776; www.cartevenezia. it; Calle dei Cristi 1731, San Polo; ⊙11am-5.30pm; ⊜Rialto-Mercato) Venice's shimmering lagoon echoes in marbled-paper earrings and artist's portfolios, thanks to the steady hands and restless imagination of *carta marmorizzata* (marbled-paper) *maestra* Rosanna Corrò. After years restoring ancient Venetian books, Rosanna began creating her original, bookish beauties: tubular statement necklaces, op-art jewellery boxes, one-of-a-kind contemporary handbags, even wedding albums.

Ca' Macana HANDICRAFTS
(Map p344; ☑041 277 61 42; www.camacana.com; Calle de le Botteghe 3172; ⊙10am-7.30pm Sun-Fri, 10am-8pm Sat; 🖬; ⊜Ca' Rezzonico) Glimpse the talents behind the Venetian Carnevale masks that so impressed Stanley Kubrick, he ordered several for his final film *Eyes Wide Shut*. Choose your papier-mâché persona from the selection of coquettish courtesan's eye-shades, chequered Casanova disguises and long-nosed plague doctors' masks – or invent your own alter ego at Ca' Macana's **mask-making workshops** (one-/two-hour per person €47/68). for individuals and families.

Chiarastella Cattana HOMEWARES
(Map p344; ☑041 522 43 69; www.chiarastella cattana.it; Salizada San Samuele 3357; ⊙10.30am-1pm & 3-7pm Mon-Sat; ⊜San Samuele) Transform any home into a thoroughly modern *palazzo* with these locally woven, strikingly original Venetian linens. Whimsical cushions feature a chubby purple rhinoceros and grumpy scarlet elephants straight out of Pietro Longhi paintings, and hand-tasselled Venetian jacquard hand towels will dry your royal guests in style. Decorators and design aficionados, save an afternoon to consider dizzying woven-to-order napkin and curtain options here.

Danghyra CERAMICS
(Map p344; ☑041 522 41 95; www.danghyra.com; Calle de le Botteghe 3220; ⊙10am-1pm & 3-7pm Tue-Sun; ⊜Ca' Rezzonico) Spare white bisque cups seem perfect for a Zen tea ceremony, but look inside: that iridescent lilac glaze is pure Carnevale. Danghyra's striking ceramics are hand-thrown in Venice with a magic touch – her platinum-glazed bowls make the simplest pasta dish appear fit for a modern doge.

Gilberto Penzo HANDICRAFTS
(Map p352; ☑041 71 93 72; www.veniceboats.com; Calle 2 dei Saoneri 2681, San Polo; ⊙9am-12.30pm & 3-6pm Mon-Sat; 🖬; ⊜San Tomà) Yes, you actually can take a gondola home in your pocket. Anyone fascinated by the models at Museo Storico Navale (p359) will go wild here, amid handmade wooden models of all kinds of Venetian boats, including some that are seaworthy (or at least bathtub worthy). Signor Penzo also creates kits so crafty types and kids can have a crack at it themselves.

★**Marina e Susanna Sent** GLASS
(Map p344; ☑041 520 81 36; www.marinaesusanna sent.com; Campo San Vio 669; ⊙10am-1pm & 1.30-6.30pm; ⊜Accademia) Wearable waterfalls and unpoppable soap-bubble necklaces are Venice style signatures, thanks to the Murano-born Sent sisters. Defying centuries-old beliefs that women can't handle molten glass, their minimalist art-glass statement jewellery is featured in museum stores worldwide, from Palazzo Grassi to MoMA. See new collections at this flagship, their

Murano studio, or the San Marco branch (at Ponte San Moise 2090).

Pied à Terre   SHOES

(Map p352; ☑ 041 528 55 13; www.piedaterre-venice.com; Sotoportego degli Oresi 60, San Polo; ⊙ 10am-12.30pm & 2.30-7.30pm; ⓢ Rialto) Rialto courtesans and their 30cm-high heels are long gone, but Venetian slippers stay stylish. Pied à Terre's colourful *furlane* (slippers) are handcrafted with recycled bicycle-tyre treads, ideal for finding your footing on a gondola. Choose from velvet, brocade or raw silk in vibrant shades of lemon and ruby, with optional piping. Don't see your size? Shoes can be custom made and shipped.

Le Burle Veneziane   JEWELLERY

(Map p344; ☑ 041 522 21 50; www.leburleveneziane.com; Piscina San Samuele 3436; ⊙ 10.30am-7.30pm; ⓢ San Samuele) The window of Monica Burcovich's shop-come-studio is filled with treasures: silk bags trimmed with vintage seed beads, feathered fascinators and dripping necklaces fashioned from the tiniest strands of microbeads, crystals and pearls. Some chokers are so finely wrought they look like sparkling pieces of lace. Monica works in the studio so you can see just how painstaking the creative process is.

Oh My Blue   JEWELLERY, HANDICRAFTS

(Map p352; ☑ 041 243 57 41; ohmyblue.it; Campo San Tomà 2865, San Polo; ⊙ 10am-7.30pm; ⓢ San Tomà) In her white-on-white gallery, switched-on Elena Rizzi showcases edgy, show-stopping jewellery, accessories and decorative objects from both local and international talent like Elena Camilla Bertellotti, Ana Hagopian and Yoko Takirai. Expect anything from quartz rings and paper necklaces, to sculptural bags and ceramics.

★ Fabricharte   CRAFTS

(Map p358; ☑ 041 200 67 43; www.fabricharte.org; Calle del Cafetier 6477/Z; ⊙ 11am-7pm Mon-Sat; ⓢ Fondamente Nove) Stacks of hand-bound books, picture frames, trays and keepsake boxes all covered in delightful, hand-stamped papers make the the window of Andreatta Andrea's workshop look like Christmas. He apprenticed at the legendary Piazzesi and now offers a unique service in Venice: bring him any well-loved book and he can rebind it for you in any of the available Raimondini papers in a day or two. He also fashions gift-worthy sketch pads and composition books, and can transform paperback books into hardbacks.

ℹ Information

EMERGENCY

For an ambulance, call ☑ 118. Call ☑ 112 or ☑ 113 for the police.

Police Headquarters (☑ 041 271 55 11; Santa Croce 500) San Marco's head police station is off the beaten track in the ex-convent of Santa Chiara, just beyond Piazzale Roma.

INTERNET ACCESS

Wi-fi access is widely available in hotels, and internet cafes are dispersed throughout the city.

MEDICAL SERVICES

Information on rotating late-night pharmacies is posted in pharmacy windows and listed in the free magazine *Un Ospite di Venezia*, available at the tourist office.

Guardia Medica (☑ 041 238 56 48) This service of night-time call-out doctors in Venice operates from 8pm to 8am on weekdays and from 10am the day before a holiday (including Sunday) until 8am the day after.

Ospedale Civile (☑ 041 529 41 11; Campo SS Giovanni e Paolo 6777; ⓢ Ospedale) Venice's main hospital; for emergency care and dental treatment.

MONEY

There are ATMs spread throughout the city, with clusters near the Rialto and Piazza San Marco.

Travelex (☑ 041 528 73 58; Piazza San Marco 142; ⊙ 9am-7pm Mon-Fri, 9am-6pm Sat, 9.20am-6pm Sun)

POST

There are post offices in every *sestiere* (district), with addresses and hours searchable at www.poste.it. The most convenient is in **Calle Larga de l'Ascension** (Map p344; Calle Larga de l'Ascension 1241; ⊙ 8.20am-1.35pm Mon-Fri, to 12.35pm Sat), just behind San Marco.

TOURIST INFORMATION

Airport Tourist Office (☑ 041 529 87 11; www.turismovenezia.it; Arrivals Hall, Marco Polo Airport; ⊙ 8.30am-7.30pm)

ℹ Getting There & Away

AIR

Most flights arrive at and depart from Marco Polo airport, 12km outside Venice, east of Mestre. Ryanair also uses **Treviso Airport** (TSF; ☑ 0422 31 51 11; www.trevisoairport.it; Via Noalese 63), about 5km southwest of Treviso and a 30km, one-hour drive from Venice.

BOAT

Anek (www.anek.gr) runs regular ferries between Venice and Greece, and **Venezia Lines**

(☎ 041 882 11 01; www.venezialines.com) runs high-speed boats to and from Croatia in summer. However, consider big-ship transport carefully – long-haul ferries and cruise ships have an outsized environmental impact on Venice's fragile lagoon aquaculture.

BUS

All buses leave from the **bus station** (Map p340) on Piazzale Roma.

Azienda del Consorzio Trasporti Veneziano (ACTV; ☎ 041 24 24; www.actv.it) Runs *vaporetti* and buses to Mestre and surrounding areas.

Azienda Trasporti Veneto Orientale (ATVO; ☎ 0421 59 46 71; www.atvo.it) Has services to destinations all over the eastern Veneto, including airport connections.

Eurolines (☎ 0861 199 19 00; www.eurolines. com) Operates a wide range of international routes.

CAR & MOTORCYCLE

The congested Trieste–Turin A4 passes through Mestre. From Mestre, take the Venice exit. From the south, take the A13 from Bologna, which connects with the A4 at Padua.

Once over the Ponte della Libertà bridge from Mestre, cars must be left at the car park at Piazzale Roma or Tronchetto; expect to pay €21 or more for every 24 hours. Parking stations in Mestre are cheaper. Car ferry 17 transports vehicles from Tronchetto to the Lido.

Avis, Europcar and Hertz all have car rental offices on Piazzale Roma and at Marco Polo airport. Several companies operate in or near Mestre train station, too.

Interparking (Tronchetto Car Park; ☎ 041 520 75 55; www.veniceparking.it; Isola del Tronchetto; per 2/3-5/5-24hr €3/5/21; ⊙24hr) Has 3957 spaces; the largest lot with the cheapest 24-hour rate. *Vaporetti* connect

directly with Piazza San Marco, while the People Mover provides connections to Piazzale Roma and the cruise terminal.

TRAIN

Trains run frequently to Venice's Stazione Santa Lucia (signed as Ferrovia within Venice). In addition, there are direct InterCity services to major points in France, Germany, Austria and Slovenia.

TO	FARE (€)	DURATION (HR)	FREQUENCY (PER HR)
Florence	29-45	2-3	1-2
Milan	20-39	2½-3½	2-3
Naples	55-120	5½-9	1
Padua	4.05-9	½-1	3-4
Rome	40-80	3½-6	1-2
Verona	8.50-23	1¾	3-4

❶ Getting Around

TO/FROM THE AIRPORT

Boat

Alilaguna (☎ 041 240 17 01; www.alilaguna.it) operates several lines that link the airport with various parts of Venice, including the Linea Blu (Blue Line, with stops at Lido, San Marco, Stazione Marittima and points in between), the Linea Rossa (Red Line, with stops at Murano and Lido) and Linea Arancio (Orange Line, with stops at Stazione Santa Lucia, Rialto and San Marco via the Grand Canal). Boats to Venice cost €15 and leave from the airport ferry dock (an eight-minute walk from the terminal).

Bus

ATVO (p381) buses run to the airport from Piazzale Roma (€6, one hour, every 30 minutes 8am to midnight).

VAPORETTO ROUTES

Here are key *vaporetto* lines and major stops, subject to seasonal change:

1 Piazzale Roma–Ferrovia–Grand Canal (all stops)–Lido and return

2 San Zaccaria–Redentore–Zattere–Tronchetto–Ferrovia–Rialto–Accademia–San Marco

3/DM Direct service from Piazzale Roma and the train station to Murano

4.1, 4.2 Circles the outside perimeter of Venice in both directions

5.1, 5.2 Follows the same route as 4.1 and 4.2, but with additional stops at Giudecca and the Lido

12 Murano–Torcello–Burano (half-hourly service) and back

N All-stops night circuit (11.30pm to 5am) for the Grand Canal, San Marco, Giudecca and the Lido

VAPORETTO

The city's main mode of public transport is *vaporetto* – Venice's distinctive water bus. Tickets can be purchased from the HelloVenezia ticket booths at most landing stations. You can also buy tickets when boarding; you may be charged double with luggage, though this is not always enforced.

Instead of spending €7 for a one-way ticket, consider a Travel Card, which is a timed pass for unlimited travel (beginning at first validation). Passes for 24/48/72 hours cost €20/30/40. A week pass costs €60. Swipe your card every time you board.

WATER TAXIS

The standard **water taxi** (Consorzio Motoscafi Venezia; Map p352; 24hr ☑ 041 522 23 03, Marco Polo airport desk ☑ 041 541 50 84; www.motoscafivenezia.it) between Marco Polo airport and Venice costs €110 for a private taxi and €25 per person for a shared taxi with up to 10 passengers. Elsewhere in Venice, official taxi rates start at €15 plus €2 per minute and €6 extra if they're called to your hotel. Night trips, extra luggage and large groups cost more. Prices are metered or negotiated in advance.

THE VENETO

Most visitors to the Veneto devote all their time to Venice itself, which is perfectly understandable – until you discover the rich variety of experiences that await just an hour or two away.

First, there are the city-states Venice annexed in the 15th century: Padua (Padova), with its pre-Renaissance fresco cycles; Vicenza, with Palladio's peerless architecture; and Verona, with its sophisticated bustle atop ancient Roman foundations. All are easily reached by train from Venice.

Then there are the wines, in particular, Valpolicella's bold Amarones. In a party mood? The hills around Conegliano produce Italy's finest bubbly: Prosecco Superiore. For harder stuff, charming Bassano del Grappa obliges with its own eponymous firewater.

On the rare day when the Adriatic wipes Venice clean of its mists, you can catch glimpses of the snowcapped Dolomites. It's hard to believe, but in less than two hours you can go from canals to the crisp Alpine clarity of Belluno and Cortina d'Ampezzo – land of idyllic hikes, razor-sharp peaks and the world's most fashion-conscious skiing.

Brenta Riviera

Every 13 June for 300 years, summer officially kicked off with a traffic jam along the Grand Canal, as a flotilla of fashionable Venetians headed to their villas along the banks of the Brenta. Every last ball gown and poker chair was loaded onto barges for dalliances that stretched until November. The party ended when Napoleon arrived in 1797, but 80 villas still strike elegant poses along the Brenta and six of them are now open to the public at various times of the year.

◉ Sights

Villa Foscari HISTORIC BUILDING
(☑ 041 520 39 66; www.lamalcontenta.com; Via dei Turisti 9, Malcontenta; admission €10; ☻ 9am-noon Tue & Sat May-Oct) The most romantic Brenta villa, the Palladio-designed Villa Foscari (1555–60) got its nickname La Malcontenta from a grand dame of the Foscari clan who was reputedly exiled here for cheating on her husband – though these bright, highly sociable salons hardly constitute a punishment. The villa was abandoned for years, but Giovanni Zelotti's frescoes have now been restored to daydream-inducing splendour.

Villa Widmann Rezzonico Foscari HISTORIC BUILDING
(☑ 041 547 00 12; www.lamalcontenta.com; Via Nazionale 420, Mira; admission €10; ☻ 9am-noon Tue & Sat May-Oct) To appreciate both gardening and Venetian-style social engineering, stop just west of Oriago at Villa Widmann Rezzonico Foscari. Originally owned by Persian-Venetian nobility, the 18th-century villa captures the Brenta's last days of rococo decadence, with Murano sea-monster chandeliers and a frescoed grand ballroom with upper viewing gallery. Head to the gallery to reach the upstairs ladies' gambling parlour where, according to local lore, villas were once gambled away in high-stakes games.

Villa Pisani Nazionale HISTORIC BUILDING
(☑ 049 50 20 74; www.villapisani.beniculturali.it; Via Doge Pisani 7, Stra; adult/reduced €7.50/3.75, park only €4.50/2.25; ☻ 9am-7pm Tue-Sun Apr-Sep, to 5pm Oct, to 4pm Nov-Mar) To keep hard-partying Venetian nobles in line, Doge Alvise Pisani provided a Versailles-like reminder of who was in charge. The 1774, 114-room Villa Pisani Nazionale is surrounded by huge gardens, a labyrinthine hedge-maze and pools to reflect the doge's glory. Here you'll find

the bathroom with a tiny wooden throne used by Napoleon; the sagging bed where new king Vittorio Emanuele II slept; and, ironically, the reception hall where Mussolini and Hitler met in 1934 under Tiepolo's ceiling depicting the *Geniuses of Peace*.

On our last visit, the poorly funded property was badly lit, so consider visiting during full daylight hours to avoid staring into darkened rooms. Temporary exhibitions are also held at the villa throughout the year, generally between March and October.

Villa Foscarini Rossi   HISTORIC BUILDING
(☑049 980 10 91; www.villafoscarini.it; Via Doge Pisani 1/2, Stra; adult/reduced €7/5; ☉9am-1pm & 2-6pm Mon-Fri, 2.30-6pm Sat & Sun Apr-Oct, 9am-1pm Mon-Fri Nov-Mar) Well-heeled Venetians wouldn't have dreamt of decamping to the Brenta without their favourite cobblers, sparking a local tradition of shoemaking. Today, 538 companies produce about 19 million pairs of shoes annually. Their lasting contribution is commemorated with a **Shoemakers' Museum** at this 18th-century villa, its collection including 18th-century slippers and kicks created for trendsetter Marlene Dietrich. Admission includes access to the villa's 17th-century *foresteria* (guesthouse), which wows with allegorical frescoes by Pietro Liberi and trompe-l'œil effects by Domenico de Bruni.

☞ Tours

Seeing the Brenta by boat reveals an engineering marvel: the ingenious hydraulic locks system developed in the 15th century to prevent river silt from being dumped into the lagoon.

★ Il Burchiello   CRUISE
(☑049 876 02 33; www.ilburchiello.it; adult/reduced half-day cruise from €55/45, full day €99/55) Watch 50 villas drift by on this modern barge. Full-day cruises run between Venice and Padua, stopping at Malcontenta, Widmann (or Barchessa Valmarana) and Pisani villas. From Venice, cruises depart from Pontile della Pietà pier on Riva degli Schiavoni (Tuesday, Thursday and Saturday). From Padua, cruises depart from Pontile del Portello pier (Wednesday, Friday and Sunday).

Half-day tours stop at one or two villas, running to Oriago from Venice (Tuesday, Thursday and Saturday) and Padua (Wednesday, Friday and Sunday), and from Oriago to Venice (Wednesday, Friday and

BRENTA BY BIKE
....
Speed past tour boats along 150km of cycling routes along the Brenta Riviera. **Veloce** (☑346 8471141; www.rentalbikeitaly.com; Via Gramsci 85, Mira; touring/mountain/racing bicycle per day €20/25/35; ☉8am-8pm) offers a pick-up and drop-off service at railway stations and hotels in many Veneto towns, including Padua, Venice and Mira. City and mountain bikes are available, along with GPS units preloaded with multilingual Brenta itineraries (€10).

Sunday) and Padua (Tuesday, Thursday and Saturday).

✖ Eating

Osteria Da Conte   MODERN VENETIAN €€
(☑049 47 95 71; www.osteriadaconte.it; Via Caltana 133, Mira; meals €25-35; ☉noon-2.30pm & 8-10.30pm Tue-Sat, noon-2.30pm Sun) An unlikely bastion of culinary sophistication lodged practically underneath an overpass, Da Conte has one of the most interesting wine lists in the region, plus creative takes on regional cuisine, from shrimps with black sesame and pumpkin purée to gnocchi in veal-cheek *ragù*. If it's on the menu, end your meal with the faultless *zabaglione*.

Da Conte lies 3.5km north of central Mira. The closest train station is Mira Mirano.

❶ Getting There & Around

ACTV's Venezia–Padova Extraurbane bus 53 leaves from Venice's Piazzale Roma about every half-hour, stopping at key Brenta villages en route to Padua.

Local Venice–Padua train services stop at Dolo (€3.30, 25 minutes, one to three per hour).

By car, take SS11 from Mestre-Venezia towards Padua and take the A4 autostrada towards Dolo/Padua.

Padua
POP 209,700

Though under an hour from Venice, Padua seems a world away with its medieval marketplaces, Fascist-era facades and hip student population. As a medieval city-state and home to Italy's second-oldest university, Padua challenged both Venice and Verona for regional hegemony. An extraordinary se-

Padua

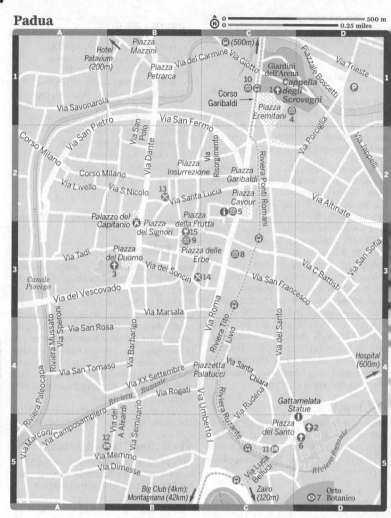

N
0   500 m
0   0.25 miles

ries of fresco cycles recalls this golden age – including in Giotto's remarkable Cappella degli Scrovegni, Menabuoi's heavenly gathering in the Baptistry and Titian's St Anthony in the Scoletta del Santo. For the next few centuries Padua and Verona challenged each other for dominance over the Veneto plains. But Venice finally settled the matter by occupying Padua permanently in 1405.

As a strategic military-industrial centre, Padua became a parade ground for Mussolini speeches, an Allied bombing target and a secret Italian Resistance hub (at its university).

⊙ Sights

★ **Cappella degli Scrovegni**   CHURCH
(Scrovegni Chapel; ☎ 049 201 00 20; www.cappelladegliscrovegni.it; Piazza Eremitani 8; adult/reduced €13/6; night ticket €8/6; ⊙ 9am-7pm, also 7-10pm various periods through year) Padua's version of the Sistine Chapel, the Cappella degli Scrovegni houses one of Italy's great Renaissance masterpieces – a striking cycle of Giotto frescoes. Dante, da Vinci and Vasari all honour Giotto as the artist who ended the Dark Ages with these paintings (1303–05), whose humanistic depiction of biblical figures was especially well suited to the chapel

Padua

◎ **Top Sights**

◎ **Sights**

🛏 **Sleeping**

🍴 **Eating**

🍷 **Drinking & Nightlife**

Enrico Scrovegni commissioned in memory of his father, who as a moneylender was denied a Christian burial.

Giotto's moving, modern approach helped change how people saw themselves: no longer as lowly vassals, but as vessels for the divine, however flawed. And where before medieval churchgoers had been accustomed to blank stares from saints perched on high thrones, Giotto introduced biblical figures as characters in recognisable settings. Onlookers gossip as middle-aged Anne tenderly kisses Joachim, and Jesus stares down Judas as the traitor puckers up for the fateful kiss. A 10-minute introductory video provides some helpful insights before you enter the church itself.

Pick up prebooked tickets at the Musei Civici agli Eremitani, where you access the chapel. Chapel visits last 15 to 20 minutes (depending on the time of year), plus another 20 minutes for the video. The 'double-turn' night-session ticket (€12) allows a 40-minute stay in the chapel and must be prebooked by phone.

Musei Civici agli Eremitani   MUSEUM
(☑049 820 45 51; Piazza Eremitani 8; adult/reduced €10/8; ⊙9am-7pm Tue-Sun) The ground floor of this monastery houses ar-
tefacts dating from Padua's Roman and pre-Roman past. Upstairs, a rambling but interesting collection boasts a few notable 14th- to 18th-century works by Bellini, Giorgione, Tintoretto and Veronese. Among the show-stoppers is a crucifix by Giotto, showing a heartbroken Mary wringing her hands as Jesus' blood drips into the empty eye sockets of a human skull.

Mary also appears in a series of dazzling paintings by 14th-century artist Guariento di Arpo, executed for the private chapel of Padua's powerful Carraresi (da Carrara) family.

Palazzo Zuckermann   GALLERY
(☑049 820 56 64; Corso di Garibaldi 33; adult/reduced €10/8; ⊙10am-7pm Tue-Sun) The ground and 1st floors of the early-20th-century Palazzo Zuckermann are home to the **Museo d'Arti Applicate e Decorative**, whose eclectic assortment of decorative and applied arts spans several centuries of flatware, furniture, fashion and jewellery. On the 2nd floor is the **Museo Bottacin**, a treasury of finely worked historic coins and medals, kept company by a modest collection of 19th-century paintings and sculpture.

Palazzo del Bò   HISTORIC BUILDING
(☑049 827 30 47; www.unipd.it/en/guidedtours; Via VIII Febbraio; adult/reduced €5/2; ⊙see website for tour times) This Renaissance *palazzo* is the seat of Padua's history-making university. Founded by renegade scholars from Bologna seeking greater intellectual freedom, the university has employed some of Italy's greatest and most controversial thinkers, including Copernicus, Galileo, Casanova and the world's first female doctor of philosophy, Eleonora Lucrezia Cornaro Piscopia (her statue graces the stairs). The 45-minute guided tours include the world's first **anatomy theatre**.

Palazzo della Ragione   HISTORIC BUILDING
(☑049 820 50 06; Piazza delle Erbe; adult/reduced €4/2; ⊙9am-7pm Tue-Sun, to 6pm Nov-Jan) Ancient Padua can be glimpsed in elegant twin squares separated by the triple-decker Gothic Palazzo della Ragione, the city's tribunal dating from 1218. Inside Il Salone (the Great Hall), frescoes by Giotto acolytes Giusto de' Menabuoi and Nicolò Miretto depict the astrological theories of Padovan professor Pietro d'Abano, with images representing the months, seasons, saints, animals and noteworthy Paduans (not necessarily in that order).

ℹ SIGHTSEE FOR LESS

A **PadovaCard** (48/72 hours €16/21) gives one adult and one child under 14 free use of city public transport and access to almost all of Padua's major attractions, including the Cappella degli Scrovegni (plus €1 booking fee; reservations essential). PadovaCards are available at Padua tourist offices, Musei Civici agli Eremitani and the hotels listed at www.padovacard.it.

The enormous 15th-century wooden horse at the western end of the hall was modelled on Donatello's majestic bronze *Gattamelata*, which still stands in Piazza del Santo. At the other end of the hall is a contemporary version of Foucault's *Pendulum*.

Duomo   CATHEDRAL

(☑ 049 65 69 14; Piazza del Duomo; baptistry €3; ⊙ 7.30am-noon & 4-7.30pm Mon-Sat, 8am-1pm & 4-8.45pm Sun & holidays, baptistry 10am-6pm) Built from a much-altered design of Michelangelo's, the whitewashed symmetry of Padua's cathedral is a far cry from its rival in Piazza San Marco. Pop in quickly for Giuliano Vangi's contemporary chancel crucifix and sculptures before taking in the adjoining 13th-century baptistry, a Romanesque gem frescoed with luminous biblical scenes by Giusto de' Menabuoi. Hundreds of male and female saints congregate in the cupola, posed as though for a school graduation photo, exchanging glances and stealing looks at the Madonna.

Basilica di Sant'Antonio   CHURCH

(Il Santo; ☑ 049 822 56 52; www.basilicadelsanto.org; Piazza del Santo; ⊙ 6.20am-7.45pm Apr-Oct, to 6.45pm Nov-Mar) **FREE** Il Santo is the soul of Padua, a key pilgrimage site and the burial place of patron saint St Anthony of Padua (1193–1231). Begun in 1232, its polyglot style incorporates rising eastern domes atop a Gothic brick structure crammed with Renaissance treasures. Behind the high altar nine radiating chapels punctuate a broad ambulatory homing in on the **Cappella del Tesoro** (Treasury Chapel), where the relics of St Anthony reside.

You'll also notice dozens of people clustering along the left transept waiting their turn to enter the **Cappella del Santo**, where Anthony's tomb is covered with requests and thanks for the saint's intercession in curing illness and recovering lost objects. The chapel itself is a light-filled Renaissance confection lined with nine panels vividly depicting the story of Anthony's life in extraordinary relief sculptures. The panels are attributed to the Padua-born Lombardo brothers and were completed around 1510.

Other notable works include the lifelike 1360s crucifix by Veronese master Altichiero da Zevio in the frescoed **Cappella di San Giacomo**; the wonderful sacristy fresco (1528) of St Anthony preaching to spellbound fish by a follower of Girolamo Tessari; and high altar reliefs by Florentine Renaissance master Donatello (1444–50; ask guards for access). Through the south door of the basilica you reach the attached monastery with its five cloisters. The oldest (13th century) is the **Chiostro della Magnolia**, so called because of the magnificent tree in its centre.

Oratorio di San Giorgio & Scoletta del Santo   CHURCH

(☑ 049 822 56 52; Piazza del Santo; adult/reduced €5/4; ⊙ 9am-12.30pm & 2.30-7pm Apr-Sep, to 5pm Oct-Mar) Anywhere else the fresco cycle of the Oratorio di San Giorgio and the paintings in the Scoletta del Santo would be considered highlights, but in Padua they must contend with Giotto's Scrovegni brilliance. This means you'll have Altichiero da Zevio and Jacopo Avanzi's jewel-like, 14th-century frescoes of St George, St Lucy and St Catherine all to yourself, while upstairs in the *scoletta* (confraternity house), Titian paintings are seldom viewed in such tranquillity.

Orto Botanico   GARDENS

(☑ 049 201 02 22; www.ortobotanicopd.it; Via dell'Orto Botanico 15; adult/reduced €10/8; ⊙ 9am-7pm daily Apr & May, 9am-7pm Tue-Sun Jun-Sep, to 6pm Tue-Sun Oct, to 5pm Tue-Sun Nov-Mar) Planted in 1545 by Padua University's medical faculty to study the medicinal properties of rare plants, Padua's World Heritage–listed Orto Botanico served as a clandestine Resistance meeting headquarters in WWII. The oldest tree is nicknamed 'Goethe's palm'; planted in 1585, it was mentioned by the great German writer in his *Voyage in Italy*. A much more recent addition is the high-tech **Garden of Biodiversity**, five interconnected greenhouses that recreate different climate zones and explore botanical and environmental themes via multimedia displays.

🛏 Sleeping

The tourist office publishes accommodation brochures and lists dozens of B&Bs, apartments and hotels online.

Ostello Città di Padova HOSTEL €
(☎049 875 22 19; www.ostellopadova.it; Via dei Aleardi 30; dm €19-23, d €46, without bathroom €40; ☺reception 7.15-9.30am & 3.30-11.30pm; 🛜) A central hostel with decent four- and six-bed dorm rooms on a quiet side street. Sheets and wi-fi are free. Breakfast is served between 7.30am and 8.30am, though there is no open kitchen. There's an 11.30pm curfew, except when there are special events, and guests must check out by 9.30am. Take bus 12 or 18, or the tram from the train station.

Belludi37 BOUTIQUE HOTEL €€
(☎049 66 56 33; www.belludi37.it; Via Luca Belludi 37; s €80, d €140-180; 🌀🛜) Graced with Flos bedside lamps and replica Danish chairs, the neutrally toned rooms at Belludi37 feature high ceilings, queen-sized beds and free minibar. Six newly opened rooms also deliver svelte bathrooms. Extra perks include a central location and helpful staff always on hand with suggestions for biking itineraries and walking tours.

Hotel Patavium HOTEL €€
(☎049 72 36 98; www.hotelpatavium.it; Via B Pellegrino 106; s €60-120, d €75-140; 🌀🛜) Smart, carpeted rooms with wide beds, flat-screen TVs and modern bathrooms define Patavium, a quick walk northwest of the city centre. Suites come with jacuzzis, while the breakfast room is a middle-class affair of candlesticks, chandeliers and corner lounge with communal TV.

🍴 Eating

Zairo ITALIAN €
(☎049 66 38 03; http://zairo.net; Prato della Valle 51; pizzas €4-9.40, meals €25; ☺noon-2pm & 7pm-midnight Tue-Sun) The fresco above the kitchen door at this sweeping, chintzy restaurant-pizzeria dates back to 1673. But you're here for Zairo's cult hit *gnocchi verdi con gorgonzola* (spinach and potato gnocchi drizzled in a decadent gorgonzola sauce), or one of its decent, spot-hitting pizzas.

Osteria dei Fabbri OSTERIA €€
(☎049 65 03 36; Via dei Fabbri 13; meals €30; ☺noon-2.30pm & 7-10.30pm Mon-Sat, noon-3pm Sun) Communal tables, wine-filled tumblers and a single-sheet menu packed with hearty dishes keep things real at dei Fab-bri. Slurp on superlative *zuppe* (soups) like sweet red-onion soup, or tuck into comforting meat dishes such as oven-roasted pork shank with Marsala, sultanas and polenta.

★ Belle Parti ITALIAN €€€
(☎049 875 18 22; www.ristorantebelleparti.it; Via Belle Parti 11; meals €50; ☺12.30-2.30pm & 7.30-10.30pm Mon-Sat) Prime seasonal produce, impeccable wines and near-faultless service meld into one unforgettable whole at this stellar fine-dining restaurant, resplendent with 18th-century antiques and 19th-century oil paintings. Seafood is the forte, with standout dishes including an arresting *gran piatto di crudità di mare* (raw seafood platter). Dress to impress and book ahead.

🍷 Drinking & Entertainment

Sundown isn't official until you've joined the crowds for a *spritz* in Piazza delle Erbe or Piazza dei Signori. Also note that Padua is the region's unofficial capital of gay and lesbian life.

Caffè Pedrocchi CAFE
(☎049 878 12 31; www.caffepedrocchi.it; Via VIII Febbraio 15; ☺8.45am-midnight Apr-Oct, to 11pm Nov-Mar) Divided into three rooms – red, white and green – the neoclassical Pedrocchi has long been a seat of intrigue and revolution, as well as a favourite of Stendhal. Soak up its esteemed history over coffee or head in for a sprightly *spritz* and decent *aperitivo* snacks.

Decorated in styles ranging from ancient Egyptian to Imperial, the building's 1st floor is home to the **Museo del Risorgimento e dell'Età Contemporanea**

TO MARKET

One of the most enjoyable activities in Padua is browsing the markets in **Piazza delle Erbe** and **Piazza della Frutta**, which operate very much as they've done since the Middle Ages. Dividing them is the Gothic Palazzo della Ragione, whose arcades, known locally as **Sotto il Salone** (www.sottoilsalone.it), rumble with specialist butchers, cheesemakers, fishmongers, *salumerie* and fresh pasta producers. The markets are open all day, every day, except Sunday, although the best time to visit is before midday.

(☑049 878 12 31; Galleria Pedrocchi 11; adult/child €4/2.50; ◔9.30am-12.30pm & 3.30-6pm Tue-Sun), which recounts local and national history from the fall of Venice in 1797 until the republican constitution of 1848.

Enoteca Il Tira Bouchon
WINE BAR

(☑049 875 21 38; www.enotecapadova.it; Sotto il Salone 23/24; ◔10am-2.30pm & 5-9pm Mon-Sat) With a guiding French hand behind the bar you can be sure of an excellent *prosecco*, Franciacorta or sauvignon at this traditional wine bar beneath Palazzo Ragione's arcades. Locals crowd in for *spunci* (bread-based snacks), *panini* and a rotating selection of 12 wines by the glass. You'll find around 300 wines on the shelves, including drops from emerging winemakers.

ℹ️ Information

Hospital (☑049 821 11 11; Via Giustiniani 1) Main public hospital.

Police Station (☑049 83 31 11; Piazzetta Palatucci 5)

Tourist Office (☑049 201 00 80; www.turismopadova.it; Vicolo Pedrocchi; ◔9am-7pm Mon-Sat) Ask about the PadovaCard (p386) here. There is a second **tourist office** (☑049 201 00 80; Piazza di Stazione; ◔9am-7pm Mon-Sat, 10am-4pm Sun) at the train station.

ℹ️ Getting There & Around

BUS

Busitalia – SITA Nord buses (☑049 820 68 34; www.fsbusitalia.it) from Venice's Piazzale Roma (€4.60, 45 minutes, one to two per hour) arrive outside Padua's train station. Check online for buses to Colli Euganei towns.

TRAIN

Train is the easiest way to reach Padua from Venice (€4 to €15, 25 to 50 minutes, one to nine per hour), Verona (€7 to €18, 45 to 90 minutes,

ℹ️ TRAVEL BY SMS

If you have a rechargeable Italian SIM card, you can use your mobile phone to purchase 75-minute tickets for use on Padua's city buses and trams. Simply text APS to the number ☑489 38 94 and wait for a confirmation SMS, which is also your electronic ticket. The €1.30 fare is automatically deducted from your phone credit. For information on all ticket types and remote payment options, see www.apsholding.it.

one to four per hour), Vicenza (€4 to €15, 15 to 25 minutes, one to five per hour) and most other Italian destinations. The station is about 500m north of Cappella degli Scrovegni.

TRAM

It is easy to get to all the sights by foot from the train and bus stations, but the city's single-branch tram running from the train station passes within 100m of all the main sights. Tickets (€1.30) are available at tobacconists and newsstands.

Vicenza
POP 113,700

When Palladio escaped an oppressive employer in his native Padua, few would have guessed the humble stonecutter would, within a few decades, transform not only his adoptive city but also the history of European architecture. By luck, a local count recognised his talents in the 1520s and sent him to study the ruins in Rome. When he returned to Vicenza, the autodidact began producing his extraordinary buildings, structures that marry sophistication and rustic simplicity, reverent classicism and bold innovation. His genius would turn Vicenza and its surrounding villas into one grand Unesco World Heritage Site. And yet, the Veneto's fourth-largest city is more than just elegant porticoes and balustrades – its dynamic exhibitions, bars and restaurants provide a satisfying dose of modern vibrancy.

◉ Sights

The heart of historic Vicenza is **Piazza dei Signori**, where Palladio lightens the mood of government buildings with his trademark play of light and shadow. Arches of dazzling white Piovene stone (a local limestone) frame shady double arcades at the Basilica Palladiana while, across the piazza, white stone and stucco grace the exposed red-brick colonnade of the 1571-designed **Loggia del Capitaniato**.

Basilica Palladiana
GALLERY

(☑0444 22 21 22; www.museicivicivicenza.it; Piazza dei Signori; temporary exhibitions €10-13; ◔temporary exhibitions only) Now a venue for world-class temporary exhibitions, the Palladian Basilica is capped with an enormous copper dome reminiscent of the hull of an upturned ship. The building, modelled on a Roman basilica, once housed the law courts and Council of Four Hundred. Palladio was

COLLI EUGANEI (EUGANEAN HILLS)

Southwest of Padua, the Euganean Hills feel a world away from the urban sophistication of Venice and the surrounding plains. To help you explore the walled hilltop towns, misty vineyards and bubbling hot springs, click onto www.parcocollieuganei.com or grab information at the Padua tourist offices. Trains serve all towns except Arquà Petrarca.

Just south of Padua lie the natural-hot-spring resorts of **Abano Terme** and **Montegrotto Terme**. They have been active since Roman times, when the Patavini built their villas on Mt Montirone. The towns are uninspiring, but the waters do cure aches and pains.

In the medieval village of **Arquà Petrarca**, look for the elegant little **house** (🖉 0429 71 82 94; www.arquapetrarca.com; Via Valleselle 4; adult/reduced €4/2; ⏰ 9am-12.30pm & 3-7pm Tue-Sun Mar-Oct, 9am-12.30pm & 2.30-5.30pm Tue-Sun Nov-Feb) where the great Italian poet Petrarch spent his final years in the 1370s.

At the southern reaches of the Euganei, you'll find **Monselice**, with its remarkable medieval castle; **Montagnana**, with its magnificent 2km defensive perimeter; and **Este**, with its rich architectural heritage and important **archaeological museum** (🖉 0429 20 85; www.atestino.beniculturali.it; Via Guido Negri 9c; adult/reduced €4/2; ⏰ 8.30am-7.30pm). Este is also home to **Este Ceramiche Porcellane** (🖉 0429 22 70; www.esteceramiche. com; Via Zanchi 22a; ⏰ 8am-noon & 2-6pm Mon, to 5.30pm Tue-Fri, by appointment Sat), one of the oldest ceramics factories in Europe.

If you want to overnight, consider staying in one of the two apartments at **Villa dei Vescovi** (🖉 049 993 04 73; www.villadeivescovi.it; Luvigliano; 3-night weekend €620-775; 🛜🅿), one of the best-preserved pre-Palladio Renaissance villas in the Veneto.

---

lucky to secure the commission in 1549 (it took its patron 50 years of lobbying the council), which involved radically restructuring the original, 15th-century *palazzo* and adding an ambitious double order of loggias, supported by Tuscan and Ionic columns topped by soaring statuary.

The building is also home to the elegant **Museo del Gioiello** (www.lineadombra.it; Piazza dei Signori; adult/reduced €6/4; ⏰ 10am-6pm Mon-Fri, 9am-7pm Sat & Sun) and its dazzling collection of historic and contemporary jewellery.

Palladio Museum MUSEUM
(Palazzo Barbarano; 🖉 0444 32 30 14; www.palladio museum.org; Contrà Porti 11; adult/reduced €6/4, or with MuseumCard; ⏰ 10am-6pm Tue-Sun) To better understand architect Andrea Palladio and his legacy, explore the frescoed halls of this modern museum. Artefacts include historical copies of Palladio's celebrated *Quattro Libri dell'Architettura* (Four Books of Architecture; 1570) and intriguing architectural models of his lauded *palazzi* and villas, as well as video footage of experts discussing various aspects of the maverick's craft and genius.

⭐**Palazzo Leoni Montanari** MUSEUM
(🖉 800 578875; www.gallerieditalia.com; Contrà di Santa Corona 25; adult/reduced €5/3, or with MuseumCard; ⏰ 10am-6pm Tue-Sun) An extraordinary collection of treasures await inside Palazzo Leoni Montanari, among them ancient pottery from Magna Graecia and grand salons filled with Canaletto's misty lagoon landscapes and Pietro Longhi's 18th-century satires. A recent addition is Agostino Fasolato's astounding *The Fall of the Rebel Angels*, carved from a single block of Carrara marble and featuring no less than 60 angels and demons in nail-biting battle. Topping it all off is a superb collection of 400 Russian icons.

Chiesa di Santa Corona CHURCH
(🖉 0444 22 28 11; Contrà di Santa Corona; adult/ reduced €3/2, or with MuseumCard; ⏰ 9am-noon & 3-6pm Tue-Sun) Built by the Dominicans in 1261 to house a relic from Christ's crown of thorns donated to the bishop of Vicenza by Louis IX of France, this Romanesque church also houses three light-filled masterpieces: Palladio's 1576 **Valmarana Chapel** in the crypt; Paolo Veronese's *Adoration of the Magi*, much praised by Goethe; and Giovanni Bellini's radiant *Baptism of Christ*, where the holy event is witnessed by a trio of Veneto beauties and a curious red bird.

⭐**Teatro Olimpico** THEATRE
(🖉 0444 22 28 00; www.olimpicovicenza.it; Piazza Matteotti 11; adult/reduced €11/8, or with MuseumCard; ⏰ 9am-5pm Tue-Sun, to 6pm early

VENICE & THE VENETO VICENZA

Vicenza

Vicenza

Jul-early Sep) Behind a walled garden lies a Renaissance marvel: the Teatro Olimpico, which Palladio began in 1580 with inspiration from Roman amphitheatres. Vincenzo Scamozzi finished the elliptical theatre after Palladio's death, adding a stage set modelled on the ancient Greek city of Thebes, with streets built in steep perspective to give the illusion of a city sprawling towards a distant horizon.

Today, Italian performers vie to make an entrance on this extraordinary stage; check the website for opera, classical and jazz performances.

Palazzo Chiericati　　　　MUSEUM
(☑ 0444 22 28 11; www.museicivicivicenza.it; Piazza Matteotti 37/39; adult/reduced €5/3; ⊙ 10am-6pm Tue-Sun early Jul-early Sep, 9am-5pm Tue-Sun rest of year) Vicenza's civic art museum occupies one of Palladio's finest buildings, designed in 1550. The ground floor, used for temporary exhibitions, is where you'll find the **Sala dal Firmamento** (Salon of the Skies) and its blush-inducing ceiling fresco of Diana and an up-skirted Helios by

Domenico Brusasorci. Highlights in the upstairs galleries include Anthony Van Dyke's allegorical *The Four Ages* and Alessandro Maganza's remarkably contemporary *Portrait of Maddalena Campiglia*. Another floor up is the private collection of the late marquis Giuseppe Roi, including drawings by Tiepolo and Picasso.

★**La Rotonda** HISTORIC BUILDING
(☑049 879 13 80; www.villalarotonda.it; Via della Rotonda 45; villa/gardens €10/5; ⊙villa 10am-noon & 3-6pm Wed & Sat mid-Mar–Oct, 10am-noon & 2.30-5pm Wed & Sat Nov–mid-Mar, gardens 10am-noon & 3-6pm Tue-Sun mid-Mar–Oct, 10am-noon & 2.30-5pm Tue-Sun Nov–mid-Mar) No matter how you look at it, this villa is a showstopper: the namesake dome caps a square base, with identical colonnaded facades on all four sides. This is one of Palladio's most admired creations, inspiring variations across Europe and the USA, including Thomas Jefferson's Monticello. Inside, the circular central hall is covered from the walls to the soaring cupola with trompe-l'œil frescoes. Catch bus 8 (€1.30, €2 on board) from in front of Vicenza's train station, or simply walk (about 25 minutes).

Villa Valmarana 'ai Nani' HISTORIC BUILDING
(☑0444 32 18 03; www.villavalmarana.com; Stradella dei Nani 8; adult/reduced €10/7; ⊙10am-12.30pm & 3-6pm Tue-Fri, 10am-6pm Sat & Sun early Mar-early Nov, by appointment rest of year) From La Rotonda, a charming footpath leads about 500m to the neoclassical elegance of Villa Valmarana 'ai Nani', nicknamed after the 17 statues of gnomes ('ai Nani') around the perimeter walls. Step inside for 1757 frescoes by Giambattista Tiepolo and his son Giandomenico. Giambattista painted the Palazzina wing with his signature mythological epics, while his offspring executed the rural, carnival and Chinese themes adorning the *foresteria*.

🛏 Sleeping

Scores of hotels in greater Vicenza are listed on the website of the **tourism board** (www.vicenzae.org) and a dozen or so B&Bs can be found at www.vitourism.it.

Ostello Olimpico HOSTEL €
(☑0444 54 02 22; www.ostellovicenza.com; Via Antonio Giuriolo 9; dm/s/d €22/30/52; ⊙reception 7.15-10am & 3.15-11.30pm; ⏝) A convenient HI youth hostel set in a fine building by the Te-

PALLADIAN HIGHLIGHTS

Basilica Palladiana (p388) Restored to its former glory after a six-year, €20-million refurbishment.

La Rotonda Palladio's most inspired design, copied the world over.

Villa di Masèr (p393) Set against a green hillside, this is Palladio's prettiest composition.

Villa Foscari (p382) River-facing facade with soaring Ionic columns that draw the eye and spirit upwards.

Palladio Museum (p389) Created by Howard Burns, the world authority on Palladio.

Teatro Olimpico (p389) Palladio's visionary elliptical theatre.

atro Olimpico. There is no curfew and both sheets and wi-fi are included in the price.

Hotel Palladio HOTEL €€
(☑0444 32 53 47; www.hotel-palladio.it; Contrà Oratorio dei Servi 25; s/d €110/170; ❄⏝) The top choice in central Vicenza, this friendly four-star hotel delivers crisp, whitewashed rooms with earthy accents and contemporary bathrooms, many of which feature generously sized showers. The lobby's stone column and rustic ceiling beams attest to the *palazzo's* Renaissance pedigree.

Relais Santa Corona HOTEL €€
(☑0444 32 46 78; www.relaissantacorona.it; Contrà di Santa Corona 19; s/d €100/150; ❄⏝) A boutique bargain, offering stylish stays in an 18th-century palace located on a street dotted with landmarks. The six rooms and two suites are soothing and soundproofed, with excellent mattresses, flat-screen TVs and uncluttered chic.

🍴 Eating

★**Sòtobotega** VENETIAN €
(☑0444 54 44 14; www.gastronomiailceppo.com; Corso Palladio 196; meals €25, set tasting menus €19.50-22; ⊙11.30am-3pm) Drop into cult-status deli **Gastronomia Il Ceppo** (☑0444 54 44 14; www.gastronomiailceppo.com; Corso Palladio 196; prepared dishes per 100g from around €2; ⊙8am-7.45pm Mon-Sat, 9am-2pm Sun) for picnic provisions, or head down into its cellar for sensational sit-down dishes like perfect house-made *bigoli* (a type of pasta) with

VENICE & THE VENETO VICENZA

A SECRET ROMAN TREASURE

Below modern Vicenza lies one of the city's lesser-known historical treasures – a **Roman criptoportico** (☑ 0444 22 66 26; larua@ctg.it; Piazza del Duomo 6; ☺ tours 10am-noon Sat & every 2nd Sun of the month, open every Sun Mar-May, last entry 11.30am) **FREE** dating back to between the late 1st century BC and early 1st century AD. Discovered during post-war reconstruction in 1954, it's the only known private *criptoportico* (covered passageway) in northern Italy. The three-sided semi-subterranean passageway once ran directly below the peristyle of a wealthy private *domus* (house), and the rooms adjacent to the *criptoportico* still contain small fragments of Roman flooring, including a rare example of hexagonal terracotta tiling studded with marble. At the end of the *criptoportico* is a medieval well, possibly used as a shelter from Hungarian invaders at the end of the 9th century.

To ensure an English-speaking guide, email ahead.

duck *ragù*. Expect no less than 500 mostly Italian wines, including local Durella grape options, and around 25 drops by the glass. Transparent floor panels reveal an ancient Roman footpath and the foundations of an 11th-century abode.

Book ahead or head in early.

★ **Al Pestello** VENETIAN €€

(☑ 0444 32 37 21; www.ristorantealpestello.it; Contrà San Stefano 3; meals €32; ☺ 7.30-10pm Mon, Wed & Thu, noon-2pm & 7.30-10pm Fri-Sun; ☎) ✐ Homely, brightly lit Al Pestello dishes out intriguing, lesser-known regional dishes like *la panà* (bread soup), red-wine braised donkey and *bresaola* 'lollies' filled with grappa-flavoured Grana Padano and mascarpone. The kitchen is obsessed with local ingredients, right down to the Colli Berici truffles, while the collection of harder-to-find *digestivi* makes for an enlightening epilogue. Book ahead.

Antico Ristorante agli Schioppi OSTERIA €€

(☑ 0444 54 37 01; www.ristoranteaglischioppi.com; Contrà Piazza del Castello 26; meals €30; ☺ noon-2pm & 7-10pm Tue-Sat; ☎) Tucked under an arcade just off Piazza del Castello lies one of the city's simplest and best restaurants. Owners Cinzia and Orlando are devotees of locally sourced products, from wild forest greens to baby river trout, but without any pretensions about it; it's just what they know best.

☕ Drinking & Nightlife

Bar Borsa BAR

(☑ 0444 54 45 83; www.barborsa.com; Basilica Palladiana, Piazza dei Signori; ☺ 5pm-midnight Mon, 10am-2am Tue-Sun; ☎) Decked out in black subway tiles and flickering candlelight, hip Borsa covers all bases, from coffee and juic-

es, to *aperitivo* and cocktail sessions. Fresh, flavoursome food options span breakfast, brunch, lunch, snacks and dinner, with DJs spinning non-commercial tunes on Fridays and Saturdays. Note: only bar service is available on Mondays.

Helmut BEER HALL

(www.facebook.com/HelmutpubVicenza; Contrà Zanella 8; ☺ 6.30pm-2am Tue-Sun) Industrial lighting, blackboard-hued walls and an antique pharmacy cabinet set the scene at new-school Helmut. Beer is the star attraction, with no less than 18 mostly European craft beers on tap, served to a smart, friendly, 30- and 40-something crowd. Sud-soaking edibles include creative burgers (€10 to €12) made with beef from lauded local butcher Damini & Affini.

Osteria al Campanile BAR

(☑ 0444 54 40 36; Piazza della Posta; ☺ 9am-2pm & 5-9pm Tue-Sun) You'll find one of Vicenza's most historic watering holes tucked beneath the Roman belltower by the cathedral. Eavesdrop on local gossip, nibble on scrumptious bite-sized *panini*, and swill unusual vintages such as the sparkling Durello, usually overshadowed by its more famous cousin, *prosecco*.

ⓘ Information

Police Station (☑ 0444 33 75 11; Viale G Mazzini 213)

Post Office (Contrà Garibaldi 1; ☺ 9am-7pm Mon-Fri)

Tourist Office (☑ 0444 32 08 54; www.vicenzae.org; Piazza Matteotti 12; ☺ 9am-1.30pm & 2-5.30pm) Ask about the good-value MuseumCard, a three-day pass (adult/reduced €15/12) that offers admission to numerous city museums.

BASSANO DEL GRAPPA, ASOLO & PALLADIO'S VILLA DI MASÈR

A road trip north from Vicenza takes you through one of Italy's most sophisticated stretches of countryside. You can visit all the key sites in a day.

Head first to Bassano del Grappa, which sits with charming simplicity on the banks of the Brenta river as it winds its way free from Alpine foothills. Located 35km northeast of Vicenza, the town is famous above all for its namesake spirit, a fiery distillation of left overs from winemaking: skins, pulp, seeds and stems. At the **Poli Museo della Grappa** (☎ 0424 52 44 26; www.poligrappa.com; Via Gamba 6; admission free, distillery guided tour €3; ⏰ museum 9am-7.30pm daily, distillery guided tours 8.30am-1pm & 2-6pm Mon-Fri), you can drink in four centuries of history of Bassano's signature grappa. Steps away is the town's most important structure, the Palladio-designed **Ponte degli Alpini** (aka Ponte Vecchio). At its eastern end is iconic drinking hole and grappa producer **Nardini** (⏰ 8.30am-9.30pm). Squeeze in for a preprandial *mezzo e mezzo* (soda water, Rabarbaro Nardini, Rosso Nardini and Cynar), then lunch with the locals at old-school **Osteria alla Caneva** (☎ 335 5423560; Via G Matteotti 34; dishes €7-15; ⏰ 9am-3pm & 5.30-9.30pm Wed-Mon) or new-school **Officina del Gusto** (Via Menarola 26; ⏰ 11am-2am Tue-Sun).

About 17km east of Bassano rises Asolo, known as the 'town of 100 vistas' for its panoramic hillside location, once the haunt of Romans and Veneti and a personal gift from Venice to Caterina, 15th-century queen of Cyprus, in exchange for her abdication. A historical hit with writers, including Pietro Bembo, Gabriele d'Annunzio and Robert Browning, its highbrow heritage outstrips its small size. Well known for its monthly Sunday **antiques market** (Antiques Market; ☎ 0423 52 46 75; www.asolo.it; Piazza Garibaldi ; ⏰ 2nd Sun of month Sep-Jun), it's overlooked by the **Rocca** (☎ 329 8508512; admission €2; ⏰ 10am-7pm Sat & Sun Apr-Jun, Sep & Oct, 10am-noon & 3-7pm Sat & Sun Jul & Aug, 10am-5pm Sat & Sun Nov-Mar), a medieval fortress that offers a breathtaking panorama of the Po Plain and mountains.

Another 5km east lies **Villa di Masèr** (Villa Barbaro; ☎ 0423 92 30 04; www.villadimaser. it; Via Barbaro 4; adult/reduced €9/7; ⏰ 10.30am-6pm Tue, Thu & Sat, 11am-6pm Sun Mar, 10am-6pm Tue-Sat, 11am-6pm Sun Apr-Oct, 11am-5pm Sat & Sun Nov-Feb; 🅿), where Palladio and Paolo Veronese conspired to create the Veneto countryside's finest monument to the *bea vita* (good life). Here, Palladio's arcaded, classically inspired exterior sets a suitable scene for his collaborator's wildly imaginative trompe l'œil architecture inside.

ⓘ Getting There & Away

There are several larger car parks skirting the historic centre, including the underground Park Verdi just north of the train station (enter from Viale dell'Ippodromo). For real-time updates on available parking spaces, see www.muoversiavicenza.it/it/parcheggi-auto.php (in Italian).

BUS

FTV (☎ 0444 22 31 15; www.ftv.vi.it) buses leave for outlying areas from the bus station, located next to the train station.

TRAIN

One to five trains arrive hourly from Venice (€6 to €16, 45 to 80 minutes) and Padua (€4 to €15, 15 to 25 minutes), while one to four trains arrive hourly from Verona (€5.40 to €16, 25 to 55 minutes).

Verona

POP 260,000

Shakespeare placed star-crossed lovers Romeo Montague and Juliet Capulet in Verona for good reason: romance, drama and fatal family feuding have been the city's hallmark for centuries. From the 3rd century BC Verona was a Roman trade centre with ancient gates, a forum (now Piazza delle Erbe) and a grand Roman arena, which still serves as one of the world's great opera venues. In the Middle Ages the city flourished under the wrathful della Scala clan, who were as much energetic patrons of the arts as they were murderous tyrants. Their elaborate Gothic tombs, the **Arche Scaligere**, are just off Piazza dei Signori.

Under Cangrande I (1308–28) Verona conquered Padua and Vicenza, with Dante,

Verona

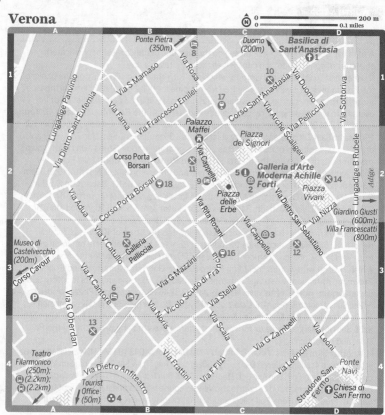

Petrarch and Giotto benefitting from the city's patronage. But the fratricidal rage of Cangrande II (1351–59) complicated matters, and the della Scala family were run out of town in 1387. Venice took definitive control in 1404, ruling until Napoleon's arrival in 1797.

The city became a Fascist control centre from 1938 to 1945, a key location for Resistance interrogation and transit point for Italian Jews sent to Nazi concentration camps. Today, the city is a Unesco World Heritage Site and a cosmopolitan crossroads, especially in summer when the 2000-year-old arena hosts opera's biggest names.

Sights

Roman Arena   RUIN

(045 800 32 04; www.arena.it; Piazza Brà; adult/reduced €10/7.50, 1st Sun of month Oct-May €1; 1.30-7.30pm Mon, 8.30am-7.30pm Tue-Sun) Built of pink-tinged marble in the 1st cen-

tury AD, Verona's Roman amphitheatre survived a 12th-century earthquake to become the city's legendary open-air opera house, with seating for 30,000 people. You can visit the arena year-round, though it's at its best during the summer opera festival. In winter months, concerts are held at the **Teatro Filarmonico** (booking 045 800 51 51; www.arena.it; Via dei Mutilati 4; box office noon-5.45pm Mon-Fri, 10am-12.45pm Sat, extended hours on show days).

Museo di Castelvecchio   MUSEUM

(045 806 26 11; Corso Castelvecchio 2; adult/reduced €6/4.50; 1.30-7.30pm Mon, 8.30am-7.30pm Tue-Sun;) Bristling with battlements along the River Adige, Castelvecchio was built in the 1350s by Cangrande II. Severely damaged by Napoleon and WWII bombings, the fortress was reinvented by architect Carlo Scarpa, who constructed bridges over exposed foundations, filled gaping holes with glass panels, and balanced a statue of

Verona

Cangrande I above the courtyard on a concrete gangplank. The complex is now home to a diverse collection of statuary, frescoes, jewellery, medieval artefacts and paintings by Pisanello, Giovanni Bellini, Tiepolo and Veronese.

Basilica di San Zeno Maggiore BASILICA
(www.chieseverona.it; Piazza San Zeno; admission €2.50; ☉8.30am-6pm Mon-Sat, 12.30-6pm Sun Mar-Oct, 10am-1pm & 1.30-5pm Mon-Sat, 12.30-5pm Sun Nov-Feb) A masterpiece of Romanesque architecture, the striped brick-and-stone basilica was built in honour of the city's patron saint. Enter through the flower-filled cloister into the nave – a vast space lined with 12th- to 15th-century frescoes. Painstaking restoration has revived Mantegna's 1457–59 *Majesty of the Virgin* altarpiece, painted with such astonishing perspective that you actually believe there are garlands of fresh fruit hanging behind the Madonna's throne.

Under the rose window depicting the Wheel of Fortune you'll find meticulously detailed 12th-century bronze doors, which include a scene of an exorcism with a demon being yanked from a woman's mouth. Beneath the main altar lies a brooding crypt,

with faces carved into medieval capitals and St Zeno's corpse glowing in a transparent sarcophagus.

Duomo CATHEDRAL
(☏ 045 59 28 13; www.chieseverona.it; Piazza Duomo; admission €2.50; ☉10am-5.30pm Mon-Sat, 1.30-5.30pm Sun Mar-Oct, 10am-1pm & 1.30-5pm Mon-Fri, to 4pm Sat, 1.30-5pm Sun Nov-Feb) Verona's 12th-century cathedral is a striking Romanesque creation, with bug-eyed statues of Charlemagne's paladins Roland and Oliver, crafted by medieval master Nicolò, on the west porch. Nothing about this sober facade hints at the extravagant 16th- to 17th-century frescoed interior with angels aloft amid trompe l'œil architecture. At the left end of the nave is the **Cartolari-Nichesola Chapel**, designed by Renaissance master Jacopo Sansovino and featuring a vibrant Titian *Assumption*.

Torre dei Lamberti TOWER
(☏ 045 927 30 27; Via della Costa 2; adult/reduced incl Galleria d'Arte Moderna Achille Forti €8/5; ☉10am-6pm Mon-Fri, last entry 5.15pm, 10am-7pm Sat & Sun, last entry 6.15pm) For panoramic views of Verona and nearby mountains, head up this 84m-high watchtower. Begun in the 12th century and finished in 1463 – too late to notice invading Venetians – it sports an octagonal bell tower whose two bells retain their ancient names: Rengo once called meetings of the city council, while Marangona warned citizens of fire. A lift whisks you up two-thirds of the way but you have to walk the last few storeys.

Full-price admission to the tower is reduced to €5 on Mondays as the adjoining Galleria d'Arte Moderna Achille Forti is closed.

★ **Galleria d'Arte Moderna
Achille Forti** MUSEUM
(Palazzo della Ragione; ☏ 045 800 19 03; www.palazzodellaragioneverona.it; Cortile Mercato Vecchio; adult/reduced €4/2.50, incl Torre dei Lamberti €8/5; ☉11am-7pm Tue-Sun Jun-Aug, 10am-6pm Tue-Fri, 11am-7pm Sat & Sun Sep-May) In the shadow of the Torre dei Lamberti, the Romanesque Palazzo della Ragione is home to Verona's jewel-box Gallery of Modern Art. Reached via the Gothic **Scala della Ragione** (Stairs of Reason), the collection of paintings and sculpture spans 1840 to 1940 and includes influential Italian artists such as Giorgio Morandi and Umberto Boccioni. Among the numerous highlights are

---

❶ MAKING THE MOST OF YOUR EURO

VeronaCard (http://turismoverona. eu; 24/72hr €15/20), available at tourist sights, tobacconists and numerous hotels, offers access to most major monuments and churches, unlimited use of town buses, plus discounted tickets to selected concerts and opera and theatre productions.

Francesco Hayez' arresting portrait *Meditazione* (Meditation), Angelo Dall'Oca's haunting *Foglie cadenti* (Falling Leaves) and Ettore Berladini's darkly humourous *I vecchi* (Old Men).

The gallery's architectural pièce de résistance is the vaulted **Cappella dei Notai** (Chapel of Notaries), bursting with late-17th- and early-18th-century biblical scenes executed by Alessandro Marchesini, Giambattista Bellotti, Santo Prunati and Louis Dorigny.

★ **Basilica di Sant'Anastasia** BASILICA
(www.chieseverona.it; Piazza di Sant'Anastasia; admission €2.50; ⊙9am-6pm Mon-Sat, 1-6pm Sun Mar-Oct, 10am-1pm & 1.30-5pm Mon-Sat, 1-5pm Sun Nov-Feb) Dating from the 13th to 15th centuries and featuring an elegantly decorated vaulted ceiling, the Gothic Chiesa di Sant'Anastasia is Verona's largest church and a showcase for local art. The multitude of frescoes is overwhelming, but don't overlook Pisanello's story-book-quality fresco *St George and the Princess* above the entrance to the **Pellegrini Chapel**, or the 1495 holy water font featuring a hunchback carved by Paolo Veronese's father, Gabriele Caliari.

★ **Giardino Giusti** GARDENS
(☎045 803 40 29; Via Giardino Giusti 2; adult/reduced €7/5; ⊙9am-8pm Apr-Sep, to 7pm Oct-Mar; ♿) Across the river from the historic centre, these sculpted gardens are considered a masterpiece of Renaissance landscaping, and named after the noble family that has tended them since opening them to the public in 1591. The vegetation is an Italianate mix of the manicured and natural, graced by soaring cypresses, one of which the German poet Goethe immortalised in his travel writings.

According to local legend, lovers who manage to find each other in the gardens' petite labyrinth are destined to stay together. If you do, whisper sweet nothings while gazing out at the city from the *belvedere* (lookout), accessed from the back of the gardens.

🎭 Festivals & Events

Estate Teatrale Veronese THEATRE, JAZZ
(www.estateteatraleveronese.it; Regaste Redentore 2) One of the best ways to experience Verona's Teatro Romano (Roman Theatre) is to attend the summer festival, when theatre (with a clear preference for Shakespeare and Goldoni), dance and jazz performances are staged.

🛏 Sleeping

For homestyle stays outside the city centre, check **Verona Bed & Breakfast** (www.bedandbreakfastverona.com).

Anfiteatro B&B B&B €
(☎347 2488462; www.anfiteatro-bedandbreakfast.com; Via Alberto Mario 5; s €60-90, d €80-130, tr €100-150) Opera divas rest up steps from the action in this 19th-century townhouse, one block from the Roman Arena and just off boutique-lined Via Mazzini. Spacious guest rooms have high wood-beamed ceilings, antique armoires for stashing purchases and divans for swooning after shows.

The charming owners also run nearby **Alla Galleria B&B** (☎347 2488462; www.bedandbreakfastallagalleria.com; Via A Cantore 4; s €65-90, d €85-130; 🛜), a tranquil, three-bedroom place with pastel hues, antique rugs and balconies.

Villa Francescatti HOSTEL €
(☎045 59 03 60; www.ostelloverona.it; Salita Fontana del Ferro 15; dm €18-20; ⊙7am-midnight; 🅿🛜) Verona's HI youth hostel occupies a 16th-century villa on a garden estate a 20-minute walk from the city centre. Rooms are off-limits from 9am to 5pm, and dinners require a reservation. Catch bus 73 (weekdays, and Saturdays until 7pm) or bus 91 (Saturdays after 7pm, Sundays and public holidays) from the train station. There's a strict midnight curfew and credit card payments are not accepted.

★ **Corte delle Pigne** B&B €€
(☎333 7584141; www.cortedellepigne.it; Via Pigna 6a; s €60-90, d €90-130, tr & q €110-150; 🅿❄🛜) In the heart of the historic cen-

ROMEO & JULIET IN VERONA

Shakespeare had no idea what he'd start when he set his (heavily derivative) tale of star-crossed lovers in Verona, but the city has seized the commercial possibilities with both hands – everything from *osterie* and hotels to embroidered kitchen aprons get the R&J branding. While the play's depiction of feuding families has genuine provenance, the lead characters themselves are fictional.

Undaunted, in the 1930s the authorities settled on a house in Via Cappello (think Capulet) as Juliet's and added a 14th-century-style balcony and a bronze statue of our heroine. You can squeeze onto the balcony itself at the altogether underwhelming **Casa di Giulietta** (Juliet's House; ☑045 803 43 03; Via Cappello 23; adult/reduced €6/4.50, or with VeronaCard; ☺1.30-7.30pm Mon, 8.30am-7.30pm Tue-Sun), or – more sensibly – see the circus from the square below, a spot framed by a slew of lovesick sticky notes.

tre, this three-room B&B is set around a quiet internal courtyard. It offers tasteful rooms and plenty of personal touches: sweet jars, luxury toiletries and even a jacuzzi for one lucky couple.

Hotel Aurora HOTEL €€
(☑045 59 47 17; www.hotelaurora.biz; Piazzetta XIV Novembre 2; d €100-250, tr €130-280; ❄ ☎) Overlooking Piazza delle Erbe, friendly Aurora offers recently renovated rooms, some with piazza views and all with classic wooden furniture and fresh, modern bathrooms. The open-air terrace makes for a perfect spot to enjoy breakfast or a lazy sundowner.

Eating

For picnic supplies, pick up fresh fruit and veg from market stalls in Piazza delle Erbe. Nearby **De Rossi** (☑045 800 24 89; Corso Porta Borsari 3; ☺7.45am-7.30pm Mon-Sat, 9.30am-7.30pm Sun) sells fresh bread. For meats and cheese, stroll 50m northeast to **Albertini** (☑045 803 10 74; Corso Sant'Anastasia 41).

Pizzeria Du de Cope PIZZA €
(☑045 59 55 62; www.pizzeriadudecope.it; Galleria Pellicciai 10; pizzas €5.50-13.50, salads €7-12; ☺noon-2.30pm & 7-11pm) Pimped with colourful wall tiles, chairs and placemats, Du de Cope is a thoroughly modern, convivial pizzeria. Peek over the counter and watch your pizza bubbling in the wood-fired oven, or ease up on the carbs with one of the high-quality salads.

★Locanda 4 Cuochi MODERN ITALIAN €€
(☑045 803 03 11; www.locanda4cuochi.it; Via Alberto Mario 12; meals €35, 3-course set menu €24; ☺7.30-10.30pm Tue, 12.30-2.30pm & 7.30-

10.30pm Wed-Sun; ☎) With its open kitchen, urbane vibe and hot-shot chefs, you're right to expect great things from the Locanda. Culinary acrobatics play second fiddle to prime produce cooked with skill and subtle twists. Whether it's perfectly crisp suckling pig with lemon and sage, or an epilogue of whipped ricotta cut with raspberry salsa and pistachio crumble, expect to swoon.

La Taverna di Via Stella VERONESE €€
(☑045 800 80 08; www.tavernadiviastella.com; Via Stella 5c; meals €30; ☺7.15-11pm Mon, 12.15-2.15pm & 7.15-11pm Wed-Sun) Brush past the haunches of prosciutto dangling over the deli bar and make your way into the dining room, decorated Tiepolo-style with rustic murals of chivalric knights and maidens. This is the place you'll want to sample traditional Veronese dishes such as *pastissada* (horse stew), *bigoli* with duck *ragù* and DOP Lessinia cheeses from Monte Veronese. Cash only for bills under €30.

★Pescheria I Masenini SEAFOOD €€€
(☑045 929 80 15; www.imasenini.com; Piazzetta Pescheria 9; meals €50; ☺7.30-10pm Tue, 12.30-2pm & 7.30-10pm Wed-Sun; ☎) Located on the piazza where Verona's Roman fish market once held sway, softly lit Masenini quietly serves up Verona's most imaginative, modern fish dishes. Inspired flavour combinations might see fresh sea bass carpaccio paired with zesty green apple and pink pepper, black-ink gnocchi schmoozing with lobster *ragù*, or sliced amberjack delightfully matched with crumbed almonds, honey, spinach and raspberries.

Shakespeare's Veneto

There is much debate about whether Shakespeare ever visited Italy, but his Italian plays are full of local knowledge. Venetian writer, architect and presenter Francesco da Mosto spoke to *Lonely Planet Traveller* magazine about the playwright's favourite Italian cities.

Verona

Verona was not thought of as a city of romance before *Romeo and Juliet* – in fact, not many people would have heard of it as it was very much in the shadow of Venice at that time. We don't know whether Romeo and Juliet existed, although Italian poet Dante did mention two feuding families, called the Montecchi and the Cappelletti. The famous balcony where Romeo is said to have declared his love to Juliet is close to Verona's main promenade – although since the balcony was apparently added to a suitably old house in 1936, it's doubtful it is the original! My favourite site in Verona is Juliet's tomb. People go there to pay tribute to Juliet and Shakespeare – even Dickens visited.

Padua

The University of Padua was one of the first in the world, and in Shakespeare's time, the city was very well known throughout Europe as a centre of learning – Galileo (of telescope fame) and Casanova (of sexual-conquest fame) are both alumni. Shakespeare used its reputation, rather than actual locations, as a backdrop for *The Taming of the Shrew* – apart from the university, he rarely mentions specific sites. The best way to experience Shakespeare's Padua is

1. Basilica di San Marco (p339) and Palazzo Ducale (p342), Venice 2. Juliet's balcony, Casa di Giulietta (p397), Verona 3. Prato della Valle, Padua (p383)

by having a stroll around the university. It feels like a little world unto itself, detached from the rest of the city. There is a marvellous wooden anatomical amphitheatre in the Medical School that was built in the 16th century, where they dissected humans and animals for the students. The life of the university runs through the city. It's lovely to walk through the portico walkways that run under the houses, and into the Prato della Valle, one of the main city squares.

Venice

Shakespeare set *Othello* in Venice, and *The Merchant of Venice* mentions the Rialto Market area several times. He even talked about gondolas and 'the tranect', which could refer to the *traghetto* ferry, which transported people from Venice to the mainland. If he did visit, Shakespeare would have spent his time wandering the streets, eavesdropping on people's conversations and observing the goings-on in shops and at the market. A walk to the Rialto is certainly evocative of that time. The Palazzo Ducale, with its magnificent Gothic facades and huge council hall, is probably what Shakespeare had in mind as the setting for the final courtroom scene in *The Merchant of Venice*, while the two bronze figures on top of the Torre dell'Orologio clock tower in Piazza San Marco are known as 'i Mori', or 'the Moors', which is a key reference in *Othello*.

VERONA'S OPERA FESTIVAL

On balmy summer nights, when 14,000 music lovers fill the Roman Arena during the opera festival and light their candles at sunset, expect goosebumps even before the performance starts. The **festival** (☑ 045 800 51 51; www.arena.it; Via Dietro Anfiteatro 6), which runs from mid-June to early September, was started in 1913 and is now the biggest open-air lyrical music event in the world. It draws international stars and the staging is legendary – highlights have included Franco Zeffirelli's lavish productions of *Carmen* and *Aida*.

Prices rise at weekends, ranging from €21 to €29 on unreserved stone steps and costing €204 on the central gold seats. Performances usually start at 8.45pm or 9pm with locals booking their dinner table for after the show. Tucking into a preshow picnic on the unreserved stone steps is fine, so decant that wine into a plastic bottle (glass and knives aren't allowed), arrive early, rent a cushion and prepare for an utterly unforgettable evening.

Drinking & Nightlife

Piazza delle Erbe is ringed with cafes and bars and fills with a fashionable drinking crowd come early evening.

★**Osteria del Bugiardo**　　　WINE BAR
(☑ 045 59 18 69; Corso Porta Borsari 17a; ⊙ 11am-midnight, to 1am Fri & Sat) Crowds converge at friendly Bugiardo for glasses of upstanding valpolicella bottled specifically for the *osteria*. Feeling peckish? Order the yellow polenta with creamy gorgonzola and salami. On weekdays from November to January, pair a powerhouse Amarone with the very local *lesso e peará* (boiled meat stew with a peppery beef, hen, bone-marrow and breadcrumb sauce).

Caffè Monte Baldo　　　WINE BAR
(☑ 045 803 05 79; Via Rosa 12; tartine €1.20; ⊙ 10am-11pm Tue-Thu, to 1am Fri, 11am-1am Sat, 11am-11pm Sun) Packed to bursting come *aperitivo* hour, wood-panelled, marble-topped Monte Baldo lures with its generous *aperitivo* bar and about 120 mostly regional wines, over 30 available by the glass. Graze on meatballs or *tartine*, tapas-sized bread artfully topped with ingredients like local *sopressa*, or cream cheese with hazelnuts and radicchio.

Antica Bottega del Vino　　　WINE BAR
(☑ 045 800 45 35; www.bottegavini.it; Vicolo Scudo di Francia 3; cicheti €2, meals €40; ⊙ noon-11pm; 🛜) While *vino* is the primary consideration at this historic, baronial-style wine bar (the cellar holds around 18,000 bottles), the linen-lined tables promise a satisfying feed. Ask the sommelier to recommend a worthy vintage for your Amarone risotto, sugar and cinnamon gnocchi, or suckling pig – some of the best wines here are bottled specifically for the *bottega*. Note that it sometimes closes in November and February.

ℹ Information

Ospedale Borgo Trento (☑ 045 812 11 11; Piazza A Stefani) Hospital northwest of Ponte Vittoria.

Police (☑ 113; Lungadige Galtarossa 11) Near Ponte Navi.

Tourist Office (☑ 045 806 86 80; www.tourism.verona.it; Via degli Alpini 9; ⊙ 9am-7pm Mon-Sat, 10am-4pm Sun) Just off Piazza Brà. Knowledgeable and helpful.

ℹ Getting There & Around

AIR

Verona-Villafranca airport (p281) is 12km outside town and accessible by ATV Aerobus to/from the train station (€6, 15 minutes, every 20 minutes 6.30am to 11.30pm). A taxi costs between €23 and €30, depending on the time of day. Flights arrive from all over Italy and some European cities, including Amsterdam, Barcelona, Berlin, Brussels, Dusseldorf, London and Paris.

BUS

The main intercity bus station is in front of the train station in the Porta Nuova area. Buses run to Padua, Vicenza and Venice.

ATV (Azienda Trasporti Verona; ☑ 045 805 79 22; www.atv.verona.it) city buses 11, 12 and 13 (bus 92 or 93 on Sundays and holidays) connect the train station with Piazza Brà. Buy tickets from newsagents and tobacconists before you board the bus (tickets valid for 90 minutes, €1.30).

TRAIN

Verona is well serviced by trains, with direct services to numerous northern Italian towns and cities, including:

➡ **Venice** (€8.60 to €23, 70 minutes to 2¼ hours, one to four hourly)

➡ **Padua** (€7 to €18, 40 to 90 minutes, one to four hourly)

➡ **Vicenza** (€5.40 to €16, 25 to 55 minutes, one to four hourly)

➡ **Milan** (€12 to €21.50, 1¼ to two hours, one to three hourly)

There are also direct international services to Austria, Germany and France.

Verona's Wine Country

A drive through Verona's hinterland is a lesson in fine wine. To the north and northwest are Valpolicella vineyards, which predate the arrival of the Romans, and east on the road to Vicenza lie the white-wine makers of Soave.

Soave

Southeast of Verona, Soave serves its namesake DOC white wine in a story-book setting. The town may be entirely encircled by medieval fortifications, including 24 bristling watchtowers, but these days strangers are more than welcome to taste the good stuff across from the old-town church at **Azienda Agricola Coffele** (☑ 045 768 00 07; www. coffele.it; Via Roma 5; wine tasting €9-12; ☉ 9am-1pm & 2.30-6.30pm Mon-Sat & by appointment).

The more adventurous can climb up to Soave's medieval **castle** (☑ 045 768 00 36; www.castellodisoave.it; adult/reduced €7/4; ☉ 9am-noon & 3-6.30pm Tue-Sun Apr-Oct, 9am-noon & 2-4pm Nov-Mar) and enjoy spectacular views over the surrounding countryside from the upper ramparts. If you have a car, strike out for **Suavia** (☑ 045 767 50 89; www. suavia.it; Via Centro 14, Fittà; ☉ 9am-1pm & 2.30-6.30pm Mon-Fri, 9am-1pm Sat & by appointment; ℗) ✐, a trailblazing winery in Fittà (about 8km north of Soave) run by the three Tessari daughters. Here, using sun-ripened Garganega grapes, the often light Soave is transformed into something altogether more complex with accents of liquorice, aniseed and fennel.

Just outside the medieval walls of Soave, **Locanda Lo Scudo** (☑ 045 768 07 66; www.lo-scudo.vr.it; Via Covergnino 9, Soave; meals €35, s/d €65/80; ☉ noon-2.30pm & 7.30-10.30pm Tue-Sat, noon-2.30pm Sun; 🐾) is half country inn and half high-powered gastronomy. Cult dishes include a risotto of scallops and porcini mushrooms, though – if it's on the menu – opt for the extraordinary *tortelloni* stuffed with local pumpkin, Grana Padano, cinnamon, mustard and Amaretto, and topped with crispy fried sage. Above the restaurant are four lovely rooms.

To reach Soave from central Verona, catch ATV bus 130 (€3.40, €4.20 on board; around 50 minutes) from Corso Porta Nuova. Purchase bus tickets at the *tabaccaio* (tobacconist) across the street at Corso Porta Nuova 10a. If driving, exit the A4 autostrada at San Bonifacio and follow the Viale della Vittoria 2km north into town. Soave's **tourist office** (☑ 045 619 07 73; Piazza Foro Boario I, Soave; ☉ 10am-5pm Mon, 9am-6pm Tue-Fri, 9am-3pm Sat & Sun Apr-Oct, 9am-5pm Tue-Fri, to 2pm Sat & Sun Nov-Mar) is just outside the medieval wall, in front of the central bus stop.

Valpolicella

Situated in the foothills of Monte Lessini, the 'valley of many cellars', from which Valpolicella gets its name, benefits from a happy microclimate created by the enormous body of Lake Garda to the west and cooling breezes from the Alps to the north. No wonder Veronese nobility got busy building weekend retreats here. Many of them, like the extraordinary Villa della Torre, still house noble wineries, while others like **Villa Spinosa** (☑ 045 750 00 93; www.villaspinosa.it; Via Colle Masua 12, Negrar; apt per 2 people €90-130, per 4 people €180-210, minimum 2-night stay; ℗) and the fabulous, family- and foodie-friendly **Agriturismo San Mattia** (☑ 045 91 37 97; www.agriturismosanmattia.it; Via Santa Giuliana 2a, Verona; s €50-65, d €80-99, apt per week €600-1190; ℗ 🏠) ✐ provide comfortable accommodation.

> ℹ **WINE TOURS**
>
> If you don't want to rent a car, **Pagus** (☑ 340 0830720, 349 1579090; www.pagusvalpolicella.net; 3½hr group tour adult/under 14yr from €60/50) offers half- and full-day tours of Valpolicella and Soave, leaving regularly from Verona. Tours include visits to unusual rural sites, impromptu rambles, lunches in local restaurants and, of course, wine tastings. Tours can also be customised.

DON'T MISS

TOP TIPPLES

Allegrini (☑ 045 683 20 11; http://allegrini.it; Via Giare 9/11, Fumane; wine tasting & cellar tour €20, tour of villa €10, tour of villa with wine tasting & snack €30-40; ☺ cellar tour & wine tasting 10.30am & 3.30pm Mon-Fri by appointment, villa tours 11am & 4pm Mon-Sat by appointment; [P]) Valpolicella aristocracy, the Allegrini family have been producing Grand crus from corvina and rondinella grapes since the 16th century.

Giuseppe Quintarelli (☑ 045 750 00 16; giuseppe.quintarelli@tin.it; Via Cerè 1, Negrar; wine tastings €20; ☺ by appointment) Giuseppe Quintarelli put the Valpolicella region on the world wine map, and the winery's Amarone remains a Holy Grail for international oenophiles. Other standout drops include Recioto, Valpolicella and Alzero.

Massimago (☑ 045 888 01 43; www.massimago.com; Via Giare 21, Mezzane di Sotto; wine tastings from €10, 2-person apt €120-150, 4-person apt €220-250; ☺ 9am-6pm Mon-Fri, by appointment Sat & Sun; [P]) Breaking the traditional mould, Camilla Chauvet concentrates on a limited range of lighter, more modern Valpolicellas at her winery-cum-lodgings, including a rosé and an unusual sparkling variety.

Valentina Cubi (☑ 045 770 18 06; www.valentinacubi.it; Località Casterna 60, Fumane; wine tastings €20; ☺ 10am-noon & 3-6pm Mon-Sat by appointment; [P]) 🍷 This teacher and winemaker is blazing a trail with one of the few certified organic wineries in the region. Subject to the quality of the year's harvest, Cubi produces one of the few 'natural', sulphate-free Valpolicellas.

Zýmē (☑ 045 770 11 08; www.zyme.it; Via Cà del Pipa 1, San Pietro in Cariano; wine tastings €15; ☺ shop 9am-5pm Mon-Sat, tastings by appointment 9am-noon & 2-6pm Mon-Sat) Celestino Gaspari's award-winning winery is famed for its striking contemporary architecture, ancient quarry-turned-cellar, and bold, big-blend wines. His lauded, full-throttle Harlequin is made using 15 local grape varieties.

◉ Sights & Activities

Five *comuni* compose the DOC quality-controlled area: Fumane, Negrar, San Pietro in Cariano, Sant'Ambrogio di Valpolicella and Marano di Valpolicella.

To reach them, follow the SS12 northwest out of Verona, veer north onto SP4 and follow the route west towards **San Pietro in Cariano**, the region's main hub. Alternatively, ATV bus 3 departs Verona's Porta Nuova for San Pietro one to three times per hour (€2.80, €3.60 on board, 43 minutes). For tourist information, and biking and hiking itineraries, visit the **Valpolicella tourist office** (☑ 045 770 19 20; www.valpolicellaweb.it; Via Ingelheim 7; ☺ 9am-1pm Mon-Fri).

Villa della Torre   HISTORIC BUILDING

(☑ 045 683 20 60; www.villadellatorre.it; Via della Torre 25, Fumane; villa guided tour €10, with wine tasting & snack €30-40; ☺ villa tours 11am & 4pm Mon-Sat by appointment; [P]) The jewel in the Allegrini crown, this historic villa dates to the mid-16th century and was built by intellectual and humanist Giulio della Torre. Numerous starchitects contributed to its construction: the classically inspired peristyle and fish pond are attributed to Giulio

Romana (of Palazzo Te fame), the chapel to Michele Sanmicheli, and the monstrous, gaping-mouthed fireplaces to Bartolomeo Ridolfi and Giovanni Battista Scultori.

Pieve di San Giorgio   CHURCH

(San Giorgio, Valpolicella; ☺ 7am-6pm) **FREE** In the tiny hilltop village of San Giorgio a few kilometres northwest of San Pietro in Cariano, you'll find this fresco-filled, cloistered 8th-century Romanesque church. Not old enough for you? In the little garden to its left you can also see a few fragments of an ancient Roman temple.

✗ Eating

★**Enoteca della Valpolicella**   VENETIAN €€

(☑ 045 683 91 46; www.enotecadellavalpolicella.it; Via Osan 47, Fumane; meals €25; ☺ noon-2.30pm Sun, noon-2.30pm & 7.30-10pm Tue-Sat) Gastronomes flock to the town of Fumane, just a few kilometres north of San Pietro in Cariano, where an ancient farmhouse has found renewed vigour as a rustically elegant restaurant. Among the more unusual dishes is a risotto made using local Recioto wine and shredded chocolate. The 700-bottle wine list is an oenophile's dream.

PROSECCO 101

What are the origins of prosecco? *Prosecco* can be traced back to the Romans. It was then known as 'Pucino' and was shipped direct to the court of Empress Livia from Aquileia, where it was produced with grapes from the Carso. During the Venetian Republic the vines were transferred to the Prosecco DOCG (quality-controlled) area, a small triangle of land between the towns of Valdobbiadene, Conegliano and Vittorio Veneto.

Describe the character of a good prosecco Straw yellow in colour with sparkling greenish reflections. The naturally formed bubbles are tiny, numerous and long-lasting in your glass. It's fragrant with fresh notes of white fruits and fresh grass. It pleases your mouth with its crispness and aromaticity. Keep in mind that these characteristics are not long-lasting – *prosecco* is meant to be drunk young.

Prosecco and the social scene Here in the Veneto we drink *prosecco* like water – sometimes it's even cheaper than water!

Mario Piccinin, sommelier and guide for Venice Day Trips (p365)

Trattoria Caprini TRATTORIA €€
(☑045 750 05 11; www.trattoriacaprini.it; Via Zanotti 9, Negrar; meals €30; ⊗noon-2.30pm & 7-10pm Thu-Tue) In the centre of Negrar, family run Caprini serves heart-warming grub you wish your mamma could make. Many items on the menu are homemade, including the delicious *lasagnetta* with hand-rolled pasta, and a *ragù* of beef, tomato, porcini and finferli mushrooms. Downstairs, beside the fire of the old *pistoria* (bakery), you can sample some 200 Valpolicella labels.

Prosecco Country

In the foothills of the Alps, **Conegliano** (pop 35,000) and **Valdobbiadene** (pop 10,560) are the toast of the Veneto. Their vine-draped hillsides produce *prosecco*, a dry, crisp white wine made in *spumante* (bubbly), *frizzante* (sparkling) and still varieties.

To explore the region properly you'll need a car of your own. The A27 heads directly north from Mestre to Conegliano, and one to four trains per hour leave from Venice to Conegliano (€5.40, one hour).

◎ Sights & Activities

Plot a tasting tour along the **Strada del Prosecco** (Prosecco Road; www.coneglianovaldobbiadene.it) from Conegliano to Valdobbiadene and drop into friendly, family-run wineries like **Azienda Agricola Frozza** (☑0423 98 70 69; www.frozza.it; Via Martiri 31, Colbertaldo di Vidor) where you can pick up bottles of top-quality bubbly for between €4 and €7. Conegliano's **tourist office** (☑0438 2 12 30; Via XX Settembre 61, Conegliano; ⊗9am-1pm Tue &

Wed, 9am-1pm & 2-6pm Thu-Sun) can also supply information and help book visits. In Conegliano itself, don't miss the eye-catching **Scuola dei Battuti** (☑0422 184 89 04; rotaryconegliano2060@gmail.com; ⊗Sala dei Battuti 10am-noon & 3-5pm Sun or by appointment), covered inside and out with 16th-century frescoes by Ludovico Pozzoserrato. This building was once home to a religious lay group known as *battuti* (beaters) for their enthusiastic self-flagellation. In the adjoining **Duomo** (⊗10am-noon & 3-7pm) are early works by Veneto artists, notably a 1492–93 altarpiece by local master Cima da Conegliano.

🛏 Sleeping & Eating

Azienda Agricola Campion FARMSTAY €
(☑0423 98 04 32; www.campionspumanti.it; Via Campion 2, San Giovanni di Valdobbiadene; s €40-45, d €65-75; ⊗tasting room 9am-noon & 2-6pm; P❄☎🏊) Why not quit worrying about the challenges of *prosecco* tasting and driving and instead bed down at this farm stay amid 14 hectares of vines in the heart of Valdobbiadene? The four rooms occupy converted farm buildings, with warm, rustic styling and the added perk of a kitchenette in each.

★Agriturismo Da Ottavio VENETIAN €
(☑0423 98 11 13; Via Campion 2, San Giovanni di Valdobbiadene; meals €15-20; ⊗noon-3pm Sat, Sun & holidays, closed Sep; ♿) ✎ *Prosecco* is typically drunk with *sopressa*, a fresh local salami, as the sparkling *spumante* cleans the palate and refreshes the mouth. There's no better way to test this than at Da Ottavio, where everything on the table, *sopressa* and *prosecco* included, is homemade by the Spada family.

Veneto Dolomites

The spiked peaks and emerald-green valleys of the Venetian Dolomites are encompassed within the 315-sq-km Parco Nazionale delle Dolomiti Bellunesi, just north of the Piave river and the historic town of Belluno. Further north, fashionably turned-out Italian snow bunnies flock to Cortina d'Ampezzo for excellent skiing in the Cinque Torri and the Parco Naturale di Fanes-Sennes-Braies (the latter sits in the neighbouring region of Trentino-Alto Adige). In summer there's excellent hiking and climbing here too.

Belluno

POP 35,350 / ELEV 390M

Perched on high bluffs above the Piave river and backed majestically by the snow-capped Dolomites, Belluno makes a scenic and strategic base to explore the surrounding mountains. The historical old town is its own attraction, mixing stunning views with Renaissance-era buildings. And you'll be happy to fuel up for hikes in the nearby mountains on the city's hearty cuisine, including Italy's most remarkable cheeses: Schiz (semisoft cow's-milk cheese, usually fried in butter) and the flaky, butter-yellow Malga Bellunense.

◉ Sights & Activities

Belluno's main pedestrian square is the Piazza dei Martiri (Martyrs' Sq), named after the four partisans hanged here in WWII. Nearby, the Piazza del Duomo is framed by the early-16th-century Renaissance Cattedrale di San Martino, the 16th-century Palazzo Rosso and the Palazzo dei Vescovi, with a striking 12th-century tower.

Parco Nazionale delle
Dolomiti Bellunesi   NATIONAL PARK

(www.dolomitipark.it) Northwest of Belluno, this magnificent national park offers trails for hikers at every level. Between late June and early September, hikers walking the six Alte Vie delle Dolomiti (high-altitude Dolomites walking trails) pass Belluno en route to mountain refuges. Iconic Route 1 starts in Belluno and, over 13 days, covers 150km of breathtaking mountain scenery to Lago di Braies in Val Pusteria to the north. Information on various hikes, themed itineraries and maps can be found on the park's website.

🛏 Sleeping & Eating

To explore hotel, B&B, camping and *agriturismo* (farm stay accommodation) options in Belluno, the Parco Nazionale and beyond, check www.infodolomiti.it.

Alla Casetta   B&B €

(☑ 0439 4 28 91; www.allacasetta.com; Via Strada delle Negre 10, Cesiomaggiore; d/tr/q €65/80/100 P @) It might take the navigation skills of an alpinist to find this patch of paradise on the Caorame river, but persevere. Hosts Christian and Amy hand-draw hiking and biking maps (the Alta Via 2 and Via Claudia Augusta bike trail are nearby), steer you towards the nearest *malga* (cheese-making hut) and point out choice fishing and kayaking spots.

Ostello Imperina   HOSTEL €

(☑ 0437 6 24 51; http://ostellovalleimperina.it Miniere di Valle Imperina; dm €25, half/full board €35/45; ⏲ 7.30am-10pm Apr-Oct) The area's only youth hostel is an exceedingly pleasant one and lies inside the Parco Nazionale delle Dolomiti Bellunesi, 35km northwest of Belluno at Rivamonte Agordino. Book ahead in high summer. To get there, take the Agordo bus (50 minutes) from Belluno.

Astor   BOUTIQUE HOTEL €€

(☑ 0437 94 37 56; www.astorbelluno.com; Piazza dei Martiri 26; d €180; P) This hotel jettisons alpine cosy in favour of city smart and super comfort. It sits, quite literally, on the edge of the historic centre, with most rooms enjoying stunning views of the valley and mountain peaks beyond. So too does the restaurant and terrace, a favourite place for an early evening *spritz*.

Al Borgo   ITALIAN €€

(☑ 0437 92 67 55; www.alborgo.to; Via Anconetta 8 meals €30-40; ⏲ noon-2.30pm Mon, noon-2.30pm & 7.30-10.30pm Wed-Sun) If you have a car or strong legs, seek out this delightful restaurant in an 18th-century villa in the hills about 3km south of Belluno. Considered the area's best, the kitchen produces everything from homemade salami and roast lamb to artisanal gelato. Wines are also skilfully chosen and grappa locally sourced.

Ristorante Terracotta   VENETO €€

(☑ 0437 29 16 92; www.ristoranteterracotta.it Borgo Garibaldi 61; lunch menu €16, meals €35-40; ⏲ 7.30-9.30pm daily, noon-2.30pm Thu-Mon) A historic home in the heart of Belluno has been converted into an intimate dining

CINQUE TORRI

At the heart of the Dolomites, just 16km west of Cortina at the confluence of the Ampezzo, Badia and Cordevole valleys, is the gorgeous area of **Cinque Torri** (www.5torri.it). It is accessible from Cortina by buses – ski shuttles in winter (free to ski-pass holders) and a Dolomiti Bus service in summer – which connect with the lifts at **Passo Falzarego**.

Hard though it is to believe, some of the fiercest fighting of WWI took place in these idyllic mountains between Italian and Austro-Hungarian troops. Now you can wander over 5km of restored trenches in an enormous open-air museum between Lagazuoi and the Tre Sassi fort. Guided tours are offered by the Gruppo Guide Alpine, and in winter you can ski the 80km **Great War Ski Tour** with the Dolomiti Superski ski pass. En route, mountain refuges like **Rifugio Scoiattoli** (☑ 333 8146960; www.5torri.it/rifugio-scoiattoli; Località Potor; meals €25-30, dm/d €58/126; ☺ 9am-9pm) at 2255m and **Rifugio Averau** (☑ 0436 46 60; www.5torri.it/rifugio-averau; Forcella Averau; meals €35-50, half-board dm/s/d €63/100/170; ☺ 9am-10pm; ☷) at 2413m provide standout lunches with great views.

room and summer courtyard. A signature seasonal menu displays care and attention and the young chef reinterprets traditional dishes with great flair. Venison carpaccio comes with mustard ice cream, gnocchi with bitter greens and crispy bacon, and a fig tart is topped with cinnamon cream.

ℹ️ Information

Tourist Office (☑ 0437 94 00 83; www.info dolomiti.it; Piazza Duomo 2; ☺ 9am-12.30pm daily, 3.30-6.30pm Mon-Sat)

ℹ️ Getting There & Away

By car, take the A27 from Venice (Mestre) – it's not the most scenic route, but avoids traffic around Treviso.

BUS

In front of the train station, **Dolomiti Bus** (☑ 0437 21 71 11; www.dolomitibus.it) offers regular service to Cortina d'Ampezzo, Conegliano and smaller mountain towns.

TRAIN

Services from Venice (€8, two to 2½ hours, five to 10 daily) run here via Treviso and/or Conegliano. Some require a change, which can add another hour.

Cortina d'Ampezzo

POP 5900 / ELEV 1224M

The Italian supermodel of ski resorts, Cortina d'Ampezzo is icy, pricey and undeniably beautiful. The town's stone church spires and pleasant cascading piazzas are framed by magnificent Alps. It doubles as a slightly less glamorous but still stunning summer base for hiking, biking and rock climbing.

 Activities

Winter crowds arrive in December for top-notch downhill and cross-country skiing and stay until late March or April, while from June until October summertime adventurers hit Cortina for climbing and hiking. Two cable cars go from Cortina's town centre to a central departure point for chairlifts, cable cars and trails. Lifts usually run from 9am to 5pm daily mid-December to April and resume June to October.

Skiing   SKIING

Ski and snowboard runs range from bunny slopes to the legendary **Staunies** black mogul run, which starts at 3000m. The Dolomiti Superski pass provides access to 12 runs in the area, or opt for a Valley pass that includes San Vito di Cadore and Auronzo/Misurina; both are sold at **Ski Pass Cortina** (☑ 0436 86 21 71; www.skipasscortina.com; Via Marconi 15; 1-/3-/7-day Valley pass €39/113/211; ☺ 8.30am-12.30pm & 3.30-7pm Mon-Sat, 8.30am-12.30pm & 5-7pm Sun winter only) or get discounted advance-purchase passes online.

Olympic Ice Stadium   SKATING

(☑ 0436 88 18 11; Via dello Stadio 1; adult/reduced incl skate rental €10/9; ☺ 10.30am-12.30pm & 3.30-5.30pm Dec-Apr) During white-outs, take a spin around this beautiful ice-skating rink built for the 1956 Winter Olympics.

Guide Alpine Cortina d'Ampezzo   HIKING, ROCK CLIMBING

(☑ 0436 86 85 05; www.guidecortina.com; Corso Italia 69a) In milder weather, guides from this reputable outfit run rock-climbing courses, mountain-climbing excursions and guided nature hikes (prices vary). In winter they also offer ad hoc courses in off-trail skiing, snowshoeing and challenging *via ferrata* (a trail with cables and ladders) climbs.

🛏 Sleeping

Prices vary widely with the seasons and spike wildly at the Christmas holidays. Many places close in April, May and/or November.

⭐ Rifugio Ospitale   CHALET €

(☑ 0436 45 85; www.ristoranteospitale.com; Via Ospitale 1; d €110; ☺ closed Jun) A 15-minute drive from Cortina, this serene and stylish place is astoundingly good value, with spectacular mountain views from its large rooms. The well-regarded restaurant has an unexpected elegance: choose from a modern communal dining table or cosy traditional *stuben* (traditional dining room). Ask the owner for the key to the beautiful fresco-filled 13th-century church below the hotel.

International Camping
Olympia   CAMPGROUND €

(☑ 0436 50 57; www.campingolympiacortina.it; Località Fiames 1; camping 2 people, car & tent €19; ☺ May-Oct; P ⌖) Sleep beneath towering pines 4km north of Cortina in Fiames, with free shuttles to town and on-site pizzeria, market, laundry and sauna.

Baita Fraina   INN €

(☑ 0436 36 34; www.baitafraina.it; Via Fraina 1, Cortina d'Ampezzo; d €100; ☺ closed May & Nov; P) Reserve ahead in the high season at this beloved, Swiss-style inn with simple but spotless rooms of knotty pine. The restaurant has a menu inspired by local ingredients.

🍴 Eating & Drinking

Cortina's pedestrian centre is ringed with pizzerias and cafes, which are your best bets for a reasonable meal. The real culinary action takes place on the surrounding slopes, where a network of *rifugi* (mountain huts) cook up some of the heartiest and homiest cuisine in the Alps.

⭐ Agriturismo El Brite de Larieto VENETO €

(☑ 368 7008083; www.elbritedelarieto.it; Passo Tre Croci, Località Larieto; meals €22-30; ☺ noon-3pm & 7-10pm, closed Thu out of season; ⌖) Located 5km northwest of Cortina on the SS48 towards Passo Tre Croci, this idyllic farm produces all its own dairy products, vegetables and much of the meat on the menu, and its *canederli* (dumplings) are a highlight.

Ristorante Da'Aurelio   GASTRONOMIC €€

(☑ 0437 72 01 18; www.da-aurelio.it; Passo Giau 5 Colle Santa Lucia; tasting menu €48, meals €45 ☺ noon-2pm & 6.30-10pm) Located at an altitude of 2175m, on the road between Cortina and Selva (SP638), elegant Da'Aurelio serves haute mountain cuisine in a classic chalet-style restaurant. Luigi 'Gigi' Dariz produces startling flavours from the freshest mountain ingredients, such as his rich yellow egg with fragrant finferli mushroom and a rack of lamb crusted with mountain herbs. There are also two comfortable rooms.

Al Camin   VENETO €€

(☑ 0436 86 20 10; www.ristorantealcamin.it; Località Alverà; meals €35-45; ☺ noon-2.30pm & 7.15-10pm) A five-minute drive up into one of Cortina's 'suburbs', this fashionable dining room fills with well-to-do locals who come for both traditional and contemporary takes on Veneto dishes. Wine is taken very seriously and the cellar has both excellent local drops and a good selection from Tuscany Piedmont, Alto Adige and Friuli.

Enoteca Cortina   WINE BAR

(www.enotecacortina.com; Via del Mercato 5 ☺ 10am-2pm & 4-9pm Mon-Sat) Pull up a stool at the rowdy front bar for a quick glass of local *soave* or *prosecco* (€3 to €6), or head out to the back room and linger under the ancient vaulted ceilings with a bottle and a selection of local cheese and prosciutto.

ℹ Information

Tourist Office (☑ 0436 86 90 86; http://cortina.dolomiti.org; Piazza Roma; ☺ 9am-1pm & 2-7.30pm Mon-Sat, 10am-1pm Sun)

ℹ Getting There & Away

The nearest train station is in Calalzo di Cadore, 35km south of Cortina. A convenient bus service departs every hour from outside the station, taking you straight to the centre of Cortina. The following companies also operate out of Cortina's **bus station** (Via G Marconi).

Cortina Express (☑ 0437 86 73 50; www.cortinaexpress.it) Daily direct services to Mestre train station (€27, 2¼ hours) and Venice airport (two hours).

Dolomiti Bus (☑ 0437 21 71 11; www.dolomitibus.it) For smaller mountain towns, Belluno and other Veneto locales.

SAD Buses (☑ 0471 45 01 11; www.sad.it) Services to Bolzano and other destinations in Alto Adige (Südtirol).

Friuli Venezia Giulia

Why Go?

With its triple-barrelled moniker, Friuli Venezia Giulia's multi-faceted nature should come as no surprise. Cultural complexity is cherished in this small, little-visited region, tucked away on Italy's far northeastern borders with Austria and Slovenia. Friuli Venezia Giulia's landscapes offer profound contrasts too, with the foreboding, perpetually snowy Giulie and Carnic Alps in the north, idyllic grapevine-filled plains in the centre, the south's beaches, Venetian-like lagoons and the curious, craggy karst that encircles Trieste.

While there's an amazing reserve of often uncrowded historical sights, from Roman ruins to Austro-Hungarian palaces, this is also a fine destination for simply kicking back with the locals, tasting the region's world-famous wines and discovering a culinary heritage that will broaden your notions of the Italian table. Serene, intriguing Trieste and friendly, feisty Udine make for great city time – they're so easy and welcoming you'll soon feel as if you're Friulian, Venezian or Giulian too.

Best Places to Eat

- La Frasca (p426)
- Orsone (p428)
- SaluMare (p414)
- Al Bagatto (p415)

Best Places to Stay

- Seven Historical Suites (p413)
- Palazzo Lantieri (p418)
- Albergo Diffuso Sauris (p430)
- Locanda Al Cappello (p425)

When to Go

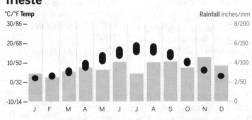

Trieste

Feb Discover the uncrowded slopes of the Carnic and Giulie Alps.

Jun Feast on prosciutto at San Daniele's Aria di Festa.

Oct Watch sails fill the horizon at Trieste's Barcolana Regatta.

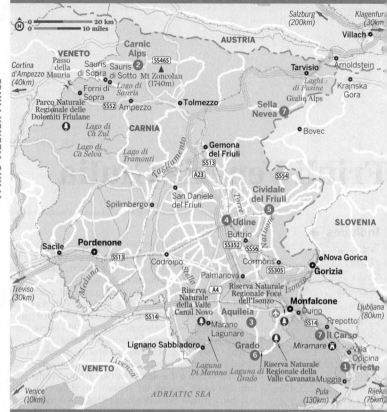

Friuli Venezia Giulia Highlights

❶ Communing with the literary ghosts in the grand cafes of **Trieste** (p415).

❷ Retreating to the wilds of the **Carnic Alps** (p430).

❸ Imagining 4th-century-AD life in the extraordinary mosaic-floored basilica at **Aquileia** (p420).

❹ Sipping Friulano and scoffing *frico* (fried cheese) at a rowdy wine bars in **Udine** (p425).

❺ Marvelling at an 8th-century Lombard chapel (p427) in **Cividale del Friuli**.

❻ Strolling the lively old town of sun-drenched beach resort **Grado** (p420).

❼ Tasting your way through the **rustic vineyards** (p426) of the Colli Orientali and the Carso.

❽ Skiing some of Europe's snowiest slopes in **Sella Nevea** (p431).

History

The semi-autonomous region of Friuli Venezia Giulia came into being as recently as 1954; its new capital, Trieste, had already traded national allegiances five times since the beginning of the century. Such is the region's history, a rollicking, often blood-stained one of boom, bust and conquest that began with the Romans in Aquileia, saw Cividale rise to prominence under the Lom-

bards, and witnessed the Venetians do their splendid thing in Pordenone and Udine. It was Austria, however, that established the most lasting foothold, with Trieste as its main seaport. While the region today is a picture of quiet prosperity, much of the 20th century was another story. War, poverty, political uncertainty and a devastating earthquake saw Friulians become the north's argest migrant population, most bound for Australia and Argentina.

ℹ Getting There & Around

Most of the region's major destinations can be reached by train or road from Venice in around two hours. **Friuli Venezia Giulia airport** (www.aeroporto.fvg.it; Via Aquileia 46, Ronchi Dei Legionari), aka Ronchi dei Legionari or Trieste No-Borders, is 33km northwest of Trieste, near Monfalcone, with daily flights from Rome, London, Munich and Frankfurt, and less-frequent services from Belgrade and Tirana. The Austrian cities of Salzburg and Graz are around four hours' drive from Udine.

Trieste

POP 205,535

Trieste, as travel writer Jan Morris once opined, 'offers no unforgettable landmark, no universally familiar melody, no unmistakable cuisine', yet it's a city that enchants many, its 'prickly grace' inspiring a cult-like roll-call of writers, travellers, exiles and misfits. Devotees come to think of its glistening belle époque cafes, dark congenial bars and even its maddening Bora wind as their own; its lack of intensive tourism can make this often feel like it's true.

Tumbling down to the Adriatic from a karstic plateau and almost entirely surrounded by Slovenia, the city is physically isolated from the rest of the Italian peninsula. Its historical singularity is also no accident. From as long ago as the 1300s, Trieste has faced east, becoming a free port under Austrian rule. The city blossomed under the 18th- and 19th-century Habsburgs; Vienna's seaside salon was also a fluid borderland where Italian, Slavic, Jewish, Germanic and even Greek culture intermingled.

◎ Sights

Most of Trieste's sights are within walking distance of the city's centre, the vast Piazza dell'Unità d'Italia, or can be accessed by Trieste's efficient bus network.

★ Castello di Miramare   CASTLE

☑ 040 22 41 43; www.castello-miramare.it; Viale Miramare; adult/reduced €6/4; ☉ 9am-7pm) Sitting on a rocky outcrop 7km from town, Castello di Miramare is Trieste's elegiac bookend, the fanciful neo-Gothic home of the hapless Archduke Maximilian of Austria. Maximilian originally came to Trieste in the 1850s as the commander-in-chief of

Austria's imperial navy, an ambitious young aristocrat known for his liberal ideas. But in 1867 he was shot by a republican firing squad in Mexico, after briefly, and rather foolishly, taking up the obsolete crown.

The castle's decor reflects Maximilian's wanderlust and the various obsessions of the imperial age: a bedroom modelled to look like a frigate's cabin, ornate orientalist salons and a red silk-lined throne room. Upstairs, a suite of rooms used by the military hero Duke Amadeo of Aosta in the 1930s is also intact, furnished in the Italian Rationalist style.

Maximilian was a keen botanist and the castle boasts 22 hectares of gardens, which burst with the colour and scent of rare and exotic trees. To get to the castle from the city centre, take bus 6 to Grignano, a 15-minute walk away.

Piazza dell'Unità d'Italia   PIAZZA

This vast public space – Italy's largest sea-facing piazza – is an elegant triumph of Austro-Hungarian town planning and contemporary civil pride. Flanked by the city's grandest *palazzi,* including Palazzo del Municipio, Trieste's 19th-century city hall, it's a good place for a drink or a chat, or simply for a quiet moment staring out at ships on the horizon.

Borgo Teresiano   NEIGHBOURHOOD

Much of the graceful city-centre area north of Corso Italia dates to the 18th-century reign of Empress Maria Theresa, including the photogenic **Canal Grande**. Reflecting centuries of religious tolerance, it's here you'll also find the mosaic-laden Serbian Orthodox **Chiesa di Santo Spiridione** (Via F Filzi) from 1868, juxtaposed with the neoclassical Catholic **Chiesa di Sant'Antonio Taumaturgo** (Via Della Zonta) from 1842. On the Via Roma bridge stands a life-sized statue

---

ℹ FVG CARD

This **discount card** (48hr/72hr/7 days €18/21/29) provides free admission to all civic museums; free transport in Udine, Lignano and on the Udine–Cividale del Friuli train; and free audio tours plus numerous discounts in the region's shops, spas, beaches and parks. The cards are available from all FVG tourist offices, some hotels and online.

Trieste

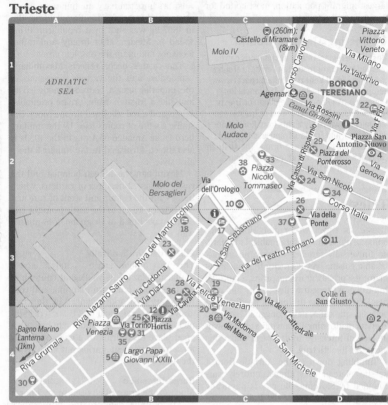

of James Joyce (Piazza Hortis is home to a similar bronze of Italo Svevo).

Castello di San Giusto
MUSEUM

(☑ 040 30 93 62; www.castellodisangiustotrieste.it; Piazza della Cattedrale 3; adult/reduced €6/4; ☺9am-5pm Tue-Sun) Once a Roman fort, this sturdy 15th-century castle was begun by Frederick of Habsburg and finished off by blow-in Venetians. The city museum is housed here, with temporary exhibitions and a well-stocked armoury. Wander around the walls for magnificent views. Bus 24 can help out if you can't face the hill.

Synagogue
SYNAGOGUE

(☑ 040 37 14 66; www.triestebraica.it; Via San Francesco d'Assisi 19; admission €3.50/2.80; ☺guided tours 10am, 11am & noon Sun) This imposing and richly decorated neoclassical synagogue, built in 1912, is testament to Trieste's once significant Jewish community. Heavily damaged during WWII, it has been meticulously restored and remains one of the most important, and profoundly beautiful, synagogues in Italy.

Arco di Riccardo
ROMAN SITE

(Via del Trionfo) The Arco di Riccardo is one of the Roman town gateways, dating from 33 BC, and looks over a pretty residential square. The gate is named for the English King Richard, who was supposed to have passed through en route from the Crusades.

Roman Theatre
ROMAN SITE

(Via del Teatro Romano) Behind Piazza dell'Unità d'Italia rise remains of the Roman theatre, which was built between the 1st and 2nd centuries AD. Concerts are held here occasionally during summer.

Museo Revoltella
MUSEUM

(☑ 040 675 43 50; www.museorevoltella.it; Via Diaz 27; adult/reduced €7/5; ☺10am-7pm Wed-Mon) This city museum was founded in

1872 and now spills into two neighbouring buildings. Baron Revoltella's original mid-19th-century house throbs with conspicuous consumption; his cup runneth over with chandeliers, ornate gilded plasterwork and flamboyant silk wallpaper. The modern Palazzo Brunner has an interesting collection of 19th- and 20th-century works by Triestine artists, including some arresting early-20th-century portraiture and busts. There's also a pretty rooftop cafe and good bookshop.

Civico Museo Sartorio MUSEUM
(☑040 30 14 79; www.museosartoriotrieste. it; Largo Papa Giovanni XXIII 1; adult/child €6/4; ☺10am-5pm Sun, morning tours Tue-Thu, afternoon tours Fri & Sat) Another significant city villa, stuffed with art, ceramics and jewellery, and featuring beautiful ceiling frescoes – some dating to the late 18th century – and a basement Roman mosaic. Don't miss the room of superb Tiepolo drawings, virtuosic and intimate in turns, or the Triptych of Santa Chiara, an exquisitely detailed, extremely intimate wooden altarpiece from the 14th century.

WORTH A TRIP

HOLOCAUST MEMORIAL

Risiera di San Sabba (📞040 82 62 02; www.risierasansabba.it; Via Palatucci 5; ⊙9am-7pm) This former rice-husking plant became a concentration camp in 1943 and has been a national monument and museum since the 1960s.

The site commemorates the 5000 people who perished here and the many thousands more who passed through on the way to Nazi forced labour and death camps. These included a great many of the city's Jewish population along with Triestine and Slovenian resistance fighters.

Although the death cells remain, most of the camp's horrific wartime structures were destroyed by the retreating German forces in 1945. The monument solemnly traces their outlines in metal and stone, their absence creating areas of reflection. A collection of prisoners' photographs, letters and other artefacts are deeply personal and vividly alive.

Take bus 8 from Trieste's train station, or bus 10 from the Riva, a 20-minute trip; from the last bus stop walk past the stadium, turning left into Via Palatucci.

Museo Joyce & Svevo　MUSEUM
(📞040 675 81 70; www.museojoycetrieste.it; 2nd fl, Via Madonna del Mare 13; ⊙9am-1pm Mon-Sat, 3-7pm Thu) FREE Joyce would enjoy the irony: his museum really belongs to friend and fellow literary great, Italo Svevo, housing a significant collection of the Triestini's first editions, photos and other memorabilia. Joyce is dealt with ephemerally, with a wall map of his haunts and homes and a Bloomsday bash in June (Svevo's birthday is also celebrated, on 19 December).

Museo della Comunità Ebraica Carlo e Vera Wagner　MUSEUM
(📞040 63 38 19; www.triestebraica.it/museo ebraicotrieste; Via del Monte 5 & 7; adult/reduced €5/3; ⊙10am-1pm Wed, 4-7pm Tue & Thu) A small, highly prized collection of liturgical items, textiles, documents and photographs, including a touching number of personal items stolen by Nazi troops in 1945. Under renovation for several years, it's recommended you call ahead to confirm opening hours.

Civico Museo Teatrale Carlo Schmidl　MUSEUM
(📞040 675 40 72; Via Rossini 4; adult/reduced €4/3; ⊙9am-5pm Tue-Sun) Trieste's long-standing cultural cred is documented at this museum, housed inside the grand Palazzo Gopcevich, with a collection that traces the city's rich musical and theatrical heritage from the 18th century onwards.

🏃 Activities

Any hint of sun sees the *triestini* flock to the concrete platforms along the water-front **Viale Miramare** (it's more pleasant than it sounds).

Bagno Marino Lanterna　SWIMMING
(📞040 30 59 22; Molo Fratelli Bandiera 3; adult €1; ⊙7.30am-7.30pm Jun-Sep, open year-round for sunbathing) For sun-worshipping and a dip in town, head to Bagno Marino Lanterna, tucked away behind the city's disused 19th-century lighthouse (it's often referred to as '*el pedocìn*' by locals). A living piece of Austro-Hungarian history, this pebbly beach is still genteelly gender-segregated.

No 2 Tram　TRAM TOUR
(www.triestetrasporti.it; Piazza Oberdan; hourly/daily ticket €1.35/4.35; ⊙departures every 20min 7am-8pm) For wonderful views, jump on this vintage tram to Villa Opicina. For most of the 5km journey from Piazza Oberdan it's a regular tram, but a funicular section tackles the steep gradient as it heads up into the Carso. It's a short but significant trip – Villa Opicina was once almost entirely Slovenian-speaking and today retains a decidedly un-Italian feel.

👉 Tours

Walking Tours　WALKING TOUR
(adult/with FVG card €9/free; ⊙10.30am Sun) Themed tours of the city centre in English. Book through the tourist office.

🎊 Festivals

Barcolana Regatta　SPORT
(www.barcolana.it) Barcolana is a major sailing spectacle with thousands of sailing boats filling the gulf on the second Sunday in October.

🛏 Sleeping

Trieste's mid- to high-end places often slash rates on weekends and can be astonishingly good value, especially compared with other Italian cities.

Forvm Boutique Hotel
BOUTIQUE HOTEL €

(📞 040 372 08 93; forvmboutiquehotel.it; Via Valdirivo 30; s/d €80/95; ❋🤖) Occupying an upper floor of a nondescript 19th-century office building, the hushed, dramatically lit lounge of this small hotel immediately soothes the weary traveller. Well that, and the complimentary welcome *aperitivo*. Rooms aren't large but are comfortable, plush and rather sexy; elegant staff are ever on hand when you need city tips or an espresso or herb tea. Breakfast costs €10 extra.

Residenzale 6a
BOUTIQUE HOTEL €

(📞 0406 72 67 15; www.residenzale6a.it; Via Santa Caterina 7; s/d €75/90; ❋🤖) Upstairs in an imposing Borgo Teresiano building, this small, cosy hotel mixes traditional furnishings with bright modern bathrooms, has a large lounge and an internal courtyard. Poetically, each of the elegant rooms is named and decorated for one of Italo Svevo's female characters.

Residence del Mare
APARTMENT €

(📞 040 30 73 46; www.residencedelmare.it; Via della Madonna del Mare 4; apt 1/2 persons €70/90; ❋🤖) If you're not after high design or pots of atmosphere, these apartments are large, very well equipped and brilliantly located. Upper floors have city views and the young staff are helpful.

★ Seven Historical Suites
BOUTIQUE HOTEL €€

(📞 040 760 08 17; www.seventrieste.com; Via F Filzi 4; apt s/d €160/180; ❋🤖) Yes, there are seven suites and they are, indeed, historical, nestled on the beamed attic floor of a grand 1884 commercial building. Still, their lavish size, a slick contemporary way with glass, marble, stone and iron, and finally, their incredible collections of Sicilian objects and antique furniture are a surprise departure for Trieste. Apart from the absolute luxury of the spaces themselves, each suite has a fully equipped kitchen stocked with beautiful ceramics, pewter and stemware, plus 24/7 access to a personal concierge.

L'Albero Nascosto
BOUTIQUE HOTEL €€

(📞 040 30 01 88; www.alberonascosto.it; Via Felice Venezian 18; s €85 d €125-145; ❋🤖) A delightful little hotel in the middle of the old town, Nascosto is a model of discreet style. Rooms are spacious and tastefully decked out with parquet floors, original artworks, books and a vintage piece or two; most also have a small kitchen corner. Breakfasts are simple but thoughtful, with local cheeses, top-quality preserves and Illy coffee.

Rooms here get snapped up; book well ahead if you can.

FRIULI VENEZIA GIULIA TRIESTE

THE DUBLINER

Think you're escaping and run into yourself. Longest way round is the shortest way home.
James Joyce, Ulysses

Stifled by the gloom and obligations of Dublin, James Joyce escaped to Trieste in 1905 with a contract to teach English at the local Berlitz language school. Along with lover (and soon wife) Nora Barnacle, the precocious but still unpublished 22-year-old arrived in a city that epitomised the twilight years of the Austro-Hungarian empire.

Trieste was a booming, brilliantly cosmopolitan place, with a polyglot creative class and no shortage of dissolute aristocrats. The gregarious Irishman wasted no time immersing himself in this fertile scene and quickly picked up the floral Triestini dialect. In between his teaching commitments, failed business ventures, family life and all-night benders, he slowly set about drafting the text of his first two ground-breaking novels, *Dubliners* and *Portrait of the Artist as a Young Man*. Perennially poor, he spent the bulk of his writing hours in the city's fin de siècle cafes, Trieste life all about him.

The Joyces remained in the city until 1915, when the outbreak of WWI forced them to relocate to neutral Zurich. Joyce returned after the war, but he was unimpressed by the brash new order and quickly made tracks for Paris. *Ulysses* may have been given form in the City of Light, but its genesis was undoubtedly in the multilingual melting pot that was pre-WWI Trieste.

Hotel Savoia Excelsior Palace
LUXURY HOTEL €€

(📋040 7 79 41; savoiaexcelsiorpalace.starhotels.com; Riva del Mandracchio 4; d €160; 🌐🛜) This glamorous 'newcomer' to Trieste's hotel scene, a classic but contemporary (and ever so slightly camp) refit of the great-boned Habsburg-era Grand Hotel, is giving the city's famed Duchi a run for its money. Grand it still is, with over 100 light-filled luxurious rooms, first-rate public areas, sea views and reasonable prices.

Hotel Vis a Vis
HOTEL €€

(📋040 760 00 11; www.hotelvisavis.net; Piazza dello Squero Vecchio 1; s/d €90/130; 🌐🛜) Vis a Vis is the Duchi's slickly modern offshoot, with smallish but luxurious, all mod-con rooms. A great choice if your tastes tend towards the contemporary, but you'd like in on the Duchi facilities.

Grand Hotel Duchi d'Aosta
LUXURY HOTEL €€€

(📋040 760 00 11; www.grandhotelduchidaosta.com; Piazza dell'Unità d'Italia 2; d €125-259; 🌐🛜🅿) There's been a hotel of sorts on this prime site since Roman times, and the Duchi remains Trieste's grand dame. Public spaces are hushed and intimate, and the rooms are opulently traditional – the way repeat visitors like them. The bathrooms might be a tad frumpy for some five-star tastes, but the moody basement pool is a good trade-off.

BUFFET, TRIESTINI STYLE

You'll be sure to eat well, in fact extremely well, at a Triestine buffet, but banish any thought of all-you-can-eat meal deals. These rowdy bar-restaurants are yet another legacy of the city's Austro-Hungarian past; if Trieste's bakeries conjure up Vienna, its buffets are Budapest all over. Usually all-day, and night, affairs, small snacks – cod or zucchini fritters, topped toasts and *panini* – are available from early morning and gobbled over lunch or at *aperitivo* time. But, hey, who's here for zucchini? Beef brisket may be a stalwart, but pork – baked, boiled, cured, stuffed into a sausage or fried – is the star attraction. Fresh grated *kren* (horseradish), *capuzi* (sauerkraut) and *patate in tecia* (mashed potatoes) are traditional accompaniments.

Eating

Trieste's long years as one of the Austro-Hungarian empire's busiest ports, along with its Slavic hinterland, are nowhere clearer than in the kitchen. Seafood is fantastic, with dishes often reminiscent of Venice, but Trieste's most characteristic culinary experience is to be had in its still thriving swag of buffets. Triestine bakeries are a scented, sweet delight: grab a *putizza* (a nut-filled brioche) to have with an excellent Illy coffee.

⭐ SaluMare
SEAFOOD €

(www.facebook.com/SaluMare; Via di Cavana 13a; meals €15; ⏰11.30am-3pm & 6.30-10.30pm Mon-Sat) This bright, buzzing reinvention of the Triestine buffet features fish and seafood. Order at the bar from a menu of small dishes: white polenta and *baccalà mantecato* (salt-cod purée) or *seppie bolito* (cuttlefish stew), prawn ceviche and anchovy butter tartines. Wash it down with a well-chosen Friulian or Veneto white.

There are plenty of reasons to linger, starting with the huge library of cookbooks and restaurant guides, a welcoming communal table and a daily delivery of international newspapers.

Buffet da Siora Rosa
BUFFET €

(📋040 30 14 60; Piazza Hortis 3; meals €25; ⏰8am-10pm Tue-Sat) Opened before WWII, the family-run Siora Rosa is one Trieste's traditional buffets. Sit outside or in the wonderfully retro interior and tuck into boiled pork, sauerkraut and other Germanic and Hungarian offerings, or opt for something fishy like *baccalà* (salted cod) with polenta.

Buffet Da Pepi
BUFFET €

(www.buffetdapepi.it; Via Cassa di Risparmio 3; meals €18; ⏰8.30am-10pm Mon-Sat) The counter here is a site of porcine carnage: legs, necks, bellies, tongues and testicles, all awaiting a slap of relish from the huge ceramic jars of mustard and a grate of *kren* (horseradish). Hot, takeaway brisket or pork rolls (€4) are great for a quick lunch.

Buffet Rudy
BUFFET €

(Via Valdirivo 32; meals €20; ⏰9am-1am Mon-Sat) Rudy has been concocting traditional boiled meats, cold cuts and beer since, oh, 1897. Come for the pork joints, served up with the house sauerkraut or just drinks and snacks at the bar (this being the beer-iest of all the buffets).

Genuino
CAFETERIA €

(www.genuino.com; Via delle Beccherie 13; dishes €4-12; ☺noon-10pm Mon-Sat) Perpetually busy Genuino packs them in for big salads, fish, wild rice and roast vegetable combination plates, seasonal soup and chicken burgers. It's fast and furious and on fast-food-style plates and trays, but rest assured everything has eco-credentials, including local wines by the glass and artisan beers.

Pirona
PASTRIES €

(Largo Barriera Vecchia 12; €3.30 per 100g; ☺7.30am-7.30pm Tue-Sat, 8am-1.30pm Sun) This jewel-box pastry shop and cafe was one of Joyce's favourites. Its nutty, spicy, boozy Triestine speciality cakes, *putizza, presnitz* and *pinza,* are particularly good.

Viezzoli
PASTRIES €

(Via della Cassa di Risparmio 7; cakes €3.50; ☺7am-8pm Mon-Sat, 8am-2pm Sun) Brave the battalion of Illy-gulping locals off to work at this cafe-bakery. Try a slice of *putizza* or another Trienstini speciality, most usually sold only as whole cakes or loaves.

Al Bagatto
SEAFOOD €€€

(☎040 30 17 71; www.albagatto.it; Via Cadorna 7; meals/degustation €55/62; ☺7.30pm-11pm Mon-Sat) This old-timer, with its dark, brooding dining room, does a Triestine seafood *degustazione – fritto misto* (fried seafood) and something involving squid ink will invariably play a part – that's daunting but delicious. The 'seasonal creative' menu is just that, or you can try ordering like the suited regulars: the freshest of fish by the *etto* (100g), weighed and filleted at the table.

Drinking & Nightlife

Trieste's historic cafes conjure times past, but remain a thriving and deeply satisfying part of daily city life (the Triestini drink twice as much coffee as the national average). Cafes, bars and buffets blur, as does what constitutes *aperitivo*. Evenings out are a refined, relaxed mix of young and old and early-evening drinks often stretch well into the night with the help of hearty buffet snacks. Via San Nicolò's bars cater to a smart after-work set, while the old town's cluster of bars are of a more boho bent. In summer there are come-and-go outdoor places along the Viale Miramare.

Buffet Kaffeehaus Romi
BAR, BAKERY

(it-it.facebook.com/eventimusicaliromi; Via Torino 30; ☺7.45am-2.30pm Mon, to 11pm Tue-Thu, to midnight Fri & Sat) This daytime bakery and cafe morphs into a bar come the evening. It's an intriguing, gently-ironic tribute to a bygone Trieste, with portraits of Imperial rulers casting their gaze over a gaggle of bearded or black-clad Triestini boys and girls. Live music happens out the back on the weekends; their Facebook page has details.

Cantina del Vescovo
WINE BAR, TAPAS

(☎344 1820600; Via Torino 32; ☺noon-12.30am Tue-Sun) Trieste's cosmopolitan gaze usually faces east, but here we have a bar that feels like you've been transported to an ultra-hip neighbourhood of Madrid. The city's most fashionable pack out this moody industrial space for bold Spanish wines, *pintxos* (tapas plates) of piquillo peppers, jamón or patatas bravas and late night burgers.

Chocolat
CAFE

(Via Cavana 15b; ☺7.30am-8pm Tue-Sat) This lovely cafe and chocolate shop makes everything in-house, including the hot chocolate slowly simmering in a great pot behind the counter and, in summer, gelato. Happily there's no surcharge for sitting at the big communal table outside on the square.

Caffè Torinese
CAFE

(Corso Italia 2; ☺7am-midnight) The smallest and, dare we say, friendliest of the historic bunch, this is an exquisite room that's just as nice for an evening tipple as a morning *capo un' b* (macchiato in a glass).

Osteria da Marino
WINE BAR

(Via della Ponte 5; ☺11am-3pm & 7pm-1am Mon-Thu, to 2.30am Fri & Sat, 7pm-midnight Sun) If you can't make it to the Carso wine region, get the owner here to ply you with indigenous grape varieties (their Vitovska selection is encyclopedic). Or just settle in with a Franciacorte sparkling or a Tuscan red and wait for the little meatballs to appear.

Buffet Al Spaceto   BUFFET
(Via Belpoggio 3a; snacks €2-3.50; ⊙ 8am-10pm
Mon-Fri, to 2.30pm Sat) An eccentric and convivial grab bag of locals gather here for
glasses of local wine and a few rounds of
whatever is on offer in the snack counter.

Caffè San Marco   CAFE
(www.caffesanmarcotrieste.eu; Via Battisti 18;
⊙ 8.30am-10.30pm Tue-Sun) Opening just before WWI, and a favourite of writers Svevo,
Saba and Joyce, this Viennese Succession giant is spectacularly decorated with theatrical mask paintings, dark chocolate-coloured
walls and miles of marble tables. Saved from
demolition in 2013, it's no longer a place of
melancholy nostalgia, but instead is a vibrant cultural hub with beautifully restored
decor, young staff and an in-cafe bookshop.

Caffè Tommaseo   BAR
(☎ 040 36 26 66; www.caffetommaseo.com; Riva III
Novembre; ⊙ 9am-10pm) Virtually unchanged
since its 1830 opening, the rich ceiling reliefs, primrose-yellow walls and Viennese
mirrors here couldn't be any more evocative.
Take coffee at the bar or sit down for a *fritto misto* (meals €30) and a chance to linger
among the ghosts.

☆ Entertainment

Teatro Verdi   OPERA
(☎ 040 672 21 11; www.teatroverdi-trieste.com; Riva
III Novembre 1) Trieste's opera house is a little
bit Scala and a little bit Fenice (thanks to a
pair of duelling architects), but wears the
mix well. Don't miss a chance to see a performance here; the Triestini are passionate
opera lovers and make a great audience.

❶ Information

Hospital (☎ 040 399 11 11; Piazza dell'Os-
pedale 2)
Police Station (☎ 040 323 58 00; Via
Hermet 7)
Tourist Office (☎ 040 347 83 12; www.
turismofvg.it; Via dell'Orologio 1; ⊙ 9am-7pm
Mon-Sat, 9am-1pm & 2-7pm Sun)

❶ Getting There & Away

AIR
Friuli Venezia Giulia airport (p409; aka Ronchi
dei Legionari or Trieste No-Borders) has direct
daily flights to and from Rome, London, Munich
and Frankfurt, and less-frequent services for
Belgrade and Tirana. Venice's Marco Polo airport
is around 1½ hours away by car or you can catch

the train to Mestre (two to three hours) and then
bus it from there.

BOAT
From mid-June to late September motor-boat
services run to and from Grado, Lignano and
points along the Istrian coast in Slovenia and
Croatia; check with the tourist office for the
current operator.
Agemar (☎ 040 36 37 37; Nuova Stazione Marittima – Molo IV; one way winter/summer deck
seat €75/90, cabin €130/165) Sells tickets for
the twice-weekly car ferry to and from Durres
in Albania, currently operated by Adria Ferries.

BUS
Bus Station (☎ 040 42 50 20; www.autostazi
onetrieste.it; Via Fabio Severo 24) National and
international buses operate from here. Destinations include Zagreb (€30, five hours, daily)
and Ljubljana (€17, 2¼ hours, daily).
APT (Azienda Provinciale Trasporti Gorizia;
☎ 800 955957; www.aptgorizia.it) Bus 51 runs
to the airport approximately every 30 minutes
between 4.30am and 10.35pm from Trieste bus
station (€4.05, one hour).
Florentia Bus (☎ 040 42 50 20; www.florentia
bus.it) Operates bus services to Ljubljana (€17,
2¾ hours, daily) and Sofia in Bulgaria (€65,
16½ hours, daily).

TRAIN
Train Station (Piazza della Libertà 8) Serves
Gorizia (€4.75, 50 minutes, hourly), Udine
(€8.75, one to 1½ hours, at least hourly),
Venice (€19.15, two hours, at least hourly) and
Rome (€81.85, 6½ to 7½ hours; most require a
change at Mestre).

❶ Getting Around

BOAT
Trieste Trasporti (☎ 800 016675; www.trieste
trasporti.it) Shuttle boats depart from the
Stazione Marittima to Muggia year-round (one
way/return €4.25/7.90, 30 minutes, six to 10
times daily). Check for other seasonal services
with the tourist office.

BUS
Trieste Trasporti (☎ 800 016675; www.
triestetrasporti.it) Bus 30 connects the train
station with Via Roma and the waterfront; bus
24 runs from the station to Castello di San
Giusto; bus 36 links Trieste bus station with
Miramare. One-hour tickets cost €1.35, all-day
€4.35.

TAXI
Radio Taxi Trieste (☎ 040 30 77 30; www.
radiotaxitrieste.it) Operates 24 hours; from the
train station to the centre will cost around €10
or a €58 flat fee to the airport.

LOCAL KNOWLEDGE

THE CARSO'S POP-UP CELLAR DOORS

Osmize predate the trendy retail pop-up phenomena by a few centuries, care of an 18th-century Austrian law that gave Carso farmers the right to sell surplus from their barns or cellars once a year (the term *osmiza* comes from the Slovenian word for 'eight', the number of days of the original licence). It's mainly vineyards that hold *osmiza* today, and farm cheeses and cured meats are always on offer too. While the Carso is known for its gutsy, innovative winemakers, *osmize* traditions still hold sway. Don't try asking for a list: finding an *osmiza* is part of the fun. Look first, along Carso roads, for the red arrows. Then look up, to gates or lintels bearing a *frasca* – a leafy branch hung ceremoniously upside down announcing that the *osmiza* is open for business. Don't forgo the chance to try the Carso's native wines: the complex, often cloudy, sometimes fierce, white Vitovska; or Terrano, aka Teran, a berry-scented red. Internationally known winemakers **Zidarich** (☎040 20 12 23; www.zidarich.it; Prepotto 23) and **Skerk** (☎040 20 01 56; www.skerk.com; Prepotto 20) do, in fact, announce *osmiza* dates on their websites, as do smaller producers **David Sardo** (☎040 229 270; www.osmize.com/samatorza/sardo-david; Samatorza 5) and **Torri di Slivia** (☎338 3515876; www.letorridislivia.net; Aurisina Cave 62). That said, you can't miss the *frasca* clustering at every crossroads in spring and autumn, and cellar visits are possible by appointment year-round.

There's a €3.50 flag fall and €6 minimum, plus a €2 surcharge between 10pm and 6am and on public holidays.

Muggia

POP 13,400

The fishing village of Muggia, 5km south of Trieste, is the only Italian settlement on the historic Istrian peninsula. Slovenia is just 4km south and Croatia (the peninsula's main occupant) a score more. With its 14th-century castle and semi-ruined walls, the port has a Venetian feel and its steep hills make for lovely views back towards Trieste.

Locals gather over jugs of wine and groaning platters of deer or boar salami at **Pane, Vine e San Daniele** (Piazza Marconi 5; salumi €8-15; ☺8am-2pm & 8pm-2am Mon-Sat) on the main square behind the port, or there are a number of same-ish seafood restaurants along the waterfront. Ferries shuttle between Muggia and Trieste.

Il Carso

If Trieste is known for its cultural idiosyncrasy, its hinterland is also fittingly distinct. Dramatically shoehorned between Slovenia and the Adriatic, the Carso (*Karst* in German, *kras* in Slovenian) is a windswept calcareous tableland riddled with caves and sinkholes. This wild landscape has long inspired myths and legend, while its geology has lent its name – karst – to geologically similar terrain around the world. It's a compelling place to visit in any season but is particularly pretty in spring, when the grey-green hills are speckled with blossom, or in autumn, when the vines and *ruje* (smoke trees) turn crimson and rust.

Sights & Activities

Grotta Gigante   CAVE
(☎040 32 73 12; www.grottagigante.it; Località Borgo Grotta Gigante 42; adult/reduced €12/9; ☺50min guided tours hourly 10am-6pm daily summer, 10am-4pm Tue-Sat winter) The area's big-ticket attraction is near Villa Opicina, 5km northeast of Trieste. At 120m high, 280m long and 65m wide, it's one of the largest and most spectacular caves that's accessible on the continent. It's easily reached from Trieste on bus 42, or by tram 2 and bus 42 in the other direction.

Castello di Duino   CASTLE
(☎040 20 81 20; www.castellodiduino.it; Frazione di Duino 32; adult/reduced €8/6; ☺9.30am-5.30pm Wed-Mon Apr-Sep, to 4pm Sat & Sun Mar, Oct & Nov) Fourteen kilometres northwest along the coast from Miramare, this 14th- and 15th-century bastion picturesquely marches down the cliff, surrounded by a verdant garden. Poet Rainer Maria Rilke was a guest here from 1911–12, a melancholy and windswept winter stay which produced the *Duino Elegies*. To get here, take bus 41 from Trieste's Piazza Oberdan.

The Rilke Trail
WALKING

(Sentiero Rilke; Frazione di Duino) FREE The path that inspired poet Rainer Maria Rilke during his stay in Duino is now an easy, even 1.7km walk from the Castello di Duino to the town of Sistiana. The extreme beauty of holyoak- and hornbeam-dotted limestone cliffs tumbling towards the sea can, like Rilke's master work, feel poetic, mystical and, when the Bora blows, profoundly existential.

There is an abudence of bird life and car parks and other facilities at both the Duino and Sistiana ends of the path.

Gorizia

POP 36,000 / ELEV 86M

Considering its serene modern incarnation, you'd never guess the turmoil of Gorizia's past. An oft-shifting border zone throughout much of its history and the scene of some of the most bitter fighting of WWI's eastern front, it was most recently an Iron Curtain checkpoint. The town's name is unmistakably Slovenian in origin and before the outbreak of WWI it was not uncommon to hear conversations in several different languages – German, Slovenian, Friulian, Italian, Venetian and Yiddish – in the main square.

Gorizia's appeal today lies in its aristocratic ambience, its unique Friulian-Slovenian cooking and its easy access to surrounding countryside, famed for its wine and rustic restaurants.

⊙ Sights

Borgo Castello
CASTLE

(☑0481 53 51 46; Borgo Castello 36; adult/reduced €6/3; ⊙10am-7pm Tue-Sun, 9.30-11.30am Mon) Gorizia's main sight is its castle, perched atop a knoll-like hill. It has some convincing re-creations and a fine wood-panelled great hall. Beneath the main fortress huddle two oddly paired museums. The tragic, gory history of Gorizia's WWI Italian-Austrian front is explored at the Museo della Grande Guerra (admission with Museo della Grande Guerra), including a to-scale re-creation of a trench. Then there's fashion: 19th- and early-20th-century finery at the Museo della Moda e delle Arti Applicate (admission with Museo della Grande Guerra). The price covers entry to Borgo Castello, the Museo della Grande Guerra and the Museo della Moda e delle Arti Applicate.

Piazza Transalpina
HISTORIC SITE

One for cold war kids. The Slovenian border – a mere formality since December 2007 – bisects the edge of Gorizia, and you can celebrate Schengen with a bit of border hopscotch at this piazza's centre, while contemplating the now crumbling fences, border posts and watchtowers.

Palazzo Coronini Cronberg
PALACE

(☑0481 53 34 85; www.coronini.it; Viale XX Settembre 14; adult/reduced €5/3; ⊙10am-1pm & 3-6pm Wed-Sun) This 16th-century residence is jammed with antiquities and is surrounded by lush gardens, which are free to visit on their own and open until 9pm in summer.

Chiesa di Sant'Ignazio
CHURCH

(Piazza della Vittoria; ⊙8am-noon & 3-7pm) Constructed from 1654 to 1724, the onion-shaped domes of this high-baroque Jesuit church watch over Gorizia's old town square.

⊨ Sleeping

★ Palazzo Lantieri
B&B €€

(☑0481 53 32 84; www.palazzo-lantieri.com; Piazza Sant'Antonio 6; s/d €80/140; P🕏🐾) This *palazzo*-stay offers light, spacious rooms in the main house or self-catering apartments in former farm buildings, all overlooking a glorious Persian-styled garden. Goethe, Kant and Empress Maria Theresa were repeat guests back in the day. Antiques fill both public and private spaces, but the charming Lantieri family are far from stuck in the past.

Their contemporary art commissions mean there's a Michelangelo Pistoletto on the ceiling and a Jannis Kounellis in the attic. Nonguests can arrange guided tours.

✕ Eating & Drinking

Cafes and bars can be found on Corso Italia and Via Terza Armata, while the old-town streets below the castle and around the covered food market (Via Verdi 30) are the best places to find casual restaurants.

Majda
GORIZIAN €

(☑0481 3 08 71; Via Duca D'Aosta 71; meals €25; ⊙noon-3pm & 7.30-11pm Mon-Sat) With a courtyard bar, friendly staff and enthusiastic decor, Majda is a happy place to sample local specialities such as ravioli filled with potato (Slovenian-style) or beetroot and local herbs, wild boar on polenta and interesting sides such as steamed wild dandelion.

Pasticceria Centrale PASTRIES €

(Via Garibaldi 4a; ☺7.30am-7.30pm) No visit to Gorizia would be complete without tasting the town's signature pastry, *gubana,* a fat snail of shortcrust filled with nuts, sultanas and spices.

Rosenbar GORIZIAN €€

(☑0481 52 27 00; www.rosenbar.it; Via Duca d'Aosta 96; meals €30; ☺noon-3pm & 7.30-10pm Tue-Sat) Rosenbar is a traditional dining room set in an airy shop front. It's known for attention to detail, in both preparation and in the always fresh and mostly organic produce they use. Along with dishes capturing Gorizia's cross-border culinary spirit, there are also a few Adriatic fish and seafood options on the menu.

Bierkeller BEER HALL

(☑0481 53 78 91; Via Lantieri 4; ☺5pm-midnight Fri-Wed) Venture down into this ancient vaulted cellar for a little piece of Bavaria, with pretzels, football on the big screen or DJs on weekends. Staff are delightful and in summer there's a pretty walled beer garden.

ⓘ Information

Tourist Office (☑0481 53 57 64; Corso Italia 9; ☺9am-6pm Mon-Sat, to 1pm Sun)

ⓘ Getting There & Away

The **train station** (Piazzale Martiri Libertà d'Italia), 2km southwest of the centre, has regular connections to and from Udine (€4.05, 30 minutes, at least hourly) and Trieste (€4.75, 50 minutes, hourly). APT (☑800 955957; www.aptgorizia.it) runs buses from the train station across to Slovenia's **Nova Gorica bus station** (€1.15, 25 minutes).

Palmanova

POP 5340

Shaped like a nine-pointed star – although you'd need an aeroplane to check – Palmanova is a defensively designed town-within-a-fortress built by the Venetians in 1593. Once common throughout Europe, these military monoliths were known as 'star forts' or *trace italienne*. So impregnable were the town's defences that Napoleon used and extended them in the late 1700s, as did the Austrians during WWI. To this day the Italian army maintains a garrison here.

◉ Sights

From hexagonal Piazza Grande, at the star's centre, six roads radiate through the old town to the defensive walls. An inviting grassy path connects the bastions and three main *porte* (gates): Udine, Cividale and Aquileia.

Civico Museo Storico MUSEUM

(☑0432 91 91 06; Borgo Udine 4; adult/reduced €2/1.50; ☺9.30am-12.30pm Tue-Sun summer, or by appointment) Head along Borgo Udine to uncover local history and weaponry from the Venetian and Napoleonic eras in the Civico Museo Storico, inside **Palazzo Trevisan**. The museum also acts as a **tourist office** (☑0432 92 48 15; ☺10am-noon) and has information on secret-tunnel tours that wind beneath the city walls.

Museo Storico Militare MUSEUM

(☑0432 92 81 75; Piazza Grande 21; ☺9am-noon Fri-Mon & 2-4pm Mon) FREE The Museo Storico Militare is inside Porta Cividale. The military museum traces the history of troops stationed in Palmanova from 1593 to WWII.

✕ Eating

La Campana d'Oro FRIULIAN €€

(☑0432 92 87 19; Borgo Udine 25b; meals €35; ☺noon-2pm Wed-Mon, 7.30-9.30pm Wed-Sat) Besides its goulash, La Campana d'Oro prepares delicate dishes such as smoked goose breast, fish soup, and fettucine with wine-soused clams, as well as simply done fish caught in nearby Marano.

ⓘ Getting There & Away

Regular buses link Palmanova with Udine (€3.30, 30 minutes) and Aquileia (€2.75, 40 minutes), leaving from Via Rota, just inside the walls.

Aquileia

POP 3500

Aquileia, off the beaten track? It certainly wasn't 2000 years ago. Colonised in 181 BC, Aquileia was once one of the largest and richest cities of the Roman Empire, at times second only to Rome, with a population of at least 100,000 at its peak. After the city was levelled by Attila's Huns in AD 452, its inhabitants fled south and west where they founded Grado and then Venice. A smaller town rose in Roman Aquileia's place in the early Middle Ages, and with the construction of the present basilica, it went on to become the largest and hugely significant Christian diocese in Europe. Conferred with a Unesco World Heritage listing in 1998, this now charmingly rural town and living museum still, rather thrillingly, guards one of the most complete, unexcavated Roman sites in Europe.

Sights

Basilica
CHURCH

(Piazza Capitolo; crypts adult/reduced €3/2.50, bell tower €2; ⊙9am-6pm Mon-Sat, from 11.30am Sun, bell tower summer only) The entire floor of the Latin cross-shaped basilica, rebuilt after an earthquake in 1348, is covered with one of the largest and most spectacular Roman-era mosaics in the world. The 760-sq-metre floor of the basilica's 4th-century predecessor is protected by glass walkways, allowing visitors to wander above the long-hidden tile work, which includes astonishingly vivid episodes from the story of Jonah and the whale, the Good Shepherd, exacting depictions of various lagoon wildlife, and portraits of wealthy Roman patrons and their quotidian business interests.

Treasures also fill the basilica's two crypts. The 9th-century Cripta degli Affreschi (Crypt of Frescoes) is adorned with faded 12th-century frescoes depicting the trials and tribulations of saints, while the Cripta degli Scavi (Excavations Crypt) reveals more mosaic floors in varying states of preservation. Some images were destroyed or badly damaged by the erection of the basilica's 73m-high bell tower, built in 1030 with stones from the Roman amphitheatre.

Roman Ruins
ROMAN SITE

Scattered remnants of the Roman town include extensive ruins of the Porto Fluviale, the old port, which once linked the settlement to the sea. It's also possible to wander among the partially restored remains of houses, roads and the standing columns of the ancient Forum on Via Giulia Augusta. Guided tours of the extraordinary Roman sights are organised by the tourist office (☑0431 91 94 91; ⊙9am-7pm summer, 9am-1pm & 2-6pm winter); otherwise, wander at will.

Museo Archeologico Nazionale
MUSEUM

(☑0431 9 10 16; www.museoarcheo-aquileia.it; Via Roma 1; adult/reduced €4/2; ⊙8.30am-7.30pm Tue-Sun) A daunting number of statues, pottery, glassware and jewellery, all locally excavated, are displayed in this museum, representing one of northern Italy's most important collections of Roman-era treasures.

Museo Paleocristiano
MUSEUM

(☑0431 9 11 31; Piazza Pirano; adult/reduced €4/2, incl Museo Archeologico Nazionale; ⊙8.30am-1.45pm Tue-Sun) FREE Part of the Museo Archeologico Nazionale, this museum houses early-Christian-era mosaics and funerary monuments gathered from the surrounding ruins.

Sleeping

Camping Aquileia
CAMPGROUND €

(☑0431 9 10 42; www.campingaquileia.it; Via Gemina 10; camping €28, d cabin €46, 4-bed bungalow €78; P☏❄) This well-maintained campground is set beside pretty fields; its comfortable new bungalows look towards the Basilica and old Roman port.

Ostello Domus Augusta
HOSTEL €

(☑0431 9 10 24; www.ostelloaquileia.it; Via Roma 25; s/d €28/46; P☏♿) A spotless if rather institutional hostel with two- to six-bed rooms and private bathrooms down the hall. Friendly, relaxed staff are helpful and happy to dole out maps and timetables.

Grado
POP 8600

A Friulian surprise, the tasteful beach resort of Grado, 14km south of Aquileia, spreads along a narrow island backed by lagoons and is linked to the mainland by a causeway. Behind the less-than-spectacular beaches you'll find a mazelike medieval centre, criss-crossed by narrow *calli* (lanes). Belle époque mansions, beach huts and thermal baths line the cheerful seafront – the greyish local sand is considered curative and used in treatments. Grado comes alive from May to September, but is also prime *passeggiata* (evening stroll) territory on any sunny Sunday.

Small *casoni* (reed huts) used by fishers dot the tiny lagoon islands. In summer some can be visited by boat. Many of the islands are, however, protected nature reserves and off limits. The tourist office (☑0431 87 71 11; Viale Dante Alighieri 66; ⊙9am-7pm summer) has the details.

On the first Sunday in July, a votive procession sails to the Santuario di Barbana (☑0431 8 04 53; www.santuariodibarbana.it), an 8th-century church on a lagoon island. Fishers have done this since 1237 when the Madonna of Barbana was claimed to have miraculously saved the town from the plague. Boats link the sanctuary with Grado; contact **Motoscafisti Gradesi** (☑ 0431 8 01 5; www.motoscafistigradesi.it; Riva Scaramuzza; ☺ daily summer, Sun only winter) for specific departures and prices.

◎ Sights

Basilica di Sant'Eufemia   BASILICA
(Campo dei Parriarchi; ☺ 8am-6pm) Grado's beautiful historic core is dominated by this lovely Romanesque basilica, dating back to AD 579; the adjoining lapidary contains 4th- to 5th-century mosaics as well as some 3rd-century Roman sarcophagi facades.

🛏 Sleeping

The town has a huge number of hotels and holiday rentals, though rooms can be scarce in summer and only bookable by the week.

Albergo Alla Spiaggia   HOTEL €€
(☑ 0431 8 48 41; www.albergoallaspiaggia.it; Via Mazzini 2; s/d €110/150; ☺ Apr-Oct; P ❋ @) The Spiaggia sports a South Beach look, set in a lovely prewar modernist building, with a fresh maritime-toned fit out. It's in a great position, wedged between pedestrian zone, historic centre and beach. Rates outside summer are great value.

🍴 Eating & Drinking

The old town's streets are known for their boisterous wine bars, casual *fritterias* and upmarket seafood restaurants.

Max'in Botega de Mar   SEAFOOD €
(www.maxingrado.it; Piazza Duca d'Aosta 7; share plates €8; ☺ 11am-3pm & 6-11pm Wed-Mon) Snack on a tartine from its extensive menu of seafood-themed toasts (€2.50-3.50 each) while downing a few lemon-infused white-wine-*spritzes* at one of its pavement tables. Still hungry? There are fish *polpettone* (meatballs) and large *crudo* plates as well. No bookings, so arrive early.

Trattoria de Toni   SEAFOOD €€
(☑ 0431 8 01 04; Piazza Duca d'Aosta 37; meals €37; ☺ noon-3pm & 6pm-10.30pm Thu-Tue) This place is undeniably old school and charmingly so, matching genial service with the best local seafood. Sample Grado's signature *boreto*, a lagoon fish stew served with white polenta, or stick with the brimming seafood pasta dishes and super fresh whole grilled fish by the gram, filleted at the table.

L'Osteria da Sandra   WINE BAR
(Campo San Niceta 16; ☺ 10am-11pm Tue-Sun) Cute hole-in-the-wall bar that attracts a local crew for an early-evening *spritzer* or three on an old-town corner. Has an excellent chilled white selection available for purchase if you're considering a picnic.

❶ Getting There & Away

Regular **SAF** (☑ 800 915303, 0432 60 81 11; www.saf.ud.it) buses link Aquileia with Grado (€1.55, 10 minutes) and Palmanova (€3.30, 45 minutes, up to eight daily); buses run between Grado and Udine (€4.75, 1¼ hours, 12 daily) via Aquileia. Trains to Venice and Trieste run to the Cervignano-Aquileia-Grado station, in Cervignano, around 15km away.

Around Grado

Beyond Grado's perpetual holiday bustle lie two picturesque nature reserves; a scant 15-minute drive will take you into a dream-like watery landscape of marsh and reeds, rich in local fauna and with intriguing examples of traditional coastal life.

◎ Sights

Riserva Naturale Regionale della Valle Cavanata   NATURE RESERVE
(☑ 0431 8 82 72; www.vallecavanata.it; ☺ 9am-3.30pm Mon, Wed & Fri, noon-6pm Sat & Sun summer, 10.30am-3.30pm Wed-Fri & Sun winter) **FREE** This reserve protects a 1920s fish-farming area and extraordinary birdlife in the east of the lagoon. More than 230 bird species have been observed, including the greylag goose and many wading birds.

Riserva Naturale Regionale Foce dell'Isonzo   NATURE RESERVE
(☑ 0432 99 81 33; www.parks.it/riserva.foce. isonzo; Isola della Cona; adult/reduced €5/3.50; ☺ 9am-5pm Fri-Wed) The final stretch of the Isonzo river's journey into the Adriatic flows through this 23.5-sq-km nature reserve where visitors can birdwatch, horse ride, cycle or walk around salt marshes and mudflats. The visitors centre also has a cafe.

Laguna di Marano

At the head of the Adriatic, sandwiched between the beach resorts of Grado and Lignano, Italy succumbs to nature – in particular birdlife – in the Laguna di Marano.

Marano Lagunare, a Roman fishing port that was later fortified, is the only settlement on the lagoon shore. Beyond the workaday docks and medieval streets, peace and quiet is ensured by two nature reserves: the 13.77-sq-km **Riserva Naturale della Foci dello Stella**, protecting the marshy mouth of the Stella river and reached by boat, and the **Riserva Naturale della Valle Canal Novo**, a 121-hectare reserve in a former fishing valley. The **visitor centre** (☑ 0431 6 75 51; www.parks.it/riserva.valle.canal.novo; Via delle Valli 2; adult/reduced €3.50/2.50; ⊙ 9am-5pm Tue-Sun), in a characteristic reed hut, is shared by the two reserves.

Pordenone

POP 51,300

Pordenone may not make it on to many travel hot lists, but that's not to say it's not the kind of place – youthful, lively – you wouldn't mind calling home. Pedestrianised Corso Vittorio Emanuele II draws an elegant curve between Piazza Cavour and the *duomo* (cathedral). Lined with an almost unbroken chain of covered *portici* (porches), the historic streetscape buzzes with smart shops and busy cafes.

◉ Sights

Duomo di San Marco CATHEDRAL
(Piazza San Marco; ⊙ 7.30am-noon & 3-7pm) The bare Romanesque-Gothic facade of the Duomo di San Marco betrays signs of frequent changes down the centuries. Inside, among the frescoes and other artworks, is the *Madonna della misericordia,* by the Renaissance master Il Pordenone (1484–1539).

Palazzo del Comune TOWN HALL
In defiance of the other-worldly, the Palazzo del Comune (Town Hall) stands facing away from the *duomo*. The 13th-century brick structure has three Gothic arches and some extravagant Renaissance additions.

Museo Civico d'Arte MUSEUM
(☑ 0434 39 29 35; www.comune.pordenone.it/museoarte; Corso Vittorio Emanuele II 51; adult/reduced €3/1; ⊙ 3.30-7.30pm Tue-Sun, 10am-1pm Sun) Located in Palazzo Ricchieri's richly decorated upper rooms is the city's modest Museo d'Arte. Its collection of Friulian and Veneto artists ranges from the 15th to the 18th centuries. The building is itself a treasure, with timber ceilings and remains of 14th-century frescoes suddenly appearing throughout.

🛏 Sleeping

Civico 22 B&B €
(☑ 335 6791330; www.bbcivico22.it; Via San Quirino 22; s/d €45/80; 🅿 🔊) You might have come to Friuli for rustic inns, but for a city pitstop this unashamedly contemporary B&B is a great choice. Three bright, white design-led rooms are housed in an assertive show of contemporary architectural taste on a quiet street. No credit cards.

🍴 Eating & Drinking

La Vecia Osteria del Moro REGIONAL €
(☑ 0434 2 86 58; www.laveciaosteriadelmoro.it; Via Castello 2; meals €35; ⊙ noon-2.30pm & 7-10.30pm Mon-Sat) La Vecia Osteria del Moro, just off the Corso near the Comune, is a vaulted den offering snacks, grills and local specialites like Venetian-style *baccalà* (cod) and snails.

Al Campanile WINE BAR
(☑ 0434 52 06 28; Vicolo del Campanile 1c; ⊙ Tue-Sun noon-11pm) The street-side barrels here make an atmospheric spot for a glass or two.

ℹ Information

Tourist Office (☑ 0434 52 03 81; Piazza XX Settembre 11; ⊙ 9am-1pm daily & 2-6pm Mon-Sat, 9am-1pm Sun summer)

ℹ Getting There & Away

Pordenone is on the Venice–Udine train line. Frequent services run to and from Udine (€4.70, 30 to 40 minutes) and Mestre (€7.40, 1¼ hours).
ATAP (☑ 800 101040; www.atap.pn.it) Runs buses to the surrounding towns.

Udine

POP 100,500 / ELEV 114M

While reluctantly ceding its premier status to Trieste in the 1950s, this confident, wealthy provincial city remains the spiritual and gastronomic capital of Friuli. Udine gives little away in its sprawling semirural suburbs, but encased inside the peripheral ring road lies an infinitely grander medieval centre: a dramatic melange of Venetian arches, Grecian statues and Roman columns. The old town is pristine, but lively. Bars here are not just for posing – kicking on is the norm.

◎ Sights

Piazza della Libertà   PIAZZA

A shimmering Renaissance epiphany materialising from the surrounding maze of medieval streets, Piazza della Libertà is dubbed the most beautiful Venetian square on the mainland. The arched **Palazzo del Comune** (Town Hall; Piazza della Libertà), also known as the Loggia del Lionello after its goldsmithing architect, Nicolò Lionello, is another clear Venetian keepsake, as is the **Loggia di San Giovanni** (Piazza della Libertà) opposite, its clock tower modelled on the one gracing Venice's Piazza San Marco.

The Arco Bollani (Bollani Arch), next to the Loggia di San Giovanni, an Andrea Palladio work from 1556, leads up to the castle used by the Venetian governors.

★ Museum of Modern and Contemporary Art   ART GALLERY

(Casa Cavazzini; ☑ 0432 41 47 72; www.udinecultura.it; Via Cavour 14; adult/reduced €5/2.50; ⊙ 10.30am-7pm Tue-Sun summer, to 5pm winter) Udine's newest museum brings together a number of bequests, creating a substantial collection of 20th-century Italian artists, including De Chirico, Morandi, Campigli and Mušič. There's also a surprise horde of notable American work, including a Willem de Kooning, Sol LeWitt and Carl Andre, all donated by the artists after the 1976 Friulian earthquake. The gallery itself is a beautiful cultural asset, its bold reconstruction designed by the late Gae Aulenti.

Discover intriguing remnants of the 16th-century building's previous lives: spectacular, previously unknown 14th-century frescoes that were uncovered during construction, and the Cavazzini family's 1930s Rationalist apartment, where you can peek at old-style gym rings in the bathroom and a formal dining room's intensely hued murals.

Cathedral   CATHEDRAL

(www.cattedraleudine.it; Piazza Duomo; ⊙ 8am-noon & 4-6pm Mon-Sat, 4-6pm Sun) The chapels of Udine's 13th-century Romanesque-Gothic cathedral house the **Museo del Duomo** (☑ 0432 50 68 30; ⊙ 9am-noon & 4-6pm Tue-Sat, 4-6pm Sun) FREE, with 13th- to 17th-century frescoes in the Cappella di San Nicolò.

Oratorio della Purità   CHURCH

(Piazza del Duomo; ⊙ 10am-noon; ask for key at the cathedral if closed) FREE The intimate Oratorio della Purità has a beautiful, dramatic ceiling painting of the Assumption by Giambattista Tiepolo, and eight biblical scenes in chiaroscuro by his son, Giandomenico, on the walls. The building was built as a theatre in 1680 but the patriarch of Aquileia ordered its transformation 80 years later, repulsed by such a devilish institution so close to a cathedral.

Castello   MUSEUM

(adult/reduced €5/2.50; ⊙ 10.30am-7pm Tue-Sun summer, to 5pm winter) Rebuilt in the mid-16th century after an earthquake in 1511, Udine's castle affords rare views of the city and snowy peaks beyond. It houses a number of different collections, all fascinating. The **Museo del Risorgimento** is both compellingly designed and set in a series of beautiful rooms while the **Museo Archeologico** highlights both locally found objects as well as the region's archaeological heyday of the late 19th-century.

The sprawling upper floors are given to the **Galleria d'Arte Antica**, which has significant work by Caravaggio (a portrait of St Francis in room 7), several stunning Tiepolos (room 10), along with lesser-known Friulian painters and religious sculpture.

Museo Diocesano and Tiepolo Galleries   ART GALLERY

(☑ 0432 2 50 03; www.musdioc-tiepolo.it; Piazza Patriarcato 1; adult/reduced €7/5; ⊙ 10am-1pm & 3-6pm Wed-Mon) The drawcards here are the two rooms featuring early frescoes by Giambattista Tiepolo, including the wonderfully over-the-top *Expulsion of the Rebellious Angels* (1726) at the apex of a grand staircase.

Museo Etnografico del Friuli   MUSEUM

(☑ 0432 27 19 20; Via Grazzano 1; admission €1; ⊙ 10.30am-5pm Tue-Sun, to 7pm summer) A small but engrossing museum of daily life, with various exhibitions devoted to the Friulian hearth, unusual spiritual practices, folk medicine, furniture production and dress. The building itself features soaring ceilings, intricate 19th-century woodwork with carved Friulian forest scenes, and its own little canal gurgling by the entrance.

🛏 Sleeping

Central Udine has a number of small, smart midrange hotels, and a couple of notable budget places. If you're driving, consider a B&B or farm stay in the surrounding suburbs or countryside. The tourist office has online listings.

Udine

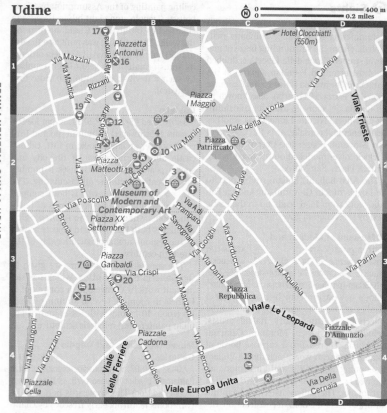

Udine

425

★ Stop & Sleep
B&B €

(☑ 339 7561610; www.stopsleepudine.com; Viale Europa Unita 101; s/d €40/55; ❄ 🛜) Don't be put off by the unprepossessing locale. This is a rare budget find and you'll be greeted by the caring, knowledgable owner. The five colourful, cutely decorated rooms occupy a top-floor apartment and have mosaic-tiled bathrooms, a full kitchen with DIY breakfast supplies and self-catering facilities. One room is en suite, while the other four rooms share two (spotless) bathrooms.

Locanda Al Cappello
GUESTHOUSE €

(http://osteriaalcappello.it; Via Paolo Sarpi 5; €65/110; ❄ 🛜) Upstairs from the stalwart spritzers are six cosy bedrooms, all individually decorated with antiques and rich colours; beautiful original beams and fireplaces feature in the larger ones. Bathrooms are both modern and atmospheric and staff give you a genuine Friulian welcome.

Hotel Clocchiatti Next
DESIGN HOTEL €€

(☑ 0432 50 50 47; www.hotelclocchiatti.it; Via Cividale 29; s/d villa €100/130, annexe €130/160; 🅿 ❄ 🛜 🏊) Two properties, one location: older-style (cheaper) rooms are in the original villa, while the contemporary steel-and-glass 'Next' rooms line up around a pool and outdoor bar in the garden. It's a pleasant walk from the centre, with easy access out of the city if you're driving.

Hotel Allegria
BOUTIQUE HOTEL €€

(☑ 0432 20 11 16; www.hotelallegria.it; Via Grazzano 18; s/d €105/135; 🅿 ❄ @) ⟋ This hotel occupies a historic town house opposite one of Udine's loveliest little churches. The rooms are large and what might be described as Udinese-organic in style, with lightwood beams, parquetry floors and shuttered windows. Quirk factor points: the hotel has a *bocciofila* (bowling area) on-site.

Eating

Udine's flavours are as intriguing as the city itself. Look out for country-style cheeses (smoked ricotta and Montasio), game, San Daniele prosciutto (ham) and delicious gnocchi and dumplings. Open-air cafes and restaurants are dotted around Piazza Matteotti and the surrounding pedestrian streets. Via Paolo Sarpi and its surrounding streets are lined with lively bars, all with bountiful enough snacks to make a meal of.

★ La Bottega del Borgo
DELI, WINE BAR €

(☑ 0432 159 09 73; www.labottegadelborgo.com; Via Grazzano 26; snacks €5-8, meals €15-18; ⊙ 8am-3pm & 4-9.30pm, bar to 11pm) This busy corner deli-winebar has such a winning way it will make you want to up sticks and settle in Udine. Locals drop in for morning coffee, pastries and bread, grab supplies for quick at-home dinners, or have things plated up to eat at the back bar area. Wine here represents Friuli's finest and there's always an elegant sparkling on offer.

Oggi
GELATERIA €

(www.oggigelato.it; Via Paolo Sarpi 3a; cones & cups €2-3.50; ⊙ 11am-10pm) If you're lucky, one of the owners of this fabulous new gelateria chain, Andrea, will be on hand to take you through Oggi's 0km ethos. The gelato here is made entirely from Friulian milk and local eggs and while there's concessions to favourite flavours and ingredients from across Italy, there's always a local special: try the *biscotto di mais* (cornmeal biscuit) and chocolate.

Antica Maddalena
FRIULIAN €

(☑ 0432 50 05 44; Via Pelliccerie 4; meals €25; ⊙ noon-3pm & 6-10pm Tue-Sat, 6-10pm Mon) This low-key restaurant, spread over two floors, is known for its quality produce. This is a great place to try *frico* (fried cheese). It's served both ways: *morbido*, a cheese-and-potato omelette, and *croccante*, its snackier crispy-fried form. *Aperitivo* time, Venetian-style seafood *stuzzichini* (snacks) can be devoured at a laneway table.

Trattoria ai Frati
FRIULIAN €€

(☑ 0432 50 69 26; Piazzetta Antonini 5; meals €25-30; ⊙ 10am-11pm Mon-Sat) A popular old-style eatery on a cobbled cul-de-sac where you can expect local specialities such as *frico*, pumpkin gnocchi with smoked ricotta, or, in season, white asparagus and fish stew. It's loved by locals for its whopper steaks and its raucous front bar.

Drinking & Nightlife

The Udinese have a reputation for being fond of a drink or three, and with such stellar wines produced in their backyard, who can blame them? Wine bars here are unpretentious though serious about their wares, with blackboards full of local drops. *Stuzzichini* (snacks) are plentiful at most bars and, if not complimentary, can be had for pocket change.

FRIULI VENEZIA GIULIA UDINE

Osteria delle Mortadele
WINE BAR

(Riva Bartolini 8; ⏱10am-10pm Mon-Sat) Yes, there's a popular restaurant out back, but it's the spill-onto-the-road front bar that will hold your interest. A rock-and-roll soundtrack, excellent wine by the glass, bountiful *stuzzichini* (snacks) and great company make this a one-drink-or-many destination.

Osteria al Barnabiti
BAR

(☑347 1747850; www.barnabiti.com; Piazza Garibaldi 3a; ⏱10am-midnight Mon-Thu, 10am-1am Fri & Sat) Fabulously eccentric decor makes this place rather memorable in a city of atmospheric bars. Great wines, grappa and cheese and meat platters complete the picture.

Leon d'Oro
BAR

(☑0432 50 87 78; 2 Via dei Rizzani; ⏱10am-3pm & 6pm-midnight Mon-Sat) A particularly good choice if the weather is balmy (or in any way warm) and the young, good-looking crowd spills out onto the corner terrace, giving it a street-party vibe. Look out for the complimentary plates of fried potatoes doing the rounds: perfect for sopping up the extra *spritz* you're bound to have here.

Al Cappello
WINE BAR

(Via Paolo Sarpi 5; ⏱10.30am-3pm & 5.30-11pm Tue-Sat, 10am-3pm & 5.30-9pm Sun in winter) Follow the locals' lead and order what may be Italy's most reasonably priced *spritz* (€1.50) through the window. *Stuzzichini* here are generous enough to constitute dinner, or you can eat well at one of the tables.

Caffè Contarena
CAFE

(Via Cavour 11; ⏱8am-9pm, to 2am Fri & Sat) Beneath the arcades of Palazzo d'Aronco, Contarena's soaring domed ceilings glitter with gold leaf and other Liberty fancy. Designed by Raimondo d'Aronco, a master of the genre and one-time local, it's a glamorous espresso stop or late-night cocktail venue, and beloved by everyone from senior citizens to students.

Caffè Caucigh
BAR

(www.caucigh.com; Via Gemona 36; ⏱7am-11pm Tue-Sun, to 1am Fri) This ornate, dark-wooded bar is a perfect Udinese compass point – it feels far more like Prague than points south. Regulars take glasses of red to the pavement for a chat with passing strangers. A calendar of jazz acts – Friuli's finest and some international surprises – play from 10pm on Friday.

RUSTIC TABLES

Friulian food is essentially rural food. Its bold flavours and earthy ingredients make the most of the seasons and of traditional *miseria* (poverty) techniques, even when it's taken way upmarket. These much-lauded country restaurants are all within an hour's drive of Udine, either in the Colli Orientali or south towards the coast.

La Frasca (☑0432 67 51 50; Viale Grado 10, Pavia di Udine; meals €35; ⏱noon-3pm & 7-10pm Thu-Tue) A *frasca* is similar to an *osmize*, a rustic place serving *salumi* (cured meats) and wine, and takes its name from the same practice of hanging a branch out as a shingle. Walter Scarbolo's relaxed roadside dining room has retained the *frasca* experience, and his fans gather for his artisan cured meats, menus that highlight a single seasonal crop, and, naturally, the wonderful Scarbolo wines.

La Subida (☑0481 6 05 31; www.lasubida.it; Via Subida, Cormons; meals €50; ⏱noon-2.30pm & 7-11pm Sat & Sun, 7-11pm Mon, Thu, Fri) A famous family-run inn, with border-crossing dishes and ingredients – rabbit, boar, flowers and berries – that bring the landscape to the plate in a very modern way. Stay over in one of their stunning forest houses and wake to birdsong and rustling leaves. Across the way there is a casual grill and terrace, with great natural orange wines (skin-contact whites) from Paraschos.

Terre e Vini (☑0481 6 00 28; www.terraevini.it; Via XXIV Maggio, Brazzano di Cormons; meals €52; ⏱noon-2.30pm Tue-Sun, 7-10pm Tue-Sat) The Felluga family are Friulian wine royalty and their cosy 19th-century *osteria* looks out over the plantings. Feast on tripe on Thursdays, salt cod on Fridays and goose stew or herbed frittata any day of the week. Book ahead for Sunday lunch.

CIVIDALE CERAMICS

Working with ancient Roman and Middle Eastern techniques, local ceramic artist Stefania Zurchi creates sculptures, reliefs and beautifully decorated utilitarian objects. Her palette evokes the Friulian landscape, moody indigos and olives cut through with the flash of bright oxide yellow and dusty pinks. Her 'girl' figures representing the seasons are highly sought after, as are her touching Madonna-and-child reliefs. The work can be found at her central Cividale del Friuli shop, **Tirare** (Via Ristori 12; ⊙9.30-12.30pm & 4-7pm Mon-Sat).

ℹ Information

Hospital (✆0432 55 21; Piazza Santa Maria della Misericordia 15) About 2km north of the centre.

Tourist Office (✆0432 29 59 72; Piazza I Maggio 7; ⊙9am-7pm Mon-Sat summer, 9am-1pm & 2-6pm winter, to 1pm Sun) Super helpful office who can book you onto local wine tours.

ℹ Getting There & Away

SAF (p421) operates buses to and from Trieste (€7.50, 1¼ hours, hourly), Aquileia (€3.30, one to 1¼ hours, up to eight daily), Lignano Sabbiadoro (€5.75, 1½ hours, eight to 11 daily) and Grado (€4.75, 1¼ hours, 12 daily).

APT (p416) buses link Udine and Friuli Venezia Giulia airport (€4.75, one hour, hourly).

Bus Station (✆0432 50 69 41; Viale Europa Unita 31)

Train Station (Viale Europa Unita) From Udine's train station services run to Trieste (€8.75, one hour), Venice (€12.15, two hours, several daily), Gorizia (€4.05, 30 minutes, hourly) and Salzburg (€24, four hours).

Cividale del Friuli

POP 11,600 / ELEV 138M

Cividale del Friuli, 15km east of Udine, may be a small town these days, but in terms of Friulian history and identity it remains hugely significant. Founded by Julius Caesar in 50 BC as Forum de Lulii (ultimately condensed into 'Friuli'), the settlement reached its apex under the Lombards, who arrived in AD 568 and usurped Roman Aquileia a couple of hundred years later. Cividale is hauntingly picturesque: rambling around its dark stone streets makes for a rewarding morning. Even better, stay to enjoy it's hearty table and cracking bars.

◉ Sights & Activities

Tempietto Longobardo   CHAPEL
(Oratorio di Santa Maria in Valle; ✆0432 70 08 67; www.tempiettolongobardo.it; Borgo Brossano; adult/reduced €4/3; ⊙10am-1pm & 3-5pm Mon-Fri, 10am-6pm Sat & Sun) Cividale's most important sight is this stunning complex that houses the only surviving example of Lombard architecture and artwork in Europe. Its ethereal stucco reliefs and choir stalls of the darkest wood are both unusual and extremely moving; some elements date as far back as the 8th century.

Ponte del Diavolo   BRIDGE
Splitting the town in two is the symbolic Devil's Bridge that crosses the emerald green Natisone river. The 22m-high bridge was first constructed in the 15th century with its central arch supported by a huge rock said to have been thrown into the river by the devil. It was rebuilt post-WWI, after it was blown up by retreating Italian troops.

Cathedral & Museo Cristiano   CATHEDRAL
(Piazza del Duomo; museo adult/reduced €4/3; ⊙museo 10am-1pm & 3-6pm Wed-Sun) This 16th-century cathedral houses the Museo Cristiano. Its 8th-century stone Altar of Ratchis is a stunning Lombard relic. Sharp-etched carvings, including a be-quiffed Jesus with one very piercing stare, dramatically pop against the smooth white background.

Bastianich   WINERY
(✆0432 70 09 43; www.bastianich.com; Via Darnazzacco 44/2, Gagliano) Joe Bastianich is a certified celebrity in the US, but his Italian vineyards, a few minutes' drive from Cividale, remain all about the wine and gracious Friulian hospitality. Pull up a stool at the new tasting room and sniff and swirl your way through drops made from the surrounding plantings and the Bastianich holdings in nearby Buttrio.

LOCAL KNOWLEDGE

WINE-TASTING TIPS

Wayne Young, a former cellar hand and currently marketing communications manager for Bastianich Wines, offers the following advice when tasting in Friuli.

Friulians are proud, hard-working, tight-knit people – they often describe themselves as cold but I disagree. They love to socialise, especially with visitors. Friuli isn't touristy, so getting attention from the outside world is a pleasure. Prepare to stop and chat and have a glass of wine or an espresso.

World Class Whites There's no other place in the world where the combination of soil, climate and the interplay between sea and mountain comes together to create whites like these. Local grape Friulano is fresh and aromatic. The sauvignon blancs are special too, and don't overlook the outstanding white blends (*uvaggi*). Reds to try: Refosco, merlot and the interesting Schioppettino.

Tasting Tips Look for wines from Ronchi di Cialla, Moschioni, Venica & Venica and Vie di Romans. And Bastianich, of course!

Stomach Liners *Frico*! It's a melted Montasio cheese pancake made with potatoes and, sometimes, bacon and onions...*awesome*.

Night Out Udine is a great little city and deserves respect. Barnabiti is a favourite: cozy and dark with great tartine (like tapas) and a wide selection of regional wines by the glass or by the bottle. Food is simple and good, and congregating outside is typical in nice weather.

Savour the complex, wildflower and honey-tinged Vespa Bianco, a 'superwhite' blended from sauvignon, chardonnay and a dash of Picolit: Friuli in a bottle. Email ahead to visit.

🍴 Eating & Drinking

Antico Leon d'Oro   FRIULIAN €
(📞0432 73 11 00; Borgo di Ponte 24; meals €22)
Eat in the courtyard of this friendly, festive place, just over the Ponte del Diavolo, and, if you're in luck, watch a polenta cook stir the pot. Dishes here couldn't be more regional: sublime d'Osvaldo *proscuitto crudo*, seasonal pasta enlivened with asparagus and *sclupit* (a mountain herb), a Friulian tasting plate of *frico*, salami and herbed frittata, and roast venison.

⭐ Orsone   GASTRONOMIC, BURGERS €€€
(📞0432 73 20 53; orsone.com; Via Darnazzacco 63, Fraz, Gagliano; meals €58, tasting menu €69, vegetarian tasting menu €59, paired wines €25) Nestled among the vines in the same valley as Bastianich's winery, this elegant dining room does a roll call of traditional dishes but there's also a definite new world sensibility at work (the bar menu takes that one step further, with American favourites such as killer burgers and lobster rolls).

The menu reads beautifully and really delivers: dishes are easy on the eye, full of bold flavours and thoughtful juxtapositions and stellar local produce. Service warm and rather theatrical, ranks up there with the best in the country. Book ahead and consider staying over in one of the B&B rooms if you want to make a night of it.

Central Caffè del Corso   CAFE
(Corso Mazzini 38; ⏰8am-11pm) *The* place on the square for an expertly made *spritzer* or coffee.

ℹ️ Information

The **tourist office** (📞0432 71 04 60; Piazza Paolo Diacono 10; ⏰10am-1pm & 3-5pm, later in summer) has information on walks around the medieval core. Look to the 'lodging and eating' section of the city's website (www.cividale.com) for a comprehensive listing of *agriturismo* and farm restaurants.

ℹ️ Getting There & Away

Ferrovie Udine Cividale (📞0432 58 18 44; www.ferrovieudinecividale.it) Private (and cute) trains connect Cividale with Udine (€2, 20 minutes), at least hourly.

HAMMING IT UP

There are two world-revered prosciuttos manufactured in Italy: the lean, deliciously nutty (and more famous) ham from Parma, and the dark, exquisitely sweet Prosciutto di San Daniele. It might come as a surprise to find that the latter – Friuli Venezia Giulia's greatest culinary gift to the world – comes from a village of only 8000 people, where it is salted and cured in 27 *prosciuttifici* (ham-curing plants) safeguarded by EU regulations.

Standards are strict. San Daniele's prosciutto is made only from the thighs of pigs raised in a small number of northern Italian regions. Salt is the only method of preservation allowed – no freezing, chemicals or other preservatives can be used. The X factor is, of course, *terroir*, the land itself. Some *prosciuttifici* claim it's the cool, resinous Alpine air meeting the Adriatic's humid, brackish breezes that define their product, others argue that it's about San Daniele's fast-draining soil: such effective ventilation makes for perfect curing conditions.

In August the town holds the **Aria di Festa**, a four-day annual ham festival when *prosciuttifici* do mass open-house tours and tastings, musicians entertain and everyone tucks in. San Daniele's tourist office has a list of *prosciuttifici* that also welcome visitors year-round; call ahead to book your tasting.

San Daniele del Friuli

POP 8200

Hilltop San Daniele sits in an undulating landscape that comes as a relief after the Venetian plains, with the Carnic Alps jutting up suddenly on the horizon. While ham is undoubtedly the town's raison d'être, it's also got a general gastronomic bent, with many good *alimentari* (grocery stores), and other culinary industries springing up, such as sustainably farmed local trout.

◉ Sights & Activities

Frescoes are one of San Daniele's fortes and you'll find some colourful examples etched by Pellegrino da San Daniele, aka Martino da Urbino (1467–1547), in the small Romanesque **Chiesa di San Antonio Abate** (Via Garibaldi). Next to the church, the **Biblioteca Guarneriana** (⌨0432 95 79 30; www.guarneriana.it; Via Roma 1; guided tours €4; ☺admission by appointment) is one of Italy's oldest and most venerated libraries. Founded in 1466, it contains 12,000 antique books, including a priceless manuscript of Dante's *Inferno*.

If you want to get out into the countryside, three cycling itineraries, each 22km, take you past pristine lakes and through the castle-dotted hills around the village; ask at the **tourist office** (⌨0432 94 07 65; Via Roma 3; ☺9.30am-noon Mon-Fri, 4-6pm Tue, Wed & Fri, 10.30am-12.30pm & 4-6pm Sat & Sun).

✕ Eating & Drinking

Bottega di Prosciutto   DELI€
(www.bottegadelprosciutto.com; Via Umberto I; ☺9am-1pm & 3-7pm, closed Mon & Wed afternoon) Levi Gregoris' prosciutto is known for its sweetness and perfume and you can buy as much as your heart and stomach desire at his Bottega di Prosciutto, as well as browsing the regional cheeses and wines and an excellent selection of pan-Italian produce.

Osteria di Tancredi   FRIULIAN €€
(⌨0432 94 15 94; www.osteriaditancredi.it; Via Sabotino 10; plates €8-10, meals €30; ☺noon-10pm Thu-Tue) Serves up Friulian classics *cjalcions* (filled pasta), *frico* and apple gnocchi in a cosy room that pares back the rustic touches to a pleasing simplicity.

Enoteca la Trappola   WINE BAR
(⌨0432 94 20 90; Via Cairoli 2) Head to dark and moody Trappola for crowd-pleasing platters of prosciutto or trout (€8) and well-priced wine by the glass with a very local, very vocal crowd.

❶ Getting There & Away

Regular buses run to San Daniele from Udine (€4.75, 45 minutes), 25km to the southeast.

North of Udine

Hit the hard north of Italy's most northeasterly region and you'll find yourself surrounded by the Carnic and Giulie Alps, the latter named after Julius Caesar. The former stretches as far west as the Dolomites and far north as the border with Austria. Meanwhile, the loftier Giulie's rugged, frigid peaks are shared with Slovenia – the Triglavski Narodni Park lies just across the border. Both areas offer excellent hiking terrain and deliver some of the loneliest, most scenic trails in Italy. As the area stands at the meeting point of three different cultures, multilingual skills can come in handy. Hikers should get ready to swap their congenial *salve* (Italian) for a *grüss gott* (German) or *dober dan* (Slovenian).

Tolmezzo & Carnia

The region known as Carnia is intrinsically Friulian (the language is widely spoken here) and named after its original Celtic inhabitants, the Carnics. Geographically, it contains the western and central parts of the Carnic Alps and presents wild and beautiful walking country flecked with curious villages.

Tolmezzo

POP 10,700 / ELEV 323M

Stunningly sited Tolmezzo is the region's capital and gateway. Pleasant rooms at **Albergo Roma** (☎0433 46 80 31; www.albergo romatolmezzo.it; Piazza XX Settembre 14; s/d €80/100; P✳@) overlook the main piazza or one of the town's many hills. An interesting detour, 6km northeast of the town, is **Illegio**, a 4th-century hill village with a still-operating 16th-century mill and dairy. Tolmezzo's **tourist office** (☎0433 4 48 98; Piazza XX Settembre 9; ⊗9am-1pm daily & 2.30-6.30pm Mon-Sat) is helpful for information on surrounding hiking trails and *agriturismi*.

SAF buses run to Udine approximately every hour (€4.05, 50 minutes) from Via Carnia Libera.

Sauris di Sotto & Sauris di Sopra

To the northwest, a minor and insanely twisted road passes the plunging Lumiei Gorge to emerge at the cobalt blue **Lago di Sauris**, an artificial lake 4km east of **Sauris di Sotto**. Another 4km on (up eight switchbacks and through a few dripping rock tunnels) is the breathtakingly pretty **Sauris di Sopra**. This twin hamlet (in German, Zahre) is an island of dark timber houses and German-speakers, known for its fine hams, sausages and locally brewed beer. There are lots of good walking trails, much fresh air and exquisite silence.

🛏 Sleeping & Eating

★**Albergo Diffuso Sauris**   APARTMENT €
(www.albergodiffusosauris.com; 2-6 bed apt €95-230) Part of the larger *alberghi diffusi* (or scattered hotels) movement in the Carnic region, the Albergo Diffuso Sauris offers various apartments within a number of refurbished village houses, all constructed in the unusual local vernacular style, with deep verandahs screened with horizontal slats.

Inside they are extremely cosy and well-equipped: live a little Carnic fantasy life, sampling Zahre beer, catching up with the village gossip and stocking up on supplies, then head 'home' to light a fire and prepare a mountain feast.

Speck Stube   DELI, FRIULIAN €
(Via Sauris di Sopra 44, Sauris di Sopra; ⊗8am-9.30pm) On one side, this village epicentre will sell you cheese, wine, the fabulous local Wolf-brand prosciutto or a bottle of wine, on the other grab your morning espresso, afternoon beer or settle in for a hearty dinner.

Tarvisio & the Giulie Alps

POP 5000

The Giulie Alps are dramatic limestone monoliths that bear more than a passing resemblance to their more famous Dolomite cousins. Though there's been some recent development of the region, including a cross-border ski lift, the area is still relatively pristine and retains a wildness often lacking in the west.

Tarvisio

Tarvisio (Tarvis, in Friulian and German) is 7km short of the Austrian border and 11km from Slovenia. Down to earth and prettily wedged into the Val Canale between the Giulie and eastern Carnic Alps, it's a good base for both winter and summer activities. Tarvisio is famous for its historic Saturday market, which has long attracted day trippers from Austria and Slovenia. It has a definite border-town buzz, though since Schengen the trade is mostly in dubious-looking leather jackets.

Activities

The area is increasingly touted for its un-crowded skiing; despite its relatively modest elevations, this is the coldest, snowiest pocket in the whole Alpine region, with heavy snowfalls not uncommon into May. The main ski centres are at Tarvisio – with a good open 4km run that promises breathtaking views and 60km of cross-country tracks – and at Sella Nevea just to the south. The **Sella Nevea** (www.sellanevea.net) resort has a number of satisfying red runs and respected freeride and backcountry skiing. In summer the hiking, caving, canoeing and windsurfing are all good.

Sleeping & Eating

The region has a number of well-priced hotels to choose from.

Hotel Edelhof   HOTEL **€€**
(☑ 0428 4 00 81; www.hoteledelhof.com; Via Armando Diaz 13; s/d €75/140; P ☏) Situated right by the lifts with large, airy rooms furnished with hand-painted wooden furniture and a basement spa. Seven-night minimum in high season.

Ristorante Italia   RESTAURANT **€**
(☑ 0428 26 37; Via Roma 131; meals €25; ⊙noon-2pm & 7-9pm Thu-Mon) A historic restaurant that fires up the *fogolar friulano*, a slow-burning stove, and serves up venison, mushroom or radicchio risotto and other hearty mountain dishes.

ⓘ Information

Tourist Office (☑ 0428 21 35; Via Roma 14; ⊙9am-1pm & 3-7pm Mon-Sat, 9am-1pm Sun winter, reduced hr summer) The helpful tourist office has trekking maps and details on Alpine conditions.

 ⓘ SKI FVG

Ski passes (1/3/6 days from €35/87/175) enable you to ski the slopes of Sella Nevea-Kani and Tarvisio, as well as some of the Austrian Arnoldstein. Both day and multi-day passes can also be used at the Friulian resorts of Piancavallo and Forni di Sopra. The Monte Canin ski lift is free to FVG Card holders, and they receive discounts on multi-day passes and equipment hire. **Promotur** (☑ 0428 65 39 15; www.promotur.org) sell passes at each of the resorts.

ⓘ Getting There & Away

Trains connect Tarvisio with Udine (€9.65, 1½ hours, up to seven daily).

Laghi di Fusine

The Laghi di Fusine (Fusine Lakes) lie within mirror-signalling distance of the Slovenian border and are perennially popular with hikers in summer and cross-country skiers and snowshoers in winter. The two lakes – Lago Superiore and Lago Inferiore – are ringed by paths and encased in the **Parco Naturale di Fusine**. For more adventurous walkers, there's a moderately challenging 11km hike up to **Rifugio Zacchi** (☑ 338 5030887; www.rifugiozacchi.it; Località Conca delle Ponze; dm €27; ⊙ Jun–mid-Sep) and across the face of Monte Mangart. In summer, bus 203 runs up here five times a day from Tarvisio (€2.10, 15 minutes).

FRIULI VENEZIA GIULIA TARVISIO & THE GIULIE ALPS

Coffee Culture

From Trapani to Tarvisio, every day begins with coffee. A quick cup from a stove-top Moka pot might be the first, but the second (third, fourth and fifth) will inevitably be from a neighbourhood bar. Italians consider these visits a moment to pause, but rarely linger. It's a stand-up sniff, swirl and gulp, a *buon proseguimento* to the barista, and on your way.

Origins

Coffee first turned up in mid-16th-century Venice, then a few years later in Trieste, care of the Viennese. While basic espresso technology made an appearance in the early 19th century, it wasn't until 1948 that Gaggia launched the first commercial machines. These reliably delivered full-bodied espresso shots with the characteristic aromatic *crema*: Italy was hooked. The machines, in fact the whole espresso ritual, spoke of a hopeful modernity as Italy reimagined itself as an urban, industrial postwar nation.

Today's Cup

Italy's superior coffee-making technology took seed around the world, carried by postwar immigrants. Global coffee culture today may embrace latte art and new brewing technologies, but in Italy tradition holds sway. Italians still overwhelmingly favour Arabica and Robusta blends with a dense *crema*, high caffeine jolt and, crucially, a price point everyone can afford. Roasts remain dark and often bitter – Italians routinely sweeten coffee – but

1. Man drinking an espresso, Piazza Navona (p83), Rome
2. Espresso coffee being made
3. Waiter delivering coffee, Perugia

Italian baristas use far less coffee per shot and ultra smooth blends. Espresso is the overwhelming order of choice and takeaway cups uncommon. Why? Clutching a coffee on the move misses coffee's dual purpose for Italians: contemplation and social belonging.

Bean Hunting

Finding your ultimate Italian espresso is trial and error, albeit enjoyable and inexpensive. Best-of lists will only get you so far: Rome's famed Caffè Sant'Eustachio, Florence's Gilli and Naples' Caffè Gambrinus will almost certainly get it right, but so too will many small town bars. Take note of *torrefazionie* (bean roasters): global giants like Trieste's Illy and Turin's Lavazza are reliable, but do seek out regional favourites, such as Verona's Giamaica, Parma's Lady, Piemonte's Caffè Vergnano and Pascucci from Le Marche.

BARISTA BASICS

→ **Caffè, espresso** Short shot of black coffee.

→ **Ristretto** Short espresso.

→ **Lungo** Long espresso.

→ **Americano** Espresso with added hot water.

→ **Macchiato** Espresso 'stained' with a little milk.

→ **Cappuccino** Espresso with steamed milk.

→ **Cappuccino scuro** Strong (dark) cappuccino.

→ **Marochino** Small cappuccino with cocoa.

→ **Latte macchiato** Dash of coffee in steamed milk.

→ **Deca** Decaf.

→ **Corretto** Spiked espresso, usually with grappa.

Emilia-Romagna & San Marino

Best Places to Eat

➡ Trattoria Ermes (p452)

➡ Ca' de Vèn (p472)

➡ All'Osteria Bottega (p444)

➡ Trattoria del Tribunale (p461)

➡ Casina del Bosco (p476)

Best Places to Stay

➡ B&B Pio (p460)

➡ Arthotel Orologio (p443)

➡ Bologna nel Cuore (p443)

➡ Alchimia B&B (p467)

➡ Foresteria San Benedetto (p457)

Why Go?

Sweeping north from the Apennines to the fertile Po Valley, Emilia-Romagna boasts some of Italy's most hospitable people, some of its most productive land and some of its most soul-satisfying food. Since antiquity, the verdant Po lowlands have sown enough agricultural riches to feed a nation and finance an unending production line of luxury cars, regal *palazzi* (mansions), Romanesque churches, and a gigantic operatic legacy (Verdi and Pavarotti, no less).

You can eat like a Roman emperor here, in the birthplace of *tagliatelle al ragù*, pumpkin-filled *cappellacci* pasta, Parma prosciutto, balsamic vinegar and *parmigiano reggiano* (Parmesan). And then there's Emilia-Romagna's treasure trove of oft-neglected destinations: vibrant Bologna with its photogenic porticoes, Ravenna with its dazzling mosaics, posh Parma, Roman frontier-town-turned-beach-resort Rimini and the hilltop micro-nation of San Marino. Wherever you go, you'll be welcomed with the customary warmth of Emilia-Romagna's people.

When to Go
Bologna

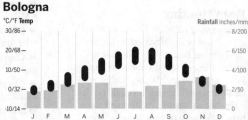

May Enjoy pleasant weather on the Po plains and avoid summer crowds on Rimini's beaches.

Jun–Aug Summer music festivals fill the agenda from Bologna to Ravenna.

Sep Ideal hiking conditions in Parco Nazionale dell'Appennino Tosco-Emiliano.

EMILIA-ROMAGNA

Bologna

POP 380,000

Fusing haughty elegance with down-to-earth grit in one beautifully colonnaded medieval grid, Bologna is a city of two intriguing halves. On one side is a hard-working, hi-tech city located in the super-rich Po valley where suave opera-goers waltz out of regal theatres and reconvene in some of the nation's finest restaurants and trattorias. On the other is a Bolshie, politically edgy city that hosts the world's oldest university and is famous for its graffiti-embellished piazzas filled with mildly inebriated students swapping Gothic fashion tips.

No small wonder Bologna has earned so many historical monikers. *La Grassa* (the fat one) celebrates a rich food legacy (*ragù* or bolognese sauce originated here). *La Dotta* (the learned one) doffs a cap to the city university founded in 1088. *La Rossa* (the red one) alludes to the ubiquity of the terracotta medieval buildings adorned with miles of porticoes, as well as the city's longstanding penchant for left-wing politics. All three names still ring true. Bologna is the kind of city where you can discuss Chomsky with a leftie newspaper-seller one minute, and eat like a king in a fine restaurant the next.

Sights

Piazza Maggiore & the Quadrilatero

All roads lead to pivotal Piazza Maggiore, flanked by the world's fifth-largest basilica and some impressive Renaissance *palazzi*.

★ **Basilica di San Petronio**   CHURCH
(Piazza Maggiore; ⊙ 7.45am-2pm & 3-6.30pm) Bologna's hulking Gothic basilica is the world's fifth-largest church, measuring 132m by 66m by 47m. Work began on it in 1390, but it was never finished and today its main facade still remains incomplete. Inside, look out for the huge sundial that stretches 67.7m down the eastern aisle. Designed in 1656 by Gian Cassini and Domenico Guglielmi, the sundial was instrumental in discovering the anomalies of the Julian calendar and led to the creation of the leap year. Original plans called for the basilica to be larger than Rome's St Peter's, but in 1561 Pope Pius

IV blocked construction by commissioning a new university on the basilica's eastern flank. If you walk along Via dell'Archiginnasio you can still see semi-constructed apses poking out oddly.

Palazzo Comunale   GALLERY
(Piazza Maggiore) FREE The palace that forms the western flank of Piazza Maggiore has been home to the Bologna city council since 1336. A salad of architectural styles, it owes much of its current look to makeovers in the 15th and 16th centuries. On the 2nd floor you'll find the *palazzo's* **Collezioni Comunali d'Arte** (☑ 051 219 36 31; adult/reduced €5/3; ⊙ 9am-6.30pm Tue-Fri, 10am-6.30pm Sat & Sun) with its interesting collection of 13th- to 19th-century paintings, sculpture and furniture. The statue of Pope Gregory XIII, the Bolognese prelate responsible for the Gregorian calendar, was placed above the main portal in 1580, while inside, Donato Bramante's 16th-century staircase was designed to allow horse-drawn carriages to ride directly up to the 1st floor. Outside the *palazzo* are photos of hundreds of partisans killed in the resistance to German occupation, many on this very spot.

Fontana del Nettuno   FOUNTAIN
(Neptune's Fountain; Piazza del Nettuno) Adjacent to Piazza Maggiore, Piazza del Nettuno owes its name to this explicit bronze statue sculpted by Giambologna in 1566. Beneath the muscled sea god, four cherubs represent the winds, and four buxom sirens, water spouting from every nipple, symbolise the four known continents of the pre-Oceania world.

Palazzo del Re Enzo   PALACE
(Piazza del Nettuno) This 13th-century palace is named after King Enzo, the illegitimate son of Holy Roman Emperor Frederick II, who was held here by papal forces between 1249 and 1272. Dating to the same period, the neighbouring **Palazzo del Podestà** (Piazza Maggiore 1) was the original residence

> ### ⓘ MAKING THE MOST OF YOUR EURO
>
> If you're visiting multiple sights, a **Bologna Welcome Card** (www.bologna welcome.com/en/richiedicard; 48hr card €20) may save you money. It offers free museum admissions and public transport (including on the BLQ airport shuttle bus) for a 48-hour period.

Emilia-Romagna & San Marino Highlights

1 Soothing your senses with opera or early evening *aperitivi* in **Parma** (p458).

2 Basking in the reflected glow of Italy's most gorgeous mosaics in **Ravenna** (p469).

3 Taking a very long, very slow and very delicious lunch in **Modena** (p448) at one of its delightfully down-to-earth eateries.

4 Cycling past the stately Castello Estense and around the muscular medieval walls of Renaissance **Ferrara** (p464).

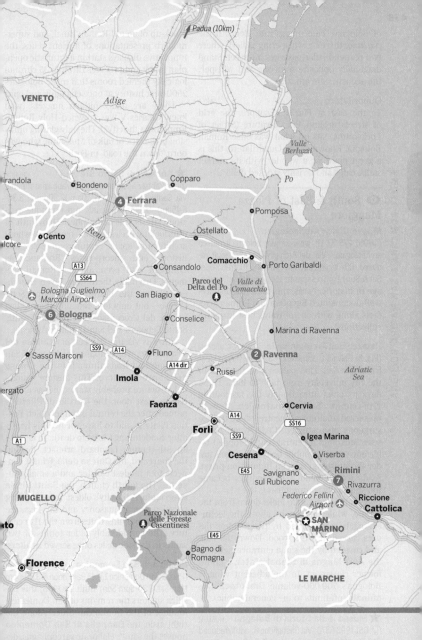

Padua (10km)

VENETO

Adige

Valle
Berluzzi

Po

Mirandola
Bondeno
Copparo
Ferrara ④
Pomposa

Cento
Ostellato
Alcore

A13
Comacchio
SS64
Consandolo
Porto Garibaldi
Bologna Guglielmo
Marconi Airport
San Biagio
Parco del
Delta del Po
Valle di
Comacchio

⑥ Bologna
Conselice

SS9   A14
Sasso Marconi
Fluno
Marina di Ravenna
A14 dir
② Ravenna
Russi
Imola
Adriatic
Sea
Faenza

A14
Cervia
Forlì
SS59   SS16
A1
Igea Marina

Cesena
Viserba
E45
Rimini
Savignano
sul Rubicone
⑦ Rivazurra
Federico Fellini
Airport
Riccione
MUGELLO
Parco Nazionale
delle Foreste
Casentinesi
SAN
MARINO
Cattolica
E45

Bagno di
Romagna
Florence
LE MARCHE

⑤ Leaving the flat lands
behind and heading out to
the **Pietra di Bismantova**
(p457) for a day of hiking.

⑥ Strolling under the
graceful porticoes, climbing
the tilted towers and indulging
in the fabled gastronomy of
Bologna (p435).

⑦ Discovering Roman
treasures and beachside
pleasures in **Rimini** (p473).

of Bologna's chief magistrate. Beneath the *palazzo*, there's a whispering gallery where two perpendicular passages intersect. Stand diagonally opposite someone and whisper: the acoustics are amazing.

Quadrilatero   AREA

To the east of Piazza Maggiore, the grid of streets around Via Clavature (Street of Locksmiths) sits on what was once Roman Bologna. Known as the Quadrilatero, this is a great place for a wander with its market stalls, cafes and lavishly stocked delis.

⦿ South & East of Piazza Maggiore

Museo Civico Archeologico   MUSEUM

(☑ 051 275 72 11; www.comune.bologna.it/museo archeologico; Via dell'Archiginnasio 2; adult/reduced €5/3; ⦿ 9am-3pm Tue-Fri, 10am-6.30pm Sat & Sun) Impressive in its breadth of coverage of historical eras, this museum displays well-documented Egyptian and Roman artefacts along with one of Italy's best Etruscan collections.

Palazzo dell'Archiginnasio   PALACE, MUSEUM

(Piazza Galvani 1; admission €3; ⦿ 9am-7pm Mon-Fri, to 2pm Sat) This palace was the seat of the city university from 1563 to 1805. These days its chief attraction is the fascinating 17th-century **Teatro Anatomico**, a well-preserved anatomical theatre where trainee surgeons once studied. Cedar-wood tiered seats surround a central marble-topped table once used for public body dissections under the sinister gaze of an Inquisition priest, ready to intervene if proceedings became too spiritually compromising.

A sculptured Apollo looks down from the ceiling, while the canopy above the lecturer's chair is supported by two skinless figures carved into the wood. Down the hall, and covered by the same entrance ticket, is the **Aula Magna di Stabat Mater**, a grand former classroom. In the adjacent wing is Bologna's 700,000-volume **Biblioteca Comunale** (off-limits to the general public).

★ Museo della Storia di Bologna   MUSEUM

(☑ 051 1993 6370; Via Castiglione 8; adult/reduced €10/7; ⦿ 10am-7pm Tue, Wed & Fri-Sun, to 10pm Thu) Walk in a historical neophyte and walk out an A-grade honours student in Bologna's golden past. This magnificent interactive museum, opened in 2012 and skillfully encased in the regal Palazzo Pepoli, is – in a word – an 'education'. Using a 3D film, a mock-up of an old Roman canal, and super-modern presentations of ancient relics, the innovative displays start in a futuristic open-plan lobby and progress through 35 chronologically themed rooms that make Bologna's 2500-year history at once engaging and epic.

There are many hidden nuggets (who knew Charles V was crowned Holy Roman Emperor in the city?). The only glaring omission is the lack of talk of Mussolini, who was born 'down the road' in Forli.

★ Abbazia di Santo Stefano   CHURCH

(http://abbaziasstefano.wix.com/abbaziasstefano; Via Santo Stefano 24; ⦿ 10am-12.30pm & 3.30-6.45pm) FREE Bologna's most unique religious site is this atmospheric labyrinth of interlocking ecclesiastical structures, whose architecture spans centuries of Bolognese history and incorporates Romanesque, Lombard and even ancient Roman elements. Originally there were seven churches – hence the basilica's nickname Sette Chiese – but only four remain intact today: Chiesa del Crocefisso, Chiesa della Trinità, Santo Sepolcro and Santi Vitale e Agricola.

Entry is via the 11th-century **Chiesa del Crocefisso**, which houses the bones of San Petronio and leads through to the **Chiesa del Santo Sepolcro**. This austere octagonal structure probably started life as a baptistery. Next door, the **Cortile di Pilato** is named after the central basin in which Pontius Pilate is said to have washed his hands after condemning Christ to death. In fact, it's an 8th-century Lombard artefact. Beyond the courtyard, the **Chiesa della Trinità** connects to a modest cloister and a small **museum**. The fourth church, the **Santi Vitale e Agricola**, is the city's oldest. Incorporating recycled Roman masonry and carvings, the bulk of the building dates from the 11th century. The considerably older tombs of two saints in the side aisles once served as altars.

Basilica di San Domenico   CHURCH

(Piazza San Domenico 13; ⦿ 9am-noon & 3.30-6pm Mon-Sat, 3.30-5pm Sun) Built in 1238, this basilica shelters the remains of San Domenico, founder of the Dominican order. Along the right aisle, the **Cappella di San Domenico** houses the saint's elaborate sarcophagus, designed by Nicola Pisano and later added to by a host of artists. Famous ghosts present here include Michelangelo, who carved the angel on the right of the altar when he was only 19, and Mozart, who spent a month at Bologna's music academy and occasionally played the church's organ.

EMILIA-ROMAGNA & SAN MARINO BOLOGNA

THE CHURCH ON THE HILL

Basilica Santuario della Madonna di San Luca (Via di San Luca 36; ⊘7am-12.30pm & 2.30-7pm Mar-Oct, to 5pm Nov-Feb) About 3.5km southwest of the city centre, the hilltop Basilica Santuario della Madonna di San Luca occupies a powerful and appropriately celestial position overlooking the teeming red-hued city below. The church houses a representation of the Virgin Mary, supposedly painted by St Luke and transported from the Middle East to Bologna in the 12th century. The 18th-century sanctuary is connected to the city walls by the world's longest portico, held aloft by 666 arches, beginning at Piazza di Porta Saragozza.

The most direct way to reach the basilica is on the **San Luca Express** (http://cityredbus. com/en/san-luca-express; adult/reduced €10/5; ⊘Thu-Sun Apr-early Nov), a tourist 'train' that leaves Piazza Maggiore six times daily, four days a week during peak tourist season. Alternatively, take bus 20 from the city centre to Villa Spada, where you can catch minibus 58 up to the sanctuary, or continue one more stop on bus 20 to the Meloncello arch and walk the remaining 2km under the arches.

⊙ Le Due Torri & University Quarter

Bolshie graffiti, communist newspaper-sellers and the whiff of last night's beer (and urine) characterise the scruffy but strangely appealing streets of the university quarter, also the site of Bologna's former Jewish ghetto.

Le Due Torri   TOWER
(The Two Towers; Piazza di Porta Ravegnana) Standing sentinel over Piazza di Porta Ravegnana, Bologna's two leaning towers are the city's main symbol. The taller of the two, the 97.6m-high **Torre degli Asinelli** (Piazza di Porta Ravegnana; admission €3; ⊘9am-7pm Apr-Sep, to 5pm Oct-Mar) is open to the public, although it's not advisable for vertigo-sufferers or owners of arthritic knees (there are 498 steps up a semi-exposed wooden staircase).

Superstitious students also boycott it: local lore says if you climb it you'll never graduate. Built by the Asinelli family between 1109 and 1119, today the tower leans 1.3m off vertical. The neighbouring 48m **Torre Garisenda** is sensibly out of bounds given its drunken 3.2m tilt.

Oratorio di Santa Cecilia   CHURCH
(Via Zamboni 15; ⊘10am-1pm & 2-6pm) This is one of Bologna's unsung gems. Inside, the magnificent 16th-century frescoes by Lorenzo Costa depicting the life and Technicolor death of St Cecilia and her husband Valeriano are in remarkably good nick, their colours vibrant and their imagery bold and unabashed.

Palazzo Poggi   PALACE, MUSEUM
(www.museopalazzopoggi.unibo.it; Via Zamboni 33; adult/reduced €5/3; ⊘10am-1pm Tue-Sun mid-Jun–mid-Sep, 10am-4pm Tue-Fri, 10.30am-5.30pm Sat & Sun mid-Sep–mid-Jun) At the university museums at Palazzo Poggi you can peruse waxwork uteri in the **Obstetrics Museum** and giant tortoise shells in the **Museum of Natural Sciences**. Further surprises are to be found in museums dedicated to ships and old maps, military architecture and physics.

Pinacoteca Nazionale   GALLERY
(www.pinacotecabologna.beniculturali.it; Via delle Belle Arti 56; adult/reduced €4/2; ⊘9am-1.30pm Tue & Wed, 2-7pm Thu-Sun) The city's main art gallery has a powerful collection of works by Bolognese artists from the 14th century onwards, including a number of important canvases by the late-16th-century Carraccis (brothers Annibale and Agostino and their cousin Ludovico). Among the founding fathers of Italian baroque art, the Carraccis were deeply influenced by the Counter-Reformation sweeping through Italy in the latter half of the 16th century. Much of their work is religious and their imagery is often highly charged and emotional.

Works to look out for include Ludovico's *Madonna Bargellini*, the *Comunione di San Girolamo* (Communion of St Jerome) by Agostino and the *Madonna di San Ludovico* by Annibale. Elsewhere in the gallery you'll find several works by Giotto, as well as Raphael's *Estasi di Santa Cecilia* (Ecstasy of St Cecilia). El Greco and Titian are also represented, but by comparatively little-known works.

Bologna

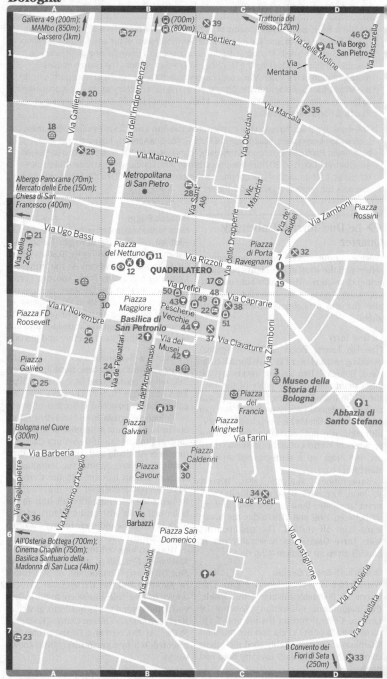

Galliera 49 (200m);
MAMbo (850m);
Cassero (1km)

📇 27

(700m)
(800m)

⊗ 39

Trattoria del
Rosso (120m)

Via Bertiera

Via delle Moline

46 ❂
🏛 41 Via Borgo
San Pietro

Via Mascarella

Via
Mentana

● 20

Via Galliera

Via dell'Indipendenza

Via Marsala

⊗ 35

Via Oberdan

18 🏛

⊗ 29

Via Manzoni

14 🏛

Albergo Panorama (70m);
Mercato delle Erbe (150m);
Chiesa di San
Francesco (400m)

Metropolitana
di San Pietro

Via Sant' Alò

28 🏛

Via delle Drapperie

Vic
Mandria

Via de'
Giudei

Via Zamboni

Piazza
Rossini

21 📇

Via Ugo Bassi

Via della Zecca

Piazza
del Nettuno

11 🏛

Via Rizzoli

Piazza
di Porta
Ravegnana

7 ❶
⊗ 32

6 ● 12 🏛 ℹ

QUADRILATERO

19 ❶

5 🏛

Via Orefici

17 ◉

Via IV Novembre

10 🏛

Piazza
Maggiore

50 🏛 48

43 🏛 49

22 ⊗

Via Caprarie

⊗ 38

Piazza FD
Roosevelt

Basilica di
San Petronio

Pescherie
Vecchie

51

26 📇

2 ❶

44 ⊗

Via dei
Musei

37 ⊗

Via Clavature

Via Zamboni

Piazza
Galileo

24 🏛

42 ◉

8 🏛

3 🏛 Museo della
Storia di
Bologna

25 📇

Via de' Pignattari

Via dell'Archiginnasio

Piazza
del
Francia

✉

❶ 1
Abbazia di
Santo Stefano

Bologna nel Cuore
(300m)

13 🏛

Piazza
Galvani

Piazza
Minghetti

Piazza
Francia

Via Barberia

Piazza
Calderini

Via Farini

Via Tagliapietre

Via Massimo d'Azeglio

Piazza
Cavour

30

⊗ 36

Vic
Barbazzi

34 ⊗
Via de' Poeti

All'Osteria Bottega (700m);
Cinema Chaplin (750m);
Basilica Santuario della
Madonna di San Luca (4km)

Piazza San
Domenico

Via Castiglione

❶ 4

Via Garibaldi

Via Cartoleria

Via Castellata

23 📇

Il Convento dei
Fiori di Seta
(250m)

⊗ 33

EMILIA-ROMAGNA & SAN MARINO BOLOGNA

◉ North & West of Piazza Maggiore

Palazzo Fava　　　　　　　　GALLERY
(☏051 1993 6305; www.genusbononiae.it; Via
Manzoni 2; adult/reduced €10/7; ◷noon-7pm
Mon, 9am-7pm Tue-Thu & Sun, to 8pm Fri & Sat)
This exhibition space encased in a Renaissance mansion is frequently the site of
blockbuster temporary art shows. Beyond
these special exhibits, the palace's biggest
draw is the group of heavily frescoed rooms
on the 1st floor, in particular the Sala di
Giasone, painted in bright naturalistic
style by the precocious young Carraccis in
the 1580s. There's also a lovely cafe on-site.

**San Colombano – Collezione
Tagliavini**　　　　　　　　　　MUSEUM
(☏051 1993 6366; www.genusbononiae.it; Via
Parigi 5; adult/reduced €7/5; ◷10am-7pm Tue-
Sun) A beautifully – repeat *beautifully* –
restored church with original frescoes and
a medieval crypt rediscovered in 2007,
the San Colombano hosts a wonderful
collection of over 80 musical instruments
amassed by the octogenarian organist, Luigi Tagliavini. Many of the assembled harp-
sichords, pianos and oboes date from the
1500s and, even more surprisingly, are still
in full working order. Listen out for regular
free concerts.

Chiesa di San Francesco　　　　CHURCH
(Piazza San Francesco; ◷6.30am-noon & 3-7pm)
Think Gothic. This dark mysterious church
was one of the first in Italy to be built in
the French Gothic style. Inside check out
the tomb of Pope Alexander V and the remarkable 14th-century marble altarpiece
depicting sundry saints and scenes from
the life of St Francis.

MAMbo　　　　　　　　　　　GALLERY
(Museo d'Arte Moderna di Bologna; www.mambo-
bologna.org; Via Don Minzoni 14; adult/reduced
€6/4; ◷noon-6pm Tue, Wed & Fri, to 8pm Thu,
Sat & Sun) Avant-gardes, atheists and people who've had their fill of dark religious
art can seek solace in one of Bologna's
newer museums (opened 2007) housed in
a cavernous former municipal bakery. Its
permanent and rotating exhibits showcase
the work of up-and-coming Italian artists.
Entrance to the permanent collection is
free the first Sunday of every month.

Bologna

🐦 Courses

**La Vecchia Scuola
Bolognese**   COOKING COURSE
(☏ 051 649 15 76; www.lavecchiascuola.com; Via
Galliera 11) It stands to reason: Bologna is a
good place to learn to cook and this is one of
several schools that offer courses for English-
speakers. Prices range from €50 for a three-
hour course to €325 for five days.

☞ Tours

Bologna's tourist office on Piazza Maggiore
offers guided, two-hour walking tours in
English (€13). Schedules change constantly,
so it's best to inquire and book directly with
the tourist office upon arrival.

City Red Bus   BUS TOUR
(www.cityredbus.com; tickets €13) Runs an hour-
long, hop-on, hop-off bus tour of the city departing from the train station several times
daily. Tickets can be bought on board.

🎇 Festivals & Events

Bologna Estate   ART
(www.bolognaestate.it; ⊙ mid-Jun–mid-Sep) A
three-month program of concerts, film projections, dance performances and much
more held in open-air venues throughout
the city. Many events are free. Tourist offices
have details.

🛏 Sleeping

Accommodation in Bologna is geared to the
business market, with a glut of midrange to
top-end hotels in the convention zone to the
north of the city. If possible, avoid the busy
spring and autumn trade-fair seasons when
hotels get heavily booked, advance reservations are essential, and standard prices (as
given in our listings) can literally double or
triple.

Albergo Panorama   PENSION €
(☏ 051 22 18 02; www.hotelpanoramabologna.it;
4th fl, Via Livraghi 1; d €70, s/d/tr/q without bath-

room €40/60/80/90; ❄️ 🛜) Tucked just off pedestrianised Via Ugo Bassi, this cheerful old-school family *pensione* has 10 spacious rooms, most with parquet and/or marble floors, and half offering lovely panoramic views of nearby *palazzi,* towers and flowery terraces. The lone room with bathroom costs €10 extra. English and French are spoken.

Albergo Centrale   HOTEL €
(🖉 051 22 51 14; www.albergocentralebologna. it; 3rd fl, Via della Zecca 2; s €48-60, d €80-88; ❄️ 🛜) Living up to its name with a perfect city-centre location, this old-fashioned hotel offers comfortable if unexceptional rooms at unbeatable rates, with parquet floors, modern furniture and an ample buffet breakfast. Take the elevator to the 3rd floor.

Albergo delle Drapperie   HOTEL €
(🖉 051 22 39 55; www.albergodrapperie.com; Via delle Drapperie 5; s €58-70, d €85-115, ste €115-140; ❄️ 🛜) Offering one of the best quality-to-price ratios in central Bologna, this hotel in the atmospheric Quadrilatero neighbourhood is snugly ensconced in the upper floors of a large building. Buzz in at ground level and climb the stairs to discover 19 attractive rooms with marble floors, wood-beamed ceilings, the occasional brick arch and colourful ceiling frescoes.

★ Arthotel Orologio   DESIGN HOTEL €€
(🖉 051 745 74 11; www.bolognarthotels.it; Via IV Novembre 10; s €90-174, d €114-205, ste €219-327; 🅿 ❄️ @ 🛜) Affiliated with the upmarket Bologna Art Hotels mini-chain, this refined pile with a prime location just off Piazza Maggiore seduces guests with its slick service, smart rooms furnished in elegant gold, blue and burgundy, swirling grey-and-white marble bathrooms, antique clocks and complimentary chocs. It also sponsors rotating art shows on the hotel walls and in the sweet piazzetta out front.

Two sister hotels within a two-block radius of the Orologio offer similarly enticing amenities: the **Arthotel Commercianti** (🖉 051 745 75 11; www.bolognahotels.it; Via de' Pignattari 11; s €100-184, d €124-215, ste €229-337; 🅿 ❄️ @ 🛜) and the more modern **Arthotel Novecento** (🖉 051 745 73 11; www.bolognarthotels.it; Piazza Galileo Galilei 4/3; s €100-184, d €124-215, ste €229-337; 🅿 ❄️ @ 🛜).

★ Bologna nel Cuore   B&B €€
(🖉 051 26 94 42; www.bolognanelcuore.it; Via Cesare Battisti 29; s €75-100, d €95-140, apt €120-125; 🅿 ❄️ 🛜) This centrally located, immaculate and well-loved B&B features a pair of bright, high-ceilinged rooms with pretty tiled bathrooms and endless mod cons, plus two comfortable, spacious apartments with kitchen and laundry facilities. Owner and art historian Maria generously shares her knowledge of Bologna and serves breakfasts featuring jams made with fruit picked near her childhood home in the Dolomites.

Enclosed garage parking is available for €20 extra per day.

Antica Residenza d'Azeglio   B&B €€
(🖉 051 644 73 89; www.anticaresidenzadazeglio. it; Via D'Azeglio 64; r €90-200; 🅿 ❄️ 🛜) It's hard not to feel at home when refined and well-travelled owner Agostino greets you in perfect English, French or Italian and shows you into your high-ceilinged 19th-century *palazzo* room, complete with well-stocked fridge and welcome bottle of wine (all included in the price). Among the five colour-themed rooms, the Camera Azzurra stands out with its delightful flowery terrace.

Perks include powerful wi-fi and air-con, plus a perfect location for those with a car. It's just paces outside Bologna's pedestrian zone, with €10-per-day garage parking out back, and an easy 10-minute walk into Piazza Maggiore.

Hotel Metropolitan   BOUTIQUE HOTEL €€
(🖉 051 22 93 93; www.hotelmetropolitan.com; Via dell'Orso 6; r €100-250; 🅿 ❄️ @ 🛜) Providing another lesson in Italian interior design, the Met doesn't miss a trick. It mixes functionality with handsome modern furnishings, injecting peace and tranquillity into its frenetic city-centre location with unexpected touches such as the superior rooms upstairs surrounding a small courtyard with olive trees. The convenient location midway between the train station and Piazza Maggiore is another plus.

Il Convento dei Fiori
di Seta   BOUTIQUE HOTEL €€
(🖉 051 27 20 39; www.silkflowersnunnery.com; Via Orfeo 34; r €99-209, ste €179-229; ❄️ 🛜) Tucked away at the south edge of town is this chic boutique hotel housed in a 14th-century convent. Most atmospheric are the four downstairs rooms, where religious-inspired frescoes share the stage with Mapplethorpe-style flower photos, snazzy modern light fixtures, linen sheets and cool mosaic-tiled bathrooms.

Prendiparte B&B

B&B €€€

(☑ 335 561 68 58, 051 58 90 23; www.prendiparte. it; Piazzetta Prendiparte 5; r €500) You will never – repeat, *never* – stay anywhere else like this. Forget the B&B tag: you don't just get a room here, you get an entire 900-year-old tower (Bologna's second tallest). The living area (bedroom, kitchen and lounge) is spread over three floors and there are nine more levels to explore, with outstanding views from the terrace up top.

The price includes breakfast, a welcome drink on the panoramic terrace and a personal tour of the tower with owner Matteo Giovanardi. For another couple of hundred euros, you can have a private dinner catered by a professional chef. Find a millionaire to shack up with and pretend you're an errant medieval prince(ss) for the night!

Eating

Gastronomic tip number one: learn the local lingo and ask for *tagliatelle al ragù*. Calling the city's signature meat sauce 'spaghetti bolognese' is like calling champagne 'fizzy wine'. Two meals into your Bologna stay and you'll start to understand why the city's known as *La Grassa*.

The university district northeast of Via Rizzoli harbours hundreds of restaurants, trattorias, takeaways and cafes catering to hard-up students and gourmet diners alike.

Stock up on victuals at the **Mercato delle Erbe** (www.mercatodelleerbe.it; Via Ugo Bassi 25; ⊙ 7am-1.15pm Mon-Sat, plus 5.30-7.30pm Mon-Wed, 4.30-7.30pm Fri), Bologna's main covered market. Alternatively, the Quadrilatero area east of Piazza Maggiore harbours a **produce market** (cnr Via delle Drapperie & Via Pescherie Vecchie; ⊙ 7am-1pm Mon-Sat, plus 4.15-7.30pm Mon-Wed, Fri & Sat) and some of the city's best-known delis.

★ Osteria dell'Orsa

ITALIAN €

(☑ 051 23 15 76; www.osteriadellorsa.com; Via Mentana 1; meals €20-25; ⊙ noon-midnight) If you were to make a list of the great wonders of Italy, hidden amid Venice's canals and Rome's Colosseum would be cheap, pretension-free *osterie* (casual taverns) like Osteria dell'Orsa, where the food is serially sublime and the prices are giveaway cheap. So what if the waiter's wearing an AC Milan shirt and the wine is served in a water glass?

Trattoria del Rosso

TRATTORIA €

(☑ 051 23 67 30; www.trattoriadelrosso.com; Via A Righi 30; meals €15-25; ⊙ noon-3pm & 7-10pm)

The Rosso, said to be the city's oldest trattoria, is a great example of what they do so well in Bologna. A bustling, workaday eatery, it serves healthy portions of home-style local fare at honest prices and without a frill in sight. Lunch specials including *primo*, *secondo*, water and coffee cost only €10.

Tamburini

BUFFET, DELI €

(www.tamburini.com; Via Caprarie 1; meals €14-18; ⊙ buffet noon-6pm, deli 8.30am-8pm Mon-Sat, 10am-6.30pm Sun) Full of swinging hams and pungent cheeses, this traditional (if touristy) delicatessen is conveniently located in the heart of the Quadrilatero. Its inexpensive grab-a-tray buffet offers visitors an easy way to test-taste multiple local specialities. Fill up on alluringly decorated cheese and meat boards, colourful salad bowls and a choice of three to four daily pasta dishes.

★ All'Osteria Bottega

OSTERIA €€

(☑ 051 58 51 11; Via Santa Caterina 51; meals €35-40; ⊙ 12.30-2.30pm & 8-10.30pm Tue-Sat) At this *osteria* truly worthy of the name, owners Daniele and Valeria lavish attention on every table between trips to the kitchen for plates of *culatello di Zibello* ham, tortellini in capon broth, pork shank in red wine reduction and other Slow Food delights. Desserts are homemade by Valeria, from the *ciambella* (Romagnola ring-shaped cake) to fresh fruit sorbets.

★ Drogheria della Rosa

TRATTORIA €€

(☑ 051 22 25 29; www.drogheriadellarosa.it; Via Cartoleria 10; meals €35-40; ⊙ noon-3pm & 7.30-11.45pm) With its wooden shelves and apothecary jars, it's not difficult to picture this place as the pharmacy it once was. Nowadays it's a charming, high-end trattoria, run by a congenial owner who gets round to every table to explain the day's short, sweet menu of superbly prepared Bolognese classics, and often bestows roses upon guests at evening's end.

Trattoria dal Biassanot

TRATTORIA €€

(☑ 051 23 06 44; www.dalbiassanot.it; Via Piella 16a; meals €28-35; ⊙ 7-10.30pm Mon, noon-2.30pm & 7-10.30pm Tue-Sat) The waiters in bow ties suggest an underlying grandiosity, but the Biassanot is about as down to earth as its earthy menu, which lists such rustic throwbacks as wild boar, goat, and veal with balsamic vinegar and mushrooms. Get in early: the check-clothed tables get busy. The pear *torta* and hot custard dessert round off proceedings very nicely.

SPAGHETTI BOLOGNESE

If you came to Emilia-Romagna in search of authentic spaghetti bolognese, you're out of luck. The name is a misnomer. Spaghetti bolognese is about as Bolognese as roast beef and Yorkshire pudding, and Bologna's fiercely traditional trattorias never list it. Instead, the city prides itself on a vastly superior meat-based sauce called *ragù*, consisting of slow-cooked minced beef simmered with pancetta, onions and carrots, and enlivened with liberal dashes of milk and wine.

So why the misleading moniker? Modern legend suggests that *ragù* may have acted as spaghetti bolognese's original inspiration when British and American servicemen passing through Emilia in WWII fell in love with the dish. Returning home after the war, they subsequently asked their immigrant Italian chefs to rustle up something similar. Details clearly got lost in translation. The 'spaghetti bolognese' eaten in contemporary London and New York is fundamentally different to Bologna's centuries-old *ragù*. First there's the sauce. Spaghetti bolognese is heavy on tomatoes while *ragù* is all about the meat. Then there's the pasta. Spaghetti bolognese is served with dry durum-wheat spaghetti from Naples taken straight from a packet. *Ragù* is spread over fresh egg-based *tagliatelle* (ribbon pasta), allowing the rich meat sauce to stick to the thick al dente strands.

Ever keen to safeguard their meat sauce from mediocrity, Bologna's chamber of commerce registered an official *ragù* recipe in 1982, although, ironically, it's still nigh on impossible to find two Bologna *ragù* that taste the same.

Osteria La Traviata OSTERIA €€

(☑051 33 12 98; www.ristorantelatraviata bologna.it; Via Urbana 5c; meals €28-43; ☺noon-2.30pm & 7.45-10.30pm Mon-Sat) Delectable locally sourced treats, from delicately fried squash blossom appetisers to desserts like homemade ricotta-walnut cake, rule the menu at this charming *osteria*. It's equally warm and welcoming on a summer evening, when tables spill out under the porticoes out front, as on a winter's night, when diners crowd inside among white stucco walls laden with framed photos and knick-knacks.

Osteria Broccaindosso OSTERIA €€

(☑051 23 41 53; Via Broccaindosso 7a; meals €13-50; ☺noon-2.30pm & 7.30pm-1am) Ever wish you could try everything on the menu? At this convivial, locally recommended *osteria*, you can. The tasting menu of appetisers alone (€13) is enough to feed most mortals, with plates of everything from *prosciutto e melone* to gorgonzola-and-pear tart. Those with gargantuan appetites can keep going (similar menus of pastas, *secondi* and desserts cost €13 to €15).

Osteria de' Poeti RISTORANTE €€

(☑051 23 61 66; www.osteriadepoeti.com; Via de' Poeti 1b; meals €30-40; ☺12.30-2.30pm daily, 7.30pm-1am Tue-Sun) In the wine cellar of a 14th-century *palazzo*, this historic eatery

makes an atmospheric spot to delve into Bologna's much-lauded cuisine. Take a table by the stone fireplace and order from the selection of traditional staples such as *tortelloni al doppio burro e salvia* (homemade ravioli with butter and sage). On Saturday nights there's live piano music from 10pm onwards.

Buca Manzoni EMILIAN €€

(☑051 27 13 07; www.bucamanzoni.it; Via Manzoni 6g; meals €25-35; ☺noon-3pm & 7-10.30pm Wed-Mon) 'We only serve proper Bolognese food here, none of that spaghetti stuff', announces your loquacious but humorous waiter. You'd better believe him. At Buca Manzoni the menu is printed in Bolognese dialect, the lasagne comes *verde* (green), and those long stringy bits of pasta are called *tagliatelle* and are nothing – dare you ask – like spaghetti.

🍷 Drinking & Nightlife

Hit the graffiti-strewn streets of the university district after sunset and the electrifying energy is enough to make a jaded 40 year old feel 20 again. Clamorous bars spill out into the street, groups of earnest drinkers sit down in circles on the hard pavement of Piazza Verdi and talented musicians jam old Thelonious Monk numbers. For a more upmarket, dressier scene head to the Quadrilatero.

DON'T MISS

BOLOGNA'S BEST GELATERIE

With some of northern Italy's hottest summer weather, and dozens of accomplished new gelato-makers graduating annually from nearby **Gelato University** (www.gelatouniversity.com), Bologna is the perfect place to indulge in Italy's favourite frozen dessert. The city's burgeoning crop of first-rate gelaterie is complemented by the world's first Gelato Museum, half an hour west of town in Anzola dell'Emilia.

Cremeria Funivia (☑ 051 656 93 65; www.cremeriafunivia.com; Piazza Cavour 1d-e; ⊗ noon-11.30pm Mon-Sat, from 11am Sun) Ask Bologna residents to name the best gelateria in town, and this place often comes out on top. Its newest branch sits directly opposite pretty Piazza Cavour. Fill a cone with house special flavours like Alice (mascarpone and chocolate) or Leonardo (pine-nut ice cream with toasted pine nuts), then head across the street and cool off under the trees.

La Sorbetteria Castiglione (www.lasorbetteria.it; Via Castiglione 44d; ⊗ 7.30am-midnight Apr-Oct, to 11pm Nov-Mar) A beloved Bologna institution since 1994, this temple to gelati is a bit peripheral to the centre but well worth the walk for decadently creamy flavours like pistachio or *gianduia* (chocolate mixed with hazelnuts).

Il Gelatauro (☑ 051 23 00 49; www.gelatauro.com; Via San Vitale 98b; ⊗ 8am-11pm) Sporting a cute logo of its namesake *gelatauro* (a bull with ice-cream-cone horns), this Calabrese-American venture keeps students from the nearby Università di Bologna pouring in day and night for exquisite flavours like ginger and cinnamon, or coffee *granite* (ices) served on homemade brioche. A take-out window stays open for an hour after the main store closes.

Galliera 49 (☑ 051 24 67 36; www.galliera49.it; Via Galliera 49b; ⊗ noon-11pm Sun-Thu, to midnight Fri & Sat) Arrive at opening time and you'll find artisan gelato-maker Lorenzo hard at work loading his morning's creations into the display case, from silky-smooth pink grapefruit sorbet to granular Sicilian-style pistachio ices to vegan and organic flavours like basil, hazelnut and almond. Free whipped cream is available; just ask!

Gelateria Gianni (www.gelateriagianni.com; Via San Vitale 2; ⊗ noon-midnight) At this centrally located favourite near the Due Torri, generous dollops of flavours such as white chocolate and cherry have brought a sweet ending to many an undergraduate date night.

Gelato Museum Carpigiani (☑ 051 650 53 06; www.gelatomuseum.com; Via Emilia 45, Anzola dell'Emilia; tours €5-20; ♿) Opened in 2012, this family-friendly museum traces the history of frozen desserts from ancient times to the present. Discover 19th-century ice cream carts, try out vintage gelato-making equipment and sample a flavour or two on the History of Gelato tour, or don an apron and create your own gelato under the expert guidance of teachers from the adjacent Gelato University.

Reserve ahead, then take TPER bus 87 from Piazza XX Settembre to the Magli stop in suburban Anzola dell'Emilia (30 minutes west of Bologna).

Zerocinquantino WINE BAR
(www.zerocinquantino.net; Via delle Pescherie Vecchie 3e; ⊗ 12.30-3pm & 6.30-11.30pm) A delightful spot for *aperitivi*, Zerocinquantino spreads out tables every evening on narrow, market-lined Via delle Pescherie Vecchie, one of Bologna's best people-watching streets. Sip a glass of local wine, accompanied by reasonably priced snacks (€1.80 to €7.50), from cheese and meat boards to marinated veggies to sandwiches served on focaccia or *piadina* (the traditional flatbread of Romagna).

Osteria del Sole BAR
(www.osteriadelsole.it; Vicolo Ranocchi 1d; ⊗ 10.30am-9.30pm Mon-Sat) The sign outside this ancient Quadrilatero dive bar – '*vino*' (wine) – tells you all you need to know. Bring in your own food, and elbow past the cacophony of smashed students, mildly inebriated grandpas and the occasional Anglo tourist for a sloppily poured glass of Chianti, Sangiovese or Lambrusco. It's a spot-on formula that's been working since 1465.

Le Stanze
WINE BAR

(www.lestanzecafe.com; Via Borgo San Pietro 1; ⊙6pm-1am) For sheer atmosphere, nothing compares to this former chapel where each of the four interior rooms has its own design concept. The *aperitivo* buffet is top-notch here, with paellas, pastas and chicken drumsticks to accompany your wine or cocktail.

Nu-Lounge Bar
BAR

(www.nu-lounge.com; Via dei Musei 6f; ⊙5.30pm-late) A swish bar in the Quadrilatero quarter, Nu-Lounge's well-groomed Italian crowd quaffs *aperitivi* while checking their reflections in the large glass windows of the porticoed terrace.

Empire English Pub
BAR

(www.empirebologna.com; Via Zamboni 24a; ⊙7pm-1am) This pungent student watering hole does a roaring trade in international beers on tap, including Guinness, Tennent's, Franziskaner, Leffe and Staropramen, spilling its patrons halfway up the colonnaded pavements.

Modo Infoshop
BAR

(www.modoinfoshop.com; Via Mascarella 24; ⊙10am-1pm & 4pm-midnight Mon-Fri, 6pm-midnight Sat & Sun) This indie bookshop with an affiliated cafe-bar next door is where postgrads sit down to write up their theses in a room decorated with *antifascismo* banners and enlivened with David Bowie on repeat. There's cheap beer, good wine and tempting chocolate brownies to enjoy.

Cassero
CLUB

(www.cassero.it; Via Don Minzoni 18; ⊙7pm-midnight Mon, Tue, Thu & Sun, to 5am Wed, Fri & Sat) Wednesday, Friday and Saturday are the big nights at this legendary (but not exclusively) gay-and-lesbian club, home of Italy's Arcigay organisation. Evenings kick off with happy hour (7pm to 8pm) at the club's Queer Garden Bar seven nights a week.

☆ Entertainment

Bologna, courtesy of its large student population, knows how to rock – but it also knows how to clap politely at the opera. The most comprehensive listings guide is *Bologna Spettacolo* (in Italian), available at newsstands or online (www.bologna spettacolo.it).

Cantina Bentivoglio
JAZZ

(www.cantinabentivoglio.it; Via Mascarella 4b; ⊙8pm-1am) Bologna's top jazz joint, the Bentivoglio is a jack of all trades. Part wine bar (choose from over 500 labels), part restaurant and part jazz club (there's live music six nights a week most of the year), this much-loved institution oozes cosy charm with its labyrinth of chambers sporting ancient brick floors, arched ceilings and shelves full of wine bottles.

In summer, it joins with three other neighbouring venues to host the annual **Salotto di Jazz**, during which revellers pour out into pedestrianised Via Mascarella for six weeks of live jazz under the stars.

Bravo Caffè
LIVE MUSIC

(www.bravocaffe.it; Via Mascarella 1; ⊙8pm-late) Hosting the university district's most dependable and varied mix of live music, Bravo begins nightly operations as a resto-bar with homemade Bolognese specialities and a 300-label wine cellar, then moves into club mode, with an eclectic mix of rock, blues, funk, pop, fusion and more.

Villa Serena
LIVE MUSIC

(www.villaserena.bo.it; Via della Barca 1; ⊙10pm-late Thu-Sat) Three floors of film screenings and music, live and canned, plus a garden for outdoor chilling.

Cinema Chaplin
CINEMA

(www.cinemachaplin.it; Piazza di Porta Saragozza 5a; admission €5-8) Screens films in English from September through May. The normal €8 admission fee is discounted to €5 on Mondays and Wednesdays.

Teatro Comunale
THEATRE

(www.tcbo.it; Largo Respighi 1) This venerable theatre, where Wagner's works were heard for the first time in Italy, is still Bologna's leading opera and classical music venue.

Oratorio di Santa Cecilia
LIVE MUSIC

(www.sangiacomofestival.it; Via Zamboni 15) The annual San Giacomo Festival brings regular free chamber-music recitals to this lovely space. Check the website or the board outside for upcoming events.

🛍 Shopping

If you came for the food, head for the Quadrilatero, a haven of family run delis and speciality food shops.

Paolo Atti
FOOD

(http://paoloatti.com; Via delle Drapperie 6; ⊙7.30am-7.15pm Mon-Sat, 10.30am-6.30pm Sun) This shop in Bologna's famed Quadrilatero neighbourhood specialises in beautifully packaged boxes of traditional Bolognese tortellini stuffed with prosciutto, *mortadella* (pork cold cut), fresh Parmesan and nutmeg. It also sells a tantalising range of baked goods, including superb artisanal *panettone* (a yeast-risen sweet bread).

La Baita   FOOD
(Via Pescheria Vecchie 3; ⊘8am-11pm, closed Sun Jun-Aug) Bologna's most famous cheese shop carries a wide selection of aged *parmigiano reggiano*, along with hams and other deli items. It doubles as a wine bar and restaurant where customers linger to people-watch at pavement tables, sipping glasses of wine and snacking on meat and cheese platters.

Gilberto   FOOD
(☑051 22 39 25; www.drogheriagilberto.it; Via delle Drapperie 5; ⊘8.30am-7.30pm Mon-Fri, to 9pm Sat) In business since 1905, this speciality food shop in Bologna's Quadrilatero district features well-stocked shelves full of wine, olive oil, truffles, marmalade and an impressive array of balsamic vinegars from Modena, along with speciality items such as chocolate tortellini.

Librerie Coop   BOOKS
(Via Orefici 19; ⊘9am-midnight) This three-level bookshop with attached cafe houses thousands of books, including many in English, French and German.

❶ Information

Ospedale Maggiore (☑051 647 81 11; Largo Nigrisoli 2) West of the city centre.
Post Office (Piazza Minghetti 4)
Tourist Office (☑051 23 96 60; www.bologna welcome.it; Piazza Maggiore 1e; ⊘9am-7pm Mon-Sat, 10am-5pm Sun) Also has an office at the airport.

❶ Getting There & Away

AIR

Bologna's **Guglielmo Marconi airport** (☑051 647 96 15; www.bologna-airport.it) is 8km northwest of the city. It's served by over two dozen airlines including Ryanair, easyJet and British Airways (daily flights to London's Stansted, Gatwick and Heathrow airports, respectively).

CAR & MOTORCYCLE

Bologna is linked to Milan, Florence and Rome by the A1 Autostrada del Sole. The A13 heads directly to Ferrara, Padua and Venice, and the A14 to Rimini and Ravenna. Bologna is also on the SS9 (Via Emilia), which connects Milan to the Adriatic coast. The SS64 goes to Ferrara.

Major car-hire companies are represented at Guglielmo Marconi airport and outside the train station. City offices include **Budget** (Via Nicolo dall'Arca 2d) and **Hertz** (Via Boldrini 4).

TRAIN

Bologna is a major transport junction for northern Italy. The high-speed train to Florence (€24) takes only 37 minutes. Other lightning-quick links include Venice (€30, 1½ hours), Milan (€40, 1¼ hours), Rome (€56, 2¼ hours) and Naples (€76, 3½ hours). Slower, less expensive trains also serve these destinations.

Frequent trains connect Bologna with cities throughout Emilia-Romagna, including Modena, Parma, Ferrara, Ravenna and Rimini.

❶ Getting Around

TO/FROM THE AIRPORT

The BLQ Aerobus, operated by **TPER** (☑051 29 02 90; www.tper.it), runs from the main train station to Guglielmo Marconi airport every 11 to 30 minutes between 5am and 11.35pm. The 20-minute journey costs €6 (tickets can be bought on board).

BICYCLE

BikeinBo (www.bikeinbo.it; Via Barontini; bike rental per day/week €15/70) will deliver a rental bike to your door anywhere in Bologna. Rates include helmet, lock, maps and front basket; an optional child seat costs €2 extra.

CAR & MOTORCYCLE

Much of the city centre is off-limits to vehicles. If you're staying downtown, your hotel can provide a ticket (€9 per 24-hour period) that entitles you to enter the ZTL (Zona a Traffico Limitato; Limited Traffic Zone) and park in designated spaces marked with blue lines.

PUBLIC TRANSPORT

Bologna has an efficient bus system, run by TPER (p448), with information booths at Bologna Centrale train station and the nearby bus station. Minibus A is the most direct of several buses that connect the train station with the city centre.

Modena

POP 186,000

If Italy were a meal, Modena would be the main course. Here, on the flat plains of the slow-flowing Po, lies one of the nation's great gastronomic centres, the creative force behind *real* balsamic vinegar, giant tortellini stuffed with tantalising fillings, sparkling

FERRARI FANTASIES & LAMBORGHINI LEGENDS

Fiats might be functional, but to appreciate the true beauty of Italian workmanship you must visit the small triangle of land between Modena and Bologna – sometimes called 'Motor Valley' – where the world's finest luxury cars, namely Ferraris and Lamborghinis, are constructed. Here, serious aficionados can bliss out for a day or two touring the region's four automotive museums, two devoted to Ferraris – including the **Museo Enzo Ferrari** (p451) in Modena – and two to Lamborghinis.

Museo Ferrari (http://museomaranello.ferrari.com; Via Ferrari 43; adult/reduced €15/13; ☉9.30am-7pm Apr-Oct, to 6pm Nov-Mar) Each year, hundreds of thousands of petrolheads make the pilgrimage to this museum in Maranello, Ferrari's home town. They come here to obsess over the world's largest collection of Ferraris, including Formula 1 exhibits, a trajectory of the cars' mechanical evolution and a revolving exhibit of 40 landmark Ferrari models. Just down the road, the company factory is off-limits to the 99.9% of the world's population that doesn't own a Ferrari.

A shuttle bus (€12) links the museum to Modena's train station and the Museo Enzo Ferrari nine times daily.

Lamborghini Museum (☎051 681 76 11; www.lamborghini.com/en/museum; Via Modena 12, Sant'Agata Bolognese; adult/reduced €13/10; ☉10am-12.30pm & 1.30-5pm Mon-Fri) Located in the village of Sant'Agata Bolognese (20km east of Modena and 35km northwest of Bologna), this museum traces the illustrious history of Lamborghini, dating back to the original 350 GT introduced in 1964. Cars on display here range from the classic Miura, Countach, Diablo and Gallardo to rare prototypes and exclusive models. Visitors who book ahead can also tour the company factory where Lamborghinis are custom-made; tours cost €40 – small change compared to the gold-on-wheels you'll be looking at.

Take bus 576 from Bologna's bus station to Sant'Agata Bolognese.

Museo Ferruccio Lamborghini (www.museolamborghini.com; Via Galliera 317, Argelato; adult/reduced €15/10, 1hr guided tour €8; ☉2.30-5.30pm Tue, 10am-1pm & 2-5.30pm Wed-Sat, 3-6.30pm Sun) Moved to its new home north of Bologna in 2013, this is a must-see museum for Lamborghini-lovers. Tour the 9000-sq-metre space on your own, checking out the Lamborghini family's personal collection of helicopters, tractors and legendary cars like the Miura SV and Countach, or reserve ahead for a personalised one-hour tour (€8, in English or Italian) with Fabio Lamborghini – a nephew of the car company's famous founder Ferruccio.

Take a train from Bologna to Funo-Centergross (€2.15, 15 minutes) then walk 20 minutes north to the museum.

Lambrusco wine and backstreets crammed with some of the best restaurants no one's ever heard of.

For those with bleached taste buds, the city has another equally lauded legacy: cars. The famous Ferrari museum (p449) is situated in the nearby village of Maranello. Modena is also notable for its haunting Romanesque cathedral and as the birthplace of the late Italian opera singer Luciano Pavarotti.

◉ Sights

Several of Modena's museums and galleries, including Galleria Estense and Musei Civici, are conveniently housed together in the Palazzo dei Musei on the western fringes of the historic centre.

★**Duomo** CATHEDRAL
(www.duomodimodena.it; Corso Duomo; ☉7am-12.30pm & 3.30-7pm) Modena's celebrated cathedral combines the austerity of the Dark Ages with throwback traditions from the Romans in a style known in Europe as Romanesque. The church stands out among Emilia-Romagna's many other ecclesial relics for its remarkable architectural purity. It is, by popular consensus, the finest Romanesque church in Italy, and in 1997 was listed as a Unesco World Heritage Site.

While not as large or spectacular as other Italian churches, the cathedral – dedicated to the city's patron saint, St Geminianus – has a number of striking features. The dark, brick-walled interior is dominated by the huge Gothic rose window (actually a

Modena

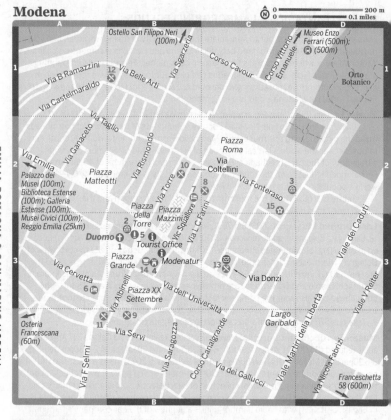

Modena

◉ Top Sights
1 Duomo... B3

◉ Sights
2 Musei del Duomo............................. B3
3 Museo della Figurina C2
4 Palazzo Comunale........................... B3
5 Torre Ghirlandina............................ B3

🛏 Sleeping
6 Hotel Cervetta 5............................... A3
7 Hotel Libertà.................................... B2

🍴 Eating
8 Hosteria Giusti................................. C2
9 Mercato Albinelli.............................. B4
10 Ristorante da Danilo B2
11 Trattoria Aldina.............................. A4
12 Trattoria Ermes B1
13 Trattoria Il Fantino........................ C3

🍷 Drinking & Nightlife
14 Caffè Concerto B3

◉ Entertainment
15 Teatro Comunale Luciano
Pavarotti..C2

13th-century addition) that shoots rays of light down the grand central apse. On the exterior facade, a series of vivid bas-reliefs depicting scenes from Genesis are the work of the 12th-century sculptor Wiligelmo. In-

terior highlights include an elaborate rood screen decorated by Anselmo da Campione and, in the crypt, Guido Mazzoni's *Madonna della pappa*, a group of five painted terracotta figures.

Torre Ghirlandina TOWER

(Corso Duomo; admission €3; ⏱9.30am-1pm & 3-7pm Tue-Fri, 9.30am-7pm Sat & Sun Apr-Sep, to 5.30pm Oct-Mar) Rising behind the cathedral is this early-13th-century, 87m tower topped with a slender Gothic spire, named after Seville's famous 'Giralda' in the early 16th century by exiled Spanish Jews. Facing it across Piazza Grande is the elegant facade of the Palazzo Comunale.

Palazzo Comunale PALACE

(Corso Duomo; admission Mon-Sat free, Sun €2; ⏱9am-7pm Mon-Sat, 9am-noon & 3-7pm Sun) Behind its elegant facade, Modena's 17th-century town hall offers several historic rooms for visitors to explore; if possible, schedule your visit to coincide with tours of the palace's balsamic-vinegar-making facility, which take place on Friday afternoons, Saturdays and Sundays.

Musei del Duomo MUSEUM

(Via Lanfranco 6; adult/child €4/3; ⏱9.30am-12.30pm & 3.30-6.30pm Tue-Sun) Tucked down an alley along the left side of the cathedral, this museum displays more captivating stonework by famed 12th-century sculptor Wiligelmo.

Galleria Estense GALLERY

(www.galleriaestense.org; Palazzo dei Musei, Piazzale Sant'Agostino 337; adult/reduced €4/2; ⏱8.30am-7.30pm Tue-Sat, 2-7.30pm Sun & Mon) Reopened in 2015 after a three-year closure (due to earthquake damage), this delightful gallery features the Este family's collection of northern Italian paintings from late medieval times to the 18th century. There are also some fine Flemish works and a canvas or two by Velázquez, Correggio and El Greco. Downstairs, the **Biblioteca Estense** (⏱9am-1.30pm Mon-Sat, plus 2.30-6.30pm Tue-Thu) FREE holds one of Italy's most valuable collections of books, letters and manuscripts, including the celebrated *Bibbia di Borso d'Este*, a masterpiece of medieval illustration.

Musei Civici MUSEUM

(City Museums; www.museicivici.modena.it/it; Palazzo dei Musei, Piazzale Sant'Agostino 337; ⏱9am-noon Tue-Fri, 10am-1pm & 4-7pm Sat & Sun) FREE Modena's jointly administered city museums, the **Museo Civico Archeologico Etnologico** and the **Museo Civico d'Arte**, are both housed in the Palazzo dei Musei. The former has some well-displayed local finds from Palaeolithic to medieval eras, as well as exhibits from Africa, Asia, Peru and New Guinea. Most interesting among the Museo Civico d'Arte's eclectic collection are the sections devoted to traditional paper-making, textiles and musical instruments. Free audio guides for both museums are available in English, French, German and Italian.

Museo Enzo Ferrari MUSEUM

(http://museomodena.ferrari.com; Via Paolo Ferrari 85; adult/reduced €15/13, incl Maranello museum €26/22; ⏱9.30am-7pm Apr-Oct, to 6pm Nov-Mar) While Maranello's Ferrari museum focuses on the supersonic cars, this museum near Modena's train station, inaugurated in 2012, celebrates Signor Enzo Ferrari himself. The memorabilia is cleverly juxtaposed in two separate buildings. The traditional house where Enzo was born in 1898 relates his life story with multilingual audio commentaries and film footage, while a slick curvaceous modern building painted in bright 'Modena yellow' acts as a gigantic car showroom, with plenty of Ferraris and Maseratis to gawp at.

A shuttle bus (day pass €12) connects to Modena's train station and the Maranello museum nine times daily.

Museo della Figurina MUSEUM

(www.museodellafigurina.it; Corso Canalgrande 103; ⏱10.30am-1pm & 3-6pm Wed-Fri, 10.30am-7pm Sat & Sun) FREE A nostalgic journey back in time for any kid that ever owned a *Panini* football sticker collection, this geeky museum is tucked away upstairs in the Palazzo Santa Margherita. It displays that precious Paolo Rossi sticker that cruelly eluded you in 1982, along with numerous other card collections, calendars and scrapbooks.

🏃 Activities

In Modena's outskirts, numerous *acetai* (producers of balsamic vinegar) and *parmigiano reggiano* (Parmesan) dairies open their doors to visitors, allowing you to observe the production process and buy direct from the source. The tourist office has a list, or you can organise a guided tour with the private agency **Modenatur** (www.modenatur.it; Via Scudari 8; ⏱2.30-6.30pm Mon, 9am-1.30pm & 2.30-6.30pm Tue-Fri).

🛌 Sleeping

Ostello San Filippo Neri HOSTEL €

(☎059 23 45 98; www.ostellomodena.it; Via Santa Orsola 48-52; dm/s/d €18.50/25/40; @ 🛜) Modena's businesslike HI hostel has 70 beds in single-sex dorms and family units. Pluses include the convenient location between the train station and downtown Modena, a guest kitchen and bar, disabled access, capacious lockers, uncrowded rooms (maximum four beds per dorm) and a bike-storage area. Rooms are closed 10am to 2pm for cleaning, but common spaces remain accessible.

Hotel Cervetta 5 · HOTEL €€

(☑ 059 23 84 47; www.hotelcervetta5.com; Via Cervetta 5; s €95-110, d €135-160; 🌐 🛜) Cervetta is about as posh as Modena gets without pampering to the convention crowd. A location adjacent to intimate Piazza Grande is complemented by quasi-boutique facilities, clean, modern bathrooms and the latest in TV technology. Fruity breakfasts and wi-fi are included; garage parking (€15) isn't.

Hotel Libertà · HOTEL €€

(☑ 059 22 23 65; www.hotelliberta.it; Via Blasia 10; s/d from €99/129; 🅿 🌐 @ 🛜) With a near-perfect mid-city location adjoining pretty Piazza Mazzini, this small hotel affiliated with the Best Western chain puts you within easy walking distance of everything. Parking costs €20 per day.

🍴 Eating

Modena would easily make a top-10 list of best Italian culinary towns. The beauty lies not just in the food, but in the way it is presented in simple, unpretentious eateries shoehorned up blind alleys or hidden inside faceless office blocks, often without signage.

Modena's produce **market** (⏱ 6.30am-2.30pm Mon-Sat year-round, plus 4.30-7pm Sat Oct-May) has its main entrance on Via Albinelli.

Trattoria Ermes · TRATTORIA €

(Via Ganaceto 89; meals €20; ⏱ noon-2.30pm Mon-Sat) In business since 1963, this fabulous, affordable little lunch spot is tucked into a single wood-panelled room at the northern edge of downtown Modena. Gregarious patron Ermes Rinaldi runs the place with his wife Bruna: she cooks, he juggles plates and orders while keeping up a nonstop stream of banter with the customers. Authentic, unpretentious Emilian cuisine at its finest.

Trattoria Aldina · TRATTORIA €

(☑ 059 23 61 06; Via Albinelli 40; meals €15-22; ⏱ noon-2.30pm Mon-Sat, plus 8-10.30pm Fri & Sat) Cloistered upstairs in a utilitarian apartment block, Aldina feels like a precious secret guarded loyally by local shoppers from the adjacent produce market. The lunch-only menu features the kind of no-nonsense homemade grub that only an Italian *nonna* raised on hand-shaped pasta could possibly concoct. There's no written menu; take what's in the pot and revel in the people-watching potential.

Trattoria Il Fantino · TRATTORIA €€

(☑ 059 22 36 46; www.gustamodena.it/ilfantino; Via Donzi 7; meals €23-29; ⏱ noon-2.30pm & 7-10.30pm Tue-Sat, noon-2.30pm Sun) Homemade Modenese miracles are forged in this low-key dining room spread with buttery yellow tablecloths and hung with jerseys and racing car photos. A mere €5 gets you an ample-sized appetiser of *parmigiano* and *salumi* (cold cuts) with Modena's famed vinegar, but make sure to save room for the divine pumpkin-stuffed ravioli, ricotta-filled tortellini, and scrumptious *secondi*.

Ristorante da Danilo · TRADITIONAL ITALIAN €€

(☑ 059 21 66 91; www.ristorantedadanilomodena.it; Via Coltellini 31; meals €25-30; ⏱ noon-3pm & 7pm-midnight Mon-Sat) Speedy waiters glide around balancing bread baskets, wine bottles and pasta dishes in this deliciously traditional dining room where first dates mingle with animated families and office groups on a birthday jaunt. Antipasti of salami, pecorino and fig marmalade are followed by delicious *secondi* of *bollito misto* (mixed boiled meats) or a vegetarian *risotto al radicchio trevigiano* (with red chicory).

★Hosteria Giusti · GASTRONOMIC €€€

(☑ 059 22 25 33; www.hosteriagiusti.it; Vicolo Squallore 46; meals €50, small half portions €35; ⏱ 12.30-2pm Tue-Sat) With only four tables, a narrow back-alley location, no real signage and a 90-minute daily opening window, this perplexingly unassuming *osteria* isn't really setting itself up for legendary status. But tentative whispers turn to exuberant shouts when regional specialities like *cotechino fritto con zabaglione al lambrusco* (fried Modena sausage with wine-flavoured egg custard) arrive at your table.

Half portions of most *primi* and *secondi* are available for those with lighter appetites.

Osteria Francescana · GASTRONOMIC €€€

(☑ 059 22 39 12; www.osteriafrancescana.it; Via Stella 22; tasting menus €170-195; ⏱ 12.30-1.30pm & 8-9.30pm Mon-Fri, 8-9.30pm Sat) You'll need to reserve three months in advance for this fabled 11-table restaurant, where food is art, decor is secondary and tasting menus top out at €195. Owner Massimo Bottura is onto his third Michelin star (earned in 2011), and

DON'T LEAVE TOWN WITHOUT TRYING...

Every Emilia-Romagna city has its gastronomic secrets, weird and wonderful local recipes that you'd be unlikely to find on the menu of your local Italian restaurant back home. Don't leave the following towns without trying these specialities.

Piacenza *Anolini in brodo* – pasta pockets filled with meat, Parmesan and breadcrumbs swimming in a rich brothlike soup.

Parma *Trippa alla Parmigiano* – slow-cooked tripe in a tomato sauce enlivened with Parmesan.

Modena *Cotechino di Modena* – pork sausage stuffed with seasoned mince and paired with lentils and mashed potatoes.

Bologna *Tagliatelle al ragù* – thick meat-heavy sauce served with wide-cut egg-based pasta.

Ferrara *Cappellacci di zucca* – ravioli-like pasta stuffed with pumpkin and nutmeg, and brushed with butter and sage.

Ravenna *Piadina* – thick unleavened bread stuffed with rocket, tomato and local soft *squacquerone* cheese.

Rimini *Brodetto* – a hearty fish soup served over lightly toasted bread.

in 2015 the restaurant leap-frogged into the number two spot on *Restaurant* magazine's influential 'World's 50 Best Restaurants' list.

For creative international cuisine with a more moderate price tag, try Bottura's equally diminutive bistro **Franceschetta 58** (☑ 059 309 10 08; www.franceschetta58.it; Via Vignolese 58; meals €35; ☺ 12.30-3pm & 7.30pm-midnight Mon-Sat), 1km southeast of the centre.

Drinking & Nightlife

A youthful bar-hopping crowd congregates along Via dei Gallucci. There's also a cluster of bars along Via Emilia near the cathedral.

Caffè Concerto CAFE, BAR
(www.caffeconcertomodena.com; Piazza Grande 26; ☺ 8am-3am) This Piazza Grande establishment manages a delicate juxtaposition between trendy (ubercontemporary decor) and old (cobbled central-square location) without appearing out of place. It wears three hats: all-day cafe, pricey restaurant and evening bar-club. The latter is its best incarnation, thanks to free bar snacks (minimum consumption €8), chilled Lambrusco and a footloose party atmosphere so often lacking in Italy's Renaissance cities.

☆ Entertainment

During July and August, outdoor concerts and ballet are staged on Piazza Grande.

Teatro Comunale Luciano Pavarotti THEATRE
(☑ 059 203 30 10; www.teatrocomunalemodena.it; Corso Canalgrande 85) It will come as no surprise that the birthplace of Pavarotti has a decent opera house. The Comunale opened in 1841 and has 900 seats and 112 boxes. Following the death of the city's exalted native son in September 2007, it was renamed in his honour.

ℹ Information

Post Office (Via Modonella 8)
Tourist Office (☑ 059 203 26 60; www.visitmodena.it; Piazza Grande 14; ☺ 2.30-6pm Mon, 9.30am-1.30pm & 2.30-6pm Tue-Sun) Provides city maps and a wealth of info about the surrounding area.

ℹ Getting There & Around

By car, take the A1 Autostrada del Sole if coming from Rome or Milan, or the A22 from Mantua and Verona.

The train station is north of the historic centre, fronting Piazza Dante. Destinations include Bologna (€3.75, 30 minutes, half-hourly), Parma (€5.20, 30 minutes, half-hourly) and Milan (regional €15, 2¼ hours, hourly/express €27.50, 1¾ hours, every two hours).

Local bus 7, operated by **SETA** (☑ 840 000216, 059 22 23 54; www.setaweb.it), links Modena's train station with Piazza Mazzini in the city centre every 10 to 15 minutes.

Like...? Try...

Like Florence? Try Bologna

Climb the 498 steps of medieval Torre degli Asinelli and the city unfurls before you like a map. There were once more than 100 such towers here, but only some 20 remain. Massimo Medica, director of Bologna's Musei Civici d'Arte Antica, explains. 'In the Middle Ages Bologna was an important city. Its university was comparable to Paris'. There wasn't the space to have a castle, so every tower belonged to a powerful family – the height showed the extent of their power. When a family was defeated, their tower would be cut.'

In the central square, Piazza Maggiore, locals and tourists recline as if at the beach. They're probably considering Bologna's other great achievement, its food. This is the home of yolky pasta: fine ribbons of *tagliatelle* entwined with *ragù* (meat sauce), *tortellini in brodo* (pork pasta parcels in a thin soup), and the artisanal ice cream of 1950s parlour La Sorbetteria Castiglione.

Like the Dolomites? Try Monti Sibillini

'On a clear day you can see Croatia from here,' says affable Maurizio Fusari, zoologist and trekking guide in the Monti Sibillini, gesturing out at the views that stretch off into the Adriatic. In this weathered mountain range, split between Umbria and Le Marche, the predominant sounds are birdsong and the swirl of the breeze, yet the wild hills are appealingly approachable. 'It's possible to reach even

1. Promontorio del Gargano (p724)
2. Bologna (p435)
3. Wildflowers near Monti Sibillini (p631)

the tallest without Alpine equipment. These are mountains for everyone.'

Walks range from gentle afternoon strolls through mountain valleys to night-time hikes to watch the sunrise, or a nine-day trek on the Grande Anello trail (120 kilometres). En route, look out for wildlife. Maurizio reels off a list: 'Wild boar, roe deer, wolves, golden eagles, peregrine falcons. Oh, and one bear. He has come here from Abruzzo. It seems he's looking for a mate.'

Like the Amalfi Coast?
Try the Gargano Promontory

The Gargano, the sea-thrusting spur of the Italian boot, was once connected to what is now Dalmatia, Croatia, across the Adriatic Sea. Knowing this makes sense of the place. It feels a region apart, with a skirt of sea so blue it makes you blink. The land is a tumultuous mix: bleached sea cliffs, dense dark-green scrub, wild orchids, pine forests and silver beaches, all of it protected and treasured as a national park. The area's uniqueness extends well into the sea, its waters punctuated with curious-looking *trabucchi*, ancient fishing traps whose origins reputedly stretch back to Phoenician times.

Vieste and Peschici are the main coastal towns, bunched-up clusters of narrow lanes and heavy limestone houses. Their pale, Arabesque buildings seem to grow out of the sea cliffs, with fierce-blue views in every direction.

In high summer, it can feel like everyone in Italy is here. Come in June and September, however, and you will experience the Gargano in its finest months, a time when the weather is seductively warm, many businesses are still open, and the carnival-like crowds are nowhere to be seen.

Reggio Emilia

POP 170,000

Often written off as an emergency pit stop on the Via Emilia, Reggio Emilia states its case as birthplace of the Italian flag – the famous red, white and green tricolour – and a convenient base for sorties south into the region's best natural attraction, the Parco Nazionale dell'Appennino Tosco-Emiliano. Those savvy enough to get out of their train/car/bus will find a cyclist-friendly city of attractive squares, grand public buildings and a leafy park. Known also as Reggio nell'Emilia, the town started life in the 2nd century BC as a Roman colony along the Via Emilia. Much of Reggio was built by the Este family during the 400 years it controlled the town, beginning in 1406.

◉ Sights

Reggio's pedestrianised city centre is an agreeable place to wander or cycle. The main sights are centred on Piazza Prampolini and adjacent Piazza San Prospero.

Duomo
CATHEDRAL

(Piazza Prampolini; ⊙8am-noon & 4-7pm) Reggio's 13th-century cathedral was first built in the Romanesque style but was given a comprehensive makeover 300 years later. Nowadays, virtually all that remains of the original is the upper half of the facade and, inside, the crypt.

Museo del Tricolore
MUSEUM

(www.musei.re.it/sedi/museo-del-tricolore; Piazza Prampolini 1; ⊙9am-noon Tue-Fri, 10am-1pm & 4-7pm Sat & Sun Sep-Jun, 9am-noon & 9-11pm Tue-Sat, 9-11pm Sun Jul & Aug) FREE In the main square, this small museum is a memorial to Reggio's proud role as birthplace of the Italian tricolour flag. At a meeting in the multi-tiered Sala del Tricolore in 1797, Napoleon's short-lived Cispadane Republic was proclaimed and the green, white and red tricolour was adopted for the first time. Next door in the 14th-century Palazzo del Comune is where the flag was actually conceived.

Palazzo dei Musei
MUSEUM

(Palazzo San Francesco; www.musei.re.it/sedi/palazzo-dei-musei; Via Spallanzani 1; ⊙9am-noon Tue-Fri, 10am-1pm & 4-7pm Sat & Sun Sep-Jun, 9am-noon & 9-11pm Tue-Sat, 9-11pm Sun Jul & Aug) FREE Formerly known as Palazzo San Francesco, the flagship of Reggio's five Musei Civici (Civic Museums) houses thematic collections of Roman archaeological finds (look out for the mosaics) and 18th-century art, along with sections dedicated to natural and municipal history.

Galleria Parmeggiani
GALLERY

(www.musei.re.it/sedi/galleria-parmeggiani; Corso Cairoli 2; ⊙9am-noon Tue-Fri, 10am-1pm & 4-7pm Sat & Sun Sep-Jun, 9-11pm Tue-Sun Jul & Aug) FREE The town's main art gallery holds some worthwhile Italian, Flemish and Spanish paintings, as well as a heterogeneous collection of costumes, arms and jewellery.

Basilica della Beata Vergine della Ghiara
CHURCH

(☑0522 43 97 07; www.musei.re.it/sedi/museo-del-santuario-della-beata-vergine-della-ghiara; Corso Garibaldi 44; ⊙by arrangement) Reggio's most important church was built in 1597 to honour the miracle of a deaf and blind boy named Marchino who regained his voice and hearing after witnessing an apparition of the Virgin Mary in front of the *Blessed Virgin of Ghiara* painting (by G Bianchi) in 1569. The Virgin has been faithfully reproduced in a chapel inside. Architecturally the basilica is classic baroque with notable paintings and frescoes by the top Emiliano artists of the period.

🛏 Sleeping

Student's Hostel della Ghiara
HOSTEL €

(☑0522 45 23 23; www.ostelloreggioemilia.it; Via Guasco 6; dm €19, d €50, without bathroom €45; ☞⌨) There's no shortage of space at Reggio's memorable HI hostel, housed in a former convent. One- to six-bed guest rooms line vast, echoing corridors, and, in summer, breakfast is served under the porticoes in the internal garden. The attached restaurant, Al Chiostro della Ghiara (www.chiostrodellaghiara.re.it; meals €18-22), serves reasonably priced meals (€18 to €22), including options for vegans, vegetarians and kids.

Cantarelli B&B
B&B €

(☑329 714 98 47; www.cantarellibandb.com; Via Monzermone 3; s/d/tr/q €50/70/90/105; ☒☞) Smack in the heart of town, Alberto Cantarelli's B&B offers three spacious and attractive antique-decorated rooms on the upper floors of his historic family home. Each room is unique, with the largest adaptable into a family suite; all come with fridge, free wi-fi and fresh pastries delivered to your door in the morning.

PARCO NAZIONALE DELL'APPENNINO TOSCO-EMILIANO

In the late 1980s Italy had half a dozen national parks. Today it has 24. One of the newest additions is **Parco Nazionale dell'Appennino Tosco-Emiliano** (www.appennino reggiano.it), a 260-sq-km parcel of land that straddles the border between Tuscany and Emilia-Romagna. Running along the spine of the Apennine mountains, the park is notable for its hiking potential, extensive beech forests and small population of wolves.

Of its many majestic peaks, the highest is 2121m **Monte Cusna**, easily scalable from the village of Civago, near the Tuscan border, on a path (*sentiero* No 605) that passes the region's best mountain hut, the **Rifugio Cesare Battisti** (☑ 0522 89 74 97; www. rifugio-battisti.it; dm incl half-board €46). The *rifugio* sits alongside one of Italy's great long-distance walking trails: the three-week, 375km-long **Grande Escursione Appennenica (GEA)**, which bisects the park in five stages from Passo della Forbici (near the Rifugio Cesare Battisti) up to its termination point just outside the park's northwest corner in Montelungo. Sections of the GEA can be done as day walks. *Trekking in the Apennines* by Gillian Price (published by Cicerone) provides an excellent detailed guide of the whole route.

One of the best gateways to the park is the village of **Castelnovo ne' Monti**, about 40km south of Reggio Emilia along the winding SS63 on a delightfully scenic ACT bus route. The large village has an ultrahelpful **tourist office** (☑ 0522 81 04 30; www.appen ninoreggiano.it; Via Roma 79e; ☉ 9am-1pm Mon-Wed, Fri & Sat) that stocks bags of free information and sells cheap maps of the region for hikers, cyclists and equestrians.

If you've arrived by bus, you can walk or take a taxi 3km from the village centre up to one of the national park's defining landmarks, the surreal **Pietra di Bismantova** (1047m), a stark limestone outcrop visible for miles around that's popular with climbers and weekend walkers. In its shadow lies the **Rifugio della Pietra** (☑ 0522 61 32 38; www. rifugiodellapietra.it; ☉ 10am-6pm Fri, 8am-10pm Sat, 8am-8pm Sun), open for food and drinks on Fridays and weekends, and the tiny **Eremo di Bismantova** monastery, which dates from 1400. From here various paths fan out to the rock's summit (25 minutes). You can also circumnavigate the rock on the lovely 5km **Anello delle Pietra** or even tackle it on a difficult *via ferrata* (trail with permanent cables and ladders) with the proper equipment.

Castelnovo ne' Monti offers a variety of overnight accommodation and restaurants, but to experience the Apennines' natural beauty, you're much better off staying at **Foresteria San Benedetto** (☑ 0522 61 17 52; www.foresteriasanbenedetto.it; ☉ s/d/tr/q €40/70/90/120, half board/full board per person extra €15/25), a simple but cosy lodge picturesquely placed at the foot of Pietra di Bismantova.

To reach Castelnovo ne' Monti on public transport, take bus 3B44 from Reggio Emilia, (€4.50, 1½ hours, every 90 minutes), operated by **SETA** (p458).

EMILIA-ROMAGNA & SAN MARINO REGGIO EMILIA

Hotel Posta
HOTEL €€

(☑ 0522 43 29 44; www.hotelposta.re.it; Piazza del Monte 2; s €85-140, d €105-190; ❄@☎) Elegant inside and out, the grand four-star Posta is housed in the 13th-century Palazzo del Capitano del Popolo, one-time residence of Reggio's governor. Rooms are individually decorated, with plenty of heavy floral fabrics, gilt-framed mirrors and antique furniture. Parking costs €12. Just around the corner, you'll find the hotel's less-expensive 16-room annexe, **Albergo Reggio** (☑ 0522 45 15 33; www.albergoreggio.it; Via San Giuseppe 7; s €60-75, d €80-105).

Eating

Reggio's central squares host a **produce market** (Piazza Prampolini; ☉ 7am-1pm Tue & Fri). Typical local snacks include *erbazzone* (herb pie with cheese or bacon) and *gnocco fritto* (fried salted dough).

Piccola Piedigrotta
PIZZA €

(☑ 0522 43 49 22; www.piccolapiedigrotta.it; Piazza XXV Aprile 1; pizzas €4.50-13; ☉ noon-2.30pm & 7pm-12.30am Tue-Sun) Reserve ahead at this very popular pizzeria that spreads out onto a spacious cobblestone square on warm summer evenings.

Caffè Arti e Mestieri GASTRONOMIC €€€

(☑ 0522 43 22 02; meals €45-50; ⊙ 7.30-10.30pm Mon, noon-2.30pm & 7.30-10.30pm Tue-Sat) Tucked back off the street around a lovely interior garden, this is Reggio's best spot for an elegant dinner. Chef Gianni d'Amato launched this new venture after his Michelin-starred Rigoletto was destroyed by the 2012 earthquake. Weekday lunch specials offer the rare chance for gourmet dining with a €10 price tag (main course, water and coffee; €13 with wine).

⭐ Entertainment

Teatro Municipale Valli PERFORMING ARTS

(www.iteatri.re.it; Piazza Martiri VII Luglio 7) Reggio's splendid neoclassical theatre – recognised as one of the finest in Italy – stages a full season of dance, opera and theatre. It's named after local-born actor Romolo Valli, who starred alongside Burt Lancaster in *The Leopard* (1963).

❶ Information

Tourist Office (☑ 0522 45 11 52; www.municipio.re.it/turismo; Via Farini 1a; ⊙ 8.30am-1pm & 2.30-6pm Mon-Sat, 9am-noon Sun)

❶ Getting There & Around

Reggio is on the Via Emilia (SS9) and A1 autostrada. The SS63 is a tortuous but scenic route that takes you southwest across the Parma Apennines to La Spezia on the Ligurian coast.

The train station is east of the town centre. Half-hourly trains serve all stops on the Milan–Bologna line, including Milan (regional/express €12.60/25.50, 1½ to 2½ hours), Parma (€2.95, 15 minutes), Modena (€2.95, 15 minutes) and Bologna (€5.80, 45 minutes).

Bus operator **SETA** (☑ 840 000216; www.setaweb.it) serves the city and region from its modern terminal just behind Reggio's train station, offering service to Apennine mountain towns such as Castelnovo ne' Monti (€4.50, 1½ hours, seven to 14 daily, route 3B44).

Parma

POP 187,000

If reincarnation ever becomes an option, pray you come back as a Parmesan. Where else do you get to cycle to work through streets virtually devoid of cars, lunch on fresh-from-the-attic prosciutto and aged *parmigiano reggiano*, quaff full-bodied Sangiovese wine in regal art-nouveau cafes, and spend sultry summer evenings listening to classical music in architecturally dramatic opera houses?

Glorying in its position as one of Italy's most prosperous cities, Parma has every right to feel smug. More metropolitan than Modena, yet less clamorous than Bologna, this is the city that gave the world Lamborghinis, a composer called Verdi and enough ham and cheese to start a deli chain. Stopping here isn't an option, it's a duty.

⊙ Sights

⭐ **Duomo** CATHEDRAL

(Piazza del Duomo; ⊙ 9am-12.30pm & 3-7pm) Another daring Romanesque beauty? Well, yes and no. Consecrated in 1106, Parma cathedral's facade is classic Lombard-Romanesque, but inside, the gilded pulpit and ornate lamp-holders scream baroque. Take note: there are some genuine treasures here. Up in the dome, Antonio da Correggio's *Assunzione della Vergine* (Assumption of the Virgin) is a kaleidoscopic swirl of cherubs and whirling angels, while down in the southern transept, Benedetto Antelami's *Deposizione* (Descent from the Cross; 1178) relief is considered a masterpiece of its type.

⭐ **Battistero** BAPTISTRY

(Piazza del Duomo; adult/reduced €6/4, combined ticket with Museo Diocesano €7; ⊙ 9am-12.30pm & 3-6.30pm) Overshadowing even the cathedral, the octagonal pink-marble baptistery on the south side of the piazza is one of the most important such structures in Italy. Its architecture is a hybrid of Romanesque and Gothic, and its construction started in 1196 on the cusp of the two great architectural eras. The interior is particularly stunning, with its interplay of pencil thin marble columns and richly coloured 13th-century frescoes in the Byzantine style, interspersed at irregular intervals with statues and bas-reliefs.

Architect and sculptor Benedetto Antelami oversaw the project and it contains his best work, including a celebrated set of figures representing the months, seasons and signs of the zodiac. The baptistery wasn't completed until 1307 thanks to several interruptions, most notably when the supply of pink Verona marble ran out.

Pinacoteca Stuard MUSEUM

(Borgo del Parmigianino 2; adult/reduced €4/2; ⊙ 10am-5pm Mon & Wed-Fri, 10.30am-6pm Sat & Sun) Giuseppe Stuard was a 19th-century Parmese art collector who amassed

500 years worth of epoch-defining art linking the Tuscan masters of the 1300s to the *novecento* romantics. In 2002 the collection was moved into a wing of this 10th-century Benedictine monastery dedicated to St Paul, where it has been artfully laid out over 24 rooms on the site of an old Roman villa.

Museo Bocchi   MUSEUM

(☑ 0521 22 82 89; www.museobocchi.it; Via Cairoli; ⊙ 10.30am-1pm Tue-Sun) FREE Don't underestimate Amedeo Bocchi, a 20th-century Parma-born artist whose painting owes a debt to the symbolism of Gustav Klimt. This museum spreads his stirring work over six rooms. Most compelling are the impressionistic studies of his beloved daughter Bianca.

Museo Diocesano   MUSEUM

(Vicolo del Vescovado 3a; admission €5, combined ticket with Battistero €7; ⊙ 9am-12.30pm & 3-6.30pm) On the other side of the square to the Duomo, in the cellars of the former bishop's palace, this museum displays statuary. Highlights include a finely sculpted Solomon and Sheba, and a 5th-century early-Christian mosaic, which was discovered under Piazza del Duomo.

Chiesa & Monastero di San
Giovanni Evangelista   CHURCH

(www.monasterosangiovanni.com; Piazzale San Giovanni; ⊙ church 9am-noon & 3-6pm daily, monastery 9-11.45am & 3-5.30pm Mon-Wed, Fri & Sat) Directly behind the Duomo, this abbey church is noteworthy for its 16th-century mannerist facade and Correggio's magnificent frescoed dome, which was highly influential for its time and inspired many later works. The adjoining monastery is known as much for the oils and unguents that its monks produce as for its Renaissance cloisters. Upstairs, a library is adorned with huge old maps that hang from the walls of a musty reading room.

Palazzo della Pilotta   MUSEUM

(Piazza della Pilotta) Looming over the manicured lawns and modern fountains of Piazza della Pace, this monumental palace is hard to miss. Supposedly named after the Spanish ball game of *pelota* that was once played within its walls, it was originally built for the Farnese family between 1583 and 1622. Heavily bombed in WWII, it has since been largely rebuilt and today houses several museums.

The most important of these, the **Galleria Nazionale** (www.gallerianazionaleparma.it; adult/reduced incl Teatro Farnese €6/3; ⊙ 8.30am-7pm Tue-Sat, to 2pm Sun), displays Parma's main art collection. Alongside works by local artists Correggio and Parmigianino, you'll find paintings by Fra' Angelico, El Greco and a piece attributed to da Vinci. Before you get to the gallery, you'll pass through the **Teatro Farnese** (☑ 0521 23 33 09; Piazzale della Pilotta 15; adult/reduced €2/1, incl Galleria Nazionale €6/3; ⊙ 8.30am-7pm Tue-Sat, to 2pm Sun), a copy of Andrea Palladio's Teatro Olimpico in Vicenza. Constructed entirely out of wood, it was almost completely rebuilt after being bombed in WWII.

For a change of period, the **Museo Archeologico Nazionale** (☑ 0521 23 37 18; www.archeobologna.beniculturali.it/parma; adult/reduced €4/2; ⊙ 9am-4.30pm Tue-Fri, 1-7pm Sat & Sun) exhibits Roman artefacts discovered around Parma and Etruscan finds from the Po valley.

Piazza Garibaldi   PIAZZA

On the site of the ancient Roman forum, Piazza Garibaldi is Parma's cobbled hub bisected by the city's main east–west artery, Via Mazzini, and its continuation, Strada della Repubblica. On the square's north side, the facade of the 17th-century **Palazzo del Governatore** (Piazza Garibaldi), these days municipal offices, sports a giant sundial, added in 1829.

Behind the palace in the **Chiesa di Santa Maria della Steccata** (Via Garibaldi 5; ⊙ 9am-noon & 3-6pm) you'll find some of Parmigianino's most extraordinary work, notably the stunning, if rather faded, frescoes on the arches above the altar. Many members of the ruling Farnese and Bourbon families lie buried here.

Parco Ducale   PARK

(⊙ 6am-midnight Apr-Oct, 7am-8pm Nov-Mar) Stretching along the west bank of the Parma river, these formal gardens seem like Parma personified – refined, peaceful and with barely a blade of grass out of place. They were laid out in 1560 around the Farnese family's **Palazzo Ducale** (☑ 0521 50 81 84; Parco Ducale 3), which now serves as headquarters of the provincial *carabinieri* (military police).

Casa Natale di Toscanini   MUSEUM

(www.museotoscanini.it; Borgo R Tanzi 13; adult/reduced €2/1; ⊙ 9am-1pm Tue, 9am-1pm & 2-6pm Wed-Sat, 2-6pm Sun) At the Parco Ducale's southeast corner, the birthplace of Italy's greatest modern conductor, Arturo

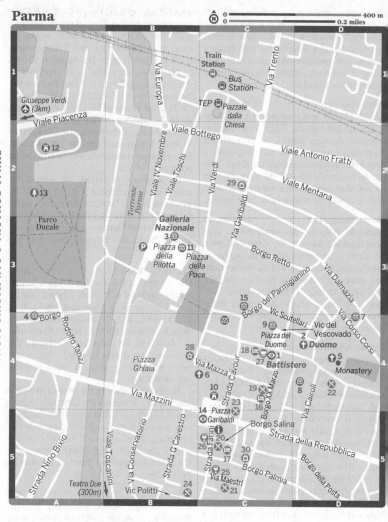

Parma

Toscanini (1867–1957), retraces his life and travels through relics and records. Of interest are his collaborations with acclaimed Italian tenor Aureliano Pertile.

La Casa del Suono MUSEUM
(www.casadelsuono.it; Piazzale Salvo d'Acquisto; adult/reduced €2/1; ⊙10am-2pm Wed-Fri, 10am-6pm Sat, 2-6pm Sun) Housed in the 17th-century Chiesa di Santa Elisabetta is this funky modern museum that focuses on the history of music technology. Review the 'ancient' 1970s tape recorders, ponder over jazz-age gramophones and stop to listen under a high-tech 'sonic chandelier'.

🛏 Sleeping

★B&B Pio B&B €
(☏ 347 776 90 65; www.piorooms.it; Borgo XX Marzo 14; s/d/q €70/80/120; 🛜) Location, comfort and hospitality all come together at this B&B run by a gregarious owner with a passion for local food and wine. Completely remodeled in 2013, four lower-floor doubles and a kitchenette-equipped upper floor suite share attractive features such as beamed ceilings, antique textiles and ultra-modern fixtures. All guests share access to a small but bright top-floor breakfast room.

Parma

Hotel Button HOTEL €
(☑ 0521 20 80 39; www.hotelbutton.it; Borgo Salina 7; s €60-80, d €80-100; ❋ @ ☎) It's easy to fall in love with the Button's simple charms: a perfect location in the heart of town, helpful front desk staff, made-to-order cappuccinos and fresh croissants (including surprisingly tasty wholegrain ones) at breakfast, spacious rooms, and a quiet sense of order and cleanliness. The low-end price tag is just icing on the cake.

Palazzo dalla Rosa Prati BOUTIQUE HOTEL €€€
(☑ 0521 38 64 29; www.palazzodallarosaprati.co.uk; Piazza del Duomo 7; r €95-140, ste €120-290, apt €130-350; ❋ ☎) Kick back like Marie Antoinette in regal digs right next to Parma cathedral. Choose among six posh and palatial renovated historic suites, ten modern apartments and one smaller, less expensive double. Corner suite 5 is especially alluring, with views into the baptistery's upper window directly across the street. Downstairs, sip wine or coffee at the modish **T-Cafe** (Strada Duomo 7; ◷ 8am-9pm Sun-Thu, to 10pm Fri & Sat).

 Eating

Parma specialities need no introduction to anyone familiar with the food of planet Earth. Both *prosciutto di Parma* (Parma ham) and *parmigiano reggiano* make ex-

cellent antipasto plates accompanied by a good Sangiovese red.

★ **Trattoria del Tribunale** TRATTORIA €
(www.trattoriadeltribunale.it; Vicolo Politi 5; meals €19-25; ◷ noon-2.30pm & 7-11pm) Run the gauntlet of ham slicers and waiters gouging lumps of *parmigiano reggiano* and settle in for a memorable meal. Start with a plate of Parma ham, proceed to the *degustazione di tortelli* (pasta pockets stuffed with chard, pumpkin and artichokes), and finish with *parmigiana di melanzane* (eggplant Parmesan) or, if you dare, *vecchia di cavallo* (horse-meat hash, a popular local dish made with minced horse meat, olive oil, onions, peppers, basil, tomatoes, celery and potatoes). Pure Parma!

Pepèn SANDWICHES €
(Borgo Sant'Ambrogio 2; sandwiches €5; ◷ 8.30am-7.30pm Tue-Sat) Join the throngs of locals pouring into this buzzing little sandwich shop, where *panini* get piled high with *prosciutto di Parma*, cheeses and countless other tasty ingredients. After seven decades, it's a dearly beloved Parma institution.

Borgo 20 MODERN ITALIAN €
(☑ 0521 23 45 65; www.borgo20.it; Borgo XX Marzo 14/16; meals €23; ◷ noon-3pm & 7.30-11pm Wed-Sun) Chef Roberto Pongolini (Michelin-

starred at his previous venture, La Cantinetta in Felino) recently downsized to create this wonderful contemporary bistro in the city centre, creating inventive culinary treats from Parma's classic local ingredients. Order à la carte from the chalkboard menu of daily specials, or let Roberto surprise you with his three-course tasting menu (€23).

Gallo d'Oro TRADITIONAL ITALIAN €€
(☑0521 20 88 46; www.gallodororistorante.it; Borgo Salina 3; meals €23-31; ☺noon-2.30pm & 7.30-11pm) Young *camerieri* (waiters) operate meat slicers, slide dexterously between tables and plonk down plates of ravioli and veal done all ways (all of them good) in the inauspiciously named 'golden chicken'. Magazine covers adorn the walls at this small bistro and the whole place emits a calm agreeable energy.

Osteria dello Zingaro OSTERIA €€
(☑0521 20 74 83; www.osteriadellozingaro.it; Borgo del Correggio 5b; meals €25-30; ☺noon-2.30pm & 7-10.30pm Mon-Sat) Hidden behind the cathedral is this local favourite. It's most famous for its horse meat (a Parma speciality), but you can also indulge in superb regional classics like *tortelli di erbette* (spinach-and-parmesan-filled pasta pockets) and *salumi misti* (six varieties of cured Parma pork), or veg out with an *insalatona pere e formaggio* (giant salad with pear, walnuts and sheep's cheese).

Osteria del Gesso EMILIAN €€
(☑0521 23 05 05; www.osteriadelgesso.it; Via Maestri 11; meals €30-35; ☺8-10.15pm Thu, 12.30-2.15pm & 8-10.15pm Fri-Tue, closed Sat & Sun summer) A familiar Italian story: family-run restaurant, great local food, charming romantic interior, laid-back (OK, slow) service and bags of atmosphere and tradition. Like most Parma restaurants, Gesso doesn't play up to tourists – it just performs naturally for people who love fantastic simple food.

🍷 Drinking & Nightlife

⭐Tabarro BAR
(www.tabarro.net; Strada Farini 5b; ☺6pm-midnight Sun-Thu, to 2am Fri & Sat) In the heart of Parma's animated Strada Farini drinking scene is this classy but friendly wine bar with tiled floors and copper counters. In warm weather, aficionados crowd the street out front, sipping fine vintages at barrels draped with tablecloths. For some fine people-watching, grab one of the pavement tables tucked across the street on Borgo Salina.

Enoteca Fontana BAR
(☑0521 28 60 37; Strada Farini 24a; ☺noon-8pm Tue-Sat) A loud, elbow-in-the-ribs type of wine bar (it gets busy!) with some tables in a room out back where you can sip wine and munch grilled *panini* while making a local friend or three.

☆ Entertainment

There are few better places in Italy to see live opera, concerts and theatre.

Teatro Regio THEATRE
(☑0521 20 39 99; www.teatroregioparma.org; Via Garibaldi 16a) Offers a particularly rich program of music and opera, even by exacting Italian standards.

Teatro Due THEATRE
(☑0521 23 02 42; www.teatrodue.org; Viale Basetti 12a) Presents the city's top drama.

🛍 Shopping

Salumeria Grisenti FOOD
(www.salumeriagrisenti.com; Borgo Giacomo Tommasini 7; ☺8.30am-1.15pm & 4.30-8pm Mon-Wed, Fri & Sat, 8.30am-1.15pm Thu) It may be smaller than some Parma delis, but this place has the triple distinction of central location, fastidious attention to quality, and continuous ownership by the same family since its founding in 1952.

Salumeria Garibaldi FOOD
(Via Garibaldi 42; ☺8am-8pm Mon-Sat) Tempting new visitors just steps from the train station is this bountiful delicatessen dating to 1829, with dangling sausages, shelves of Lambrusco wines, slabs of Parma ham and wheel upon wheel of *parmigiano reggiano*.

ℹ Information

Police Station (☑0521 21 94; Borgo della Posta 14)
Post Office (Via Melloni 4B)
Tourist Office (☑0521 21 88 89; www.turismo.comune.parma.it; Piazza Garibaldi; ☺1-7pm Mon, 9am-7pm Tue-Sat, 9am-1pm & 2-6pm Sun)

ℹ Getting There & Away

Parma's **Giuseppe Verdi Airport** (☑0521 95 15 11; www.parma-airport.it; Via Licinio Ferretti) is a mere 3km from the city centre. Ryanair offers thrice-weekly flights to London Stansted, along with service to Trapani and Cagliari. Bus 6 links to the train station.

From Piazzale dalla Chiesa in front of Parma's train station, **TEP** (☑ 0521 21 41; www.tep.pr.it) operates buses throughout the region.

Parma is on the A1 connecting Bologna and Milan, and just east of the A15, which runs to La Spezia. Via Emilia (SS9) passes right through town.

There are trains once or twice hourly to Milan (regional/express €10.70/23, 1¼ to 1¾ hours), Bologna (€7.10, one to 1¼ hours), Modena (€5.20, 30 minutes) and Piacenza (€5.20, 40 minutes, half-hourly).

🛈 Getting Around

Traffic is banned from the historic centre, so park your car just outside at **Parcheggio Toschi** (www.apcoa.it/parking-in/parma/toschi.html; per hr/24hr €1.90/10.70; ⊘ 24hr) and rent a bike next door at **Parma Punto Bici** (punto bici@infomobility.pr.it; Viale Toschi 2; bike rental per hr/24hr/48hr €0.70/10/15, tandem €1.80/20/30; ⊘ 9am-1pm & 3-7pm Mon-Sat, 10am-1pm & 2.30-7.30pm Sun). Alternatively, if staying overnight in the city centre, ask your hotel for a parking pass, which will allow you to drive and park in Parma's ZTL (Limited Traffic Zone).

Busseto & Verdi Country

During the 'golden age of opera' in the second half of the 19th century, only Wagner came close to emulating Giuseppe Verdi, Italy's operatic genius who was born in the tiny village of Roncole Verdi in 1813. You can discover his extraordinary legacy starting in the town of Busseto (35km northwest of Parma), a pleasant place with enough sights for a decent musical day out.

◎ Sights

★ **Museo Nazionale Giuseppe Verdi**　　　MUSEUM
(www.museogiuseppeverdi.it; Via Provesi 35; adult/reduced €9/7; ⊘ 10am-6.30pm Tue-Sun Apr-Oct, shorter hours Nov-Mar) Take a trip through the rooms of this fine country-mansion-turned-museum on the outskirts of the small town of Busseto, which cleverly maps out the story of Verdi's life through paintings, music and audio guides (included in the price). As you explore, you'll undoubtedly recognise numerous stanzas from classic operas such as *Il Trovatore* and *Aida*, still fresh after two centuries.

Teatro Verdi　　　THEATRE
(Piazza Verdi; adult/reduced €4/3; ⊘ 9.30am-12.30pm & 3-6pm Tue-Sun Apr-Oct, to 5pm Nov-Mar) This stately theatre on Busseto's aptly named Piazza Verdi was built in 1868, although Verdi himself initially pooh-poohed the idea. It opened with a performance of his masterpiece *Rigoletto*.

Casa Natale di Giuseppe Verdi　　　MUSEUM
(www.casanataleverdi.it; Via della Processione 1, Roncole Verdi; adult/reduced €5/4; ⊘ 9.30am-1pm & 2.30-6pm Tue-Sun Apr-Oct, shorter hours Nov-Mar) The humble cottage where Giuseppe Verdi was born in 1813 is now a small museum. Grab a tablet at the entrance to take advantage of recently introduced multimedia exhibits highlighting the composer's life and music. It's in the hamlet of Roncole Verdi, 5km southeast of Busseto.

Casa Barezzi　　　MUSEUM
(www.museocasabarezzi.it; Via Roma 119, Busseto; adult/reduced €4/3; ⊘ 10am-12.30pm & 3-6.30pm Tue-Sun) This museum in the centre of Busseto is encased in the home of composer Verdi's patron and was the site of Verdi's first concert. It's lovingly curated and filled with Verdi memorabilia including papers, furnishings and valuable recordings.

Villa Verdi　　　MUSEUM
(www.villaverdi.org; Via Verdi 22, S Agata di Villanova sull'Arda; adult/reduced €9/5; ⊘ 9.30-11.45am & 2.30-6.15pm Tue-Sun Apr-Oct, shorter hours Nov-Mar) Verdi's villa, where he composed many of his major works, is 5km northwest of Busseto. Verdi lived and worked here from 1851 onwards. Guided visits through the furnishings and musical instruments should be booked in advance online.

🛈 Information

Busseto Tourist Office (☑ 0524 9 24 87; www.bussetolive.com; Piazza Verdi 10, Busseto; ⊘ 9.30am-1pm & 3-5.30pm Tue-Sun) Sells combo tickets for the Casa Natale, Casa Barezzi and Teatro Verdi for €10, or Villa Verdi plus Casa Barezzi for €11.

🛈 Getting There & Away

Train service from Parma to Busseto (€3.75, 30 to 45 minutes) requires a change in Fidenza. Alternatively, **TEP** (www.tep.pr.it; Piazzale Carlo Alberto della Chiesa; ⊘ 8.10am-12.50pm & 2.15-4.40pm Mon-Fri) offers direct but slow bus service between the two towns (1½ hours, one to three daily) on its route 2106.

EMILIA-ROMAGNA & SAN MARINO BUSSETO & VERDI COUNTRY

Piacenza

POP 100,300

Named 'pleasant place' (Placentia) by the Romans, Piacenza soon proved itself to be an important strategic location as well. Just short of the regional border with Lombardy, the contemporary city is perfect day-trip fodder. Its picturesque centre reveals a beautiful Gothic town hall and a couple of august churches.

⊙ Sights

Piazza dei Cavalli
PIAZZA

Dominated by Palazzo Gotico, the impressive 13th-century town hall, Piacenza's main square is named after its two baroque equestrian statues, cast by the Tuscan sculptor Francesco Mochi between 1612 and 1625. Depicted here are the Farnese dukes Alessandro and Ranuccio, gallantly seated astride martial bronze horses.

Duomo
CATHEDRAL

(Piazza del Duomo 33; ⊙ 7am-noon & 4-7pm) An ultra-dark church even by Italian standards, Piacenza's cold, dungeonlike cathedral is classic Romanesque. If you can strain your eyes hard enough, you'll make out the two-dozen pillars that hold up the roof and the heavenly frescoes by Morazzone and Guercino that adorn it. One of a trio of classic Romanesque cathedrals in Emilia, it rose (like Parma's) from the ruins of the devastating 1117 earthquake.

Ricci Oddi Galleria d'Arte Moderna
GALLERY

(☑ 0523 32 07 42; www.riccioddi.it; Via San Siro 13; adult/reduced €5/3.50; ⊙ 9.30am-12.30pm & 3-6pm Tue-Fri & Sun, 9.30am-12.30pm & 4-10pm Sat) Piacenza's hidden secret is this modern art collection amassed by local aficionado, Ricci Oddi, in the early 20th century. Well-lit and cleverly laid out over a purpose-built gallery, the collection catalogues various artistic schools (Emilian, Lombard) and stylistic movements (symbolism, *novecento*) from the 1830s to the 1930s. Jumping out at you are Giovanni Boldini's *Ritratto di Signora* and Amedeo Bocchi's light-filled *La Colazione del Mattino*.

Palazzo Farnese
MUSEUM

(www.musei.piacenza.it; Piazza Cittadella 29; adult/reduced €6/4.50; ⊙ 10am-1pm & 3-6pm Tue-Thu, to 7pm Fri-Sun) On the northern edge of the *centro storico* (historic centre), this vast palace was started in 1558 but never fully completed. It now houses the Pinacoteca, an art gallery, along with minor museums of archaeology, carriages, Italian unification and ceramics.

❶ Information

Tourist Office (☑ 0523 49 20 01; www.comune.piacenza.it; Piazza dei Cavalli 10; ⊙ 10am-1pm & 3-7pm) Handily placed in central Piazza dei Cavalli.

❶ Getting There & Around

There are half-hourly trains to/from Milan (regular/high-speed €6.70/14, 45 minutes to one hour), Parma (€5.20/11.50, 25 to 40 minutes) and Bologna (€10.70/22.50, 1¼ to two hours).

Piacenza is just off the A1 linking Milan and Bologna and the A21 joining Brescia and Turin. Via Emilia (SS9) also runs past on its way to Rimini and the Adriatic Sea.

SETA (☑ 840 000216; www.setaweb.it) runs frequent buses between the train station and Piazza dei Cavalli (€1.20, five minutes).

Ferrara

POP 135,000

A heavyweight Renaissance art city peppered with colossal palaces and still ringed by its intact medieval walls, Ferrara jumps out at you like an absconded Casanova (he once stayed here) on the route between Bologna and Venice. But, like any city situated in close proximity to *La Serenissima*, it is continually overlooked. As a result, Venice avoiders will find Ferrara's bike-friendly streets and frozen-in-time *palazzi* relatively unexplored and deliciously tranquil.

Historically Ferrara was once the domain of the powerful Este clan, rivals to Florence's Medici in power and prestige, who endowed the city with its signature building – a huge castle complete with moat positioned slap-bang in the city centre. Ferrara suffered damage from bombing raids during WWII, but its historical core remains intact. Of particular interest is the former Jewish ghetto, the region's largest and oldest, which prevailed from 1627 until 1859.

⊙ Sights

Renaissance palaces reborn as museums are Ferrara's tour de force. Also check out the intricate old town with its one-time Jewish ghetto. Note that most museums are closed on Monday.

If you're sticking around for a while, you'll save money with a **MyFE Ferrara Tourist Card** (www.myfecard.it/en; 2-/3-/6-day card €10/12/18), which offers free museum admissions, exemption from Ferrara's hotel tourist tax and discounts at some hotels and restaurants.

⭐ **Castello Estense**   CASTLE
(www.castelloestense.it;   Viale   Cavour; adult/reduced €8/6; ☺ 9.30am-5.30pm Tue-Sun Sep-May, 9am-1.30pm & 3-7pm Tue-Sun Jun-Aug) Complete with moat and drawbridge, Ferrara's towering castle was commissioned by Nicolò II d'Este in 1385. Initially it was intended to protect him and his family from the town's irate citizenry, who were up in arms over tax increases, but in the late 15th century it became the family's permanent residence. Although sections are now used as government offices, a few rooms, including the royal suites, are open for viewing.

Highlights are the **Sala dei Giganti** (Giants' Room), **Salone dei Giochi** (Games Salon), **Cappella di Renée de France** and the claustrophobic **dungeon**. It was here in 1425 that Duke Nicolò III d'Este had his young second wife, Parisina Malatesta, and his son, Ugo, beheaded after discovering they were lovers, providing the inspiration for Robert Browning's 'My Last Duchess'.

Linked to the castle by an elevated passageway, the 13th-century crenellated **Palazzo Municipale** (admission free; ☺ 9am-2pm Mon-Fri) was the Este family home until they moved next door to the castle. Nowadays, it's largely occupied by administrative offices but you can wander around its twin courtyards.

⭐ **Palazzo dei Diamanti**   PALACE, MUSEUM
(Corso Ercole I d'Este 21) Named after the spiky diamond-shaped ashlar stones on its facade, the late-15th-century 'diamond palace' was built for Sigismondo d'Este. It houses Ferrara's **Pinacoteca Nazionale** (www.pinacoteca ferrara.it; Corso Ercole I d'Este 21; adult/reduced €4/2; ☺ 9am-2pm Tue-Sun, to 7pm Thu), where you can contemplate the genius of the 16th- to 17th-century 'Ferrara school', spearheaded by artists with odd nicknames such as Guercino (the squinter) and Il Maestro degli Occhi Spalancati (master of the wide-open eyes). Free audio guides enhance the experience. High-profile special exhibits are held in the adjacent **Spazio Espositivo** (adult/reduced €11/9; ☺ 10am-8pm).

FERRARA'S CITY WALLS

Only Lucca in Tuscany can claim a more complete set of walls than Ferrara, though with a total circumference of 9km, Ferrara's are longer. Adorned with a well-marked set of paths, unbroken on the northern and eastern sections, the walls make a pleasant walking or cycling loop.

Duomo   CATHEDRAL
(Piazza Cattedrale; ☺ 7.30am-noon & 3.30-6.30pm Mon-Sat, 7.30am-12.30pm & 3.30-7pm Sun) The outstanding feature of the pink-and-white 12th-century cathedral is its three-tiered marble facade, combining Romanesque and Gothic styles on the lower and upper tiers respectively. Much of the upper level is a graphic representation of *The Last Judgment*, and heaven and hell (notice the four figures clambering out of their coffins). Astride a pair of handsome lions on either side of the main doorway squats an oddly secular duo, mouths agape at the effort of holding up the pillars.

Museo della Cattedrale   MUSEUM
(www.artecultura.fe.it/152; Via San Romano; adult/reduced €6/3; ☺ 9.30am-1pm & 3-6pm Tue-Sun) This museum houses various artefacts from Ferrara's Duomo, including a serene *Madonna* by Jacopo della Quercia, a couple of vigorous Cosimo Tura canvases, and some witty bas-reliefs illustrating the months of the year.

Museo del Risorgimento e della Resistenza   MUSEUM
(www.artecultura.fe.it/147; Corso Ercole I d'Este 19; adult/reduced €4/2; ☺ 9.30am-1pm & 3-6pm Tue-Sun) Next door to Pinacoteca Nazionale, this small museum exhibits documents, proclamations and posters from the Italian unification movement and WWII, as well as numerous uniforms, guns and hand grenades.

Casa Romei   PALACE, MUSEUM
(Via Savonarola 30; adult/reduced €3/1.50; ☺ 8.30am-2pm Sun-Wed, 2-7.30pm Thu-Sat) This palace was once owned by Giovanni Romei, a top administrator to the Este clan – and his importance shows in the architecture. The austere brick exterior hides a peaceful inner patio (once part of an adjacent monastery). On the 1st floor is a 16th-century apartment

Ferrara

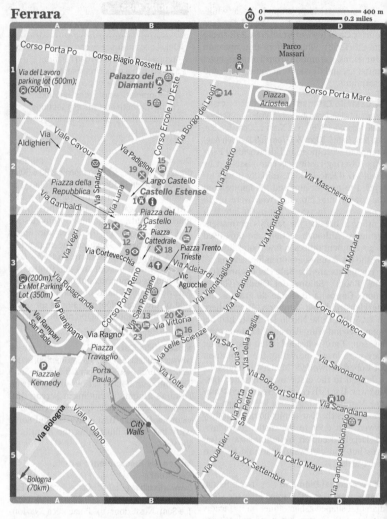

preserved in its original state. There's plenty of art and frescoes dotted around.

Palazzo Schifanoia
PALACE, MUSEUM

(www.artecultura.fe.it/159; Via Scandiana 23; adult/reduced €3/2; ⊙9.30am-6pm Tue-Sun) Dating to 1385, the Este's 14th-century pleasure palace suffered significant earthquake damage in May 2012, but its highlight – the Salone dei Mesi (Room of the Months) – remains open to visitors. Inside you'll find Ferrara's most famous frescoes, executed by Francesco del Cossa in 1470, which depict the months, seasons and signs of the zodiac and constitute

an exceptionally fine and cohesive example of secular Renaissance art.

Covered by the same ticket is the nearby Museo Lapidario (Via Camposabbionario; ⊙9.30am-6pm Tue-Sun), with its small collection of Roman and Etruscan stele, tombs and inscriptions.

Palazzo Massari
PALACE, MUSEUM

(Corso Porta Mare 9) This early Renaissance palace houses three museums: the Museo Giovanni Boldini, dedicated solely to Ferrara-born Giovanni Boldini; the Museo dell'Ottocento, focusing on 19th-

Ferrara

century art; and the **Museo d'Arte Moderna e Contemporanea Filippo de Pisis**, half of which is devoted to its namesake modern Ferraranese painter. Unfortunately, due to damage sustained during Emilia-Romagna's 2012 earthquake, the palace will remain closed at least until 2017. In the meantime, many of Boldini's and di Pisis' works are on display at the Castello Estense.

🎎 Festivals & Events

Il Palio   SPORTS
(www.paliodiferrara.it; ⊗ May) On the last Sunday of May each year, the eight *contrade* (districts) of Ferrara compete in a horse race that momentarily turns Piazza Ariostea into medieval bedlam. Claimed to be the oldest race of its kind in Italy, Ferrara's Palio was first held in 1259, and was officially enshrined as an annual competition in 1279.

🛏 Sleeping

Le Stanze di Torcicoda   B&B €
(☑ 380 9068718; www.lestanze.it; Vicolo Mozzo Torcicoda 9; s €55-70, d €80-100; ❄🕾) Tucked down a crooked lane in Ferrara's old Jewish quarter, this cosy, long-established B&B offers four rooms of varying sizes in a late 14th-century house. Owner Pietro Zanni keeps things environmentally friendly with organic-leaning breakfasts, green cleaning products and services for cyclists including an enclosed bike garage.

Locanda Borgonuovo   B&B €
(☑ 0532 21 11 00; www.borgonuovo.com; Via Cairoli 29; s €60-70, d €90-100; P❄🕾) Just around the corner from the Duomo, this little gem is Italy's oldest B&B. Four refined rooms

and three apartments, each decorated with antiques, come with polished wood floors, minibars, safes, flat-screen TVs and wi-fi. Enjoy breakfast in the elegant upstairs sitting room, or retire to the frondy central patio. Parking costs €10, and guests have free access to bikes.

Albergo degli Artisti   GUESTHOUSE €
(☑ 0532 76 10 38; www.albergoartisti.it; Via Vittoria 66; s/d €40/60, without bathroom €28/50; 🕾) Ferrara's most economical option offers immaculate rooms at an unbeatable price on a back alley within a five-minute walk of the Duomo and Castello Estense. Attractive common spaces include a sunny upstairs terrace and a teeny but cheerful guest kitchen. Book ahead for the three rooms with bathroom. No breakfast.

★ Alchimia B&B   B&B €€
(☑ 0532 186 46 56; www.alchimiaferrara.it; Via Borgo dei Leoni 122; s €70-80, d €110-120; P❄@🕾) Occupying a lovingly remodelled 15th-century home with a spacious, green backyard, this classy six-room B&B seamlessly blends beamed high ceilings with modern comforts such as memory-foam beds, electric tea kettles, state-of-the-art bathrooms, fantastic air-con, rock-solid wi-fi and self-serve wine fridges. Local artists' work graces the walls, guests get free parking and loaner bikes, and pets stay free.

Albergo Annunziata   HOTEL €€
(☑ 0532 20 11 11; www.annunziata.it; Piazza della Repubblica 5; r €94-194, ste €134-204; P❄@🕾) At this top-notch, centrally located four-star hotel, romantics can be forgiven for having Casanova apparitions (the man himself once

stayed here). Six of the sharp modernist rooms with mosaic bathrooms come with direct views of Castello Estense. Guests enjoy free use of bikes, along with a breakfast that's often described as Italy's best, while kids love the complimentary table football.

Hotel de Prati HOTEL €€
(☑ 0532 24 19 05; www.hoteldeprati.com; Via Padiglioni 5; s €50-85, d €80-120, ste €120-150; ❄) Smarter than the average three-star hotel, de Prati charms with its central location, antique furniture and friendly owner. Wrought-iron bedsteads reign upstairs while downstairs public rooms are enlivened by contemporary art.

 ## Eating

Like all Emilian cities, Ferrara has its gastronomic nuances. Don't leave town without trying *cappellacci di zucca*, a hat-shaped pasta pouch filled with pumpkin and herbs, and brushed with sage and butter. Delicious! *Salama da sugo* is a stewed pork sausage, while *pasticcio di maccheroni* is an oven-baked macaroni pie topped with Parmesan. Even Ferrarese bread is distinctive, shaped into a crunchy twisted knot.

★ **Osteria del Ghetto** OSTERIA €€
(☑ 0532 76 49 36; www.osteriadelghetto.it; Via Vittoria 26; meals €25-30; ☺ noon-2.30pm & 7.30-10.30pm Tue-Sun) An understated jewel amid the winding streets of Ferrara's old Jewish ghetto, this *osteria* leads you through a nondescript downstairs bar up to a bright upstairs dining room embellished with striking modern murals. The excellent menu mixes Ferrara staples like *cappellacci di zucca* with a less-predictable fish menu.

Trattoria da Noemi TRATTORIA €€
(☑ 0532 76 90 70; www.trattoriadanoemi.it; Via Ragno 31a; meals €28-35; ☺ noon-3pm & 7.30-11pm Wed-Mon) All of Ferrara's classic dishes are delivered *con molto amore* (with much love) at this back-alley eatery named after the hardworking, independent-spirited mother of proprietor Maria Cristina Borgazzi. Arrive early (yes, it's busy) to get some of the city's best *cappellacci di zucca*, grilled meats and macaroni pie. Enough said!

Osteria Quattro Angeli TRADITIONAL ITALIAN €€
(☑ 0532 21 18 69; www.osteriaquattroangeli.it; Piazza Castello 10; meals €27; ☺ 8am-1am Tue-Sun) Relax beneath fat, sausage-shaped salamis opposite the castle and demolish enormous portions of Ferrara classics supplement-

ed by cuts of local cured meat. Come 6pm, the tented section out front becomes a busy *aperitivi* bar, upping the noise levels and heightening the atmosphere.

Osteria Savonarola OSTERIA €€
(☑ 0532 20 02 14; Piazza Savonarola 18; meals €23-31; ☺ 12.30-3.30pm & 7pm-midnight Tue-Sun) Friendly, efficient service and outdoor seating on an arcaded pavement with prime Castello Estense views make this an enjoyable warm-weather spot for lunch or dinner. The menu is classically Ferrarese, and prices are easy on the wallet.

Al Brindisi OSTERIA €€
(www.albrindisi.net; Via Adelardi 11; meals €15-50; ☺ 11am-midnight Tue-Sun) The oldest *osteria* in the world (according to Guinness), this scruffy-meets-stylish wine bar was already an established drinking den in 1435. Titian drank here, while the soon-to-be Pope John Paul II dropped by 550 years later. Succinct pasta dishes are well supplemented by wine drawn from racks that are thick with a healthy coating of Ferrara dust.

Il Don Giovanni GASTRONOMIC €€€
(☑ 0532 24 33 63; www.ildongiovanni.com; Corso Ercole I d'Este 1; meals €55-70; ☺ 8-10pm Mon, 12.30-2pm & 8-10pm Tue-Sat) This highly acclaimed eatery specialises in fresh-caught fish from the Adriatic, vegetables harvested from the restaurant's own garden, eight varieties of bread baked daily and a wine list featuring over 600 Italian and international labels. The menu is an imaginative feast of unconventional concoctions; guinea-fowl-stuffed pasta and roast eel stand out.

ⓘ Information

Police Station (☑ 0532 29 43 11; Corso Ercole I d'Este 26)

Post Office (Viale Cavour 27)

Tourist Office (☑ 0532 20 93 70; www.ferrarainfo.com; ☺ 9am-6pm Sep-May, 9am-1.30pm & 2.30-6pm Jun-Aug) In Castello Estense's courtyard.

ⓘ Getting There & Around

Ferrara Bus & Fly (☑ 0532 194 44 44; www.ferrarabusandfly.it) offers direct transfers eight times daily between Bologna's Guglielmo Marconi airport and Ferrara (€15, one hour).

From Ferrara's train station, 1.5km west of the centre, trains run frequently to Bologna (€4.60, 30 to 50 minutes, half-hourly), Ravenna (€6.40, one to 1½ hours, hourly) and other destinations throughout Emilia-Romagna.

TPER (☑ 0532 59 94 11; www.tper.it) operates frequent local buses along Viale Cavour between the train station and the centre (€1.50, five minutes). For Castello Estense, get off at Cavour Giardini.

Most traffic is banned from the city centre. Free 24-hour parking is available at the **Ex Mof** (cnr Corso Isonzo & Via Darsena) and **Via del Lavoro** (Via del Lavoro) parking lots (south of the *centro storico* and behind the train station, respectively). For a comprehensive list of parking options, see www.ferraratua.com.

Get in the saddle and join the hundreds of other pedallers in one of Italy's most cycle-friendly cities. Many places, such as **Pirani e Bagni** (☑ 0532 77 21 90; Piazzale Stazione 2; bike rental per hr/3hr/day €2/5/7; ⊘ 4.45am-8pm Mon-Fri) beside the train station and **Ferrara Store** (www.ferrara-store.it/bike-rental-in-ferrara. html; Piazza della Repubblica 23/25; per hour/day €2.50/10; ⊘ 7.30am-7pm) near Castello Estense, rent bikes. The tourist office can provide info on the region's well-developed network of bike routes; look for the spiral-bound *Bike Book*, which details itineraries throughout Ferrara and the Po Delta.

Ravenna

POP 160,000

For mosaic lovers, Ravenna is an earthly paradise. Spread out over several churches and baptisteries around town is one of the world's most dazzling collections of early Christian mosaic artwork, enshrined since 1996 on Unesco's World Heritage list. Wandering through the unassuming town centre today, you'd never imagine that for a three-century span beginning in 402, Ravenna served as capital of the Western Roman Empire, chief city of the Ostrogoth Kingdom of Italy and nexus of a powerful Byzantine exarchate. During this prolonged golden age, while the rest of the Italian peninsula flailed in the wake of Barbarian invasions, Ravenna became a fertile art studio for skilled craftsmen, who covered the city's terracotta brick churches in heart-rendingly beautiful mosaics.

Ravenna's brilliant 4th- to 6th-century gold, emerald and sapphire masterpieces will leave you struggling for adjectives. A suitably impressed Dante once described them as a 'symphony of colour' and spent the last few years of his life admiring them. Romantic toff Lord Byron added further weight to Ravenna's literary credentials when he spent a couple of years here before decamping to Greece.

◎ Sights

Ravenna revolves around its eight Unesco World Heritage Sites (seven scattered about town, one 5km to the southeast). A *biglietto cumulativo* (combo ticket, €9.50) grants access to five of the sites: San Vitale, Galla Placidia, Sant-Apollinare Nuovo, Museo Arcivescovile and Battistero Neoniano. Two others (Sant'Apollinare in Classe and Mausoleo di Teodorico) require individual tickets, while the Battistero degli Ariani is free. The website www.ravennamosaici.it gives more information.

★**Basilica di San Vitale**　　　CHURCH
(Via Fiandrini; 5-site combo ticket €9.50; ⊘ 9am-7pm Apr-Sep, 9am-5.30pm Mar & Oct, 9.30am-5pm Nov-Feb) Sometimes, after weeks of trolling around dark Italian churches, you can lose your sense of wonder. Not here! The lucid mosaics that adorn the altar of this ancient church consecrated in 547 by Archbishop Massimiano invoke a sharp intake of breath in most visitors. Gaze in wonder at the rich greens, brilliant golds and deep blues bathed in shafts of soft yellow sunlight.

The mosaics on the side and end walls inside the church represent scenes from the Old Testament: to the left, Abraham prepares to sacrifice Isaac in the presence of three angels, while the one on the right portrays the death of Abel and the offering of Melchizedek. Inside the chancel, two magnificent mosaics depict the Byzantine emperor Justinian with San Massimiano and a particularly solemn and expressive Empress Theodora, who was his consort.

★**Mausoleo di Galla Placidia**　　　HISTORIC BUILDING
(Via Fiandrini; 5-site combo ticket €9.50, plus summer-only surcharge €2; ⊘ 9am-7pm Apr-Sep, 9am-5.30pm Mar & Oct, 9.30am-5pm Nov-Feb) In the same complex as Basilica di San Vitale, the small but equally incandescent Mausoleo di Galla Placidia was constructed for Galla Placidia, the half-sister of Emperor Honorius, who initiated construction of many of Ravenna's grandest buildings. The mosaics here are the oldest in Ravenna, probably dating from around AD 430.

★**Basilica di Sant'Apollinare Nuovo**　　　CHURCH
(Via di Roma; 5-site combo ticket €9.50; ⊘ 9am-7pm Apr-Sep, 9.30am-5.30pm Mar & Oct, 10am-5pm Nov-Feb) An old legend states that Pope Gregory the Great once ordered the

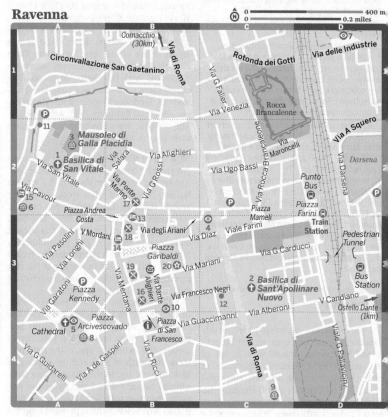

Ravenna

Apollinare's mosaics to be blackened as they were distracting worshippers from prayer. A millennium and a half later, the dazzling Christian handiwork is still having the same effect. It's almost impossible to take your eyes off the 26 white-robed martyrs heading towards Christ with his Apostles on the right (south) wall. On the opposite side, an equally expressive procession of virgins bears similar offerings for the Madonna.

The basilica dates originally from the 560s and its architectural fusion of Christian east and west can be seen in its marble porticoes and distinctive conical bell tower.

Museo Arcivescovile   MUSEUM
(Piazza Arcivescovado; 5-site combo ticket €9.50; ⊙9am-7pm Apr-Sep, 9.30am-5.30pm Mar & Oct, 10am-5pm Nov-Feb) A museum with a difference, this religious gem is on the 2nd floor of the Archiepiscopal Palace. It hides two not-to-be-missed exhibits: an exquisite ivory throne carved for Emperor Maximilian by Byzantium craftsmen in the 6th century (the surviving detail is astounding); and the stunning collection of mosaics in the 5th-century chapel of San Andrea, which has been cleverly incorporated into the museum's plush modern interior.

Battistero Neoniano   RELIGIOUS SITE
(Piazza del Duomo; 5-site combo ticket €9.50; ⊙9am-7pm Apr-Sep, 9.30am-5.30pm Mar & Oct, 10am-5pm Nov-Feb) Roman ruins aside, this is Ravenna's oldest intact building, constructed over the site of a former Roman baths' complex in the late 4th century. Built in an octagonal shape, as was the custom with all Christian baptisteries of this period, it was originally attached to a church (since destroyed). The mosaics, which thematically depict Christ being baptised by St John the Baptist in the River Jordan, were added at the end of the 5th century.

★ Basilica di Sant'Apollinare in Classe   CHURCH
(Via Romea Sud; adult/reduced €5/2.50, Sun morning free; ⊙8.30am-7.30pm) This signature early Christian basilica, lighter than Ravenna's other churches, is situated 5km southeast of town in the former Roman port of Classe. Its magnificent central apse mosaic, featuring Ravenna's patron Sant'Apollinare flanked by sheep juxtaposed against a stunningly green landscape, is surmounted by a brilliant star-spangled triumphal arch displaying symbols of the four evangelists.

Other mosaics in the apse depict Byzantine Emperor Constantine IV (652–685) and biblical figures such as Abel and Abraham. The basilica – architecturally the city's most 'perfect' – was built in the early 6th century on the burial site of Ravenna's patron saint, who converted the city to Christianity in the 2nd century.

To get here, take a local train to Classe (€1.30, five minutes), one stop in the direction of Rimini, or catch bus 4 opposite the train station.

Mausoleo di Teodorico   TOMB
(Via delle Industrie 14; adult/reduced €4/2; ⊙8.30am-5.30pm Oct-Mar, to 7pm Apr-Sep) Historically and architecturally distinct from Ravenna's other Unesco sites (there are no mosaics here), this two-storey mausoleum was built in 520 for Gothic king Teodorico, who ruled Italy as a Byzantine viceroy. It is notable for its Gothic design features and throwback Roman construction techniques: the huge blocks of stone were not cemented by any mortar. At the heart of the mausoleum is a Roman porphyry basin recycled as a sarcophagus. It's 2km from the city centre; take bus 5.

Battistero degli Ariani   BAPTISTERY
(Via degli Ariani; ⊙8.30am-4.30pm Nov-Mar, to 7.30pm Apr-Oct) `FREE` The gratis entry here (unique among Ravenna's Unesco sites) is no reflection of the quality of the artistry inside. The baptistery's breathtaking dome mosaic, depicting the baptism of Christ encircled by the 12 Apostles, was completed over a period of years beginning in the 5th century.

Museo d'Arte della Città di Ravenna   GALLERY
(www.mar.ra.it; Via di Roma 13; adult/reduced €9/7; ⊙9am-6pm Tue-Fri, to 7pm Sat & Sun) Arranged in a converted 15th-century monastery abutting a public garden, Ravenna's permanent art collection is backed up by regular temporary expos. The ground floor features some rather fetching modern mosaics, first brought together in the 1950s, including one (Le coq bleu) based on a design by Marc Chagall.

Domus dei Tappeti di Pietra   MUSEUM
(www.domusdeitappetidipietra.it; Via Gianbattista Barbiani; adult/reduced €4/3; ⊙10am-5pm Mon-Fri, to 6pm Sat & Sun) Not nearly as impressive as the Unesco site mosaics, but still worth a look for serious aficionados, these

6th-century floor mosaics from a 14-room late-Roman palace were only unearthed in 1993–94. Restored but incomplete, they show considerable artistic merit, and are decorated with geometric and floral designs.

Tomba di Dante   TOMB

(Via D Alighieri 9; ⊙10am-6pm Apr-Oct, to 4pm Nov-Mar) FREE A son of Florence, Italy's *Sommo Poeta* (supreme poet), Dante Alighieri, was expelled from the city of his birth in 1302 for political reasons and spent many years 'on the run'. He finally sought refuge in Ravenna, where he died in 1321. As a perpetual act of penance, Florence still supplies the oil for the lamp that burns continually in his tomb.

Courses

Gruppo Mosaicisti   COURSE

(www.gruppomosaicisti.it; Via Fiandrini 8) Tucked around the side of San Vitale, this school offers a variety of mosaic-making courses, for beginners, experienced artists and those involved in professional restoration work.

Mosaic Art School   COURSE

(www.mosaicschool.com; Via Francesco Negri 14) Offers five-day intensive mosaic-making courses for all skill levels.

Festivals & Events

Ravenna hosts one of Italy's top classical-music events, and jazz fans are well served by the Ravenna Jazz (www.erjn.it/ravenna) festival every May.

Ravenna Festival   MUSIC

(www.ravennafestival.org) Renowned Italian conductor Riccardo Muti has close ties with Ravenna and is intimately involved with this classical-music festival each year. Concerts are staged in June and July at venues all over town, including the Teatro Alighieri (www.teatroalighieri.org; Via Mariani 2). Ticket prices start at €15.

Sleeping

★ M Club Deluxe   B&B €

(☑333 9556466; www.m-club.it; Piazza Baracca 26; s €70-90, d €80-100, ste €130-150; P ❄ ���) Two minutes from San Vitale's gorgeous mosaics, industrious young owner Michael Scapini Mantovani has converted this old family home into a luxurious B&B. Historical touches (ancient beamed ceilings, a stuffed crocodile brought from Ethiopia by a great uncle, Michael's father's decades-old

collection of *National Geographics*) coexist with countless modern conveniences, including super-comfy beds and wi-fi routers in every room.

Ostello Dante   HOSTEL €

(☑0544 42 11 64; www.hostelravenna.com; Via Nicolodi 12; dm €18-20, s €28, d €52; @ ��) A good option for solo travellers and cyclists, Ravenna's handy HI hostel is in a modern building 1km east of the train station. It's closed between noon and 2.30pm; there's also an 11.30pm night lock-up, but night owls can leave a €20 deposit for a 'night key'. Take bus 1, 70 or 75 from the train station.

Hotel Centrale Byron   HOTEL €

(☑0544 21 22 25; www.hotelbyron.com; Via IV Novembre 14; s €58-65, d €75-100; P ❄ @ �) You can't beat the Byron's location, in the car-free, wonderfully ingratiating streets of central Ravenna. It's no lie to say you could lob a football from the window of your clean, modern room into beautiful Piazza del Popolo.

Albergo Cappello   BOUTIQUE HOTEL €€

(☑0544 21 98 13; www.albergocappello.it; Via IV Novembre 41; r €139-189; P ❄ @ �) Colour-themed rooms come in three categories (deluxe, suite and junior suite) at this finely coiffed seven-room boutique hotel smack in the town centre. Murano glass chandeliers, original 15th-century frescoes and coffered ceilings are set against modern fixtures and flat-screen TVs. The ample breakfast features pastries from Ravenna's finest *pasticceria*. There's also an excellent restaurant and wine bar attached.

Eating & Drinking

La Piadina del Melarancio   FAST FOOD €

(☑331 1586246; www.ilmelarancio.it; Via IV Novembre 31; piadinas €3.50-5; ⊙11.30am-8.30pm Mon-Fri, to 10pm Sat & Sun) This simple city-centre spot is a great place to try Romagna's classic snack food: a hot, fresh *piadina* (stuffed flatbread). Fillings range from *squacquerone* cheese with caramelised figs to sausage, mozzarella and tomato sauce. Place your order at the front counter and wait until your number's called.

★ Ca' de Vèn   RISTORANTE €€

(☑0544 3 01 63; www.cadeven.it; Via Corrado Ricci 24; meals €25-35; ⊙noon-2.30pm & 6-10pm Tue-Sun) Old men and their dogs swap oenological tips with wine snobs in this cavernous wine-bar-cum-restaurant beautified with frescoed vaulting and floor-to-ceiling shelves stuffed with bottles, books and other curiosities. Settle in over excellent *aperitivi* and, when the room starts to spin, decamp to the wood-panelled back hall for delectable Romagnola specialities like *squacquerone* cheese pudding with crunchy ham.

Osteria dei Battibecchi
OSTERIA €€

(☑ 0544 21 95 36; www.osteriadeibattibecchi.it; Via della Tesoreria Vecchia 16; meals €23-32; ⊗12.30-3pm & 7pm-midnight) Simple Romagnola food done right is the hallmark of this Slow Food–recommended local favourite – from the basket of warm *piadina* bread that comes unbidden to your table, through scrumptious plates of pasta, grilled vegetables, meat and fish, to homemade desserts like *zuppa inglese* (liqueur-soaked ladyfingers layered with custard and chocolate sauce).

La Gardela
TRATTORIA €€

(☑ 0544 21 71 47; www.ristorantelagardela.com; Via Ponte Marino 3; meals €20-30; ⊗noon-2.30pm & 7-10.30pm Fri-Wed) Economical prices, formidable home cooking and an attractive front terrace that's good for people watching mean this bustling trattoria can be crowded, but in a pleasant, gregarious way. Professional waiters glide by with plates of Italian classics: think risottos, pasta with *ragù*, and good grilled meats and fish. Fixed-price menus including water and coffee (but not wine) start at €15.

ℹ Information

Post Office (Piazza Garibaldi 1)

Tourist Office (☑ 0544 3 54 04; www. turismo.ravenna.it; Piazza Caduti per la Libertà 2; ⊗8.30am-7pm Mon-Sat, 10am-6pm Sun) Helpful office whose offerings include the 'Taste Routes' map granting discounts at local restaurants.

ℹ Getting There & Around

Frequent trains connect with Bologna (€7.10, one to 1½ hours), Ferrara (€6.40, 1¼ hours), Rimini (€4.60, one hour) and the south coast.

Ravenna is on a branch (A14 dir) of the main east-coast A14 autostrada. The SS16 (Via Adriatica) heads south to Rimini and on down the coast. The main car parks are east of the train station and north of the Basilica di San Vitale; for a comprehensive map of parking options, see www.cesostapervoi.it.

Local buses operated by **START** (☑ 0544 68 99 11; http://startromagna.it; single/24hr ticket €1.30/3) depart from Piazza Farini. **Punto Bus** (Piazza Farini; ⊗6.30am-7.30pm Mon-Sat, from 7.30am Sun), inside the train station, provides bus information and tickets.

In town, cycling is popular. Rent bikes just outside Ravenna's train station at **Cooperativa Sociale la Formica** (Piazza Farini; bikes per hr/day €1.50/12; ⊗7am-7pm Mon-Fri). Alternatively, use the free 'C'entro in Bici' bike-hire service sponsored by Ravenna's main tourist office: simply present photo ID and tourist office staff will provide you with a key to unlock one of the free yellow bikes stored at racks throughout the city. Return the bike at least half an hour before closing time to reclaim your photo ID.

Rimini

POP 146,000

Roman relics, jam-packed beaches, hedonistic nightclubs and the memory of film director and native son Federico Fellini make sometimes awkward bedfellows in seaside Rimini. Although there's been a settlement here for over 2000 years, Rimini's coast was just sand dunes until 1843, when the first bathing establishments took root next to the ebbing Adriatic. The beach huts gradually morphed into a megaresort that was sequestered by a huge nightclub scene in the 1990s. Despite some interesting history, Fellini-esque movie memorabilia and a decent food culture, 95% of Rimini's visitors come for its long, boisterous, sometimes tacky beachfront.

Once a thriving Latin colony known as Ariminum, Rimini changed hands like a well-worn library book in the Middle Ages when periods of Byzantine, Lombard and Papal rule culminated in the roguish reign of Sigismondo Malatesta in the 15th century. But the worst was to come. Rimini got whacked more than any other Italian city during WWII, when bombing raids were followed by the brutal 'Battle of Rimini', during which an estimated 1.5 million rounds of Allied ammunition were fired on the German-occupied city.

◉ Sights

Piazza Cavour is Rimini's main square, containing the city's finest *palazzi*, including the 16th-century **Palazzo del Municipio**, reconstructed after being razed during WWII, and the 14th-century Gothic **Palazzo del Podestà**. The palaces aren't open to the public, but provide an attractive backdrop to the modern-day to-ings and fro-ings in the square.

Rimini

Rimini

Keep your eyes open for Rimini's brand-new Fellini Museum, under construction at the time of research and scheduled to open as early as 2016 in the modern wing of Rimini's Museo della Città.

★ **Tempio Malatestiano**   CHURCH
(Via IV Novembre 35; ⊙8.30am-12.30pm & 3.30-7pm Mon-Sat, 9am-1pm & 3.30-7pm Sun) Built originally in 13th-century Gothic style and dedicated to St Francis, Rimini's cathedral was radically transformed in the mid-1400s into a Renaissance Taj Mahal for the tomb of Isotta degli Atti, beloved mistress of roguish ruler Sigismondo Malatesta. Sigismondo hired Florentine architect Leon Battista Alberti to redesign the church in 1450, and the resulting edifice, while incomplete, is replete with Alberti's grandiose Roman-inspired touches, along with elements that glorify Sigismondo and Isotta, including numerous medallions bearing the two lovers' initials.

Alberti's grand project was interrupted and eventually abandoned as Sigismondo's popularity and influence waned in the 1460s. Sigismondo, known disparagingly as the 'Wolf of Rimini' thanks to his aggressive military campaigns, came into direct conflict with Pope Pius II, who burned his effigy in Rome and condemned him to hell for a litany of sins that included rape, murder, incest, adultery and severe oppression of the people. Sigismondo lost most of his territory in subsequent battles with Papal forces and died in 1468. His sarcophagus rests near Isotta's inside the church.

★ **Museo della Città** MUSEUM
(www.museicomunalirimini.it/musei/museo_citta; Via Tonini 1; adult/reduced €6/4; ⊙8.30am-1pm & 4-7pm Tue-Sat, 10am-12.30pm & 3-7pm Sun Sep-May, 2-11pm Tue-Sat, 5-11pm Sun Jun-Aug) This rambling museum is best known for its Roman section. Spread over several rooms with excellent bilingual (Italian/English) signage are finds from two nearby Roman villas, including splendid mosaics, a rare and exquisite representation of fish rendered in coloured glass, and the world's largest collection of Roman surgical instruments. Other highlights include the colourful and imaginative doodlings of Federico Fellini, whose *Libro dei miei sogni* (Book of My Dreams) is on display here.

Museum tickets also include admission to the adjacent **Domus del Chirurgo** (Piazza Ferrari), a recently excavated Roman villa with several fine floor mosaics still partially intact.

★ **Ponte di Tiberio** LANDMARK
The majestic five-arched Tiberius' Bridge dates from AD 21. In Roman times it marked the start of the Via Emilia – the important arterial road between the Adriatic Coast (at Rimini) and the Po River valley (at Piacenza) – which linked up here with the Via Flaminia from Rome. These days, the bridge still connects Rimini's city centre to the old fishing quarter of Borgo San Giuliano and rests on its original foundations consisting of an ingenious construction of wooden stilts.

Arco di Augusto LANDMARK
(Corso d'Augusto) This Roman triumphal arch, the oldest of its kind in northern Italy, was commissioned by Emperor Augustus in 27 BC and stands an impressive 17m high on modern-day Corso d'Augusto. It was once the end point of the ancient Via Flaminia that linked Rimini with Rome. Buildings that had grown up around the arch were demolished in 1935 to improve its stature.

Borgo San Giuliano AREA
Just over the Ponte di Tiberio, Rimini's old fishing quarter has been freshened up and is now a colourful patchwork of cobbled lanes, trendy trattorias, wine bars and trim terraced houses (read: prime real estate). Look out for the numerous murals.

Castel Sismondo MUSEUM
(Piazza Malatesta; admission €2; ⊙3-6pm Tue-Sun) Also known as the Rocca Malatestiana, Rimini's classic Renaissance castle was de-signed by the great military leader himself, Sigismondo Malatesta. The outside looks promising, but sadly the only interior access is to a subterranean room with Italian-only displays on the Malatesta family's two dozen castles in the local region.

 Activities

Beaches
Rimini's beaches are like a slice of California in Italy. Spend 10 minutes on the promenade in August and you'll realise that all kinds of new trends kick off here – wacky or otherwise. You'll see Nordic beach-walkers, office workers getting a reiki massage, gym enthusiasts pumping iron, clubbers in search of a hangover cure, computer geeks surfing on their sun loungers, and more.

In peak season it's hard to see the sand through all the assembled umbrellas, sun loungers, amusement parks and crowded beach bars. Suffice it to say there's 40km of it, mostly backed by clamorous hotel development.

Theme Parks
In a beach resort, garish theme parks are an inevitable by-product, and Rimini has its fair share. For details on 11 parks in the Rimini area, including **Italia in Miniatura** (☑0541 73 67 36; www.italiainminiatura.com; Via Popilia 239; adult/child €22/16; ⊙9am-7pm Apr–mid-Sep, 9.30am-sunset mid-Sep–Mar; ⊛), with its scale models of Italy's major sights, and **Aquafàn** (www.aquafan.it; Via Ascoli Piceno 6, Riccione; adult/child €28/20; ⊙10am-6.30pm Jun–mid-Sep; ⊛), the area's biggest water park, see the Riviera dei Parchi website (www.rivieradeiparchi.it).

🛏 **Sleeping**
Ironically for a city with more than 1200 hotels, finding accommodation can be tricky. In July and August places can be booked solid and prices are sky-high, especially as many proprietors insist on full board. In winter a lot of places simply shut up shop.

Hotel Villa Lalla HOTEL €
(☑0541 5 51 55; www.villalalla.com; Viale V Veneto 22; s €36-54, d €59-124; Ᵽ⊛@) A few blocks in from the beach, this family run place offers great rates outside the peak summer season. Superior rooms are more welcoming than standards, with squeaky clean beige, brown and white decor. From mid-June to mid-September when the restaurant's open,

half or full board is a steal at €8 extra per meal. Guests get free use of bikes.

Sunflower City Backpacker Hostel HOSTEL €
(📞 0541 2 51 80; www.sunflowerhostel.com; Viale Dardanelli 102; dm €14-32, s €26-64, d €42-86; @ 🛜) Run by three ex-backpackers, the Sunflower welcomes travellers with laundry and cooking facilities, retro Austin Powers–style wallpaper, an in-house bar and organised pub crawls. It's in a leafy residential district halfway between the train station and the beach. Exuding an even livelier party vibe, Sunflower's beachside branch (📞 0541 37 34 32; Via Siracusa 25; dm €15-34, d €44-94; ⏰ Mar-Oct) (high season only) has its own stage with live music in summer.

Hotel de Londres HOTEL €€
(📞 0541 5 01 14; www.hoteldelondres.it; Viale Vespucci 24; s €70-157, d €80-175, ste €135-229; 🅿️ 🛜) This well-appointed little place near the beach offers enough thoughtful extras to usurp the competition. Making a stopover worthwhile are the rooftop spa, small gymnasium, flowery terrace and free bikes.

⭐ **Grand Hotel** HISTORIC HOTEL €€€
(📞 0541 5 60 00; www.grandhotelrimini.com; Parco Federico Fellini; s €114-343, d €149-449, ste €286-546; 🅿️ ❄️ @ 🛜 ♒) Rimini's only five-star hotel is as much a monument as a place to stay. Despite a 1920 fire and serious damage incurred during WWII, it has remained true to its 1908 roots with rooms clad in authentic 18th-century Venetian antiques. Beloved by Fellini, the hotel has lured many other celebs with its pool, private beach and elegant communal areas.

🍴 Eating

Rimini's cuisine is anchored by the *piadina* and *pesce azzurro* (oily fish), especially sardines and anchovies. The favourite tipple is Sangiovese wine.

⭐ **Casina del Bosco** SANDWICHES €
(http://casinadelbosco.it; Via Beccadelli 15; piadina €4.80-7.50; ⏰ 11am-1am) A beloved Rimini institution, this sweet eatery just in from the beach serves some of the best and most diverse *piadine* in town, stuffed with fillings that range from ham, gorgonzola and grilled vegetables to salted ricotta with caramelised figs. Warm, efficient service and alfresco seating across from Parco Federico Fellini are just icing on the cake.

⭐ **La Marianna** SEAFOOD €€
(📞 0541 2 25 30; www.trattorialamarianna.it; Viale Tiberio 19, Borgo San Giuliano; meals €28-40; ⏰ 12.30-2.30pm & 7.30-11.30pm) New owners have lovingly preserved the recipes and traditions of this former inn just north of the old Roman bridge, which has welcomed travellers for over a century. Turquoise-aproned waiters zip between the covered front terrace and the marble-tiled dining room, brandishing exquisite platters of fried and grilled fish, along with pasta specials such as shrimp, artichoke and ricotta ravioli.

⭐ **Osteria De Borg** OSTERIA €€
(📞 0541 5 60 74; www.osteriadeborg.it; Via Forzieri 12; meals €25-35, pizzas €7.50-11; ⏰ 12.30-2.30pm & 7.30-11.30pm) A homey *osteria* in the old fishing quarter, this place is all about simple, honest food made with local ingredients and served in unpretentious surroundings. Second courses revolve around meat, from local *mora romagnola* pork to meatballs with stuffed zucchini to steaks grilled on an open fire with rosemary and sea salt. In the evenings there's also wood-fired pizza.

Abocar (Due Cucine) MODERN ITALIAN €€
(📞 0541 2 22 79; http://abocarduecucine.it; Via Farini 13; meals €33-43; ⏰ 7.30-11.30pm Tue-Sun) For a romantic dinner, head to this elegant newcomer with pretty internal garden, opened in 2014 by the son of fabled local restaurateur Tonino Il Lurido (owner of one of Fellini's former haunts). Three carefully crafted tasting menus – revolving around fish, meat or a combination of the two – offer a daily changing feast of innovative Italian flavours.

🍷 Drinking & Nightlife

Rimini's drinking action spins on two hubs: the Marina Centro neighbourhood along the seafront, and the buzzy cluster of bars surrounding the brick triple archway of the old *pescheria* (fish market) off Piazza Cavour; the latter is especially active around *aperitivo* time.

Caffè Cavour CAFE
(Piazza Cavour 13; ⏰ 7am-midnight Wed-Mon) Early risers bump into the remnants of last night's dance marathons in this swish cafe on Rimini's main square. Mornings are for cappuccinos, evenings for *aperitivi*, the plush leather seats inside for anytime.

RIMINI'S CLUBBING SCENE

Some come to Rimini in search of Roman relics. Others seek out its lavish modern night-clubs. Rimini first garnered a reputation for mega-hip nightclubbing in the 1990s when an electric after-dark scene took off in the hills of **Misano Monte** and **Riccione** several kilometres to the south of the city centre. Far from being a tacky re-run of Torremolinos or Magaluf, Rimini's new clubs quickly established themselves as modish, fashionable affairs that appealed to a broader age demographic than the 18 to 30 dives of yore. That's not to say they were boring.

Discoteca Baia Imperiale (www.baiaimperiale.net; Via Panoramica 36, Gabicce Mare; ⊙10pm-4am) With eight dance floors, Baia Imperiale is one of Europe's largest clubs, and even the stone-cold sober agree that it's one of the world's most beautiful – dripping with marble staircases, pools, and assorted obelisks and statues of Roman emperors.

Cocoricò (www.cocorico.it; Viale Chieti 44, Riccione; ⊙11pm-5.30am) Dancing under Cocoricò's glass pyramid, 2000 clammy strangers quickly become friends to the sounds of techno, house and underground. World-famous DJs pop in on Fridays and Saturdays, while drag queens enliven the scene on 'Tunga party' nights. In summer Cocoricò also hosts poolside dance parties at the nearby Aquafàn water park.

Byblos (www.byblosclub.com; Via Pozzo Castello 24, Misano Adriatico; ⊙10pm-5am Fri & Sat) Feeling more like a hedonistic Beverly Hills house party than a club, this converted villa complex with swimming pool, restaurant and highly acclaimed DJs fills up with ridiculously beautiful people.

Disco Bar Coconuts (www.coconuts.it; Lungomare Tintori 5; ⊙11.30pm-4am) This popular nightspot on the Marina Centro waterfront exudes a summer-beach-party atmosphere, with palm trees sprouting from its wooden deck.

EMILIA-ROMAGNA & SAN MARINO RIMINI

Rockisland BAR
(www.rockislandrimini.net; Via Largo Boscovich; ⊙5pm-late Tue-Sun; 🛜) Perched on stilts over the Adriatic at the far end of the marina pier, Rockisland is the place for beer, sunset cocktails, live rock music and bikers with beards.

Barge IRISH PUB
(www.thebarge.eu; Lungomare Tintori 13; ⊙noon-3am) A magnet for modish 20-somethings, this seafront pub offers an irresistible combo: draught Guinness, regular DJs and frequent live music.

Il Vecchio e Il Mare BAR
(Via Pisacane 10; ⊙5pm-midnight Tue-Sun) One of several lively bars surrounding the historic fish market, this rustic place stands out for its enticing boards of meat and fish appetisers, served free with any drink order of €7 or more at *aperitivo* time.

ⓘ Information

Ospedale Infermi (☏0541 70 51 11; Viale Settembrini 2) Located 2.5km southeast of the centre.

Police Station (☏0541 43 61 11; Corso d'Augusto 192)

Post Office (Via Gambalunga 40)

Tourist Office (☏0541 5 33 99; www.rimini turismo.it) Waterfront (☏0541 5 69 02; Piazzale Fellini 3; ⊙8.30am-7pm Mon-Sat Easter-Oct, to 6pm Nov-Easter); Train Station (☏0541 5 13 31; Piazzale Cesare Battisti 1; ⊙8.15am-6.45pm Mon-Sat)

ⓘ Getting There & Away

Rimini's **Federico Fellini International Airport** (www.riminiairport.com), 8km south of the city centre, offers direct flights to/from Germany with Air Berlin and to/from Russia with Transaero, Ural Airlines and various charter carriers.

Benedettini (☏0549 90 38 54; www.bened ettinispa.com) and **Bonelli Bus** (☏0541 66 20 69; www.bonellibus.it) operate 12 buses daily from Rimini's train station to San Marino (€5, 50 minutes).

By car, you have a choice of the A14 (south into Le Marche or northwest towards Bologna and Milan) or the toll-free but very busy SS16.

Hourly trains run down the coast to the ferry ports of Ancona (from €6.75, one to 1¼ hours) and Bari (Intercity/Frecciabianca €51.50/62.50, 4¾ to six hours). Up the line, they serve Ravenna (€4.60, one hour, hourly) and Bologna (from €9.50, one to 1½ hours, half-hourly).

ⓘ Getting Around

START (http://startromagna.it; single/24hr ticket €1.30/4.50) operates Rimini's public transport system. Local bus 9 runs between Rimini's train station and the airport (25 minutes). For Riccione (30 minutes), catch local bus 11 from the train station or along the *lungomare* (seafront promenade); it leaves every 12 to 20 minutes between 5.20am and 1.15am.

You can hire bikes and scooters from kiosks on Piazzale Kennedy.

SAN MARINO

Of the world's 196 independent countries, San Marino is the fifth smallest and – arguably – the most curious. How it exists at all is something of an enigma. A sole survivor of Italy's once powerful city-state network, this landlocked micronation clung on long after the more powerful kingdoms of Genoa and Venice folded. And still it clings, secure in its status as the world's oldest surviving sovereign state and its oldest republic (since AD 301). San Marino also enjoys one of the planet's highest per capita GDPs.

Measuring 61 sq km, the country is larger than many outsiders imagine, being made up of nine municipalities each hosting its own settlement. The largest 'town' is Dogana (on the bus route from Italy), a place 99.9% of the two million annual visitors skip on their way through to the Città di San Marino, the medieval settlement on the slopes of 750m-high Monte Titano that was added to the Unesco World Heritage list in 2008.

Though San Marino is old and commands some astounding views, it retains a curious lack of intimacy and (dare we say) soul.

⊙ Sights & Activities

Città di San Marino's highlights are its spectacular views, its Unesco-listed streets, and a stash of rather bizarre museums dedicated to vampires, torture, wax dummies and strange facts (pick up a list in the tourist office). Ever popular in summertime is the hourly changing of the guard (⊘hourly 9.30am-12.30pm & 3.30-4.30pm Mon-Fri, hourly 10.30am-5.30pm Sat & Sun Jun–mid-Sep) in Piazza della Libertà.

Torre Cesta
CASTLE

(Seconda Torre; www.museidistato.sm/mtc; Via Salita alla Cesta; admission €4; ⊘8am-8pm mid-Jun–mid-Sep, 9am-5pm mid-Sep–mid-Jun) Dominating the skyline and offering superb views towards Rimini and the coast, the Cesta cas-

tle dates from the 13th century and sits atop 750m Monte Titano. Today you can walk its ramparts and peep into its four-room museum devoted to medieval armaments.

Torre Guaita
CASTLE

(Prima Torre; www.museidistato.sm/mtg; Via Salita alla Rocca; admission €4; ⊘8am-8pm mid-Jun–mid-Sep, 9am-5pm mid-Sep–mid-Jun) The oldest and largest of San Marino's castles, Torre Guaita dates from the 11th century. It was used as a prison as recently as 1975.

Museo di Stato
MUSEUM

(www.museidistato.sm/mds; Piazza Titano 1; ⊘8am-8pm mid-Jun–mid-Sep, 9am-5pm mid-Sep–mid-Jun) **FREE** San Marino's best museum by far is the well-laid-out if disjointed state museum displaying art, history, furniture and culture.

🛏 Sleeping & Eating

Hotel Titano
HOTEL €€

(☑0549 99 10 07; www.hoteltitano.com; Contrada del Collegio 31; r €78-175, ste €119-236; P ❋ @ ☎) Smack in the centre of Città di San Marino, the Titano is San Marino's best all-rounder, with a tearoom, fine-view restaurant (La Terraza) and enough mod cons to justify a four-star rating.

🛍 Shopping

Azienda Filatelica-Numismatica
SOUVENIRS

(www.aasfn.sm; Piazza Garibaldi 5; ⊘8.30am-6.15pm Mon-Fri, 9am-1.30pm & 2-6pm Sat & Sun) Collectors can pick up rare San Marino stamps and coins at this small shop. There's a mailbox just outside for mailing those 'proof-you've-been-there' postcards.

ⓘ Information

Tourist Office (☑0549 88 23 90; www.visitsanmarino.com; Contrada Omagnano 20, Città di San Marino; ⊘8.30am-6pm Mon-Fri, 9am-1.30pm & 2-6pm Sat & Sun) You can get your passport stamped with a San Marino visa for €5 here.

ⓘ Getting There & Away

Bonelli Bus (p477) and Benedettini (p477) operate 12 buses daily to/from Rimini (one way €5, 50 minutes), arriving at Piazzale Calcigni. The SS72 leads up from Rimini.

Leave your car at one of Città di San Marino's numerous car parks and walk up to the *centro storico*. Alternatively, park at car park 11 and take the **funivia** (Cable Car; return €4.50; ⊘7.50am-sunset Sep-Jun, to 1am Jul & Aug).

Florence & Tuscany

Includes ➡

Best Places to Eat

➡ La Leggenda dei Frati (p510)

➡ 5 e Cinque (p509)

➡ Enoteca I Terzi (p524)

Best Wine Tastings

➡ Le Volpi e l'Uva (p513)

➡ Antinori nel Chianti Classico (p527)

➡ Osticcio (p541)

Why Go?

Florence (Firenze in Italian) and Tuscany (Toscana) are the perfect introduction to Italy's famed *dolce vita*. Life is sweet around leading lady Florence, a fashionable urbanite known for her truly extraordinary treasure trove of world-class art and architecture, and a seasonally driven cuisine emulated the world over. Away from the city the pace slows as magnificent landscapes and the gentle heartbeat of the seasons cast their seductive spell.

This part of Italy has been working on its remarkable heritage since Etruscan times, meaning there's mountains to see and do. Explore a World Heritage Site in the morning, visit a vineyard in the afternoon and bunk down in a palatial villa or overwhelmingly rural *agriturismo* (farm stay accommodation) with indigenous black pigs at night. Renaissance paintings and Gothic cathedrals? Check. Spectacular trekking and sensational Slow Food? Yep. Hills laden with vines and ancient olive groves? More than you can possibly imagine.

When to Go
Florence

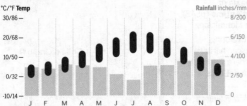

May & Jun Wildflower-adorned landscapes beg outdoor action, be it walking, cycling or horse riding.

Jul Not as madbusy as August (avoid) and with music festivals aplenty.

Sep–Nov Grapes and olives are harvested; forests yield white truffles and porcini mushrooms.

Florence & Tuscany Highlights

1 Swooning over Florence's treasures: the world's finest collection of Renaissance paintings at the **Uffizi** (p492) and the dome of Brunelleschi's **Duomo** (p483).

2 Pedalling and picnicking atop stone city walls encircling **Lucca** (p565).

3 Getting lost in medieval Pisa and scaling its iconic **Leaning Tower** (p558) at sunset.

4 Setting sail for the Mediterranean isle of **Elba** (p554), and sleeping on a wine estate scented with orange blossoms.

5 Vineyard-hopping through **Chianti** (p526) and lunching at an Antinori family estate.

6 Gorging on Gothic architecture and almond biscuits in **Siena** (p518).

7 Being spellbound by Gregorian chants in the compelling **Abbazia di Sant'Antimo** (p542), near Montalcino.

8 Exploring Etruscan heritage in southern Tuscany's **Città del Tufa** (p547).

9 Marvelling at frescoes in Cappella Bacci and the beautiful Tuscan square Piazza Grande in **Arezzo** (p570).

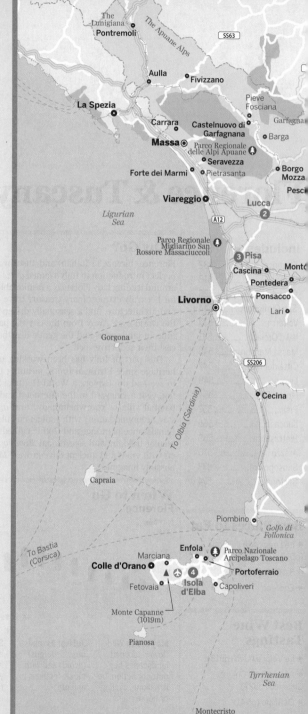

FLORENCE

POP 377,200

Return time and again and you still won't see it all. Stand on a bridge over the Arno river several times in a day and the light, mood and view changes every time. Surprisingly small as it is, Florence (Firenze) looms large on Europe's 'must-sees' list. Host to the tourist masses that flock here to feast on world-class art, Tuscany's largest city buzzes with romance and history. Towers and palaces evoke a thousand tales of its medieval past; designer boutiques and artisan workshops pearl its streets; and the local drinking and dining scene is second to none. Cradle of the Renaissance and home of Machiavelli, Michelangelo and the Medici, Florence is magnetic, romantic and brilliantly absorbing.

History

Controversy continues over who founded Florence. The most commonly accepted story tells us that Emperor Julius Caesar founded Florentia around 59 BC, but archaeological evidence suggests the presence of an earlier village founded by the Etruscans of Fiesole around 200 BC.

In the 12th century Florence became a free *comune* (town council), ruled by 12 *priori* (consuls) assisted by the Consiglio di Cento (Council of One Hundred), drawn mainly from the merchant class. Agitation among different factions led to the appointment of a foreign governing *podestà* (magistrate) in 1207.

A plague in 1348 halved the city's population and in 1378 the government was rocked by a revolt by the city's *ciompi* (wool workers), who sought a greater voice in the *comune*'s decision-making processes. Though initially successful, the major and minor guilds soon closed ranks to re-establish the old order, with members of the Medici family – bankers to the pope – taking a major role in the city's government.

In 1434, Cosimo il Vecchio (the Elder, also known simply as Cosimo de' Medici, 1389–1464) became Florence's de facto ruler. His eye for talent saw a constellation of artists such as Alberti, Brunelleschi, Lorenzo Ghiberti, Donatello, Fra' Angelico and Fra' Filippo Lippi flourish.

The rule of Lorenzo il Magnifico (1469–92), Cosimo's grandson, ushered in the most glorious period of Florentine civilisation and of the Italian Renaissance. His court fostered a flowering of art, music and poetry, turning Florence into Italy's cultural capital. Not long before Lorenzo's death, the Medici bank failed and the family was driven out of Florence. The city fell under the control of Savonarola, a Dominican monk who led a puritanical republic, burning the city's wealth on his 'Bonfire of the Vanities'. His lure proved to be short-lived, and after falling from favour he was tried as a heretic and executed in 1498.

After the Spanish defeated Florence in 1512, Emperor Charles V married his daughter to Lorenzo's great-grandson Alessandro de' Medici, whom he made duke of Florence in 1530. Seven years later Cosimo I, one of the last truly capable Medici rulers, took charge, becoming grand duke of Tuscany after Siena fell to Florence in 1569.

In 1737 the grand duchy of Tuscany passed to the French House of Lorraine, which retained control, apart from a brief interruption under Napoleon, until it was incorporated into the Kingdom of Italy in 1860. Florence briefly became the national capital but Rome assumed the mantle permanently in 1870.

ℹ PLAN AHEAD: THE FIRENZE CARD

The Firenze Card (www.firenzecard.it; €72) is valid for 72 hours and covers admission to some museums, villas and gardens in Florence, as well as unlimited use of public transport and free wi-fi across the city. Its biggest advantage is reducing queuing time in high season – museums have a separate queue for cardholders. The downside of the Firenze Card is it only allows one admission per museum, plus you need to visit an awful lot of museums to justify the cost.

Buy the card online (and collect upon arrival in Florence) or buy in Florence at tourist offices or ticketing desks of the Uffizi (Entrance 2), Palazzo Pitti, Palazzo Vecchio, Museo del Bargello, Cappella Brancacci, Basilica di Santa Maria Novella and Giardino Bardini. If you're an EU citizen, your card also covers under 18s travelling with you.

Florence

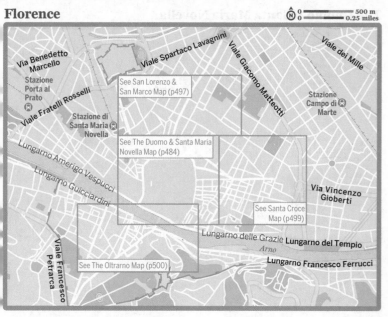

The city was severely damaged during WWII and was ravaged by floods in 1966. Since 1997 Florence's world-class Uffizi Gallery has been engaged in its biggest-ever expansion – a €65 million investment project, dubbed the 'Nuovi Uffizi project'. Its end date remains a mystery.

Sights

Florence's major sights lie in the geographic, historic and cultural heart of the city – the tight grid of streets between Piazza del Duomo and Piazza della Signoria.

Piazza Duomo

One ticket gets you up the cupola and *campanile* (bell tower) of the Duomo, and into the baptistry and the Grande Museo del Duomo; buy it at Piazza di San Giovanni 7 and use within 24 hours.

★ **Duomo**   CATHEDRAL
(Cattedrale di Santa Maria del Fiore; Map p484; www.operaduomo.firenze.it; Piazza del Duomo; ☺10am-5pm Mon-Wed & Fri, to 4.30pm Thu, to 4.45pm Sat, 1.30-4.45pm Sun) **FREE** Florence's Duomo is the city's most iconic landmark. Capped by Filippo Brunelleschi's red-tiled

cupola, it's a staggering construction whose breathtaking pink, white and green marble facade and graceful *campanile* (bell tower) dominate the medieval cityscape. Sienese architect Arnolfo di Cambio began work on it 1296, but construction took almost 150 years and it wasn't consecrated until 1436. In the echoing interior, look out for frescoes by Vasari and Zuccari and look up to 44 stained-glass windows.

The Duomo's neo-Gothic facade was designed in the 19th century by architect Emilio de Fabris to replace the uncompleted original, torn down in the 16th century. The oldest and most clearly Gothic part of the cathedral is its south flank, pierced by Porta dei Canonici (Canons' Door), a mid-14th-century High Gothic creation (you enter here to climb up inside the dome).

After the visual wham-bam of the facade, the sparse decoration of the cathedral's vast interior, 155m long and 90m wide, comes as a surprise – most of its artistic treasures have been removed over the centuries according to the vagaries of ecclesiastical fashion, and many will be on show in the sparkling new Grande Museo del Duomo. The interior is also

The Duomo & Santa Maria Novella

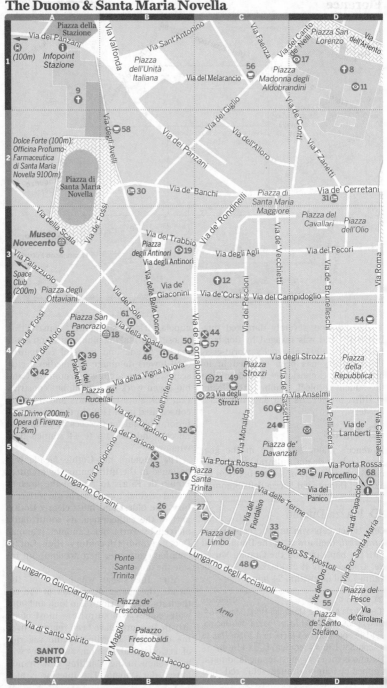

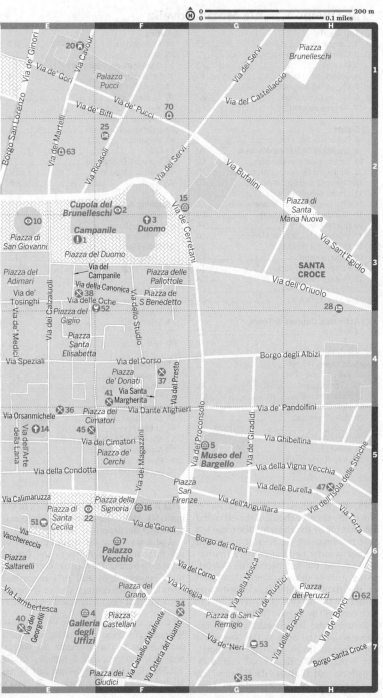

The Duomo & Santa Maria Novella

unexpectedly secular in places (a reflection of the sizeable chunk of the cathedral not paid for by the church): down the left aisle two immense frescoes of equestrian statues portray two *condottieri* (mercenaries) – on the left Niccolò da Tolentino by Andrea del Castagno (1456), and on the right Sir John Hawkwood (who fought in the service of Florence in the 14th century) by Uccello (1436).

Between the left (north) arm of the transept and the apse is the **Sagrestia delle Messe** (Mass Sacristy), its panelling a marvel of inlaid wood carved by Benedetto and Giuliano da Maiano. The fine bronze doors were executed by Luca della Robbia – his only known work in the material. Above the doorway is his glazed terracotta *Resurrezione* (Resurrection).

A stairway near the main entrance of the cathedral leads down to the **Cripta Santa Reparata** (crypt), where excavations between 1965 and 1974 unearthed parts of the 5th-century Chiesa di Santa Reparata that originally stood on the site.

★ **Cupola del Brunelleschi** LANDMARK
(Brunelleschi's Dome; Map p484; www.opera duomo.firenze.it; Duomo, Piazza del Duomo; adult/child incl campanile & baptistry €15/3; ⊙8.30am-7pm Mon-Fri, to 5.40pm Sat) When Michelangelo went to work on St Peter's

in Rome, he reportedly said: 'I go to build a greater dome, but not a fairer one'. One of the finest masterpieces of the Renaissance, the cupola crowning the Duomo is a feat of engineering and one that cannot be fully appreciated without climbing its 463 interior stone steps. It was built between 1420 and 1436 to a design by Filippo Brunelleschi, and is a staggering 91m high and 45.5m wide.

Taking his inspiration from Rome's Pantheon, Brunelleschi arrived at an innovative engineering solution – a distinctive octagonal shape of inner and outer concentric domes resting on the drum of the cathedral rather than the roof itself – allowing artisans to build from the ground up without needing a wooden support frame. Over four million bricks were used in the construction, all of them laid in consecutive rings in horizontal courses using a vertical herringbone pattern.

The climb up the spiral staircase is relatively steep, and should not be attempted if you are claustrophobic. Make sure to pause when you reach the balustrade at the base of the dome, which gives an aerial view of the octagonal *coro* (choir) of the cathedral below and the seven round stained-glass windows (by Donatello, Andrea del Castagno, Paolo Uccello and Lorenzo Ghiberti) that pierce the octagonal drum.

Look up and you'll see flamboyant late-16th-century frescoes by Giorgio Vasari and Federico Zuccari, depicting the *Giudizio universale* (Last Judgment).

As you climb, snapshots of Florence can be spied through small windows. The final leg – a straight, somewhat hazardous flight up the curve of the inner dome – rewards with an unforgettable 360-degree panorama of one of Europe's most beautiful cities.

Buy tickets from the Duomo ticket office at Piazza San Giovanni 7, opposite the baptistry's northern entrance.

★ **Campanile**　　　　　　　TOWER
(Map p484; www.operaduomo.firenze.it; Piazza del Duomo; adult/child inc cathedral dome & baptistry €15/3; ☺8.30am-7.30pm) The 414-step climb up the cathedral's 85m-tall campanile, begun by Giotto in 1334, rewards with a staggering city panorama. The first tier of bas-reliefs around the base of its elaborate Gothic facade are

---

ⓘ SAVVY ADVANCE PLANNING

➡ To cut costs, visit on the first Sunday of the month when admission to state museums, including the Uffizi and Galleria dell'Accademia, is free.

➡ Cut queues by booking tickets in advance for the Uffizi and Galleria dell'Accademia.

➡ The Uffizi, Galleria dell'Accademia and most other state museums are shut on Monday – the perfect day for visiting the hidden gem of Museo di Orsanmichele.

➡ Catch contemporary art (for free) on Thursday evening at Palazzo Strozzi.

➡ Reserve a tour of the Vasari corridor (on Ponte Vecchio) and tickets for Cappella Brancacci and Cappella dei Magi.

➡ Book family-friendly tours and/or art workshops at Palazzo Vecchio and Museo Novecento.

➡ Buy tickets for springtime's Maggio Musicale Fiorentino festival.

---

copies of those carved by Pisano depicting the Creation of Man and the *attività umane* (arts and industries). Those on the second tier depict the planets, the cardinal virtues, the arts and the seven sacraments. The sculpted Prophets and Sibyls in the upper-storey niches are copies of works by Donatello and others.

Grande Museo del Duomo　　MUSEUM
(Cathedral Museum; Map p484; www.ilgrande museodelduomo.it; Piazza del Duomo 9; adult/child incl cathedral bell tower, cupola & baptistry €15/3; ☺9am-7pm) This impressive museum safeguards sacred and liturgical treasures from the *duomo*, baptistry and bell tower. Awe-inspiring highlights include Ghiberti's original 15th-century masterpiece, *Porta del Paradiso* (Gates of Paradise) – gloriously golden, 16m-tall gilded bronze doors designed for the eastern entrance to the Baptistry – as well as those he sculpted for the northern entrance. The best-known work is Michelangelo's *La Pietà*, a work he sculpted when he was almost 80 and intended for his own tomb.

Battistero di San Giovanni LANDMARK
(Baptistry; Map p484; Piazza di San Giovanni; adult/child incl cupola, campanile & museum €15/3; ⊗8.15-10.15am & 11.15am-7pm Mon-Sat, 8.30am-2pm Sun & 1st Sat of month) This 11th-century baptistry is a Romanesque, octagonal striped structure of white-and-green marble with three sets of doors, conceived as panels on which to tell the story of humanity and the Redemption. Most celebrated of all are Lorenzo Ghiberti's gilded bronze doors at the eastern entrance, the *Porta del Paradiso* (Gate of Paradise). What you see today are copies – the originals are in the Grande Museo del Duomo.

◉ Piazza della Signoria & Around

Piazza della Signoria PIAZZA
(Map p484; Piazza della Signoria) The hub of local life since the 13th century, Florentines flock here to meet friends and chat over early-evening *aperitivi* at historic cafes. Presiding over everything is **Palazzo Vecchio**, Florence's city hall, and the 14th-century **Loggia dei Lanzi**, an open-air gallery showcasing Renaissance sculptures, including Giambologna's *Rape of the Sabine Women* (c 1583), Benvenuto Cellini's bronze *Perseus* (1554) and Agnolo Gaddi's *Seven Virtues* (1384–89).

In centuries past, townsfolk congregated on the piazza whenever the city entered one of its innumerable political crises. The people would be called for a *parlamento* (a people's plebiscite) to rubber-stamp decisions that frequently meant ruin for some ruling families and victory for others. Scenes of great pomp and circumstance alternated with those of terrible suffering: it was here that vehemently pious preacher-leader Savonarola set fire to the city's art – books, paintings, musical instruments, mirrors, fine clothes and so on – during his famous 'Bonfire of the Vanities' in 1497, and where he was hung in chains and burnt as a heretic, along with two other supporters, a year later.

The same spot where both fires burned is marked by a bronze plaque embedded in the ground in front of Ammannati's **Fontana de Nettuno** (Neptune Fountain) with pin-headed bronze satyrs and divinities frolicking at its edges. More impressive are the equestrian statue of Cosimo I by Giambologna in the centre of the piazza, the much-photographed copy of Michelangelo's *David* guarding the western entrance to the Palazzo Vecchio since 1910 (the original stood here until 1873), and two copies of important Donatello works – *Marzocco,* the heraldic Florentine lion (for the original, visit the Museo del Bargello), and *Giuditta e Oloferne* (Judith and Holofernes; c 1455; original inside Palazzo Vecchio).

The Loggia dei Lanzi at the piazza's southern end owes its name to the Lanzichenecchi (Swiss bodyguards) of Cosimo I, who were stationed here.

★**Palazzo Vecchio** MUSEUM
(Map p484; ☑055 276 82 24; www.musefir enze.it; Piazza della Signoria; museum adult/reduced €10/8, tower €10/8, archaeology tour €2, museum & tower €14/12; ⊗museum 9am-midnight Fri-Wed, to 2pm Thu summer, 9am-7pm Fri-Wed, to 2pm Thu winter; tower 9am-9pm Fri-Wed, to 2pm Thu summer, 10am-5pm Fri-Wed, to 2pm Thu winter) This fortress palace, with its crenellations and 94m-high tower, was designed by Arnolfo di Cambio between 1298 and 1314 for the *signoria* (city government). It remains the seat of the city's power, home to the mayor's office and the municipal council. From the top of the **Torre d'Arnolfo** (tower), you can revel in unforgettable rooftop views. Inside, Michelangelo's *Genio della Vittoria* (Genius of Victory) sculpture graces the Salone dei Cinquecento, a magnificent painted hall created for the city's 15th-century ruling Consiglio dei Cinquecento (Council of 500).

During their short time in office the nine *priori* (consuls) – guild members picked at random – of the signoria lived in the palace. Every two months nine new names were pulled out of the hat, ensuring ample comings and goings.

In 1540 Cosimo I made the palace his ducal residence and centre of government, commissioning Vasari to renovate and decorate the interior. What impresses is the 53m-long, 22m-wide **Salone dei Cinquecento** with swirling battle scenes, painted floor to ceiling by Vasari and his apprentices. These glorify Florentine victories by Cosimo I over arch-rivals Pisa and Siena: unlike the Sienese, the Pisans are depicted bare of armour (play 'Spot

ℹ️ MUSEUM TICKETS

In July, August and other busy periods such as Easter, long queues are a fact of life at Florence's key museums – if you haven't prebooked your ticket you could well end up standing in line for four hours or so.

For a fee of €3 per ticket (€4 for the Uffizi and Galleria dell'Accademia), tickets to nine *musei statali* (state museums) can be reserved, including the Uffizi, Galleria dell'Accademia (where *David* lives), Palazzo Pitti, Museo del Bargello and the Cappelle Medicee. In reality, the only museums where prebooking is vital are the Uffizi and Accademia – to organise your ticket, go online or call **Firenze Musei** (Florence Museums; ☎ 055 29 48 83; www.firenzemusei.it), with ticketing desks (open 8.30am to 7pm Tuesday to Sunday) at the Uffizi and Palazzo Pitti.

At the Uffizi, signs point prebooked-ticket holders to the building opposite the gallery where tickets can be collected; once you've got the ticket you go to Door 1 of the museum (for prebooked tickets only) and queue again to enter the gallery. It's annoying, but you'll still save hours of queuing time overall.

Admission to all state museums, including the Uffizi and Galleria dell'Accademia, is free on the first Sunday of each month and also on 18 February, the day Anna Maria Louisa de' Medici (1667–1743) died. The last of the Medici family, it was she who bequeathed the city its vast cultural heritage.

EU passport holders aged under 18 and over 65 get into Florence's state museums for free, and EU citizens aged 18 to 25 pay half-price. Have your ID with you at all times. Note that museum ticket offices usually shut 30 minutes before closing time.

---

the Leaning Tower'). To top off this unabashed celebration of his own power, Cosimo had himself portrayed as a god in the centre of the exquisite panelled ceiling – but not before commissioning Vasari to raise the original ceiling 7m in height. It took Vasari and his school, in consultation with Michelangelo, just two years (1563–65) to construct the ceiling and paint the 34 gold-leafed panels. The effect is mesmerising.

Off this huge space is the **Chapel of SS Cosmas and Damian**, home to Vasari's 1557–58 triptych panels of the two saints depicting Cosimo the Elder as Cosmas (right) and Cosimo I as Damian (left). Next to the chapel is the **Sala di Leo X**, the private suite of apartments of Cardinal Giovanni de' Medici, the son of Lorenzo Il Magnifico, who became pope in 1513.

Upstairs, the private apartments of Eleonora and her ladies-in-waiting bear the same heavy-handed decor, blaring the glory of the Medici. The ceiling in the **Camera Verde** (Green Room) by Ridolfo del Ghirlandaio was inspired by designs from Nero's Domus Aurea in Rome. The **Sala dei Gigli,** named after its frieze of fleur-de-lis, representing the Florentine Republic, is home to Donatello's original *Judith and Holofernes*.

The **Sala delle Carte Geografiche** (Map Room) houses Cosimo I's fascinating collection of 16th-century maps charting everywhere in the known world at the time, from the polar regions to the Caribbean.

On rain-free days, end with a 418-step hike up the palace's striking **Torre d'Arnolfo**. No more than 25 people are allowed at any one time and you have just 30 minutes to lap up the brilliant city panorama.

Gucci Museo MUSEUM
(Map p484; www.gucci.com; Piazza della Signoria 10; adult/child €7/free, after 5pm €5; ⊙10am-8pm, to 11pm Thu) Strut through the chic cafe and icon store to reach this museum. It tells the tale of the Gucci fashion house, from the first luggage pieces in Gucci's signature beige fabric emblazoned with the interlocking 'GG' logo to the 1950s red-and-green stripe and beyond. Don't miss the 1979 Cadillac Seville with gold Gs on the hubcaps and Gucci fabric upholstery. Displays continue to present day. In the final room exhibiting men's loafers, look in the mirrors (to admire your own feet and inferior footwear).

The Uffizi

JOURNEY INTO THE RENAISSANCE

Navigating the Uffizi's chronologically-ordered art collection is straightforward enough: knowing which of the 1500-odd masterpieces to view before gallery fatigue strikes is not. Swap coat and bag (travel light) for floor plan and audioguide on the ground floor, then meet 16th-century Tuscany head-on with a walk up the *palazzo's* magnificent bust-lined staircase (skip the lift – the Uffizi is as much about masterly architecture as art).

Allow four hours for this journey into the High Renaissance. At the top of the staircase, on the 2nd floor, show your ticket, turn left and pause to admire the full length of the first corridor sweeping south towards the Arno river. Then duck left into room 2 to witness first steps in Tuscan art – shimmering altarpieces by **Giotto** ❶ et al. Journey through medieval art to room 8 and **Piero della Francesca's** ❷ impossibly famous portrait, then break in the corridor with playful **ceiling art** ❸. After Renaissance heavyweights **Botticelli** ❹ and **da Vinci** ❺, meander past the Tribuna (potential detour) and enjoy the daylight streaming in through the vast windows and panorama of the **riverside second corridor** ❻. Lap up soul-stirring views of the Arno, crossed by Ponte Vecchio and its echo of four bridges drifting towards the Apuane Alps on the horizon. Then saunter into the third corridor, pausing between rooms 25 and 34 to ponder the entrance to the enigmatic Vasari Corridor. End on a high with High Renaissance maestro **Michelangelo** ❼.

The Ognissanti Madonna
Room 2
Draw breath at the shy blush and curvaceous breast of Giotto's humanised Virgin (*Maestà*; 1310) – so feminine compared with those of Duccio and Cimabue painted just 25 years before.

Portraits of the Duke & Duchess of Urbino
Room 8
Revel in realism's voyage with thes[e] uncompromising, warts-and-all portraits (1472–75) by Piero della Francesca. No larger than A3 size, they originally slotted into a portabl[e] hinged frame that folded like a boo[k]

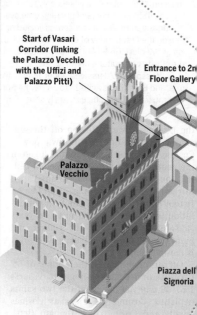

Start of Vasari Corridor (linking the Palazzo Vecchio with the Uffizi and Palazzo Pitti)

Entrance to 2n[d] Floor Gallery

Palazzo Vecchio

Piazza dell[a] Signoria

Grotesque Ceiling Frescoes
First Corridor
Take time to study the make-believe monsters and most unexpected of burlesques (spot the arrow-shooting satyr outside room 15) waltzing across this eastern corridor's fabulous frescoed ceiling (1581).

JUERGEN RICHTER/GETTY IMAGES ©

The Genius of Botticelli
Room 10–14

The miniature form of *The Discovery of the Body of Holofernes* (c 1470) makes Botticelli's early Renaissance masterpiece all the more impressive. Don't miss the artist watching you in *Adoration of the Magi* (1475), left of the exit.

View of the Arno

Indulge in intoxicating city views from this short glassed-in corridor – an architectural masterpiece. Near the top of the hill, spot one of 73 outer towers built to defend Florence and its 15 city gates below.

Second Corridor

Tribuna

First Corridor

Arno River

Entrance to Vasari Corridor

VALUE LUNCHBOX

Try the Uffizi rooftop cafe or – better value – gourmet *panini* at 'Ino (www. ino-firenze.com; Via dei Georgofili 3-7r).

Doni Tondo
Room 35

The creator of *David*, Michelangelo, was essentially a sculptor and no painting expresses this better than *Doni Tondo* (1506–08). Mary's muscular arms against a backdrop of curvaceous nudes are practically 3D in their shapeliness.

Third Corridor

Tribuna

No room in the Uffizi is so tiny or so exquisite. It was created in 1851 as a 'treasure chest' for Grand Duke Francesco and in the days of the Grand Tour, the Medici Venus here was a tour highlight.

Annunciation
Room 15

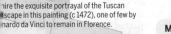

...mire the exquisite portrayal of the Tuscan ...scape in this painting (c 1472), one of few by ...nardo da Vinci to remain in Florence.

MATTER OF FACT

The Uffizi collection spans the 13th to 18th centuries, but its 15th- and 16th-century Renaissance works are second to none.

★ **Galleria degli Uffizi** GALLERY
(Uffizi Gallery; Map p484; www.uffizi.firenze.
it; Piazzale degli Uffizi 6; adult/reduced €8/4, incl
temporary exhibition €12.50/6.25; ⊙8.15am-
6.50pm Tue-Sun) Home to the world's greatest collection of Italian Renaissance art,
Florence's premier gallery occupies the vast
U-shaped Palazzo degli Uffizi, built between
1560 and 1580 to house government offices.
The collection, bequeathed to the city by
the Medici family in 1743 on condition that
it never leave Florence, contains some of
Italy's best-known paintings including Piero
della Francesco's profile portaits of the Duke
and Duchess of Urbino and room full of
masterpieces by Sandro Botticelli.

The gallery is undergoing a €65 million
refurbishment (the Nuovi Uffizi project)
that will eventually see the doubling of exhibition space and possibly a new exit loggia designed by Japanese architect Arato
Isozaki. A number of revamped rooms are
open, but until the project is completed
(date unknown) expect some halls to be
closed and the contents of others changed.

The world-famous collection, displayed
in chronological order, spans the gamut of
art history from ancient Greek sculpture to
18th-century Venetian paintings. But its core
is the Renaissance collection.

Visits are best kept to three or four hours
maximum. When it all gets too much, head
to the rooftop cafe (aka the terraced hanging garden, where the Medici clan listened
to music performances on the square below)
for fresh air and fabulous views.

➧ *Tuscan Masters: 13th to 14th Centuries*

Arriving in the *Primo Corridoio* (First
Corridor) on the 2nd floor, the first seven
rooms – closed for renovation at the time of
writing – are dedicated to pre-Renaissance
Tuscan art. Among the 13th-century Sienese
works displayed are three large altarpieces from Florentine churches by Duccio di
Buoninsegna, Cimabue and Giotto. These
clearly reflect the transition from the Gothic
to the nascent Renaissance style. Note the
overtly naturalistic realism overtones in Giotto's portrayal of the Virgin Mary and saints
in the *Madonna di Ognissanti*.

Moving into Siena in the 14th century, the
highlight is Simone Martini's shimmering
Annunciazione (1333), painted with Lippo
Memmi and setting the Madonna in a sea of
gold. Also of note is the *Madonna in trono
con il Bambino in trono e otto angeli* (Madonna with Child and Saints; 1340) by Piet-

ro Lorenzetti, which demonstrates a realism
similar to Giotto's; unfortunately both Pietro
and his artistic brother Ambrogio died from
the plague in Siena in 1348.

Masters in 14th-century Florence paid
as much attention to detail as their Sienese
counterparts: savour the realism and and
extraordinary gold-leaf work of the *Pietà
di San Remigio* (1360–65) by gifted Giotto
pupil, Giottino.

➧ *Renaissance Pioneers*

In Room 8, Piero della Francesca's famous
profile portraits (1465) of the crooked-nosed,
red-robed duke and duchess of Urbino are
wholly humanist in spirit: the former painted from the left side as he'd lost his right eye
in a jousting accident, and the latter painted
a deathly stone-white, reflecting the fact the
portrait was painted posthumously. Don't
miss the reverse side featuring the duke and
duchess immortalised with the Virtues.

Carmelite monk Fra' Filippo Lippi had an
unfortunate soft spot for earthly pleasures,
scandalously marrying a nun from Prato.
Search out his self-portrait as a podgy friar
in *Incoronazione Maringhi* (Coronation of
the Virgin; 1439–47) and don't miss his later
Madonna con Bambino e due angeli (Madonna and Child with Two Angels; 1460–65),
an exquisite work that clearly influenced his
pupil, Sandro Botticelli.

Another related pair, brothers Antonio
and Piero del Pollaiolo, fill Room 9, where
their seven cardinal and theological values
of 15th-century Florence – commissioned
for the merchant's tribunal in Piazza della
Signoria – radiate energy. More restrained
is Piero's *Portrait of Galeazzo Maria Sforza*
(1471).

The only canvas in the theological and
cardinal virtues series not to be painted by
the Pollaiolos is *Fortitude* (1470), the first
documented work by Botticelli.

➧ *Botticelli Room*

The spectacular Sala del Botticelli, numbered as Rooms 10 to 14, but in fact one
large hall, is one of the Uffizi's hot spots and
is always packed. Of the 15 works by the
Renaissance master known for his ethereal
figures, *La nascita di Venere* (The Birth of
Venus; c 1485), *Primavera* (Spring; c 1482),
the deeply spiritual *Annunciazione di
Cestello* (Cestello Annunciation; 1489–90),
the *Adorazione dei Magi* (Adoration of
the Magi; 1475) featuring the artist's self-
portrait (look for the blond-haired guy, ex-

treme right, dressed in yellow), and the *Madonna del Magnificat* (Madonna of the Magnificat; 1483) are the best known. True aficionados rate his twin set of miniatures depicting a sword-bearing Judith returning from the camp of Holofernes and the discovery of the decapitated Holofernes in his tent (1495–1500) as among his finest works.

➡ Leonardo Room

Room 15 displays three early Florentine works by Leonardo da Vinci: the incomplete *Adorazione dei Magi* (Adoration of the Magi; 1481–82), drawn in red earth pigment (removed for restoration at the time of writing); his *Annunciazione* (c 1475–80); and *The Baptism of Christ* (1470-75).

➡ La Tribuna

The Medici clan stashed away their most precious masterpieces in this exquisite octagonal-shaped treasure trove (Room 18), created by Francesco I between 1581 and 1586. Designed to amaze and perfectly restored to its original exquisite state, a small collection of classical statues and paintings adorn its walls, upholstered in crimson silk, and 6000 mother-of-pearl shells painted with crimson varnish encrust the domed ceiling.

➡ High Renaissance to Mannerism

Passing through the loggia or *Secondo Corridoio* (Second Corridor), visitors enjoy wonderful views of Florence before entering the *Terzo Corridoio* (Third Corridor). Rooms 24 to 34 were closed at the time of writing as part of the massive ongoing expansion and reorganisation of the Uffizi.

Michelangelo dazzles with the *Doni Tondo*, a depiction of the Holy Family that steals the High Renaissance show in Room 35. The composition is unusual – Joseph holding an exuberant Jesus on his muscled mother's shoulder as she twists round to gaze at him, the colours as vibrant as when they were first applied in 1506-08. It was painted for wealthy Florentine merchant Agnolo Doni (who hung it above his bed) and bought by the Medici for Palazzo Pitti in 1594.

➡ 1st-Floor Galleries

As part of the ongoing Nuovi Uffizi expansion project, the Uffizi has already added 1800 sq metres of gallery space to its vast repertoire and expansion continues well into 2015. Head downstairs to the 1st-floor galleries where Rooms 46 to 55 display the Uffizi's collection of 16th- to 18th-century works by foreign artists, including Rembrandt (room 49); Rubens and Van Dyck share room 55. The next 10 rooms give to a nod to antique sculpture, before moving back into the 16th century with Andrea del Sarto (Rooms 57 and 58) and Raphael (Room 66) whose *Madonna del cardellino* (Madonna of the Goldfinch; 1505–06) steals the show. Raphael painted it during his four-year sojourn in Florence.

Rooms 90 to 94 feature works by Caravaggio, deemed vulgar at the time for his direct interpretation of reality. *The Head of Medusa* (1598–99), commissioned for a ceremonial shield, is supposedly a self-portrait of the young artist who died at the age of 39. The biblical drama of an angel steadying the hand of Abraham as he holds a knife to his son Isaac's throat in Caravaggio's *Sacrifice of Isaac* (1601–02) is glorious in its intensity.

★ **Museo del Bargello**   MUSEUM
(Map p484; www.polomuseale.firenze.it; Via del Proconsolo 4; adult/reduced €4/2; ◷8.15am-4.50pm summer, to 1.50pm winter, closed 1st, 3rd & 5th Sun & 2nd & 4th Mon of month) It was behind the stark walls of Palazzo del Bargello, Florence's earliest public building, that the *podestà* meted out justice from the late 13th century until 1502. Today the building safeguards Italy's most comprehensive collection of Tuscan Renaissance sculpture with some of Michelangelo's early works and a hall full of Donatello's pieces. Michelangelo was just 21 when a cardinal commissioned him to create the drunken grape-adorned Bacchus (1496–97), displayed in Bargello's downstairs **Sala di Michelangelo**. Unfortunately the cardinal didn't like the result and sold it to a banker. Other Michelangelo works to look out for here include the marble bust of *Brutus* (c 1539–40), the *David/Apollo* from 1530–32 and the large, uncompleted roundel of the *Madonna and Child with the Infant St John* (aka the *Tondo Pitti*; 1503–05).

After Michelangelo left Florence for the final time in 1534, sculpture was dominated by Baccio Bandinelli (his 1551 *Adam and Eve*, created for the *duomo*, is displayed in the Sala di Michelangelo) and Benvenuto Cellini (look for his playful 1548–50 marble *Ganimede* in the same room).

On the 1st floor, to the right of the staircase, is the **Sala di Donatello**. Here, in the majestic Salone del Consiglio Generale where the city's general council met, works by Donatello and other early 15th-century sculptors can be admired. Originally on the facade of Chiesa di Orsanmichele and now within a tabernacle at the hall's far end, Donatello's wonderful *St George* (1416–17) brought a new sense of perspective and movement to Italian sculpture. Also look for the bronze bas-reliefs created by Brunelleschi and Ghiberti for the Baptistry doors competition.

Yet it is Donatello's two versions of *David*, a favourite subject for sculptors, which really fascinate: Donatello fashioned his slender, youthful dressed image in marble in 1408 and his fabled bronze between 1440 and 1450. The latter is extraordinary – the more so when you consider it was the first freestanding naked statue to be sculpted since classical times.

Criminals received their last rites before execution in the palace's 1st-floor **Cappella del Podestà**, also known as the Mary Magdalene Chapel, where Hell and Paradise are frescoed on the walls, as are stories from the lives of Mary of Egypt, Mary Magdalene and John the Baptist. These remnants of frescoes by Giotto were not discovered until 1840, when the chapel was turned into a storeroom and prison.

The 2nd floor moves into the 16th century with a superb collection of terracotta pieces by the prolific della Robbia family, including some of their best-known works, such as Andrea's *Ritratto idealizia di fanciullo* (Bust of a Boy; c 1475) and Giovanni's *Pietà* (1514). Instantly recognisable, Giovanni's works are more elaborate and flamboyant than either father Luca's or cousin Andrea's, using a larger palette of colours.

Museo Galileo
MUSEUM

(Map p500; ☎055 26 53 11; www.museo galileo.it; Piazza dei Giudici 1; adult/reduced/family €9/5.50/22; ☺9.30am-6pm Wed-Mon, to 12.30pm Tue) On the river next to the Uffizi in 12th-century Palazzo Castellani – look for the sundial telling the time on the pavement outside – is this state-of-the-art science museum, named after the great Pisa-born scientist who was invited by the Medici court to Florence in 1610 (don't miss two of his fingers and a tooth displayed here).

◉ Around Piazza della Repubblica

Chiesa e Museo di Orsanmichele
CHURCH, MUSEUM

(Map p484; Via dell'Arte della Lana; ☺church 10am-5pm, museum 10am-5pm Mon) **FREE** This unusual and inspirational church, with a Gothic tabernacle by Andrea Orcagna, was created when the arcades of an old grain market (1290) were walled in and two storeys added during the 14th century. Its exterior is decorated with niches and tabernacles bearing statues. Representing the patron saints of Florence's many guilds, the statues were commissioned in the 15th and 16th centuries after the *signoria* ordered the city's guilds to finance the church's decoration.

These statues represent the work of some of the greatest Renaissance artists. Only copies adorn the building's exterior today, but all the originals except one are beautifully displayed in the church's little-known, light and airy museum, open only on Monday in two floors above the church.

Via de' Tornabuoni
LANDMARK

(Map p484) Renaissance palaces and Italian fashion houses border Via de' Tornabuoni, the city's most expensive shopping strip. Named after a Florentine noble family (which died out in the 17th century), it is referred to as the 'Salotto di Firenze' (Florence's Drawing Room). At its northern end is **Palazzo Antinori** (Map p484; Piazza Antinori 3) (1461–69), owned by the aristocratic Antinori family (known for wine production) since 1506. Opposite, huge stone steps lead up to 17th-century **Chiesa di San Gaetano** (Map p484).

Chiesa di Santa Trìnita
CHURCH

(Map p484; Piazza Santa Trinita; ☺8am-noon & 4-5.45pm Mon-Sat, 8-10.45am & 4-5.45pm Sun) Built in Gothic style and later given a Mannerist facade, this 14th-century church shelters some of the city's finest frescoes: Lorenzo Monaco's *Annunciation* (1422) in **Cappella Bartholini Salimbeni** and eye-catching frescoes by Ghirlandaio depicting the life of St Francis of Assisi in **Cappella Sassetti**, right of the altar. The frescoes were painted between 1483 and 1485 and feature portraits of illustrious Florentines of the time; pop a €0.50 coin in the slot to illuminate the frescoes for two minutes.

Palazzo Strozzi GALLERY

(Map p484; ☑ 055 246 96 00; www.palazzo strozzi.org; Piazza degli Strozzi; adult/reduced €10/8, 2 tickets for price of 1 6-11pm Thu; ☉9am-8pm Tue, Wed & Fri-Sun, to 11pm Thu) This 15th-century Renaissance mansion was built for wealthy merchant Filippo Strozzi, one of the Medicis' major political and commercial rivals. Today it hosts exciting art exhibitions. There's always a buzz about the place, with young Florentines congregating in the courtyard Café Apollo (run by Florentine designer Roberto Cavalli). Art workshops and other activities aimed squarely at families make the gallery a firm favourite with pretty much everyone.

Museo Marino Marini GALLERY

(Map p484; Piazza San Pancrazio 1; adult/reduced €6/4; ☉10am-5pm Wed-Sat & Mon) Deconsecrated in the 19th century, Chiesa di San Pancrazio is home to this small art museum displaying sculptures, portraits and drawings by Pistoia-born sculptor Marino Marini (1901-80). But the highlight is the **Cappella Rucellai** with a tiny scale copy of Christ's Holy Sepulchre in Jerusalem – a Renaissance gem designed by Leon Battista Alberti. The chapel was built between 1458 and 1467 for the tomb of wealthy Florentine banker and wool merchant, Giovanni Ruccellai.

◉ Santa Maria Novella

Basilica di Santa Maria Novella CHURCH

(Map p484; www.chiesasantamarianovella.it; Piazza di Santa Maria Novella 18; adult/reduced €5/3.50; ☉9am-5.30pm Mon-Thu, 11am-5.30pm Fri, 9am-5pm Sat, 1-5pm Sun) The striking green-and-white marble facade of Santa Maria Novella fronts an entire monastical complex, comprising romantic church cloisters and a frescoed chapel. The basilica itself is a treasure chest of artistic masterpieces, climaxing with frescoes by Domenico Ghirlandaio. The lower section of the basilica's striped marbled facade is transitional from Romanesque to Gothic; the upper section and the main doorway (1456-70) were designed by Leon Battista Alberti.

As you enter, look straight ahead to see Masaccio's superb fresco *Holy Trinity* (1424-25), one of the first artworks to use the then newly discovered techniques of perspective and proportion. Hanging in the central nave is a luminous painted *Crucifix* by Giotto (c 1290).

The first chapel to the right of the altar, **Cappella di Filippo Strozzi**, features spirited late-15th-century frescoes by Filippino Lippi (son of Fra' Filippo Lippi) depicting the lives of St John the Evangelist and St Philip the Apostle.

Behind the main altar is the **Cappella Maggiore** with Domenico Ghirlandaio's frescoes. Those on the right depict the life of John the Baptist; those on the left illustrate scenes from the life of the Virgin Mary. The frescoes were painted between 1485 and 1490, and are notable for their depiction of Florentine life during the Renaissance. Spot portraits of Ghirlandaio's contemporaries and members of the Tornabuoni family, who commissioned them.

To the far left of the altar, up a short flight of stairs, is the **Cappella Strozzi di Mantova,** covered in 14th-century frescoes by Niccolò di Tommaso and Nardo di Cione depicting paradise, purgatory and hell. The altarpiece (1354-57) here was painted by the latter's brother Andrea, better known as Andrea Orcagna.

From the church, walk through a side door into the serene **Chiostro Verde** (Green Cloister; 1332-62), part of the vast monastical complex occupied by Dominican friars who arrived in Florence in 1219 and settled in Santa Maria Novella two years later. The tranquil cloister takes its name from the green earth base used for the frescoes on three of the cloister's four walls. On its north side is the spectacular **Cappellone degli Spagnoli** (Spanish Chapel), originally the friars' chapter house and named as such in 1566 when it was given to the Spanish colony in Florence. The chapel is covered in extraordinary frescoes (c 1365-67) by Andrea di Bonaiuto. The vault features depictions of the Resurrection, Ascension and Pentecost, and on the altar wall are scenes of the *Via Dolorosa, Crucifixion* and *Descent into Limbo*. On the right wall is a huge fresco of *The Militant and Triumphant Church* – look in the foreground for a portrait of Cimabue, Giotto, Boccaccio, Petrarch and Dante. Other frescoes in the chapels depict the *Triumph of Christian Doctrine*, 14 figures symbolising the Arts and Sciences, and the Life of St Peter.

By the side of the chapel, a passage leads into the **Chiostro dei Morti** (Cloister of the Dead), a cemetery existent well before the arrival of the Dominicans to Santa Maria Novella. The tombstones embedded in the walls and floor date to the 13th and 14th centuries.

On the west side of the Chiostro Verde, another passage leads to the 14th-century **Cappella degli Ubriachi** and a large **refectory** (1353–54) featuring ecclesiastical relics and a 1583 *Last Supper* by Alessandro Allori.

There are two entrances to the Santa Maria Novella complex: the main entrance to the basilica or through the tourist office opposite the train station on Via dei Panzani; Firenze Card holders are obliged to use the latter.

★ **Museo Novecento**   MUSEUM
(Museum of the 20th Century; Map p484; ☑055 28 61 32; www.museonovecento.it; Piazza di Santa Maria Novella 10; adult/reduced €8.50/4; ☉10am-6pm Mon-Wed, to 2pm Thu, to 9pm Fri, to 8pm Sat & Sun) Don't allow the Renaissance to distract from Florence's fantastic modern art museum, in a 13th-century palazzo previously used as a pilgrim shelter, hospital and school. A well-articulated itinerary guides visitors through modern Italian painting and sculpture from the early 20th century to the late 1980s. Installation art makes effective use of the outside space on the 1st-floor loggia. Fashion and theatre get a nod on the 2nd floor, and the itinerary ends with a 20-minute cinematic montage of the best films set in Florence.

☉ San Lorenzo

Basilica di San Lorenzo   BASILICA
(Map p484; Piazza San Lorenzo; admission €4.50, incl Biblioteca Medicea Laurenziana €7; ☉10am-5.30pm Mon-Sat, plus 1.30-5pm Sun winter) Considered one of Florence's most harmonious examples of Renaissance architecture, this unfinished basilica was the Medici parish church and mausoleum. It was designed by Brunelleschi in 1425 for Cosimo the Elder and built over an earlier 4th-century church. In the solemn interior look out for Brunelleschi's austerely beautiful **Sagrestia Vecchia** (Old Sacristy) with its sculptural decoration by Donatello. Michelangelo was commissioned to design the facade in 1518, but his design in white Carrara marble was never executed, hence the building's rough unfinished appearance.

Inside, columns of *pietra serena* (soft grey stone) crowned with Corinthian capitals separate the nave from the two aisles. Donatello, who was still sculpting the two bronze pulpits (1460–67) adorned with panels of the Crucifixion when he died, is buried in the chapel featuring Fra' Filippo Lippi's *Annunciation* (c 1450).

Biblioteca Medicea Laurenziana   LIBRARY
(Medici Library; Map p484; www.bml.firenze.sbn.it; Piazza San Lorenzo 9; admission €3, incl basilica €7; ☉9.30am-1.30pm Mon-Sat) Beyond the Basilica di San Lorenzo ticket office lie peaceful cloisters framing a garden with orange trees. Stairs lead up the loggia and the Biblioteca Medicea Laurenziana, commissioned by Giulio de' Medici (Pope Clement VII) in 1524 to house the extensive Medici library (started by Cosimo the Elder and greatly added to by Lorenzo Il Magnifico). The extraordinary staircase in the vestibule, intended as a 'dark prelude' to the magnificent **Sala di Lettura** (Reading Room), was designed in by Michelangelo.

Museo delle Cappelle Medicee   MAUSOLEUM
(Medici Chapels; Map p484; ☑055 29 48 83; www.polomuseale.firenze.it; Piazza Madonna degli Aldobrandini; adult/reduced €6/3; ☉8.15am-1.50pm, closed 2nd & 4th Sun & 1st, 3rd & 5th Mon of month) Nowhere is Medici conceit expressed so explicitly as in the Medici Chapels. Adorned with granite, marble, semi-precious stones and some of Michelangelo's most beautiful sculptures, it is the burial place of 49 dynasty members. Francesco I lies in the dark, imposing **Cappella dei Principi** (Princes' Chapel) alongside Ferdinando I and II and Cosimo I, II and III. Lorenzo Il Magnifico is buried in the graceful **Sagrestia Nuova** (New Sacristy), which was Michelangelo's first architectural work.

It is also in the sacristy that you can swoon over three of Michelangelo's most haunting sculptures: *Dawn and Dusk* on the sarcophagus of Lorenzo, Duke of Urbino; *Night and Day* on the sarcophagus of Lorenzo's son Giuliano (note the unfinished face of 'Day' and the youth of the sleeping woman drenched in light aka 'Night'); and *Madonna and Child,* which adorns Lorenzo's tomb.

Palazzo Medici-Riccardi   PALACE
(Map p484; ☑055 276 03 40; www.palazzo-medici.it; Via Cavour 3; adult/reduced €7/4; ☉8.30am-7pm Thu-Tue) Cosimo the Elder entrusted Michelozzo with the design of the family's townhouse in 1444. The result was this palace, a blueprint that influenced the construction of Florentine family residences such as Palazzo Pitti and Palazzo Strozzi.

San Lorenzo & San Marco

The upstairs chapel, **Cappella dei Magi**, is covered in a wonderfully detailed frescoes (c 1459–63) by Benozzo Gozzoli, a pupil of Fra' Angelico, and is one of the supreme achievements of Renaissance painting.

◉ San Marco

★ Galleria dell'Accademia   GALLERY
(Map p497; www.polomuseale.firenze.it; Via Ricasoli 60; adult/reduced €8/4; ☺8.15am-6.50pm Tue-Sun) A queue marks the door to this gallery, built to house one of the Renaissance's most iconic masterpieces, Michelangelo's *David*. But the world's most famous statue is worth the wait. The subtle detail of the real thing – the veins in his sinewy arms, the leg muscles, the change in expression as you move around the statue – *is* impressive. Carved from a single block of marble, Michelangelo's most famous work was his most challenging – he didn't choose the marble himself and it was veined.

And when the statue of the nude boy-warrior, depicted for the first time as a man in the prime of life rather than a young boy, assumed its pedestal in front of Palazzo Vecchio on Piazza della Signoria in 1504, Florentines immediately adopted it as a powerful emblem of Florentine power, liberty and civic pride.

Michelangelo was also the master behind the unfinished *San Matteo* (St Matthew; 1504–08) and four *Prigioni* ('Prisoners' or 'Slaves'; 1521–30), also displayed in the gallery. The Prisoners seem to be writhing and struggling to free themselves from the marble; they were meant for the tomb of Pope Julius II, itself never completed. Adjacent rooms contain paintings by Andrea Orcagna, Taddeo Gaddi, Domenico Ghirlandaio, Filippino Lippi and Sandro Botticelli.

★ Museo di San Marco   MUSEUM
(Map p497; www.polomuseale.firenze.it; Piazza San Marco 1; adult/reduced €4/2; ☺8.15am-

1.50pm Mon-Fri, 8.15am-4.50pm Sat & Sun, closed 1st, 3rd & 5th Sun & 2nd & 4th Mon of month) At the heart of Florence's university area sits **Chiesa di San Marco** and adjoining 15th-century Dominican monastery where both gifted painter Fra' Angelico (c 1395–1455) and the sharp-tongued Savonarola (1452–1498) piously served God. Today the monastery, aka one of Florence's most spiritually uplifting museums, showcases the work of Fra' Angelico. After centuries of being known as 'Il Beato Angelico' (literally 'The Blessed Angelic One') or simply 'Il Beato' (The Blessed), the Renaissance's most blessed religious painter was made a saint by Pope John Paul II in 1984.

Enter via Michelozzo's **Cloister of Saint Antoninus** (1440). Turn immediately right to enter the **Sala dell'Ospizio** (Pilgrims' Hospital) where Fra' Angelico's attention to perspective and the realistic portrayal of nature comes to life in a number of major paintings, including the *Deposition of Christ* (1432).

Giovanni Antonio Sogliani's fresco *The Miraculous Supper of St Domenic* (1536) dominates the former monks' refectory in the cloister; and Fra' Angelico's huge *Crucifixion and Saints* fresco (1441–42) decorates the former chapterhouse. But it is the 44 monastic cells on the 1st floor that are the most haunting: at the top of the stairs, Fra' Angelico's most famous work, *Annunciation* (c 1440), commands all eyes.

A stroll around each of the cells reveals snippets of many more religious reliefs by the Tuscan-born friar, who decorated the cells between 1440 and 1441 with deeply devotional frescoes to guide the meditation of his fellow friars. Most were executed by Fra' Angelico himself, others by aides under his supervision, including Benozzo Gozzoli. Among several masterpieces is the magnificent *Adoration of the Magi* in the cell used by Cosimo the Elder as a meditation retreat (Nos 38 to 39). Quite a few of the frescoes are gruesome: the cell of San Antonino Arcivescovo features Jesus pushing open the door of his sepulchre, squashing a nasty-looking devil in the process.

Contrasting with the pure beauty of these frescoes are the plain rooms that Savonarola called home from 1489. Rising to the position of prior at the Dominican convent, it was from here that the fanatical monk railed against luxury, greed and corruption of the clergy. Kept as a kind of shrine to the turbulent priest, they house a portrait, a few personal items, the linen banner Savonarola carried in processions and a grand marble monument erected by admirers in 1873.

◉ Santa Croce

Basilica di Santa Croce　　CHURCH, MUSEUM
(Map p499; www.santacroceopera.it; Piazza di Santa Croce; adult/reduced €6/4; ☉9.30am-5.30pm Mon-Sat, 2-5.30pm Sun) The austere interior of this Franciscan basilica is a shock after the magnificent neo-Gothic facade enlivened by varying shades of coloured marble. Most visitors come to see the tombs of Michelangelo, Galileo and Ghiberti inside this church, but frescoes by Giotto in the chapels right of the altar are the real highlights. The basilica was designed by Arnolfo di Cambio between 1294 and 1385 and owes its name to a splinter of the Holy Cross donated by King Louis of France in 1258.

◉ The Oltrarno

Literally 'beyond the Arno', the atmospheric Oltrarno takes in all of Florence south of the river and is the traditional home of the city's artisanal workshops.

Ponte Vecchio　　BRIDGE
(Map p500) Dating to 1345, Ponte Vecchio was the only Florentine bridge to survive destruction at the hands of retreating German forces in 1944. Above the jewellers' shops on the eastern side, the **Corridoio Vasariano** (Vasari corridor) is a 16th-century passageway between the Uffizi and Palazzo Pitti that runs around, rather than through, the medieval **Torre dei Mannelli** at the bridge's southern end. The first documentation of a stone bridge here, at the narrowest crossing point along the entire length of the Arno, dates from 972.

Basilica di Santo Spirito　　CHURCH
(Map p500; Piazza Santo Spirito; ☉9.30am-12.30pm & 4-5.30pm Thu-Tue) FREE The facade of this Brunelleschi church, smart on Florence's most shabby-chic piazza, makes a striking backdrop to open-air concerts in summer. Inside, the basilica's length is lined with 38 semicircular chapels (covered with a plain wall in the 1960s), and a colonnade of grey *pietra forte* Corinthian columns injects monumental grandeur. Artworks to look for include Domenico di Zanobi's *Madonna of the Relief* (1485) in the Cappella Velutti, in

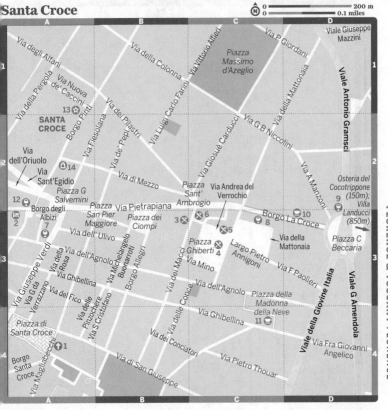

Santa Croce

Santa Croce

which the Madonna wards off a little red devil with a club.

Filippino Lippi's poorly lit *Madonna with Child and Saints* (1493–94) is in the **Cappella Nerli** in the right transept.

The main altar, beneath the central dome, is a voluptuous baroque flourish, rather out of place in Brunelleschi's characteristically spare interior.

Don't miss the door next to **Capella Segni** in the left aisle leading to the sacristy,

The Oltrarno

200 m
0.1 miles

SAN FREDIANO

SANTO SPIRITO

Gnam (150m); Berberè (200m)

Culinaria Bistrot (150m); Ostello Tasso (450m)

Desinare (300m)

See The Duomo & Santa Maria Novella Map (p484)

Porta San Niccolò (400m); La Bottega del Buon Caffè (700m)

ZEB (300m); Piazzale Flò (800m)

Porta San Miniato (200m); Piazzale Michelangelo (700m)

Forte di Belvedere (200m); Museo delle Porcellane (350m)

Piazza del Carmine

Borgo San Frediano

Piazza N Sauro

Borgo della Stella

Via Santa Monaca

Via dell'Ardiglione

Via de' Serragli

Via Sant'Agostino

Via della Chiesa

Via del Campuccio

Via delle Caldaie

Borgo Tegolaio

Via Romana

Via Santa Maria

Via Mazzetta

Piazza San Felice

Via Maggio

Via de' Serragli

Giardino Torrigiani

Lungarno Guicciardini

Piazza degli Scarlatti

Via di Santo Spirito

Piazza de' Frescobaldi

Palazzo Frescobaldi

Ponte Santa Trinita

Borgo SS Apostoli

Lungarno degli Acciaiuoli

Corridoio Vasariano

Piazza della Signoria

Via de' Neri

Piazza Castellani

Piazza della Signoria

Piazza dei Giudici

Piazza Mentana

Lungarno Generale Diaz

Arno

Lungarno Torrigiani

Via de' Bardi

Costa Scarpuccia

Costa di San Giorgio

Vicolo della Cava

Via Stracciatella

Piazza Santa Felicità

Piazza di Santa Maria Soprarno

Piazza de' Rossi

Via de' Bardi

Via de' Barbadori

Via de' Ramaglianti

Via Guicciardini

Borgo San Jacopo

Vicolo della Cava

Piazza della Passera

Via de' Velluti

Via dello Sprone

Via Maggio

Via Michelozzi

Piazza Santo Spirito

Sdrucciolo de' Pitti

Sdrucciolo de' Pitti

Via Sguazza

Via de' Velluti

Piazza dei Pitti

Palazzo Pitti

1

2

3

4

5

6

7

8

9

10

11

12

13

14

15

16

17

18

19

20

21

22

23

24

25

The Oltrarno

where you'll find a poignant wooden crucifix attributed by some experts to Michelangelo. Michelangelo used to visit the hospital inside the neighbouring monastery at night to study the anatomy of corpses yet to be buried, hence his donation of the exquisitely sculptured Christ – or so the story goes.

Cappella Brancacci CHAPEL
(Map p500; ☑ 055 276 82 24; http://museicivici fiorentini.comune.fi.it; Piazza del Carmine 14; adult/reduced €6/4.50; ☺ 10am-5pm Wed-Sat & Mon, 1-5pm Sun) Fire in the 18th century all but destroyed 13th-century **Basilica di Santa Maria del Carmine**, but fortunately it spared the magnificent frescoes in this chapel – a treasure of paintings by Masolino da Panicale, Masaccio and Filippino Lippi commissioned by rich merchant Felice Brancacci upon his return from Egypt in 1423. The entrance to the chapel is to the right of the main church entrance. Only 30 people are allowed in at any one time and visits are limited to 30 minutes in high season.

Palazzo Pitti MUSEUM
(Map p500; www.polomuseale.firenze.it; Piazza dei Pitti; ☺ 8.15am-6.50pm Tue-Sun, reduced hours winter) Commissioned by banker Luca Pitta and designed by Brunelleschi in 1457, this vast Renaissance palace was later bought by the Medici family. Over the centuries, it served as the residence of the city's rulers until the Savoys donated it to the state in 1919. Nowadays it houses an impressive silver museum, a couple of art museums and a series of rooms recreating life in the palace during House of Savoy times.

Giardino di Boboli GARDENS
(Map p500; Piazza dei Pitti; adult/reduced incl Museo degli Argenti, Museo delle Porcellane & Galleria del Costume €7/3.50; ☺ 8.15am-7.30pm summer, reduced hours winter) Behind Palazzo Pitti, the Boboli Gardens were laid out in the mid-16th century to a design by architect Niccolò Pericoli. At the upper, southern limit, beyond the box-hedged rose garden and Museo delle Porcellane, fantastic views over the Florentine countryside infold.

Giardino Bardini GARDENS
(Map p500; www.bardinipeyron.it; entrances at Via de' Bardi 1r & Costa di San Giorgio 2; adult/reduced €8/6; ☺ 10am-7pm Tue-Sun) This garden was named after art collector Stefano Bardini (1836–1922), who bought the villa in 1913 and restored its medieval garden. It has all the features of a quintessential Tuscan garden including artificial grottos, an orangery, marble statues and fountains. Inside the villa is the 2nd-floor **Museo Pietro Annigoni** displaying works by the Italian painter Pietro Annigoni (1910–88), the **Museo Roberto Capucci** showcasing Capucci-designed haute couture on the 4th floor; and temporary exhibitions plus a wonderful roof terrace to gaze down on the city on the 3rd floor.

> ❶ **GARDEN STROLL**
>
> An easy footpath leads from Giardino di Boboli to Giardino Bardini, which are a mere five-minute walk apart. The gate between the two shuts at 5pm.

LOCAL KNOWLEDGE

CLET STREET ART

Should you notice something gone awry with street signs in Oltrarno – on a No Entry sign, a tiny black figure stealthily sneaking away with the white bar for example – you can be sure it is the work of CLET, Florence's most talked-about and admired street artist who quietly beavers away in his Oltrarno studio on Via dell'Olmo creating stickers that end up on street signs all over the city. Occasionally the French-born artist creates even more of a stir in his adopted city with a piece of installation art, like the time he installed, in the black of night, a life-sized figurine entitled *Uomo Comune* (Common Man) on Ponte alle Grazie (to which the city authorities turned a blind eye for a week before removing it).

April and May. with the garden's flower beds of azaleas, peonies and wisteria in bloom, are lovely months to visit, as is June with its flowering irises. The garden restaurant, La Leggenda Dei Frati (p510), with stone loggia overlooking the Florentine skyline, is one of the most romantic spots in the city to dine.

Piazzale Michelangelo　　　VIEWPOINT
(📷13) Turn your back on the bevy of ticky-tacky souvenir stalls flogging *David* statues and boxer shorts and take in the spectacular city panorama from this vast square, pierced by one of Florence's two *David* copies. Sunset here is particularly dramatic. It's a 10-minute uphill walk along the serpentine road, paths and steps that scale the hillside from the Arno and Piazza Giuseppe Poggi; from Piazza San Niccolò walk uphill and bear left up the long flight of steps signposted Viale Michelangelo. Or take bus 13 from Stazione di Santa Maria Novella.

Forte di Belvedere　　　FORTRESS, GALLERY
(www.museicivicifiorentini.comune.fi.it; Via di San Leonardo 1; adult/reduced €5/3; ⊙variable) Forte di Belvedere is a rambling fort designed by Bernardo Buontalenti for Grand Duke Ferdinando I at the end of the 16th century. From the massive bulwark soldiers kept watch on four fronts – as much for internal security as to protect the Palazzo Pitti as against foreign attack. Today the fort hosts seasonal art exhibitions, well worth a peek if only to revel in the sweeping city panorama that can be had from the fort.

🎓 Courses

Florence has zillions of schools running courses in Italian language, culture and cuisine. **Context Travel** (www.contexttravel. com) organises fresco-painting workshops.

Cucina Lorenzo de' Medici　　COOKING COURSE
(Map p497; www.cucinaldm.com; Via dell'Ariento Piazza del Mercato Centrale) Shiny new state-of-the-art cooking school with 16 work stations in the fabulously bustling food mall above Florence's central food market; cooking classes (€90 to €130, three hours) and cooking demonstrations with tastings (€38, 1½ hours) around the chef's table. Sign up online or in situ at the information desk in the food mall.

Desinare　　　COOKING COURSE
(☑055 22 11 18; www.desinare.it; Via dei Serragli 234r) Shop for and cook a typical Tuscan meal, learn about Italian cheeses or master the art of pasta-making at this recommended (and super-stylish) school near Boboli Gardens. Superb kitchen shop and tastings at the 'chef's table' too in the showroom of interior designer Riccardo Barthel.

🧭 Tours

City Sightseeing Firenze　　　BUS TOUR
(Map p497; ☑055 29 04 51; www.firenze.city-sightseeing.it; Piazza della Stazione 1; adult 1/2/3 days €20/25/30) Explore Florence by red open-top bus, hopping on and off at 15 bus stops around the city. Tickets, sold by the driver, are valid for 24 hours.

★500 Touring Club　　　DRIVING TOUR
(www.500touringclub.com; Via Gherardo Silvani 149a) Hook up with Florence's 500 Touring Club for a guided tour in a vintage motor – with you behind the wheel! Every car has a name in this outfit's fleet of gorgeous vintage Fiat 500s from the 1960s (Giacomo is the playboy, Anna the feminist girl and so on). Motoring tours are guided – hop in your car and follow the leader – and themed – families love the picnic trip, couples wine tasting.

March to November tours need to be booked well in advance.

De Gustibus　　　TOUR
(☑340 579 62 07; www.de-gustibus.it) This umbrella association for local farms in the surrounding Florentine countryside organises

extremely tasty tours to small family-run organic farms. Tours are invariably themed – wine, truffles, olive oil – and can be by car, on foot or bicycle. Check its website or Facebook page for details of upcoming tours.

ArtViva WALKING TOUR
(Map p484; ☑ 055 264 50 33; www.italy.artviva.com; Via de' Sassetti 1; per person from €25) One-to three-hour city walks led by historians or art history graduates: tours include the Uffizi, the Original David tour and an adult-only 'Sex, Drugs & the Renaissance' art tour.

Curious Appetite TOUR
(www.curiousappetitetravel.com) Private and group, food and wine tastings led by Italian-American Coral Lelah. Tastings last 3½ hours, cost from €65 per person (minimum four people) and are themed: at the market, craft cocktails and *aperitivi*, Italian food and wine pairings, and artisan gelato.

Accidental Tourist TOUR
(☑ 055 69 93 76; www.accidentaltourist.com) Become an Accidental Tourist (membership €10), then sign up for a wine tour (€60), cooking class (€70), gourmet picnic (€35) and so on; tours happen in and around Florence.

🎊 Festivals & Events

Festa di Anna Maria Medici CULTURAL
(☉18 Feb) Florence's Feast of Anna Maria Medici marks the death in 1743 of the last Medici, Anna Maria, with a costumed parade from Palazzo Vecchio to her tomb in the Cappelle Medicee.

Scoppio del Carro FIREWORKS
A cart of fireworks is exploded in front of the cathedral at 11am on Easter Sunday.

Maggio Musicale Fiorentino PERFORMING ARTS
(www.operadifirenze.it) Italy's oldest arts festival features world-class performances of theatre, classical music, jazz and dance; April to June.

Festa di San Giovanni RELIGIOUS
(☉24 Jun) Florence celebrates its patron saint, John, with a *calcio storico* (historic football) match on Piazza di Santa Croce and fireworks over Piazzale Michelangelo.

🛏 Sleeping

Florence is unexpectedly small, rendering almost anywhere in the centre convenient. Budget hotels are clustered around the Santa Maria Novella train station and Mercato Centrale in neighbouring San Lorenzo.

🛏 Around Piazza del Duomo & Piazza della Signoria

Hotel Cestelli HOTEL €
(Map p484; ☑ 055 21 42 13; www.hotelcestelli.com; Borgo SS Apostoli 25; d €70-100, without bathroom s €40-60, d €50-80; ☉closed 4 weeks Jan-Feb, 2-3 weeks Aug; ☏) Housed in a 12th-century *palazzo* a stiletto hop from fashionable Via de' Tornabuoni, this intimate eight-room hotel is a gem. Rooms reveal an understated style, tastefully combining polished antiques with spangly chandeliers, vintage art and silk screens. Owners Alessio and Asumi are a mine of local information and are happy to share their knowledge. No breakfast.

★ Hotel Scoti PENSION €€
(Map p484; ☑ 055 29 21 28; www.hotelscoti.com; Via de' Tornabuoni 7; s/d €75/130; ☏) Wedged between the designer stores on Florence's smartest shopping strip, this hidden *pensione* is a splendid mix of old-fashioned charm and value for money. Its 16 traditionally styled rooms are spread across the 2nd floor of a towering 16th-century *palazzo*, with some offering lovely rooftop views. The star of the show, though, is the frescoed lounge from 1780. Breakfast €5.

Hotel Davanzati HOTEL €€
(Map p484; ☑ 055 28 66 66; www.hoteldavanzati.it; Via Porta Rossa 5; s/d €132/199; ✲@☏♿) Twenty-odd steps lead up to this swish hotel. A labyrinth of 27 enchanting rooms, frescoes and modern comforts, it has bags of charisma – and that includes Florentine brothers Tommaso and Riccardo, and father Fabrizio, who run the show (Grandpa Marcello surveys proceedings). Laptop, Nespresso coffee machine and 300 free movies on the TV in every room; iPads and playstations to borrow at reception.

Hotel Perseo HOTEL €€
(Map p484; ☑ 055 21 25 04; www.hotelperseo.it; Via de' Cerretani 1; s €130, d €155-210; ✲@☏♿) Perseo is a perfect family choice with its 20 large rooms, down-to-earth decor and friendly hosts, New Zealander Louise and Italian husband Giacinto. Top-floor rooms smooch with the rooftops and gorgeous *duomo* views. Should you not find (black) No 1 on the street, look for red No 23. Book online for the cheapest rates.

★ Antica Torre di Via de' Tornabuoni 1
BOUTIQUE HOTEL €€€

(Map p484; ☎ 055 265 81 61; www.tornabuoni1. com; Via de' Tornabuoni 1; d from €200; 🖸🏠) Just steps from the Arno, inside the beautiful 14th-century Palazzo Gianfigliazzi, is this raved-about hotel. Its 20 rooms are stylish, spacious and contemporary. But what completely steals the show is the stunning rooftop breakfast terrace – easily the best in the city. Sip cappuccino and swoon over Florence graciously laid out at your feet.

Hotel Torre Guelfa
HISTORIC HOTEL €€€

(Map p484; ☎ 055 239 63 38; www.hoteltorre guelfa.com; Borgo SS Apostoli 8; d/tr €240/270; 🖸@🏠) If you wanna kip in a Real McCoy Florentine *palazzo* without breaking the bank, this 31-room hotel with fortress-style facade is the address. Scale its 13th-century, 50m-tall tower – Florence's tallest privately owned *torre* – for a sundowner overlooking Florence and you'll be blown away. Rates are practically halved in low season.

🛏 Santa Maria Novella

Ostello Archi Rossi
HOSTEL €

(Map p497; ☎ 055 29 08 04; www.hostelarchi rossi.com; Via Faenza 94r; dm €25-32; ⊙ closed Dec; @🏠) Guests' paintings and artwork brighten this busy hostel near Santa Maria Novella train station. Bright white dorms have three to nine beds and must be evacuated between 10.30am and 2.30pm for cleaning. Guests can use washing machines, frozen meal dispensers and microwaves. No curfew but guests have to ring the bell after 2am.

Hotel Azzi
HOTEL €€

(Locanda degli Artisti; Map p497; ☎ 055 21 38 06; www.hotelazzi.com; Via Faenza 56/88r; d €120-150, tr €160-180, q €180-210; 🖸🏠) The five-minute walk from the train station only adds to the convenience of this 24-room hotel. It has been around a while and furnishings are old-style. But triple and quadruple rooms in particular are enormous – brilliant for families – and the kids' corner with toys in the lounge, library full of books and summer terrace are welcome touches.

Hotel L'O
DESIGN HOTEL €€€

(Map p484; ☎ 055 27 73 80; www.hotelorologio florence.com; Piazza di Santa Maria Novella 24; d from €375; 🅿🖸@🏠) The type of seductive address James Bond would feel right at home in, this super-stylish hotel oozes panache. Designed as a showcase for the (very wealthy) owner's (exceedingly expensive) luxury wristwatch collection, L'O (the hip take on its full name, Hotel L'Orologio) has four stars, rooms named after watches and clocks pretty much everywhere. Don't be late...

🛏 San Lorenzo & San Marco

★ Academy Hostel
HOSTEL €

(Map p484; ☎ 055 239 86 65; www.academy hostel.eu; Via Ricasoli 9r; dm €32-36, s/d €42/100, d without bathroom €85; 🖸@🏠) This classy 10-room, 40-bed hostel sits on the 1st floor of Baron Ricasoli's 17th-century *palazzo*. The inviting lobby area was once a theatre and 'dorms' sport maximum four or six beds, high moulded ceilings and brightly coloured lockers. The terrace is a perfect spot to chill. No credit cards for payments under €100.

Hotel Orto de' Medici
HOTEL €€

(Map p497; ☎ 055 48 34 27; www.ortodei medici.it; Via San Gallo 30; d from €184; 🖸@🏠) This three-star hotel in San Marco redefines elegance with its majestic high ceilings, chic oyster-grey colour scheme and contemporary furnishings, offset to perfection by the historic *palazzo* in which it languishes. Hunt down the odd remaining 19th-century fresco, and don't miss the garden complete with lemon trees in terracotta pots and rambling ivy. To really splurge, go for a room with its own flowery terrace.

Hotel Morandi alla Crocetta
BOUTIQUE HOTEL €€

(Map p497; ☎ 055 234 47 47; www.hotelmorandi. it; Via Laura 50; s/d €105/170; 🅿🖸🏠) This medieval-convent-turned-hotel away from the madding crowd in San Marco is a stunner. Rooms are refined and traditional in look – think antique furnishings, wood beams and oil paintings – with a quiet, old-world ambience. Pick of the bunch is frescoed room No 29, the former chapel.

🛏 Santa Croce

★ Hotel Dalí
HOTEL €

(Map p484; ☎ 055 234 07 06; www.hoteldali.com; Via dell'Oriuolo 17; d €90, s/d without bathroom €40/70, apt from €95; 🅿🏠) A warm welcome from hosts Marco and Samanta awaits at this lovely small hotel. A stone's throw from the Duomo, it has 10 sunny rooms, some overlooking a leafy inner courtyard, decorated in a low-key modern way and equipped with kettles, coffee and tea. No breakfast, but – miraculous for downtown Florence – free parking in the rear courtyard.

The icing on the cake is a trio of gorgeous self-catering apartments – one with a Duomo view – sleeping two, four or six.

Hotel Orchidea
HOTEL €

(Map p499; ☑ 055 248 03 46; www.hotelorchidea florence.it; Borgo degli Albizi 11; s/d with shared bathroom €60/80) This old-fashioned *pensione* in the mansion where the Donati family roosted in the 13th century (Dante's wife, Gemma, was allegedly born in the tower) is charm personified. Its seven rooms with sink and shared bathroom are simple, but their outlook is five-star. Many guests return each May/June simply to enjoy the 100-year-old wisteria in bloom. No breakfast; free tea and coffee-making facilities.

Villa Landucci
B&B €€

(☑ 055 66 05 95; www.villalanducci.it; Via Luca Landucci 7; d/tr €130/150; P 🖥 📶) Five elegant and refreshingly spacious rooms are named after Tuscan wines at this gourmet-themed B&B, a short walk away from Santa Croce. The best in the house, 'Bolgheri' and 'Chianti', open onto the well-tended garden with veggie patch, magnolia tree, age-old palm and kids' play area. Breakfast is predominantly organic and free parking is a rarity.

Borrow a bicycle (reserve in advance) to pedal the 500m to Piazza del Duomo. Debora, a sommelier, and partner Matteo, who created the place, are founts of knowledge when it comes to dining well, and they can organise wine-tasting and food tours for guests.

🛏 The Oltrarno

★ Ostello Tasso
HOSTEL €

(☑ 055 060 20 87; www.ostellotassofirenze.it; Via Villani 15; dm €30-32, s/d €37/70; @ 🖥) Hostelling in Florence got a whole load more stylish with the opening of this chic crash pad, a two-minute walk from the tasty eateries of Piazza Tasso. Coloured bed linen and floor rugs give three- to six-bed dorms a boutique charm, the courtyard garden is a dream, and DJs spin tunes in the hip lounge bar (open to nonguests too). Rates include breakfast, locker, sheets and towel.

★ Palazzo Guadagni Hotel
HOTEL €€

(Map p500; ☑ 055 265 83 76; www.palazzogua dagni.com; Piazza Santo Spirito 9; d €150, extra bed €45; ❄ 🖥) This romantic hotel overlooking Florence's liveliest summertime square is legendary – Zefferelli shot scenes from *Tea with Mussolini* here. Housed in an artfully revamped Renaissance palace, it has 15 spacious if old-fashioned rooms and an impossibly romantic loggia terrace with wicker chairs and predictably dreamy views. Off season, double room rates drop to as low as €90.

Hotel La Scaletta
HOTEL €€

(Map p500; ☑ 055 28 30 28; www.hotella scaletta.it; Via Guicciardini 13; d €124-174, ste €194-214) An austere air wafts through this maze of a hotel, hidden in a 15th-century *palazzo* near Palazzo Pitti. But rooms – the priciest ones peeping down on Boboli Gardens – are spacious, and the view from the dreamy roof terrace is absolutely fabulous. Savour a summertime breakfast or early evening drink here and congratulate yourself on finding one of the best deals in town.

Palazzo Belfiore
APARTMENT €€

(Map p500; ☑ 055 26 44 15; www.palazzo belfiore.it; Via dei Velluti 8; d €160-185; 🖥) The smartly painted taupe door with shiny black knocker reflects the contemporary twist on the historic at this stylish residence, at home in a Renaissance *palazzo* on the Oltrarno. Its seven apartments with kitchen are spacious and swish, with a complimentary newspaper of your choice to start each day. Upon request, breakfast can be delivered (for an additional cost).

★ SoprArno Suites
GUESTHOUSE €€€

(Map p500; ☑ 055 046 87 18; www.soprarno suites.com; Via Maggio 35; d from €230; 🖥) A brilliant addition to the hotel scene, this boutique address squirrelled away in an Oltrarno courtyard creates an intimate home-from-home vibe while making it very clear each guest is special. Each of the 11 designer rooms are exquisitely dressed in vintage objets d'art and collectibles – the passion of Florentine owner Matteo and his talented Florence-born, British-raised wife Betty Soldi (herself a calligrapher and graphic designer).

Several have bathtubs with clawed feet, some are inspired by what remains of original 19th-century ceiling frescoes, and every room has a kettle, a fridge, a minibar and a DVD player (no telly). Breakfast around the shared table makes a grand start to the day.

Eating

Quality ingredients and simple execution are the hallmarks of Florentine cuisine, climaxing with the fabulous *bistecca alla fiorentina,* a huge slab of T-bone steak rubbed with olive oil, seared on the char-grill, garnished with salt and pepper and served *al sangue* (bloody).

Other typical dishes include *crostini* (toast topped with chicken-liver pâté or other toppings), *ribollita* (a thick vegetable, bread and bean soup), *pappa al pomodoro* (bread and tomato soup) and *trippa alla fiorentina* (tripe cooked in a rich tomato sauce).

Hip Santa Croce and increasingly gentrified Oltrarno are packed with great dining addresses.

Piazza del Duomo to Piazza della Signoria

★ Osteria Il Buongustai   OSTERIA €
(Map p484; Via dei Cerchi 15r; meals €15; ⊙11.30am-3.30pm Mon-Sat) Run with breathtaking speed and grace by Laura and Lucia, this place is unmissable. Lunchtimes heave with locals who work nearby and savvy students who flock here to fill up on tasty Tuscan homecooking at a snip of other restaurant prices. The place is brilliantly no frills – expect to share a table and pay in cash; no credit cards.

★ Mariano   SANDWICHES €
(Map p484; Via del Parione 19r; panini €3-5; ⊙8am-3pm & 5-7.30pm Mon-Fri, 8am-3pm Sat) Our favourite for its simplicity, around since 1973. Sunrise to sunset this brick-vaulted, 13th-century cellar gently buzzes with Florentines propped at the counter sipping coffee or wine or eating salads and *panini.* Come here for a coffee-and-pastry breakfast, light lunch, *aperitivo* or *panino* to eat on the move.

Look for the green neon 'pizzicheria' up high on the outside facade and the discrete 'alimentari' sign above the entrance.

Trattoria Marione   TRATTORIA €
(Map p484; ☑055 21 47 56; Via della Spada 27; meals €25; ⊙noon-3pm & 7-11pm) For the quintessential 'Italian dining' experience, Marione is gold. It's busy, it's noisy, it's 99.9% local and the cuisine is right out Nonna's Tuscan kitchen. No one appears to speak English so go for Italian – the tasty excellent-value traditional fare is worth it. If you don't get a complimentary *limoncello* with the bill you clearly failed the language test.

'Ino   SANDWICHES €
(Map p484; www.inofirenze.com; Via dei Georgofili 3r-7r; panini €5-8; ⊙11.30am-4.30pm summer, noon-3.30pm Mon-Fri, 11.30am-4.30pm Sat & Sun winter) 🖋 Artisan ingredients sourced locally and mixed creatively by passionate gourmet Alessandro Frassica is the secret behind

---

BEST GELATERIE

Florentines take gelato seriously and there's healthy rivalry among local *gelaterie artigianale* (makers of handmade gelato), who strive to create the city's creamiest, most flavourful and freshest ice cream. Flavours are seasonal and a cone or tub costs around €2/3/4/5 per small/medium/large/maxi.

Vivoli (Map p484; Via dell'Isola delle Stinche 7; tubs €2-10; ⊙7.30am-midnight Tue-Sun summer, to 9pm winter) Inside seating makes this ice-cream and cake shop stand out. Pistachio, pear and caramel, and chocolate with orange are crowd favourites. Pay at the cash desk then trade your receipt for your choice. No cones, only tubs.

Grom (Map p484; www.grom.it; cnr Via del Campanile & Via delle Oche; cones €2.50-4.50, tubs €2.50-5.50; ⊙10am-midnight summer, to 11pm winter) Rain, hail or shine, queues run halfway down the street at this sweet address; many ingredients are organic. Tasty hot chocolate and milkshakes too.

Gelateria La Carraia (Map p500; Piazza Nazario Sauro 25r; cones/tubs €1.50-6; ⊙11am-11pm summer, to 10pm winter) One glance at the constant line out the door of this bright green-and-citrus shop with exciting flavours (ricotta and pear, zuppa inglese, the best mint in town), and know you're at a Florentine favourite.

Carabé (Map p497; www.gelatocarabe.com; Via Ricasoli 60r; ⊙10am-midnight, closed mid-Dec–mid-Jan) Traditional Sicilian gelato, granita (sorbet) and brioche (Sicilian ice-cream sandwich); handy address if you're waiting in line to see *David.*

FARM TO TABLE

Culinaria Bistrot (☎ 055 22 94 94; www.de-gustibus.it/en; Piazza Torquato Tasso 13; meals €20; ⊗ 12.30-2.30pm & 6-11.30pm Wed-Mon) No dining address in Florence captures the culinary magic of 'farm to table' dining quite like this San Frediano bistro, an instant charmer with its exposed red-brick vaulted ceiling. French chef Jacques Pachoud only works with organic produce from local farms to cook up memorable Tuscan and Mediterranean dishes.

Titillate tastebuds with a traditional Tuscan tasting platter of local salami and/or cheese (€10 to €13), then move onto a chicken and prune tajine perhaps or a pork cheek and bean *cocotte* (casserole).

Also known as Culinaria di De Gustibus, the bistro is the business card of **De Gustibus** (p502), an organisation established to promote sustainable food and wine tourism through tastings, lunches, tours and other tempting foodie events and happenings. Farmers in the network supply the bistro with its astonishing choice of superb-quality local products.

La Bottega del Buon Caffè (☎ 055 553 56 77; www.borgointhecity.com; Lungarno Benvenuto Cellini 69r; 4-course lunch menu €60, 6-course tasting menus €80 & €95 (€125 & €145 with wine); ⊗ 12.30-3pm & 7.30-10.30pm Tue-Sat, 12:30-3pm Sun) Farm to table is the philosophy of this Michelin-starred restaurant where head chef Antonello Sardi mesmerises diners from the stunning open kitchen. Veg and herbs arrive from the restaurant's own farm, Borgo Santa Pietro, in the Sienese hills. Breads and *foccacia* (the nut version is heavenly) are homemade and the olive oil used (special production from Vinci) is clearly only the best.

From the complimentary amuse-bouche (pecorino cheese mousse served on a broad bean leaf with rosemary blossom) to the leapy pink radish dipped in salted butter that accompanies Sardi's creative take on traditional chicken-liver paté, ingredients are overwhelmingly fresh, green and natural.

this gourmet sandwich bar near the Uffizi. Create your own combo, pick from dozens of fun house specials or go for a tasting platter (salami, cheese, pecorini).

End with chocolate *degustazione* (tasting) – the chocolate peppered with olive oil and lemon zest is sensational.

Cantinetta dei Verrazzano TUSCAN €
(Map p484; Via dei Tavolini 18-20; focaccia from €3; ⊗ 8am-9pm summer, 8am-4pm Mon-Sat, 10am-4.30pm Sun winter) A *forno* (baker's oven) and *cantinetta* (small cellar) make a heavenly match. Sit down at a marble-topped table, sip wine from the Verrazzano family's Chianti estate and tuck into traditional *focaccia* or a mixed cold-meat platter.

★**Obicà** ITALIAN €€
(Map p484; ☎ 055 277 35 26; www.obica.com; Via de' Tornabuoni 16; 1/2/3 mozzarella €13/20/30, pizza €9.50-17, taglierini €4.50-19.50; ⊗ noon-4pm & 6.30-11.30pm Mon-Fri, noon-11pm Sat & Sun) Given its exclusive location in Palazzo Tornabuoni, this designer address is naturally ubertrendy – even the table mats are upcycled from organic products. Taste different

mozzarella cheeses in the cathedral-like interior or snuggle beneath heaters on sofa seating in the elegant, star-topped courtyard. At *aperitivo* hour nibble on *taglierini* (tasting boards loaded with cheeses, salami, deep fried veg and so on).

🍴 Santa Maria Novella

Il Latini TRATTORIA €€
(Map p484; ☎ 055 21 09 16; www.illatini.com; Via dei Palchetti 6r; meals €30; ⊗ 12.30-2.30pm & 7.30-10.30pm Tue-Sun) A veteran guidebook favourite built around traditional *crostini* (toast), Tuscan meats, fine pasta and roasted meats served at shared tables. There are two dinner seatings (7.30pm and 9pm), with service ranging from charming to not so charming. Reservations mandatory.

★**L'Osteria di Giovanni** TUSCAN €€€
(Map p484; ☎ 055 28 48 97; www.osteriadigiovanni.it; Via del Moro 22; meals €50; ⊗ 7-10pm Mon-Fri, noon-3pm & 7-10pm Sat & Sun) Cuisine at this smart neighbourhood eatery is sumptuously Tuscan. Imagine truffles, tender steaks and pastas such as *pici al sugo di salsiccia*

e cavolo nero (thick spaghetti with a sauce of sausage and black cabbage). Throw in a complimentary glass of *prosecco* and you'll want to return time and again.

🍴 San Lorenzo & San Marco

★ Mercato Centrale   TUSCAN €

(Map p497; 📞 055 239 97 98; www.mercato centrale.it; Piazza del Mercato Centrale 4; dishes €7-15; ⊙10am-1am, food stalls noon-3pm & 7pm-midnight; 🛜) Meander the maze of stalls crammed with fresh produce at Florence's oldest and largest food market, on the ground of a 19th-century iron-and-glass structure. Then head up to the shiny new 1st floor – a vibrant food fair with dedicated bookshop, cookery school, bar and stalls cooking up steaks, grilled burgers, vegetarian dishes, pizza, gelato, pastries and pasta. Load up and find a free table.

★ Trattoria Mario   TUSCAN €

(Map p497; www.trattoria-mario.com; Via Rosina 2; meals €20; ⊙noon-3.30pm Mon-Sat, closed 3 weeks Aug) Arrive by noon to ensure a stool around a shared table at this noisy, busy, brilliant trattoria – a legend that retains its soul (and allure with locals) despite being in every guidebook. Charming Fabio, whose grandfather opened the place in 1953, is front of house while big brother Romeo and nephew Francesco cook with speed in the kitchen.

Monday and Thursday are tripe days, and Friday is fish. Whatever the day, local Florentines flock here for a brilliantly blue *bistecca alla fiorentina*. No advance reservations, no credit cards.

Pugi   BAKERY €

(Map p497; www.focacceria-pugi.it; Piazza San Marco 9b; ⊙7.45am-8pm Mon-Sat, closed 2 weeks mid-Aug) The inevitable line outside the shop says it all. This bakery is a Florentine favourite for pizza slices and chunks of *schiacciata* (Tuscan flatbread) baked up plain, spiked with salt and rosemary, or topped or stuffed with whatever delicious edible goodie's in season. Grab a number, drool over the savoury (and sweet) treats demanding to be devoured, and wait for them to call your number.

Should you be queueing to see *David*, Pugi is a perfect two-minute hop from the Galleria dell'Accademia.

Da Nerbone   MARKET €

(Map p497; Piazza del Mercato Centrale, Mercato Centrale; ⊙7am-2pm Mon-Sat) Forge your way past cheese, meat and sausage stalls on the ground floor of Florence's Mercato Centrale to join the lunchtime queue at Nerbone, in the biz since 1872. Go local and order *trippa alla fiorentina* (tripe and tomato stew) or follow the crowd with a feisty *panini con bollito* (a hefty boiled-beef bun, dunked in the meat's juices before serving). Eat standing up or fight for a table.

Antica Trattoria da Tito   TRATTORIA €€

(📞 055 47 24 75; www.trattoriadatito.it; Via San Gallo 112r; meals €30; ⊙lunch & dinner Mon-Sat) The 'No well done meat here' sign, strung in the window, says it all: the best of Tuscan culinary tradition is the only thing this iconic

---

TRIPE: FAST-FOOD FAVOURITE

When Florentines fancy a fast munch on the move, they flit by a *trippaio* – a cart on wheels or mobile stand – for a tripe *panino* (sandwich). Think cow's stomach chopped up, boiled, sliced, seasoned and bunged between bread.

Bastions of good old-fashioned Florentine tradition, *trippai* still going strong include the cart on the southwest corner of **Mercato Nuovo** (p514), **L'Antico Trippaio** (Map p484; Piazza dei Cimatori; ⊙vary), **Pollini** (Map p499; Piazza Sant'Ambrogio; ⊙variable) and hole-in-the-wall **Da Vinattieri** (Map p484; Via Santa Margherita 4; panini €4.50; ⊙10am-7.30pm Mon-Fri, to 8pm Sat & Sun). Pay up to €4.50 for a *panino* with tripe doused in *salsa verde* (pea-green sauce of smashed parsley, garlic, capers and anchovies) or garnished with salt, pepper and ground chilli. Alternatively, opt for a bowl (€5.50 to €7) of *lampredotto* (cow's fourth stomach chopped and simmered for hours).

The pew-style seating at staunchly local **Osteria del Cocotrippone** (📞 055 234 75 27; Via Vincenzo Gioberti 140; meals €25; ⊙noon-2.30pm & 7-10.30pm) in the off-centre Beccaria neighbourhood is not a coincidence: Florentines come here to venerate the offal side of their city's traditional cuisine. The *trippa alla fiorentina* (tripe in tomato sauce) and *L'Intelligente* (fried brain and zucchini) are local legends.

trattoria serves. In business since 1913, Da Tito does everything right – tasty Tuscan dishes like onion soup and wild-boar pasta, served with friendly gusto and hearty goodwill to a local crowd. Don't be shy to enter.

✗ Santa Croce

★ All'Antico Vinaio
OSTERIA €

(Map p484; ☑ 055 238 27 23; www.allantico vinaio.com; Via dei Neri 65r; tasting platters €8-30, focaccia €5-7; ☺ 10am-4pm & 6-11pm Tue-Sat, noon-3.30pm Sun) The crowd spills out the door of this noisy Florentine thoroughbred. Push your way to the tables at the back and pray for a pew to taste cheese and salami in situ. Or join the queue at the deli counter for a well-stuffed focaccia (€5 to €7) wrapped in waxed paper to take away – quality is outstanding. Pour yourself a glass of wine (€2) while you wait.

Mercato di Sant'Ambrogio
MARKET €

(Map p499; Piazza Ghiberti; ☺ 7am-2pm Mon-Sat) Outdoor food market with an intimate, local flavour.

Semel
SANDWICHES €

(Map p499; Piazza Ghiberti 44r; panini €3.50-5; ☺ 11.30am-3pm) Florentines swear by this pocket-sized sandwich bar opposite Sant'Ambrogio food market. There is no fixed menu, rather an impossible-to-decide choice of six gourmet combos, crafted with love by passionate owner and *panini* king Marco Paparozzi. Wash it down with a glass of water or wine, and pride yourself on snagging one of the cheapest, tastiest lunches in town.

Il Pizzaiuolo
PIZZA €

(Map p499; ☑ 055 24 11 71; Via dei Macci 113r; pizzas €5-10; ☺ 12.30-2.30pm & 7.30pm-midnight Mon-Sat, closed Aug) Young Florentines flock to The Pizza Maker to nosh Neapolitan thick-crust pizzas hot from the wood-fired oven. Bookings essential for dinner.

Brac
VEGETARIAN €

(Map p484; ☑ 055 094 48 77; www.libreriabrac. net; Via dei Vagellai 18r; meals €20; ☺ noon-midnight, closed 2 weeks mid-Aug; ☑) This hipster cafe-bookshop – a hybrid dining-*aperitivi* address – cooks up inventive, home-style and strictly vegetarian and/or vegan cuisine. Its decor is recycled vintage with the odd kid's drawing thrown in for that intimate homey touch; and the vibe is artsy.

★ Il Teatro del Sale
TUSCAN €€

(Map p499; ☑ 055 200 14 92; www.teatrodelsale. com; Via dei Macci 111r; lunch/dinner/weekend brunch €15/20/30; ☺ 11am-3pm & 7.30-11pm Tue-Sat, 11am-3pm Sun, closed Aug) Florentine chef Fabio Picchi is one of Florence's living treasures who steals the Sant'Ambrogio show with this eccentric, good-value members-only club (everyone welcome, annual membership €7) inside an old theatre. He cooks up weekend brunch, lunch and dinner, culminating at 9.30pm in a live performance of drama, music or comedy arranged by his wife, artistic director and comic actress Maria Cassi.

Dinners are hectic: grab a chair, serve yourself water, wine and antipasti and wait for the chef to yell out what's about to be served before queuing at the glass hatch for your *primo* (first course) and *secondo* (second course). Note this is the only Picchi restaurant to serve pasta! Dessert and coffee are laid out buffet-style just prior to the performance.

Trattoria Cibrèo
TUSCAN €€

(Map p499; www.edizioniteatrodelsalecibreo firenze.it; Via dei Macci 122r; meals €30; ☺ 12.50-2.30pm & 6.50-11pm Tue-Sat, closed Aug) Dine here and you'll instantly understand why a queue gathers outside before it opens. Once inside, revel in top-notch Tuscan cuisine: perhaps *pappa al pomodoro* (a thick soupy mash of tomato, bread and basil) followed by *polpettine di pollo e ricotta* (chicken and ricotta meatballs). No reservations, no credit cards, no coffee, no pasta and arrive early to snag a table.

✗ The Oltrarno

★ 5 e Cinque
VEGETARIAN €

(Map p500; ☑ 055 274 15 83; Piazza della Passera 1; meals €25; ☺ 10am-10pm Tue-Sun) The hard work and passion of a photography and antique dealer is behind this highly creative, intimate eating space adored by every savvy local. Cuisine is vegetarian with its roots in Genova's kitchen – '5 e Cinque' (meaning '5 and 5') is a chickpea sandwich from Livorno and the restaurant's *cecina* (traditional Ligurian flat bread made from chickpea flour) is legendary.

★ Gnam
BURGERS €

(☑ 055 22 39 52; www.gnamfirenze.it; Via di Camaldoli 2r; meals from €10; ☺ noon-3pm & 6pm-midnight) Bread arrives at the table in

DON'T MISS

SILVER SPOON DINING

In Fabbrica (☎ 347 5145468; http://www.pampaloni.com/restaurant/; Via del Gelsomino 99; meal €45; ⊗ 8-10.30pm Wed-Sat) 1.5km south of Porto Romana along Via Senese on the Oltrarno, fuses Florence's outstanding tradition of craftsmanship with its equally fine cuisine. Meaning 'In the Factory', In Fabbrica is just that. By day, workers from third-generation Florentine silver house Pampaloni lunch here. Come dusk, the speakeasy canteen opens its doors to culturally curious diners.

Tables are laid with silver cutlery and majestic candelabras, waiters wear white gloves, and there are two fixed menus – one Italian, one Japanese. Advance reservations essential.

a brown paper bag and fries are served in a miniature copper cauldron at this green, artisanal burger joint in San Frediano. Ingredients are seasonal, locally sourced and organic – and there are vegetarian and gluten-free burgers as well as the traditional beefy variety. Delicous homemade soups also, to eat in or takeaway.

Berberè
PIZZA €

(☎ 055 238 29 46; www.berberepizza.it; Piazza dei Nerli 1; pizza €6.50-13; ⊗ noon-2.30pm & 7pm-midnight Fri-Sun, 7pm-midnight Mon-Thu) Florence's stunning new kid on the block, this modern pizza space in San Frediano is an inspirational cocktail of perfect pizza, delicious craft beers brewed by small producers and striking contemporary interior design. Grab a stool at the white marble bar and pick from 14 pizza types – several are vegetarian – made with organic flour and live yeast. Reservations essential.

Gustapizza
PIZZA €

(Map p500; Via Maggio 46r; pizza €4.50-8; ⊗ 11.30am-3pm & 7-11pm Tue-Sun) This unpretentious pizzeria near Piazza Santa Spirito redefines the word 'packed'. Arrive early to grab a bar stool at a wooden-barrel table and pick from seven pizza types.

Tamerò
ITALIAN €

(Map p500; ☎ 055 28 25 96; www.tamero.it; Piazza Santa Spirito 11r; meals €20; ⊗ noon-3pm & 7pm-2am Tue-Sun) A happening address on Florence's hippest square: admire pasta

cooks at work in the open kitchen while you wait for a table – the chances are you'll have to. A buoyant, party-loving crowd flocks here to fill up on imaginative fresh pasta, giant salads and copious cheese/salami platters. Decor is trendy industrial and weekend DJs spin sets from 10pm.

S.Forno
BAKERY €

(Map p500; Via Santa Monaco 3r; ⊗ 7.30am-7.30pm) Shop for fresh breads, bespoke *panini* and gourmet products stacked on vintage shelves at this hip bakery with baker Angelo at the helm.

La Casalinga
TRATTORIA €

(Map p500; ☎ 055 21 86 24; www.trattorialacasalinga.it; Via de' Michelozzi 9r; meals €25; ⊗ noon-2.30pm & 7-10pm Mon-Sat) Family run and locally loved, this busy unpretentious place is one of Florence's cheapest trattorias. Don't be surprised if Paolo, the patriarch figure who conducts the mad-busy show from behind the bar, relegates you behind locals in the queue: it's a fact of life, and eventually you'll be rewarded with hearty Tuscan dishes, cooked to exacting perfection.

★ Il Santo Bevitore
TUSCAN €€

(Map p500; ☎ 055 21 12 64; www.ilsantobevitore.com; Via di Santo Spirito 64-66r; meals €40; ⊗ 12.30-2.30pm & 7.30-11pm, closed Aug) Reserve or arrive dot-on 7.30pm to snag the last table at this ever-popular address, an ode to stylish dining where gastronomes dine by candlelight in a vaulted, whitewashed, bottle-lined interior. The menu is a creative reinvention of seasonal classics, different for lunch and dinner: purple cabbage soup with mozzarella cream and anchovy syrup, acacia honey *bavarese* (firm, creamy mousse) with Vin Santo–marinated dried fruits.

La Leggenda dei Frati
TUSCAN €€€

(Map p500; ☎ 055 068 05 45; www.laleggendadeifrati.it; Costa di San Giorgio 6, Villa Bardini; menus €55 & €70, meals €60; ⊗ lunch & dinner Tue-Sun) This is summer's hottest address. At home in the historic garden house of Villa Bardini, the Legend of Friars (run by the highly regarded Saporito brothers, previously in Castellina in Chianti) enjoys the most romantic terrace with view in Florence. Veggies are plucked fresh from the vegetable patch, tucked between waterfalls and ornamental beds in Giardino Bardini, and contemporary art jazzes up the classical interior.

Cuisine is Tuscan, gastronomic and well worth the vital advance reservation.

🍷 Drinking & Nightlife

Florence's drinking scene is split between *enoteche* (increasingly hip wine bars that invariably make great eating addresses too), trendy lounge bars with lavish *aperitivo* buffets (predinner drinks with nibbles from around 7pm to 10pm) and straightforward cafes that double as lovely lunch venues. For craft beer, Berberé (p510) is excellent.

🍷 Piazza del Duomo to Piazza della Signoria

Coquinarius   WINE BAR
(Map p484; www.coquinarius.com; Via delle Oche 11r; crostini & carpacci €4, meals €35; ⊘noon-10.30pm) With its old stone vaults, scrubbed wooden tables and refreshingly modern air, this *enoteca* run by the dynamic and charismatic Nicolas is spacious and stylish. The wine list features bags of Tuscan greats and unknowns, and outstanding *crostini* and *carpacci* (cold sliced meats) ensure you don't leave hungry.

TOP CAFES

Good cafes are a dime a dozen in Florence. Prime squares to sit and people-watch from a pavement terrace are Piazza della Repubblica, Piazza Santo Spirito and Piazza della Signoria. Note: a coffee drunk standing at the bar is dramatically cheaper than one drunk sitting down.

Caffè Rivoire (Map p484; Piazza della Signoria 4; ⊘7am-11pm Tue-Sun) This golden oldie with unbeatable people-watching terrace has produced some of the city's most exquisite chocolate since 1872. Black-jacketed barmen with ties set the formal tone.

Gilli (Map p484; www.gilli.it; Piazza della Repubblica 39r; ⊘7.30am-1.30am) The most famous of historic cafes on the city's old Roman forum, Gilli has been serving utterly delectable cakes, chocolates, fruit tartlets and *millefoglie* (sheets of puff pastry filled with rich vanilla or chocolate Chantilly cream) to die for since 1733 (it moved to this square in 1910 and sports a beautifully preserved art-nouveau interior).

L'Arte del Sogno (Map p499; ☑ 055 012 02 93; Borgo La Croce 24-26r; ⊘9am-7.30pm Mon-Fri, to 11pm Sat) Be it a mug of cinnamon-spiced milk, cappuccino or the most outrageous coffee imagineable with every cream-nut-chocolate topping going, this contemporary coffee house and tea room is just divine, darling. The choice of hot chocolate, tea and infusions – not to mention cookies, cakes, muffins and tarts – is equally impressive. Tables strung together from upcycled gilded picture frames and driftwood add an appealing artsy vibe.

Café Apollo (Map p484; Piazza Strozzi; ⊘8.30am-8pm Fri-Wed, to 11pm Thu) High-vaulted ceiling, sleek black Panton chairs, excellent coffee and unelevated prices seduce a mixed crowd at this artsy hangout in Palazzo Strozzi on Florence's most designer-chic street. It's run by the same team as Caffè Giacosa (Map p484; www.caffegiacosa.it; Via della Spada 10r; ⊘7.45am-8.30pm Mon-Fri, 8.30am-8.30pm Sat, 12.30-8pm Sun) of Roberto Cavelli fame across the road, and the chocolate-swirled cappuccino is among the best in town.

News Cafe (Map p484; ☑ 055 21 11 68; Via del Giglio 59) There is one fun reason to have a coffee at this San Lorenzo cafe – for a one-off cappuccino made by barista Marco. Designs drawn on the frothy milk depend on mood and whim, but the unelevated price is a constant – €1.20/2.10 standing up/sitting down.

Le Murate Caffè Letterario (Map p499; ☑ 055 234 68 72; www.lemurate.it; Piazza delle Murate Firenze; ⊘9am-1am) This artsy cafe-bar in Florence's former jail is where literati meet to talk, create and perform over coffee, drinks and light meals. The literary cafe hosts everything from readings and interviews with authors – Florentine, Italian and international – to film screenings, debates, live music and art exhibitions. Tables are built from recycled window frames and in summer everything spills outside into the brick courtyard.

THE PERFECT HANG-OUT

Ditta Artigianale (Map p484; ☎ 055 274 15 41; www.dittaartigianale.it; Via dei Neri 32r; ⏰ 8am-10pm Mon-Thu, 8am-midnight Fri, 9.30am-midnight Sat, 9.30am-10pm Sun; 🛜) With industrial decor and welcoming laid-back vibe, ingenious coffee roastery–cafe-bar Ditta Artigianale rocks. Behind the bar is well-travelled Florentine barista Francesco Sanapo and gin queen Cecilia who together shake and mix what the city's most compelling hybrid is famed for – first-class coffee and outstanding gin cocktails.

Brunch is served from 10am to 4pm, and a gourmet *aperitivo* kicks in at 7pm, making it a perfect place to hang out whatever the time of day.

La Terrazza
BAR

(Map p484; www.continentale.it; Vicolo dell'Oro 6r; ⏰ 2.30-11.30pm Apr-Sep) This rooftop bar with wooden-decking terrace accessible from the 5th floor of the Ferragamo-owned Hotel Continentale is as chic as one would expect of a fashion-house hotel. Its *aperitivo* is a modest affair, but who cares with that fabulous, drop-dead-gorgeous panorama of one of Europe's most beautiful cities. Dress the part or feel out of place.

Slowly
LOUNGE, BAR

(Map p484; www.slowlycafe.com; Via Porta Rossa 63r; ⏰ 6.30pm-3am Mon-Sat, closed Aug) Sleek and sometimes snooty, this lounge bar with a candle flickering on every table is known for its glam interior, Florentine Lotharios and lavish fruit-garnished cocktails – €10 including buffet during the bewitching *aperitivo* 'hour' (6.30pm to 10pm). Ibiza-style lounge tracks dominate the turntable.

Amblé
BAR, CAFE

(Map p484; ☎ 055 26 85 28; Piazzetta dei del Bene 7a; ⏰ 10am-10pm Mon-Sat, noon-10pm Sun) You need to know about this cafe-bar, a hop and a skip from Ponte Vecchio, to find it. Salvaged vintage tables and chairs – all for sale – create a hip, shabby-chic look and the tiny terrace feels well away from the madding crowd on summer evenings. From the river head down Viccolo dell'Oro to the Continentale hotel, and turn left along the alleyway that runs parallel to the river.

Procacci
CAFE

(Map p484; www.procacci1885.it; Via de' Tornabuoni 64r; ⏰ 10am-8pm Mon-Sat) The last remaining bastion of genteel old Florence on Via de' Tornabuoni, this tiny cafe was born in 1885 as a delicatessen serving truffles in its repertoire of tasty morsels. Bite-sized *panini tartufati* (truffle pâté rolls) remain the thing to order, best accompanied by a glass of *prosecco*.

YAB
CLUB

(Map p484; www.yab.it; Via de' Sassetti 5r; ⏰ 9pm-4am Oct-May) Pick your night according to your age and tastes at this disco club, around since the 1970s behind Palazzo Strozzi.

🍷 Santa Maria Novella

Shake Café
CAFE

(Map p484; ☎ 055 29 53 10; www.shakecafe.bio; Via degli Avelli 2r; ⏰ 7am-8pm) Handily close to the train station, this self-service juice bar has a perfect people-watching pavement terrace on car-free Piazza Santa Maria Novella. Its fruit-powered juices and smoothies include fabulous combos such as pineapple, fennel, celery, mint, chicory and liquorice. Unusually for Florence, Shake Café also makes cappuccinos with soya, almond or rice milk. Salads, wraps, sandwiches and gelati stave off hunger pangs.

Sei Divino
WINE BAR

(Borgo d'Ognissanti 42r; ⏰ 6pm-2am Wed-Mon) This stylish wine bar tucked beneath a red-brick vaulted ceiling is privy to one of Florence's most happening *aperitivo* scenes. It plays music, hosts occasional exhibitions and in summertime the pavement action kicks in. *Aperitivi* 'hour' (with copious banquet) runs 7pm to 10pm.

Space Club
CLUB

(www.spaceclubfirenze.com; Via Palazzuolo 37r; admission incl 1 drink €16; ⏰ 10pm-4am) Sheer size alone at this vast club in Santa Maria Novella impresses – dancing, drinking, video-karaoke in the bar, and a mixed student-international crowd.

🍷 Santa Croce

Kitsch
BAR

(Map p499; www.kitschfirenze.com; Viale A Gramsci 5; ⏰ 6.30pm-2.30am; 🛜) Cent-conscious Florentines love this American-styled bar for its lavish spread at *aperitivi* time – €10 for a drink and sufficient nibbles to not need dinner. It sports a dark-red theatrical interior and a bright 20s- to early-30s crowd out for a good time. DJ sets set the place rocking after dark. **Kitsch Devx** (Map p497; Via San Gallo 22r; ⊘6pm-2am) is its twin sister.

Drogheria LOUNGE, BAR
(Map p499; www.drogheriafirenze.it; Largo Annigoni 22; ⊘10am-2am) Be it rain, hail or shine, this is a lovely contemporary address in Santa Croce. Inside, it is a large space with dark wood furnishings and comfy leaf-green armchairs, perfect for lounging for hours on end. Come spring, the action moves outside onto the terrace, aplomb on the huge square across from Sant'Ambrogio market.

Lion's Fountain IRISH PUB
(Map p499; www.thelionsfountain.com; Borgo degli Albizi 34r; ⊘10am-2am) If you have the urge to hear more English than Italian – or local bands play for that matter – this is the place. Plump on a pretty pedestrian square, Florence's busiest Irish pub buzzes in summer when the beer-loving crowd spills across most of the square. Live music.

Bamboo CLUB
(Map p499; ☑335 43 44 84; www.bamboolounge club.com; Via Giuseppe Verdi 59r; ⊘7pm-4am Thu-Sat) A hipster crowd looks beautiful in this Santa Croce newcomer, a lounge and dance club with chintzy red seating, steely grey bar and a mix of hip hop and R&B on the turntable. Dress up, look good to get in.

🍴 The Oltrano

⭐**Le Volpi e l'Uva** WINE BAR
(Map p500; www.levolpieluva.com; Piazza dei Rossi 1; ⊘11am-9pm Mon-Sat) This unassuming wine bar hidden away by Chiesa di Santa Felicità remains as appealing as the day it opened over a decade ago. Its food and wine pairings are first-class – taste and buy boutique wines by 150 small producers from all over Italy, matched perfectly with cheeses, cold meats and the best *crostini* in town. Wine-tasting classes too.

Il Santino WINE BAR
(Map p500; Via di Santo Spirito 60r; ⊘12.30-11pm) This pocket-sized wine bar is packed every evening. Inside, squat modern stools contrast with old brick walls, but the real action is outside, from around 9pm, when the buoyant wine-loving crowd spills onto the street.

Volume BAR
(Map p500; www.volumefirenze.com; Piazza Santo Spirito 3r; ⊘9am-1.30am) Armchairs, recycled and upcycled vintage furniture, books to read, juke box, crepes and a tasty choice of nibbles with coffee or a light lunch give this hybrid cafe-bar-gallery real appeal – all in an old hat-making workshop with tools and wooden moulds strewn around. Watch for various music, art and DJ events and happenings.

ZEB WINE BAR
(www.zebgastronomia.com; Via San Miniato 2r; ⊘noon-3pm Sun-Tue, noon-3pm & 7.30-10.30pm Thu-Sat) Local gastronomes adore this modern, minimalist *enoteca* at the foot of the hill leading up to Piazzale Michelangelo, in village-like San Niccolò. Post-panorama, sit around the deli-style counter and indulge in a delicious choice of cold cuts and creative Tuscan dishes prepared by passionate chef Alberto Navari and his *mamma* Giuseppina.

Flò LOUNGE
(☑055 65 07 91; www.flofirenze.com; Piazzale Michelangelo 84; ⊘7.30pm-late summer) Without a doubt the hottest and hippest place to be seen in the city on sultry summer nights is Flò, a truly ab fab seasonal lounge bar that pops up each May on Piazzale Michelangelo. Different themed lounge areas include a dance floor, and VIP area (where you have no chance of reserving a table unless you're in the Florentine in-crowd).

⭐ Entertainment

La Cité LIVE MUSIC
(Map p500; www.lacitelibreria.info; Borgo San Frediano 20r; ⊘8am-2am Mon-Sat, 3pm-2am Sun; 🔊) A hip cafe-bookshop with an eclectic choice of vintage seating, La Cité makes a wonderful, intimate venue for live music – jazz, swing, world music – and book readings.

Jazz Club JAZZ
(Map p499; Via Nuovo de' Caccini 3; ⊘10.30pm-2am Tue-Sat, closed Jul & Aug) Catch salsa, blues, Dixieland and world music as well as jazz at Florence's top jazz venue.

Opera di Firenze OPERA
(☑055 277 9350; www.operadifirenze.it; Piazzale Vittorio Gui, Viale Fratelli Rosselli; ⊘box office 2-6pm Mon, 10am-6pm Tue-Sat) Florence's striking new opera house with glittering contemporary geometric facade sits on the

green edge of city park Parco delle Cascine. Its three thoughtfully designed and multi-functional concert halls seat an audience of 5000 and play host to the springtime Maggio Musicale Fiorentino.

🛍 Shopping

Tacky mass-produced souvenirs (boxer shorts emblazoned with David's packet) are everywhere, not least at the city's two main markets, Mercato Centrale (p508) and Mercato Nuovo (Map p484; Loggia Mercato Nuovo; ⊙8.30am-7pm Mon-Sat), awash with cheap imported handbags and other leather goods. But for serious shoppers keen to delve into a city synonymous with craftsmanship since medieval times, there are plenty of workshops and boutiques to visit. Leather goods, jewellery, hand-embroidered linens, designer fashion, perfume, marbled paper, wine, puppets and gourmet foods all make quality souvenirs.

★Officina Profumo-Farmaceutica
di Santa Maria Novella   BEAUTY, GIFTS
(www.smnovella.it; Via della Scala 16; ⊙9.30am-7.30pm) In business since 1612, this perfumery-pharmacy began life when the Dominican friars of Santa Maria Novella

began to concoct cures and sweet-smelling unguents using medicinal herbs cultivated in the monastery garden. The shop today sells a wide range of fragrances, skin-care products, ancient herbal remedies and preparations alongside teas, herbal infusions, liqueurs, scented candles, organic olive oil, chocolate, honey and cookies.

★& Company   ARTS, CRAFTS
(Map p500; http://andcompanyshop.tumblr.com/; Via Maggio 60r; ⊙10.30am-1pm & 3-6.30pm Mon-Sat) This mesmerising Pandora's box of beautiful objects and paper creations is the love child of Florence-born, British-raised calligrapher and graphic designer Betty Soldi and her vintage-loving husband, Matteo Perduca. Together the pair have created an extraordinary boutique showcasing their own customised cards and upcycled homewares alongside work by other designers. Souvenir shopping at its best!

Letizia Fiorini   GIFTS, HANDICRAFTS
(Map p484; Via del Parione 60r; ⊙10am-7pm Tue-Sat) This charming shop is a one-woman affair – Letizia Fiorini sits at the counter and makes her distinctive puppets by hand in between assisting

SHOP TO EAT

Shopping for culinary products is a sheer joy in foodie Florence, a city where locals live to eat. Mercato Centrale (p508) aside, these are Florentines' favourites for food shopping. Don't miss the splendid array of conserved vegetables and other homemade treats on sale at Il Teatro del Sale (p509).

La Bottega Della Frutta (Map p484; Via dei Federighi 31r; ⊙8.30am-7.30pm Mon-Sat, closed Aug) Follow the trail of knowing Florentines, past the flower-and veg-laden bicycle parked outside, into this enticing food shop bursting with boutique cheeses, organic fruit and veg, biscuits, chocolates, conserved produce, excellent-value wine et al. Mozzarella oozing raw milk arrives fresh from Eboli in Sicily every Tuesday, and if you're looking to buy olive oil this is the place to taste. Simply ask Elisabeta or husband Francesco.

Eataly (Map p484; ☑055 015 36 01; Via de' Martelli 22r; ⊙10am-10.30pm) Eataly shops are as much about learning about food as shopping for it, and the Florence branch is no exception. Grab a free audioguide at the information desk (near the exit) and peruse aisles laden with coffee, biscuits, conserved vegetables, pasta, rice, olive oil while listening to Renaissance tales. Many products are local and/or organic; most are by small producers.

Dolce Forte (www.dolceforte.it; Via della Scala 21; ⊙10am-1pm & 3.30-7.45pm Wed-Sat & Mon, 3.30-7.45pm Tue) Elena is the passion and knowledge behind this astonishing chocolate shop that sells only the best. Think black-truffle-flavoured chocolate, an entire cherry, stone and all, soaked in grappa and wrapped in white chocolate or – for the ultimate taste sensation – formaggio di fossa (a cheese from central Italy) soaked in sweet wine and enrobed in dark chocolate.

customers. You'll find Pulcinella (Punch), Arlecchino the clown, beautiful servant girl Colombina, Doctor Peste (complete with plague mask), cheeky Brighella, swashbuckling Il Capitano and many other characters from traditional Italian puppetry.

Giulio Giannini e Figlio   HANDICRAFTS

(Map p500; www.giuliogiannini.it; Piazza dei Pitti 37r; ☺10am-7pm Mon-Sat, 11am-6.30pm Sun) This quaint old shopfront has watched Palazzo Pitti turn pink with the evening sun since 1856. One of Florence's oldest artisan families, the Gianninis – bookbinders by trade – make and sell marbled paper, beautifully bound books, stationery and so on. Don't miss the workshop upstairs.

Mrs Macis   FASHION

(Map p499; Borgo Pinti 38r; ☺4-7.30pm Mon, 10.30am-1pm & 4-7.30pm Tue-Sat) Workshop and showroom of the talented Carla Macis, this eye-catching boutique – dollhouse-like in design – specialises in very feminine 1950s, '60s and '70s clothes and jewellery made from new and recycled fabrics. Every piece is unique and fabulous.

Grevi   FASHION

(Map p484; www.grevi.com; Via della Spada 11-13r; ☺10am-2pm & 3-8pm Mon-Sat) It was a hat made by Siennese milliner Grevi that actress Cher wore in the film *Tea with Mussolini*; ditto Maggie Smith in *My House in Umbria* (2003). So if you want to shop like a star for a hat by Grevi, this hopelessly romantic boutique is the address. Hats range in price from €30 to unaffordable for many.

Boutique Nadine   VINTAGE

(Map p484; www.boutiquenadine.com; Via de' Benci 32r; ☺2.30-7.30pm Mon, 10.30am-7.30pm Tue-Sat, 2-7pm Sun) There is no more elegant and quaint address to shop for vintage clothing, jewellery, homewares and other pretty little trinkets. From the wooden floor and antique display cabinets to the period changing cabin, Nadine's attention to detail is impeccable. Find a second, riverside boutique near Ponte Vecchio at Lungarno Acciaiuoli 22r.

Aprosio & Co   ACCESSORIES, JEWELLERY

(Map p484; www.aprosio.it; Via della Spada 38; ☺10am-7pm Mon-Fri, 10.30am-7.30pm Sat) Ornella Aprosio fashions teeny tiny glass and crystal beads into dazzling pieces of jewellery, hair accessories, animal-shaped

brooches, handbags, even glass-flecked cashmere. It is all quite magical.

Marioluca Giusti   HOMEWARES

(Map p484; www.mariolucagiusti.com; Via della Vigna Nuova 88r; ☺10am-7.30pm Mon-Sat, 11am-7.30pm Sun) The voluptuous jugs, beakers, glasses and other elegant tableware items in this eye-catching boutique look like glass – but are not! Everything created by Florentine designer Marioluca Giusti is, in fact, crafted from acrylic, melamine or other synthetic material. Young, fresh and a mix of pop and vintage in style, the homewares here make great gifts to take home.

Scriptorium   CRAFTS

(Map p484; Via dei Pucci 4; ☺9.30am-7.30pm Mon-Fri, 9.30am-1pm Sat) A mooch around this upmarket boutique is worth it, if only to dip into the utterly cinematic courtyard of Palazzo Pucci in which it's hidden. Scriptorium crafts exquisite leather boxes and books, calligraphy nibs and pens, and old-world wax seals in every colour under the sun.

ⓘ Information

EMERGENCY

Police Station (Questura; ☑English-language service 055 497 72 68, 055 4 97 71;

http://questure.poliziadistato.it; Via Zara 2;
⏲24hr) Should you have a theft or other unfortunate incident to report, the best time to visit the city's police station is between 9am and 2pm weekdays when the foreign-language service – meaning someone speaks who English – kicks in.

MEDICAL SERVICES

24-Hour Pharmacy (Stazione di Santa Maria Novella) This pharmacy inside Florence's central train station opens 24 hours. There is usually at least one member of staff who speaks English.

Dr Stephen Kerr: Medical Service (✆055 28 80 55, 335 8361682; www.dr-kerr.com; Piazza Mercato Nuovo 1; ⏲3-5pm Mon-Fri, or by appointment 9am-3pm Mon-Fri) Resident British doctor.

Hospital (Ospedale di Santa Maria Nuova; ✆055 2 75 81; Piazza di Santa Maria Nuova 1)

TOURIST INFORMATION

Airport Tourist Office (✆055 31 58 74; www.firenzeturismo.it; Via del Termine, Aeroporto Vespucci; ⏲9am-7pm Mon-Sat, to 2pm Sun)

Infopoint Stazione (Map p484; ✆055 21 22 45; www.firenzeturismo.it; Piazza della Stazione 5; ⏲9am-7pm Mon-Sat, to 2pm Sun)

Central Tourist Office (✆055 29 08 32; www.firenzeturismo.it; Via Cavour 1r; ⏲9am-6pm Mon-Sat)

Getting There & Away

AIR

Tuscany's main international airport is in Pisa (p563) and offers flights to most major European cities.

Florence Airport (Aeroport Vespucci; ✆055 306 13 00; www.aeroporto.firenze.it; Via del Termine) Also known as Amerigo Vespucci or Peretola airport, 5km northwest of the city centre; domestic and European flights.

BUS

Services from the Sita bus station, just west of Piazza della Stazione, are limited; the train is better. Destinations include the following:

Greve in Chianti (€4.20, one hour, hourly)

San Gimignano (via Poggibonsi; €7.20, 1¼ hours, 14 daily)

Siena (€7.80, 1¼ hours, at least hourly)

CAR & MOTORCYCLE

Florence is connected by the A1 northwards to Bologna and Milan, and southwards to Rome and Naples. The A11 links Florence with Pistoia, Lucca, Pisa and the coast, but most locals use the FI-PI-LI dual carriageway. Another dual carriageway, the S2, links Florence with Siena.

TRAIN

Florence's central train station is Stazione di Santa Maria Novella. Tickets are sold in the main ticketing hall; skip the permanently long queue by buying tickets from the touch-screen automatic ticket-vending machines; machines have an English option and accept cash and credit cards.

Florence is on the Rome–Milan line. Services include:

TO	FARE (€)	DURATION (HR)	FREQUENCY
Bologna	24	1-1¾	every 15 mins
Lucca	7.20	1½-1¾	half-hourly
Milan	29-53	2¼-3½	hourly
Pisa	8	¾-1	half-hourly
Rome	43-52	1¾-4¼	half-hourly
Venice	50-60	2¾-4½	two per hour

ℹ Getting Around

TO/FROM THE AIRPORT
Bus

A shuttle (single/return €6/8, 25 minutes) travels between Florence airport and Florence's Stazione di Santa Maria Novella train station every 30 minutes between 6am and 11.30pm (5.30am to 11pm from the city centre).

A shuttle bus (single/return €6/8, 20 minutes) links Florence bus station and Florence airport every 30 minutes between 6am and 8pm, then hourly from 8.30pm until 11.30pm (from 5.30am to 12.30am from the airport).

Terravision (www.terravision.eu; one way €4.99, 70 minutes) and **Autostradale** (www.airportbusexpress.it; one way €5, 80 minutes, hourly) run buses to Pisa airport from the bus stops outside Florence's Stazione di Santa Maria Novella on Via Alamanni (under the digital station clock). Buy tickets online, on board and in Pisa at the Pisa Airport Information Desk in the arrivals hall.

Taxi

A taxi between Florence Airport and town costs a flat rate of €20 (€23 on Sunday and holidays, €22 between 10pm and 6am) plus €1 per bag.

Train

Regular trains link Florence's Stazione di Santa Maria Novella with the central train station in Pisa, Pisa Centrale (€8, 1½ hours, at least hourly from 4.30am to 10.25pm), from where the PisaMover shuttle bus (€1.30, eight minutes) continues to Pisa International Airport.

FIESOLE DAY TRIPPER

A visit to Fiesole provides the perfect excuse to head for the hills. Perched 9km northeast of the city, this hilltop village has seduced for centuries with its cooler air, olive groves, scattering of Renaissance-styled villas and spectacular views of the plain. Boccaccio, Marcel Proust, Gertrude Stein and Frank Lloyd Wright, among others, raved about it.

Morning

Founded in the 7th century BC by the Etruscans, Fiesole was the most important city in northern Etruria and its **Area Archeologica** (www.museidifiesole.it; Via Portigiani 1; adult/reduced Fri-Sun €10/6, Mon-Thu €8/4; ☉10am-7pm summer, shorter hours winter), off central square Piazza Mino di Fiesole. Buy a ticket at the **tourist office** (☏055 596 13 11, 055 596 13 23; www.fiesoleforyou.it; Via Portigiani 3, Fiesole; ☉10am-6.30pm summer, to 5.30pm winter), a couple of doors away, then meander around the ruins of a small Etruscan temple, Roman baths and an archaeological museum. Later, pause on the stone steps of the 1st-century-BC Roman amphitheatre, summer stage to Italy's oldest open-air festival, **Estate Fiesolana** (www.estatefiesolana.it).

Afterwards, pop into the neighbouring **Museo Bandini** (www.museidifiesole.it; Via Dupré; adult/reduced €5/3, with Area Archeologica ticket free; ☉10am-7pm summer, shorter hours winter) to view early Tuscan Renaissance art, including fine medallions (c 1505–20) by Giovanni della Robbia and Taddeo Gaddi's luminous *Annunciation* (1340–45).

From the museum, a 300m walk along Via Giovanni Dupré brings you to the **Fondazione Primo Conti** (☏055 59 70 95; www.fondazioneprimoconti.org; Via Giovanni Dupré 18; admission €3; ☉9am-2pm Mon-Fri) where the eponymous avant-garde 20th-century artist lived and worked. Inside hang more than 60 of his paintings, and the views from the garden are inspiring. Ring to enter.

Lunch with a View

Meander back to Piazza Mino di Fiesole, host to an antiques market on the first Sunday of each month, where cafe and restaurant terraces tempt. The pagoda-covered terrace of **Villa Aurora** (☏055 5 93 63; www.villaurora.net; Piazza Mino da Fiesole 39; meals €30; ☉noon-2.30pm & 7-10.30pm), around since 1860, is the classic choice. For rustic Tuscan partaken at a shared table, **Vinandro** (☏055 5 91 21; www.vinandrofiesole.com; Piazza Mino da Fiesole 33; meals €25; ☉noon-midnight) is popular, but not a patch on **La Reggia degli Etruschi** (☏055 5 93 85; www.lareggiadeglietruschi.com; Via San Francesco; meals €30; ☉7-9.30pm Mon-Wed, 12.30-1.30pm & 7-9.30pm Thu-Sun), an outstanding dine with swoon-worthy views where knowing Florentines lunch on Sunday.

Afternoon

Stagger around **Cattedrale di San Romolo** (Piazza Mino di Fiesole; ☉7.30am-noon & 3-5pm) FREE, begun in the 11th century. A terracotta statue of San Romolo by Giovanni della Robbia guards the entrance inside.

Afterwards, make your way up steep walled **Via San Francesco** and be blown away by the beautiful panorama of Florence that unfolds from the terrace adjoining 15th-century **Chiesa e Convento di San Francesco**. The tourist office has brochures outlining several short trails (1km to 3.5km) fanning out from here.

Aperitivo

Join Florentines for an early evening drink at **JJ Hill** (☏055 5 93 24; Piazza Mino da Fiesole 40; ☉6pm-midnight Mon-Wed, 5pm-1am Thu-Sat, 5-11pm Sun), or fire up the romantic in you with a 2½-hour, 21km guided bike ride at sunset (€45) with **FiesoleBike** (☏345-33 50 926; www.fiesolebike.it; Piazza Mino da Fiesole). This creative bike rental/guiding outfit is run with passion by local lad Giovanni Crescioli (a qualified biking and hiking guide); his tour departs daily from Piazza Mino di Fiesole at 5pm in season (book online).

Getting There & Around

ATAF bus 7 (€1.20, 20 minutes, every 15 minutes) goes from Florence's Piazza San Marco uphill to Piazza Mino di Fiesole.

BICYCLE & SCOOTER

Milleunabici (www.bicifirenze.it; Piazza della Stazione; 1hr/5hr/1 day €2/5/10; ⊙10am-7pm Mar-Oct) Violet coloured bikes to rent in front of Stazione di Santa Maria Novella; leave ID as a deposit.

Florence by Bike (www.florencebybike. com; Via San Zanobi 54r; 1hr/5hr/1 day €3/9/14; ⊙9am-1pm & 3.30-7.30pm Mon-Sat, 9am-5pm Sun summer, closed Sun winter) Top-notch bike shop with bike rental (city, mountain, touring and road bikes), itinerary suggestions and organised bike tours (two-hour photography tours of the city by bike, and day trips to Chianti).

CAR & MOTORCYCLE

Nonresident traffic is banned from the historic centre of Florence for most of the week and our advice is to avoid the irksome bother of having a car in the city. Motorists staying in hotels within the limited traffic zone are allowed to drive to their hotel to drop off luggage, but must tell reception their car registration number and the time they were in no-cars-land (there's a two-hour window) so the hotel can organise a permit. If you transgress, a fine of around €150 will be sent to you (or the car-hire company you used).

Away from the historic centre, there is free parking around Piazzale Michelangelo. Paying car parks can be found around Fortessa da Basso and in the Oltrarno beneath Piazzale di Porta Romana.

PUBLIC TRANSPORT

Buses and electric minibuses run by public transport company ATAF serve the city. Most buses start/terminate at the bus stops opposite the southeastern exit of Stazione di Santa Maria Novella. Tickets valid for 90 minutes (no return journeys) cost €1.20 (€2 on board) and are sold at kiosks, tobacconists and at the **ATAF ticket & information office** (Map p497; ☑199 10 42 45, 800 42 45 00; www.ataf.net; Piazza della Stazione, Stazione di Santa Maria Novella; ⊙6.45am-8pm Mon-Sat) inside the main ticketing hall at Santa Maria Novella train station.

A travel pass valid for 1/3/7 days costs €5/12/18. Upon boarding, time-stamp your ticket (punch on board) or risk an on-the-spot €50 fine. One tramline is up and running; more are meant to follow in 2017.

TAXI

Pick one up at the train station or call ☑055 42 42.

CENTRAL TUSCANY

When people imagine classic Tuscan countryside, they usually conjure up images of central Tuscany. However there's more to this popular region than gently rolling hills, sun-kissed vineyards and artistically planted avenues of cypress trees. Truth be told, the real gems are the historic towns and cities, most of which are medieval and Renaissance time capsules magically transported to the modern day.

Siena

POP 54,126

The rivalry between historic adversaries Siena and Florence continues to this day, and participation isn't limited to the locals – most travellers tend to develop a strong preference for one over the other. These allegiances often boil down to aesthetic preference: while Florence saw its greatest flourishing during the Renaissance, Siena's enduring artistic glories are largely Gothic.

History

Legend tells us that Siena was founded by the son of Remus, and the symbol of the wolf feeding the twins Romulus and Remus is as ubiquitous in Siena as it is in Rome. In reality the city was probably of Etruscan origin, although it didn't begin to grow into a proper town until the 1st century BC, when the Romans established a military colony here called Sena Julia.

In the 12th century, Siena's wealth, size and power grew along with its involvement in commerce and trade. Its rivalry with neighbouring Florence grew proportionately, leading to numerous wars during the first half of the 13th century between Guelph Florence and Ghibelline Siena. Eventually, Siena was forced to ally with its rival in 1270.

In the ensuing century the city was ruled by the Consiglio dei Nove (Council of Nine, a bourgeois group constantly bickering with the aristocracy) and enjoyed its greatest prosperity.

A plague outbreak in 1348 killed two-thirds of Siena's 100,000 inhabitants and led to a period of decline that culminated in the city being handed over to Cosimo I de' Medici, who barred the inhabitants from operating banks and thus severely curtailed its power.

This centuries-long economic downturn in the wake of the Medici takeover was a blessing in disguise, as the lack of funds meant that it was subject to very little re-development or new construction. This led to the historic centre's inclusion on Unesco's World Heritage List as it is the living embod-iment of a medieval city.

◎ Sights

★ **Piazza del Campo** FOUNTAIN

This sloping piazza, popularly known as Il Campo, has been Siena's civic and social centre since being staked out by the ruling Consiglio dei Nove in the mid-12th century. It was built on the site of a Roman mar-ketplace, and its pie-piece paving design is divided into nine sectors to represent the number of members of that ruling council.

In 1346 water first bubbled forth from the Fonte Gaia (Happy Fountain; Piazza del Campo) in the upper part of the square. Today, the fountain's panels are reproductions; the se-verely weathered originals, sculpted by Ja-copo della Quercia in the early 15th century, are on display in the Complesso Museale Santa Maria della Scala.

The Campo is the heart of the city. Its magnificent pavement acts as a carpet on which students and tourists picnic and re-lax, and the cafes around the perimeter are the most popular *aperitivo* spots in town.

Palazzo Comunale HISTORIC BUILDING

(Palazzo Pubblico; Piazza del Campo; ◎10am-7pm summer, to 6pm winter) The restrained, 14th-century Palazzo Comunale serves as the grand centrepiece of the square in which it sits – notice how its concave facade mirrors the opposing convex curve. From the *palaz-zo* soars a graceful bell tower, the Torre del Mangia (Palazzo Comunale, Piazza del Campo; admission €10; ◎10am-7pm summer, to 4pm win-ter), 102m high and with 500-odd steps. The views from the top are magnificent.

★ **Museo Civico** MUSEUM

(Palazzo Comunale, Piazza del Campo; adult/reduced €9/8; ◎10am-7pm summer, to 6pm winter) Siena's most famous museum occu-pies rooms richly frescoed by artists of the Sienese school. Commissioned by the gov-erning body of the city, rather than by the Church, many – unusually – depict secular subjects. The highlight is Simone Martini's celebrated *Maestà* (Virgin Mary in Majesty; 1315) in the Sala del Mappamondo (Hall of the World Map). It features the Madonna

beneath a canopy surrounded by saints and angels, and is Martini's first known work.

★ **Duomo** CATHEDRAL

(www.operaduomo.siena.it; Piazza del Duomo; summer/winter €4/free, when floor displayed €7; ◎10.30am-7pm Mon-Sat,1.30-6pm Sun summer, 10.30am-5.30pm Mon-Sat, 1.30-5.30pm Sun win-ter) Siena's cathedral is one of Italy's most awe-inspiring churches. Construction start-ed in 1215 and over the centuries many of Italy's top artists have contributed: Gio-vanni Pisano designed the intricate white, green and red marble facade; Nicola Pisano carved the elaborate pulpit; Pinturicchio painted some of the frescoes; Michelange-lo, Donatello and Gian Lorenzo Bernini all produced sculptures. Buy tickets from the duomo ticket office (www.operaduomo.siena. it; Piazza del Duomo; ◎10.30am-7pm summer, to 5.30pm winter).

Museo dell'Opera del Duomo MUSEUM

(www.operaduomo.siena.it; Piazza del Duomo 8; admission €7; ◎10.30am-7pm summer, to 5.30pm winter) The collection here showcases art-works that formerly adorned the cathedral, including 12 statues of prophets and philos-ophers by Giovanni Pisano that originally stood on the facade. Many of the statues were designed to be viewed from ground level, which is why they look so distorted as they crane uncomfortably forward. The mu-seum's highlight is Duccio di Buoninsegna's striking *Maestà* (1311), which was painted on both sides as a screen for the *duomo*'s high altar. Buy tickets from the *duomo* ticket office.

Siena

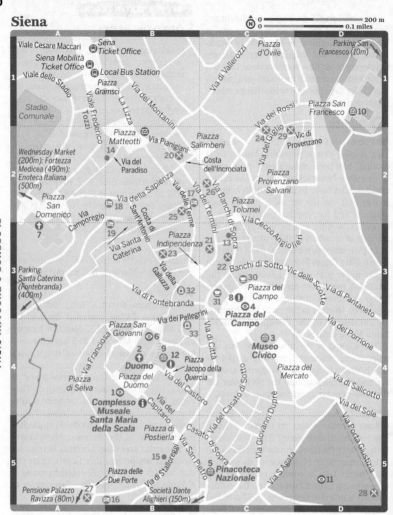

Siena Map

- Viale Cesare Maccari
- Sena Ticket Office
- Siena Mobilità Ticket Office
- Local Bus Station
- Viale dello Stadio
- Piazza Gramsci
- Via dei Montanini
- Piazza d'Ovile
- Parking San Francesco (10m)
- Via di Vallerozzi
- Via dei Rossi
- Piazza San Francesco **10**
- Stadio Comunale
- La Lizza
- Viale Frederico Tozzi
- Piazza Matteotti
- Via Pianigiani
- Piazza Salimbeni
- **24** Via del Giglio **29** Vic di Provenzano
- **14**
- **20**
- Wednesday Market (200m); Fortezza Medicea (490m); Enoteca Italiana (500m);
- Via del Paradiso
- Costa dell'Incrociata
- Piazza Provenzano Salvani
- Piazza San Domenico
- **7**
- Via della Sapienza
- **18**
- Costa di Sant'Antonio
- Via Camporegio
- **19**
- **17**
- **26**
- Via dei Termini
- Via delle Terme
- **25**
- Piazza Tolomei
- Via Banchi di Sopra
- Via Cecco Angiolieri
- Via Santa Caterina
- Piazza Indipendenza
- **23**
- **21**
- **13**
- **22** Banchi di Sotto
- Vic delle Scotte
- Via di Pantaneto
- Parking Santa Caterina (Fontebranda) (400m)
- Via della Galluzza
- Via di Fontebranda
- **32**
- **30**
- **31**
- **8**
- **4**
- Piazza del Campo
- **Piazza del Campo**
- Via dei Pellegrini
- **33**
- Via del Porrione
- Piazza San Giovanni **6**
- **2**
- **9**
- **12**
- Piazza Jacopo della Quercia
- Via di Città
- **Museo Civico**
- **3**
- Via di Salicotto
- Via Franciosa
- **Duomo**
- Piazza del Duomo
- Via del Castoro
- Piazza del Mercato
- Via del Sole
- Piazza di Selva
- **1**
- **Complesso Museale Santa Maria della Scala**
- Via del Capitano
- Via del Casato di Sotto
- Casato di Sopra
- Via Giovanni Duprè
- Via Porta Giustizia
- Piazza di Postierla
- **15**
- **5**
- **Pinacoteca Nazionale**
- Piazza delle Due Porte
- Pensione Palazzo Ravizza (80m) **27**
- **16**
- Società Dante Alighieri (150m)
- Via di Stalloreggi
- Via San Pietro
- Via S.Agata
- **11**
- **28**

Battistero di San Giovanni
LANDMARK

(Piazza San Giovanni; admission €4; ☉10.30am-7pm summer, to 5.30pm winter) The Baptistery is lined with frescoes and centres around a hexagonal marble font by Jacopo della Quercia, decorated with bronze panels depicting the life of St John the Baptist by artists including Lorenzo Ghiberti (*Baptism of Christ* and *St John in Prison*) and Donatello (*The Head of John the Baptist Being Presented to Herod*). Buy tickets from the *duomo* ticket office.

Cripta
CHRISTIAN

(Piazza San Giovanni; admission incl audioguide €6; ☉10.30am-7pm summer, to 5.30pm winter) Remarkably, this now-atmospheric, vaulted space was filled with debris until 1999 (with the rubbish having been deposited in the 1300s). Now you'll see 180 sq metres of 13th century *pintura a secco*; these 'dry paintings' (also called 'mural paintings') contrast with frescoes which are painted on wet plaster, making them more durable. Buy tickets from the *duomo* ticket office.

Siena

FLORENCE & TUSCANY SIENA

Panorama del Facciatone   TOWER
(Piazza del Duomo 8; ☺10.30am-7pm summer, to 5.30pm winter) For an unforgettable view of Siena's unique cityscape, haul yourself up the 131-step, narrow corkscrew stairway to the **Panorama del Facciatone**. Entrance is included in the Museo dell'Opera ticket.

★**Complesso Museale Santa Maria della Scala**   BUILDING
(www.santamariadellascala.com; Piazza del Duomo 1; adult/reduced €9/8; ☺10.30am-6.30pm Wed-Mon summer, to 4.30pm winter) This former hospital, parts of which date from the 13th century, was built as a hospice for pilgrims travelling the Via Francigena pilgrimage trail. Its highlight is the upstairs *Pellegrinaio* (Pilgrims' Hall), with vivid 15th-century frescoes by Lorenzo Vecchietta, Priamo della Quercia and Domenico di Bartolo lauding the good works of the hospital and its patrons.

The building is now a cultural centre and houses three museums. The pick is the atmospheric Archaeological Museum set in the basement tunnels. Also don't miss the medieval *fienile* (hayloft) on level three, which showcases Jacopo della Quercia's original sculptures from Siena's central Fonte Gaia fountain.

★**Pinacoteca Nazionale**   GALLERY
(Via San Pietro 29; adult/reduced €4/2; ☺8.15am-7.15pm Tue-Sat, 9am-1pm Sun & Mon) An extraordinary collection of Gothic masterpieces from the Sienese school sits inside the once grand but now sadly dishevelled 14th-century Palazzo Buonsignori. The pick of the collection is on the 2nd floor, including magnificent works by Duccio di Buoninsegna, Simone Martini, Niccolò di Segna, Lippo Memmi, Ambrogio and Pietro Lorenzetti, Bartolo di Fredi and Taddeo di Bartolo.

The collection demonstrates the gulf cleaved between artistic life in Siena and Florence in the 15th century. While the Renaissance flourished 70km to the north, Siena's masters and their patrons remained firmly rooted in the Byzantine and Gothic precepts borne of the early 13th century. Religious images and episodes predominate, typically pasted lavishly with gold and generally lacking any of the advances in painting (perspective, emotion, movement) that artists in Florence were exploring. That's not to say that the works here are second-rate – many are among the most beautiful and important creations of their time.

Artworks to hunt out include Duccio's *Madonna and Child* (Room 2), *Madonna with Child and Four Saints* (Room 4) and

ℹ️ MUSEUM PASS & COMBINED TICKETS

If you are planning to visit Siena's major monuments, save money with a combined pass:

➜ **OPA SI Pass** (Duomo, Museo dell'Opera, Battistero di San Giovanni, Cripta and Oratorio di San Bernardino; March to October €12, November to February €8, valid for three days) Purchase this pass at the duomo ticket office (p519).

➜ **Museo Civico and Museale Santa Maria della Scala** (combined ticket €13) Available at both museums.

➜ **Museo Civico, Museale Santa Maria della Scala and Torre del Mangia** (combined ticket €20) Available at all three museums.

Santa Maria Maddalena (Room 5); Simone Martini's *Madonna della Misericordia* and *Madonna with Child* (both in Room 4), *Madonna and Child* (Room 6) and *Blessed Agostino* altarpiece (Room 6); Lippo Memmi's *Adoration of the Magi* (Room 6); Ambrogio Lorenzetti's luminous *Annunciation* and *Madonna with Child* (both in Room 8); Pietro Lorenzetti's *Madonna Enthroned with Saint Nicholas and the Prophet Elia* and *Crucifixion* (both in Room 8); and Taddeo di Bartolo's *The Annunciation of the Virgin Mary* (Room 11).

The gallery occasionally rearranges its exhibits; we've cited the room numbers at time of writing.

Chiesa di San Domenico CHURCH
(Piazza San Domenico; ⊙9am-12.30pm & 3-7pm) **FREE** St Catherine was welcomed into the Dominican fold within this imposing church and its **Cappella di Santa Caterina** is adorned with frescoes by Il Sodoma depicting events in her life. Catherine died in Rome but her head was returned to Siena – it's clearly visible in a 15th-century tabernacle above the altar in a signed *cappella* near the gift shop.

Oratorio di San Bernardino GALLERY
(Piazza San Francesco 10; admission €3; ⊙10.30am-1.30pm & 3-5.30pm mid-Mar–Oct) Nestled in the shadow of the huge Gothic church of San Francesco, this 15th-century oratory is dedicated to St Bernardino

and decorated with Mannerist frescoes by Il Sodoma, Beccafumi and Pacchia. Upstairs, the small **Museo Diocesano di Arte Sacra** has some lovely paintings, including *Madonna del Latte* (Nursing Madonna, c 1340) by Ambrogio Lorenzetti.

 Courses

Scuola Leonardo da Vinci LANGUAGE COURSE
(☑0577 24 90 97; www.scuolaleonardo.com; Via del Paradiso 16; per 1/2 weeks €200/360) Italian-language school with supplementary cultural programs.

Società Dante Alighieri LANGUAGE COURSE
(☑0577 4 95 33; www.dantealighieri.com; Via Tommaso Pendola 37; per 1/2 weeks €210/380) Language and cultural courses southwest of the city centre.

Tuscan Wine School COURSE
(☑0577 22 17 04; www.tuscanwineschool.com; Via di Stalloreggi 26; ⊙11am-6.30pm Mon-Sat Mar-Oct) Daily two-hour wine-tasting classes introducing Italian and Tuscan wines (€40).

👉 Tours

Centro Guide Turistiche Siena e Provincia CULTURAL TOUR
(☑0577 4 32 73; www.guidesiena.it; Galleria Odeon, Via Banchi di Sopra 31; ⊙10am-1pm & 3-5pm Mon-Fri) The pick of the tours offered by this association of accredited guides are the 90-minute Classical Siena Walking Tour (€20, 11am Monday to Saturday), which features key historical and cultural landmarks, and the 90-minute Secret Siena Walk (€20, 11am Sunday), which takes in both Siena's streets and the *duomo*'s crypt. Prices include admission fees.

The tours, in English and Italian, depart from outside the tourist office in the Piazza Duomo. You can buy tickets from the guide, there's no need to book and children under 12 are free. The centre also operates private guided tours in Siena and throughout the region (three/six hours €140/260).

✨ Festivals & Events

Accademia Musicale Chigiana MUSIC
(www.chigiana.it) The Accademia Musicale Chigiana presents three highly regarded concert series featuring classical musicians from around the world: Micat in Vertice from November to April, Settimana Musicale Senese in July and Estate Musicale Chigiana in July and August.

IL PALIO

Dating from the Middle Ages, this spectacular annual event stages a series of colourful pageants and a frenetic horse race on 2 July and 16 August. Ten of Siena's 17 *contrade* (town districts) compete for the coveted *palio* (silk banner). Each *contrada* has its own traditions, symbol and colours plus its own church and *palio* museum.

The race is staged in the Campo. From about 5pm, representatives from each *contrada* parade in historical costume, bearing their individual banners. The actual race kicks off at 7.45pm in July and 7pm in August. For scarcely one exhilarating minute, the 10 horses and their bareback riders tear three times around a temporary dirt racetrack with a speed and violence that makes spectators' hair stand on end.

Join the crowds in the centre of the Campo at least four hours before the start if you want a place on the rails, but be aware that once there you won't be able to leave until the race has finished. Alternatively, the cafes in the Campo sell places on their terraces; these cost between €350 and €400 per ticket, and can be booked through the tourist office up to one year in advance.

During the Palio, hotels raise their rates between 10% and 50% and they enforce a minimum-stay requirement.

🛏 Sleeping

★ Hotel Alma Domus   HOTEL €

(📞0577 4 41 77; Via Camporegio 37; s €40-52, d €60-€122; ❄🛜♿) Your chance to sleep in a convent: Alma Domus is owned by the church and is still home to several Dominican nuns. The economy rooms, although supremely comfortable, are styled very simply. But the superior ones are positively sumptuous, with pristine bathrooms, pared-down furniture and bursts of magenta and lime. Many have mini-balconies with uninterrupted views of the *duomo*.

Antica Residenza Cicogna   B&B €

(📞0577 28 56 13; www.anticaresidenzacicogna.it; Via delle Terme 76; s €70-95, d €95-115, ste €120-155; ❄@🛜) You get a true feel for Siena's history in this exquisite 13th century palazzo. Tiled floors, ornate lights and painted ceilings meet tones of yellow ochre and (suitably) burnt sienna. The best of the fabulous suites is named after landscape painter Paesaggi, where bucolic views sit in panels above your head, and a tiny blue passageway winds to the bathroom.

Alle Due Porte   B&B €

(📞0577 28 76 70; www.sienatur.it; Via di Stalloreggi 51; d/tr €85/110; ❄🛜) Taking its name from the nearby city gate, this well-located B&B has loads of character and a real 'home away from home' vibe. It's set on the 1st floor of a rebuilt 12th-century tower house and offers three rooms (two with air-con) full of typically Tuscan features such as beams and metal bed frames.

★ Pensione Palazzo Ravizza   BOUTIQUE HOTEL €€

(📞0577 28 04 62; www.palazzoravizza.it; Pian dei Mantellini 34; d €80-220, ste €180-320; 🅿❄@🛜) Heritage features and luxurious flourishes combine at this Renaissance-era *palazzo* to create an irresistible hotel. Frescoed ceilings, stone staircases and gilt mirrors meet elegant furnishings, wooden shutters and (from some bedrooms) captivating views. The greenery-framed rear garden is utterly delightful; settle down in a wicker chair here, gaze out towards the hills and you may never want to leave.

Castel Pietraio   HISTORIC HOTEL €€

(📞0577 30 00 20; www.castelpietraio.it; Strada di Strove 33, Monteriggioni; s €90, d €120-165) Castel Pietraio is a sleep spot that's simply too good to miss. The medieval castle is owned by Barone Neri Del Nero and bedrooms, in the adjoining outbuildings, are rich in aristocratic trappings with Carrara-marble bathrooms and chestnut beams. The wine cellar, meanwhile, is stocked with the Baron's own DOCG Chianti and DOC Vin Santo. It's 15km west of Siena.

Campo Regio Relais   BOUTIQUE HOTEL €€€

(📞0577 22 20 73; www.camporegio.com; Via della Sapienza 25; d €220-400, ste €450; ❄🛜) The decor in each of the six, individually styled rooms here is exquisite – expect anything from old mahogany to fine linen, 18th-century antiques to art nouveau. Breakfast is served in the sumptuously decorated lounge or on the terrace, with a sensational view across higgledy-piggledy rooftops to Torre del Mangia and the *duomo*.

Castello delle Serre
BOUTIQUE HOTEL €€€

(☑ 338 5040811; www.castellodelleserre.com; Piazza XX Settembre 1, Serre di Rapolano; d €225-265, ste €275-395; P ✳ @ 🛜 ☲) The prospect of spending the night in this fabulous medieval castle makes the 40km trip east from Siena well worth the effort. Meticulously restored by the Italian-American Gangale family, it features huge rooms and a swish pool area. For a once-in-a-lifetime experience, book into the deluxe suite in the turret where a private terrace commands suitably regal views.

✕ Eating

Morbidi
DELI €

(www.morbidi.com; Via Banchi di Sopra 75; lunch buffet €12; ⊙ 8am-8pm Mon-Thu, to 9pm Fri & Sat) Possibly the classiest cheap feed in Siena: set in the stylish basement of Morbidi's deli, the lunch buffet on offer here is excellent. For a mere €12, you can join the well-dressed locals sampling antipasti, salads, risottos, pastas and a dessert of the day. Bottled water is supplied, wine and coffee cost extra. Buy your ticket upstairs before heading down.

Consorzio Agrario di Siena
DELI €

(www.capsi.it; Via Pianigiani 13; ⊙ 8am-8.30pm Mon-Sat, 9.30am-8pm Sun) Operating since 1901, this farmer's co-op is a rich emporium of food and wine, much of it locally produced. There's a small bar area where you can purchase and eat a slab of freshly cooked pizza (€12 to €14.30 per kg).

Grom
GELATERIA €

(www.grom.it; Via Banchi di Sopra 11; gelato €2.50-5.50; ⊙ 11am-midnight summer, to 11pm winter) Delectable gelato with flavours that change with the seasons; many of the ingredients are organic or Slow Food–accredited. They do milkshakes too.

Kopa Kabana
GELATERIA €

(www.gelateriakopakabana.it; Via dei Rossi 52-55; gelato €1.90-4.50; ⊙ 11am-8pm mid-Feb–mid-Nov, later hours in warm weather) Come here for fresh gelato made by self-proclaimed ice-cream master Fabio (we're pleased to concur).

★ Enoteca I Terzi
TUSCAN €€

(☑ 0577 4 43 29; www.enotecaiterzi.it; Via dei Termini 7; meals €35-40; ⊙ 11am-1am summer,

11am-4pm & 6.30pm-midnight winter, closed Sun) A favourite for many locals who head to this historic *enoteca* to linger over lunches, *aperitivi,* and casual dinners featuring top-notch Tuscan *salumi* (cured meats), delicate handmade pasta and wonderful wines.

Nonna Gina
OSTERIA €€

(☑ 0577 28 72 47; www.osterianonnagina.com; Pian dei Mantellini 2; meals €25-35; ⊙ 12.30-2.30pm & 7.30-10.30pm Tue-Sun) The atmosphere is pure Siena-neighbourhood-*osteria*: gingham tablecloths; postcards tacked to the rafters; pictures of Palio jockeys on the walls. The menu speaks of fine local traditions too: piles of local meat form the *antipasto toscano*, the house red is a very decent Chianti, while the ingredients of the 'secret sauce' covering the plump, cheese-filled gnocchi will never be revealed.

La Compagnia dei Vinattieri
TUSCAN €€

(☑ 0577 23 65 68; www.vinattieri.net; Via delle Terme 79; antipasto platter €7-9, meals €35; ⊙ noon-10pm, closed late Feb-late Mar) Duck down the stairs to enjoy a quick glass of wine and a meat or cheese platter in this cellar, or settle in for a leisurely meal; perhaps trying *radicchio* pie with Gorgonzola and walnuts, guinea fowl ravioli, or Tuscan-style cuttlefish stuffed with spinach. To drink? Choose something from a wine list 1000-strong.

Grotta Santa Caterina
da Bagoga
TUSCAN €€

(☑ 0577 28 22 08; www.bagoga.it; Via della Galluzza 26; meals €35; ⊙ noon-3pm & 7-10pm Tue-Sat, 12-3pm Sun) Pierino Fagnani ('Bagoga'), one of Siena's most famous Palio jockeys, swapped his saddle for an apron in 1973 and has been operating this much-loved restaurant ever since. Traditional Tuscan palate-pleasers feature on the menu, and are best showcased in the four-course *tipico* (€35) or *degustazione* (€50 with wine) menus. Book ahead.

Tre Cristi
SEAFOOD €€€

(☑ 0577 28 06 08; www.trecristi.com; Vicolo di Provenzano 1; 4-course tasting menus €35-45, 6-course menus €65; ⊙ 12.30-2.30pm & 7.30-10pm Mon-Sat) Seafood restaurants are thin on the ground in this meat-obsessed region, so the long existence of Tre Cristi (it's been around since 1830) should be heartily celebrated. The menu here is as elegant as the decor, and touches such as a complimentary glass of *prosecco* at the start of the meal add to the experience.

🍷 Drinking

Enoteca Italiana   WINE BAR
(www.enoteca-italiana.it; Fortezza Medicea, Piazza Libertà 1; ⊘noon-midnight Wed-Sat, to 7.30pm Mon & Tue) The former munitions cellar and dungeon of this Medici fortress has been artfully transformed into a classy *enoteca* that carries more than 1500 Italian labels. You can take a bottle with you, ship a case home or just enjoy a glass in the attractive courtyard or vaulted interior. There's usually food available, too.

Caffè Fiorella   CAFE
(www.torrefazionefiorella.it; Via di Città 13; ⊘7am-8pm Mon-Sat) Squeeze into this tiny, heart-of-the-action space to enjoy some of Siena's best coffee. In summer, the coffee *granita* with a dollop of cream is a wonderful indulgence.

Bar Il Palio   CAFE
(Piazza del Campo 47; ⊘8am-midnight) Arguably the best coffee on the central Campo square; drink it standing at the bar or suffer the financial consequences.

🛍 Shopping

Panificio Il Magnifico   FOOD
(www.ilmagnifico.siena.it; Via dei Pellegrini 27; ⊘7.30am-7.30pm Mon-Sat) Lorenzo Rossi is Siena's best baker, and his *panforte*, *ricciarelli* (sugar-dusted chewy almond biscuits) and *cavallucci* (almond biscuits made with Tuscan *millefiori* honey) are a weekly purchase for most local households. Try them at his bakery and shop behind the *duomo*, and you'll understand why.

Il Pellicano   CERAMICS
(☎340 5974038; www.siena-ilpellicano.it; Via Diacceto 17a; ⊘10.30am-7pm summer, hours vary in winter) Elisabetta Ricci has been making traditional hand-painted Sienese ceramics for over 30 years. She shapes, fires and paints her creations, often using Renaissance-era styles or typical *contrade* designs. Elisabetta also conducts lessons in traditional ceramic techniques.

Wednesday Market   MARKET
(⊘7.30am-1pm) Spreading around Fortezza Medicea and towards the Stadio Comunale, this is one of Tuscany's largest markets and is great for cheap clothing; some food is also sold. An antiques market is held here on the third Sunday of each month.

ℹ Information

Hospital (☎0577 58 51 11; www.ao-siena.toscana.it; Viale Bracci) Just north of Siena at Le Scotte.

Police Station (☎0577 20 11 11; Via del Castoro 6)

Tourist Office (☎0577 28 05 51; www.terresiena.it; Piazza del Duomo 1; ⊘9am-6pm daily summer, 10am-5pm Mon-Sat, to 1pm Sun winter) Provides free Siena city maps, reserves accommodation, organises car and scooter hire, and sells train tickets (commission applies). Also takes bookings for day tours.

ℹ Getting There & Away

BUS

Siena Mobilità (www.sienamobilita.it), part of the **Tiemme** (www.tiemmespa.it) network, runs services between Siena and other parts of Tuscany. It has a **ticket office** (☎0577 20 42 25; www.tiemmespa.it; Piazza Gramsci; ⊘6.30am-7.30pm Mon-Fri, 7am-7.30pm Sat & Sun) underneath the main bus station in Piazza Gramsci; there's also a left-luggage office here (per 24 hours €5.50).

Routes operated, Monday to Saturday include:
Arezzo (€6.60, 1½ hours, eight daily)
Colle di Val d'Elsa (€3.40, 30 minutes, hourly) With onward connections for Volterra (€2.75, four daily)
Florence (€7.80, 1¼ hours, frequent)
Montalcino (€4.90, 70 minutes, six daily)
Montepulciano (€6.60, 1½ hours, two daily)
Pienza (€5.50, 70 minutes, two daily)
Rome Fiumicino Airport (€22, 3¾ hours, two daily)
San Gimignano (€6, one to 1½ hours, 10 daily)

Services to Montalcino, Montepulciano and Pienza depart from outside the train station.

Sena (www.sena.it) also has a **ticket office** (☎0861 1991900; Piazza Gramsci; ⊘8.30am-7.45pm Mon-Sat) underneath the Piazza Gramsci bus station; its routes include:
Milan (€25, 4¼ hours, three daily)
Perugia (€15, 1½ hours, two daily)
Rome (€25, 3½ hours, nine daily)
Turin (€40, 7¼ hours, two daily)
Venice (€24, 5½ hours, two daily)

CAR & MOTORCYCLE

For Florence, take the RA3 (Siena–Florence *superstrada*) or the more scenic SR222.

TRAIN

Siena's rail links aren't extensive; handy direct services include:
Florence (€10, 1½ hours, hourly)
Grosseto (€9, 1½ hours, eight daily)

ℹ️ Getting Around

TO/FROM THE AIRPORT

A Siena Mobilità bus travels between Pisa airport and Siena (one way/return €13/26, two hours), leaving Siena at 7.10am and Pisa at 11.45am. Buy tickets at least one day in advance online or at the bus station.

BUS

Siena Mobilità operates city bus services (per 90 minutes €1.10). Buses 8 and 9 run between the train station and Piazza Gramsci.

CAR & MOTORCYCLE

There's a Limited Traffic Zone (ZTL) in the historic centre, although visitors can drop off luggage at their hotel, then get out (reception must report your licence number or risk a fine).

Large, conveniently located car parks are at Stadio Comunale and around Fortezza Medicea, both north of Piazza San Domenico. Hotly contested free street parking (look for white lines) is available in Viale Vittorio Veneto, on the southern edge of Fortezza Medicea.

Most car parks charge €2 per hour. For more information surf www.sienaparcheggi.com.

Chianti

The ancient vineyards in this postcard-perfect part of Tuscany produce the grapes used in Chianti Classico (www.chianticlassico.com), a Sangiovese-dominated drop sold under the Gallo Nero (Black Cockerel/Rooster) trademark. As well as giving this region its identity, wine also shapes the landscape – a place almost unchanged since ancient times where you'll also encounter historic olive groves, honey-coloured stone farmhouses, dense forests, graceful Romanesque *pieve* (rural churches), Renaissance villas and imposing stone castles built in the Middle Ages by Florentine and Sienese warlords.

Split between the provinces of Florence (Chianti Fiorentino) and Siena (Chianti Senese), Chianti is usually accessed via the SR222 (Via Chiantigiana) and is criss-crossed by a picturesque network of *strade provinciale* (provincial roads) and *strade secondaria* (secondary roads), some of which are unsealed, narrow and difficult to navigate. A good road map is *Le strade del Gallo Nero* (€2.50), available at newsstands in the region.

Greve in Chianti

POP 14,035

Some 26km south of Florence, Greve is the main town in the Chianti Fiorentino. It's the hub of the local wine industry and has an amiable market-town air, an attractive central square, and tasty eateries and *enoteche*.

Greve's annual wine fair is held in the first or second week of September – book accommodation well in advance.

🍴 Eating & Drinking

⭐ **Mangiando Mangiando**   TUSCAN €€

(📞 0558 54 63 72; www.mangiandomangiando.it; Piazza Matteotti 80; meals €30; ☺ noon-3pm & 7-10pm Feb-Dec, closed Thu) When an eatery gives as proud prominence to its list of producers as it does its menu, you know the dishes should be local and good. So it proves in this cheerful, casual eatery, where Tuscan standards (think rich beef pasta) accompany flavoursome soups, and Chianti Classico (€4.50) and Riserva (€5.50) come by the glass.

Enoteca Falorni   WINE BAR

(www.enotecafalorni.it; Galleria delle Cantine 2; ☺ 11.30am-5.30pm Mon, Thu & Fri, to 7.30pm Sat & Sun) Enoteca Falorni is the biggest in Chianti, stocking more than 1000 wines, with 100 different varieties available for tasting, including Toscana IGTs ('Super Tuscans'), top DOCs and DOCGs, Vin Santo and grappa. Buy a prepaid wine card costing €10 to €25 from the central bar, stick it into one of the many taps and out trickles your tipple of choice.

ℹ️ Information

Tourist Office (📞 0558 54 62 99; info@turismo.greveinchianti.eu; Piazza Matteotti 11; ☺ 10am-7pm summer, reduced hours winter) On Greve's main square.

ℹ️ Getting There & Around

BUS

SITA buses travel between Greve and Florence (€3.30, one hour, hourly).

CAR & MOTORCYCLE

Find free parking on Piazza della Resistenza. On Fridays, don't park overnight in the paid spaces on Piazza Matteotti – your car will be towed to make room for Saturday market stalls.

TUSCANY'S CELEBRITY BUTCHER

The small town of Panzano in Chianti, 10km south of Greve in Chianti, is known coun-try-wide as the home of **L'Antica Macellerìa Cecchini** (www.dariocecchini.com; Via XX Luglio 11; ⊙9am-4pm), a butcher's shop owned and run by the extrovert **Dario Cecchini**. This Tuscan celebrity has carved out a niche for himself as a poetry-spouting guardian of the *bistecca* (steak) and other Tuscan meaty treats, and he operates three eateries clus-tered around the *macellerìa*: **Officina della Bistecca** (🖉0558 5 21 76; Via XX Luglio 11; set menu €50; ⊙sittings at 1pm & 8pm), with a set menu built around the famous *bistecca*; **Solociccia** (🖉0558 5 27 27; Via Chiantigiana 5; set menus €30 & €50; ⊙sittings at 1pm, 7pm & 9pm daily), where guests sample meat dishes other than steak; and **Dario DOC** (Via XX Luglio 11; burger €10-15, light menu €20; ⊙noon-3pm Mon-Sat), his casual lunchtime-only eatery. Book ahead for the Officina and Solociccia.

Around Greve in Chianti

The vine-etched hills around Greve are idyl-lic, classic wine-making territory with ample opportunity to explore ancient villages and prestigious wine estates.

⊙ Sights & Activities

★**Antinori nel Chianti Classico**   WINERY
(🖉0552 35 97 00; www.antinorichianticlassico. it; Via Cassia per Siena 133, Località Bargino; tour & tasting €25-50, bookings essential; ⊙10am-6pm summer, to 5pm winter) Visiting this cellar com-plex is a James Bond–esque experience. Get cleared at the gated, guarded entrance, ap-proach a sculptural main building that's set into the hillside then explore an exquisitely designed winery full of architectural flour-ishes and state-of-the-art equipment. Your one-hour guided tour (English and Italian) finishes with a tutored tasting of three An-tinori wines beside the family museum.

At the stylish bar beside the shop you can taste 16 different wines (€4 to €9 per tasting); have a sommelier-led 'guided tast-ing' of three wines (€9 or €12); or simply drink a glass of wine (ranging from €7 for a Marchese Antinori 2009 to €35 for a Solaia 2009). Afterwards, you can also enjoy lunch in the **Rinuccio 1180** (p528) restaurant.

Bargino is 20km northwest of Greve via the SS222, SP3 and SS2.

Badia a Passignano   WINERY
(www.osteriadipassignano.com; Badia a Passigna-no) It doesn't get much more atmospheric: an 11th-century abbey, owned by Benedic-tine monks and set amid vineyards run by the legendary Antinori dynasty. The four-hour 'Antinori at Badia a Passignano' tour (€150, two daily, Monday to Saturday) includes a vineyard and cellar visit and a

meal in the estate's **Osteria di Passignano** (🖉0558 07 12 78; www.osteriadipassignano.com; Via di Passignano 33, Badia a Passignano; meals €60; ⊙12.15-2.15pm & 7.30-10pm Mon-Sat) res-taurant, with four signature Antinori wines.

Other options include visits to the Tig-nanello vineyard (where the grapes for the Tignanello and Solaia Super Tuscans are grown), and tours of the cellars and tastings of four wines (€80; one tour daily Monday to Saturday). Bookings are essential for tours.

Or, just turn up at the estate's wine shop, **La Bottega** (www.osteriadipassignano.com; Ba-dia di Passignano; ⊙10am-7.30pm, closed Sun), to taste and buy Antinori wines and olive oil. Badia a Passignano is 7km west of Greve.

Castello di Verrazzano   WINERY
(🖉0558 5 42 43; www.verrazzano.com; Via Citille, Greti; tours €16-115) This castle 3km north of Greve was once home to Giovanni da Verraz-zano (1485–1528), who explored the North American coast and is commemorated in New York by the Verrazano Narrows bridge. Today it presides over a 220-hectare historic wine estate offering a wide range of tours.

Each tour incorporates a short visit to the historic wine cellar and gardens plus tast-ings of the estate's wines (including its flag-ship Chianti Classico) and other products; perhaps honey, olive oil or balsamic vine-gar. The 'Classic Wine Tour' (€16, 1½ hours, 10am to 3pm Monday to Friday) includes a tasting of several wines; the 'Chianti Tradi-tion Tour' (€34, 2½ hours, 11am Monday to Friday) includes a tasting of wine and gas-tronomic specialities; while the 'Wine and Food Experience' (€58, three hours, noon Monday to Friday) includes a four-course lunch with estate wines. Tour bookings are essential.

CYCLING CHIANTI

Exploring Chianti by bicycle is a true highlight. The Greve in Chianti **tourist office** (p526) publishes a brochure listing walking and cycling routes; rent bicycles from **Ramuzzi** (☑ 055 85 30 37; www.ramuzzi.com; Via Italo Stecchi 23; touring bike per day/week €35/220, scooter per day/week €55/290; ⊙ 9am-1pm & 3-7pm Mon-Fri, 9am-1pm Sat).

Several companies offer guided cycling tours from Florence:

Florence By Bike (☑ 0554 8 89 92; www.florencebybike.it) Tour of northern Chianti (one day) with lunch and wine tasting (€83; four per week March to October).

I Bike Italy (☑ 342 9352395; www.ibike italy.com) Two-day tour including accommodation, breakfast, lunch and dinner (€375; mid-March to October).

I Bike Tuscany (☑ 335 812 07 69; www. ibiketuscany.com) Year-round, one-day tours (€155) for all levels, includes transports from Florence to Chianti.

🛌 Sleeping

Ostello del Chianti   HOSTEL €

(☑ 0558 05 02 65; www.ostellodelchianti.it; Via Roma 137, Tavarnelle Val di Pesa; dm €16, d/q €50/70; ⊙ reception 8.30-11am & 4pm-midnight, hostel closed Nov–mid-Mar; P @ 🛜) This is one of Italy's oldest hostels and though it occupies an ugly building in the less-than-scenic town of Tavarnelle Val di Pesa, the friendly staff and bargain prices compensate. Dorms max out at six beds and bike hire can be arranged for €8 per day. Breakfast costs €2. Florence is easily accessed by SITA bus (€3.30, one hour).

Fattoria di Rignana   AGRITURISMO €€

(☑ 0558 5 20 65; www.rignana.it; Via di Rignana 15, Rignana; d fattoria €110, without bathroom €95, d villa €140; P @ 🛜 ☒) A chic, historic farmhouse with its very own bell tower rewards you for the drive up the long, rutted road. You'll also find glorious views, a large swimming pool and a very decent eatery. Choose between elegant rooms in the 17th-century villa and rustic ones in the *fattoria* (farmhouse). It's 4km from Badia a Passignano and 10km west of Greve.

Villa Il Poggiale   BOUTIQUE HOTEL €€

(☑ 0558 2 83 11; www.villailpoggiale.it; Via Empolese 69, San Casciano in Val di Pesa; d €150-170, ste €195-350; P ❄ @ 🛜 ☒) Accommodation in Chianti is often prohibitively expensive, but this hilltop Renaissance-era villa bucks the trend. Spacious rooms have four-poster beds and frescoed ceilings, a spa sits downstairs and the swimming pool commands wraparound views. Just the place, after a day's sighseeing, to savour the complimentary afternoon tea. Villa Il Poggiale is 20km northwest of Greve.

Villa I Barronci   HOTEL €€€

(☑ 0558 2 05 98; www.ibarronci.com; Via Sorripa 10, San Casciano in Val di Pesa; d €190-250; P ❄ @ 🛜 ☒ 🍴) Exemplary service, superb amenities and high comfort levels ensure this modern country hotel is one to remember. You can relax in the bar, rejuvenate in the spa, laze by the pool or head off for easy day trips to Volterra, San Gimignano and Siena. The villa is 20km northwest of Greve, and 15km south of Florence.

🍴 Eating & Drinking

Rinuccio 1180   TUSCAN €€

(☑ 0552 35 97 20; www.antinorichianticlassico.it; Via Cassia per Siena 133, Bargino; meals €35, tasting platters €10-15; ⊙ noon-4pm) Imagine lunching inside a glass box on a terrace with an intoxicating 180-degree Dolby-esque surround of hills, birdsong and pea-green vines. This is what the starlet of the Chianti dining scene, set on the über-high-tech Antinori wine estate in Bargino, is all about. Cuisine is Tuscan, modern, seasonal and sassy. The wine list is (naturally) fabulous. Book ahead.

La Cantinetta di Rignana   TUSCAN €€

(☑ 0558 5 26 01; www.lacantinettadirignana. com; Rignana; meals €40; ⊙ noon-3pm & 7-10pm Wed-Mon summer, hours vary winter) You might wonder, as you settle onto the terrace here, whether you've found your perfect Chianti lazy lunch location. A historic mill forms the backdrop, vine-lined hills roll off to the horizon and rustic dishes are full of local ingredients and packed with flavour. It's 4km from Badia a Passignano at the end of an unsealed road.

La Locanda di Pietracupa   TUSCAN €€

(☑ 0558 07 24 00; www.locandapietracupa.com; Via Madonna di Pietracupa 31, San Donato in Poggio; meals €40; ⊙ 12.30-2.30pm & 7.30-9.30pm daily summer, closed Tue winter; 🛜) Exquisitely presented dishes showcasing local ingredients are the hallmarks of this elegant but un-stuffy eatery, 20km southwest of Greve in Chianti. The regularly changing menu might feature beef with a Chianti Classico reduction, pigeon with truffle vinaigrette or *tagliolini* studded with zucchini flowers.

The bedrooms (single/double €80/95) are also suitably refined; expect candy-striped satins and pared-down wrought-iron beds.

L'Antica Scuderia   TUSCAN €€

(☑0558 07 16 23; www.ristorolanticascuderia.com; Via di Passignano 17, Badia a Passignano; meals €45, pizzas €8-15; ◷12.30-2.30pm & 7.30-10.30pm Wed-Mon) If you fancy eating on a garden terrace overlooking one of the Antinori vineyards, this casual eatery may well fit the bill. Lunch features antipasti, pastas and traditional grilled meats, while dinner sees plenty of pizza-oven action. Kids love the playground set; adults love the fact that it's at the opposite end of the garden.

Castellina in Chianti

POP 2879

Established by the Etruscans and fortified by the Florentines in the 15th century as a defensive outpost against the Sienese, Castellina in Chianti is now a major centre of the wine industry. To taste some of the local product, head to **Antica Fattoria la Castellina** (Via Ferruccio 26; ◷10.30am-12.30pm & 2.30-5.30pm), the town's best-known wine shop.

◉ Sights & Activities

Museo Archeologico del Chianti Senese   MUSEUM

(www.museoarcheologicochianti.it; Piazza del Comune 18; adult/reduced €5/3; ◷10am-6pm daily Apr, May, Sep & Oct, 11am-7pm Jun-Aug, 10am-5pm Sat & Sun Nov-Mar) Etruscan archaeological finds from the local area are on display at this museum in the town's medieval *rocca* (fortress). Room 4 showcases artefacts found in the 7th-century-BC **Etruscan Tombs of Montecalvario** (Ipogeo Etrusco di Monte Calvario; ◷24hr) FREE, which are located on the northern edge of town off the SR222.

Via delle Volte   WALKING

From Castellina's southern car park, follow Via Ferruccio or the panoramic path next to the town's eastern defensive walls. These lead to the atmospheric Via delle Volte, an arched medieval passageway that was originally used for ancient sacred rites and later enclosed with a roof and incorporated into the Florentine defensive structure.

🛏 Sleeping & Eating

Il Colombaio   B&B €

(☑0577 74 04 44; www.albergoilcolombaio.it; Via Chiantigiana 29; d €90; P🐾🛜🏊) A tasteful conversion has turned this 14th-century farmhouse on the edge of Castellina into a stylish *albergo* with a rich heritage feel: tapestry-covered chairs frame lace curtains and oil paintings; a vast stone sink graces the lounge. Breakfast is served in the vaulted wine cellar or on the terrace; perhaps linger over it before a dip in the pool.

Ristorante Albergaccio   TUSCAN €€€

(☑0577 74 10 42; www.albergacciocast.com; Via Fiorentina 63, Castellina in Chianti; 4/5 courses €58/68, 3-course kids menu €27; ◷12.30-2.30pm & 7.30-9.30pm, closed parts of Dec-Mar; 🍷) Albergaccio bills its culinary approach as 'the territory on the table' and local, seasonal and organic produce certainly hold sway here. The style is innovative and upmarket, the 320-strong wine list is well priced and the eatery is rightly popular with local and international foodies. It's 1km northeast of Castellina on the San Donato in Poggio road.

ℹ Information

Tourist Office (☑0577 74 13 92; www.turismo.comune.castellina.si.it; Via Ferruccio 40; ◷10am-noon & 3-6pm daily Jun-Oct, Tue, Thu, Sat & Sun only Mar-May, reduced hours winter) Provides maps and books visits to wineries and cellars.

ℹ Getting There & Around

BUS

Siena Mobilità (www.sienamobilita.it) buses travel between Castellina and Siena (€3.40, 35 minutes, seven daily Monday to Saturday).

CAR & MOTORCYCLE

The most convenient car park is at the southern edge of town off Via IV Novembre (€1/5 per hour/day).

Florence

Chianti
Fiorentino

CHIANTI

Castello di
Verrazzano

Antinori
nel Chianti
Classico

Badia a
Passignano

Greve in Chianti

Panzano in Chianti

La Locanda di
Pietracupa

Volpaia

Radda in Chianti

Castellina in
Chianti

Castello
di Ama

Chianti
Senese

Castello
di Brolio

Siena

JOHN ELK/GETTY IMAGES ©

Wine Tour of Chianti

Tuscany has more than its fair share of highlights, but few can match the glorious indulgence of a leisurely drive through Chianti. On offer is an intoxicating blend of scenery, acclaimed restaurants and ruby-red wine.

From **Florence**, take the *superstrada* (expressway) towards Siena, exit at Bargino and follow the signs to **Antinori nel Chianti Classico** (p527), a state-of-the-art wine estate featuring an architecturally innovative ageing cellar. Take a tour, prime your palate with a wine tasting and enjoy lunch in the estate's Rinuccio 1180 restaurant.

Head southeast along the SS2, SP3 and SS222 (Via Chiantigiana) towards Greve in Chianti. Stop at historic **Castello di Verrazzano** (p527) for a tasting en route.

On the next day, make your way to **Greve in Chianti** to test your new-found knowledge over a self-directed tasting at Enoteca Falorni (p526). For lunch, eat a Tuscan-style burger at Dario DOC (p527) in **Panzano in Chianti** or linger over lunch at La Locanda di Pietracupa (p528). Your destination in the afternoon should be **Badia a Passignano** (p527), an 11th-century, still-functioning Vallombrosian abbey surrounded by an Antinori wine estate. Enjoy a tasting in the *enoteca* (wine bar) and consider staying for an early pizza dinner at L'Antica Scuderia (p529) opposite the abbey, where you'll be able to watch the sun set over the vineyards.

On day three, pop into the pretty hilltop hamlet of **Volpaia** near **Radda in Chianti** and take a tour of the Castello di Volpaia p532) cellars before relaxing over lunch at the innovative Ristorante Albergaccio (p529) in **Castellina in Chianti**.

On the final day, head towards **Siena**. Along the way, take a guided tour of the **Castello di Brolio** (p532), ancestral home of the aristocratic Ricasoli family. Their wine estate is the oldest in Italy, so be sure to sample some Baron Ricasoli Chianti Classico at the estate's *cantina* (cellar) or over lunch in its *osteria* (casual tavern). Afterwards, investigate award-winning wines and contemporary art at **Castello di Ama** (p532).

DANITA DELIMONT/GETTY IMAGES ©

Top: Vineyards in Chianti
Bottom: Castello di Verrazzano

Radda in Chianti & Around

POP 1666

Pretty Radda's age-old streets fan out from its central square, where the shields and escutcheons of the 16th-century **Palazzo del Podestà** add drama to the scene. A historic wine town, it's an appealing base for visits to classic Tuscan vineyards and striking sculpture parks.

◉ Sights & Activities

Castello di Brolio CASTLE

(☑ 0577 73 02 80; www.ricasoli.it; garden, chapel & crypt €5, guided tours €8; ⊙ 10am-7pm Apr-Oct, guided tours every 30min 10.30am-12.30pm & 2.30-5pm Tue-Sun) The ancestral estate of the aristocratic Ricasoli family dates from the 11th century and is the oldest winery in Italy. Currently home to the 32nd baron, it opens its formal garden, panoramic terrace and museum to day-trippers, who often adjourn to the on-site *osteria* for lunch after a guided tour of the castle's small but fascinating museum.

Occupying three rooms in the castle's tower, the museum is dedicated to documenting the life of the extravagantly mustachioed Baron Bettino Ricasoli (1809–80), the second prime minster of the Republic of Italy and a true polymath (scientist, farmer, winemaker, statesman, businessman). A leading figure in the Risorgimento, one of his other great claims to fame is inventing the formula for Chianti Classico that is enshrined in current DOC regulations.

The *castello's* chapel dates from the early 14th century; below it is a crypt where generations of Ricasolis are interred. The estate produces wine and olive oil, and the huge terrace commands a spectacular view of the vineyards and olive groves. The Classic Tour (€25, two hours, Monday, Wednesday and Friday at 10am, plus 3pm March to June) takes in the wine-making facilities and features a tasting, while the Vineyard Tour (€45, two hours, 3.30pm Tuesday and Thursday) sees you exploring the estate's different *terroirs* and sampling vintages beside the vines.

A *bosco inglese* (English garden) surrounds the estate, in it (near the car park) you'll find the estate's **Osteria del Castello** (☑ 0577 73 02 90; 4-course tasting menu with wines €50; ⊙ noon-2.30pm & 7.30-9.30pm Fri-Wed late-Mar–Oct). Just outside the estate's entrance gates, on the SP484, is a modern cantina (⊙ 9am-7.30pm Mon-Fri & 10am-7pm Sa & Sun Apr to mid-Oct) where you can taste the Castello di Brolio's well-regarded Chianti Classico.

Castello di Ama SCULPTURE

(☑ 0577 74 60 31; www.castellodiama.com; Località Ama; guided tours €15, with wine & oil tasting €35; ⊙ by appointment year-round) At Castello di Ama centuries-old wine-making traditions meet cutting-edge contemporary art. As well as producing internationally famous wines such as 'L'Apparita' Merlot, this estate also features a sculpture park showcasing 13 impressive site-specific pieces by artists including Louise Bourgeois, Chen Zhen, Anish Kapoor, Kendell Geers and Daniel Buren. It's 9km south of Radda, near Lecchi in Chianti

Parco Sculture del Chianti SCULPTURE

(Chianti Sculpture Park; ☑ 0577 35 71 51; www.chiantisculpturepark.it; Località La Fornace; adult/child €10/5; ⊙ 10am-dusk Apr-Oct, by appointment Nov-Mar; ⓘ) More than 25 site-specific contemporary artworks are tucked into this 13-acre wood, meaning you'll encounter abstract humans, cube clusters and multi-coloured cows amid the foliage. Between June and August weekly sunset Jazz and Opera concerts are staged in the park's white Carrara marble and black Zimbabwean granite amphitheatre. Look out for Hitchcock, Fellini and Charlie Chaplin amid the 'spectators'.

The park is 16km south of Radda. While here, detour to the nearby village of **Pievasciata**, whose streets are home to an increasing number of site-specific contemporary international artworks (check to see if Yu Zhaoyang's hilarious *Town Ostriches* are still next to the cypress trees).

Castello di Volpaia WINERY

(☑ 0577 73 80 66; www.volpaia.it; Località Volpaia) Wines, olive oils, vinegars and honey have been produced for centuries at this wine estate based in the medieval hilltop hamlet of Volpaia (the name is misleading, as there's no actual castle here). Book ahead to enjoy a tasting and tour of the estate's cellars (€11), or pop into its *enoteca* (noon to 7pm Thursday to Tuesday), which is inside the hamlet's main tower.

🛏 Sleeping

★ **Villa Sassolini** BOUTIQUE HOTEL €€€

(☑ 0559 70 22 46; www.villasassolini.it; Largo Moncioni, Località Moncioni; d €200-345, ste €325-443, dinner €50; ⊘ closed Nov–mid-Mar; ❀ ☎ ☒) It's hard to top the romantic credentials of this gorgeous hotel set in dense forest on the border of Chianti and the Valdarno. Luxe rooms, an intimate restaurant and a spectacular pool terrace are three of many elements contributing to an utterly irresistible package; proximity to the Valdarno's designer clothing outlet stores being another. It's 25km east of Radda.

✖ Eating & Drinking

★ Ristorante La Bottega   TUSCAN €€
(☑ 0577 73 80 01; www.labottegadivolpaia.it; Piazza della Torre 1, Volpaia; meals €25; ⊘ noon-2.30pm & 7.30-9.30pm Wed-Mon Easter-Jan) *Cucina contadina* (food from the farmers' kitchen) is the mainstay of this pretty restaurant run by the Barucci family – the kitchen garden is right outside and Mum Gina is likely to have made the soup or pasta (her *ribollita* is famous). And what better place to eat it than an outdoor, tree-shaded terrace with sweeping views of Chianti's hills.

Osteria Le Panzanelle   TUSCAN €€
(☑ 0577 73 35 11; www.lepanzanelle.it; Lucarelli; meals €35; ⊘ 12.30-2pm & 7.30-9pm Tue-Sun, closed part of Jan & Feb) An ideal lunch stop en route from Chianti to Siena, this roadside inn serves traditional Tuscan dishes in its garden and downstairs bar-dining room. The menu changes monthly, reflecting what is in season. Find it 5km south of Panzano in Chianti, right next to the SP2 to Radda in Chianti. Bookings are advisable.

Val d'Elsa

A convenient base for visiting the rest of Tuscany, this valley stretching from Chianti to the Maremma national park ticks many of the boxes on every Tuscan 'must-do' list, with ample opportunity to enjoy fine food, wine, museums and scenery.

San Gimignano

POP 7768

As you crest the nearby hills, the 14 towers of this walled hill town look like a medieval Manhattan. Originally an Etruscan village, the settlement was named after the bishop of Modena, San Gimignano, who is said to have saved the city from Attila the Hun. It became a *comune* in 1199 and was very prosperous due in part to its location on the Via Francigena – building a tower taller than

---

ⓘ SAN GIMIGNANO CENT SAVER

Two combined tickets save you money. The first (adult/reduced €6/5) gives admission to the Museo Civico, the **Museo Archeologico & Spezieria di Santa Fina** (Via Folgore da San Gimignano 11; adult/reduced €6/5; ⊘ 9.30am-6.30pm summer, 11am-5pm winter) and the town's small **Ornithological Museum** (☑ 0577 94 13 88; Via Quercecchio; adult/child €1.50/1; ⊘ 11am-5.30pm Apr-Sep). The second (adult/reduced €6/3) gets you into the Collegiata and **Museo d'Arte Sacra** (Piazza Pecori 1; adult/child €3.50/2; ⊘ 10am-7pm Mon-Fri, to 5pm Sat, 12.30-7pm Sun summer, 10am-4.30pm Mon-Sat, 12.30-4.30pm Sun winter). Both tickets can be bought at the respective participating sights.

---

those built by one's neighbour (there were originally 72) became a popular way for the town's prominent families to flaunt their power and wealth. In 1348 plague wiped out much of the population and weakened the local economy, leading to the town's submission to Florence in 1353.

Today, not even the plague could deter the swarms of summer day trippers, lured here by the town's palpable sense of history, intact medieval streetscapes and enchanting rural setting.

◉ Sights

★ Collegiata   CHURCH
(Duomo or Basilica di Santa Maria Assunta; Piazza del Duomo; adult/reduced €4/2; ⊘ 10am-7pm Mon-Fri, to 5pm Sat, 12.30-7pm Sun summer, to 4.30pm daily winter) Parts of San Gimignano's Romanesque cathedral were built in the second half of the 11th century, but its remarkably vivid frescoes, depicting episodes from the Old and New Testaments, date from the 14th century. Look out, too, for the Cappella di Santa Fina, near the main altar – a Renaissance chapel adorned with naive and touching frescoes by Domenico Ghirlandaio depicting the life of one of the town's patron saints. These featured in Franco Zeffirelli's 1999 film *Tea with Mussolini*.

Entry is via the side stairs and through a loggia that was originally covered and functioned as the baptistry. Once in the main space, face the altar and look to your left

San Gimignano

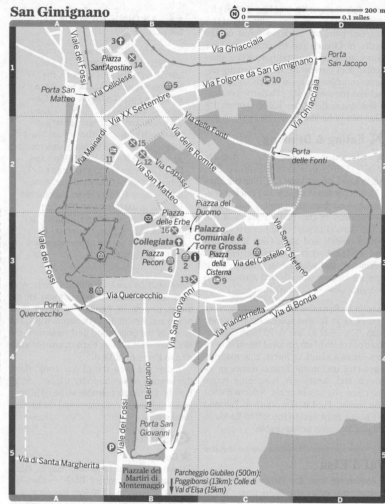

(north). On the wall are scenes from Genesis and the Old Testament by Bartolo di Fredi, dating from around 1367. The top row runs from the creation of the world through to the forbidden fruit scene. This in turn leads to the next level and fresco, the expulsion of Adam and Eve from the Garden of Eden, which has sustained some war damage. Further scenes include Cain killing Abel, and the stories of Noah's ark and Joseph's coat. The last level continues with the tale of Moses leading the Jews out of Egypt, and the story of Job.

On the right (south) wall are scenes from the New Testament by the workshop of Simone Martini (probably led by Lippo Memmi, Martini's brother-in-law), which were completed in 1336. Again, the frescoes are spread over three levels, starting in the six lunettes at the top. Starting with the Annunciation, the panels work through episodes such as the Epiphany, the presentation of Christ in the temple and the massacre of the innocents on Herod's orders. The subsequent panels on the lower levels summarise the life and death of Christ, the Resurrection

San Gimignano

and so on. Again, some have sustained damage, but most are in good condition.

On the inside wall of the front facade, extending onto adjoining walls, is Taddeo di Bartolo's striking depiction of the Last Judgment – on the upper-left side is a fresco depicting *Paradiso* (Heaven) and on the upper-right *Inferno* (Hell). The fresco of San Sebastian under them is by Benozzo Gozzoli.

The church is commonly known as the Collegiata, a reference to the college of priests which originally managed it.

★ Palazzo Comunale & Torre Grossa   MUSEUM

(Museo Civico; ☑ 0577 99 03 12; Piazza del Duomo 2; adult/reduced €6/5; ⊙9am-6.30pm summer, 11am-5pm winter) The 12th-century Palazzo Comunale is home to the **Camera del Podestà**, with its meticulously restored and slightly saucy cycle of frescoes by Memmo di Filippuccio – in this morality tale the rewards of marriage are shown in the scenes of the husband and wife naked in the bath and in bed. Be sure to climb the 218 steps of the *palazzo*'s 54m Torre Grossa for a spectacular view over the town and surrounding countryside.

The *palazzo*'s **Sala di Dante** is where the great poet Dante Alighieri addressed the town's council in 1299, urging it to support the Guelph cause. The room (also known as the Sala del Consiglio) is home to Lippo Memmi's early 14th-century *Maestà,* which portrays the enthroned Virgin and Child surrounded by angels, saints and local dignitaries – the kneeling noble in red-and-black stripes was the *podestà* (chief magistrate) of the time. Other frescoes portray jousts, hunting scenes and castles. Gadget fans are likely to enjoy the augmented reality glasses which superimpose digital medieval characters over the frescoes; hire them from the gift shop.

Upstairs is a small but charming pinacoteca. Highlights are two large *Annunciation* panels (1482) by Filippino Lippi, *Madonna of Humility Worshipped by Two Saints* (1466) and *Madonna and Child with Saints* (1466) by Benozzo Gozzoli, and an altarpiece by Taddeo di Bartolo (1401) illustrating the life of St Gimignano.

Chiesa di Sant'Agostino   CHURCH

(Piazza Sant'Agostino; ⊙7am-noon & 3-7pm summer, to 6pm winter) FREE This late-13th-century church is best known for Benozzo Gozzoli's charming fresco cycle illustrating the life of St Augustine. You'll find it behind the altar – putting €0.50 in the slot provides better illumination. Gozzoli also painted the fresco featuring San Sebastian on the north wall, which shows the saint protecting the citizens of San Gimignano during the 1464 plague. What makes the image highly unusual is that he's helped by a bare-breasted Virgin Mary; this symbolises her maternal love for humanity.

Museo del Vino   MUSEUM

(www.sangimignanomuseovernaccia.com; Parco della Rocca; ⊙11.30am-6.30pm Apr-Oct) FREE San Gimignano's famous wine, Vernaccia, is celebrated in this small museum next to the *rocca* (fortress). Exhibits trace the history of the product and the surrounding land; there's also an *enoteca* where you can buy glasses of local vintages to enjoy on a terrace with a panoramic view.

☞ Tours

★ Vernaccia di San Gimignano Vineyard Visit   WINERY

(€20; ⊙5-7pm Tue & Thu Apr-Oct) These highly enjoyable tastings of local foods and wines are delivered by English-speaking guides. Book at the tourist office at least a day in advance.

OFF THE BEATEN TRACK

VIA FRANCIGENA

Devise a holiday with a difference by walking or driving parts of the Via Francigena, a medieval pilgrimage route connecting Canterbury with Rome. In central Tuscany, the route goes past or through San Gimignano, Monteriggioni, San Quirico d'Orcia and Radicófani, among other towns. Globalmap publishes *Via Francigena in Toscana* (€8), an excellent 1:50,000 hiking map with detailed routes and information about accommodation for pilgrims; tourist offices and bookshops sell the map. Online, find route maps and GPS coordinates at www.francigenalibrari. beniculturali.it.

 Festivals & Events

Ferie delle Messi   CULTURAL
(www.cavalieridisantafina.it) A June pageant (usually the third weekend) evoking the town's medieval past through re-enacted battles, archery contests and plays.

Festival Barocco di San Gimignano   MUSIC
A high-quality season of Baroque music concerts in September and early October. Check www.sangimignano.com for details.

🛏 Sleeping

⭐ **Al Pozzo dei Desideri**   APARTMENT €
(✆370 3102538, 0577 90 71 99; www.alpozzo deidesideri.it; Piazza della Cisterna 32; d/tr/q €110/120/160; ❄🛜) Three rooms-with-a-view (two over the countryside and one over the town's main piazza) are on offer in this gorgeous 13th-century building; expect marble bathrooms, drapes and warm stone walls. All have a fridge and tea- and coffee-making facilities. There's no breakfast, but this is town-centre Tuscany: there's a good cafe close by.

Foresteria Monastero di San Girolamo   HOSTEL €
(✆0577 94 05 73; www.monasterosangirolamo.it; Via Folgore da San Gimignano 30; s/tw €43/75; ℗) This is a first-rate backpacker choice. Run by friendly Benedictine Vallumbrosan nuns, it has basic but comfortable rooms sleeping two to five people; all have attached bathrooms. Parking and kitchen use are availa-ble for a small fee. Book in advance at www. monasterystays.com, as it's usually full.

If you don't have a reservation, arrive between 9am and noon or between 3.30pm and 5.30pm and ring the monastery bell (the one closer to the town centre), rather than the Foresteria one, which is never answered.

⭐ **Il Paluffo**   AGRITURISMO €€
(✆0571 66 42 59; www.paluffo.com; via Citerna 144, near Lucardo; B&B d €160, 4-/6-person apt per week €1890/2300; ℗❄@🛜🏊) ◿ Hidden in the hills 20km north of San Gimignano sits the kind of luxurious, innovative, ecological *agriturismo* that you remember for a very, very long time. At Il Paluffo an inspired conversion of a centuries-old olive farm has seen the former fermentation room transformed into a book-packed, two-story lounge with vast sofas and a kooky feature fireplace.

Bedrooms feature 18th-century frescoes, polished wooden shutters and age-speckled mirrors. Bathrooms are jaw-dropping, with circular tubs, mezzanine showers, and wood from old wine barrels lining the floors.

Staff can arrange wine tasting and truffle hunting, cookery courses cover everything from pasta making to Tuscan dinner parties. Add a luscious bio-filtered swimming pool, an honesty bar stacked with Tuscan wines, a courtyard dotted with lemon trees, and terraces where valley views stretch as far San Gimignano's towers, and you have a dream stay.

Hotel L'Antico Pozzo   BOUTIQUE HOTEL €€
(✆0577 94 20 14; www.anticopozzo.com; Via San Matteo 87; s €80-95, d €90-180; ❄@🛜) The sense of heritage here is irresistible: stone arches and winding stairs lead to an intimate breakfast terrace; chic, spacious bedrooms are often replete with cornices and crowned with networks of beams. The posher rooms are named after poets and graded – Dante, a high-ceilinged beauty rich in polished woods, is the best. Naturally.

🍴 Eating & Drinking

San Gimignano is known for its *zafferano* (saffron). You can purchase meat, vegetables, fish and takeaway food at the Thursday morning market in and around Piazzas Cisterna, Duomo and Erbe.

Dal Bertelli   SANDWICHES €
(Via Capassi 30; panini €4-6, glasses of wine €2; ⏰1-7pm Mar-early Jan) The Bertelli family has lived in San Gimignano since 1779, and its

current patriarch is fiercely proud of both his heritage and his sandwiches. Salami, cheese, bread and wine is sourced from local artisan producers and it's sold in generous portions in a determinedly un-gentrified space with marble work surfaces, wooden shelves and curious agricultural implements dangling from stone walls.

Gelateria Dondoli GELATERIA €

(www.gelateriadipiazza.com; Piazza della Cisterna 4; gelati €2.50-5; ⊘9am-11pm summer, to 7.30pm winter) Think of it less as ice cream, more as art. Former gelato world champion Sergio Dondoli is a member of Italy's Ice Cream World Championship team (of course there's such a thing). Among his most famous creations are *Crema di Santa Fina* (saffron cream) gelato and Vernaccia sorbet.

★**Locanda Sant'Agostino** TUSCAN €€

(✆0577 94 31 41; www.locandasantagostino.net; Piazza Sant'Agostino 15; meals €30; ⊘12.30-2.30pm & 7-10pm Thu-Tue) It's a bit like eating in an Italian grandmother's kitchen: bundles of wheat hang from the ceiling; knick-knacks stack the shelves and the cooking is sublime. Homemade *pici* (thick, hand-rolled pasta) might come with wild-boar *ragù*, while truffles feature strongly – like the servings of Vernaccia wine, they're dished out with an admirably generous hand.

Perucà TUSCAN €€

(✆0577 94 31 36; www.peruca.eu; Via Capassi 16; meals €30; ⊘12.30-2pm & 7.30-10pm Tue-Sun mid-Feb–early Dec, open Mon Apr-Sep) The owner is as knowledgeable about regional food and wine as she is enthusiastic, and the food is excellent. Try the house speciality of *fagottini del contadino* (ravioli with *pecorino*, pears and saffron cream) with a glass of Fattoria San Donato's Vernaccia – it's a match made in heaven.

❶ Information

Tourist Office (✆0577 94 00 08; www.sangimignano.com; Piazza del Duomo 1; ⊘9am-1pm & 3-7pm summer, 9am-1pm & 2-6pm winter) An extremely helpful office which organises tours, supplies maps and has information on the *Strada del Vino Vernaccia di San Gimignano* (Wine Road of the Vernaccia of San Gimignano). It also offers accommodation booking on its website.

❶ Getting There & Away

BUS

The **bus station** (Piazzale dei Martiri di Montemaggio) neighbours the police station at Porta San Giovanni. The tourist office sells bus tickets.

Florence (€6.80, 1¼ to two hours, 14 daily) Change at Poggibonsi.

Siena (€6, one to 1½ hours, 10 daily Monday to Saturday)

Volterra (€6, 1½ hours, four daily Monday to Saturday) Change at Colle di Val d'Elsa.

CAR & MOTORCYCLE

From Florence and Siena, take the Siena–Florence *superstrada*, then the SR2 and finally the SP1 from Poggibonsi Nord. From Volterra, take the SR68 east and follow the turn-off signs north to San Gimignano on the SP47.

The cheapest parking option (per hour/24 hours €1.50/6) is Parcheggio Giubileo on the southern edge of town; the most convenient is Parcheggio Montemaggio next to Porta San Giovanni (per hour/24 hours €2/20).

TRAIN

The closest train station is at Poggibonsi (by bus €2.50, about 30 minutes, frequent).

Volterra

POP 10,760

Volterra's well-preserved medieval ramparts give the windswept town a proud, forbidding air that author Stephenie Meyer deemed ideal for the discriminating tastes of the planet's principal vampire coven in her wildly popular book series *Twilight*. Fortunately, the reality is considerably more welcoming, as any wander through the winding cobbled streets attests.

◉ Sights

★**Museo Etrusco Guarnacci** MUSEUM

(Via Don Minzoni 15; adult/reduced combined ticket €10/6; ⊘9am-7pm summer, 10am-4.30pm winter) The vast collection of Etruscan artefacts exhibited here makes this one of Italy's most impressive collections. Found locally, they include some 600 funerary urns carved mainly from alabaster and tufa – perhaps the pick is the *Urn of the Sposi*, a strikingly realistic terracotta rendering of an elderly couple. The finds are displayed according to subject and era; the best examples (those dating from later periods) are on the 2nd and 3rd floors.

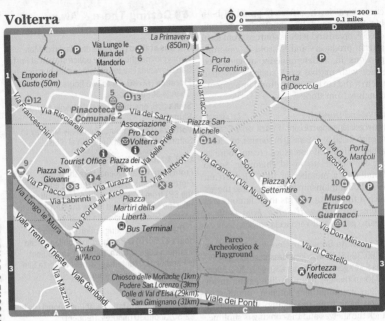

Volterra

Cattedrale di Santa Maria Assunta
CATHEDRAL

(Duomo di Volterra; Piazza San Giovanni; ⊙8am-noon & 2-7pm summer, to 5pm winter) A handsome coffered ceiling is the most striking single feature of the *duomo*, which was built in the 12th and 13th centuries and remodelled in the 16th. The Chapel of Our Lady of Sorrows, on the left as you enter from Piazza San Giovanni, has two sculptures by Andrea della Robbia and a small fresco of the *Procession of the Magi* by Benozzo Gozzoli.

In front of the *duomo*, a 13th-century baptistry (Piazza San Giovanni) features a small marble font (1502) by Andrea Sansovino.

★Pinacoteca Comunale
GALLERY

(Via dei Sarti 1; adult/reduced combined ticket €10/6; ⊙9am-7pm summer, 10am-4.30pm winter) Local, Sienese and Florentine art holds sway in this modest collection in the Palazzo Minucci Solaini. Taddeo di Bartolo's *Madonna Enthroned with Child* (1411) is exquisite, while Rosso Fiorentino's *Deposition from the Cross* (1521) appears strikingly, surprisingly, modern.

Ecomuseo dell'Alabastro   MUSEUM
(Via dei Sarti 1; adult/reduced combined ticket €10/6; ⊙9am-7pm summer, 10am-4.30pm winter) As befits a town that's hewn the precious material from nearby quarries since Etruscan times, Volterra is the proud possessor of an alabaster museum. It's an intriguing exploration of everything related to the rock, from production and working to commercialisation. Contemporary creations feature strongly, there are also choice examples from Etruscan times onwards as well as a re-created artisan's workshop.

Roman Theatre   ARCHAEOLOGICAL SITE
(Via Francesco Ferrucci; admission €3.50; ⊙10.30am-5.30pm summer, 10am-4.30pm winter) One of Italy's finest and best-preserved Roman theatres makes for an evocative site, with its grassy ranks of seating and towering columns. It was commissioned in the 1st century BC and could hold up to 2000 spectators. Today the sloping seating area (*cavea*), orchestra pit and stage are still clearly discernible. If you're not that keen on Roman ruins, though, do note there's a great view of the theatre from (free to access) Via Lungo Le Mura del Mandorlo.

Tours

★**Volterra by Night**   WALKING TOUR
(www.volterratur.it/en; adult/child €10/free; ⊙weekly mid-Jun–mid-Sep) Fabulously atmospheric, in-the-dark meanderings amid Volterra's improbably small alleyways and Gothic architecture. Tours last 90 minutes, start at 9.30pm, and have to be booked by 4pm the same day.

New Moon Tour   WALKING TOUR
(☑0588 8 60 99; www.newmoonofficialtour. com; tours €30) Fans of Stephenie Meyer's *Twilight* series adore discovering the clock tower, alleyways and arches that Edward and Bella career around in the *New Moon* vampire novel. These evening tours tend to run twice-monthly in April and May, and weekly in July and August. Tickets must be pre-booked – the price includes an *aperitivo* and a surprise or two...

Festivals & Events

Volterra AD 1398   CULTURAL
(www.volterra1398.it; day pass adult/reduced €10/6) On the third and fourth Sundays of

GALLERIA CONTINUA

It may seem strange to highlight contemporary art in this medieval time capsule of a town, but there's good reason. **Galleria Continua** (☑0577 94 31 34; www.galleriacontinua.com; Via del Castello 11; ⊙10am-1pm & 2-7pm Mon-Sat) is one of the best commercial art galleries in Europe, showing the work of big-name artists such as Ai Weiwei, Daniel Buren, Carlos Garaicoa, Moataz Nasr, Kendell Geers and Sophie Whettnall.

Spread over three venues (an old cinema, a medieval tower and a medieval vaulted cellar), the gallery is one of San Gimignano's most compelling attractions.

August, the citizens of Volterra roll back the calendar some 600 years, take to the streets in period costume and celebrate all the fun of a medieval fair.

Sleeping

★**Podere San Lorenzo**   AGRITURISMO €
(☑0588 3 90 80; www.agriturismo-volterra.it; Via Allori 80; B&B d €100, 2-/3-/4-bed apt without breakfast €105/135/160; ❀❋) In this tranquil model of slow tourism you dip straight into a rural idyll. An alluring spring-fed biological swimming pool sits steps away from an enviable veg garden; apartments (two with private terraces) and rooms are chock-full of history – in the oldest the 'new' beams are 500 years old. Gourmet dinners (per person €30 including wine) are served in a former 12th-century chapel.

Walking, biking and hands-on olive-oil production opportunities are available, as are cooking classes given by chef Mariana (per person €100). It's set on an olive farm some 3km outside Volterra. Arriving on the SS68 from Siena, Florence and San Gimignano, you'll pass a sculpture of a red circle at the entrance to town and should then turn right into the narrow lane after the car saleyard.

La Primavera   B&B €
(☑0588 8 72 95; www.affittacamere-laprimavera. com; Via Porta Diana 15; s/d/tr €50/75/100; ⊙mid-Apr–mid-Nov; ℗❋) Fittingly for a former alabaster workshop, some of the bedrooms in this home-style B&B feature vast carved fireplaces. Otherwise this is a cosy

① VOLTERRA CENT SAVER

A *biglietto cumulativo* (combined ticket) costing €10/6 per adult/reduced covers admission to Volterra's Museo Etrusco Guarnacci, the Pinacoteca Comunale and the Ecomuseo dell'Alabastro.

affair, with a communal lounge, pretty garden, polished parquet floors and soothing pastel colour schemes – choose from violet, yellow, green or blue. It's just outside the city walls, a 10-minute walk from Piazza dei Priori. No credit cards.

Chiosco delle Monache HOSTEL €
(☑ 0588 8 66 13; www.ostellovolterra.it; Via del Teatro 4, Località San Girolamo; dm €18, B&B s/d €53/69; ☺ mid-Mar–Oct; ⓟⓡ) Opened in 2009 after a major renovation, this excellent private hostel occupies a 13th-century monastery complete with a frescoed refectory where breakfast is served. Airy rooms overlook the cloisters and have good beds and bathrooms; dorms sleep up to six. Breakfast (for those in dorms) costs €6. It's 1km away from the centre of town.

✗ Eating & Drinking

L'Incontro CAFE €
(Via G Matteotti 18; sandwiches €2.50-3.50; ☺ 7am-1am Thu-Tue; ⓡ) L'Incontro's rear *salone* is a top spot to grab a quick antipasto plate or *panino* for lunch, and its front bar area is always crowded with locals enjoying a coffee or *aperitivo*. The house-baked biscuits are noteworthy – try the chewy and nutty *brutti mai buoni* ('ugly but good') or its alabaster-coloured cousin, *ossi di morto* (bones of the dead).

La Carabaccia TUSCAN €€
(☑ 0588 8 62 39; www.lacarabacciavolterra.it; Piazza XX Settembre 4-5; meals €25; ☺ noon-2.30pm & 7.30-9.30pm, closed Mon Oct-Easter; ✐) Sisters Sara, Lalla and Patrizia have put their heart and soul into this fantastic trattoria with a country-style interior and attractive front terrace. It's the city's best lunch option and is named after a humble Tuscan vegetable soup (one of the specialities of the house). The small menu changes daily according to the pick of the offerings from local producers.

Caffè dei Fornelli CAFE, BAR
(☑ 0588 8 05 96; www.caffedeifornelli.it; Piazza dei Fornelli 3; ☺ 9am-11pm, closed Thu in winter) The city's bohemian set congregates here, drawn by genial host Carlo Bigazzi, cheap house wine (€1.50 per glass), live jazz, poetry readings and exhibitions. The cafe interior is pleasant, but the most sought-after tables are on the street outside.

🔒 Shopping

Volterra's centuries-old heritage as an alabaster mining and working town ensures plenty of shops specialise in hand-carved alabaster items. The **Cooperativa Artieri dell'Alabastro** (www.artierialabastro.it; Piazza dei Priori 5; ☺ 10am-6pm) showcases the impressive work of 23 local alabaster artisans in a roomy town-centre shop. The showroom of craftsman **Paolo Sabatini** (www.paolosabatini.com; Via G Matteotti 56; ☺ variable) is a smaller, more intimate affair. To watch alabaster being carved, head to **Alab'Arte** (www.alabarte.com; Via Orti San Agostino 28; ☺ 10am-12.30pm & 3-6pm Mon-Sat).

Emporio del Gusto FOOD
(Via San Lino 2; ☺ 7.30am-1pm & 5-8pm Wed-Fri, 7.30am-1pm Tue, 9.30am-1pm Sat) A feast of local goodies stacks the shelves in this *comune*-sponsored food co-op. Look out for olive-oil products (including toiletries), fresh milk and yoghurt, cheese, vegetables, locally grown saffron, truffles, pasta, bread and wine.

Fabula Etrusca JEWELLERY
(www.fabulaetrusca.it; Via Lungo Le Mura del Mandorlo 10; ☺ 10am-7pm Easter-Christmas) Distinctive pieces in 18-carat gold – many based on Etruscan designs – are handmade in this workshop on the city's northern walls.

① Information

Tourist Office (☑ 0588 8 60 99; www.volterra tur.it; Piazza dei Priori 19; ☺ 9.30am-1pm & 2-6pm) The extremely efficient tourist office provides free maps, offers a free hotel-booking service and rents out an audioguide tour of the town.

① Getting There & Around

BUS

The bus station is in Piazza Martiri della Libertà. Buy tickets at newsagents or the **Associazione Pro Loco Volterra** (☑ 0588 8 61 50; www.provolterra.it; Piazza dei Priori 10; ☺ 9.30am-

12.30pm & 3-6pm, hours can vary). Bus services are reduced on Sundays.

CPT (www.cpt.pisa.it) buses connect Volterra with Pisa (€6.10, two hours, up to 10 Monday to Saturday).

You'll need to go to Colle di Val d'Elsa (€2.75, 50 minutes, four Monday to Saturday) to catch one of four connecting services (Monday to Saturday) to San Gimignano (€3.40, 35 minutes), Siena (€3.40, two hours) and Florence (€8.35, two hours).

CAR & MOTORCYCLE

Volterra is accessed via the SR68. A ZTL applies in the historic centre. The most convenient car park is beneath Piazza Martiri della Libertà (per hour/day €1.50/11).

Val d'Orcia & Val di Chiana

These two valleys are showcases of classic Tuscan scenery – the landscape of the Val d'Orcia is so magnificent that it is protected as a Unesco World Heritage Site.

Montalcino & Around

POP 5127

This town is defined by the fruit of vines – it's known globally as the home of one of the world's great wines, Brunello di Montalcino. A remarkable number of *enoteche* line its medieval streets.

◎ Sights

Fortezza HISTORIC BUILDING
(Piazzale Fortezza; courtyard free, ramparts adult/child €4/2; ⊙9am-8pm Apr-Oct, 10am-6pm Nov-Mar) This imposing 14th-century structure was expanded under the Medici dukes and now dominates the town's skyline. You can sample and buy local wines in its *enoteca* (tasting of two/three/five Brunellos €9/13/19) and also climb up to the fort's ramparts. Buy a ticket for the ramparts at the bar.

**Museo Civico e Diocesano
d'Arte Sacra** MUSEUM
(☑0577 84 60 14; Via Ricasoli 31; adult/reduced €4.50/3; ⊙10am-1pm & 2-5.30pm Tue-Sun) Occupying the former convent of the neighbouring **Chiesa di Sant'Agostino**, this collection of religious art from the town and surrounding region includes a triptych by Duccio and a *Madonna and Child* by Simone Martini. Other artists represented

include the Lorenzetti brothers, Giovanni di Paolo and Sano di Pietro.

Poggio Antico WINERY
(☑0577 84 80 44; www.poggioantico.com; ⊙cantina 10am-6pm, restaurant noon-2.30pm & 7-9.30pm Tue-Sun, closed Sun evening winter) Located 5km outside Montalcino on the road to Grosseto, Poggio Antico is a superb foodie one-stop-shop. It makes award-winning wines (try its Brunello Altero or Riserva), conducts free cellar tours in Italian, English and German, offers paid tastings (approx €25 depending on wines) and has an on-site restaurant (meals €40). Book tours in advance.

🛏 Sleeping

★ Il Palazzo B&B €
(☑0577 84 91 10; www.ilpalazzomontalcino.it; Via Panfilo Dell'Oca 23; d €75-80; P⊙) Il Palazzo manages to both immerse you in aristocratic surroundings and make you feel cosily at home. The rambling 500-year-old building features ornate tile floors, beams, sumptuous tapestries and antique chairs. But it's the friendly welcome and the almost incidental nature of the splendour that really delights. The rates are ridiculously good too.

Hotel Vecchia Oliviera HOTEL €€
(☑0577 84 70 28; www.vecchiaoliviera.com; Via Landi 1; s €70-85, d €120-190; P❊☂☲) Chandeliers, elegant armchairs, polished wooden floors and rich rugs lend this converted oil mill a refined air. The pick of the 11 rooms comes with hill views and a jacuzzi, the pool is in an attractive garden setting, and the terrace has wrap-around views.

🍴 Eating & Drinking

★ Il Leccio TUSCAN €€
(☑0577 84 41 75; www.illeccio.net; Costa Castellare 1, Sant'Angelo in Colle; meals €40; ⊙noon-3pm & 7-10pm) Sometimes simple dishes are the hardest to perfect, and perfection is the only term to use when discussing this trattoria in Brunello heartland. Watching the chef make his way between his stove and kitchen garden to gather produce for each order puts a whole new spin on the word 'fresh', and both the results and the house Brunello are spectacular.

Osticcio WINE BAR
(www.osticcio.it; Via Matteotti 23; antipasto plates €7-18, meals €37; ⊙noon-4pm & 7-11pm Fri-Wed, plus noon-7pm Thu summer) In a town overflowing with *enoteche*, this is definitely one

ABBAZIA DI SANT'ANTIMO

The beautiful, Romanesque **Abbazia di Sant'Antimo** (www.antimo.it; Castelnuovo dell'Abate; ⏱10.15am-12.30pm & 3-6.30pm Mon-Sat, 9.15-10.45am & 3-6pm Sun) lies in an isolated valley just below the village of Castelnuovo dell'Abate, 11km from Montalcino. It's Romanesque exterior features stone carvings set in the bell tower and apsidal chapels. Visit in the morning when the sun – streaming through the windows – creates a surreal atmosphere, or at night when it's lit up. The real highlight though is when the monks perform Gregorian chants during daily services; check its website for times.

of the best. A huge selection of Brunello and its more modest sibling Rosso di Montalcino accompanies tempting dishes such as marinated anchovies, *cinta senese* (Tuscan pork) crostini, and pasta with pumpkin and pecorino. The panoramic view, meanwhile, almost upstages it all.

Fiaschetteria Italiana 1888 CAFE
(Piazza del Popolo 6; ⏱7.30am-midnight, closed Thu winter) You could take a seat in the slender square outside this atmosphere-laden *enoteca*-cafe, but then you'd miss its remarkable 19th-century decor – all brass, mirrors and ornate lights. It's been serving coffee and glasses of Brunello to locals since 1888 (hence the name) and is still chock-full of charm.

ℹ Information

Tourist Office (☏0577 84 93 31; www.prolocomontalcino.com; Costa del Municipio 1; ⏱10am-1pm & 2-5.50pm) The tourist office is just off the main square and can book cellar-door visits and accommodation.

ℹ Getting There & Away

BUS

Regular Siena Mobilità buses (€5, 1½ hours, six daily Monday to Saturday) run to/from Siena.

CAR & MOTORCYCLE

From Siena, take the SS2 (Via Cassia) after Buonconvento, then turn off onto the SP45. Find parking around the Fortezza (€1.50 per hour).

Pienza

POP 2125

The road to Montepulciano might pass right through Pienza, but that doesn't detract from this pretty town's astonishing appeal. A sleepy hamlet until Enea Silvio Piccolomini (later Pius II) decided to rebuild it in magnificent Renaissance style, Pienza today is top of the tourist charts: summer weekends here are particularly busy, with tourists outnumbering locals by a ratio of around 50:1. Come midweek if possible.

Unesco added Pienza's historic centre to its World Heritage list in 1996, citing the revolutionary vision of urban space realised in Piazza Pio II and the buildings around it.

⊙ Sights

Piazza Pio II PIAZZA
Stand in this magnificent square and spin 360 degrees. You've just taken in an overview of Pienza's major monuments. Gems of the Renaissance constructed in a mere three years between 1459 and 1462, they're arranged according to the urban design of Bernardo Rossellino, who applied the principles of Renaissance town planning devised by his mentor, Leon Battista Alberti.

The space available to Rossellino was limited, so to increase the sense of perspective and dignity of the great edifices he'd been commissioned to design, he set them off at angles to the cathedral around a magnificently paved piazza. It was a true masterstroke.

🛏 Sleeping & Eating

★**Cavalierino** AGRITURISMO €
(☏0578 75 87 33; www.cavalierino.it; Via di Poggiano 17; 4-person apt per night/week from €180/1100; P🅿🛜🌊) The first thing that strikes you about Cavalierino is the peace. In this hilltop, supremely stylish, organic *agriturismo* wicker furniture and contemporary paintings blend artfully with bright rooms and terracotta floors. The top-floor bedrooms offer bewitching views of snaking rows of vines; the pool and sauna add to the appeal, as do the washing machines, well-stocked kitchens (including coffee makers) and racks of luxury toiletries. Cavalierino is midway between Pienza and Montepulciano.

★ **La Bandita**
Townhouse   BOUTIQUE HOTEL €€€
(☑0578 74 90 05; www.labanditatownhouse.com;
Corso Il Rossellino 111; r €250-495, ste €350-695;
P❄@🛜🅿) There's something irresistible
about La Bandita, where 12 dreamily luxurious rooms sit inside a Renaissance-era convent – here age-old stone walls meet sleek
leather sofas and suspended beds. But the
real joy is the ambition: to give guests a taste
of Tuscan village life. Its heart-of-Pienza setting helps, as does a gorgeous communal
lounge and a laid-back wine bar.

Osteria Sette di Vino   TUSCAN €
(☑0578 74 90 92; Piazza di Spagna 1; meals €20;
⊙12.30-2.30pm & 7.30-10pm Thu-Tue) Known
for its *zuppa di pane e fagioli* (bread and
white-bean soup), *bruschette* and range of
local *pecorino* cheese, this simple place is
run by the exuberant Luciano, who is immortalised as Bacchus in a copy of Caravaggio's famous painting hanging above the
main counter. There's a clutch of tables inside and a scattering outside – book ahead.

Pummarò   PIZZA €
(Via del Giglio 4; slice €2.50, pizza €6-10; ⊙noon-
11pm Tue-Sun; 🛜🍴) Look for brightly painted bicycles in a laneway off Via Rossellino
and you'll find this teensy pizzeria, which
is a great place to source a cheap and quick
snack. There's an innovative range of all-veg-
etable offerings; the *pizza pummarò* (with
cherry tomatoes, *mozzarella di bufala* and
basil) is superb.

ℹ Information

Tourist Office (☑0578 74 99 05; info.
turismo@comune.pienza.si.it; Corso Rossellino
30; ⊙10am-1pm & 2-5pm Wed-Mon summer,
10am-4pm Sat & Sun winter) Located on the
ground floor of Palazzo Borgia.

ℹ Getting There & Away

BUS
Two Siena Mobilità buses run Monday to Saturday between Siena and Pienza (€5.50, 70
minutes); nine travel to/from Montepulciano
(€2.50). The bus stops are just off Piazza Dante
Alighieri. Buy tickets at one of the nearby bars.

Montepulciano
POP 14,290
Exploring this reclaimed narrow ridge of
volcanic rock will push your quadriceps
to failure point. When this happens, self-

medicate with a generous pour of the highly
reputed Vino Nobile while drinking in spectacular views over the Val di Chiana and Val
d'Orcia.

◎ Sights

★ **Il Corso**   STREET
Montepulciano's main street – called in
stages Via di Gracciano, Via di Voltaia, Via
dell'Opio and Via d'Poliziano – climbs up the
eastern ridge of the town from Porta al Prato and loops to meet Via di Collazzi on the
western ridge. To reach the centre of town
(Piazza Grande) take a dog-leg turn into Via
del Teatro.

In Piazza Savonarola, up from the Porta
al Prato, is the Colonna del Marzocca (Piazza Savonarola), erected in 1511 to confirm
Montepulciano's allegiance to Florence. The
splendid stone lion, squat as a pussycat atop
this column is, in fact, a copy; the original
is in the town's Museo Civico. The late-
Renaissance Palazzo Avignonesi (Via di
Gracciano nel Corso 91) is at No 91; other notable buildings include the Palazzo di Bucelli
(Via di Gracciano nel Corso 73) at No 73 (look for
the recycled Etruscan and Latin inscriptions
and reliefs on the lower facade), and Palazzo Cocconi (Via di Gracciano nel Corso 70) at
No 70.

Continuing uphill, you'll find Michelozzo's
Chiesa di Sant'Agostino (Piazza Michelozzo;
⊙9am-noon & 3-6pm), with its lunette above
the entrance holding a terracotta Madonna
and Child, John the Baptist and St Augustine. Opposite, the Torre di Pulcinella (Piazza Michelozzo), a medieval tower house, is
topped by the town clock and the hunched
figure of Pulcinella (Punch of Punch and
Judy fame), which strikes the hours. After passing historic Caffè Poliziano (Via di
Voltaia 27; ⊙7am-8pm Mon-Thu, to 10pm Fri, to
11pm Sat, to 9pm Sun; 🛜), the Corso continues
straight ahead and Via del Teatro veers off
to the right.

★ **Palazzo Comunale**   PALACE
(Piazza Grande; terrace/tower €3/5; ⊙10am-6pm
summer) Built in the 14th-century in Gothic
style and remodelled in the 15th century by
Michelozzo, the Palazzo Comunale still functions as the town hall. The main reasons to
head inside are to drink in the extraordinary
views from the panoramic terrace and the
tower – from the latter you can see as far
as Pienza, Montalcino and even, on a clear
day, Siena.

Museo Civico
MUSEUM, ART GALLERY

(www.museocivicomontepulciano.it; Via Ricci 10; adult/reduced €5/3; ⏰ 10am-1pm & 3-6pm Tue-Sun summer, Sat & Sun only winter) Montepulciano's modest museum and pinacoteca have recently had a curatorial dream come true: a painting in their collections has been attributed to Caravaggio. The masterpiece is a characteristic Portrait of a Gentleman. Worth the entrance fee alone, it's accompanied by high-tech, touch-screen interpretation, which allows you to explore details of the painting, its restoration and diagnostic attribution.

Courses & Tours

★ Strada del Vino Nobile di Montepulciano
TOUR

(☑ 0578 71 74 84; www.stradavinonobile.it; Piazza Grande 7) The office of the Strada del Vino Nobile di Montepulciano organises tours and courses, including cooking courses (€60 to €180), vineyard tours (€30 to €115), Slow Food tours (€100 to €155), wine-tasting lessons (€40) and walking tours in the vineyards culminating in a wine tasting (€45 to €60). Book in advance at its information office in Piazza Grande.

★ Festivals & Events

Bravio delle Botti
CULTURAL

(www.braviodellebotti.com; ⏰ Aug) Members of the city's eight *contrade* push 80kg wine barrels uphill in this race held on the last Sunday in August. There are also Renaissance-themed celebrations during the week before.

Sleeping

Camere Bellavista
HOTEL €

(☑ 0578 75 73 48; www.camerebellavista.it; Via Ricci 25; d €75-100; [P][🐾]) As this excellent budget hotel is four stories tall and sits on the edge of the old town, the views live up to its name. The styling is heritage rustic with exposed beams, hefty wooden furniture, brass bedsteads and smart new bathrooms. The owner isn't resident, so phone ahead to be met with the key. No breakfast.

★ Locanda San Francesco
B&B €€

(☑ 0578 75 87 25; www.locandasanfrancesco.it; Piazza San Francesco 3; d €160-250; [P][❄][@][🐾]) There's only one downside to this B&B: once you check into this supremely welcoming, 14th century *palazzo*, you might never want to go. The feel is elegant but also homely:

refined furnishings meet well-stocked bookshelves; restrained fabrics are teamed with fluffy bathrobes. The best room has superb views over the Val d'Orcia on one side and the Val di Chiana on the other.

Fattoria San Martino
AGRITURISMO €€

(☑ 0578 71 74 63; www.fattoriasanmartino.it; Via di Martiena 3; r €140-180; ⏰ closed Dec-Easter; [P][🐾][🏊][👪]) 🍃 Dutch-born Karin and Italian Antonio met when working in Milan's high-velocity fashion industry, but eventually decided organic farming was more to their liking than haute couture. The homespun-chic rooms in this rebuilt 12th-century farmhouse and purpose-built annexe are sure to please, as will the all-vegetarian meals (dinner €35 plus wine), pretty garden, biological filtered pool and emphasis on sustainability.

✕ Eating & Drinking

Osteria Acquacheta
TUSCAN €€

(☑ 0578 71 70 86; www.acquacheta.eu; Via del Teatro 2; meals €25; ⏰ 12.15-4pm & 7.30-10.30pm Wed-Mon) Hugely popular with locals and tourists alike, this bustling *osteria* specialises in *bistecca alla fiorentina* (chargrilled T-bone steak), which comes to the table in huge, lightly seared and exceptionally flavoursome slabs (don't even *think* of asking for it to be served otherwise). Lunch sittings are at 12.15pm and 2.15pm; dinner at 7.30pm and 9.15pm – book ahead.

★ La Grotta
RISTORANTE €€€

(☑ 0578 75 74 79; www.lagrottamontepulciano.it; Via San Biagio 15; meals €44, 6-course tasting menu €48; ⏰ 12.30-2.30pm & 7.30-10pm Thu-Tue, closed mid-Jan–mid-Mar) The ingredients, and sometimes dishes, may be traditional, but the presentation is full of refined flourishes – artfully arranged Parmesan shavings and sprigs of herbs crown delicate towers of pasta, vegetables and meat. The service is exemplary and the courtyard garden divine. It's just outside town on the road to Chiusi.

ℹ Information

Tourist Office (☑ 0578 75 73 41; www.prolocomontepulciano.it; Piazza Don Minzoni 1; ⏰ 9.30am-12.30pm & 3-6pm Mon-Sat, 9.30am-12.30pm Sun) Reserves last-minute accommodation (in person only), offers internet access (€3.50 per hour), supplies town maps, can advise on mountain bike and scooter rental (€25 to €50) and sells bus and train tickets (€1 commission applies for train tickets).

ⓘ Getting There & Around

BUS
The bus station is next to car park No 5. Siena Mobilità runs four buses daily between Siena and Montepulciano (€6.60, one hour) stopping at Pienza (€2.50) en route. There are three services per day to/from Florence (€11.20, 90 minutes).

Regular buses connect with Chiusi-Chianciano Terme (€3.40, 40 minutes), from where you can catch a train to Florence (€12.90, two hours, frequent) via Arezzo (€6.40, 50 minutes).

CAR & MOTORCYCLE
Coming from Florence, take the Valdichiana exit off the A1 (direction Bettole-Sinalunga); from Siena, take the Siena–Bettole–Perugia autostrada.

A ZTL applies in the historic centre. The most convenient car park is at Piazza Don Minzoni (€1.30 per hour April to October, free November to March), from where minibuses (€1) weave their way up the hill to Piazza Grande.

SOUTHERN TUSCANY

With its landscape of dramatic coastlines, mysterious Etruscan sites and medieval hilltop villages, this little-visited pocket of Tuscany offers contrasts galore. It's a region created for the Italy connoisseur.

Massa Marittima

POP 8665

Drawcards at this tranquil hill town include an eccentric yet endearing jumble of museums, an extremely handsome central piazza and largely intact medieval streets that are blessedly bereft of tour groups.

Briefly under Pisan domination, Massa Marittima became an independent *comune* in 1225 but was swallowed up by Siena a century later. The 1348 plague, followed by the decline of the town's lucrative mining industry 50 years later, reduced it to the brink of extinction. It was brought back to life by the draining of surrounding marshes (formerly a malarial risk) and the re-establishment of mining in the 18th century.

◎ Sights

The town's main sights are in the Città Vecchia (Old Town).

THE FERTILITY TREE

A rather risqué surprise lurks beneath the loggia of a former 13th-century wheat store. Its public drinking fountain, **Fonte dell'Abbondanza** (Fountain of Abundance), is now decommissioned. But it's the extraordinary fresco known as the **Albero della Fecondità** (Via Ximenes, off Piazza Garibaldi) FREE (Fertility Tree) that might make you blush. Look closely to see what type of fruit the tree bears!

★**Cattedrale di San Cerbone**   CATHEDRAL
(Piazza Garibaldi; ☉noon-7pm summer, to 6pm winter) Presiding over photogenic Piazza Garibaldi (aka Piazza Duomo), Massa Marittima's asymmetrically positioned 13th-century *duomo* is dedicated to St Cerbonius, the town's patron saint, who's always depicted surrounded by a flock of geese. Inside, don't miss the freestanding *Maestà* (Madonna and Child enthroned in majesty; 1316) attributed by some experts to Duccio di Buoninsegna.

Museo di Arte Sacra   MUSEUM
(Museum of Sacred Art; ☑0566 90 19 54; www.museiartesacra.net; Corso Diaz 36; adult/reduced €5/3; ☉10am-1pm & 3-6pm Tue-Sun summer, 11am-1pm & 3-5pm Tue-Sun winter) Housed in the former monastery of San Pietro all'Orto, this museum houses a splendid *Maestà* (c 1335-37) by Ambrogio Lorenzetti and sculptures by Giovanni Pisano that originally adorned the *duomo's* facade. The collection of primitive grey alabaster bas-reliefs also came from the *duomo*, but date from an earlier era.

Museo Archeologico   MUSEUM
(Piazza Garibaldi 1; adult/reduced €3/1.50; ☉10am-12.30pm & 3.30-7pm Tue-Sun summer, 10am-12.30pm & 3-5pm Tue-Sun winter) The 13th-century **Palazzo del Podestà** houses a dusty archaeological museum where the noteworthy exhibit is *La Stele del Vado all'Arancio,* a simple but compelling stone stela (funeral or commemorative marker) dating from the 3rd millennium BC.

Torre del Candeliere   TOWER
(Candlestick Tower; Piazza Matteotti; adult/child €3/2; ☉10am-1pm & 3-6pm Tue-Sun summer, 11am-1pm & 2.30-4.30pm Tue-Sun winter) Climb

WORTH A TRIP

PARCO REGIONALE DELLA MAREMMA

This spectacular **regional park** (www.parco-maremma.it; park admission adult/reduced €10/5) incorporates the Uccellina mountain range, a 600-hectare pine forest, marshy plains and a 20km stretch of unspoiled coastline. The main **visitor centre** (☑0564 40 70 98; Via del Bersagliere 7-9, Alberese; ☺8am-6pm mid-Jun–mid-Sep, to 4pm mid-Sep–mid-Nov, to 2pm mid-Nov–mid-Jun) is in Alberese, on the park's northern edge.

Park access is limited to 13 signed walking trails, varying in length from 2.5km to 13km; the most popular is A2 ('Le Torri'), a 5.8km walk to the beach. The entry fee (paid at the visitor centre) varies according to whether a park-operated bus transports you from the visitor centre to your chosen route. From 15 June to 15 September the park can only be visited on a guided tour due to possible bushfire threat.

As well as the walking trails, there are four guided mountain-bike tours (€20 to €25, two to six hours) and a guided 2½-hour canoe tour (adult/child €16/10); book these at the visitor centre. Private operators run horse and pony treks in the park – contact **Il Gelsomino** (☑0564 40 5 133; www.ilgelsomino.com; Via Strada del Barbicato 4, Alberese; treks from €30) or **Circolo Ippico Uccellina** (☑334 9797181; www.circoloippicouccellina.it; Località Collecchio 38, Magliano in Toscana; per half-/full day from €55/95).

to the top of this 13th-century, 74m-high tower for stupendous views over the old town.

🛏 Sleeping

★ La Fattoria di Tatti   B&B €

(☑0566 91 20 01; www.tattifattoria.it; Via Matteotti 10, Tatti; s €60-80, d €90-115; ☺closed Nov–mid-Mar; ℗@) La Fattoria di Tatti is imposing – one of those stately Tuscan farmhouses that ranges over four floors. Its weathered 18th-century walls shelter eight simple but stylish rooms, while its position at the summit of the hilltop village of Tatti, 25km southeast of Massa Marittima, ensures mesmerising valley views.

Manager Maria prepares a delicious breakfast and guests are welcome to use the kitchen at other times. A nearby playground and pizzeria/trattoria make it an ideal choice for families.

Podere Riparbella   AGRITURISMO €€

(☑0566 91 55 57; www.riparbella.com; Località Sopra Pian di Mucini; s €82-92, d €164; ☺closed early Jan–mid-Apr; ℗☎) ✎ The Swiss owners of this 46-hectare estate, 5km outside town, have built an ecologically sustainable farm operation where they cultivate grapes and olives, and make jams. The 11 guest rooms are in a charming old building with communal lounge and terrace. A delicious four-course dinner uses home-grown and local products and is included in the price. No credit cards.

🍴 Eating

Il Bacchino   DELI €

(Via Moncini 8; ☺9am-10pm summer, 10am-1pm & 4-7.30pm Tue-Sat winter) Owner Magdy Lamei may not be a local (he's from Cairo), but it would be hard to find anyone else as knowledgeable and passionate about local artisanal produce. Come here to taste local wines, or to stock up on picnic provisions including jams, cheese and cured meats.

★ La Tana del Brillo Parlante   TUSCAN €€

(☑0566 90 12 74; www.latanadeibrilli.it; Vicolo del Ciambellano 4; meals €32; ☺noon-2.30pm & 7-10pm Thu-Tue Dec-Oct) In this enchanting space rustic trinkets are lit by fairy lights. It's billed as the 'smallest *osteria* in Italy' and seats a mere 10 people (another six can squeeze onto tiny alley tables outside). The food ticks every box on the Slow Food check list, featuring deliciously authentic Maremmese dishes. In summer and at weekends, book well in advance. No credit cards.

ℹ Information

Tourist Office (☑0566 90 27 56; www.altamaremmaturismo.it; Via Todini 3; ☺9.30am-1pm & 2-6.30pm Tue-Sun) Down a side street beneath the Museo Archeologico.

ℹ Getting There & Away

BUS

The bus station is on Piazza del Risorgimento, 800m down the hill from Piazza Garibaldi. Monday to Saturday, there are four buses to/

from Grosseto (€4, 1¼ hours) and one to Siena (€5.50, two hours). To get to Volterra change in Monterotondo Marittimo. **Massa Veternensis** (Piazza Garibaldi 18) sells both bus and train tickets.

There's a convenient car park (€1 per hour during the day, free at night) close to Piazza Garibaldi; head up the hill and you'll find it on your left. Or continue further downhill to the free car park on Piazzetta di Borgo.

The nearest train station is in Follonica, 22km southwest of Massa, and is served by a regular shuttle bus (€2.60, 25 minutes, 10 daily).

Città del Tufa

The picturesque towns of Pitigliano, Sovana and Sorano form a triangle enclosing a dramatic landscape where, since Etruscan times, local buildings have been constructed from the volcanic porous rock called tufa. This inland area is called the Città del Tufa (City of the Tufa) or, less commonly, the Paese del Tufa (Land of the Tufa).

Hot and dusty post-exploration, replicate the Romans with a refreshing dip in thermal, mineral-rich, open-air waters in the village of Terme di Saturnia, 35km from Sorano and 26km from Pitigliano. To track down the springs, look for the telltale sign of cars parked roadside just south of the village turn-off (or spy the Cascate del Gorello signs), then wander down the dirt path to a magnificent cluster of open-air pools with waters a constant 37.5°C. Alternatively, you can indulge in the upmarket option at luxury spa **Terme di Saturnia** (☑ 0564 60 01 11; www.termedisaturnia.it; day admission €25, after 2pm €20; ☉ 9.30am-7pm summer, to 5pm winter), 3km downhill from the village of the same name.

Pitigliano
POP 3878

Check your car mirrors before screeching to a halt and indulging in an orgy of photography on the approach to this spectacularly sited hilltop stronghold, surrounded by gorges on three sides to create a natural bastion completed to the east by a constructed fortress. Within the Old Town, twisting stairways disappear around corners, cobbled alleys bend tantalisingly out of sight beneath graceful arches and quaint stone

houses are crammed next to each other in a higgledy-piggledy fashion.

Originally built by the Etruscans, who left a rich legacy of tombs and *vie cave* (sunken roads) that remain to this day, Pitigliano came under Roman rule before becoming a fiefdom of the wealthy Aldobrandeschi and Orsini families; the Orsins, who were from Rome, enlarged the fortress, reinforced the defensive walls and built an imposing aqueduct. Their rule came to an end in 1608 when the town was absorbed into the grand duchy of Tuscany under Cosimo I de' Medici.

◉ Sights & Activities

There's a fine walk from Pitigliano to Sovana (8km) that incorporates parts of the *vie cave* hewn out of tufa in the valleys below Pitigliano. The enormous passages – up to 20m deep and 3m wide – are popularly believed to be sacred routes linking Etruscan necropolises and other religious sites. For a description and map, go to www.trekking.it and download the pdf in the Maremma section.

La Piccola Gerusalemme MUSEUM
(Little Jerusalem; ☑ 0564 61 42 30; www.lapiccola gerusalemme.it; Vicolo Manin 30; adult/reduced €4/3; ☉ 10am-1pm & 2.30-6pm summer, 10am-noon & 3-5pm winter) Head down Via Zuccarelli and turn left at a sign indicating 'La Piccola Gerusalemme' to visit this fascinating time-capsule of Pitogliano's rich but sadly near-extinct Jewish culture. It incorporates a tiny, richly adorned synagogue (established in 1598 and one of only five in Tuscany), ritual bath, kosher butcher, bakery, wine cellar and dyeing workshops.

Museo Civico Archeologico di Pitigliano MUSEUM
(☑ 0564 61 40 67; Piazza della Fortezza; adult/reduced €3/2; ☉ 10am-5pm Mon, Thu & Fri, to 6pm Sat & Sun Jun-Aug, 10am-5pm Sat & Sun Easter-May) Head up the stone stairs to this small but well-run museum which has rich displays of finds from local Etruscan sites. Highlights include some huge intact *bucchero* (black earthenware pottery) urns dating from the 6th century BC and a collection of charming pinkish-cream clay oil containers in the form of small deer.

🍴 Sleeping & Eating

★ **Le Camere del Ceccottino** PENSION €€
(☑ 0564 61 42 73; www.ceccottino.com; Via Roma 159; r €80-150; ✳🕸) Owned and operated

A FINE WINE DETOUR

Terenzi (☑ 0564 59 96 01; www.terenzi.eu; Località Montedonico, Scansano) was awarded the prestigious 'Emerging Winery of the Year' accolade in Gambero Rosso's 2013 *Vini d'Italia* (Wines of Italy) guide. This wine estate is located on a scenic road just outside the town of Scansano, a 50-minute drive from Pitigliano on a secondary route to Grosseto.

It's best known for its Morellino di Scansano DOCG, a ruby-red Sangiovese with berry and violet overtones that can be tasted over a meal at the winery's **restaurant** (meals €35; ⊙ noon-3pm, closed Wed in winter) or purchased at its **cantina** (per 3 wines €10-20; ⊙ 9.30am-7.30pm summer, 10am-6pm Sat & Sun 9.30am-1pm & 2-5.30pm Mon-Fri winter). There's even a **locanda** (d €110-155, ste €140-175; P ❋ 🛜 ❄) for travellers wanting to soak up wonderful views and wine over a few days.

by the extremely helpful Chiara and Alessandro, who also run a nearby *osteria* and *enoteca* of the same name, this *pensione* boasts an excellent location near the *duomo* and four immaculately maintained and well-equipped rooms. Opt for the superior or prestige room if possible, as the standard versions are a little small. No breakfast.

La Rocca　TUSCAN, WINE BAR €
(Piazza della Repubblica 92; panino €4, meals €28; ⊙ 10am-3am Tue-Sat, to midnight Sun) Generous pourings of local wine, including Pitigliano's very own DOC white, are on offer at this cavernous wine bar, tucked away at the far end of Piazza della Repubblica, near the panoramic viewpoint. The range of *prodotti tipici* (typical local products) is impressive – choose from rustic pastas, antipasti platters and *panini* stuffed with cured meats and *pecorino* cheese.

★ Il Tufo Allegro　TUSCAN €€
(☑ 0564 61 61 92; www.iltufoallegro.com; Vicolo della Costituzione 5; meals €22-70; ⊙ noon-1.30pm Thu-Mon & 7.30-9.30pm Wed-Mon Mar-Dec) The aromas emanating from the kitchen door off Via Zuccarelli should be enough to draw you down the stairs and into the cosy dining rooms, which are carved out of tufa. Chef Domenico Pichini's menus range from traditional to modern, and all of his creations rely heavily on local produce for inspiration. It's near La Piccola Gerusalemme museum.

❶ Information

Tourist Office (☑ 0564 61 71 11; www.comune. pitigliano.gr.it; Piazza Garibaldi 12; ⊙ 10am-12.30pm & 3.30-6pm Tue-Sat summer, 10am-12.30pm & 3-5.30pm Fri & Sat, 10am-12.30pm Sun winter) In the piazza just inside the Old City's main gate.

❶ Getting There & Away

Tiemme (www.tiemmespa.it) buses leave from Via Santa Chiara, just off Piazza Petruccioli. Most buses run Monday to Saturday; buy tickets at Bar Guastini on Piazza Petruccioli. Services include Siena (€8.50, three hours, one daily) and Sovana (€1.50, 10 to 20 minutes, one daily).

Sovana

POP 100

Built by the Romans, this postcard-pretty village with a cobbled main street hides away two austerely beautiful Romanesque churches, a museum showcasing a collection of ancient gold coins, and Etruscan treasures.

◎ Sights

Parco Archeologico 'Città del Tufa'　ARCHAEOLOGICAL SITE
(Necropoli di Sovana; www.leviecave.it; admission €5; ⊙ 10am-7pm summer, to 5pm Sat & Sun Nov & Mar) At Tuscany's most significant Etruscan tombs, 1.5km east of town, signs in Italian and English guide you around four elaborate burial sites. The headline exhibit is the **Tomba Ildebranda**, named after Gregory VII, which still preserves traces of its carved columns and stairs. The **Tomba dei Demoni Alati** (Tomb of the Winged Demons) features a headless, recumbent terracotta figure.

🛏 Sleeping & Eating

★ Taverna Etrusca　HOTEL €
(☑ 0564 61 41 13; www.tavernaetrusca.com; Piazza del Pretorio 16; d €80-90, meals €20-60; 🛜) Sovana's rich heritage can certainly be felt in these stylish lodgings. Twisting wooden stairs lead to stately rooms made atmos-

pheric by artful lighting and stone walls. Downstairs, refined modern Tuscan cuisine is served in a shaded courtyard garden and brick-and-beam dining room. The 30-page *carta dei vini* features both Sovana and Morellino di Scansano DOC wines.

❶ Getting There & Away

Monday and Saturday, Tiemme buses travel to/from Pitigliano (€1.50, 10 to 20 minutes, one daily) and Sorano (€1.50, 15 minutes, one or two daily).

Sorano & Around

POP 3506

Sorano sits dramatically astride a rocky outcrop overlooking the Lente river and gorge. Below, *cantine* (cellars) are dug out of tufa, snug against a tantalising series of terraced gardens, many part-hidden from view.

◉ Sights & Activities

Fortezza Orsini   FORT
(☑ 0564 63 34 24; admission €4; ☉ 10am-1pm & 3-7pm Tue-Sun summer (open daily Aug), till 6pm Oct,10am-1pm & 2-5pm Sat & Sun Mar) Work on this massive fortress started in the 11th century. Today it still stands sentinel over the town, its sturdy walls linking two bastions surrounded by a dry moat. The highlight of any visit is undoubtedly a guided tour of the evocative subterranean passages (11am and 3.30pm), which are noticeably chilly even in the height of the Tuscan summer.

**Area Archeologica di
Vitozza**   ARCHAEOLOGICAL SITE
(☉ 10am-dusk) FREE More than 200 caves pepper a high rock ridge here, making it one of the largest troglodyte dwellings in Italy. The complex was first inhabited in prehistoric times. To explore the site, you'll need two hours and sturdy walking shoes. It's 3 miles due east of Sorano, near the hamlet of San Quírico; follow signs from the SR74.

CENTRAL COAST & ELBA

Livorno

POP 160,512

Tuscany's second-largest city is a quintessential port town. Though first impressions are unlikely to be kind, this is a 'real' city that really does grow on you.

Its seafood is the best on the Tyrrhenian coast, its historic quarter threaded with Venetian-style canals is shabby-chic, and pebbly beaches stretch south from the town's belle époque seafront. Be it a short stay between ferries or a day trip from Florence or Pisa, Livorno (Leghorn in English) is understated but worth the trip.

◉ Sights & Activities

★ Terrazza Mascagni   STREET
(Viale Italia; ☉ 24-hr) FREE No trip to Livorno is complete without a stroll along (and photo shoot of) this dazzling terrace with stone balustrades that sweeps gracefully along the seafront, in a dramatic chessboard flurry of black-and-white checks. When it was built in the 1920s it was called Terrazza Ciano after the leader of the Livorno fascist movement; it now bears the name of Livorno-born opera composer Pietro Mascagni (1863–1945).

★ Piccola Venezia   AREA
Piccola Venezia (Little Venice) is crossed with small canals built during the 17th century using Venetian methods of reclaiming land from the sea. At the heart sits the remains of the Medici-era **Fortezza Nuova** (New Fort; ☉ 24hr) FREE. Canals link it with the waterfront **Fortezza Vecchia** (Old Fort; ☉ 24hr) FREE, built 60 years before the Fortezza Nuova. The waterways are huge fun to explore; either from canal-side footpaths or by tour boat: panoramas emerge of faded, peeling apartments draped with brightly coloured washing, interspersed with waterside cafes.

🛏 Sleeping

Camping Miramare   CAMPGROUND €
(☑ 0586 58 04 02; www.campingmiramare.it; Via del Littorale 220; camping 2 people, car & tent €32-65; ▦ ▦) Be it a tent pitched beneath trees or a deluxe version with wooden terrace and sun-loungers on the stony beach, this campground – open year-round thanks to its village of mobile homes, maxi caravans and bungalows – has it all. Rates out of summer are at least 50% lower. Find the site 8km south of town in Antignano.

★ Hotel al Teatro   BOUTIQUE HOTEL €€
(☑ 0586 89 87 05; www.hotelalteatro.it; Via Mayer 42; s/d €85/110; ᴘ ❄ @ 🛜) With its marble staircase, antique furniture, tapestries and individually designed rooms, this irresistible eight-room address is one of Tuscany's

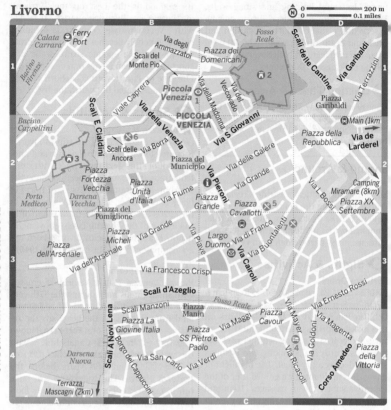

FLORENCE & TUSCANY LIVORNO

Livorno

Livorno

loveliest urban hotels. But the real stunner is the gravel garden out back where guests can lounge on green wicker furniture beneath a breathtakingly beautiful, 350-year-old magnolia tree.

Grand Hotel Palazzo   HISTORIC HOTEL €€
(☏0586 26 08 36; www.grandhotelpalazzo.com; Viale Italia 195, nr Terrazza Mascagni; d €150-190, ste €350-400; P❋@☎☎) This shimmering ship of a 19th-century seafront palace, with 123 perfectly thought-out rooms and glistening sea views, is belle époque Livorno relived. Dip into the rooftop infinity pool then indulge in a sunset *aperitivo* and panoramic sea view. Dining in its rooftop garden restaurant, face to face with the sea and the islet of Gorgona, is equally glam.

Eating

Sampling traditional *cacciucco*, a remarkable mixed seafood stew, is reason enough to visit Livorno.

★**La Barrocciaia**　　　OSTERIA €
(☎0586 88 26 37; www.labarrocciaia.it; Piazza Cavallotti 13; meals €20; ☺11am-3pm & 6-11pm Tue-Sat) Locals speak of La Barrocciaia with reverence – partly because of a homely interior that's alive with banter, but also because of the simple but superb food. The menu fluctuates, with stews often majoring on wild boar, octopus or squid; the pasta might come smothered in crab, while the chocolate and pear tart is one heck of a dessert.

Mercato Centrale　　　MARKET €
(Via Buontalenti; ☺6am-2pm Mon-Sat) For foodie nirvana, get lost in Livorno's magnificent late-19th-century Mercato Centrale, a 95m-long neoclassical food market that miraculously survived Allied WWII bombing. Arresting both gastronomically and architecturally, the market is a gargantuan maze of food stalls bursting with local produce, including the most astonishing fish and seafood.

Surfer Joe's Diner　　　AMERICAN €
(☎0586 80 92 11; www.surferjoe.it/diner; Terrazza Mascagni; meals €15-30; ☺11am-midnight Sun-Thu, to 1am Fri & Sat, shorter hours winter) What a burst of dynamism this zesty surf bar on the seafront adds to Livorno's drinking and dining scene. American burgers, onion rings, pancakes and smoothies form its culinary core; 1950s diner is its 'look'; and surf music is its idol. A huge terrace licked by the sea breeze and shaded with bamboo huts is the icing on the cake.

L'Ancora　　　SEAFOOD €€
(☎0586 8 14 01; www.ristoranteancoralivorno. com; Scali delle Ancora 10; meals €35; ☺noon-2.30pm & 7-10.30pm summer, Wed-Mon winter) L'Ancora's canalside terrace is the white-hot ticket in good weather, though settling for a table in the 17th-century, barrel-ceilinged, brick boat house is hardly a hardship. You can get *cacciucco* here, but the *carbonara di mare* (seafood and pasta in white sauce) is the family's pride and joy.

ℹ Information

Tourist office (☎0586 89 42 36; www.costa deglietruschi.it; Via Pieroni 16; ☺8.30am-5pm summer, 9.30am-3.30pm winter) Hands out free maps and books boat tours.

ℹ Getting There & Away

BOAT
Regular ferries for Sardinia and Corsica depart from the **Stazione Marittima** at Calata Carrara; ferries to Capraia use the smaller Porto Mediceo near Piazza dell'Arsenale. Boats to Spain and Sicily, plus some Sardinia services, use Porto Nuovo, 3km north.

Corsica Ferries (☎825 095095 per min €0.15; www.corsica-ferries.it) Two to seven services per week to Bastia, Corsica (from €30, four hours) and Golfo Aranci, Sardinia (from €50, six to ten hours).

Grimaldi Lines (www.grimaldi-ferries.com) Weekly sailings to/from Barcelona (from €35, 21 hours) and Tangiers, Morocco (from €80, 58 hours).

Moby (www.moby.it) Year-round, runs at least two services a day to Olbia, Sardinia (from €48, seven to 10 hours). Plus in the summer, several crossings a week to Bastia, Corsica (from €30, four hours).

Toremar (www.toremar.it) Several crossings per week, year round to Capraia (€17, 2¾ hours).

CAR
The A12 runs past the city and the SS1 connects Livorno with Rome. Find car parks near the waterfront.

TRAIN
From the **main train station** on Piazza Dante walk westwards (straight ahead) along Viale Carducci, Via de Larderel, then Via Grande into central Piazza Grande, Livorno's main square.
Florence (€10, 1½ hours, hourly)
Pisa (€3, 15 minutes, two to four per hour)
Rome (from €19, three to four hours, 12 daily)

ℹ Getting Around

CTT Nord (www.livorno.cttnord.it) has a service (bus 1) from the main train station to Porto Mediceo (€1.20, on board €1.70) via Piazza Grande. If you're catching a ferry to Sardinia or Corsica, take bus 1 to Piazza Grande then bus 5 from Via Cogorano, just off Piazza Grande.

RICHARD I'ANSON/GETTY IMAGES ©

RUSSELL MOUNTFORD/GETTY IMAGES ©

Duomo (p483), Florence
city's most iconic landmark took almost 150
years to complete.

Lucca (p565)
most every turn there is a pavement terrace
the alfresco.

Tuscan landscapes
many rolls out gently undulating hills and
sun-kissed vineyards surrounding medieval and
Renaissance villages.

Sweet treats
many is a paradise for foodies, especially those
with a sweet tooth.

RICHARD I'ANSON/GETTY IMAGES ©

Isola d'Elba

Napoleon would think twice about fleeing Isola d'Elba (the island of Elba) today. Dramatically more congested now than when the emperor was charitably dumped here in 1814 (poor thing), the island is an ever-glorious haven of beach-laced coves, vineyards, azure waters, hairpin-bend motoring and mind-bending views crowned by the peak of Monte Capanne. Given the rugged terrain, hiking, biking and sea kayaking are big.

With the exception of high season (actually only August), when the island's beaches and roads are jam-packed, Elba is a Robinson Crusoe–style paradise. In springtime, early summer and autumn, when grapes and olives are harvested, there are plenty of tranquil nooks on this stunningly picturesque, 28km-long, 19km-wide island protected by the **Parco Nazionale Arcipelago Toscano**, Europe's largest protected marine area.

❶ Getting There & Around

Elba is a one-hour ferry crossing from Piombino on the mainland to Portoferraio (at least hourly, passenger/car and driver €14/55). Unless it's August or a summer weekend, there's no need to book tickets in advance.

Car is the easiest way to get around Elba; **Twn Rent** (☑ 0565 91 46 66; www.twn-rent.it; Viale Elba 32) in Portoferraio rents cars and scooters. The island's southwest coast offers the most dramatic and scenic motoring.

Portoferraio

POP 12,027

Known to the Romans as Fabricia and later Ferraia (since it was a port for iron exports), this small harbour was acquired by Cosimo I de' Medici in the mid-16th century, when the fortifications took shape.

Portoferraio can be a hectic place in high season, but wandering the streets and steps of the historic centre, indulging in the exceptional eating options and bargaining for sardines with fisherfolk at the old port more than make up for the squeeze.

◉ Sights & Activities

Old Town AREA

The Old Town's spiderweb of narrow streets and alleys staggers uphill from the old harbour to Portoferraio's defining twinset of forts, **Forte Falcone** and the salmon-pink

Forte Stella (Via della Stella; adult/reduced €2/1.50; ⊙ 9am-7pm Easter-Sep), revealing deserted 16th-century ramparts to wander and seagulls freewheeling overhead.

From central square Piazza Cavour head uphill along Via Garibaldi to the foot of the monumental **Scalinata Medici**, a fabulous mirage of 140 wonky stone steps cascading up through every sunlit shade of amber to the dimly lit, 17th-century **Chiesa della Misericordia** (Via della Misericordia; ⊙ 8am-5pm). Inside is Napoleon's death mask. Continue to the top of the staircase to reach the forts and **Villa dei Mulini**, where Napoleon lived when in Elba.

Museo Nazionale della Residenza Napoleoniche MUSEUM

(Villa dei Mulini; Piazzale Napoleone; adult/reduced €5/3; ⊙ 9am-7pm Mon & Wed-Sat, to 1pm Sun) **Villa dei Mulini** was home to Napoleon during his stint in exile on this small isle. With its Empire-style furnishings, splendid library, fig-tree-studded Italianate gardens and unbeatable sea view, the emperor didn't want for creature comforts – contrast this with the simplicity of the camp bed and travelling trunk he used when on campaigns.

🛏 Sleeping

Half-board is usually the only option in August and many hotels close between November and Easter. The best places to stay are a short drive from the town centre.

Rosselba Le Palme CAMPGROUND €

(☑ 0565 93 31 01; www.rosselbalepalme.it; Ottone; adult €14-23, tent €6-55, car €1-6; ⊙ mid-Apr–Sep; P 🐾 🕏 🖶) Set around a botanical garden backed by Mediterranean forest, few campsites are as leafy or large. The beach is a 400m walk between trees while accommodation ranges from simple pitches and cute wooden chalets to 'glamping' tents with bathtubs and villa apartments. Find the ground 9km east of Portoferraio near Ottone.

Villa Ombrosa HOTEL €

(☑ 0565 91 43 63; www.villaombrosa.it; Via Alcide de Gasperi 3, Portoferraio; d from €95, half-board per person €60-126; P 🕏 🖶) One of the few hotels in town and open year-round, three-star Ombrosa looks out to sea and the pinprick islet of Lo Scoglietto. Decor is a jumble of styles, but summer rates include a lounger and umbrella on Ghiaie Beach across the street. Rooms with sea views tout pocket-

TOP ELBA BEACH SPOTS

It pays to know your *spiagge* (beaches), given that the ones along Elba's 147km of coastline embrace every shade of sand, pebble and rock. The quietest, most select beaches are tucked in rocky coves and involve a steep clamber down from the street. Parking is invariably roadside and scant.

Enfola

Just 6km west of Portoferraio, it's not so much the grey pebbles as the outdoor action that lures the crowds here. There are pedalos to rent, a diving school and a family-friendly 2.5km-long circular hiking trail around the green cape. The **Parco Nazionale dell'Arcipelago Toscano visitor centre** (Tuscan Archipelago National Park; ☑ 0565 91 94 11; www.islepark.it; Enfola; ⊘ 10.30am-1.30pm & 2.30-4.30pm summer only) is also here.

Sansone & Sorgenta

This twinset of cliff-ensnared white-shingle and pebble beaches stands out for its turquoise, crystal-clear waters just made for snorkelling. By car from Portoferraio, follow the SP27 to Enfola. Parking can be challenging.

Morcone, Pareti & Innamorata

Find this trio of charming sandy-pebble coves framed by sweet-smelling pine and eucalyptus trees some 3km south of Capoliveri, on the southeastern part of the island. Rent a kayak and paddle out to sea from Innamorata, the wildest of the three; or fine dine and stay overnight on Pareti beach at **Hotel Stella Maris** (☑ 0565 96 84 25; www.albergostellamaris.it; Pareti; half-board per person d €70-125; ℗ ✲), one of the few island hotels to sit on the sand.

Colle d'Orano & Fetovaia

The standout highlight of these two gorgeous swaths of golden sand on Elba's western coast is the dramatic drive – not to be missed – along the SP25 that links the two. Legend has it that Napoleon frequented Colle d'Orano to sit and swoon over his native Corsica visible across the water. Heavenly scented maquis (herbal scrubland) covers the promontory protecting sandy Fetovaia, where nudists flop on nearby granite rocks known as Le Piscine.

sized balconies and the breakfast pastries are light as air.

Hotel e Ristorante Mare HOTEL €€
(☑ 0565 93 30 69; www.hotelmare.org; Magazzini; d €125-180, half-board per person €55-110; ⊘ summer; ✲ @ 🛜 🛥 🛝) The setting is secluded and gorgeous: on the edge of a tiny, crab-claw harbour that's 9km east of Portoferraio by car. A crisp blue-and-white striped colour scheme lends things a nautical air, while the rooftop terrace, pool and waterfront restaurant are reminiscent of being on an ocean liner, something enhanced by spectacular views across a grand, sweeping bay.

 Eating

★ **Il Castagnacciao** PIZZA €
(Via del Mercato Vecchio 13; pizza €4.50-7; ⊘ 10am-2.30pm & 5-10.30pm Thu-Tue, to midnight summer) They work the pizza chef so hard here the dining room sometimes has a smoky tinge.

To go local, start with a lip-smacking plate of *torta di ceci* (chickpea 'pizza'), then watch your rectangular, thin-crust supper go in and out of the wood-fired oven. But save space for dessert – *castagnaccio* (chestnut 'cake') baked over the same flames.

Caffescondido TRATTORIA €€
(Via del Carmine 65; meals €25; ⊘ noon-2pm & 7-9.30pm Mon-Sat) This Slow Food–endorsed trattoria, footsteps from pretty Piazza Gramsci, makes for the perfect getaway from the waterfront crowds. Options are simple – just a handful of *primi* (first courses) and *secondi* (second courses) are chalked on the blackboard, which usually stars a local classic such as *baccalà alla marinese* (saltcod with potatoes) or *polpo brisco* (octopus). No credit cards.

Bitta 20 SEAFOOD €€€
(☑ 0565 93 02 70; Calata Mazzini 20; meals €45; ⊘ noon-2.30pm & 7-11pm) Portoferraio's best

DON'T MISS

GOURMET ESCAPES

Estates producing Isola d'Elba's ubiquitous fine wine and olive oil provide idyllic sleeping spots.

Tenuta La Chiusa (☑ 0565 93 30 46; www.tenutalachiusa.it; Magazzini 93; 2 people per week €450-850, up to 5 people per wk €750-1300; P ⊞) Some 8km east of Portoferraio, Tenuta La Chiusa is Elba's oldest wine-making estate, and is also where Napoleon stayed the night upon landing on Elba in 1814. Right on the seashore, it is stunning – offering a 17th-century farmhouse, an 18th-century villa, 8 hectares of vineyards, olive groves, palm trees and 10 apartments, some on the beach in former peasants' cottages.

Self-catering accommodation (minimum stay one week) has a simple charm; guests can buy olive oil and wine at reception; and, should you not fancy cooking, an excellent eatery is a two-minute shore-side stroll away at tiny Magazzini harbour. The estate also organises wine-tasting in its cellar.

Agriturismo Due Palme (☑ 0565 93 30 17, 338 7433736; www.agriturismoelba.it; Via Schiopparello 28, Schiopparello; d €50-70, 4-person house per week €720-900) Utterly tranquil, despite being just a few minutes from the Portoferraio–Magazzini road, this idyllic agriturismo's five traditionally styled former workers' cottages are dotted amid orange and lemon trees and 100-year old olive groves. The estate was founded by the welcoming Fabrizio's grandfather, and is the only olive plantation on Elba to produce quality-stamped IGP olive oil.

Guests can taste and buy the silky fresh-green oil (€19 per litre) and are invariably tempted to sample some oranges. Tree-shaded deck chairs, a BBQ and an astonishingly flowery garden heighten the charm.

chef has relocated to this bright, white harbour-side eatery, where a long strip of tables overlooks a string of bobbing yachts. White tablecloths and smart service combine with sublime fish and seafood cooked with a fabulous dose of creativity. Which all makes it very popular – book.

ⓘ Information

Tourist office (☑ 0565 91 46 71; www.isoleditoscana.it; Calata Italia 44; ☺ 9am-7pm Mon-Sat, 10am-1pm & 3-6pm Sun summer, 9am-5pm Mon-Thu, 9am-1pm Fri winter) Helpful staff have abundant information on walking and biking on the island. Find the office on the seafront, near the ferry docks.

Marciana & Marciana Marina

POP 2246

Unlike many modern cookie-cutter marinas, the attractive seaside resort of Marciana Marina, 18km west of Portoferraio, has character and history to complement its pretty pebble beaches. From the port a 9km mountain road corkscrews inland to Marciana, the island's oldest and highest village (375m) from where a half-day walking trail leads to the island's most important pilgrimage site. End back in the hilltop village with a quintessential Slow Food lunch to remember

at **Osteria del Noce** (☑ 0565 90 12 84; www.osteriadelnoce.it; Via della Madonna 14; meals €25; ☺ noon-2pm & 7-9.30pm late-Mar–Sep).

◉ Sights & Activities

Santuario della Madonna del Monte   CHAPEL
(☺ dawn-dusk) Park at the entrance to Marciana and head 40 minutes out of the village on foot along Via delle Fonti and its continuations, Via delle Coste and Via dei Monti, to this much-altered 11th-century church. Inside is a stone upon which a divine hand is said to have painted an image of the Virgin, believed to have miraculous powers.

It is an invigorating uphill hike along an old mule track bordered by scented parasol pines, chestnut trees, wild sage and thyme. The coastal panorama that unfolds as you get higher is remarkable. Once you reach the hilltop chapel (627m), drink like Napoleon did from the old stone fountain across from the church – look for the plaque commemorating his visit here on horseback in 1814. Next, continue five minutes along the footpath to play 'I Spy Corsica'.

★ **Cabinovia Monte Capanne**   FUNICULAR
(Cableway; ☑ 0565 90 10 20; www.cabinovia-isoladelba.it; single/return €12/18; ☺ 10am-1pm & 2.20-6pm Apr-Sep, to 5pm Oct) If you only have time

for one road trip from Portoferraio, make it this. Some 750m south of Marciana on the Poggio road, this cable car sees you climbing into an open, barred basket – imagine riding in a canary-yellow parrot cage – to be whisked up to the summit of Elba's highest point, Monte Capanne (1018m).

After 20 minutes, scramble around the rocky peak to savour an astonishing 360-degree panorama of Elba, the Tuscan Archipelago, the Etruscan Coast and Corsica 50km away. The scent of *la macchia* (Mediterranean scrub) is heavenly. Hikers can buy a one-way ticket and walk back down – a 1½-hour hike along a rocky but well-marked path.

NORTHWESTERN TUSCANY

There is more to this green corner of Tuscany than Italy's iconic Leaning Tower. Linger over lunches of rustic regional specialities, and meander through medieval hilltop villages and along ancient pilgrim routes. Even the largest towns – university hub Pisa and 'love at first sight' Lucca – have an air of tranquillity and tradition that positively begs the traveller to stay for a few days of cultural R&R. This is snail-paced Italy, impossible not to love.

Pisa

POP 88,627

Once a maritime power to rival Genoa and Venice, Pisa now draws its fame from an architectural project gone terribly wrong. But the world-famous Leaning Tower is just one of many noteworthy sights in this compact and compelling city. Education has fuelled the local economy since the 1400s, and students from across Italy still compete for places in its elite university and research schools. This endows the centre of town with a vibrant and affordable cafe and bar scene, and balances an enviable portfolio of well-maintained Romanesque buildings, Gothic churches and Renaissance piazzas with a lively street life dominated by locals rather than tourists.

History

Possibly of Greek origin, Pisa became an important naval base under Rome and remained a significant port for many centuries. The city's so-called golden days began late in the 9th century when it became an independent maritime republic and a rival of Genoa and Venice. The good times rolled on into the 12th and 13th centuries, by which time Pisa controlled Corsica, Sardinia and most of the mainland coast as far south as Civitavecchia. Most of the city's finest buildings date from this period, when the distinctive Pisan-Romanesque architectural style flourished.

Pisa's support for the Ghibellines during the tussles between the Holy Roman Emperor and the pope brought the city into conflict with its mostly Guelph Tuscan neighbours, including Siena, Lucca and Florence. The real blow came when Genoa's fleet defeated Pisa in devastating fashion at the Battle of Meloria in 1284. After the city fell to Florence in 1406, the Medici encouraged great artistic, literary and scientific endeavours and re-established Pisa's university. Galileo Galilei, the city's most famous son, later taught here.

◉ Sights

Many visitors to Pisa arrive by train at Stazione San Rossore and don't get any further than neighbouring Piazza dei Miracoli. Those in the know arrive or depart using Pisa's Stazione Centrale allowing casual discovery of the *centro storico* (historic centre).

ⓘ TOWER & COMBO TICKETS

Buy tickets for the Leaning Tower from one of two well-signposted ticket offices: the main **ticket office** (www.opapisa.it; Piazza dei Miracoli; ⊘ 8am-8pm summer, 10am-5pm winter) behind the tower or the smaller office inside **Museo delle Sinópie** (p560).

To guarantee your visit to the tower and to save the long queue in high season, buy tickets in advance online – they can be purchased up to 20 days in advance but no later than one day before visiting.

Ticket offices in Pisa also sell combination tickets covering admission to the Baptistry, Camposanto and Museo delle Sinópie: a ticket covering one/two/three sights costs €5/7/8 (reduced €3/4/5). Admission to the cathedral is free, but you need to show a ticket – either for one of the other sights or a cathedral coupon distributed at ticket offices.

Pisa

⊙ Piazza dei Miracoli

No Tuscan sight is more immortalised in kitsch souvenirs than the iconic tower teetering on the edge of this gargantuan piazza, which is called both the **Campo dei Miracoli** (Field of Miracles) and **Piazza del Duomo** (Cathedral Sq). The piazza's expansive green lawns provide an urban carpet on which Europe's most extraordinary concentration of Romanesque buildings – in the form of the cathedral, baptistry and tower – are arranged. With two million visitors every year, crowds are the norm, many arriving by tour bus from Florence for a whirlwind visit.

★ Leaning Tower   TOWER
(Torre Pendente; www.opapisa.it; Piazza dei Miracoli; admission €18; ⊙ 9am-8pm summer, 10am-5pm winter) One of Italy's signature sights, the Torre Pendente truly lives up to its name, leaning a startling 3.9 degrees off the vertical. The 56m-high tower, officially the Duomo's *campanile* (bell tower), took almost 200 years to build, but was already listing when it was unveiled in 1372. Over time, the tilt, caused by a layer of weak subsoil, stead-

FLORENCE & TUSCANY PISA

ily worsened until it was finally halted by a major stabilisation project in the 1990s.

Building began in 1173 under the supervision of architect Bonanno Pisano, but his plans came a cropper almost immediately. Only three of the tower's seven tiers had been built when he was forced to abandon construction after it started leaning. Work resumed in 1272, with artisans and masons attempting to bolster the foundations but failing miserably. They kept going, though, compensating for the lean by gradually building straight up from the lower storeys. But once again work had to be suspended – this time due to war – and construction wasn't completed until the second half of the 14th century.

Over the next 600 years, the tower continued to tilt at an estimated 1mm per year. By 1993 it stood 4.47m out of plumb, more than 5 degrees from the vertical. To counter this, steel braces were slung around the third storey and joined to steel cables attached to neighbouring buildings. This held the tower in place as engineers began gingerly removing soil from below the northern foundations. After some 70 tonnes of earth had been extracted from the northern side, the tower sank to its 18th-century level and, in the process, rectified the lean by 43.8cm. Experts believe that this will guarantee the tower's future for the next three centuries.

Access to the Leaning Tower is limited to 40 people at a time – children under eight are not allowed in/up and those aged eight to 10 years must hold an adult's hand. To avoid disappointment, book in advance online or go straight to a ticket office when you arrive in Pisa to book a slot for later in the day. Visits last 30 minutes and involve a steep climb up 300-odd occasionally slippery steps. All bags, handbags included, must be deposited at the free left-luggage desk next to the central ticket office – cameras are about the only thing you can take up.

★ **Duomo** CATHEDRAL
(www.opapisa.it; Piazza dei Miracoli; ⊙10am-8pm summer, 10am-12.45pm & 2-5pm winter) FREE
Pisa's magnificent Romanesque Duomo was begun in 1064 and consecrated in 1118. Its striking tiered exterior, with cladding of green-and-cream marble bands, gives on to a vast columned interior capped by a gold wooden ceiling. The elliptical dome, the first of its kind in Europe at the time, was added in 1380.

Note that while admission is free, you'll need an entrance coupon from the ticket office or a ticket from one of the other Piazza dei Miracoli sights.

The cathedral, which served as a blueprint for subsequent Romanesque churches in Tuscany, was paid for with spoils from a 1063 naval battle that the Pisans fought against an Arab fleet off Palermo. To mark the victory, and symbolise Pisa's domination of the Mediterranean, the cathedral was Europe's largest when it was completed.

The main facade – not finished until the 13th century – has four exquisite tiers of columns diminishing skywards, while the echoing interior, 96m long and 28m high, is propped up by 68 hefty granite columns in classical style. The wooden ceiling, decorated with 24-carat gold, is a legacy from the period of Medici rule.

Before setting foot in the cathedral, study the three pairs of 16th-century bronze doors at the main entrance. Designed by the school of Giambologna to replace the wooden originals destroyed (along with most of the cathedral interior) by fire in 1596, the doors are quite spellbinding – hours can be spent deciphering the biblical scenes illustrating the immaculate conception of the Virgin and birth of Christ (central doors), the road to Calvary and crucifixion of Christ, and the Ministry of Christ. Kids can play spot the rhino.

Inside, don't miss the extraordinary early-14th-century octagonal pulpit in the north aisle. Sculpted from Carrara marble by Giovanni Pisano and featuring nude and heroic figures, its depth of detail and heightening of feeling brought a new pictorial expressionism and life to Gothic sculpture. Pisano's work forms a striking contrast to the controversial 2001 pulpit and altar by Italian sculptor Giuliano Vangi.

★ **Battistero** RELIGIOUS SITE
(Baptistry; www.opapisa.it; Piazza dei Miracoli; adult/reduced €5/3, combination ticket with Camposanto & Museo delle Sinópie 2/3 sights €7/8 (reduced €4/5); ⊙8am-8pm summer, 10am-5pm Nov-Feb) Pisa's unusual round baptistry has one dome piled on top of another, each roofed half in lead, half in tiles, and topped by a gilt bronze John the Baptist (1395). Construction began in 1152, but it was remodelled and continued by Nicola and Giovanni Pisano more than a century later and finally completed in the 14th century. Inside, the hexagonal marble pulpit (1260) by Nicola Pisano is the highlight.

The lower level of arcades is Pisan-Romanesque; the pinnacled upper section and dome are Gothic.

Pisan scientist Galileo Galilei (who, so the story goes, came up with the laws of the pendulum by watching a lamp in Pisa's cathedral swing), was baptised in the octagonal font (1246). Don't leave without climbing to the **Upper Gallery** to listen to the custodian demonstrate the double dome's remarkable acoustics and echo effects, every half-hour on the hour/half-hour.

Camposanto CEMETERY
(www.opapisa.it; Piazza dei Miracoli; adult/reduced €5/3, combination ticket with Battistero & Museo delle Sinópie 2/3 sights €7/8 (reduced €4/5); ⊙8am-8pm summer, 10am-5pm winter) Soil shipped from Calvary during the Crusades is said to lie within the white walls of this hauntingly beautiful, final resting place for many prominent Pisans, arranged around a garden in a cloistered quadrangle. During WWII, Allied artillery destroyed many of the cloisters' frescoes, but a couple were salvaged and are now displayed in the **Sala Affreschi** (Frescoes Room). Most notable is the Triumph of Death (1336–41), a remarkable illustration of Hell attributed to 14th-century painter Buonamico Buffalmacco.

Museo delle Sinópie MUSEUM
(www.opapisa.it; Piazza dei Miracoli; adult/reduced €5/3, combination ticket with Battistero or Camposanto €7/5, Battistero & Camposanto €8/5; ⊙8am-7.30pm summer, 10am-4.30pm winter) Home to some fascinating frescoes, this museum safeguards several *sinópie* (preliminary sketches), drawn by the artists in red-earth pigment on the walls of the

ℹ️ HOW TO FALL IN LOVE WITH PISA

Sure, the iconic Leaning Tower is the reason everyone wants to go to Pisa. But once you've put yourself through the Piazza dei Miracoli madness (littered lawns, football-playing school groups, photo-posing pandemonium…), there's a good chance you'll simply want to get out of town.

To avoid leaving Pisa feeling oddly deflated by one of Europe's great landmarks, save the Leaning Tower and its oversized square for the latter part of the day – or, better still, an enchanting visit after dark (mid-June to August) when the night casts a certain magic on the glistening white monuments and the tour buses have long gone.

Upon arrival, indulge instead in peaceful meanderings along the Arno river, over its bridges and through Pisa's medieval heart. Discover the last monumental wall painting **Keith Haring** (www.keithcafe.com; Via Zandonai 4; ⏰7am-11pm; 🐾) did before he died; enjoy low-key architectural and artistic genius at the riverside **Palazzo Blu** (p561) and Pisan-Gothic **Chiesa di Santa Maria della Spina** on Lungarno Gambacorti (built between 1230 and 1223 to house a reliquary of a thorn from Christ's crown); and lunch with locals at **Sottobosco** (p563) or **Osteria Bernardo** (p562).

And only once you've fallen in love with the other Pisa, head for the tower.

Camposanto in the 14th and 15th centuries before the frescoes were overpainted. The museum is a compelling study in fresco painting, with short films and scale models filling in the gaps.

Museo dell'Opera del Duomo MUSEUM

(www.opapisa.it; Piazza dei Miracoli) Currently closed for extensive renovation, this museum is a repository for works of art once displayed in the cathedral and baptistry. Collection highlights include Giovanni Pisano's ivory carving of the *Madonna and Child* (1299), made for the cathedral's high altar, and his mid-13th-century *Madonna del colloquio,* originally from a gate of the *duomo.* Possibly even more memorable is the museum's tranquil cloister garden with stunning, crowd-free views of the Leaning Tower.

◉ Along the Arno

Away from the crowded heavyweights of Piazza dei Miracoli, along the Arno river banks, Pisa comes into its own. Splendid *palazzi*, painted a multitude of hues, line the southern *lungarno* (riverside embankment), from where shopping boulevard Corso Italia legs it to the central train station, Stazione Centrale.

Pisa's medieval heart lies north of the water: from riverside **Piazza Cairoli**, with its bars and gelaterie, meander along Via Cavour and lose yourself in ancient backstreets. A daily fresh-produce market fills **Piazza delle Vettovaglie**, ringed with 15th-century porticoes and cafe terraces.

Palazzo Blu GALLERY

(www.palazzoblu.it; Lungarno Gambacorti 9; ⏰10am-7pm Tue-Fri, to 8pm Sat & Sun) FREE Facing the river is this magnificently restored, 14th-century building that has a striking dusty-blue facade. Inside, its over-the-top 19th-century interior decoration is the perfect backdrop for the Foundation Pisa's art collection – predominantly Pisan works from the 14th to the 20th centuries, plus various temporary exhibitions.

Museo Nazionale di San Matteo MUSEUM

(Piazza San Matteo in Soarta; adult/reduced €5/2.50; ⏰8.30am-7.30pm Tue-Sat, to 1.30pm Sun) This inspiring repository of medieval masterpieces sits in a 13th-century Benedictine convent on the Arno's northern waterfront boulevard. The museum's collection of paintings from the Tuscan school (c 12th to 14th centuries) is notable, with works by Lippo Memmi, Taddeo Gaddi, Gentile da Fabriano and Ghirlandaio. Don't miss Masaccio's *St Paul,* Fra' Angelico's *Madonna of Humility* and Simone Martini's *Polyptych of Saint Catherine.*

✨ Festivals & Events

Luminaria di San Ranieri LIGHT SHOW

(⏰16 Jun) The night before Pisa's patron saint's day is magical: thousands upon thousands of candles and blazing torches light up the river and riverbanks while fireworks bedazzle the night sky.

Regata Storica di San Ranieri
SPORTS

(⊙17 Jun) The Arno comes to life with a rowing regatta to commemorate the city's patron saint.

Palio delle Quattro Antiche Repubbliche Marinare
CULTURAL

(Regatta of the Four Ancient Maritime Republics) The four historical maritime rivals – Pisa, Venice, Amalfi and Genoa – take turns to host this historic regatta in early June; in 2017 it sails into Pisa.

Gioco del Ponte
CULTURAL

(⊙Jun) During Gioco del Ponte (Game of the Bridge), two teams in medieval costume battle it out over the Ponte di Mezzo; last Sunday in June.

🛏 Sleeping

Hostel Pisa Tower
HOSTEL €

(☏050 520 24 54; www.hostelpisatower.it; Via Piave 4; dm €20-25; @🛜) This super-friendly hostel occupies a suburban villa a couple of minutes' walk from Piazza dei Miracoli. It's bright and cheery, with colourful decor, female and mixed dorms, communal kitchen, and a summer-friendly terrace overlooking a small grassy garden. Dorms are named, meaning you can sleep with Galileo, Mona Lisa, Leonardo or Michelangelo.

Royal Victoria Hotel
HOTEL €€

(☏050 94 01 11; www.royalvictoria.it; Lungarno Pacinotti 12; d €95-170, tr €105-180; ❄🛜🅿) This doyen of Pisan hotels, run by the Piegaja family since 1837, offers old-world luxury accompanied by warm, attentive service. Its 38 rooms exude a shabby-chic spirit with their Grand Tour antiques, although renovations are imminent. Don't miss an *aperitif* flopped on a sofa on the 4th-floor terrace, packed with potted plants. Garage parking/bike hire €20/15 per day, breakfast €5.

Hotel Bologna
HOTEL €€

(☏050 50 21 20; www.hotelbologna.pisa.it; Via Giuseppe Mazzini 57; d/tr €148/188; 🅿❄🛜🅿) Placed well away from the Piazza dei Miracoli mayhem, this elegant four-star mansion hotel is an oasis of peace and tranquillity. Its big, bright rooms have wooden floors and colour-coordinated furnishings – some are frescoed. Kudos for the small terrace and cypress-shaded garden out the back – delightful for lazy summertime breakfasts. Reception organises bike/scooter hire; courtyard parking for motorists €12 per night.

Hotel Relais dell'Orologio
HOTEL €€€

(☏050 83 03 61; www.hotelrelaisorologio.com; Via della Faggiola 12-14; d €150-240; ❄🛜) Something of a honeymoon venue, Pisa's dreamy five-star hotel occupies a tastefully restored 14th-century fortified tower housed in a quiet backstreet. Some rooms have original frescoes and the flowery patio restaurant is a welcome retreat from the crowds. Book online to bag the cheapest deal – non-refundable, early-booking rates are best value.

🍴 Eating

⭐L'Ostellino
SANDWICHES €

(Piazza Felice Cavallotti 1; panini €3-6; ⊙11.30am-4.30pm Mon-Fri, to 6pm Sat & Sun) For a buster-size gourmet *panino* (sandwich) wrapped in crunchy waxed paper, this miniscule deli and *panineria* (sandwich shop) with just a handful of tables delivers. Take your pick from dozens of different combos written by hand on the blackboard (*lardo di colonnata* with figs or cave-aged pecorino with honey and walnuts are sweet favourites), await construction, then hit the green lawns of Piazza dei Miracoli to picnic with the crowds.

Pizzeria Il Montino
PIZZA €

(☏050 59 86 95; www.pizzeriailmontino.com; Vicolo del Monte 1; pizzas €6-8, foccacine €2.50-4; ⊙10.30am-3pm & 5-10pm Mon-Sat) There is nothing flash or fancy about this down-to-earth pizzeria, an icon among Pisans, student or sophisticate alike. Take away or order at the bar then grab a table, inside or out, and munch on house specialities such as *cecina* (chickpea pizza), *castagnaccio* and *spuma* (sweet, nonalcoholic drink). Or go for a *focaccine* (small flat roll) filled with salami, pancetta or *porchetta* (suckling pig).

Hidden in a back alley, the quickest way to find Il Montino is to head west along Via Ulisse Dini from the northern end of Borgo Stretto (opposite the Lo Sfizio cafe at Borgo Stretto 54) to Piazza San Felice where it is easy to spot, on your left, a telling blue neon 'Pizzeria' sign.

Osteria Bernardo
TUSCAN €€

(☏050 57 52 16; www.osteriabernardo.it; Piazza San Paolo all'Orto 1; meals €35; ⊙8-11pm Tue-Sat, 12.30-2.30pm & 8-11pm Sun) This small bistro on one of Pisa's loveliest squares, well away from the madding Leaning Tower crowd, is the perfect fusion of easy dining and gourmet excellence. Its menu is small – just four or five dishes to choose from for each course – and cuisine is creative. The wild-boar *pappardelle* (wide flat pasta strips) scented with chocolate is a great change from the norm.

biOsteria 050 — VEGETARIAN €€

(☑ 050 54 31 06; www.biosteria050.it; Via San Francesco 36; meals €25-30; ⊗ 12.30-2.30pm & 7.30-10.30pm Tue-Sat, 7.30-10.30pm Mon & Sun; ☑) ⚡ Everything that Marco and Raffaele at Zero Cinquanta cook up is strictly seasonal, local and organic, with products from farms within a 50km radius of Pisa. Feast on dishes like risotto with almonds and asparagus or go for one of the excellent-value lunch specials.

Drinking

Most drinking action takes place on and around Piazza delle Vettovaglie and the university on cafe-ringed Piazza Dante Alighieri, always packed with students.

Sottobosco — CAFE

(www.sottoboscocafe.it; Piazza San Paolo all'Orto; ⊗ 10am-midnight Tue-Fri, noon-1am Sat, 7pm-midnight Sun) This creative cafe with books for sale and funky furnishings induces love at first sight. Tuck into a doughnut and cappuccino at a glass-topped table filled with artists' crayons perhaps, or a collection of buttons. Lunch dishes (salads, pies and pasta) are simple and homemade, and come dusk, jazz bands play or DJs spin tunes.

Bazeel — BAR

(www.bazeel.it; Lungarno Pacinotti 1; ⊗ 7.30am-2am) A dedicated all-rounder, Bazeel is a hot spot from dawn to dark. Laze over breakfast, save cents with a great-value buffet lunch (two/three courses €8/10) or hang out with the A crowd over a generous *aperitivo* spread, live music and DJs. Its chapel-like interior is nothing short of fabulous, as is its pavement terrace out front. Check its Twitter feed for what's on.

Salza — CAFE

(Borgo Stretto 44; ⊗ 8.15am-8pm Tue-Sun) This old-fashioned cake shop has been tempting Pisans into sugar-induced wickedness since 1898. It's an equally lovely spot for a cocktail – anytime.

ⓘ Information

Tourist Office (☑ 050 4 22 91; www.pisaunica terra.it; Piazza Vittorio Emanuele II 16; ⊗ 10am-1pm & 2-4pm)

ⓘ Getting There & Away

AIR

Pisa International Airport (Galileo Galilei Airport; ☑ 050 84 93 00; www.pisa-airport. com) Tuscany's main international airport, a 10-minute drive south of Pisa; flights to most major European cities.

BUS

Pisan company **CPT** (☑ 050 50 55 02; www.cpt. pisa.it; Piazza Sant'Antonio 1; ⊗ ticket office 7am-8.15am Mon-Fri, to 8pm Sat & Sun) runs buses to/from Volterra (€6.10, two hours, up to 10 daily) and Livorno (€2.75, 55 minutes, half-hourly to hourly).

CAR

Pisa is close to the A11 and A12. The SCG FI-PI-LI (SS67) is a toll-free alternative for Florence and Livorno, while the north–south SS1, the Via Aurelia, connects the city with La Spezia and Rome.

TRAIN

There is a handy **left luggage office** (Deposito Bagagli; 1st 12hr €4, subsequent 12hr €2; ⊗ 6am-9pm) at **Pisa Centrale** (Piazza della Stazione) train station – not to be confused with north-of-town Pisa San Rossore station. Regional train services to/from Pisa Centrale:

Florence (€8, 1¼ hours, frequent)

Livorno (€2.50, 15 minutes, frequent)

Lucca (€3.40, 30 minutes, every 30 minutes)

Viareggio (€3.40, 15 minutes, every 20 minutes)

ⓘ Getting Around

TO/FROM THE AIRPORT
Train

PisaMover shuttle buses link the airport with Pisa Centrale train station (€1.80, eight minutes, every 10 minutes). From December 2015 this shuttlebus service will be replaced by a super-speedy, fully automated rail link called PisaMover; check the Pisa airport website for details.

Bus

The LAM Rossa (red) bus line (€1.10, 10 minutes, every 10 to 20 minutes) passes through the city centre and the train station en route to/from the airport. Buy tickets from the blue ticket machine, next to the bus stops to the right of the train station exit.

Taxi

A taxi between the airport and city centre costs around €10. To book, call **Radio Taxi Pisa** (☑ 050 54 16 00; www.cotapi.it).

Lucca

FLORENCE & TUSCANY LUCCA

200 m
0.1 miles

Via dei Bacchettoni

Baluardo San Salvatore

Porta Elisa

Baluardo della Libertà

Orto Botanico

Via del Giardino Botanico

Baluardo San Regolo

Via San Michelletto

Via della Quarquonia

Via Paoli

Via Elisa

Piazza San Francesco

Via Santa Chiara

Via del Fosso

Via San Nicolao

Porta San Gervasio

Via del Fosso

Via Rosi

Via Santa Gemma Galgani

Via della Fratta

Piazza San Pietro

Via Dell'Angelo Custode

Piazza Santa Maria

Via Fillungo

Via della Quarquonia

Piazza Santa Maria

Piazza Anfiteatro

Via Canuleia

Via Guinigi

Torre Guinigi

Via Santa Croce

Via Della Rosa

Piazza Antelminelli

Passeggiata delle Mura

Via della Cavallerizza

Piazza Scarpellini

Piazza San Frediano

Via Mordini

Via Sant'Andrea

Piazza del Carmine

Piazza dei Servi

Piazza San Martino

Museo della Cattedrale

Cattedrale di San Martino

Via degli Angeli

Via Battisti

Via Buia

Via Fillungo

Via del Moro

Via Santa Lucia

Piazza San Michele

Via Cenami

Via del Battistero

Via Vallisneri

Piazza San Giovanni

Via del Molinetto

Piazza San Bernardini

Via San Giorgio

Via Tegrini

Via di Poggio

Corte Campana

Via Vittorio Emanuele II

Via Veneto

Piazza Napoleone

Piazza del Giglio

Orto Botanico

Passeggiata della Mura

Via Delle Conce

Via Santa Giustina

Via del Toro

Piazza Sant'Agostino

Via Galli Tassi

Via San Paolino

Via San Donato

Piazza San Romano

Baluardo Santa Croce

Porta San Donato

Piazzale San Donato

Piazzale Verdi

Piazzale Boccherini

Mura

Lucca

BICYCLE

Many hotels rent bikes. Otherwise, stands at the northern end of Via Santa Maria and other streets off Piazza dei Miracoli rent four-wheel rickshaws for up to three/six people (€10/15 per hour) and regular bicycles (€3 per hour).

CAR & MOTORCYCLE

Parking costs up to €2 per hour; don't park in the historic centre's Limited Traffic Zone (ZTL). There's a free car park outside the zone on Lungarno Guadalongo near the Fortezza di San Gallo on the south side of the Arno.

Lucca

POP 86,204

Lovely Lucca endears itself to everyone who visits. Hidden behind imposing Renaissance walls, its cobbled streets, handsome piazzas and shady promenades make it a perfect destination to explore by foot – as a day trip from Florence or in its own right. At the day's end, historic cafes and restaurants tempt visitors to relax over a glass or two of Lucchesi wine and a slow progression of rustic dishes prepared with fresh produce from nearby Garfagnana.

History

Founded by the Etruscans, Lucca became a Roman colony in 180 BC and a free *comune* (self-governing city) during the 12th century, when it enjoyed a period of prosperity based on the silk trade. In 1314 it briefly fell under the control of Pisa but under the leadership of local adventurer Castruccio Castracani degli Antelminelli, the city regained its freedom and remained an independent republic for almost 500 years.

Napoleon ended all this in 1805, when he created the principality of Lucca and placed his sister Elisa in control. Twelve years later the city became a Bourbon duchy, before being incorporated into the Kingdom of Italy. It miraculously escaped being bombed during WWII, so the fabric of the historic centre has remained unchanged for centuries.

⊙ Sights

Stone-paved Via Fillungo, with its fashion boutiques and car-free mantra, threads its way through the medieval heart of the old city. East is one of Tuscany's loveliest piazzas, oval cafe-ringed **Piazza Anfiteatro**, so-called after the amphitheatre that was here in Roman times. Spot remnants of the amphitheatre's brick arches and masonry on the exterior walls of the medieval houses ringing the piazza.

City Wall   HISTORIC SITE

Lucca's monumental *mura* (wall) was built around the old city in the 16th and 17th centuries and remains in almost perfect condition. It superceded two previous walls, the first built from travertine stone blocks as early as the 2nd century BC. Twelve metres high and 4.2km long, today's ramparts are crowned with a tree-lined footpath looking down on the *centro storico* and out towards the Apuane Alps. This path is a favourite location for the locals' daily *passeggiata* (traditional evening stroll).

Children's playgrounds, swings and picnic tables beneath shady plane trees add

LOCAL KNOWLEDGE

A WALLTOP PICNIC

When in Lucca, picnicking atop its city walls – on grass or at a wooden picnic table – is as lovely (and typical) a Lucchesi lunch as any.

Buy fresh-from-the-oven pizza and focaccia with a choice of fillings and toppings from fabulous 'n' famed bakery **Forno Amedeo Giusti** (Via Santa Lucia 20; pizzas & filled focaccias per kg €9-16; ⊘ 7am-7.30pm Mon-Sat, 4-7.30pm Sun), then nip across the street for a bottle of Lucchesi wine and Garfagnese *biscotti al farro* (spelt biscuits) at **Antica Bodega di Prospero** (Via Santa Lucia 13; ⊘ 9am-1pm & 4-7.30pm); look for the old-fashioned shop window fabulously stuffed with sacks of beans, lentils and other local pulses.

Complete the perfect picnic with a slice of *buccellato*, a traditional sweet bread loaf with sultanas and aniseed seeds, baked by **Taddeucci** (www.taddeucci.com; Piazza San Michele 34; buccellato per 300/600/900g loaf €4.50/9/13.50; ⊘ 8.30am-7.45pm, closed Thu winter) since 1881. Or seduce taste buds with truffles, white chocolate spread and other heavenly chocolate creations from **Caniparoli** (www.caniparolicioccolateria.it; Via San Paolino 96; ⊘ 9.30am-1pm & 3.30-7.30pm Mon-Sat, to 7pm Sun), the best *cioccolateria* (chocolate maker) in town.

Swill down the picnic with your pick of Italian craft beers at microbrewery **De Cervesia** (Via Fillungo 90; ⊘ 10am-1pm & 3.30-7.30pm Tue-Sat), with a small shop on Lucca's main shopping street and a tap room for serious tasting (open 5pm to 10pm Tuesday to Sunday) a few blocks away at Via Michele Rosi 20. Should a shot of something stronger be required to aid digestion, nip into historic pharmacy **Antica Farmacia Massagli** (Piazza San Michele; ⊘ 9am-7.30pm) for a bottle of China elixir, a heady liqueur of aromatic spices and herbs first concocted in 1855.

a buzz of activity to Baluardo San Regolo, Baluardo San Salvatore and Baluardo Santa Croce – three of the 11 bastions studding the way. Older kids kick footballs around on the green lawns of Baluardo San Donato.

★ **Cattedrale di San Martino** CATHEDRAL
(www.museocattedralelucca.it; Piazza San Martino; adult/reduced €3/2, with museum & Chiesa e Battistero dei SS Giovanni & Reparata €7/5; ⊘ 9.30am-5pm Mon-Fri, to 6pm Sat, 11.30am-5pm Sun) Lucca's predominantly Romanesque cathedral dates to the 11th century. Its stunning facade was constructed in the prevailing Lucca-Pisan style and designed to accommodate the pre-existing *campanile* (bell tower). The reliefs over the left doorway of the portico are believed to be by Nicola Pisano, while inside, treasures include the **Volto Santo** (literally, Holy Countenance) crucifix sculpture and a wonderful 15th-century tomb in the **sacristy**. The cathedral interior was rebuilt in the 14th and 15th centuries with a Gothic flourish.

Legend has it that the *Volto Santo,* a simply fashioned image of a dark-skinned, life-sized Christ on a wooden crucifix, was carved by Nicodemus, who witnessed the crucifixion. In fact, it has been dated to the 13th century. A major object of pilgrimage, the sculpture is carried through the streets every 13 September at dusk during the **Luminaria di Santa Croce**, a solemn torchlit procession marking its miraculous arrival in Lucca.

The cathedral's many other works of art include a magnificent *Last Supper* by Tintoretto above the third altar of the south aisle and Domenico Ghirlandaio's 1479 *Madonna Enthroned with Saints*. This impressive work by Michelangelo's master is currently located in the sacristy. Opposite lies the exquisite, gleaming marble tomb of Ilaria del Carretto carved by Jacopo della Quercia in 1407. The young second wife of the 15th-century lord of Lucca, Paolo Guinigi, Ilaria died in childbirth aged only 24. At her feet lies her faithful dog.

★ **Museo della Cattedrale** MUSEUM
(www.museocattedralelucca.it; Piazza San Martino; adult/reduced €4/3, with cathedral sacristy & Chiesa e Battistero dei SS Giovanni & Reparata €7/5; ⊘ 10am-6pm) The cathedral museum safeguards elaborate gold and silver decorations made for the cathedral's Volto Santo, including a 17th-century crown and a 19th-century sceptre.

★ **Torre Guinigi** TOWER
(Via Guinigi; adult/reduced €4/3; ⊘ 9.30am-6.30pm summer, 10.30am-4.30pm winter) The

bird's-eye view from the top of this medieval, 45m-tall red-brick tower adjoining 14th-century **Palazzo Guinigi** is predictably magnificent. But what impresses even more are the seven oak trees planted in a U-shaped flower bed at the top of the tower. Legend has it that upon the death of powerful Lucchese ruler Paolo Guinigi (1372–1432) all the leaves fell off the trees. Count 230 steps to the top.

Chiesa e Battistero dei SS Giovanni e Reparata
CHURCH

(Piazza San Giovanni; adult/reduced €4/3, with cathedral museum & sacristy €7/5; ⊙10am-6pm summer, 10am-5pm Sat & Sun winter) The 12th-century interior of this deconsecrated church is a hauntingly atmospheric setting for summertime opera recitals; buy tickets in advance inside the church. In the north transept, the Gothic baptistry crowns an archaeological area comprising five building levels going back to the Roman period. Don't miss the hike up the red-brick bell tower.

Palazzo Pfanner
PALACE

(www.palazzopfanner.it; Via degli Asili 33; palace or garden adult/reduced €4.50/4, both €6/5; ⊙10am-6pm Apr-Nov) Fire the romantic in you with a stroll around this beautiful 17th-century palace where parts of *Portrait of a Lady* (1996) starring Nicole Kidman and John Malkovich were shot. Its baroque-styled garden – the only one of substance within the city walls – enchants with ornamental pond, lemon house and 18th-century statues of Greek gods posing between potted lemon trees. Summertime chamber music concerts hosted here are absolutely wonderful.

Climb the grand outdoor staircase to the frescoed and furnished *piano nobile* (main reception room), home to Felix Pfanner, an Austrian émigré who first brought beer to Italy – and brewed it in the mansion's cellars from 1846 until 1929. From the copperpots strung above the hearth in the kitchen to the dining-room table laid for lunch, the rooms vividly evoke daily life in an early 18th-century Lucchese *palazzo* (mansion).

Chiesa di San Michele in Foro
CHURCH

(Piazza San Michele; ⊙7.40am-noon & 3-6pm summer, 9am-noon & 3-5pm winter) One of Lucca's many architecturally significant churches, this glittering Romanesque edifice marks the spot where the city's Roman forum was. The present building with exquisite wedding-cake facade was constructed on the site of its 8th-century precursor over 300 years, beginning in the 11th century. Crowning the structure is a figure of the archangel Michael slaying a dragon. Inside the dimly lit interior, don't miss Filippino Lippi's 1479 painting of Sts Helen, Jerome, Sebastian and Roch (complete with plague sore) in the south transept.

Festivals & Events

Lucca Summer Festival MUSIC
(www.summer-festival.com; ⊙Jul) This month-long festival brings rock and pop stars to Lucca.

Sleeping

⭐**Piccolo Hotel Puccini** HOTEL €
(☑0583 5 54 21; www.hotelpuccini.com; Via di Poggio 9; s/d €75/100; ❄🖥) In a brilliant central location, this welcoming three-star hotel hides behind a discreet brick exterior. Its small guest rooms are attractive with wooden floors, vintage ceiling fans and colourful, contemporary design touches. Breakfast, optional at €3.50, is served at candlelit tables behind the small reception area. Rates are around 30% lower in winter.

Ostello San Frediano HOSTEL €
(☑0583 46 99 57; www.ostellolucca.it; Via della Cavallerizza 12; dm/d €23/68; ⊙mid-Feb–Dec; 🖥) Slap-bang in the centre of walled Lucca, inside a historic building, hostellers won't get closer to the action than this. Top notch in comfort and service, this HI-affiliated hostel with 141 beds in voluminous rooms is serviced with a bar and grandiose dining room (breakfast €5, lunch or dinner €11). Non-HI members can buy a welcome stamp for €2.

⭐**Locanda Vigna Ilaria** B&B €€
(☑0583 33 20 91; www.locandavignailaria.it; Via della Pieve Santo Stefano 967c, St Alessio; d/q €110/120; 🅿) Those on a Tuscan road trip or who love easy parking will be smitten with this stone house in a wealthy surburb, 4km north of Lucca's walled city in St Alessio (dump the car, then meander along green lanes, past vast villas bathed in olive groves). The *locanda* (inn) has five rooms furnished with a mix of old, new and upcycled – lots of wine boxes!

2italia APARTMENT €€
(☑392 996 02 71; www.2italia.com; Via della Anfiteatro 74; apt for 2 adults & up to 4 children €190; 🖥📶) Not a hotel but several family-friendly

self-catering apartments overlooking Piazza Anfiteatro, with a communal kids' playroom in the attic. Available on a nightly basis (minimum two nights), the project is the brainchild of well-travelled parents-of-three, Kristin (English) and Kaare (Norwegian). Spacious apartments sleep up to six, have a fully equipped kitchen and washing machine, and come with sheets and towels.

Alla Corte degli Angeli   BOUTIQUE HOTEL €€€
(☑ 0583 46 92 04; www.allacortedegliangeli. com; Via degli Angeli 23; s/d/ste €150/250/400; ✵@☎) This boutique hotel sits in a couple of 15th-century townhouses, with stylish beamed lounge leading to 21 sunny rooms adorned with frescoed ceilings, patches of exposed brick and landscape murals. Every room is named after a different flower, and up-to-the-minute bathrooms have jacuzzi tubs and power-jet showers. Breakfast €10.

Eating

Da Felice   PIZZA €
(www.pizzeriadafelice.it; Via Buia 12; focaccias €1-3, pizza slices €1.30; ⊙ 11am-8.30pm Mon, 10am-8.30pm Tue-Sat) This buzzing spot behind Piazza San Michele is where the locals come for wood-fired pizza, *cecina* (salted chickpea pizza) and *castagnacci* (chestnut cakes). Eat in or take away, *castagnaccio* comes wrapped in crisp white paper, and my it's good married with a chilled bottle of Moretti beer.

Grom   GELATERIA €
(www.grom.it; Via Fillungo 56; cone €2.20-3.30; ⊙ 11.30am-10pm Sun-Thu, to 11pm or midnight Fri & Sat) Natural and organic is the philosophy of this master ice-cream maker. Join the line of locals for a tub of caramel and pink Himalayan salt, yoghurt, tiramisu or seasonal fruit sorbet.

Trattoria da Leo   TRATTORIA €
(☑ 0583 49 22 36; Via Tegrimi 1; meals €25; ⊙ 12.30-2pm & 7.30-10.30pm Mon-Sat) A much-loved veteran, Leo is famed for its friendly ambience and cheap food – ranging from plain-Jane acceptable to grandma delicious. Arrive in summer to snag one of 10 checked-tableclothed tables crammed beneath parasols on the narrow street outside. Otherwise, it's noisy dining inside among typically nondescript 1970s decor. No credit cards.

★ **Ristorante Giglio**   TUSCAN €€
(☑ 0583 49 40 58; www.ristorantegiglio.com; Piazza del Giglio 2; meals €35; ⊙ 12.30-2pm & 7.30-10pm Thu-Mon, 7.30-10pm Wed) Don't let the tacky plastic-covered pavement terrace deter. Splendidly at home in the frescoed 18th-century Palazzo Arnolfini, Giglio is stunning. Dine at white-tableclothed tables, sip a complimentary *prosecco*, watch the fire crackle in the marble fireplace and savour traditional Tuscan with a modern twist: think fresh artichoke salad served in an edible parmesan-cheese wafer 'bowl', or risotto simmered in Chianti.

Local Food Market   DELI €€
(☑ 0583 31 10 77; Via San Paolino 116; meals €30; ⊙ 10am-11.30pm Tue-Sun) This bright modern address is hidden in a courtyard, complete with potted lemon plants and tables in the sun. In keeping with the seemingly latest trend sweeping through Tuscany, Local Food Market is just that – an upmarket food market, deli and health food shop where you can eat between shelves stacked high with local Tuscan products.

Port Ellen Clan   TUSCAN €€
(☑ 0583 49 39 52; www.portellenclan.com; Via del Fosso 120; meals €30; ⊙ 7.30pm-1am Wed-Fri, noon-3pm & 7.30pm-1am Sat & Sun) 'Ristorante, Enoteca, Design Ideas' is the strapline of this romantic candlelit space named after the town in the Scottish Hebrides where the owner holidays. Cuisine is imaginative with homemade *tortelli* stuffed with stewed oxtail and pork tenderloin with fennel mash jostling for attention on the creative menu. Excellent artisan beer and whisky list.

ℹ Information

Tourist Office (☑ 0583 58 31 50; www.lucca itinera.it; Piazzale Verdi; ⊙ 9am-7pm summer, to 5pm winter) Free hotel reservations, left-luggage service (two bags €2.50/4.50/7 per hour/half-day/day) and guided city tours in English departing daily at 2pm (€10, two hours).

ℹ Getting There & Away

BUS

From the bus stops around Piazzale Verdi, Vaibus runs services throughout the region, including to Pisa airport (€3.40, 45 minutes to one hour, 30 daily) and Castelnuovo di Garfagnana (€4.20, 1½ hours, eight daily).

CAR & MOTORCYCLE

The A11 runs westwards to Pisa and Viareggio and eastwards to Florence. The easiest parking is Parcheggio Carducci, just outside Porta Sant'Anna. Within the walls, most car parks are for residents only, indicated by yellow lines. Blue lines indicate where anyone can park (€2 per hour).

TRAIN

The station is south of the city walls: take the path across the moat and through the dark, grungy tunnel under Baluardo San Colombano.

Florence (€7.20, 1¼ to 1¾ hours, hourly)
Pisa (€3.40, 30 minutes, every half hour)
Viareggio (€3.40, 25 minutes, hourly)

🚴 Getting Around

Rent wheels (ID required) to pedal the 4.2km circumference of Lucca's romantic city walls from a couple of outlets on Piazza Santa Maria, or try the following:

Tourist Center Lucca (🏠 0583 49 44 01; www.touristcenterlucca.com; Piazzale Ricasoli 203; bike per hour/3hr/day €4/8/12; ⊗ 8.30am-7.30pm summer, 9am-6pm winter) Exit the train station and bear left to find this handy bike rental outlet, with kids' bikes, tandems, trailers and various other gadgets. It also has left-luggage facilities.

Pietrasanta

POP 24,237

Often overlooked by Tuscan travellers, this refined art town is an unexpected and beautiful surprise. Its bijou historic heart, originally walled, is car-free and loaded with tiny art galleries, workshops and fashion boutiques – perfect for a day's amble broken only by lunch.

Founded in 1255 by Guiscardo da Pietrasanta, *podestà* of Lucca, Pietrasanta was seen as a prize by Genoa, Lucca, Pisa and Florence, all of whom jostled for possession of its marble quarries and bronze foundries. Florence predictably won and Leo X (Giovanni de' Medici) took control in 1513, putting the town's famous quarries at the disposal of Michelangelo, who came here in 1518 to source marble for the facade of Florence's San Lorenzo. The artistic inclination of Pietrasanta dates from this time, and today it is the home of many artists, including internationally lauded Colombian-born sculptor Fernando Botero, whose work can be seen here.

CARNIVAL IN VIAREGGIO

Italy's beach-loving hoi polloi pack out the coastal strip known as the **Versilian Riviera**, which legs it north from the major town of Viareggio to the regional border with Liguria. Frolicking on the long sandy beach and lapping up the seafront's line-up of 1920s art-nouveau facades aside, the main reason to visit Viareggio is for its flamboyant, four-week Mardi Gras **Carnevale** (http://viareggio.ilcarnevale.com) in February, second only to Venice for party spirit.

👁 Sights

From Pietrasantra train station (Piazza della Stazione) head straight across Piazza Carducci to the old city gate and onto the central square, **Piazza del Duomo**.

Duomo di San Martino   CATHEDRAL
(Piazza del Duomo; ⊗ variable) It is impossible to miss Pietrasanta's attractive cathedral, dating from 1256, on the central square. Its distinctive 36m-tall, red-brick bell tower is actually unfinished; the red brick was meant to have a marble cladding.

Chiesa di Sant'Agostino   CHURCH
(Piazza del Duomo; ⊗ variable) The far end of Piazza del Duomo is dominated by the 13th-century stone hulk of this deconsecrated church. Once dedicated to St Augustine, the Romanesque space hosts seasonal art exhibitions today.

Museo dei Bozzetti   MUSEUM
(🏠 0584 79 55 00; www.museodeibozzetti.it; Via Sant'Agostino 1; ⊗ 9am-1pm & 2-7pm Tue-Fri, 2-7pm Sat, 4-7pm Sun) **FREE** Inside the convent adjoining Chiesa di Sant'Agostino dozens of moulds of famous sculptures cast or carved in Pietrasanta are showcased by this small museum.

Via della Rocca   VIEWPOINT
(Piazza del Duomo) Next to Chiesa di Sant'Agostino, a steep path known as Via della Rocca leads up to what remains of Piatrasanta's ancient fortifications. The crenelled city walls date to the early 1300s and what remains of **Palazzo Guinigi** was built as a residence for *signore* of Lucca, Paolo Guinigi, in 1408. Views of the city and the deep-blue Mediterranean beyond are predictably worth the short climb.

🛏 Sleeping & Eating

⭐ **Le Camere di Filippo**   B&B €€
(📞 0584 7 00 10; www.filippolondon.it; Via Stagio Stagi 22; d €120-150; 🅿 ❄ @ 🛜) A fabulous address with two kitchens and four fantastic rooms, each with a different colour scheme and crisp design.

⭐ **Filippo**   TUSCAN €€
(📞 0584 7 00 10; http://ristorantefilippo.com; Via Stagio Stagi 22; meals €40; ⏱ 12.30-2.30pm & 7.30pm-2am, closed Mon winter) 🍴 This exceptional foodie address never disappoints. From the homemade bread (all six or so varieties) and focaccia brought warm to your table throughout the course of your meal, to the contemporary fabric on the walls, giant wicker lampshades and modern open kitchen, this bistro is chic. Cuisine is seasonal and as creative as the interior design.

🍷 Drinking

L'Enoteca Marcucci   WINE BAR
(📞 0584 79 19 62; www.enotecamarcucci.it; Via Garibaldi 40; ⏱ 10am-1pm & 5pm-1am Tue-Sun) Taste fine Tuscan wine on bar stools at high wooden tables or beneath big parasols on the street outside. Whichever you pick, the distinctly funky, artsy spirit of Pietrasanta's best-loved *enoteca* enthrals.

❶ Getting There & Away

Regional train services include:

Lucca (with change of train in Pisa or Viareggio; €5.90, one hour, every 30 minutes)

Pisa (€4.30, 30 minutes, every 30 minutes)

Viareggio (€2.50, 10 minutes, every 10 minutes)

EASTERN TUSCANY

The eastern edge of Tuscany is beloved by film directors who've immortalised its landscape and medieval hilltop towns in several critically acclaimed and visually splendid films. Yet the region remains refreshingly bereft of tourist crowds and offers uncrowded trails for those savvy enough to explore here.

Arezzo

POP 99,232

Arezzo may not be a Tuscan centrefold, but those parts of its historic centre that survived merciless WWII bombings are compelling – the city's central square is as beautiful as it appears in Roberto Benigni's classic film *La vita è bella* (Life is Beautiful).

Once an important Etruscan town, Arezzo was later absorbed into the Roman Empire. A free republic as early as the 10th century, it supported the Ghibelline cause in the violent battles between pope and emperor and was eventually subjugated by Florence in 1384.

Today, the city is known for its churches, museums and fabulously sloping **Piazza Grande**, across which a huge antiques fair spills during the first weekend of each month. Come dusk, Arentini (locals of Arezzo) spill along the length of shop-clad Corso Italia for the ritual *passeggiata* (evening stroll).

👁 Sights

⭐ **Cappella Bacci**   CHURCH
(📞 0575 35 27 27; www.pierodellafrancesca.it; Piazza San Francesco; adult/reduced €8/5; ⏱ 9am-6.30pm Mon-Fri, to 5.30pm Sat, 1-5.30pm Sun) This chapel, in the apse of 14th-century **Basilica di San Francesco**, safeguards one of Italian art's greatest works: Piero della Francesca's fresco cycle of the *Legend of the True Cross*. Painted between 1452 and 1466, it relates the story of the cross on which Christ was crucified. Only 25 people are allowed in every half-hour, making advance booking (by telephone or email) essential in high season. The ticket office is down the stairs by the basilica's entrance.

This medieval legend is as entertaining as it is inconceivable. The illustrations follows the story of the tree that Seth plants on the grave of his father, Adam, and from which the True Cross is made. Another scene shows the long-lost cross being rediscovered by Helena, mother of the emperor Constantine; behind her, the city of Jerusalem is represented by a medieval view of Arezzo. Other scenes show the victory of Heraclius over the Persian king Khosrau, who had been accused of stealing the cross; Constantine sleeping in a tent on the eve of his battle with Maxentius (note Piero's masterful depiction of the nocturnal light); and Constantine carrying the cross into battle.

Two of the best-loved scenes depicts the meeting of the Queen of Sheba and King Solomon. In the first half she is kneeling on a bridge over the Siloam River and meeting with the king; she and her attendants are depicted wearing rich Renaissance-style

Arezzo

gowns. In the second half, King Solomon's palace seems to be modelled on the designs of notable architect Leon Battista Alberti.

★ **Chiesa di Santa Maria della Pieve**   CHURCH

(Corso Italia 7; ⊗8am-12.30pm & 3-6.30pm) FREE This 12th-century church – Arezzo's oldest – has an exotic Romanesque arcaded facade adorned with carved columns, each uniquely decorated. Above the central doorway are 13th-century carved reliefs called *Cyclo dei Mesi* representing each month of the year. The plain interior's highlight – removed for restoration work at the time of writing – is Pietro Lorenzetti's polyptych *Madonna and Saints* (1320–24), beneath the semidome of the apse. Below the altar is a 14th-century silver bust reliquary of the city's patron saint, San Donato.

Arezzo

Duomo di Arezzo   CATHEDRAL

(Cattedrale di SS Donato e Pietro; Piazza del Duomo; ⊗7am-12.30pm & 3-6.30pm) FREE Construction started in the 13th century but Arezzo's

ⓘ AREZZO CENT SAVER

A combined ticket (adult/reduced €12/7) covers admission to Cappella Bacci, Museo Archeologico Nazionale and Museo di Casa Vasari.

cathedral wasn't completed until the 15th century. In the northeast corner, left of the intricately carved main altar, is an exquisite fresco of *Mary Magdalene* (c 1459) by Piero della Francesca. Also notable are five glazed terracottas by Andrea della Robbia and his studio. Behind the cathedral is the pentagonal **Fortezza Medicea** (1502) atop the crest of one of Arezzo's two hills – the *duomo* was built on the crest of the other.

Museo Archeologico Nazionale 'Gaio Cilnio Mecenate' MUSEUM

(www.museistataliarezzo.it; Via Margaritone 10; adult/reduced €6/3; ◷8.30am-7.30pm, to 1.30pm Nov) Overlooking the remains of a Roman amphitheatre that seated up to 10,000 spectators, this museum in a 14th-century convent building exhibits Etruscan and Roman artefacts. The highlight is the *Cratere di Euphronios,* a 6th-century-BC Etruscan vase with vivid scenes showing Hercules in battle. Also of note is an exquisite tiny portrait of a bearded man from the second half of the 3rd century AD, executed in chrysography whereby a fine sheet of gold is engraved then encased between two glass panes.

Museo di Casa Vasari MUSEUM

(Vasari House Museum; www.museistataliarezzo. it; Via XX Settembre 55; adult/reduced €4/2; ◷9am-7pm Mon & Wed-Sat, to 1pm Sun) Built and sumptuously decorated by Arezzo-born painter, architect and art historian Giorgio Vasari (1511–74), this museum is where Vasari lived and worked, and where the original manuscript of his *Lives of the Most Excellent Painters, Sculptors and Architects* (1550) – still in print under the title *The Lives of the Artists* – is kept. End on the bijou, Renaissance-style roof garden with flower beds, box hedges and fountain in its centre. To get into the museum, ring the bell.

Festivals & Events

Fiera Antiquaria di Arezzo ANTIQUES

(Arezzo Antique Fair) Tuscany's most famous antiques fair is held in Piazza Grande on the first Sunday and preceding Saturday of every month.

Sleeping

Palazzo dei Bostoli B&B €

(☑334 1490558; www.palazzobostoli.it; Via G Mazzini 1; s/d €55/75; ❄☺) This old-fashioned place offers five simple but comfortable rooms on the 2nd floor of a 13th-century *palazzo* near Piazza Grande. Breakfast – a coffee and *cornetto* (croissant) – is served at a bar on nearby Corso Italia.

Casa Volpi HOTEL €

(☑0575 35 43 64; www.casavolpi.it; Via Simone Martini 29; s/d €65/95; Ⓟ@☺⊕) This 18th-century manor is a delicious 1.5km bicycle ride away from the cobbled streets of downtown Arezzo (the hotel lends wheels to guests). Its 15 rooms are decorated in a clasical style, with plenty of original features – beamed ceilings, red-brick flooring, parquet – to charm. Family-run, the hotel restaurant spills in to the pretty garden in summer. Breakfast €9.

Eating

★ Antica Osteria Agania TUSCAN €

(☑0575 29 53 81; www.agania.com; Via G Mazzini 10; meals €25; ◷noon-3pm & 6-10.30pm Tue-Sun) Agania has been around for years and her fare is die-hard traditional – the tripe and *grifi con polenta* (lambs' cheeks with polenta) are sensational. But it is timeless, welcoming addresses like this, potted fresh herbs on the doorstep, that remain the cornerstone of Tuscan dining. Begin with *antipasto misto* (mixed appetisers) followed by your choice combo of six pastas and eight sauces.

Agania's *pici* (fat spaghetti) with wild-boar sauce is legendary. Arrive by 1pm to beat the crowd of regulars or join the crowd waiting outside.

La Bottega di Gnicche SANDWICHES €

(www.bottegadignicche.com; Piazza Grande 4; panini €3.50-5; ◷11am-8pm Thu-Tue) Choose from a delectable array of artisan meats and cheeses to stuff in a *panini* at this old-fashioned *alimentari* (grocery store) on Arezzo's main piazza. Eat next to canary-yellow bags of artisan Martelli pasta stacked up on the front porch, or perch on a stool inside.

ⓘ Information

Tourist Office (☑0575 40 19 45; www. benvenutiadarezzo.it; Palazzo Comunale, Via Ricasoli; ◷10am-1pm & 2-7pm Mon-Fri, 10am-

1pm Sat & Sun Jun-Sep, to 4pm Oct-May)
Find a branch (Piazza della Repubblica 22-23;
⊘10.30am-12.30pm & 2-4pm) of the tourist
office to the right as you exit the train station.

Una Vetrina per Arezzo e Le Sue Vallate
(✆0575 182 27 70; ⊘9am-7pm) Private tourist
office on the *scala mobile* leading up to Piazza
del Duomo; toilet facilities (€0.50).

❶ Getting There & Away

BUS
Siena Mobilità (www.sienamobilita.it) serves
Siena (€6.80, 1½ hours, seven daily). **Etruria
Mobilità** (www.etruriamobilita.it) buses serve
Sansepolcro (€4.10, one hour, hourly) and
Cortona (€3.40, one hour, frequent). Buy
tickets from the ticket office to the left as you
exit the train station; buses leave from the bay
opposite.

CAR & MOTORCYCLE
To drive here from Florence, take the A1; the
SS73 heads west to Siena. Parking at the train
station costs €2 per hour.

TRAIN
Arezzo is on the Florence–Rome train line, and
there are frequent services to Florence (€8, 1½
hours) and Rome (€14 to €26.50, two hours).
There are also hourly regional services to Cortona (€3.40, 20 minutes).

Sansepolcro
POP 16,109

This 'hidden gem' is a town that truly deserves the description. Its historic centre is
littered with *palazzi* and churches squirrel-
ling away Renaissance works of art or bejewelled with exquisite terracotta Andrea della
Robbia medallions. Spend a day wandering
from dimly lit church to church, following in
the footsteps of Sansepolcro's greatest son,
Renaissance artist Piero della Francesca.

◉ Sights

★Museo Civico   MUSEUM
(www.museocivicosansepolcro.it; Via Niccolò Aggiunti 65; adult/reduced €8/5; ⊘10am-1.30pm &
2.30-7pm summer, 10am-1pm & 2.30-6pm winter)
The town's flagship museum is home to a
small but top-notch collection of artworks,
including three Piero della Francesca masterpieces: *Resurrection* (1458–74), the *Madonna della Misericordia* polyptych (1445–
56) and *Saint Julian* (1455–58). Admire also
works by the studio of Andrea della Robbia:
a polychrome terracotta called *The Nativity
and Adoration of the Shepherds* (1485) and

a beautiful tondo (circular sculpture) known
as the *Virgin and Child with Manetti Coat
of Arms* (1503).

Cattedrale di San Giovanni
Evangelista   CATHEDRAL
(Duomo di Sansepolcro; Via Giacomo Matteotti
4; ⊘10am-noon & 4-7pm) Sansepolcro's 14th-
century *duomo* contains an *Ascension* by
Perugino, a *Resurrection* by Raffaellino del
Colle and a polyptych by Niccolò di Segna
that is thought to have influenced Piero's
Resurrection. Left of the main altar is the
striking *Il Volto Santo* (Sacred Face), a
wooden crucifix with a wide-eyed Christ in
a blue gown that dates to the 9th century,
and – nearby – a beautiful ceramic tabernacle (unfortunately badly chipped) by Andrea
della Robbia.

Leaving the cathedral, turn right onto Piazza Garabaldi to admire the 16 medallions
by Andrea della Robbia on the facade of
Palazzo Preterio.

🛏 Sleeping & Eating

Da Ventura, Fiorentino and Guidi all offer a
couple of B&B rooms up top as well as memorable dining.

★Ristorante Da Ventura   TUSCAN €€
(✆0575 74 25 60; www.albergodaventura.it; Via
Niccolò Aggiunti 30; meals €25; ⊘12.30pm-
2.15pm & 7.30-9.45pm Tue-Sat) This old-world
eatery is a culinary joy. Trolleys laden with
fiesty joints of pork, beef stewed in Chianti
Classico and roasted veal shank are pushed
from table to table, bow-tied waiters intent
on piling plates high. The veal filet topped
with wafer-thin slices of *lardo di colonnata* and the veal carpaccio with black truffle
shavings are glorious.

Ristorante Fiorentino   ITALIAN €€
(✆0575 74 20 33; www.ristorantefiorentino.it;
Via Luca Pacioli 60; meals €35; ⊘noon-3pm &
7.30-10.30pm Thu-Tue) An iconic address, this
grandiose dining room dates to 1807. Sweep
up the marble staircase and into a historic world of glass chandeliers, Renaissance
wooden coffered ceiling and original fireplace. Food is traditional with an occasional
modern twist.

🍷 Drinking

Enoteca Guidi   WINE BAR
(✆0575 74 19 07; www.locandaguidi.it; Via Luca
Pacioli 44-46; meals €20; ⊘11am-midnight Thu-
Tue) Owner Saverio presides over the teensy

VAL DI CHIANA

Driving south from Arezzo to Cortona, allow time to linger in the Val di Chiana, a wide green valley punctuated by gently rolling hills crowned with medieval villages. Its prized agricultural land is rich in orchards and olive groves, and it is from here that Tuscany's famed Chianina cows – one of the oldest breeds of cattle in the world and the essential ingredient in Tuscany's signature dish, *bistecca alla fiorentina* – originate.

The place to sink your teeth into the iconic T-bone steak is the picturesque walled town of **Castiglion Fiorentino** (population 13,386), crowned with the impressively restored Cassero, a bulky medieval fortress with panoramic views of the Val di Chiana both from grassy green grounds and the top of its half-ruined medieval **torre** (Cassero; adult/reduced €3/1.50; ⏱10am-6pm Fri-Sun summer, 10am-12.30pm & 3.30-6pm Fri-Sun winter). The only lunch address, without a doubt, is locally venerated **Ristorante Da Muzzicone** (☎348 935 66 16, 0575 65 84 03; Piazza San Francesco 7; Meals €30; ⏱12.15-2.15pm & 7.30-9.30pm), where succulent, cooked-to-perfection beef (€45 per kilogram) is chargrilled over a wood fire at one end of a large barn-like interior. If T-bone is not your cup of tea, there are grilled beef fillets in green pepper sauce or balsamic vinegar to tempt. In summer, tables spill onto the pretty square outside. Reservations essential.

If you're in the valley on the third Sunday in June, don't miss Castiglion Fiorentino's **Palio dei Rioni** – Siena's Palio on a smaller scale – which sees jockeys on horseback race around Piazza Garibaldi.

enoteca and rear dining space where simple meals are served. Enjoy a local artisan beer or some *vino* (everything from local drops to fashionable Super Tuscans).

ℹ️ Information

Tourist Office (☎0575 74 05 36; www.valtiberinatoscana.it; Via Giacomo Matteotti 8; ⏱9.30am-1pm & 2.30-6.30pm summer, shorter hours winter; 📶)

ℹ️ Getting There & Away

BUS

Etruria Mobilità (www.etruriamobilita.it) buses link Sansepolcro with Arezzo (€4.20, one hour). **Sulga** (www.sulga.it) operates a daily service to Rome and Fiumicino Airport (€19.50, 3½ to 4¼ hours); check schedules and buy tickets online. Buses use the bus station off Via G Marconi, near Porta Fiorentina.

CAR & MOTORCYCLE

A ZTL (Limited Traffic Zone) applies within the city walls; find free parking just outside.

Cortona

POP 22,607

Rooms with a view are the rule rather than the exception in this spectacularly sited hilltop town. In the late 14th century Fra' Angelico lived and worked here, and fellow artists Luca Signorelli and Pietro da Cortona were both born within the walls – all are repre-

sented in the Museo Diocesano's collection. More recently, the town featured in *Under the Tuscan Sun*, the soap-in-the-sun book and subsequent film recounting author Frances Mayes' experience in restoring a villa and forging a new life here.

👁 Sights

⭐ **Museo Diocesano** MUSEUM
(Piazza del Duomo 1; adult/reduced €5/3; ⏱10am-7pm Tue-Sun summer, to 5pm Tue-Sun winter) Little is left of the original Romanesque character of Cortona's cathedral, rebuilt several times in a less-than-felicitous fashion. Fortunately, its wonderful artworks have been saved and displayed in this museum. Highlights include a moving *Crucifixion* (1320) by Pietro Lorenzetti and two beautiful works by Fra' Angelico: *Annunciation* (1436) and *Madonna with Child and Saints* (1436–37). Room 1 features a remarkable Roman sarcophagus decorated with a frenzied battle scene between Dionysus and the Amazons.

Museo dell'Accademia Etrusca MUSEUM
(MAEC; www.cortonamaec.org; Piazza Signorelli 9; adult/reduced €10/7; ⏱10am-7pm summer, to 5pm Tue-Sun winter) The plain facade of 13th-century Palazzo Casali was added to the original building in the 17th century. Inside, this fascinating museum displays substantial local Etruscan and Roman finds, Renaissance globes, 18th-century decorative arts and contemporary paintings. The Etrus-

can collection is the highlight, particularly those objects excavated from the tombs at Sodo, just outside town.

Fortezza del Girifalco   LANDMARK
(Via per Santa Margherita; adult/child €3/1.50; ⏰10am-1pm & 3-6pm Sat & Sun May & Jun, 10am-1pm & 4-7pm Jul-Sep) There's a stupendous view over the Val di Chiana to Lago Trasimeno in Umbria from the remains of this Medici fortress atop the highest point in town.

Festivals & Events

Giostra dell'Archidado   CULTURAL
(www.giostraarchidado.com; ⏰May or Jun) A full week of medieval merriment (the date varies to coincide with Ascension Day) culminates in a crossbow competition.

Cortonantiquaria   FAIR
(www.cortonantiquaria.it; ⏰late Aug or early Sep) Cortona's well-known antiques market sets up in the beautiful 18th-century halls of Palazzo Vagnotti.

Sleeping

★ Casa Chilenne   B&B €
(☑0575 60 33 20; www.casachilenne.com; Via Nazionale 65; d €110; ✦@�) Run by San Franciscan Jeanette and her Cortonese husband Luciano, this welcoming B&B scales a narrow townhouse on Cortona's main pedestrian street. Five spacious rooms have access to a small rooftop terrace, complete with bijou cooking area and chairs to lounge on. Breakfast is a feast, served around beautifully dressed tables.

La Corte di Ambra   B&B €€
(☑0575 178 82 66; www.cortonaluxuryrooms.com; Via Benedetti 23; d €150-300; ✦@�) Squirrelled away in Palazzo Fierli-Petrella, this contemporary guesthouse has five luxurious rooms with whitewashed beamed ceilings, chandelier lighting and beautiful linens in mellow neutral tones. En suite bathrooms are up-to-the-minute and – unusually for a Renaissance Tuscan palace – the B&B has a lift; one room is genuinely wheelchair-friendly.

Eating & Drinking

Pedestrian main street Via Nazionale has plenty of places to linger over coffee or cocktails. For wine- and olive-oil tasting, not to mention tempting rounds of cheese aged in *farro* (spelt) or straw, pop into I Tre Toscani (Via Dardano 35).

Pasticceria Banchelli   PASTRIES €
(☑0575 60 10 52; Via Nazionale 11; ⏰10am-8pm Tue-Sun) For sinful cakes with coffee, this cake shop with cafe has been the place to go since 1930.

Fiaschetteria La Fett'unta   TUSCAN €
(☑0575 63 05 82; www.winebarcortona.com; Via Giuseppe Maffei 3; meals €15) This tiny, deli-style *fiaschetteria* (wine bar) with tempting cold cuts and pre-prepared dishes sitting beneath glass, begging to be gobbled up, cooks up first-class budget dining. Service is overwhelmingly friendly, there's a kids' corner, and traditional Tuscan cuisine – fresh from the kitchen of big sister Osteria del Teatro across the street – is spot-on.

La Bucaccia   TUSCAN €€
(☑0575 60 60 39; www.labucaccia.it; Via Ghibellina 17; meals €32, set tasting menu €29; ⏰12.45-3pm & 7-10.30pm Tue-Sun) Cortona's finest address, this gourmet gem is at home in the old medieval stable of a Renaissance *palazzo*. Cuisine is Tuscan and Cortonese – much meat and handmade pasta (chestnut ravioli!) – and the cheese course is superb, thanks to owner Romano Magi who ripens his own. Dedicated gourmets won't be able to resist the six *pecorino* types to taste with fruit sauces, salsas and honeys.

Caffè degli Artisti   CAFE
(Via Nazionale 18) This vintage cafe on Cortona's pedestrian main street is wonderful for mellowing out over an aromatic pot of white, black or green leaf tea.

Information

Tourist Office (☑0575 63 72 21; www.comunedicortona.it; Piazza Signorelli; ⏰9am-12.30pm Mon, Wed & Fri, 9am-12.30pm & 3-5.30pm Tue & Thu)

Getting There & Around

Car is by far the easiest way to access hilltop Cortona. The nearest train station is 6km southwest in Camucia, accessible via bus (€1.40, 15 minutes, hourly). Camucia train station has no ticket office, only machines (if you need assistance purchasing tickets, go to the station at Terontola, 7km south of Camucia, instead). Destinations include:

Arezzo (€3.40, 25 minutes, hourly)
Florence (€10.20, 1¾ hours, hourly)
Rome (€11.15, 2¾ hours, eight daily)

Umbria & Le Marche

Why Go?

For years Italophiles have waxed lyrical about Tuscany's natural, artistic and culinary wonders, without so much as a passing nod to its neighbours, Umbria and Le Marche. How they have missed out! This phenomenally beautiful yet unsung region is Italy in microcosm: olive groves, vineyards, sun-ripened wheat fields stippled with wildflowers and hills plumed with cypress trees rolling gently west to the snow-dusted Apennines and east to the glittering Adriatic. In between, castle-topped medieval hill towns await, glowing like honey in the fading light of sundown.

The region scores highly on the artistic front, too, as the birthplace of Renaissance masters Raphael and Perugino, and sprightly composer Rossini. St Francis of Assisi, St Benedict and St Valentine all hail from here, making a pilgrimage to this area a profoundly spiritual one. So next time you glance at the map and your eyes alight on old-favourite Tuscany, why not press on east? You won't regret it.

Best Places to Eat

➡ La Taverna (p586)
➡ Osteria Eat Out (p600)
➡ Tempio del Gusto (p609)
➡ Ristorante Vespasia (p611)

Best Places to Stay

➡ B&B San Fiorenzo (p584)
➡ Alla Madonna del Piatto (p597)
➡ B&B La Magnolia (p614)
➡ La Cuccagna (p602)

When to Go
Perugia

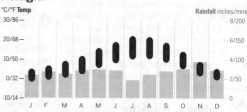

Feb Celebrate all things truffle at Norcia's Mostra Mercato del Tartufo Nero festival.

May Make for Le Marche's beaches, as wildflowers bloom on the Piano Grande.

Jun & Jul Get lost in music at the Spoleto Festival and Perugia's Umbria Jazz.

UMBRIA

Italy's green heart, Umbria is a land unto itself, the only Italian region that borders neither the sea nor another country. Removed from outside influences, it has kept alive many of Italy's old-world traditions. You'll see grandmothers in aprons making pasta by hand and front doors that haven't been locked in a century.

Separated from Le Marche by the jagged spine of the Monti Sibillini, it contrasts wild, in-your-face beauty with the gentle fall and rise of overlapping hills and wildflower-flecked meadows. The Etruscans, Romans and medieval feuding families have left their indelible imprint on its pretty hill towns, where history seems to creep up on you at every corner – from the Gothic wonder of Orvieto to Assisi's saintly calling.

Foodies are in their element here, with the rich earthiness of the *tartufo* (truffle), fine cured meats from Norcia and full-bodied local wines finding their way onto menus.

History

Umbria is named in honour of its first inhabitants, the Umbri tribe who settled east of the Tiber around 1000 BC, establishing the towns of Spoleto, Gubbio and Assisi. They jockeyed for regional supremacy with the Etruscans to the west of the river – the founders of Perugia and Orvieto – until the 3rd century BC, when the Romans came marching through, conquering them both.

Following the collapse of the Western Roman Empire, the region spent much of the Middle Ages being fought over by Holy Roman Empire advocates (Ghibellines) and supporters of the Pope (Guelphs). Intriguingly, it was during this turbulent period that peace-loving St Francis came to prominence in Assisi.

Eventually the region became one of the Papal States, though this was not to its long-term benefit. Indeed, historians like to say that time stopped in Umbria in 1540 when the pope imposed a salt tax. The resulting war brought Umbrian culture to a standstill, which is partly why the medieval hearts of Umbrian towns are so well preserved.

Perugia has a strong artistic tradition. In the 15th century it was home to fresco painters Bernardino Pinturicchio and his master Pietro Vannucci (known as Perugino), who would later teach Raphael. Its cultural tradition continues to this day in the form of the University of Perugia and the famous Università per Stranieri (University for Foreigners), which teaches Italian, art and culture to thousands of students from around the world.

USEFUL WEBSITES ON UMBRIA

Bella Umbria (www.bellaumbria.net) Accommodation and restaurant listings for Umbria. Search for festivals and events by location or date.

Regione Umbria (www.regioneumbria.eu) The official Umbrian tourist website.

Sistema Museo (www.sistemamuseo.it) Get the inside scoop on Umbria's museums and upcoming events.

Umbria Online (www.umbriaonline.com) Find information on accommodation, events and itineraries across Umbria.

🛈 Getting Around

While having your own wheels certainly makes it easier to reach those off-the-radar hill towns and rural corners of Umbria, it is possible to get to many places by public transport with a little pre-planning.

Buses head from Perugia to most towns in the area; check at the tourist office or the bus station for exact details. **Trenitalia** (Ferrovie dello Stato; ☑ 892021; www.trenitalia.com) sparsely criss-crosses Umbria, but the regional bus company **Umbria Mobilità** (☑ 075 963 70 01; www.umbriamobilita.it) fills in the blanks.

Your first port of call for mountain biking and road cycling itineraries should be http://bikeinumbria.it.

Perugia

POP 162,100

Lifted by a hill above a valley patterned with fields, where the river Tiber runs swift and clear, Perugia is Umbria's petite and immediately likeable capital. Its *centro storico* (historic centre) rises in a helter-skelter of cobbled alleys, arched stairways and piazzas framed by magnificent *palazzi* (mansions). History seeps through every shadowy corner of these streets and an aimless wander through them can feel like time travel.

Back in the 21st century, Perugia is a party-loving, pleasure-seeking university city, with

Umbria &
Le Marche
Highlights

1 Making the spiritual pilgrimage in the footsteps of a peace-seeking saint to Assisi's **Basilica di San Francesco** (p594).

2 Gazing at endless acres of spring wildflowers or trekking up the snow-capped peaks of **Monti Sibillini** (p631).

3 Spelunking your way through a forest of stalactites at **Grotte di Frasassi** (p626), Europe's largest cave.

4 Swimming, chilling and eating just-caught shellfish by the Adriatic in coastal **Parco del Conero** (p621).

5 Savouring towering views on a rickety ride up Monte Ingino aboard Gubbio's **Funivia Colle Eletto** (p603).

6 Cashing in your golden ticket for a chocolate-factory tour at **Casa del Cioccolato Perugina** (p582).

7 Slipping into the relaxed groove of lake life: swimming, cycling and sipping locally grown wines at **Lago Trasimeno** (p589).

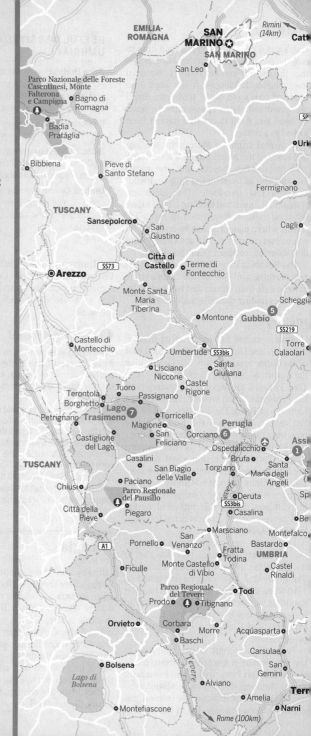

Perugia

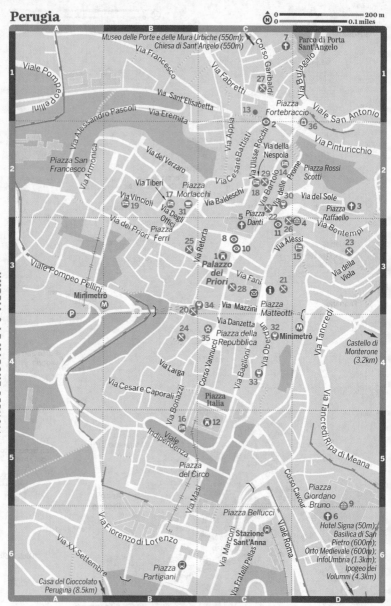

students pepping up the nightlife and filling cafe terraces. The hopping summer event line-up counts one of Europe's best jazz festivals. Together with its spiritual sister Assisi, Perugia is a candidate for European Capital of Culture 2019. Watch this space.

Sights

Piazza IV Novembre
PIAZZA

In Perugia all roads seem to lead to Piazza IV Novembre, once the meeting point for the ancient Etruscan and Roman civilisations. In the medieval period, it was the political

Perugia

centre of Perugia. Now people from all walks of life gather here to chat, slurp gelato and watch street entertainers or the odd budding opera singer.

★ **Palazzo dei Priori** PALACE
(Corso Vannucci) Flanking Corso Vannucci, this Gothic palace, constructed between the 13th and 14th centuries, is architecturally striking with its tripartite windows, ornamental portal and fortress-like crenellations. It was formerly the headquarters of the local magistracy, but now houses the city's main art gallery, the Galleria Nazionale dell'Umbria. Also of note is the Nobile Collegio del Cambio (Exchange Hall; www.perugiacittamuseo.it; Palazzo dei Priori, Corso Vannucci 25; admission €4.50, incl Nobile Collegio della Mercanzia €5.50; ⊙9am-12.30pm & 2.30-5.30pm Mon-Sat, 9am-1pm Sun), Perugia's medieval money exchange, with its Perugino frescoes.

The extravagantly adorned money exchange has three rooms: the Sala dei Legisti (Legist Chamber), with 17th-century wooden stalls carved by Giampiero Zuccari; the Sala dell'Udienza (Audience Chamber),

with outstanding Renaissance frescoes by Perugino; and the Chapel of San Giovanni Battista, painted by a student of Perugino's, Giannicola di Paolo. Nearby sits the Nobile Collegio della Mercanzia (Merchant's Hall; www.perugiacittamuseo.it; Palazzo dei Priori, Corso Vannucci 15; admission €1.50, incl Nobile Collegio del Cambio €5.50; ⊙9am-1pm & 2.30-5.30pm Tue-Sat, 9am-1pm Sun summer, reduced hours winter), showcasing a 14th-century audience chamber with exquisite wood panelling.

The Sala dei Notari (Notaries' Hall; Piazza IV Novembre; ⊙9am-1pm & 3-7pm Tue-Sun) FREE was built between 1293 and 1297 and is where the nobility met. The arches supporting the vaults are Romanesque, covered with frescoes depicting biblical scenes and Aesop's fables. To reach the hall, walk up the steps from Piazza IV Novembre.

Galleria Nazionale dell'Umbria GALLERY
(☎075 5866 8410; Palazzo dei Priori, Corso Vannucci 19; adult/reduced €6.50/3.25; ⊙8.30am-7.30pm Tue-Sun) Umbria's foremost art gallery is housed in Palazzo dei Priori on the city's main strip. Its collection, one of central

Italy's richest, numbers almost 3000 works, ranging from Byzantine-inspired 13th-century paintings to Gothic works by Gentile da Fabriano and Renaissance masterpieces by hometown heroes Pinturicchio and Perugino.

Cattedrale di San Lorenzo CATHEDRAL
(Piazza IV Novembre; ⊘7.30am-noon & 3.30-6.45pm Mon-Sat, 8am-1pm & 4-7pm Sun) Overlooking Piazza IV Novembre is Perugia's stark medieval cathedral. A church has stood here since the 900s, but the version you see today was begun in 1345 from designs created by Fra Bevignate. Building continued until 1587, although the main facade was never completed. Inside you'll find dramatic late Gothic architecture, an altarpiece by Signorelli and sculptures by Duccio. The steps in front of the facade are where seemingly all of Perugia congregates; they overlook the piazza's centrepiece, the delicate pink-and-white marble **Fontana Maggiore** (Great Fountain; Piazza IV Novembre).

Another of Fra Bevignate's designs, the fountain was completed in 1278 by famous sculptors Nicola and Giovanni Pisano. Bas-relief statues grace the polygonal basin, representing scenes from the Old Testament, the founding of Rome, the seven 'liberal arts', the signs of the zodiac, and a griffin and lion. The griffin is the symbol of Perugia and the lion that of the Guelphs, the Middle Ages faction that favoured rule by the papacy over rule by the Holy Roman Empire.

Museo Archeologico Nazionale dell'Umbria MUSEUM
(Piazza Giordano Bruno 10; adult/reduced €4/2; ⊘8.30am-7.30pm Tue-Sun, 10am-7.30pm Mon) The convent adjoining the Chiesa di San Domenico is home to a superior collection of Etruscan and prehistoric artefacts – carved funerary urns, coins and Bronze Age statuary – dating as far back as the 16th century BC. The *Cippo Perugino* (Perugian Memorial Stone) has the longest Etruscan-language engraving ever found, offering a rare window into this obscure culture.

Casa del Cioccolato Perugina MUSEUM
(ⓘ075 527 67 96; www.perugina.it; Van San Sisto 207, Loc San Sisto; adult/reduced €9/7; ⊘9am-1pm & 2-5.30pm Mon-Fri, plus 10am-4pm Sa Mar-May, Aug & Oct-Dec; ⓘ) **FREE** To visit the Wonka-esque world of Perugian chocolate, call ahead to latch onto a 1¼-hour guided tour (in Italian or English, times vary). After visiting the museum, you'll wend your way through an enclosed sky bridge, watching as the white-outfitted Oompa Loompas, er, factory workers go about their chocolate-creating business.

Check the website for the calendar of three- to four-hour chocolate-making workshops. Held at 10am and 3.30pm on Saturdays, they cost between €55 and €65. Drive through the gates of the humorously nondescript factory entrance marked Nestlé, or take the bus to San Sisto.

Basilica di San Pietro BASILIC
(Borgo XX Giugno 74; ⊘8am-noon & 3.30-6pm) South of the town centre, past the Porta di San Pietro, this 10th-century basilica's interior is an incredible mix of gilt and marble and contains a *Pietà* (a painting of the dead Christ supported by the Madonna) by Perugino. For a glimpse into gardens past, take a stroll or picnic at the serene **Orto Medievale** (Borgo XX Giugno 74; ⊘8am-5pm Mon-Fri) **FREE** gardens, behind the basilica.

During the medieval period, monasteries often created gardens reminiscent of the Garden of Eden and biblical stories, with plants that symbolised myths and sacred stories. Numbered locations through this garden include the Cosmic Tree, symbolising the ancestor of all trees; the Tree of Light and Knowledge; and the Tree of Good and Evil.

Rocca Paolina FORT, GARDENS
(Piazza Italia) **FREE** At the southern end of Corso Vannucci is tiny **Giardini Carducci**, with expansive views across the city's spires to the countryside and cypress-cloaked hills beyond. The gardens stand atop a once-massive 16th-century fortress, now known as Rocca Paolina. Built by Pope Paolo III Farnese in the 1540s, the fortress was built over entire sections of a formerly wealthy neighbourhood.

Now used as the throughway for the *scale mobili* (escalators), its nooks and crannies are venues for art exhibits, and the last weekend of the month sees Perugia's antiques market held here.

Casa Museo di Palazzo Sorbello MUSEUM
(www.casamuseosorbello.org; Piazza Piccinino 9; adult/reduced €5/3; ☺ guided tours 10.30am-2pm & 3-6pm, shorter hours winter) A few steps from the Piazza IV Novembre, this exquisite 17th-century mansion, once owned by the noble Sorbello family, has recently been restored to its frescoed, gilt-clad, chandelier-lit 18th-century prime. Guided tours (in Italian) let you admire the family's almost ludicrously opulent collection of art, porcelain, embroidery and manuscripts.

Capella di San Severo CHAPEL
(Piazza Raffaello; adult/reduced €3/2; ☺ 10am-1.30pm & 2.30-6pm Tue-Sun) Walking for a couple of minutes northeast from Piazza IV Novembre brings you to this rather bland, boxy-looking church. Your efforts will be rewarded, however, once you step inside and find the chapel decorated with Raphael's lush *Trinity with Saints* (thought by many to be his first fresco), painted during the artist's residence in Perugia (1505–08).

Ipogeo dei Volumni HISTORIC SITE
(Via Assisana 53, Località Ponte San Giovanni; adult/reduced €3/1.50; ☺ 9am-1pm & 3.30-6.30pm) About 5km southeast of the city, the Ipogeo dei Volumni is a 2nd-century-BC underground Etruscan burial site, holding the funerary urns of the Volumni, a local noble family. The surrounding grounds are a massive expanse of partially unearthed burial chambers, with several buildings housing the artefacts that haven't been stolen over the years.

Take a train from Piazza Italia to Ponte San Giovanni and walk west from there. By car, take the Bonanzano exit heading south on the E45.

Pozzo Etrusco HISTORIC SITE
(Etruscan Well; Piazza Danti 18; adult/reduced €3/2; ☺ 10am-1.30pm & 2.30-6pm Tue-Sun summer, 11am-1.30pm & 2.30-5pm winter) Just north of Piazza IV Novembre, you can venture down into a 37m-deep well. Dating from the 3rd century BC, it was the main water reservoir of the Etruscan town, and, more recently, a source of water during WWII bombing raids.

Chiesa di San Domenico CHURCH
(Piazza Giordano Bruno; ☺ 7am-noon & 4-7pm) Erected in the early 14th century, Umbria's largest church is an imposing vision, with a 17th-century interior lit by immense stained-glass windows. The church's pride and joy is the Gothic tomb of Pope Benedict XI, who died after eating poisoned figs in 1304.

Arco Etrusco HISTORIC SITE
(Etruscan Arch) At the end of Via Ulisse Rocchi, facing Piazza Fortebraccio and the Università per Stranieri, are the ancient city's Etruscan gates dating from the 3rd century BC. The upper part is Roman and bears the inscription 'Augusta Perusia'.

Chiesa di Sant'Agostino CHURCH
(Piazza Lupattelli; ☺ 10am-1pm & 5.30-7pm Mon-Sat, 8am-12.30pm Sun) North of the Università per Stranieri, along Corso Garibaldi, this formerly magnificent church still boasts a beautiful 16th-century choir by sculptor Baccio d'Agnolo. However, small signs forlornly mark the places where artworks once hung before they were carried off to France by Napoleon's troops.

Chiesa di Sant'Angelo CHURCH
(Via Sant'Angelo; ☺ 9am-5pm) North along Corso Garibaldi, Via del Tempio branches off to one of Italy's oldest churches, the Romanesque Chiesa di Sant'Angelo, parts of which date back to the 5th century. It stands on the foundations of an even older Roman temple.

Museo delle Porte e delle Mura Urbiche MUSEUM
(Museum of the City Walls and Gates; Porta Sant' Angelo; adult/reduced €3/2; ☺ 10.30am-1.30pm & 3-6pm Tue-Sun) Next door to the Chiesa di Sant'Angelo, in the 14th-century Porta Sant'Angelo, the city's largest medieval gateway, this museum whisks you through the history of the city's defences. Even more engrossing are the sweeping views of Perugia from this vantage point.

🎓 Courses

Università per Stranieri LANGUAGE COURSE
(☑ 075 5 74 61; www.unistrapg.it; Piazza Fortebraccio 4) This is Italy's foremost academic institution for foreigners, offering courses in language, literature, history, art, music, opera and architecture. One-, three- and six-month language courses start at €400 a month; intensive courses in summer cost €600 a month.

DON'T MISS

ALL THAT JAZZ

Umbria Jazz (www.umbriajazz.com) Ever since making its debut in 1973, Perugia's swinging 10-day July festival, Umbria Jazz, has put the city firmly on the world jazz map, with such headline acts as BB King, Van Morrison, James Brown, Sting, Chet Baker and, more recently, Herbie Hancock and Diana Krall.

The Arena Santa Giuliana hosts most performances, but events are also held at other venues, including the Teatro Morlacchi and Galleria Nazionale dell'Umbria. Tickets go for anything between €15 and €120. There's also a winter edition, held in late December and early January. See the website for details.

✯ Festivals & Events

Check www.bellaumbria.net or www.regioneumbria.eu for details on Perugia's gazillions of festivals, concerts, summer outdoor film screenings and *sagre* (traditional festivals).

Eurochocolate FOOD
(www.eurochocolate.com) Perugia celebrates the cocoa bean over nine days in mid-October. More than a million chocolate lovers flock here for choc-crazy exhibitions, cookery classes, giant chocolate sculptures and – the real reason everyone is here – to hoover up the free samples.

🛏 Sleeping

★ **B&B San Fiorenzo** B&B €
(☑ 393 3869987; www.sanfiorenzo.com; Via Alessi 45; r €70-120; 🖥📶) Buried in Perugia's medieval maze of a centre is this charming 15th-century *palazzo*, where Luigi and Monica make you welcome in one of three unique rooms. A Florentine architect has carefully incorporated mod cons and marble bathrooms into spacious quarters with brick vaulting, lime-washed walls and antique furnishings, including an apartment with an 11th-century well shower and a 13th-century tower room.

Breakfast is a handsome spread, with homemade cakes, fresh fruit and decent cappuccino. Incidentally, the church of the same name that sits opposite once harboured Raphael's *Ansidei Madonna* altarpiece, now in London's National Gallery.

Little Italy HOSTEL €
(☑ 075 966 19 97; www.littleitalyhostel.it; Via della Nespola 1; dm €18-20, d €35; 🖥) History and cutting-edge design cavort at this slick newcomer to the backpacker scene. Pair the central location with modern dorms and rooms housed in a revamped 11th-century church (complete with original vaults and frescoes), a focus on Italian food and design and a chilled-out bar, and you are looking at one neat place to stay.

Alla Maison di Alessia B&B €
(☑ 345 0784208; www.allamaisondialessia.it; Via Bartolo 55-61; per week s €300-360, d €525-600; 🖥📶) Alessia and Enrico have waved magic wands over this historic house, where rooms are rented by the week. There are just four rooms – three doubles with kitchenettes and one single – but each has been lovingly dressed in chalk-box pastel shades and with eye-catching details. Breakfast is a sweet affair playing up Italian produce.

Hotel Signa HOTEL €
(☑ 075 572 41 80; www.hotelsigna.it; Via del Grillo 9; s €37-58, d €47-80, tr €80-90, q €98-120; ❄🖥📶) Slip down an alley off Corso Cavour to reach Signa, one of Perugia's best budget picks. The petite rooms are simple, bright and well kept; many have balconies with cracking views of the city and countryside. Rooms at the cheaper end of the scale have shared bathrooms. Breakfast costs an extra €6.50. The owner, Mario, hands out maps and tips freely.

Hotel Morlacchi GUESTHOUSE €
(☑ 075 572 03 19; www.hotelmorlacchi.it; Via Tiberi 2; s €40-60, d €60-80, tr €80-90; 🖥) A friendly, old-school guesthouse near Piazza IV Novembre. The cosy, low-ceilinged rooms, spread over several floors of a 17th-century townhouse, are modest but comfortable with antiques and original artworks. Breakfast costs €6 extra per person.

Primavera Minihotel HOTEL €
(☑ 075 572 16 57; www.primaveraminihotel.it; Via Vincioli 8; s €45-55, d €70-100; ❄🖥📶) This petite, welcoming hotel is tucked in a quiet corner of the *centro storico*. Magnificent views complement the bright rooms, decorated with period furnishings and characterful features like exposed stone, beams and wood floors. Breakfast costs €5 to €8 extra. There's no lift, so be prepared to schlep your bags up steps.

Castello di Monterone
HOTEL €€€

(✆075 572 42 14; www.castellomonterone.com; Strada Montevile 3; s €136-162, d €180-330; P🅿❄@🈂) Ever fancied spending the night in a medieval castle? This is the real Mc-Coy, with all the turreted, ivy-clad, vaulted trappings you would imagine. The individually designed rooms have been finished to great effect, with exposed stone, wooden furniture, handmade wrought-iron beds and antiques. A pool with sweeping views over the rolling countryside and a first-rate restaurant add to its appeal.

Castello di Monterone is situated 3.2km east of the centre; see the website for exact directions.

Hotel Brufani Palace
HERITAGE HOTEL €€€

(✆075 573 25 41; www.brufanipalace.com; Piazza Italia 12; s €120-180, d €150-293, ste €300-533; P❄@🈂🍴) From its hilltop perch, the five-star Hotel Brufani Palace has captivating views of the valley below and the hills beyond. The hotel itself matches this initial impression with frescoed public rooms, impeccably decorated bedrooms with marble bathrooms, a garden terrace for summer dining, and helpful trilingual staff. You can swim over Etruscan ruins in the subterranean fitness centre. There's access for disabled guests.

Eating

Perugia has a staggering number of places to eat. The first days the mercury rises above 15°C or so (usually in March), dozens of open-air locales spring up along and around Corso Vannucci.

Al Mangiar Bene
PIZZA €

(✆075 573 10 47; www.almangiarbene.com; Via della Luna 21; pizzas €6-12, meals €25-35; ⊙12.30-2.45pm & 7.30-10.45pm, closed Sun & Mon lunch; 🍴) 🌱 Tucked down a narrow alley, this subterranean restaurant sources nearly all its ingredients locally from organic suppliers, from its pasta flour to the tender cuts of beef, thinly sliced and served with rocket or truffle. Pizza and calzone are baked in a hearth-like brick oven. Even the beer and wines are organic. There's also an €8.50 children's menu.

Fressco
CAFE €

(✆075 573 41 80; www.fressco.com; Via del Sole 2; snacks €2-6; ⊙9.30am-9.30pm Mon-Sat) Fresh indeed, this laid-back cubby hole of a juice bar and cafe is run single-handedly by a cheery guy from Istanbul named Kahraman. It's hip and wholesome, with a menu given over to cold-pressed juices and smoothies, salads, flat-bread sandwiches and soups. A top spot for kicking back with breakfast or a snack.

Pizzeria Mediterranea
PIZZA €

(Piazza Piccinino 11/12; pizzas €4.50-12; ⊙12.30-2.30pm & 7.30-11.30pm; 🍴) A classic pizzeria with a wood-fired oven and bustling atmosphere, this popular spot does the best pizzas in town. Served bubbling hot, they come with light, Neapolitan-style bases and flavoursome toppings. Expect queues at the weekend.

Ristorante dal Mi'Cocco
UMBRIAN €

(✆075 573 25 11; Corso Garibaldi 12; set meals €13; ⊙1-3pm & 8-10.30pm Tue-Sun) Don't ask for a menu because there isn't one. Diners

---

TOP FIVE UMBRIAN DELICACIES

Once something of a culinary backwater, much of the world is now playing catch up with Umbria's Slow Food commitment in a region where three-hour dinners, organic produce and locavore dining have long been part of daily life. Eat like an Umbrian by sampling these dishes on your travels:

Cinghiale Richly gamey but tender, wild boar is often served over pasta or stewed in sauce.

Tartufi Umbrian black truffles give menus an earthy edge, especially in the autumn harvest months.

Lenticchie These small, thin lentils from Castelluccio are at their best in a thick soup topped with bruschetta and virgin olive oil.

Piccione Umbrians readily order pigeon, often from the highest-end restaurants. The delicate poultry was a mainstay for townsfolk under siege in the Middle Ages.

Farro Spelt and emmer wheats still grace tables today. Classic *zuppa di farro* (spelt soup) is rich, nutty and distinctly Umbrian, perfect for a warm lunch on a cold day in the hills.

get a set menu of a starter, main course, side dish and dessert. You may receive asparagus risotto in May or *tagliatelle* with peas and ham in November. It's extremely popular with students, so it's best to call ahead.

Covered Market
MARKET €

(Piazza Matteotti; ⊙ 7am-1.30pm Mon-Fri, 7.30am-1.30pm & 4.30-7.30pm Sat) Found below a rather desultory craft and tourist-tat market, you can buy fresh produce, bread, cheese and meat here. Head through the arched doorway to the immediate right of the tourist office.

★ La Taverna
ITALIAN €€

(☑ 075 572 41 28; www.ristorantelataverna.com; Via delle Streghe 8; meals €30-40; ⊙ 12.30-3pm & 7.30-11pm) Way up there on the Perugia dining wish list, La Taverna consistently wins the praise of local foodies. Chef Claudio cooks market-fresh produce with flair and precision, while waiters treat you like one of the *famiglia*.

Brick vaults and candlelit tables create an intimate backdrop for season-rooted dishes, from homemade pasta with black truffles to herb-crusted lamb, all paired with superb wines.

Osteria a Priori
OSTERIA €€

(☑ 075 572 70 98; www.osteriaapriori.it; Via dei Priori 39; meals €30; ⊙ 12.30-2.30pm & 7.30-10pm Mon-Sat) ✒ Located above an *enoteca* (wine bar), this fashionable *osteria* (casual tavern) specialises in local wines and fresh regional cuisine prepared with seasonal ingredients. Umbrian cheeses and cured meats feature alongside truffles, roast meats and autumnal mushrooms. Weekday lunch is a snip at €9. Reservations recommended.

Wine Bartolo Hosteria
OSTERIA €€

(☑ 075 571 60 27; Via Bartolo 30; meals €20-35; ⊙ dinner Thu-Tue) Descend a staircase into a hobbit-like burrow where walls of wine bottles surround a handful of cosy tables underneath a low brick ceiling. The food is winningly fresh and inspired by the seasons, along the lines of *taglierini* (a type of pasta) with Norcia black truffles and Chianina beef stewed with Sangiovese.

Il Gufo
UMBRIAN €€

(☑ 075 573 41 26; Via della Viola 18; meals €25-35; ⊙ 8pm-1am Tue-Sat) The owner-chef gathers ingredients from local markets and cooks up whatever is fresh and in season. Go for robustly seasoned dishes such as wild boar

with fennel or pappardelle with rabbit *ragù* (meat-and-tomato sauce).

Drinking & Nightlife

Much of Perugia's nightlife parades outside the cathedral and around Fontana Maggiore, where local and foreign students gather to chat, flirt and play guitars and drums. Grab a gelato and go for a people-watching *passeggiata* (evening stroll) to watch the street theatre unfold.

As day fades into dusk at *aperitivo* hour in summer, locals spill out onto pavement terraces and patios with far-reaching views across the surrounding valley and hills.

Kundera
BAR

(Via Gugliemo Oberdan 23; ⊙ 6.30pm-midnight) Follow the lead of students and clued-up locals by heading to this artsy little bar for *aperitivo* time, when €5 gets you a drink (cocktails included) and a tasty platter of appetisers – you can even ask for the gluten-free option. Snag a table on the terrace when it's warm.

Sandri
CAFE €

(Corso Vannucci 32; pastries €2.50; ⊙ 7.30am-11pm) This city institution has been serving coffee and cake since 1860. Its delicately frescoed, chandelier-lit interior provides the perfect backdrop for exquisite-looking pastries, chocolates and cakes, enticingly presented in floor-to-ceiling cabinets.

Bottega del Vino
WINE BAR

(Via del Sole 1; ⊙ noon-3pm & 7pm-midnight Mon-Sat) A fire or candles burn romantically on the terrace, while inside live jazz and hundreds of bottles of wine lining the walls add to the romance of the setting. You can taste dozens of Umbrian wines, which you can purchase with the help of sommelier-like experts.

Il Sole
BAR

(Via delle Rupe 1; ⊙ 12.30-3pm & 7.30-10.30pm Tue-Sun) Better for drinking than dining, Il Sole is all about the engrossing view over town, country and wooded hill from its terrace. It's a beautiful spot for a sundowner.

Caffè Morlacchi
CAFE

(Piazza Morlacchi 6/8; ⊙ 8am-1am Mon-Sat, 4-10pm Sun; 🛜) Students, professors and all comers flock to this vibrantly coloured, blissfully relaxed hang-out for coffee by day and cocktails to the backbeat of DJ tunes by night.

Lunabar Ferrari
BAR

(Via Scura 1/6; ☺8am-1.30am) This lounge bar spins together frescoed plaster walls and luxuriant rugs with modern art and crazy chandeliers. Go for the cocktails, DJ sets and *aperitivo* buffet (€6) from 6.30pm to 9.30pm.

Entertainment

When the student population grows, some of the clubs on the outskirts of town run a bus to Palazzo Gallenga, starting around 11pm. Students hand out flyers on Corso Vannucci, so check with them or ask at the steps. Most clubs get going around midnight, so it's worth remembering that the *scale mobili* stop running at 2am.

Cinema Teatro del Pavone
CINEMA

(☑075 572 81 53; www.teatrodelpavone.it; Corso Vannucci 67) Dating back to 1717, the grand theatre plays host to not only films but also musical performances and special events.

Shopping

Via Oberdan, the main boulevard Corso Vannucci and the steep Via Sant'Ercolano, wedged between the high townhouses of the *centro storico*, are dotted with boutiques, music shops, bookstores and jewellers.

Augusta Perusia Cioccolato e Gelateria
FOOD

(www.cioccolatoaugustaperusia.it; Via Pinturicchio 2; ☺10.30am-6.30pm Mon-Sat; 🖼) Giordano worked for Perugina for 25 years. In 2000, he opened his own shop, creating delectable morsels from the old tradition, including *baci* (hazelnut 'kisses' covered in chocolate) from the original Perugian recipe.

ℹ Information

Banks line Corso Vannucci; all have ATMs.

InfoUmbria (☑329 6514942; www.umbriabest. com; Via della Pallotta 5; ☺9am-1pm & 2.30-6.30pm Mon-Fri, 9am-1pm Sat) Also known as InfoTourist, it offers information on all of Umbria and is a fantastic resource for *agriturismi* (farm stay accommodation).

Ospedale Perugia (☑075 57 81; Piazzale Menghini 1)

Post Office (Piazza Matteotti 1; ☺8.20am-7.05pm Mon-Fri, 8am-12.35pm Sat)

Tourist Office (☑075 573 64 58; http:// turismo.comune.perugia.it; Piazza Matteotti 18; ☺9am-6.30pm Mon-Sat, to 2.30pm Sun) Housed in the 14th-century Loggia dei Lanari, Perugia's main tourist office has stacks of info on the city, maps (€0.50) and up-to-date bus and train timetables.

ℹ Getting There & Away

AIR

Aeroporto Sant'Egidio (PEG; ☑075 59 21 41; www.airport.umbria.it; Via dell'Aeroporto, Sant'Egidio), 12km east of the city, is small and easy to navigate, with daily **Ryanair** (www. ryanair.co.uk) flights (except on Saturdays) to London Stansted.

BUS

Umbria Mobilità (p577) operates all intercity buses, which leave from Piazza Partigiani in the city's south (take the *scale mobili* through the Rocca Paolina from Piazza Italia). Services go to the following destinations. (Note that it's better to travel to Florence by train.)

TO	FARE (€)	DURATION	FREQUENCY
Assisi	4.20	45min	9 daily
Castiglione del Lago	6.10	1hr	9 daily
Deruta	3.60	30min	13 daily
Florence	13.50	2hr	1 daily
Gubbio	5.50	1¼hr	10 daily
Todi	6.10	1¼hr	9 daily
Torgiano	3	30min	9 daily

CAR & MOTORCYCLE

From Rome, leave the A1 at the Orte exit and follow the signs for Terni. Once there, take the SS3bis/E45 for Perugia. From the north, exit the A1 at Valdichiana and take dual-carriageway SS75 for Perugia. The SS75 to the east connects the city with Assisi.

Rental companies have offices at the airport and train station.

> **GOING TO ROME?**
>
> Sulga (☑800 099661; www.sulga.it) Blue-and-white Sulga buses link the bus station on Piazza Partigiani with Terminal 3 at Rome's Fiumicino (FCO) airport (€22, 3¼ hours); they depart at 6.30am, 8am, 9am and 2.30pm from Monday to Saturday, and 7.30am and 8.30am on Sunday. The same buses also run to Rome's Tiburtina train station (€17, 2½ hours, five daily). Several buses stop in Deruta and Todi. Check the website for details.

TRAIN

In the southwest of town, Perugia's main **train station** (☎ 075 963 78 91; Piazza Vittorio Veneto) has trains running to the following destinations.

TO	FARE (€)	DURATION	FREQUENCY
Arezzo	7-12	1hr	every 2 hours
Assisi	2.50	20min	hourly
Florence	13.50-20	2hr	every 2 hours
Orvieto	7-15	1¾-3hr	10 daily
Rome	11-23	2¼-3½hr	17 daily
Spello	3	30min	hourly

ⓘ Getting Around

If you're not carrying too much luggage, the simplest way of getting from Perugia's intercity bus station to the town centre is by hopping aboard the *scale mobili* linking Piazza Partigiani with Piazza Italia. There are also *scale mobili* from the car park at the Piazzale della Cuppa outside the city walls up to the Via dei Priori.

TO/FROM THE AIRPORT

Umbria Mobilità (p577) runs a frequent bus service from the airport to Perugia (€3, 30 minutes) and Assisi (€3, 20 minutes); you'll need the exact change. Tickets are a third cheaper if you buy them from the airport bar.

Alternatively, a shuttle bus (€8) leaves from Piazza Italia for the airport about two hours before each flight, stopping at the train station. The tourist office has exact timetables. From the airport, buses leave once everyone is on board.

A taxi costs approximately €30.

BUS

It's a steep 1.5km climb from Perugia's train station, so a bus is highly recommended (and essential for those with luggage). The bus takes you to Piazza Italia. Tickets cost €1.50 from the train-station kiosk or €2 on board. Validate your ticket on board to avoid a fine. A 10-ticket pass costs €12.90.

CAR & MOTORCYCLE

Perugia is humorously difficult to navigate and most of the city centre is only open to residential or commercial traffic.

The city has several fee-charging car parks (€0.80 to €1.60 per hour, 24 hours a day). Piazza Partigiani and the Mercato Coperto are the most central and convenient. There's also a free car park at Piazza Cupa.

MINIMETRÒ

These single-car people-movers traverse between the train station and Pincetto (just off Piazza Matteotti) every minute. A €1.50 ticket works for the bus and Minimetrò. From the train station facing the tracks, head right up a long platform.

TAXI

Available from 6am to 2am (24 hours from July to September); call ☎ 075 500 48 88 to arrange pick-up. A ride from the city centre to the main train station will cost about €10 to €15. Tack on €1 for each suitcase.

Torgiano

POP 6510

Vineyards and olive groves sweep up to thi medieval walled town on a hilltop perc overlooking the confluence of the Chiasci and Tiber rivers. Torgiano has an irresistibl draw for gastronomes: it's renowned for it thick, green extra-virgin olive oil and spicy peppery red wines, such as Rubesco Ross DOC, produced with 70% Sangiovese grapes

◉ Sights

Museo del Vino   MUSEUM
(Wine Museum; www.lungarotti.it/fondazione muvit; Corso Vittorio Emanuele 31; adult/reduce incl Museo dell'Olio e dell'Olio €7/5; ⊙10am 6pm daily summer, to 5pm & closed Mon winter The Museo del Vino takes a thematic romp through viticulture in a 20-room, 17th-cen tury mansion. Greek, Etruscan and Roman ceramics, jugs and vessels, glassware and various wine-making implements race you from the Bronze Age to the present, cover ing topics such as wine as medicine and its role in mythology. A wine tasting and audio guide is included in the ticket price.

Museo dell'Olivo e dell'Olio   MUSEUM
(www.lungarotti.it/fondazione/moo; Via Garibal di 10; adult/reduced incl Museo del Vino €7/5 ⊙10am-6pm daily summer, to 5pm & closed Mor winter) Showcasing mills, presses and crafts the Museo dell'Olivo e dell'Olio is an ode to olive oil and its symbolic, medicinal and di etary uses.

⌂ Sleeping & Eating

Al Grappolo d'Oro   HOTEL €
(☎ 075 98 22 53; www.algrappolodoro.net; Via Principe Umberto 24; s/d €60/90; ﾟ☀❄☎) The view across vineyards from the tree-rimmed pool is soothingly beautiful at this

bijou hotel in the centre of town. Smartly furnished 19th-century rooms are bright, serene and kept spotlessly clean. There's free bike hire if you fancy pedalling off into the countryside. Breakfast is included.

Ristorante Siro   ITALIAN €€
(☎075 98 20 10; www.hotelsirotorgiano.it; Via Giordano Bruno 16; meals €20-30; ◷noon-2.30pm & 7-9.30pm) Overflowing with regulars, this convivial, picture-plastered restaurant is big on old-school charm. The mixed antipasti starter for two would feed a small family. Next, loosen a belt notch for gnocchi cooked in Rubesco wine sauce, and mains like wild boar stew and butter-soft steaks.

🛈 Getting There & Away

Umbria Mobilità (p577) *extraurbano* buses head to Perugia (€3, 30 minutes, nine daily).

Lago Trasimeno

A splash of inky blue on the hilly landscape, Lago Trasimeno is where Umbria spills over into Tuscany. Italy's fourth-largest lake is a prime spot if you want to tiptoe off the well-trodden trail for a spell and slip into the languid rhythm of lake life. Around this 128 sq km lake, silver-green olive groves, vines, woods of oak and cypress and sunflower fields frame castle-topped medieval towns, such as Castiglione del Lago and Passignano, which are draped along its shores like a daisy chain. A gentle and unhurried ambience hangs over the lake's trio of islands – Maggiore, Minore and Polvese – all wonderfully relaxing escapes.

Hannibal destroyed the Roman army here in 217 BC, and the lake's numerous fortifications attest to its strategic position and turbulent past.

◉ Sights & Activities

Dotted with nature reserves and crisscrossed with well-signposted trails, Lago Trasimeno begs outdoor escapades. For the inside scoop on activities from hiking and cycling to sailing and wine tasting, visit www.lagotrasimeno.co.uk.

Ask at any of the tourist offices around the lake or in Perugia for a booklet of walking and horse-riding tracks. Horse-riding centres offering beautiful hacks into the surrounding countryside include **Le Case Rosse dei Montebuono** (☎075 528 85 56; www.lecaserosse.com; Località Case Sparse 15), inland to the southeast of the lake.

One of the best places to base yourself is **Castiglione del Lago**, which has a fine beach where you can lounge, swim, windsurf, or hire a pedalo or kayak, as well as a sprinkling of cultural attractions. A covered passageway connects **Palazzo della Corgna** (Piazza Gramsci; adult/reduced incl Rocca del Leone €5/4; ◷9am-7pm, shorter hours winter), a 16th-century ducal palace housing frescoes by Giovanni Antonio Pandolfi and Salvio Savini, with the 13th-century **Rocca del Leone** fortress, a stellar example of medieval military architecture.

The lake's main inhabited island – **Isola Maggiore**, near Passignano – was reputedly a favourite with St Francis. The hilltop **Chiesa di San Michele Arcangelo** contains a crucifixion painted by Bartolomeo Caporali dating from around 1460. You can also visit the mostly uninhabited island and environmental lab at **Isola Polvese** on a day trip with Fattoria Il Poggio.

🛌 Sleeping

★ **Fattoria Il Poggio**   HOSTEL €
(☎075 965 95 50; www.fattoriaisolapolvese.com; Isola Polvese; dm/d/apt/q €20/56/80/90, meals €15; ◷Mar-Oct, reception closed 3-7pm; @🛜🏊♿) It's a HI youth hostel but you'd never know it. Nestled in gardens on the tranquil islet of Isola Polvese, this eco-minded farmstead has bright, spick-and-span rooms and gorgeous lake views. If you don't mind catching the ferry back to the hostel by 7pm, you'll be rewarded handsomely with a family style meal prepared with organic produce and homegrown herbs. Buffet breakfast costs €5.

The people who run the place are lovely. If you want to go canoeing or fishing, learn about macrobiotic cooking or sign up for a reiki or yoga course, just say the word.

La Casa sul Lago   HOSTEL €
(☎075 840 00 42; www.lacasasullago.com; Via del Lavoro 25, Torricella di Magione; dm €18, r per person €25-30, meals €15; 🅿@🛜♿) This is one of central Italy's top-rated hostels. The private rooms could be in a three-star hotel, and guests have access to every amenity known to hostelkind: bicycles and wi-fi (both free!), games, home-cooked meals, an outdoor pool and a garden with hammocks strung between the trees for whiling away a lazy afternoon – all within 50m of the lake.

DON'T MISS

WINE & OLIVE OIL TASTING

Vines and olives thrive in the microclimate of Lago Trasimeno, which yields some top-quality DOC (Denominazione di origine controllata) red and white wines, as well as gold-green DOP (Denominazione d'origine protetta) olive oils. You can pick up a bottle anywhere, but you'll get more out of a tasting at one of the *cantine* (wineries) that open their doors to visitors.

Cantine Giorgio Lungarotti (☑ 075 988 66 49; http://lungarotti.it; Viale Giorgio Lungarotti 2; ⏱ 9am-12.30pm & 3-6pm Mon-Fri, 9.30am-1pm & 3.30-6pm Sat) The Lungarottis, who operate most of the wineries around here, are the closest thing Umbria has to a ruling noble family these days. At their Torgiano wine estate, Cantine Giorgio Lungarotti, you can take a spin of their cellars and taste the fruits of their labours. A basic €12 tasting gets you three wines: a full-bodied Rubino red, a citrusy, straw-coloured Torre di Giano white and Grifone, a fresh, floral rosé.

For the more expensive tastings (€18 to €25), they'll crack open some of their best bottles. All tastings are accompanied by Umbrian bread and extra-virgin olive oil. Stock up on Lungarotti wine, olive oil, balsamic vinegar and brandy in the *enoteca* (wine bar).

Strada del Vino Colli del Trasimeno (☑ 075 84 74 11; www.stradadelvinotrasimeno.it) The Strada del Vino (Wine Route) of the Colli del Trasimeno (Trasimeno Hill district) is made for slow touring, taking in *cantine* and cellars offering tastings (you almost always need to call ahead), farms and *agriturismi* (farm stay accommodation), where you can sleep off the overindulgence. Visit the website for the low-down on five mapped wine-related itineraries, or pick up a brochure at the tourist office in Castiglione del Lago.

Il Torrione
B&B €

(☑ 075 95 32 36; www.iltorrionetrasimeno.com; Via delle Mura 4, Castiglione del Lago; s €55, d & apt €80) Romance abounds at this artistically minded tranquil retreat. Each room is decorated with artworks painted by the owner, and a private flower-filled garden – complete with a 16th-century tower and chaise longues from which to watch the sun set – overlooks the lake. Rent the tower room (up a flight of pirate-ship stairs) for an intimate private apartment.

Franco is your kind host; he will pick you up/drop you off at the station for free on request.

La Torre
HOTEL €

(☑ 075 95 16 66; www.latorretrasimeno.com; Via Vittorio Emanuele 50, Castiglione del Lago; s €40-70, d €45-100; ❄ 🐾) Housed in a lovingly renovated, whitewashed *palazzo* in Castiglione's historic centre, La Torre extends a warm family welcome. The spotless, old-style rooms are decorated in florals and a chalk box of pastels. Breakfast is delicious but costs €6 extra.

Camping Badiaccia
CAMPGROUND €

(☑ 075 965 90 97; www.badiaccia.com; Via Pratovecchio 1, Badiaccia; camping 2 people, car & tent €23-27; 🅿 @ 🐾 🐟 🐾) Right on the lakefront, this tree-shaded campground is kid heaven, with a playground, pizzeria, tennis courts, a private beach, two pools, mini golf and loads of activities to keep the *bambini* (and their parents) amused. Kayaks, bikes and pedalos are available for hire.

✗ Eating

Specialities of the Trasimeno area include *fagiolina* (little white beans), carp in *porchetta* (cooked in a wood oven with garlic, fennel and herbs) and *tegemacchio,* a kind of soupy stew of the best varieties of local fish, cooked in olive oil, white wine and herbs.

DivinPeccato
TRATTORIA €€

(☑ 075 968 01 18; www.ristorantedivinpeccato. com; Via Trasimeno 95, Panicarola; meals €30-35; ⏱ 12.30-2pm & 7.30-9.30pm Thu-Sun, 7.30-9.30pm Mon & Tue) Chef Nicola works culinary magic at this wonderful trattoria, well worth the 10km trek south of Castiglione del Lago. Homemade bread is an appetising lead to a menu fizzing with seasonal oomph – think duck breast in strawberry sauce, and wild boar and ravioli in porcini sauce. Sommelier Mirko pairs the food with fine Umbrian wines drawn from the cellar. Perfection.

Ristorante Monna Lisa
UMBRIAN €€

(☑ 075 95 10 71; www.ristorantemonnalisa.com; Via del Forte 2, Castiglione del Lago; meals €30-35; ⏱ 12.30-2.30pm & 7.30-10.30pm Thu-Tue) You

DETOUR TO DERUTA

Deruta's pride and joy is majolica ceramics. The blue-and-yellow metallic-oxide glazing technique imported from Majorca in the 15th century has been the mainstay of the local industry ever since.

For the best-quality stuff, eschew factory mass productions, which are cheaper and lower quality, in favour of the real deal at smaller workshops rooted in centuries-old tradition.

At **Maioliche Nulli** (☑ 075 97 23 84; www.maiolichenulli.com; Via Tiberina 142; ☉ 9am-8pm), Rolando Nulli creates each item by hand, while his brother Goffredo finishes them with intricate paintings, specialising in classic medieval designs. If they're not busy and you ask nicely in Italian, they might even bring you downstairs and teach you to throw a bowl on the wheel.

Get a taste for the genuine article and trace the history of pottery in Deruta from the 14th to 20th centuries at the **Museo Regionale della Ceramica** (Largo San Francesco; adult/reduced €5/4; ☉ 10.30am-1pm & 3-6pm Wed-Sun), housed in the former Franciscan convent.

L'Antico Forziere (☑ 075 972 43 14; www.anticoforziere.it; Via della Rocca 2; s/d/ste €75/100/150, incl half board €100/170/230, meals €30-40; ☉ restaurant 12.30-2pm & 8-10pm Tue-Sun; P ❋ ☎ ☎ ❸), a 17th-century farmhouse turned stylishly rustic *agriturismo* (farm stay accommodation), resides in the dozy hamlet of *Casalina*, just south of Deruta. Here twin-brother celebrity chefs Stefano and Andrea Rodella wow foodies with their culinary high-wire theatrics. Their inventive menu brims with season-inspired, artistically assembled showstoppers like hare ravioli with beet tops and zest of orange, and saddle of suckling pig marinated in bitter cocoa and served with crispy artichokes – all washed down with excellent wines.

Buses connect the town with Perugia (€3.60, 30 minutes, 13 daily).

can imagine Mona Lisa giving a wry smile of approval to the food served at this intimate, art-strewn restaurant in the heart of town. You, too, will be smiling about specialities like *fagiolina*, carpaccio of wild boar on rocket and rich stews prepared with Trasimeno lake fish. The *spaghetti alle vongole* (spaghetti with clams) deserves a gold star, too.

La Cantina   UMBRIAN €€
(☑ 075 965 24 63; Via Vittorio Emanuele 91, Castiglione del Lago; meals €20-30; ☉ noon-11.30pm) Sunset is the prime time for lake viewing from the flowery terrace of this old-town restaurant, housed in a converted 17th-century olive mill. A fire warms the brick-vaulted interior in the cooler months. It does terrific wood-oven pizza for pocket-money prices, as well as local fare like trout with *fagiolina*.

❶ Information

Tourist Office (☑ 075 965 24 84; info@iat. castiglione-del-lago-pg.it; Piazza Mazzini 10, Castiglione del Lago; ☉ 10.30am-1pm & 3.30-7pm Mon-Fri, 9am-1pm & 3.30-7pm Sat, 9am-1pm Sun) Advises on *agriturismi* and activities

like cycling and water sports, and has an impressive collection of maps.

❶ Getting There & Around

BICYCLE
You can hire bikes at most campgrounds or at **Cicli Valentini** (☑ 075 95 16 63; www. ciclivalentini.it; Via Firenze 68b, Castiglione del Lago; per half/full day €8/10, per week €49; ☉ 9am-1pm & 3.30-8pm Mon-Sat).

BUS
Umbria Mobilità (p577) buses link Perugia with Passignano (€4.20, one hour, 10 daily) and Castiglione del Lago (€6.10, one hour, nine daily).

CAR & MOTORCYCLE
Two major highways skirt the lake: the SS71, which heads from Chiusi to Arezzo on the west side (in Tuscany); and SS75bis, which crosses the north end of the lake, heading from the A1 in Tuscany to Perugia.

FERRY
Umbria Mobilità (p577) ferry services run from late March to late September. Hourly ferries head from San Feliciano to Isola Polvese (€6 return, 10 minutes), Tuoro to Isola Maggiore (€6 return, 10 minutes), Castiglione del Lago to

ALL SAINTS

As saintly performances go, Umbria has a star-studded cast. Besides being the much-venerated birthplace of St Francis, the region has given rise to two other greats: St Benedict and the Casanova of the saint world, St Valentine. St Benedict, founder of the Benedictine rule and western monasticism, was born in 480 AD in **Norcia**. St Valentine, meanwhile, was a bishop from **Terni**, allegedly martyred on 14 February 273 AD. His remains are entombed in the **Basilica di San Valentino**, now a much-loved wedding venue and the scene of a great feast on St Valentine's Day. Want to impress someone special? You could draw back your cupid bow and bring them here for a romantic weekend – it sure beats a bunch of petrol station roses. For inspiration, visit www.sanvalentinoterni.it.

Isola Maggiore (€8.10 return, 30 minutes) and Passignano to Isola Maggiore (€7.30 return, 25 minutes). Ferries stop running around 7pm.

TRAIN

Services run roughly hourly from Perugia to Passignano (€3, 28 minutes) and Castiglione del Lago (€4.40 to €12.60, 65 minutes to 1½ hours), and once daily to Torricella (€2.40, 25 minutes).

Todi

POP 16,900

A collage of soft-stone houses, *palazzi* and belfries pasted to a hillside, Todi looks freshly minted for a fairy tale. Wandering its steeply climbing backstreets is like playing a game of medieval snakes and ladders. The pace of life inches along, keeping time with the wildflowers and vines that seasonally bloom and ripen in the valley below.

Like rings around a tree, Todi's history can be read in layers: the interior walls show Todi's Etruscan and even Umbrian influence, the middle walls are an enduring example of Roman know-how, and the 'new' medieval walls boast of Todi's economic stability and prominence during the Middle Ages.

⊙ Sights

Piazza del Popolo   PIAZZA

Just try to walk through the Piazza del Popolo without feeling compelled to sit on the medieval building steps and write a postcard home. The 13th-century Palazzo del Capitano links to the Palazzo del Popolo to create what is now the Museo Civico e Pinacoteca Comunale. The **cathedral** (☏ 075 894 30 41; Piazza del Popolo; ⊙ 10am-1pm & 3.30-6pm Mon-Sat, to 7.30pm Sun), at the northwestern end of the square, has a magnificent rose window.

Chiesa di Santa Maria della Consolazione   CHURCH

(Via della Consolazione; ⊙ 9.30am-12.30pm & 3-6.30pm Wed-Mon, shorter hours winter) The postcard home you've just written most likely features Todi's famed church, the late-Renaissance masterpiece Chiesa di Santa Maria della Consolazione. Inside, architecture fans can admire its geometrically perfect Greek cross design, and outside, its soaring cupola-topped dome.

Museo Civico e Pinacoteca Comunale   MUSEUM

(Piazza del Popolo; adult/reduced €4/2.50; ⊙ 10am-1.30pm & 3-6pm Tue-Sun) Housed in the striking Palazzo del Capitano, this museum features an elegant triple window. It holds a fine (if hardly overwhelming) collection of paintings, and a rather more successful archaeological section with lots of old coins and ceramics.

Tempio di San Fortunato   CHURCH

(Piazza Umberto 1; ⊙ 9am-1pm & 3-7pm Tue-Sun, shorter hours winter) The lofty medieval Tempio di San Fortunato has frescoes by Masolino da Panicale, and contains the tomb of Beato Jacopone, Todi's beloved patron saint. Inside, make it a point to climb the **Campanile di San Fortunato** (adult/reduced €2/1.50; ⊙ 10am-1pm & 3-6.30pm Tue-Sun), where views of the hills and castles surrounding Todi await.

✦ Festivals & Events

Todi Festival   CULTURAL

(www.todifestival.it) Held for 10 days each August, this festival brings together a mix of classical and jazz concerts, theatre, ballet and art exhibitions.

NARNI – THE MAGICAL HEART OF ITALY

Like Greenwich or the North Pole, Narni is a place best known for where it is, almost slap-bang at the geographical centre of Italy. You can walk to a stone marking the exact spot just outside the town. But Narni has a lot more going for it than merely being the answer to a trivia question. It boasts one of the finest medieval town centres in Umbria, with a collection of churches, piazzas, *palazzi* and fortresses that are quite magical – and fittingly so, given that CS Lewis used the Roman name for the town (plucked at random from an ancient atlas) for his own fictional magical kingdom of Narnia.

The town lies 21km south of Todi, just east of the A1 autostrada (from the south take the Magliano Sabina exit; from the north the Orte exit) and is well served by buses from Terni (€3, 30 minutes) and Orvieto (€6.90, 1½ hours).

🛏 Sleeping

San Lorenzo Tre   B&B €
(☑ 075 894 45 55; www.sanlorenzo3.it; Via San Lorenzo 3; d €75-110, ste €130-150; @) Five generations of the same family have lived at this 17th-century abode. Awaiting guests are rooms full of character, with polished brick floors, delicately painted beams and carefully chosen antiques. There's no TV, but there are books to browse, in keeping with the blissfully laid-back vibe. Breakfasts are home-cooked and the garden terrace has magical views. There's no lift.

★ Il Ghiottone Umbro   B&B €€
(☑ 075 894 84 44, 339 1321509; www.ilghiottone umbro.com; Frazione San Giorgio 45, Vocabolo Molino; r €95-120) What a delight! Danish duo Thomas and Lisbeth bring together old-stone farmhouse charm with Scandi cool at their gorgeous boutique B&B. The rooms combine historic features like beams and tiles with bursts of original detail: canopy beds, free-standing tubs and Nordic designer furnishings. Breakfast is a second-to-none spread of muesli, fresh fruits and juices, homemade pastries and other imaginative treats.

Thomas and Lisbeth are passionate cooks and bring their love of seasonal, regional food to their cookery courses, which range from three (€550) to six (€1110) days.

Fonte Cesia   BOUTIQUE HOTEL €€
(☑ 075 894 37 37; www.fontecesia.it; Via Lorenzo Leonj 3; s €90-120, d €90-145, ste €175-220; P❄@) Just south of the main square, this renovated 17th-century *palazzo* has great old-world charm. The rooms are a bit small, but come with elegant antique touches, and some have views of the surrounding hills. The suites step up the romance – one has a jacuzzi tub, another a canopy bed.

🍴 Eating

Bar Pianegiani   GELATERIA €
(Corso Cavour 40; ⊙6am-midnight Tue-Sun) Around 50 years of tradition has created the world's most perfect gelato. Try the black cherry (*spagnola*) or hazelnut (*nocciola*).

Vineria San Fortunato   UMBRIAN €
(☑ 075 372 11 80; www.vineriasanfortunato.it; Piazza Umberto I 5; meals €25; ⊙10am-2am Thu-Tue) Wine lovers are in their element at this slick, vaulted wine bar, where Umbrian and Tuscan wines are perfectly matched with delicious tasting platters of *salumi e formaggi* (cold meats and cheeses) and season-driven day specials, simple as tender lamb and olive stew and *strangozzi* pasta with asparagus. The little terrace overlooks the Tempio di San Fortunato. *Aperitivo* is from 6pm to 8pm.

Pizzeria Ristorante Cavour   PIZZA €€
(☑ 075 894 37 30; Corso Cavour 21; meals €20-30; ⊙noon-3.30pm & 7-11pm) If it's a fine day, bypass the brick-vaulted interior and head straight outside to the terrace for towering views. Try the thin-crust pizza or house specialities like fettuccine with goose *ragù*.

ℹ Information

Post Office (Piazza Garibaldi 4; ⊙8.20am-1.35pm Mon-Fri, 8.20am-12.35pm Sat)
Tourist Office (☑ 075 894 25 26; www.regioneumbria.eu; Piazza del Popolo 38; ⊙9.30am-1pm & 3-6pm Mon-Sat, 10am-1pm Sun) Helpful tourist office on the main square.

ℹ Getting There & Away

Umbria Mobilità (p577) operates buses between Todi and Perugia (€6.90, 1¼ hours, nine daily).

By car, Todi is easily reached on the SS-3bis-E45, which runs between Perugia and Terni, or take the Orvieto turn-off from A1 (the Milan–Rome–Naples route).

Trains run to Perugia (€5.10, 50 minutes, 18 daily). Although the train station is 3km away, city bus C (€2, eight minutes) coincides with arriving trains, and operates every other hour on Sunday.

Assisi

POP 27,400

As if cupped in celestial hands, with the plains spreading picturesquely below and Monte Subasio rearing steep and wooded above, the mere sight of Assisi in the rosy glow of dusk is enough to send pilgrims' souls spiralling to heaven. It is at this hour, when the pitter-patter of daytripper footsteps have faded and the town is shrouded in saintly silence, that the true spirit of St Francis of Assisi, born here in 1181, can be felt most keenly.

◉ Sights

★ **Basilica di San Francesco**　　　BASILICA
(www.sanfrancescoassisi.org; Piazza di San Francesco; ⊙upper church 8.30am-6.45pm, lower church & tomb 6am-6.45pm) FREE Visible for miles around, the Basilica di San Francesco is the crowning glory of Assisi's Unesco World Heritage ensemble. It's divided into an upper church, the **Basilica Superiore**, with a celebrated cycle of Giotto frescoes, and beneath, the lower older **Basilica Inferiore**, where you'll find frescoes by Cimabue, Pietro Lorenzetti and Simone Martini. Also here, in the **Cripta di San Francesco** is St Francis' elaborate and monumental tomb.

The Basilica Superiore, which was built immediately after the lower church between 1230 and 1253, is home to one of Italy's most famous works of art – a series of 28 frescoes depicting the life of St Francis. Vibrant and colourful, they are generally attributed to a young Giotto, though some art historians contest this, claiming that stylistic discrepancies suggest that they were created by several different artists.

From outside the upper church, stairs lead down to the Romanesque Basilica Inferiore, whose half-light and architectural restraint beautifully embody the ascetic, introspective spirit of Franciscan life. Divine works by Giotto and fellow Sienese and Florentine masters Cimabue, Pietro Lorenzetti and Simone Martini decorate the main body of the church and side-chapels, representing an artistic weathervane for stylistic developments across the ages.

The basilica has its own **information office** (☏075 819 00 84; www.sanfrancescoassisi.org; Piazza di San Francesco 2; ⊙9am-noon & 2-5.30pm Mon-Sat), opposite the entrance to the lower church, where you can schedule an hour-long tour in English or Italian, led by a resident Franciscan friar. To avoid disappointment at busy times, either call or email ahead (booking@sanfrancescoassisi.org).

Rocca Maggiore　　　　　　　　FORT
(Via della Rocca; adult/reduced €5.50/3.50; ⊙10am-7pm, shorter hours winter) Dominating the city is the massive 14th-century Rocca Maggiore, an oft-expanded, pillaged and rebuilt hill-fortress offering 360-degree views of Perugia to the north and the surrounding valleys below. Walk up winding staircases and claustrophobic passageways to reach the archer slots that served Assisians as they went medieval on Perugia.

Basilica di Santa Chiara　　　BASILICA
(Piazza Santa Chiara; ⊙6.30am-noon & 2-7pm summer, to 6pm winter) Built in a 13th-century Romanesque style, with steep ramparts

Assisi

Assisi

Basilica di San Francesco

8 | 1 | Basilica di San Francesco
Piazza Superiore di San Francesco

i | Basilica di San Francesco Information Office

14 | Via San Giacomo

18

6

7

5 | i

3

9 | Corso Mazzini
Via Acro dei Priori

17 | Via San Rufino
19 | Via S Gabriele dell'Addolorata

4 | Piazza San Rufino

11 | Via Eremo delle Carceri

Piazza Matteotti
APM Bus Station

10 | Viale Umberto I
13 | Via Galeazzo Alessi
APM (250m)

2 | Piazza Santa Chiara
Via S Chiara

12 | Via Sant'Antonio
Via Sant'Agnese

15 | Via Portica
16 | Via B da Quintavalle

Piazza del Comune
Via Macelli Vecchi

Piazza Garibaldi
Via Antonio Crisofani

Piazza Vescovado

Via San Paolo
Via Aluigi
Via Capobove
Via S Maria delle Rose
Via del Colle
Via della Rocca

Via Giotto
Via Brizi
Via San Croce
Via Metastasio
Via San Francesco
Via Giorgetti
Via Fontebella
Via del Fosso Cupo
Via Don Giovanni Rossi
Via Borgo San Pietro

Viale Vittorio Emanuele

Via S Apollinare
Via Porta Moiano

Via D Stella
V Frate Elia
Porta San Pietro

Piazza Unità d'Italia
Intercity Bus Station

Viale G Marconi

Basilica di Santa Maria degli Angeli (4km)
Ostello della Pace (2.5km)

Chiesa di San Damiano (1.5km)

Alla Madonna del Piatto (8km)
Via Villamena
Via Porta Perlici

Eremo delle Carceri (3.5km)

Vicolo Bovi

200 m
0.1 miles

CHURCH TOUR

Basilica di San Francesco

➡ **Length** 1½ hours

➡ **See Basilica di San Francesco** (p594)

Entering the Romanesque lower church, immediately to your left is the Cappella di San Martino, bearing the imprint of Sienese genius Simone Martini, whose 10-piece fresco cycle (1313–1318) spells out the life and deeds of St Martin of Tours. Pietro Lorenzetti's frescoes depicting The Passion of Christ (1320) dance across the walls of the left transept, while Cimabue's Madonna Enthroned with Child, St Francis and Four Angels (1289) will hold you captive in the right transept. The vault above the high altar showcases the quadriptych allegorical marvel of the Quattro Vele (1315–20), an ode to St Francis' virtues of poverty, chastity and obedience, alongside a fresco showing the saint's apotheosis. Descend to the crypt to the Tomb of St Francis. Hidden for almost 600 years, it was discovered in 1818 following a 52-day dig, and painstakingly restored in 2011.

Steps lead from the courtyard to the upper church, the brighter twin of the two, lit by a cosmatesque rose window. In the nave draw your gaze heavenwards to cross-rib vaults shimmering with tiny stars like a midnight sky. The walls are a giant canvas for one of the world's greatest works of art: the 28-fresco cycle Life of St Francis (1297–1300), widely attributed to Florentine master Giotto, though this is still a bone of contention for art historians. Contemplate emotive works such as the *Renunciation of Worldly Goods*, *Miracle of the Spring* and *Death and Ascension of St Francis*. Painted in the spirit of artistic devotion, they are a fascinating window on the life of the poverty-preaching saint. Above them, frescoes depicting scenes from the Old and New Testament unfold, from the *Creation of the World* through to the *Three Marys at the Sepulchre*. Decay and oxidation have reduced Cimabue's frescoes (1280) in the apse and transepts to ghostly silhouettes, rendering them all the more enigmatic; The Crucifixion shows St Francis kneeling below the cross.

and a striking pink-and-white facade, this church is dedicated to St Clare, a spiritual contemporary of St Francis and founder of the Sorelle Povere di Santa Chiara (Order of the Poor Ladies), now known as the Poor Clares. She is buried in the church's crypt, alongside the Crocifisso di San Damiano, a Byzantine cross before which St Francis was praying when he heard from God in 1205.

Basilica di Santa Maria degli Angeli   CHURCH

(Santa Maria degli Angeli; ⏱ 6.15am-12.50pm & 2.30-7.30pm) That enormous domed church you can see as you approach Assisi along the Tiber Valley is the 16th-century Basilica di Santa Maria degli Angeli, the seventh largest church in the world, some 4km west and several hundred metres further down the hill from old Assisi. Built between 1565 and 1685, its vast ornate confines house the tiny, humble Porziuncola Chapel, where St Francis first took refuge having found his vocation and given up his worldly goods,

and which is generally regarded as the place where the Franciscan movement started. St Francis died at the site of the Cappella del Transito on 3 October 1226.

Eremo delle Carceri   RELIGIOUS SITE

(⏱ 6.30am-7pm summer, to 6pm winter) FREE In around 1205 St Francis chose these caves above Assisi as his hermitage, where he could retire to contemplate spiritual matters and be at one with nature. The *carceri* (isolated places, or 'prisons') along Monte Subasio's forested slopes are as peaceful today as in St Francis' time, even though they're now surrounded by various religious buildings.

Take a contemplative walk or picnic under the oaks. It's a 4km drive (or walk) east of Assisi, and a dozen nearby hiking trails are well signposted.

Chiesa di San Damiano   CHURCH

(Via San Damiano; ⏱ 10am-noon & 2-6pm summer, to 4.30pm winter) It's a 1.5km olive-tree-lined stroll southeast of the centre to the church where St Francis first heard the voice of God and where he wrote his *Canticle of the Creatures*. The serene surroundings are popular with pilgrims.

Foro Romano　ARCHAEOLOGICAL SITE
(Roman Forum; Via Portica; adult/reduced €4/2.50, with Rocca Maggiore €8/5; ⏰10am-1pm & 2.30-6pm summer, to 5pm winter) On Piazza del Comune, just around the corner from the tourist office, is the entrance to the town's partially excavated Roman Forum, while on the piazza's northern side is the well-preserved facade of a 1st-century Roman temple, the **Tempio di Minerva** (Temple of Minerva; ⏰7.30am-noon & 2-7pm Mon-Sat, 8.30am-noon & 2-7pm Sun) FREE, hiding a rather uninspiring 17th-century church.

Duomo di San Rufino　CHURCH
(Piazza San Rufino; ⏰8am-1pm & 2-7pm summer, to 6pm winter) The 13th-century Romanesque church, remodelled by Galeazzo Alessi in the 16th century, contains the fountain where St Francis and St Clare were baptised. The facade is festooned with grotesque figures and fantastic animals.

Chiesa Nuova　CHURCH
(Piazza Chiesa Nuova; ⏰7am-12.30pm & 3-7pm summer, to 6pm winter) Just southeast of the Piazza del Comune, this domed church is a peaceful place for contemplation. It was built by King Philip III of Spain in the 1600s on the spot reputed to be the house of St Francis' family. A bronze statue of the saint's parents stands outside.

🏃 Activities

To really feel the spirituality of Assisi, do as St Francis did and make the pilgrimage into the surrounding wooded hills. Many make the trek to **Eremo delle Carceri** or **Santuario di San Damiano** on foot. The tourist office has several maps, including a route that follows in St Francis' footsteps to Gubbio (18km). A popular spot for hikers is nearby **Monte Subasio**. Local bookshops sell walking and mountain-biking guides and maps for the area.

Bicycle rentals are available at **Angelucci Andrea Cicli Riparazione Noleggio** (☎075 804 25 50; www.angeluccicicli.it; Via Risorgimento 54a; bike rental per hr/day €5/20) in Assisi's suburb of Santa Maria degli Angeli.

🎊 Festivals & Events

The **Festa di San Francesco** falls on 3 and 4 October and is the main religious event in the city. **Settimana Santa** (Easter Week) is celebrated with processions and performances.

Festa di Calendimaggio　CULTURAL
(www.calendimaggiodiassisi.com) This festival takes a joyous leap into spring with flamboyant costumed parades, jousting and other medieval fun. It starts the first Wednesday after 1 May.

🛏 Sleeping

Keep in mind that in peak periods such as Easter, August and September, and during the Festa di San Francesco, you will need to book accommodation well in advance. The tourist office has a list of private rooms, religious institutions (of which there are 17), flats and *agriturismi* in and around Assisi.

⭐ **Alla Madonna del Piatto**　AGRITURISMO €
(☎075 819 90 50; www.incampagna.com; Via Petrata 37; d €85-105; ⏰Mar-Nov; P🐾) 🌿 Waking up to views of meadows and olive groves sweeping up to Assisi is bound to put a spring in your step at this ecofriendly *agriturismo*, less than 15 minutes' drive from the basilica. Each of the six rooms has been designed with care, love and character, with wrought-iron beds, antique furnishings and intricate handmade fabrics.

If you can tear yourself away from the vine-draped terrace, hook onto one of the intimate cooking classes, which Letizia runs (in Italian or English) twice a week. Start the day in local markets and finish it off with a feast of your own creation. Six-hour classes cost €120 per person. There's a minimum two-night stay. It's 8km north of Assisi – take the SS444 and turn left when you see the sign for Petrata.

St Anthony's Guesthouse　B&B €
(☎075 81 25 42; atoneassisi@tiscali.it; Via Galeazzo Alessi 10; s/d/tr €45/65/85; ⏰Mar–mid-Nov; P) Look for the iron statue of St Francis feeding the birds and you've found your Assisian oasis – a peaceful convent run by sweet sisters. Rooms are spartan but welcoming and six have balconies with breathtaking views. Olive-tree-shaded gardens and an 800-year-old breakfast room make this a heavenly choice. There is a two-night minimum stay and an 11pm curfew.

The Saint of Assisi

That someone could found a successful movement based on peace, love, compassion, charity and humility in any age is remarkable; that Francis Bernardone was able to do it in war-torn 13th-century Umbria was nothing short of a miracle. But then again, in his early years Francis was very much a man of the times – and anything but saintly.

Not-So-Humble Beginnings

Born in Assisi in 1181, the son of a wealthy cloth merchant and a French noblewoman, Francis was a worldly chap: he studied Latin, spoke passable French, had a burning fascination with troubadours and spent his youth carousing. In 1202 Francis joined a military expedition to Perugia and was taken prisoner for nearly a year until his father paid ransom. Following a spate of ill health, he enlisted in the army of the Count of Brienne and was Puglia-bound in 1205 when a holy vision sparked his spiritual awakening.

Life & Death

Much to the shock, horror and ridicule of his rich, pleasure-seeking friends, Francis decided to renounce all his possessions in order to live a humble, 'primitive' life in imitation of Christ, preaching and helping the poor. He travelled widely around Italy and beyond, performing miracles such as curing the sick, communicating with animals, spending hermit-like months praying in a cave, and founding monasteries. Before long, his wise words and good deeds had attracted a faithful crowd of followers.

St Francis asked his followers to bury him in Assisi on a hill known as Colle

d'Inferno (Hell Hill), where people were executed at the gallows until the 13th century, so as to be in keeping with Jesus, who had died on the cross among criminals and outcasts.

Saintly Spots

Today various places claim links with St Francis, including Greccio in Lazio where he supposedly created the first (live) nativity scene in 1223; Bevagna in Umbria where he is said to have preached to the birds; and La Verna in Tuscany where he received the stigmata shortly before his death at the age of 44. He was canonised just two years later, after which the business of 'selling' St Francis began in earnest. Modern Assisi, with its glorious churches and thriving souvenir industry, seems an almost wilfully ironic comment on Francis' ascetic and spiritual values.

TOP ST FRANCIS SITES

➡ **Assisi** (p594) His home town and the site of his birth and death, his hermitage, his chapel, the first Franciscan monastery and the giant basilica containing his tomb.

➡ **Gubbio** (p602) Where the saint supposedly brokered a deal between the townsfolk and a man-eating wolf – Francis tamed the wolf with the promise that it would be fed daily.

➡ **Rome** Francis was given permission by Pope Innocent III to found the Franciscan order at the Basilica di San Giovanni in Laterano (p109).

1. View of Assisi
2. Basilica di San Giovanni in Laterano (p109), Rome
3. Interior of the Basilica di San Francesco (p594), Assisi

JON ARNOLD IMAGES/GETTY IMAGES ©

LONELY PLANET IMAGES/GETTY IMAGES ©

SIR FRANCIS CANKER/GETTY IMAGES ©

Ostello della Pace
HOSTEL €

(☑ 075 81 67 67; www.assisihostel.com; Via Valecchie 177; dm €18, d €40-50; ☺ 1 Mar-8 Nov & 27 Dec-6 Jan; P@☎) Snug below the city walls and housed in a beautifully converted 17th-century farmhouse, this hostel is a charmer. The dorms and handful of private rooms are kept spick and span and the well-tended gardens have magical views of Assisi, crowned by the dome of its famous basilica. Find it just off the road coming in from Santa Maria degli Angeli.

Hotel Ideale
B&B €€

(☑ 075 81 35 70; www.hotelideale.it; Piazza Matteotti 1; s €60-100, d €110-150; P❄☎❄) Ideal indeed, this welcoming family-run B&B sits plumb on Piazza Matteotti. Many of the bright, high-ceilinged rooms open onto balconies with uplifting views over the rooftops to the valley beyond. Breakfast is done properly, with fresh pastries, fruit, cold cuts and frothy cappuccino, and is served in the garden when the weather's fine.

Hotel Alexander
HOTEL €€

(☑ 075 81 61 90; www.hotelalexanderassisi.it; Piazza Chiesa Nuova 6; s €60-80, d €99-140; ❄☎) On a small cobbled piazza by the Chiesa Nuova, Hotel Alexander offers nine spacious rooms and a communal terrace with wonderful rooftop views. The modern decor – pale wooden floors and earthy brown tones – contrasts well with the wood-beamed ceilings and carefully preserved antiquity all around.

Nun Assisi
BOUTIQUE HOTEL €€€

(☑ 075 815 51 50; www.nunassisi.com; s €240-390, d €290-440, ste €330-750; P@❄❄) This former convent has been reborn as a super-stylish boutique hotel, with a clean, modern aesthetic and whisper-quiet gardens planted with olive trees. Stone arches and beams provide flair in pared-down rooms with virginal white walls and flat-screen TVs. The restaurant puts a contemporary spin on seasonal Umbrian fare, and the gorgeous subterranean spa is snuggled within 1st-century Roman ruins.

Residenza D'Epoca San Crispino
HISTORIC HOTEL €€€

(☑ 075 815 51 24; www.assisibenessere.it; Via Sant'Agnese 11; r €180-220; @❄) Big on medieval charm, this 14th-century mansion has soul-stirring views of Assisi from its gardens and a free shuttle whisking you to its private spa. Each generously sized suite is different, but all have oodles of character, with original vaulting and eye-catching features such as fireplaces, four-poster beds and antique trappings. Basilica di Santa Chiara is close by. Breakfast is included.

🍴 Eating & Drinking

Piadina Biologica
SANDWICHES €

(Via Giotto 3; ☺ 9.30am-8pm Mon-Sat) 🍴 Stop by for tasty and wholesome organic *piadine* (flat-bread sandwiches). It even does organic wine from €2 per glass.

Pizzeria da Andrea
PIZZA €

(Via San Rufino 26; pizza & snacks €1.30-2.50; ☺ 8.30am-9pm) The go-to place on the square for perfectly thin, crisp *pizza al taglio* (by the slice) and *torta al testo* (filled Umbrian flat bread) for a fistful of change.

★ Osteria Eat Out
UMBRIAN €€

(☑ 075 81 31 63; www.nunassisi.com; Via Eremo delle Carceri 1a; meals €35-50; ☺ 12.30-2.30pm & 7.30-10.30pm Tue-Sun) With such astounding views and minimalist-chic interiors, you might expect Nun Assisi's glass-fronted restaurant to prefer style over substance. Not so. Polished service and an exciting wine list are well matched with seasonal Umbrian cuisine flavoured with home-grown herbs. Dishes such as *umbricelli* pasta (spaghetti's Umbrian sister) with fresh truffle and fillet of Chianina beef are big on flavour and easy on the eye.

Osteria dei Priori
UMBRIAN €€

(☑ 075 81 21 49; Via Giotto 4; meals €25-35, 2-course day menu €18; ☺ 12.30-2.30pm & 7.30-10pm Tue-Sun) This wonderfully cosy *osteria* believes wholeheartedly in sourcing the best local ingredients. Tables draped in white linen are gathered under brick vaults. Presuming you've booked ahead, you're in for quite a treat: Umbrian specialities like *norcina* (pasta in a creamy mushroom-sausage sauce) and rich wild-boar stew are brilliantly fresh, full of flavour and beautifully presented.

La Locanda del Podestà
UMBRIAN €€

(☑ 075 81 65 53; www.locandadelpodesta.it; Via San Giacomo 6; meals €20-30; ☺ noon-2.45pm & 7-9.30pm Thu-Tue) This inviting cubby hole of a restaurant is big on old-world charm, with low arches and stone walls. Distinctly Umbrian dishes such as *torta al testo* with prosciutto and truffle-laced *strangozzi* pasta are expertly matched with regional wines. Friendly service adds to the familiar vibe.

Ristorante Metastasio ITALIAN €€

(☑ 075 81 65 25; Via Metastasio 9; meals €25-35; ☺ noon-2.30pm & 7-9.30pm) Sunset makes the terrace of this restaurant a magnet – the valley below Assisi spreads picturesquely before you. The food is good, too, particularly spot-on pasta dishes such as pappardelle with porcini and wild boar.

Bibenda Assisi WINE BAR

(www.bibendaassisi.it; Via Nepis 9; ☺ 11.30am-11pm Wed-Mon; 🖃) Everyone has been singing the praises of this rustic-chic wine bar recently. Here you can try regional *vini* with tasting plates of local *salumi e formaggi*. Nila will talk you through the wine list.

❶ Information

Post Office (Porta San Pietro; ☺ 8.20am-1.45pm Mon-Fri, to 12.45pm Sat)

Tourist Office (☑ 075 813 86 80; www.assisi. regioneumbria.eu; Piazza del Comune 22; ☺ 9.30am-7pm daily summer, 8am-2pm & 3-6pm Mon-Fri, 9am-7pm Sat, 9am-6pm Sun winter) Stop by here for maps, leaflets and info on accommodation.

❶ Getting There & Around

BUS

Umbria Mobilità (p577) runs buses to Perugia (€4.20, 45 minutes, nine daily) and Gubbio (€6.10, 70 minutes, 11 daily) from Piazza Matteotti. **Sulga** (☑ 075 500 96 41; www.sulga.it) buses leave from Porta San Pietro for Naples (€25, 5¼ hours, one daily at 1.45pm) and Rome's Stazione Tiburtina (€18.50, 3¼ hours, two daily).

CAR & MOTORCYCLE

From Perugia take the SS75, exit at Ospedalicchio and follow the signs. In town, daytime parking is all but banned. Central car parks for the old town include Piazza Giovanni Paolo II (€1.25 per hour) and Piazza Matteotti (€1.30 per hour).

TAXI

For a taxi, call ☑ 075 81 31 00.

TRAIN

Assisi is on the Foligno–Terontola train line with regular services to Perugia (€2.40, 24 minutes, hourly). You can change at Terontola for Florence (€14.85 to €22.50, two to three hours, 11 daily) and at Foligno for Rome (€10 to €22, two to three hours, 14 daily). Assisi's train station is 4km west in Santa Maria degli Angeli; shuttle bus C (€1.30, 13 minutes) runs between the train station and Piazza Matteotti every 30 minutes. Buy tickets from the station *tabaccaio* (tobacconist's shop) or in town.

Spello

POP 8620

Sometimes it seems like it's just not possible for the next Umbrian town to be prettier than the last. And then you visit Spello, a higgledy-piggledy ensemble of honey-coloured houses spilling down a hillside, guarded by three stout Roman gates and chess-piece towers.

Come summer, the green-fingered locals try to outdo each other with their billowing hanging baskets and flowerpots, filling the streets with a riot of colour and scent.

⊙ Sights

A leisurely stroll is the best way to click into Spello's easygoing groove. Begin at Porta Consolare, which dates from Roman times, then head towards Piazza Matteotti, the heart of Spello.

Chiesa di Santa Maria Maggiore CHURCH

(Piazza Matteotti; ☺ 8.30am-12.30pm & 3-7pm, shorter hours winter) The impressive 12th-century Chiesa di Santa Maria Maggiore houses the town's real treat. In its **Cappella Baglioni**, Pinturicchio's beautiful frescoes of the life of Christ are in the right-hand corner as you enter. Even the floor, dating back to 1566, is a masterpiece.

Chiesa di Sant'Andrea CHURCH

(Piazza Matteotti; ☺ 8am-7pm) You can admire Pinturicchio's *Madonna with Child and Saints* in the gloomy Chiesa di Sant'Andrea.

Chiesa di San Severino RELIGIOUS SITE

(near the Arco Romano) To see the view of all views, head up past the Arco Romano to the Chiesa di San Severino. The active Capuchin monastery is closed to the public but its Romanesque facade is so stunning you'll have trouble deciding whether you'd like to gaze at its architecture or the bucolic countryside view below.

🎊 Festivals & Events

Corpus Domini RELIGIOUS

The people of Spello celebrate this feast in June (the Sunday 60 days after Easter) by skilfully decorating the main street with fresh flowers in colourful designs. Come on the Saturday evening before the Sunday procession to see the floral fantasies being laid out (from about 8.30pm). The Corpus procession begins at 11am on Sunday.

🛏 Sleeping

Agriturismo il Bastione
AGRITURISMO €

(☑ 340 5973402; www.agriturismoilbastione.it; Via Fontemonte 3; d €85-125, incl half-board €135-175; @ 🐾) What a delight this medieval farmstead is! On the slopes of 1290m Monte Subasio and surrounded by olive trees, the *agriturismo* has stirring views over patchwork plains and hills. The rooms and suites have a cosily rustic flavour, with wrought-iron beds, beams and stone walls. Dinner, served in the barrel-vaulted restaurant, is a feast of homegrown produce. You could easily hole up here for a day or two to cycle (mountain bikes are available), ride horses or hike through the Monte Subasio nature park to Assisi, around 6km distant.

La Residenza dei Cappuccini
B&B €

(☑ 331 4358591; www.residenzadeicappuccini.it; Via Cappuccini 5; d €65-88; 🕾) Up a steep, winding lane lies this little gem of a B&B, which plays up the historic charm with its atrium of exposed stone and beams. All rooms come with kitchenettes and a DIY breakfast basket. Loveliest of all is Saio, with its own fireplace. If you fancy a hack in the hills, the owners can arrange for you to go horse riding.

Palazzo Bocci
HISTORIC HOTEL €€

(☑ 0742 30 10 21; www.palazzobocci.com; Via Cavour 17; s €54-80, d €77-118, ste €115-136; P ❋ 🕾 🐾) Within the walls of this 17th-century *palazzo*'s lavishly frescoed salon, you get a real sense of Spello's history.

OFF THE BEATEN TRACK

A GREAT RURAL ESCAPE

La Cuccagna (☑ 075 92 03 17; http://lacuccagna.com; Frazione Santa Cristina 22; d €110-140; P 🅿 ❋ ✔) You'll find it tough to drag yourself away from the spirit-lifting views from the garden patio and olive-tree-fringed pool at this high-on-a-hill B&B. Sarah and Salvatore's beautifully restored country home is pin-drop peaceful and big on rustic charm, with rooms fitted out with original beams and stone walls. Organic produce makes its way onto the breakfast table.

They also arrange everything from pizza-making workshops to olive-picking holidays. The B&B is midway between Perugia and Gubbio – see the website for precise directions.

Quarters are understated yet elegant, with tiled floors and beams or ceiling murals. There's a garden terrace with soothingly lovely country views and a restaurant ensconced in a 14th-century mill, which makes the most of Umbrian produce such as Norcia truffles.

🍴 Eating & Drinking

Osteria del Buchetto
OSTERIA €€

(☑ 0742 30 30 52; Via Cappuccini 19; meals €25-30; ⊙ 1-3pm & 7.30-11pm Thu-Sat, 1-3pm Sun) You eat on a raised platform with romantic views of the valley towards Assisi at this *osteria*, right at the top of town near the Roman arch. The food is proudly local, and lingering is positively encouraged. Perhaps start with the *strangozzi* pasta with truffles (or, if in season, asparagus), and move on to the speciality – expertly grilled steaks.

Enoteca Properzio
WINE BAR

(☑ 0742 30 15 21; www.enotecaproperzio.com; Palazzo dei Canonici, Piazza Matteotti 8; sharing plates from €10; ⊙ noon-midnight Tue-Sun) At the most charming *enoteca* in town, you can try a half-dozen Umbrian wines while snacking on cheese, prosciutto and bruschetta, then stock up on an enticing array of regional specialities (*salumi*, Spello olive oil, *strangozzi* pasta and the like).

❶ Information

Tourist Office (Pro Loco; ☑ 0742 30 10 09; www.prospello.it; Piazza Matteotti 3; ⊙ 9.30am-12.30pm & 3.30-5.30pm) Has town maps, a list of accommodation options and walking maps, including an 8km walk across the hills to Assisi.

❶ Getting There & Away

CAR & MOTORCYCLE
Spello is on the SS75 between Perugia and Foligno.

TRAIN
There are services at least hourly to Perugia (€3, 30 minutes) and Assisi (€1.70, 10 minutes). If the station is unstaffed, buy your tickets at the self-service ticket machine. It's a 10-minute walk into town.

Gubbio

POP 32,400

While most of Umbria feels soft, warm and rounded by the millennia, Gubbio is angular, sober, imposing and medieval through

Gubbio

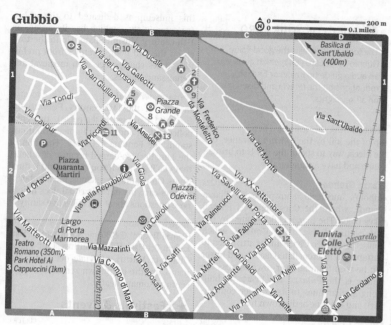

and through. Perched on the steep slopes of Monte Ingino, the Gothic buildings wend their way up the hill towards Umbria's closest thing to a theme-park ride: its open-air *funivia* (cable car).

◉ Sights

★**Funivia Colle Eletto** VIEWPOINT
(adult/reduced return €6/5; ⊙9am-8pm daily summer, 10am-5pm Thu-Tue winter) Although the **Basilica di Sant'Ubaldo** (⊙8am-7pm) **FREE**, perched high up on Monte Ingino, is a perfectly lovely church, the real adventure is reaching it on the *funivia*, as exhilarating as any roller coaster. The word *funivia* suggests an enclosed cable car, but it's actually a ski lift of sorts, whisking visitors up the mountain in precarious-looking metal baskets.

In order to board you have to stand on a red dot and then get thrown into a basket by the operator as it whizzes past – health and safety be damned. Once the giddiness has worn off, you can watch Gubbio, which moments before had seemed so impossibly hilly, gradually transform into a flat little toy town far below. The entire valley spreads picturesquely before you from the top.

The basilica, which can't help but come as a bit of an anticlimax after the approach,

Gubbio

displays the body of St Ubaldo, the 12th-century bishop of Gubbio, in a glass coffin above the altar. It also has a small museum dedicated to the **Corsa dei Ceri**, the town's most popular festival, where you can see the massive statues that are carried through the streets during this festival. There's a cafe on top of the hill by the *funivia* entrance, but the nicest way to spend the day is to bring a picnic and have a wander.

Piazza Grande   PIAZZA

Gubbio's medieval showpiece is Piazza Grande, where the Corsa dei Ceri festival takes place. The piazza is dominated by the 14th-century **Palazzo dei Consoli**, which houses the Museo Civico and is attributed to Gattapone – its crenellated facade and tower can be seen from all over town. Across the square is the **Palazzo del Podestà**, built along similar lines to its grander counterpart, and now the active town hall.

Museo Civico   MUSEUM

(Piazza Grande; adult/reduced €5/2.50; ⊙10am-1.30pm & 2.30-6pm, shorter hours winter) Housed in the Palazzo dei Consoli, this museum displays the Eugubian Tablets, discovered in 1444. Dating from between 300 and 100 BC, these seven bronze tablets are the best existing example of the ancient Umbrian script. Upstairs is a picture gallery featuring works from the Gubbian school, while downstairs – and accessed round the back – is a small archaeological museum.

Via Federico da Montefeltro   AREA

Walk up Via Ducale to the Via Federico da Montefeltro where you'll encounter a triumvirate of ancientness, beginning at the 13th-century pink **cathedral** (Via Federico da Montefeltro; donations welcome; ⊙10am-5pm), with a fine 12th-century stained-glass window and a fresco attributed to Bernardino Pinturicchio. Opposite, the 15th-century **Palazzo Ducale** (adult/reduced €5/2.50; ⊙8.30am-7.30pm) was built by the Duke of Montefeltro's family as a scaled-down version of their grand *palazzo* in Urbino. Next door is the **Museo Diocesano** (adult/reduced €5/3; ⊙10.30am-6pm Tue-Sun), an art gallery tracing 2000 years of ecclesiastical history.

Museo della Maiolica a Lustro   MUSEUM

(Via Dante 24; admission €5; ⊙9am-1pm & 3.30-7pm) Just below the Funivia Colle Eletto, this museum is dedicated to the *a lustro* ceramic style, which has its origins in 11th-century Muslim Spain. Up in the tower, on the 2nd floor, ceramics from prehistoric times share space with medieval and Renaissance pieces.

Fontana dei Pazzi   FOUNTAIN

In front of the 14th-century **Palazzo del Bargello** (⊙closed to the public), the city's police station and prison in medieval times, stands the Fontana dei Pazzi (Fountain of the Lunatics), so-named because of a belief that you'll go mad if you run around it three times. On summer weekends, the number of visitors carrying out this ritual does indeed pose questions about the collective sanity!

Teatro Romano   ARCHAEOLOGICAL SITE

(Roman Theatre; ⊙8.30am-7.30pm Apr-Sep, 8am-1.30pm Oct-Mar) **FREE** Southwest of Piazza Quaranta Martiri, off Viale del Teatro Romano, are the overgrown remains of a 1st-century Roman theatre.

★ Festivals & Events

Corsa dei Ceri   CULTURAL

(www.ceri.it) The 'Candles Race' is a centuries-old event held each year on 15 May to commemorate the city's patron saint, Sant'Ubaldo. It starts at 5.30am and involves three teams, each carrying a *cero* (massive wooden pillars weighing about 400kg, each bearing a statue of a 'rival' saint) and racing through the city's streets. This is one of Italy's liveliest festivals and has put Gubbio on the map.

Palio della Balestra   CULTURAL

On the last Sunday in May, Gubbio gets out its medieval crossbows for its annual archery competition with regional rival Sansepolcro. The festival carries over all year in tourist shops alive with rather scary-looking crossbow paraphernalia.

⌂ Sleeping

Residenza di Via Piccardi   HISTORIC HOTEL €

(☎075 927 61 08; www.residenzadiviapiccardi.it; Via Piccardi 12; s/d €40/60; ☜) Step through the arched gate into the romantic garden of this period residence. Share an amorous breakfast for two in the garden or cook up a simple dinner in the hotel's kitchen. Family owned, the medieval stone building has cosy rooms decorated in cheery florals, with all the basic comforts.

Relais Ducale
HOTEL €€

(☑ 075 922 01 57; www.relaisducale.com; Via Galeotti 19; s €75-105, d €85-175; @) You'll need to be in shape to stay here, as this hotel is a stiff walk up the hill and two flights of steps, but it's worth it. Set in a converted annexe of the Ducale Palace, its rooms are utterly charming, with polished wood floors and antique furnishings; one even has a barrel-vaulted stone ceiling. The flowery terrace overlooks Piazza della Signoria.

Park Hotel Ai Cappuccini
BOUTIQUE HOTEL €€€

(☑ 075 92 34; www.parkhotelaicappuccini.it; Via Tifernate; s €130-190, d €170-270, meals €40-50; P❄🕸🏊) Silence still hangs like a monk's habit over this stunningly converted 17th-century monastery, which skilfully intertwines history with contemporary comfort. Rooms are classically elegant, with fine fabrics and lots of polished wood. Its own art gallery, an excellent restaurant serving Mediterranean cuisine, an indoor pool and spa and beautiful gardens all make this one of the top places to stay in town.

✗ Eating

For a quick pastry or pizza, try the snack bars on Corso Garibaldi and Via dei Consoli.

Picchio Verde
ITALIAN €

(☑ 075 927 66 49; www.ristorantepicchioverde.com; Via Savelli della Porta 65; meals €15-25; ⊘9am-2pm & 7-10.30pm Wed-Mon) Huddled away in the old town, the 'green woodpecker' attracts a faithful local following for its cosy vaulted interior, authentic food and modest prices. Homemade pasta (try the *mezzelune* – semicircular pasta – stuffed with braised hare) segues smoothly into mains of meat grilled to perfection over an open fire. The two-course lunch including wine, water and coffee is a snip at €15.

Taverna del Lupo
UMBRIAN €€

(☑ 075 927 43 68; www.tavernadellupo.it; Via Ansidei 21; meals €35-45; ⊘noon-2pm & 7.30-9pm Thu-Tue; 🎵) Soft light casts flattering shadows across the barrel-vaulted interior of Gubbio's most sophisticated restaurant, serving Umbrian cuisine with a pinch of creativity and a dash of medieval charm. It's a class act, with tables draped in white linen and polished service. Flavours ring true in specialities like ravioli in asparagus-and-porcini sauce and tender capon with truffles, expertly matched with wines.

OH CHRISTMAS TREE!

Listed by the *Guinness Book of Records* in 1991 and flicked on by Pope Francis from the Vatican in 2014, Gubbio's shimmering, 650m-high whopper of a Christmas tree is officially the world's biggest. Spreading up the slopes of Monte Ingino and topped by a shooting star, its 300 photovoltaic-powered lights are visible from miles away and draw visitors to the medieval town in their thousands between 7 December (Immaculate Conception) and 6 January (Epiphany). For details of this year's light fantastic event, visit www.alberodigubbio.com.

❶ Information

Post Office (☑ 075 927 39 25; Via Cairoli 11; ⊘8.20am-7.05pm Mon-Fri, 8.20am-12.35pm Sat)

Tourist Office (☑ 075 922 06 93; www.comune.gubbio.pg.it; Via della Repubblica 15; ⊘8.30am-1.45pm & 3.30-6.30pm Mon-Fri, 9am-1pm & 3-6.30pm Sat & Sun) Sells the Gubbio Turisticard and rents out multilingual audio guides (€3).

❶ Getting There & Around

Gubbio has no train station but Umbria Mobilità (p577) buses run to Perugia (€5.50, 1¼ hours, 10 daily) from Piazza Quaranta Martiri.

By car, take the SS298 from Perugia or the SS76 from Ancona, and follow the signs.

Spoleto
POP 39,300

Presided over by a formidable medieval fortress and backed by the broad-shouldered Apennines, their summits iced with snow in winter, Spoleto is visually stunning. The hill town is also something of a historical picnic: the Romans left their mark in the form of grand arches and an amphitheatre; the Lombards made it the capital of their duchy in 570, building it high and mighty and leaving it with a parting gift of a Romanesque cathedral in the early 13th century.

Today, the town has winged its way into the limelight with its mammoth Festival dei Due Mondi, a 17-day summer feast of opera, dance, music and art.

WORTH A TRIP

PARCO REGIONALE DEL MONTE CUCCO

A memorable road trip on the Umbria-Le Marche border, just 13km east of Gubbio, is the SS3 that wends along the eastern fringes of **Parco Regionale del Monte Cucco** (www.discovermontecucco.it), a gorgeous swathe of wildflower-speckled meadows, gentle slopes brushed with beech, yew and silver fir trees, deep ravines splashed by waterfalls and karst cave systems, all topped off by the oft snowcapped hump of 1566m Monte Cucco. The winding road affords mood-lifting views on almost every corner, passing quaint mountain hamlets and woods where wolves, lynx and wild boar roam. The park beckons outdoor escapades and the website gives the low-down on everything from its 120km of marked hiking trails to mountain biking, horse riding, hang-gliding and cross-country skiing.

The big deal for spelunkers is **Grotta Monte Cucco** (☑075 917 10 46; www.grotta montecucco.umbria.it; Via Valentini 39, Costacciaro; discovery tour adult/reduced €12/10; ☺info point 9am-1pm Fri-Sun May-Jun & Sep-Nov, 9am-1pm & 4-6pm daily Jul & Aug, tours 10am & 3pm daily Jul & Aug, by request rest of year), one of Europe's most spectacular limestone caves, with a 30km maze of galleries reaching up to 900m deep. Those up for a challenge can delve into its underground forest of stalactites and stalagmites on a guided two- to three-hour discovery tour. For more details on the caves and park, stop by the info point in the nearby village of Costacciaro.

◉ Sights

Rocca Albornoziana   FORT, MUSEUM
(Piazza Campello; adult/reduced €7.50/6.50; ☺9.30am-7.30pm) Rising high and mighty on a hilltop above Spoleto, the Rocca, a glowering 14th-century former papal fortress, is now a fast, scenic escalator ride from Via della Ponzianina. The fortress contains the **Museo Nazionale del Ducato**, which traces the history of the Spoleto duchy through a series of Roman, Byzantine, Carolingian and Lombard artefacts, from 5th-century sarcophagi to Byzantine jewellery.

Museo Archeologico   MUSEUM
(Via S Agata; adult/reduced €4/2; ☺8.30am-7.30pm) Down in the centre of town, Spoleto's pride and joy is its archaeological museum, located on the western edge of Piazza della Libertà. It showcases a well-curated collection of Roman and Etruscan finds from the area, spread over four floors.

You can step outside to view the mostly intact 1st-century **Teatro Romano** (Roman theatre), which often hosts live performances during the summer; check with the museum or the tourist office.

Museo Carandente   MUSEUM
(www.palazzocollicola.it; Piazza Collicola; adult/reduced €4/3; ☺10.30am-1pm & 3.30-7pm Wed-Mon) The town's premier collection of modern art is named after its late former director and noted art critic, Giovanni Carandente, and

has been significantly revamped. The collection is dominated by works of late-20th-century Italian artists, including the sculptor Leonardo Leoncillo.

Casa Romana   HISTORIC BUILDING
(Roman House; Via di Visiale; adult/reduced €3/2; ☺11am-7pm Wed-Mon) This excavated Roman house isn't exactly Pompeii, but it gives visitors a peek into what a typical home of the area would have looked like in the 1st century BC. Just to the south, near the Piazza Fontana, stand the remains of the **Arco di Druso e Germanico** (Arch of Drusus and Germanicus) (named for the sons of Emperor Tiberius), which once marked the entrance to the Roman forum.

Duomo di Spoleto   CATHEDRAL
(Piazza del Duomo; ☺8.30am-12.30pm & 3.30-7pm) A flight of steps sweeps down to Spoleto's pretty pale-stone cathedral, originally built in the 11th century using huge blocks of salvaged stones from Roman buildings for its slender bell tower. A 17th-century remodelling saw a striking Renaissance porch added. The rainbow swirl of mosaic frescoes in the domed apse was executed by Filippo Lippi and his assistants.

Lippi died before completing the work and Lorenzo de' Medici travelled to Spoleto from Florence and ordered Lippi's son, Filippino, to build a mausoleum for the artist. This now stands in the right transept of the cathedral.

Museo del Tessile e del Costume   MUSEUM

(Museum of Textiles and Costumes; Via delle Terme; adult/reduced €3/2; ⊙3.30-7pm Sat & Sun) Housed in the Palazzo Rosari-Spada, this museum holds a collection of antique noble finery from the 15th to the 20th century, donated from the wardrobes of some of the area's leading families.

Chiesa di San Pietro   CHURCH

(Località San Pietro; ⊙9am-6.30pm) An hour-long stroll can be made along the Via del Ponte to the Ponte delle Torri. Cross this bridge and follow the lower path, Strada di Monteluco, to reach Chiesa di San Pietro, whose 13th-century facade is liberally be-decked with sculpted animals.

Ponte delle Torri   BRIDGE

Many people literally draw breath the first time they glimpse the medieval Ponte delle Torri, a 10-arch bridge that leaps spectacu-larly across a steeply wooded gorge – a scene beautifully captured by Turner in his 1840 oil painting. The bridge was erected in the 14th century on the foundations of a Roman aqueduct.

⚜ Festivals & Events

Spoleto Festival   PERFORMING ARTS

(www.festivaldispoleto.it; ⊙late Jun–mid-Jul) The Italian-American composer Gian Carlo Menotti conceived the Festival dei Due Mondi (Festival of Two Worlds) in 1958. Now simply known as the Spoleto Festival, it has given the town a worldwide reputation. Events at the 17-day festival range from op-era and theatre performances to ballet and art exhibitions. For details and tickets, visit the website.

🛏 Sleeping

Stop by the tourist office for info on *affitta-camere* (rooms for rent), hostels, campsites and *agriturismi* in the surrounding area. Prices rocket during the festival and drop considerably during low season; good deals can often be snapped up at the following places by prebooking online.

Much of the pedestrianised old town is off-limits to traffic – hotels generally give you a free pass to park outside the medieval walls.

★ L'Aura   B&B €

(☑0743 4 46 43; Piazza Torre dell'Olio 5; s €40-50, d €60-70; [P][@][🛜]) You'll feel as snug as an Italian bug at this cute B&B on the top floor

DON'T MISS

A WALK WITH A VIEW

Giro dei Condotti Beginning at the Rocca fort, the 6km Giro dei Condotti walk is an irresistible draw for pho-tographers, keen walkers and anyone who appreciates a jaw-dropping view. It leads along the ramparts and over the staggering 10-arch Ponte delle Torri, before taking you along sun-dappled woodland trails to a lookout with a clas-sic postcard view of the bridge, valley and fortress-crowned hilltop. Be sure to wear flat, comfortable shoes.

of a 200-year-old *palazzo*. Claudia makes you welcome and gives excellent tips on Spoleto. It's a tidy, homey place, with bright, wood-beamed rooms and a terrace overlook-ing rooftops to the hills beyond. There's no lift, so be prepared to schlep your bags up the stairs (there are a few flights).

Albergo Villa Cristina   GUESTHOUSE €

(☑0743 4 80 36; www.albergovillacristina.com; Via Collerisana 15; s €40-70, d €60-110; [P][🛜][🍴]) Anna Maria is the little ray of sunshine brighten-ing up this guesthouse, lodged in a lovingly restored 18th-century country home, with dreamy views out over cypress-plumed hill-sides from its garden terrace. Traditional-style, tiled-floor rooms are kept spick and span. Homemade cakes and honey are served with bread, ricotta and fresh coffee at breakfast. It's a 15-minute walk west of town.

Hotel dei Duchi   HOTEL €

(☑0743 4 45 41; www.hoteldeiduchi.com; Viale Giacomo Matteotti 4; s €75-85, d €100-110, tr €125; [P][❄][@][🛜]) Next to a tidy park just outside the old town, this is a purpose build rather than a renovation. So although the rooms are spacious, contemporary and well kept, they aren't exactly oozing old-world charm. Its elevated position gives it fine views of the countryside and, slightly closer to home, the Roman theatre from the terrace.

Hotel San Luca   BOUTIQUE HOTEL €€

(☑0743 22 33 99; www.hotelsanluca.com; Via Interna delle Mura 21; ⊙s €85-120, d €120-190; [P][❄][@][🛜][🍴]) Once a convent and now a heavenly boutique hotel, the San Luca has polished service and refined interiors to ri-val any of the five-stars in Umbria, yet the atmosphere is relaxed enough to cater to

Spoleto

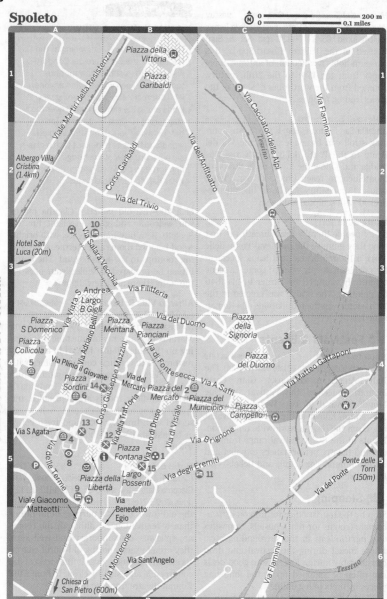

UMBRIA & LE MARCHE SPOLETO

cyclists and walkers. Pastel tones and antique furnishings inside complement the manicured 17th-century garden. The homemade cakes are the stars of the breakfast buffet.

Palazzo Leti   GUESTHOUSE €€€
(☏ 0743 22 49 30; www.palazzoleti.com; Via degli Eremiti 10; s €120-180, d €135-240; ℗ ❄ @ 🛜 🐾) In the southeast part of town facing the hills, this beautifully converted 13th-century noble

Spoleto

palace exudes romance and charm down to the last detail, from the delicate breakfast china to the historical oak and wrought-iron furnishings. With the view and perfect silence, you'll feel like you're staying in the country, but you're a three-minute walk from the centre of Spoleto.

✕ Eating

★ **Tempio del Gusto**   ITALIAN €€
(☑ 0743 4 71 12; www.iltempiodelgusto.com; Via Arco di Druso 11; meals €25-40; ⊙ Fri-Wed) Intimate, inventive and unmissable, Tempio del Gusto is fine dining without the Michelin-starred price tag. The food here speaks volumes about a chef who believes in sourcing, cooking and presenting with real pride and purpose. Eros Patrizi is the whiz behind the stove. Freshly made pasta, a trio of smoked fish, herb-crusted pork – every dish strikes a perfect balance.

Il Pentagramma   UMBRIAN €€
(☑ 0743 22 31 41; www.ristorantepentagramma. com; Via Tommaso Martani 6; meals €25-35; ⊙ 12.30-2.30pm & 7.30-10.30pm Tue-Sun) The menu has an operatic flourish at Il Pentagramma and you may well find yourself rhapsodising about the food dished up in the cosy stone-walled interior or on the terrace. The seasons shine in dishes from ricotta-stuffed zucchini flowers to wild-boar-filled tortellini and *strangozzi* with black truffle, all well matched with Umbrian wines.

Ristorante Apollinaire   UMBRIAN €€
(☑ 0743 22 32 56; www.ristoranteapollinare.it; Via S Agata 14; meals €25-40; ⊙ 12.30-2.30pm & 7.30-10.30pm Wed-Sun) Flair and creativity meets Umbrian tradition at Apollinaire, where the chef brings nous and an artistic eye for detail to winningly fresh produce. On the menu you might find seasonal showstoppers like homemade *strangozzi* pasta with chilli and parsley or rack of lamb with hazelnut sauce and aubergine purée. You are constantly enveloped in low wood-beamed ceilings and candlelight flickering against brick.

Sabatini   ITALIAN €€
(☑ 0743 4 72 30; www.ristorantesabatinispoleto.it; Corso Mazzini 52-54; meals €25-30; ⊙ 11am-midnight Tue-Sun) Forget studying the menu – just go for one of the daily tasting menus and loosen a belt notch for dish after delectable dish. This is home cooking at its best with a pinch of seasonality – simple as 24-month dry-cured prosciutto sliced by hand, black pork fillet cooked with Sagrantino and red onion, and *millefoglie* of pistachio and whipped cream.

❶ Information

Post Office (Viale Giacomo Matteotti 2; ⊙ 8.20am-7.05pm Mon-Fri, to 12.35pm Sat)

Tourist Office (☑ 0743 21 86 20; www. visitspoleto.it; Piazza della Libertà 7; ⊙ 9am-1.30pm & 3-7pm Mon-Sat, 10am-1pm Sun)

❶ Getting There & Around

Umbria Mobilità (p577) buses run frequently to Norcia (€6.30, 50 minutes, seven daily).

Trains from the main station connect with Rome (€8.50 to €17.50, 1½ hours, hourly), Perugia (€4.80, one hour, nine daily) and Assisi (€3.70, 40 minutes, hourly). From the train station, about 1km from the centre, take city bus A, B or C for €1.30 to the Piazza della Libertà (make sure the bus reads 'Centro').

By car, the city lies on the E45 and is an easy connection via the SS209 to the Valnerina.

Norcia & the Valnerina

After the thigh-challenging hill towns of western and northern Umbria, the flatter, less elevated prospects of Norcia can come as a relief. You'll still need to do something to work up an appetite, however. The merest mention of Norcia sends Italian gastronomes into raptures about the earthy delights of its *tartufo nero* (black truffle) and the prized

UMBRIA & LE MARCHE NORCIA & THE VALNERINA

salumi from its acorn-fed pigs, both of which feature prolifically on restaurant menus and in shop windows.

Crisp mountain air, picture-book medieval looks and the town's spiritual claim to fame as the birthplace of St Benedict are other reasons for lingering here. Norcia's other great draw is its proximity to the rugged, exhilarating wilderness of **Monti Sibillini** (p631). Almost as scenic is Norcia's own valley, the steep-sided Valnerina valley, freckled with wildflowers in summer, which is best explored on a meandering drive along the SS209.

◉ Sights

Often devastated by earthquakes – the last major rumble was in 1979 – Norcia's petite, walled centre is a joy to explore on foot. Its medieval buildings have been seriously patched up over the years, but the town has preserved its charm.

Piazza San Bendetto   PIAZZA

On the centrepiece Piazza San Benedetto, a statue of Norcia's famous son, St Benedict, with hand outstretched in blessing, stands proud. The saint and his twin sister, St Scholastica, were born here to a well-to-do family in 480 AD. Next to the Basilica di San Benedetto is the 14th-century **Palazzo Comunale**, with a striking portico and belfry, while opposite lies the **Castellina**, a 16th-century papal fortress.

Basilica di San Benedetto   CHURCH

(Piazza San Benedetto; ☉9am-6pm) St Benedict and St Scholastica were apparently born in the Roman crypt of the 13th-century Basilica di San Benedetto. The church's pale, delicate facade gives way to a calm, contemplative interior, where monks often shuffle past bearing prayer books. Each day at 7.45pm, the monks attend a Gregorian chant; visitors are also welcome to attend. Filippo Napoletano's early-17th-century frescoes depict scenes from the life of the saint.

🛏 Sleeping & Eating

Corte Belvoir   B&B €€

(☎334 8473696; www.cortebelvoir.com; Via dell'Ospedale, Località Grotti; d €90-160) Squirrelled away in the Monti Sibillini National Park, this B&B lodged in a 500-year-old manor is a find. A hill lifts it above the plains and grants views deep into the mountains. The generously sized rooms brim with wood-beamed, stone-walled romance, and your kind hosts – Alessandro and Rossana – go out of their way to make your stay that extra bit special.

It's located on the Via dell'Ospedale, 4km southeast of the town centre.

★Palazzo Seneca   HISTORIC HOTEL €€€

(☎0743 81 74 34; www.palazzoseneca.com; Via Cesare Battisti 12; s €160-176, d €180-300, ste €450-700; P✳🖵) In family hands since 1850, Palazzo Seneca gives guests a tantalising glimpse of the high life. You can truly feel like you're living in a palace here, even if just for a night or two, playing chess in a leather chair in front of the fireplace or having a soothing aromatherapy massage in the subterranean spa.

Four-poster beds and marble bathrooms meld seamlessly with ancient stone walls and oak floors, and the accompanying Ristorante Vespasia is a gourmet delight. See

---

HUNTERS & GATHERERS

Gastronomically speaking, Norcia is a town of hunters and gatherers. As the country's cured-meat capital, its shops brim with delectable pork and wild-boar prosciutto, salami and sausages. In fact, the word *norcineria* has become synonymous with 'butcher' throughout Italy.

Pigs aren't the only animals that like to snuffle around in the undergrowth of the surrounding oak woods, however. The area is also one of the region's largest producers of the elusive *tartufo nero* (black truffle), unearthed by dogs led by a *cavatore*, or truffle hunter. Should you wish to embark on your own tuber treasure hunt, Palazzo Seneca offers truffle-hunting packages, or ask the tourist office to put you in touch with local guides heading out in search of culinary gold.

If you're here on the last weekend in February or the first weekend in March, you're in for a treat at the **Mostra Mercato del Tartufo Nero** (www.neronorcia.it; ☉Feb/Mar) festival, where thousands turn out to taste and buy wonderful truffles and *salumi* direct from the producers.

the website for special themed packages, covering everything from cookery classes to truffle hunting.

Trattoria dal Francese TRATTORIA €€
(☑ 0743 81 62 90; Via Riguardati 16; meals €30; ☺ noon-2.30pm & 6.30-9pm Sat-Thu) Maybe it's its presence in many of the Italian 'best restaurant' guides that keeps this trattoria permanently packed or perhaps it's the quality of the food, which is a cut above most places even in this renowned foodie town. It's in Norcia, so expect a menu packed with piggy products (salami, ham, sausages), truffles and cheese.

★ **Ristorante Vespasia** UMBRIAN €€€
(☑ 0743 81 74 34; www.palazzoseneca.com; Via Cesare Battisti 10; meals €50-110; ☺ noon-3pm & 7-10pm) Set in a 16th-century *palazzo,* the elegantly simple furnishings here complement the understated gourmet cuisine. Try excellent homemade pasta with truffles or porcini mushrooms, or locally grown saffron to accompany risotto and local pork. Herbs come from its own garden. In warmer months, dine in the garden to jazz or blues.

ℹ Information

Casa del Parco (☑ 0743 82 81 73; www. sibillini.net; Piazza San Benedetto; ☺ 9.30am-12.30pm & 4-7pm, shorter hours winter) Has tourist information about the area, including Monti Sibillini.

ℹ Getting There & Around

Buses run to and from Spoleto (€6.30, 50 minutes, seven daily) and Perugia (€8.60, two hours, one daily).

By car, from Spoleto, take the SS209 to the SS396. The closest train station is in Spoleto.

Orvieto

POP 21,100

Sitting astride a volcanic plug of rock above fields streaked with vines, and olive and cypress trees, Orvieto is visually stunning from the first. Like the love child of Rome and Florence, nestled midway between the two cities, history hangs over the cobbled lanes, medieval piazzas and churches of this cinematically beautiful city. And few churches in Italy can hold a candle to its wedding cake of a Gothic cathedral, which frequently elicits gasps of wonder at its layers of exquisite detail.

PIANO GRANDE

What sounds like a finely tuned instrument is in fact a lyrical landscape. Tucked in the far-eastern corner of Umbria, between Castelluccio and Norcia, the Piano Grande is a 1270m-high plain flanked by the bare-backed peaks of the Apennines. When the snow melts, it gives way to a springtime eruption of wildflowers more beautiful than any Monet painting, its canvas embroidered red, gold, violet and white with poppies, cornflowers, wild tulips, daisies, crocuses and narcissi. It's a florist's heaven, a hay-fever sufferer's hell and an endless source of camera-clicking fascination for walkers, who flock here for serendipitous strolls through the meadows.

⊙ Sights

Duomo di Orvieto CATHEDRAL
(☑ 0763 34 24 77; www.opsm.it; Piazza Duomo 26; admission €3; ☺ 9.30am-6pm Mon-Sat, 1-5.30pm Sun, shorter hours winter) Nothing can prepare you for the visual feast that is Orvieto's soul-stirring Gothic cathedral. Dating to 1290, it sports a black-and-white banded exterior fronted by what is perhaps the most astonishing facade to grace any Italian church, a mesmerising display of rainbow frescoes, jewel-like mosaics, bas-reliefs and delicate braids of flowers and vines.

The building took 30 years to plan and three centuries to complete. It was started by Fra Bevignate and later additions were made by Sienese master Lorenzo Maitani, Andrea Pisano (of Florence Cathedral fame) and his son Nino Pisano, Andrea Orcagna and Michele Sanicheli.

Of the art on show inside, it's Luca Signorelli's magnificent *Giudizio Universale* that draws the crowds. The artist began work on the vast fresco in 1499 and over the course of the next four years covered every inch of the **Cappella di San Brizio** with a swirling and, at times, grotesque depiction of the Last Judgment. Michelangelo is said to have taken inspiration from the work. Indeed, to some, Michelangelo's masterpiece runs a close second to Signorelli's creation.

On the other side of the transept, the **Cappella del Corporale** houses a 13th-century altar cloth stained with blood that

Orvieto

UMBRIA & LE MARCHE ORVIETO

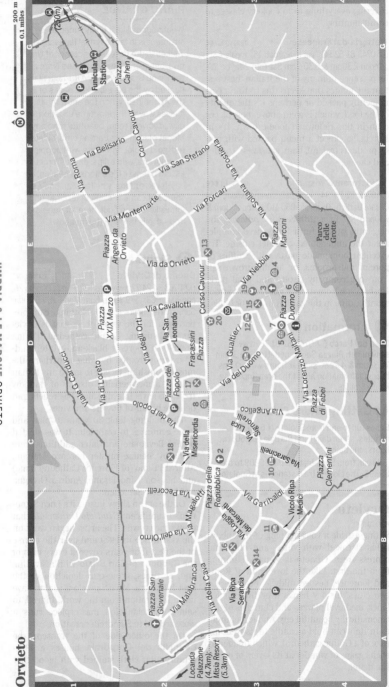

Orvieto

miraculously poured from the communion bread of a priest who doubted the transubstantiation.

Museo dell'Opera del Duomo di Orvieto
MUSEUM

(☎0763 34 24 77; www.museomodo.it; Piazza Duomo 26; admission €5; ☺9.30am-7pm) Housed in the former papal palace, this museum contains a fine collection of religious relics from the cathedral, as well as Etruscan antiquities and paintings by artists such as Arnolfo di Cambio and the three Pisanos (Andrea, Nino and Giovanni).

Orvieto Underground
HISTORIC SITE

(www.orvietounderground.it; Piazza Duomo 24; adult/reduced €6/5; ☺tours 11am, 12.15pm, 4pm & 5.15pm daily) The coolest place in Orvieto (literally), this series of 440 caves has been used for millennia by locals for various purposes, including as WWII bomb shelters, refrigerators, wells and, during many a pesky Roman or barbarian siege, as dovecotes to trap the usual one-course dinner: pigeon (still seen on local restaurant menus as *palombo*).

The 45-minute tours (with English-speaking guides) leave from in front of the tourist office.

Museo Claudio Faina e Civico
MUSEUM

(www.museofaina.it; Piazza Duomo 29; adult/reduced €4.50/3; ☺9.30am-6pm) Stage your own archaeological dig at this fantastic museum opposite the Duomo di Orvieto. It houses one of Italy's foremost collections of Etruscan artefacts, including plenty of stone sarcophagi and terracotta pieces,

as well as some significant Greek ceramic works.

Torre del Moro
HISTORIC BUILDING

(Moor's Tower; Corso Cavour 87; adult/reduced €2.80/2; ☺10am-8pm) From the Piazza Duomo, head northwest along Via del Duomo to Corso Cavour and the 13th-century Torre del Moro. Climb all 250 steps for sweeping views of the city.

Chiesa di San Giovenale
CHURCH

(Piazza San Giovenale; ☺8am-12.30pm & 3.30-6pm) At the western end of town is this stout little church, constructed in the year 1000. Its Romanesque-Gothic art and frescoes from the later medieval Orvieto school are an astounding contrast. Just to the north, you can enjoy towering views of the countryside from the town walls.

Museo Archeologico Nazionale
MUSEUM

(Palazzo Papale, Piazza Duomo; adult/reduced €3/1.50; ☺8.30am-7.30pm) Ensconced in the medieval Palazzo Papale, the archaeological museum holds plenty of interesting artefacts, some over 2500 years old. Etruscan ceramics, necropolis relics, bronzes and frescoed chamber tombs are among the items on display.

Chiesa di Sant'Andrea
CHURCH

(Piazza della Repubblica; ☺8.30am-12.30pm & 3.30-7.30pm) This 12th-century church, with its curious decagonal bell tower, presides over the Piazza della Repubblica, once Orvieto's Roman Forum and now lined with cafes. It lies at the heart of what remains of the medieval city.

UMBRIA & LE MARCHE ORVIETO

ℹ MORE FOR YOUR EURO

The **Carta Unica Orvieto** (adult/ reduced €20/17) permits entry to the town's nine main attractions (including the Duomo and its Cappella di San Brizio, Museo Claudio Faina e Civico, Orvieto Underground, Torre del Moro and Museo dell'Opera del Duomo). It also includes a round trip on the funicular and unlimited rides on city buses. It can be purchased at many of the attractions, the tourist office, the Piazza Cahen tourist office and the railway station.

🎉 Festivals & Events

Palombella RELIGIOUS

(☸ Pentecost Sun) For traditionalists, this rite has celebrated the Holy Spirit and good luck since 1404. For animal rights activists, the main event celebrates nothing more than scaring the living crap out of a bewildered bird. Take one dove, cage it, surround the cage with a wheel of exploding fireworks, and hurtle the cage 300m down a wire towards the cathedral steps. If the dove lives (it usually does), the couple most recently married in the cathedral becomes its caretakers.

Umbria Jazz Winter MUSIC

(www.umbriajazz.com; ☸ late Dec-early Jan) This celebration of cool musical styles jazzes up the dull patches of winter, with a great feast and party on New Year's Eve.

🛏 Sleeping

It's always a good idea to book ahead in summer, on weekends, or if you're planning to come over New Year, when the Umbria Jazz Winter festival is in full swing.

★ B&B La Magnolia B&B €

(☎ 0763 34 28 08, 349 4620733; www.bblamagnolia.it; Via del Duomo 29; d €60-90; ❄) Tucked down a sidestreet north of the Duomo (the sign is easily missed), this light-filled Renaissance residence has delightful rooms and apartments, an English-speaking owner, a large shared kitchen and a balcony overlooking the rooftops. The owner Serena can tell you all about Orvieto – whatever you want to know, just ask.

B&B Ripa Medici B&B €

(☎ 0763 34 13 43; www.ripamedici.it; Vicolo Ripa Medici 14; d/apt €70/80; ❄ 🛜 🚻) Hugging the cliff walls on the edge of the old town, this B&B takes the concept of room with a view to a whole new level, gazing longingly out across undulating countryside. The rooms have been given a pinch of romance, with antique furnishings and canopy beds, while the beamed apartment offers even more space and a kitchen. Owner Sabrina's home-cooked breakfasts are a delight.

B&B Michelangeli B&B €

(☎ 0763 39 38 62; www.bbmichelangeli.com; Via Saracinelli 22; s €60-100, d €70-160; ℗) A spacious guesthouse, with bright, nicely kept rooms scattered with homely trinkets, and a well-stocked kitchen where you can knock up a speedy pasta dish should you so wish. We love the beautiful wood carvings and wrought-iron beds.

★ Misia Resort BOUTIQUE HOTEL €€

(☎ 0763 34 23 36; Località Rocca Ripesena 51/52; s €80, d €130-160; ❄ 🛜 🚻) You won't regret going the extra mile to this boutique hotel on the rocks, with fabulous views of Orvieto from its hilltop hamlet perch. This stunning country house conversion has been designed with the utmost taste. The light, spacious rooms in soft, earthy tones come with stylish vintage touches – a chesterfield sofa here, a distressed wood beam there.

They say that a hotel is only as good as its host, and Giorgio is as good as they get, welcoming you with a glass of wine and whipping up delicious breakfasts. Misia sits 6km west of Orvieto.

Hotel Duomo HOTEL €€

(☎ 0763 34 18 87; www.orvietohotelduomo.com; Vicolo di Maurizio 7; s €70-90, d €100-130, ste €120-160; ℗ ❄ 🛜 🚻) Orvieto's captivating Duomo is almost close enough to touch at Hotel Duomo, where the church bells will most likely be your wake-up call. This Liberty-style *palazzo*, where Orvieto-born artist Livio Orazio Valentini has left his bold, abstract imprint on the refined, neutral-hued rooms (all have marble bathrooms), has service both discreet and polite.

🍴 Eating

Pasqualetti GELATERIA €

(Piazza Duomo 14; cones €2.50-3.50; ☸ 11am-8pm) This gelateria serves mouth-watering gelato, plus there are plenty of tables on the piazza for you to gaze at the magnificence of the cathedral while you gobble.

A TASTE OF ORVIETO

If you're keen to slip on an apron and get behind the stove, Orvieto's the place. At **Ristorante Zeppelin** (p615), English-speaking chef Lorenzo Polegri whips up an Umbrian feast at his one-day cookery classes, where you'll learn to prepare specialities such as wild-boar *ragù* and hand-rolled *umbricelli* pasta (spaghetti's Umbrian sister). He also prepares a five-course menu as the culinary climax of truffle hunts, and runs market mornings and tours of local *pecorino* (sheep's-milk cheese), olive oil and wine producers. Daily prices range from €50 to €120 per person and full details are given on the website.

Decugnano dei Barbi (☑0763 30 82 55; www.decugnanodeibarbi.com; Località Fossatello 50) 🍃 estate, perched above vineyards 18km east of Orvieto, offers unique tastings and four-hour cookery classes. The winery can trace its viticultural lineage back 800 years and the lovely master sommelier Anna Rita will guide you through its cellars and talk you through a tasting of its minerally whites and full-bodied Orvieto Classico reds. Or sign up in advance to assemble a four-course meal together with Rosanna, paired (naturally) with homegrown wines and served in the atmospheric surrounds of a converted chapel.

Trattoria del Moro Aronne TRATTORIA €€
(☑0763 34 27 63; www.trattoriadelmoro.info; Via San Leonardo 7; meals €25-30; ☺noon-2.30pm & 7.30-9.30pm Wed-Mon) This welcoming trattoria has a convivial feel, authentic food and honest prices. The focus is on traditional cooking and strong regional flavours. Warm up with a goat cheese and fig marmalade starter before hitting your stride with a healthy cut of grilled beef.

Trattoria dell'Orso TRATTORIA €€
(☑0763 34 16 42; Via della Misericordia 18; meals €25-35; ☺noon-2pm & 7.30-9.30pm Wed-Sat, noon-2pm Sun) As the owner of Orvieto's oldest restaurant, Gabriele sees no need for such modern fancies as written menus; instead he reels off the day's dishes as you walk in the door. Go with his recommendations – perhaps the *zuppa di farro* (spelt soup) followed by fettuccine with porcini – as he knows what he's talking about. Be prepared to take your time.

Ristorante Zeppelin UMBRIAN €€
(☑0763 34 14 47; www.ristorantezeppelin.it; Via Loggia dei Mercanti 34; meals €25-30; ☺12.30-2.30pm & 7.30-9.30pm; ☑🐾) This natty place has a cave-like vaulted interior, jazz on the stereo, cheek-by-jowl tables and a model Zeppelin suspended from the ceiling. The inimitable Lorenzo brings Umbrian food to the table, including such local delights as homemade *umbricelli* pasta and wild boar stewed in a black olive, cherry tomato and cocoa sauce.

Le Grotte del Funaro UMBRIAN €€
(☑0763 34 32 76; www.grottedelfunaro.it; Via Ripa Serancia 41; pizza €4-8.50, meals €25-35; ☺noon-

3pm & 7pm-midnight) What could be more romantic – well, at least in a *Snow White* fairytale kind of way – than dining in a proper underground grotto? But this restaurant has more going for it than novelty factor alone. Alfredo and Sandra make a cracking kitchen duo, preparing wood-oven pizzas alongside Umbrian dishes like truffle-ricotta-filled ravioli and braised Chianina beef.

I Sette Consoli ITALIAN €€€
(☑0763 34 39 11; www.isetteconsoli.it; Piazza Sant'Angelo 1a; meals around €45, 6-course tasting menu €42; ☺12.30-3pm & 7.30-10pm closed Wed, and dinner Sun) This refined restaurant walks the culinary high wire in Orvieto, with inventive, artfully presented dishes, from pasta so light it floats off the fork to beautifully cooked pigeon casserole with minced hazelnuts and cherry-beer sauce. In good weather, try to get a seat in the garden, with the *duomo* in view. Dress for dinner and book ahead.

🍷 Drinking

Vinosus WINE BAR
(Piazza Duomo 15; ☺11am-4pm & 7pm-midnight Tue-Sun) In photo-op range of the cathedral's northwest wall is this wine bar and eatery. Try the cheese platter with local honey and pears for an elegant addition to wine.

☆ Entertainment

Teatro Mancinelli THEATRE
(☑0763 34 04 93; www.teatromancinelli.com; Corso Cavour 122; adult/reduced €2/1, show tickets €15-60; ☺theatre visits 10am-6pm Wed-Sat, 3-6pm Sun) The theatre plays host to Umbria Jazz

ORVIETO'S WINE COUNTRY

Now famed for its white DOC vintages, Orvieto's wine-growing potential was first spotted by the Etruscans more than 2000 years ago. They were attracted not just by the ideal soil and climate, but also by the soft tufa rock that underpins much of the landscape from which deep cool cellars could be (and indeed still are) cut to allow the grapes to ferment. From the Middle Ages onwards, Orvieto became known across Italy and beyond for its super-sweet gold-coloured wines. Today these have largely given way to drier vintages, such as Orvieto and Orvieto Classico.

To really immerse yourself in the world of viticulture, spend a night or two at the **Locanda Palazzone** (✆ 0763 39 36 14; www.locandapalazzone.com; Località Rocca Ripesena; ste d €230-340, q €340-410), a highly respected winery a few kilometres outside Orvieto that also rents out rather stylish suites in a restored medieval farmhouse.

in winter but offers everything from ballet and opera to folk music and Pink Floyd tributes throughout the year. If you're not able to catch a performance, it's worth a visit to see the allegorical frescoes and tufa walls.

ⓘ Information

Farmacia del Moro (✆ 0763 34 41 00; Corso Cavour 89; ◔9am-1pm & 4-8pm Mon-Fri) Posts 24-hour pharmacy information.

Police Station (✆ 0763 3 92 11; Piazza Cahen)

Post Office (Via Largo M Ravelli; ◔8.20am-7.05pm Mon-Fri, to 12.35pm Sat)

Tourist Office (✆ 0763 34 17 72; www.orvieto.regioneumbria.eu; Piazza Duomo 24; ◔8.15am-1.50pm & 4-7pm Mon-Fri, 10am-1pm & 3-6pm Sat & Sun) In summer, you can buy funicular, bus and Carta Unica Orvieto tickets here.

ⓘ Getting There & Away

BUS

Buses depart from the station on Piazza Cahen, stopping at the train station, and include services to Todi (€5.50, two hours, one daily) and Terni (€7.60, two hours, twice daily).

TRAIN

Connections include Rome (€7.50 to €17, 1¼ hours, hourly), Florence (€15.40 to €22.50, 1½ to 2½ hours, hourly) and Perugia (€7.10 to €15.60, 1¾ to 2½ hours, hourly).

CAR & MOTORCYCLE

Orvieto is on the Rome–Florence A1, while the SS71 heads north to Lago Trasimeno. There's plenty of metered parking on Piazza Cahen and in designated areas outside the city walls, including Campo della Fiera.

ⓘ Getting Around

A century-old **funicular** (tickets €1.30; ◔every 10min 7.15am-8.30pm Mon-Sat, every 15min 8am-8.30pm Sun) creaks up the wooded hill from the train station west of the centre to Piazza Cahen. The fare includes a bus ride from Piazza Cahen to Piazza Duomo.

Bus 1 runs up to the old town from the train station (€1.30), bus A connects Piazza Cahen with Piazza Duomo and bus B runs to Via Garibaldi.

LE MARCHE

From the white-pebble, cliff-backed bays along the Adriatic to sloped hill towns and the high-rise mountain ranges of Monti Sibillini, Le Marche is one of Italy's little-known treasures.

It's inland where Le Marche really shines. Urbino, Raphael's hometown, presents a smorgasbord of Renaissance art and history up and down its vertical streets. Pale but lovely Ascoli Piceno has beauty and history in bounds. Equally walkable is Macerata, with a famous open-air opera theatre and festival. Covering its western reaches, and bleeding over into neighbouring Umbria, is the wild and wonderful Parco Nazionale dei Monti Sibillini.

History

The first well-known settlers of Le Marche were the Piceni tribe, whose 3000-year-old artefacts can be seen in the Museo Archeologico in Ascoli Piceno. The Romans invaded the region early in the 3rd century BC, and dominated it for almost 700 years. After they fell, Le Marche was sacked by the Goths, Vandals, Ostrogoths and, finally, the Lombards.

In the 8th century AD, Pope Stephen II decided to call upon foreigners to oust the ungodly Lombards. The first to lead the charge of the Frankish army was Pepin the Short, but it was his rather tall son Charlemagne who finally took back control from the Lombards for good. On Christmas Day in 800, Pope Leo III crowned him Emperor of the Holy Roman Empire.

After Charlemagne's death, Le Marche entered into centuries of war, anarchy and general Dark Ages mayhem. In central Italy, two factions developed: the Guelphs (who backed papal rule) and the Ghibellines (supporting the emperor). The Guelph faction eventually won out and Le Marche became part of the Papal States. It stayed that way until Italian unification in 1861.

ℹ Getting There & Around

Drivers have two options on the coastline: the A14 autostrada (main highway) or the SS16 *strada statale* (state highway). Inland roads are either secondary or tertiary and much slower. Regular trains ply the coast on the Bologna–Lecce line and spurs head to Macerata and Ascoli Piceno.

Ancona

POP 102,500

Often brushed aside as being just another of Italy's bolshie, gritty port towns, Ancona is no beauty at first glance from the ferry, it's true. But there's more to Ancona than meets the superficial eye, and to simply bypass it is to miss much. In the old town, crowned by the *duomo*, you can peel back layers of history of the city founded by Greek settlers from Syracuse around 387 BC, admiring Roman ruins, the rich stash of its archaeological museum and its Renaissance *palazzi*, which glow softly in the evening light. Linger long enough in its hilltop parks overlooking the Adriatic and lively boulevards and cafe-rimmed piazzas and you'll see a more likeable side to Le Marche's seafront capital, promise.

◉ Sights

★ **Museo Archeologico**
Nazionale delle Marche   MUSEUM
(Via Ferretti 6; adult/reduced €4/2; ⊙8.30am-7.30pm Tue-Sun) Housed in the beautiful 16th-century **Palazzo Ferretti**, where the ceilings are covered with original frescoes and bas-reliefs, this museum presents a fascinating romp through time, from the Palaeolithic period to the Middle Ages. Although not as well curated as it could be (English

---

MONUMENTAL ANCONA

North of Piazza Dante Alighieri, at the far end of the port, is the **Arco di Traiano** (Trajan's Arch), erected in 115 BC by Apollodorus of Damascus in honour of the Roman Emperor Trajan. Luigi Vanvitelli's grand **Arco Clementino** (Clementine's Arch), inspired by Apollodorus' arch and dedicated to Pope Clement XII, is further on, near Molo Rizzo.

Head south along the coastal road and, after about 750m, you'll come across the enormous **Mole Vanvitelliana** (⊡ info 071 222 50 31; waterfront), designed by Luigi Vanvitelli in 1732 for Pope Clementine. Just past the pentagonal building, on Via XXIX Settembre, is the baroque **Porta Pia**, built as a monumental entrance to the town in the late 18th century at the request of Pope Pius VI.

---

information is sorely lacking), persevere, as this museum holds real treasures.

Among them are Neolithic flint daggers, richly embellished Attic vases, Etruscan votive bronzes, Celtic gold (the torques are stunning) and a pristine copy of the famous bronzes of Pergola (50–30 BC). Keep an eye out, too, for the *Venus of Frasassi*, a statuette of a buxom dame, 8.7cm tall, carved from stalactite 28,000 years ago.

Chiesa di San Domenico   CHURCH
(Piazza del Plebiscito; ⊙10am-noon & 4-8pm) Flanked by cafes, the elegant Piazza del Plebiscito has been Ancona's meeting spot since medieval times. It's dominated by this baroque church, containing the superb *Crucifixion* by Titian and *Annunciation* by Guercino. That gigantic statue in front is Pope Clement XII, who was honoured by the town for giving it free port status. The nearby fountain is from the 19th century.

Cattedrale di San Ciriaco   CATHEDRAL
(Piazzale del Duomo; ⊙8am-noon & 3-7pm summer, to 6pm winter) A stiff but scenic climb up from the old town, Ancona's perkily domed cathedral commands sweeping views of the city and port from its hilltop perch. Guarded by two marble lions, the cathedral sits grandly atop the site of an ancient pagan temple and is a potpourri of Byzantine,

Ancona

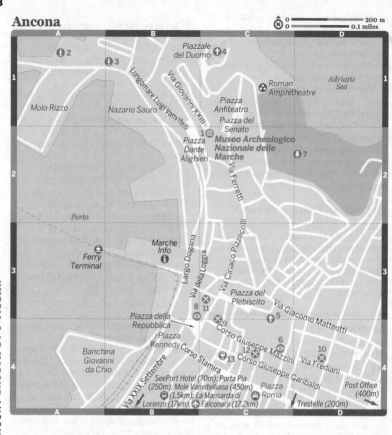

Ancona

◉ Top Sights
1 Museo Archeologico Nazionale
   delle Marche C2

◉ Sights
2 Arco Clementino A1
3 Arco di Traiano B1
4 Cattedrale di San Ciriaco C1
5 Chiesa di San Domenico C3
6 Fontana del Calamo C4
7 Parco del Cardeto D2
8 Teatro delle Muse B3

✕ Eating
9 Enopolis C4
10 Mercato delle Erbe D4
11 Osteria del Pozzo C3
12 Pizzeria Bontà Delle Marche C4

☕ Drinking & Nightlife
13 Liberty Cocktail Lounge C4

Romanesque and Gothic architectural features.

Wandering downhill from here along Piazza Anfiteatro, you will glimpse the remains of the city's **Roman amphitheatre**, believed to have been built during the reign of Emperor Augustus.

Fontana del Calamo   FOUNTAIN
(Corso Mazzini) Head along Corso Mazzini to see the 16th-century Fontana del Calamo, its 13 masked spouts supposedly representing effigies of those who had been beheaded.

Teatro delle Muse   THEATRE
(☏071 5 25 25; www.teatrodellemuse.org; Via della Loggia) On Piazza della Repubblica, this ornate theatre was built in 1826 and has a neoclassical facade that melds with Greek friezes portraying Apollo and the Muses.

🛌 Sleeping

⭐ **La Mansarda di Lorenzo**   APARTMENT €
(☎ 333 5051307; cirioni.lorenzo@gmail.com;
Via Cuneo 1, Falconara Marittima; apt €56-80;
P❄🛜🅿) Handily placed near the airport
yet still peaceful, this penthouse apartment
is a delight – spacious, immaculate, homely
and run by the affable Lorenzo. It's kitted
out with lounge and dining areas, the com-
fiest of beds, a huge terrace and a proper
kitchen with breakfast goodies. Give Lorenzo a call and he'll even pick you up from the
airport.

Trestelle   B&B €
(☎ 345 4562337; www.bbtrestelle.it; Via San Martino 10; s/d/tr €40/70/110; ❄🛜) This welcoming B&B is right in the thick of things,
a three-minute amble from Piazza Roma.
Rooms are simple yet modern and immaculately kept, with tiled floors and the odd
burst of colour.

Grand Hotel Passetto   HOTEL €€
(☎ 071 3 13 07; www.hotelpassetto.it; Via Thaon
de Revel 1; s €90-140, d €130-203, ste €180-255;
P❄@🛜🏊) Near Ancona's white-shingle
beach, a 20-minute walk east of the centre, this hotel has a genteel atmosphere, a
relaxing pool area and incredible sea views.
The light rooms are done out with parquet
floors and crisp white linen; the best have
four-poster beds and the suite has its own
jacuzzi. Substantial discounts are offered on
weekends and around holidays.

SeePort Hotel   BOUTIQUE HOTEL €€
(☎ 071 971 51 00; www.seeporthotel.com; Rupi di
Via XXIX Settembre 12; d €120-170, ste €245-265)
A breath of fresh air to Ancona's hotel scene,
the SeePort gazes wistfully out across the
harbour and the Adriatic. Housed in a clever conversion of a 1950s concrete block, the
crisp minimalist interiors have subtle nods
to the sea and the light-drenched, parquet-
floored rooms are among the town's most
stylish. The highly regarded restaurant dishes up Le Marche cuisine.

🍴 Eating

Corso Garibaldi and Corso Mazzini are
packed with restaurants, gelaterie and by-
the-slice pizza places, some of which can be
fiercely packed at lunchtime (aim to arrive
early).

HIGH ABOVE ANCONA

Parco del Cardeto (www.parcodel
cardeto.it; ⏰ 8.30am-8.30pm summer,
8am-5.30pm winter) The din of central
Ancona fades to a distant hum from this
park straddling the hill behind the city,
with broad views across the rooftops of
the old town to the port and the Adriatic.
The pine shade and sea breezes up here
are refreshing in summer. Fortifications,
a 19th-century lighthouse and a Napoleonic-era cemetery can be found in its
grounds.

Pizzeria Bontà Delle Marche   PIZZA €
(☎ 071 5 57 76; Via Benincasa 7; pizza slice around
€1.50; ⏰ 10.30am-2.45pm & 4.30-10.30pm Mon-
Sat, 4.30-11pm Sun; 🅿) For good, honest, sub-
€5 grub, you can't beat this place, where
the pizzas fly bubbling hot out of the oven
quicker than you can say *delizioso!* They're
served *al taglio* (by the slice) or whole to
take away.

Mercato delle Erbe   MARKET €
(Piazza dell'Erbe; ⏰ 7.30am-1pm & 5-8pm Mon-
Wed, Fri & Sat, 7.30am-1pm Thu) Going strong
since 1926, this market hall does a brisk
trade in fresh produce, pastries and bread,
cheese, *salumi* and other picnic goodies.

Osteria del Pozzo   OSTERIA €€
(☎ 071 207 39 96; Via Bonda 2; meals €25-35;
⏰ noon-2.30pm & 7.30-10pm Mon-Sat) Unless
you've booked ahead, you'll be lucky to grab
one of the cheek-by-jowl tables at this inviting *osteria*, which overflows with regulars.
They are here for the spot-on seafood –
generous helpings of pasta with shellfish,
beautifully cooked sea bass and the like –
all washed down with inexpensive house
wine.

Enopolis   ITALIAN €€
(☎ 071 207 15 05; www.enopolis.it; Corso Mazzini 7;
meals €35-45; ⏰ 9.30am-3.30pm & 6.30pm-mid-
night Wed-Mon) A visit to this restaurant and
enoteca is worth it simply for the tour of
the labyrinthine cellars of the 18th-century
Palazzo Jona. You can sit among contemporary art or next to an ancient well as you
sample fresh fish (the main event) along
with recommended wines for each course.

🍷 Drinking

Piazza del Plebiscito is one of the most relaxed spots for an alfresco drink, with tables set up on the pretty square.

Liberty Cocktail Lounge   BAR
(Via Traffico 7-10; ⊙ 11am-1.30am Mon, Tue & Thu-Sat, 5pm-1.30am Wed & Sun) Hidden on a back alley and identified only by a discreet sign, this art-deco-inspired cafe is an atmospheric spot to kick off a night with a cocktail (€8). Tiffany glass lamps and a bohemian crowd will make you want to paint the scene and sell it as a framed poster.

🛈 Information

Farmacia Centrale (☑ 071 20 27 46; Corso Mazzini 1)

Marche Info (☑ 071 35 89 91; www.comune. ancona.it; Via della Loggia 50; ⊙ 9am-2pm & 3-7pm, shorter hours winter) Within the ferry terminal, this is the tourist office for Ancona Le Marche province. Stop by for leaflets, maps, itineraries and more.

Police Station (☑ 071 2 28 81; Via Giovanni Gervasoni 19) South of the city centre.

Post Office (Largo XXIV Maggio; ⊙ 8.20am-7.05pm Mon-Fri, 8.20am-12.35pm Sat)

🛈 Getting There & Away

AIR

Falconara Airport (☑ 071 2 82 71; www. ancona-airport.com) Situated 19km west of Ancona, Falconara Airport is small and easy to navigate. Major airlines that fly into Ancona include Lufthansa, Alitalia and Ryanair; the latter operates daily flights to London Stansted.

BUS

Most buses leave from Piazza Cavour, inland from the port (it's a five-minute walk east of the seafront, along Corso Giuseppe Garibaldi), except for a few going to Falconara and Portonovo, which originate at the train station.

TO	FARE (€)	DURATION	FREQUENCY
Falconara airport	5	45min	hourly
Jesi	2.85	45min	hourly
Macerata	3.75	1½hr	12 daily
Numana	2.35	45min	hourly
Portonovo	2	30min	9 daily Jun-Aug
Recanati	2.65	1¼hr	hourly
Senigallia	3.75	1hr	hourly

CAR & MOTORCYCLE

Ancona is on the A14, linking Bologna with Bari. The SS16 coastal road runs parallel to the autostrada and is a pleasant, toll-free alternative if you're not looking to get anywhere fast. The SS76 connects Ancona with Perugia and Rome.

There's plenty of parking, which gets steadily more expensive the closer to the centre you get (€1.20 to €2.70 per hour). At the multistorey Parcheggio Degli Archi near the train station it's just €2 to park all day.

You'll find all the major car hire companies at the airport, including **Europcar** (☑ 071 916 22 40; www.europcar.it), **Maggiore** (☑ 071 918 88 05), **Avis** (☑ 071 5 22 22; www.avis.com) and **Hertz** (☑ 071 207 37 98; www.hertz.com).

FERRY

Ferries operate to Greece, Croatia, Albania and Turkey.

TRAIN

Ancona is on the Bologna–Lecce line. Check whether you're taking a Eurostar service, as there can be a substantial supplement.

TO	FARE (€)	DURATION	FREQUENCY
Bari	44.50-55.50	3¾-4¾hr	hourly
Bologna	15-32	1¾-2¾hr	twice hourly
Florence	49.50-68	2¾-3¼hr	hourly
Milan	56-81	3¼-4hr	hourly
Pesaro	4.35-12	27-56min	twice hourly
Rome	16.70-38	3-4hr	every 2hr

🛈 Getting Around

TO/FROM THE AIRPORT

There is a frequent train service between Castelferreti station, opposite the terminal, and Ancona (15 to 25 minutes, €1.75). Alternatively, Conero bus runs the Aerobus Raffaelo roughly hourly from Piazza Cavour to the airport (from 6am to 10pm Monday to Saturday, shorter hours on Sunday). The trip costs €5 one way and takes around 30 minutes. The airport **taxi service** (☑ 071 91 82 21) can take you to central Ancona (around €40).

BUS

About six **Conero Bus** (www.conerobus.it) services, including buses 1/3, 1/4 and 1/5, connect the main train station with the centre (Piazza Cavour), while bus 12 connects the main station with the ferry port (€1.30); look for the

WORTH A TRIP

THE FLYING HOUSE OF LORETO

Straddling a hilltop and visible from afar, Loreto is absorbed entirely by its bauble-domed **Basilica della Santa Casa** (Piazza della Madonna; ⏱6.15am-7pm). While the original basilica started in 1468 was Gothic, Renaissance additions have made today's basilica an architectural masterpiece, with its riot of gold-leafed halos, impressive frescoes and religious triptychs. Inside stands the elaborate marble **Santa Casa di Loreto**, or the Holy House shrine, where pilgrims flock to glimpse a jewel-encrusted black statue of the Virgin and pray in the candlelit twilight. The chapel is allegedly where Jesus was raised as a child. Legend has it a host of angels winged the chapel over from Nazareth in 1294 after the Crusaders were expelled from Palestine.

If you fancy staying the night in the calm, pretty old town, 18th-century townhouse **B&B Antica Maison** (☎366 1754341; www.anticamaison.net; Via Francesco Asdrubali 24; s/d/tr €55/70/90; ❄🛜) brims with charming features like beams and four-poster beds. Fausta and Livio extend a very warm welcome. Foodie pilgrims won't want to miss out on the grilled meats prepared with a gourmet twist at Michelin-starred **Ristorante Andreina** (☎071 97 01 24; www.ristoranteandreina.it; Via Buffolareccia 14 ; menus €55-75; ⏱noon-3pm & 8-10.30pm Thu-Mon).

Loreto can be easily reached by train from Ancona (€2.65, 20 minutes, hourly).

bus stop with the big signpost displaying Centro and Porto.

TAXI

Call ☎071 4 33 21 at the train station or ☎071 20 28 95 in the town centre.

Parco del Conero

Only minutes from Ancona but a world unto itself, Parco del Conero is stunning, with limestone cliffs razoring above the cobalt-blue Adriatic and crescent-shaped, white pebble bays backed by fragrant woods of pine, oak, beech, broom and oleander trees. Walking trails thread through the 60 sq km park, which is a conservation area. Remarkably still off the radar for many travellers, the park retains a peaceful, unspoilt air found nowhere else along Le Marche's coastline. Its highest peak is 572m Monte Conero, which takes a spectacular nosedive into the sea. The vineyards that taper down its slopes produce the excellent, full-bodied Rosso Conero red wine.

Parco del Conero encompasses the cliff-backed seaside resorts of **Portonovo**, **Sirolo** and **Numana**, all of which make fine bases for exploring. Boat trips from Portonovo and Sirolo are the best way to cove hop.

🛏 Sleeping

Camping Internazionale　CAMPGROUND €
(☎071 933 08 84; www.campinginternazionale.com; Via San Michele 10, Sirolo; camping 2 people, car & tent €26-48, for sea view add €4-8; ⏱mid-

May–mid-Sep; @🛜❄👶) Shaded in the trees just a few metres from the scenic beaches below Sirolo, this full-service campsite is replete with swimming pool, pizzeria, bar, grocery store and children's club with plenty of activities to keep the little ones amused. Free walking tours of the park are offered in summer.

⭐ **Acanto Country House**　GUESTHOUSE €€
(☎071 933 11 95; www.acantocountryhouse.com; Via Ancarano 18, Sirolo; s €70, d €100-140, ste €110-150; P❄🛜❄) Set back from Sirolo's beaches and surrounded by cornfields, meadows and olive groves, this converted farmhouse is a gorgeous country escape, taking in the full sweep of the coast. Named after flowers like peony and rose, rooms have been designed with the utmost attention to detail, with gleaming wood floors, exposed stone and embroidered bedspreads.

There's an outdoor pool and jacuzzi for a relaxing bubble, and the owners are more than happy to oblige whether you want to hire a bike or make use of the barbecue area.

🍴 Eating

La Torre　SEAFOOD €€
(☎071 933 07 47; www.latorrenumana.it; Via la Torre 1, Numana; meals €30-40; ⏱12.30-2.30pm & 7.30-10.30pm Mon-Sat, 12.30-3pm Sun) Floor-to-ceiling glass walls maximise the wraparound sea views from this sleek, industrial-chic restaurant, with bare wood floors, crisp white tablecloths and exposed silver pipework. Choose from brilliantly fresh sushi, antipasti

and artistically presented mains, mostly – surprise, surprise – with a seafood slant. It's hugely popular with the locals.

Il Molo SEAFOOD €€

(☑ 071 80 10 40; www.ilmolo.it; Spaggia di Portonovo, Portonovo; meals €30; ☺ noon-2.30pm & 7.30pm-late daily Jun-Aug, Wed-Mon Apr, May, Sep & Oct) Whatever splashes around in the sea around Monte Conero lands on the menu at Il Molo, generously supplied by the local fishermen who show up here each morning with their fresh catches. Expect various inventive combinations of pasta and shellfish.

❶ Information

Tourist Office (☑ 071 933 18 79; www.parcodelconero.com; Via Peschiera 30, Sirolo; ☺ 9am-1pm & 4-7pm mid-Jun–mid-Sep, 9am-1pm Mon-Sat Mar–mid-Jun & mid-Sep–Dec) For information on the park or to arrange guided tours.

❶ Getting There & Away

Buses from Ancona run sporadically throughout the year, peaking in July and August, but the area is much easier to explore with your own set of wheels.

Urbino

POP 15,500

Raphael's Renaissance 'hood, the vibrant university town of Urbino is often the first stop on a trip to Le Marche and understandably so. The patriarch of the Montefeltro family, Duca Federico da Montefeltro, created the hippest art scene of the 15th century here, gathering the great artists, architects and scholars of his day to create a sort of think tank. The town's splendour was made official by Unesco, which deemed the entire city centre a World Heritage Site in 1998.

◉ Sights

Palazzo Ducale PALACE, MUSEUM

(www.palazzoducaleurbino.it; adult/reduced all 3 museums €12/9.50; ☺ 8.30am-7.15pm Tue-Sun, to 2pm Mon) A microcosm of Renaissance architecture, art and history, the Palazzo Ducale contains the **Galleria Nazionale delle Marche** (adult/reduced €12/9.50; ☺ 8.30am-7.15pm Tue-Sun, to 2pm Mon), **Museo Archeologico** and **Museo della Ceramica**. The museum triptych is housed within Federico da Montefeltro's palace. The duke enlisted the foremost artists and architects of the age

to create this whimsically turreted Renaissance masterpiece.

In the Galleria Nazionale delle Marche, a monumental staircase, one of Italy's first, leads to the *piano nobile* (literally 'noble floor') and the Ducal Apartments. Piero della Francesca was one of the artists employed by the duke, and his work, *The Flagellation*, adorns the duke's library. The collection also includes a large number of drawings by Federico Barocci, as well as stunning Renaissance works by Raphael, Titian and Signorelli.

From Corso Garibaldi you get the best view of the complex, with its unusual Facciata dei Torricini, a three-storey loggia in the form of a triumphal arch, flanked by circular towers.

Duomo di Urbino CATHEDRAL

(☺ 7.30am-1pm & 2-8pm) Rebuilt in the early 19th century in neoclassical style, the interior of Urbino's *duomo* commands much greater interest than its austere facade. Particularly memorable is Federico Barocci's *Last Supper*. The basilica's **Museo Diocesano Albani** (www.museodiocesanourbino.it; admission €3; ☺ 9.30am-1pm & 2.30-6.30pm Wed-Mon) contains religious artefacts, vestments and more paintings, including Andrea da Bologna's *Madonna del Latte* (Madonna Breastfeeding).

Casa Natale di Raffaello MUSEUM

(Via Raffaello 57; adult/reduced €3.50/2.50; ☺ 9am-7pm Mon-Sat, 10am-1pm & 3-6pm Sun) North of the Piazza della Repubblica you'll find the 15th-century house where Raphael was born in 1483 and spent his first 16 years. On the 1st floor is possibly one of Raphael's first frescoes, a Madonna with child. The museum takes a touching look at Raphael's family life.

Above all, the museum homes in on the influence of his father, Giovanni Santi, who was a court painter and taught his talented young son all he knew.

Casa della Poesia MUSEUM

(Palazzi Odasi, Via Valerio 1; ☺ 3-6.30pm Mon & Thu, 9am-1pm Wed & Fri, 10.30am-6.30pm Sat & Sun) FREE South of the piazza, this brand new cultural space in the Renaissance Palazzo Odasi is dedicated to controversial expat American poet Ezra Pound, a seminal figure in the early modernism movement. Centred on a lovely arcaded inner courtyard, it hosts everything from art and photography exhibitions to readings and talks.

Urbino

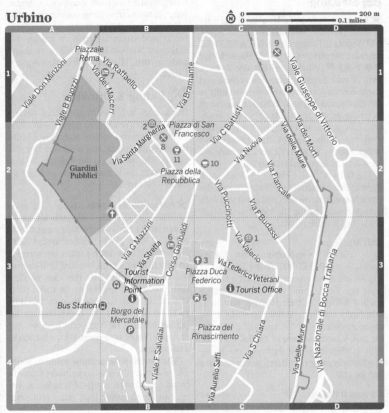

Oratorio di San Giovanni   CHURCH
(Via Barocci 31; admission €2.50; ⏰10am-1pm
& 3-6pm Mon-Sat, 10am-1pm Sun) This 14th-
century church features brightly coloured
frescoes by Lorenzo and Giacomo Salimbeni.

🎎 Festivals & Events

The city swings into summer at the **Urbino
Jazz Festival** in June, when performances are held all over town. This is followed
by the **International Festival of Ancient
Music** in July and the **Festa dell'Aqui-
lone**, a kite festival, on the first weekend in
September.

Festa dell'Duca   CULTURAL
(⏰3rd Sun Aug) The city time-travels back to
the Middle Ages, with medieval fun hitting
the streets in the shape of a costumed procession and the re-enactment of a tournament on horseback.

Urbino

★**Locanda della Valle Nuova** FARMSTAY €
(☑0722 33 03 03; www.vallenuova.it; La Cappella 14, Sagrata di Fermignano; d €56, apt €90-150, half-board per person €30; ⊘late May-early Nov; 🅿@🛜🏊) 🏊 What a delight this organic farm is, with bright, immaculate rooms and lovely, soothing views across wooded hills to the mountains beyond. Whether you want to rustle up an Italian feast with a cookery class, go horse riding or learn basket-weaving, Giulia, one of the owners, will oblige. She is also a terrific cook and dinners are a feast of homegrown goodies.

The farm is 16km south of Urbino (follow signs to Fermignano, then Sagrata), but the English-speaking owners will assist you with transport and visiting the local towns. Minimum stay is three nights.

B&B Albornoz B&B €
(☑347 2987897; www.bbalbornoz.com; Via dei Maceri 23; s €50, d €70-80; 🛜🍴) Wedged in a quiet old-town corner, this B&B has boutique flavour. A spiral staircase links three studios full of designer touches, with murals, funky lighting and bold artworks, from the monochromatic 'You and Me' to the floral, lilac-kissed romance of 'Osaka'. All come with kitchenettes and espresso machines. The friendly owners will squeeze in an extra bed for €20.

Albergo Italia HOTEL €€
(☑0722 27 01; www.albergo-italia-urbino.it; Corso Garibaldi 32; s €50-70, d €80-120; ❄🛜) Set behind the Palazzo Ducale, the Italia could not be better positioned. Modern and well designed, the shuttered townhouse is restfully quiet and staff are genuinely friendly. In warmer months, take breakfast on the balcony.

Urbino Resort AGRITURISMO €€
(www.tenutasantigiacomoefilippo.it; Via San Giacomo in Foglia 7, Pantiere; s €108-132, d €120-175, ste €180-240, meals €30-40; 🅿❄🛜🍴) 🏊 And relax... You can't help but unwind the minute you check into this gorgeous country abode, surrounded by vineyards and gardens fragrant with flowers and herbs. Spread across six stylishly converted stone farm buildings, the wood-floored rooms are individually designed – some are decorated in soothing pastels with Laura Ashley fabrics, others are slick and contemporary. An infinity pool overlooking the hills, a spa offering treatments from massage to shiatsu, hikes in the surrounding countryside and a lakefront restaurant that uses organic, farm-fresh produce in its creative cuisine will make you want to linger here more than a night or two. The resort sits 13km north of Urbino.

🍴 Eating & Drinking

Don't miss Italy's only homicidal pasta – *strozzapreti* (priest stranglers) – available in most restaurants. One legend has it that the shredded pasta was designed to choke priests who would eat for nothing at local restaurants, so if you happen to wear the collar – be careful.

★**Antica Osteria da la Stella** OSTERIA €€
(☑0722 32 02 28; www.anticaosteriadalastella.com; Via Santa Margherita 1; meals €25-40; ⊘12.30-2.30pm & 7.30-10.30pm Tue-Sat, 12.30-2.30pm Sun) Duck down a quiet side street to this rustically elegant, beamed 15th-century inn once patronised by the likes of Piero della Francesca. Legendary in these parts, Osteria de la Stella puts its own inventive twist on seasonal food. Every dish strikes perfect balance, be it gnocchi with porcini-and-quail sauce or venison with wild berries and polenta.

The owners take genuine pride in sourcing, and everything is homemade, from the bread served with syrup-thick balsamic vinegar to the dreamily light pasta and petits fours.

Osteria L'Angolo Divino OSTERIA €€
(☑0722 32 75 59; www.angolodivino.com; Via Sant'Andrea 14; meals €30; ⊘noon-2.30pm & 7-10.30pm Tue-Sun) This subterranean *osteria* oozes atmosphere. Arched brick alcoves overflow with wine bottles, which are available for tastings. On the menu are simple but perfectly flavoured pasta specialities, including gnocchi with truffle and better-than-it-sounds *pasta nel sacco* (pasta in a sack, or fresh pasta coated with eggs and breadcrumbs).

Tartufi Antiche Bontà WINE BAR
(Via Raffaello Sanzio 35; ⊘10am-8pm Tue-Sun) 🏊 You'll find fresh truffles year round alongside a mouthwatering array of other local specialities at this deli-*enoteca*. Venture downstairs to sample the best of the region's *vino* with a tasting plate of *salumi e formaggi*.

Caffè Centrale CAFE
Piazza della Repubblica; ⊘ 6.30am-2am) Popular with Urbino's students, this is the best of the piazza cafes. Its outdoor tables get a relaxing dose of afternoon sun. Pastries, sandwiches and gelato are served any time of day, and aperitivi accompany late-afternoon drinks.

❶ Information

Tourist Information Point (☑ 0722 26 31; Piazza Mercatale; ⊘ 9am-6pm) At the entrance of the lift (one-way tickets €0.50; ⊘ 7am-8pm) into town (this lift cuts out a five- to 10-minute uphill walk to the old town). Free wi-fi.

Tourist Office (☑ 0722 26 13; Via Puccinotti 3; ⊘ 9am-1pm & 2.30-5.30pm Mon-Sat, 9am-1pm Sun) Pick up a free map and the miniguide *Urbino City of Art* for €5.

❶ Getting There & Around

BUS
Adriabus (☑ 800 664332, 0722 37 67 38; www.adriabus.eu) runs an hourly service daily between Urbino and Pesaro (€3.10, one hour), from where you can pick up a train for Bologna.
Shuttle buses operate from Piazza della Repubblica and Piazza Mercatale.

CAR
Most vehicles are banned from the walled city. There are car parks outside the city gates, including the main one at Borgo del Mercatale. Parking costs €1.50 per hour.

TAXI
For a taxi, call ☑ 0722 25 50.

TRAIN
There is no train service to Urbino (pick up trains in Pesaro, about 35km away).

Pesaro
POP 94,600

Look beyond the concrete high-rise hotels and the crowds of bronzed holidaymakers jostling for towel space on the beach in August, and you'll find a lot to like about Pesaro.
The town's setting is perfect, with beaches of fine golden sand fringing the Adriatic, a backdrop of undulating hills, and a pretty old town centred on the cafe-rimmed Piazza del Popolo, where the Renaissance Palazzo Ducale stands proud. The composer Rossini was so fond of his home town that he left it all of his possessions when he died (be sure to check out Casa Rossini while you're here).

◉ Sights & Activities

Pesaro has four major beach areas – the Blue Flag–awarded **Levante**, **Ponente**, **Baia Flaminia** and the **free beach**. Levante and Ponente are the jam-packed hotel-fronted beaches, so for more elbow room head to the free beach *(spiaggia libera)* to the south of the city, under Monte Ardizio.

Casa Rossini MUSEUM
(Via Rossini 34; combined ticket incl entry to Musei Civici adult/reduced €9/7.50; ⊘ 10am-1pm & 4.30-7.30pm Tue-Sun) In 1792 famous composer Rossini was born in a typical Pesaro townhouse that is now the Casa Rossini. His mother was a singer, his father a horn player and the young lad was composing when he was knee-high to a grasshopper. Prints, personal items and portraits provide an insight into the life of the virtuoso and his operas, such as the jaunty *Barber of Seville*.

Musei Civici MUSEUM
(www.museicivicipesaro.it; Piazza Toschi Mosca 29; combined ticket incl entry to Casa Rossini adult/reduced €9/7.50; ⊘ 10am-1pm & 4-7.30pm Tue-Sun, shorter hours winter) Opened in the 1860s, just after Italian reunification, the town's original art gallery is now the Musei Civici, which also showcases Pesaro's 700-year-old pottery tradition with one of Italy's best collections of majolica ceramics.

✸ Festivals & Events

Rossini Opera Festival MUSIC
(☑ 0721 380 02 94; www.rossinioperafestival.it; Via Rossini 24; ⊘ box office during festival 10am-noon & 4-6.30pm) This two-week festival in August is a love letter to Pesaro's local legend. Productions of Rossini's operas and concerts are staged at the Teatro Rossini and Adriatic Arena. Tickets go for anything between €20 and €150, with substantial student and last-minute discounts.

⊨ Sleeping & Eating

Most hotels close from October to Easter. Though many places are uninspiring 1960s concrete blocks, you can find some charmers if you look hard enough.

Marinella CAMPGROUND €
(☑ 0721 5 57 95; www.campingmarinella.it; SS16 km244; camping 2 people, car & tent €26.50-39.50; ⊘ Easter-Sep; ☏▥) Drift off in your seaside tent to the sound of waves breaking on the beach. A pizzeria is on site, as well as

a minimarket, beach volleyball and lots of child-friendly activities.

Hotel Clipper
HOTEL €€

(☑ 0721 3 09 15; www.hotelclipper.it; Viale Guglielmo Marconi 53; s €39-99, d €49-169, tr €74-189; P ❄ 🖟 🗟 ➡) In the capable hands of the friendly Gasparini family, Clipper is literally steps from the beach and a five-minute stroll from the centre. The bright and breezy rooms are well kept and have balconies; it's worth shelling out an extra €5 per night for a sea view. Rates include bike rental and beach towels.

L'Angolo di Mario
SEAFOOD, PIZZA €€

(☑ 0721 6 58 50; http://angolodimario.it; Via Nazario Sauro; pizza €2.50-10, meals €25-35; ☺ noon-3pm & 7-11.30pm, closed Mon) L'Angolo di Mario couples sea views with contemporary decor, pleasant service and great food. Bag a table on the terrace to gaze out across the Adriatic as you dig into well-heaped plates of mussels and clams or seafood pasta, before mains of grilled fish or beef. It also does a mean pizza.

☆ Entertainment

Teatro Rossini
THEATRE

(☑ 0721 3 24 82; www.enteconcerti.it; Via Rossini) This theatre was renamed in the composer's honour, and its grand ceiling and ornate box seats make it a breathtaking spot to catch a concert, especially during the Rossini Opera Festival.

ℹ Information

Tourist Office (☑ 0721 6 93 41; www.turismo.pesarourbino.it; Piazzale della Libertà 11; ☺ 9am-1pm & 3-6.30pm Mon-Sat, 9am-1pm Sun) Has excellent information in English, with maps, hotels and sights.

ℹ Getting There & Around

BUS

The main bus station is on Piazza Matteotti, with regular buses to Ancona (€5.15, 1¼ hours, four daily). **Adriabus** (☑ 0722 37 67 38, 0800 664332; www.adriabus.eu) operates a twice-daily service to Rome (€40, 4¾ hours) and hourly buses to Urbino (€3.10, one hour).

TRAIN

Pesaro is on the Bologna–Lecce train line and you can reach Rome (€19.40 to €45, 3½ to 5¾ hours, nine daily) by changing trains at Falconara Marittima, just before Ancona. There are at least hourly services to Ancona (€4.35 to €10.40, 35 to 50 minutes), Rimini (€3.75 to

€9, 16 to 32 minutes) and Bologna (€10.70 to €21.50, 1¼ to 2¼ hours). The train station is on the western edge of town, about 2km from the beach.

Grotte di Frasassi

Grotte di Frasassi
CAV

(☑ 0732 9 00 80; www.frasassi.com; adult/reduce €15.50/13.50; ☺ 10am-6pm, to 5pm winter) I September 1971 a team of climbers stumble across a hole in the hill country around Gen ga. On closer inspection, this 'hole' turned out to be one of the biggest cave system in Europe, the Grotte di Frasassi, which i today Le Marche's unmissable geologica marvel.

The fast-flowing river Sentino has gouged out this karst wonderland, which can be admired on a 70-minute tour through its warren of chambers and tunnels. Tours in English depart at roughly 11.15am, 12.45pm 2.45pm and 4.15pm daily, but it's worth calling ahead to double-check times. Wea comfortable shoes and bring an extra layer as the 14°C temperature can feel nippy in summer.

On a tour you'll take in the greatest hits o the cave's rock stars. First up is the Ancona Abyss, a cavernous 200m-high, 180m-long chamber, which – as your guide will point out – would comfortably accommodate Milan Cathedral. Your gaze will be drawn to a fairy forest of dripping stalactites and gian stalagmites reaching up to 20m in length some 1.4 million years in the making. High lights here include Niagara, a petrified cas cade of pure calcite and a crystallized lake In the so-called Gran Canyon, look out for parallel stalactites resembling pipe organs and waxy stalagmites that rise up like melt ed candles .

To reach the caves from Ancona, take the SS76 off the A14 and look for the Genga-Sassoferrato exit. The car park, 1.5km east of the cave entrance at San Vittore Terme is where you buy your tickets and catch the shuttle bus to the caves. The closest train station, Genga San Vittore Terme, is also next to the car park and ticket office.

Macerata
POP 42,000

Straddling low-rise hills, Macerata combines charming hill-town scenery with the verve of student life – its university is one o

Europe's oldest, dating to 1290. Its old town, a jumbled maze of cobblestone streets and honey-coloured *palazzi*, springs to life in summer for a month-long opera festival.

Sights & Activities

Arena Sferisterio THEATRE

0733 23 07 35; www.sferisterio.it; Piazza Mazzini 10; adult/reduced €3/2, incl guided tour €5/4; 9am-4pm Mon, 9am-1pm & 3-7pm Tue-Sun, guided tours noon & 5pm) One of Europe's most stunning outdoor theatres is the neoclassical Arena Sferisterio, a grand colonnaded affair resembling an ancient Roman arena, which was built between 1820 and 1829. Its acoustics are second to none. From mid-July to mid-August it's the backdrop for the **Macerata Opera Festival** (www.sferisterio.it), one of Italy's foremost musical events, attracting the cream of the operatic world.

Loggia dei Mercanti HISTORIC BUILDING

(Piazza della Libertà) The historic centre is presided over by the Renaissance Loggia dei Mercanti on Piazza della Libertà. Built in 1505 for Cardinal Alessandro Farnese, the soon-to-be Pope Paul III, the arcaded building housed travelling merchants selling their wares.

Musei Civici di Palazzo Buonaccorsi MUSEUM

0733 25 63 61; www.maceratamusei.it; Via Don Minzoni 24; adult/reduced €3/2; 10am-6pm Tue-Sun) Macerata's museums cluster in the Musei Civici di Palazzo Buonaccorsi. The collections are spread over three floors.

On the ground floor is the **Museo delle Carozza**, housing an extensive collection of 18th- to 20th-century coaches. Stepping up to the 1st floor brings you to the city's **Arte Antica** collection, with works dating from the 13th to the 19th centuries, while the 2nd floor is dedicated to Arte Moderna, with several rooms given over to Macerata-born painter Ivo Pannaggi, a driving force behind Italian futurism in the 1920s and '30s.

Sleeping

Albergo Arena HOTEL €

0733 23 09 31; www.albergoarena.com; Vicolo Sferisterio 16; s €50-85, d €65-100; P ※ @ ⑦) Bang in the heart of the old town, this shuttered stone house offers modest, spotlessly kept rooms. It's a welcoming base for exploring the historic centre.

ⓘ EXTREME CAVING

Speleo Avventura (0732 9 72 11; www.frasassi.com; 2hr-blue/3hr-red course €35/45) To up the adventure ante considerably at the Grotte di Frasassi, sign up for a course with Speleo Avventura to pass across 30m chasms and crawl on your hands and knees along narrow passages and tunnels. There are two versions: blue (easy-ish) and red (hard, as you'll be going right into the cave's bowels). Book at least a week in advance. Happy spelunking.

Hotel Arcadia HOTEL €

0733 23 59 61; www.harcadia.it/dove.htm; Via Matteo Ricci 134; s/d/tr/q €40/60/80/100; P ※ ⑦) On a quiet lane not far from the cathedral, the Arcadia gives three-star comfort and a genuinely warm welcome at wallet-friendly prices. The pick of the rooms sport a contemporary look, with warm hues, parquet floors and flat-screen TVs. Light sleepers should be aware that the walls are quite thin.

★**Le Case** AGRITURISMO €€

(0733 23 18 97; www.ristorantelecase.it; Via Mozzavinci 16/17; s/d/ste €90/120/210, meals €40-90; P ※ ⑦ ⛱ ⚐) 🍴 A drive lined with cypress trees sweeps up to this country manor and organic farm, nestled in glorious isolation 9km west of Macerata. The pale-hued, wood-floored rooms combine an air of discreet luxury with original trappings like beams, flagstone floors and antique furnishings, and you'll sleep like a log given the pin-drop peace here.

A spa area and an indoor pool overlooking rolling hills, two gourmet restaurants, including Michelin-starred L'Enoteca, and farmyard animals to please the kids all make this an outstanding pick. Homemade jams, breads and tarts make their way onto the breakfast table. Staff will happily squeeze in a cot or an extra bed if you ask.

To reach Le Case, head north of Macerata to Villa Potenza, then follow the signs near the chapel for Le Case; full directions are given on the website.

Eating & Drinking

Osteria dei Fiori OSTERIA €€

(0733 26 01 42; www.osteriadeifiori.it; Via Lauro Rossi 61; meals €25-30; noon-3.30pm &

7-10.30pm Mon-Sat; 🖉🏠) This *osteria* has a homely, low-key vibe and alfresco seating in summer. The cuisine is season-focused, but the creative menu might include, say, spaghetti with spring chicory and hazelnuts, followed by roasted rabbit with fennel and coffee-aniseed ice cream. Kids and vegetarians are well catered for.

Trattoria da Ezio   TRATTORIA €€

(🖉 0733 23 23 66; www.trattoriadaezio.eu; Via Giovanni Mario Crescimbeni 65; meals €25-30; ⊙ noon-2.30pm & 7.30-9.30pm Tue-Sat; 🖉) A trattoria in the classic mould, da Ezio has been bubbling and stirring since 1957. The look and homely vibe have changed little since then and neither has the slow-food menu – making the most of freshly made pasta and farm-fresh meat and veggies. There are good vegetarian options.

★ L'Enoteca   ITALIAN €€€

(🖉 0733 23 18 97; www.enotecalecase.it; Via Mozzavinci 16/17; meals €50-60, tasting menus €45-90; ⊙ 8pm-10pm Wed-Sat) 🍽 Worth the trek to the countryside, Le Case's Michelin-starred restaurant has enough gourmet panache to keep foodies coming from afar. Beams and exposed stone create a rustically elegant scene. Meat reared on the organic farm, foraged herbs and flowers and garden veg all go into Michele Biagiola's menus created with love, precision and a razor-sharp eye for detail.

Choose a wine from the 1700-bottle list to pair with such gastronomic showstoppers as apple cake with sticky pork ribs and ginger gelato or *tortelli* stuffed with tender guinea fowl.

Caffè Venanzetti   CAFE

(Galleria Scipione, Via Gramsci 21/23; ⊙ 7am-9pm Mon-Sat) High ceilings and an old-world wood-mirror decor make this cafe a visual treat to go with delectable pastries and a mighty fine cappuccino.

☆ Entertainment

Teatro Lauro Rossi   THEATRE

(🖉 0733 23 35 08; Piazza della Libertà) Teatro Lauro Rossi is an elegant theatre built in 1774 for the musical enjoyment of the nobility. It now also allows well-dressed riff-raff to attend. It stages everything from classical music concerts to comedies, contemporary plays and dance productions.

ℹ Information

Post Office (Via Gramsci 44; ⊙ 8.20am-7.05pm Mon-Fri, 8.20am-12.35pm Sat)

Tourist Office (🖉 0733 23 48 07; www.turismo.provinciamc.it; Corso della Repubblica 32; ⊙ 9am-1pm & 3-6pm Mon-Sat, 9am-1pm Sun) Pick up info on Macerata and its surrounds and book tours here.

ℹ Getting There & Around

BUS

Services head to Rome (€23.50, four hours, six daily) and Civitanova Marche (€2.25, one hour, hourly). Timetables for local buses are available at the bus terminal.

CAR & MOTORCYCLE

The SS77 connects the city with the A14 to the east and roads for Rome in the west. There is paid parking (€1.20 per hour) from 8am to 8pm skirting the city walls and free parking at the Giardini Diaz, where the buses arrive.

TRAIN

From the **train station** (🖉 0733 24 03 54; Piazza XXV Aprile 8/10) there are good connections to Ancona (€5.60, 1¼ hours, hourly) and Rome (€16.20 to €33.60, four to five hours, eight daily). To reach Ascoli Piceno (€8.30, 1¾ to 2¼ hours, 10 daily), change trains in San Benedetto del Tronto and Civitanova Marche. Bus 6 links the station with the Piazza della Libertà in the city centre.

Ascoli Piceno

POP 49,900

With a continuous history dating from the Sabine tribe in the 9th century, Ascoli (as it's known locally) is like the long-lost cousin of ancient Rome and a small *Marchigiani* village, heavy on history and food. Weary legs will appreciate its lack of hills and all travellers will appreciate its historical riches, excellent pinacoteca, one of Italy's unsung perfect piazzas and the calorific *olive all'ascolana*, a veal-stuffed fried-olive treat.

◉ Sights

The town's Vecchio Quartiere (Old Quarter) stretches from Corso Mazzini (the main thoroughfare of the Roman-era settlement) to the Castellano river. Its main street is the picturesque Via delle Torri, which eventually becomes Via Solestà; it's a perfect spot to wander round.

⭐ Piazza del Popolo

PIAZZA

The harmonious and simply lovely Piazza del Popolo has been Ascoli's *salotto* (sitting room) since Roman times. The rectangular square is flanked on the west by the 13th-century Palazzo dei Capitani del Popolo. Built in the same famed travertine stone used throughout the region for centuries, the 'Captain's Palace' was the headquarters for the leaders of Ascoli. The statue of Pope Paul III above the main entrance was erected in recognition of his efforts to bring peace to the town.

Chiesa di San Francesco

CHURCH

(Piazza del Popolo; ⊗ 7am-12.30pm & 3.30-8pm) This beautiful church was started back in 1262 as an homage to a visit from St Francis himself. In the left nave is a 15th-century wooden cross that miraculously made it through a 1535 fire at the Palazzo dei Capitani, and has reputedly spilled blood twice since. Virtually annexed to the church is Loggia dei Mercanti, built in the 16th century by the powerful guild of wool merchants to hide their rough-and-tumble artisan shops.

Pinacoteca

MUSEUM

(www.ascolimusei.it; Piazza Arringo; adult/reduced €8/5; ⊗ 10am-7pm Tue-Sun summer, to 5pm winter) Gathered around a tree-shaded courtyard, the second-largest art gallery in Le Marche sits inside the 17th-century Palazzo Comunale. It boasts an outstanding display of art, sculpture and religious artefacts; there are 400 works in total, including paintings by Van Dyck, Titian and Rembrandt, and a stunning embroidered 13th-century papal cape worn by Ascoli-born Pope Nicholas IV.

Your ticket also gives you entry to two small collections in Ascoli's old quarter: the Galleria d'Arte Contemporanea (Corso Mazzini 90; adult/reduced €8/5, incl Pinacoteca & Museo dell'Arte Ceramica; ⊗ 10am-7pm Tue-Sun summer, to 5pm winter) and the Museo dell'Arte Ceramica (☑ 0736 29 82 13; Piazza San Tommaso; adult/reduced €8/5, incl Pinacoteca & Galleria d'Arte Contemporanea; ⊗ 10am-7pm Tue-Sun summer, to 5pm winter), which has displays on the major Italian pottery towns, including Deruta, Faenza and Genoa.

Duomo della Città di Ascoli Piceno

CATHEDRAL

(Piazza Arringo; ⊗ 8am-noon & 4-8pm) Topped by a pair of mismatched towers, Ascoli's *duomo* was built in the 16th century over a medieval building and dedicated to St Emidio, patron saint of the city. In the Cappella del Sacramento is the *Polittico*, a polyptych executed in 1473 by Carlo Crivelli. The crypt of Sant Emidio has a set of mosaics any ceramicist will appreciate.

Next to the cathedral and something of a traffic barrier today, the *battistero* (baptistry) has remained unchanged since it was constructed in the 11th century.

Chiesa di San Pietro Martire

CHURCH

(Piazza Ventidio Basso; ⊗ 7.30am-12.30pm & 3.30-7pm) The 14th-century Chiesa di San Pietro Martire is dedicated to the saint who founded the Dominican community at Ascoli. The chunky Gothic structure houses the Reliquario della Santa Spina, containing what is said to be a thorn from Christ's crown.

Torre degli Ercolani

HISTORIC BUILDING

(Via dei Soderini) This 40m-high tower, west of the Chiesa di San Pietro Martire, is the tallest of the town's medieval towers. Palazzetto Longobardo, a 12th-century Lombard-Romanesque defensive position and now the Ostello dei Longobardi youth hostel, abuts the tower. Just to the north is the well-preserved Ponte Romano, a single-arched Roman bridge.

Museo Archeologico

MUSEUM

(Piazza Arringo; adult/reduced €4/2; ⊗ 8.30am-7.30pm Tue-Sun) Ascoli's archaeological museum holds a small collection of tribal artefacts from Piceni and other European people dating back to the first centuries AD.

🎉 Festivals & Events

Fritto Misto all'Italiana

FOOD

(www.frittomistoallitaliana.it; ⊗ late Apr) This four-day festival of fried food aims to 'debunk the prejudice that it's unhealthy'. After a few hours spent grazing stalls packed with heavy-duty treats – *cannoli* from Sicily, *panzerotti* from Puglia and, of course, fried stuffed Ascoli olives – your body may not agree, although your taste buds will have had a blast.

Quintana

CULTURAL

(www.quintanadiascoli.it; ⊗ late Jul/early Aug) This is one of Italy's most famous medieval festivals, and for good reason. Expect thousands of locals dressed in typical medieval garb: knights in armour, flag-throwers and ladies in flamboyant velvet robes. Processions and flag-waving contests take place throughout July and August, but the big draw is the Quintana joust, when the town's six *sestieri* (districts) face off.

🛏 Sleeping

For a town of such modest proportions, Ascoli Piceno has an extraordinary number of charming hotels, many of which offer early booking discounts. Stop by the tourist office for lists of apartments, *agriturismi* and B&Bs.

Villa Fortezza   B&B €

(☑ 328 4131656; www.villafortezza.it; Via Fortezza Pia 5; s €40-80, d €70-100, q €120; 🅿 ❋ 🛜 🐾) On its hilltop perch above the old town near the fort and reached by a seemingly never-ending flight of steps, this villa is a delight. Salvatore, your kindly host, does his best to welcome you in his art-strewn home, where individually designed, parquet-floored rooms swing from classic to contemporary. A tree-shaded garden, gorgeous views and homemade *dolci* (sweets) at breakfast clinch the deal.

★ Hotel Palazzo dei Mercanti   HISTORIC HOTEL €€

(☑ 0736 25 60 44; www.palazzodeimercanti.it; Corso Trento e Trieste 35; r €90-190; 🅿 🛜) This 16th-century *palazzo* was once part of the Sant'Egido convent. Today you'll count your blessings in rooms done out in soothing pastel tones and hand-crafted furniture, with nice touches like tea and coffee and bathrobes (handy for the spa's whirlpool, sauna and hammam). The *palazzo* manages the delicate task of combining original stone-vaulted interiors with a fresh, contemporary aesthetic.

Palazzo Guiderocchi   BOUTIQUE HOTEL €€

(☑ 0736 25 97 10; www.palazzoguiderocchi.com; Via Cesare Battisti 3; s €65-100, d €70-110, ste €130-170; 🅿 ❋ 🛜) Not many places offer the history, atmosphere and comfort of this 16th-century *palazzo*. Beautifully gathered around an inner courtyard, it retains the romance of vaulted ceilings on the 1st floor, low wood-beamed ceilings on the 2nd, and frescoes and several original doors throughout. During slow months, palatial rooms can be an absolute steal.

🍴 Eating & Drinking

★ Degusteria 25 Doc & Dop   ITALIAN €

(☑ 0736 31 33 24; Via Panichi 3; meals €15; ⊙ 11am-midnight Tue-Sun) Strings of garlic and chilli dangle from the ceiling of this convivi-al deli-*enoteca,* where the locals squeeze in or spill out onto the terrace for fine wines and tasting plates of regional *salumi,* cheese and, of course, *olive all'ascolana.* Decent daily specials are rustled up for €6.

Our tip: go for *aperitivo,* which is one of the best in town. For €7 you'll get a drink an appetising sample of the three dishes of the day and a mini feast of regional specialities.

Bella Napoli   PIZZA €

(☑ 0736 25 70 30; Via dei Bonaparte 18; pizza €4.50-9; ⊙ 7-11pm) Yep, the name might make you want to leg it in the opposite direction pronto, but bear with us. Unlike its touristville name, this pizzeria is as authentic as they come. It's jam-packed on weekend nights with locals digging into monster-sized pizzas, including the double-whammy UFO (two pizzas, one on top of the other, with the filling in the middle).

Il Desco   MEDITERRANEAN €€

(☑ 0736 25 07 57; www.ildescoristorante.it; Via Vidacilio 10; meals €30-40; ⊙ noon-5pm & 7.30pm-midnight Tue-Sat, noon-5pm Sun) Funky chandeliers, high vaults and white distressed wood create a country-chic backdrop at this gorgeously styled *palazzo*. When the weather warms, diners spill out into the garden courtyard, lit by tealights. A clever use of herbs elevates seasonal specialities, from homemade fettuccine with artichokes and bacon, to fillet of sea bass with zucchini and almonds. It's all delicious.

Piccolo Teatro   ITALIAN €€

(☑ 0736 26 15 74; www.alpiccoloteatro.it; Via Goldoni 2; meals €25-35; ⊙ 11.30am-11pm Tue-Sun) This barrel-vaulted restaurant blends historic charm with a dash of style. Tables draped in white linen set the scene for wonderfully light pasta and season-driven dishes – from artichoke tart with fondue of Castelmagno cheese and smoked bacon chips to *coniglio in porchetta* (rolled rabbit stuffed with herbs) with plump Ascoli olives.

Caffè Meletti   CAFE

(Piazza del Popolo 20; ⊙ 7.30am-10pm Tue-Thu, to 11.30pm Fri-Sun) From the elegant shade of this cafe's portico you can sip a coffee or a glass of the famous homemade *anisette* (anise-flavoured liqueur) with *olive all'ascolana* as you gaze onto the piazza. The cafe, founded in 1904, was once a popular haunt for the likes of Ernest Hemingway and Jean-Paul Sartre.

ℹ Information

Police Station (☑ 0736 35 51 11; Viale della Repubblica 8)

Post Office (Via Crispi 2; ⏱ 8.20am-7.05pm Mon-Fri, 8.20am-12.35pm Sat)

Tourist Office (☑ 0736 25 30 45; turismo@ comune.ascolipiceno.it; Piazza Arringo 7; ⏱ 9am-6.30pm Mon-Fri, 9am-1pm & 3-6.30pm Sat, 10am-6pm Sun) Well stocked with maps and leaflets on Ascoli's sights and hiking in the surrounds and Monti Sibillini. It also rents out bikes for €2/4 per half/full day.

ℹ Getting There & Away

BUS

Services leave from Piazzale della Stazione, in front of the train station in the new part of town, east of the Castellano river. **START** (☑ 0736 33 80 28; www.startspa.it) runs buses to Rome (€14.50, three hours, eight daily) and Civitanova Marche (€5.15, two hours, 12 daily).

TRAIN

Connections to Ancona (€8.30, two hours, 16 daily) often involve a change in Porto d'Ascoli. Trains to Macerata (€7.55, 2¼ hours, 12 daily) require one or two changes. The station is a 15-minute walk east of the centre.

Monti Sibillini

Straddling the Le Marche–Umbria border in rugged splendour, the **Parco Nazionale dei Monti Sibillini** never looks less than extraordinary, whether visited in winter, when its peaks are dusted with snow, or in summer, when its meadows are carpeted with poppies and cornflowers. The 70,000-hectare national park covers some of the most dramatic landscapes in central Italy, with glacier-carved valleys, beautifully preserved hilltop hamlets, quiet beech forests where deer roam, and mountains, 10 of which tower above 2000m.

The park is a magnet for anyone seeking outdoor adventure or a brush with wildlife, with an expansive network of walking trails criss-crossing the area. *Rifugi* (mountain huts) welcome hikers every few kilometres with hearty meals and warm beds; most open summer only and details are available at all local tourist offices. There's a terrifically scenic driving loop around the mountains, which visitors can easily reach from Norcia (in Umbria) or Ascoli Piceno, Macerata or Ancona. From the southwest, start in Norcia, heading to **Castelluccio**. Follow signs to Montemonaco, Montefortino and Aman-

dola. Just past **Montefortino**, take the road marked for Madonna dell'Ambro, which will take you to the **Gola dell'Infernaccio**, Monti Sibillini's waterfall masterpiece. Backtrack to Montefortino and continue on the circle.

Although not technically in the Monti Sibillini National Park, the largest and prettiest town is **Sarnano**, on the SS78, which leads to **Sasso Tetto**, the main ski area in Monti Sibillini. From the main ski area, the road drops down to Lago Fiastra. To continue on an equally stunning drive, circle around to the SS209 through the Valnerina in Umbria.

🏃 Activities

Perched like an eyrie on a 1452m hilltop and ringed by the mighty summits of the Apennines, **Castelluccio** is a lone ranger of a village, with just 150 inhabitants admiring its jaw-dropping backdrop on a daily basis. Technically in Umbria, although only just, it makes a terrific base for hiking in the park. It's famous for its *lenticchie* (small, sweet lentils), and *pecorino* and ricotta cheeses, but it's the location that brings in visitors. The Casa del Parco (p611) in Norcia has information on walking and other activities, including paragliding, mountain biking and horse riding, in the surrounding area.

🛏 Sleeping & Eating

Taverna di Castelluccio   GUESTHOUSE €
(☑ 0743 82 11 58; www.tavernacastelluccio.it; Via Dietro la Torre 8; s/d/tr €52.50/80/115, incl half-board €70/116/159; 🐾) One of Castelluccio's few hotels, this abode has bright, pleasantly simple rooms, some with gorgeous Piano Grande views. A good night's sleep is guaranteed and the resident goats might be your wake-up call. It's worth forking out the extra for half-board, as the food (thick lentil soup, homemade pasta, grilled lamb and the like) is superb.

Hotel Paradiso   HOTEL €
(☑ 0737 84 74 68; www.sibillinihotels.it; Piazza Umberto I, Amandola; s/d/ste/q €40/72/120/120, incl half-board €60/120/160/240; 🅿🐾🚲) It's not easy to find or to reach, but this hilltop retreat is worth the trek for the view alone. With 48 spick-and-span rooms (most with balconies), a restaurant serving solid Umbrian home cooking (breakfast €5, lunch or dinner €20), a romantic arched walkway and bike rental, this is a cracking base for a mountain holiday.

La Citadella
AGRITURISMO €

(☑ 0736 85 63 61; www.cittadelladeisibillini.it; Località Citadella, Montemonaco; s/d €50/100, incl half-board €65/130; P 🛜 🌊 🐾) Goat bells are likely to be your wake-up call at this serene *agriturismo* just north of the village of Montemonaco. Rooms are pretty simple, but with a great restaurant serving local, homegrown fare, a mountain-facing swimming pool and easy access to the walks of the Monti Sibillini, you probably won't be spending too much time in them. Minimum stay two nights.

Agriturismo La Filomena
AGRITURISMO €

(☑ 0734 84 40 17; www.agriturismolafilomena.it; Frazione Collina 11, Montefortino; d €58-65, per week €240-800; P 🛜 🌊 🐾) Crouched at the foot of Monte Fortino and spread across several renovated houses and barns, this *agriturismo* is the real McCoy. There's a tranquil pool for whiling away lazy afternoons, nature trails to ramble, a barbecue area and cellars for sampling Le Marche wines. The apartments are big on charm (some even have fireplaces) and all have well-equipped kitchens.

ⓘ Information

The official park website (www.sibillini.net) has a wealth of information on where to say, what to do and how to get around. There are also 11 Casa del Parco visitor information centres, including at Norcia (p611) and **Amandola** (☑ 0736 84 85 98; Chiostro di San Francesco, Largo Leopardi 4; ⊙ 10am-12.30pm & 3.30-6.30pm).

ⓘ Getting There & Away

Monti Sibillini is best reached by bus from Ascoli Piceno or Macerata. Services are busiest when school is in session, so they can be spotty for tourists. Check with tourist offices in Ascoli or Macerata, or with the bus companies: **Contram** (☑ 0737 6 34 01; www.contram.it) in Macerata and Start (p631) in Ascoli Piceno.

The nearest train stations are in Ascoli Piceno to the south and Tolentino to the north.

Sarnano

Spilling photogenically down a hillside, its medieval heart a maze of narrow cobbled lanes, Sarnano looks every inch the Italian hill-town prototype – particularly when its red-brick facades glow warmly in the late-afternoon sun. It is a charming and hospitable base for exploring the Monti Sibillini range.

The **Sarnano tourist office** (☑ 0733 65 71 44; Largo Ricciardi 1; ⊙ 9am-1pm Mon-Sat, plus 3-6pm Tue-Thu) has walking and climbing information and details of accommodation in the park.

🛏 Sleeping & Eating

★ Agriturismo Serpanera
AGRITURISMO €€

(☑ 334 1220242; www.serpanera.com; Contrada Schito 447; apt per day €79-169, per week €429-1239; P ❄ 🌊 🐾) 🥐 Quite the rural idyll, this 17th-century farmhouse snuggles deep among 10 hectares of orchards, vines and woodlands. Besides its spotless apartments, the eco-savvy *agriturismo* invites lingering with its gorgeous views of Sarnano to Monti Sibillini beyond, a pool overlooking rolling hills, a spa, barbecue area, nature trails and horse riding. Your affable hosts, Marco and Cristiana, whip up delicious breakfasts with farm-fresh produce.

The *agriturismo* is a five-minute drive from Sarnano on the SP78; see the website for full directions.

Le Clarisse
OSTERIA €€

(☑ 345 4959389; www.osterialeclarisse.it; Via Mazzini 240; meals €15-38; ⊙ noon-3pm & 7.30-10pm) Right in the centre of town, Le Clarisse is an *osteria* in the classic mould, serving whatever is fresh and seasonal (with an emphasis on regional truffles) in a warm brick-walled, candlelit interior.

Abruzzo & Molise

Best Mountain Towns

➡ Pescocostanzo (p640)

➡ Scanno (p641)

➡ Chieti (p646)

➡ Pacentro (p640)

Best Hikes

➡ Sentiero della Libertà
(p637)

➡ Corno Grande (p636)

➡ Monte Amaro (p644)

➡ Monte Tranquillo (p644)

Why Go?

Bisected by the spinal Apennines mountains, Abruzzo and
Molise make up Italy's forgotten quarter. Natural attractions
rather than cultural colossi are the primary draw here. A
major national park building effort in the 1990s created an
almost unbroken swathe of protected land that stretches
from the harsh, isolated Monti della Laga in the north to the
round-topped Majella mountains further south.

Dotted in their midst are some of Italy's most eerily picturesque mountain villages. Indeed, sometimes a visit here
feels like a trip back to the 1950s, to a world of wheezing
trains, ruined farmhouses and pastoral poppy-filled fields.
All this is good news for prospective walkers who share
the region's ample paths with sheep dogs, mountain goats,
abundant bird life and the odd, rarely sighted, human being.

Sulmona is the best base for mountain excursions, Pescara on the Adriatic coast satisfies those with traditional
beach urges, while little-explored Molise invites stopovers
in coastal Termoli.

When to Go
L'Aquila

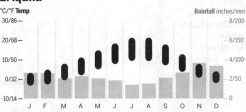

Jan & Feb Grab
some skis or a
snowboard and
head to one of the
Abruzzo–Molise
ski areas.

Jul Sulmona
boasts jousting
during its medie-
val festival, while
Pescara hosts a
major jazz festival.

May, Jun & Sep
Wildflowers,
pleasant summer
sun – perfect
conditions for
hiking.

Abruzzo & Molise Highlights

1 Breathing in the pure mountain air of **Pescocostanzo** (p640), a small town with big mansions.

2 Taking a walk through history on the Sentiero della Libertà in the **Parco Nazionale della Majella** (p640).

3 Keeping an eye out for rare Marsican bears while hiking in the **Parco Nazionale d'Abruzzo, Lazio e Molise** (p643).

4 Feeling the call of the wild as you climb **Corno Grande** (p636), summit of the Gran Sasso and the Apennines' highest peak.

5 Finding a fine family-run trattoria in the little-visited *centro storico* (historic centre) of **Isernia** (p648).

6 Catching a bus up through the craggy **Gole di Sagittario** (p643) gorge between Sulmona and Scanno.

7 Double-taking at hyper-realistic Roman busts in the **Museo Archeologico Nazionale dell'Abruzzo** (p646) in Chieti.

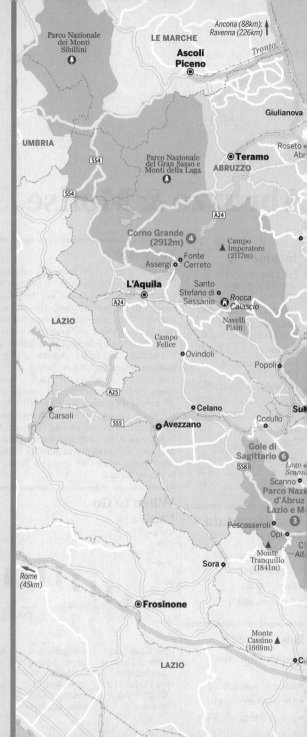

Ancona (88km);
Ravenna (226km)

LE MARCHE

Tronto

Ascoli Piceno

Parco Nazionale dei Monti Sibillini

Giulianova

UMBRIA

Roseto
Abr

SS4

Parco Nazionale del Gran Sasso e Monti della Laga

Teramo

ABRUZZO

SS4

A24

Corno Grande (2912m) **4**

Campo Imperatore (2117m)

Assergi
Fonte Cerreto

L'Aquila

Santo Stefano di Sessanio

Rocca Calascio

A24

LAZIO

Navelli Plain

Campo Felice

Ovindoli

Popoli

A25

Celano

Su

Carsoli

SS5

Avezzano

Cocullo

Gole di Sagittario **6**

SS83

Lago Scann

Scanno

Parco Nazi d'Abruz Lazio e M

Rome (45km)

Pescasseroli

Opi **3**

C
Alf

Monte Tranquillo (1841m)

Sora

Frosinone

Monte Cassino (1669m)

C

LAZIO

0
40 km
0
20 miles

Ferries to Croatia

Adriatic
Sea

Pescara
Pescara
Airport

7 Chieti

A14

Riserva
Naturale di
Punta Aderci

Vasto

Vasto
Marino

SS16

Termoli

Ferries to Isole Tremiti

Campomarino

Parco
Nazionale
del Gargano

onte
naro
793m)

2

o Nazionale
lla Majella
entro

Casoli

Lago di
Sangro

Portocannone

A14

San
Severo
(50km)

Montecilfone

Trigno

San Martino
in Pensilis

o Taranta
Peligna

Palena

Bosco di
Sant'Antonio

1 Pescocostanzo

Rivisondoli

SS17

SS16

SS650

Agnone

Ururi

Biferno

Lago di
Guardialfiera

SS647

Castel di
Sangro

Pietrabbondante

Samnite
Theatre-Temple
Complex

Riserva
Collemeluccio

MOLISE

SS87

Fortore

Alfadena

Abbazia di
San Vincenzo
al Volturno

La Pineta
Paleolithic Village

Lago di
Occhito

PUGLIA

MOLISE

5 Isernia

Campobasso

o Venafro

Campitello
Matese

Altilia

Saepinum

Sepino

Lago
del Matese

SS87

CAMPANIA

Benevento
(36km)

ABRUZZO

Best known for its dramatic mountain scenery, Abruzzo's landscape is surprisingly diverse. A vast plain extends east of Avezzano, the coastline is flat and sandy, and there are ancient forests in the Parco Nazionale d'Abruzzo, Lazio e Molise.

Many towns retain a medieval look, while the numerous hilltop castles and isolated, sometimes abandoned, *borghi* (medieval towns) exude a sinister charm, lending credence to Abruzzo's fame as an ancient centre of magic, and the land of a thousand castles.

Parco Nazionale del Gran Sasso e Monti della Laga

About 20km northeast of L'Aquila, the Gran Sasso massif is the centrepiece of the Parco Nazionale del Gran Sasso e Monti della Laga, one of Italy's largest national parks. The park's predominant feature is its jagged rocky landscape through which one of Europe's southernmost glaciers, the Calderone, cuts its course. It's also a haven for wildlife, home to an estimated 40 wolves, 350 chamois and six pairs of royal eagles. Hiking trails criss-cross the park and atmospheric castles and medieval towns crown the foothills.

🏃 Activities

The small village of Fonte Cerreto near Assergi is the main gateway to the Gran Sasso. From here a funivia (cable car; ☑ 0862 60 61 43; Mon-Fri €10, Sat & Sun €15; ☉ 8am-5pm Mon-Sat, to 6pm Sun, closed May) runs up to Campo Imperatore (2117m), a high windswept plateau 27km long that is known as Italy's 'Little Tibet'. Up top, there's hiking in summer and skiing in winter. For more information contact the park office (☑ 0862 6 05 21; www.gransassolagapark.it; Via del Convento 1; ☉ 9am-1pm & 2-6pm), which occupies the premises of an old monastery in Assergi.

One of the most popular trekking routes is the climb up to Corno Grande, which, at 2912m, is the Apennines' highest peak. The 9km *via normale* starts in the main parking area at Campo Imperatore and ascends 782m. Allow five to seven hours for the round trip. The trail is graded EE (experienced hiker). It should be clear of snow from early June to late September/early October. If attempting the ascent, or any other serious route, be sure to arm yourself with the CAI 1:25,000 map *Gran Sasso d'Italia* (€10).

🛏 Sleeping

The park has a network of *rifugi* (mountain huts) for walkers. Otherwise, there is a handful of hotels near the *funivia* base station, including Hotel Nido dell'Aquila (☑ 0862 60 68 40; www.nidodellaquila.it; Fonte Cerreto; d/tr €99/194; 🅿 🛜 ❄️), which has a pool and restaurant.

At the top of the cable-car lift, the Rifugio Campo Imperatore (☑ 0862 40 00 00; www.rifugiocampoimperatore.it; Campo Imperatore; half-board from €60; 🛜 ❄️) is the hotel where Mussolini was briefly imprisoned in 1943 before his dramatic rescue by German paratroopers. It's windswept but well run.

❶ Getting There & Away

Fonte Cerreto is just off the A24 motorway (clearly signposted). AMA buses connect with L'Aquila (€1.20, 40 minutes, six daily).

Sulmona

POP 25,200

An underdog city of good honest restaurants and half-discovered mountain magic, Sulmona sits strategically on a plateau in the middle of three national parks making it, unequivocally, the best base for outdoor excursions in Abruzzo. It's easy to reach from Pescara or Rome, and simple to navigate once you arrive (trails fan out from the city limits). The city's minor fame stems from its Roman affiliations – the Roman poet Ovid was born here in 43 BC. It is also known within Italy for its *confetti* – the almond sweets, not the wedding paper.

👁 Sights

Most sights are on or near the main street, Corso Ovidio, which runs southeast from the Villa Comunale park to Piazza Garibaldi, Sulmona's main square. A five-minute stroll away is Piazza XX Settembre, with its statue of Ovid – a popular meeting point.

Piazza Garibaldi PIAZZA

The large town square is home to Sulmona's extensive Wednesday and Saturday morning market: you'll find fresh fish, veg, fruit and flowers as well as the ubiquitous *porchetta* van, selling pork in a roll. Along Corso Ovidio is a striking series of arches, all that remains of a 13th-century aqueduct. In the centre of the piazza, the Renaissance Fontana del Vecchio (Fountain of the Old One)

THE FREEDOM TRAIL

During WWII, with the Allies advancing swiftly through southern Italy, the inmates at one of the country's most notorious POW camps – Fonte d'Amore (Campo 78), 5km north of Sulmona – began to sniff freedom.

Their excitement wasn't unfounded. When the Italian government surrendered in September 1943, the camp's Italian guards deserted their posts and promptly disappeared. Their boots were quickly filled by German soldiers invading Italy from the north but, in the confusion of the changeover, many POWs escaped.

Using the Apennines as a natural refuge, the prisoners fanned out into the surrounding mountains. With the help of local partisans, most fled east across the Majella range from German-occupied Sulmona to Casoli on the Sangro river, which had been held by the Allies since September 1943. The rugged and dangerous escape route – nicknamed the Sentiero della Libertà (Freedom Trail; www.ilsentierodellaliberta.it) – was used multiple times by escaped Allied POWs during the exceptionally cold winter of 1943–44, when the Allied advance was temporarily halted by German troops dug in along the Gustav Line (a fortified defensive line built by the Germans across central Italy in 1943 to stem the Allied advance).

Having to negotiate well-guarded checkpoints and rugged mountainous terrain, not all the escapees made it. On a windswept mountain pass known as Guado di Coccia, halfway between Campo di Giove and the small mountain village of Palena, a stone monument memorialises Ettore De Conti, an Italian partisan captured and executed by the Germans in September 1943. It acts as an enduring symbol of the underground resistance.

Today, the Sentiero della Libertà has been turned into a historic long-distance hiking trail that cuts across the peaks and plateaus of the Parco Nazionale della Majella. Well signposted with red and white markers, the 60km-long path starts at the eastern suburbs of Sulmona and is usually tackled over three to four days with stops in Campo di Giove and Taranta Peligna. Since 2001, a commemorative communal march along the trail has been held in late April attracting up to 700 people. See the Sentiero della Libertà website (Italian only) for entry details.

The foreboding fences and watchtowers of the now disused Campo 78 still rise above the village of Fonte d'Amore.

is said by some to depict Solimo, the founder of Sulmona.

To the northeast, the 14th-century Chiesa di San Filippo Neri displays its impressive Gothic portal against a backdrop of often snow-covered mountains.

Museo Dicesano di Arte Sacra MUSEUM
(📞 0864 21 29 62; admission €3.15; ⏰ 9am-1pm & 3.30-6.30pm Tue-Sun) On Piazza Garibaldi, housed in the former Santa Chiara convent, this small museum has an eclectic collection of religious and contemporary art. A highlight is a detailed *presepe* (nativity scene) depicting 19th-century Sulmona.

Palazzo dell'Annunziata PALACE
(Corso Ovidio) The most impressive of Sulmona's *palazzi* (mansions), founded in 1320 but rebuilt many times over, sits above a 1st-century-BC Roman *domus* (villa). The building has a harmonious blend of Gothic and Renaissance architecture. Inside is the four-in-one Museo Civico (📞 0864 21 02 16; ⏰ 9am-1pm & 4-6.30pm) FREE with sections dedicated to archeology, religious art, Abruzzese-Molisiano culture and the remains of said Roman *domus*. On the same complex is the heavily baroque Chiesa della SS Annunziata.

Cattedrale di San Panfilo CATHEDRAL
(Piazza del Duomo; ⏰ 7.30am-noon & 3-7pm) Slightly out of the centre, the Gothic-meets-baroque cathedral is like many things in Sulmona – understated and underrated. The fantastically restored interior guards some precious old artefacts, including a 14th-century wooden crucifix. The highlight, however, is a subterranean room (opened in 2009) containing the relics of hermit turned pope, Pietro da Morrone (1215–96), including his slippers and a piece of his heart.

ABRUZZO & MOLISE SULMONA

Museo dell'Arte Confettiera MUSEUM

(☑ 0864 21 00 47; www.pelino.it; Via Stazione Introdacqua 55; ⊙ 9am-12.30pm & 3.30-6.30pm Mon-Sat) **FREE** This museum is housed in the **Fabbrica Confetti Pelino**, Sulmona's most famous manufacturer of *confetti*. The reconstructed 16th-century laboratory looks more like an old-time science lab than a sweet-making plant. It's about 1km from Porta Napoli, at the southern end of Corso Ovidio.

Festivals & Events

Giostra Cavalleresca di Sulmona CULTURAL

(www.giostrasulmona.it) On the last weekend in July, local horse riders gallop around Piazza Garibaldi in this medieval tournament. A week later, the competition is opened up to riders from across Europe in the **Giostra Cavalleresca d'Europa**.

🛏 Sleeping

★ Legacy Casa Residencia B&B €

(☑ 377 9766036; www.legacycasaresidencia.com; Vico dell'Ospedale 54; d/apt €75/105; 🅿 ❄ 🛜) A beautifully curated and professionally run B&B right in the centre of Sulmona with a choice of double rooms or mini apartments. All the accommodation skilfully combines convenience and comfort with the distinct sense that you're in the heart of traditional Italy.

Albergo Ristorante Stella HOTEL €

(☑ 0864 5 26 53; www.hasr.it; Via Panfilo Mazara 18; s/d €55/75; 🅿 ❄ @ 🛜) A bright little three-star place in the *centro storico*, the Stella offers 10 airy, modern rooms and a smart, ground-floor restaurant-wine bar (meals €15 to €25). Discounts of around 20% are available for stays of more than one night.

🍴 Eating & Drinking

Sulmona is a mine of good honest trattorias where you can hunt down the typical Abruzzo pasta *spaghetti alla chitarra*, a long egg pasta made with a unique guitar-like cutter.

★ Il Vecchio Muro ABRUZZESE €

(☑ 0864 5 05 95; www.vecchiomuro.it; Via M D'Eramo 20; meals €20-25; ⊙ 12.45-2.30pm & 7.45-10.30pm, closed Wed Oct-Apr) Possibly the best restaurant in Sulmona (no mean feat), the 'old wall' is notable for its fantastic pizza (dinner only) and unique *cacio e pepe* (spaghetti with cheese and black pepper), which is served in an edible basket made from

Parmesan. Other dishes, especially those involving sausage and mushroom, offer a good back up. You can eat either inside, or outside in a covered garden.

Pensavo Peggio OSTERIA €€

(☑ 0864 3 20 25; Via Barbato 1; meals €25; ⊙ 12.30-2.30pm & 7.30-10.30pm) A restaurant with an ironic sense of humour – *pensavo peggio* means 'worse than I thought'. However, the food is top-notch at this atmospheric stone-walled *cantina* with open kitchen grill, and is served with breezy Sulmonan gusto. Of particular note is the ravioli in a veal, spinach and cheese sauce.

Ristorante Clemente ABRUZZESE €€

(☑ 0864 21 06 79; Vico Quercia 5; meals €25; ⊙ noon-3pm & 7.30-11pm Fri-Wed) Photos of family members on the wall remind you that this is a proud, family-run restaurant. The menu is based on the cornerstones of Abruzzese cooking, using seasonal products to produce delicious meals.

Il Bolognino CAFE

(Piazza SS Annunziata 2; ⊙ 7am-11pm Wed-Mon) Long opening hours make this place a master of many trades. Drop in for a breakfast *cornetto* (croissant), an afternoon *pausa* (tea snack), evening tapas, or beer over a Pearl Jam tribute night. The bar is perched right in the main square and the clientele is traditionalist mixed with trendy.

ℹ Information

Tourist Office (☑ 0864 5 32 76; www.abruzzoturismo.it; Corso Ovidio 208; ⊙ 9am-1pm & 5.30-7.30pm) *Molto* helpful staff. The office also sells local bus tickets.

ℹ Getting There & Away

BUS

Buses leave from a confusing array of points, including Villa Comunale, the hospital and beneath Ponte Capograssi. The tourist office will point you in the right direction.

ARPA (☑ 800 762622; www.arpaonline.it) Buses go to and from L'Aquila (€12.60, 1½ hours, nine daily).

SATAM (☑ 0871 34 49 76; www.gruppolapanoramica.it/satam/) Runs services to Pescara (€7, one hour, four daily) and other nearby towns, plus four daily services to Naples (€18, 2½ hours).

TRAIN

Trains link with L'Aquila (€4.80, one hour, 10 daily), Pescara (€4.80, 1¼ hours, 16 daily) and

Rome (€10.50, 2¾ hours, 10 daily). The train station is 2km northwest of the historic centre; the half-hourly bus A runs between the two.

Around Sulmona

Located 5km north of Sulmona at the foot of the Monte Morrone, the village of **Badia** and its environs are filled with religious significance.

Sights

Abbazia di Santo Spirito Al Morrone

RELIGIOUS SITE

(📞 0864 3 28 49; ⏱ 9am-3pm Mon-Fri) **FREE**
It's hard to miss this massive abbey in Badia close to the sheer western slopes of the Monte Morrone. Notable for its monumental staircase, religious frescoes and old pharmacy, its main sights can be seen on a guided tour available in either Italian or English. The abbey also hosts regular art expos and music concerts. Like many religious sites in the area, the abbey owes its existence to the hermit who became Pope Celestine V (aka Pietro da Morrone) whose 'great refusal' (abdication) caused political furor in the late 13th century.

The abbey was built as a seat for the Celestine order in the 1200s. Damaged in an earthquake in 1706 it later became a prison. Today, after several restorations, it houses local government offices and the HQ of Majella national park.

Eremo di Sant'Onofrio al Morrone

RELIGIOUS SITE

This cliff-clinging hermitage with its 15th-century frescoes, narrow oratory and arched porticoes literally cowers under a massive rock face in the Morrone Mountains. It was here in a grotto beneath the present church that Pietro da Morrone was apparently told he was to become pope in 1294. It's a steep 20-minute walk from a car park just outside Badia to reach the hermitage. The views of Sulmona and the Valle Peligna below are superb.

Opening hours vary; check ahead with the tourist office in Sulmona.

Sanctuario di Ercole Curino

ARCHAEOLOGICAL SITE

FREE Sitting below the Sant'Onofrio hermitage, this sanctuary was originally thought to be the erstwhile house of Sulmona-born poet Ovid when it was first uncovered in

---

L'AQUILA: THE SLOW RECOVERY

Over half a decade on from the devastating 6.3 magnitude earthquake in 2009 that killed 309 people and rendered 65,000 homeless, L'Aquila's skyline is still dotted with cranes and scaffolding. The notoriously sluggish revival has been dogged by squabbling and scandal, a controversy that peaked in 2012 when six scientists and an official were convicted of multiple counts of manslaughter for failing to warn residents of the quake risk. Their convictions were overturned in 2014.

For the time being, L'Aquila's once august city centre remains a building site with cordoned off streets and impassable 'red zones'. Not surprisingly, reviving the city's historic buildings has taken second place to rehousing L'Aquila's residents, though a sprinkling of new bars and restaurants has breathed new life into some areas.

A landmark was passed in May 2015 when the restored **Basilica di San Bernardino** (Via San Bernardino; ⏱ 7am-12.30pm & 3-7.30pm) was reopened. No stranger to seismic upheaval, the church has been rebuilt once before (in baroque style) following an earthquake in 1703. Also open for viewing is the city's impressive **Fontana delle 99 Cannelle** (Fountain of 99 Spouts).

L'Aquila's finest sight, the **Basilica di Santa Maria di Collemaggio** (Piazzale di Collemaggio) remains closed, although you can admire its two-tone jewel-box walls from the outside. In 2014 the church, which guards the mausoleum of Pope Celestine V, was allocated €12 million to restore its badly damaged interior. Optimists are suggesting it may reopen as early as 2016.

Putting a time frame on the rest of L'Aquila's revival is difficult. An estimated 485 historical buildings were damaged in the quake and forecasters are suggesting that a minimum of €600 million will be required to restore them to their former glory. Given the financial deadlock to date, it's unlikely the city will return to anything like business as usual before 2021.

the 1950s, but statues later found confirmed it as a Roman-era shrine to Hercules. The sanctuary's former foundations cover a couple of mountainside terraces. There's also a preserved mosaic floor sheltered in a wooden hut.

Parco Nazionale della Majella

History, geology and ecology collide in 750-sq-km Parco Nazionale della Majella, Abruzzo's most diverse park where wolves roam in giant beech woods, ancient hermitages speckle ominous mountains, and 500km of criss-crossing paths and a handful of ski areas cater to the hyperactive. Monte Amaro, the Apennines' second-highest peak, surveys all around it from a lofty 2793m-high vantage point.

From Sulmona the two easiest access points are **Campo di Giove** (elevation 1064m), a small skiing village 18 tortuous kilometres to the southeast, and the lovely town of Pescocostanzo, 33km south of Sulmona along the SS17.

Pescocostanzo

ELEV 1400M

Set amid verdant highland plains, Pescocostanzo is practically Alpine, a surprisingly grand hilltop town whose historical core has changed little in more than 500 years. Much of the cobbled centre dates from the 16th and 17th centuries when it was an important town on the 'Via degli Abruzzi', the main road linking Naples and Florence.

Sights & Activities

Of particular note is the **Collegiata di Santa Maria del Colle**, an atmospheric church that combines a superb Romanesque portal with a lavish baroque interior. Nearby, **Piazza del Municipio** is flanked by a number of impressive *palazzi,* including **Palazzo Comunale**, with its distinctive clock tower, and **Palazzo Fanzago**, designed by the great baroque architect Cosimo Fanzago in 1624; look out for the carved wooden dragons under the roof.

History apart, Pescocostanzo also offers skiing on **Monte Calvario** and summer hiking in the **Bosco di Sant'Antonio**, a nature reserve characterised by its beech forest, 9km northwest of Pescocostanzo.

Sleeping & Eating

★**Albergo La Rua** HOTEL €
(☑ 0864 64 00 83; www.larua.it; Via Rua Mozza 1; d €85; 🛜) Hikers should head straight for this charming little hotel in the historic centre. The look is country cosy, with low wood-beamed ceilings and a stone fireplace, and the superfriendly owners are a mine of local knowledge on the town's distinctive domestic architecture, fine jewellery and dialect.

Le Torri Hotel HOTEL €€
(☑ 0864 64 20 40; www.letorrihotel.it; Via del Vallone 4; s €80-140, d €100-160; ✳@🛜) This stylish and enticing hotel, in a *palazzo* once owned by a baron, has large, comfortable rooms with wooden floors, antique furnishings and inviting white bedspreads.

★**Ristorante da Paolino** ITALIAN €€
(☑ 0864 64 00 80; www.ristorantedapaolino. com; Strada Vulpes 34; meals €30; ⏱1-3pm & 8pm-midnight Tue-Sun) A bustling and popular little inn-restaurant in the heart of the village near Palazzo Fanzago; be sure to book ahead. Pasta dishes make full use of local seasonal ingredients such as truffles and chestnuts, and you can follow up with rabbit, veal or beef – and a creamy pudding.

Il Gallo di Pietra ABRUZZESE €€
(☑ 0864 64 20 40; www.ilgallodipietra.it; Via del Vallone 4; meals €35; ⏱11am-2pm & 7-11pm Mon-Sat) Attached to Le Torri Hotel; you can dine alfresco in the garden or beside the fire in the cosy indoor restaurant. The menu features the enticing flavours of Abruzzese and Neapolitan cuisine.

ⓘ Information

Tourist Office (☑ 0864 64 14 40; Vico delle Carceri; ⏱9am-1pm & 3-6pm Mon-Fri Sep-Jun, 9am-1pm & 4-7pm daily Jul & Aug) Off the central Piazza del Municipio. Also see the Parco Nazionale della Majella's comprehensive website (www.parcomajella.it).

ⓘ Getting There & Away

Buses run from Sulmona to Pescocostanzo (€4, one hour, three daily) via Castel di Sangro, and to Campo di Giove (€2.30, 45 minutes, three daily).

Pacentro

In a region not lacking in attractive hilltop villages, Pacentro stands out. Set on a knoll above the Sulmona plateau in the foothills of the Parco Nazionale della Majella, this

TAKE TO THE PISTES

Abruzzo and Molise might lack the glamour of the northern Alps, but skiing is enthusiastically followed and there are resorts across the regions (bank on about €35 for a daily ski pass).

➤ **Campitello Matese** In Molise's Monti del Matese, Campitello offers 40km of pistes, including 15km for cross-country skiers.

➤ **Campo di Giove** At the foot of the Parco Nazionale della Majella, this resort offers Abruzzo's highest skiing, at 2350m.

➤ **Campo Felice** A small resort 40km south of L'Aquila with 40km of pistes (30km downhill, 10km cross-country).

➤ **Campo Imperatore** Twenty-two kilometres of mainly downhill pistes and more than 60km of cross-country trails in the Parco Nazionale del Gran Sasso e Monti della Laga.

➤ **Ovindoli Monte Magnola** One of Abruzzo's biggest ski resorts, with 30km of downhill pistes and 50km of cross-country trails.

➤ **Pescasseroli** A popular outpost deep in the Parco Nazionale d'Abruzzo , Lazio e Molise with 30km of downhill slopes.

➤ **Pescocostanzo** Good for ski hiking as well as downhill skiing. It's celebrated for its medieval architecture.

➤ **Roccaraso-Rivisondoli** Near Pescocostanzo, this is one of the best-equipped resorts, with 28 ski lifts, two cable cars and more than 100km of ski slopes.

compact village, with its three slim Renaissance towers similar to those in Tuscany's San Gimignano, has never expanded far beyond its medieval boundaries and remains free of the unsightly modern sprawl that encircles some of its bigger neighbours. Largely off the standard tourist circuit and – unlike Pescocostanzo and Scanno – not affiliated with a ski resort, its pleasantly dishevelled streets remain quiet and authentic. It's a good place to mingle with the locals, taste home cooking in low-key trattorias, or use as a base for some nearby national park walks.

Pacentro's 20th-century history was decidedly chequered. During WWII, the village's population was forcibly evicted by Germans soldiers who subsequently looted the settlement before beating a hasty retreat. When the conflict ended, many local families emigrated (including the paternal grandparents of the pop singer, Madonna), leaving Pacentro depopulated and economically depressed for a generation.

If the émigrés were to return today, they would be surprised to see a village on the rebound. Of interest to modern visitors is the 14th-century **Cantelmo Castle** with its famous three towers, the mannerist-meets-baroque **Chiesa Santa Maria della Misericordia**, and a slew of grand nobles' houses that beautify the lanes between Piazza del Popolo and Piazza Umberto I.

Pacentro lies 10km east of Sulmona along the SS487. Regular ARPA (p638) buses run between the two towns (€2.40, 30 minutes, nine daily).

Scanno

POP 1990

A tangle of steep alleyways and sturdy, greystone houses, Scanno is a dramatic and atmospheric *borgo* (medieval town), known for its finely worked filigree gold jewellery. For centuries a centre of wool production, it is one of the few places in Italy where you can still see women wearing traditional dress – especially during the week-long **costume festival** (www.costumediscanno.org) held at the end of April. The somewhat sombre but imposing costumes were famously photographed by Cartier-Bresson in 1951. They comprise a full black skirt and bodice with puffed sleeves, a headdress of braided fabric topped with an angular cap, and filigree jewellery including star-shaped charms, given as betrothal gifts by shepherds before they departed on the long *transhumanza* (sheep migration).

Be sure to take the exhilarating drive or bus ride up to Scanno from Sulmona

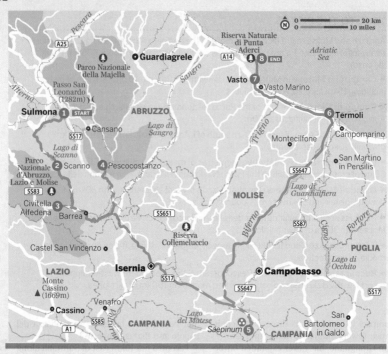

Driving Tour
Cut to the Heart

START SULMONA
END RISERVA NATURALE DI PUNTA ADERCI
LENGTH 245KM TO 310KM; ONE WEEK

An oasis in the mountainous terrain of southern Abruzzo, **1 Sulmona** is the place to start. With its attractive historic centre, welcoming vibe and great trattorias, it's the archetypal Italian town. Check out the market stalls on Piazza Garibaldi and join the locals on their *passeggiata* (evening stroll) along Corso Ovidio. After a night in Sulmona, push on southward to hilltop **2 Scanno**. It's a slow, scenic ride that takes you through the breathtaking Gole di Sagittario, a rocky gorge that squeezes the road like a natural vice, and up past the beautiful Lago di Scanno. Scanno's dramatic appearance has made it something of a tourist attraction, but visit out of summer and you'll find it a tranquil spot.

From Scanno, the next leg takes you into the national parks. From Lago di Barrea you can head deep into the magnificent Parco Nazionale d'Abruzzo, Lazio e Molise, the most popular of Abruzzo's three national parks, and set up camp in **3 Civitella Alfedena**. Or you can head north and take the long way round to pretty **4 Pescocostanzo** in the Parco Nazionale della Majella. Either way, spend a couple of days exploring the surrounding mountains. Once you've recharged your batteries, continue on past Isernia to take a look at the well-preserved Roman ruins at **5 Saepinum**.

After the mountains, it's time to hit the coast and top up your tan at **6 Termoli**, or further up the road at **7 Vasto**, both popular Adriatic resorts. From Termoli, the Isole Tremiti are just a day trip away. But if the crowds get too much (and they might in summer), go north to the Spiaggia di Punta Penna, a lovely beach in the **8 Riserva Naturale di Punta Aderci**.

through the rocky Gole di Sagittario, a WWF reserve and gorge, and past tranquil Lago di Scanno, where there's a scattering of bars and cafes, and you can hire boats in summer.

🛏 Sleeping & Eating

⭐ Il Palazzo
B&B €

(☑ 0864 74 78 60; Via Ciorla 25; r €60-90; P 🛜) This elegant and gently welcoming B&B spans seven rooms on the 2nd floor of an old *palazzo* in the *centro storico*. The rooms are stylishly decorated with antique furnishings, and breakfast is served under a frescoed ceiling.

Hotel Belvedere
HOTEL €

(☑ 0864 7 43 14; www.belvederescanno.it; Piazza Santa Maria della Valle 3; s/d €35/70; P 🛜) In a good location on Scanno's main piazza, this pleasant hotel offers spick-and-span modern rooms decked out with parquet and polished wood trimmings. Also offers half and full board.

Pizzeria Trattoria Vecchio Mulino
TRATTORIA €

(☑ 0864 74 72 19; Via Silla 50; pizzas/meals €7/25; ☺ noon-3pm & 7pm-midnight, closed Wed winter) This old-school eatery is a good bet for a classic wood-fired pizza, lentil soups and pasta liberally sprinkled with local saffron. In summer the pretty streetside terrace provides a good perch from which to people-watch.

ℹ Information

Tourist Office (☑ 0864 7 43 17; Piazza Santa Maria della Valle 12; ☺ 9am-1pm & 3-6pm Mon & Thu, 9am-1pm Tue, Wed & Fri year-round, plus 9am-1pm & 3-6pm Sat & Sun Apr-Oct) In the village centre.

ℹ Getting There & Away

ARPA (☑ 800 762622; www.arpaonline.it) Buses run to and from Sulmona (€3.20, one hour, seven daily).

Parco Nazionale d'Abruzzo, Lazio e Molise

Italy's second-oldest national park is also one of its most ecologically rich. Established by royal decree in 1923, it began as a modest 5-sq-km reserve that, little by little, morphed into the 440-sq-km protected area it is today. The evolution wasn't easy. The park was temporarily abolished in 1933 by the Mussolini government. It returned to the fold in 1950 only to face further encroachment from housing construction, road building and ski developers.

Despite a long history battling political, bureaucratic and hunting interests, the park has managed to remain at the forefront of Italy's conservation movement, successfully initiating a host of campaigns to reintroduce and protect wild animals such as the Abruzzo chamois, Apennine wolf, lynx, deer and – most notably – Marsican bear (the park has Italy's largest surviving enclave of these threatened animals).

Today the park extends over three regions, with over half of it covered in thick beech forest. Thanks to its long history, it receives more visitors than other parks – around two million annually.

◉ Sights & Activities

Right in the middle of the park, the red-roofed town of Pescasseroli has the open airy feel of a large village. Narrow streets and medieval churches suggest a rich history, but the lure of the wilderness is never far away. The Centro di Visita di Pescasseroli (☑ 0863 911 32 21; Viale Colli d'Oro; adult/child €6/4; ☺ 10am-6.30pm Apr-Aug, 10am-5.30pm Sep-Mar) has a small museum, a clinic for sick animals, and a resident bear and wolf, but it's limited and charges a steep entry fee. For a better rundown of the park's flora and fauna, head 17km southeast to Civitella Alfedena, whose wolf museum doubles as an info centre.

Situated on a hilltop 6km from Pescasseroli is Opi, a *borgo più bella d'Italia* (one of Italy's most beautiful towns). It's one of the highest settlements in the park and makes an attractive base. The little Centro Visita del Camoscio (Opi; ☺ 10am-1pm & 3-7pm Sat & Sun, daily July & Aug) FREE, a wildlife sanctuary, studies the Apennine chamois; it has a viewpoint from which you can see the animals roaming.

On the park's eastern edge and about 17km from Opi is the picturesque Lago di Barrea with the venerable and handsome town of Barrea positioned on a rocky spur above the lake.

At nearby Civitella Alfedena, a seductive hamlet reached via a bridge across the lake, you can study the local flora and fauna at the Museo del Lupo Appenninico (Wolf Centre; ☑ 0864 89 01 41; Via Santa Lucia; admission

WALKING & WILDLIFE

With about 150 well-marked routes, signalled by white and red marks daubed on trees and rocks, the Parco Nazionale d'Abruzzo, Lazio e Molise is a mecca for hikers. Trails range from easy family jaunts to multiday hikes over rocky peaks and exposed highlands. The best time to go is between June and September, although access to some of the busier routes around Pescasseroli is often limited in July and August. To book entry to trails, contact the **Centro di Visita** (p643) in Pescasseroli or the **Museo del Lupo Appenninico** (p643) in Civitella Alfedena.

Don't set off without the official hiking map (€12) available at all local tourist offices. Note that the time estimates given are one way only.

Two of the area's most popular hikes are the climbs up Monte Amaro (2793m; Route F1) and Monte Tranquillo (1841m; Route C3). The **Monte Amaro route**, a 2¼-hour hike, starts from a car park 7km southeast of Pescasseroli (follow the SS83 for about 2km beyond Opi) and rises steeply up to the peaks where you're rewarded with stupendous views over the Valle del Sangro. There's quite a good chance of spotting a chamois on this walk.

The **Monte Tranquillo route** takes about 2½ hours from a starting point 1km south of Pescasseroli (follow signs for the Hotel Iris and Centro Ippico Vallecupa). If you still have your breath at the top, you can continue northwards along the Rocca Ridge before descending down to Pescasseroli from the north. This beautiful but challenging 19.5km circuit takes six or seven hours.

You may be lucky enough to spot an **Apennine wolf** or a **Marsican brown bear** on your hike: this might sound like a scary prospect, but the animals are extremely shy, the only possible threat being from a female bear protecting her cubs. Lynx, chamois, roe deer, wild boar, golden eagles and peregrine hawks also inhabit the park, and flora includes the rare lady's slipper orchid.

€3; ☺10am-1.30pm & 3-6.30pm), which has an impressive amount of information (in Italian only) on the wolf and its role in myth and literature, as well as an extensive photo gallery that will help you identify everything from rare orchids to chamois. Try to spot the two wolves who regularly trot through their large enclosure at the free **Area Faunistica del Lupo** behind the museum. To see a rare lynx, follow the signs from the museum to the **Area Faunistica delle Lince**.

Hiking opportunities abound, whether you want to go it alone or with an organised group. There are numerous outfits offering guided excursions, including **Ecotur** (☎0863 91 27 60; www.ecotur.org; Via Piave 9, Pescasseroli), which organises treks, bike rides and various other activities.

Between May and October, the **Centro Ippico Vallecupa** (☎0863 91 04 44; www.agriturismomaneggiovallecupa.it; Via della Difesa, Pescasseroli; rides 1hr/full day €20/80) offers guided horse rides in the park.

🛏 Sleeping & Eating

★**Albergo Antico Borga La Torre**   HOTEL €
(☎0864 89 01 21; www.albergolatorre.com; Via Castello 3, Civitella Alfedena; s €30-50, d €32-60; P@) Housed in an atmospheric 18th-century *palazzo* in Civitella Alfedena's medieval centre, this attractive and spotless hotel is popular with hikers. It also runs a small restaurant serving hot, fortifying food, after which the owner might treat you to his homemade and eye-wateringly strong *digestivo*.

B&B La Sosta   B&B €
(☎0863 91 60 57; Via Marsicana 17, Opi; per person €25; P) This delightful B&B on the main road below Opi is run with passionate care by a hospitable elderly couple. There are six very clean, smart rooms, a sunny terrace, and excellent access to the nearby mountains. The breakfasts are quite special too, with cakes and lashings of homemade jam. Excellent value.

Campeggio Wolf   CAMPGROUND €

(✆0864 89 03 60; Via Sotto i Cerri, Civitella Alfedena; camping per person €5-6.50, tent €5-6, car €3-4; ☺May-Sep) This camping ground is a fairly simple affair but has free hot showers.

Il Duca degli Abruzzi   ITALIAN €€

(✆0863 91 10 75; www.ilducadegliabruzzi.it; Piazza Duca degli Abruzzi, Pescasseroli; meals €25) This handsome hotel-restaurant is located on a quiet square in Pescasseroli's *centro storico*. Everything is homemade: try the truffle pasta or potato gnocchi, and follow up with baked cod or grilled pork, washed down with Montepulciano d'Abruzzo.

❶ Getting There & Away

Pescasseroli, Civitella Alfedena and other villages in the national park are linked by daily buses to Avezzano (€5, 1½ hours), from where you can change for L'Aquila, Pescara and Rome. Buses also head to Castel di Sangro (€3.90, 1¼ hours), where there are connections to Sulmona and Naples.

Pescara

POP 123,100

Abruzzo's largest city is a heavily developed seaside resort with one of the biggest marinas on the Adriatic. The city was heavily bombed during WWII and much of the city centre was reduced to rubble. It's a lively place with an animated seafront, especially in summer, but unless you're coming for the 16km of sandy beaches, there's no great reason to hang around. One sight not to miss is the Museo delle Genti d'Abruzzo, which has plenty that will appeal to kids too.

◉ Sights

Pescara's main attraction is its long stretch of beachfront, and the shopping precinct around pedestrianised Corso Umberto. From Piazzale della Repubblica, the beach is a short walk down Corso Umberto. The only vaguely old streets in Pescara are on the south side of the Aterno-Pescara river occupying the site of the former Roman town of Aternum.

Museo delle Genti d'Abruzzo   MUSEUM

(✆085 451 00 26; www.gentidabruzzo.it; Via delle Caserme 24; adult/reduced €6/3; ☺hours vary) Located on a quiet road parallel to the river on the opposite bank from the centre, this wonderful museum illustrates Abruzzo peasant culture. The information is mainly in Italian, but the objects speak eloquently for themselves. There are shepherds' capes, carnival masks, outlandish silver saddle pommels and even a conical stone hut, and the section on Scanno costume and jewellery is outstanding. Altogether this amounts to a moving exploration of a lost way of life. Opening hours are changeable; check the website for the current schedule.

Museo Casa Natale Gabriele D'Annunzio   MUSEUM

(✆0865 6 03 91; Corso Manthonè 116; admission €2; ☺9am-1.30pm) The birthplace of controversial fascist poet Gabriele D'Annunzio is small but excellently curated with furniture, documents, photos and his death mask displayed in a polished glass case.

Museo d'Arte Moderna Vittoria Colonna   GALLERY

(✆085 428 37 59; Via Gramsci 26; adult/reduced €6/4; ☺9.30am-1.30pm & 4-8pm) Near the seafront, one block back from the beach, this gallery has a Picasso and a Miró among its small collection of modern art.

⁂ Festivals & Events

Pescara Jazz   MUSIC

(www.pescarajazz.com) This international jazz festival is held in mid-July at the Teatro D'Annunzio. In the past it has featured big-name stars including Keith Jarrett, Herbie Hancock and Stan Getz.

⊨ Sleeping & Eating

Hotel Alba   HOTEL €

(✆085 38 91 45; www.hotelalba.pescara.it; Via Michelangelo Forti 14; s €50-80, d €75-120, tr €135-150; P❋@) A glitzy three-star place, the Alba provides comfort and a central location. Rooms vary but the best sport polished wood, firm beds and plenty of sunlight. Rates are lowest at weekends and garage parking costs €10.

Hotel Victoria   HOTEL €€

(✆085 37 41 32; www.victoriapescara.com; Via Piave 142; s/d €95/135; P❋@☎) A top-notch hotel in a handsome building in the city centre, the Victoria is a memorable place with impressionist paintings etched onto bedroom doors, curvaceous balconies and an excellent downstairs cafe. Best of all, though, is the service, which goes above and beyond the call of duty. Bonuses include a business centre and a spa.

Caffè Letterario CAFE €

(☑ 085 6 42 43; Via delle Caserme 62; lunch €7-12; ⏱ 9am-6pm Sun-Wed, 9am-3am Thu-Sat) This popular lunchtime spot has huge floor-to-ceiling windows and exposed-brick walls. The menu is chalked up on a daily board, and typically comprises a few mains and several vegetable side dishes. There's live music Thursday to Saturday nights.

Ristorante Marechiaro da Bruno SEAFOOD €€

(☑ 085 421 38 49; www.ristorantemarechiaro.eu; Lungomare Matteotti 70; meals €25-30; ⏱ noon-3pm & 7-11pm Thu-Tue) With a prime position on the seafront, the speciality here is bound to be seafood – in all shapes and sizes. It's a lively place, smarter than its neighbours, with suited waiters and white linen, and there's an impressive array of pizzas at night.

ℹ Information

Tourist Office (☑ 085 422 54 62; www.proloco.pescara.it; Piazzale della Repubblica; ⏱ 9am-1pm & 3-6pm Oct-May, 9am-1pm & 4-7pm Jun-Sep) Tourist information centre at Piazzale della Repubblica.

ℹ Getting There & Away

AIR

Pescara Airport (☑ 899 130310; www.abruzzoairport.com) Pescara airport is 3km out of town and easily reached by bus 38 (€1.10, 20 minutes, every 15 minutes) from in front of the train station. Ryanair flies to London Stansted and Alitalia to Milan and Rome-Fiumicino.

BOAT

Agenzia Sanmar (☑ 0854 451 08 73; www.sanmar.it; Stazione Marittima Banchina Sud) Contact Agenzia Sanmar at the port for ferry information and tickets to Croatia.

SNAV (☑ 071 207 61 16; www.snav.it) From mid-July to early August, a daily SNAV jetfoil runs to the islands on Croatia's Dalmatian coast, including Hvar. One-way tickets for the 5¾-hour journey cost from €69 per person.

BUS

ARPA (☑ 800 762622; www.arpaonline.it) Buses leave from Piazzale della Repubblica for L'Aquila (€8, two hours, 10 daily), Sulmona (€6, one hour, 11 daily), Naples (€26, 4½ hours, four daily), Rome (€17, 2¾ hours, 11 daily) and towns throughout Abruzzo and Molise.

TRAIN

Direct trains run to Ancona (from €9.40, 1¼ to two hours, 20 daily), Bari (from €32, three hours, 16 daily), Rome (from €12.80, four hours, six daily) and Sulmona (€4.80, 1¼ hours, 16 daily).

Chieti

POP 54,300

Overlooking the Aterno valley, Chieti is a sprawling hilltop town with roots dating back to pre-Roman times when, as capital of the Marrucini tribe, it was known as Teate Marrucinorum. Later, in the 4th century BC, it was conquered by the Romans and incorporated into the Roman Republic.

The commune of Chieti splits into two parts: Chieti Scalo is the new commercial district, while hilltop Chieti is of more interest to travellers thanks to its two fine archaeology museums.

◉ Sights

★ Museo Archeologico Nazionale dell'Abruzzo MUSEUM

(☑ 0871 40 43 92; www.archeoabruzzo.beniculturali.it; Villa Frigerj; adult/reduced €4/2; ⏱ 9am-8pm Tue-Sat, 10.30am-8pm Sun) Housed in a neoclassical villa in the Villa Comunale park, the Museo Archeologico Nazionale displays a comprehensive collection of local finds, including the 6th-century-BC *Warrior of Capestrano,* considered the most important pre-Roman find in central Italy. Mystery surrounds the identity of the warrior but there are some who reckon it to be Numa Pompilo, the second king of Rome and successor to Romulus.

The museum also showcases 5th-century-BC funerary steles, an impressive coin collection and some colossal statues – including that of a seated Hercules – dating from the 1st century BC.

Complesso Archeologico la Civitella MUSEUM

(☑ 0871 6 31 37; www.lacivitella.it; Via Pianell; adult/reduced €4/2; ⏱ 9am-8pm Tue-Sat, 9am-2pm Sun) The Complesso Archeologico la Civitella is a modern museum built around a Roman amphitheatre. Exhibits chart the history of Chieti and include weapons and pottery dating back to the Iron Age.

🛏 Sleeping

Grande Albergo Abruzzo HOTEL €

(☑ 0871 4 19 40; www.albergoabruzzo.it; Via Asinio Herio 20; r from €80; ☐🐾) Well-located with panoramic views of coast and mountains, the Grande's rooms are more dusty than grand these days, but there are other perks such as the outdoor terrace, on-site restaurant and free parking.

❶ Information

Tourist Office (☑0871 6 36 40; Via Spaventa 47; ◷8am-1pm & 4-7pm Mon-Sat Jul-Sep, 8am-1pm Mon-Sat plus 3-6pm Tue, Thu & Fri Oct-Jun) Chieti's helpful tourist office can provide information and accommodation lists for the town and surrounding area.

❶ Getting There & Away

ARPA (p646) buses (€2.20, 20 minutes, three to four an hour) link Chieti with Pescara. Get off at the top of town in Chieti.

Vasto & Around

POP 39,800

On Abruzzo's southern coast, the hilltop town of Vasto has an atmospheric medieval quarter and superb sea views. Much of the *centro storico* dates from the 15th century, a golden period in which the city was known as 'the Athens of the Abruzzi'; it is also distinguished as the birthplace of the poet Gabriele Rossetti.

Two kilometres downhill is the blowzy resort of **Vasto Marina**, a strip of hotels, restaurants and campgrounds fronting a long sandy beach. About 5km further north along the coast is the beautiful **Spiaggia di Punta Penna** and the **Riserva Naturale di Punta Aderci** (www.puntaderci.it), a 285-hectare area of uncontaminated rocky coastline, ideal for long beach walks, swimming and diving.

In summer the action is on the beach at Vasto Marina. Up in the old town, interest revolves around the small historic centre, with its landmark **Castello Caldoresco**, located on Piazza Rossetti, and the low-key Romanesque **Cattedrale di San Giuseppe** (☑0873 36 71 93; Piazza Pudente; ◷8.30am-noon & 4.30-7pm). The Renaissance Palazzo d'Avalos hosts four museums, including the **Museo Archeologico** (☑0873 36 77 73; Piazza Pudente; admission €3; ◷9.30am-12.30pm & 4-7pm Sat & Sun, daily Jun-Aug).

Sunrise Agri Food (☑0873 6 93 41; Loggia Amblingh 51; mains €6.50-8.50; ◷noon-3pm & 7.30pm-midnight Wed-Mon) is a friendly, slightly brash little place with swoon-worthy Adriatic views and delicious home cooking, including sumptuous risottos.

The train station (Vasto-San Salvo) is about 2km south of Vasto Marina. Trains run frequently to Pescara (€4.80, one hour) and Termoli (from €2.60, 15 minutes). From the station take bus 1 or 4 for Vasto Marina and the town centre (€1.10).

MOLISE

Of Italy's 20 regions, Molise probably ranks 20th in terms of name recognition. In fact, until 1970, it was part of Abruzzo, the adjacent region it closely resembles. Mountains and hills rather than people crowd the interior, while flatter plains guard a short 35km stretch of Adriatic coast. Although Isernia and Campobasso are the largest cities, you'll probably encounter your brightest epiphanies in coastal Termoli, a higgledy-piggledy old town characterised by its *trabucchi* (fishing platforms). Molise has suffered steady depopulation since the late 19th century, adding to its sense of isolation.

Fair-weather travellers beware: in March 2015 the small Molise village of Capracotta received one of the highest ever recorded amounts of snowfall in a 24-hour period (an astounding 2.56m).

Campobasso

POP 51,000

Molise's regional capital and main transport hub is a sprawling, uninspiring city with little to recommend it. However, if you do find yourself passing through, the pocket-sized *centro storico* is worth a quick look.

Although rarely open, the Romanesque churches of **San Bartolomeo** (Salita San Bartolomeo) and **San Giorgio** (Viale della Rimembranza) are fine examples of their genre. Further up the hill, at the top of a steep tree-lined avenue, sits **Castello Monforte** (☑0874 6 32 99; ◷9am-1pm & 3.30-6.30pm Tue-Sun) **FREE**. Ceramics found in the castle are now on show at the small **Museo Sannitico** (Samnite Museum; ☑0874 41 22 65; Via Chiarizia 12; ◷9am-1.30pm & 2-5.30pm) **FREE**, along with artefacts from local archaeological sites.

For a spot of lunch, **Trattoria La Grotta di Zi Concetta** (☑0874 31 13 78; Via Larino 9; meals €25; ◷noon-2pm & 7.30-10.30pm Mon-Fri) is an old-school trattoria serving delicious homemade pasta and superb meat dishes.

The **tourist office** (☑0874 41 56 62; Piazza della Vittoria 14; ◷8.30am-1.30pm Mon-Fri, plus 3-5.30pm Mon & Wed) can provide further information on the city and surrounding province.

Unless you're coming from Isernia, Campobasso is best reached by bus. Services link with Termoli (€3.20, 1¼ hours, 10 daily), Naples (€9.80, 2¾ hours, four daily on weekdays) and Rome (€12.10, three hours, five daily). Up to 14 daily trains run to/from Isernia (€3.10, one hour).

Saepinum

A hidden Molise treasure, the Roman ruins of Saepinum (☉9am-7pm) FREE are among the best preserved and least visited in the country. Unlike Pompeii and Ostia Antica, which were both major ports, Saepinum was a small provincial town of no great importance. It was originally established by the Samnites but the Romans conquered it in 293 BC, paving the way for an economic boom in the 1st and 2nd centuries AD. Some 700 years later, it was sacked by Arab invaders.

The walled town retains three of its four original gates and its two main roads, the *cardus maximus* and the *decamanus*. Highlights include the forum, basilica and theatre, near to which the Museo Archeologico Vittoriano (admission €2; ☉9.30am-1pm & 3-6.30pm Tue-Sun) displays artefacts unearthed on the site.

It's not easy to reach Saepinum by public transport, but the bus from Campobasso to Sepino (€1.20, six daily weekdays) generally stops near the site at Altilia, although it's best to ask the driver.

Isernia

POP 22,000

Surrounded by remote, sparsely populated hills, Isernia doesn't make a huge impression. Earthquakes and a massive WWII bombing raid spared little of its original *centro storico*, although the humble old town retains an authentic tourist-free Italian feel and hides some decent trattorias.

The main historical draw is La Pineta, a 700,000-year-old village – one of Europe's oldest – unearthed by road workers in 1979. Excavations are ongoing and in 2014, archaeologists found the tooth of a young child dated to around 586,000 years ago. The dusty Museo Paleolitico di Isernia (☎0865 41 05 00; Corso Marcelli 48; admission €2; ☉8.30am-7pm) includes artefacts dug up at La Pineta, including piles of elephant and rhino bones, fossils and stone tools.

If you want to stay the night, Hotel Sayonara (☎0865 5 09 92; www.sayonara.is.it; Via G Berta 131; s/d €55/85; ❄) is a reasonable option near the train station. Rooms are rather spartan, but staff try their best to help and there's a pleasant downstairs restaurant and gelateria. For dinner hit Osteria O'Pizzaiuolo (☎0865 41 27 76; Corso Marcelli 214; pizzas €6, meals €20-25) in the old town for epic *cavatelli* pasta with sausage and broccoli, or beef with black truffles.

Isernia's tourist office (☎0865 39 92; 6th fl, Palazzo della Regione, Via Farinacci 9; ☉8am-2pm Mon-Sat) can provide accommodation lists.

From the bus terminus next to the train station on Piazza della Repubblica, Azienda di Trasporti Molisana (☎0864 6 47 44; www.atm-molise.it) runs buses to Campobasso (€3.50, 50 minutes, eight daily) and Termoli (€4.90, 1½ hours, six daily). Get tickets from Bar Ragno d'Oro on Piazza della Repubblica.

Trains connect Isernia with Sulmona (€7.45, three to four hours, two daily), Campobasso (€3.10, one hour, 14 daily), Naples (€6.75, two hours, five daily) and Rome (€11.30, two hours, six daily).

Termoli

POP 32,600

Despite its touristy trattorias and brassy bars, Molise's top beach resort retains a winning, low-key charm. At the eastern end of the seafront, the pretty *borgo antico* (old town) juts out to sea like a massive pier, dividing the sandy beach from Termoli's small harbour. From the seawall you'll see several typical Molisiano *trabucchi*.

The town's most famous landmark, Frederick II's 13th-century Castello Svevo (☎0875 71 23 54; ☉by request), guards entry to the tiny *borgo* – a tangle of narrow streets, pastel-coloured houses and souvenir shops. From the castle, follow the road up and come to Piazza Duomo and Termoli's majestic 12th-century cathedral (☎0875 70 80 25; ☉7.30-11.50am & 4.30-8pm). A masterpiece of the Puglian-Romanesque architecture style, the cream-coloured facade features a striking round-arched central portal.

🛏 Sleeping

Locanda Alfieri   B&B €
(☑ 0875 70 81 13; www.locandalfieri.com; Via Duomo 39; s incl breakfast €40-55, d incl breakfast €75-110; 🅿 📶) A 'diffused hotel' with rooms scattered throughout the *centro storico*, this is a great base from which to explore Termoli, the Isole Tremiti and Molise. Room styles vary from 'creative' traditional to modern-chic (some with ubercool showers with mood lighting).

★ Residenza Sveva   HOTEL €€
(☑ 0875 70 68 03; www.residenzasveva.com; Piazza Duomo 11; s €69-79, d €89-119; 🅿 📶) This elegant *centro storico* 'diffused hotel' has its reception on Piazza Duomo, near the cathedral, but the 21 rooms are squeezed into several *palazzi* in the *borgo*. The style is summery with plenty of gleaming blue tiles and traditional embroidery. There's also an excellent, elegant seafood restaurant (open Wednesday to Sunday) on site.

🍴 Eating

La Sacrestia   ITALIAN €
(☑ 0875 70 56 03; Via Ruffini 48-50; pizzas €7-8, meals €25; ⊙noon-3pm & 7pm-1am daily summer, Wed-Mon winter) This is one of the better restaurants in the lively area between Corso Nazionale and Via Fratelli Brigida. Sit streetside or in the brick-vaulted interior and chow down on knockout pizza or fresh-off-the-boat seafood.

Ristorante Da Nicolino   SEAFOOD €€
(☑ 0875 70 68 04; www.ristorantenicolino.it; Via Roma 3; meals €35; ⊙12.30-2.45pm & 7.30-10.45pm Fri-Wed) Well regarded by locals, this discreet restaurant near the entrance to the old town serves the best seafood in town. Highly recommended is the *brodetto di pesce* (fish soup).

ℹ Information

Tourist Office (☑ 0875 70 39 13; www.termoli.net; 1st fl, Piazza Bega 42; ⊙8am-2pm & 3-6pm Mon & Wed, 8am-2pm Tue, Thu & Fri) Helpful but hard to find, Termoli's tourist office is tucked away in a dodgy-looking car park behind a small shopping gallery, 100m east of the train station.

ℹ Getting There & Away

BOAT

Termoli is the only port with year-round ferries to the Isole Tremiti. **Tirrenia Navigazione** (☑ 0875 70 53 43; www.tirrenia.it; tickets €16-20) runs a year-round ferry and **Navigazione Libera del Golfo** (☑ 0875 70 48 59; www.navlib.it; round-trip €36.50; ⊙Apr-Sep) operates a quicker hydrofoil. Buy tickets online or at the port.

BUS

Termoli's bus station is beside Via Martiri della Resistenza. Various companies have services to/from Campobasso (€3.20, 1¼ hours, 10 daily), Isernia (€4.90, 1½ hours, six daily), Pescara (€5.40, 1¾ hours, two daily) and Rome (€15.50, 3¾ hours, five daily).

TRAIN

Direct trains serve Bologna (from €43.50, four to 5½ hours, 10 daily), Lecce (from €29, 3½ to 4½ hours, 10 daily) and stations along the Adriatic coast.

Albanian Towns

Several villages to the south of Termoli form an Albanian enclave that dates back to the 15th century. These include **Portocannone**, **San Martino in Pensilis** and Ururi. Although the inhabitants shrugged off their Orthodox religion in the 18th century, they still speak a version of Albanian that's incomprehensible to outsiders.

However, it's for their riotous and partisan *carressi* (chariot races) that the villages are best known. Each year Ururi (3 May), Portocannone (the Monday after Whit Sunday, seven weeks after Easter) and San Martino in Pensilis (30 April) stage a no-holds-barred chariot race. The chariots (more like carts) are pulled by bulls and hurtle around a traditional course, urged on by villagers on horseback. Bear in mind that, dramatic as these festivals are, they're in no way geared to tourists.

Getting to these villages is quite a trial without your own transport, but **ATM** (☑ 0874 6 47 44; www.atm-molise.it) runs daily buses to all three from the bus station at Termoli.

Naples & Campania

Why Go?

Campania could be a multi–Academy Award winner, scooping up everything from Best Cinematography to Best Original Screenplay. Strewn with temples, castles and palaces, the region bursts with myths, legends and anecdotes – Icarus plunged to his death in the Campi Flegrei, sirens lured sailors off Sorrento, and Wagner put quill to paper in lofty Ravello.

Campania's cast includes some of Europe's most fabled destinations, from haunting Pompeii and Herculaneum to celebrity-studded Capri and Positano. At its heart thumps bad-boy Naples, a love-it-or-loathe-it sprawl of operatic *palazzi* (mansions) and churches, mouthwatering markets and art-crammed museums. Beyond its hyperactive streets lies a wonderland of lush bay islands, faded fishing villages and wild mountains. Seductive, vivacious and often contradictory – welcome to Italy at its passionate best.

Best Places to Eat

➡ L'Ebbrezza di Noè (p669)

➡ President (p692)

➡ Il Focolare (p682)

➡ Donna Rosa (p700)

Best Places to Stay

➡ Hotel Palazzo Murat (p699)

➡ Hotel Luna Convento (p703)

➡ Hotel Caruso (p704)

➡ Hotel Piazza Bellini (p666)

When to Go
Naples

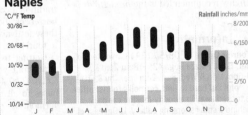

Easter Follow the faithful at mystical Easter processions in Sorrento and Procida.

May Naples celebrates culture with its event-packed Maggio dei Monumenti festival.

Sep Hit the coast for warm, languid days without the maddening August crowds.

NAPLES

POP 989,110

Italy's most misunderstood city is also one of its most intriguing – an exhilarating mess of bombastic baroque interiors, cocky baristas and subterranean ruins. Contradiction is the catchphrase here, a place where anarchy and grit sidle up beside glorious churches, tranquil cloisters and dignified seaside castles. Naples' *centro storico* (historic centre) is a Unesco World Heritage Site, its museums lay claim to some of Europe's finest archaeology and art, and its gilded royal palaces make Rome look positively provincial.

History

According to legend, traders from Rhodes established the city on the island of Megaris (where Castel dell'Ovo now stands) in about 680 BC. Originally called Parthenope, in honour of the siren whose body had earlier washed up there (she drowned herself after failing to seduce Ulysses), it was eventually incorporated into a new city, Neapolis, founded by Greeks from Cumae (Cuma) in 474 BC. However, within 150 years it was in Roman hands, becoming something of a VIP resort favoured by emperors Pompey, Caesar and Tiberius.

After the fall of the Roman Empire, Naples became a duchy, originally under the Byzantines and later as an independent dukedom, until it was captured in 1139 by the Normans and absorbed into the Kingdom of the Two Sicilies. The Normans, in turn, were replaced by the German Swabians, whose charismatic leader Frederick II injected the city with new institutions, including its university.

The Swabian period came to a violent end with the victory of Charles I of Anjou at the 1266 battle of Benevento. The Angevins did much for Naples, promoting art and culture, building Castel Nuovo and enlarging the port, but they were unable to stop the Spanish Aragons taking the city in 1442. However, Naples continued to prosper. Alfonso I of Aragon, in particular, introduced new laws and encouraged the arts and sciences.

In 1503 Naples was absorbed by Spain, which sent viceroys to rule as virtual dictators. Despite Spain's heavy-handed rule, Naples flourished artistically and acquired much of its splendour. Indeed, it continued to bloom when the Spanish Bourbons re-established Naples as the capital of the Kingdom of the Two Sicilies in 1734. Aside from a Napoleonic interlude under Joachim Murat (1806–15), the Bourbons remained until they were unseated by Garibaldi and the Kingdom of Italy in 1860.

Modern Struggles & Achievements

Naples was heavily bombed in WWII, and the effects can still be seen on many monuments around the city. Since the war, Campania's capital has continued to suffer. Endemic corruption and the re-emergence of the Camorra have plagued much of the city's postwar resurrection, reaching a nadir in the years following a severe earthquake in 1980. In 2011 the city's sporadic garbage-disposal crisis flared up again, leading frustrated residents to set fire to uncollected rubbish in the streets.

Despite these tribulations, the winds of change are blowing. In recent years, Naples' young and visionary mayor, Luigi de Magistris, has introduced numerous schemes aimed at making Italy's third-largest city cleaner and greener. Among these is the pedestrianisation of Naples' famous Lungomare (seafront). New ideas and innovation are driving a growing number of youth-run enterprises and businesses, while the city's famous art-themed metro launched another two show-stopping, starchitect-designed stations in 2015.

◉ Sights

◉ Centro Storico

The three east–west *decumani* (main streets) of Naples' *centro storico* follow the original street plan of ancient Neapolis. Most of the major sights are grouped around the busiest two of these classical thoroughfares: 'Spaccanapoli' (consisting of Via Benedetto Croce, Via San Biagio dei Librai and Via Vicaria Vecchia) and Via dei Tribunali. North of Via dei Tribunali, Via della Sapienza, Via Anticaglia and Via Santissimi Apostoli make up the quieter third *decumanus*.

★ **Complesso Monumentale di Santa Chiara**   BASILICA, MONASTERY

(Map p658; ☑ 081 551 66 73; www.monastero disantachiara.eu; Via Santa Chiara 49c; basilica free, Complesso Monumentale adult/reduced €6/4.50; ◷ basilica 7.30am-1pm & 4.30-8pm, Complesso Monumentale 9.30am-5.30pm Mon-Sat, 10am-2.30pm Sun; Ⓜ Dante) Vast, Gothic and cleverly deceptive, the mighty **Basilica di Santa Chiara** stands at the heart of this tranquil

Naples & Campania Highlights

1 Channelling the ancients on the ill-fated streets of **Pompeii** (p687).

2 Being bewitched by Capri's ethereal **Grotta Azzurra** (p678).

3 Walking with the gods on the **Amalfi Coast** (p699).

4 Re-evaluating artistic ingenuity in Naples' **Cappella Sansevero** (p654).

5 Lunching by lapping waves on pastel-hued **Procida** (p683).

6 Indulging in a little thermal therapy on **Ischia** (p680).

7 Attending a concert at Ravello's dreamy **Villa Rufolo** (p704).

8 Exploring Naples' underworld on a **Tunnel Borbonico** (p665) tour.

9 Pretending you're royalty at the **Reggia di Caserta** (p674).

10 Admiring ancient Hellenic ingenuity in **Paestum** (p708).

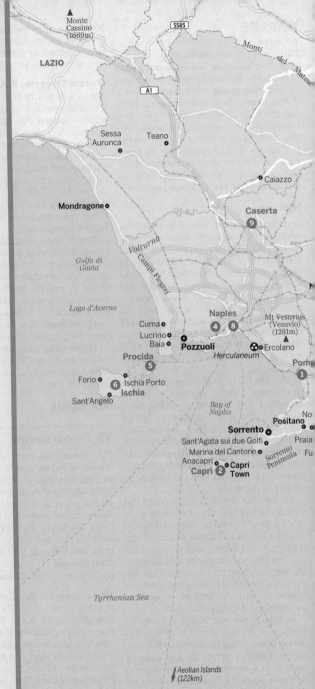

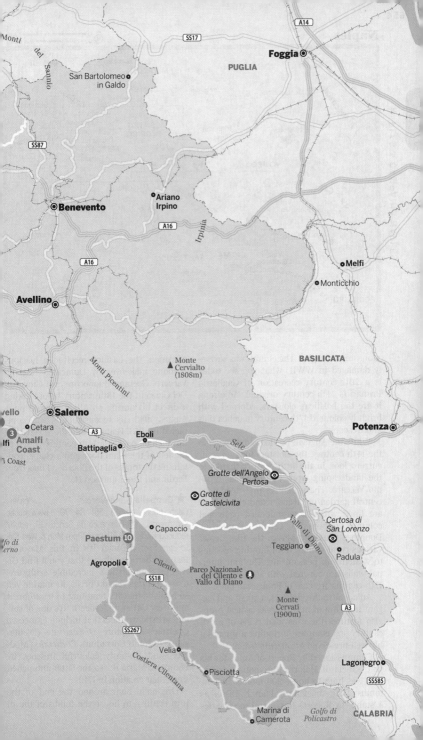

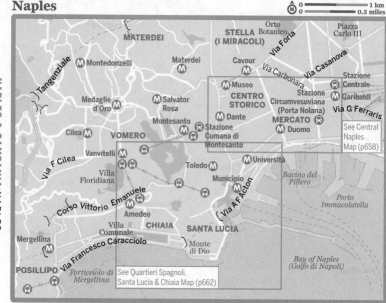

monastery complex. The church was severely damaged in WWII: what you see today is a 20th-century recreation of Gagliardo Primario's 14th-century original. Adjoining it are the basilica's cloisters, adorned with brightly coloured 17th-century majolica tiles and frescoes.

While the Angevin porticoes date back to the 14th century, the cloisters took on their current look in the 18th century thanks to the landscaping work of Domenico Antonio Vaccaro. The walkways that divide the central garden of lavender and citrus trees are lined with 72 ceramic-tiled octagonal columns connected by benches. Painted by Donato e Giuseppe Massa, the tiles depict various rural scenes, from hunting sessions to vignettes of peasant life. The four internal walls are covered with soft, whimsical 17th-century frescoes of Franciscan tales.

Adjacent to the cloisters, a small and elegant museum of mostly ecclesiastical props also features the excavated ruins of a 1st-century spa complex, including a remarkably well-preserved *laconicum* (sauna).

Commissioned by Robert of Anjou for his wife Sancia di Maiorca, the monastic complex was built to house 200 monks and the tombs of the Angevin royal family. Dissed as a 'stable' by Robert's ungrateful son Charles

of Anjou, the basilica received a luscious baroque makeover by Domenico Antonio Vaccaro, Gaetano Buonocore and Giovanni Del Gaizo in the 18th century before taking a direct hit during an Allied air raid on 4 August 1943. Its reconstruction was completed in 1953. Features that did survive the fire include part of a 14th-century fresco to the left of the main door and a chapel containing the tombs of the Bourbon kings from Ferdinand I to Francesco II.

★ Cappella Sansevero   CHAPEL
(Map p658; ☎ 081 551 84 70; www.museo sansevero.it; Via Francesco de Sanctis 19; adult/reduced €7/5; ⊗ 9.30am-6.30pm Mon & Wed-Sat, to 2pm Sun; ⓜ Dante) It's in this Masonic-inspired baroque chapel that you'll find Giuseppe Sanmartino's incredible sculpture, *Cristo velato* (Veiled Christ), its marble veil so realistic that it's tempting to try to lift it and view Christ underneath. It's one of several artistic wonders that include Francesco Queirolo's sculpture *Disinganno* (Disillusion), Antonio Corradini's *Pudicizia* (Modesty) and riotously colourful frescoes by Francesco Maria Russo, the latter untouched since their creation in 1749.

Originally built around the end of the 16th century to house the tombs of the di

Sangro family, the chapel was given its current baroque fit-out by Prince Raimondo di Sangro, who, between 1749 and 1766, commissioned the finest artists to adorn the interior. In Queirolo's *Disinganno*, the man trying to untangle himself from a net represents Raimondo's father, Antonio, Duke of Torremaggiore. After the premature death of his wife, Antonio abandoned the young Raimondo, choosing instead a life of travel and hedonistic pleasures. Repentant in his later years, he returned to Naples and joined the priesthood. His attempt to free himself from sin is represented in Queirolo's masterpiece.

Even more poignant is Antonio Corradini's *Pudicizia*, whose veiled female figure pays tribute to Raimondo's mother, Cecilia Gaetani d'Aquila d'Aragona. Raimondo was only 11 months old when she died, and the statue's lost gaze and broken plaque represent a life cruelly cut short.

The chapel's original polychrome marble flooring was badly damaged in a major collapse involving the chapel and the neighbouring Palazzo dei di Sangro in 1889. Designed by Francesco Celebrano, the flooring survives in fragmentary form in the passageway leading off from the chapel's right side. The passageway leads to a staircase, at the bottom of which you'll find two meticulously preserved human arterial systems – one of a man, the other of a woman. Debate still circles the models: are the arterial systems real or reproductions? And if they are real, just how was such an incredible state

of preservation achieved? More than two centuries on, the mystery surrounding the alchemist prince lives on.

Chiesa del Gesù Nuovo   CHURCH
(Map p658; ☎ 081 551 86 13; Piazza del Gesù Nuovo; ⊗ 7.15am-12.45pm & 4-8pm Mon-Sat, 7am-2pm & 4-9pm Sun; Ⓜ Dante) The extraordinary Chiesa del Gesù Nuovo is an architectural Kinder Surprise. Its shell is the 15th-century, Giuseppe Valeriani–designed facade of Palazzo Sanseverino, converted to create the 16th-century church. Inside, piperno-stone sobriety gives way to a gob-smacking blast of baroque that could make the Vatican blush: a vainglorious showcase for the work of top-tier artists such as Francesco Solimena, Luca Giordano and Cosimo Fanzago.

Chiesa e Chiostro di San
Gregorio Armeno   CHURCH, CLOISTER
(Map p658; ☎ 081 420 63 85; Via San Gregorio Armeno 44; ⊗ 9.30am-noon Mon-Fri, to 1pm Sat & Sun; ☐ C55 to Via Duomo) Overstatement knows no bounds at this richly ornamented 16th-century monastic complex. The church packs a visual punch with its lavish wood and papier-mâché choir stalls, sumptuous altar by Dionisio Lazzari, and Luca Giordano's masterpiece fresco *The Embarkation, Journey and Arrival of the Armenia Nuns with the Relics of St Gregory*. Excess gives way to soothing tranquillity in the picture-perfect cloisters, accessible through the gate on Vico Giuseppe Maffei.

NAPLES IN...

Two Days
Start with a burst of colour in the cloister of the **Basilica di Santa Chiara** (p651), get breathless over the astounding *Cristo velato* (Veiled Christ) in the **Cappella Sansevero** (p654), then head underground on a **Napoli Sotterranea** tour (p665). After lunch, take in Lanfranco's dome fresco in the Duomo, meditate on a Caravaggio masterpiece at **Pio Monte della Misericordia** (p656), then simply kick back in bohemian Piazza Bellini. Next morning, explore ancient treasures at the **Museo Archeologico Nazionale** (p657), then head up to the **Certosa e Museo di San Martino** (p659), for extraordinary baroque interiors, Neapolitan art and a sweeping panorama. Cap the night on the fashionable, bar-packed streets of Chiaia.

Four Days
Spend the morning of day three cheek-to-crater with **Mt Vesuvius** (p686), then ponder its bone-chilling fury at **Herculaneum** (p684) or **Pompeii** (p686). Alternatively, spend the day at Caserta's mammoth royal pad **Reggia di Caserta** (p674). On day four, head up to the **Palazzo Reale di Capodimonte** (p661) to eye up the bounty of artistic masterpieces inside, then head underground on a guided tour of the otherworldly **Catacomba di San Gennaro** (p666). Top it all off with a romantic evening shouting 'bravo' at the luscious **Teatro San Carlo** (p670).

ℹ **BEFORE YOU EXPLORE**

If you're planning to blitz the sights, the **Campania Artecard** (800 60 06 01; www. campaniartecard.it) is an excellent investment. A cumulative ticket that covers museum admission and transport, it comes in various forms. The Naples three-day ticket (adult/reduced €21/12) gives free admission to three participating sites, a 50% discount on others and free use of public transport in the city. Other handy options include a 7-day 'Tutta la Regione' ticket (€34), which offers free admission to five sites and discounted admission to others in areas as far afield as Caserta, Ravello (Amalfi Coast) and Paestum. The latter does not cover transport. Cards can be purchased online, at the dedicated Artecard booth inside the tourist office at Stazione Centrale, or at participating sites and museums.

Complesso Monumentale di San Lorenzo Maggiore ARCHAEOLOGICAL SITE
(Map p658; ☑ 081 211 08 60; www.sanlorenzo maggiorenapoli.it; Via dei Tribunali 316; church admission free, excavations & museum adult/reduced €9/7; ☺ 9.30am-5.30pm; ☐ C55 to Via Duomo) Architecture and history buffs shouldn't miss this richly layered religious complex, its commanding basilica deemed one of Naples' finest medieval buildings. Aside from Ferdinando Sanfelice's petite facade, the Cappella al Rosario and the Cappellone di Sant'Antonio, its baroque makeover was stripped away last century to reveal its austere, Gothic elegance. Beneath the basilica, a sprawl of extraordinary ruins will transport you back two millennia.

Pio Monte della Misericordia CHURCH, MUSEUM
(Map p658; ☑ 081 44 69 44; www.piomontedella misericordia.it; Via dei Tribunali 253; adult/reduced €7/5; ☺ 9am-2pm Thu-Tue; ☐ C55 to Via Duomo) The 1st floor of this octagonal, 17th-century church delivers a small, satisfying collection of Renaissance and baroque art, including works by Francesco de Mura, Giuseppe de Ribera, Andrea Vaccaro and Paul van Somer. It's also home to contemporary artworks by Italian and foreign artists, each inspired by Caravaggio's masterpiece *Le Sette Opere di Misericordia* (The Seven Acts of Mercy), considered by many to be the most important painting in Naples. You'll find it above the main altar in the ground-floor chapel.

★ **Duomo** CATHEDRAL
(Map p658; ☑ 081 44 90 65; Via Duomo 149; baptistry €1.50; ☺ cathedral 8.30am-1.30pm & 2.30-8pm Mon-Sat, 8.30am-1.30pm & 4.30-7.30pm Sun, baptistry 8.30am-1pm Mon-Sat, 8.30am-12.30pm & 5-6.30pm Sun; ☐ C55 to Via Duomo) Whether you go for Giovanni Lanfranco's fresco in the **Cappella di San Gennaro** (Chapel of St Janarius), the 4th-century mosaics in the baptistry, or the thrice-annual miracle of San Gennaro, do not miss Naples' cathedral. Kick-started by Charles I of Anjou in 1272 and consecrated in 1315, it was largely destroyed in a 1456 earthquake, with copious nips and tucks over the subsequent centuries.

Among these is the gleaming neo-Gothic facade, only added in the late 19th century. Step inside and you'll immediately notice the central nave's gilded coffered ceiling, studded with late-mannerist art. The high sections of the nave and the transept are the work of baroque overachiever Luca Giordano.

Off the right aisle, the 17th-century Cappella di San Gennaro (also known as the Chapel of the Treasury) was designed by Giovanni Cola di Franco and completed in 1637. The most sought-after artists of the period worked on the chapel, creating one of Naples' greatest baroque legacies. Highlights here include Giuseppe de Ribera's gripping canvas *St Gennaro Escaping the Furnace Unscathed* and Giovanni Lanfranco's dizzying dome fresco. Hidden away in a strongbox behind the altar is a 14th-century silver bust in which sit the skull of San Gennaro and the two phials that hold his miraculously liquefying blood.

The next chapel eastwards contains an urn with the saint's bones and a cupboard full of femurs, tibias and fibulas. Below the high altar is the **Cappella Carafa**, a Renaissance chapel built to house yet more of the saint's remains.

Off the left aisle lies the 4th-century **Basilica di Santa Restituta**, subject to an almost complete makeover after the earthquake of 1688. From it you can access the **Battistero di San Giovanni in Fonte**. Western Europe's oldest baptistry, it's encrusted with fragments of glittering 4th-century mosaics. Alas, the Duomo's subterranean archaeological zone, which includes fascinating remains of Greek and Roman buildings and roads, remains closed indefinitely.

MADRE
GALLERY

(Museo d'Arte Contemporanea Donnaregina; ☑ 081 1931 3016; www.madrenapoli.it; Via Settembrini 79; adult/reduced €7/3.50, Mon free; ⊙ 10am-7.30pm Mon & Wed-Sat, to 8pm Sun; Ⓜ Piazza Cavour) When *Madonna and Child* overload hits, reboot at Naples' museum of modern and contemporary art. Start on level three – the setting for temporary exhibitions – before hitting the permanent collection of painting, sculpture and installations from prolific 20th- and 21st-century artists on level two. Among these are Olafur Eliasson, Shirin Neshat and Julian Beck, as well as Italian heavyweights Mario Merz and Michelangelo Pistoletto. Specially commissioned installations from the likes of Francesco Clemente, Anish Kapoor and Rebecca Horn cap things off on level one.

★ Museo Archeologico Nazionale
MUSEUM

(Map p658; ☑ 081 442 21 49; http://cir. campania.beniculturali.it/museoarcheologiconazionale; Piazza Museo Nazionale 19; adult/reduced €8/4; ⊙ 9am-7.30pm Wed-Mon; Ⓜ Museo, Piazza Cavour) Naples' National Archaeological Museum serves up one of the world's finest collections of Graeco-Roman artefacts. Originally a cavalry barracks and later a seat of the city's university, the museum was established by the Bourbon king Charles VII in the late 18th century to house the antiquities he inherited from his mother, Elisabetta Farnese, as well as treasures looted from Pompeii and Herculaneum. Star exhibits include the celebrated *Toro Farnese* (Farnese Bull) sculpture and a series of awe-inspiring mosaics from Pompeii's Casa del Fauno.

Before tackling the collection, consider investing in the *National Archaeological Museum of Naples* (€12), published by Electa; if you want to concentrate on the highlights, audioguides (€5) are available in English. It's also worth calling ahead to ensure that the galleries you want to see are open, as staff shortages often mean that sections of the museum close for part of the day.

The basement houses the Borgia collection of Egyptian relics and epigraphs (closed indefinitely on our last visit). The ground-floor Farnese collection of colossal Greek and Roman sculptures features the *Toro Farnese* and a muscle-bound *Ercole* (Her-

cules). Sculpted in the early 3rd century AD and noted in the writings of Pliny, the *Toro Farnese*, probably a Roman copy of a Greek original, depicts the humiliating death of Dirce, Queen of Thebes. Carved from a single colossal block of marble, the sculpture was discovered in 1545 near the Baths of Caracalla in Rome and was restored by Michelangelo, before eventually being shipped to Naples in 1787. *Ercole* was discovered in the same Roman excavations, albeit without his legs. When they turned up at a later dig, the Bourbons had them fitted.

If you're short on time, take in both these masterpieces before heading straight to the mezzanine floor, home to an exquisite collection of mosaics, mostly from Pompeii. Of the series taken from the Casa del Fauno, it is *La battaglia di Alessandro contro Dario* (The Battle of Alexander against Darius) that really stands out. The best-known depiction of Alexander the Great, the 20-sq-metre mosaic was probably made by Alexandrian craftsmen working in Italy around the end of the 2nd century BC.

Beyond the mosaics, the **Gabinetto Segreto** (Secret Chamber) contains a small but much-studied collection of ancient erotica. Pan is caught in the act with a nanny goat in the collection's most famous piece – a small and surprisingly sophisticated statue taken from the Villa dei Papiri in Herculaneum. You'll also find a series of nine paintings depicting erotic positions – a menu for brothel patrons.

Originally the royal library, the enormous **Sala Meridiana** (Great Hall of the Sundial) on the 1st floor is home to the *Farnese Atlante*, a statue of Atlas carrying a globe on his shoulders, as well as various paintings from the Farnese collection. Look up and you'll find Pietro Bardellino's riotously colourful 1781 fresco depicting the (short-lived) triumph of Ferdinand IV of Bourbon and Marie Caroline of Austria in Rome.

The rest of the 1st floor is largely devoted to fascinating discoveries from Pompeii, Herculaneum, Boscoreale, Stabiae and Cuma. Among them are whimsical wall frescoes from the Villa di Agrippa Postumus and the Casa di Meleagro, extraordinary bronzes from the Villa dei Papiri, as well as ceramics, glassware, engraved coppers and Greek funerary vases.

Mercato di Porta Nolana
MARKET

(Porta Nolana; ⊙ 8am-6pm Mon-Sat, to 2pm Sun; Ⓜ Garibaldi) Naples at its most vociferous and

Central Naples

400 m
0.2 miles

Catacomba di Gennaro (1km);
Palazzo Reale di Capodimonte (2km)

Museo
Museo Archeologico
Nazionale

Piazza Museo
Nazionale 4

Via Tommasi

Via Broggia

Via Enrico Pessina

Piazza
Dante

Via Bellini

Via Santa Maria di Costantinopoli

Piazza
del Gesù
Nuovo

Via Port'Alba

Via Pignasecca

Piazza
Carità

Via Toledo

Via S Anna dei Lombardi

Via D Lioy

Via S Gaudioso

Via F del Giudice

Via del Sole

Piazza
Luigi
Miraglia

Cappella
Sansevero

Via San Sebastiano

Via San Domenico Maggiore

Vico San Domenico Maggiore

Piazza San Domenico Maggiore

Via Benedetto Croce

Complesso
Monumentale
di Santa Chiara

Via Santa Chiara

Via Mezzocannone

Largo
Giusso

Via San Geronimo

Vico
Donnaromita

Via G Paladino

Vico S Nicola al Nilo

Vico S Severino

Via B Capasso

See Quartieri Spagnoli, Santa Lucia & Chiara Map (p662)

Piazzetta
Orefici

Via dei Cimbri

Via d'Alagno

Duomo

Piazza
Nicola
Amore

Via Duomo

Via Scialoja

Via Santa Maria Vecchia

CENTRO
STORICO

Via San Biagio dei Librai

Via San Gregorio Armeno

Via San Paolo

Via Atri

Via d'Anticaglia

Vico Giganti

Via Duomo

Vico Zuroli

Vico della Pace

Via della Zite

Via del Tribunali

Via S Nicola dei Caserti

Via P Colletta

Via dell'Annunziata

Via C Miri

Via Santissimi Apostoli

Via Pisanelli

Via PS Mancini

Via Duchesca

Via Carbonara

Piazza
Principe
Umberto

Corso Novara

Via Firenze

Stazione
Centrale

Garibaldi

Piazza
Garibaldi

Garibaldi

Stazione
Circumvesuviana
(Piazza Garibaldi)

Terminal Bus
Metropark

Eccellenze Campane
(1km)

Via G Pica

Via S Cosmo Fuori Porta Nolana

Stazione
Circumvesuviana
(Porta Nolana)

Corso G Garibaldi

Via C Carmignano

Via Sopramuro

Via Nolana

Via Lavinaio

Via A de Pace

Vico Barre

Via G Savarese

Piazza del
Mercato

Piazza
Masaniello

Chiesa di
Santa Maria del
Carmine

Via D Carmine

Piazza
G Pepe

Via Amerigo Vespucci

Via E Cosenz

Vico S Giovanni

Calata della Marinella

Calata Villa del Popolo

Via Nuova Marina

SITA Sud
Bus Stop (180m)

Via Sant'Eligio

Via Duca di San Donato

MERCATO

Corso Umberto I

Via Ranieri

Vicolo Sedil
Capuano

Duomo

Via A Vicaria

Piazza
Bellini

Via Santa Maria di Costantinopoli

Via del Porto

Via Volabra

Via Donnalbina

Via Vespri

Central Naples

intense, the Mercato di Porta Nolana is a heady, gritty street market where bellowing fishmongers and greengrocers collide with fragrant delis and bakeries, industrious Chinese traders and contraband cigarette stalls. Dive in for anything from buxom tomatoes and mozzarella to golden-fried street snacks, cheap luggage and bootleg CDs.

The market's namesake is medieval city gate **Porta Nolana**, which stands at the head of Via Sopramuro. Its two cylindrical towers, optimistically named Faith and Hope, support an arch decorated with a bas-relief of Ferdinand I of Aragon on horseback.

◉ Vomero

Visible from all over Naples, the stunning Certosa di San Martino is the one compelling reason to take the funicular up to middle-class Vomero (*vom*-e-ro).

★ **Certosa e Museo di San Martino**   MONASTERY, MUSEUM
(Map p662; ☑081 229 45 68; www.polo musealenapoli.beniculturali.it; Largo San Martino 5; adult/reduced €6/3; ☺8.30am-7.30pm Thu-Tue; Ⓜ Vanvitelli, ⓕ Montesanto to Morghen) The high point (quite literally) of the Neapolitan baroque, this charterhouse-turned-museum was founded as a Carthusian monastery in the 14th century. Centred on one of the most beautiful cloisters in Italy, it has been decorated, adorned and altered over the centuries by some of Italy's finest talent, most importantly Giovanni Antonio Dosio in the 16th century and baroque master Cosimo

Fanzago a century later. Nowadays, it's a superb repository of Neapolitan artistry.

The monastery's church and the rooms that flank it contain a feast of frescoes and paintings by some of Naples' greatest 17th-century artists, among them Francesco Solimena, Massimo Stanzione, Giuseppe de Ribera and Battista Caracciolo. In the nave, Cosimo Fanzago's inlaid marble work is simply extraordinary.

Adjacent to the church, the **Chiostro dei Procuratori** is the smaller of the monastery's two cloisters. A grand corridor on the left leads to the larger **Chiostro Grande** (Great Cloister). Originally designed by Dosio in the late 16th century and added to by Fanzago, it's a sublime composition of Tuscan-Doric porticoes, marble statues and vibrant camellias. The skulls mounted on the balustrade were a light-hearted reminder to the monks of their own mortality.

Just off the Chiostro dei Procuratori, the small **Sezione Navale** documents the history of the Bourbon navy from 1734 to 1860, and features a small collection of beautiful royal barges. The **Sezione Presepiale** houses a whimsical collection of rare Neapolitan *presepi* (nativity scenes) from the 18th and 19th centuries, including the colossal 18th-century Cuciniello creation, which covers one wall of what used to be the monastery's kitchen. The **Quarto del Priore** in the southern wing houses the bulk of the picture collection, as well as one of the museum's most famous pieces, Pietro Bernini's tender *Madonna col Bambino e San Giovannino*

THE ART OF THE NEAPOLITAN PRESEPE

Christmas nativity cribs may not be exclusive to Naples, but none match the artistic brilliance of the *presepe napoletano* (Neapolitan nativity crib). What sets the local version apart is its incredible attention to detail, from the lifelike miniature *prosciutti* (hams) in the tavern to the lavishly costumed *pastori* (crib figurines or sculptures) adoring the newborn Christ.

For the nobility and bourgeoisie of 18th-century Naples, the *presepe* provided a convenient marriage of faith and ego, becoming as much a symbol of wealth and good taste as a meditation on the Christmas miracle. The finest sculptors were commissioned and the finest fabrics used. Even the royals got involved: Charles III of Bourbon consulted the esteemed *presepe* expert, Dominican monk Padre Rocco, on the creation of his 5000-*pastore* spectacular, still on show at the Palazzo Reale. Yet even this pales in comparison to the up-sized Cuciniello crib on display at the Certosa e Museo di San Martino (p659), considered the world's greatest.

Centuries on, the legacy continues. The craft's epicentre is the *centro storico* street of Via San Gregorio Armeno (Map p658; C55 to Via Duomo), its clutter of shops and workshops selling everything from doting donkeys to kitsch celebrity caricatures. Serious connoisseurs, however, will point you towards the very few workshops that completely handcraft their *pastori* the old-fashioned way. Among the latter are Ars Neapolitana (Map p658; 392 537 71 16; Via dei Tribunali 303; 10am-6.30pm Mon-Fri, to 3pm Sat, plus 10am-6.30pm Sat & Sun late Oct-early Jan; C55 to Via Duomo) and La Scarabattola (p671), both in the *centro storico*.

(Madonna and Child with the Infant John the Baptist).

A pictorial history of Naples is told in Immagini e Memorie di Napoli (Images and Memories of Naples). Here you'll find portraits of historic characters; antique maps, including a 35-panel copper map of 18th-century Naples in Room 45; and rooms dedicated to major historical events such as the Revolt of the Masaniello (Room 36) and the plague (Room 37). Room 32 boasts the beautiful *Tavola Strozzi* (Strozzi Table); its fabled depiction of 15th-century maritime Naples is one of the city's most celebrated historical records.

You will need to book in advance to access the Certosa's imposing Sotterranei Gotici (Gothic basement), open to the public on Saturday and Sunday at 11.30am (with guided tour in Italian) and 4.30pm (without guided tour). The austere vaulted space is home to about 150 marble sculptures and epigraphs, including a statue of St Francis of Assisi by 18th-century master sculptor Giuseppe Sanmartino. To book a visit, email accoglienza.sanmartino@beniculturali.it at least two weeks in advance.

Castle Sant'Elmo CASTLE, MUSEUM
(Map p662; 081 558 77 08; www.coopculture.it; Via Tito Angelini 22; adult/reduced €5/2.50; castle 8.30am-7.30pm Wed-Mon, museum 9am-7pm Wed-Mon; Vanvitelli, Montesanto to Morghen) Star-shaped Castel Sant'Elmo was originally a church dedicated to St Erasmus. Some 400 years later, in 1349, Robert of Anjou turned it into a castle before Spanish viceroy Don Pedro de Toledo had it further fortified in 1538. Used as a military prison until the 1970s, it's now famed for its jaw-dropping panorama, and for its Museo del Novecento, dedicated to 20th-century Neapolitan art.

Via Toledo & Quartieri Spagnoli

Galleria di Palazzo Zevallos Stigliano GALLERY
(Map p662; 081 42 50 11; www.palazzozevallos.com; Via Toledo 185; adult/reduced €5/3; 10am-6pm Tue-Fri, to 8pm Sat & Sun; Municipio) Built for a Spanish merchant in the 17th century and reconfigured in belle époque style by architect Luigi Platania in the early 20th century, Palazzo Zevallos Stigliano houses a compact yet stunning collection of Neapolitan and Italian art spanning the 17th- to early-20th centuries. Star attraction is Caravaggio's mesmerising swan song, *The Martyrdom of St Ursula* (1610). Completed weeks before the artist's lonely death, the painting depicts a vengeful king of the Huns piercing the heart of his unwilling virgin bride-to-be, Ursula.

◉ Santa Lucia & Chiaia

Palazzo Reale   PALACE, MUSEUM
(Royal Palace; Map p662; ☑ 081 40 05 47; www.
sbapsae.na.it/cms; Piazza del Plebiscito 1; adult/
reduced €4/3; ⊗ 9am-8pm Thu-Tue; ☐ R2 to Via
San Carlo, Ⓜ Municipio) Envisaged as a 16th-
century monument to Spanish glory (Naples
was under Spanish rule at the time), the
magnificent Palazzo Reale is home to the
Museo del Palazzo Reale, a rich and eclectic collection of baroque and neoclassical
furnishings, porcelain, tapestries, sculpture
and paintings, spread across the palace's
royal apartments.

Among the many highlights is the Teatri-
no di Corte, a lavish private theatre created
by Ferdinando Fuga in 1768 to celebrate the
marriage of Ferdinand IV and Marie Caroline of Austria. Incredibly, Angelo Viva's statues of Apollo and the Muses set along the
walls are made of papier mâché.

In Sala (Room) XII, there's the 16th-
century canvas *Gli esattori delle imposte*
(The Tax Collectors) by Dutch artist Marinus
Claesz Van Raymerswaele. Sala XIII used to
be Joachim Murat's study in the 19th century but was used as a snack bar by Allied
troops in WWII. Meanwhile, what looks like
a waterwheel in Sala XXIII is actually a nifty
rotating reading desk made for Marie Caroline by Giovanni Uldrich in the 18th century.

The Cappella Reale (Royal Chapel) houses an 18th-century *presepe napoletano* (Neapolitan nativity crib). Fastidiously detailed,
its cast of *pastori* (crib figurines) were
crafted by a series of celebrated Neapolitan
artists, including Giuseppe Sanmartino,
creator of the *Cristo velato* (Veiled Christ)
sculpture in the Cappella Sansevero.

The palace is also home to the Biblioteca
Nazionale (National Library; Map p662; ☑ 081
781 91 11; www.bnnonline.it; ⊗ 8.30am-7pm Mon-
Fri, to 2pm Sat, papyri exhibition closes 2pm Mon-
Sat; ☐ R2 to Via San Carlo, Ⓜ Municipio) FREE,
its own priceless treasures including at least
2000 papyri discovered at Herculaneum and
fragments of a 5th-century Coptic Bible. The
National Library's beautiful Biblioteca Lucchesi Palli (Lucchesi Palli Library; closed
Saturday), designed by some of Naples'
most celebrated 19th-century craftspeople,
is home to numerous fascinating artistic
artefacts, including letters by composer Giuseppe Verdi. Bring photo ID to enter the
Biblioteca Nazionale.

MeMus   MUSEUM
(Museum & Historical Archive of the Teatro San Car-
lo; Map p662; http://memus.squarespace.com;
Palazzo Reale, Piazza del Plebiscito; adult/reduced
€6/5, incl Palazzo Reale €10/5; ⊗ 9.30am-5pm
Mon, Tue & Thu-Sat, to 2pm Sun; ☐ R2 to Via San
Carlo, Ⓜ Municipio) Located inside the Palazzo
Reale (purchase tickets at the palace ticket
booth), modern museum MeMus documents the history of Europe's oldest working
opera house, the Teatro San Carlo (p670).
The collection includes costumes, sketches,
instruments and memorabilia, displayed in
annually changing themed exhibitions. One
interactive, immersive exhibit allows visitors
to enjoy the music of numerous celebrated
composers with accompanying visuals by
artists who have collaborated with the opera
house, among them William Kentridge.

Castel Nuovo   CASTLE, MUSEUM
(Map p662; ☑ 081 795 77 22; Piazza Municipio;
admission €6; ⊗ 9am-7pm Mon-Sat, last entry
6pm; Ⓜ Municipio) Locals know this 13th-
century castle as the Maschio Angioino
(Angevin Keep) and its Cappella Palatina
is home to fragments of frescoes by Renaissance maverick Giotto; they're on the splays
of the Gothic windows. You'll find Roman
ruins under the glass-floored Sala dell'Ar-
meria (Armoury Hall), and a collection of
mostly 17th- to early-20th-century Neapolitan paintings on the upper floors. The top
floor houses the more interesting works, including landscape paintings by Luigi Crisco-
nio and a watercolour drawing by architect
Carlo Vanvitelli.

Castel dell'Ovo   CASTLE
(Map p662; ☑ 081 795 45 93; Borgo Marinaro;
⊗ 8am-6.45pm Mon-Sat, to 1.45pm Sun; ☐ 128 to
Via Santa Lucia) FREE Built by the Normans in
the 12th century, Naples' oldest castle owes
its name (Castle of the Egg) to Virgil. The
Roman scribe reputedly buried an egg on
the site where the castle now stands, warning that when the egg breaks, the castle
(and Naples) will fall. Thankfully, both are
still standing, and walking up to the castle's
ramparts will reward you with a breathtaking panorama.

◉ Capodimonte & La Sanità

★ Palazzo Reale di Capodimonte   MUSEUM
(☑ 081 749 91 11; www.polomusealenapoli.beni
culturali.it; Via Miano 2; adult/reduced €7.50/3.75;
⊗ 8.30am-7.30pm Thu-Tue; ☐ R4, 178 to Via

Quartieri Spagnoli, Santa Lucia & Chiaia

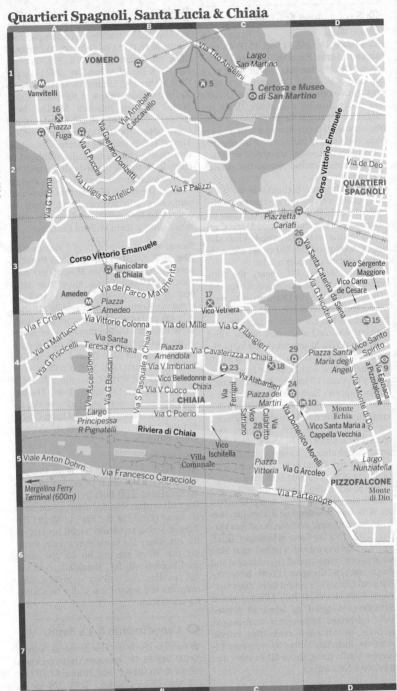

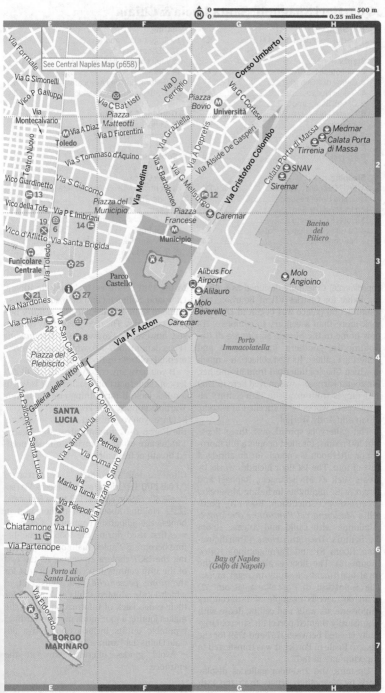

See Central Naples Map (p658)

Via Formale

Via G Simonelli

Vico P Galluppi

Via Montecalvario

Via C Battisti

Piazza Matteotti

Via A Diaz

Via D Fiorentini

Toledo

Via S Tommaso d'Aquino

Via S Giacomo

Vico Giardinetto

Vico della Tofa

Via P E Imbriani

Via Santa Brigida

Vico d'Afflitto

Funicolare Centrale

Via Nardones

Via Chiaia

Piazza del Plebiscito

Via C Console

SANTA LUCIA

Via Santa Lucia

Via Petronio

Via Cuma

Via Marino Turchi

Via Palepoli

Via Chiatamone

Via Lucilio

Via Partenope

Porto di Santa Lucia

Via Eldorado

BORGO MARINARO

Bay of Naples (Golfo di Napoli)

Via D Cerriglio

Piazza Bovio

Via G C Cortese

Corso Umberto I

Università

Via Graziella

Via A Depretis

Via Alside De Gasperi

Via Cristoforo Colombo

Via Medina

Via S Bartolomeo

Via G Melisurgo

Piazza del Municipio

Piazza Francese

Municipio

Parco Castello

Alibus For Airport

Alilauro

Molo Beverello

Caremar

Via A F Acton

Porto Immacolatella

Molo Angioino

Bacino del Piliero

Calata Porta di Massa

Medmar

Calata Porta di Massa

Tirrenia

SNAV

Siremar

Via San Carlo

Galleria della Vittoria

Via Pallonetto Santa Lucia

Via Santa Lucia

Via Nazario Sauro

Quartieri Spagnoli, Santa Lucia & Chiaia

Capodimonte) Originally designed as a hunting lodge for Charles VII of Bourbon, this monumental palace was begun in 1738 and took more than a century to complete. It's now home to the **Museo Nazionale di Capodimonte**, southern Italy's largest and richest art gallery. Its vast collection – much of which Charles inherited from his mother, Elisabetta Farnese – was moved here in 1759 and ranges from exquisite 12th-century altarpieces to works by Botticelli, Caravaggio, Titian and Andy Warhol.

The gallery is spread over three floors and 160 rooms; for most people, a full morning or afternoon is enough for an abridged best-of tour. The 1st floor includes works by greats such as Michelangelo, Raphael and Titian, with highlights including Masaccio's *Crocifissione* (Crucifixion; Room 3), Botticelli's *Madonna col Bambino e due angeli* (Madonna with Child and Angels; Room 6), Bellini's *Trasfigurazione* (Transfiguration; Room 8) and Parmigianino's *Antea* (Room 12). The floor is also home to the royal apartments, a study in regal excess. The **Salottino di Porcellana** (Room 52) is an outrageous example of 18th-century chinoiserie, its walls and ceiling dense with whimsically themed porcelain 'stucco'. Originally created between 1757 and 1759 for the Palazzo Reale in Portici, it was transferred to Capodimonte in 1867.

Upstairs, the 2nd-floor galleries display work by Neapolitan artists from the 13th to the 19th centuries, including de Ribera, Giordano, Solimena and Stanzione. It's also home to some spectacular 16th-century Belgian tapestries. The piece that many come to see, however, is Caravaggio's *Flagellazione* (Flagellation; 1607–10), which hangs in reverential solitude in Room 78.

If you have any energy left, the small gallery of modern art on the 3rd floor is worth a quick look, if for nothing else than Andy Warhol's poptastic *Mt Vesuvius*.

Once you've finished in the museum, the **Parco di Capodimonte** – the palace's 130-hectare estate – provides a much-needed breath of fresh air.

Cimitero delle Fontanelle CEMETERY
(⌨ 081 1970 3197; cimiterofontanelle.com; Via Fontanelle 80; ⊙ 9am-4pm; 🚌 C51 to Via Fontanelle) **FREE** Holding about eight million human bones, the ghoulish Fontanelle Cemetery was first used during the 1656 plague, before becoming Naples' main burial site during the 1837 cholera epidemic. At the end of the 19th century it became a hot spot for the *anime pezzentelle* (poor souls) cult, in which locals adopted skulls and prayed for their souls. Lack of information at the site makes joining a tour much more rewarding; reputable outfits include Cooperativa Sociale Onlus 'La Paranza' (p666).

Avoid guides offering tours at the entrance.

👉 Tours

Tunnel Borbonico HISTORIC SITE

(Map p662; ☎ 081 764 58 08, 366 2484151; www.
tunnelborbonico.info; Vico del Grottone 4; 75min
standard tour adult/reduced €10/5; ☉ standard
tour 10am, noon, 3.30pm & 5.30pm Fri-Sun; 🚇 R2
to Via San Carlo) Traverse five centuries along
Naples' engrossing Bourbon Tunnel. Conceived by Ferdinand II in 1853 to link the
Palazzo Reale to the barracks and the sea,
the never-completed escape route is part
of the 17th-century Carmignano Aqueduct
system, itself incorporating 16th-century
cisterns. An air-raid shelter and military
hospital during WWII, this underground
labyrinth rekindles the past with evocative
wartime artefacts. The standard tour doesn't
require booking, though the Adventure Tour
(80 minutes; adult/reduced €15/10) and
adults-only Speleo Tour (2½ hours; €30) do.
Tours also depart from Tunnel Borbonico's
second entrance, reached through the Parcheggio Morelli (Via Domenico Morelli 40)
parking complex in Chiaia.

Napoli Sotterranea ARCHAEOLOGICAL SITE

(Underground Naples; Map p658; ☎ 081 29 69
44; www.napolisotterranea.org; Piazza San Gaetano
68; adult/reduced €10/8; ☉ English tours 10am,
noon, 2pm, 4pm & 6pm; 🚇 C55 to Via Duomo) This
evocative guided tour leads you 40m below
street level to explore Naples' ancient labyrinth of aqueducts, passages and cisterns.

Kayak Napoli KAYAKING

(☎ 331 9874271; www.kayaknapoli.com; tours €20-
30; 🚇 140 to Via Posillipo) 🛶 Popular kayak
tours along the Neapolitan coastline, gliding
past often-inaccessible ruins, neoclassical
villas and luscious gardens, as well as into
secret sea grottoes. Tours cater to rookie and
experienced paddlers, with day and night
options. Meet at Via Posillipo 68 (Baia delle
Rocce Verdi) in the Posillipo neighbourhood.
Tours are subject to weather and should be
booked ahead.

🎉 Festivals & Events

Festa di San Gennaro RELIGIOUS

The faithful flock to the Duomo to witness
the miraculous liquefaction of San Gennaro's blood on the Saturday before the first
Sunday in May. Repeat performances take
place on 19 September and 16 December.

Maggio dei Monumenti CULTURAL

(☉ May) A month-long cultural feast, with
concerts, performances, exhibitions, guided
tours and other events across Naples.

Wine & The City WINE

(www.wineandthecity.it; ☉ May) A two-week
celebration of regional *vino*, with free wine

THE SUBTERRANEAN CITY

Mysterious shrines, secret passageways, forgotten burial crypts: it might sound like the
set of an Indiana Jones film, but it's actually what lurks beneath Naples' loud and greasy
streets. Subterranean Naples is one of the world's most thrilling urban wonderlands;
a silent, mostly undiscovered sprawl of cathedral-like cisterns, pin-thin conduits, catacombs and ancient ruins.

Speleologists (cave specialists) estimate that about 60% of Neapolitans live and work
above this network, known in Italian as the *sottosuolo* (underground). Since the end
of WWII, some 700 cavities have been discovered, from original Greek-era grottoes to
palaeo-Christian burial chambers and royal Bourbon escape routes. According to the
experts, there are over 3 million square feet of caves, caverns and tunnels under the
modern city.

Naples' dedicated caving geeks are quick to tell you that their underworld is one of the
largest and oldest on earth. Sure, Paris might claim a catacomb or two, but its subterranean offerings don't come close to this giant's 2500-year history.

And what a history it is. Naples' most famous saint, San Gennaro, was interred in the
Catacomba di San Gennaro in the 5th century. A century later, in 536, Belisario and his
troops caught Naples by surprise by storming the city through the city's ancient tunnels.
According to legend, Alfonso of Aragon used the same trick in 1442, undermining the
city walls by using an underground passageway leading into a tailor's shop and straight
into town. Even the city's dreaded Camorra has got in on the act. In 1992 the notorious
Stolder clan was busted for running a subterranean drug lab, with escape routes heading
straight to the pad of the clan boss.

CATACOMBA DI SAN GENNARO

An evocative otherworld of tombs, corridors and broad vestibules, the **Catacomba di San Gennaro** (☎ 081 744 37 14; www.catacombedinapoli.it; Via Capodimonte 13; adult/reduced €8/5; ⏱ 1hr tours every hour 10am-5pm Mon-Sat, to 1pm Sun; 🚌 R4, 178 to Via Capodimonte) are Naples' oldest and most sacred catacombs. Not only home to 2nd-century Christian frescoes and 5th-century mosaics, they harbour the oldest known image of San Gennaro as the protector of Naples. Indeed, it was the interment of the saint's body here in the 5th century that turned this city of the dead into a Christian pilgrimage site.

Tours of the catacomb are run by the **Cooperativa Sociale Onlus 'La Paranza'** (☎ 081 744 37 14; www.catacombedinapoli.it; Via Capodimonte 13; ⏱ information point 10am-5pm Mon-Sat, to 1pm Sun; 🚌 R4 to Via Capodimonte), the ticket office of which is to the left of the **Chiesa di Madre di Buon Consiglio** (☎ 081 741 00 06; Via Capodimonte 13; ⏱ 8am-12.30pm & 5-7pm Mon-Sat, 9am-1pm & 5-7pm Sun; 🚌 R4 to Via Capodimonte), a snack-sized replica of St Peter's in Rome completed in 1960. The cooperative also runs a fascinating walking tour called *Il Miglio Sacro* (The Holy Mile), which explores the neighbouring Sanità district. See its website for details.

tastings and cultural events in palaces, museums, boutiques and eateries throughout the city.

Napoli Teatro Festival   THEATRE
(www.napoliteatrofestival.it; ⏱ Jun) Three weeks of local and international theatre and performance art, staged in conventional and unconventional venues.

🛏 Sleeping

From funky B&Bs and cheery hostels to old-school seafront luxury piles, slumber options in Naples are varied, plentiful and relatively cheap. For maximum atmosphere, consider the *centro storico,* where you'll have many of the city's sights on your doorstep.

🛏 Centro Storico

Cerasiello B&B   B&B €
(☎ 338 9264453, 081 033 09 77; www.cerasiello.it; Via Supportico Lopez 20; s €40-60, d €55-80, tr €70-95, q €85-105; ❄ 🛜; Ⓜ Piazza Cavour, Museo) This gorgeous B&B consists of four rooms with private bathroom, an enchanting communal terrace and an ethno-chic look melding Neapolitan art with North African furnishings. The stylish kitchen offers a fabulous view of the Certosa di San Martino, a view shared by all rooms (or their bathroom) except Fuoco (Fire), which looks out at a beautiful church cupola.

Although technically in the Sanità district, the B&B is a short walk from Naples' *centro storico.* Bring €0.20 for the lift.

Casa Latina   B&B €
(Map p658; ☎ 338 9264453; www.bbcasalatina.it; Vico Cinquesanti 47; s €40-55, d €55-75, tr €70-90, q €85-100; ❄ 🛜; Ⓜ Piazza Cavour) Creativity and style flow through this crisp new B&B, accented with eclectic lighting, boho photography, a fully equipped kitchen and a tranquil terrace. All four rooms are soothing and contemporary, with original architectural detailing and fetching bathrooms with recycled terracotta basins. One upper-level room features a tatami-style bed and banquettes, the latter transforming into extra bed space (ideal for young families).

Hostel of the Sun   HOSTEL €
(Map p662; ☎ 081 420 63 93; www.hostelnapoli.com; Via G Melisurgo 15; dm €18-22, s €30-35, d €60-80; ❄ @ 🛜; Ⓜ Municipio) HOTS is an ultra-friendly hostel near the hydrofoil and ferry terminals. Located on the 7th floor (have €0.05 for the lift), it's a bright, sociable place with multicoloured dorms, a casual in-house bar (with cheap cocktails between 8pm and 11pm) and – a few floors down – a series of hotel-standard private rooms, seven with en suite bathrooms.

★ Hotel Piazza Bellini   BOUTIQUE HOTEL €€
(Map p658; ☎ 081 45 17 32; www.hotelpiazzabellini.com; Via Santa Maria di Costantinopoli 101; d from €100; ❄ @ 🛜; Ⓜ Dante) Only steps from buzzing Piazza Bellini, this sharp, contemporary hotel occupies a 16th-century *palazzo,* its mint white spaces spiked with original majolica tiles and the work of emerging artists. Rooms offer pared-back cool, with designer fittings,

chic bathrooms and mirror frames drawn straight onto the wall. Rooms on the 5th and 6th floors have panoramic terraces.

Decumani Hotel de Charme
BOUTIQUE HOTEL €€

(Map p658; ☑ 081 551 81 88; www.decumani.it; Via San Giovanni Maggiore Pignatelli 15; s €99-124, d €99-164; ❄@🛜; Ⓜ Università) This classic boutique hotel occupies the former *palazzo* of Cardinal Sisto Riario Sforza, the last bishop of the Bourbon kingdom. Simple, stylish rooms feature high ceilings, parquet floors, 19th-century furniture, and modern bathrooms with spacious showers. Deluxe rooms crank up *la dolce vita* with personal hot tubs. The *pièce de résistance*, however, is the property's breathtaking baroque salon.

⌷ Via Toledo & Quartieri Spagnoli

Nardones 48
APARTMENT €

(Map p662; ☑ 338 8818998; www.nardones48. it; Via Nardones 48; small apt €60-72, large apt €80-120; ❄🛜; Ⓡ R2 to Via San Carlo) White-on-white Nardones 48 serves up seven smart mini-apartments in a historic Quartieri Spagnoli building. The five largest apartments, each with mezzanine bedroom, accommodate up to four; the two smallest, each with a sofa bed, accommodate up to two. Three apartments boast a panoramic terrace, and all have modern kitchenette, flat-screen TV and contemporary bathroom with spacious shower.

La Ciliegina Lifestyle Hotel
BOUTIQUE HOTEL €€

(Map p662; ☑ 081 1971 8800; www.cilieginahotel. it; Via PE Imbriani 30; d €150-250, junior ste €200-350; ❄@🛜; Ⓜ Municipio) An easy walk from the hydrofoil terminal, this chic, contemporary slumber spot is a hit with fashion-conscious urbanites. Spacious white rooms are splashed with blue and red accents, each with top-of-the-range Hästens bed, flat-screen TV and marble-clad bathroom with water-jet Jacuzzi shower (one junior suite has a Jacuzzi tub).

Hotel Il Convento
HOTEL €€

(Map p662; ☑ 081 40 39 77; www.hotelil convento.com; Via Speranzella 137a; s €50-93, d €65-140; ❄🛜; Ⓜ Municipio) This lovely hotel in the Quartieri Spagnoli is a soothing blend of antique Tuscan furniture, well-stocked bookshelves and candle-lit stairs. Rooms are cosy and elegant, combining creamy

tones and dark woods with patches of 16th-century brickwork. For €80 to €180 you get a room with a private roof garden. The hotel is wheelchair accessible.

⌷ Santa Lucia & Chiaia

B&B Cappella Vecchia
B&B €

(Map p662; ☑ 081 240 51 17; www.cappella vecchia11.it; Vico Santa Maria a Cappella Vecchia 11; s €50-80, d €75-110, tr €90-140; ❄@🛜; 🚌 C24 to Piazza dei Martiri) Run by a super-helpful young couple, this B&B is a first-rate choice in the smart, fashionable Chiaia district. Rooms are simple and upbeat, with funky bathrooms, vibrant colours, and Neapolitan themes. There's a spacious communal area for breakfast, and free internet available 24/7. Check the website for special offers.

Grand Hotel Vesuvio
HOTEL €€€

(Map p662; ☑ 081 764 00 44; www.vesuvio.it; Via Partenope 45; s/d €280/310; ❄@🛜; 🚌 128 to Via Santa Lucia) Known for hosting legends – past guests include Rita Hayworth and Humphrey Bogart – this five-star heavyweight is a decadent mélange of dripping chandeliers, period antiques and opulent rooms. Count your lucky stars while drinking a martini at the rooftop restaurant.

✕ Eating

Pizza and pasta are the staples of Neapolitan cuisine. Pizza was created here and nowhere will you eat it better. Seafood is another local speciality and you'll find mussels and clams served in many dishes. Neapolitan street food is equally delicious. *Misto di frittura* – zucchini flowers, deep-fried potato and aubergine – makes for a great snack, especially if eaten from paper outside a tiny streetside stall. It's always sensible to book a table if dining at a restaurant on a Friday or Saturday night. Also note that many eateries close for two to four weeks in August, so check before heading out.

✕ Centro Storico

★ Pizzeria Gino Sorbillo
PIZZA €

(Map p658; ☑ 081 44 66 43; www.accademia dellapizza.it; Via dei Tribunali 32; pizzas from €3.30; ⊗ noon-3.30pm & 7pm-1am Mon-Sat; Ⓜ Dante) Day in, day out, this cult-status pizzeria is besieged by hungry hordes. While debate may rage over whether Gino Sorbillo's pizzas are the best in town, there's no doubt that his giant, wood-fired discs – made using organic flour and tomatoes – will have you licking finger tips and whiskers. Head in super early or prepare to queue.

Salumeria
BISTRO €

(Map p658; ☏ 081 1936 4649; www.salumeria upnea.it; Via San Giovanni Maggiore Pignatelli 34/35; sandwiches from €3.70, charcuterie platters from €5.90; ⊗10am-midnight, closed Wed Sep-May; 🛜; 🚇Dante) The latest project for UpNea, a dynamic team known for hip arts events, this bistro-bar covers all bases, from coffee and house-baked morning muffins, to soups, salads, charcuterie boards and insanely good *panini* and hamburgers. The menu focuses on top-quality local produce; even the ketchup is made in-house using DOP Piennolo tomatoes from Vesuvius. Libations include Petragnola craft beers.

La Campagnola
NEAPOLITAN €

(Map p658; ☏ 081 45 90 34; Via dei Tribunali 47; meals €18; ⊗ 12.30-4pm & 7-11.30pm; 🛜; 🚇Dante) Boisterous and affable, this spruced-up Neapolitan stalwart dishes unfussed, soul-coaxing classics. Daily specials include a killer *genovese* (pasta with a slow-cooked lamb, tomato and onion *ragù*) on Thursday, while week-round classics include hearty *salsiccia con friarielli* (pork sausage with Neapolitan bitter greens). If there's still room to move, conclude with the rum-soaked *babà*.

La Taverna di Santa Chiara
NEAPOLITAN €€

(Map p658; ☏ 339 8150346; Via Santa Chiara 6; meals €25; ⊗12.30-3pm & 7-11pm Wed-Mon; 🛜; 🚇Dante) Gragnano pasta, Agerola pork, Benevento *latte nobile:* this intimate, two-level eatery is healthily obsessed with small, local producers and Slow Food ingredients. The result is a beautiful, seasonal journey across Campania. For an inspiring overview, order the *antipasto misto* (mixed antipasto), then tuck into lesser-known classics like *zuppa di soffritto* (spicy meat stew) with a glass of smooth house *vino*.

★Eccellenze Campane
NEAPOLITAN €€

(☏081 20 36 57; www.eccellenzecampane.it; Via Benedetto Brin 49; pizza from €6, meals €30; ⊗7am-11pm Sun-Fri, to midnight Sat; 🚌116, 192, 460, 472, 475) This is Naples' answer to Turin-based food emporium Eataly, an impressive, contemporary showcase for top-notch Campanian comestibles. The sprawling space is divided into various dining and shopping sections, offering everything from beautifully charred pizzas and light *fritture* (fried snacks) to finer-dining seafood, coveted Sal

Da Riso pastries, craft beers and no shortage of take-home pantry treats. A must for gastronomes.

✕ Via Toledo & Quartieri Spagnoli

Pintauro
PASTRIES €

(Map p662; ☏ 348 7781645; Via Toledo 275; sfogliatelle €2; ⊗9am-8pm Mon-Sat, 9.30am-2pm Sun, closed mid-Jul–early Sep; 🚇Municipio) Of Neapolitan *dolci* (sweets), the cream of the crop is the *sfogliatella,* a shell of flaky pastry stuffed with creamy, scented ricotta. This local institution has been selling *sfogliatelle* since the early 1800s, when its founder supposedly brought them to Naples from their culinary birthplace on the Amalfi Coast.

Trattoria San Ferdinando
NEAPOLITAN €€

(Map p662; ☏ 081 42 19 64; Via Nardones 117; meals €27; ⊗noon-3pm Mon-Sat, 7.30-11pm Tue-Fri; 🚌R2 to Via San Carlo, 🚇Municipio) Hung with theatre posters, cosy San Ferdinando pulls in well-spoken theatre types and intellectuals. For a Neapolitan taste trip, ask for a rundown of the day's antipasti and choose your favourites for an *antipasto misto* (mixed antipasto). Seafood standouts include a delicate *seppia ripieno* (stuffed squid), while the homemade desserts make for a satisfying dénouement.

✕ Vomero

Friggitoria Vomero
FAST FOOD €

(Map p662; ☏081 578 31 30; Via Domenico Cimarosa 44; snacks from €0.20; ⊗9.30am-2.30pm & 5-9.30pm Mon-Fri, to 11pm Sat; 🚠Centrale to Piazza Fuga) The stuff of legend, this spartan snack bar makes some of the city's most scrumptious *fritture* (deep-fried snacks). Crunch away on tempura-style aubergines and spinach, *zeppole* (doughnuts), *frittatine di maccheroni* (fried pasta and egg) and *supplì di riso* (rice balls). Located opposite the funicular, it's a handy pit stop before legging it to the Certosa di San Martino.

✕ Santa Lucia & Chiaia

Muu Muzzarella Lounge
NEAPOLITAN €

(Map p662; Vico II Alabardieri 7; dishes €7-14; ⊗12.30pm-1.30am Tue-Sat, 6.30am-1.30am Sun; 🛜; 🚌C24 to Riviera di Chiaia) Pimped with milking-bucket lights and cow-hide patterned cushions, playful, contemporary Muu is all about super-fresh Campanian mozzarella, from cheese and charcuterie platters to creative dishes like buffalo bocconcini with creamy pesto and crunchy apple. Leave room for the chef's secret-recipe white-chocolate cheesecake, best paired with a glass of Guappa (buffalo-milk liqueur).

⭐ **L'Ebbrezza di Noè** NEAPOLITAN €€

(Map p662; ☑ 081 40 01 04; www.lebbrezzadinoe.com; Vico Vetriera 9; meals €37; ⊗ 8.30pm-midnight Tue-Sun; Ⓜ Piazza Amedeo) A wine shop by day, 'Noah's Drunkenness' transforms into an intimate culinary hot spot by night. Slip inside for *vino* and conversation at the bar, or settle into one of the bottle-lined dining rooms for seductive, market-driven dishes like house special *paccheri fritti* (fried pasta stuffed with aubergine and served with fresh basil and a rich tomato sauce).

Ristorantino dell'Avvocato NEAPOLITAN €€

(Map p662; ☑ 081 032 00 47; www.ilristorantinodellavvocato.it; Via Santa Lucia 115-117; meals €40; ⊗ noon-3pm & 7.30-11pm, lunch only Mon & Sun; 🛜; ☐ 128 to Via Santa Lucia) This elegant yet welcoming restaurant has quickly won the respect of Neapolitan gastronomes. Apple of their eye is affable lawyer turned head chef Raffaele Cardillo, whose passion for Campania's culinary heritage merges with a knack for subtle, refreshing twists – think gnocchi with fresh mussels, clams, crumbed pistachio, lemon, ginger and garlic.

✖ Capodimonte & La Sanità

Pizzeria Starita PIZZA €

(☑ 081 557 36 82; Via Materdei 28; pizzas from €3.50; ⊗ noon-4pm & 7pm-midnight Mon-Sat, 7pm-midnight Sun; Ⓜ Materdei) The giant fork and ladle hanging on the wall at this historic pizzeria were used by Sophia Loren in *L'Oro di Napoli*, and the kitchen made the *pizze fritte* sold by the actress in the film. While the 60-plus pizza varieties include a tasty *fiorilli e zucchine* (zucchini, zucchini flowers and *provola*), our allegiance remains to its classic marinara.

Drinking & Nightlife

The city's student and alternative drinking scene is around the piazzas and alleyways of the *centro storico*. For a something more chic hit the cobbled lanes of upmarket Chiaia. While some bars operate from 8am, most open from around 5.30pm and close around 2am.

Clubs usually open at 10.30pm or 11pm but don't fill up until after midnight. Many close in summer (July to September), some transferring to out-of-town beach locations. Admission charges vary, but expect to pay between €5 and €30, which may or may not include a drink.

Caffè Gambrinus CAFE

(Map p662; ☑ 081 41 75 82; www.grancaffegambrinus.com; Via Chiaia 12; ⊗ 7am-1am Sun-Thu, to 2am Fri, to 3am Sat; ☐ R2 to Via San Carlo, Ⓜ Municipio) Grand, chandeliered Gambrinus is Naples' oldest and most venerable cafe. Oscar Wilde knocked back a few here and Mussolini had some of the rooms shut to keep out left-wing intellectuals. The prices may be steep, but the *aperitivo* nibbles are decent and sipping a *spritz* or a luscious *cioccolata calda* (hot chocolate) in its belle époque rooms is something worth savouring.

Spazio Nea CAFE

(Map p658; ☑ 081 45 13 58; www.spazionea.it; Via Constantinopoli 53; ⊗ 9am-2am; 🛜; Ⓜ Dante) Aptly skirting bohemian Piazza Bellini, this whitewashed gallery features its own cafe-bar speckled with books, flowers, cultured crowds and alfresco seating at the bottom of a baroque staircase. Eye up exhibitions of contemporary Italian and foreign art, then kick back with a *caffè* or a Cynar *spritz*. Check Nea's Facebook page for upcoming readings, live music gigs or DJ sets.

Enoteca Belledonne BAR

(Map p662; ☑ 081 40 31 62; www.enotecabelledonne.com; Vico Belledonne a Chiaia 18; ⊗ 10am-2pm & 4.30pm-2am Tue-Sat, 6.30pm-1am Mon & Sun; 🛜; ☐ C24 to Riviera di Chiaia) Exposed-brick walls, ambient lighting and bottle-lined shelves set a cosy scene at Chiaia's best-loved wine bar – just look for the evening crowd spilling out onto the street. Swill, sniff and eavesdrop over a list of well-chosen, mostly Italian wines, including 30 by the glass. The decent grazing menu includes charcuterie and cheese (€16), crostini (from €6) and *bruschette* (€7).

Galleria 19 CLUB

(Map p658; www.galleria19.it; Via San Sebastiano 19; ⊗ 11pm-5am Tue-Sat; Ⓜ Dante) Set in a long, cavernous cellar scattered with chesterfields and industrial lamps, this popular *centro storico* club draws a uni crowd early in the week and 20- and 30-somethings on Friday and Saturday. Tunes span electronica, commercial and house. Check the website for upcoming events.

⭐ Entertainment

Options run the gamut from nail-biting football games to world-class opera. For cultural listings check www.incampania.it. Tickets for most cultural events are available from ticket agency **Box Office** (Map p662; ☎081 551 91 88; www.boxofficenapoli.it; Galleria Umberto I 17; ⊙9.30am-8pm Mon-Fri, 9.30am-1.30pm & 4.30-8pm Sat; 🚇R2 to Piazza Trieste e Trento) or the box office inside bookshop **Feltrinelli** (Map p662; ☎081 032 23 62; www.azzurro service.net; Piazza dei Martiri 23; ⊙11am-2pm & 3-8pm Mon-Sat; 🚇C24 to Piazza dei Martiri).

Teatro San Carlo OPERA, BALLET
(Map p662; ☎081 797 23 31; www.teatrosan carlo.it; Via San Carlo 98; ⊙box office 10am-5.30pm Mon-Sat, to 2pm Sun; 🚇R2 to Via San Carlo) One of Italy's top opera houses, the San Carlo stages opera, ballet and concerts. Bank on €50 for a place in the sixth tier, €100 for a seat in the stalls or – if you're under 30 and can prove it – €30 for a place in a side box. Ballet tickets range from €35 to €80, with €20 tickets for those under 30.

Centro di Musica Antica Pietà de' Turchini CLASSICAL MUSIC
(Map p662; ☎081 40 23 95; www.turchini.it; Via Santa Caterina da Siena 38; funicularCentrale to Corso Vittorio Emanuele) Classical-music buffs are in for a treat at this beautiful deconsecrated church, an evocative setting for concerts of mostly 17th- to 19th-century Neapolitan works. Tickets usually cost €10 (reduced €7).

Lanificio 25 LIVE MUSIC
(Map p658; www.lanificio25.it; Piazza Enrico De Nicola 46; admission €5-10; ⊙9pm-late Fri & Sat;

🚇Garibaldi) This Bourbon-era wool factory and 15th-century cloister is now a burgeoning party and culture hub, strung with coloured lights and awash with video projections. Live music (usually from 10pm) is the mainstay, with mostly Italian outfits playing indie, rock, world music, electronica and more to an easy, arty, cosmopolitan crowd.

Football

Naples' football team, Napoli, is the third-most supported in the country after Juventus and Milan, and watching it play at the **Stadio San Paolo** (Piazzale Vincenzo Tecchio; 🚇Napoli Campi Flegrei) is a highly charged rush. The season runs from late August to late May, with seats costing between €20 and €100. Book tickets at Azzurro Service in bookshop Feltrinelli, at Box Office or from some tobacconists, and don't forget your photo ID. On match days, tickets are also available at the stadium itself.

🛍 Shopping

Tramontano ACCESSORIES
(Map p662; ☎081 41 48 37; www.tramontano.it; Via Chiaia 143-144; ⊙10am-1.30pm & 4-8pm Mon-Sat; 🚇C24 to Piazza dei Martiri) Tramontano has a solid rep for its exquisitely crafted Neapolitan leather goods, from glam handbags and preppy satchels to duffels and totes. Each year, a new bag is added to the Rock Ladies' Collection, inspired by a classic song, whether it's Patti Smith's 'Kimberley' or Creedence Clearwater Revival's 'Proud Mary'.

E. Marinella FASHION
(Map p662; ☎081 764 42 14; www.marinellana poli.it; Via Riviera di Chiaia 287; ⊙8am-8pm Mon-Sat, 9am-1pm Sun; 🚇C25 to Riviera di Chiaia, C24 to Piazza dei Martiri) One-time favourite of Luchino Visconti and Aristotle Onassis, this pocket-sized, vintage boutique is the place for prêt-

-porter and made-to-measure silk ties in striking patterns and hues. Match them with an irresistible selection of luxury accessories, including shoes, vintage colognes, and scarves for female style queens.

La Scarabattola   CRAFTS

(Map p658; ☑ 081 29 17 35; www.lascarabattola.it; Via dei Tribunali 50; ⊙ 10.30am-2pm & 3.30-7.30pm Mon-Fri, 10am-6pm Sat; ☐ C55 to Via Duomo) Not only do La Scarabattola's handmade sculptures of *magi* (wise men), devils and Neapolitan folk figures constitute Jerusalem's official Christmas crèche, the artisan studio's fans include fashion designer Stefano Gabbana and Spanish royalty. Figurines aside, sleek ceramic creations (think Pulcinella-inspired place-card holders) refresh Neapolitan folklore with contemporary style.

❶ Information

Loreto-Mare Hospital (Ospedale Loreto-Mare; ☑ 081 254 27 01, emergency 081 254 27 43; Via A Vespucci 26; ☐ 154, ☐ 1, 2, 4) Central-city hospital with an emergency department.

Pharmacy (Stazione Centrale; ⊙ 7am-9pm Mon-Sat, to 8pm Sun) Inside the train station.

Police Station (Questura; ☑ 081 794 11 11; Via Medina 75; Ⓜ Università) Has an office for foreigners. To report a stolen car, call ☑ 081 79 41 43.

TOURIST OFFICES

Head to the following tourist bureaux for information and a map of the city:

Tourist Information Office (Map p658; ☑ 081 551 27 01; Piazza del Gesù Nuovo 7; ⊙ 9am-5pm Mon-Sat, to 1pm Sun; Ⓜ Dante) Tourist office in the *centro storico*.

Tourist Information Office (Map p658; ☑ 081 26 87 79; Stazione Centrale; ⊙ 8.30am-7.30pm; Ⓜ Garibaldi) Tourist office inside Stazione Centrale (Central Station).

Tourist Information Office (Map p662; ☑ 081 40 23 94; Via San Carlo 9; ⊙ 9am-5pm Mon-Sat, to 1pm Sun; ☐ R2 to Via San Carlo, Ⓜ Municipio) Tourist office at Galleria Umberto I, directly opposite Teatro San Carlo.

WEBSITES

In Campania (www.incampania.com) Campania's official tourist website.

Napoli Unplugged (www.napoliunplugged. com) Informative website covering sights, events, news and practicalities.

❶ Getting There & Away

AIR

Capodichino, 7km northeast of the city centre, is southern Italy's main airport, linking Naples with most Italian and several European cities, as well as New York. Budget carrier Easyjet operates several routes to/from Capodichino, including London, Paris, Brussels and Berlin.

BOAT
Ferry Terminals

Naples, the bay islands and the Amalfi Coast are served by a comprehensive ferry network. There are several ferry and hydrofoil terminals in central Naples.

Molo Beverello (Map p662) Right in front of Castel Nuovo; services fast ferries and hydrofoils for Capri, Sorrento, Ischia (both Ischia Porto and Forio) and Procida. Some hydrofoils for Capri, Ischia, Procida and Sicily's Aeolian Islands also leave from Mergellina, 5km west.

Molo Angioino (Map p662) Right beside Molo Beverello; services slow ferries for Sicily, the Aeolian Islands and Sardinia.

Calata Porta di Massa (Map p662) Beside Molo Angioino; services slow ferries to Ischia, Procida and Capri.

FERRIES

DESTINATION (FROM NAPLES – CALATA PORTA DI MASSA & MOLO ANGIOINO)	FERRY COMPANY	PRICE (€)	DURATION	DAILY FREQUENCY (HIGH SEASON)
Capri	Caremar	12.70	80 min	3
Ischia (Ischia Porto)	Caremar	11.20 / 11.30	80/75 min	6/6
Procida	Caremar	12.20	60 min	6
Aeolian Islands	Siremar / SNAV (summer only)	from 50 to 150	10½/4½ hr	2 weekly/1 daily
Milazzo (Sicily)	Siremar	from 57	17 hr	2 weekly
Palermo (Sicily)	SNAV / Tirrenia	from 50 / from 32	10¼–11¾ hr	1 to 2/1 daily
Cagliari (Sardinia)	Tirrenia	from 49	16¼ hr	2 weekly

HYDROFOILS & HIGH-SPEED FERRIES

DESTINATION (FROM NAPLES – MOLO BEVERELLO)	FERRY COMPANY	PRICE (€)	DURATION (MIN)	DAILY FREQUENCY (HIGH SEASON)
Capri	Caremar/Navigazione Libera del Golfo/SNAV	17.80/19/ 20.10	45–50	4/8/17
Ischia (Casamicciola Terme & Forio)	Caremar/Alilauro/ SNAV	17.60/18.70/ 18.60	50–65	4/7/8
Procida	Caremar/SNAV	13.20/15.90	40	8/4
Sorrento	Alilauro/Navigazione Libera del Golfo	12.30/12.30	35–40	5/1

Ferry Services

Ferry services are pared back considerably in the winter, and adverse sea conditions may affect sailing schedules.

The tables list hydrofoil and ferry destinations from Naples. The fares, unless otherwise stated, are for a one-way, high-season, deck-class single.

Tickets for shorter journeys can be bought at the ticket booths on Molo Beverello, Calata Porta di Massa or at Mergellina. For longer journeys try the offices of the ferry companies or a travel agent.

Hydrofoil and ferry companies are:
Caremar (☏081 551 38 82; www.caremar.it)
Alilauro (☏081 497 22 01; www.alilauro. it) Runs up to five daily hydrofoils between Naples and Sorrento (€12.30, 40 minutes).
SNAV (☏081 428 55 55; www.snav.it)
Medmar (☏081 333 44 11; www.medmar group.it)
Siremar (☏081 497 29 99; www.siremar.it)
Tirrenia (☏892 123; www.tirrenia.it)

BUS

Most national and international buses now leave from **Terminal Bus Metropark** (Map p658; ☏800 650006; Corso Arnaldo Lucci; ⓂGaribaldi), located on the south side of Stazione Centrale. The bus station is home to **Biglietteria Vecchione** (☏081 563 03 20; Corso Arnaldo Lucci, Terminal Bus Metropark; ◷6.30am-7.30pm Mon-Sat; ⓂGaribaldi), a ticket agency selling national and international bus tickets.

Terminal Bus MetroPark serves numerous bus companies offering regional services, the most useful of which is SITA Sud. Connections from Naples include Amalfi and Positano.

CAR & MOTORCYCLE

Naples is on the Autostrada del Sole, the A1 (north to Rome and Milan) and the A3 (south to Salerno and Reggio di Calabria). The A30 skirts Naples to the northeast, while the A16 heads across the Apennines to Bari.

On approaching the city, the motorways meet the Tangenziale di Napoli, a major ring road around the city. The ring road hugs the city's northern fringe, meeting the A1 for Rome in the east and continuing westwards towards the Campi Flegrei and Pozzuoli.

TRAIN

Naples is southern Italy's rail hub and on the main Milan–Palermo line, with good connections to other Italian cities and towns.

National rail company **Trenitalia** (☏892021; www.trenitalia.com) runs regular services to Rome (2nd class €11.80 to €43, 70 minutes to 2¾ hours, up to 49 daily).

High-speed private rail company **Italo** (☏06 07 08; www.italotreno.it) also runs daily services to Rome (2nd class €15 to €39, 70 minutes, up to 15 daily). Not all Italo services stop at Roma Termini, with many stopping at Roma Tiburtina instead.

Circumvesuviana (☏800 211388; www.eavs rl.it) operates frequent train services to Sorrento (€4.50, 66 minutes) via Ercolano (€2.50, 16 minutes), Pompei (€3.20, 35 minutes) and other towns along the coast, departing from Naples' Porta Nolana and stopping at Piazza Garibaldi station, adjacent to Stazione Centrale.

From late May to October, express tourist train Campania Express runs three times daily between Porta Nolana and Piazza Garibaldi stations in Naples and Sorrento. The only stops en route are Ercolano and Pompei. One-day return tickets (€15, €10 for Artecard holders) can be purchased at the stations, online at www.eavs rl.it or www.campaniartecard/grandtour, or by phone on 800 600 601.

Ferrovia Cumana (www.sepsa.it) trains leave from Stazione Cumana di Montesanto on Piazza Montesanto, 500m southwest of Piazza Dante, running to Pozzuoli (€1.30, 22 minutes, every 20 minutes) and other Campi Flegrei locations beyond, including Lucrino (€2.50, 29 minutes) and Fusaro (€3.20, 33 minutes).

CAMPI FLEGREI

Stretching west of Posillipo Hill to the Tyrrhenian Sea, the Campi Flegrei (Phlegraean or 'Fiery' Fields) is home to some of Campania's most remarkable – and overlooked – Graeco-Roman ruins. Gateway to the area is the port town of Pozzuoli. Established by the Greeks around 530 BC, its most famous resident is the **Anfiteatro Flavio** (☑ 848 80 02 88; Via Nicola Terracciano 75; adult/reduced €4/2; ☺ 9am-1hr before sunset Wed-Mon; Ⓜ Pozzuoli, ℝ Cumana to Pozzuoli), Italy's third-largest ancient Roman amphitheatre.

A further 6km west, Baia was once a glamorous Roman holiday resort frequented by sun-seeking emperors. Fragments of this opulence linger among the 1st-century ruins of the **Parco Archeologico di Baia** (☑ 081 868 75 92; www.coopculture.it; Via Sella di Baia; adult/reduced €4/2 Sat & Sun, Tue-Fri free; ☺ varied; ⛿ EAV to Baia, ℝ Cumana to Fusaro), its mosaics, stuccoed *balneum* (bathroom) and imposing Tempio di Mercurio once part of a sprawling palace and spa complex. While the ruins are free on weekdays, weekend visitors need to purchase their tickets at the fascinating **Museo Archeologico dei Campi Flegrei** (Archaeological Museum of the Campi Flegrei; ☑ 081 523 37 97; cir.campania.beniculturali.it/museoarcheologicocampiflegrei; Via Castello 39; admission Sat & Sun €4, Tue-Fri free; ☺ 9am-2pm Tue-Sun, last entry 1pm; ⛿ EAV to Baia), a further 2km south along the coast.

Yet another 2km south, in the sleepy town of Bacoli, lurks the magical **Piscina Mirabilis** (Marvellous Pool; ☑ 333 6853278; Via Piscina Mirabilis; donation appreciated; ☺ varied, closed Mon; ℝ Cumana to Fusaro, then EAV bus to Bacoli), the world's largest Roman cistern. You'll need to call the custodian to access the site, but it's well worth the effort. Bathed in an eerie light and featuring 48 soaring pillars and a barrel-vaulted ceiling, the so-called 'Marvellous Pool' is more subterranean cathedral than giant water tank. While entrance is free, show your manners by offering the custodian a €2 or €3 tip.

Both the Ferrovia Cumana and Naples' metro line 2 serve Pozzuoli, and the town is also connected to Ischia and Procida by frequent car and passenger ferries. To reach Baia, take the Ferrovia Cumana train to Fusaro station, walk 150m north, turning right into Via Carlo Vanvitelli (which eventually becomes Via Bellavista). The ruins are 750m to the east. To reach Bacoli, catch a Bacoli-bound EAV Bus from Fusaro.

Unfortunately, the Campi Flegrei's second-rate infrastructure and unreliable public transport, plus the fickle opening times of its sites, make pre-trip planning a good idea. Contact the **tourist office** (☑ 081 526 14 81; www.infocampiflegrei.it; Largo Matteotti 1a; ☺ 9am-3pm Mon-Fri; Ⓜ Pozzuoli, ℝ Cumana to Pozzuoli) in Pozzuoli for updated information on the area's sights and opening times, or consider exploring the area with popular local tour outfit **Yellow Sudmarine** (p687).

🛈 Getting Around

TO/FROM THE AIRPORT

Airport shuttle bus Alibus connects the airport to Piazza Garibaldi (Stazione Centrale) and Molo Beverello (€3 from selected tobacconists, €4 on board; 45 minutes; every 20 minutes).

Official taxi fares from the airport are as follows: €23 to a seafront hotel or to Mergellina hydrofoil terminal, €19 to Piazza Municipio or Molo Beverello ferry terminal, and €16 to Stazione Centrale.

BUS

In Naples, buses are operated by city transport company **ANM** (☑ 800 639525; www.anm.it). There's no central bus station, but most buses pass through Piazza Garibaldi.

CAR & MOTORCYCLE

Vehicle theft, anarchic traffic and illegal parking 'attendants' make driving in Naples a bad option. Furthermore, much of the city centre is closed to nonresident traffic for much of the day.

East of the city centre, there's a 24-hour car park at Via Brin (€1.30 for the first four hours, €7.20 for 24 hours).

FUNICULAR

Three services connect central Naples to Vomero, while a fourth connects Mergellina to Posillipo.

METRO

Line 1 Runs from Garibaldi (Stazione Centrale) to Vomero and the northern suburbs via the city centre. Useful stops include:

WORTH A TRIP

REGGIA DI CASERTA

The one compelling reason to stop at the otherwise nondescript town of Caserta, 30km north of Naples, is to gasp at the colossal, World Heritage-listed **Reggia di Caserta** (Palazzo Reale; ☎ 0823 27 71 11; www.reggiadicaserta.beniculturali.it; Viale Douhet 22, Caserta; adult/reduced €12/6; ⏱ palace 8.30am-7.30pm Wed-Mon, park 8.30am-1hr before sunset Wed-Mon, Giardino Inglese 8.30am-2hr before sunset Wed-Mon Jun-Aug, reduced hours rest of year; ☒ Caserta). With film credits including *Mission: Impossible 3* and the interior shots of Queen Amidala's royal residence in *Star Wars Episode 1: The Phantom Menace* and *Star Wars Episode 2: Attack of the Clones*, this former royal residence is Italy's monumental swan song to the baroque. The complex began life in 1752 after Charles VII ordered a palace to rival Versailles. Neapolitan Luigi Vanvitelli was commissioned for the job and built a palace bigger than its French rival. With its 1200 rooms, 1790 windows, 34 staircases and 250m-long facade, it was reputedly the largest building in 18th-century Europe.

Vanvitelli's immense staircase leads up to the royal apartments, lavishly decorated with frescoes, art, tapestries, period furniture and crystal. The apartments are also home to the Mostra Terrea Motus, an underrated collection of international modern art commissioned after the region's devastating earthquake in 1980.

To clear your head afterwards, explore the elegant landscaped park, which stretches for some 3km to a waterfall and fountain of Diana. Within the park is the famous Giardino Inglese (English Garden), a romantic oasis of intricate pathways, exotic flora, pools and cascades. Bicycle hire (€4) is available at the back of the palace building, as are pony and trap rides (€50 per 30 minutes, up to five people).

If you're feeling peckish, consider skipping the touristy palace cafeteria for local cafe **Martucci** (☎ 0823 32 08 03; Via Roma 9, Caserta; pastries from €1.50, sandwiches from €3.50, salads €7.50; ⏱ 5am-10.30pm Sun-Thu, to midnight Fri & Sat). Located 250m east of the palace. it has great coffee freshly made *panini* and substantial cooked-to-order meals.

Regular trains connect Naples to Caserta (€3.90, 35 to 50 minutes) from Monday to Saturday, with reduced services on Sunday. Caserta train station is located directly opposite the palace grounds. If you're driving, follow the signs for the Reggia.

Duomo and Università (southern edge of the *centro storico*), Municipio (hydrofoil and ferry terminals), Toledo (Via Toledo and Quartieri Spagnoli), Dante (western edge of the *centro storico*) and Museo (National Archaeological Museum).

Line 2 Runs from Gianturco to Garibaldi (Stazione Centrale) and on to Pozzuoli. Useful stops include: Piazza Cavour (La Sanità and northern edge of *centro storico*), Piazza Amedeo (Chiaia) and Mergellina (Mergellina ferry terminal). Change between lines 1 and 2 at Garibaldi or Piazza Cavour (known as Museo on Line 1).

Line 6 A light-rail service running between Mergellina and Mostra.

TAXI

Official taxis are white and have meters; always ensure the meter is running. There are taxi stands at most of the city's main piazzas or you can call one of the following taxi cooperatives. See the taxi company websites for a comprehensive list of fares.

Consortaxi (☎ 081 22 22; www.consortaxi. com)

Consorzio Taxi Napoli (☎ 081 88 88; www. consorziotaxinapoli.it)

Radio Taxi Napoli (☎ 081 556 44 44; www. radiotaxinapoli.it)

BAY OF NAPLES

Capri

POP 12,200

A stark mass of limestone rock rising sheerly through impossibly blue water, Capri (*capri*) is the perfect microcosm of Mediterranean appeal – a smooth cocktail of vogueish piazzas and cool cafes, Roman ruins, rugged seascapes and holidaying VIPs. While it's also a popular day-trip destination, consider staying a couple of nights to explore beyond Capri Town and its uphill rival Anacapri. It's here, in Capri's hinterland, that the island really seduces with its overgrown vegetable plots, sun-bleached stucco and indescribably beautiful walking trails.

◎ Sights

◎ Capri Town & Around

Whitewashed buildings, labyrinthine laneways, and luxe boutiques and cafes: Capri Town personifies upmarket Mediterranean chic.

Piazza Umberto I   PIAZZA

Located beneath the clock tower and framed by see-and-be-seen cafes, this showy, open-air salon is central to your Capri experience, especially in the evening when the main activity in these parts is dressing up and hanging out. Be prepared for the cost of these front-row seats – the moment you sit down for a drink, you're going to pay handsomely for the grandstand views (around €6 for a coffee and €16 for a couple of glasses of white wine).

Chiesa di Santo Stefano   CHURCH

(Piazza Umberto I; ⊗8am-8pm) Overlooking Piazza Umberto I, this baroque 17th-century church boasts a well-preserved marble floor (taken from Villa Jovis) and a statue of San Costanzo, Capri's patron saint. Note the pair of languidly reclining patricians in the chapel to the south of the main altar, who seem to mirror some of the mildly debauched folk in the cafes outside. Beside the northern chapel is a reliquary with a saintly bone that reputedly saved Capri from the plague in the 19th century.

★ Villa Jovis   RUIN

(Jupiter's Villa; Via A Maiuri; admission €2; ⊗11am-3pm, closed Tue 1st-15th of month, closed Sun rest of month) A 45-minute walk east of Capri along Via Tiberio, Villa Jovis was the largest and most sumptuous of the island's 12 Roman villas and Tiberius' main Capri residence. A vast pleasure complex, now reduced to ruins, it famously pandered to the emperor's debauched tastes, and included imperial quarters and extensive bathing areas set in dense gardens and woodland.

The villa's spectacular location posed major headaches for Tiberius' architects. The main problem was how to collect and store enough water to supply the villa's baths and 3000-sq-metre gardens. The solution they eventually hit upon was to build a complex canal system to transport rainwater to four giant storage tanks, whose remains you can still see today.

The stairway behind the villa leads to the 330m-high **Salto di Tiberio** (Tiberius' Leap), a sheer cliff from where, as the story goes, Tiberius had out-of-favour subjects hurled into the sea. True or not, the stunning views are real enough; if you suffer from vertigo, tread carefully.

A shortish but steep walk from the villa, down Via Tiberio and Via Matermània, is the **Arco Naturale** – a huge rock arch formed by the pounding sea; you can time this walk to take in lunch at cave restaurant **Le Grotelle** (🖉081 837 57 19; Via Arco Naturale 13; meals around €28; ⊗noon-2.30pm & 7-11pm Jul & Aug, noon-2.30pm & 7-11pm Fri-Wed Jun & Sep, noon-2.30pm Fri-Wed Apr, May & Oct).

Certosa di San Giacomo   MONASTERY

(🖉081 837 62 18; Viale Certosa 40; admission €4; ⊗9am-2pm Tue-Sun, plus 5-8pm summer) Founded in 1363, this picturesque monastery is generally considered to be the finest remaining example of Caprese architecture and today houses a school, a library, a temporary exhibition space and a museum with some evocative 17th-century paintings. Be sure to look at the two cloisters, which have a real sense of faded glory (the smaller is 14th century, the larger 16th century).

To get here take Via Vittorio Emanuele, east of Piazza Umberto I, which meanders down to the monastery.

Giardini di Augusto   GARDENS

(Gardens of Augustus; admission €1; ⊗9am-1hr before sunset) Escape the crowds by seeking out these colourful gardens near the Certosa di San Giacomo. Founded by Emperor Augustus, they rise in a series of flowered terraces to a lookout point offering breathtaking views over to the **Isole Faraglioni**, a group of three limestone stacks that rise out of the sea.

◎ Anacapri & Around

Delve beyond the Villa San Michele di Axel Munthe and the souvenir stores and you'll discover that Capri Town's more subdued sibling is, at heart, the laid-back rural village that it's always been.

★ Seggiovia del Monte Solaro   CABLE CAR

(🖉081 837 14 38; www.capriseggiovia.it; single/return €7.50/10; ⊗9.30am-5pm summer, to 3.30pm winter) A fast and painless way to reach Capri's highest peak, Anacapri's Seggiovia del Monte Solaro chairlift whisks you

Capri

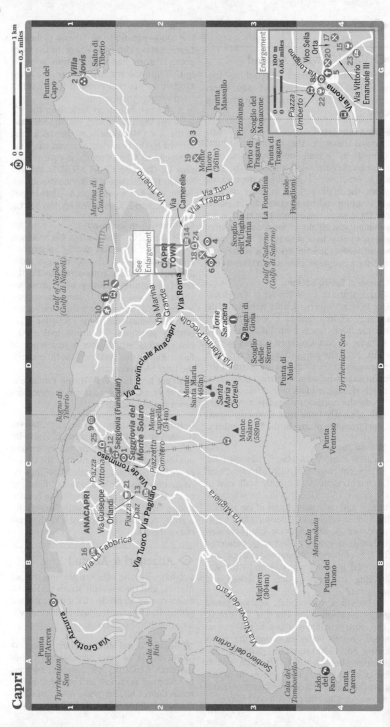

Capri

to the top of the mountain in a beautiful ride of just 12 minutes. The views from the top are outstanding – on a clear day, you can see the entire Bay of Naples, the Amalfi Coast and the islands of Ischia and Procida.

Villa San Michele di Axel Munthe
MUSEUM, GARDENS

(☏081 837 14 01; www.villasanmichele.eu; Via Axel Munthe 34; admission €7; ☉9am-6pm summer, reduced hours rest of year) The former home of Swedish doctor, psychiatrist and animal-rights advocate Axel Munthe, San Michele di Axel Munthe should be included on every visitor's itinerary. Built on the site of the ruins of a Roman villa, the gardens make a beautiful setting for a tranquil stroll, with pathways flanked by immaculate flowerbeds. There are also superb views from here, plus some fine photo props in the form of Roman sculptures.

If you are here between July and September, you may be able to catch one of the classical concerts that take place in the gardens. Check the Axel Munthe Foundation website (www.sanmichele.org) for the current program and reservation information.

⚲ Activities

★ Banana Sport
BOATING

(☏081 837 51 88; Marina Grande; 2hr/day rental €90/200; ☉May-Sep) Located on the eastern edge of the waterfront, Banana Sport hires out five-person motorised dinghies, allowing you to explore secluded coves and grottoes. You can also visit the popular swimming spot **Bagno di Tiberio** (€10), a small inlet west of Marina Grande; it's said that Tiberius once swam here.

Sercomar
DIVING

(☏081 837 87 81; www.capriseaservice.com; Via Colombo 64, Marina Grande; ☉Apr-Oct; ⌖) Sercomar offers various diving packages costing from €100 for a single dive (maximum of three people) to €150 for an individual dive and €350 for a four-session beginner's course. It also organises children's snorkelling classes from €35 for 30 minutes (12 years and over).

⌖ Sleeping

Capri's accommodation is top-heavy, with plenty of four- and five-star hotels and fewer budget options. As a general rule, the further you go from Capri Town, the less you'll pay. Camping is forbidden.

Always book ahead. Hotel space is at a premium during the summer, and many places close in winter, typically between November and March.

★ Hotel Villa Eva
HOTEL €€

(☏081 837 15 49; www.villaeva.com; Via La Fabbrica 8; d €110-180, tr €160-210, apt per person €55-70; ☉Easter-Oct; ✳@☎✉⌖) Nestled amid fruit and olive trees in the countryside near Anacapri, Villa Eva is an idyllic retreat, complete with swimming pool, lush gardens and

DON'T MISS

GROTTA AZZURRA

Glowing in an ethereal blue light, the bewitching **Grotta Azzurra** (Blue Grotto; admission €13; ⊙9am-1hr before sunset) is Capri's most famous single attraction.

The grotto had long been known to local fishermen when it was rediscovered by two Germans – writer Augustus Kopisch and painter Ernst Fries – in 1826. Subsequent research, however, revealed that Emperor Tiberius had built a quay in the cave around AD 30, complete with a nymphaeum. Remarkably, you can still see the carved Roman landing stage towards the rear of the cave.

Measuring 54m by 30m and rising to a height of 15m, the grotto is said to have sunk by up to 20m in prehistoric times, blocking every opening except the 1.3m-high entrance. And this is the key to the magical blue light. Sunlight enters through a small underwater aperture and is refracted through the water; this, combined with the reflection of the light off the white sandy seafloor, produces the vivid blue effect to which the cave owes its name.

The easiest way to visit is to take a **tour** (☑081 837 56 46; www.motoscafisticapri.com; Private Pier 0, Marina Grande; tickets online €12, in person €14) from Marina Grande; tickets include the return boat trip and a rowing boat into the cave, with the admission fee paid separately. Allow a good hour.

The grotto is closed if the sea is too choppy and swimming in it is forbidden, although you can swim outside the entrance – get a bus to Grotta Azzurra, take the stairs down to the right and dive off the small concrete platform. When visiting, keep in mind that the singing 'captains' are included in the price, so don't feel any obligation if they push for a tip.

sunny rooms and apartments. Whitewashed domes, terracotta floors, stained-glass windows and vintage fireplaces add character, while the location ensures peace and quiet.

The only drawback is that it's tricky to get to: take the Grotta Azzurra bus from Anacapri and ask the driver where to get off, or cough up for a taxi.

Hotel Gatto Bianco HOTEL €€
(☑081 837 51 43; www.gattobianco-capri.com; Via Vittoria Emanuele III 32; s €100-170, d €150-230; ⊙Apr-Nov; ❄@❸) This gracious hotel dates from 1953 and boasts leafy courtyards and terraces and a fluffy white cat – presumably from a long lineage. The light-filled rooms are decorated in traditional style with stunning blue-and-yellow majolica tiling, a tasteful colour scheme and verdant views.

Casa Mariantonia BOUTIQUE HOTEL €€
(☑081 837 29 23; www.casamariantonia.com; Via Guiseppe Orlandi 80; d €120-280; ⊙Apr-Oct; ❢❄❸❅) This fabulous boutique retreat counts Jean-Paul Sartre and Alberto Moravia among its past guests, which may well give you something to muse over while you are enjoying the tranquil beauty of the surroundings. Rooms deliver restrained elegance in soothing tones and there are

private terraces with garden views. The in-house restaurant is set in a lemon grove.

Grand Hotel Quisisana HOTEL €€€
(☑081 837 07 88; www.quisi.com; Via Camerelle 2; r/ste from €330/850; ⊙Easter-Oct; ❢❄❸❅) Boasting a five-star luxury rating, the Quisisana is Capri's most prestigious address and just few espadrille-clad steps from La Piazzetta (Piazza Umberto I). A hotel since the 19th century, it's a bastion of unapologetic opulence, with two swimming pools, a fitness centre and spa, restaurants, bars and subtropical gardens. Rooms are suitably palatial, with cool colour schemes and classy furniture.

Capri Palace HOTEL €€€
(☑081 978 01 11; www.capripalace.com; Via Capodimonte 2b; d/ste from €500/1000; ⊙Apr-Oct; ❢❄❸❅) A VIP favourite (Gwyneth Paltrow, Liz Hurley and Naomi Campbell have all chilled here), the super-slick Capri Palace is the hotel of the moment. Its stylish Mediterranean interior is enlivened with eye-catching contemporary art and its guest rooms are never less than lavish – some even have their own terraced garden and private plunge pool.

For stressed guests, the health spa is said to be the island's best. Note that there's a three-night minimum stay in high season.

✕ Eating

Many restaurants, like the hotels, close over winter.

Raffaele Buonacore   FAST FOOD €

(☑ 081 837 78 26; Via Vittorio Emanuele III 35; snacks €1-6; ⊙ 6am-5pm Mar-Oct; ⊜) Ideal for a quick fill-up, this popular and down-to-earth snack bar does a roaring trade in savoury and sweet treats, including frittatas, *panini* (sandwiches), pastries, waffles and legendary ice cream. Hard to beat, though, are the delicious *sfogliatelle* (cinnamon-infused ricotta in a puff-pastry shell, €1) and the feather-light speciality *caprilu al limone* (lemon and almond cakes).

★ È Divino   ITALIAN €

(☑ 081 837 83 64; Vico Sella Orta; meals €20; ⊙ 1-3pm & 7.30pm-midnight Tue-Sun) Look hard for the sign: this slow-food restaurant is a well-kept secret. Step inside and you find yourself in what resembles a traditional sitting room; the only hints that this is a restaurant are the tantalising aromas and the distant tinkle of glasses. The menu changes daily, according to whatever is fresh from the garden or market.

La Rondinella   ITALIAN €€

(☑ 081 837 12 23; www.ristorantepizzerialarond inella.com; Via Giuseppe Orlandi 295; meals €30; ⊙ noon-2.30pm & 7-11.30pm Fri-Mon) La Rond-inella has a relaxed, rural feel and remains one of Anacapri's better restaurants; apparently Graham Greene had a favourite corner table here. The menu features a number of Italian classics such as *saltimbocca alla romana* (veal slices with ham and sage).

Il Geranio   SEAFOOD €€€

(☑ 081 837 06 16; www.geraniocapri.com; Via G Matteotti 8; meals €50; ⊙ noon-3pm & 7-11.30pm Apr-Oct) Time to pop the question, celebrate an anniversary or quell those pre-departure blues? The terrace here has stunning views over the pine trees to the sea and beyond to the extraordinary Isole di Faraglioni rocks. Seafood is the house speciality, particularly the salt-baked fish. Other good choices include octopus salad and linguini with saffron and mussels. Dress to impress.

OFF THE BEATEN TRACK

SOOTHING ISLAND HIKES

Away from the boutiques, yachts and bikinis, Capri offers some soul-lifting hikes. Favourite routes include from Arco Naturale to the Punta dell'Arcera (1.2km, 1¼ hours), best tackled in this direction to avoid a final climb up to Arco Naturale. Another popular route is from Anacapri to Monte Solaro (2km, two hours), the island's highest point. If you don't fancy an upward trek, take the *seggiovia* (chairlift) up and walk down.

Running along the island's oft-over-looked western coast, the Sentiero dei Fortini (Path of the Small Forts; 5.2km, three hours), which connects Punta dell'Arcera near the Grotta Azzurra to Punta Carena, promises more bucolic bliss. For the best effect, start at Punta dell'Arcera so you can end your hike with sunset drinks at Punta Carena. Capri's tourist offices can provide information and maps of the island's various trails.

🍷 Drinking & Nightlife

Capri's nightlife is a showy business. The main activity is dressing up and hanging out, ideally at one of the cafes on La Piazzetta (Piazza Umberto 1). Aside from the cafes, the nightlife here is fairly staid, with surprisingly few nightclubs, given the penchant for the locals to glitz up and strut their stuff.

Pulalli   WINE BAR

(☑ 081 837 41 08; Piazza Umberto I, Capri Town; ⊙ noon-3pm & 7pm-11.30pm daily Aug, closed Tue Sep-Jul) Climb the clock-tower steps to the right of the tourist office and your reward is this lofty local hang-out where fabulous wine meets a discerning selection of cheese, charcuterie, and more substantial fare such as *risotto al limone* (lemon risotto). Try for a seat on the terrace or, best of all, the coveted table on its own balcony.

Caffè Michelangelo   CAFE

(Via Giuseppe Orlandi 138, Anacapri; ⊙ 8am-1am) It's not that flashy, but the position of the delightful Caffè Michelangelo, on a street flanked by tasteful shops and near two lovely piazzas, makes it a perfect spot for indulging in a little people-watching-and-cocktail-sipping time. Large, cushioned chairs and a raised terrace add to the kick-back appeal.

Taverna Anema e Core CLUB

(✆081 837 64 61; www.anemaecore.com; Vico Sella Orta 39E, Capri Town; ⊙noon-11pm Apr-Oct) Lying beyond a humble exterior is one of the island's most famous nightspots, run by the charismatic Guido Lembo. This smooth and sophisticated bar-club attracts an appealing mix of super-chic and casually dressed punters, here for the relaxed atmosphere and regular live music, including unwaveringly authentic Neapolitan guitar strumming and singing.

 Shopping

If you're not in the market for a new Rolex or Prada bag, look out for ceramic work, lemon-scented perfume and *limoncello* (lemon liqueur). For perfume don't miss **Carthusia I Profumi di Capri** (✆081 837 53 35; www. carthusia.it; Via F Serena 28, Capri Town; ⊙9am-6pm) in Capri Town; for *limoncello* head up to Anacapri and **Limoncello di Capri** (✆081 837 29 27; www.limoncello.com; Via Capodimonte 27, Anacapri; ⊙9am-7.30pm).

If you *are* in the market for a new Rolex or Prada bag, head to Via Vittorio Emanuele and Via Camerelle.

ⓘ Information

Post Office (Via Roma 50; ⊙8am-6.30pm Mon-Fri, to 12.30pm Sat)

Tourist Office (✆081 837 06 34; www. capritourism.com; Banchina del Porto, Marina Grande) Can provide a map of the island (€1) with town plans of Capri and Anacapri. For hotel listings and other useful information, ask for a free copy of *Capri è*.

RESOURCES

Capri (www.capri.com) User-friendly site covering everything from hotel bookings and attractions to ferry times.

Capri Tourism (www.capritourism.com) Official website of Capri's tourist office.

ⓘ Getting There & Away

See Naples, Sorrento and specific Amalfi Coast towns for details of ferries and hydrofoils to the island.

Note that some companies require you to pay a small supplement for luggage, typically around €2.

ⓘ Getting Around

BUS

Sippic (✆081 837 04 20; Bus Station, Via Roma, Capri Town; tickets €1.80) Runs regular buses to/from Marina Grande, Anacapri and Marina Piccola. It also operates buses from Marina Grande to Anacapri and from Marina Piccola to Anacapri.

Staiano Autotrasporti (✆081 837 24 22; www.staianotourcapri.com; Bus Station, Via Tommaso, Anacapri; tickets €1.80, day tickets €8.60) Buses serve the Grotta Azzurra and Faro di Punta Carena.

SCOOTER

Ciro dei Motorini (✆081 837 80 18; www. capriscooter.com; Via Marina Grande 55, Marina Grande; per 2/24hr €30/65) For scooter hire at Marina Grande, stop here.

FUNICULAR

Funicular (tickets €1.80; ⊙6.30am-12.30am) Connects Marina Grande to Capri Town. Single tickets cost €1.80.

TAXI

From Marina Grande, a **taxi** (✆ in Anacapri 081 837 11 75, in Capri Town 081 837 66 57) costs around €20 to Capri and €25 to Anacapri; from Capri to Anacapri costs about €20.

Ischia

POP 62,200

Sprawling over 46 sq km, Ischia (iss-*kyah*) is the biggest and busiest island in the bay. It's a lush concoction of sprawling spa towns, mud-wrapped Germans and ancient relics. Also famous for its thermal waters, it has some fine beaches and spectacular scenery.

Most visitors stay on the touristy north coast, but go inland and you'll find a rural landscape of chestnut forests, dusty farms and earthy hillside villages.

◉ Sights

★**Castello Aragonese** CASTLE

(Aragon Castle; ✆081 991 959, 081 992 834; Rocca del Castello, Ischia Ponte; adult/reduced €10/6; ⊙9am-90min before sunset) The elegant 15th-century Ponte Aragonese connects Ischia Ponte to Castello Aragonese, a sprawling, magnificent castle perched high and mighty on a rocky islet. While Syracusan tyrant Gerone I built the site's first fortress in 474 BC, the bulk of the current structure dates from the 1400s, when King Alfonso of Aragon gave the older Angevin fortress a thorough makeover, building the fortified bastions, current causeway and access ramp cut into the rock.

★ **La Mortella**   GARDENS

Place of the Myrtles; ☑ 081 98 62 20; www.lamor ella.it; Via F Calese 39, Forio; adult/reduced €12/7; ☺ 9am-7pm Tue, Thu, Sat & Sun Apr-early Nov) Designed by Russell Page and inspired by the Moorish gardens of Spain's Alhambra, La Mortella is recognised as one of Italy's finest botanical gardens and is well worth a couple of hours of your time. Stroll among terraces, pools, palms, fountains and more than 1000 rare and exotic plants from all over the world. The lower section of the garden is humid and tropical, while the upper level features Mediterranean plants.

🏊 Activities

Unlike Capri, Ischia has some great beaches. From chic Sant'Angelo on the south coast, water taxis reach the sandy **Spiaggia dei Maronti** and the intimate cove of **Il Sorgeto** (Via Sorgeto; ☺ Apr-Oct), with its steamy thermal spring. Sorgeto can also be reached on foot down a poorly signposted path from the village of Panza.

★ **Negombo**   SPA

(☑ 081 98 61 52; www.negombo.it; Baia di San Montano, Lacco Ameno; admission all day €32, from 2pm €20; ☺ 8.30am-7pm late Apr-Oct) This is the place to come for a dose of pampering. Part spa resort, part botanical wonderland, with more than 500 exotic plant species, Negombo's combination of Zen-like thermal pools, hammam, contemporary sculpture and private beach on the Baia di San Montano tends to draw a younger crowd than many other Ischian spa spots.

Geo-Ausfluge   HIKING

(Geo-Ausfluge; ☑ English spoken 081 90 30 58; www.eurogeopark.com; walks €17-26) Unlike Capri and Procida, Ischia is not easily accessible to hikers. If you're interested in exploring the hinterland, Italian geologist Aniello Di Lorio conducts a selection of walks throughout the island ranging from three to five hours, including lunch, with various collection points in Ischia; pick up in Casamicciola and Panza costs a further €9 return.

Ischia Diving   DIVING

(☑ 081 98 18 52; www.ischiadiving.net; Via Iasolino 106, Ischia Porto; single dive €40) This well-established diving outfit offers some attractively priced dive packages, like five dives including equipment for €185.

🛏 Sleeping

Most hotels close in winter and prices normally drop considerably among those that stay open.

Hotel Noris   HOTEL €

(☑ 081 99 13 87; www.norishotel.it; Via A Sogliuzzo 2, Ischia Ponte; d €50-85; ☺ Easter-Oct; ❊ 🛜) This place has a great price and a great position within easy strolling distance of the Ponte sights. The comfy, decent-size rooms have small balconies and are decked out in fresh colours. Breakfast is the standard, albeit slightly more expansive, Continental buffet. Bonus points are due for the special parking deal with the public car park across the way.

Camping Mirage   CAMPGROUND €

(☑ 081 99 05 51; www.campingmirage.it; Via Maronti 37, Spiaggia dei Maronti, Barano d'Ischia; camping per 2 people, car & tent €45; ☺ Easter-Oct; 🅿 ♿) Located on Spiagga dei Maronti, one of Ischia's best beaches, and within walking distance of Sant'Angelo, this shady campground offers 50 places, showers, laundry facilities, a bar and a restaurant dishing up local special *tubettoni, cozze e pecorino* (pasta with mussels and sheep's cheese).

Albergo il Monastero   HOTEL €€

(☑ 081 99 24 35; www.albergoilmonastero.it; Castello Aragonese, Rocca del Castello, Ischia Ponte; s €90, d €135-190; ☺ Easter-Oct; ❊) The former monks' cells still have a certain appealing sobriety about them, featuring dark-wood furniture, white walls, vintage terracotta tiles and no TV (don't worry – the views are sufficiently prime time). Elsewhere there is a pleasing sense of space and style, with vaulted ceilings, chic plush sofas and antiques. The hotel restaurant has an excellent reputation.

★ **Hotel Semiramis**   HOTEL €€

(☑ 081 90 75 11; www.hotelsemiramisischia.it; Spiaggia di Citara, Forio; d €140-180; ☺ late Apr-Oct; 🅿 ❊ 🛜 ♿) A few minutes' walk from the Poseidon spa complex, this bright hotel has a tropical-oasis feel with its central pool surrounded by lofty palms. Rooms are large and beautifully tiled in the traditional yellow-and-turquoise pattern, and the garden is glorious, featuring fig trees, vineyards and distant sea views.

WORTH A TRIP

IL FOCOLARE: A SLOW FOOD WONDER

Tucked away in the hills above Casamicciola Terme is one restaurant verified foodies cannot afford to miss – Il Focolare (☎ 081 90 29 44; www.trattoriailfocolare.it; Via Creajo al Crocefisso 3, Barano d'Ischia; meals €30; ⏱ 12.30-2.45pm & 7.30-11.30pm Jun-Oct, 12.30-2.45pm Wed, 7.30-11.30pm Sat & Sun Nov-May). Forget *spaghetti alle vongole* (spaghetti with clams) – this proud Slow Food stalwart celebrates all things turf. Indeed, it's one of the best spots to savour the island's legendary *coniglio all'Ischitana* (a claypot-cooked local rabbit with garlic, onion, tomatoes, wild thyme and white wine), a dish that needs to be booked two days in advance.

If you haven't pre-ordered the rabbit, don't fret – the daily menu brims with beautiful, seasonal dishes, from *tagliatelle al ragù di cinghiale* (ribbon-shaped pasta with wild boar ragout) to a sublime *antipasto misto*, where you might get anything from *rotolino di zucchini* (fried, bread-crumbed zucchini filled with buffalo mozzarella) to *terrina di parmigiano tartufata con i funghi* (think porcini-mushroom crème brûlée).

To get here, catch bus 16 from Piazza Marina in Casamicciola Terme and ask the driver to let you off at the restaurant (it's the last stop). From June to November, the last bus back to town departs at around 12.40am; from December to May the last service departs at 7.30pm.

✗ Eating

Seafood aside, Ischia is famed for its rabbit, which is bred on inland farms. Another local speciality is *rucolino* – a green liquorice-flavoured liqueur made from *rucola* (rocket).

★ Montecorvo
ITALIAN **€€**

(☎ 081 99 80 29; www.montecorvo.it; Via Montecorvo 33, Forio; meals €30; ⏱ 12.30-3.30pm & 7.30pm-1am, closed lunch Jul & Aug) At this extraordinary place part of the dining room is tunnelled into a cave and the terrace looks as though it belongs in a jungle. Owner Giovanni prides himself on the special dishes he makes daily, with an emphasis on grilled meat and fish, and the menu also includes a good range of pasta and vegetable antipasti.

You will need more than a good compass to find this spot, hidden amid lush foliage outside Forio and fronted by pines, a waterfall and steep steps. Fortunately, it is well signposted.

Ristorante da Ciccio
ITALIAN **€€**

(☎ 081 99 16 86; Via Luigi Mazzella 32, Ischia Ponte; meals €25; ⏱ noon-3.30pm & 7.30-11.30pm, closed Tue Dec-Feb) Sublime seafood and charming host Carlo make this atmospheric place a winner. Highlights include *tubattone* pasta with clams and pecorino cheese, a zesty mussel soup topped with fried bread and *peperoncino* (chilli), and a delicious chocolate and almond cake. Tables spill out onto the pavement in summer, from where there are fabulous castle views.

Ristorante Pietratorcia
ITALIAN **€€**

(☎ 081 90 72 32; www.ristorantepietratorcia.it; Via Provinciale Panza 267, Forio; set menu from €28; ⏱ 11am-11pm Tue-Sun Apr-Oct) Enjoying a bucolic setting among tumbling vines, wild fig trees and rosemary bushes, this A-list winery is a foodie's nirvana. Tour the old stone cellars, sip a local drop and eye up the delectable degustation menu. Offerings include fragrant bruschetta and cheeses, hearty Campanian sausages and spicy *salumi* (charcuterie).

ℹ Information

Ischia Online (www.ischiaonline.it) Good all-around website including sights, hotels and ferry times.

Tourist Office (☎ 081 507 42 11; www.infoischiaprocida.it; Corso Sogliuzzo 72, Ischia Porto; ⏱ 9am-2pm & 3-8pm Mon-Sat) A slim selection of maps and brochures.

ℹ Getting There & Away

Regular hydrofoils and ferries run to/from Naples. You can also catch hydrofoils direct to Capri (€19.80, 50 minutes). Ischia is also connected to Procida by hydrofoil (€8 to €9.20, 15 minutes) and ferry (€7.10, 15 to 30 minutes).

ℹ Getting Around

The island's main bus station is located in Ischia Porto. There are two principal lines: the CS (Circolo Sinistro, or Left Circle), which circles the island anticlockwise, and the CD line (Circolo Destro, or Right Circle), which travels in a clockwise direction, passing through each town and departing every 30 minutes. Buses pass near all hotels and campsites. A single ticket, valid for 90 minutes, costs €1.90; an all-day, multi-use ticket is €6; a two-day ticket €10; three days €13; and one week €26. Taxis and micro-taxis (scooter-engined three-wheelers) are also available.

You can do this small island a favour by not bringing your car. If you want to hire a car or a scooter for a day, there are plenty of hire companies. **Balestrieri** (☑ 081 98 56 91; www. autonoleggiobalestrieri.it; Via Iasolino 35, Ischia Porto) hires out cars and scooters (per day/week €20/140) and they also have mountain bikes (€15 per day). You can't take a hired vehicle off the island.

Procida

POP 10,800

Dig out your paintbox: the Bay of Naples' smallest island (and its best-kept secret) is a soulful blend of hidden lemon groves, weathered fishing folk and pastel-hued houses. August aside – when beach-bound mainlanders flock to its shores – its narrow sun-bleached streets are the domain of the locals.

◉ Sights & Activities

The best way to explore the island (a mere 4 sq km) is on foot or by bike. However, the island's narrow roads can be clogged with cars – one of its few drawbacks.

From panoramic Piazza dei Martiri, the village of **Corricella** tumbles down to its marina in a riot of pinks, yellows and whites. Further south, a steep flight of steps leads down to **Chiaia** beach, one of the island's most beautiful.

All pink, white and blue, little **Marina di Chiaiolella** has a yacht-stocked marina, old-school eateries and a languid disposition. Nearby, the **Lido** is a popular beach.

Abbazia di San Michele Arcangelo

CHURCH, MUSEUM

(☑ 334 8514028, 334 8514252; associazionemillen nium@virgilio.it; Via Terra Murata 89, Terra Murata; admission €3; ⊙10am-1pm & 3-6pm) Soak in the dizzying bay views at the belvedere before exploring the adjoining Abbazia di San Michele Arcangelo. Built in the 11th century and remodelled between the 17th and 19th centuries, this one-time Benedictine abbey houses a small museum with some arresting pictures done in gratitude by shipwrecked sailors, plus a church with a spectacular coffered ceiling and an ancient Greek alabaster

basin converted into a font, and a maze of catacombs that leads to a tiny secret chapel.

Barobe & Gommoni

BICYCLE RENTAL

(☑ 339 7163303; Via Roma 134, Marina Grande; per day €10; ⁂) The bicycles for hire here are one of the best ways to explore the island. Small, open micro-taxis can also be hired for two to three hours for around €35, depending on your bargaining prowess.

Blue Dream Yacht Charter Boating

BOATING

(☑ 339 5720874, 081 896 05 79; www.bluedream charter.com; Via Vittorio Emanuele 14, Marina Grande; per week from €1500) If you have 'champagne on the deck' aspirations, you can always charter your very own yacht from here. Sleeps six.

✦ Festivals & Events

Procession of the Misteri

RELIGIOUS

Good Friday sees a colourful procession when a wooden statue of Christ and the Madonna Addolorata, along with life-size plaster and papier-mâché tableaux illustrating events leading to Christ's crucifixion, are carted across the island. Men dress in blue tunics with white hoods, while many of the young girls dress as the Madonna.

🛏 Sleeping

Bed & Breakfast La Terrazza

B&B €

(☑ 081 896 00 62; Via Faro 26, Marina Grande; s €50-70, d €75-90; ⊙Easter-Oct) An extremely attractive budget option, where the rooms are decked out with paintings, metal lamps, tiles and antiques. Take time out on the terracotta-floored terrace – thus the B&B's name – where you can lie back on a lounger and enjoy the sunset. Homemade breakfasts are served up here.

★ Hotel La Vigna

BOUTIQUE HOTEL €€

(☑ 081 896 04 69; www.albergolavigna.it; Via Principessa Margherita 46, Terra Murata; d €150-180, ste €180-230; ⊙Easter-Oct; ⁂ @ ⑦) Enjoying a fabulous cliff-side location with a delightful garden and in-house spa, this 18th-century villa is a delight. Five of the spacious, simply furnished rooms offer direct access to the garden. Superior rooms (€180 to €200) feature family-friendly mezzanines, while the main perk of the suite is the bedside hot tub: perfect for romancing couples.

Casa Sul Mare

HOTEL €€

(☑ 081 896 87 99; www.lacasasulmare.it; Salita Castello 13, Marina Corricella; r €125-170;

⊘Easter-Oct; ✦☎) A fabulous place with the kind of evocative views that helped make *The Talented Mr Ripley* such a memorable film. Overlooking the picturesque Marina Corricella, near the ruined Castello d'Avalos, the rooms are elegant, with exquisite tiled floors, wrought-iron bedsteads and a warm Mediterranean colour scheme.

Eating

Da Giorgio   TRATTORIA €
(☑081 896 79 10; Via Roma 36, Marina Grande; meals €18; ⊘noon-3pm & 7-11.30pm Mar-Oct; ➔) These folks try hard to please, with a reasonably priced menu, welcoming window boxes and inexpensive beer. The menu holds few surprises, but the ingredients are fresh; try the *antipasto di mare* (€10) or *gnocchi alla sorrentina* (gnocchi in a tomato, basil and pecorino cheese sauce).

Fammivento   SEAFOOD €€
(☑081 896 90 20; Via Roma 39, Marina Grande; meals €25; ⊘noon-12.30am Tue-Sat, noon-3pm Sun Apr-Oct) Get things going with the *frittura di calamari* (fried squid), then try the *fusilli carciofi e calamari* (pasta with artichokes and calamari). For a splurge, go for the house speciality of *zuppa di crostaci e moluschi* (crustacean and mollusc soup).

ℹ Information

Pro Loco (☑081 810 19 68; www.proloco procida.it; Via Roma, Stazione Marittima, Marina Grande; ⊘9.30am-6pm) Located at the Ferry & Hydrofoil Ticket Office, this modest office has sparse printed information but should be able to advise on activities and the like.

ℹ Getting There & Around

Procida is linked to Ischia by ferry (€7.10, 15 to 30 minutes) and hydrofoil (€8 to €9.20, 15 minutes). Ferries run to Pozzuoli (€7, 20 minutes) and both ferries and hydrofoils sail to Naples.

There is a limited bus service (€1), with four lines radiating from Marina Grande. Bus L1 connects the port and Via Marina di Chiaiolella.

SOUTH OF NAPLES

Ercolano & Herculaneum

Ercolano is an uninspiring Neapolitan suburb that's home to one of Italy's best-preserved ancient sites: Herculaneum. A superbly conserved Roman fishing town, Herculaneum is smaller and less daunting than Pompeii, allowing you to visit without that nagging itch that you're bound to miss something.

◉ Sights

★ Ruins of Herculaneum   ARCHAEOLOGICAL SITE
(☑081 732 43 27; www.pompeiisites.org; Corso Resina 187, Ercolano; adult/reduced €11/5.50, incl Pompeii €20/10; ⊘8.30am-7.30pm summer, to 5pm winter; 🚆Circumvesuviana to Ercolano-Scavi) Upstaged by its larger rival, Pompeii, Herculaneum harbours a wealth of archaeological finds, from ancient advertisements and stylish mosaics to carbonised furniture and terror-struck skeletons. Indeed, this superbly conserved Roman fishing town of 4000 inhabitants is easier to navigate than Pompeii, and can be explored with a map and audioguide (€6.50).

From the site's main gateway on Corso Resina, head down the walkway to the ticket office (at the bottom on your left). Ticket purchased, follow the walkway to the actual entrance to the ruins (*scavi*).

Herculaneum's fate runs parallel to that of Pompeii. Destroyed by an earthquake in AD 62, the AD 79 eruption of Mt Vesuvius saw it submerged in a 16m-thick sea of mud that essentially fossilised the city. This meant that even delicate items, such as furniture and clothing, were discovered remarkably well preserved. Tragically, the inhabitants didn't fare so well; thousands of people tried to escape by boat but were suffocated by the volcano's poisonous gases. Indeed, what appears to be a moat around the town is in fact the ancient shoreline. It was here in 1980 that archaeologists discovered some 300 skeletons, the remains of a crowd that had fled to the beach only to be overcome by the terrible heat of clouds surging down from Vesuvius.

The town itself was rediscovered in 1709 and amateur excavations were carried out intermittently until 1874, with many finds carted off to Naples to decorate the houses of the well-to-do or ending up in museums. Serious archaeological work began again in 1927 and continues to this day, although with much of the ancient site buried beneath modern Ercolano it's slow going. Indeed, note that at any given time some houses will invariably be shut for restoration.

➡ Casa d'Argo

(Argus House) This noble house would originally have opened onto Cardo II (as yet
unearthed). Onto its porticoed, palm-treed
garden open a *triclinium* (dining room) and
other residential rooms.

➡ Casa dello Scheletro

(House of the Skeleton) The modest Casa dello Scheletro features five styles of mosaic
flooring, including a design of white arrows
at the entrance to guide the most disorien-
tated of guests. In the internal courtyard,
don't miss the skylight, complete with the
remnants of an ancient security grill. Of the
house's mythically themed wall mosaics,
only the faded ones are originals; the others
now reside in Naples' Museo Archeologico
Nazionale (p657).

➡ Terme Maschili

(Men's Baths) The Terme Maschili were the
men's section of the **Terme del Foro** (Forum
Baths). Note the ancient latrine to the left of
the entrance before you step into the *apodyterium* (changing room), complete with
bench for waiting patrons and a nifty wall
shelf for sandal and toga storage.

While those after a bracing soak would
pop into the *frigidarium* (cold bath) to the
left, the less stoic headed straight into the
tepadarium (tepid bath) to the right. The
sunken mosaic floor here is testament to
the seismic activity preceding Mt Vesuvius'
catastrophic eruption. Beyond this room lies
the *caldarium* (hot bath), as well as an exercise area.

➡ Decumano Massimo

Herculaneum's ancient high street is lined
with shops, and fragments of advertisements – listing everything from the weight
of goods to their price – still adorn the walls.
Note the one to the right of the Casa del
Salone Nero. Further east along the street,
a crucifix found in an upstairs room of the
Casa del Bicentenario (Bicentenary House)
provides possible evidence of a Christian
presence in pre-Vesuvius Herculaneum.

➡ Casa del Bel Cortile

(House of the Beautiful Courtyard) Inside the
Casa del Bel Cortile lie three of the 300 skeletons discovered on the ancient shore by archaeologists in 1980. Almost two millennia
later, it's still poignant to see the forms of
what are understood to be a mother, father
and young child huddled together in the
last, terrifying moments of their lives.

➡ Casa di Nettuno e Anfitrite

(House of Neptune and Amphitrite) This aristocratic pad takes its name from the extraordinary mosaic in the *nymphaeum* (fountain
and bath). The warm colours in which the
sea god and his nymph bride are depicted
hint at how lavish the original interior must
have been.

➡ Casa del Tramezzo di Legno

(House of the Wooden Partition) Unusually, this
house features two atria, which likely belonged to two separate dwellings that were
merged in the 1st century AD. The most
famous relic here is a wonderfully well-
preserved wooden screen, separating the
atrium from the *tablinum*, where the owner
talked business with his clients. The second
room off the left side of the atrium features
the remains of an ancient bed.

➡ Casa dell'Atrio a Mosaico

(House of the Mosaic Atrium; ⊘ closed for restoration) An ancient mansion, the House of the
Mosaic Atrium harbours extensive floor tilework, although time and nature have left the
floor buckled and uneven. Particularly noteworthy is the black-and-white chessboard
mosaic in the atrium.

➡ Casa del Gran Portale

(House of the Large Portal) Named after the elegant brick Corinthian columns that flank
its main entrance, the House of the Large
Portal is home to some well-preserved wall
paintings.

➡ Casa dei Cervi

(House of the Stags) Closed indefinitely on our
last visit, the Casa dei Cervi is an imposing
example of a Roman noble family's house
that, before the volcanic mud slide, boasted
a seafront address. Constructed around a
central courtyard, the two-storey villa contains murals and some beautiful still-life
paintings. Waiting for you in the courtyard
is a diminutive pair of marble deer assailed
by dogs, and an engaging statue of a drunk-
en, peeing Hercules.

Terme Suburbane   ARCHAEOLOGICAL SITE

(Suburban Baths; ⊘ closed for restoration) Marking Herculaneum's southernmost tip is the
1st-century-AD Terme Suburbane, one of
the best-preserved Roman bath complexes
in existence, with deep pools, stucco friezes
and bas-reliefs looking down upon marble
seats and floors. This is also one of the best
places to observe the soaring volcanic depos-
its that smothered the ancient coastline.

MAV   MUSEUM
(Museo Archeologico Virtuale; ☑ 081 1980 6511; www.museomav.com; Via IV Novembre 44; adult/reduced €7.50/6, optional 3D documentary €4; ⊙ 9am-5.30pm daily Mar-Sep, reduced hours rest of year;☒ Circumvesuviana to Ercolano-Scavi) Using high-tech holograms and computer-generated recreations, this 'virtual archaeological museum' brings ruins like Pompeii's forum and Capri's Villa Jovis back to virtual life. Especially fun for kids, it's a useful place to comprehend just how impressive those crumbling columns once were. The museum is on the main street linking Ercolano-Scavi train station to the ruins of Herculaneum.

✖ Eating

Viva Lo Re   NEAPOLITAN **€€**
(☑ 081 739 02 07; www.vivalore.it; Corso Resina 261; meals €35; ⊙ noon-4pm & 8.30-late Tue-Sat, noon-4pm Sun; ☒ Circumvesuviana to Ercolano-Scavi) Located 500m southeast of the ruins of Herculaneum on Corso Resina – dubbed the Miglio d'oro (Golden Mile) for its once-glorious stretch of 18th-century villas – Viva Lo Re is a stylish, inviting osteria, where vintage prints and bookshelves meet a superb wine list, gracious staff and gorgeous, revamped regional cooking.

ℹ Information

Tourist Office (Via IV Novembre 44; ⊙ 9am-5.30pm Mon-Sat; ☒ Circumvesuviana to Ercolano-Scavi) Ercolano's new tourist office is located in the same building as MAV, between the Circumvesuviana Ercolano-Scavi train station and the Herculaneum ruins.

ℹ Getting There & Away

You can reach Ercolano by Circumvesuviana train, which run frequently from Naples (€2.50, 17 minutes) and Sorrento (€3.40, 48 minutes). Alight at Ercolano-Scavi station, from where the ruins are an 800m walk southwest on Via IV Novembre.

By car take the A3 from Naples, exit at Ercolano Portico and follow the signs to car parks near the site's entrance.

Mt Vesuvius

Looming over the Bay of Naples, stratovolcano **Mt Vesuvius** (☑ 081 239 56 53; adult/reduced €10/8; ⊙ 9am-6pm Jul & Aug, to 5pm Apr-Jun & Sep, to 4pm Mar & Oct, to 3pm Nov-Feb, ticket office closes 1hr before the crater) has blown its top more than 30 times. Its violent outburst in AD 79 not only drowned Pompeii in pumice and pushed the coastline back several kilometres but also destroyed much of the mountain top, creating a huge caldera and two new peaks. The most destructive explosion after that of AD 79 was in 1631, while the most recent was in 1944.

What redeems this slumbering menace is the spectacular panorama from its crater, which takes in Naples, its world-famous bay, and part of the Apennine mountains. From Piazzale Stazione Circumvesuviana, outside Ercolano-Scavi train station, **Vesuvio Express** (☑ 081 739 36 66; www.vesuvioexpress.it; Piazzale Stazione Circumvesuviana, Ercolano; return incl admission to summit €20; ⊙ every 40min, 9.30am to 4pm) runs shuttle buses up to the summit car park. From here, an 860m path (best tackled in trainers, with sweater in tow) leads up to the crater (roughly a 25-minute climb). From Pompeii, **Busvia del Vesuvio** (☑ 340 9352616; www.busviadelvesuvio.com; Via Villa dei Misteri, Pompeii; return incl entry to summit adult/reduced €22/7; ⊙ 9am-4pm) runs hourly shuttle services between Pompei-Scavi-Villa dei Misteri train station (steps away from the Ruins of Pompeii) and Boscoreale Terminal Interchange, from where a 4WD-style bus continues the journey up the slope to the summit car park.

Vesuvius itself is the focal point of the **Parco Nazionale del Vesuvio** (Vesuvius National Park; www.epnv.it), which offers nine nature walks around the volcano. A simple map of the trails can be downloaded from the park's website. Alternatively, **Naples Trips & Tours** (☑ 349 7155270; www.naplestripsandtours.com; guided tour €50) runs a daily horse-riding tour of the park (weather permitting). Running for three to four hours, the tour includes transfers to/from Naples or Ercolano-Scavi Circumvesuviana station, helmet, saddle, guide and (most importantly) coffee.

If travelling by car, exit the A3 at Ercolano Portico and follow signs for the Parco Nazionale del Vesuvio.

Note that when weather conditions are bad the summit path is shut and bus departures are suspended.

Pompeii

POP 25,365

Each year about 2.5 million people pour in to wander the eerie shell of ancient Pompeii, a once thriving commercial centre. Not only an evocative glimpse into Roman life, the ruins provide a stark reminder of the malign forces that lie deep inside Mt Vesuvius.

◉ Sights

★ Ruins of Pompeii ARCHAEOLOGICAL SITE

(☎ 081 857 53 47; www.pompeiisites.org; entrances at Porta Marina, Piazza Esedra & Piazza Anfiteatro; adult/reduced €11/5.50, incl Herculaneum €20/10; ⊘ 8.30am-7.30pm summer, to 5pm winter) The ghostly ruins of ancient Pompeii (Pompei in Italian) make for one of the world's most engrossing archaeological experiences. Much of the site's value lies in the fact that the town wasn't simply blown away by Vesuvius in AD 79 but buried under a layer of *lapilli* (burning fragments of pumice stone). The result is a remarkably well-preserved slice of ancient life, where visitors can walk down Roman streets and snoop around millennia-old houses, temples, shops, cafes, amphitheatres, and even a brothel.

The origins of Pompeii are uncertain, but it seems likely that it was founded in the 7th century BC by the Campanian Oscans. Over the next seven centuries the city fell to the Greeks and the Samnites before becoming a Roman colony in 80 BC.

In AD 62, a mere 17 years before Vesuvius erupted, the city was struck by a major earthquake. Damage was widespread and much of the city's 20,000-strong population was evacuated. Fortunately, many had not returned by the time Vesuvius blew, but 2000 men, women and children perished nevertheless.

After its catastrophic demise, Pompeii receded from the public eye until 1594, when the architect Domenico Fontana stumbled across the ruins while digging a canal. Exploration proper, however, didn't begin until 1748. Of Pompeii's original 66 hectares, 44 have now been excavated. Of course that doesn't mean you'll have unhindered access to every inch of the Unesco-listed site – expect to come across areas cordoned off for no apparent reason, a noticeable lack of clear signs, and the odd stray dog. Audio guides are a sensible investment (€6.50, cash only) and a good guidebook will also help – try *Pompeii*, published by Electa Napoli.

In recent years, the site has suffered a number of high-profile incidents due to bad weather. Most recently, heavy rain caused the wall of an ancient shop to collapse in March 2014. Maintenance work is ongoing,

 ⓘ TOURS

You'll almost certainly be approached by a guide outside the *scavi* (excavations) ticket office: note that authorised guides wear identification tags. If considering a guided tour of the ruins, reputable tour operators include **Yellow Sudmarine** (☎ 329 1010328, 334 1047036; www. yellowsudmarine.com; 2hr Pompeii guided tour €110) and **Walks of Italy** (www. walksofitaly.com; 2½hr Pompeii guided tour €52), both of which also offer excursions to other areas of Campania.

but progress is beset by political, financial and bureaucratic problems.

➤ **Terme Suburbane**

Just outside ancient Pompeii's city walls, this 1st-century-BC bathhouse is famous for several erotic frescoes that scandalised the Vatican when they were revealed in 2001. The panels decorate what was once the *apodyterium* (changing room). The room leading to the colourfully frescoed *frigidarium* (cold-water bath) features fragments of stuccowork, as well as one of the few original roofs to survive at Pompeii. Beyond the *tepadarium* (tepid bath) and *caldarium* (hot bath) rooms are the remains of a heated outdoor swimming pool.

➤ **Porta Marina**

The ruins of Pompeii's main entrance is at Porta Marina, the most impressive of the seven gates that punctuated the ancient town walls. A busy passageway now, as it was then, it originally connected the town with the nearby harbour, hence the gateway's name. Immediately on the right as you enter the gate is the 1st-century-BC **Tempio di Venere** (Temple of Venus), formerly one of the town's most opulent temples.

➤ **Foro**

(Forum) A huge grassy rectangle flanked by limestone columns, the *foro* was ancient Pompeii's main piazza, as well as the site of gladiatoral battles before the Anfiteatro was constructed. The buildings surrounding the forum are testament to its role as the city's hub of civic, commercial, political and religious activity.

➤ **Basilica**

The basilica was the 2nd-century-BC seat of Pompeii's law courts and exchange. Their

Tragedy in Pompeii

24 AUGUST AD 79

8am Buildings including the **Terme Suburbane** ❶ and the **foro** ❷ are still undergoing repair after an earthquake in AD 63 caused significant damage to the city. Despite violent earth tremors overnight, residents have little idea of the catastrophe that lies ahead.

Midday Peckish locals pour into the **Thermopolium di Vetutius Placidus** ❸. The lustful slip into the **Lupanare** ❹, and gladiators practise for the evening's planned games at the **anfiteatro** ❺. A massive boom heralds the eruption. Shocked onlookers witness a dark cloud of volcanic matter shoot some 14km above the crater.

3pm–5pm Lapilli (burning pumice stone) rains down on Pompeii. Terrified locals begin to flee; others take shelter. Within two hours, the plume is 25km high and the sky has darkened. Roofs collapse under the weight of the debris, burying those inside.

25 AUGUST AD 79

Midnight Mudflows bury the town of Herculaneum. Lapilli and ash continue to rain down on Pompeii, bursting through buildings and suffocating those taking refuge within.

4am–8am Ash and gas avalanches hit Herculaneum. Subsequent surges smother Pompeii, killing all remaining residents, including those in the **Orto dei Fuggiaschi** ❻. The volcanic 'blanket' will safeguard frescoed treasures like the **Casa del Menandro** ❼ and **Villa dei Misteri** ❽ for almost two millennia.

TOP TIPS

» Visit in the afternoon
» Allow three hours
» Wear comfortable shoes and a hat
» Bring drinking water
» Don't use flash photography

Terme Suburbane
The *laconicum* (sauna), *caldarium* (hot bath) and large, heated swimming pool weren't the only sources of heat here; scan the walls of this suburban bathhouse for some of the city's raunchiest frescoes.

Villa di Diomede

Casa del Poeta Tragico

Porta Ercolano

Ca Fa

Tempio di Apollo

Basilica

Porta Marina

Terme del Foro

Macellum

Teatro Grande

Quadriportico dei Teatri

Porta di Stabia

Teatro Piccolo

Foro
An ancient Times Square of sorts, the forum sits at the intersection of Pompeii's main streets and was closed to traffic in the 1st century AD. The plinths on the southern edge featured statues of the imperial family.

a dei Misteri

...e to the world-famous *Dionysiac Frieze* ...o. Other highlights at this villa include ...pe l'oeil wall decorations in the *cubiculum* ...room) and Egyptian-themed artwork in the ...num (reception).

Lupanare
The prostitutes at this brothel were often slaves of Greek or Asian origin. Mattresses once covered the stone beds and the names engraved in the walls are possibly those of the workers and their clients.

Thermopolium di Vetutius Placidus
The counter at this ancient snack bar once held urns filled with hot food. The *lararium* (household shrine) on the back wall depicts Dionysus (the god of wine) and Mercury (the god of profit and commerce).

...ei
...j

...ta del
...suvio

> #### EYEWITNESS ACCOUNT
>
> Pliny the Younger (AD 61–c 112) gives a gripping, first-hand account of the catastrophe in his letters to Tacitus (AD 56–117).

Porta di Nola

Casa della Venere in Conchiglia

Porta di Sarno

(7)

Grande Palestra

(3) (6) (5)

...io
...de

a del
...andro
...welling most ...belonged to the ...of Poppaea ...a, Nero's second ...A room to the left ...atrium features ...War paintings ...polychrome ...c of pygmies ...g down the Nile.

Orto dei Fuggiaschi
The Garden of the Fugitives showcases the plaster moulds of 13 locals seeking refuge during Vesuvius' eruption – the largest number of victims found in any one area. The huddled bodies make for a moving scene.

Anfiteatro
Magistrates, local senators and the games' sponsors and organisers enjoyed front-row seating at this veteran amphitheatre, home to gladiatorial battles and the odd riot. The parapet circling the stadium featured paintings of combat, victory celebrations and hunting scenes.

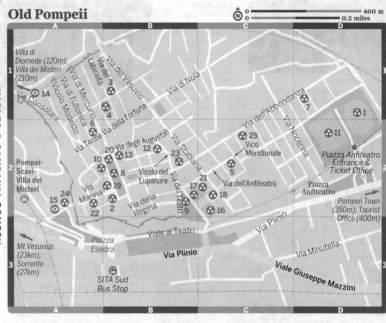

Old Pompeii

semicircular apses would later influence the design of early Christian churches.

➡ Tempio di Apollo

(Temple of Apollo) The oldest and most important of Pompeii's religious buildings, the Tempio di Apollo largely dates to the 2nd century BC, including the striking columned portico. Fragments remain of an earlier version dating to the 6th century BC.

➡ Tempio di Giove

(Temple of Jupiter) One of the two flanking triumphal arches of the Tempio di Giove still remains.

➡ Granai del Foro

(Forum Granary) The Granai del Foro is now used to store hundreds of amphorae and a number of body casts that were made in the late 19th century by pouring plaster into the hollows left by disintegrated bodies. Among these casts is a pregnant slave; the belt around her waist would have displayed the name of her owner.

➡ Macellum

The *macellum* was the city's main produce market. The circular area in the centre was the *tholos*, a covered space in which fish and seafood were sold. Surviving market frescoes reveal some of the goods for sale, including prawns.

➡ **Lupanare**

Ancient Pompeii's only dedicated brothel, Lupanare is a tiny two-storey building with five rooms on each floor. Its collection of raunchy frescoes was a menu of sorts for clients. The walls in the rooms are carved with graffiti – including declarations of love and hope written by the brothel workers – in various languages.

➡ **Foro Triangolare**

The verdant Foro Triangolare would originally have overlooked the sea.

➡ **Teatro Grande**

The 2nd-century-BC Teatro Grande was a huge 5000-seat theatre carved into the lava mass on which Pompeii was originally built.

➡ **Quadriportico dei Teatri**

Behind the Teatro Grande's stage, the porticoed Quadriportico dei Teatri was initially used for the audience to stroll between acts, and later as a barracks for gladiators.

➡ **Teatro Piccolo**

Also known as the Odeion, the Teatro Piccolo was once an indoor theatre renowned for its acoustics.

➡ **Tempio di Iside**

(Temple of Isis) The pre-Roman Tempio di Iside was a popular place of cult worship.

➡ **Casa del Menandro**

Better preserved than the larger Casa del Fauno, luxurious Casa del Menandro has an outstanding, elegant peristyle (a colonnade-framed courtyard) beyond its beautifully frescoed atrium. On the peristyle's far right side a doorway leads to a private bathhouse, lavished with exquisite frescoes and mosaics. The central room off the far end of the peristyle features a striking mosaic of the ancient Greek dramatist Menander, after which the rediscovered villa was named.

➡ **Via dell'Abbondanza**

(Street of Abundance) The Via dell'Abbondanza was ancient Pompeii's Main Street. The elevated stepping stones allowed people to cross the street without stepping into the waste that washed down the thoroughfare.

➡ **Terme Stabiane**

At this typical 2nd-century-BC bath complex, bathers would enter from the vestibule, stop off in the vaulted *apodyterium* (changing room), and then pass through to the *tepidarium* (warm room) and *caldarium* (hot room). Particularly impressive is the stuccoed vault in the men's changing room, complete with whimsical images of *putti* (winged babies) and nymphs.

➡ **Casa della Venere in Conchiglia**

(House of the Venus Marina) Casa della Venere in Conchiglia harbours a lovely peristyle looking onto a small, manicured garden. It's here in the garden that you'll find the striking Venus fresco after which the house is named.

➡ **Anfiteatro**

(Amphitheatre) Gladiatorial battles thrilled up to 20,000 spectators at the grassy *anfiteatro*. Built in 70 BC, it's the oldest known Roman amphitheatre in existence.

➡ **Grande Palestra**

Lithe ancients kept fit at the Grande Palestra, an athletics field with an impressive portico dating to the Augustan period. At its centre, and closed off to public access, lie the remains of a swimming pool.

➡ **Casa del Fauno**

(House of the Faun) Covering an entire *insula* (city block) and boasting two atria at its front end (humbler homes had one), Pompeii's largest private house is named after the delicate bronze statue in the *impluvium* (rain tank). It was here that early excavators found Pompeii's greatest mosaics, most of which are now in Naples' Museo Archeologico Nazionale (p657). Valuable on-site survivors include a beautiful, geometrically patterned marble floor.

➡ **Casa del Poeta Tragico**

(House of the Tragic Poet) Hidden behind scaffolding when we visited, the Casa del Poeta Tragico features the world's first known 'beware of the dog' (*cave canem*) warnings.

➡ **Casa dei Vettii**

The Casa dei Vettii is home to a famous depiction of Priapus with his gigantic phallus balanced on a pair of scales...much to the anxiety of many a male observer.

Villa dei Misteri ARCHAEOLOGICAL SITE

This recently restored, 90-room villa is one of the most complete structures left standing in Pompeii. The dionysiac frieze, the most important fresco still on site, spans the walls of the large dining room. One of the biggest and most arresting paintings from the ancient world, it depicts the initiation of a bride-to-be into the cult of Dionysus, the Greek god of wine.

A farm for much of its life, the villa's *vino*-making area is still visible at the northern end.

Follow Via Consolare out of the town through Porta Ercolano. Continue past Villa di Diomede, turn right, and you'll come to Villa dei Misteri.

🛏 Sleeping & Eating

The ruins are best visited on a day trip from Naples, Sorrento or Salerno; once the excavations close for the day, the area around the site becomes decidedly seedy. Most of the restaurants near the ruins are characterless affairs set up for feeding busloads of tourists. Down in the modern town are a few decent restaurants serving excellent local food.

If you'd rather eat at the ruins, the on-site cafeteria peddles the standard choice of *panini*, pizza slices, salads, hot meals and gelato.

★ **President**   CAMPANIAN €€

(☑081 850 72 45; www.ristorantepresident.it; Piazza Schettini 12; meals €35; ⏱noon-4pm & 7pm-midnight, closed Mon Oct-Apr; 🚆FS to Pompei, 🚆Circumvesuviana to Pompei Scavi-Villa dei Misteri) With its dripping chandeliers and gracious service, the Michelin-starred President feels like a private dining room in an Audrey Hepburn film. At the helm is charming owner-chef Paolo Gramaglia, whose passion for local produce, history and culinary creativity translates into bread made to ancient Roman recipes, slow-cooked snapper paired with tomato puree and sweet-onion gelato, and deconstructed *pastiera* (sweet Neapolitan tart).

❶ Information

Tourist Office (☑081 850 72 55; Via Sacra 1; ⏱8.30am-3.30pm Mon-Fri) Located in the centre of the modern town.

❶ Getting There & Away

To reach the ruins by Circumvesuviana train from either Naples (€3.20, 36 minutes) or Sorrento (€2.80, 30 minutes), alight at Pompeii-Scavi-Villa dei Misteri station, located beside the main entrance at Porta Marina.

Busvia del Vesuvio (p686) shuttle buses to Vesuvius depart from outside the Pompei-Scavi-Villa dei Misteri train station.

To get here by car, take the A3 from Naples. Use the Pompeii exit and follow signs to Pompeii Scavi. Car parks (approximately €5 per hour) are clearly marked and vigorously touted.

Sorrento

POP 16,500

On paper, cliff-straddling Sorrento is a place to avoid – a package-holiday centre with few must-see sights and no beach to speak of. In reality, it's a strangely appealing place, its laid-back southern Italian charm resisting all attempts to swamp it in graceless development.

Dating to Greek times and known to Romans as Surrentum, it's ideally situated for exploring the surrounding area: to the west the best of the peninsula's unspoiled countryside and, beyond that, the Amalfi Coast; to the north, Pompeii and the archaeological sites; offshore, the fabled island of Capri.

According to Greek legend, it was in Sorrento's waters that the mythical sirens once lived. Sailors of antiquity were powerless to resist the beautiful song of these charming maidens-cum-monsters, who would lure them and their ships to their doom. Homer's Ulysses escaped by having his oarsmen plug their ears with wax and by strapping himself to his ship's mast as he sailed past.

🅞 Sights

Museo Correale   MUSEUM

(☑081 878 18 46; www.museocorreale.it; Via Correale 50; admission €7; ⏱9.30am-6.30pm Tue-Sat, to 1.30pm Sun) East of the city centre, this museum is well worth a visit, whether you're a clock collector, an archaeological egghead or into embroidery. In addition to the rich assortment of 17th- to 19th-century Neapolitan art and crafts, there are Japanese, Chinese and European ceramics, clocks, furniture and, on the ground floor, Greek and Roman artefacts.

Chiesa di San Francesco   CHURCH

(Via San Francesco; ⏱8am-1pm & 2-8pm) Located next to the Villa Comunale Park, this is one of Sorrento's most beautiful churches. Surrounded by bougainvillea and birdsong, the evocative cloisters have an Arabic portico and interlaced arches supported by octagonal pillars. The church is most famous, however, for its summer program of concerts featuring world-class performers from the classical school. If this strikes a chord, check out the schedule at the tourist office. There are also regular art exhibitions.

Museo Bottega della Tarsia Lignea   MUSEUM

(☑081 877 19 42; www.museomuta.it; Via San Nicola 28; adult/reduced €8/5; ⏱10am-6.30pm

Sorrento

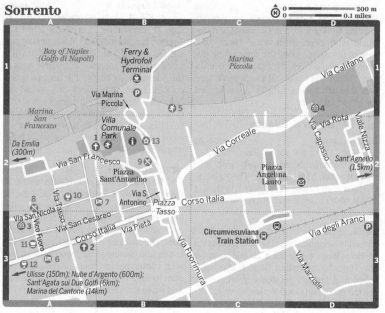

Apr-Oct, to 5pm Nov-Mar) Since the 18th century, Sorrento has been famous for its *intarsio* furniture, made with elaborately designed inlaid wood. Some wonderful examples can be found in this museum, housed in an 18th-century palace, complete with beautiful frescoes. There's also an interesting collection of paintings, prints and photographs depicting the town and surrounding area in the 19th century.

Duomo CATHEDRAL
(Corso Italia; ⊙ 8am-12.30pm & 4.30-9pm) To get a feel for Sorrento's history, stroll down Via Pietà from Piazza Tasso and past two medieval palaces en route to the cathedral, with its striking exterior fresco, triple-tiered bell tower, four classical columns and elegant majolica clock. Take note of the striking marble bishop's throne (1573) and the beautiful wooden choir stalls decorated in the local *intarsio* style.

🏃 Activities

★ Sic Sic BOATING
(☑ 081 807 22 83; www.nauticasicsic.com; Marina Piccola; ⊙ May-Oct) Seek out the best beaches by rented boat, with or without a skipper. This outfit rents a variety of motor boats, starting at around €40 per hour or €100 per day. It also organises boat excursions, wedding shoots and similar.

Bagni Regina Giovanna SWIMMING

Sorrento lacks a decent beach, so consider heading to Bagni Regina Giovanna, a rocky beach with clear, clean water about 2km west of town, set among the ruins of the Roman Villa Pollio Felix. It's possible to walk here (follow Via Capo), although you'll save your strength if you get the SITA bus headed for Massa Lubrense.

Festivals & Events

Sant'Antonino RELIGIOUS

(⊙14 Feb) The city's patron saint, Sant'Antonino, is remembered annually with processions and huge markets. The saint is credited with having saved Sorrento during WWII when Salerno and Naples were heavily bombed.

Settimana Santa RELIGIOUS

Famed throughout Italy; the first procession of Holy Week takes place at midnight on the Thursday preceding Good Friday, with robed and hooded penitents in white; the second occurs on Good Friday, when participants wear black robes and hoods to commemorate the death of Christ.

Sleeping

Most accommodation is in the town centre or clustered along Via Capo, the coastal road west of the centre. Be sure to book early for the summer season.

Ulisse HOSTEL €

(☑ 081 877 47 53; www.ulissedeluxe.com; Via del Mare 22; dm €30, d €60-120; P ❄ 🛜) Although it calls itself a hostel, the Ulisse is about as far from a backpackers' pad as a hiking boot from a stiletto. Most rooms are plush, spacious affairs with swish if rather bland fabrics, gleaming floors and large en suite bathrooms. There are two single-sex dorms, and quads for sharers. Breakfast is included in some rates but costs €10 with others.

Casa Astarita B&B €

(☑ 081 877 49 06; www.casastarita.com; Corso Italia 67; d €90-130, tr €110-150; ❄ 🛜) Housed in a 16th-century *palazzo* on Sorrento's main strip, this charming B&B has a colourful, eclectic look with original vaulted ceilings, brightly painted doors and majolica-tiled floors. Its six simple but well-equipped rooms surround a central parlour, where breakfast is served on a large rustic table.

Nube d'Argento CAMPGROUND €

(☑ 081 878 13 44; www.nubedargento.com; Via Capo 21; camping per 2 people, car & tent €38, 2-person bungalows €60-85, 4-person bungalows €90-120; ⊙Mar-Dec; @ ❄ 🏠) This inviting campground is an easy 1km drive west of the Sorrento city centre. Pitches and wooden chalet-style bungalows are spread out beneath a canopy of olive trees – a source of much-needed summer shade – and the facilities are excellent. Kids in particular will enjoy the open-air swimming pool, table-tennis table, slides and swings.

★**Hotel Cristina** HOTEL €€

(☑ 081 878 35 62; www.hotelcristinasorrento.it; Via Privata Rubinacci 6, Sant'Agnello; s €130, d €150, tr €180, q €200; ⊙Mar-Oct; ❄ 🛜 ❄) Located high above Sant'Agnello, this hotel has superb views, particularly from the swimming pool. The spacious rooms have sea-view balconies and combine inlaid wooden furniture with contemporary flourishes like Philippe Starck chairs. There's an in-house restaurant and a free shuttle bus to/from Sorrento's Circumvesuviana train station.

La Tonnarella HOTEL €€

(☑ 081 878 11 53; www.latonnarella.com; Via Capo 31; d €120-140, ste €240-350; ⊙Apr-Oct & Christmas; P ❄ @ 🛜) A splendid choice – but not for minimalists – La Tonnarella is a dazzling canvas of majolica tiles, antiques, chandeliers and statues. Rooms, most with their own balcony or small terrace, continue the sumptuous classical theme with traditional furniture and discreet mod cons. The hotel also has its own private beach, accessible by lift, and a highly regarded terrace restaurant.

Hotel Astoria HOTEL €€

(☑ 081 807 40 30; www.hotelastoriasorrento.com; Via Santa Maria delle Grazie 24; s €50-110, €70-170; ❄ 🛜) This renovated classic has the advantage of being located in the heart of the *centro storico*. Overall, it's an excellent choice. The interior sparkles with colourful glossy tiles and blue and buttercup-yellow paintwork. The large enclosed back terrace is a delight, with seats set under orange and lemon trees and colourful tiled murals lining the back wall.

Eating

A local speciality to look out for is *gnocchi alla sorrentina* (gnocchi baked in tomato sauce with mozzarella).

★ **Da Emilia** TRATTORIA €
(☑ 081 807 27 20; Via Marina Grande 62; meals €20; ⊙ noon-2.30pm & 7pm-midnight; 🖼) Founded in 1947 and still run by the same family, this is a homely yet atmospheric joint overlooking the fishing boats in Marina Grande. There's a large informal dining room, complete with youthful photos of former patron Sophia Loren, a scruffily romantic terrace and a menu of straightforward, no-fail dishes such as mussels with lemon.

Inn Bufalito ITALIAN €€
(☑ 081 365 69 75; www.innbufalito.it; Vico Fuoro 21; meals €25; ⊙ 11am-midnight; 🖼🖼) 🎵 Owner Franco Coppola (no relation to the movie man) exudes a real passion for showcasing local produce – the restaurant is a member of the Slow Food Movement. A mozzarella bar as well as a restaurant, this effortlessly stylish place boasts a menu including delights such as Sorrento-style cheese fondue and buffalo-meat *carpaccio*.

Ristorante il Buco ITALIAN €€€
(☑ 081 878 23 54; www.ilbucoristorante.it; Rampa Marina Piccola 5; meals €60; ⊙ 12.30-2.30pm & 7.30-11pm Thu-Tue Feb-Dec) Housed in a former monks' wine cellar, this dress-up restaurant offers far-from-monastic cuisine. The emphasis is on innovative regional cooking, so expect modern combos such as pasta with rockfish sauce, or *treccia* (local cheese) and prawns served on capers with tomato and olive sauce. In summer there's outdoor seating near one of the city's ancient gates. Reservations recommended.

🍷 **Drinking & Nightlife**

Cafè Latino CAFE, BAR
(☑ 081 878 37 18; Vico Fuoro 4a; ⊙ 10am-1am summer) Think locked-eyes-over-cocktails time. This is the place to impress your date with cocktails (from €7) on the terrace, surrounded by orange and lemon trees. Sip a Mary Pickford (rum, pineapple, *grenadino* and maraschino) or a glass of chilled white wine. If you can't drag yourselves away, you can also eat here (meals around €30).

Bollicine WINE BAR
(☑ 081 878 46 16; Via Accademia 9; ⊙ 7.30pm-2am) The wine list at this unpretentious bar with a dark, woody interior includes all the big Italian names and a selection of interesting local labels. If you can't decide what to go for, the amiable bar staff will advise you.

There's also a small menu of *panini*, bruschettas and one or two pasta dishes.

English Inn PUB
(☑ 081 807 43 57; www.englishinn.it; Corso Italia 55; ⊙ 9am-2am) The vast upstairs garden terrace, with its orange trees and dazzle of bougainvillea, is a delight and attracts a mainly expat crowd, who head here for the disco beats and karaoke nights, accompanied by Guinness on tap. The party atmosphere continues late into the night, while the bacon-and-eggs breakfast is a suitable reviver.

☆ **Entertainment**

Teatro Tasso THEATRE
(☑ 081 807 55 25; www.teatrotasso.it; Piazza Sant'Antonino; incl a cocktail €25; ⊙ Sorrento Musical 9.30pm summer) The southern-Italian equivalent of a London old-time music hall, Teatro Tasso is home to the *Sorrento Musical*, a sentimental 75-minute revue of Neapolitan classics such as 'O Sole Mio' and 'Trona a Sorrent'.

ℹ **Information**

Main Tourist Office (☑ 081 807 40 33; www.sorrentotourism.com; Via Luigi de Maio 35; ⊙ 8.30am-8pm Mon-Sat, 9am-1pm Sun Jul-Sep) In the Circolo dei Forestieri (Foreigners' Club). Ask for the useful publication *Surrentum*.

Post Office (Corso Italia 210)

ℹ **Getting There & Away**

BOAT

Sorrento is the main jumping-off point for Capri and also has good ferry connections to Naples, Ischia and Amalfi coastal towns. All ferries and hydrofoils depart from the port at Marina Piccola, where you buy your tickets.

Caremar (p672) Runs ferries to Capri (€14.70, 25 minutes, 4 daily).

Alilauro (p672) Runs up to five daily hydrofoils between Naples and Sorrento (€12.30, 40 minutes).

BUS

Curreri (☑ 081 801 54 20; www.curreriviaggi.it) Runs eight daily services to Sorrento from Naples Capodichino airport (75 minutes). Buses depart from outside the arrivals hall and arrive in Piazza Angelina Lauro. Buy tickets (€10) on board.

SITA Sud (p697) Buses serve Naples, the Amalfi Coast and Sant'Agata, leaving from the bus stop across from the entrance of the Circumvesuviana train station. Buy tickets at the station bar or from shops bearing the SITA sign.

TRAIN

Sorrento is the last stop on the Circumvesuviana (p672) train line from Naples. Trains run every half-hour for Naples (one hour 10 minutes; €4.50), via Pompeii (30 minutes; €2.80) and Ercolano (50 minutes; €3.40).

❶ Getting Around

Local bus lines B and C run to/from the port at Marina Piccola (€1).

For a **taxi**, call ☑ 081 878 22 04 or ☑ 081 877 24 84.

West of Sorrento

The countryside west of Sorrento is the very essence of southern Italy. Tortuous roads wind their way through hills covered in olive trees and lemon groves, passing through sleepy villages and tiny fishing ports. There are magnificent views at every turn, the best being from Sant'Agata sui Due Golfi and the high points overlooking Punta Campanella, the westernmost point of the Sorrento Peninsula.

Sant'Agata sui Due Golfi

Perched high in the hills above Sorrento, sleepy Sant'Agata sui due Golfi commands spectacular views of the Bay of Naples on one side and the Bay of Salerno on the other (hence its name, Saint Agatha on the Two Gulfs). The best viewpoint is the **Convento del Deserto** (☑ 081 878 01 99; Via Deserto; ⊙ gardens 8am-7pm, lookout 10am-noon & 5-7pm summer, 10am-noon & 3-5pm winter), a Carmelite convent 1.5km uphill from the village centre.

Agriturismo La Tore (☑ 081 808 06 37; www.letore.com; Via Pontone 43; s €60-70, d €90-130, dinner €25-35; ⊙ Easter-early Nov; P@🗺🎝) is a wonderful organic farm with seven barnlike rooms that sleep six. In the winter, a self-contained apartment is also available. A short drive (or a long walk) from the village, the rustic farmhouse hidden among fruit trees and olive groves has a lovely setting. Conveniently, the owners can also organise a shuttle-bus pick-up from Naples' Capodichino airport or Stazione Centrale.

From Sorrento, there's a pretty 3km (approximately one hour) trail up to Sant'Agata. SITA Sud buses leave roughly every hour to two hours from the Circumvesuviana train station.

Marina del Cantone

From Sorrento, follow the coastal road round to **Termini**. Stop a moment to admire the views before continuing on to **Nerano**, from where a beautiful hiking trail leads down to the stunning **Bay of Ieranto**, one of the coast's top swimming spots, and the tranquil, unassuming village of **Marina del Cantone**.

◉ Sights & Activities

A popular diving destination, the protected waters here are part of an 11-sq-km marine reserve called the **Punta Campanella**, its underwater grottoes lush with flora and fauna.

Nettuno Diving   DIVING
(☑ 081 808 10 51; www.sorrentodiving.com; Via Vespucci 39; 🖝) Dive the depths of this marine reserve with a PADI-certified outfit that runs underwater activities for all ages and abilities. These include snorkelling excursions, beginner's courses, cave dives and immersions off Capri and the Li Galli islands. Costs start at €25 (children €15) for a day-long outing to the Baia di Ieranto. It can also organise reasonably priced accommodation.

🛏 Sleeping & Eating

Villaggio Residence
Nettuno   CAMPGROUND, APARTMENT €
(☑ 081 808 10 51; www.villaggionettuno.it; Via A Vespucci 39; camping per 2 people, tent & car €41, bungalows €130-185, apt €190; ⊙ Mar-early Nov; P🌼@🗺🎝) Marina's campground, in the terraced olive groves by the entrance to the village, offers an array of accommodation options, including campsites, mobile homes and (best of all) apartments in a 16th-century tower for two to five people. It's a friendly, environmentally sound place with excellent facilities and a comprehensive list of activities.

Lo Scoglio   ITALIAN €€€
(☑ 081 808 10 26; www.hotelloscoglio.com; Piazza delle Sirene 15, Massa Lubrense; meals €60; ⊙ 12.30-5pm & 7.30-11pm) The only marina restaurant directly accessible from the sea, Lo Scoglio is a favourite of visiting celebs. The food is top notch (and priced accordingly). Although you can eat *fettucine al bolognese* and steak here, you'd be sorry to miss the superb seafood. Options include a €30 antipasto of raw seafood and *spaghetti al riccio* (spaghetti with sea urchins).

ℹ Getting There & Around

SITA Sud (p697) runs regular buses between Sorrento and Marina del Cantone from the Circumvesuviana train station in Sorrento.

AMALFI COAST

Stretching about 50km along the southern side of the Sorrento Peninsula, the Amalfi Coast (Costiera Amalfitana) is one of Europe's most breathtaking. Cliffs terraced with scented lemon groves sheer down into sparkling seas; sherbet-hued villas cling precariously to unforgiving slopes while sea and sky merge in one vast blue horizon.

Yet its stunning topography has not always been a blessing. For centuries after the passing of Amalfi's glory days as a maritime superpower (from the 9th to the 12th centuries), the area was poor and its isolated villages were regular victims of foreign incursions, earthquakes and landslides. But it was this very isolation that first drew visitors in the early 1900s, paving the way for the advent of tourism in the latter half of the century. Today the Amalfi Coast is one of Italy's premier tourist destinations, a favourite of cashed-up jet-setters and love-struck couples.

The best time to visit is in late spring or early autumn. In summer the coast's single road (SS163) gets very busy and prices are inflated; in winter much of the coast simply shuts down.

ℹ Getting There & Away

BOAT

Boat services to the Amalfi Coast towns are generally limited to the summer tourist season, from April/May to October. In July and August, it's a good idea to book tickets in advance, especially if travelling between the Amalfi Coast and Capri.

BUS

SITA Sud (☑ 089 40 51 45; www.sitasud trasporti.it) operates a frequent, year-round service along the SS163 between Sorrento and Amalfi via Positano, and from Amalfi to Salerno.

CAR & MOTORCYCLE

If driving from the north, exit the A3 autostrada at Vietri sul Mare and follow the SS163 along the coast. From the south, leave the A3 at Salerno and head for Vietri sul Mare and the SS163.

TRAIN

From Naples you can take either the Circumvesuviana to Sorrento or a Trenitalia train to Salerno, then continue along the Amalfi Coast, eastwards or westwards, by SITA Sud bus.

Positano

POP 3900

The pearl in the pack, Positano is the coast's most photogenic and expensive town. Its steeply stacked houses are a medley of peaches, pinks and terracottas, and its near-vertical streets (many of which are, in fact, staircases) are lined with vogueish shop displays, jewellery stalls, elegant hotels and smart restaurants. Look closely, though, and you'll find reassuring signs of everyday reality – crumbling stucco, streaked paintwork and even, on occasion, a faint whiff of drains.

An early visitor, John Steinbeck, wrote in May 1953 in *Harper's Bazaar*: 'Positano bites deep. It is a dream place that isn't quite real when you are there and becomes beckoningly real after you have gone.' More than 60 years on, his words still ring true.

◎ Sights

Chiesa di Santa Maria Assunta CHURCH
(Piazza Flavio Gioia; ◷ 8am-noon & 4-9pm) This church, with its colourful majolica-tiled dome, is the most famous and, let's face it, pretty much the only sight in Positano. If you are visiting at a weekend you will probably have the added perk of seeing a wedding; it's one of the most popular churches in the area for exchanging vows.

Step inside to see a delightful classical interior, with pillars topped with gilded Ionic capitals and winged cherubs peeking from above every arch.

Above the main altar is a 13th-century Byzantine Black Madonna and Child. During restoration works of the square and the crypt, a Roman villa was discovered; still under excavation, it is closed to the public.

🏃 Activities

Although Spiaggia Grande is no one's dream beach, with greyish sand covered by legions of brightly coloured umbrellas, the water's clean and the setting is striking. Hiring a chair and umbrella in the fenced-off areas costs around €20 per person per day, but the crowded public areas are free.

Positano

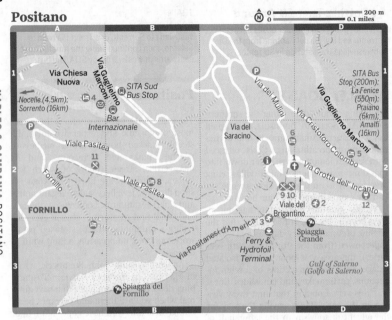

Positano

★ **Blue Star**   BOATING
(☑ 089 81 18 88; www.bluestarpositano.it; Spiaggia
Grande; ⊗ 8.30am-9pm) Operating out of a kiosk on Spiaggia Grande, Blue Star hires out
small motorboats for €60 per hour (€200
for four hours). Consider heading for the archipelago of Li Galli, the four small islands
where, according to Homer, the sirens lived.
The company also organises popular and
fun yacht excursions to Capri and the Grotta
dello Smeraldo (€60).

L'Uomo e il Mare   BOATING
(☑ 089 81 16 13; www.gennaroesalvatore.it;
⊗ 9am-8pm) An Italian-English couple offers
a range of tours, including Capri and Amalfi day trips (from €55), out of a kiosk near

the ferry terminal. They also run a romantic sunset cruise to Li Galli, complete with
champagne (€30).

🛏 Sleeping

Positano is a glorious place to stay, but be
aware that prices are, overall, high. Like
everywhere on the Amalfi Coast it gets very
busy in summer, so book ahead, particularly
on weekends and in July and August. Ask at
the tourist office about rooms or apartments
in private houses.

Villa Nettuno   HOTEL €
(☑ 089 87 54 01; www.villanettunopositano.it; Viale
Pasitea 208; s/d €70/85; ⊗ year-round) Hidden
behind a barrage of perfumed foliage, Vil-

la Nettuno oozes charm. Go for one of the original rooms in the 300-year-old part of the building with heavy rustic decor and a communal terrace. Rooms in the renovated part of the villa lack the same character.

Hostel Brikette   HOSTEL €
(☑089 87 58 57; www.hostel-positano.com; Via Marconi 358; dm €24-50, d €65-145, apt €80-220; ☺year-round; ✳☎) The Brikette is a bright, cheerful place with wonderful views and a range of sleeping options, from dorms to doubles and apartments. Conveniently, it also offers a daily hostelling option that allows day trippers use of the hostel's facilities, including showers, wi-fi and left luggage, for €10. Breakfast isn't included.

Pensione Maria Luisa   PENSION €
(☑089 87 50 23; www.pensionemarialuisa.com; Via Fornillo 42; d €70-80, with sea view €95; ☺Mar-Oct; @☎) The Maria Luisa is a friendly old-school *pensione*. Rooms feature shiny blue tiles and simple, no-frills decor; those with private balconies are well worth the extra €15 for the bay views. If you can't bag a room with a view, there's a small communal terrace offering the same sensational vistas. Breakfast is an additional €5.

La Fenice   B&B €€
(☑089 87 55 13; www.lafenicepositano.com; Via Guglielmo Marconi 4; d €140; ☺Easter-Oct; ⛱) With hand-painted Vietri tiles, white walls and high ceilings, the rooms here are simple but stylish; most have their own balcony or terrace. The views are stunning, but it feels very homely and not super posh. As with everywhere in Positano, you'll need to be good at stomping up and down steps to stay here.

Hotel California   HOTEL €€
(☑089 87 53 82; www.hotelcaliforniapositano.it; Via Cristoforo Colombo 141; d €160-195; ☺Easter-Oct; Ⓟ✳☎) Ignore the incongruous name: this Hotel California is housed in a grand 18th-century palace, its facade washed in soothing pinks and yellows. The rooms in the older part of the house are magnificent, with original ceiling friezes; new rooms are spacious and luxuriously decorated. Breakfast is served on a glorious and leafy front terrace.

★Hotel Palazzo Murat   HOTEL €€€
(☑089 87 51 77; www.palazzomurat.it; Via dei Mulini 23; d €180-270; ☺May–mid-Jan; ✳@☎) Hidden behind an ancient wall from the tourists who surge along its pedestrian thoroughfare daily, this magnificent hotel occupies the 18th-century *palazzo* that the one-time king of Naples used as his summer residence. Rooms – five (more expensive) in the original part of the building, 25 in the newer section – are decorated with sumptuous antiques, original oil paintings and glossy marble.

WALK THE COAST

Rising steeply from the coast, the densely wooded Lattari mountains provide some stunning walking opportunities. An extraordinary network of paths traverses the craggy, precipitous peaks, climbing to remote farmhouses through wild and beautiful valleys. It's tough going, though – long ascents up seemingly endless flights of steps are almost unavoidable.

The best-known walk, the 12km Sentiero degli Dei (Path of the Gods; three to six hours), follows the steep, often rocky paths linking Positano to Praiano. Marked by red-and-white stripes daubed on rocks and trees, it's a spectacular, mountain-top trail punctuated by caves, dizzying terraces and deep valleys framed by the brilliant blue of the sea. The walk starts in the centre of Praiano, where the tourist office can provide maps and guidance. Just downhill and on the same side is Alimentari Rispoli, where you can buy bread, cheeses, meat, drinks and fruit for the hike (tip: bring a pen knife as sandwiches aren't made on site). Also, don't forget to bring plenty of water and comfortable walking shoes for the journey.

Hiking maps can be downloaded at www.amalficoastweb.com. Another reliable regional hiking map is the CAI (Club Alpino Italiano; Italian Alpine Club) *Monti Lattari, Penisola Sorrentina, Costiera Amalfitana: Carta dei Sentieri* (€9) at 1:30,000. If you prefer a guided hike, there are a number of reliable local guides including American **Frank Carpegna** (www.positanofrankcarpegna.com), a longtime resident here, and **Zia Lucy** (www.zialucy.it).

Eating

Most restaurants, bars and trattorias, many of which are unashamedly touristy, close over winter, making a brief reappearance for Christmas and New Year.

La Brezza
CAFE €

(☑089 87 58 11; www.labrezzapositano.it; Via Regina Giovanna 2; snacks around €6; ☺9am-1am; 🛜) With a steely grey-and-white interior, free internet and wi-fi, and a terrace with views over the sea and quay, this is the best beachfront place for *panini* or snacks. There are regular art exhibitions and a daily 'happy hour' (6pm to 8pm), with drinks accompanied by complimentary light eats.

★ Donna Rosa
ITALIAN €€

(☑089 81 18 06; www.drpositano.com; Via Montepertuso 97-99, Montepertuso; meals from €40; ☺noon-2.30pm & 7-11.30pm Mon, Tue & Thu-Sun Apr-Dec, closed lunch Aug) This is one of the Amalfi Coast's most reputable restaurants, located in mountainside Montepertuso, above Positano. Once a humble trattoria and now run by Rosa's daughter Raffaella, the lineage is set to continue with Raffaella's daughter Erika, who studied with Jamie Oliver in London. The celebrity chef dined here on his honeymoon and declared it one of his favourite restaurants.

Next2
RISTORANTE €€

(☑089 812 35 16; www.next2.it; Viale Pasitea 242; meals €45; ☺6.30-11.30pm) Understated elegance meets creative cuisine at this contemporary set-up. Local and organic ingredients are put to impressive use in beautifully presented dishes such as ravioli stuffed with aubergine, and prawns and sea bass with tomatoes and lemon-scented peas. Desserts are wickedly delicious, and the alfresco sea-facing terrace is summer perfection.

La Cambusa
SEAFOOD €€

(☑089 81 20 51; www.lacambusapositano.com; Piazza A Vespucci 4; meals €40; ☺noon-midnight Mar-Nov) This restaurant, run by amiable Luigi, is on the front line, which, given the number of cash-rich tourists in these parts, could equal high prices for less than average food. Happily, that is not the case here. The locals still rate La Cambusa as a top place for seafood. Go for simple spaghetti with clams, oven-baked sea bass or splash out with the Mediterranean lobster. There is a good selection of side dishes, like roasted artichokes, and the position is Positano at its best.

Drinking & Nightlife

Generally speaking, Positano's nightlife is genteel, sophisticated and safe.

Music on the Rocks
CLUB

(☑089 87 58 74; www.musicontherocks.it; Via Grotte dell'Incanto 51; cover €10-30; ☺10pm-late) This is one of the town's few genuine nightspots and one of the best clubs on the coast. Music on the Rocks is dramatically carved into the tower at the eastern end of Spiaggia Grande. Join the flirty, good-looking crowd and some of the region's top DJs spinning mainstream house and reliable disco.

ℹ Information

Post Office (Via Marconi 318)

Tourist Office (☑089 87 50 67; Via del Saracino 4; ☺9am-7pm Mon-Sat, to 2pm Sun summer, 9am-4pm Mon-Sat winter) Can provide lots of information; expect to pay for walking maps and similar.

RESOURCES

Positano (www.positano.com) Information on sights, activities, accommodation, transport and more in Positano and along the Amalfi Coast.

ℹ Getting There & Away

BOAT

Positano has excellent ferry connections to the coastal towns and Capri from April to October.

Alicost (☑089 87 14 83; www.alicost.it) Operates three daily services to Amalfi (€8, 20 minutes), with one continuing to Salerno (€12, 75 minutes). It also runs one daily service to Capri (€19.20, 50 minutes) and two daily services to Sorrento (€16, 40 minutes).

TraVelMar (☑089 87 29 50; www.travelmar.it) Runs six daily ferries to Amalfi (€8, 25 minutes) and Salerno (€12, 70 minutes).

Lucibello (☑089 87 50 32; www.lucibello.it) Operates three daily services to Capri (€18.50, 50 minutes).

NLG (☑081 552 07 63; www.navlib.it) Sails once daily service to Capri (€19.20, 30 minutes).

BUS

SITA Sud (p697) runs frequent buses to/from Amalfi (€2.50, 40 to 50 minutes) and Sorrento (€2.50, one hour). Buses drop you off at one of two main bus stops: arriving from Sorrento and the west, opposite Bar Internazionale; arriving from Amalfi and the east, at the top of Via Cristoforo Colombo. To get into town from the former, follow Viale Pasitea; from the latter (a far shorter route), take Via Cristoforo Colombo. When departing, buy bus tickets at Bar Internazionale or, if headed east, from the *tabaccheria* (tobacconist) at the bottom of Via Colombo.

ⓘ Getting Around

Getting around Positano is largely a matter of walking. If your knees can handle it, there are dozens of narrow alleys and stairways that make walking relatively easy and joyously traffic-free.

Otherwise, **Flavio Gioia** (☑ 089 81 18 95; www.flaviogioia.com; Via Cristoforo Colombo 49) local buses follow the lower ring road every half-hour. Stops are clearly marked and you can buy your ticket (€1.20) on board. The Flavio Gioia buses pass by both SITA bus stops. There are also around 14 daily buses up to Montepertuso and Nocelle.

Praiano & Furore

An ancient fishing village, **Praiano** has one of the coast's most popular beaches, Marina di Praia. From the SS163 (next to the Hotel Continental), take the steep path that leads down the side of the cliffs to a tiny inlet with a small stretch of coarse sand and deep-blue water.

Respected local dive outfit **Centro Sub Costiera Amalfitana** (☑ 089 81 21 48; www.centrosub.it; Via Marina di Praia; dives from €80; 🐟) runs lessons for adults and children over eight, as well as night dives and full diving days exploring the area's coral, marine life and grottoes.

Stunningly set on a cliffside overlooking Marina di Praia, **Hotel Onda Verde** (☑ 089 87 41 43; www.hotelondaverde.com; Via Terramare 3, Praiano; d €110-230; ⊗ Apr-Nov; ❋ 🖤) is a sound slumber option, its rooms a smart, soothing combo of satin bedheads, elegant Florentine-style furniture and majolica-tiled floors. The restaurant also comes highly recommended.

A few kilometres further on, **Marina di Furore** sits at the bottom of what's known as the fjord of Furore, a giant cleft that cuts through the Lattari mountains. The main village, however, stands 300m above, in the upper Vallone del Furore. A one-horse place that sees few tourists, it breathes a distinctly rural air despite the colourful murals and unlikely modern sculpture.

To get to upper Furore by car follow the SS163 and then the SS366 signposted to Agerola; from Positano, it's 15km. Otherwise, regular SITA Sud buses depart from the bus terminus in Amalfi (€1.60, 25 minutes, at least three daily).

Amalfi

POP 5430

Believe it or not, pretty little Amalfi, with its sun-filled piazzas and small beach, was once a maritime superpower with a population of more than 70,000. For one thing, it's not a big place – you can easily walk from one end to the other in about 20 minutes. For another, there are very few historical buildings of note. The explanation is chilling – most of the old city, and its populace, simply slid into the sea during an earthquake in 1343.

Just around the headland, neighbouring Atrani is a picturesque tangle of whitewashed alleys and arches centred on a lively, lived-in piazza and popular beach.

◉ Sights

★**Cattedrale di Sant'Andrea** CATHEDRAL
(☑ 089 87 10 59; Piazza del Duomo; ⊗ 7.30am-7.45pm) A melange of architectural styles, Amalfi's cathedral, one of the few relics of the town's past as an 11th-century maritime superpower, makes a striking impression at the top of its sweeping flight of stairs. Between 10am and 5pm entrance is through the adjacent **Chiostro del Paradiso** (☑ 089 87 13 24; Piazza del Duomo; adult/reduced €3/1; ⊗ 9am-7pm), a 13th-century cloister.

The cathedral dates in part from the early 10th century and its stripey facade has been rebuilt twice, most recently at the end of the 19th century. Although the building is a hybrid, the Sicilian Arabic-Norman style predominates, particularly in the two-tone masonry and the 13th-century bell tower. The huge bronze doors also merit a look; first of their type in Italy, they were commissioned by a local noble and made in Syria before being shipped to Amalfi. Less impressive is the baroque interior, although the altar features some fine statues and there are some interesting 12th- and 13th-century mosaics.

Museo della Carta MUSEUM
(☑ 089 830 45 61; www.museodellacarta.it; Via delle Cartiere 23; admission €4; ⊗ 10am-6.30pm daily Mar-Oct, 10am-3.30pm Tue, Wed & Fri-Sun Nov-Feb) Amalfi's paper museum is housed in a rugged, cave-like 13th-century paper mill (the oldest in Europe). It lovingly preserves the original paper presses, which are still in full working order, as you'll see during the 15-minute guided tour (in English), which explains the original cotton-based paper

---

NOCELLE

A world apart from self-conscious Positano, the tiny, left-alone mountain village of Nocelle (450m) affords some of the most spectacular views on the entire coast. A stop on the Sentiero degli Dei hiking route, it's a sleepy, silent place where not much ever happens, much to the delight of its very few residents. If you can't pull yourself away, consider checking in at **Villa della Quercia** (☑ 089 812 34 97; www.villadellaquercia.com; Via Nocelle 5; r €70-80; ☺ Apr-Oct; ☎), a former monastery with a heavenly panorama. If peckish, tuck into delicious, regional dishes at **Trattoria Santa Croce** (www.ristorantesantacrocepositano.com; Via Nocelle 19; ☺ noon-2.30pm & 7-11pm Apr-Oct), a reliable low-key nosh spot in the main part of the village.

The easiest way to get to Nocelle is by local bus from Positano (€1.20, 30 minutes, 14 daily). If you're driving, follow the signs from Positano. Hikers tackling the Sentiero degli Dei might want to stop off as they pass through.

---

production and the later wood-pulp manufacturing. Afterwards you may well be inspired to pick up some of the stationery sold in the gift shop, alongside calligraphy sets and paper pressed with flowers.

Grotta dello Smeraldo   CAVE
(admission €5; ☺ 9.30am-4pm) Four kilometres west of Amalfi, this grotto is named after the eerie emerald colour that emanates from the water. Stalactites hang down from the 24m-high ceiling, while stalagmites grow up to 10m tall. Buses regularly pass the car park above the cave entrance (from where you take a lift or stairs down to the rowing boats). Alternatively, **Coop Sant'Andrea** (☑ 089 87 29 50; www.coopsantandrea.com; Lungomare dei Cavalieri 1) runs boats from Amalfi (€10 return, plus cave admission). Allow 1½ hours for the return trip.

🏃 Activities

Amalfi Marine   BOATING
(☑ 329 2149811; www.amalfiboats.it; Spiaggia del Porto, Lungomare dei Cavalieri) Run by American local resident Rebecca Brooks, Amalfi Marine hires out boats (without a skipper

from €250 per day, per boat; maximum six passengers). It also organises day-long excursions along the coast and to the islands (from €45 per person).

🎉 Festivals & Events

Every 24 December and 6 January, divers from all over Italy make a pilgrimage to the ceramic *presepe* (nativity scene) submerged in the Grotta dello Smeraldo.

The **Regatta of the Four Ancient Maritime Republics**, which rotates between Amalfi, Venice, Pisa and Genoa, is held on the first Sunday in June. Amalfi's turn comes round again in 2017.

🛏 Sleeping

Albergo Sant'Andrea   HOTEL €
(☑ 089 87 11 45; www.albergosantandrea.it; Via Duca Mansone l; s/d €60/90; ☺ Mar-Oct; ☀☎) Enjoy the atmosphere of busy Piazza del Duomo from the comfort of your own room. This modest two-star has basic rooms with brightly coloured tiles and coordinating fabrics. Double glazing has helped cut down the piazza hubbub, which can reach fever pitch in high season – this is one place to ask for a room with a (cathedral) view.

Residenza del Duca   HOTEL €€
(☑ 089 873 63 65; www.residencedelduca.it; Via Duca Mastalo II 3; s €70, d €130; ☺ Mar-Oct; ☀) This family-run hotel has just six rooms, all of them light, sunny, and prettily furnished with antiques, majolica tiles and the odd chintzy cherub. The jacuzzi showers are excellent. Call ahead if you are carrying heavy bags, as it's a seriously puff-you-out-climb up some steps to reach here and a luggage service is included in the price. Room 2 is a particular winner, with its French windows and stunning views.

Hotel Lidomare   HOTEL €€
(☑ 089 87 13 32; www.lidomare.it; Largo Duchi Piccolomini 9; s/d €65/145; ☺ year-round; ☀☎) Family run, this old-fashioned hotel has real character. The large, luminous rooms have an air of gentility, with their appealingly haphazard decor, vintage tiles and fine antiques. Some have jacuzzi bathtubs, others have sea views and a balcony, some have both. Rather unusually, breakfast is laid out on top of a grand piano.

Hotel Centrale   HOTEL €€
(☑ 089 87 26 08; www.amalfihotelcentrale.it; Largo Duchi Piccolomini 1; d €100-120; ☺ Easter-Oct;

🔊) This is one of the best-value hotels
malfi. The entrance is on a tiny little pi-
, in the *centro storico,* but many of the
ll but tastefully decorated rooms over-
Piazza del Duomo. The aquamarine
mic tiling lends it a vibrant, fresh look
the views from the rooftop terrace are
nificent.

lotel Luna Convento HOTEL €€€
89 87 10 02; www.lunahotel.it; Via Pantaleone
ite 33; s €250-300, d €270-320, ste €460-620;
ster-Oct; P ❄ @ 🔊 ☕) This former con-
: was founded by St Francis in 1222 and
been a hotel for some 170 years. Rooms
he original building are in the former
iks' cells, but there's nothing poky about
bright tiles, balconies and seamless sea
vs. The newer wing is equally beguiling,
religious frescoes over the bed. The
stered courtyard is magnificent.

Eating

?ansa CAFE €
89 87 10 65; www.pasticceriapansa.it; Piaz-
el Duomo 40; cornetti & pastries from €1.50;
am-10pm Wed-Mon) A marbled and mir-
d 1830 cafe on Piazza del Duomo where
k-bow-tied waiters serve a great Italian
ikfast: freshly made *cornetti* and deli-
isly frothy cappuccino.

•atro TRATTORIA €€
89 87 24 73; Via E Marini 19; meals €25;
.30am-3pm & 6.30-11pm, closed Wed; 🖐)
•erb no-fuss trattoria tucked away in
atmospheric backstreets of the *centro*
ico (Via E Marini is reached via Salita
;i Orafi). Seafood specialities include *pe-
spada il teatro* (swordfish in a tomato,
er and olive-oil sauce), plus there are
d vegetarian options, including *scialat-
: al teatro* (pasta with tomatoes and
ergines).

Arcate ITALIAN €€
89 87 13 67; www.learcate.net; Largo Orlan-
Buonocore, Atrani; pizzas from €6, meals €25;
2.30-3pm & 7.30-11.30pm Tue-Sun Sep-Jun, dai-
l & Aug) On a sunny day, it's hard to beat
dreamy location: at the far eastern point
he harbour overlooking the beach, with
ini's ancient rooftops and church tower
ind you. Huge white parasols shade the
awl of tables, while the dining room is a
ie-walled natural cave. Pizzas are served
ight; daytime fare includes risotto with
'ood and grilled swordfish.

The food is good, but it's a step down
from the setting.

⭐**Marina Grande** SEAFOOD €€€
(📋 089 87 11 29; www.ristorantemarinagrande.com;
Viale Delle Regioni 4; tasting menu lunch/dinner
€25/60, meals €45; ⊘ noon-3pm & 6.30-11pm Tue-
Sun Mar-Oct) 🍴 Run by the third generation
of the same family, this beachfront restaurant serves fish so fresh it's almost flapping.
It prides itself on its use of locally sourced
organic produce, which, in Amalfi, means
high-quality seafood.

🛈 Information

Post Office (Corso delle Repubbliche Marinare
31) Next door to the tourist office.
Tourist Office (📋 089 87 11 07; www.amalfi
touristoffice.it; Corso delle Repubbliche
Marinare 33; ⊘ 9am-1pm & 2-6pm Mon-Sat)

🛈 Getting There & Away

BOAT

Between April and October there are daily sailings to/from Amalfi.

Alicost (p700) Operates three daily services to
Positano (€8, 20 minutes), with two stopping in
Capri (€20.80, 80 minutes) and Sorrento (€17,
60 minutes).

TraVelMar (p700) Runs ferries to Positano
(€8, 25 minutes, seven daily), Minori (€3, 10
minutes, six daily), Maiori (€3, 15 minutes,
six daily) and Salerno (€8, 35 minutes, seven
daily).

NLG (p700) Sails once daily service to Positano (€8, 15 minutes) and Capri (€21.30, 80
minutes).

BUS

SITA Sud (p697) runs frequent daily services
from Piazza Flavio Gioia to Sorrento (€3.40, 100
minutes) via Positano (€2.20, 50 minutes), as
well as to Ravello (€1.60, 25 minutes) and Salerno (€2.80, 1¼ hours). Buy tickets and check
current schedules at Bar Il Giardino delle Palme,
opposite the bus stop.

Ravello

POP 2500

Sitting high in the hills above Amalfi, refined
Ravello is a polished town almost entirely
dedicated to tourism. Boasting impeccable
bohemian credentials (Wagner, DH Lawrence and Virginia Woolf all lounged here),
it's today known for its ravishing gardens
and stupendous views, the best in the world
according to former resident Gore Vidal.

Most people visit on a day trip from Amalfi – a nerve-tingling 7km drive up the Valle del Dragone – although to best enjoy Ravello's romantic other-worldly atmosphere you'll need to stay overnight.

The **tourist office** (☑ 089 85 70 96; www. ravellotime.it; Via Roma 18; ⊙ 9am-7pm) has information on the town and its walking trails.

◉ Sights & Activities

Cathedral
CATHEDRAL

(Piazza Duomo; museum €3; ⊙ 8.30am-noon & 5.30-8.30pm) Forming the eastern flank of Piazza Duomo, the cathedral was built in 1086 but has since undergone various makeovers. The facade is 16th century, but the central bronze door, one of only about two dozen in the country, dates from 1179; the interior is a late-20th-century interpretation of what the original must once have looked like.

Of particular interest is the striking pulpit, supported by six twisting columns set on marble lions and decorated with flamboyant mosaics of peacocks and other birds. Note also how the floor is tilted towards the square – a deliberate measure to enhance the perspective effect. Entry is via the cathedral museum.

★ Villa Rufolo
GARDENS

(☑ 089 85 76 21; www.villarufolo.it; Piazza Duomo; adult/reduced €5/3; ⊙ 9am-5pm) To the south of Ravello's cathedral, a 14th-century tower marks the entrance to this villa, famed for its beautiful cascading gardens. Created by a Scotsman, Scott Neville Reid, in 1853, they are truly magnificent, commanding divine panoramic views packed with exotic colours, artistically crumbling towers and luxurious blooms. Note that the gardens are at their best from May till October; they don't merit the entrance fee outside those times.

The villa was built in the 13th century for the wealthy Rufolo dynasty and was home to several popes as well as king Robert of Anjou. Wagner was so inspired by the gardens when he visited in 1880 that he modelled the garden of Klingsor (the setting for the second act of the opera *Parsifal*) on them. Today the gardens are used to stage concerts during the town's classical-music festival.

Villa Cimbrone
GARDENS

(☑ 089 85 80 72; www.villacimbrone.com; Via Santa Chiara 26; adult/reduced €7/4; ⊙ 9am-7.30pm summer, to sunset winter) Some 600m south of Piazza Duomo, the Villa Cimbrone is worth a wander, if not for the 11th-century villa itself (now an upmarket hotel), then for the fabulous views from the delightful gardens. They're best admired from the Belvedere of Infinity, an awe-inspiring terrace lined with classical-style statues and busts.

★✦ Festivals & Events

★ Ravello Festival
PERFORMING ARTS

(☑ 089 85 83 60; www.ravellofestival.com; ⊙ Jun-Sep) Between late June and early September, the Ravello Festival – established in 1953 – turns much of the town centre into a stage. Events range from orchestral concerts and chamber music to ballet performances; film screenings and exhibitions are held in atmospheric outdoor venues, most notably the famous overhanging terrace in the Villa Rufolo gardens.

⌊▦ Sleeping

Agriturismo Monte Brusara
AGRITURISMO €

(☑ 089 85 74 67; www.montebrusara.com; Via Monte Brusara 32; s/d €45/90; ⊙ year-round) An authentic working farm, this mountainside *agriturismo* is located a tough half-hour walk of about 1.5km from Ravello's centre (call ahead to arrange to be picked up). It is especially suited to families – children can feed the pony while you sit back and admire the views – or to those who simply want to escape the crowds. The three rooms are comfy but basic, the food is fabulous and the owner is a charming, garrulous host. Half-board is also available.

Hotel Villa Amore
PENSION €€

(☑ 089 85 71 35; www.villaamore.it; Via dei Fusco 5; s/d €65/120; ⊙ May-Oct; @) This welcoming family-run *pensione* is the best choice in town by price. Tucked down a quiet lane, it has modest, homey rooms and sparkling bathrooms. All rooms have a balcony and some have bathtubs. The restaurant is a further plus, its terrace boasting (still more) fabulous views: the food's good and prices are reasonable (around €25 for a meal).

★ Hotel Caruso
HOTEL €€€

(☑ 089 85 88 01; www.hotelcaruso.com; Piazza San Giovanni del Toro 2; s €575-720, d €757-976; ⊙ Apr-Nov; P ✷ 🖨 🖀) There can be no better place to swim than the Caruso's sensational infinity pool. Seemingly set on the edge of a precipice, its blue waters merge with sea and sky to magical effect. Inside, the sublimely restored 11th-century *palazzo* is no less impressive, with Moorish arches doubling as window frames, 15th-century vaulted ceilings and high-class ceramics.

Eating

Babel CAFE €€
(✏ 089 85 86 215; Via Trinità 13; meals €20; ⊙ 11am-11pm) A cool little white-painted deli-cafe serving high-quality, affordable salads, bruschetta, cheese and meat boards and an excellent range of local wines. There's a jazz soundtrack, and a little gallery selling unusually stylish ceramic tiles.

Da Salvatore ITALIAN €€
(✏ 089 85 72 27; www.salvatoreravello.com; Via della Republicca 2; meals €28; ⊙ noon-3pm & 7.30-10pm Tue-Sun) Located just before the bus stop, Da Salvatore has nothing special by way of decor, but the view, from both the dining room and the large terrace, is very special indeed. Dishes include creative options like tender squid on a bed of pureed chickpeas with spicy *peperoncino*.

In the evening, part of the restaurant is transformed into an informal pizzeria, serving some of the best wood-fired pizza you will taste anywhere this side of Naples.

❶ Getting There & Away

SITA Sud (p697) operates regular daily buses from Piazza Flavio Gioia in Amalfi (€1.60, 25 minutes).

By car, turn north about 2km east of Amalfi. Vehicles are not permitted in Ravello's pedestrianised town centre and the metered parking around it is costly: €5 an hour and only payable by credit card.

South of Amalfi

From Amalfi to Salerno

The 26km drive to Salerno, though less exciting than the 16km stretch westwards to Positano, is exhilarating and dotted with a series of small towns, each with their own character and each worth a brief look.

Three and a half kilometres east of Amalfi, or a steep 1km-long walk down from Ravello, **Minori** is a small workaday town, popular with holidaying Italians. If you're a sweet tooth, pit stop at **Gambardella** (✏ 089 87 72 99; www.gambardella.it; Piazza Cantilena 7; pastries from €1.50), a *pasticceria* (pastry shop) peddling exemplary treats, including *torta di ricotta e pera* (ricotta and pear tart).

Further along, **Maiori** is the coast's biggest resort, a brassy place full of large seafront hotels, restaurants and beach clubs.

Just beyond **Erchie** and its beautiful beach, **Cetara** is a picturesque tumbledown fishing village with a reputation as a gastronomic highlight. Tuna and anchovies are the local specialities, appearing in various guises at **Al Convento** (✏ 089 26 10 39; www.alconvento.net; Piazza San Francesco 16; meals €25; ⊙ 12.30-3pm & 7-11pm summer, closed Wed winter), a sterling seafood restaurant near the small harbour. Particularly delicious is the spaghetti served with anchovies and wild fennel.

Shortly before Salerno, the road passes through **Vietri sul Mare**, the ceramics capital of Campania. Pop into **Ceramica Artistica Solimene** (✏ 089 21 02 43; www.ceramicasolimene.it; Via Madonna degli Angeli 7; ⊙ 9am-7pm Mon-Fri, 10am-1pm & 4-7pm Sat), a vast ceramics factory outlet with an extraordinary glass-and-ceramic facade by Italian architect Paoli Soleri, a former student of American architect Frank Lloyd Wright.

Salerno

POP 139,000

Upstaged by the glut of postcard-pretty towns along the Amalfi Coast, Campania's second-largest city is actually a pleasant surprise. A decade of civic determination has turned this major port and transport hub into one of southern Italy's most liveable cities, and its small but buzzing *centro storico* is a vibrant mix of medieval churches, tasty trattorias and good-spirited, bar-hopping locals.

Originally an Etruscan and later a Roman colony, Salerno flourished with the arrival of the Normans in the 11th century. Robert Guiscard made it the capital of his dukedom in 1076 and, under his patronage, the Scuola Medica Salernitana was renowned as one of medieval Europe's greatest medical institutes. More recently, it was left in tatters by the heavy fighting that followed the 1943 landings of the American 5th Army, just south of the city.

◉ Sights

★ **Duomo** CATHEDRAL
(Piazza Alfano; ⊙ 9am-6pm Mon-Sat, 4-6pm Sun) You can't miss the looming presence of Salerno's impressive cathedral, widely considered to be the most beautiful medieval church in Italy. Built by the Normans in the

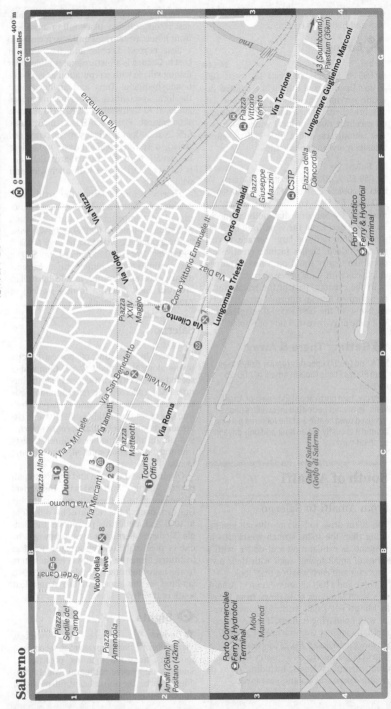

Salerno

0 ⓝ
0 ———— 400 m
0 ———— 0.2 miles

Via Dalmazia

Via Nizza

Via Velia

Piazza Alfano

Duomo 1 🏛

Piazza Sedile del Campo

Piazza Amendola

Via del Canali

5 🏨

Via S Michele

Via Mercanti

Via Duomo

Vicolo della Neve

8 🍴

3 🏛
2 🏛

Piazza Matteotti

Tourist Office ℹ

Via Iannelli

Via San Benedetto

6 🍴

Via Velia

Piazza XXIV Maggio

Via Volpe

Corso Vittorio Emanuele II

4 🏛
7 🍴
Via Cilento

Ⓜ

Via Roma

Via Diaz

Lungomare Trieste

Corso Garibaldi

Piazza Giuseppe Mazzini

🅒 CSTP

Piazza Vittorio Veneto
🏛

Via Torrione

Piazza della Concordia

Lungomare Guglielmo Marconi

A3 (Southbound);
Paestum (36km)

Porto Turistico
Ferry & Hydrofoil
Terminal

Gulf of Salerno
(Golfo di Salerno)

Porto Commerciale
Ferry & Hydrofoil
Terminal

Molo Manfredi

Amalfi (26km);
Positano (42km)

Irno

alerno

century and later aesthetically remod-
d in the 18th century, it sustained severe
nage in a 1980 earthquake. It is dedicated
an Matteo (St Matthew), whose remains
e reputedly brought to the city in 954
now lie beneath the main altar in the
lted crypt.

ake special note of the magnificent
n entrance, the 12th-century **Porta dei
ni**, named after the marble lions at the
of the stairway. It leads through to a
utiful, harmonious courtyard, surround-
oy graceful arches and overlooked by a
-century bell tower. Carry on through
huge bronze doors (similarly guarded
ions), which were cast in Constantinople
he 11th century. When you come to the
e-aisled interior, you will see that it is
ely baroque, with only a few traces of the
final church. These include parts of the
usept and choir floor and the two raised
oits in front of the choir stalls. Through-
the church you can see extraordinarily
uiled and colourful 13th-century mosaic
k.

n the right-hand apse, don't miss the
pella delle Crociate (Chapel of the
sades), containing stunning frescoes and
e wonderful mosaics. It was so named
ause crusaders' weapons were blessed
e. Under the altar stands the tomb of
-century pope Gregory VII.

tello di Arechi   CASTLE
089 296 40 15; www.ilcastellodiarechi.it; Via
edetto Croce; adult/reduced €5/2.50; ⊙9am-
Tue-Sat, to 6.30pm Sun summer, to 5pm
Sun winter) Hop on bus 19 from Piazza
V Maggio to visit Salerno's most famous

landmark, the forbidding Castello di Arechi,
dramatically positioned 263m above the city.
Originally a Byzantine fort, it was built by
the Lombard duke of Benevento, Arechi II,
in the 8th century and subsequently modified by the Normans and Aragonese, most
recently in the 16th century.

The views of the Gulf of Salerno and the
city rooftops are spectacular; you can also
visit a permanent collection of ceramics,
arms and coins. If you are here during summer, ask the tourist office for a schedule of
the annual series of concerts staged here.

Museo Virtuale della Scuola
Medica Salernitana   MUSEUM
(☑089 257 61 26; www.museovirtualescuola
medicasalernitana.beniculturali.it; Via Mercanti
74; adult/reduced €3/1; ⊙9.30am-1pm Tue-Wed,
9.30am-1pm & 5-8pm Thu-Sat, 10am-1pm Sun; ⊡)
Slap bang in Salerno's historic centre, this
engaging museum deploys 3D and touch-
screen technology to explore the teachings
and wince-inducing procedures of Salerno's
once-famous, now-defunct medical institute. Established around the 9th century,
the school was the most important centre
of medical knowledge in medieval Europe,
reaching the height of its prestige in the
11th century. It was closed in the early 19th
century.

Museo Pinacoteca Provinciale   MUSEUM
(☑089 258 30 73; www.museibiblioteche.
provincia.salerno.it; Via Mercanti 63; adult/reduced
€3/1.50; ⊙9am-7.45pm Tue-Sun) **FREE** Art enthusiasts should seek out the Museo Pinacoteca Provinciale, located deep in the heart of
the historic quarter. Spread throughout six
galleries, the museum houses a collection
dating from the Renaissance right up to the
first half of the 20th century.

🛏 Sleeping

Ostello Ave Gratia Plena   HOSTEL €
(☑089 23 47 76; www.ostellodisalerno.it; Via dei
Canali; dm/s/d €16/45/65; ⊙year-round; @ 🖎)
Housed in a 16th-century convent, Salerno's
excellent HI hostel is right in the heart of
the *centro storico*. Inside there's a charming central courtyard and a range of bright
rooms, from dorms to great bargain doubles
with private bathroom. The 2am curfew is
for dorms only.

Hotel Montestella   HOTEL €€
(☑089 22 51 22; www.hotelmontestella.it; Corso Vittorio Emanuele II 156; s/d/tr €75/100/110;

year-round; ✳@🛜) Within walking distance of just about anywhere worth going to, the Montestella is on Salerno's main pedestrian thoroughfare, halfway between the *centro storico* and train station. The rooms are spacious and comfortable, with blue carpeting and patterned wallpaper, while the public spaces have a fresh, modern look. It's one of the best midrange options in town.

✕ Eating

★ Vicolo della Neve ITALIAN €
(📞089 22 57 05; www.vicolodellaneve.it; Vicolo della Neve 24; meals €20; ⏱7-11.30pm Thu-Tue) A city institution on a scruffy street, this is the archetypal *centro storico* trattoria, with brick arches, fake frescoes and walls hung with works by local artists. The menu is, similarly, unwaveringly authentic, with pizzas and *calzones, peperoni ripieni* (stuffed peppers) and a top-notch *parmigiana di melanzane* (baked aubergine). It can get incredibly busy: book well in advance.

Pizza Margherita ITALIAN €
(📞089 22 88 80; Corso Garibaldi 201; pizzas/buffet from €5/6.50, lunch menu €8.50; ⏱12.30-3.30pm & 7.30pm-midnight; 👶) It looks like a bland, modern canteen, but this is, in fact, one of Salerno's most popular lunch spots. Locals regularly queue for the lavish lunchtime buffet that, on any given day, might include buffalo mozzarella, salami, mussels in various guises and a range of salads.

If that doesn't appeal, the daily lunch menu (pasta, main course, salad and half a litre of bottled water) is chalked up on a blackboard, or there's the regular menu of pizzas, pastas, salads and main courses.

La Cantina del Feudo ITALIAN €€
(📞089 25 46 96; Via Velia 45; meals €28; ⏱noon-2pm & 7-11pm Tue-Sun; 🍴) Frequented by locals in the know, this restaurant is tucked up a side street off the pedestrian *corso*. The menu changes daily, but the emphasis is on vegetable dishes like white beans with chicory, noodles and turnip tops, and ravioli stuffed with cheese. The interior has a rural trattoria feel and there's a terrace for alfresco dining.

ℹ Information

Post Office (Corso Garibaldi 203)
Tourist Office (📞089 23 14 32; Lungomare Trieste 7; ⏱9am-1pm & 3-7pm Mon-Sat) Has limited information.

ℹ Getting There & Away

BOAT

Between April and October there are daily sailings to/from Salerno.
Caremar (Map p662; 📞02 577 65 871; www.caremar.it) Runs a daily hydrofoil to/from Capri (€18.30, 50 minutes).
Alicost (p700) Runs several daily hydrofoils to/from Capri (€21, 50 minutes), Amalfi (€8, 20 minutes) and Positano (€12, 30 minutes).
Departures are from the Porto Turistico, 200m down the pier from Piazza della Concordia. You can buy tickets from the booths by the embarkation point.

Departures for Capri leave from Molo Manfredi at the Porto Commerciale.

BUS

SITA Sud (p697) Buses for Amalfi (€2.80, 1¼ hours, at least hourly) depart from Piazza Vittorio Veneto, beside the train station, stopping en route at Vietri sul Mare, Cetara, Maiori and Minori. Tickets are available inside the train station.
CSTP (📞089 48 70 01; www.cstp.it) Bus 50 runs from Piazza Vittorio Veneto to Pompeii (€2.80, 70 minutes, 15 daily). For Paestum take bus 34 from the CSTP bus stop on Piazza della Concordia (€3.40, one hour and 20 minutes, 12 daily).

CAR & MOTORCYCLE

Salerno is on the A3 between Naples and Reggio di Calabria; the A3 is toll-free from Salerno south. If you want to hire a car, there's a **Europcar** (📞089 258 07 75; www.europcar.com; Via Clemente Mauro 18) agency between the train station and Piazza della Concordia.

TRAIN

Salerno is a major stop on southbound routes to Calabria, and the Ionian and Adriatic Coasts. From the station in Piazza Vittorio Veneto there are regular trains to Naples (€9, 35 minutes, half-hourly) and Rome (Intercity, from €21, three hours, hourly).

ℹ Getting Around

Walking is the most sensible option; from the train station it's a 1.2km walk along Corso Vittorio Emanuele II to the historic centre.

Paestum

Paestum, or Poseidonia as the city was originally called (in honour of Poseidon, the Greek god of the sea), was founded in the 6th century BC by Greek settlers and fell under Roman control in 273 BC. It became an important trading port and remained so until the fall of the Roman Empire, when periodic outbreaks of malaria and savage Saracen raids led its weakened citizens to abandon the town.

Its ancient temples are utterly unmissable, not to mention an easy day trip from Salerno or Agropoli. For more information on Paestum and the Costiera Cilentana, drop into the local **tourist office** (✆0828 81 10 16; www.infopaestum.it; Via Magna Crecia 887; ✆9am-1.30pm & 2.30-7pm Mon-Sat).

◉ Sights

Paestum's Temples   ARCHAEOLOGICAL SITE
(✆0828 81 10 23; incl museum adult/reduced €10/5; ✆8.45am-7.45pm, last entry 7pm Jun & Jul, as early as 3.35pm Nov) A Unesco World Heritage Site, these temples are among the best-preserved monuments of Magna Graecia, the Greek colony that once covered much of southern Italy. Rediscovered in the late 18th century, the site as a whole wasn't unearthed until the 1950s. Lacking the tourist mobs that can sully better-known archaeological sites, the place has a wonderful serenity. Take sandwiches and prepare to stay at least three hours. In spring the temples are particularly stunning, surrounded by scarlet poppies.

Buy your tickets in the museum, just east of the site, before entering from the main entrance on the northern end. The first structure is the 6th-century-BC **Tempio di Cerere** (Temple of Ceres); originally dedicated to Athena, it served as a Christian church in medieval times.

As you head south, you can pick out the basic outline of the large rectangular forum, the heart of the ancient city. Among the partially standing buildings are the vast domestic housing area and, further south, the amphitheatre; both provide evocative glimpses of daily life here in Roman times. In the former houses you'll see mosaic floors, and a marble *impluvium* that stood in the atrium and collected rainwater.

The **Tempio di Nettuno** (Temple of Neptune), dating from about 450 BC, is the largest and best preserved of the three temples at Paestum; only parts of its inside walls and roof are missing. Almost next door, the so-called basilica (in fact, a temple to the goddess Hera) is Paestum's oldest surviving monument. Dating from the middle of the 6th century BC, it's a magnificent sight, with nine columns across and

18 along the sides. Ask someone to take your photo next to one of the columns: it's a good way to appreciate the scale.

Save time for the **museum** (✆0828 81 10 23; ✆8.30am-7.30pm, last entry 6.45pm, closed 1st & 3rd Mon of month), which covers two floors and houses a collection of fascinating, if weathered, metopes (bas-relief friezes). This collection includes 33 of the original 36 metopes from the Tempio di Argiva Hera (Temple of Argive Hera), situated 9km north of Paestum, of which virtually nothing else remains. The star exhibit is the 5th-century-BC fresco Tomba del Truffatore (Tomb of the Diver), thought to represent the passage from life to death with its frescoed depiction of a diver in mid-air. The fresco was discovered in 1968 inside the lid of the tomb of a young man, alongside his drinking cup and oil flasks, which he would perhaps have used to oil himself for wrestling matches. Rare for the period in that it shows a human form, the fresco expresses pure delight in physicalilty, its freshness and grace eternally arresting. Below the diver, a symposium of men repose languidly on low couches and brandish drinking cups.

🍴 Sleeping & Eating

⭐**Casale Giancesare**   B&B **€**
(✆333 1897737, 0828 72 80 61; www.casale-gianc esare.it; Via Giancesare 8; s €65-120, d €65-120, apt per week €600-1300; ✆year-round; ⓟ❄@ 🛜🏊) A 19th-century former farmhouse, this elegantly decorated stone-clad B&B is run by the delightful Voza family, who will happily ply you with their homemade wine and *limoncello*. It's located 2.5km from the glories of Paestum and surrounded by vineyards and olive and mulberry trees; views are stunning, particularly from the swimming pool.

Nonna Sceppa   ITALIAN **€€**
(✆0828 85 10 64; Via Laura 53; meals €35; ✆12.30-3pm & 7.30-11pm Fri-Wed; 🛗) Seek out the superbly prepared, robust dishes at Nonna Sceppa, a family-friendly restaurant that's gaining a reputation throughout the region for excellence. Dishes are firmly seasonal and, during summer, concentrate on fresh seafood like the refreshingly simple grilled fish with lemon. Other popular choices include risotto with zucchini and artichokes, and spaghetti with lobster.

❶ Getting There & Away

The best way to get to Paestum by public transport is to take **CSTP** (☑ 089 48 70 01; www.cstp.it) bus 34 from Piazza della Concordia in Salerno.

Regular trains link Salerno with Paestum (€2.70, 32 minutes). From Paestum station, walk straight ahead through the stone arch and up via Porta Sirena; it's a pleasant 10-minute walk.

If you're driving, you could take the A3 from Salerno and exit for the SS18 at Battipaglia. More pleasant is the Litoranea, the minor road that hugs the coast. From the A3 take the earlier exit for Pontecagnano and follow the signs for Agropoli and Paestum.

COSTIERA CILENTANA

Southeast of the Gulf of Salerno, the coastal plains begin to give way to wilder, jagged cliffs and unspoilt scenery, a taste of what lies further on in the stark hills of Basilicata and the wooded peaks of Calabria. Inland, dark mountains loom over the remote highlands of the Parco Nazionale del Cilento e Vallo di Diano, one of Campania's best-kept secrets.

Several destinations on the Cilento coast are served by the main rail route from Naples to Reggio di Calabria. Check Trenitalia (p956) for fares and times.

By car take the SS18, which connects Agropoli with Velia via the inland route, or the SS267, which hugs the coast.

Agropoli

POP 20,700

Located just south of Paestum, Agropoli is a busy summer resort, but otherwise a pleasant, tranquil town that makes a good base for exploring the Cilento coastline and park. While the shell is a fairly faceless grid of shop-lined streets, the kernel, the historic city centre, is a fascinating tangle of narrow cobbled streets with ancient churches, venerable residents and a castle with superb views.

◉ Sights

Il Castello   CASTLE
(◉ 10am-8pm) **FREE** Built by the Byzantines in the 5th century, the castle was strengthened during the Angevin period, the time of the Vespro War bloodbath. It continued to be modified, and only part of the original defensive wall remains. It's an enjoyable walk here through the historic centre, and you can wander the ramparts and enjoy magnificent views of the coastline and town.

🛏 Sleeping & Eating

Anna   B&B, APARTMENT €
(☑ 0974 82 37 63; www.bbanna.it; Via S Marco 28-30, Agropoli; d €75-90; ☯ year-round; P 🌐) A great location, across from the town's sweeping sandy beach, this trim budget choice is known locally for its restaurant, where you can salivate over homemade morning *cornetti*. The rooms are large and plain with small balconies; specify a sea view to enjoy the sun setting over Sorrento. Sunbeds and bicycles can be hired for a minimal price.

Anna   PIZZA €
(☑ 0974 82 37 63; www.ristorantepizzeriaanna.it; Lungomare San Marco 32; meals from €15, pizzas from €4; ☯ 11am-midnight) At the city-centre end of the promenade, this has been a locals' favourite for decades. Family run, with a small B&B upstairs, Anna is best known for its pizzas, especially since a British broadsheet named Anna's *sorpresa* the best pizza in Italy in 2010, its seven-slice selection including mussels, aubergines, zucchini, marinated pork, ham, prawns and spicy sausage.

❶ Getting There & Away

CSTP (☑ 089 48 70 01; www.cstp.it) operates several buses daily to Agropoli from Salerno (€3.90, 75 to 80 minutes) and Paestum (€2.20, 20 minutes). If driving from Paestum, head south along the SS18.

Parco Nazionale del Cilento e Vallo di Diano

Stretching from the coast up to Campania's highest peak, Monte Cervati (1900m), and beyond to the regional border with Basilicata, the Parco Nazionale del Cilento e Vallo di Diano is Italy's second-largest national park. A little-explored area of barren heights and empty valleys, it's the perfect antidote to the holiday mayhem on the coast.

For further information stop by the tourist office (p709) in Paestum. For guided hiking opportunities, contact **Gruppo Escursionistico Trekking** (☑ 0975 7 25 86; www.getvallodidiano.it; Via Provinciale 29, Silla di Sassano) or **Associazione Trekking Cilento** (☑ 0974 84 33 45; www.trekkingcilento.it; Via Cannetiello 6, Agropoli).

Sights & Activities

★ Grotte di Castelcivita   CAVE

(☑ 0828 77 23 97; www.grottedicastelcivita.com; Piazzale N Zonzi, Castelcivita; adult/reduced €10/8; ⊙ standard tours 10.30am, noon, 1.30pm & 3pm Mar-Oct, plus 4.30pm & 6pm Apr-Sep; P ♿) The grottoes are fascinating otherworldly caves that date from prehistoric times: excavations have revealed that they were inhabited 42,000 years ago, making them the oldest known settlement in Europe. Take a jacket, and leave the high heels at home, as paths are wet and slippery. Hard hats, and a certain level of fitness and mobility, are required. Located 40km southeast of Salerno, the complex is refreshingly non-commercial.

Although it extends over 4800m, only around half of the complex is open to the public. The one-hour tour winds around extraordinary stalagmites and stalactites, and a mesmerising play of colours, caused by algae, calcium and iron that tint the naturally sculpted rock shapes. The tour culminates in a cavernous lunar landscape – think California's Death Valley in miniature – called the Caverna di Bertarelli (Bertarelli Cavern). The caves are still inhabited – by bats – so no flash photos for fear of blinding them.

Grotte di Pertosa   CAVE

(☑ 0975 39 70 37; www.grottedipertosa-auletta. it; Pertosa; guided visits adult/reduced 100min €20/15, 75min €16/13, 60min €13/10; ⊙ 9am-7pm Apr & May, 10am-7pm Jun-Aug, 10am-6pm Sep, reduced hours rest of year; P ♿) (Re)discovered in 1932, the Grotte di Pertosa date back 35 million years. Used by the Greeks and Romans as places of worship, the caves burrow for some 2500m, with long underground passages and lofty grottoes filled with stalagmites and stalactites. The first part of the tour takes part as a boat (or raft) ride on the river; you disembark just before the waterfall (phew!) and continue on foot for around 800m, surrounded by marvellous rock formations and luminous crystal accretions.

Certosa di San Lorenzo   MONASTERY

(☑ 0975 77 74 45; Padula; adult/reduced €4/2; ⊙ 9am-7pm Wed-Mon) One of the largest monasteries in southern Europe, the Certosa di San Lorenzo dates from 1306 and covers 250,000 sq metres. Numerologists can swoon at the following: 320 rooms and halls, 2500m of corridors, galleries and hallways, 300 columns, 500 doors, 550 windows, 13 courtyards, 100 fireplaces, 52 stairways and 41 fountains – in other words, it is *huge*.

You won't have time to see everything, be sure to visit the highlights, including the vast central courtyard (a venue for summer classical-music concerts), the magnificent wood-panelled library, frescoed chapels, and the kitchen with its grandiose fireplace and famous tale: apparently this is where the legendary 1000-egg omelette was made in 1534 for Charles V. Unfortunately, the historic frying pan is not on view!

Within the monastery you can also peruse the modest collection of ancient artefacts at the **Museo Archeologico Provinciale della Lucania Occidentale** (☑ 0975 7 71 17; ⊙ 8am-1.15pm & 2-3pm Tue-Sat, 9am-1pm Sun) FREE.

🍴 Sleeping & Eating

★ Agriturismo i Moresani   AGRITURISMO €

(☑ 0974 90 20 86; www.imoresani.com; Località Moresani; d €90-110; ⊙ Mar-Oct; ❄ 🛜 🏊) If you are seeking utter tranquility, head to this *agriturismo* 1.5km west of Casal Velino. The setting is bucolic: rolling hills in every direction, interspersed with grapevines, grazing pastures and olive trees. Family run, the 18-hectare farm produces its own *caprino* goat's cheese, wine, olive oil and preserves. Rooms have cream- and earth-coloured decor and surround a pretty private garden.

Trattoria degli Ulivi   ITALIAN €

(☑ 334 2595091; www.tavolacaldadegliulivi.it; Viale Certosa, Padula; menus from €12; ⊙ Sun-Sat 11am-4pm) If you've worked up an appetite walking the endless corridors of the Certoza de San Lorenzo then this restaurant – located just 50m to the west – is the place to come. The decor is canteen-like, but the daily specials are affordable, tasty and generously proportioned. It serves snacks as well as four-course blow-out lunches.

Vecchia Pizzeria Margaret   PIZZA €

(☑ 0975 33 00 00; Via Luigi Curto, Pollo; pizza from €3) Fabulous wheels of pizza, cooked in a wood-fired oven; it also dishes up antipasti and pasta dishes. Service is fast and friendly, and prices are low. You'll find the restaurant just east of the river, near the hospital.

ℹ Getting There & Away

Public transport in the area is lacking and inconvenient. To get the best out of the park and the surrounding region, you will need a car. Car rental companies include Europcar (p708) in Salerno and **Alba Rent Car** (☑ 0974 82 80 99; Via A De Gasperi 82; per day from €50) in Agropoli.

1. Parco Archeologico di Baia (p673), Campi Flegrei 2. Remains of a statue in Pompeii 3. Tempio di Nettuno (p709), Paestum 4. Ancient mosaic in Casa di Nettuno e Anfitrite (p685), Herculaneum

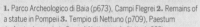

Historical Riches

Few Italian regions can match Campania's historical legacy. Colonised by the ancient Greeks and loved by the Romans, it's a sun-drenched repository of A-list antiquities, from World Heritage wonders to lesser-known archaeological gems.

Paestum

Great Greek temples never go out of vogue and those at Paestum (p708) are among the greatest outside Greece itself. With the oldest structures stretching back to the 6th century BC, this place makes Rome's Colosseum feel positively modern.

Herculaneum

A bite-sized Pompeii, Herculaneum (p684) is even better preserved than its nearby rival. This is the place to delve into the details, from once-upon-a-time shop advertisements and furniture, to vivid mosaics, even an ancient security grille.

Pompeii

Short of stepping into the Tardis, Pompeii (p686) is your best bet for a little time travel. Locked in ash for centuries, its excavated streetscapes offer a tangible, encounter with the ancients and their daily lives, from luxury homes to a racy brothel.

Subterranean Naples

Eerie aqueducts, mysterious burial crypts and ancient streetscapes: beneath Naples' hyperactive streets lies a wonderland of Graeco-Roman ruins. For a taste, head below the Complesso Monumentale di San Lorenzo Maggiore (p645) or follow the leader on a tour of the evocative Catacombe di San Gennaro.

Campi Flegrei

The Phlegraean Fields (p673) simmer with ancient clues. Roam where emperors bathed at the Parco Archeologico di Baia, sneak into a Roman engineering marvel at the Piscina Mirabilis, or spare a thought for doomed martyrs at the Anfiteatro Flavio.

Puglia, Basilicata & Calabria

Includes ➡

Why Go?

The Italian boot's heel (Puglia), instep (Basilicata) and toe (Calabria) are where you can witness the so-called Mezzogiorno (southern Italy) in all its throbbing intensity. This is a land of drying washing on weather-worn balconies, speeding scooters and dilapidated *centro storicos* (historic centres) that haven't yet qualified for a Unesco listing. Though the south's more down-to-earth cities lack the extensive tourist infrastructure of northern Italy, there's prettiness amid the grittiness.

Head to Lecce for an eye full of baroque magnificence, or soon-to-be European Capital of Culture Matera and its remarkable cave houses. Other southern secrets have yet to seep out: the intricate mosaic floor of Otranto cathedral and the Amalfi-like luminescence of Maratea have figured little in most travellers' itineraries to date. Equally underplayed is the simple yet epic *cucina povera* (peasant food) and the wild national parks (including Pollino, Italy's largest).

Best Unesco World Heritage Sites

➡ Matera (p749)

➡ Monte Sant'Angelo (p727)

➡ Castel del Monte (p724)

Best Magna Graecia Museums

➡ Museo Nazionale di Reggio Calabria (p766)

➡ Tavole Palatine (p756)

➡ Museo Nazionale Archeologico di Taranto (p747)

When to Go
Bari

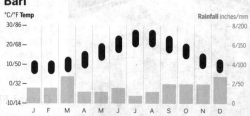

Apr–Jun Spring wildflowers are blooming: a perfect time for hiking in the mountains.

Jul & Aug Summer is beach weather and the best party time for festivals and events.

Sep & Oct No crowds, mild weather and wild mushrooms galore.

PUGLIA

Puglia is Italy's ascendant region, a place where savvy travellers bored or worn down by the crowds of Campania and Tuscany escape for something a bit less frenetic and manicured. Top of the list for prospective newcomers is the food. Puglia's *cucina povera* is about as earthy as Italian cuisine gets without eating it straight out of the soil. Then there's the exuberant architecture, best summarised by the word 'baroque' and exhibited in all its finery in the glittering 'Florence of the South', Lecce, and its smaller sibling, Gallipoli.

With the longest coastline of any region in mainland Italy, Puglia is larger than many people realise. In the north, the spur of land sticking out into the Adriatic is occupied by the balmy microclimates of the Gargano peninsula, a kind of miniature Amalfi with fewer poseurs. The Italian boot's 'stiletto' hosts the land of Salento, a dry scrubby region famous for its wines, and bloodthirsty Greek and Turkish history. In between lies the Valle d'Itria, a karstic depression populated by vastly contrasting medieval towns that have little in common apart from their haunting beauty.

Of the larger cities, Brindisi, an erstwhile Roman settlement, is one of the major departure points for Greece (by ferry), while Puglia's largest metropolis, Bari, has a university and trendier inclinations.

History

At times Puglia feels and looks Greek – and for good reason. This tangible legacy dates from when the Greeks founded a string of settlements along the Ionian coast in the 8th century BC. A form of Greek dialect (Griko) is still spoken in some towns southeast of Lecce. Historically, the major city was Taras (Taranto), settled by Spartan exiles who dominated until they were defeated by the Romans in 272 BC.

The long coastline made the region vulnerable to conquest. The Normans left their fine Romanesque churches, the Swabians their fortifications and the Spanish their flamboyant baroque buildings. No one, however, knows exactly the origins of the extraordinary 16th-century conical-roofed stone houses, the *trulli,* unique to Puglia.

Apart from invaders and pirates, malaria was long the greatest scourge of the south, forcing many towns to build away from the coast and into the hills. After Mussolini's seizure of power in 1922, the south became the frontline in his 'Battle for Wheat'. This initiative was aimed at making Italy self-sufficient when it came to food, following the sanctions imposed on the country after its conquest of Ethiopia. Puglia is now covered in wheat fields, olive groves and fruit arbours.

Bari

POP 320,200

If Lecce is the south's Florence, Bari is its Bologna, a historic but youthful town with a high percentage of students lending it a cooler and hipper edge. More urban than its neighbours Lecce and Brindisi, with grander boulevards and a more active nightlife, Bari supports a large university, a recently renovated opera house and municipal buildings that sparkle with a hint of northern grandiosity.

Some time-poor travellers skip over Bari on their way to Puglia's big-hitter, Lecce (the towns have a long-standing rivalry, especially over soccer), but Bari doesn't lack history or culture. The slower-paced old town contains the bones of St Nicholas (aka Santa Claus) in its Basilica di San Nicola, along with a strapping castle and plenty of unfussy trattorias that arguably plug the delicious local nosh – *cucina barese* – better than anywhere else in Puglia.

As the second-largest town in southern Italy, Bari is a busy port with connections to Greece, Albania and Croatia, and sports an international airport used by popular budget airlines.

ⓘ Dangers & Annoyances

Once notorious for petty crime, Bari has cleaned up its act of late. Nonetheless, take all of the usual precautions: don't leave anything in your car; don't display money or valuables; and watch out for bag-snatchers on scooters. Be particularly careful in Bari Vecchia's dark streets at night.

◉ Sights

Most sights are in or near the atmospheric old town, Bari Vecchia, a medieval labyrinth of tight alleyways and graceful piazzas. It fills a small peninsula between the new port to the west and the old port to the southeast, cramming in 40 churches and more than 120 shrines.

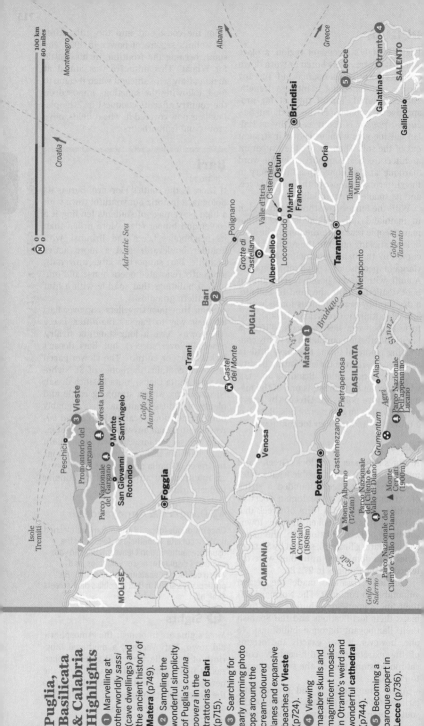

Puglia, Basilicata & Calabria Highlights

① Marvelling at otherworldly *sassi* (cave dwellings) and the ancient history of **Matera** (p749).

② Sampling the wonderful simplicity of Puglia's *cucina povera* in the trattorias of **Bari** (p715).

③ Searching for early morning photo ops around the cream-coloured lanes and expansive beaches of **Vieste** (p724).

④ Viewing macabre skulls and magnificent mosaics in Otranto's weird and wonderful **cathedral** (p744).

⑤ Becoming a baroque expert in **Lecce** (p736).

100 km
60 miles

Croatia
Montenegro
Albania
Greece

Adriatic Sea

MOLISE

Isole Tremiti

Peschici
③ Vieste
Promontorio del Gargano
Parco Nazionale del Gargano
Foresta Umbra
④ Monte Sant'Angelo
San Giovanni Rotondo
◉ **Foggia**

Golfo di Manfredonia

Trani
Castel del Monte

Venosa

CAMPANIA

Monte Cervialto (1808m)

Castelmezzano
Pietrapertosa

◉ **Potenza**
Monte Alburno (1742m)
Parco Nazionale del Cilento e Vallo di Diano
Monte Cervati (1900m)

BASILICATA

Sele
Agri
Sinni

Grumentum
Aliano
Parco Nazionale Dell'appennino Lucano

Parco Nazionale del Cilento e Vallo di Diano

Golfo di Salerno

Bari **②**
PUGLIA

Polignano
Grotte di Castellana
Alberobello
Locorotondo
Valle d'Itria
Cisternino
Ostuni
Martina Franca

Matera ①

Bradano
Basento

Metaponto

Taranto

Golfo di Taranto

Oria
◉ **Brindisi**

Tarantine Murge

⑤ Lecce
Galatina
Gallipoli
SALENTO
Otranto **④**

Ionian Sea

Tyrrhenian Sea

Crotone
Capo Colonna

Le Castella

Golfo di Squillace

San Giovanni in Fiore

Lago di Cecita o Mucone

Parco Nazionale della Sila

Camigliatello Silano

CALABRIA

Cosenza

Sibari

Parco Nazionale del Pollino

Monti di Orsomarso (1987m)

Diamante

North Tyrrhenian Coast

Paola

Tyrrhenian Coast

Ionian Coast

Pizzo

Golfo di Sant'Eufemia

Tropea

Capo Vaticano

Golfo di Gioia

South Tyrrhenian Coast

Scilla

Messina

Villa San Giovanni

7 **Reggio di Calabria**

8 Parco Nazionale dell'Aspromonte

Gerace

Locri

Tyrrhenian Sea

Aeolian Islands

SICILY

6 Hiking on sinuous paths through vibrant Mediterranean foliage up to a massive statue of Jesus in the hills above **Maratea** (p758).

7 Admiring 2500-year-old Greek statues fashioned in bronze in the **Museo Nazionale di Reggio Calabria** (p766).

8 Enjoying walking and solitude in the wilds of the mysterious **Parco Nazionale dell'Aspromonte** (p765).

Bari

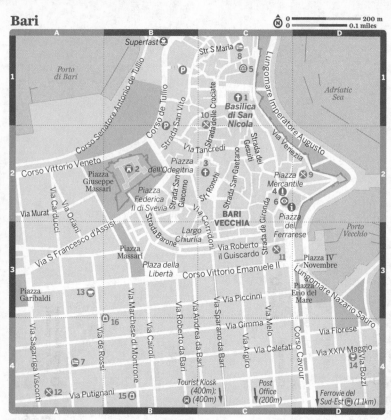

Bari

◎ Top Sights
1 Basilica di San Nicola C1

◎ Sights
2 Castello Svevo B2
3 Cathedral C2
4 Colonna della Giustizia C2
    Museo del Succorpo della
    Cattedrale .... (see 3)
5 Museo Nicolaiano C1
6 Piazza Mercantile C2

⊜ Sleeping
7 B&B Casa Pimpolini A4
8 Santa Maria del Buon Consiglio C1

⊗ Eating
9 La Locanda di Federico D2
10 Maria delle Sgagliozze C1
11 Paglionico Vini e Cucina C3
12 Terranima A4

⊖ Drinking & Nightlife
13 Caffè Borghese A3
14 Nessun Dorma D4

⊜ Shopping
15 Enoteca Vinarius de Pasquale B4
16 Il Salumaio B4

Castello Svevo   CASTLE
(Swabian Castle; ☑ 083 184 00 09; Piazza Federico II di Svevia; adult/reduced €3/1.50; ⊗ 8.30am-7.30pm Thu-Tue) **FREE** The Normans originally built over the ruins of a Roman fort, then

Frederick II built over the Norman castle, incorporating it into his design – the two towers of the Norman structure still stand. The bastions, with corner towers overhanging the moat, were added in the 16th century during Spanish rule, when the castle was a magnificent residence.

★ **Basilica di San Nicola** BASILICA
(www.basilicasannicola.it; Piazza San Nicola; ☺7am-8.30pm Mon-Sat, to 10pm Sun) Bari's signature basilica was one of the first Norman churches to be built in southern Italy, and is a splendid example of Puglian-Romanesque architecture. Dating to the 12th century, it was originally constructed to house the relics of St Nicholas (better known as Father Christmas), which were stolen from Turkey in 1087 by local fishing folk. Today, it is an important place of pilgrimage for both Catholics and Orthodox Christians.

St Nicholas' remains, which are said to emanate a miraculous manna liquid with special powers, are ensconced in a shrine in the beautiful vaulted crypt. Above, the interior is huge and simple with a decorative 17th-century wooden ceiling. The magnificent 13th-century ciborium over the altar is Puglia's oldest. Other items related to the basilica, including chalices, vestments and crests, are displayed in the new-ish **Museo Nicolaiano** (Strada Vanese 1; ☺11am-6pm Thu-Tue) **FREE** nearby.

Cathedral CATHEDRAL
(Piazza dell'Odegitria; ☺8am-12.30pm & 4-7.30pm Mon-Sat, 5-8.30pm Sun) Built over the original Byzantine church, the 11th-century Romanesque cathedral, dedicated to San Sabino, is technically Bari's most important church, although its fame pales alongside San Nicola. Inside, the plain walls are punctuated with deep arcades and the eastern window is a tangle of plant and animal motifs. The highlight lies in the subterranean **Museo del Succorpo della Cattedrale** (admission €1; ☺9.30am-4pm Sun-Wed), where recent excavations have revealed remnants left over from an ancient Christian basilica and various Roman ruins. These include parts of a 2nd-century Roman road, the floor mosaic from a 5th-century palaeo-Christian basilica featuring octopuses, fish and plant motifs, and elements of a 9th-century Byzantine church. Talk about history in layers!

Piazza Mercantile PIAZZA
This beautiful piazza is fronted by the Sedile, the headquarters of Bari's Council of Nobles. In the square's northeast corner is the **Colonna della Giustizia** (Column of Justice; Piazza Mercantile), where debtors were once tied and whipped.

 **Festivals & Events**

Festa di San Nicola RELIGIOUS
(☺7-9 May) The Festival of St Nicholas is Bari's biggest annual shindig, celebrating the 11th-century arrival of St Nicholas' relics from Turkey. On the first evening a procession leaves Castello Svevo for the Basilica di San Nicola. The next day there's a deafening fly-past and a fleet of boats carries the statue of St Nicholas along the coast.

That evening – and the next – ends with a massive fireworks display. It's a jolly, crowded family affair, attended by many Russian visitors who come to view the relics.

Sleeping

Most hotel accommodation here tends to be bland and overpriced, aimed at business clientele. B&Bs are generally a better option.

Santa Maria del Buon Consiglio B&B $
(☎388 2227366; www.santamariadelbuon consiglio.com; Via Forno Santa Scolastica 1-3; s €35-70, d €60-100, tr €85-90; ✳🖥) A graciously hosted B&B in the heart of old Bari near the port. Rooms have rough-cast stone walls and four-poster beds with drapes.

B&B Casa Pimpolini B&B $
(☎080 521 99 38; www.casapimpolini.com; Via Calefati 249; s €45-60, d €70-80; ✳@) This lovely B&B in the new town is within easy walking distance to shops, restaurants and Bari Vecchia. The rooms are warm and welcoming, and the homemade breakfast is a treat. Great value.

Villa Romanazzi Carducci HOTEL $
(☎080 542 74 00; www.villaromanazzi.com; Via Capruzzi 326; s/d from €59/69; 🅿✳🖥🏊) The one hotel in Bari daring to show some flair, the Villa Romanazzi near the train station is run by the French Accor group. Businesslike rooms are modern and clean-lined, but the real bonuses are in the extras: gardens embellished with statues, a picturesque swimming pool (summer only), an enormous fitness centre, a spa and a decent restaurant with excellent breakfasts.

Eating

★ **Paglionico Vini e Cucina** OSTERIA $
(☎338 2120391; Strada Vallisa 23; meals €20; ☺noon-3pm & 7-11pm Mon-Sat, noon-3pm Sun) Run by the Paglionico family for more than a century, this 100% Italiano *osteria* (casual tavern) is an absolute classic. There's no menu, just a chalkboard displaying what's

cooking that day. It's all fine salt-of-the-earth Puglian cuisine – the *riso, patate e cozze* (oven-baked rice, potatoes and mussels) is particularly good. The owners and waiters are brusque but brilliant.

Maria delle Sgagliozze
PUGLIAN $

(Strada delle Crociate; snacks €1; ⊙from 5pm) Octogenarian Maria dispenses the legendary Barese street food *sgagliozze* (deep-fried polenta cubes) from the front of her house. Sprinkle them with a pinch of salt and Bob's your uncle!

Terranima
PUGLIAN $$

(✎080 521 97 25; www.terranima.com; Via Putignani 213/215; meals €25-30; ⊙11.30am-3.30pm & 6.30-10.30pm Mon-Sat, 11.30am-3.30pm Sun) Peep through the lace curtains into the cool interior of this rustic trattoria where worn flagstone floors and period furnishings make you feel like you're dining in someone's front room. The menu features fabulous regional offerings such as veal, lemon and caper meatballs, and *sporcamuss*, a sweet flaky pastry.

La Locanda di Federico
PUGLIAN $$

(✎080 522 77 05; www.lalocandadifederico.com; Piazza Mercantile 63-64; meals €30; ⊙10.30am-3.30pm & 7pm-midnight) With domed ceilings, archways and medieval-style artwork on the walls, this restaurant oozes atmosphere. The menu is typical Puglian, starring dishes such as *orecchiette con le cime di rape* ('little ears' pasta with turnip tops) and prawns with pancetta. The people-watching is equally good – if you can take your eyes off the food.

 ## Drinking & Nightlife

Nessun Dorma
COCKTAIL BAR

(www.nessundormabari.it; Via Fiume 3; ⊙11am-midnight Sun-Thu, 11am-3am Fri & Sat) This new aptly named bar (*nessun dorma* means 'nobody sleeps') behind the Teatro Petruzzelli stays open late at weekends with live music and DJ sets. The interior is mega-chic with plush sofas and fashionable furnishings. It also serves American-style food.

Caffè Borghese
CAFE

(✎080 524 21 56; Corso Vittorio Emanuele II 22; ⊙8am-2am Tue-Sun) You'll experience genuine hospitality and friendly service at this small refined cafe that has a faintly Parisian air. With an all-day menu, it serves some pretty good food starting with breakfast, but, with its casual tables and bustling bar,

it works best for a morning coffee, an afternoon *pausa* (break) or an evening cocktail.

 ## Shopping

Designer shops and the main Italian chains line Via Sparano da Bari, while delis and gourmet food shops are located throughout the city.

Il Salumaio
FOOD

(✎080 521 93 45; www.ilsalumaio.it; Via Piccinni 168; ⊙8.30am-2pm & 4.30-9pm Mon-Sat) Breathe in the delicious smell of fine regional produce at this venerable delicatessen.

Enoteca Vinarius de Pasquale
WINE

(✎080 521 31 92; Via Marchese di Montrone 87; ⊙8am-2pm & 4-8.30pm Mon-Sat) Stock up on Puglian wines such as Primitivo di Manduria at this gorgeous old shop, founded in 1911.

 ## Information

From Piazza Aldo Moro, in front of the main train station, streets heading north will take you to Corso Vittorio Emanuele II, which separates the old and new parts of the city.

Hospital (✎080 559 11 11; Piazza Cesare)

Morfimare Travel Agency (✎080 578 98 15; www.morfimare.it; Corso de Tullio 36-40) For ferry bookings.

Police Station (✎080 529 11 11; Via Murat 4)

Post Office (Piazza Umberto I 33/8)

Tourist Office (✎080 524 22 44; Piazza del Ferrarese 29; ⊙10am-1pm & 4-7pm) New office opened in 2014. There are also kiosks at the train station and airport.

 ## Getting There & Away

AIR

Bari's **Palese airport** (www.aeroportidipuglia.it), 10km northwest of the city centre, is served by a host of international and budget airlines, including easyJet, Alitalia and Ryanair.

Pugliairbus (http://pugliairbus.aeroportidipuglia.it) connects Bari airport with Foggia airport and Brindisi airport. It also has a service from Bari airport to Matera (€6, 1¼ hours, five daily), Vieste (€20, 2¾ hours, four daily) and Taranto (€9.50, 1¼ hours, two daily).

BOAT

Ferries run from Bari to Albania, Croatia, Greece and Montenegro. All boat companies have offices at the ferry terminal, accessible on bus 20 from the main train station. Fares vary considerably among companies and it's easier to book with a travel agent such as Morfimare The main companies and their routes are as follows:

Jadrolinija (📞080 527 54 39; www.jadrolinija. hr; Nuova Stazione Marittima di Bari) Ferries to Dubrovnik in Croatia. Up to six times a week in summer.

Montenegro Lines (📞382 3031 1164; www. montenegrolines.net; Corso de Tullio 36) To Bar in Montenegro.

Superfast (📞080 528 28 28; www.superfast. com; Corso di Tullio 6) To Corfu, Igoumenitsa and Patras in Greece. Departs at 7.30pm.

Ventouris Ferries (📞for Albania 080 521 27 56, for Greece 080 521 76 99; www.ventouris. gr; Nuova Stazione Marittima di Bari) Regular ferries to Corfu, Cephalonia and Igoumenitsa (Greece) and daily ferries to Durrës (Albania).

BUS

Intercity buses leave from two main locations. From Via Capruzzi, south of the main train station, **SITA** (📞080 579 01 11; www.sitabus.it) covers local destinations. **Ferrovie Appulo-Lucane** (📞080 572 52 29; http://ferrovie appulolucane.it) buses serving Matera (€4.90, 1¼ hours, six daily) also depart from here, plus **Marozzi** (📞080 556 24 46; www.marozzivt.it) buses for Rome (from €34.50, six hours, eight daily – note that the overnight bus departs from Piazza Moro) and other long-distance destinations.

Buses operated by **Ferrovie del Sud-Est** (FSE; 📞080 546 21 11; www.fseonline.it) leave from Largo Ciaia, south of Piazza Aldo Moro and service the following locations:

Alberobello (€4.90, 1¼ hours, hourly); continues to Locorotondo (€5.60, 1 hour 35 minutes) and Martina Franca (€5.60, 1 hour 50 minutes)

Grotte di Castellana (€2.80, one hour, five daily)

Taranto (€8.40, 1¾ to 2¼ hours, frequent)

TRAIN

A web of train lines spreads out from Bari. Note that there are fewer services on the weekend.

From the **main train station** (📞080 524 43 86), Trenitalia trains go to Puglia and beyond:

TO	FARE	DURATION (HRS)	FREQUENCY
Brindisi	€8.40	1	frequent
Foggia	€9	1	frequent
Milan	€66.50	7-10	every 4hrs
Rome	€54	4	every 4hrs

Ferrovie Appulo-Lucane (p721) serves two main destinations:

TO	FARE	DURATION (HRS)	FREQUENCY
Matera	€4.90	1½	12 daily
Potenza	€10.50	4	4 daily

Ferrovie del Sud-Est trains leave from the southern side of the station where they have their own separate ticket office.

TO	FARE	DURATION (HRS)	FREQUENCY
Albero-bello	€4.90	1½	hourly
Martina Franca	€5.60	2	hourly
Taranto	€8.40	2½	9 daily

🛈 Getting Around

Central Bari is compact – a 15-minute walk will take you from Piazza Aldo Moro to the old town. For the ferry terminal, take bus 20 (tickets €1.50) from Piazza Moro.

Street parking is migraine-inducing. There's a large parking area (€1) south of the main port entrance; otherwise, there's a large multistorey car park between the main train station and the FSE station. Another car park is on Via Zuppetta opposite Hotel Adria.

TO/FROM THE AIRPORT

For the airport, take the **Tempesta shuttle bus** (www.autoservizitempesta.it) from the main train station (€4, 30 minutes, hourly), with pickups at Piazza Garibaldi and the corner of Via Andrea da Bari and Via Calefati. Alternatively, normal city bus 16 covers the same route and a trip is much cheaper (€1), though marginally slower (40 minutes). A taxi trip from the airport to town costs around €24.

Around Bari

The *Terra di Bari* (land of Bari') surrounding the capital is rich in olive groves and orchards, and the region has an impressive architectural history with some magnificent cathedrals, an extensive network of castles along its coastline, charming seaside towns like Trani and the mysterious inland Castel del Monte.

Trani

POP 53,900

Known as the 'Pearl of Puglia', beautiful Trani has a sophisticated feel, particularly

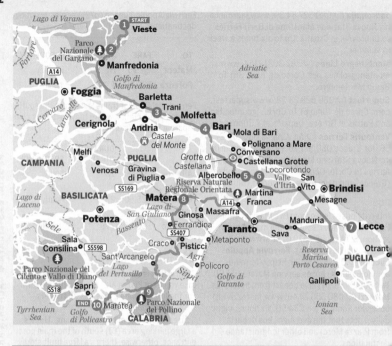

Driving Tour
Italy's Authentic South

START VIESTE
END MARATEA
LENGTH 650KM TO 700KM; ONE WEEK

Consider a gentle start in lovely, laid-back
1 Vieste with its white sandy beaches and
medieval backstreets, but set aside half a day
to hike or bike in the lush green forests of the
2 Parco Nazionale del Gargano (p724).
Follow the coastal road past dramatic cliffs,
salt lakes and flat farming land to **3 Trani**,
with its impressive seafront cathedral and
picturesque port, before spending a night in
4 Bari, where you'll find hip bars and salt-
of-the-earth trattorias. The next day head to
5 Alberobello, home to a dense neighbourhood of extraordinary cone-shaped stone
homes called *trulli*; consider an overnight
trulli stay.

Stroll around one of the most picturesque
centro storico (historic centres) in southern

Italy at **6 Locorotondo**. Hit the road and
cruise on to lively baroque **7 Lecce**, where
you can easily chalk up a full day exploring
the sights, shops and flamboyantly fronted
palazzi and churches, including the Basilica
di Santa Croce.

Day five will be one to remember. Nothing
can prepare you for Basilicata's **8 Matera**,
where *sassi* (former cave dwellings) are a
dramatic reminder of the town's poverty-
stricken past. After days of pasta, *fave* beans
and *cornetti* (Italian croissants), it's high time
for some exercise on the trails of the spectacular **9 Parco Nazionale del Pollino**. Finally,
wind up the trip with more walking or a day of
beach slothing at the spread out coastal town
of **10 Maratea** with its surrounding seaside
resorts, medieval village and cosmopolitan
harbour offset by a thickly forested and
mountainous interior.

n summer when well-heeled visitors pack
he array of marina-side bars. The marina is
he place to promenade and watch the white
achts and fishing boats in the harbour,
vhile the historic centre, with its medieval
hurches, glossy limestone streets and faded
et charming *palazzi* is an enchanting area
> explore. But it's the cathedral, pale against
he deep-blue sea, that is the town's most ar-
esting sight.

◉ Sights

athedral
CATHEDRAL
¹iazza del Duomo; campanile €3; ⊙8.30am-
¹.30pm & 3.30-7pm Mon-Sat, 9am-12.30pm &
9pm Sun) The dramatic seafront cathedral
dedicated to St Nicholas the Pilgrim, fa-
¹ous for being foolish. The Greek Christian
andered through Puglia, crying '*Kyrie
eison*' (Greek for 'Lord, have mercy'). First
ought to be a simpleton, he was revered
ter his death (aged 19) after several mir-
les attributed to him occurred. Below the
urch is the crypt, a forest of ancient col-
nns where the bones of St Nicholas are
pt beneath the altar. You can also visit the
mpanile (bell tower).

Construction of the cathedral started in
97 on the site of a Byzantine church and
.s completed in the 13th century. The
¹gnificent original bronze doors (now dis-
ayed inside) were cast by Barisano da Tra-
an accomplished 12th-century artisan.

The interior of the cathedral reflects typi-
Norman simplicity and is lined by colon-
des. Near the main altar are the remains
a 12th-century floor mosaic, stylistically
ilar to that in Otranto.

stle
CASTLE
0883 50 66 03; www.castelloditrani.benicultur
¹; Piazza Manfredi 16; admission €3; ⊙8.30am-
¹) Two hundred metres north of the ca-
dral is Trani's other major landmark,
vast, almost modernist Swabian castle
lt by Frederick II in 1233. Charles V later
¹ngthened the fortifications; it was used
¹ prison from 1844 to 1974.

¹issanti Church
CHURCH
Ognissanti; ⊙hours vary) Built by the
ghts Templar in the 12th century, this
rch is where Norman knights swore alle-
¹ce to Bohemond I of Antioch, their lead-
¹efore setting off on the First Crusade.

ⓘ TRAVELLING EAST

Puglia is the main jumping-off point for
onward travel to Greece, Croatia and Albania. The two main ports are Bari and
Brindisi, from where you can catch ferries to Vlorë and Durrës in Albania, Bar
in Montenegro, and Cephalonia, Corfu,
Igoumenitsa and Patras in Greece. Fares
from Bari to Greece are generally more
expensive than those from Brindisi.
Taxes are usually from €9 per person
and €12 per car. High season is generally the months of July and August, with
reduced services in low season. Tariffs
can be up to one-third cheaper in low
season.

Scolanova Church
CHURCH
(☑ 0883 48 17 99; Via Scolanova 23; ⊙hours vary)
This church was one of four former synagogues in the ancient Jewish quarter, all of
which were converted to churches in the
14th century. Inside is a beautiful Byzantine
painting of Madonna dei Martiri.

🛏 Sleeping

Albergo Lucy
HOTEL $
(☑ 0883 48 10 22; www.albergolucy.com; Piazza
Plebiscito 11; d/tr/q from €75/95/115; ※ ◉) Located in a restored 17th-century *palazzo*
overlooking a leafy square and close to the
shimmering port, this family run place oozes charm and is great value. Bike hire and
guided tours are available. Breakfast isn't
served, but there are plenty of cafes a short
stroll away.

B&B Centro Storico Trani
B&B $
(☑ 0883 50 61 76; www.bbtrani.it; Via Leopardi
28; s €35-50, d €50-70, tr €70-80) This simple,
old-fashioned B&B inhabits an old backstreet monastery and is run by an elderly
couple. It's basic, but the rooms are large
and 'Mama' makes a mean *crostata* (jam
tart).

Hotel Regia
HOTEL $$
(☑ 0883 58 44 44; www.hotelregia.it; Piazza del
Duomo 2; s €120-130, d €130-150; ※ ◉) A lone
building facing the cathedral, the 18th-
century Palazzo Filisio houses this charming
hotel with understated grandeur. Rooms
are sober and stylish, and the location is
stupendous.

✗ Eating

★ **Corteinfiore** SEAFOOD **$$**
(☑ 0883 50 84 02; www.corteinfiore.it; Via Ognis-santi 18; meals €30; ⊙ 12.30-2.15pm & 8-10.15pm Tue-Sun) Romantic, urbane, refined. The wooden decking, buttercup-yellow table-cloths and marquee-conservatory setting are refreshing, while the wines are excellent and the cooking delicious. It also has modern and attractive rooms (from €100) decked out in pale colours.

La Darsena SEAFOOD **$$**
(☑ 0883 48 73 33; Via Statuti Marittimi 98; meals €30; ⊙ noon-3pm & 8-11.30pm Tue-Sun) Re-nowned for its seafood, swish La Darsena is housed in a waterfront *palazzo*. Outside tables overlook the port while inside, photos of old Puglia cover the walls beneath a huge wrought-iron dragon chandelier.

❶ Information

From the train station, Via Cavour leads through Piazza della Repubblica to Piazza Plebiscito and the public gardens. Turn left at Piazza della Repubblica for the harbour and cathedral.

Tourist Office (☑ 0883 58 88 30; www.traniweb.it; 1st fl, Palazzo Palmieri, Piazza Trieste 10; ⊙ 8.30am-1.30pm Mon, Wed & Fri, 8.30am-1.30pm & 3.30-5.30pm Tue & Thu) Located 200m south of the cathedral. Offers free guided walking tours most days at 8pm.

❶ Getting There & Away

STP (☑ 0883 49 18 00; www.stpspa.it) has fre-quent bus services to Bari (€4.20, 45 minutes). Services depart from **Bar Stazione** (Piazza XX Settembre 23), which also has timetables and tickets.

Trani is on the main train line between Bari (€3.10, 30 to 45 minutes, frequent) and Foggia (€6.30, 40 to 50 minutes, frequent).

Castel del Monte

★ **Castel del Monte** CASTLE
(☑ 0883 56 99 97; www.casteldelmonte.benicultur ali.it; adult/reduced €5/2.50; ⊙ 9am-6.30pm Oct-Mar, 10.15am-7.45pm Apr-Sep) You'll see Castel del Monte, an unearthly geometric shape on a hilltop, from miles away. Mysterious and perfectly octagonal, it's one of southern Italy's most talked-about landmarks and a Unesco World Heritage Site.

No one knows why Frederick II built it – there's no nearby town or strategic cross-roads. It was not built to defend anything, as it has no moat or drawbridge, no arrow slits, and no trapdoors for pouring boiling oil on invaders.

Some theories claim that, according to mid-13th-century beliefs in geometric sym-bolism, the octagon represented the union of the circle and square, of God-perfection (the infinite) and human-perfection (the fi-nite). The castle was therefore nothing less than a celebration of the relationship be-tween humanity and God.

The castle has eight octagonal towers. Its interconnecting rooms have decorative marble columns and fireplaces, and the doorways and windows are framed in coral-lite stone. Many of the towers have washing rooms with what are thought to be Europe's first flushing loos – Frederick II, like the Arab world he admired, set great store by cleanliness.

To get to the castle without a car, take the Ferrovia Bari-Nord train from Bari to Andria, then bus number 6 from Andria station to the castle (35 minutes, five daily, April to October only). The castle is about 35km from Trani.

Promontorio del Gargano

The coast surrounding this expansive prom-ontory seems permanently bathed in a pink-hued, pearly light, providing a painterly contrast to the sea, which softens from in-tense to powder blue as the evening draws in. It's one of Italy's most beautiful areas, en-compassing white limestone cliffs, fairy-tale grottoes, sparkling sea, ancient forests, rare orchids and tangled, fragrant maquis (dense scrub vegetation).

Once connected to what is now Dalmatia (in Croatia), the 'spur' of the Italian boot has more in common with the land mass across the sea than with the rest of Italy. Creeping urbanisation was halted in 1991 by the cre-ation of the Parco Nazionale del Gargano (www.parcogargano.gov.it) FREE. Aside from its magnificent national park, the Gargano is home to pilgrimage sites and the lovely sea-side towns of Vieste and Peschici.

Vieste
POP 13,900

Like a young belle who's beautiful without even realising it, the town of Vieste clings modestly to a spectacular promontory on the Gargano peninsula resembling a cross between Naples and Dubrovnik with a bit of Puglian magic mixed in. The narrow alleys of the old town, decorated with lines of drying clothes and patrolled by slinking cats and the odd friendly dog, are an atmospheric place day or night, off-season or on. Wedged up against the old town is the equally unpretentious new town, ghostly in winter, but packed with holidaying humanity in summer, especially during the *passeggiata* (evening stroll).

Vieste is strategically placed atop the steep Pizzomunno cliffs between two sweeping sandy beaches. The gritty harbour offers water sports, while the surrounding Parco Nazionale del Gargano is revered for cycling and hiking. All things considered, it's one of the south's most complete all-in-one destinations.

Sights

Vieste is primarily a beach resort, but the steep, skinny alleys of the old town are your ticket for entry to another, more tranquil world. The castle built by Frederick II is occupied by the military and closed to the public.

Chianca Amara · HISTORIC SITE
(Bitter Stone; Via Cimaglia) Vieste's most gruesome sight is this worn and polished stone where thousands were beheaded when Turks sacked Vieste in the 16th century.

Museo Malacologico · MUSEUM
(☑ 0884 70 76 88; Via Pola 8; ☺ 9.30am-12.30pm & 4-8pm Apr-Oct) **FREE** This esoteric shell museum has four rooms of fossils and molluscs, some enormous and all beautifully patterned and coloured. Note the seasonal opening hours.

Cathedral · CATHEDRAL
(Via Duomo; ☺ 7.30am-noon & 4-11pm) Built by the Normans on the ruins of a Vesta temple, the cathedral is in Puglian-Romanesque style with a fanciful tower that resembles a cardinal's hat. Of note are its beautiful paintings, swirling interior columns and Latin-inscribed altar.

La Salata · HISTORIC SITE
(☑ 0854 70 66 35; adult/child €5/free; ☺ 5.30pm & 8.15pm Mon-Fri Jun-Sep, by appointment Oct-May) This palaeo-Christian graveyard dating from the 4th to 6th centuries AD is 9km out of town. Inside the cave, tier upon tier of narrow tombs are cut into the rock wall; others form shallow niches in the cave floor. Guided tours are mandatory.

Activities

Superb sandy beaches surround the town: in the south are Spiagga del Castello, Cala San Felice and Cala Sanguinaria; due north, head for the area known as La Salata. Diving is popular around the promontory's rocky coastline, which is filled with marine grottoes.

From May to September fast boats zoom to the Isole Tremiti. For hiking ideas, pick up a *Guida al Trekking sul Gargano* brochure from the tourist office. A section of walk 4 is doable from Vieste. It starts 2.5km south of town off the Lungomare Enrico Mattei, where a track cuts up through olive groves into increasingly wild terrain.

Centro Ormeggi e Sub · BOATING
(☑ 0884 70 79 83; Lungomare Vespucci) Offers diving courses and rents out sailing boats and motorboats.

Tours

Several companies offer tours of the caves that pock the Gargano coast – a three-hour tour costs around €13.

Explora Gargano · CYCLING
(☑ 0884 70 22 37; www.exploragargano.it; Vieste-Peschici km 5.5; hiking and mountain biking half-day from €70, quad tours and jeep safari per day from €50) To get off the beach for a day or two, take one of the many tours on offer at Explora Gargano. As well as hiking and mountain biking in the Foresta Umbra, it offers quad tours and jeep safaris.

Motobarca Desirèe · BOAT TOUR
(www.grottemarinegargano.com; Lungomare Vespucci; adult/child €15/7; ☺ Apr-Oct) Boat tours of the various caves, arches and *trabucchi* (Puglian fishing structures) that characterise the Gargano coast. Trips are spectacular, though the boats can get crowded. Two departures a day (9am and 2.30pm); buy tickets port-side.

Sleeping

★ B&B Parallelo 41 · B&B $
(☑ 0884 35 50 09; www.bbparallelo41.it; Via Forno de Angelis 3; r from €70; ❈ @ ❞) Beautiful small B&B in the midst of the old town where four recently renovated rooms have been decorated with hand-painted ceilings, luxurious beds and super-modern bathrooms. Breakfasts consist of a substantial buffet, and the reception area acts as a mini-information centre for a slew of local activities.

THE RICH FLAVOURS OF CUCINA POVERA

In Italy's less wealthy 'foot', traditional recipes have been born out of economic necessity rather than through celebrity chefs with fancy ideas. Local people used whatever ingredients were available to them, plucked directly from the surrounding soil and seas, and kneaded and blended using recipes passed down through generations. The result is called *cucina povera* (literally 'food of the poor'), which, thanks to a recent global obsession with farm-to-table purity, has become increasingly popular.

If there is a mantra for *cucina povera*, it is 'keep it simple'. Pasta is the south's staple starch. Made with durum wheat rather than eggs, it is most commonly sculpted into *orecchiette* or 'little ears' and doused with various toppings, many of which include a mixture of readily available vegetables. Aubergine, mushrooms, tomatoes, artichokes and olives grow abundantly in southern climes and they're all put to good use in the dishes.

Meat, though present in southern cooking, is used more sparingly than in the north. Lamb and horse meat predominate and are usually heavily seasoned. Unadulterated fish is more common, especially in Puglia, which has a longer coastline than any other mainland Italian region. Popular fish dishes incorporate mussels, clams, octopus (in Salento), swordfish (in northern Calabria), cod and prawns.

A signature Puglian *primi* (first course) is *orecchiette con cima di rape*, a gloriously simple blend of rapini (a bitter green leafy veg with small broccoli-like shoots) mixed with anchovies, olive oil, chilli peppers, garlic and *pecorino*. Another popular *orecchiette* accompaniment is *ragù di carne di cavallo* (horse meat), sometimes known as *ragù alla barese*. Bari is known for its starch-heavy *riso, patate e cozze*, a surprisingly delicious marriage of rice, potatoes and mussels that is baked in the oven. Another wildly popular vegetable is wild chicory, which, when combined with a broad bean purée, is reborn as *fave e cicorie*.

Standard cheeses of the south include *burrata*, which has a mozzarella-like shell and a gooey centre, and *pecorino di filiano*, a sheep's-milk cheese from Basilicata. There are tons of bread recipes, but the horn-shaped crusty bread from Matera is king.

Campeggio Capo Vieste CAMPGROUND $
(✆ 0884 70 63 26; www.capovieste.it; Vieste-Peschici km 8; camping 2 people, car & tent €33, 1-bedroom bungalow €77-164; ☺ Mar-Oct; ☻) This tree-shaded campground is right by a sandy beach at La Salata, around 8km from Vieste and accessible by bus. Activities include tennis and a sailing school.

Hotel Seggio HOTEL $$
(✆ 0884 70 81 23; www.hotelseggio.it; Via Veste 7; d €120, half-board €150; ☺ Apr-Oct; P ❄ @ ☎ ☻) A butter-coloured, 17th-century, family-run *palazzo* in the town's historic centre. Steps spiral down to a dreamy pool and sunbathing terrace with an ocean backdrop. The 30 rooms are plain but modern.

✗ Eating

★ **Vecchia Vieste** PUGLIAN $
(✆ 0884 70 70 83; Via Mafrolla 32; meals €20-25, tasting menu €25; ☺ noon-3pm & 7-11pm) The best in Vieste can be found in the stony cavernous interior of this modest restaurant that sells what is possibly the best home-made, hand-shaped *orecchiette* in Puglia (and that's saying something). Try it topped with the obligatory *cima di rape* (rapini – a bitter green leafy veg – with anchovies, olive oil, chilli peppers, garlic and *pecorino*). The very reasonably priced *menù degustazione* comes with four courses.

Osteria Al Duomo OSTERIA $$
(✆ 0884 70 82 43; www.osterialduomo.it; Via Alessandro III 23; meals €25; ☺ noon-3pm & 7-11pm Mar-Nov) Tucked away in a picturesque narrow alley in the heart of the old town, this welcoming *osteria* has a cosy cave-like interior and outdoor seating under a shady arbour. Homemade pastas with seafood sauces feature prominently.

Taverna Al Cantinone TRADITIONAL ITALIAN $$
(✆ 0884 70 77 53; Via Mafrolla 26; meals €25-30; ☺ noon-3pm & 7-11pm Wed-Mon) Run by a charming Italian-Spanish couple who have a passion for cooking. The food is exceptional and exquisitely presented, and the menu changes with the seasons.

ℹ️ Information

Post Office (Via Vittorio Veneto)

Tourist Office (☑ 0884 70 88 06; Piazza Kennedy; ⊙8am-8pm Mon-Sat) You can weigh yourself down with useful brochures here.

ℹ️ Getting There & Around

BOAT

Vieste's port is to the north of town, about a five-minute walk from the tourist office. In summer, several companies, including Linee Marittime Adriatico (p729), head to the Isole Tremiti (€27 to €30, 1½ hours). Tickets can be bought port-side.

BUS

From Piazzale Manzoni, where intercity buses terminate, a 10-minute walk east along Viale XXIV Maggio, which becomes Corso Fazzini, brings you into the old town and the Marina Piccola's attractive promenade. In summer buses terminate at Via Verdi, a 300m walk from the old town down Via Papa Giovanni XXIII.

SITA (☑ 0881 35 20 11; www.sitabus.it) buses run between Vieste and Foggia (€7, 2¾ hours, four daily) via Manfredonia. There are also services to Monte Sant'Angelo (€5) via Manfredonia, but **Ferrovie del Gargano** (☑ 0881 58 72 11; www.ferroviedelgargano.com) buses have a direct daily service to Monte Sant'Angelo (€6.30, two hours) and frequent services to Peschici (€1.70, 35 minutes).

From May to September, **Pugliairbus** (☑ 080 580 03 58; http://pugliairbus.aeroportidipuglia. it) runs a service to the Gargano, including Vieste, from Bari airport (€20, 3½ hours, four daily).

Monte Sant'Angelo

POP 13,300 / ELEV 796M

One of Europe's most important pilgrimage sites, this isolated mountain-top town has an extraordinary atmosphere. Pilgrims have been coming here for centuries – and so have the hustlers, pushing everything from religious kitsch to parking spaces.

The object of devotion is the Santuario di San Michele. Here, in AD 490, St Michael the Archangel is said to have appeared in a grotto to the Bishop of Siponto. He left behind his scarlet cloak and instructions not to consecrate the site as he had already done so. During the Middle Ages, the sanctuary marked the end of the Route of the Angel, which began in Mont St-Michel (in Normandy) and passed through Rome. In 999 the Holy Roman Emperor Otto III made a pilgrimage to the sanctuary to pray that prophecies about the end of the world in the year 1000 would not be fulfilled. His prayers were answered, the world staggered on and the sanctuary's fame grew. The sanctuary has been a Unesco World Heritage Site since 2011.

👁️ Sights

The town's serpentine alleys and jumbled houses are perfect for a little aimless ambling. Look out for the different shaped *cappelletti* (chimney stacks) on top of the neat whitewashed houses.

⭐ **Santuario di San Michele** CAVE
(Via Reale Basilica; ⊙7am-8pm Jul-Sep, 7am-1pm & 2.30-8pm Apr-Jun & Oct, 7am-1pm & 2.30-7pm Nov-Mar) FREE Over the centuries this sanctuary has expanded to incorporate a large complex of religious buildings that overlay its original shrine. The double-arched entrance vestibule at street level stands next to a distinctive octagonal bell tower built by Carlo I of Naples in 1282. As you descend the staircase inside, look for the 17th-century pilgrims' graffiti. The grotto/shrine where St Michael is said to have left a footprint in stone is located at the bottom of the staircase. Because of St Michael's footprint it became customary for pilgrims to carve outlines of their feet and hands into the stone. Etched Byzantine bronze and silver doors, cast in Constantinople in 1076, open into the grotto itself. Inside, a 16th-century statue of the Archangel Michael covers the site of St Michael's footprint.

Tomba di Rotari HISTORIC SITE
(admission €1; ⊙10am-1pm & 3-7pm Apr-Oct) A short flight of stairs opposite the Santuario di San Michele leads to a 12th-century baptistry with a deep sunken basin for total immersion. You enter the baptistry through the facade of the Chiesa di San Pietro with its intricate rose window squirming with serpents – all that remains of the church, destroyed in a 19th-century earthquake. The Romanesque portal of the adjacent 11th-century Chiesa di Santa Maria Maggiore has some fine bas-reliefs.

Castle HISTORIC SITE
(Largo Roberto Giuscardo 2; admission €2; ⊙9.30am-1pm & 2.30-7pm) At the highest point of Monte Sant'Angelo is this rugged bijou, a Norman castle with Swabian and Aragonese additions as well as panoramic views.

TRABUCCHI

Hang around the coastal towns and villages of Abruzzo, Molise and northern Puglia and you'll soon become adept at spotting *trabucchi*. These old-fashioned wooden fishing platforms that jut out into the sea have a long history, possibly stretching back to Phoenician times. Made entirely of local pine wood they are located on rocky promontories where their complex nets trap fish swimming close to the shoreline.

There are two types of *trabucchi* on Italy's Adriatic coast. Those in Abruzzo and Molise usually inhabit shallow waters, necessitating a narrow wooden walkway to connect the platform (usually equipped with a small wooden hut) with the shore. The *trabucchi* on the Gargano peninsula in Puglia, on the other hand, are sited over deeper drop-offs meaning the platforms are generally connected directly to the shoreline.

Trabucchi are protected as historic monuments in Parco Nazionale del Gargano, where numerous examples embellish the shore between Vieste and Peschici. Most are still used by fishers and some have been turned into fish restaurants where – if you're lucky – you can watch your meal being caught before you eat it. A good *trabucco* to try is Il Trabucco da Mimi in Peschici.

Sleeping & Eating

Hotel Michael
HOTEL $

(☑ 0884 56 55 19; www.hotelmichael.com; Via Basilica 86; s/d €60/80; 🐾) A small hotel with shuttered windows, located on the main street across from the Santuario di San Michele, this traditional place has spacious rooms with extremely pink bedspreads. Ask for a room with a view.

Casa li Jalantuúmene
TRATTORIA $$

(☑ 0884 56 54 84; www.li-jalantuumene.it; Piazza de Galganis 5; meals €40; ⊘ 12.30-2.15pm & 7.30-10.30pm Wed-Mon) This renowned restaurant has an entertaining and eccentric chef, Gegè Mangano, and serves excellent fare. It's intimate, there's a select wine list and, in summer, tables spill onto the piazza. There are also four suites on site (€130), decorated in traditional Puglian style.

❶ Getting There & Away

Ferrovie del Gargano (☑ 0882 22 89 60; www.ferroviedelgargano.com) Has a direct bus service from Vieste (€6.30, two hours, five daily). Buy your tickets from Bar Esperia next to Santuario di San Michele; buses leave from Corso Vittorio Emanuele.

SITA (☑ 0881 35 20 11; www.sitasudtrasporti.it) Buses run from Foggia (€4.90, 1¾ hours, four daily) and Vieste via Manfredonia. They leave from Corso Vittorio Emanuele in Monte Sant'Angelo.

Peschici

POP 4400

Perched above a turquoise sea and tempting beach, Peschici, like Vieste, is another cliff-clinging Amalfi lookalike. Its tight-knit old walled town of Arabesque whitewashed houses acts as a hub to a wider resort area. The small town gets crammed in summer, so book in advance. Boats zip across to the Isole Tremiti in high season.

Sleeping & Eating

Locanda al Castello
B&B $

(☑ 0884 96 40 38; www.peschicialcastello.it; Via Castello 29; s €35-70, d €70-120; 🅿🌀🐾) Staying here is like entering a large, welcoming family home. It's by the cliffs with fantastic views. Enjoy hearty home cooking in the restaurant (meals €18) while the owners' kids run around playing football – indoors!

Baia San Nicola
CAMPGROUND $

(☑ 0884 96 42 31; www.baiasannicola.it; Localita Punta San Nicola; adult €7-10, tent €6-11, 2-person bungalow per week €420-720; ⊘ mid-May–mid-Oct) The best campground in the area, 2km south of Peschici towards Vieste, Baia San Nicola is on a pine-shaded beach, offering camping, bungalows, apartments and myriad amenities.

★ Il Trabucco da Mimi
SEAFOOD $$

(☑ 0884 96 25 56; www.altrabucco.it; Localita Punta San Nicola; meals €30-40; ⊘ 12.30-2.30pm & 7.30-10.30pm Easter-Oct) For the ultimate in fresh fish you can't beat eating at a *trabucco* (the traditional wooden fishing platforms lining the coast). Watch the fishing process in operation – you can even help out – and dine on the catch. The decor here is simple and rustic and you'll pay for the experience – but it's worth it. It also hosts live jazz.

Porta di Basso   SEAFOOD **$$**
(☑ 0884 91 53 64; www.portadibasso.it; Via Colombo 38; meals €30-40; ⊙ noon-2.30pm & 7-11pm Fri-Wed) 🍴 Superb views of the ocean drop away from the floor-to-ceiling windows beside intimate alcove tables at this elegant clifftop restaurant. The menu of fresh local seafood changes daily. Close to the restaurant, two extremely stylish suites with fantastic sea views offer *albergo-diffuso*-style accommodation (€110 to €120).

ℹ Information

Tourist Office (☑ 0884 91 53 62; Via Magenta 3; ⊙ 8am-2pm & 5-9pm Mon-Sat Apr-Oct, 8am-2pm Mon-Fri, 9am-noon & 4-7pm Sat Nov-Mar)

ℹ Getting There & Away

The bus terminal is beside the sportsground, uphill from the main street, Corso Garibaldi.

Ferrovie del Gargano (p727) buses run frequent daily services between Peschici and Vieste (€1.70, 35 minutes).

From April to September, ferry companies, including **Linee Marittime Adriatico** (☑ 0884 96 20 23; www.collegamentiisoletremiti.com; Corso Garibaldi 32), serve the Isole Tremiti (adult €24 to €27, child €14 to €16, one to 1½ hours, one daily).

Foresta Umbra

The 'Forest of Shadows' is the Gargano's enchanted interior – thickets of tall, epic trees interspersed with picnic spots bathed in dappled light. It's the last remnant of Puglia's ancient forests: Aleppo pines, oaks, yews and beech trees shade the mountainous terrain. More than 65 different types of orchid have been discovered here, and the wildlife includes roe deer, wild boar, foxes, badgers and the increasingly rare wild cat. Walkers and mountain bikers will find plenty of well-marked trails within the forest's 5790 sq km.

⊙ Sights & Activities

The small visitor centre in the middle of the forest houses a **museum and nature centre** (SP52bis; admission €1.20; ⊙ 9am-7pm mid-Apr–mid-Oct) with fossils, photographs, and stuffed animals and birds. Half-day guided hikes (per person €10), bike hire (per hour/day €5/25) and walking maps (€2.50) are available here. The centre is on SP52bis, close to the junction with SP528.

There are 15 official trails in the park ranging from 0.5km to 13.5km in length. Several of them start near the visitor centre and the adjacent Laghetto Umbra, including path 9, which can be done as a loop returning on a military road. A park leaflet provides a map and trail descriptions.

🛏 Sleeping

Rifugio Sfilzi   B&B **$**
(☑ 340 6315260; www.rifugiosfilzi.com; SP528; adult/child €35/17) In the middle of the Foresta Umbra a few kilometres north of the visitor centre towards Vico di Gargano, this cosy *rifugio* (mountain hut) offers eight rooms with three- and four-bed configurations, making them ideal for groups or families. It also has a small shop selling locally made products such as jams and oils, and a cafe-restaurant with fantastic homemade cake and coffee.

La Chiusa delle More   B&B **$$$**
(☑ 330 543766; www.lachiusadellemore.it; r €200-240; ⊙ May-Oct; 🅿 ❄ 🤖 🏊) La Chiusa delle More offers an escape from the cramped coast. An attractive stone-built *agriturismo* (farm stay accommodation), only 1.5km from Peschici, it's set in a huge olive grove, and you can dine on home-grown produce, borrow mountain bikes and enjoy panoramic views from your poolside lounger. Note there is a three-night minimum stay.

Isole Tremiti

POP 500

This beautiful archipelago of three islands, 36km offshore, is a picturesque sight of raggedy cliffs, sandy coves and thick pine woods, surrounded by the glittering dark-blue sea.

Unfortunately the islands are no secret, and in July and August some 100,000 holidaymakers descend on the archipelago. At this time it's noisy, loud and hot. If you want to savour the islands' tranquillity, visit during the shoulder season. In the low season most tourist facilities close down and the few permanent residents resume their quiet and isolated lives.

The islands' main facilities are on San Domino, the largest and lushest island, which was formerly used to grow crops. It's ringed by alternating sandy beaches and limestone cliffs, while the inland is covered in thick maquis flecked with rosemary and foxglove. The centre harbours a nondescript small town with several hotels.

Small San Nicola island is the traditional administrative centre; a castle-like cluster of medieval buildings rises up from its rocks. The third island, Capraia, is uninhabited.

Most boats arrive at San Domino. Small boats regularly make the brief crossing to San Nicola (€6 return) in high season; from October to March a single boat makes the trip after meeting the boat from the mainland.

◉ Sights & Activities

San Domino   ISLAND

Head to San Domino for walks, grottoes and coves. It has a pristine, marvellous coastline and the islands' only sandy beach, **Cala delle Arene**. Alongside the beach is the small cove **Grotta dell'Arene**, with calm clear waters for swimming.

You can also take a boat trip (€12 to €15 from the port) around the island to explore the grottoes: the largest, **Grotta del Bue Marino**, is 70m long. A tour around all three islands costs €15 to €17. Diving in the translucent sea is another option with **Tremiti Diving Center** (☑ 337 648917; www.tremitidivingcenter.com; Via Federico 2). There's an undemanding, but enchanting, walking track around the island, starting at the far end of the village.

San Nicola   ISLAND

Medieval buildings thrust out of San Nicola's rocky shores, the same pale-sand colour as the barren cliffs. In 1010, Benedictine monks founded the **Abbazia e Chiesa di Santa Maria** here; for the next 700 years the islands were ruled by a series of abbots who accumulated great wealth.

Although the church retains a weather-worn Renaissance portal and a fine 11th-century floor mosaic, its other treasures have been stolen or destroyed throughout its troubled history, which has seen various religious orders come and go, including the Benedictines, the Cistercians and the Lateran Canons. The only exceptions are a painted wooden Byzantine crucifix brought to the island in AD 747 and a black Madonna, probably transported here from Constantinople in the Middle Ages.

Capraia   ISLAND

The third of the Isole Tremiti, Capraia (named after the wild caper plant) is uninhabited. Bird life is plentiful, with impressive flocks of seagulls. There's no organised transport, but trips can be negotiated with local fishing folk.

🛏 Sleeping & Eating

In summer you'll need to book well ahead and many hotels insist on full board. Camping is forbidden.

La Casa di Gino   B&B **$$**

(☑ 0882 46 34 10; www.hotel-gabbiano.com; Piazza Belvedere; s/d €100/150; ✺) A tranquil accommodation choice on San Nicola, away from the frenzy of San Domino, this B&B run by the Hotel Gabbiano has stylish white-on-white rooms.

Hotel Gabbiano   HOTEL **$$**

(☑ 0882 46 34 10; www.hotel-gabbiano.com; Piazza Belvedere; r €100-130; ✺🕾) An established icon on San Nicola and run for more than 30 years by a Neapolitan family, this smart hotel has pastel-coloured rooms with balconies overlooking the town and the sea. It also has a seafood restaurant, spa and gym.

Architiello   SEAFOOD **$$**

(☑ 0882 46 30 54; www.ristorantearchitiello carolina.com; Via Salita delle Mura, San Nicola; meals €25; ☉ Apr-Oct) A class act with a seaview terrace, this place specialises in – what else? – fresh fish.

❶ Getting There & Away

Boats for the Isole Tremiti depart from several points on the Italian mainland: Manfredonia, Vieste and Peschici in summer, and Termoli in nearby Molise year-round.

Valle d'Itria

Between the Ionian and Adriatic coasts rises the great limestone plateau of the Murgia (473m). It has a strange karst geology: the landscape is riddled with holes and ravines through which small streams and rivers gurgle, creating what is, in effect, a giant sponge. At the heart of the Murgia lies the idyllic Valle d'Itria. Here you will begin to spot curious circular stone-built houses dotting the countryside, their roofs tapering up to a stubby and endearing point. These are *trulli*, Puglia's unique rural architecture. It's unclear why the architecture developed in this way; one popular story says that it was so the dry-stone constructions could be quickly dismantled, to avoid payment of building taxes.

The rolling green valley is criss-crossed by dry-stone walls, vineyards, almond and olive groves, and winding country lanes. This is the part of Puglia most visited by foreign tourists and is the best served by hotels and luxury *masserias* (working farms) or manor farms. Around here are also many of Puglia's self-catering villas; to find them, try websites such as www.tuscanynow.com, www.ownersdirect.co.uk, www.holidayhomesin italy.co.uk and www.trulliland.com.

Grotte di Castellana

Grotte di Castellana   CAVE
(☑080 499 82 21; www.grottedicastellana.it; Piazzale Anelli; admission €15; ⊙9am-6pm Mar-Oct, by prior appointment Nov-Feb) Don't miss these spectacular limestone caves, 40km southeast of Bari and Italy's longest natural subterranean network. The interlinked galleries, first discovered in 1938, contain an incredible range of underground landscapes, with extraordinary stalactite and stalagmite formations – look out for the jellyfish, the bacon and the stocking. The highlight is the Grotta Bianca (White Grotto), an eerie white alabaster cavern hung with stiletto-thin stalactites.

There are two tours in English: a 1km, 50-minute tour that doesn't include the Grotta Bianca (€10, on the half-hour); and a 3km, two-hour tour (€15, on the hour) that does include it. The temperature inside the cave averages 18°C so take a light jacket.

Visit, too, the Museo Speleologico Franco Anelli (☑080 499 82 30; ⊙9.30am-1pm & 3.30-6.30pm mid-Mar–Oct, 10am-1pm Nov–mid-Mar) FREE or the Osservatorio Astronomico Sirio (☑080 499 82 13; admission €4; ⊙guided visits only by appointment), with its telescope and solar filters allowing for maximum solar-system visibility.

ⓘ Getting There & Away

The grotto can be reached by rail from Bari on the FSE Bari–Taranto train line, but not all trains stop at Grotte di Castellana. However, all services stop at Castellana Grotte (€2.80, 50 minutes, roughly hourly), 2km before the grotto, from where you can catch a local bus (€1.10) to the caves.

Alberobello

POP 11,000
Unesco World Heritage Site Alberobello resembles an urban sprawl – for gnomes. The

Zona dei Trulli on the western hill of town is a dense mass of 1500 beehive-shaped houses, white-tipped as if dusted by snow. These dry-stone buildings are made from local limestone; none are older than the 14th century. Inhabitants do not wear pointy hats, but they do sell anything a visitor might want, from miniature *trulli* to woollen shawls.

The town is named after the primitive oak forest Arboris Belli (beautiful trees) that once covered this area. It's an amazing place, but also something of a tourist trap – from May to October busloads of tourists pile into *trullo* homes, drink in *trullo* bars and shop in *trullo* shops.

If you park in Lago Martellotta, follow the steps up to Piazza del Popolo, where the Belvedere Trulli lookout offers fabulous views over the whole higgledy-piggledy picture.

◉ Sights

Rione Monti   NEIGHBOURHOOD
Within the old town quarter of Rione Monti more than 1000 *trulli* cascade down the hillside, most of which are now souvenir shops. The area is surprisingly quiet and atmospheric in the late evening, once the gaudy stalls have been stashed away.

Rione Aia Piccola   NEIGHBOURHOOD
On the eastern side of Via Indipendenza is Rione Aia Piccola. This neighbourhood is much less commercialised than Rione Monti, with 400 *trulli*, many still used as family dwellings. You can climb up for a rooftop view at many shops, although most do have a strategically located basket for donations.

Trullo Sovrano   MUSEUM
(☑080 432 60 30; Piazza Sacramento; admission €1.50; ⊙10am-6pm) In the modern part of town, the 18th-century Trullo Sovrano is the only two-floor *trullo*, built by a wealthy priest's family. It's a small museum providing an insight into *trullo* life, with sweet, rounded rooms that include a re-created bakery, bedroom and kitchen. The souvenir shop here has a wealth of literature on the town and surrounding area, plus Alberobello recipe books.

🛏 Sleeping

It's a unique experience to stay in your own *trullo*, though some people might find Alberobello too touristy to use as a base.

MASSERIAS: LUXURY ON THE FARM

Masserias are unique to southern Italy. Modelled on the classical Roman villa, these for-tified farmhouses – equipped with oil mills, cellars, chapels, storehouses and accommo-dation for workers and livestock – were built to function as self-sufficient communities. These days, they still produce the bulk of Italy's olive oil, but many have been converted into luxurious hotels, *agriturismi* (farm stay accommodation), holiday apartments or restaurants. Staying in a *masseria* is a unique experience, especially when you can dine on home-grown produce.

Il Frantoio (☑ 0831 33 02 76; www.masseriailfrantoio.it; SS16, km 874; d €180-240, ste €250; P @) Stay at this charming, whitewashed farmhouse, where the owners still live and work producing high-quality organic olive oil. (Or else book yourself in for one of the marathon eight-course lunches – the food is superb.) Owner Armando takes guests for a tour of the farm each evening in his 1949 Fiat. Il Frantoio lies 5km outside Ostuni along the SS16 in the direction of Fasano. You'll see the sign on your left-hand side when you reach the km 874 sign.

Masseria Torre Coccaro (☑ 080 482 93 10; www.masseriatorrecoccaro.com; Contrada Coccaro 8; d €430-520, ste €614-1365; ❄ @ ☎ ⛱) For pure luxury, stay at this superchic yet countrified *masseria*. There's a glorious spa set in a cave, a beach-style swimming pool, cooking courses on offer and a restaurant (meals €90) dishing up home-grown produce. It's around 10km from Locorotondo.

Masseria Maizza (www.masseriatorremaizza.com; d €460–558, ste €678–1522; ❄ @ ☎ ⛱) Around 10km from Locorotondo is Masseria Maizza. It is a luxurious farm-complex conversion but is contemporary and glamorous, and aimed at couples. There is a balmy beach club (about 4km away) and neighbouring golf course. It also runs cookery courses.

Borgo San Marco (☑ 080 439 57 57; www.borgosanmarco.it; Contrada Sant'Angelo 33; d from €165; P ❄ ☎ ⛱) Once a *borgo* (medieval town), this *masseria* has 16 rooms, a spa in the orchard and is traditional with a bohemian edge. Nearby are some frescoed rock churches. It's 8km from Ostuni; to get here take the SS379 in the direction of Bari, exiting at the sign that says 'SC San Marco–Zona Industriale Sud Fasano', then follow the signs. Note: there's a four-night minimum stay in July, and seven-night minimum in August.

Casa Albergo Sant'Antonio HOTEL $
(☑ 080 432 29 13; www.santantonioalbergo.it; Via Isonzo 8a; s/d/tr/q €50/76/95/110; ☎) Excel-lent value right in the heart of the Rione Monti neighbourhood, this simple hotel is in an old monastery and located next to a unique *trulli*-style church with a conical roof. Rooms are relatively monastic and spartan, but will do the trick for the un-fussy.

Camping dei Trulli CAMPGROUND $
(☑ 080 432 36 99; www.campingdeitrulli.com; Via Castellana Grotte; camping 2 people, car & tent €26.50, bungalows per person €25-40, trulli €30-60; P @ ⛱) This campground, 1.5km out of town, has some nice tent sites, a restaurant, a market, two swimming pools, tennis courts and bicycle hire. You can also rent *trulli* off the grounds.

Trullidea TRULLO $$
(☑ 080 432 38 60; www.trullidea.it; Via Monte San Gabriele 1; 2-person trullo €99-150; ☎) Fifteen renovated, quaint, cosy and atmospheric *trulli* in Alberobello's *trulli* zone available on a self-catering, B&B, or half- or full-board basis.

🍴 Eating

Trattoria Terra Madre ITALIAN $
(☑ 080 432 38 29; www.trattoriaterramadre.it; Piazza Sacramento 17; meals €18.50; ⊙ 8-11pm Tue-Sun; 🍴) 🌿 Run by the charming peo-ple from Charming Tours, this ambitious venture slavishly honours the farm-to-table ethos – most of what you eat will have been plucked within sight of your plate from the organic garden outside. The vegetable an-tipasto is epic, ditto the chickpea soup and stuffed artichokes. The place is educational

too: various alcoves in the restaurant explain the harvesting and processing techniques.

La Cantina TRADITIONAL ITALIAN **$$**
(☑080 432 34 73; www.ilristorantelacantina.it; cnr Corso Vittorio Emanuele & Vico Lippolis; meals €25; ☺noon-3pm & 8-11.30pm Wed-Mon) Although tourists have discovered this place, located to the side of a little Doric temple, it has maintained the high standards established back in 1958. There are just seven tables (book ahead), and staff serve delicious meals made with fresh seasonal produce.

Il Poeta Contadino TRADITIONAL ITALIAN **$$$**
(☑080 432 19 17; www.ilpoetacontadino.it; Via Indipendenza 21; meals €65; ☺noon-2.30pm & 7-10.30pm Tue-Sun Feb-Dec) Located just outside the main throng, the dining room here has a medieval banquet feel with its sumptuous decor and chandeliers. Dine on a poetic menu that includes the signature dish, broad bean purée with *cavatelli* (rod-shaped pasta) and seafood.

❶ Information

Tourist Office (☑080 432 51 71; Via Garibaldi; ☺8am-1pm Mon, Wed & Fri, 8am-1pm & 3-6pm Tue & Thu) Just off the main square. There is another tourist information office (☑080 432 28 22; www.prolocoalberobello.it; Monte Nero 1; ☺9am-7.30pm) in the Zona dei Trulli.

❶ Getting There & Away

Alberobello is easily accessible from Bari (€4.90, 1½ hours, hourly) on the FSE Bari–Taranto train line. From the station, walk straight ahead along Via Mazzini, which becomes Via Garibaldi, to reach Piazza del Popolo.

Locorotondo

POP 14,200

Locorotondo is endowed with a whisper-quiet pedestrianised *centro storico,* where everything is shimmering white aside from the blood-red geraniums that tumble from the window boxes. Situated on a hilltop on the Murge Plateau, it's a *borgo più bella d'Italia* (www.borghitalia.it) – that is, it's rated as one of the most beautiful towns in Italy. There are few 'sights' as such – rather, the town itself is a sight. The streets are paved with smooth ivory-coloured stones, with the church of Santa Maria della Graecia as their sunbaked centrepiece.

From Villa Comunale, a public garden, you can enjoy panoramic views of the surrounding valley. You enter the historic quarter directly across from here.

Not only is this deepest *trulli* country, it's also the liquid heart of the Puglian wine region. Sample some of the local *spumante* at Cantina del Locorotondo (☑080 431 16 44; www.locorotondodoc.com; Via Madonna della Catena 99; ☺9am-1pm & 3-7pm).

🛏 Sleeping

Truddhi TRULLO **$**
(☑080 443 13 26; www.trulliresidence.it; Contrada da Trito 292; d €65-80, apt €100-150, per week from €450-741; **P ❄**) This charming cluster of 10 self-catering *trulli* in the hamlet of Trito near Locorotondo is surrounded by olive groves and vineyards. It's a tranquil place and you can take cooking courses (per day €80) with Mino, a lecturer in gastronomy.

★**Sotto le Cummerse** APARTMENT **$$**
(☑080 431 32 98; www.sottolecummerse.it; Via Vittorio Veneto 138; apt incl breakfast €82-298; **❄ ❄**) At this *albergo diffuso* you'll stay in tastefully furnished apartments scattered throughout the *centro storico*. The apartments are traditional buildings that have been beautifully restored and furnished. Excellent value and a great base for exploring the region.

🍴 Eating

★**Quanto Basta** PIZZA **$**
(☑080 431 28 55; Via Morelli 12; pizza €6-7; ☺7.30-11.30pm Tue-Sun) Craft beer and pizza make an excellent combination, no more so than at Quanto Basta in the old town with its wooden tables, soft lighting and stone floors.

La Taverna del Duca TRATTORIA **$$**
(☑080 431 30 07; www.tavernadelducascatigna.it; Via Papadotero 3; meals €35; ☺noon-3pm & 7.30pm-midnight Tue-Sat, noon-3pm Sun & Mon) In a narrow side street off Piazza Vittorio Emanuele, this well-regarded trattoria serves local classics such as *orecchiette* with various vegetable sidekicks.

❶ Information

Tourist Office (☑080 431 30 99; www.prolo colocorotondo.it; Piazza Vittorio Emanuele 27; ☺10am-1pm & 3-6pm Mon-Fri, 10am-1pm Sat) Offers free internet access.

❶ Getting There & Away

Locorotondo is easily accessible via frequent trains from Bari (€5.60, 1½ to two hours) on the FSE Bari–Taranto train line.

Martina Franca

POP 49,800

The old quarter of this town is a picturesque scene of winding alleys, blinding white houses and blood-red geraniums. There are graceful baroque and rococo buildings here too, plus airy piazzas and curlicue ironwork balconies that almost touch above the narrow streets.

This town is the highest in the Murgia, and was founded in the 10th century by refugees fleeing the Arab invasion of Taranto. It only started to flourish in the 14th century when Philip of Anjou granted tax exemptions (*franchigie,* hence Franca); the town became so wealthy that a castle and defensive walls, complete with 24 solid bastions, were built.

◉ Sights & Activities

The best way to appreciate Martina Franca's beauty is to wander around the narrow lanes and alleyways of the *centro storico.*

Passing under the baroque Arco di Sant'Antonio at the western end of pedestrianised Piazza XX Settembre, you emerge into Piazza Roma, dominated by the imposing, 17th-century rococo Palazzo Ducale (Piazza Roma 32; ⊙9am-1pm Mon-Fri, 9.30am-12.30pm Sat & Sun) FREE, whose upper rooms have semi-restored frescoed walls and host temporary art exhibitions.

From Piazza Roma, follow the fine Corso Vittorio Emanuele, with baroque townhouses, to reach Piazza Plebiscito, the centre's baroque heart. The piazza is overlooked by the 18th-century Basilica di San Martino, its centrepiece a statue of city patron, St Martin, swinging a sword and sharing his cloak with a beggar.

Walkers can ask for the free *Carta dei Sentieri del Bosco delle Pianelle* brochure at the tourist office, which maps out 10 walks in the nearby Bosco delle Pianelle (around 10km west of town). This lush woodland is part of the larger 1206-hectare Riserva Naturale Regionale Orientata, populated with lofty trees, wild orchids, and a rich and varied bird life, including kestrels, owls, buzzards, hoopoe and sparrow hawks.

Festivals & Events

Festival della Valle d'Itria   MUSIC

This annual music festival (late July to early August) features international performances of opera, classical music and jazz. For information, contact the Centro Artistico Musicale Paolo Grassi (☑080 480 51 00; www.festivaldellavalleditria.it; ⊙10am-1pm Mon-Fri) in the Palazzo Ducale.

▥ Sleeping

B&B San Martino   B&B $

(☑080 48 56 01; http://xoomer.virgilio.it/bed-and-breakfast-sanmartino; Via Abate Fighera 32; d €40-120; ❀) A stylish B&B in a historic palace with rooms overlooking gracious Piazza XX Settembre. The rooms have exposed stone walls, shiny parquet floors, wrought-iron beds and small kitchenettes.

Villaggio In   APARTMENT $$

(☑080 480 59 11; www.villaggioincasesparse.it; Via Arco Grassi 8; apt €75-170, per week €420-1050; ❀⊛) These charming apartments with arched ceilings are located in original *centro storico* homes. The rooms are large, painted in pastel colours and decorated with antiques and country frills. A variety of apartments are on offer, sleeping from two to six people.

✕ Eating

Gran Caffè   CAFE $

(Piazza XX Settembre 7; snacks €1-4; ⊙7am-2am) Quintessential Italian cafe. Sit. People-watch. Sip coffee. Nibble croissants. Repeat.

La Piazzetta Garibaldi   OSTERIA $$

(☑080 430 49 00; Piazza Garibaldi; meals €24-28; ⊙noon-3pm & 7.30pm-midnight Thu-Tue) A highly recommended green-shuttered *osteria* in the *centro storico.* Delicious aromas entice you into the cave-like interior and the *cucina tipica* menu of typical Pugliese food doesn't disappoint. Worthy of a long lunch.

Ciacco   PUGLIAN $$

(☑080 480 04 72; Via Conte Ugolino; meals €30; ⊙12.30-2.30pm & 8-11pm Tue-Sun) Dive into the historic centre to find Ciacco, a traditional restaurant with white-clad tables and a cosy fireplace, serving up Puglian cuisine in a modern key. It's tucked down a narrow pedestrian lane a couple of streets in from the Chiesa del Carmine.

ⓘ Information

Tourist Office (☏ 080 480 57 02; Piazza XX Settembre 3; ⏱ 9am-1pm Mon-Fri, plus 4.30-7pm Tue & Thu, 9am-12.30pm Sat) The tourist office is to the right of the Arco di Sant'Antonio just before you enter the old town.

ⓘ Getting There & Around

The FSE train station is downhill from the historic centre. From the train station, go right along Viale della Stazione, continue along Via Alessandro Fighera to Corso Italia, then continue to the left along Corso Italia to Piazza XX Settembre.

FSE (☏ 080 546 21 11) trains run to/from the following destinations:

Bari €5.60, two hours, hourly

Lecce €7.70, two hours, five daily

Taranto €2.40, 40 minutes, frequent

FSE buses run to Alberobello (€1, 30 minutes, five daily Monday to Saturday).

Ostuni

POP 32,500

Chic Ostuni shines like a pearly white tiara, extending across three hills with the magnificent gem of a cathedral as its sparkling centrepiece. It's the end of the *trulli* region and the beginning of the hot, dry Salento. With some excellent restaurants, stylish bars and swish yet intimate places to stay, it's packed in summer.

⊙ Sights

Ostuni is surrounded by olive groves, so this is the place to buy some of the region's DOC 'Collina di Brindisi' olive oil – either delicate, medium or strong – direct from producers.

Cathedral　　　　　　　　　　　CATHEDRAL
(Via Cattedrale; admission €1; ⏱ 9am-1pm & 3-7pm) Ostuni's dramatic 15th-century cathedral has an unusual Gothic-Romanesque facade with a frilly rose window and an inverted gable.

**Museo di Civiltà Preclassiche
della Murgia**　　　　　　　　　　MUSEUM
(☏ 0831 33 63 83; Via Cattedrale 15; ⏱ 10am-1pm Tue-Fri, 10am-1pm & 4-7pm Sat & Sun) FREE Located in the Convento delle Monacelle, the museum's most famous exhibit is the 25,000-year-old star of the show: Delia. She was pregnant at the time of her death and her well-preserved skeleton was found in a local cave. Many of the finds here come from the Palaeolithic burial ground, now the **Parco Archeologico e Naturale di Arignano**

(☏ 0831 30 39 73), which can be visited by appointment.

🏃 Activities

The surrounding countryside is perfect for cycling. **Ciclovagando** (☏ 330 985255; www.ciclovagando.com; Via di Savoia 19, Mesagne; half-/full-day €30/40), based in Mesagne, 30km south of Ostuni, organises guided tours. Each tour covers approximately 20km and departs daily from various towns in the district, including Ostuni and Brindisi. For an extra €15 you can sample typical Puglian foods on the tour.

🎊 Festivals & Events

La Cavalcata　　　　　　　　　RELIGIOUS
Ostuni's annual feast day is held on 26 August, when processions of horsemen dressed in glittering red-and-white uniforms (resembling Indian grooms on their way to be wed) follow the statue of Sant'Oronzo around town.

🛏 Sleeping

Le Sole Blu　　　　　　　　　　B&B $
(☏ 0831 30 38 56; www.webalice.it/solebluostuni; Corso Vittorio Emanuele II 16; s €30-40, d €60-80) Located in the 18th-century (rather than medieval) part of town, Le Sole Blu only has one room available: it's large and has a separate entrance, but the bathroom is tiny. However, the two self-catering apartments nearby are excellent value.

★ La Terra　　　　　　　　　　HOTEL $$
(☏ 0831 33 66 51; www.laterrahotel.it; Via Petrarolo; d €130-170; 🅿 ❄ 🛜) This former 13th-century palace offers atmospheric and stylish accommodation with original niches, dark-wood beams and furniture, and contrasting light stonework and whitewash. The result is a cool contemporary look. The bar is as cavernous as they come – it's tunnelled out of a cave.

🍴 Eating

Osteria Piazzetta Cattedrale　OSTERIA $$
(☏ 0831 33 50 26; www.piazzettacattedrale.it; Via Arcidiacono Trinchera 7; meals €30-40; ⏱ 12.30-3pm & 7pm-12.30am Wed-Mon) Just beyond the arch opposite Ostuni's cathedral is this tiny little hostelry serving up magical food in an atmospheric setting. The menu includes plenty of vegetarian options.

PUGLIA, BASILICATA & CALABRIA VALLE D'ITRIA

Osteria del Tempo Perso
OSTERIA $$

(☑ 0831 30 33 20; www.osteriadeltempoperso. com; Gaetano Tanzarella Vitale 47; meals €30; ⊗ 12.30-3pm & 7.30-11pm Tue-Sun) A sophisticated rustic restaurant in a cave-like former bakery, this laid-back place serves great Puglian food, specialising in roasted meats. To get here, face the cathedral's south wall and turn right through the archway into Largo Giuseppe Spennati, then follow the signs.

Porta Nova
MODERN ITALIAN $$$

(☑ 0831 33 89 83; www.ristoranteportanova.com; Via G Petrarolo 38; meals €45; ⊗ 1-3.30pm & 7-11pm) This restaurant has a wonderful location on the old city wall. Revel in the rolling views from the terrace or relax in the elegant interior while you feast on top-notch local cuisine, with seafood the speciality.

❶ Information

Tourist Office (☑ 0831 30 12 68; Corso Mazzini 8; ⊗ 9am-1pm & 5-9pm Mon-Fri, 5.30-8.30pm Sat & Sun) Located off Piazza della Libertà; can organise guided visits of the town in summer, and bike rental.

❶ Getting There & Around

STP Brindisi (p743) buses run to Brindisi (€3.10, 50 minutes, six daily) and to Martina Franca (€2.10, 45 minutes, three daily), leaving from Piazza Italia in the newer part of Ostuni.

Trains run frequently to Brindisi (€4, 25 minutes) and Bari (€9, 50 minutes). A half-hourly local bus covers the 2.5km between the station and town.

Lecce
POP 95,000

If Puglia were a movie, Lecce would be cast in the starring role. Bequeathed with a generous stash of baroque buildings by its 17th-century architects, the city has a completeness and homogeneity that other southern Italian metropolises lack. Indeed, so distinctive is Lecce's architecture that it has acquired its own moniker, *barocco leccese* (Lecce baroque), an expressive and hugely decorative incarnation of the genre replete with gargoyles, asparagus columns and cavorting gremlins. Swooning 18th-century traveller Thomas Ashe thought it 'the most beautiful city in Italy', but the less-impressed Marchese Grimaldi said the facade of Basilica di Santa Croce made him think a lunatic was having a nightmare.

Either way, it's a lively, graceful but relaxed university town with some decent Puglian restaurants, and a strong tradition for papier-mâché making. Both the Adriatic and Ionian Seas are within easy access and it's a great base from which to explore the Salento.

◉ Sights

Lecce has more than 40 churches and at least as many *palazzi*, all built or renovated between the 17th and 18th centuries, giving the city an extraordinary cohesion. Two of the main proponents of *barocco leccese* were brothers Antonio and Giuseppe Zimbalo, who both had a hand in the fantastical Basilica di Santa Croce.

★ Basilica di Santa Croce
CHURCH

(☑ 0832 24 19 57; www.basilicasantacroce.eu; Via Umberto I; ⊗ 9am-noon & 5-8pm) It seems that hallucinating stonemasons have been at work on the basilica. Sheep, dodos, cherubs and beasties writhe across the facade. Throughout the 16th and 17th centuries, a team of artists under Giuseppe Zimbalo laboured to work the building up to this pitch. Look for Zimbalo's profile on the facade. The interior is more conventionally Renaissance and deserves a look, once you've drained your camera batteries outside. Zimbalo also left his mark in the former Convento dei Celestini, just north of the basilica, which is now the **Palazzo del Governo**, the local government headquarters.

Piazza del Duomo
PIAZZA

Piazza del Duomo is a baroque feast, the city's focal point and a sudden open space amid the surrounding enclosed lanes. During times of invasion the inhabitants of Lecce would barricade themselves in the square, which has conveniently narrow entrances. The 12th-century **cathedral** (crypt €1; ⊗ 8.30am-12.30pm & 4-8.30pm) is one of Giuseppe Zimbalo's finest works; he was also responsible for the 68m-high bell tower.

The cathedral is unusual in that it has two facades, one on the western end and the other, more ornate, facing the piazza. It's framed by the 15th-century **Palazzo Vescovile** (Episcopal Palace; Piazza del Duomo) and the 18th-century Seminario, designed by Giuseppe Cino. The latter hosts a library of old books and the **Museo Diocesano di Arte Sacra** (Piazza del Duomo; admission €1; ⊗ 9.30am-12.30pm & 5.30-8.30pm), home to religious art.

Lecce

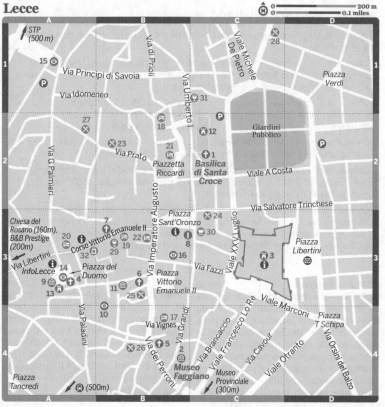

PUGLIA, BASILICATA & CALABRIA LECCE

LECCE'S NOTABLE CHURCHES

Lecce's unique baroque style is perhaps best seen in its churches; the city harbours dozens of them.

Chiesa di Sant'Irene (Corso Vittorio Emanuele II; ⏰7.30-11am & 4-6pm) The interior of 17th-century Chiesa di Sant'Irene contains a magnificent pair of mirror-image baroque altarpieces facing each other across the transept.

Chiesa di Santa Chiara (Piazza Vittorio Emanuele II; ⏰9.30-11.30am daily, plus 4.30-6.30pm Mon-Sat) A notable baroque church with every niche a swirl of twisting columns and ornate statuary. The ceiling is classic Leccese papier-mâché.

Chiesa di San Matteo (Via dei Perroni 29; ⏰7.30-11am & 4-6pm) Located 200m to the south of Chiesa di Santa Chiara. It's the last work of Giuseppe Zimbalo.

Chiesa del Rosario (Via Libertini; ⏰8am-1pm & 4-8pm) Instead of the intended dome roof, this church ended up with a quick-fix wooden one following architect Zimbalo's death before the building was completed.

Chiesa dei SS Nicolò e Cataldo (Via San Nicola; ⏰9am-noon Sep-Apr) The Chiesa dei SS Nicolò e Cataldo, near the main city gate Porta Napoli, was built by the Normans in 1180. It got caught up in the city's baroque frenzy and was revamped in 1716 by the prolific Cino, who retained the Romanesque rose window and portal.

★Museo Faggiano — MUSEUM

(☎360 722448; www.museofaggiano.it; Via Grandi 56/58; admission €3; ⏰9.30am-1pm & 4-8pm) Breaking the floor to replace sewer pipes led the owner of this private home to the chance discovery of an archaeological treasure trove. Layers of history are revealed beneath the floors starting with the Messapii culture in around the 5th century BC and progressing through Roman crypts, medieval walls, Jewish insigna and Knights Templar symbolism in a rooftop tower. You have to see it to believe it!

Museo Provinciale — MUSEUM

(☎0832 68 35 03; Viale Gallipoli 28; ⏰8.30am-7.30pm Mon-Sat, to 1.30pm Sun) FREE This museum stylishly covers 10,000 years of history, from Palaeolithic and Neolithic bits and bobs to a handsome display of Greek and Roman jewels, weaponry and ornaments. The stars of the show are the Messapians, whose jaunty Mycenaean-inspired jugs and bowls date back 2500 years.

Roman Amphitheatre — HISTORIC SITE

(Piazza Sant'Oronzo; ⏰10am-noon & 5-7pm May-Sep) Below the ground level of the piazza is this restored 2nd-century-AD amphitheatre, discovered in 1901 by construction workers. It was excavated in the 1930s to reveal a perfect horseshoe with seating for 15,000. It was closed and a little overgrown at last visit.

MUST — GALLERY

(www.mustlecce.it; Via degli Ammirati 11; admission €3; ⏰10am-1.30pm & 2.30-7.30pm) This beautiful conversion of the Monastery of Santa Chiara houses the work of local artists and has a great view of a Roman amphitheatre from the back window. It was being renovated at last visit but should have reopened by the time you read this, with an extended remit to cover local history.

Colonna di Sant'Oronzo — MONUMENT

(Piazza Sant'Oronzo) Two Roman columns once marked the end of the Appian Way in Brindisi. When one of them crumbled in 1582 some of the pieces were rescued and subsequently donated to Lecce (the base and capital remain in Brindisi). The old column was rebuilt in 1666 with a statue of Lecce's patron saint placed on top. Sant'Oronzo is venerated for supposedly saving the city of Brindisi from a 1656 plague.

Museo Teatro Romano — HISTORIC SITE

(☎0832 27 91 96; Via degli Ammirati; adult/reduced €3/2; ⏰9.30am-1.30pm & 5-7.30pm Mon-Fri, 9.30am-1.30pm Sat) Uncovered in the 1930s, this small Roman theatre has well-preserved russet-coloured Roman mosaics and frescoes.

Castello di Carlo V — CASTLE

(☎0832 24 65 17; admission €5; ⏰9am-8.30pm Mon-Fri, 9.30am-8.30pm Sat & Sun) This 16th-century castle was built around a

12th-century Norman tower to the orders of Spain's Charles V and consists of two concentric trapezoidal structures. It's been used as a prison, a court and a military headquarters; now you can wander around the baronial spaces and visit the on-site papier-mâché museum.

Courses

Awaiting Table
COOKING
(www.awaitingtable.com; day/week course €195/1895) Silvestro Silvestori's splendid culinary and wine school provides day or weeklong courses with market shopping, tours, tastings, noteworthy lecturers – and lots of hands-on cooking. Book well in advance as courses fill up rapidly.

Sleeping

★ Palazzo Rollo
APARTMENT $
(☑ 0832 30 71 52; www.palazzorollo.it; Corso Vittorio Emanuele II 14; s/d €65/85; 🅿 🌐 @) Stay in a 17th-century palace – the Rollo family seat for more than 200 years. The three grand B&B suites (with kitchenettes) have high curved ceilings and chandeliers. Downstairs, contemporary-chic studios open onto an ivy-hung courtyard. The rooftop garden has wonderful views.

Palazzo Belli B&B
B&B $
(☑ 380 7758456; www.palazzobelli.it; Corso Vittorio Emanuele II 33; s/d €60/80; 🛜) A wonderfully central, elegant and well-priced option located in a fine mansion near the cathedral. Rooms have marbled floors and wrought-iron beds. Breakfast is served in the nearby All'Ombra del Barocco bar.

Azzurretta B&B
GUESTHOUSE $
(☑ 0832 24 22 11; www.hostelecce.com; Via Vignes 2; d/tr €70/85; 🅿 🛜) The friendly brother of the owner of Centro Storico B&B runs this artier version located within the same building; ask for the large double with a balcony, wooden floors and a vaulted ceiling. Massage is available in your room or on the roof terrace. You get a cafe voucher for breakfast.

The brothers also have a tiny studio flat, which is a little dark but a good option if you're self-catering on a budget.

B&B Idomeneo 63
B&B $
(☑ 333 9499838; www.bebidomeneo63.it; Via Idomeneo 63; s/d/tr €50/80/95; 🛜) You'll be looked after like a VIP at this wonderfully curated B&B in the midst of Lecce's marvellous baroque quarter, complete with six colour-coded rooms and a funky entrance lounge. Decked out boutique-hotel style, but incorporating some older baroque features (stone ceiling arches), the real treat here is in the little extras such as breakfast, which is delivered on a tray to your room every morning. The upper suite has a roof terrace.

Centro Storico B&B
B&B $
(☑ 328 8351294, 0832 24 27 27; www.centrostoricolecce.it; Via A Vignes 2; s/d €40/60; 🅿 🌐 🛜) This friendly and efficient B&B located in a historic palace features big rooms, double-glazed windows and pleasantly old-fashioned decor. The huge rooftop terrace has sun loungers and views. Cafe vouchers are provided for breakfast, and there are also coffee-and-tea-making facilities.

B&B Prestige
B&B $
(☑ 349 7751290; www.bbprestige-lecce.it; Via Libertini 7; s/d/tr €70/80/110; 🅿 @ 🛜) On the corner of Via Santa Maria del Paradiso in the historic centre, the rooms at this lovely B&B are light, airy and beautifully finished. The communal sun-trap terrace has views over San Giovanni Battista church.

Risorgimento Resort
HOTEL $$
(☑ 0832 24 63 11; www.risorgimentoresort.it; Via Imperatore Augusto 19; d €115-220, ste €215-355; 🅿 🌐 @ 🛜) A warm welcome awaits at this stylish five-star hotel in the centre of Lecce. The rooms are spacious and refined with high ceilings, modern furniture and contemporary details reflecting the colours of the Salento, and the bathrooms are enormous. There's a restaurant, wine bar and rooftop garden.

Patria Palace Hotel
HOTEL $$
(☑ 0832 24 51 11; www.patriapalacelecce.com; Piazzetta Riccardi 13; r from €155; 🅿 🌐 @ 🛜) This sumptuous hotel is traditionally Italian with large mirrors, dark-wood furniture and wistful murals. The location is wonderful, the bar gloriously art deco with a magnificent carved ceiling, and the shady roof terrace has views over the Basilica di Santa Croce.

Eating

★ Trattoria Il Rifugio della Buona Stella
PUGLIAN $
(☑ 366 4373192; www.ilrifugiodellabuonastella.it; Via Prato 28; meals €14-20; ⏱ 12.15-3pm & 7.15-11.30pm Wed-Mon) A third-generation family restaurant in a gorgeous Leccese building with sandy stone walls and medieval decor, this wonderful trattoria serves fine food at

PAPIER-MÂCHÉ ART

Lecce is famous for its papier-mâché art *(cartapesta)*. Statues and figurines are sculpted out of a mixture of paper and glue before being painted and used to adorn churches and other public buildings. Lecce's *cartapesta* culture originated in the 17th century when glue and paper offered cheap raw materials for religious artists who couldn't afford expensive wood or marble. Legend has it that the first exponents of the art were Leccese barbers who shaped and chiseled their morphing statues in between haircuts.

These days the art is still practiced in Lecce and you'll see a number of traditional workshops such as La Cartapesta di Claudio Riso (☑0832 24 34 10; Corso Vittorio Emanuele II 27) scattered around the old town centre. Also worth perusing is the papier-mâché museum inside the Castello di Carlo V (p738) and the decorative papier-mâché ceiling inside the Chiesa di Santa Chiara (p738).

sale-of-the-century prices (*secondi* from €6.50!). Start off with the homemade bread, proceed to pasta with swordfish and rapini, and hit the jackpot with the grilled sausages.

A bottle of Salentino red wine should satisfy most alcohol cravings.

Gelateria Natale   GELATERIA $
(www.natalepasticceria.it; Via Trinchese 7a; ⊘7am-11pm Mon-Fri, 7.30am-1am Sat & Sun) Lecce's best ice-cream parlour also has an array of fabulous confectionery.

Trattoria di Nonna Tetti   TRATTORIA $
(☑0832 24 60 36; Piazzetta Regina Maria 28; mains €8-12; ⊘11am-2pm & 7-11pm Mon-Sat) A warmly inviting restaurant, popular with all ages and budgets, this trattoria serves a wide choice of traditional dishes. Try the most emblematic Puglian dish here – braised wild chicory with a purée of boiled dried broad beans, along with *contorni* (side dishes) like *patate casarecce* (homemade thinly sliced fries).

Trattoria le Zie – Cucina Casareccia   TRATTORIA $
(☑0832 24 51 78; Viale Costadura 19; meals €20-23; ⊘noon-3pm & 7-11pm Tue-Sat, 7-11pm Sun) Ring the bell to gain entry to this place that feels like a private home, with its patterned cement floor tiles, desk piled high with papers, and charming owner Carmela Perrone. In fact, it's known locally as simply le Zie (the aunts). Here you'll taste true *cucina povera*, including horse meat done in a *salsa piccante* (spicy sauce). Booking is a must.

La Torre di Merlino   PIZZA, ITALIAN $$
(☑0832 24 20 91; Via Giambattista del Tufo 10; meals €30-38; ⊘12.30-3pm & 8pm-1am Tue-Sun) It's hard to imagine that anyone couldn't be satisfied by the Merlino's all-encompassing

menu, which includes the best pizza in Lecce washed down with craft beer, some stalwart Puglian pasta dishes, and innovative modern main courses (involving black truffles, rabbit and raw red prawns marinated in lemon). Creative but not pretentious.

Alle due Corti   PUGLIAN $$
(☑0832 24 22 23; www.alleduecorti.com; Via Prato 42; meals €20-23; ⊘12.45-2.15pm & 7.45-11pm Mon-Sat) For a taste of sunny Salento, check out this no-frills, fiercely traditional restaurant. The seasonal menu is classic Puglian, written in a dialect that even some Italians struggle with. Go for the real deal with a dish of *ciceri e tria* (crisply fried pasta with chickpeas).

 Drinking

Via Imperatore Augusto is full of bars, and on a summer's night it feels like one long party. Wander along to find somewhere to settle.

★**Enoteca Mamma Elvira**   WINE BAR
(Via Umberto I 19; ⊘11am-midnight) All you need to know about emerging Salento wine will be imparted by the hip but friendly staff at this cool new joint near the Santa Croce church. Taster glasses are dispatched liberally if you order a few snacks.

All'Ombra del Barocco   WINE BAR
(www.allombradelbarocco.it; Corte dei Cicala 9; ⊘8am-1am) This cool restaurant-cafe-wine bar, next door to the Liberrima bookshop, has a range of teas, cocktails and *aperitivi*. It's open for breakfast and also hosts musical events; the modern cooking is well worth a try. Tables fill the little square outside, an ideal place from which to watch the *passeggiata*.

Caffè Alvino CAFE
(Piazza Sant'Oronzo; ⊗7am-8pm Wed-Mon; 🖭)
Treat yourself to great coffee and *pasticciotto* (custard pie) at this iconic chandeliered cafe in Lecce's main square; it has a hard-to-ignore display of cakes.

ⓘ Information

The historic centre's twin main squares are Piazza Sant'Oronzo and Piazza del Duomo, linked by pedestrianised Corso Vittorio Emanuele II.

Puglia Blog (www.thepuglia.com) An informative site run by Fabio Ingrosso with articles on culture, history, food, wine, accommodation and travel in Puglia.

Hospital (📞0832 66 11 11; Via San Cesario) About 2km south of the centre on the Gallipoli road.

InfoLecce (📞0832 52 18 77; www.infolecce. it; Piazza del Duomo 2; ⊗9.30am-1.30pm & 3.30-7.30pm Mon-Sat, from 10am Sun) Independent and helpful tourist information office. Has guided tours and bike rental (per hour/ day €3/15).

Police Station (📞0832 69 11 11; Viale Otranto 1)

Post Office (Piazza Libertini)

Tourist Office (📞0832 68 29 85; Corso Vittorio Emanuele II 16; ⊗9am-1pm & 4-8pm) One of three main government-run offices. The others are in Castello di Carlo V (📞0832 24 65 17; Castello di Carlo V; ⊗9am-8.30pm Mon-Fri, 9.30am-8.30pm Sat & Sun) and Piazza Sant'Oronzo (📞0832 24 20 99; Piazza Sant'Oronzo; ⊗9.30am-1.30pm & 3.30-7.30pm).

ⓘ Getting There & Away

BUS

The city bus terminal is located to the north of Porta Napoli.

Pugliairbus (http://pugliairbus.aeroportidi puglia.it) Runs to Brindisi airport (€7.50, 40 minutes, nine daily).

STP (📞0832 35 91 42; www.stplecce.it) Runs buses to Brindisi (€6.30, 35 minutes, nine daily), Gallipoli (€2.80, 1¼ hours, frequent) and Otranto (€2.80, two hours, frequent) from the **STP bus station** (📞800 430346; Viale Porta D'Europa).

TRAIN

The main train station, 1km southwest of Lecce's historic centre, runs frequent services.

TO	FARE	DURATION
Bari	€9	1½ -2 hr
Bologna	€59.50	7½-9½ hr
Brindisi	€2.80	30 mins
Naples	€53.10	5½ hr (transfer in Caserta)
Rome	€66	5½-9 hr

FSE trains head to Otranto, Gallipoli and Martina Franca; the ticket office is located on platform 1.

Brindisi

POP 89,800

Like all ports, Brindisi has its seamy side, but it's also surprisingly slow-paced and balmy, particularly the palm-lined Corso Garibaldi, which links the port to the train station, and the promenade stretching along the interesting seafront.

The town was the end of the ancient Roman road Via Appia, down whose length trudged weary legionnaires and pilgrims, crusaders and traders, all heading to Greece and the Near East. These days little has changed except that Brindisi's pilgrims are now sun-seekers rather than soul-seekers.

◎ Sights

Museo Archeologico Provinciale Ribezzo MUSEUM
(📞0831 56 55 08; Piazza del Duomo 8; adult/reduced €5/3; ⊗9.30am-1.30pm Tue-Sat, plus 3.30-6.30pm Tue, Thu & Sat) This superb museum covers several floors with well-documented exhibits (in English), including some 3000 bronze sculptures and fragments in Hellenistic Greek style. There are also terracotta figurines from the 7th century, underwater archaeological finds, and Roman statues and heads (not always together).

Roman Column MONUMENT
(Via Colonne) The gleaming white column above a sweeping set of sun-whitened stairs leading to the waterfront promenade marks the imperial Via Appia terminus at Brindisi. Originally there were two columns, but one was presented to the town of Lecce back in 1666 as thanks to Sant'Oronzo for having relieved Brindisi of the plague.

Brindisi

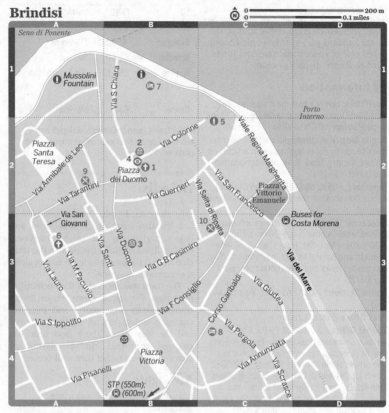

Cathedral   CATHEDRAL
(Piazza del Duomo; ⊘8am-9pm Mon-Fri & Sun, to noon Sat) This 11th-century cathedral was substantially remodelled after an earth-

quake in 1743. You can see how the original Romanesque structure may have looked by studying the nearby Porta dei Cavalieri Templari, a fanciful portico with pointy arches – all that remains of a medieval Knights Templar's church that once also stood here.

**Tempio di San Giovanni
al Sepolcro**   CHURCH
(Via San Giovanni) The Knights Templar's secondary church is a square brown bulk of Norman stone conforming to the circular plan the Templars so loved.

Palazzo Granafei-Nervegna   MUSEUM
(Via Duomo 20; ⊘10am-1pm & 5-8pm Tue-Sun) **FREE** A 16th-century Renaissance-style palace named for the two different families who owned it. The building is of interest because it houses the huge ornate capital that used to sit atop one of the Roman columns that marked the end of the Appian Way (the rest of the column is in Lecce). Also on site

---

is a salubrious cafe and the archaeological remains of a Roman *domus* (house).

Sleeping

Grande Albergo Internazionale HOTEL **$$**
(☑ 0831 52 34 73; www.albergointernazionale.it; Viale Regina Margherita 23; s/d €100/160; P ❀ ☎) Built in 1870 for English merchants en route to Bombay and the Raj, the Internazionale offers grandeur, albeit of the rather faded variety. It has great harbour views, large rooms with grandly draped curtains, and stately common areas, but modern gadgetry takes second place to history here. Look out for off-season online room deals.

Hotel Orientale HOTEL **$$**
(☑ 0831 56 84 51; www.hotelorientale.it; Corso Garibaldi 40; s/d €75/130; P ❀ ☎) This sleek, modern hotel overlooks the long palm-lined *corso*. Rooms are pleasant, the location is good and it has a small fitness centre, private car park and (rare) cooked breakfast option.

✕ Eating

Trattoria Pantagruele TRATTORIA **$$**
(☑ 0831 56 06 05; Via Salita di Ripalta 1; meals €30; ☺ noon-3pm & 7.30-11.30pm Mon-Fri, 7.30-11.30pm Sat) Named after French writer François Rabelais' satirical character, this charming trattoria three blocks from the waterfront serves up excellent fish and grilled meats.

Il Giardino PUGLIAN **$$**
(☑ 0831 56 40 26; Via Tarantini 14-18; meals €30; ☺ 12.30-2.30pm & 7.30-10.30pm Tue-Sat, 12.30-2.30pm Sun) Established more than 40 years ago in a restored 15th-century *palazzo*, sophisticated Il Giardino serves refined seafood and meat dishes in a delightful garden setting.

ℹ Information

The new port is east of town, across the Seno di Levante at Costa Morena, in a bleak industrial wilderness.

The old port is about 1km from the train station along Corso Umberto I, which leads into Corso Garibaldi where there are numerous cafes, shops, ferry companies and travel agencies.

Antono Perrino Hospital (☑ 0831 53 71 11) Southwest of the centre; take the SS7 for Mesagne.

Post Office (Piazza Vittoria)

Tourist Office (☑ 0831 52 30 72; www.viaggiareinpuglia.it; Viale Regina Margherita 44; ☺ 9am-8.30pm Tue-Sun) Has a wealth of information and brochures on the area. If you are interested in pedal power, pick up *Le Vie Verdi* map, which shows eight bicycling routes in the Brindisi area, ranging from 6km to 30km.

ℹ Getting There & Away

AIR

From **Salento Airport** (BDS; ☑ 0831 411 74 06; www.aeroportidipuglia.it), Brindisi's small airport, there are domestic flights to Rome, Naples and Milan. Airlines include Alitalia and easyJet. There are also direct flights from London Stansted with Ryanair.

BOAT

Ferries, all of which take vehicles, leave Brindisi for Greece and Albania.

Ferry companies have offices at Costa Morena (the newer port), which is 4km from the train station. A free bus connects the two.

Grimaldi Lines (☑ 0831 54 81 16; www.grimaldi-lines.com; Costa Morena Terminal) Daily ferries to Igoumenitsa and Patras in Greece.

Red Star Ferries (☑ 0831 57 52 89; www.directferries.co.uk/red_star_ferries.htm; Costa Morena Terminal) To Vlorë in Albania.

BUS

There are regular SITA buses to Lecce (€6.30, 35 minutes, nine daily).

Pugliairbus (http://pugliairbus.aeroportidipuglia.it) Has services to Bari airport (€10, 1¾ hours) and Lecce (€7.50, 40 minutes) from Brindisi's airport.

Ferrovie del Sud-Est buses serving local towns leave from Via Bastioni Carlo V, in front of the train station.

Marozzi (☑ 0831 52 16 84) Runs to Rome's Stazione Tiburtina (€37.50 to €40, six to seven hours, four daily) from Viale Arno.

STP Brindisi (www.stpbrindisi.it) Buses go to Ostuni (€3.10, 50 minutes, six daily) and Lecce (€2.80, 45 minutes, two daily), as well as towns throughout the Salento. Most leave from Via Bastioni Carlo V, in front of the train station.

TRAIN

The train station has regular services to the following destinations:
Bari from €8.40, one hour
Lecce from €2.80, 30 minutes
Milan from €99.50, 8½ to 11 hours
Rome from €70, eight to twelve hours
Taranto from €4.90, one hour

ℹ Getting Around

Major and local car-rental firms are represented at the airport. To reach the airport by bus, take the STP-run **Cotrap** bus (✆ 800 232042; www.stpbrindisi.it; single ticket €1) from Via Bastoni Carlo V.

A free **minibus** connects the train station and old ferry terminal with Costa Morena. It departs two hours before boat departures. You'll need a valid ferry ticket.

Southern & Western Salento

The Penisola Salentina, better known simply as Salento, is hot, dry and remote, retaining a flavour of its Greek past. It stretches across Italy's heel from Brindisi to Taranto and down to Santa Maria di Leuca. Here the lush greenery of Valle d'Itria gives way to flat, ochre-coloured fields hazy with wildflowers in spring, and endless olive groves.

Galatina

POP 27,300

With a charming historic centre, Galatina, 18km south of Lecce, is at the core of the Salentine Peninsula's Greek past. It is almost the only place where the ritual *tarantismi* (spider music) is still practised. The tarantella folk dance evolved from this ritual, and each year on the feast day of St Peter and St Paul (29 June), it is performed at the (now deconsecrated) church.

◉ Sights

Basilica di Santa Caterina d'Alessandria CHURCH
(◷ 8am-12.30pm & 4.30-6.45pm Apr-Sep, 8am-12.30pm & 3.45-5.45pm Oct-Mar) Most people come to Galatina to see the incredible 14th-century Basilica di Santa Caterina d'Alessandria. Its interior is a kaleidoscope of frescoes and is absolutely beautiful, with a pure-white altarpiece set against the frenzy of frescoes. It was built by the Franciscans, whose patron was Frenchwoman Marie d'Enghien de Brienne.

Married to Raimondello Orsini del Balzo, the Salentine's wealthiest noble, Marie had plenty of cash to splash on interior decoration. The gruesome story goes that Raimondello (who is buried here) climbed Mount Sinai to visit relics of Santa Caterina (St Catherine). Kissing the dead saint's hand, he bit off a finger and brought it back as a holy relic.

It is not clear who the artists Marie employed really were; they could have been

itinerant painters down from Le Marche and Emilia or southerners who'd absorbed the latest Renaissance innovations on trips north. Bring a torch.

🛏 Sleeping

Samadhi AGRITURISMO
(✆ 0836 60 02 84; www.agricolasamadhi.com; Via Stazione 116; r with/without bathroom €119/99; ❄ 🔇 😑) ✐ Soothe the soul with a stay at Samadhi, located around 7km east of Galatina in tiny Zollino. It's on a 10-hectare organic farm and the owners are multilingual. As well as ayurvedic treatments and yoga courses, there's a vegan restaurant offering organic meals. Check the website for upcoming retreats and courses.

❶ Getting There & Away

FSE runs frequent trains between Lecce and Galatina (€2.10, 30 minutes), and Galatina and Zollino (€1, eight minutes).

Otranto

POP 5540

Bloodied and bruised by an infamous Turkish massacre in 1480, Otranto's story is best told in its amazing cathedral where the bones of 813 martyrs are displayed in a glass case behind the altar. Less macabre is the cathedral's other jaw-dropper, its medieval mosaic floor that rivals the famous early Christian mosaics of Ravenna in its richness and historical significance.

Lying deep in Italy's stiletto, Otranto has back-heeled quite a few invaders over the centuries and been brutally kicked by others – most notably the Turks. Sleuth around its compact old quarter and you can peel the past off in layers – Greek, Roman, Turkish and Napoleonic. These days the town is a generally peaceful place, unless you're fighting for beach space at the height of summer.

◉ Sights

★ Cathedral CATHEDRAL
(✆ 0836 80 27 20; Piazza Basilica; ◷ 7am-noon daily, plus 3-7pm Apr-Sep, 3-6pm Oct-Mar) Mosaics, skulls, crypts and biblical-meets-tropical imagery: Otranto's cathedral is like no other in Italy. The church was built by the Normans in the 11th century, though it's been given a few facelifts since. Covering the entire floor is its pièce de résistance, a vast 12th-century mosaic of a stupendous tree of life balanced on the back of two elephants.

The mosaic was created by a young monk called Pantaleone in 1165, whose vision of heaven and hell encompassed an amazing (con)fusion of the classics, religion and plain old superstition, including Adam and Eve, Diana the huntress, Hercules, King Arthur, Alexander the Great, and a menagerie of monkeys, snakes and sea monsters.

Beguiled by the well-preserved floor, most people forget to look up at the beautiful wooden coffered ceiling.

The beauty of the floor contrasts sharply with the ghoulishly fascinating **Cappella Mortiri** (Chapel of the Dead), where the bones and skulls of 813 Otranto martyrs beheaded by the invading Turks peer out of seven tall glass cases. The stone upon which the grisly deed was allegedly carried out is preserved behind the altar.

If the bones haven't freaked you out, the church also has a dungeon-like crypt to explore.

Castello Aragonese Otranto   CASTLE
(www.castelloaragoneseotranto.it; Piazza Castello; adult/child €2/free; ☉9am-1pm & 3-7pm) This squat, thick-walled fort, with the Charles V coat of arms above the entrance, has great views from the ramparts. There are some faded original murals and original cannonballs on display.

Chiesa di San Pietro   CHURCH
(Via San Pietro; ☉10am-noon & 3-6pm) Vivid Byzantine frescoes decorate the interior of this church, which was being restored at the time of writing. Follow the signs from Castello Aragonese Otranto; if it's closed, ask for the key at the cathedral.

🏃 Activities

There are some great beaches north of Otranto, especially **Baia dei Turchi**, with its translucent blue water. South of Otranto a spectacular rocky coastline makes for an impressive drive down to Castro. To see what goes on underwater, **Scuba Diving Otranto** (☏0836 80 27 40; www.scubadiving.it; Via Francesco di Paola 43) offers day or night dives as well as introductory courses and diving courses.

🛏 Sleeping

Balconcino d'Oriente   B&B $
(☏0836 80 15 29; www.balconcinodoriente.com; Via San Francesco da Paola 71; d €60-120, tr €80-150; P✴) This B&B has an African–Middle Eastern theme throughout with colourful bed linens, African prints, Moroccan lamps

and orange colour washes on the walls. The downstairs restaurant serves traditional Italian meals (€20 to €24).

★ Palazzo Papaleo   HOTEL $$
(☏0836 80 21 08; www.hotelpalazzopapaleo.com; Via Rondachi 1; r €97-249; P✴@🔊) 🍴 Located next to the town cathedral, this sumptuous hotel was the first to earn the EU Eco-label in Puglia. Aside from its ecological convictions, the hotel has magnificent rooms with original frescoes, exquisitely carved antique furniture and walls washed in soft greys, ochres and yellows. Soak in the panoramic views while enjoying the rooftop spa. The staff are exceptionally friendly.

Palazzo de Mori   B&B $$
(☏0836 80 10 88; www.palazzodemori.it; Bastione dei Pelasgi; s/d €105/140; ☉Apr-Oct; ✴@) 🍴 In Otranto's historic centre, this charming B&B serves breakfast on the sun terrace overlooking the port. The rooms are decorated in soothing white on white.

🍴 Eating

La Bella Idrusa   PIZZA $
(☏0836 80 14 75; Via Lungomare degli Eroi; pizzas €5; ☉7pm-midnight Thu-Tue) You can't miss this pizzeria right by the huge Porta Terra in the historic centre. Despite the tourist-trap location, the food doesn't lack authenticity. And it's not just pizzas on offer: seafood standards are also served.

L'Altro Baffo   SEAFOOD $$
(☏0836 80 16 36; www.laltrobaffo.com; Cenobio Basiliano 23; meals €30-40; ☉11am-3pm & 6pm-midnight Tue-Sun) This elegant modern restaurant near the castle – on a side street signed towards the cathedral – dishes up seafood with a contemporary twist. Try the raw fish tasting plate or the Otranto classic: *polipo alla pignata* (octopus stewed in a clay pot).

ℹ Information

Tourist Office (☏0836 80 14 36; Via del Porto; ☉9am-1pm & 3-7pm) Down in the new port area.

ℹ Getting There & Away

Otranto can be reached from Lecce by FSE train (€3.50, 1¼ hours). It is on a small branch line, which necessitates changing in Maglie and sometimes Zollino too. Services are reduced on Sundays.

DRAMATIC COASTLINE

For a scenic road trip, the drive south from Otranto to Castro takes you along a wild and beautiful coastline. The coast here is rocky and dramatic, with cliffs falling down into the sparkling, azure sea; when the wind is up you can see why it is largely treeless. Many of the towns here started life as Greek settlements, although there are few monuments to be seen. Further south, the resort town of Santa Maria di Leuca is the tip of Italy's stiletto and the dividing line between the Adriatic and Ionian Seas.

Gallipoli

POP 21,100

Like Taranto, Gallipoli is a two-part town: the modern hub is based on the mainland, while the older *centro storico* inhabits a small island that juts out into the Ionian Sea. With a raft of serene baroque architecture usurped only by Lecce, it is, arguably, the prettiest of Salento's smaller settlements.

The old town, ringed by the remains of its muscular 14th-century walls is the best place to linger. It's punctuated by several baroque chapels, a traditional fishing port, a windswept sea drive, and narrow lanes barely wide enough to accommodate a Fiat *cinquecento* (500).

◉ Sights & Activities

Gallipoli has some fine beaches, including the Baia Verde, just south of town. Nature enthusiasts will want to take a day trip to Parco Regionale Porto Selvaggio, about 20km north – a protected area of wild coastline with walking trails amid the trees and diving off the rocky shore.

Cattedrale di Sant'Agata   CATHEDRAL
(Via Antonietta de Pace; ⊙hours vary) On the island, Gallipoli's 17th-century cathedral is a baroque beauty that could compete with anything in Lecce. Not surprisingly, Giuseppe Zimbalo, who helped beautify Lecce's Santa Croce basilica, worked on the facade. Inside, it's lined with paintings by local artists.

Frantoio Ipogeo   HISTORIC SITE
(☑338 1363063; Via Antonietta de Pace 87; admission €1.50; ⊙10am-noon) This is only one

of some 35 olive presses buried in the tufa rock below the town. It was here, between the 16th and early 19th centuries, that local workers pressed Gallipoli's olive oil, which was then stored in one of the 2000 cisterns carved beneath the old town.

Museo Civico   MUSEUM
(☑0833 26 42 24; Via Antonietta de Pace 108; admission €1; ⊙10am-12.30pm Tue-Sun, plus 3.30-6pm Tue, Thu, Sat & Sun) Founded in 1878, this dusty museum is a 19th-century time capsule featuring fish heads, ancient sculptures, a 3rd-century-BC sarcophagus and other weird stuff.

Farmacia Provenzana   HISTORIC BUILDING
(Via Antonietta de Pace; ⊙8.30am-12.30pm & 4.30-8.30pm Sun-Fri) A beautifully decorated pharmacy dating from 1814.

🛏 Sleeping

Insula   B&B $
(☑366 3468357; www.bbinsulagallipoli.it; Via Antonietta de Pace 56; s €40-80, d €60-150; ⊙Apr-Oct; ❄@) A magnificent 15th-century building houses this memorable B&B. The five rooms are all different but share the same princely atmosphere with exquisite antiques, vaulted high ceilings and cool pastel paintwork.

Hotel Palazzo del Corso   HOTEL $$$
(☑0833 26 40 40; www.hotelpalazzodelcorso.it; Corso Roma 145; r from €239; P❄@🛜❄) This beautiful luxury hotel is actually in the new town, but is worth forking out for if you fancy a bit of regal treatment. There's a fantastic terrace complete with a small swimming pool, a gym, and large comfortable rooms that have enough defining features (carpets, interesting furniture, wall paintings) to prevent them from looking too corporate.

🍴 Eating

Caffè Duomo   CAFE $
(Via Antonietta de Pace 72; desserts €9; ⊙7.30am-1am) For good Gallipoli *spumone* (layered ice cream with candied fruit and nuts) and refreshing *granite* (ices made with coffee, fresh fruit or locally grown pistachios and almonds), head to Caffè Duomo.

La Puritate   TRATTORIA $$$
(☑0833 26 42 05; Via S Elia 18; meals €45; ⊙12.30-3pm & 8-11.30pm) *The* place for fish in the old town, with large windows and sea views. Follow the practically obligatory seafood antipasti with delicious *primi* (first

courses). Anything involving fish is good, especially the prawns, swordfish and tuna. It's popular and quite formal. Reservations are recommended.

ℹ Information

Tourist Office (☏0833 26 25 29; Via Antonietta de Pace 86; ⊙8am-9pm summer, 8am-1pm & 4-9pm Mon-Sat winter) Near the cathedral in the old town.

ℹ Getting There & Away

FSE buses and trains head direct to Lecce (€4.20, one hour, four daily).

Taranto

POP 193,100

The once splendiferous Greek-Spartan colony of Taras is, today, a city of two distinct parts – a mildewed *centro storico* on a small artificial island protecting a lagoon (the Mar Piccolo), and a swankier new city replete with wide avenues laid out in a formal grid. The contrast between the two is sudden and sharp: the diminutive old town with its muscular Aragonese castle harbours a downtrodden, vaguely abandoned air, while the larger new city is busier, plusher and bustling with commerce.

Not generally considered to be on the tourist circuit, Taranto is rimmed by modern industry, including a massive steelworks, and is home to Italy's second biggest naval base after La Spezia. Thanks to an illustrious Greek and Roman history, it has been bequeathed with one of the finest Magna Graecia museums in Italy. For this reason alone, it's worth a stopover.

◉ Sights

Taranto's medieval town centre is one of southern Italy's least-dressed-up-for-tourism historic quarters. It is perched on the small narrow island dividing the Mar Piccolo (Small Sea) and the Mar Grande (Big Sea). This odd geography means that blue sea and sky surround you wherever you go.

★ Museo Nazionale Archeologico di Taranto
MUSEUM

(☏099 453 21 12; www.museotaranto.it; Via Cavour 10; adult/reduced €5/2.50; ⊙8.30am-7.30pm) In the new town is one of Italy's most important archaeological museums, exploring ancient Taras. It houses, among other artefacts, the largest collection of Greek terracotta figures in the world. Also on exhibit are fine collections of 1st-century-BC glassware, classic black-and-red Attic vases and stunning jewellery, such as a 4th-century-BC bronze and terracotta crown.

Cathedral
CATHEDRAL

(Via Duomo; ⊙8am-noon & 4.30-7.30pm) The 11th-century cathedral is one of Puglia's oldest Romanesque buildings and an extravagant treat. It's dedicated to San Cataldo, an Irish monk who lived and was buried here in the 7th century; the **Capella di San Cataldo** is a baroque riot of frescoes and polychrome marble inlay.

Castello Aragonese
CASTLE

(☏099 775 34 38; www.castelloaragonese taranto.it; Piazza Castello; ⊙9.30am-10pm) **FREE** Guarding the swing bridge that joins the old and new parts of town, this impressive 15th-century structure was once a prison and is currently occupied by the Italian navy, which has restored it. Multilingual and free guided tours are led by naval officers throughout the day. Opposite are the two remaining columns of the ancient **Temple of Poseidon** (Piazza Castello).

✶ Festivals & Events

Le Feste di Pasqua
RELIGIOUS

Taranto is famous for its Holy Week celebrations – the biggest in the region – when bearers in Ku Klux Klan–style robes carry icons around the town. There are three processions: the Perdoni, celebrating pilgrims; the Addolorata (lasting 12 hours but covering only 4km); and the Misteri (even slower at 14 hours to cover 2km).

▬ Sleeping

Affittacamere Sparta
B&B $

(☏329 2345262; www.bebsparta.it; Via Principe Amedeo 5; s €45-55, d €65-70, tr €80-85; ✳☞) These meticulously refurbished apartments are arranged on the ground floor of this otherwise utilitarian building on the western edge of the new town. The decor is ultra-comfortable with kitchenettes, power showers and mood lighting. Clever Greek-Sparta touches provide interesting design accents. Vouchers are provided for a light Italian breakfast in a cafe around the corner.

Hotel Akropolis
HOTEL $$

(☏099 470 41 10; www.hotelakropolis.it; Vico Seminario 3; s/d €105/145; ✳@☞) A rare ray of light in the crumbling old town, this

Taranto

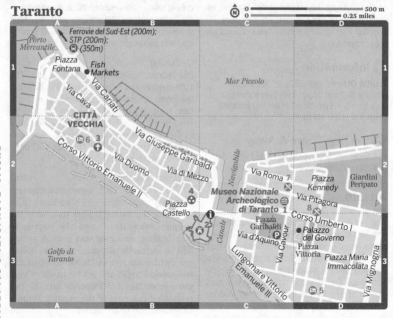

Taranto

◎ Top Sights

◎ Sights

🛏 Sleeping

✴ Eating

converted medieval *palazzo* has been made into a hotel with a heavy Greek theme. Improbably (considering the grungy surroundings), there are 13 stylish cream-and-white rooms, beautiful original maiolica-tiled floors and tremendous views from the rooftop terrace.

The downstairs bar and restaurant is enclosed in stone, wood and glass, and has atmospheric curtained alcoves.

✗ Eating & Drinking

★ Trattoria-Pizzeria
Amici Miei   PIZZA, ITALIAN $
(📞 099 400 44 70; Via Ciro Giovinazzi 18; meals €18-22; ⊙ noon-3pm & 7-11pm) The aptly named Amici Miei (my friends) is suitably friendly and renowned for its mega-sized portions that don't scrimp on taste. On top of all that, the warm homemade bread is divine, the wine measures are exceedingly generous, and staff sometimes serve complimentary dishes of freshly fried chips!

Trattoria al Gatto Rosso   TRATTORIA $$
(📞 099 452 98 75; www.ristorantegattorosso.com; Via Cavour 2; meals €30-35; ⊙ noon-3pm & 7.30-11pm Tue-Sun) A relaxed and unpretentious trattoria with a real touch of class – heavy tablecloths, deep wine glasses and the like. It is located in the new town and is very popular with discerning business types.

ℹ Information

Taranto splits neatly into three. The old town is on a tiny island, lodged between the northwest port and train station and the new city to the southeast. Italy's largest steel plant occupies the city's entire western half. The grid-patterned new city contains the banks, and most hotels and restaurants. The **tourist office** (📞 099 453

23 97; Corso Umberto I 113; ⊘9am-3pm) is at the side of the Castello Aragonese.

ℹ Getting There & Around

BUS

Buses heading north and west depart from Porto Mercantile. **FSE** (☑ 080 546 21 11; www.fseonline.it) buses go to Bari (€5.80, 1¾ to 2¼ hours, frequent). Infrequent **SITA** (☑ 899 325204; www.sitabus.it) buses leave for Matera (€5.20, 1¾ hours, one daily). **STP** (☑ 080 975 26 19; www.stpspa.it) and FSE buses go to Lecce (€5.80, two hours, four daily).

Marozzi (☑ 080 5799 0111; www.marozzivt.it) has express services serving Rome's Stazione Tiburtina (€43, six hours, three daily). **Autolinee Miccolis** (☑ 099 470 44 51; www.miccolis-spa.it) serves Naples (€23, four hours, three daily) via Potenza (€15, two hours).

The bus **ticket office** (⊘ 6am-1pm & 2-7pm) is at Porto Mercantile.

TRAIN

Trenitalia and FSE trains go to the following destinations:

Bari €8.40, 1¼ hours, frequent

Brindisi €4.90, one hour, frequent

Rome from €50.50, six hours, five daily

AMAT (☑ 099 452 67 32; www.amat.taranto.it) buses run between the train station and the new city.

BASILICATA

Basilicata has an otherworldly landscape of tremendous mountain ranges, dark forested valleys and villages so melded with the rock faces that they seem to have grown there. Its isolated yet strategic location on routes linking ancient Rome to the eastern Byzantine empire has seen it successively invaded, pillaged, plundered, abandoned and neglected.

In the north the landscape is a fertile zone of gentle hills and deep valleys – once covered in thick forests, now cleared and cultivated with wheat, olives and grapes. The purple-hued mountains of the interior are impossibly grand and a wonderful destination for hikers and naturalists, particularly the soaring peaks of the Lucanian Apennines and the Parco Nazionale del Pollino.

On the coast, Maratea is one of Italy's most chic seaside resorts. However, Matera is Basilicata's star attraction, the famous *sassi* (former cave dwellings) of the city presiding over a rugged landscape of ravines and grottoes. Its ancient cave dwellings tell a tale of poverty, hardship and struggle, and its history is best immortalised in writer Carlo Levi's superb book *Christ Stopped at Eboli* – a title suggesting Basilicata was beyond the hand of God, a place where pagan magic still existed and thrived.

Today, Basilicata is attracting a slow but steadily increasing trickle of tourists. For those wanting to experience a raw and unspoilt region of Italy, Basilicata's remote atmosphere and wild landscape will appeal.

History

Basilicata spans Italy's instep with slivers of coastline touching the Tyrrhenian and Ionian Seas. It was known to the Greeks and Romans as Lucania (a name still heard today) after the Lucani tribe who lived here as far back as the 5th century BC. The Greeks also prospered, settling along the coastline at Metapontum and Erakleia, but things started to go wrong under the Romans, when Hannibal, the ferocious Carthaginian general, rampaged through the region.

In the 10th century, the Byzantine Emperor Basilikòs (976–1025) renamed the area, overthrowing the Saracens in Sicily and the south and reintroducing Christianity. The pattern of war and overthrow continued throughout the Middle Ages as the Normans, Hohenstaufens, Angevins and Bourbons constantly tussled over its strategic location, right up until the 19th century. As talk of the Italian unification began to gain ground, Bourbon-sponsored loyalists took to Basilicata's mountains to oppose political change. Ultimately, they became the much-feared bandits of local lore who make scary appearances in writings from the late 19th and early 20th centuries. In the 1930s, Basilicata was used as a kind of open prison for political dissidents – most famously the painter, writer and doctor Carlo Levi – sent into exile to remote villages by the fascists.

Matera

POP 60,500 / ELEV 405M

Stand in the right spot at a viewpoint overlooking Matera's huddled *sassi*, and it's not difficult to imagine you've been teleported back to the Holy Land circa 100 BC. At once epic and cinematic, the 'Città Sotterranea', as it's known, perches on the upper reaches of the steep-sided Gravina gorge and its timeless urban landscape has often been used to evoke biblical scenes in films and TV.

The old town, with its unique *sassi*, is split into two sections – the Sasso Barisano and the Sasso Caveoso – separated by a ridge upon which sits Matera's gracious *duomo* (cathedral). The houses' rock-grey facades once hid grimy, filthy abodes, but since the 1980s, Matera has been a city on the rebound filled with an increasing number of cafes and restaurants, and primed for tourism. With 9000 years of continuous human habitation, the place hides layer upon layer of history.

History

Matera is said to be one of the world's oldest towns, dating back to the Palaeolithic Age and inhabited continuously for around 7000 years. The simple natural grottoes that dotted the gorge were adapted to become homes, and an ingenious system of canals regulated the flow of water and sewage. In the 8th century the caves became home to Benedictine and Basilian monks; the earliest cave paintings date from this period.

The prosperous town became the capital of Basilicata in 1663, a position it held until 1806 when the power moved to Potenza. In the decades that followed, an unsustainable increase in population led to the habitation of unsuitable grottoes – originally intended as animal stalls – even lacking running water. The dreadful conditions fostered a tough and independent spirit: in 1943, Matera became the first Italian city to rise up against German occupation.

By the 1950s more than half of Matera's population lived in the *sassi*, typical caves sheltering families with an average of six children. The infant mortality rate was 50%. In his poetic and moving memoir, *Christ Stopped at Eboli,* Carlo Levi describes how children would beg passers-by for quinine to stave off the deadly malaria. Such publicity finally galvanised the authorities into action and in the late 1950s about 15,000 inhabitants were forcibly relocated to new government housing schemes.

◉ Sights & Activities

The two *sasso* districts – the more restored, northwest-facing **Sasso Barisano** and the more impoverished, northeast-facing **Sasso Caveoso** – are both extraordinary, riddled with serpentine alleyways and staircases, and dotted with frescoed *chiese rupestri* (cave churches) created between the 8th and 13th centuries. Today Matera contains some 3000 habitable caves.

The *sassi* are accessible from several points. There's an entrance off Piazza Vittorio Veneto, or take Via delle Beccherie to Piazza del Duomo and follow the tourist itinerary signs to enter either Barisano or Caveoso. Sasso Caveoso is also accessible from Via Ridola.

For a great photograph, head out of town for about 3km on the Taranto–Laterza road and follow signs for the *chiese rupestri*. This takes you up on the Murgia Plateau to the belvedere, from where you have fantastic views of the plunging ravine and Matera.

◉ Sasso Barisano

Chiesa di Madonna delle Virtù &
Chiesa di San Nicola del Greci CHURCH
(Via Madonna delle Virtù; ⊘10am-1.30pm Mon-Fri, 10am-1.30pm & 3-6pm Sat & Sun) **FREE** This monastic complex is one of the most important monuments in Matera and is composed of dozens of caves spread over two floors. Chiesa di Madonna delle Virtù was built in the 10th or 11th century and restored in the 17th century. Above it, the simple Chiesa di San Nicola del Greci is rich in frescoes. The complex was used in 1213 by Benedictine monks of Palestinian origin.

★**Chiesa San Pietro Barisano** CHURCH
(Piazza San Pietro Barisano; adult/reduced €3/2, joint ticket with Chiesa di Santa Lucia alle Malve & Chiesa di Santa Maria d'Idris €6/4.50; ⊘10am-7pm Apr-Oct, 10am-2pm Nov-Mar) Below this church is an ancient honeycomb of niches where corpses were placed for draining, while at the entrance level are 15th- and 16th-century frescoes. The empty frame of the altarpiece graphically illustrates the town's troubled recent history: the church was plundered when Matera was partially abandoned in the 1960s and '70s.

◉ Sasso Caveoso

Chiesa di San Pietro Caveoso CHURCH
(Piazza San Pietro Caveoso; ⊘Mass 7pm Mon-Sat, 11am & 7pm Sun) **FREE** The only church in the *sassi* not dug into the tufa rock, Chiesa di San Pietro Caveoso was originally built in 1300 and has a 17th-century Romanesque-baroque facade.

Chiesa di Santa Maria d'Idris CHURCH
(Piazza San Pietro Caveoso; adult/reduced €3/2, joint ticket with Chiesa San Pietro Barisano & Chiesa

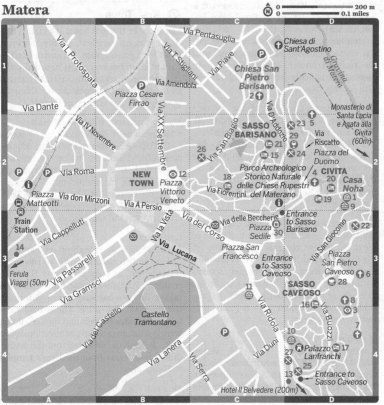

PUGLIA, BASILICATA & CALABRIA MATERA

Matera

di Santa Lucia alle Malve €6/4.50; ⊙10am-1pm & 2.30-7pm Tue-Sun Apr-Oct, 10.30am-1.30pm Tue-Sun Nov-Mar) Dug into the Idris rock, this church has an unprepossessing facade, but the narrow corridor communicating with the recessed church of San Giovanni in Monterrone is richly decorated with 12th- to 17th-century frescoes.

Chiesa di Santa Lucia alle Malve   CHURCH
(Rione Malve; adult/reduced €3/2, joint ticket with Chiesa San Pietro Barisano & Chiesa di Santa Maria d'Idris €6/4.50; ⊙10am-1pm & 2.30-7pm Apr-Oct, 10.30am-1.30pm Tue-Sun Nov-Mar) Built in the 8th century to house a Benedictine convent, this church has a number of 12th-century frescoes, including an unusual breastfeeding Madonna.

Casa-Grotta di Vico Solitario   HISTORIC SITE
(admission €2; ⊙9.30am-late) For a glimpse of life in old Matera, visit this historic *sasso* off Via Bruno Buozzi. There's a bed in the middle, a loom, a room for manure and a section for a pig and a donkey. You also have access to a couple of neighbouring caves: in one, a black-and-white film depicts gritty pre-restoration Matera.

Museo della Scultura Contemporanea   MUSEUM
(MUSMA; ☑366 9357768; www.musma.it; Via San Giacomo; adult/reduced €5/3.50; ⊙10am-2pm Tue-Sun, plus 4-8pm Sat & Sun Apr-Sep, 10am-2pm Tue-Sun Oct-Mar) Housed in Palazzo Pomarici, MUSMA is a fabulous contemporary sculpture museum. The setting – deeply recessed caves and frescoed palace rooms – is extraordinary and the works themselves absorbing. You can also book a tour to visit the **Cripta del Peccato Originale** (Crypt of Original Sin), which is located 7km south of Matera and has well-preserved frescoes from the late 8th century. It's known as the Sistine Chapel of the cave churches and the frescoes depict dramatic Old Testament scenes.

★**Casa Noha**   MUSEUM
(☑0835 33 54 52; Recinto Cavone 9; suggested donation €4; ⊙10am-6pm Wed-Sun) Buffing itself up for its European Capital of Culture status in 2019, Matera opened this brilliant multimedia exhibit in February 2014. Hosted in several rooms of a 16th-century family home, it relates the sometimes painful social history of the town and its *sassi*, warts and all. The presentation is made using films projected onto various walls and lasts approximately 20 minutes.

◉ New Town

The focus of the new town is Piazza Vittorio Veneto, an excellent, bustling meeting point for a *passeggiata*. It's surrounded by elegant churches and richly adorned *palazzi* with their backs to the *sassi*: an attempt by the bourgeois to block out the shameful poverty the *sassi* once represented.

Museo Nazionale d'Arte Medievale e Moderna della Basilicata   MUSEUM
(☑0835 31 42 35; Palazzo Lanfranchi; adult/reduced €2/1; ⊙9am-8pm Thu-Tue) The stars of the show here are Carlo Levi's paintings, including the panoramic mural *Lucania '61* depicting peasant life in biblical Technicolor. There's also some centuries-old sacred art from the *sassi*.

Cathedral   CATHEDRAL
(Piazza del Duomo) Set high up on a spur between the two natural bowls of the *sassi*, the subdued, graceful exterior of the 13th-century Puglian-Romanesque cathedral makes the neo-baroque excess within all the more of a surprise. The ornate capitals, sumptuous chapels and tons of gilding were getting an extensive renovation at last visit. Pediments mounted on the cathedral's altars came from the Greek temples at Metaponto.

Museo Nazionale Ridola   MUSEUM
(☑0835 31 00 58; Via Ridola 24; adult/reduced €2.50/1.25; ⊙9am-8pm Tue-Sun, 2-8pm Mon) This impressive collection includes local Neolithic finds and some remarkable Greek pottery, such as the *Cratere Mascheroni*, a huge urn more than 1m high.

Palombaro Lungo   HISTORIC SITE
(Piazza Vittorio Veneto; guided tour €3; ⊙10am-1pm & 3-6pm) Being a troglodyte city, much of Matera's beauty is obscured in caves or underground, including this giant cistern, which is, arguably, as magnificent as a subterranean cathedral. Lying under the city's main square with arches carved out of the existing rock, it is mind-boggling in its scale and ingenuity. Multilingual guides explain its conception and history. Tours last 25 minutes.

☞ Tours

There are plenty of official guides for the *sassi* – try www.sassiweb.it.

MATERA ON THE REBOUND

Recently named 2019 European City of Culture, Matera has taken huge strides in burying the unpleasant ghosts of its past. In the 1950s and '60s, the town and its ancient cave-houses were ingloriously considered to be the shame of Italy, a giant slum where malaria was rampant and a desperate populace subsisted on or below the breadline. After years of political squabbling, Matera's inhabitants were eventually evacuated (some forcibly) and resettled in a burgeoning new town higher up the gorge. Neglected and uncared for, the old town and its *sassi* (former cave dwellings) fell into a steep decline. By the 1980s old Matera was a virtual ghost town, an unholy mess of unlivable abodes.

Help came with a three-pronged attack of film-making, tourism and Unesco intervention. Italian director, Pier Paolo Pasolini was one of the first to put Matera on the map, making use of the town's biblical landscapes in his 1964 movie, *The Gospel According to St Matthew*. The success of the film and its eerie backdrops inspired others, including Hollywood heavyweights such as Mel Gibson, who arrived in Matera in 2004 to film *The Passion of the Christ*.

Celluloid fame led to a trickle of curious tourists and this, in turn, fuelled an increasing desire among Italians to clean up the once dilapidated *sassi* and showcase their historical value for future generations. In 1993, Unesco gave the town an extra boost when it named Matera's *sassi* and rupestrian churches a World Heritage Site. Progress has been rapid since. Bars and restaurants now inhabit once abandoned cave-houses and meticulous restoration work has saved ancient frescoes from almost certain decay.

Priming itself for 2019, Matera is in the process of restoring its 13th-century cathedral. In 2014 the town also opened a new interactive museum, Casa Noha, which tells the story of Matera's recent past in blunt, uncensored detail, and the *sassi* provided a backdrop in 2015 for the remaking of the movie *Ben Hur*, starring Morgan Freeman and Jack Huston.

Ferula Viaggi
TOUR

(☑ 0835 33 65 72; www.ferulaviaggi.it; Via Cappelluti 34; ◔ 9am-1.30pm & 3.30-7pm Mon-Sat) Excellent and informative guided tours of the *sassi*, plus tours that include tastings or cookery courses, and also hiking and cycling tours into the Parco della Murgia Materana. Ferula Viaggi also runs Bike Basilicata, which rents bikes and helmets, and supplies a road book and map so you can head off on your own.

Altieri Viaggi
TOUR

(www.altieriviaggi.it; Via Ridola 61) Runs 50-minute tours in an Ape Calessino (auto rickshaw) around the *sassi* for €15, plus plenty of other trips, including hiking.

🎉 Festivals & Events

Sagra della Madonna della Bruna
RELIGIOUS

(◔ 2 Jul) The colourful Procession of Shepherds parades ornately decorated papier-mâché floats around town. The finale is the *assalto al carro,* when the crowd descends on the main cart and tears it to pieces.

Gezziamoci
MUSIC

(www.onyxjazzclub.com; ◔ last week Aug) This jazz festival happens in the *sassi* and surrounding Parco della Murgia Materana.

🛏 Sleeping

La Dolce Vita B&B
B&B $

(☑ 0835 31 03 24; www.ladolcevitamatera.it; Rione Malve 51; r €80; ☎) 🅿 This delightful, ecofriendly B&B in Sasso Caveoso has self-contained apartments with solar panels and recycled rainwater for plumbing. Accommodation is cool, comfortable and homey. Owner Vincenzo is passionate about Matera and is a mine of information on the *sassi*.

Il Vicinato
B&B $

(☑ 0835 31 26 72; www.ilvicinato.com; Piazzetta San Pietro Caveoso 7; s/d €60/80; ❉☎) This B&B enjoys a great, easy-to-find location. Rooms are decorated in clean modern lines, with views across to Idris rock and the Murgia Plateau. As well as the standard rooms, there's a room with a balcony, and a small apartment, each with an independent entrance.

EXPLORING MATERA'S GORGE

In the picturesque landscape of the Murgia Plateau, the Matera Gravina cuts a rough gouge in the earth, a 200m-deep canyon pockmarked with abandoned caves and villages and roughly 150 mysterious *chiese rupestri* (cave churches). The area is protected as the Parco della Murgia Materana, an 80-sq-km wild park formed in 1990 and, since 2007, included in Matera's Unesco World Heritage Site. You can hike from the *sassi* into the gorge; steps lead down from the parking place near the Monasterio di Santa Lucia (Via Madonna delle Virtù). At the bottom of the gorge you have to ford a river and then climb up to the belvedere (Taranto–Laterza road) on the other side; this takes roughly two hours.

Cave churches accessible from the belvedere include San Falcione, Sant'Agnese and Madonna delle Tre Porte. The belvedere is connected by road to the Jazzo Gattini visitor centre (☐ 0835 33 22 62; ⊙ 9.30am-1pm Nov-Mar, 9.30am-2.30pm & 4-6.30pm Apr-Oct) encased in an old sheepfold. Guided hikes can be organised here plus walks to the nearby Neolithic village of Murgia Timone. For longer forays into the park, including a long day trek to the town of Montescaglioso, consider a guided hike with Ferula Viaggi (p753).

Beware: paths and river crossings in the park can be treacherous during and after bad weather.

Sassi Hotel
HOTEL $

(☐ 0835 33 10 09; www.hotelsassi.it; Via San Giovanni Vecchio 89; s/d €70/90; ❄️@) The first hotel in the *sassi* is set in an 18th-century rambling edifice in Sasso Barisano with some rooms in caves and some not. Singles are small but doubles are gracefully furnished. The balconies have superb views of the cathedral.

★ Hotel Il Belvedere
HOTEL $$

(☐ 0835 31 17 02; www.hotelbelvedere.matera.it; Via Casalnuovo 133; d from €130; 🛜) Looks can be deceptive – especially in Matera. This cave boutique looks unremarkable from its streetside perch on the edge of the Sasso Caveoso, but you'll feel your jaw start to drop as you enter its luxurious entrails and spy the spectacle of Old Matera sprawling below a jutting terrace. Cavernous rooms sport mosaics, mood lighting and curtained four-poster beds.

Hotel in Pietra
BOUTIQUE HOTEL $$

(☐ 0835 34 40 40; www.hotelinpietra.it; Via San Giovanni Vecchio 22; s/d/ste from €50/115/185; ❄️@🛜) The lobby of this hotel is set in a former 13th-century chapel complete with soaring arches, while the eight rooms combine soft golden stone with the natural cave interior. Furnishings are Zen-style with low beds, and the bathrooms are super stylish and include vast sunken tubs.

Locanda di San Martino
HOTEL $$

(☐ 0835 25 66 00; www.locandadisanmartino.it; Via Fiorentini 71; d €89-200; ❄️🛜❄️) The main lure of this Sasso Caveoso hotel is its Roman-themed spa complete with swimming pool in a subterranean cave. Cave accommodation, with niches and rustic brick floors, is set around a warren of cobbled paths and courtyards. The spa costs an extra €10 for guests, €20 for nonguests.

Palazzo Viceconte
HOTEL $$

(☐ 0835 33 06 99; www.palazzoviceconte.it; Via San Potito 7; d €95-140, ste €139-350; ❄️@🛜) You won't have trouble spotting the palatial features at this 15th-century *palazzo* near the cathedral with superb views of the *sassi* and gorge. The hotel is elegantly furnished and the rooftop terrace has panoramic views. Be king (or queen) for a day (or more) amid the courtyards, salons, frescoed ceilings and antiques.

★ Palazzo Gattini
HOTEL $$$

(☐ 0835 33 43 58; www.palazzogattini.it; Piazza del Duomo 13; d/ste €260/390; P❄️@🛜❄️) Setting a high standard and living up to it, the Gattini is the former palatial home of Matera's most noble family and the city's plushest hotel. If the erstwhile nobility could see the palace's 20 luxuriously refurbished rooms today, they'd probably give enthusiastic nods of approval. Beautiful stone walls combine with expensive fittings and expansive common areas, including a spa, restaurant, terrace and coffee shop.

Eating

Terrazza Rivelli
ITALIAN $

(☑0835 31 26 13; Via Ridola 47; meals €15-20; ⊙11.30am-3.30pm & 7-11.30pm Wed-Mon) There are two terraces here – one out front and one on the roof – plus seating in several semiformal but relaxed dining rooms inside. Food is typical southern Italian with some Puglian influences, such as *orecchiette*. Waiters get you off to a good start with a basket of classic Basilicata bread – possibly the finest in all Italy.

Oi Marì
PIZZA $

(☑0835 34 61 21; Via Fiorentini 66; pizzas from €5; ⊙8.30pm-11.45pm daily, plus 1-3pm Sat & Sun) In Sasso Barisano, this lofty and convivial cavern is styled as a Neapolitan pizzeria. It has a great, cheery atmosphere with excellent, substantial pizzas to match, as well as *primi* of the day.

Stone
INTERNATIONAL $

(☑0835 33 99 68; Via San Biagio 23; meals €20-24; ⊙7pm-6am) Stone is where you go to find young company or late-night grub (or both). Cavernous (like everywhere in Matera), its brightly lit interior has been given a lounge-lizard makeover with suspended glass floors and luxuriant furnishings.

The noise level rises as the night progresses, but there are plenty of alcoves if you wish to escape the TV soccer, loquacious DJs and out-of-town trendies clustered around the aperitif buffet. The food is good (you can't go wrong with the pizza), but the cocktails are better.

Le Botteghe
TRATTORIA $

(☑0835 34 40 72; www.lebotteghematera.it; Piazza San Pietro; meals €18.50-23; ⊙1-2.30pm & 8-11.30pm Thu-Tue) In Sasso Barisano, this is a classy but informal restaurant set in arched whitewashed rooms. Try delicious local specialities like *fusilli mollica e crusco* (pasta and fried bread with local sweet peppers).

★Soul Kitchen
MODERN ITALIAN $$

(☑0835 31 15 68; www.ristorantesoulkitchen.it; Via Casalnuovo 27; meals €30-35; ⊙12.15-2.45pm & 7.15-11.15pm Fri-Wed) If you thought Basilicata was somehow lagging behind the rest of Italy in the food stakes, you clearly haven't been to Soul Kitchen. New in 2013, this cavernous restaurant with sharp colour accents (grab a pew on the mezzanine) epitomises Matera's ambitious drive to reinvent its image. Dishes are recognisably Basilicatan, but

with modern twists, and are presented with artistic aplomb.

Baccanti
TRADITIONAL ITALIAN $$$

(☑0835 33 37 04; www.baccantiristorante.com; Via Sant'Angelo 58-61; meals €50; ⊙1-3.30pm & 8-11.30pm Tue-Sat, 1-4pm Sun) As classy as a cave can be. The design is simple glamour against the low arches of the cavern, while the dishes are delicate and complex, using local ingredients, and the gorge views are sublime.

Drinking & Nightlife

★Vicolo Cieco
WINE BAR

(☑338 8550984; Via Fiorentini 74; ⊙11am-3am) Matera's new hipster inclinations are on show at this wine-bar cum cafe in a typical cave-house off Sasso Barisano's main drag. The decor is whimsical to say the least – picture retro jukeboxes, a wall-mounted Scalextric track, chairs cut in half and glued to the wall in the name of art, and a knife-and-fork chandelier! The wine and music selections are excellent and there are also great snacks (cheese boards and *panini*).

Keiv
CAFE, BAR

(Via Bruno Ruccini 184; ⊙8.30am-2am) The new cooler face of the *sassi* is evident at this cafe that metamorphoses into a lounge bar in the early evening. Giant mirrors decorated by local artists enlarge a comfortable space where DJs spin discs on Friday and Saturday nights.

🛍 Shopping

Geppetto
CRAFTS

(Piazza Sedile 19; ⊙9.30am-1pm & 3.30-8pm) This craft shop stands out amongst the tawdrier outlets selling tufa lamps and tiles. Its speciality is the *cuccù*, a brightly painted ceramic whistle in the shape of a cockerel, which was once prized by Matera's children. The whistles were traditionally considered a symbol of good luck and fertility.

ℹ Information

The maps *Carta Turistica di Matera* and *Matera: Percorsi Turistici* (€1.50), available from various travel agencies, bookstores and hotels around town, describe a number of itineraries through the *sassi* and the gorge.

Basilicata Turistica (www.aptbasilicata.it) The official tourist website has useful information on history, culture, attractions and sights.

Hospital (☑0835 25 31 11; Via Montescaglioso) About 1km southeast of the centre.

Parco Archeologico Storico Naturale delle Chiese Rupestri del Materano (☎0835 33 61 66; www.parcomurgia.it; Via Sette Dolori; ☻9.30am-6.30pm) For info on Parco della Murgia Materana.

Police Station (☎0835 37 81; Via Gattini)

Post Office (Via Passarelli; ☻8am-6.30pm Mon-Fri, to 12.30pm Sat)

Sassiweb (www.sassiweb.it) Another informative website on Matera.

Tourist Office (Piazza Matteotti 2; ☻9am-8pm Mon & Wed-Fri, 9am-7pm Tue, 10am-7pm Sat) Matera's main tourist office is next to the exit for the underground train station.

❶ Getting There & Away

BUS

The bus station is north of Piazza Matteotti, next to the subterranean train station.

Grassani (☎0835 72 14 43; www.grassani.it) Serves Potenza (€5.50, 1½ hours, four daily). Buy tickets on the bus.

Marino (www.marinobus.it) Runs two services daily to Naples (€22, 4½ hours).

Marozzi (☎06 225 21 47; www.marozzivt. it) Runs three daily buses to Rome (€34, 6½ hours). A joint SITA and Marozzi service leaves daily for Siena, Florence and Pisa, via Potenza. Advance booking is essential.

Pugliairbus (☎080 580 03 58; http://pugliair bus.aeroportidipuglia.it) Operates a service to Bari airport (€6, 1¼ hours, four daily).

SITA (☎0835 38 50 07; www.sitabus.it) Goes to Taranto (€5.70, two hours, six daily) and Metaponto (€2.90, one hour, up to five daily) and many small towns in the province. Buy tickets from newspaper kiosks on Piazza Matteotti.

TRAIN

Ferrovie Appulo-Lucane (FAL; ☎0835 33 28 61; http://ferrovieappulolucane.it) runs regular trains (€4.90, 1½ hours, 12 daily) and buses (€4.90, 1½ hours, six daily) to Bari. For Potenza, take a FAL bus to Ferrandina and connect with a Trenitalia train, or head to Altamura to link up with FAL's Bari–Potenza run.

Metaponto

In stark contrast to the dramatic Tyrrhenian coast, Basilicata's Ionian coast is a listless, flat affair dotted with large tourist resorts. A brief respite is provided by the Greek ruins at Metaponto (known as Metapontum to the Greeks), which, with their accompanying museums, bring alive the enormous influence of Magna Graecia in southern Italy.

While the modern town of Metaponto is pretty grim, the two main archaeological sites and the local museum are well worth a visit. The sites have proven particularly valuable to archaeologists who, by studying their undisturbed ruins, have managed to map the entire ancient urban plan. Settled by Greeks in the 8th and 7th centuries BC, Metaponto's most famous resident was Pythagoras, who founded a school here after being banished from Crotone (in Calabria) in the 6th century BC. After Pythagoras died, his house and school were incorporated into the Temple of Hera (known as the Tavole Palatine), whose elegantly ruined columns remain.

◉ Sights

★**Tavole Palatine**   ARCHAEOLOGICAL SITE
(Palatine Tables; ☻9am-1hr before sunset) **FREE**
The remains of the Temple of Hera – 15 columns and sections of pavement – are Metaponto's most impressive sight. They're known as the Tavole Palatine (Palatine Tables), since knights, or paladins, are said to have gathered here before heading to the Crusades. The ruins are 3km north of town, just off the highway – to find them, follow the slip road for Taranto onto the SS106.

Museo Archeologico Nazionale   MUSEUM
(☎0835 74 53 27; Via Aristea 21; admission €2.50; ☻9am-8pm Tue-Sun, 2-8pm Mon) This small but important museum looks like it could do with a good dusting; nevertheless, the artefacts from the nearby Greek ruins of Metaponto are well laid out.

Parco Archeologico   ARCHAEOLOGICAL SITE
(☻9am-1hr before sunset) **FREE** Not to be confused with the Tavole Palatine, the Parco Archeologico is a larger, if less impressive collection of Metaponto ruins that contains the remains of a Greek theatre and the Doric Tempio di Apollo Licio.

The park is 2km northeast of the Museo Archeologico Nazionale – from the museum, walk in a straight line down Via Aristea, pass through the town square and go straight ahead at the traffic circle.

❶ Getting There & Away

SITA buses run from Matera to Metaponto (€2.90, one hour, up to five daily). The town is also on the Taranto–Reggio train line with connections to Potenza (€5.75, 1½ hours) and Naples (€13.85, four hours).

Potenza

POP 68,600 / ELEV 819M

Basilicata's regional capital, Potenza, has been ravaged by earthquakes (the last in 1980) and, as the highest town in the Basilicata region, it broils in summer and shivers in winter. You may find yourself passing through as it's a major transport hub.

Potenza's few sights are in the old centre, at the top of the hill. To get there, take the elevators from Piazza Vittorio Emanuele II. The ecclesiastical highlight is the ca-thedral, erected in the 12th century and rebuilt in the 18th. The elegant Via Pretoria, flanked by a boutique or two, makes a pleasant traffic-free stroll, especially during the *passeggiata*.

In central Potenza, B&B Al Convento (☑ 097 12 55 91; Largo San Michele Arcangelo 21; s/d €55/80; ❄@☎) is a great accommodation choice housing a mix of polished antiques and design classics.

The town centre straddles a high ridge, east to west. To the south lie the main Trenitalia and Ferrovie Appulo-Lucane train stations, connected to the centre by buses 1 and 10.

Grassani (☑ 0835 72 14 43) has buses to Matera (€5.30, 1½ hours, four daily). SITA (☑ 0971 50 68 11; www.sitabus.it) has daily buses to Melfi, Venosa and Maratea. Buses leave from Via Appia 185 and also stop near the Scalo Inferiore Trenitalia train station. Liscio (☑ 097 15 46 73; www.autolineeliscio.it) buses serve various cities including Rome (€24, 4½ hours, three daily).

There are regular train services from Potenza to Foggia (from €6, 2¼ hours), Salerno (from €6, 1¾ hours) and Taranto (from €8.20, two hours). For Bari (from €10.50, four hours, four daily), take the Ferrovie Appulo-Lucane (☑ 0971 41 15 61; http://ferrovie appulolucane.it) train at Potenza Superiore station.

Appennino Lucano

The Appennino Lucano (Lucanian Apennines) bite Basilicata in half like a row of jagged teeth. Sharply rearing up south of Potenza, they protect the lush Tyrrhenian coast and leave the Ionian shores gasping in the semi-arid heat. The area is protected by the Parco Nazionale Dell'Appennino Lucano, the newest of Italy's 24 national parks, inaugurated in 2007.

ℹ SOUTHERN SUNDAYS

True to Mediterranean tradition, Sunday remains a day of rest in southern Italy, turning many smaller settlements into ghost towns. Shops close, some restaurants take at least part of the day off, and many bus routes and some train routes don't function at all. Unless you have access to your own transport, this is a good day to stay put in a larger city, veg on a beach, or go for a long walk in the countryside.

Aside from its sharp mountain terrain, the park's most iconic site is the Roman ruins of Grumentum, 75km south of Potenza just outside the town of Grumento Nova. The Parco Archeologico di Grumentum (admission incl museum €2.50; ☉9am-1hr before sunset) is sometimes known as Basilicata's 'Little Pompeii'. The large site contains remains of a theatre, an amphitheatre, Roman baths, a forum, two temples and a *domus* with mosaic floors. There's also an interesting museum (☑0975 6 50 74; admission incl archaeological site €2.50; ☉9am-8pm Tue-Sun, 2-8pm Mon).

Castelmezzano & Pietrapertosa

The two mountaintop villages of Castelmezzano (elevation 985m) and Pietrapertosa (elevation 1088m), ringed by the Lucanian Dolomites are spectacular. They are Basilicata's highest villages and are often swathed in cloud, making you wonder why anyone would build here – in territory best suited to goats.

Castelmezzano is surely one of Italy's most theatrical villages: the houses huddle along an impossibly narrow ledge that falls away in gorges to the Caperrino river. Pietrapertosa is even more amazing: the Saracen fortress at its pinnacle is difficult to spot as it is carved out of the mountain.

You can 'fly' between these two dramatic settlements courtesy of Il Volo dell'Angelo (The Angel Flight; ☑ Castelmezzano 0971 98 60 42, Pietrapertosa 0971 98 31 10; www.volodellangelo. com; singles €35-40, couples €63-72; ☉May-Sep), two heart-in-mouth ziplines where you are suspended, belly down, in a cradle harness, and whizzed via cables across an abyss. The Peschiera line that runs between Castelmezzano and Pietrapertosa is one of the world's longest (1452m) and fastest (120km/h). Daredevils only!

You can spend a night in Pietrapertosa at a delightful B&B, **La Casa di Penelope e Cirene** (☑0971 98 30 13; Via Garibaldi 32; d from €70). Dine at the authentic Lucano restaurant **Al Becco della Civetta** (☑0971 98 62 49; www.beccodellacivetta.it; Vicolo I Maglietta 7; meals €25; ⊖Wed-Mon) in Castelmezzano, which also offers traditionally furnished, simple whitewashed rooms (doubles €80).

You'll need your own vehicle to visit Castelmezzano and Pietrapertosa.

Basilicata's Western Coast

Resembling a mini Amalfi, Basilicata's Tyrrhenian coast is short but sweet. Squeezed between Calabria and Campania's Cilento peninsula, it shares the same beguiling characteristics: hidden coves and pewter sandy beaches backed by majestic coastal cliffs. The SS18 threads a spectacular route along the mountains to the coast's star attraction: the charming seaside settlements of Maratea.

Maratea

POP 5220

Contrasting sharply with Basilicata's rugged isolated interior, Maratea is the antithesis of the rest of the region. This disparate collection of placid coastal villages inhabits a narrow 32km-long strip on the Tyrrhenian Sea sandwiched between Calabria and Campania. Embellished with lush vegetation, sheltered coves and well-tended cliff-side villages, Maratea's latent joys are not dissimilar to those on the Amalfi – but there are fewer people enjoying them (and notably fewer non-Italians). Climb endless steps to lofty viewpoints, poke around ancient hilltop churches (44 of them), sip cappuccinos in diminutive drop-dead-gorgeous piazzas, and watch the sun render the sea turquoise, blue and aquamarine.

ℹ Orientation

What is usually referred to as Maratea is actually a collection of small settlements split into several parts, some of them walkable if you're relatively fit and the weather cooperates. Maratea's main train station sits roughly in the middle.

The Porto is clustered around a small harbour and is about a 10-minute walk below the station (towards the sea). The 'village' of Fiumicello is in the same direction, but reached by turning right rather than left once you've passed under the railway bridge. The main historic centre, known as Maratea Borgo, is perched in the hills behind. A bus leaves every 30 minutes or so from the station, or you can walk up a series of steps and paths (approximately 5km; the town is always visible). It has plenty of cafes and places to eat. The Marina di Maratea is located 5km south along the coast and has its own separate train station. The village of Acquafredda is 8km in the other direction, kissing the border of Campania.

⊙ Sights & Activities

The deep green hillsides that encircle this tumbling conurbation offer excellent walking trails, providing a number of easy day trips to the surrounding hamlets of Acquafredda and Fiumicello, with its small sandy beach. The **tourist office** (☑0973 03 03 66; Piazza Vitolo 1; ⊖8am-2pm & 3-6pm) in Maratea Borgo's main square dispenses an excellent map.

Statue of Christ the Redeemer   STATUE
The symbol of Maratea and viewable from multiple vantage points along the coast is this 22m-high statue of Christ with his arms outstretched (completed in 1965). Slightly smaller than the similar Christ the Redeemer statue in Rio de Janeiro, this one is made of concrete with a Carrara marble covering and sits atop 644m-high Monte San Biagio.

A dramatic winding asphalt road leads to the top, although it's more fun to walk the steep path (# I) that starts off Via Cappuccini in Maratea Borgo.

The statue faces inland towards the **Basilica di San Biagio** opposite.

Maratea Superiore   RUIN
FREE The ruins of the original settlement of Maratea, supposedly founded by the Greeks, are situated at a higher elevation than the current village on a rocky escarpment just below the Christ the Redeemer statue. Abandoned houses with trees growing in their midst have long been given over to nature.

Marvin Escursioni   BOAT TOUR
(☑338 8777899; Porto di Maratea; half-day boat trips €25) Operator based in the Porto di Maratea offering half-day boat tours (morning or afternoon) that include visits to surrounding grottoes and coves.

🛏 Sleeping

★**Locanda delle Donne Monache** HOTEL $$
(☑0973 87 74 87; www.locandamonache.com; Via Mazzei 4; r €130-310; ☺Apr-Oct; P🅿❄@🛜🏊) Overlooking the medieval *borgo*, this exclusive hotel is in a converted 18th-century convent with a suitably lofty setting. It's a hotchpotch of vaulted corridors, terraces and gardens fringed with bougainvillea and lemon trees. The rooms are elegantly decorated in pastel shades and – bonus – there's a panoramic outdoor pool and tempting offers of cooking classes.

Hotel Villa Cheta Elite HOTEL $$
(☑0973 87 81 34; www.villacheta.it; Via Timpone 46; r €140-264; ☺Apr-Oct; P🅿❄🛜) Set in an art nouveau villa at the entrance to the hamlet of Acquafredda, this hotel is like a piece of plush Portofino towed several hundred kilometres south. Enjoy a broad terrace with spectacular views, a fabulous restaurant and large rooms where antiques mix seamlessly with modernities. Bright Mediterranean foliage fills sun-dappled terraced gardens.

🍴 Eating

★**La Caffetteria** CAFE $
(Piazza Buraglia; panini from €4; ☺7.30am-2am summer, to 10pm winter) The outdoor seating at this delightful cafe in Maratea Borgo's central piazza is ideal for dedicated people-watching. The cafe serves homemade snacks throughout the day.

Lanterna Rossa SEAFOOD $$
(☑0973 87 63 52; Porto; meals €40; ☺10.30am-3.30pm & 7.30pm-midnight Wed-Mon Feb-Dec) Head for this terrace overlooking the port to dine on exquisite seafood. Highly recommended is the signature dish, *zuppa di pesce* (fish soup). The Bar del Porto sits beneath it serving ice cream and coffee.

Il Sacello MODERN ITALIAN $$$
(☑0973 87 61 39; Via Mazzei 4; meals €30-50; ☺12.30-2.30pm & 7.30-10.30pm) High-flying fine dining, quite literally, as you overlook the red rooftops of Maratea Borgo and the lovely swimming pool beautifying this restaurant, which is part of the Locanda delle Donne Monache hotel. The food is Italian fare given a modern touch. Try the rabbit with *cavatelli*, the beef tartare or the sweeter-than-sweet desserts including *cannoli*.

ℹ Getting There & Around

Maratea is easily accessed via the coastal train line. InterCity and regional trains on the Rome–Reggio line stop at Maratea train station. Some slower trains stop at Marina di Maratea.

Local buses (€1.10) connect the coastal towns and Maratea train station with Maratea Borgo, running more frequently in summer. Some hotels offer pick-ups from the station.

CALABRIA

If a Vespa-riding, siesta-loving, chaotically unadorned version of Italy still exists, you'll probably find it in Calabria, the 'toe' that kicks Sicily into the Tyrrhenian Sea. Scarred by recurrent earthquakes and lacking a Matera or Lecce to give it high-flying tourist status, this is a land of throwbacks and traditions, sheltered by craggy mountains and burdened with a long history of poverty, Mafia activity and emigration (the few travellers you do meet are often Americans retracing family roots). If you're only going to visit Italy once in your life, it's unlikely that Calabria will be top of your list. But if you're intent on seeing a candid and uncensored version of *la dolce vita* that hasn't been dressed up for tourist consumption, look no further *ragazzi*.

Calabria's gritty cities are of patchy interest. More alluring is its attractive Tyrrhenian coastline dotted with some surprisingly picturesque towns and villages (Tropea and Scilla stand out). The mountainous centre is dominated by three national parks, none of them particularly well-explored. Easily the region's biggest snare are its Greek artefacts collected from ruins, archaeological sites and ancient shipwrecks and catalogued in some truly impressive museums.

History

Traces of Neanderthal, Palaeolithic and Neolithic life have been found in Calabria, but the region only became internationally important with the arrival of the Greeks in the 8th century BC. They founded a colony at what is now Reggio di Calabria. Remnants of this colonisation, which spread along the Ionian coast with Sibari and Crotone as the star settlements, are still visible. However, the fun didn't last for the Greeks and in 202 BC the cities of Magna Graecia all came under Roman control. The Romans did irreparable

PARCO NAZIONALE DEL POLLINO

Italy's largest national park, the Pollino National Park (www.parcopollino.it), straddles Basilicata and Calabria and covers 1960 sq km. It acts like a rocky curtain separating the region from the rest of Italy and has the richest repository of flora and fauna in the south.

The park's most spectacular areas are Monte Pollino (2248m), Monti di Orsomarso (1987m) and the canyon of the Gole del Raganello. The mountains, often snowbound, are blanketed by forests of oak, alder, maple, beech, pine and fir. The park is most famous for its ancient *pino loricato* trees, which can only be found here and in the Balkans. The oldest specimens reach 40m in height.

The park has a varied landscape, from deep river canyons to alpine meadows, and is home to rare stocks of roe deer, wild cats, wolves, birds of prey (including the golden eagle and Egyptian vulture) and the endangered otters, *Lutra lutra*.

Good hiking maps are scarce. The *Carta Excursionistica del Pollino Lucano* (scale 1:50,000), produced by the Basilicata tourist board, is a useful driving map. The large-scale *Parco Nazionale del Pollino* map shows all the main routes and includes some useful information on the park, its flora and fauna and the park communities. Both maps are free and can be found in local tourist offices.

Your own vehicle is useful in Pollino. However, from the north there's a daily SLA Bus (✆0973 2 10 16; www.slasrl.it) between Naples and Rotonda, while SAM Autolinee (✆0973 66 21 06; www.samautolinee.com) buses operate around some of Basilicata's Pollino villages.

Basilicata

In Basilicata the park's main centre is Rotonda (elevation 626m), which houses the official park office, Ente Parco Nazionale del Pollino (✆0973 66 93 11; Via delle Frecce Tricolori 6; ⊙8am-2pm Mon-Fri, plus 3-5.30pm Mon & Wed). Interesting villages to explore include the unique Albanian villages of San Paolo Albanese and San Costantino Albanese. These isolated and unspoilt communities fiercely maintain their mountain culture and the Greek liturgy is retained in the main churches. For local handicrafts visit the town of Terranova di Pollino for wooden crafts, Latronico for alabaster and Sant'Arcangelo for wrought iron.

geological damage destroying the countryside's handsome forests. Navigable rivers became fearsome *fiumare* (torrents) dwindling to wide, dry, drought-stricken river beds in high summer.

Calabria's fortified hilltop communities weathered successive invasions by the Normans, Swabians, Aragonese and Bourbons, and remained largely undeveloped. Although the 18th-century Napoleonic incursion and the arrival of Garibaldi and Italian unification inspired hope for change, Calabria remained a disappointed, feudal region and, like the rest of the south, was racked by malaria. A by-product of this tragic history was the growth of banditry and organised crime. Calabria's Mafia, known as the 'ndrangheta (from the Greek for heroism or virtue), inspires fear in the local community, but tourists are rarely the target of its aggression. For many, the only answer has been to get out and, for at least a century, Calabria has seen its young people emigrate in search of work.

Northern Tyrrhenian Coast

The good, the bad and the ugly line the region's western seashore.

The Autostrada del Sole (A3) is one of Italy's great coastal drives. It twists and turns through mountains, past huge swathes of dark-green forest and flashes of cerulean-blue sea. But the Italian penchant for cheap summer resorts has taken its toll here and certain stretches are blighted by shoddy hotels and soulless stacks of flats.

In the low season most places close. In summer many hotels are full, but you should have an easier time with the camping sites.

Praia a Mare

POP 6820

Praia a Mare, which lies just short of the border with Basilicata, is the start of a stretch of wide, pebbly beach that continues south for about 30km to Cirella and Diamante.

The chalet-style Picchio Nero (☎ 0973 9 31 70; www.hotelpicchionero.com; Via Mulino 1; s/d incl breakfast €65/78; ℗) in Terranova di Pollino, with its Austrian-style wooden balconies and recommended restaurant, is a popular hotel for hikers. It's family run, cosy and friendly, has a small garden and can help arrange excursions.

Two highly recommended restaurants include Luna Rossa (☎ 0973 9 32 54; Via Marconi 18; meals €35; ⊗ Thu-Tue) in Terranova di Pollino – where creative local specialities are rustled up simply and with real flair in a rustic wood-panelled building providing breathtaking views – and Da Peppe (☎ 0973 66 12 51; Corso Garibaldi 13; meals €25-35; ⊗ noon-3pm & 7.30-11pm Tue-Sun) in Rotonda, which uses wonderful local meat and woodland products such as truffles and mushrooms.

Calabria

Civita was founded by Albanian refugees in 1746. Other towns worth visiting are Castrovillari, with its well-preserved 15th-century Aragonese castle, and Morano Calabro (look up the beautiful MC Escher woodcut of this town). Naturalists should also check out the wildlife museum Centro Il Nibbio (☎ 0981 3 07 45; Vico II Annunziata 11; admission €4; ⊗ 10am-1pm & 4-8pm summer, 10am-1pm & 3-6pm winter) in Morano, which explains the Pollino ecosystem.

White-water rafting down the spectacular Lao river is popular in the Calabrian Pollino. Centro Lao Action Raft (☎ 0985 2 14 76; www.laoraft.it; Via Lauro 10/12) in Scalea can arrange rafting trips as well as canyoning, trekking and mountain-biking. Ferula Viaggi (p753) in Matera runs mountain-bike excursions and treks into the Pollino.

The park has a number of *agriturismi*. Tranquil Agriturismo Colloreto (☎ 347 3236914; www.colloreto.it; s/d €28/56), near Morano Calabro, is in a remote rural setting, gorgeous amid rolling hills. Rooms are comfortable and old-fashioned with polished wood and flagstone floors. Also in Calabria, Locanda di Alia (☎ 0981 4 63 70; www.alia.it; Via Ietticelle 55; s/d €90/120; ℗ ✳ ✵) in Castrovillari offers bungalow-style accommodation in a lush green garden; it's famous for an outstanding restaurant, where you can sample delectable local recipes featuring peppers, pork, figs, anise and honey.

This flat, leafy grid of a town sits on a wide pale-grey beach, looking out to an intriguing rocky chunk off the coast: the Isola di Dino.

Just off the seafront is the tourist office (☎ 0985 7 25 85; Via Amerigo Vespucci 6; ⊗ 8am-1pm), which has information on the Isola di Dino sea caves. Alternatively, expect to pay around €5 for a guided tour from the old boys who operate off the beach.

Autolinee Preite (☎ 0984 41 30 01; www.autoservizipreite.it) operates buses to Cosenza (€5.40, two hours, 10 daily). SITA (☎ 0971 50 68 11; www.sitabus.it) goes north to Maratea and Potenza. Regular trains also pass through for Paola and Reggio di Calabria.

Aieta & Tortora

Precariously perched, otherworldly Aieta and Tortora must have been difficult to reach pre-asphalt. Rocco (☎ 0973 2 29 43; www.roccobus.it) buses serve both villages, 6km and 12km from Praia respectively. Aieta is higher than Tortora and the journey

constitutes much of the reward. When you arrive, walk up to the 16th-century Palazzo Spinello at the end of the road and take a look into the ravine behind it – it's a stunning view.

Diamante

POP 5400

This fashionable seaside town, with its long promenade, is central to Calabria's famous *peperoncino* (chilli), the conversation-stalling spice that so characterises the region's cuisine. In early September a hugely popular chilli-eating competition takes place. Diamante is also famed for the bright murals that contemporary local and foreign artists have painted on the facades of the old buildings. For the best seafood restaurants, head for the seafront at Spiaggia Piccola.

Autolinee Preite (☎ 0984 41 30 01; www.autoservizipreite.it) buses between Cosenza and Praia a Mare stop at Diamante.

Paola

POP 16,900

Paola is worth a stop to see its holy shrine. The large pilgrimage complex is above a sprawling small town where the dress of choice is a tracksuit and the main activity is hanging about on street corners. The 80km of coast south from here to Pizzo is mostly overdeveloped and ugly. Paola is the main train hub for Cosenza, about 25km inland.

Watched over by a crumbling castle, the **Santuario di San Francesco di Paola** (☑ 0982 58 25 18; ☺ 6am-1pm & 2-6pm) FREE is a curious, empty cave with tremendous significance to the devout. The saint lived and died in Paola in the 15th century and the sanctuary that he and his followers carved out of the bare rock has attracted pilgrims for centuries. The cloister is surrounded by naive wall paintings depicting the saint's truly incredible miracles. The original church contains an ornate reliquary of the saint. Also within the complex is a modern basilica, built to mark the second millennium. Black-clad monks hurry about.

There are several hotels near the train station, but you'll be better off staying in towns further north along the coast.

Cosenza

POP 69,800 / ELEV 238M

Cosenza epitomises the unkempt charm of southern Italy. It is a no-nonsense workaday town where tourists are incidental and local life, with all its petty dramas, takes centre stage. The modern city centre is a typically chaotic Italian metro area that serves as a transport hub for Calabria and a gateway to the nearby mountains of Sila National Park. The old town, stacked atop a steep hill, has a totally different atmosphere. Time-warped and romantically dishevelled, its dark weathered alleys are full of drying clothes on rusty balconies, old curiosity shops and the freshly planted shoots of an arty renaissance.

◉ Sights

In the new town, pedestrianised Corso Mazzini provides a pleasant respite from the chaotic traffic and incessant car honking. The thoroughfare serves as an **open-air museum** with numerous sculptures lining the *corso*, including *Saint George and the Dragon* by Salvador Dalí.

In the old town, head up the winding, charmingly dilapidated Corso Telesio, which has a raw Neapolitan feel to it and is lined with ancient tenements and antiquated shopfronts, including shops housing an instrument maker and a Dickensian shoe mender. The side alleys are a study in urban decay. At the top, the 12th-century **cathedral** (Piazza del Duomo; ☺ 8am-noon & 3-7.30pm) was rebuilt in restrained baroque style in the 18th century. In a chapel off the north aisle is a copy of an exquisite 13th-century Byzantine Madonna.

Head further along the *corso* to Piazza XV Marzo, an appealing square fronted by the Palazzo del Governo and the handsome neoclassical **Teatro Rendano** (Piazza XV Marzo).

From Piazza XV Marzo, follow Via Paradiso, then Via Antonio Siniscalchi for the route to the down-at-heel Norman **castle** (Piazza Frederico II), left in disarray by several earthquakes. It's closed for restoration, but the view merits the steep ascent.

Cosenza's culture is low-key, but you can piece bits of it together at the recently refurbished **Galeria Nazionale** (Via G V Gravina; ☺ 10am-6pm Tue-Sun) FREE, with its Renaissance-baroque art from the Neapolitan school. Close by, the new-ish **Museo dei Brettii e degli Enotri** (www.museodei brettiiedeglienotri.it; Salita S Agostino 3; admission €3; ☺ 9am-1pm & 4.30-7.30pm Tue-Fri, 10am-1pm & 4.30-7.30pm Sat & Sun) is essentially an archaeological museum displaying finds from the Bronze Age–Enotri culture and the Brettii people who founded Cosenza in the 4th century BC.

⊨ Sleeping

B&B Via dell'Astrologo   B&B $
(☑ 338 9205394; www.viadellastrologo.com; Via Rutilio Benincasa 16; r €60-95; 🕾) A gem in the historic centre, this small B&B is tastefully decorated with polished wooden floors, white bedspreads and good-quality artwork. Brothers Mario and Marco, the venue's owners, are a mine of information on Cosenza and Calabria in general.

Royal Hotel   HOTEL $
(☑ 0984 41 21 65; www.hotelroyalsas.it; Viale delle Medaglie d'Oro 1; s/d/tr €55/65/75; 🅿 ❋ @ 🕾) Probably the best all-round hotel, the Royal is a short stroll from Corso Mazzini and has just moved digs to a brand new building. Rooms are fresh and businesslike, if a little bland.

Hotel Excelsior HOTEL **$**
(☑ 0984 47 43 83; www.htlexcelsior.it; Piazza Matteotti; s/d/tr €50/70/90; ✴@🛜) One of the few decent central options, the Excelsior has an old-school feel, although regular renovations have kept the place comfortable and up to date.

Eating

Gran Caffè Renzelli CAFE **$**
(Corso Telesio 46; cakes from €1.20; ⊘7am-9pm Mon-Sat) This venerable cafe behind the *duomo* has been run by the same family since 1803 when the founder arrived from Naples and began baking gooey cakes and desserts. Sink your teeth into *torroncino torrefacto* (a confection of sugar, spices and hazelnuts) or *torta telesio* (made from almonds, cherries, apricot jam and lupins).

L'Osteria degli Amici ITALIAN **$$**
(☑ 0984 79 58 93; Via Trento 49; meals €22-28; ⊘11am-3pm & 7pm-midnight) There's no sea in Cosenza, but the seafood is, ironically, rather good at this venerable small restaurant just off the city's main pedestrian street. With Sicily so close you can't go wrong with the *linguine alle vongole* (pasta and clams, a Sicilian speciality).

Ristorante Calabria Bella CALABRIAN **$$**
(☑ 0984 79 35 31; www.ristorantecalabriabella.it; Piazza del Duomo; meals €25; ⊘12.30-3pm & 7.15pm-midnight) Traditional Calabrian cuisine, such as *grigliata mista di carne* (mixed grilled meats), is regularly dished up at this cosy restaurant in the old town.

ℹ Orientation

The main drag, Corso Mazzini, runs south from Piazza Bilotti (formerly known as Piazza Fera), near the bus station, and intersects Viale Trieste before meeting Piazza dei Bruzi. Head further south and cross the Busento river to reach the old town.

ℹ Getting There & Around

AIR
Lamezia Terme airport (Sant'Eufemia Lamezia, SUF; ☑ 0968 41 43 33; www.sacal.it; Cosenza), 63km south of Cosenza, at the junction of the A3 and SS280 motorways, links the region with major Italian cities. The airport is served by Ryanair, easyJet and charters from northern Europe. A shuttle leaves the airport every 20 minutes for the airport train station, where there are frequent trains to Cosenza (€5.80, one hour).

BUS
The main **bus station** (☑ 0984 41 31 24) is northeast of Piazza Bilotti. Services leave for Catanzaro (€4.80, 1¾ hours, eight daily) and towns throughout La Sila. **Autolinee Preite** (☑ 0984 41 30 01; www.autoservizipreite.it) has buses heading daily along the north Tyrrhenian coast; **Autolinee Romano** (☑ 0962 2 17 09; www.autolineeromano.com) serves Crotone as well as Rome and Milan.

TRAIN
Stazione Nuova (☑ 0984 2 70 59) is about 2km northeast of the centre. Regular trains go to Reggio di Calabria (from €14.60, 2¾ hours) and Rome (from €52.40, four to six hours), both usually with a change at Paola, and Naples (from €16.90, three to four hours), as well as most destinations around the Calabrian coast.

Regular buses link the centre and the main train station, although they follow a roundabout route.

Parco Nazionale della Sila

'La Sila' is a big landscape, where wooded hills create endless rolling views. It's dotted with small villages and cut through with looping roads that make driving a test of your-digestion.

It's divided into three areas covering 130 sq km: the Sila Grande, with the highest mountains; the strongly Albanian Sila Greca (to the north); and the Sila Piccola (near Catanzaro), with vast forested hills.

The highest peaks, covered with tall Corsican pines, reach 2000m – high enough for thick snow in winter. This makes it a popular skiing destination. In summer the climate is coolly alpine, spring sees carpets of wildflowers and there's mushroom hunting in autumn. At its peak is the Bosco di Gallopani (Forest of Gallopani). There are several beautiful lakes, the largest of which is Lago di Cecita o Mucone near Camigliatello Silano. There is also plenty of wildlife here, including the light-grey Apennine wolf, a protected species.

During August, Sila in Festa takes place, featuring traditional music. Autumn is mushroom season, when you'll be able to frequent mushroom festivals, including the Sagra del Fungo in Camigliatello Silano.

◉ Sights & Activities

La Sila's main town, San Giovanni in Fiore (1049m), is named after the founder of its beautiful medieval abbey. Today, the abbey houses a home for the elderly and the **Museo Demologico** (☑0984 97 00 59; Abbazia Forense; admission €1.50; ☺8.30am-6.30pm, closed Sun Oct-May) exhibiting tools from the town's strong artisan culture. The attractive old centre is famous for its Armenian-style handloomed carpets and tapestry; you can visit the studio and shop of carpet maker **Domenico Caruso** (☑0984 99 27 24; www.scuolatappeti.it; Via A Gramsci 195).

A popular ski-resort town with 6km of slopes, **Camigliatello Silano** (1272m) looks much better under snow. A few lifts operate on Monte Curcio, about 3km to the south. Around 5.5km of slopes and a 1500m lift can be found near **Lorica** (1370m), on gloriously pretty Lago Arvo – the best place to camp in summer.

Scigliano (620m) is a small hilltop town located west of the Sila Piccola section of the park and 75km south of Cosenza; it has a superb B&B.

🛏 Sleeping

⭐ B&B Calabria
B&B **$**

(☑349 8781894; www.bedandbreakfastcalabria.it; Via Roma 9, Frazione Diano, Scigliano; s/d/t/q €35/60/75/80; ☺Apr-Nov) This B&B in the mountains has five comfortable rooms, all with separate entrances. Owner Raffaele is a great source of information on the region and can recommend places to eat, visit and go hiking. Rooms have character and clean modern lines and there's a wonderful terrace overlooking endless forested vistas. Mountain bikes available.

The B&B is west of the national park in the village of Scigliano, about an hour south of Cosenza by train.

Hotel Aquila & Edelweiss
HOTEL **$$**

(☑0984 57 80 44; www.hotelaquilaedelweiss.com; Viale Stazione 15, Camigliatello Silano; s/d €80/120; P☀@) This three-star hotel in Camigliatello Silano has a stark and anonymous exterior but it's in a good location and the rooms are cosy and comfortable.

Park Hotel 108
HOTEL **$$**

(☑0521 64 81 08; www.hotelpark108.it; Via Nazionale 86, Lorica; r €95-135; P☎) Situated on the hilly banks of Lago Arvo, surrounded by dark-green pines. The rooms here are decorated in classic bland-hotel style – but who cares about decor with views like this!

🛍 Shopping

La Sila's forests yield wondrous wild mushrooms, both edible and poisonous.

Antica Salumeria Campanaro
FOOD

(Piazza Misasi 5, Camigliatello Silano) Sniff around the Antica Salumeria Campanaro; it's a temple to all things fungoid, as well as an emporium of fine meats, cheeses, pickles and wines.

ℹ Information

Good-quality information in English is scarce. You can try the national park **visitors centre** (☑0984 53 71 09) at Cupone, 10km from Camigliatello Silano, or the **Pro Loco tourist office** (☑0984 57 81 59; Via Roma; ☺9.30am-12.30pm & 3.30-6.30pm Wed-Mon) in Camigliatello Silano. A useful internet resource is the official park website (www.parcosila.it). The people who run B&B Calabria in the park are extremely knowledgeable and helpful.

For a map, you can use *La Sila: Carta Turistico-Stradale ed Escurionistica del Parco Nazionale* (€7). *Sila for 4* is a miniguide in English that outlines a number of walking trails in the park. The map and booklet are available at tourist offices.

ℹ Getting There & Away

You can reach the park's two main hubs, Camigliatello Silano and San Giovanni in Fiore, via regular Ferrovie della Calabria buses from Cosenza or Crotone.

Ionian Coast

With its flat coastline and wide sandy beaches, the Ionian coast has some fascinating stops from Sibari to Santa Severina, with some of the best beaches on the coast around Soverato. However, the coast has borne the brunt of some ugly development and is mainly a long, uninterrupted string of resorts, thronged in the summer months and shut down from October to May.

It's worth taking a trip inland to visit Santa Severina, a spectacular mountain-top town, 26km northwest of Crotone. The town is dominated by a Norman castle and is home to a beautiful Byzantine church.

Le Castella

This town is named for its impressive 16th-century Aragonese **castle** (admission €3; ☺9am-midnight summer, 9am-1pm & 3-6pm winter), a vast edifice linked to the mainland by a short causeway. The philosopher Pliny said that Hannibal constructed the first tower. Evidence shows it was begun in the 4th century BC, designed to protect Crotone in the wars against Pyrrhus.

Le Castella is south of a rare protected area, Capo Rizzuto, along this coast, rich not only in nature but also in Greek history. For further information on the park, try www.riservamarinacaporizzuto.it.

With around 15 campgrounds near Isola di Capo Rizzuto to the north, this is the Ionian coast's prime camping area. Try La Fattoria (☑0962 79 11 65; Via del Faro; camping 2 people, car & tent €23, bungalow €60; ☑Jun-Sep), 1.5km from the sea. Otherwise, Da Annibale (☑0962 79 50 04; Via Duomo 35; s/d €50/70; P꩜@☎) is a pleasant hotel in town with a splendid fish restaurant (meals €30; ☑noon-3pm & 7.30-11pm).

For expansive sea views dine at bright and airy Ristorante Micomare (☑0962 79 50 82; www.ristorantemicomare.it; Via Vittoria 7; meals €20-25; ☑noon-3pm & 7.30-11pm).

Gerace

POP 2830

A spectacular medieval hill town, Gerace is worth a detour for the views alone – on one side the Ionian Sea, on the other, dark, interior mountains. About 10km inland from Locri on the SS111, it has Calabria's largest Romanesque cathedral. Dating from 1045, later alterations have not robbed it of its majesty.

For a taste of traditional Calabrian cooking, the modest and welcoming Ristorante A Squella (☑0964 35 60 86; Viale della Resistenza 8; meals €20) makes for a great lunchtime stop that serves reliably good dishes, specialising in seafood and pizzas. Afterwards you can wander down the road and admire the views.

Further inland is Canolo, a small village seemingly untouched by the 20th century. Buses connect Gerace with Locri and also Canolo with Siderno, both of which link to the main coastal railway line.

Parco Nazionale dell'Aspromonte

Most Italians think of the Parco Nazionale dell'Aspromonte (www.parcoaspromonte.gov. it) as a hiding place used by Calabrian kidnappers in the 1970s and '80s. It's still rumoured to contain 'ndrangheta strongholds, but as a tourist you're unlikely to encounter any murky business. The national park, Calabria's second-largest, is startlingly dramatic, rising sharply inland from Reggio. Its highest peak, Montalto (1955m), is dominated by a huge bronze statue of Christ and offers sweeping views across to Sicily.

Subject to frequent mudslides and carved up by torrential rivers, the mountains are nonetheless awesomely beautiful. Underwater rivers keep the peaks covered in coniferous forests and ablaze with flowers in spring. It's wonderful walking country and the park has several colour-coded trails.

Extremes of weather and geography have resulted in some extraordinary villages, such as Pentidàttilo and Roghudi, clinging limpet-like to the craggy, rearing rocks and now all but deserted. It's worth the drive to explore these eagle-nest villages. Another mountain eyrie with a photogenic ruined castle is Bova, perched at 900m above sea level. The drive up the steep, dizzying road to Bova is not for the faint-hearted, but the views are stupendous.

Maps are scarce. Try the national park office (☑0965 74 30 60; www.parcoaspromonte. gov.it; Via Aurora; ☑9am-1pm Mon-Fri, plus 3-5pm Tue & Thu) in Gambarie, the Aspromonte's main town and the easiest approach to the park. The roads are good and many activities are organised from here – you can ski and it's also the place to hire a 4WD; ask around in the town.

It's also possible to approach from the south, but the roads aren't as good. The co-operative Naturaliter (☑347 3046799; www. naturaliterweb.it), based in Condofuri, is an excellent source of information, and can help arrange walking and donkey treks and place you in B&Bs throughout the region. Co-operativa San Leo (☑347 3046799), based in Bova, also provides guided tours and accommodation. In Reggio di Calabria, you can book treks and tours with Misafumera (☑0965 67 70 21; www.misafumera.it; Via Nazionale 306d; weeklong treks €260-480).

Hotel Centrale (☑0965 170 00 43; www. hotelcentrale.net; Piazza Mangeruca 22; s/d incl half-board €60/70; P꩜☎) in Gambarie is a large, all-encompassing place reminiscent of a ski hotel in the Italian Dolomites. It has a decent restaurant, a comprehensive modern spa, recently renovated wood-finished rooms and the best cafe in town. It's located right at the bottom of the ski lift.

To reach Gambarie, take ATAM (p768) city bus 319 from Reggio di Calabria (€1, 1½ hours, up to six daily). Most of the roads inland from Reggio eventually hit the SS183 road that runs north to the town.

Reggio di Calabria

POP 185,900

Port, transport nexus and the main arrival and departure point for Sicily, Reggio is an ostensibly unimpressive city with one big get-out-of-jail card: its fabulous national museum, which guards some of the finest artefacts of Magna Graecia you're ever likely to see.

The city's mishmash of architecture is a result of its geographic placement in a major earthquake zone. The last big quake in 1908 triggered a tsunami that claimed over 100,000 lives. By Italian standards, little of historical merit remains, although the *lungomare* sea drive, with its views of smouldering Mt Etna across the Messina Strait, is, arguably, one of the most animated places in Italy for an evening *passeggiata*.

Despite struggles with civic corruption and infiltration from the 'ndrangheta (Calabrian mafia), Reggio has bravely attempted to improve its image in recent years with plans to rehabilitate its port and waterfront (as yet unrealised). Fortunately, there's no need to rehabilitate the food. Reggio hides some of Calabria's best salt-of-the-earth restaurants. You can work up an appetite for them by hiking in the nearby Parco Nazionale dell'Aspromonte, or exploring the coastline at nearby seaside escapes along the Tyrrhenian and Ionian coasts.

⊙ Sights

★ Museo Nazionale di Reggio Calabria
MUSEUM

(📞0965 81 22 55; www.archeocalabria.benicul turali.it; Piazza de Nava 26; adult/reduced €5/3; ⊙9am-8pm) Emerging from an interminable renovation (since 2009), southern Italy's finest museum is now partly reopened. More importantly it is displaying what are probably the world's finest examples of ancient Greek sculpture: the Bronzi di Riace, two extraordinary bronze statues discovered on the seabed near Riace in 1972 by a snorkelling chemist from Rome.

You'll have to stand for three minutes in a decontamination chamber (an experience in itself) to see the bronzes, but, after four

years in 'storage', they don't disappoint. Larger than life, they depict the Greek obsession with the body; inscrutable, determined and fierce, their perfect form is more godlike than human. The finest of the two has ivory eyes and silver teeth parted in a faint *Mona Lisa* smile. No one knows who they are – whether human or god – and even their provenance is a mystery. They date from around 450 BC; it's believed they're the work of two artists.

In the same room as the bronzes is the 5th-century-BC bronze *Philosopher's Head*, the oldest-known Greek portrait in existence. Also on display are impressive exhibits from Locri, including statues of Dioscuri falling from his horse.

Most of the rest of the exhibits were still locked away as of early 2015. Phone ahead for the latest information. Admission prices could change.

🛌 Sleeping

Finding a room should be easy, even in summer, since most visitors pass straight through en route to Sicily.

B&B Casa Blanca
B&B $

(📞347 9459210; www.bbcasablanca.it; Via Arcovito 24; s €50-60, d €70-90, apt €105-120; ❊❀🉐) A little gem in Reggio's heart, this 19th-century *palazzo* has spacious rooms gracefully furnished with romantic white-on-white decor. There's a self-serve breakfast nook, a small breakfast table in each room and two apartments available. Great choice.

Hotel Continental
HOTEL $

(📞0965 81 21 81; www.hotelcontinentalrc.it; Via Vincenzo Florio 10; r from €59; 🅿❀🉐) Right next to the port, the Continental does a brisk trade in overnight travellers bound for Sicily. The decor holds no surprises, but the service is exceedingly polite and professional. A breakfast buffet can be procured for an extra €6.

🍴 Eating & Drinking

Cèsare
GELATERIA $

(Piazza Indipendenza; ⊙6am-1am) The most popular gelateria in town is in a modest green kiosk at the end of the *lungomare* (seafront promenade).

★ La Cantina del Macellaio
TRATTORIA $$

(📞0965 2 39 32; www.lacantinadelmacellaio.com; Via Arcovito 26; meals €25; ⊙7.30-11.30pm Mon-Sat, noon-3pm & 8-11pm Sun) One of the best

Reggio di Calabria

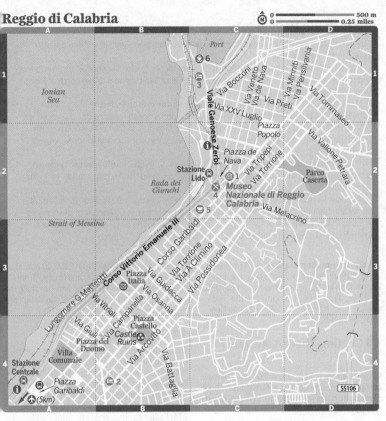

restaurants in Calabria with epic risotto (with apple and almonds), *ragù* (meat and tomato sauce) and grilled veal. The mostly Calabrian wines are equally impressive, as is the service.

Caffe Matteotti CAFE
(www.caffematteotti.it; Corso Vittorio Emanuele III 39; ⊙7am-2am Tue-Sun) The stylish white tables and chairs on the terrace here offer sea views with your *aperitivi*. This is also a prime people-watching spot.

ⓘ Information

Walk northeast along Corso Garibaldi for the tourist office, shopping and other services. The *corso* has long been a de facto pedestrian zone during the ritual *passeggiata*.

Hospital (☏ 0965 39 71 11; Via Melacrino)
Police Station (☏ 0965 41 11 11; Corso Garibaldi 442)
Post Office (Via Miraglia 14)

ⓘ ONWARD TO SICILY

Reggio di Calabria is the gateway to Sicily and its main port, Messina. There are also boats to the Aeolian Islands.

Note that there are two main departure ports for Sicily: the Stazione Marittima in Reggio di Calabria, and the ferry port in the town of Villa San Giovanni, 14km north of Reggio and easily accessible by train.

The main car ferry from Reggio's Stazione Marittima is operated by Meridiano (✆0965 81 04 14; www.meridianolines.net), which runs a dozen ferries a day on weekdays (three to four on weekends). Ferries run either to Messina or Tremestieri (8km south of Messina). The crossing takes 25 to 30 minutes; cars cost €10 and foot passengers €1.50.

The other main ferry company is Uscita Lines (✆0965 2 95 68; www.uscitalines.it), which runs passenger-only boats to Messina (€3.50) and the Aeolian Islands, including Stromboli (€41.70) and Vulcano (€22.10).

The car ferries from Villa San Giovanni are run by Caronte & Tourist (✆800 627414; www.carontetourist.it). There are 36 crossings a day. Cars cost €37 and foot passengers €3.50. The crossing is a speedy 20 minutes. This is also the port used by Trenitalia's train-ferry; carriages are pulled directly onto the ferry.

Tourist Information Kiosk (Viale Genovese Zerbi; ◷9am-noon & 4-7pm) There are also information kiosks at both the airport (✆0965 64 32 91; airport; ◷9am-5pm) and the Stazione Centrale (✆0965 2 71 20; Stazione Centrale; ◷9am-5pm).

ⓘ Getting There & Away

AIR

Reggio's **airport** (REG; ✆0965 64 05 17; www. aeroportodellostretto.it) is at Ravagnese, about 5km south. It has Alitalia flights to Rome, Milan and Turin.

BUS

Most buses terminate at the Piazza Garibaldi bus station, in front of the Stazione Centrale. Several different companies operate to towns in Calabria and beyond. Regional trains are more convenient than bus services to Scilla and Tropea.

ATAM (✆800 433310; www.atam-rc.it) Serves the Aspromonte Massif, with bus 127 to Gambarie (€1.10, 1½ hours, six daily).

Lirosi (✆0966 5 79 01) Serves Rome (€36, eight hours, two daily).

CAR & MOTORCYCLE

The A3 ends at Reggio, via a series of long tunnels. If you are continuing south, the SS106 hugs the coast around the 'toe', then heads north along the Ionian Sea.

TRAIN

Trains stop at **Stazione Centrale** (✆0965 89 20 21), the main train station at the town's southern edge. Of more use to ferry foot passengers and those visiting the Museo Nazionale is the Stazione Lido, near the harbour. There are frequent trains to Milan (from €156, 10 hours), Rome (from €61, 7½ hours) and Naples (from €39, four hours). Regional services run along the coast to Scilla and Tropea, and also to Catanzaro and less frequently to Cosenza and Bari.

ⓘ Getting Around

Orange local buses run by ATAM cover most of the city including regular buses between the port and Piazza Garibaldi outside Stazione Centrale. The Università–Aeroporto bus 27 runs from Piazza Garibaldi to the airport and vice versa (15 minutes, hourly). Buy your ticket at ATAM offices, tobacconists or news stands.

Southern Tyrrhenian Coast

North of Reggio, along the coast-hugging Autostrada del Sole (A3), the scenery rocks and rolls to become increasingly beautiful and dramatic, if you can ignore the shoddy holiday camps and unattractive developments that sometimes scar the land. Like the northern part of the coast, it's mostly quiet in winter and packed in summer.

Scilla

POP 5160

In Scilla, cream-, ochre- and earth-coloured houses cling on for dear life to the jagged promontory, ascending in jumbled ranks to the hill's summit, which is crowned by a castle and, just below, the dazzling white confection of the Chiesa Arcipretale Maria Immacolata. Lively in summer and serene in low season, the town is split in two by the tiny port. The fishing district of Scilla Chianalea, to the north, harbours small hotels and restaurants off narrow lanes, lapped by the sea. It can only be visited on foot.

Scilla's high point is a rock at the northern end, said to be the lair of Scylla, the mythical six-headed sea monster who drowned sailors as they tried to navigate the Strait of Messina. Swimming and fishing off the town's glorious white sandy beach is somewhat safer today. Head for **Lido Paradiso** from where you can squint up at the castle while sunbathing on the sand.

◉ Sights

Castello Ruffo   CASTLE
(☑ 0956 70 42 07; admission €1.50; ⊗ 8.30am-7.30pm) An imposing hilltop fortress, this castle has at times been a lighthouse and a monastery. It houses a *luntre,* the original boat used for swordfishing, and on which the modern-day *passarelle* (a special swordfish-hunting boat equipped with a 30m-high metal tower) is based.

⏁ Sleeping

Le Piccole Grotte   B&B $
(☑ 338 2096727; www.lepiccolegrotte.it; Via Grotte 10; d €90-120; ☀ ☎) In the picturesque Chianalea district, this B&B is housed in a 19th-century fisher's house beside steps leading to the crystal-clear sea. Rooms have small balconies facing the cobbled alleyway or the sea. The same people run **La Locandiera** (☑ 0965 75 48 81; www.lalocandiera.org; Via Zagari 27; d €60-100; ☀ ☎), another sea-facing B&B just around the corner.

Hotel Principe di Scilla   HOTEL $$
(☑ 0965 70 43 24; www.ubais.it; Via Grotte 2; ste €150-180; ☀ ☎) Get lulled to sleep by the sound of lapping waves in this grand old family residence on Scilla's seafront. Two suits of armour guard the front door, while inside, six individually themed suites are stuffed with countless antiques.

✕ Eating & Drinking

Bleu de Toi   SEAFOOD $$
(☑ 0965 79 05 85; www.bleudetoi.it; Via Grotte 40; meals €30-35; ⊗ noon-3pm & 8pm-midnight Wed-Mon) Soak up the atmosphere in the Chianalea district at this little restaurant. It has a terrace over the water and excellent seafood dishes, including Scilla's renowned swordfish.

Dali City Pub   BAR
(Via Porto; ⊗ noon-midnight) On the beach in Scilla town, this popular bar has a Beatles tribute corner (appropriately named the Cavern) and has been going strong since 1972.

❶ Getting There & Away

Scilla is on the main coastal train line. Frequent trains run to Reggio di Calabria (€2.40, 30 minutes). The train station is a couple of blocks from the beach.

Capo Vaticano

There are spectacular views from this rocky cape, with its beaches, ravines and limestone sea cliffs. Birdwatchers' spirits should soar. Around 7km south of Tropea, Capo Vaticano has a lighthouse, built in 1885, which is close to a short footpath from where you can see as far as the Aeolian Islands. Capo Vaticano beach is one of the balmiest along this coast.

Tropea

POP 6780
Tropea, a puzzle of lanes and piazzas, is famed for its captivating prettiness, dramatic position and sunsets the colour of amethyst. It sits on the Promontorio di Tropea, which stretches from Nicotera in the south to Pizzo in the north. The coast alternates between dramatic cliffs and icing-sugar-soft sandy beaches, all edged by translucent sea. Unsurprisingly, hundreds of Italian holidaymakers descend here in summer. If you hear English being spoken, it is probably from Americans visiting relatives: enormous numbers left the region for America in the early 20th century.

Despite the mooted theory that Hercules founded the town, it seems this area has been settled as far back as Neolithic times. Tropea has been occupied by the Arabs, Normans, Swabians, Anjous and Aragonese, as well as being attacked by Turkish pirates. Perhaps they were all after the town's famous red onions, so sweet they can be turned into marmalade.

◉ Sights

Cathedral
(⊗ 6.30-11.30am & 4-7pm) The beautiful Norman cathedral has two undetonated WWII bombs near the door: it's believed they didn't explode due to the protection of the town's patron saint, Our Lady of Romania. A

PUGLIA, BASILICATA & CALABRIA SOUTHERN TYRRHENIAN COAST

FOOTPRINTS OF MAGNA GRAECIA

Long before the Romans colonised Greece, the Greeks were colonising southern Italy. Pushed out of their homelands by demographic, social and political pressures, the nebulous mini-empire they created between the 8th and 3rd centuries BC was often referred to as Magna Graecia by the Romans in the north. Many Greek-founded cities were located along the southern coast of present-day Puglia, Basilicata and Calabria. They included (west to east) Locri Epizephiri, Kroton, Sybaris, Metapontum and Taras (now Taranto).

Magna Graecia was more a loose collection of independent cities than a coherent state with fixed borders, and many of these cities regularly raged war against each other. The most notable conflict occurred in 510 BC when the athletic Krotons attacked and destroyed the hedonistic city of Sybaris (from which the word 'sybaritic' is derived).

Magna Graecia was the 'door' through which Greek culture entered Italy influencing its language, architecture, religion and culture. Though the cities were mostly abandoned by the 5th century AD, the Greek legacy lives on in the Griko culture of Calabria and the Salento peninsula, where ethnic Greek communities still speak Griko, a dialect of Greek.

Remnants of Magna Graecia can be seen in numerous museums and architectural sites along Calabria's Ionian coast.

Sibari

Museo Archeologico Nazionale delle Sibaritide (☑0981 7 93 91; Via Casoni, Casa Blanca; admission €2; ⏰9am-7.30pm Tue-Sun) Founded around 730 BC and destroyed by the Krotons in 510 BC, Sybaris was rebuilt twice: once as Thuni by the Greeks in 444 BC, and again in 194 BC by the Romans who called it Copia. Evidence of all three cities can be seen at this archaeological site and its museum located 5km southeast of the modern beach resort of Sibari. Serious flooding affected the site in 2013, meaning the park suffers periodic closures. Check ahead.

Crotone

Museo Archeologico Nazionale di Crotone (☑0962 90 56 25; Via Risorgimento 120, Crotone; admission €2; ⏰9am-7pm Tue-Sun) Founded in 710 BC, the powerful city state of Kroton was known for its sobriety and high-performing Olympic athletes. Crotone's museum is located in the modern town, while the main archaeological site is at Capo Colonna, 11km to the southeast.

Locri

Museo Nazionale di Locri Epizephiri (☑0964 39 00 23; admission €4; ⏰9am-7pm Tue-Sun) Situated 3km south of modern-day Locri, the Greek colony of Locri Epizephiri was founded in 680 BC and abandoned in the 5th century AD. The archaeological site is large and quite overgrown, although the attached museum is better curated. Reliefs from the on-site **Temple of Marasà** depicting Dioscuri falling from his horse are on display at the **Museo Nazionale di Reggio Calabria** (p766).

Byzantine icon of the Madonna (1330) hangs above the altar – she is also credited with protecting the town from the earthquakes that have pummelled the region.

Santa Maria dell'Isola　　CHURCH
The town overlooks Santa Maria dell'Isola, a medieval church with a Renaissance make over, which sits on its own rocky little island, although centuries of silt have joined it to the mainland.

Sleeping

⭐**Donnaciccina**　　B&B $$
(☑0963 6 21 80; www.donnaciccina.com; Via Pellic-cia 9; s €55-120, d €70-170, apt €112-240; ✳@🛜) Overlooking the main *corso,* this delightful B&B has retained a tangible sense of history with its carefully selected antiques, canopy beds and terracotta tiled floors. There's also a self-catering apartment perfectly positioned on the cliff overlooking the sea, and a chatty parrot in reception.

Residenza il Barone
B&B $$

(☎ 0963 60 71 81; www.residenzailbarone.it; Largo Barone; ste €140-200; ❄@☎) This graceful *palazzo* has six suites decorated in masculine neutrals and tobacco browns, with dramatic modern paintings by the owner's brother adding pizazz to the walls. There's a computer in each suite and you can eat breakfast on the small roof terrace with views over the old city and out to sea.

✕ Eating

Al Pinturicchio
TRADITIONAL ITALIAN $

(☎ 0963 60 34 52; Via Dardona, cnr Largo Duomo; meals €16-22; ⊘ 7.30pm-midnight) Recommended by the locals, this restaurant in the old town has a romantic ambience, candlelit tables and a menu of imaginative dishes.

Osteria del Pescatore
SEAFOOD $

(☎ 0963 60 30 18; Via del Monte 7; meals €20-25; ⊘ 7.30pm-midnight Thu-Tue) Swordfish *(spada)* is a speciality on this part of the coast and it rates highly on the menu at this simple seafood place tucked away in the backstreets.

❶ Information

Tourist Office (☎ 0963 6 14 75; Piazza Ercole; ⊘ 9am-1pm & 4-8pm) In the old town centre.

❶ Getting There & Away

Trains run to Pizzo-Lamezia (€2.40, 30 minutes, 12 daily), Scilla (€4.60, 1¼ hours, frequent) and Reggio (from €6.40, 1¾ hours, frequent). **SAV** (☎ 0963 6 11 29) buses connect with other towns on the coast.

Pizzo
POP 9240

Stacked high up on a sea cliff, pretty little Pizzo is the place to go for *tartufo*, a death-by-chocolate ice-cream ball, and to see an extraordinary rock-carved grotto church. It's a popular and cheerful tourist stop. Piazza della Repubblica is the epicentre, set high above the sea with great views. Settle here at one of the many gelateria terraces for an ice-cream fix.

◉ Sights

Chiesa di Piedigrotta
CAVE

(admission €2.50; ⊘ 9am-1pm & 3-7.30pm) The Chiesa di Piedigrotta is an underground cave full of carved stone statues. It was carved into the tufa rock by Neapolitan ship-

wreck survivors in the 17th century. Other sculptors added to it and it was eventually turned into a church. Later statues include the less-godly figures of Fidel Castro and John F Kennedy. It's a bizarre, one-of-a-kind mixture of mysticism, mystery and kitsch. Buy tickets at the restaurant above the cave.

Chiesa Matrice di San Giorgio
CHURCH

(Via Marconi) In town, the 16th-century Chiesa Matrice di San Giorgio, with its dressed-up Madonnas, houses the tomb of Joachim Murat, the French-born former king of Naples, brother-in-law of Napoleon and well-known European dandy.

Castello Murat
CASTLE

(☎ 0963 53 25 23; adult/reduced €2.50/1.50; ⊘ 9am-1pm & 3pm-midnight Jun-Sep, 9am-1pm & 3-7pm Oct-May) This neat little 15th-century castle is named for Joachim Murat, supporter of Napoleon Bonaparte. He was captured in Pizzo and sentenced to death for treason in 1815. Inside the castle, you can see his cell and the details of his grisly end by firing squad, which is graphically illustrated with waxworks. Although Murat was the architect of enlightened reforms, the locals showed no great concern when he was executed.

🛏 Sleeping & Eating

Armonia B&B
B&B $

(☎ 0963 53 33 37; www.casaarmonia.com; Via Armonia 9; s/d without bathroom €45/60; @) Run by the charismatic Franco in his 18th-century family home, this B&B has a number of rooms (with shared bathroom). The sea views are spectacular.

Ristorante Don Diego di Pizzo
PIZZA $

(☎ 340 892 44 69; www.dondiegoristorante.com; Via M Salomone 243; meals €20-25; ⊘ noon-3pm & 7pm-midnight Wed-Mon) Fantastic views from a panoramic terrace and food to match. The restaurant is particularly known for its pizza.

❶ Getting There & Away

Pizzo is just off the major A3 autostrada. There are two train stations. Vibo Valentia-Pizzo is located 4km south of town on the main Rome–Reggio di Calabria line. A bus service connects you to Pizzo. Pizzo-Lamezia is south of the town on the Tropea–Lamezia Terme line. Shuttle buses (€2) connect with trains or you can walk for 20 minutes along the coast road.

Surprises of the South

In the Mezzogiorno, the sun shines on a magical landscape: dramatic cliffs and sandy beaches fringed with turquoise seas; wild rocky mountains and gentle forested slopes; rolling green fields and flat plains. Sprinkled throughout are elegant *palazzi* (mansions), *masserias* (working farms), ancient cave-dwellings and gnome-like stone huts.

Promontorio del Gargano

Along with its charming seaside villages, sandy coves and crystalline blue waters, the Gargano (p724) is also home to the Parco Nazionale del Gargano. It's perfect for hikers, nature trippers and beach fiends alike.

Valle d'Itria

In a landscape of rolling green hills, vineyards, orchards and picture-pretty fields, conical stone huts called *trulli* sprout from the ground en masse in the Disneyesque towns of Alberobello (p731) and Locorotondo (p733).

Salento

In Salento, hot, dry plains covered in wildflowers and olive groves reach towards the gorgeous beaches and waters of the Ionian and Adriatic Seas. It's the unspoilt 'heel' of Italy, with Lecce (p736) as its sophisticated capital.

Matera

The ancient cave city of Matera (p749) has been inhabited since Palaeolithic times. Explore the tangled alleyways, admire frescoes in rock churches, and sleep in millennia-old *sassi* (former cave dwellings).

Parco Nazionale dell'Aspromonte

In this wild park (p765), narrow roads lead to hilltop villages such as spectacularly sited Bova. Waterfalls, wide riverbeds, jagged cliffs and sandstone formations form the backdrop to a landscape made for hiking.

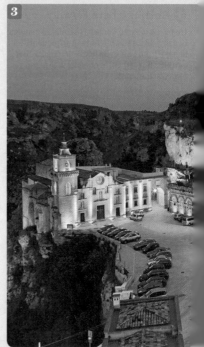

1. Promontorio del Gargano 2. Conical *trulli* houses, Alberobello, Valle d'Itria 3. View over Matera 4. Basilica di Santa Croce (p736), Lecce, Salento

Sicily

Why Go?

More of a sugar-spiked espresso than a milky cappuccino, Sicily rewards visitors with an intense, bittersweet experience. Overloaded with art treasures and natural beauty, undersupplied with infrastructure, and continuously struggling against Mafia-driven corruption, Sicily's complexities sometimes seem unfathomable. To really appreciate this place, come with an open mind – and a healthy appetite. Despite the island's perplexing contradictions, one factor remains constant: the high quality of the cuisine.

After 25 centuries of foreign domination, Sicilians are heirs to an impressive cultural legacy, from the refined architecture of Magna Graecia to the Byzantine splendour and Arab craftsmanship of the island's Norman cathedrals and palaces. This cultural richness is matched by a startlingly diverse landscape that includes bucolic farmland, smouldering volcanoes and kilometres of island-studded aquamarine coastline.

Best Places to Eat

➡ Ferro di Cavallo (p785)

➡ A Putia delle Cose Buone (p820)

➡ Osteria Antica Marina (p812)

➡ Ristorante Crocifisso (p824)

Best Places to Stay

➡ Pensione Tranchina (p839)

➡ Henry's House (p820)

➡ Hotel Signum (p799)

When to Go
Palermo

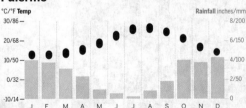

Easter Colourful religious processions and marzipan lambs in every bakery window.

May Wildflowers, dreamy coastal walking and Syracuse's festival of classic drama.

Sep Warm weather and seaside fun without summer prices.

History

Sicily's most deeply ingrained cultural influences originate from its first inhabitants – the Sicani from North Africa, the Siculi from Latium (Italy) and the Elymni from Greece. The subsequent colonisation of the island by the Carthaginians (also from North Africa) and the Greeks, in the 8th and 6th centuries BC respectively, compounded this cultural divide through decades of war when powerful opposing cities struggled to dominate the island.

Although part of the Roman Empire, Sicily didn't truly come into its own until after the Arab invasions of AD 831. Trade, farming and mining were all fostered under Arab influence and Sicily soon became an enviable prize for European opportunists. The Normans, desperate for a piece of the pie, invaded in 1061 and made Palermo the centre of their expanding empire and the finest city in the Mediterranean.

Impressed by the cultured Arab lifestyle, King Roger squandered vast sums on ostentatious palaces and churches, and encouraged a hedonistic atmosphere in his court. But such prosperity – and decadence (Roger's grandson, William II, even had a harem) – inevitably gave rise to envy and resentment and, after two centuries of pleasure and profit, the Norman line was extinguished. The kingdom passed to the austere German House of Hohenstaufen with little opposition from the seriously eroded and weakened Norman occupisers.

In the centuries that followed, Sicily passed to the Holy Roman Emperors, Angevins (French) and Aragonese (Spanish) in a turmoil of rebellion and revolution that continued until the Spanish Bourbons united Sicily with Naples in 1734 as the Kingdom of the Two Sicilies. Little more than a century later, on 11 May 1860, Giuseppe Garibaldi planned his daring and dramatic unification of Italy from Marsala on Sicily's western coast.

Reeling from this catalogue of colonisers, Sicilians struggled in poverty-stricken conditions. Unified with Italy, but no better off, nearly one million men and women emigrated to the USA between 1871 and 1914 before the outbreak of WWI.

Ironically, the Allies (seeking Mafia help in America for the re-invasion of Italy) helped in establishing the Mafia's stranglehold on Sicily. In the absence of suitable administrators, they invited the undesirable *mafioso* (Mafia boss) Don Calógero Vizzini to do the job. When Sicily became a semi-autonomous region in 1948, Mafia control extended right to the heart of politics and the region plunged into a 50-year silent civil war. It only started to emerge from this after the anti-Mafia maxi-trials of the 1980s, in which Sicily's revered magistrates Giovanni Falcone and Paolo Borsellino hauled hundreds of Mafia members into court, leading to important prosecutions.

The assassinations of Falcone and Borsellino in 1992 helped galvanise Sicilian public opposition to the Mafia's inordinate influence, and while organised crime lives on, the thuggery and violence of the 1980s has diminished. A growing number of businesses refuse to pay the extortionate protection money known as the *pizzo*, and there continue to be important arrests, further encouraging those who would speak out against the Mafia. On the political front, anti-Mafia crusaders currently serve in two of the island's most powerful positions: Palermo mayor Leoluca Orlando and Sicilian governor Rosario Crocetta. Nowadays the hot topics on everyone's mind are the island's continued economic struggles and Sicily's role as the gateway for the flood of immigrants from northern Africa.

ⓘ Getting There & Away

BOAT

Regular car and passenger ferries cross the strait between Villa San Giovanni (Calabria) and Messina, while hydrofoils connect Messina with Reggio di Calabria.

Sicily is also accessible by ferry from Naples, Genoa, Civitavecchia, Salerno, Cagliari, Malta and Tunisia. Prices rise between June and September, when advanced bookings may also be required.

ROUTE	ADULT FARE FROM (€)	DURATION (HRS)
Civitavecchia–Palermo	63	14
Genoa–Palermo	68	21
Malta–Pozzallo	33	1¾
Naples–Catania	42	11
Naples–Palermo	53	10
Naples–Trapani	94	7
Reggio di Calabria–Messina	3.50	35min
Tunis–Palermo	42	11

SICILY HISTORY

Sicily Highlights

1 Joining the ranks of impeccably dressed opera-goers at elegant Teatro Massimo in **Palermo** (p778).

2 Climbing Europe's most active volcano in the afternoon, and returning to buzzing nightlife in **Catania** (p808).

3 Marvelling at the majesty of the Doric temple in **Segesta** (p839).

4 Watching international stars perform against Mt Etna's breathtaking backdrop at summer festivals in **Taormina** (p804).

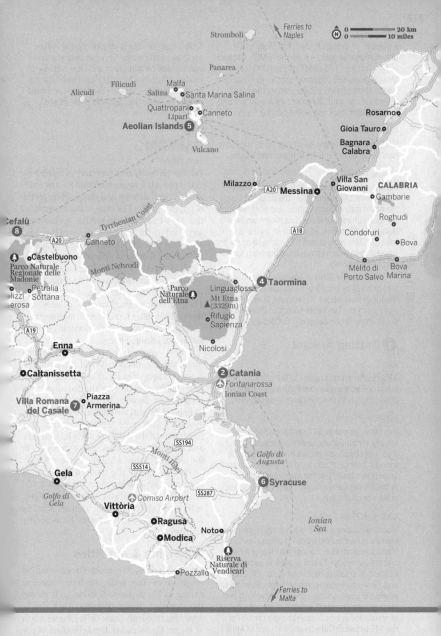

5 Observing Stromboli's volcanic fireworks and hiking to your heart's content on the stunningly scenic **Aeolian Islands** (p792).

6 Stepping back in time at an ancient Greek theatre performance in **Syracuse** (p815).

7 Admiring prancing wild beasts and dancing bikini-clad gymnasts on the mosaic floors of **Villa Romana del Casale** (p827).

8 Being dazzled by Byzantine mosaics and splendid coastal sunsets in **Cefalù** (p790).

AIR

A number of airlines fly direct to Sicily's four international airports – Palermo (PMO), Catania (CTA), Trapani (TPS) and Comiso (CIY) – although many still require a transfer in Rome or Milan. Alitalia (www.alitalia.com) is the main Italian carrier, while **Ryanair** (www.ryanair.com) is the leading low-cost airline serving Sicily.

BUS

SAIS Trasporti (www.saistrasporti.it) runs long-haul services to Sicily from Rome and Naples.

TRAIN

For travellers originating in Rome and points south, InterCity trains cover the distance from mainland Italy to Sicily in the least possible time, without a change of train. If coming from Milan, Bologna or Florence, your fastest option is to take the ultra-high-speed Frecciarossa as far as Naples, then change to an InterCity train for the rest of the journey.

All trains enter Sicily at Messina, after being transported by ferry from Villa San Giovanni at the toe of Italy's boot. At Messina, trains branch west along the Tyrrhenian coast to Palermo, or south along the Ionian coast to Catania.

ⓘ Getting Around

AIR

Alitalia offers direct flights to the offshore islands of Pantelleria (from Palermo and Trapani) and Lampedusa (from Palermo and Catania).

BUS

Bus services within Sicily are provided by a variety of companies. Buses are usually faster if your destination involves travel through the island's interior; trains tend to be cheaper (and sometimes faster) on the major coastal routes. In small towns and villages tickets are often sold in bars or on the bus.

CAR & MOTORCYCLE

Having your own vehicle is advantageous in the interior, where public transit is often slow and limited. Autostradas connect the major cities and are generally of good quality, especially the A18 and A20 toll roads, running along the Ionian and Tyrrhenian coasts, respectively. Even so, the island's highways have suffered some high-profile problems in recent years – most notably the landslide-induced collapse of a key section of the A19 between Catania and Palermo in April 2015 (still under repair at the time of research). Drive defensively; the Sicilians are some of Italy's most aggressive drivers, with a penchant for overtaking on blind corners, holding a mobile phone in one hand while gesticulating wildly with the other!

TRAIN

Sicily's train service is very efficient along the north and east coasts. Services to towns in the interior tend be infrequent and slow, although if you have the time the routes can be very picturesque. InterCity trains are the fastest and most expensive, while the *regionale* is the slowest.

PALERMO

POP 657,000

Palermo is a city of decay and of splendour and – provided you can handle its raw energy, deranged driving and chaos – has plenty of appeal. Unlike Florence or Rome, many of the city's treasures are hidden, rather than scrubbed up for endless streams of tourists.

At one time an Arab emirate and seat of a Norman kingdom, Palermo became Europe's grandest city in the 12th century, then underwent another round of aesthetic transformations during 500 years of Spanish rule. The resulting treasure trove of palaces, castles and churches has a unique architectural fusion of Byzantine, Arab, Norman, Renaissance and baroque gems.

While some of the crumbling *palazzi* (mansions) bombed in WWII are being restored, others remain dilapidated; turned into shabby apartments, the faded glory of their ornate facades is just visible behind strings of brightly coloured washing. The evocative history of the city remains very much part of the daily life of its inhabitants, and the dusty web of backstreet markets in the old quarter has a Middle Eastern feel.

The flip side is the modern city, a mere 15-minute stroll away, parts of which could be neatly jigsawed and slotted into Paris, with a grid system of wide avenues lined by seductive shops and handsome 19th-century apartments.

◉ Sights & Activities

Via Maqueda is the main street, running north from the train station, changing names to Via Ruggero Settimo as it passes the landmark Teatro Massimo, then finally widening into leafy Viale della Libertà north of Piazza Castelnuovo, the beginning of the city's modern district.

◉ Around the Quattro Canti

The busy intersection of Corso Vittorio Emanuele and Via Maqueda is known as the **Quattro Canti**. Forming the civic heart of

Palermo, this crossroads divides the historic nucleus into four traditional quarters – Albergheria, Capo, Vucciria and La Kalsa.

★ **Fontana Pretoria**   FOUNTAIN
This huge and ornate fountain, with tiered basins and sculptures rippling in concentric circles, forms the centrepiece of **Piazza Pretoria**, a spacious square just south of the Quattro Canti. The city bought the fountain in 1573; however, the flagrant nudity of the provocative nymphs proved too much for Sicilian church-goers attending Mass next door, and they prudishly dubbed it the Fountain of Shame.

La Martorana   CHURCH
(Chiesa di Santa Maria dell'Ammiraglio; Piazza Bellini 3; adult/reduced €2/1; ⊘ 9.30am-1pm & 3.30-5.30pm Mon-Sat, 9-10.30am Sun) On the southern side of Piazza Bellini, this luminously beautiful 12th-century church was endowed by King Roger's Syrian emir, George of Antioch, and was originally planned as a mosque. Delicate Fatimid pillars support a domed cupola depicting Christ enthroned amid his archangels. The interior is best appreciated in the morning, when sunlight illuminates magnificent Byzantine mosaics.

Chiesa Capitolare di San Cataldo   CHURCH
(Piazza Bellini 3; admission €2.50; ⊘ 9.30am-12.30pm & 3-6pm) This 12th-century church in Arab-Norman style is one of Palermo's most striking buildings. With its dusky-pink bijou domes, solid square shape, blind arcading and delicate tracery, it illustrates perfectly the synthesis of Arab and Norman architectural styles. The interior, while more austere, is still beautiful, with its inlaid floor and lovely stone-and-brickwork in the arches and domes.

◉ **Albergheria**

Southwest of the Quattro Canti is Albergheria, a rather shabby, rundown district once inhabited by Norman court officials, now home to a growing number of immigrants who are attempting to revitalise its dusty backstreets. The top tourist draws here are the Palazzo dei Normanni (Norman Palace) and its exquisite chapel, both at the neighbourhood's far western edge.

★ **Palazzo dei Normanni &**
Cappella Palatina   PALACE, CHAPEL
(www.fondazionefedericosecondo.it; Piazza Indipendenza 1; adult/reduced Fri-Mon €8.50/6.50, Tue-Thu €7/5; ⊘ 8.15am-5.40pm Mon-Sat, to 1pm Sun, Royal Apartments closed Tue-Thu, chapel closed 9.45-11.15am Sun) This venerable palace dates to the 9th century but owes its current look (and name) to a major 12th-century Norman makeover, during which spectacular mosaics were added to its **Royal Apartments** and priceless jewel of a chapel, the Cappella Palatina. Designed by Roger II in 1130, the chapel glitters with stunning gold mosaics, its aesthetic harmony further enhanced by the inlaid marble floors and wooden *muqarnas* ceiling, a masterpiece of Arabic-style honeycomb carving that reflects Norman Sicily's cultural complexity.

The chapel is Palermo's top tourist attraction. Note that queues are likely, and that you'll be refused entry if you're wearing shorts, a short skirt or a low-cut top. The top level of the palace's three-tiered loggia houses Sicily's regional parliament and the Royal Apartments, including the mosaic-lined Sala dei Venti, and Sala di Ruggero II, King Roger's magnificent 12th-century bedroom. These latter attractions are only open to visitors Friday through Monday.

Chiesa di San Giovanni degli
Eremiti   CHURCH
(☑ 091 651 50 19; Via dei Benedettini 16; adult/reduced €6/3; ⊘ 9am-6pm Mon-Sat, 9am-1pm Sun) This remarkable, five-domed remnant of Arab-Norman architecture occupies a magical little hillside in the middle of an otherwise rather squalid neighbourhood. Surrounded by a garden of citrus trees, palms, cacti and ruined walls, it's built atop a mosque that itself was superimposed on an earlier chapel. The peaceful Norman cloisters outside offer lovely views of the Palazzo dei Normanni.

★ **Mercato di Ballarò**   MARKET
(⊘ 7am-7pm Mon-Sat, to 1pm Sun) Snaking for several city blocks southeast of Palazzo dei Normanni is Palermo's busiest street market, which throbs with activity well into the early evening. It's a fascinating mix of noises, smells and street life, and the cheapest place for everything from Chinese padded bras to fresh produce, fish, meat, olives and cheese – smile nicely for a taste.

◉ **Capo**

Northwest of Quattro Canti is the Capo neighbourhood, another densely packed web of interconnected streets and blind alleys.

SICILY

Palermo

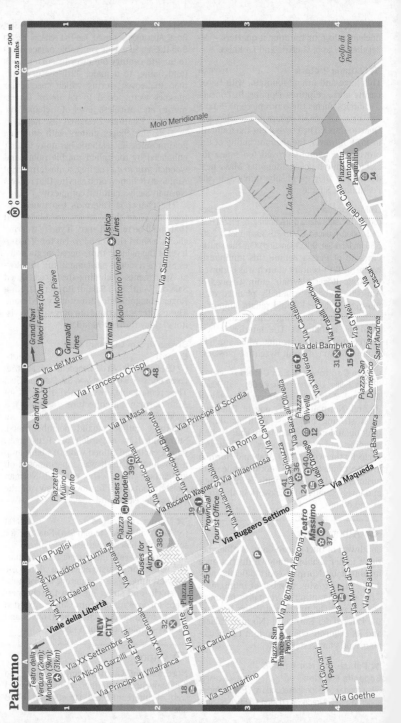

0.25 miles
500 m

Teatro della
Verdura (2km);
Mondello (9km);
(31km)

**NEW
CITY**

Viale della Libertà

Via Puglisi

Via XX Settembre

Via Nicolò Garzilli

Via Principe di Villafranca

Via Achimede

Via Isidoro la Lumia

Via A Gaetario

Via Torrearsa

Via E Parisi

Via XII Gennaio

Via Dante

Piazza
Castelnuovo

Via Carducci

Via Sammartino

Via Goethe

Via Giovanni
Pacini

Piazzetta
Mulino a
Vento

Buses to
Mondello

Piazza
Sturzo

Buses for
Airport

Via Emerico Amari

Via la Masa

Via Principe di Belmonte

Via Riccardo Wagner

Via Francesco Crispi

Via Principe di Scordia

Via Roma

Via Mariano Stabile

Via Villaermosa

Via Cavour

Via Ruggero Settimo

Provincial
Tourist Office

Via Pignatelli Aragona

Via Francesco di Paola

Piazza San

Via Volturno

Via Mura di S Vito

Via G Battista

Via del Mare

Grandi Navi
Veloci

Grimaldi
Lines

Tirrenia

Ustica
Lines

Molo Piave

Molo Vittorio Veneto

Molo Meridionale

Via Sammuzzo

La Cala

Via dei Bambinai

Via Castello

Via Fratelli Cianciolo

Via G Meli

Piazza
Sant'Andrea

Piazza San
Domenico

Via Bandiera

Via Maqueda

VUCCIRIA

Piazza
Olivella

Via Bara all'Olivella

Via dell'Orologio

Via Valverde

Via Spinuzza

Piazzetta
Antonio
Pasqualino

Golfo di
Palermo

Via della Cala

Via
Cassari

**Teatro
Massimo**

Grandi Navi
Veloci Ferries (50m)

SICILY

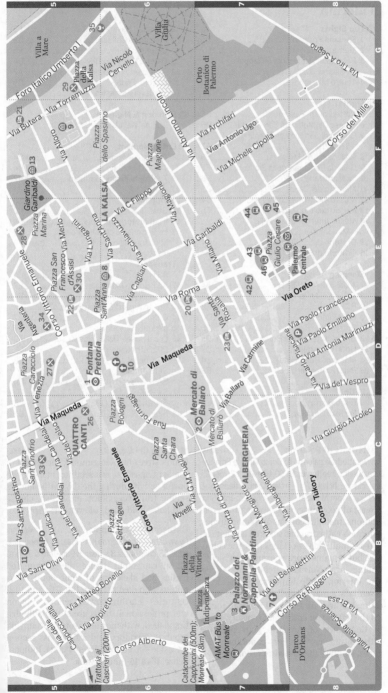

CAPO

11

Piazza Sant'Agostino

Via Sant'Agostino

Via Sant'Oliva

Via delle Cappuccine

Via Papireto

Via Matteo Bonello

Via Judica

Via del Candelai

Via Candelai

Via Venezia

Via Maqueda

QUATTRO CANTI

26

33

27

Piazza Caracciolo

Piazza Sant'Onofrio

Via del Celso

Piazza Sett'Angeli

5

Corso Vittorio Emanuele

Piazza Santa Chiara

Piazza Bologni

Via Novelli

Via G M Puglia

Via Porta di Castro

ALBERGHERIA

Via A Mongitore

Via Mongitore

Via Albergheria

Via del Benedettini

Corso Tükory

3 **Palazzo dei Normanni & Cappella Palatina**

Piazza Indipendenza

Piazza della Vittoria

Corso Rè Ruggero

Via Brasa

Parco D'Orleans

Viale delle Scienze

Corso Alberto

Trattoria ai Cascinari (200m)

Catacombe dei Cappuccini (500m); Monreale (8km)

AMAT Bus to Monreale

1 **Fontana Pretoria**

6 10

Via Maqueda

2 **Mercato di Ballarò**

Mercato di Ballarò

Via Ballarò

Rua Formaggi

Via Argenteria

Via Roma

20

Via Santa Rosalia

Via Santa

Via Carmine

23

Via del Vespro

Via Giorgio Arcoleo

42

Via Oreto

Via Carlo Pisacane

Via Paolo Francesco

Via Paolo Emiliano

Via Antonia Marinuzzi

46

43

Piazza Giulio Cesare

Palermo Centrale

44

45

47

Via Milano

Via Garibaldi

Via Magione

Piazza Magione

Via C Filippo

Via Schiavuzzo

Via Sant'Anna

8

Piazza Sant'Anna

30

22

Piazza San Francesco d'Assisi

Via Merlo

Piazza Marina

Giardino Garibaldi

28

Corso Vittorio Emanuele

34

Via Cagliari

Via Lungarini

13

LA KALSA

Piazza dello Spasimo

Via Alloro

9

29

Piazza della Kalsa

21

Via Butera

Via Torremuzza

Via Nicolò Cervello

Via Abramo Lincoln

Villa a Mare

Foro Italico Umberto I

35

Villa Giulia

Orto Botanico di Palermo

Via Tiro A Segno

Via Archifari

Via Antonio Ugo

Via Michele Cipolla

Corso dei Mille

Palermo

Cattedrale di Palermo CATHEDRAL

(www.cattedrale.palermo.it; Corso Vittorio Emanuele; cathedral free, tombs €1.50, treasury €2, roof €5, all-inclusive ticket €7; ⊙ royal tombs, treasury & roof 9am-4pm Mon-Sat, tombs only 9am-1pm Sun) A feast of geometric patterns, ziggurat crenellations, maiolica cupolas and blind arches, Palermo's cathedral has suffered aesthetically from multiple reworkings over the centuries, but remains a prime example of Sicily's unique Arab-Norman architectural style. The interior, while impressive in scale, is essentially a marble shell whose most interesting features are the royal Norman tombs (to the left as you enter) and treasury, home to Constance of Aragon's gem-encrusted 13th-century crown. For panoramic city views, climb to the cathedral's roof.

Mercato del Capo MARKET

Capo's street market, running the length of Via Sant'Agostino, is a seething mass of colourful activity during the day, with vendors selling fruit, vegetables, meat, fish, cheese and household goods of every description.

Catacombe dei Cappuccini CATACOMB

(www.catacombepalermo.it; Piazza Cappuccini; adult €3, child under 8yr free; ⊙ 9am-1pm & 3-6pm) These catacombs house the mummified bodies and skeletons of some 8000 Palermitans who died between the 17th and 19th centuries. Earthly power, gender, religion and professional status are still rigidly distinguished, with men and women occupying separate corridors, and a first-class section set aside for virgins. From Piazza Indipendenza, it's a 15-minute walk.

◎ Vucciria

Once a notorious den of Mafia activity, the Vucciria retains a grungy, authentic edge. In the evenings, it becomes a mecca for bar-hopping and seriously down-to-earth street food. It's also home to some of Palermo's finest baroque artwork.

Museo Archeologico Regionale MUSEUM
(☑091 611 68 05; www.regione.sicilia.it/beniculturali/salinas; Piazza Olivella 24) This splendid, wheelchair-accessible museum has been undergoing renovations since 2010, with no dependable reopening date in sight. Situated in a Renaissance monastery surrounding a gracious courtyard, it houses some of Sicily's most valuable Greek and Roman artefacts, including the museum's crown jewel, a series of original decorative friezes from the temples at Selinunte.

Oratorio di Santa Cita CHAPEL
(www.ilgeniodipalermo.com; Via Valverde; admission €4, joint ticket incl Oratorio di San Domenico €6; ⊘9am-2pm Mon-Sat Nov-Mar, to 6pm Apr-Oct) This 17th-century chapel showcases the breathtaking stuccowork of Giacomo Serpotta, who famously introduced rococo to Sicilian churches. Note the elaborate *Battle of Lepanto* on the entrance wall. Depicting the Christian victory over the Turks, it's framed by stucco drapes held by hundreds of naughty cherubs modelled on Palermo's street urchins. Serpotta's virtuosity also dominates the side walls, where sculpted white stucco figures hold gilded swords, shields and a lute, and a golden snake (Serpotta's symbol) curls around a picture frame.

Oratorio di San Domenico CHAPEL
(www.ilgeniodipalermo.com; Via dei Bambinai 2; admission €4, joint ticket incl Oratorio di Santa Cita €6; ⊘9am-2pm Mon-Sat Nov-Mar, to 6pm Apr-Oct) Dominating this small chapel is Anthony Van Dyck's fantastic blue-and-red altarpiece, *The Virgin of the Rosary with St Dominic and the Patronesses of Palermo*. Van Dyck completed the work in Genoa in 1628, after leaving Palermo in fear of the plague. Also gracing the chapel are Giacomo Serpotta's amazingly elaborate stuccoes (1710–17), vivacious and whirling with figures. Serpotta's name meant 'lizard' or 'small snake', and he often included these signature reptiles in his work; see if you can find one!

◎ La Kalsa

Due to its proximity to the port, La Kalsa was subjected to carpet bombing during WWII, leaving it derelict and rundown. Mother Teresa considered it akin to the shanty towns of Calcutta and established a mission here. Certain areas of La Kalsa, especially the part nearest the Quattro Canti, have undergone extensive renovation in recent years – for example, the former stock exchange has been converted into a high-end hotel. However, the neighbourhood still feels scruffy around the edges, with a decaying ambience that some will find intriguing, others off-putting.

Galleria Regionale della Sicilia MUSEUM
(Palazzo Abatellis; ☑091 623 00 11; www.regione.sicilia.it/beniculturali/palazzoabatellis; Via Alloro 4; adult/reduced €8/4; ⊘9am-6.30pm Tue-Fri, to 1pm Sat & Sun) Housed in the stately 15th-century Palazzo Abatellis, this fine museum features works by Sicilian artists from the Middle Ages to the 18th century. Its greatest treasure is *Triunfo della Morte* (Triumph of Death), a magnificent fresco in which Death is represented as a demonic skeleton mounted on a wasted horse, brandishing a wicked-looking scythe while leaping over his hapless victims.

Galleria d'Arte Moderna MUSEUM
(☑091 843 16 05; www.galleriadartemoderna palermo.it; Via Sant'Anna 21; adult/reduced €7/5; ⊘9.30am-6.30pm Tue-Sun) This lovely, wheelchair-accessible museum is housed in a sleekly renovated 15th-century *palazzo*, which metamorphosed into a convent in the 17th century. Divided over three floors, the wide-ranging collection of 19th- and 20th-century Sicilian art is beautifully displayed. There's a regular program of modern-art exhibitions here, as well as an excellent bookshop and gift shop. English-language audio guides cost €4.

Museo dell'Inquisizione MUSEUM
(Piazza Marina 61; adult/reduced palace or prison €5/2.50, both €7.50/5; ⊘10am-6pm) Housed in the lower floors and basements of the 14th-century Palazzo Chiaromonte Steri, Palermo's newest museum offers a chilling but fascinating look at the legacy of the Inquisition in Palermo. Thousands of 'heretics' were detained here between 1601 and 1782; the honeycomb of former cells has been painstakingly restored to reveal multiple layers of their graffiti and artwork (religious

and otherwise). Excellent guided visits of the prison and the palace itself are available in English with advance notice.

Museo Internazionale delle Marionette
MUSEUM

(☑091 32 80 60; www.museomarionettepalermo.it; Piazzetta Antonio Pasqualino 5; adult/reduced €5/3; ⊘9am-1pm & 2.30-6.30pm Mon-Sat) This whimsical museum houses over 3500 marionettes, puppets, glove puppets and shadow figures from Palermo, Catania and Naples, as well as from further-flung places such as Japan, Southeast Asia, Africa, China and India. Occasional puppet shows (adult/child €10/5) are staged on the museum's top floor in a beautifully decorated traditional theatre complete with hand-cranked music machine.

◉ New City

North of Piazza Giuseppe Verdi, Palermo elegantly slips into cosmopolitan mode. Here you'll find fabulous neoclassical and art nouveau buildings hailing from the last golden age of Sicilian architecture, along with late-19th-century mansion blocks lining the broad boulevard of Viale della Libertà.

★ Teatro Massimo
THEATRE

(☑tour reservations 091 605 32 67; www.teatro massimo.it; Piazza Giuseppe Verdi; guided tours adult/reduced €8/5; ⊘9.30am-5.30pm) Palermo's grand neoclassical opera house took over 20 years to complete and has become one of the city's iconic landmarks. The closing scene of *The Godfather: Part III*, with its visually stunning juxtaposition of high culture, crime, drama and death, was filmed here. Guided 25-minute tours are offered throughout the day in English, Spanish, French and Italian.

✹ Festivals & Events

Festino di Santa Rosalia
RELIGIOUS

(U Fistinu; www.santarosaliapalermo.it; ⊘10-15 Jul) Palermo's biggest annual festival celebrates patron saint Santa Rosalia, beloved for having saved the city from a 17th-century plague. The most colourful festivities take place on the evening of 14 July, when the saint's relics are paraded aboard a grand chariot from the Palazzo dei Normanni through the Quattro Canti to the waterfront, where fireworks and general merriment ensue.

🛏 Sleeping

Budget options can be found around Via Maqueda and Via Roma in the vicinity of the train station. Midrange and top-end hotels are concentrated further north. Parking usually costs an extra €10 to €15 per day.

★ B&B Amélie
B&B €

(☑091 33 59 20; www.bb-amelie.it; Via Prinicipe di Belmonte 94; s €40-60, d €60-80, tr €90-100; ✷@☞) On a pedestrianised New City street a stone's throw from Teatro Politeama, the affable, multilingual Angela has converted her grandmother's spacious 6th-floor flat into a cheery B&B. Rooms are colourfully decorated, and the corner triple has a sunny terrace. Angela, a native Palermitan, generously shares her local knowledge and serves a tasty breakfast featuring homemade cakes and jams.

★ Palazzo Pantaleo
B&B €

(☑091 32 54 71; www.palazzopantaleo.it; Via Ruggero Settimo 74h; s/d/ste €80/100/140; 🅿☞) Offering unbeatable comfort and a convenient location, Giuseppe Scaccianoce's classy B&B occupies the top floor of an old *palazzo* half a block from Piazza Politeama, hidden from the busy street in a quiet courtyard with free parking. Five rooms and one spacious suite feature high ceilings, marble, tile or wooden floors, soundproof windows and modern bathrooms.

Hotel Orientale
HOTEL €

(☑091 616 57 27; www.albergoorientale.191.it; Via Maqueda 26; s €30-40, d €40-60, d without bathroom €30-45; ✷☞) This *palazzo*'s grand marble stairway and arcaded courtyard, complete with motor scooters, potted plants and strung-up washing, provide an evocative introduction to Palermo's most atmospherically faded old-school budget hotel. Breakfast is served under the lovely frescoed ceiling in the library. The Ballarò market and train station are both just around the corner.

A Casa di Amici Hostel
HOSTEL €

(☑091 765 46 50; www.acasadiamici.com; Via Dante 57; dm €14-23, d €40-70; ✷☞) Vibrant, friendly and filled with artwork left by former guests, this funky hostel-cum-guesthouse is a great choice. Beds are in mixed or single-sex dorms, or in several imaginatively decorated, music-themed rooms, complemented by a kitchen and yoga room. Multilingual owner Claudia provides helpful

SICILIAN PUPPET THEATRE

Since the 18th century, the Opera dei Pupi (traditional Sicilian puppet theatre) has been enthralling adults and children alike. The shows are a mini theatrical performance with some puppets standing 1.5m high – a completely different breed from the glove puppet popular in the West. These characters are intricately carved from beech, olive or lemon wood with realistic-looking features; flexible joints ensure they have no problem swinging their swords or beheading dragons.

Effectively the soap operas of their day, Sicilian puppet shows expounded the deepest sentiments of life – unrequited love, treachery, thirst for justice and the anger and frustration of the oppressed. The swashbuckling tales centre on the legends of Charlemagne's heroic knights, Orlando and Rinaldo, with an extended cast including the fair Angelica, the treacherous Gano di Magonza and forbidding Saracen warriors. Good puppeteers are judged on the dramatic effect they can create – lots of stamping feet and a gripping running commentary – and on their speed and skill in directing the battle scenes. See a perfromance at **Cuticchio Mimmo** (p787) or **Piccolo Teatro dei Pupi** (p821).

maps and advice, and also runs the **A Casa di Amici B&B** (☏ 091 58 48 84; www.acasadiamici.com; Via Volturno 6; s €20-40, d €40-60; ✳☏) behind Teatro Massimo.

B&B Panormus   B&B €

(☏ 091 617 58 26; www.bbpanormus.com; Via Roma 72; s €45-70, d €60-83, tr €75-120; ✳☏) Popular for its keen prices, charming host and convenient location between the train station and the Quattro Canti, this B&B offers five high-ceilinged rooms decorated in elegant Liberty style, each with double-glazed windows, flat-screen TV and a private bathroom down the passageway.

Butera 28   APARTMENT €€

(☏ 333 3165432; www.butera28.it; Via Butera 28; apt per day €70-180, per week €450-1200; ✳☏⚑) Delightful multilingual owner Nicoletta rents 11 comfortable apartments in the 18th-century Palazzo Lanzi Tomasi, the last home of Giuseppe Tomasi di Lampedusa, author of *The Leopard*. Units range from 30 to 180 sq metres, most sleeping a family of four or more. Four apartments face the sea, most have laundry facilities and all have well-equipped kitchens.

Massimo Plaza Hotel   HOTEL €€

(☏ 091 32 56 57; www.massimoplazahotel.com; Via Maqueda 437; r €100-250; ℗✳☏) Boasting a prime location along Palermo's newly pedestrianised Via Maqueda, this older hotel is a Palermo classic. Seven of the 15 rooms boast full-on views of the iconic Teatro Massimo across the street. The included breakfast (continental or American) can be delivered directly to your room at no extra charge, and enclosed parking costs €15 per day.

Grand Hotel Piazza Borsa   HOTEL €€€

(☏ 091 32 00 75; www.piazzaborsa.com; Via dei Cartari 18; s €126-199, d €169-219, ste €370-813; ℗✳@☏) Grandly situated in Palermo's former stock exchange, this four-star hotel encompasses three separate buildings housing 127 rooms. Nicest are the high-ceilinged suites with jacuzzis and windows facing Piazza San Francesco. Parking costs €18 per 24-hour period.

🍴 Eating

Sicily's ancient cuisine is a mixture of spicy and sweet flavours, epitomised in the aubergine-based *caponata* and the Palermitan classic *bucatini con le sarde* (hollow tube-shaped noodles with sardines, wild fennel, raisins, pine nuts and breadcrumbs). Cakes, marzipan confections and pastries are all works of art – don't miss the ubiquitous and sinfully delicious *cannoli* (tubes of pastry filled with sweetened ricotta).

Restaurants rarely start to fill up before 9pm. For cheap eats, visit Palermo's markets, wander the tangle of alleys east and south of Teatro Massimo, or spend a Saturday evening snacking with locals at the street food carts in Piazza Caracciolo in the Vucciria district.

Many places close on Sunday, especially in the evening.

★ Ferro di Cavallo   TRATTORIA €

(☏ 091 33 18 35; www.ferrodicavallopalermo.it; Via Venezia 20; meals €15-17; ⏱11.30am-3.30pm Mon-Sat, plus 7.45-11.30pm Wed-Sat) Tables line the footpath and caricatures of the owners beam down from bright-red walls at this cheerful family-run trattoria near the

DON'T MISS

PALERMO'S STREET FOOD

If you were taught that it was bad manners to eat in the street, you can break the rule in good company here. The mystery is simply how Palermo is not the obesity capital of Europe given just how much eating goes on! Palermitans are at it all the time: when they're shopping, commuting, discussing business, romancing...basically at any time of the day. What they're enjoying is the *buffitieri* – little hot snacks prepared at stalls and meant to be eaten on the spot.

Kick off the morning with *pane e panelle*, Palermo's famous chickpea fritter sandwich – great for vegetarians and a welcome change from a sweet custard-filled croissant. If you like, ask for it with a few *crocchè*, potato croquettes flavoured with fresh mint, also cheekily nicknamed *cazzilli* (little penises). Then again, you might want to go for some *sfincione* (a spongy, oily pizza topped with onions and caciocavallo cheese). In summer, locals also enjoy a freshly baked brioche filled with ice cream or *granite* (crushed ice mixed with fresh fruit, almonds, pistachios or coffee).

From 4pm onwards the snacks become decidedly more carnivorous and you may just wish you hadn't read the following translations: how about some barbecued *stigghiola* (goat intestines filled with onions, cheese and parsley), for example? Or a couple of *pani ca meusa* (bread rolls stuffed with ricotta and/or sautéed beef spleen)? You'll be asked if you want your roll *schietta* (single) or *maritata* (married). If you choose *schietta*, the roll will only have ricotta in it before being dipped into boiling lard; choose *maritata* and you'll get the beef spleen as well.

You'll find street food stalls all over town. Classic spots include Piazza Caracciolo in the Vucciria district, **Francu u Vastiddaru** (Corso Vittorio Emanuele 102; sandwiches €1.50-3.50; ⊙8am-late) and **Friggitoria Chiluzzo** (Piazza della Kalsa; sandwiches €1.50-2; ⊙8.30am-3pm Mon-Sat) in the Kalsa, and the no-name *pane e panelle* cart on Piazza Carmine in Ballarò market.

If you want expert guidance, check out the low-key guided tours offered by **Palermo Street Food** (www.palermostreetfood.com) and **Streat Palermo** (www.streatpalermo. it). Both offer the chance to wander Palermo's backstreets with a knowledgeable local guide, stopping for a taste (or two or three) at the city's most authentic hang-outs.

Quattro Canti. Nothing costs more than €8 on the straightforward à la carte menu. It's a great place to try Sicilian classics like *pasta con le sarde* (pasta with sardines, pine nuts, raisins and wild fennel); save room for the excellent *cannoli* (€2).

⭐**Trattoria Ai Cascinari**   SICILIAN €
(✓091 651 98 04; Via d'Ossuna 43/45; meals €20-25; ⊙12.30-2.30pm Tue-Sun, plus 8-10.30pm Wed-Sat) Yes, it's a bit out of the way, but this friendly neighbourhood trattoria, 1km north of the Cappella Palatina, is a long-standing Palermitan favourite, and deservedly so. It's especially enjoyable on Sunday afternoons, when locals pack the labyrinth of back rooms, as waiters perambulate non-stop with plates of scrumptious seasonal antipasti, fresh seafood and desserts from Palermo's beloved Pasticceria Cappello.

⭐**Pasticceria Cappello**   PASTICCERIA €
(www.pasticceriacappello.it; Via Giosuè Carducci 22; desserts from €2; ⊙7.30am-9.30pm Thu-Tue) One of Palermo's finest bakeries, Cappello is fa-

mous for its *setteveli* (seven-layer chocolate-hazelnut cake), invented here and now copied all over Palermo. Its display case brims with countless other splendid pastries and desserts, including the *delizia di pistacchio* (a pistachio cake topped with creamy icing and a chocolate medallion) and treats such as *cannoli* and *sfogliatelle*.

Bisso Bistrot   BISTRO €
(✓328 1314595, 091 33 49 99; Via Maqueda 172; meals €14-17; ⊙9am-midnight Tue-Sun) Frescoed walls, high ceilings and reasonably priced appetisers, *primi* and *secondi* greet diners at this historic Liberty-style bookstore at the northwest corner of the Quattro Canti, recently converted into a classy but casual bistro. Lunch and dinner menus range from traditional Sicilian pasta, meat and fish dishes to sardine burgers, with cafe service in the mornings and afternoons.

Pizzeria Frida   PIZZA €
(www.fridapizzeria.it; Piazza Sant'Onofrio 37; pizzas €4.50-11; ⊙7.30pm-midnight, closed Tue) With

footpath tables under umbrella awnings on a low-key Capo piazza, this local favourite makes pizzas in a variety of shapes, including *quadri* (square pizzas) and *vulcanotti* (named after famous volcanoes and looking the part). Toppings include Sicilian specialities like tuna, capers, pistachios, mint, aubergines and ultra-fresh ricotta.

Osteria Mangia & Bevi   SICILIAN €
(☑ 091 507 39 43; www.osteriamangiaebevi.it; Largo Cavalieri di Malta 18; meals €19-29; ⊗ 1-3pm & 8-11pm Tue-Sun) Despite its somewhat contrived aesthetics – waiters clad in traditional Sicilian *coppole* (caps), checked shirts and suspenders – this Capo district eatery with pavement seating delivers delicious spruced-up renderings of humble Sicilian classics, including the trademark *mangia e bevi* (grilled green onions wrapped in bacon) and *pasta fritta* (pasta with tomato sauce, Parmesan and breadcrumbs served in little frying pans).

★ **Trattoria Il Maestro del Brodo**   TRATTORIA €€
(☑ 091 32 95 23; Via Pannieri 7; meals €22-31; ⊗ 12.30-3.30pm Tue-Sun, plus 8-11pm Fri & Sat) This no-frills trattoria in the Vucciria offers delicious soups, an array of ultrafresh seafood and a sensational antipasto buffet (€8) featuring a dozen-plus homemade delicacies: *sarde a beccafico* (stuffed sardines), aubergine *involtini* (roulades), smoked fish, artichokes with parsley, sun-dried tomatoes, olives and more.

Osteria Ballarò   SICILIAN €€
(☑ 091 791 01 84; www.osteriaballaro.it; Via Calascibetta 25; meals €30-45; ⊗ 12.15-3.15pm & 7-11.30pm) A hot new foodie address, this classy restaurant-cum-wine bar marries an atmospheric setting with fantastic island cooking. Bare stone columns, exposed brick walls and vaulted ceilings set the stage for delicious seafood *primi,* local wines and memorable Sicilian *dolci* (sweets). Reservations recommended. For a faster eat, you can snack on street food at the bar or take away from the hole-in-the-wall counter outside.

🍸 Drinking & Nightlife

Palermo's liveliest clusters of bars can be found along Via Chiavettieri in the Vucciria neighbourhood (just northwest of Piazza Marina) and in the Champagneria district east of Teatro Massimo, centred on Piazza Olivella, Via Spinuzza and Via Patania.

Higher-end bars and dance venues are concentrated in the newer part of Palermo. In summer, many Palermitans decamp to Mondello by the sea.

Kursaal Kalhesa   BAR
(☑ 091 616 00 50; www.facebook.com/kursaal kalhesa; Foro Umberto I 21; ⊗ 6.30pm-1am Tue-Sun) Recently reopened after a restyling, Kursaal Kalhesa has long been a noted city nightspot. Touting itself as a restaurant, wine bar and jazz club, it draws a cool, in-the-know crowd who come to hang out over *aperitivi,* dine alfresco or catch a gig under the high vaulted ceilings. It's in a 15th-century *palazzo* on the city's sea walls.

⭐ Entertainment

The daily paper *Il Giornale di Sicilia* has a listing of what's on. Another excellent resource is www.balarm.it.

Teatro Massimo   OPERA
(☑ box office 091 605 35 80; www.teatromassimo. it; Piazza Giuseppe Verdi) Ernesto Basile's six-tiered art-nouveau masterpiece is Europe's third-largest opera house and one of Italy's most prestigious, right up there with La Scala in Milan and La Fenice in Venice. With lions flanking its grandiose columned entrance and an interior gleaming in red and gold, it stages opera, ballet and music concerts from September to June.

Cuticchio Mimmo   THEATRE
(☑ 091 32 34 00; www.figlidartecuticchio.com; Via Bara all'Olivella 95; ⊗ 6.30pm Sat & Sun Sep-Jul) This puppet theatre is a charming low-tech choice for children (and adults), staging traditional shows with fabulous handcrafted puppets.

Teatro di Verdura   PERFORMING ARTS
(☑ 091 765 19 63; Viale del Fante 70; ⊗ mid-Jun–Sep) A summer-only program of ballet and music in the lovely gardens of the Villa Castelnuovo, about 6km north of the city centre. Take Viale della Libertà to Viale Diana to Viale del Fante. There's a delightful open-air bar that opens during shows.

Teatro Politeama Garibaldi   PERFORMING ARTS
(☑ 091 607 25 11; Piazza Ruggero Settimo; ⊗ Oct-Jun) This grandiose theatre is a popular venue for opera, ballet and classical music, staging afternoon and evening concerts. It's home to Palermo's symphony orchestra, the **Orchestra Sinfonica Siciliana** (☑ 091 607 25 32; www.orchestrasinfonicasiciliana.it).

🛍 Shopping

Via Bara all'Olivella is good for arts and crafts.

Il Laboratorio Teatrale HANDICRAFTS
(Via Bara all'Olivella 48-50; ☺10am-1pm & 4-7pm Tue-Sat) A true artists' workshop, this enchanting space is where the Cuticchio family constructs puppets for its famous theatre across the street. High-quality puppets dating from the late 1800s to the present are displayed here, and are available for purchase by serious enthusiasts.

Miniature Alfio Ferlito ARTS
(🖉339 5416016; Via Bara all'Olivella 60; ☺9am-1pm & 4-7pm Mon-Sat) Working out of his appropriately tiny shop, artisan Alfio Ferlito crafts beautiful miniature renditions of houses, furniture, people, traditional Sicilian horse-drawn carts and more.

Le Ceramiche di Caltagirone CERAMICS
(www.leceramichedicaltagirone.it; Via Cavour 114; ☺9am-1pm & 4-8pm Mon-Sat, 9am-1pm Sun) This little shop near Teatro Massimo specialises in tiles and pottery from Caltagirone, the ceramics capital of southeastern Sicily. There's a good selection from a variety of artists, even if prices are a bit higher than you'd pay at the source.

Gusti di Sicilia FOOD & DRINK
(www.gustidisicilia.com; Via Emerico Amari 79; ☺8.30am-11pm Mon-Sat, 8.30am-2pm & 6-11pm Sun) Whether for gifts or personal souvenirs, this is a stellar spot to stock up on beautifully packaged Sicilian edibles, from tins of tuna to jars of *caponata*, capers and marmalade to bottles of wine and olive oil to unexpected treasures like *pasta con le sarde* sauce.

ℹ Information

EMERGENCY
For an ambulance, call 🖉118 or 🖉091 666 55 28.
Questura (🖉091 21 01 11; Piazza della Vittoria 8) Main police station.

MEDICAL SERVICES
Ospedale Civico (🖉091 666 11 11; www.arnascivico.it; Piazza Nicola Leotta) Emergency facilities.

TOURIST INFORMATION
Municipal Tourist Office (🖉091 740 80 21; promozioneturismo@comune.palermo.it; Piazza Bellini; ☺8.30am-6.30pm Mon-Sat) The most reliable of Palermo's city-run information booths. Others at Piazza Castelnuovo, the Port of Palermo and Mondello are only intermittently staffed, with unpredictable hours.
Provincial Tourist Office (🖉091 58 51 72; informazionituristiche@provincia.palermo.it; Via Principe di Belmonte 92; ☺8.30am-2pm & 2.30-7pm Mon-Fri, to 6pm Sat) On a pedestrianised street in the New City.
Tourist Information – Falcone-Borsellino Airport (🖉091 59 16 98; ☺8.30am-7.30pm Mon-Fri, 8.30am-6pm Sat) Downstairs in the arrivals hall.

ℹ Getting There & Away

AIR
Falcone-Borsellino Airport (🖉091 702 02 73; www.gesap.it) is at Punta Raisi, 31km west of Palermo.

Alitalia flies from Palermo to destinations throughout Europe. Several cut-rate carriers also offer flights to/from Palermo, including Ryanair, Volotea, Vueling and easyJet. Falcone-Borsellino is the hub airport for regular domestic flights to the islands of Pantelleria and Lampedusa.

BOAT
The ferry terminal is located just east of the corner of Via Francesco Crispi and Via Emerico Amari.
Grandi Navi Veloci (GNV; 🖉091 58 74 04, 010 209 45 91; www.gnv.it; Calata Marinai d'Italia) Runs ferries from Palermo to Civitavecchia, Genoa, Naples and Tunis.
Grimaldi Lines (🖉081 49 64 44, 091 611 36 91; www.grimaldi-lines.com; Via del Mare) Twice-weekly ferries from Palermo to Salerno (from €55, 10 to 12 hours) and Tunis (from €42, 11 to 14 hours).
Siremar (🖉091 749 33 15; www.siremar.it; Via Francesco Crispi 118) Car ferries (€18.35, three hours, one daily) and hydrofoils (€23.55, 1½ hours, two daily) from Palermo to Ustica.
Tirrenia (🖉344 0920924; www.tirrenia.it; Calata Marinai d'Italia) Ferries to Cagliari (from €49, 12 hours, Saturday only) and Naples (from €52, 10 hours, daily).
Ustica Lines (🖉092 387 38 13; www.usticalines.it; Molo Vittorio Veneto) From late June to early September, operates one daily hydrofoil to Lipari (€39.80, four hours), Stromboli (€55.20, 5¼ hours) and other points in the Aeolian Islands.

BUS
Offices for all bus companies are located within a block or two of Palermo Centrale train station. The two main departure points are the **Piazzetta Cairoli bus terminal** (Piazzetta Cairoli), just

AROUND PALERMO

A few kilometres outside Palermo's city limits, the beach town of Mondello and the dazzling cathedral of Monreale are both worthwhile day trips. Just offshore, Ustica makes a great overnight or weekend getaway.

Mondello's long, sandy beach became fashionable in the 19th century, when people came to the seaside in their carriages, prompting the construction of the huge art nouveau pier that still graces the waterfront. Most of the beaches near the pier are private (two sun loungers and an umbrella cost €10 to €20); however, there's a wide swath of public beach opposite the centre of town with all the requisite pedaleos and jet skis for hire. Given its easygoing seaside feel, Mondello is an excellent base for families. To get here, take bus 806 (€1.40, 30 minutes) from Piazza Sturzo in Palermo.

Cattedrale di Monreale (☑ 091 640 44 03; Piazza del Duomo; admission to cathedral free, north transept €2, terrace €2; ☉8.30am-12.45pm & 2.30-5pm Mon-Sat, 8-10am & 2.30-5pm Sun), in the hills 8km southwest of Palermo, is considered the finest example of Norman architecture in Sicily, incorporating Norman, Arab, Byzantine and classical elements. Inspired by a vision of the Virgin, it was built by William II in an effort to outdo his grandfather Roger II, who was responsible for the cathedral in Cefalù and the Cappella Palatina in Palermo. The interior, completed in 1184 and executed in shimmering mosaics, depicts 42 Old Testament stories. Outside the cathedral, the **cloister** (adult/reduced €6/3; ☉9am-6.30pm Mon-Sat, 9am-1pm Sun) is a tranquil courtyard with a tangible oriental feel. Surrounding the perimeter, elegant Romanesque arches are supported by an exquisite array of slender columns alternately decorated with mosaics. To reach Monreale, take AMAT bus 389 (€1.40, 35 minutes, every 1¼ hours) from Piazza Indipendenza in Palermo or AST's Monreale bus (one way/return €1.90/3, 40 minutes, hourly Monday to Saturday) from in front of Palermo Centrale train station.

The 8.7-sq-km island of **Ustica** was declared Italy's first marine reserve in 1986. The surrounding waters are a playground of fish and coral, ideal for snorkelling, diving and underwater photography. To enjoy Ustica's wild coastline and dazzling grottoes without the crowds try visiting in June or September. There are numerous dive centres, hotels and restaurants on the island, as well as some nice hiking. To get here from Palermo, take the once-daily car ferry (€18.35, three hours) or the faster, twice-daily hydrofoils (€23.55, 1½ hours) operated by **Siremar** (p788). For more details on Ustica, see Lonely Planet's *Sicily* guide.

south of the train station's eastern entrance, and **Via Paolo Balsamo**, due east of the train station.

AST (Azienda Siciliana Trasporti; ☑ 091 680 00 32; www.aziendasicilianatrasporti.it; New Bus Bar, Via Paolo Balsamo 32) Services to southeastern destinations including Ragusa (€13.50, four hours, four daily Monday to Saturday, two on Sunday).

Autoservizi Tarantola (☑ 092 43 10 20; New Bus Bar, Via Paolo Balsamo 32) Buses from Palermo to Segesta (one way/return €7/11.20, 80 minutes, three daily).

Cuffaro (☑ 091 616 15 10; www.cuffaro.info; Via Paolo Balsamo 13) Services to Agrigento (€9, two hours, three to eight daily).

SAIS Autolinee (☑ 091 616 60 28; www.sais autolinee.it; Piazza Cairoli) To/from Catania (€15, 2¾ hours, eight to 10 daily) and Messina (€16, 2¾ hours, three to six daily).

SAIS Trasporti (☑ 091 617 11 41; www.saistrasporti.it; Via Paolo Balsamo 20) Thriceweekly overnight service to Rome (€37, 12 hours).

Salemi (☑ 091 772 03 47; www.autoservizi salemi.it; Piazza Cairoli) Several buses daily to Marsala (€9.40, 2½ hours) and Trapani's Birgi airport (€11, 1¾ hours).

Segesta (☑ 091 616 79 19; www.segesta.it; Piazza Cairoli) Services to Trapani (€8.60, two hours, at least 10 daily). Also sells Interbus tickets to Syracuse (€12, 3¼ hours, two to three daily).

CAR & MOTORCYCLE

Palermo is accessible on the A20-E90 toll road from Messina and the A19-E932 from Catania via Enna. Trapani and Marsala are also easily accessible from Palermo by motorway (A29), while Agrigento and Palermo are linked by the SS121, a good state road through the island's interior.

❶ DISRUPTION TO THE A19

In April 2015, a viaduct on the A19 auto-strada between Palermo and Catania collapsed, disrupting traffic between Sicily's two major cities. As this book went to press, crews were at work repairing the damage, but the 17km-long section of the highway between Scillato and Tremonzelli (62km to 79km southeast of Palermo) remained closed indefinitely, with traffic diverted onto the much slower SS643 through Polizzi Generosa. Until repairs on the A19 are complete, the train remains a more direct and efficient way to travel between Palermo and Catania.

Most major auto hire companies are represented at the airport. You'll often save money by booking your rental online before leaving home. Given the city's chaotic traffic and expensive parking, and the excellent public transit from Palermo's airport, you're generally better off postponing rental car pick-up until you're ready to leave the city.

TRAIN

From Palermo Centrale station, just south of the centre at the foot of Via Roma, regular trains leave for Messina (from €11.80, 2¾ to 3½ hours, hourly), Agrigento (€8.30, 2¼ hours, eight to 10 daily) and Cefalù (€5.15, 45 minutes to one hour, hourly). There are also three to six direct trains daily to Catania (€12.50, 2¾ hours), plus InterCity trains to Reggio di Calabria, Naples and Rome.

❶ Getting Around

TO/FROM THE AIRPORT

Prestia e Comandè (☑ 091 58 63 51; www.prestiaecomande.it) runs a half-hourly bus service from the airport to the centre of town (one way/return €6.30/11), with stops outside Teatro Politeama Garibaldi (35 minutes) and Palermo Centrale train station (50 minutes). Buses are parked to the right as you exit the airport arrivals hall. Buy tickets at the kiosk adjacent to the bus stop. Return journeys to the airport run with similar frequency, picking up at the same points.

A slower option is the twice-hourly Trinacria Express train (€5.80, one hour) from Punta Raisi station (just downstairs from the arrivals hall) to Palermo Centrale.

A taxi from the airport to downtown Palermo costs €40 to €45.

BUS

Palermo's orange, white and blue city buses, operated by **AMAT** (☑ 848 800817, 091 35 01 11; www.amat.pa.it), are frequent but often crowded and slow. The free map handed out at Palermo tourist offices details all the major bus lines; most stop at the train station. Tickets, valid for 90 minutes, cost €1.40 if pre-purchased from *tabaccheria* (tobacconists) or AMAT booths, or €1.80 on board the bus. A day pass costs €3.50.

Three small buses – Linea Gialla, Linea Verde and Linea Rossa (€0.52 for 24-hour ticket) – operate in the narrow streets of the *centro storico* (historic centre) and can be useful if you're moving between tourist sights.

CAR & MOTORCYCLE

Driving is frenetic in the city and best avoided, if possible. Use one of the staffed car parks around town (€12 to €20 per day) if your hotel lacks parking.

TYRRHENIAN COAST

The coast between Palermo and Milazzo is studded with popular tourist resorts attracting a steady stream of holidaymakers, particularly between June and September. The best of these is Cefalù, a resort second only to Taormina in popularity. Just inland lie the two massive natural parks of the Madonie and Nebrodi mountains.

Cefalù

POP 14,300

This popular holiday resort wedged between a dramatic mountain peak and a sweeping stretch of sand has the lot: a great beach; a truly lovely historic centre with a grandiose cathedral; and winding medieval streets lined with restaurants and boutiques. Avoid the height of summer when prices soar, beaches are jam-packed and the charm of the place is tainted by bad-tempered drivers trying to find a car park.

◉ Sights

★**Duomo di Cefalù**   CATHEDRAL
(☑ 092 192 20 21; Piazza del Duomo; ☺ 8am-7pm Apr-Sep, 8am-5pm Oct-Mar) Cefalù's cathedral is one of the jewels in Sicily's Arab-Norman crown, only equalled in magnificence by the Cattedrale di Monreale and Palermo's Cappella Palatina. Filling the central apse, a towering figure of Christ All Powerful is the focal point of the elaborate Byzantine mosaics

CEFALÙ'S BACKYARD PLAYGROUND

Due south of Cefalù, the 40,000-hectare **Parco Naturale Regionale delle Madonie** incorporates some of Sicily's highest peaks, including the imposing Pizzo Carbonara (1979m). The park's wild, wooded slopes are home to wolves, wildcats, eagles and the near-extinct ancient Nebrodi fir trees that have survived since the last ice age. Ideal for hiking, cycling and horse trekking, the park is also home to several handsome mountain towns, including **Castelbuono**, **Petralia Soprana** and **Petralia Sottana**.

The region's distinctive rural cuisine includes roasted lamb and goat, cheeses, grilled mushrooms and aromatic pasta with *sugo* (meat sauce). A great place to sample these specialities is **Nangalarruni** (✆ 0921 67 14 28; www.hostariananangalarruni.it; Via delle Confraternite 10; fixed menus €25-35; ☺ 12.30-3pm & 7-10pm, closed Wed winter) in Castelbuono.

For park information, contact the Ente Parco delle Madonie in **Cefalù** (p792) or **Petralia Sottana** (✆ 0921 68 40 11; Corso Paolo Agliata 16; ☺ 8am-2pm & 3-7pm Mon-Fri, 3-7pm Sat, 10.30am-1pm & 4.30-7pm Sun).

Bus service to the park's main towns is limited; to fully appreciate the Madonie, you're better off hiring a car for a couple of days.

– Sicily's oldest and best preserved, predating those of Monreale by 20 or 30 years.

La Rocca
VIEWPOINT

(adult/child €4/2; ☺ 8am-7pm May-Sep, 9am-4pm Oct-Apr) Looming over the town, this imposing rocky crag is the site where the Arabs built their citadel, occupying it until the Norman conquest in 1061 forced them down to the port below. To reach the summit, follow signs for Tempio di Diana from the corner of Corso Ruggero and Vicolo Saraceni. The 30- to 45-minute route climbs the **Salita Saraceno**, a winding staircase, through three tiers of city walls before emerging onto rock-strewn upland slopes with spectacular coastal views.

🏃 Activities

Cefalù's crescent-shaped beach, just west of the medieval centre, is lovely, but in the summer get here early to find a patch for your umbrella and towel. You can escape with a boat tour along the coast during the summer months with agencies along Corso Ruggero, including **Visit Sicily Tours** (✆ 339 2284053, 0921 92 50 36; www.visitsicilytours.com; Corso Ruggero 83; half-day boat tour adult/child €30/15) (right next door to the tourist office).

🛏 Sleeping

Dolce Vita
B&B €

(✆ 0921 92 31 51; www.dolcevitabb.it; Via Bordonaro 8; s €25-60, d €45-110) This popular B&B has one of the loveliest terraces in town, complete with deck chairs overlooking the sea and a barbecue for those warm balmy

evenings. Rooms are airy and light, with comfy beds, though the staff's lackadaisical attitude can detract from the charm.

Scirocco Bed & Breakfast
B&B €

(✆ 0392 644 41 31; www.sciroccobeb.com; Piazza Garibaldi 8; s €30-60, d €60-90; ❄ 🛜) Convenient location and spectacular views are the two big selling points at this relatively new B&B halfway between the train station and the cathedral. Friendly Romanian owner Nicole offers four comfortable and bright upper-floor guest rooms, crowned by a rooftop terrace that's perfect for watching the sun set over the Tyrrhenian Sea or monitoring cafe life on Piazza Garibaldi directly below.

Hotel Kalura
HOTEL €€

(✆ 0921 42 13 54; www.hotelkalura.com; Via Vincenzo Cavallaro 13; s €55-109, d €79-189, 4-person apt €115-249; 🅿 ❄ @ 🛜 ♿) East of town on a rocky outcrop, this German-run, family oriented hotel has its own pebbly beach, restaurant and fabulous pool. Most rooms have sea views, and the hotel staff can arrange loads of activities, including mountain biking, hiking, canoeing, pedalos, diving and dance nights. It's a 20-minute walk into town.

🍴 Eating & Drinking

⭐ Ti Vitti
SICILIAN €€

(✆ 0921 92 15 71; www.ristorantetivitti.com; Via Umberto I 34; meals €35-45; ☺ noon-3pm & 6.30-11pm Wed-Mon) Named after a Sicilian card game, this fine restaurant specialises in fresh-from-the-market fish dishes, locally sourced treats such as basilisco mushrooms from the nearby Monte Madonie, and some of the best *cannoli* you'll find anywhere on the planet. For something more casual, head to its affiliated pizzeria, **Bottega Ti Vitti** (http://bottegativitti.com; Lungomare Giardina 7; pizza, salads & burgers €5-10; ⊙10am-midnight, closed Tue Nov-Apr), whose waterfront setting is perfect for sunset *aperitivi*.

Locanda del Marinaio SEAFOOD €€
(☑0921 42 32 95; Via Porpora 5; meals €30-40; ⊙noon-2.30pm & 7-11pm Wed-Mon) Fresh seafood rules the chalkboard menu at this excellent new eatery along the old town's main waterfront thoroughfare. Depending on the season, you'll find dishes such as red tuna carpaccio with toasted pine nuts, shrimp and zucchini on a bed of velvety ricotta, or grilled octopus served with thyme-scented potatoes, all accompanied by an excellent list of Sicilian wines.

La Galleria SICILIAN, CAFE €€
(☑0921 42 02 11; www.lagalleriacefalu.it; Via Mandralisca 23; meals €25-40; ⊙12.30-3pm & 7-11pm Fri-Wed) This is about as hip as Cefalù gets. Functioning as a restaurant, cafe and occasional gallery space, La Galleria has an informal vibe, a bright internal courtyard and an innovative menu that mixes standard *primi* and *secondi* with a range of all-in-one dishes (€14 to €16) designed to be meals in themselves.

❶ Information

Ente Parco delle Madonie (☑0921 92 33 27; www.parcodellemadonie.it; Corso Ruggero 116; ⊙8am-6pm Mon-Sat) Knowledgeable staff supply information about the Parco Naturale Regionale delle Madonie.

Hospital (☑0921 92 01 11; www.fondazione sanraffaelegiglio.it; Contrada Pietrapollastra) On the main road out of town in the direction of Palermo.

Questura (☑0921 92 60 11; Via Roma 15)

Tourist Office (☑0921 42 10 50; strcefalu@ regione.sicilia.it; Corso Ruggero 77; ⊙9am-8pm Mon-Sat) English-speaking staff, lots of leaflets and good maps.

❶ Getting There & Away

The best way to get to and from Cefalù is by rail. Hourly trains go to Palermo (€5.15, 45 minutes to 1¼ hours) and virtually every other town on the coast.

AEOLIAN ISLANDS

The Aeolian Islands are a little piece of paradise. Stunning cobalt sea, splendid beaches, some of Italy's best hiking and an awe-inspiring volcanic landscape are just part of the appeal. The islands also have a fascinating human and mythological history that goes back several millennia; the Aeolians figured prominently in Homer's *Odyssey,* and evidence of the distant past can be seen everywhere, most notably in Lipari's excellent archaeological museum.

The seven islands of Lipari, Vulcano, Salina, Panarea, Stromboli, Alicudi and Filicudi

MILAZZO: GATEWAY TO THE AEOLIAN ISLANDS

DESTINATION	COST (€) HYDROFOIL/FERRY	DURATION HYDROFOIL/FERRY
Alicudi	29/20	3¼ / 6hr
Filicudi	24/18	2½ / 5hr
Lipari	16/13	50min / 2hr
Panarea	18/14	2¼ / 5hr
Salina	19/15	1¾ / 3¼hr
Stromboli	22/17	2¾ / 6hr
Vulcano	15/12	45min / 1½hr

Most ferries to the Aeolian Islands run from Milazzo. To reach Milazzo's ferry terminal, you have a few options: from Milazzo's train station, take AST local bus 5 (€1.20, 10 minutes, at least hourly); from Catania's Fontanarossa airport, take a **Giuntabus** (☑090 67 57 49, 090 67 37 82; www.giuntabustrasporti.com) express bus (€15, two hours, two to four daily) or book a shuttle (€25, two hours, reservation required) with **Alibrando** (☑090 928 85 85; www.eolie booking.com/navetta). In addition, Giuntabus offers direct bus service from Messina Centrale train station (€4.20, 50 minutes, hourly Monday through Saturday, six on Sunday). All will drop you just outside Milazzo's ferry terminal.

are part of a huge 200km volcanic ridge that runs between the smoking stack of Mt Etna and the threatening mass of Vesuvius above Naples. Collectively, the islands exhibit a unique range of volcanic characteristics, which earned them a place on Unesco's World Heritage list in 2000. The islands are mobbed with visitors in July and August, but out of season things remain delightfully tranquil.

❶ Getting There & Away

Both **Ustica Lines** (www.usticalines.it) and **Siremar** (www.siremar.it) run hydrofoils year-round from Milazzo, the mainland city closest to the islands. Almost all boats stop first at Vulcano and Lipari, then continue to the ports of Santa Marina and/or Rinella on Salina island. Beyond Salina, boats either branch off east to Panarea and Stromboli, or west to Filicudi and Alicudi. Ustica Lines also operates limited year-round service to the islands from Messina and Reggio Calabria.

Ustica Lines and Siremar's hydrofoil schedules complement each other nicely, with one company or the other providing service nearly hourly to the main islands of Vulcano, Lipari and Salina. Frequency of service on all routes increases in the summer. Note that hydrofoils are sometimes cancelled due to heavy seas.

Both Siremar and **NGI Traghetti** (☏090 928 40 91; www.ngi-spa.it) also run car ferries from Milazzo to the islands; they're slightly cheaper, but slower and less regular than the hydrofoils.

Additional seasonal services include Ustica Lines hydrofoils from Palermo (once daily late June to early September), Siremar ferries from Naples (twice weekly April to September) and **SNAV** (☏081 428 55 55; www.snav.it) hydrofoils from Naples (daily July to early September, plus weekends in June).

❶ Getting Around

BOAT

Siremar and Ustica Lines both operate year-round, inter-island hydrofoil services. Siremar also offers inter-island ferry links. Ticket offices with posted timetables can be found close to the docks on all islands.

CAR & SCOOTER

You can take your car to Lipari, Vulcano or Salina by ferry, or garage it at Milazzo or Messina on the mainland from €12 per day. The islands are small, with narrow, winding roads. You'll often save money (and headaches) by hiring a scooter on site, or better yet, exploring the islands on foot.

---

❶ FERRYING TO THE AEOLIANS FROM NAPLES

An atmospheric way to reach the Aeolians is via the twice weekly ferry from Naples. Set off at 8pm and you'll awake to the sight of a smoking Stromboli at dawn. Comfortable private cabins with bunk beds, writing desk and hot showers cost only a bit extra (€85 for a single cabin versus €55 for a standard seat, or €141 versus €111 for two people), and full meals (including *cannoli*!) are served on board at reasonable prices. The boat continues beyond Stromboli to Panarea, Salina, Lipari and Vulcano.

Lipari

POP 11,200 / ELEV 602M

Lipari is the Aeolians' thriving hub, both geographically and functionally, with regular ferry and hydrofoil connections to all other islands. Lipari town, the largest urban centre in the archipelago, is home to the islands' only tourist office and most dependable banking services, along with enough restaurants, bars and year-round residents to offer a bit of cosmopolitan buzz. Meanwhile, the island's rugged shoreline offers excellent opportunities for hiking, boating and swimming.

As evidenced by its fine archaeological museum and the multi-layered ruins strewn about town, Lipari has been inhabited for some 6000 years. The island was settled in the 4th millennium BC by Sicily's first known inhabitants, the Stentinellians, who developed a flourishing economy based on obsidian, a glassy volcanic rock. Commerce subsequently attracted the Greeks, who used the islands as ports on the east–west trade route, and pirates such as Barbarossa (or Redbeard), who sacked the city in 1544.

Lipari's two harbours, Marina Lunga (where ferries and hydrofoils dock) and Marina Corta (700m south, used by smaller boats) are linked by a bustling main street, Corso Vittorio Emanuele, flanked by shops, restaurants and bars. Overlooking the colourful snake of day trippers is Lipari's clifftop citadel, surrounded by 16th-century walls.

Lipari Town

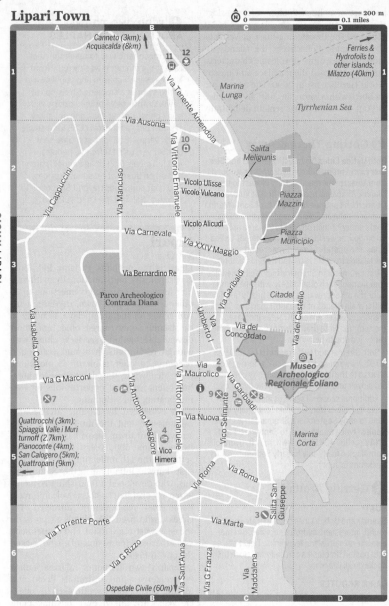

◉ Sights & Activities

★ **Museo Archeologico Regionale Eoliano**   MUSEUM

(☏ 090 988 01 74; www.regione.sicilia.it/benicul turali/museolipari; Castello di Lipari; adult/reduced €6/3; ⊗ 9am-6.30pm Mon-Sat, 9am-1pm Sun) A must-see for Mediterranean history buffs, Lipari's archaeological museum boasts one of Europe's finest collections of ancient finds. Especially worthwhile are the Sezione Preistorica, devoted to locally discovered artefacts from the Neolithic and Bronze Ages

Lipari Town

⊙ Top Sights
1 Museo Archeologico Regionale
Eoliano.. D4

✪ Activities, Courses & Tours
2 Da Massimo/Dolce Vita..................... C4
3 Diving Center La Gorgonia C6

⊜ Sleeping
4 Diana Brown B5
5 Enzo Il Negro C4
6 Hotel Oriente B4

✖ Eating
7 E Pulera A4
8 Gilberto e Vera C4
9 Kasbah C4

⊚ Shopping
10 La Formagella.......................................B2

⊙ Transport
11 Guglielmo Urso Local Bus
Stop B1
12 Siremar B1
Siremar & Ustica Lines
Ticket Office .... (see 12)
Ustica Lines .... (see 12)

to the Graeco-Roman era, and the Sezione Classica, whose highlights include ancient shipwreck cargoes and the world's largest collection of miniature Greek theatrical masks.

★ **Quattrocchi**   VIEWPOINT

Lipari's best coastal views are from a celebrated viewpoint known as Quattrocchi (Four Eyes), 3km west of town. Follow the road for Pianoconte and look on your left about 300m beyond the turn-off for Spiaggia Valle i Muria. Stretching off to the south, great, grey cliffs plunge into the sea, while in the distance plumes of sinister smoke rise from the dark heights of neighbouring Vulcano.

★ **Spiaggia Valle i Muria**   BEACH

Lapped by clean waters and surrounded by sheer cliffs, this dark, pebbly beach on Lipari's southwestern shore is a dramatically beautiful swimming and sunbathing spot. From the signposted turn-off, 3km west of Lipari town towards Pianoconte, it's a steep 15-minute downhill walk; come prepared with water and sunscreen. In good weather, Lipari resident **Barni** (☑349 1839555, 339 8221583) sells refreshments from his rustic

cave-like beach bar, and provides ultrascenic boat transfers to and from Lipari's Marina Corta (€5/10 one way/return).

Diving Center La Gorgonia   DIVING

(☑090 981 26 16; www.lagorgoniadiving.it; Salita San Giuseppe; per dive with rented/personal equipment €50/30, courses €55-750) This outfit offers courses, boat transport, equipment hire and general information about scuba diving and snorkelling around Lipari. See the website for a complete price list.

Eastern Beaches

On Lipari's eastern shore, sunbathers and swimmers head a few kilometres north of Lipari town to bask on **Spiaggia di Canneto**. Further north near the island's abandoned pumice mines is pebbly **Spiaggia della Papesca**, nicknamed **Spiaggia Bianca** for the white pumice dust that used to cover it; residual pumice still gives the sea its limpid turquoise colour.

☞ Tours

Numerous agencies in town, including the dependable **Da Massimo/Dolce Vita** (☑090 981 30 86; www.damassimo.it; Via Maurolico 2), offer boat tours to the surrounding islands. Prices are around €25 for a circuit around Vulcano, €30 for a tour of Salina, €40 to visit Filicudi and Alicudi, €40 for a day trip to Panarea and Stromboli, and €75 to €80 for a late afternoon trip to Stromboli, including a guided hike up the mountain at sunset and a late-night return to Lipari.

🛏 Sleeping

Lipari is the Aeolians' best-equipped base for island-hopping, with plenty of places to stay, eat and drink. Note that prices soar in summer; avoid August if possible.

★ **Diana Brown**   B&B €

(☑338 640 75 72, 090 981 25 84; www.dianabrown.it; Vico Himera 3; s €30-70, d €40-80, tr €50-100; ❋🛜) Tucked down a narrow alley, South African Diana's delightful rooms sport tile floors, abundant hot water and welcome extras such as kettles, fridges, clothes-drying racks and satellite TV. Units downstairs are darker but have built-in kitchenettes. There's a sunny breakfast terrace and solarium with deck chairs, plus a book exchange and laundry service. Optional breakfast costs €5 extra per person.

WORTH A TRIP

COASTAL HIKES

Lipari's rugged northwestern coastline offers excellent walking opportunities. Most accessible is the pleasant hour-long stroll from Quattropani to Acquacalda along Lipari's north shore, which affords spectacular views of Salina and a distant Stromboli. Take the bus to Quattropani (€2.40, 25 minutes), then simply proceed downhill on the main road 5km to Acquacalda, where you can catch the bus (€1.55) back to Lipari.

More strenuous, but equally rewarding in terms of scenery, is the three- to four-hour hike descending steeply from Pianoconte (€1.90, 15 minutes by bus) down past the old Roman baths of Terme di San Calogero to the western shoreline, then skirting the clifftops along a flat stretch before climbing steeply back to Quattropani.

Enzo Il Negro   GUESTHOUSE €

(☑090 981 31 63; www.enzoilnegro.com; Via Garibaldi 29; s €40-50, d €60-90; ❄🕸) Family run for decades, this down-to-earth guesthouse near picturesque Marina Corta offers spacious, tiled, pine-furnished rooms with fridges. Two panoramic terraces overlook the rooftops, the harbour and the castle walls.

Hotel Oriente   HOTEL €

(☑090 981 14 93; www.hotelorientelipari.com; Via Marconi 35; s €40-70, d €60-100; 🅿❄🕸) This centrally located, older hotel will either charm you with its quirkiness or drive you crazy with its clutter. Just 100m west of the centre, its rooms are rather bland and faded, but the common spaces drip with character, from the spacious citrus-filled courtyard, to the eclectically decorated breakfast room and bar, to the in-house museum of antique Sicilian paraphernalia.

🍴 Eating & Drinking

Fish abound in the waters of the archipelago and include tuna, mullet, cuttlefish and sole, all of which end up on local menus. Try *pasta all'eoliana*, a simple blend of the island's excellent capers with olives, olive oil, anchovies, tomatoes and basil.

Bars are concentrated along Corso Vittorio Emanuele and down by Marina Corta.

Gilberto e Vera   SANDWICHES €

(www.gilbertoevera.it; Via Garibaldi 22-24; sandwiches €5; ⊗8am-2pm & 4pm-midnight Mar-Nov) This straightforward shop sells two dozen varieties of sandwiches, all costing €5 and served with a smile. Sicilian ingredients such as capers, olives, aubergine and tuna all make frequent appearances. Long opening hours make this the perfect spot to purchase early morning hiking or beach-hopping provisions, or to sip a mid-afternoon or late evening glass of wine on the streetside terrace.

Kasbah   MODERN SICILIAN, PIZZA €€

(☑090 981 10 75; www.kasbahcafe.it; Vico Selinunte 45; pizzas €6-8, meals €30-36; ⊗7-10pm, closed Wed Oct-Apr) Tucked down narrow Vico Selinunte, with a window where you can watch the chefs at work, this place serves everything from fancy pasta, fish and meat dishes to simple wood-fired pizzas (try the Kasbah, with smoked swordfish, rocket, lemon and black pepper). The stylish dining room with its grey linen tablecloths is complemented by a more casual outdoor terrace.

E Pulera   MODERN SICILIAN €€

(☑090 981 11 58; www.pulera.it; Via Isabella Conti; meals €35-45; ⊗7.30-10pm May-Oct) With its serene garden setting, low lighting, artsy tile-topped tables and exquisite food – from tuna carpaccio with blood oranges and capers to *cassata* (sponge cake, ricotta, marzipan, chocolate and candied fruit) served with sweet Malvasia wine for dessert – E Pulera makes an upscale but relaxed choice for a romantic dinner.

🛍 Shopping

La Formagella   FOOD & DRINK

(Via Vittorio Emanuele 250; ⊗7.30am-9pm May-Oct, shorter hours rest of year) You simply can't leave the Aeolian Islands without a small pot of capers and a bottle of sweet Malvasia wine. You can get both, along with meats, cheeses and other delicious goodies, at this gourmet grocery-deli just around the corner from the hydrofoil dock.

ℹ Information

Corso Vittorio Emanuele is lined with ATMs. The other islands have relatively few facilities, so it's best to sort out your finances here before moving on.

Ospedale Civile (☑090 988 51 11; Via Sant'Anna) First-aid and emergency services.

Police Station (☑090 981 13 33; Via Marconi)

Tourist Office (☑ 090 988 00 95; infopointeo lie@regione.sicilia.it; Via Maurolico 17; ⊙ 9am-1.30pm Mon-Fri, plus 4.30-7pm Mon, Wed & Fri) Lipari's sporadically staffed office provides information covering all of the Aeolian Islands.

❶ Getting There & Around

BOAT

Lipari is the Aeolians' transport hub. The main port is Marina Lunga, where you'll find a joint **Siremar & Ustica Lines ticket office** (Marina Lunga; ⊙ 5.45-8.30am, 9.30am-2pm & 3-8.30pm) at the head of the hydrofoil jetty. Timetable information is displayed here.

Year-round ferries and hydrofoils serve Milazzo and all the other Aeolian islands; less frequent services include year-round hydrofoils to Messina and ferries to Naples, and summer-only hydrofoil services to Palermo. Websites for **Ustica Lines** (☑ 090 981 24 48; www.usticalines.it) and **Siremar** (☑ 090 981 10 17; www.siremar.it) have complete schedules and price details.

BUS

Autobus Guglielmo Urso (☑ 090 981 10 26; www.ursobus.com/orariursobus.pdf) runs buses around the island roughly hourly from its **bus stop** adjacent to Marina Lunga. The Linea Urbana follows the eastern shoreline, making stops at Canneto (€1.30) and Acquacalda (€1.55), while the Linea Extraurbana climbs to the western highland settlements of Pianoconte (€1.90) and Quattropani (€2.40). Discounts are available for round-trip journeys or multiple rides (six-/10-/20-ride tickets from €7/10.50/20.50).

CAR & MOTORCYCLE

Several places around town rent bicycles (€10 to €15 per day), scooters (€15 to €50) and cars (€30 to €80), including **Da Marcello** (☑ 090 981 12 34; www.noleggiodamarcello.com; Via Sottomonastero) down by the ferry dock.

Vulcano

POP 720 / ELEV 500M

Vulcano is a memorable place, not least because of the vile smell of sulphurous gases. Once you escape the drab and dated tourist centre, Porto di Levante, the island has a delightfully tranquil, unspoilt quality. Beyond the well-marked trail to the looming Fossa di Vulcano, the landscape gives way to rural simplicity with vineyards, birdsong and a surprising amount of greenery. The island is worshipped by Italians for its therapeutic mud baths and hot springs, and its black beaches and weird steaming landscape make for an interesting day trip.

Boats dock at Porto di Levante. To the right, as you face the island, are the mud baths and the small Vulcanello peninsula; to the left is the volcano. Straight ahead is Porto di Ponente, 700m west, where you will find the Spiaggia Sabbia Nera (Black Sand Beach).

⚹ Activities

★ Fossa di Vulcano   WALKING

FREE Vulcano's top attraction is the straightforward trek up its 391m volcano (no guide required). Start early if possible and bring a hat, sunscreen and water. Follow the signs south along Strada Provinciale, then turn left onto the zigzag gravel track that leads to the summit. It's about an hour's scramble to the lowest point of the crater's edge (290m).

Laghetto di Fanghi   HOT SPRING

(www.geoterme.it; admission €2, incl visit to faraglione €2.50, shower €1, towel €2.60; ⊙ 7am-7pm mid-Mar–Oct) Backed by a *faraglione* (rock tower) and stinking of rotten eggs, Vulcano's harbourside pool of thick, coffee-coloured sulphurous gloop isn't exactly a five-star beauty farm. But the warm (28°C) mud is considered an excellent treatment for rheumatic pains and skin diseases, and rolling around in it can be fun if you don't mind smelling funny for a few days. Keep the mud away from your eyes and hair, as the sulphur is acidic and can damage the cornea.

Sicily in Kayak   KAYAKING

(☑ 329 5381229; www.sicilyinkayak.com) This outfit offers kayaking tours around Vulcano and the other Aeolians, ranging in length from half a day to an entire week.

Beaches

At Porto di Ponente, on the far side of the peninsula from Porto di Levante, the dramatic and only mildly commercialised black-sand beach of Spiaggia Sabbia Nera curves around a pretty bay. It is one of the few sandy beaches in the archipelago. A smaller, quieter black-sand beach, Spiaggia dell'Asina, can be found on the island's southern side near Gelso.

🛏 Sleeping & Eating

Unless you're here for the walking and the mud baths, Vulcano is not a great place for an extended stay; the town is pretty soulless and the sulphurous fumes really do smell. However, there are some good options for those who choose to stick around.

SICILY VULCANO

Casa Arcada B&B, APARTMENT €
(☑347 6497633; www.casaarcada.it; Via Provinciale 178; B&B per person €30-55, d apt per week €420-770; ❈❸) Conveniently located at the volcano's edge, 20m back from the main road between the port and the crater path, this sweet whitewashed complex offers bed and breakfast in five immaculate tile-floored rooms with air-con and mini-fridges, along with weekly rental apartments. The communal upstairs sun terrace affords lovely views up to the volcano and across the water to Lipari.

★ **La Forgia Maurizio** SICILIAN €€
(☑339 1379107; Strada Provinciale 45, Porto di Levante; meals €30-35; ⊘noon-3pm & 7-11pm) The owner of this devilishly good restaurant spent 20 winters in Goa, India; Eastern influences sneak into the menu of Sicilian specialities, and several items are vegan- and/or vegetarian-friendly. Don't miss the *liquore di kumquat e cardamom,* Maurizio's homemade answer to *limoncello.* The multicourse tasting menu is an excellent deal at €30 including wine, water and dessert.

❶ Getting There & Around

BOAT
Vulcano is an intermediate stop between Milazzo and Lipari; both Siremar and Ustica Lines run multiple vessels in both directions throughout the day. The trip to or from Lipari takes only 10 minutes, making Vulcano an easy and popular day-trip destination.

CAR & MOTORCYCLE
Nolo Sprint da Luigi (☑347 7600275; http://vulcano-luigi-rent.com; Porto di Levante; bicycle/scooter/car per day from €5/20/40) Rent some wheels from this well-signposted outfit near the port. Multilingual owners Luigi and Nidra offer tips for exploring the island and also rent out an apartment (€40 to €70) in Vulcano's tranquil interior.

Salina

POP 2200 / ELEV 962M
Ah, green Salina! In stark contrast to sulphur-stained Vulcano and lava-blackened Stromboli, Salina's twin craters of Monte dei Porri and Monte Fossa delle Felci – nicknamed *didyme* (twins) by the ancient Greeks – are lushly wooded and invitingly verdant, a result of the numerous freshwater springs on the island.

Wildflowers, thick yellow gorse bushes and serried ranks of grapevines carpet the hillsides in vibrant colours and cool greens, while its high coastal cliffs plunge dramatically towards beaches. The famous Aeolian capers grow plentifully here, as do the grapes used for making Malvasia wine.

◉ Sights & Activities

Pollara VILLAGE
Don't miss a trip to sleepy Pollara, sandwiched dramatically between the sea and the steep slopes of an extinct volcanic crater on Salina's western edge. The gorgeous beach here was used as a location in the 1994 film *Il postino,* although the land access route to the beach has since been closed due to landslide danger.

★ **Monte Fossa delle Felci** HIKING
For jaw-dropping views, climb to the Aeolians' highest point, Monte Fossa delle Felci (962m). The two-hour ascent starts from the **Santuario della Madonna del Terzito**, an imposing 19th-century church at Valdichiesa, in the valley separating the island's two volcanoes. Up top, gorgeous perspectives unfold on the symmetrically arrayed volcanic cones of Monte dei Porri, Filicudi and a distant Alicudi.

Wineries
Outside Malfa there are numerous wineries where you can try the local Malvasia wine. Signposted off the main road, **Fenech** (☑090 984 40 41; www.fenech.it; Via Fratelli Mirabilo 41) is an acclaimed producer whose 2012 Malvasia won awards at five international competitions. Another important Malvasia is produced at the luxurious Capofaro (p799) resort on the 13-acre Tasca d'Almerita estate, between Malfa and Santa Marina.

🛏 Sleeping & Eating

The island remains relatively undisturbed by mass tourism, yet offers some of the Aeolians' finest hotels and restaurants. Accommodation can be found in Salina's three main towns: Santa Marina Salina on the east shore, Malfa on the north shore and Rinella on the south shore, as well as in Lingua, a village adjoining ancient salt ponds 2km south of Santa Marina. Note that many hotels have their own excellent restaurants.

★ **A Cannata** PENSION €€
(☑090 984 31 61; www.acannata.it; Via Umberto,
Lingua; r per person incl breakfast €40-90, incl
half-board €75-125; 🕾) Newly remodelled in
classic Aeolian style, with peach-coloured
stucco, cheerful blue doors, and floors
clad in gorgeous reproductions of historic tiles, this family-run *pensione* offers
25 spacious units, many (along with the
breakfast terrace) overlooking Lingua's
picturesque salt lagoon. Don't miss half-
board at its Slow Food–acclaimed **restaurant** (☑090 984 31 61; Via Umberto I 13, Lingua;
meals €35; ⊗12.30-2.30pm & 7.30-10pm), featuring menus built around fresh-caught
seafood and home-grown veggies and
herbs.

Hotel Mamma Santina BOUTIQUE HOTEL €€
(☑090 984 30 54; www.mammasantina.it; Via
Sanità 40, Santa Marina Salina; d €110-190;
⊗Apr-Oct; 🕸@🕾🏊) A labour of love for its
architect owner, this boutique hotel has
inviting rooms decorated with pretty tiles
in traditional Aeolian designs. Many of
the sea-view terraces come equipped with
hammocks, and on warm evenings the attached restaurant (meals €35 to €40) has
outdoor seating overlooking the glowing
blue pool and landscaped garden.

★ **Hotel Signum** BOUTIQUE HOTEL €€€
(☑090 984 42 22; www.hotelsignum.it; Via
Scalo 15, Malfa; d €150-550, ste €450-700;
🕸🕾🏊) Hidden in Malfa's hillside lanes
is this alluring labyrinth of antique-clad
rooms, peach-coloured stucco walls, tall
blue windows and vine-covered terraces with full-on views of Stromboli. The
attached wellness centre, **Salus Per Aq-
uam** (Wellness Center; ☑090 984 42 22; www.
hotelsignum.it; Via Scalo 15, Malfa; admission
€30, treatments extra; ⊗Apr-Sep), a stunning
pool and one of the island's best-regarded
restaurants make this the perfect place to
unwind for a few days in utter comfort.

Capofaro BOUTIQUE HOTEL €€€
(☑090 984 43 30; www.capofaro.it; Via Faro
3, Malfa; d €190-350, ste €330-690; ⊗late
Apr-early Oct; 🕸@🕾🏊) Immerse yourself
in luxury at this five-star boutique resort
halfway between Santa Marina and Malfa,
surrounded by well-tended Malvasia vineyards and a picturesque lighthouse. The
20 rooms all have sharp white decor and
terraces looking straight out to smoking

Stromboli. Tennis courts, poolside mas-
sages, wine tasting and vineyard visits
complete this perfect vision of island chic.

★ **Da Alfredo** SANDWICHES €
(Piazza Marina Garibaldi, Lingua; granite €2.60,
sandwiches €9-13; ⊗9am-11pm) Salina's most
atmospheric option for an affordable
snack, Alfredo's place is renowned all over
Sicily for its *granite:* ices made with coffee, fresh fruit or locally grown pistachios
and almonds. It's also worth a visit for its
pane cunzato (open-faced sandwiches
piled high with tuna, ricotta, aubergine,
tomatoes, capers and olives); split one
with a friend – they're huge!

🛍 Shopping

**Laboratorio di Ceramiche
Artistiche** CERAMICS
(www.ceramichesalina.it; Via Piccolo Torrente,
Malfa; ⊗8am-noon & 2-7pm) Gorgeous multicoloured floor tiles, many of them one-
of-a-kind historic pieces from the Naples
area, are displayed here on shelves, walls
and throughout the large gravel courtyard. Overseas shipping can be arranged.

ℹ Information

Banca Nuova Bank with ATM; bear right along
the waterfront as you exit the boat docks.

ℹ Getting There & Around

BOAT
Hydrofoils and ferries serve Santa Marina Sali-
na and Rinella from Lipari and the other islands.
You'll find ticket offices in both ports.

BUS
CITIS (☑090 984 41 50; www.trasportisalina.
it) runs buses every hour or two in the low
season (more frequently in summer) from
Santa Marina Salina to Lingua and Malfa. In
Malfa, make connections for Rinella, Pollara,
Valdichiesa and Leni. Fares are €1.90 to €2.90
depending on your destination. Timetables are
posted online, and at ports and bus stops.

CAR & MOTORCYCLE
Above Santa Marina Salina's port, **Antonio
Bongiorno** (☑338 3791209; www.rentbon-
giorno.it; Via Risorgimento 222, Santa Marina
Salina) rents bikes (per day from €8), scooters
(€25 to €30) and cars (€60 to €70). Several
agencies in Rinella offer similar services – look
for signs at the ferry dock.

Delightful Desserts

From citrus-scented pastries filled with ricotta, to ice cream served on a brioche, to the marzipan fruits piled in every confectioner's window, Sicily celebrates the joys of sugar morning, noon and night.

Multicultural Roots

People from the Arabs to the Aztecs have influenced Sicily's culture of sweets: the former introduced sugar cane; the latter's fiery hot chocolate so impressed the Spaniards that they brought it to Sicily. The land also supplied inspiration, from abundant citrus, almond and pistachio groves to Mt Etna's snowy slopes, legendary source of the first *granita*.

Sweet Sicilian Classics

The all-star list of Sicilian desserts starts with *cannoli*, crunchy pastry tubes filled with sweetened ricotta, garnished with chocolate, crumbled pistachios or a spike of candied citrus. Vying for the title of Sicily's most famous dessert is *cassata*, a coma-inducing concoction of sponge cake, cream, marzipan, chocolate and candied fruit. Feeling more adventurous? How about an *'mpanatigghiu*, a traditional Modican pastry stuffed with minced meat, almonds, chocolate and cinnamon?

A SUGAR-FUELLED ISLAND SPIN

➡ **Pasticceria Cappello** Renowned for its *setteveli*, a velvety seven-layer chocolate cake. (p786)

➡ **Da Alfredo** Dreamy *granite* made with almonds and wild strawberries. (p799)

➡ **Ti Vitti** Divine *cannoli* featuring fresh-from-the-sheep ricotta from the Madonie Mountains. (p791)

➡ **Dolceria Bonajuto** Aztec-influenced chocolate with vanilla and hot peppers. (p825)

➡ **Gelati DiVini** Outlandish ice-cream flavours including Marsala wine, wild fennel and olive oil. (p826)

➡ **Maria Grammatico** Marzipan fruit, almond pastries and toasted-nut *torrone*. (p838)

GILAS/GETTY IMAGES ©

1. Display of marzipan fruit 2. *Cassata* siciliana 3. *Cannoli*
4. Granita made with prickly pear fruit

JANNHUIZENGA/GETTY IMAGES ©

Stromboli

POP 400 / ELEV 924M

Stromboli's perfect triangle of a volcano juts dramatically out of the sea. It's the only island whose smouldering cone is permanently active, attracting a steady stream of visitors like moths to its massive flame. Volcanic activity has scarred and blackened the northwest side of the island, while the eastern side is untamed, ruggedly green and dotted with low-rise whitewashed houses.

The youngest of the Aeolian volcanoes, Stromboli was formed a mere 40,000 years ago and its gases continue to send up an almost constant spray of liquid magma, a process defined by vulcanologists as *attività stromboliana* (Strombolian activity). The volcano's most dramatic recent activity involved major lava flows that burst forth between June and December 2014, creating a new mass of hardened lava rock below the volcano's northeast crater and cancelling tours to the summit for several months. Several other significant eruptions have occurred in recent years: on 27 February 2007, two new craters opened on the volcano's summit; on 5 April 2003, the village of Ginostra was showered with rocks up to 4m wide; and on 30 December 2002, a tsunami caused damage to Stromboli town, injuring six people and closing the island to visitors for a few months.

Boats arrive at Porto Scari, downhill from the main town of Stromboli at the island's northeastern corner. Accommodation is concentrated within a 2km radius of the port, while San Vincenzo church, the meeting point for guided hikes up the volcano, is a short walk up the Scalo Scari to Via Roma.

◉ Sights & Activities

★ Stromboli Crater VOLCANO

For nature lovers, climbing Stromboli is one of Sicily's not-to-be-missed experiences. Since 2005 access has been strictly regulated: you can walk freely to 400m, but need a guide to continue any higher. Organised treks depart daily (between 3.30pm and 6pm, depending on the season), timed to reach the summit (924m) at sunset and to allow 45 minutes to observe the crater's fireworks.

The climb itself takes 2½ to three hours, while the descent back to Piazza San Vincenzo is shorter (1½ to two hours). All told, demanding five- to six-hour trek up to the top and back; you'll need to have proper walking shoes, a backpack that allows free movement of both arms, clothing for cold and wet weather, a change of T-shirt, a handkerchief to protect against dust (wear glasses not contact lenses), a torch, 1L to 2L of water and some food. If you haven't got any of these, **Totem Trekking** (☑ 090 986 57 52; www.totemtrekkingstromboli.com; Piazza San Vincenzo 4; ⊙ 9.30am-1pm & 3.30-7pm) hires out all the necessary equipment, including boots (€6), backpacks (€5), hiking poles (€4), torches (€3) and windbreakers (€5).

★ Sciara del Fuoco Viewpoint VIEWPOINT

(Trail of Fire) An alternative to scaling Stromboli's summit is the hour-long climb to this viewpoint (400m, no guide required), which directly overlooks the Sciara del Fuoco (the blackened laval scar running down Stromboli's northern flank) and offers fabulous if more distant views of the crater's explosions. Bring plenty of water, and a torch if walking at night. The trail (initially a switchbacking road) starts in Piscità, 2km west of Stromboli's port; halfway up, you can stop for pizza at L'Osservatorio (p803).

La Sirenetta Diving DIVING

(☑ 347 5961499, 338 8919675; www.lasirenetta diving.it; Via Marina 33; ⊙ Jun–mid-Sep) Offers diving courses and accompanied dives, opposite the beach at La Sirenetta Park Hotel.

Beaches

Stromboli's black sandy beaches are the best in the Aeolian archipelago. The most accessible and popular swimming and sunbathing is at **Ficogrande**, a strip of rocks and black volcanic sand about a 10-minute walk northwest of the hydrofoil dock. Further-flung beaches worth exploring are at **Piscità** to the west and **Forgia Vecchia**, about 300m south of the port.

⚐ Tours

Magmatrek (☑ 090 986 57 68; www.magmatrek. it; Via Vittorio Emanuele) has experienced, multilingual vulcanological guides who lead regular treks (maximum group size 20) up to the crater every afternoon (per person €28). It can also put together tailor-made treks for individual groups. Other agencies charging identical prices include **Stromboli Adventures** (☑ 090 98 62 64; www.stromboli adventures.it; Via Vittorio Emanuele), **Quota 900** (☑ 090 98 62 51; www.quota900stromboli.com; Via

Roma) and **Il Vulcano a Piedi** (☑ 349 2126428, 090 98 61 44; www.ilvulcanoapiedi.it; Via Pizzillo).

Società Navigazione Pippo (☑ 338 9857883, 090 98 61 35; pipponav.stromboli@libero. it; Porto Scari) is among the numerous boat companies at Porto Scari offering 2½-hour daytime circuits of the island (€25), 1½-hour sunset excursions to watch the Sciara del Fuoco from the sea (€20) and evening trips to Ginostra village on the other side of the island for dinner or *aperitivi* (€25).

🛏 Sleeping

Over a dozen places offer accommodation, including B&Bs, guesthouses and fully fledged hotels.

★**Casa del Sole**   GUESTHOUSE €
(☑ 090 98 63 00; www.casadelsolestromboli.it; Via Cincotta; dm €25-30, s €30-50, d €60-100) This cheerful Aeolian-style guesthouse is only 100m from a sweet black-sand beach in Piscità, the tranquil neighbourhood at the west end of town. Dorms, private doubles and a guest kitchen all surround a sunny patio, overhung with vines, fragrant with lemon blossoms, and decorated with the masks and stone carvings of sculptor-owner Tano Russo. Call for free pick-up (low season only) or take a taxi (€10) from the port 2km away.

Albergo Brasile   PENSION €
(☑ 090 98 60 08; www.strombolialbergobrasile.it; Via Soldato Cincotta; d €70-90; ☺ Easter-Oct; ❄) About 2km from the boat dock in peaceful Piscità, this laid-back *pensione* has cool, white rooms, a pretty entrance courtyard with lemon and olive trees, and a roof terrace that commands views of the sea and the volcano. Two larger rooms with air-con cost extra. Half-board is sometimes available (and required) in July and August.

✕ Eating & Drinking

★**L'Osservatorio**   PIZZA €
(☑ 338 1097830, 090 945 08 56; pizzas €7-12; ☺ 10.30am-late) Sure, you could eat a pizza in town, but come on – you're on Stromboli! Make the 45-minute, 2km uphill trek west of town to this pizzeria and you'll be rewarded with exceptional volcano views from an expansive panoramic terrace, best after sundown.

La Bottega del Marano   DELI €
(Via Vittorio Emanuele; snacks from €2; ☺ 8.30am-1pm & 4.30-8pm Mon-Sat) The per-

OFFSHORE ISLANDS

Sicily is an island lover's paradise, with more than a dozen offshore islands scattered in the seas surrounding the main island. Beyond the major Aeolian Islands of Lipari, Vulcano, Stromboli and Salina covered in this guide, you can detour to the smaller Aeolians: **Panarea**, **Filicudi** and **Alicudi**. Alternatively, cast off from Sicily's western coast to the slow-paced **Egadi Islands** or the remote, rugged volcanic island of **Pantelleria**. South of Agrigento, the sand-sprinkled **Pelagic Islands** of Lampedusa, Linosa and Lampione offer some fantastic beaches. **Ustica Lines** (☑ 0923 87 38 13; www.usticalines.it) and **Siremar** (☑ 091 749 33 15; www.siremar. it) provide hydrofoil and/or ferry service to all of these islands. For complete information about the Egadi Islands and the lesser Aeolian islands, including where to sleep and eat, see Lonely Planet's *Sicily* guide.

fect source for volcano-climbing provisions or a self-catering lunch, this reasonably priced neighbourhood grocery, five minutes west of the trekking agency offices, has a well-stocked deli case full of meats, cheeses, olives, artichokes and sun-dried tomatoes, plus shelves full of wine and awesomely tasty fresh-baked focaccias.

★**Punta Lena**   SICILIAN €€
(☑ 090 98 62 04; Via Marina 8; meals €34-40; ☺ 12.15-2.30pm & 7-10.30pm early May–mid-Oct) For a romantic outing, head to this family run waterfront restaurant with cheerful blue decor, fresh flowers, lovely sea views and the soothing sound of waves lapping in the background. The food is as good as you'll get anywhere on the island, with signature dishes including fresh seafood and spaghetti *alla stromboliana* (with wild fennel, cherry tomatoes and breadcrumbs).

Pardès   WINE BAR
(Via Vittorio Emanuele 81; ☺ 10.30am-2.30pm & 6-10pm mid-Mar–Oct; ☎) This wine bar/cafe has pleasant seating indoors and on an outdoor terrace where you can sip coffee or wine while using its wi-fi (it's one of the few places on the island with reliable internet access).

ℹ️ Information

Bring enough cash for your stay on Stromboli. Many businesses don't accept credit cards, and the village's lone ATM on Via Roma is sometimes out of service. Internet access is limited and slow; your best bet for wi-fi is the wine bar/cafe Pardès (p803), five to 10 minutes west of Stromboli's main church.

ℹ️ Getting There & Away

Ustica Lines (☑ 090 98 60 03; www.ustica lines.it) and **Siremar** (☑ 090 98 60 16; www. siremar.it) offer hydrofoil service to/from Lipari (€16.80, 50 minutes to 1¾ hours), Salina (€15.50, one hour) and all the other Aeolian islands. Ticket offices for both companies are at Stromboli's port. Siremar also operates one direct early morning hydrofoil from Milazzo (€22.45, 1¼ hours), along with twice weekly ferry service to Naples and the other Aeolians. Another option is to visit Stromboli on an all-inclusive day trip from Lipari.

IONIAN COAST

Magnificent, overdeveloped, crowded – and exquisitely beautiful – the Ionian coast is among Sicily's most popular tourist destinations and home to 20% of the island's population. Moneyed entrepreneurs have built their villas and hotels up and down the coastline, eager to bag a spot on Sicily's version of the Amalfi Coast. Above it all towers the muscular peak of Mt Etna (3329m), puffs of smoke billowing from its snow-covered cone.

Taormina

POP 11,100 / ELEV 204M

Spectacularly situated on a terrace of Monte Tauro, with views westwards to Mt Etna, Taormina is a beautiful small town, reminiscent of Capri or an Amalfi coastal resort. Over the centuries, Taormina has seduced an exhaustive line of writers and artists, aristocrats and royalty, and these days it's host to a international arts festival that packs the town with international visitors.

Perched on its eyrie, Taormina is sophisticated, chic and comfortably cushioned by some serious wealth – far removed from the banal economic realities of other Sicilian towns. But the charm is not manufactured. The capital of Byzantine Sicily in the 9th century, Taormina is an almost perfectly preserved medieval town, and, if you can tear yourself away from the shopping and sunbathing, it has a wealth of small but perfect tourist sites. Taormina is also a popular resort with gay men.

Be warned that in July and August the town and its surrounding beaches swarm with tourists.

👁 Sights

A short walk uphill from the bus station brings you to Corso Umberto I, a pedestrianised thoroughfare that traverses the length of the medieval town and connects its two historic town gates, Porta Messina and Porta Catania.

⭐ Teatro Greco   RUIN

(☑ 0942 2 32 20; Via Teatro Greco; adult/reduced €8/4; ⊙ 9am-1hr before sunset) Taormina's premier sight is this perfect horseshoe-shaped theatre, suspended between sea and sky, with Mt Etna looming on the southern horizon. Built in the 3rd century BC, it's the most dramatically situated Greek theatre in the world and the second largest in Sicily (after Syracuse). In summer, it's used to stage international arts and film festivals.

⭐ Corso Umberto   AREA

Taormina's chief delight is wandering this pedestrian-friendly thoroughfare, lined with stylish boutiques and Renaissance palaces. Midway down, pause to revel in stunning panoramic views of Mt Etna and the coast from **Piazza IX Aprile** and visit the charming rococo **Chiesa San Giuseppe** (Piazza IX Aprile; ⊙ 9am-7pm). Continue west through **Torre dell'Orologio**, the 12th-century clock tower, into **Piazza del Duomo**, home to an ornate baroque fountain (1635) that sports Taormina's symbol, a two-legged centaur with the bust of an angel.

Villa Comunale   PARK

(Parco Duchi di Cesarò; Via Bagnoli Croce; ⊙ 9am-midnight summer, 9am-sunset winter) To escape the crowds, wander down to these stunningly sited public gardens. Created by Englishwoman Florence Trevelyan, they're a lush paradise of tropical plants and delicate flowers. There's also a children's play area.

Castelmola   VILLAGE

For eye-popping views of the coastline and Mt Etna, head for this hilltop village above Taormina, crowned by a ruined castle. Either walk (one hour) or take the hourly Interbus service (one way/return €1.90/3, 15 minutes). While you're up here, stop in for almond wine at **Bar Turrisi** (⏱9am-2am), a four-level bar with some rather cheeky decor.

Isola Bella   ISLAND
Southwest of Lido Mazzarò is the minuscule Isola Bella, set in a stunning cove with fishing boats. You can walk here in a few minutes but it's more fun to rent a small boat from Mazzarò and paddle round Capo Sant'Andrea.

🏃 Activities

Lido Mazzarò   BEACH
Many visitors to Taormina come only for the beach scene. To reach Lido Mazzarò, directly beneath Taormina, take the **funivia** (cable car; Via Luigi Pirandello; single ticket/day pass €3/10; ⏱every 15min 8.45am-1.30am Mon, 7.45am-1.30am Tue-Sun). This beach is well serviced with bars and restaurants; private operators charge a fee for umbrellas and deck chairs (usually about €10 per person per day).

Nike Diving Centre   DIVING
(📱339 1961559; www.diveniketaormina.com) Opposite Isola Bella, this dive centre offers a wide range of courses for children and adults.

🎊 Festivals & Events

In addition to Taormina's well-established festivals, other recently launched summer cultural events include the **Taormina Opera Festival** (www.taorminafestival.org; ⏱mid-Jul–mid-Sep), **Italian Opera Taormina** (www.italian operataormina.com; ⏱May-Oct) and **Taormina Lirica** (www.taorminalirica.it; ⏱Jun & Sep).

Taormina FilmFest   FILM
(www.taorminafilmfest.it; ⏱mid-Jun) Hollywood big shots arrive in mid-June for a week of film screenings, premieres and press conferences at the Teatro Greco.

Taormina Arte   PERFORMING ARTS
(www.taormina-arte.com; ⏱Jun-Sep) From June to September, this festival features opera, dance, theatre and music concerts with an impressive list of international names.

🛏 Sleeping

Taormina has plenty of luxurious accommodation although some less expensive places can be found. Many hotels offer discounted parking (from €10) at Taormina's two public parking lots.

Isoco Guest House   GUESTHOUSE €
(📱0942 2 36 79; www.isoco.it; Via Salita Branco 2; s €70-98, d €80-120; ⏱Mar-Nov; ❄@🅿) Charming and well-travelled multilingual owner Michele Scimone runs this welcoming, gay-friendly guesthouse. Each room is dedicated to an artist, from Botticelli to graffiti pop designer Keith Haring. Breakfast is served around a large table on the upstairs patio, while a pair of sunny terraces offer stunning sea views and a hot tub. Multinight or prepaid stays earn the best rates.

Hostel Taormina   HOSTEL €
(📱0942 62 55 05; www.hosteltaormina.com; Via Circonvallazione 13; dm €18-23, r €49-85; ❄🅿) Friendly and laid-back, this year-round hostel occupies a house with pretty tiled floors and a roof terrace commanding panoramic sea views. It's a snug, homey set-up with accommodation in three dorms, a private room and a couple of apartments. There's also a communal kitchen, a relaxed vibe, and the owners go out of their way to help.

Villa Nettuno   PENSION €
(📱0942 2 37 97; www.hotelvillanettuno.it; Via Pirandello 33; s €38-44, d €60-78, breakfast €4; ❄🅿) A throwback to another era, this conveniently located salmon-pink *pensione* has been run by the Sciglio family for seven decades. Its low prices reflect a lack of recent updates, but the pretty gardens, complete with olive trees and potted geraniums, and the sea views from the breakfast terrace, offer a measure of charm you won't find elsewhere at this price.

B&B Le Sibille   B&B €
(📱349 7262862; www.lesibille.net; Corso Umberto 187a; d €70-110, 4-person apt €110-140; ⏱Apr-Oct; @🅿) This B&B wins points for its prime location on Taormina's pedestrian thoroughfare and its rooftop breakfast terrace. Three doubles with small balconies overlooking Corso Umberto are complemented by a pair of modern apartments done up with Ikea furniture and colourfully tiled bathrooms. Light sleepers beware: the street below can get noisy with holidaymakers!

⭐Hotel Villa Belvedere   HOTEL €€€
(📱094 22 37 91; www.villabelvedere.it; Via Bagnoli Croce 79; d €211-511; ⏱Mar-late Nov; ❄@🅿🏊) Built in 1902, the jaw-droppingly pretty Villa Belvedere was one of the original grand hotels, well-positioned with fabulous views and luxuriant gardens, which are a particular highlight. There is also a swimming pool

Taormina

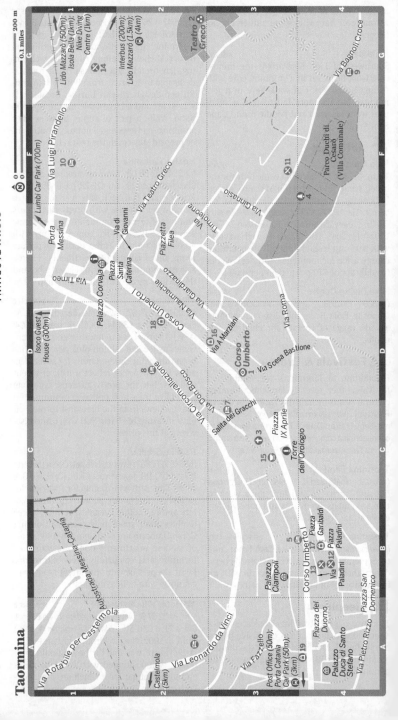

Via Rotabile Per Castelmola Autostrada Messina-Catania

Castelmola (5km)

Via Leonardo da Vinci

Via Fazzello

Post Office (50m); Porta Catania Car Park (50m); (3km)

Piazza del Duomo

Palazzo Duca di Santo Stefano

Via Pietro Rizzo

Piazza San Domenico

Palazzo Ciampoli

Corso Umberto I

Via Paladini

Piazza Paladini

Piazza Garibaldi

Lumbi Car Park (700m)

Porta Messina

Via Timeo

Palazzo Corvaja

Piazza Santa Caterina

Via di Giovanni

Piazzetta Filea

Isoco Guest House (300m)

Via Luigi Pirandello

Via Teatro Greco

Via Timoleone

Via Gimnasio

Corso Umberto I

Via Naumachie

Via Giardinazzo

Via Circonvallazione

Via Don Bosco

Salita dei Gracchi

Piazza IX Aprile

Torre dell'Orologio

Corso Umberto I

Via A Marziani

Corso Umberto I

Via Scesa Bastione

Via Roma

Parco Duchi di Cesarò (Villa Comunale)

Lido Mazzarò (500m); Isola Bella (2km); Nike Diving Centre (1km)

Interbus (200m); Lido Mazzarò (1.5km); (4km)

Teatro 2 Greco

Via Bagnoli Croce

Taormina

with a 100-year-old palm tree rising from a small island in the middle.

Casa Cuseni
B&B €€€

(☑094 22 83 62; www.casacuseni.com; Via Leonardo da Vinci 5; d €150, ste €250) Pre-booking is essential at this early-20th-century villa once frequented by Tennessee Williams, DH Lawrence, Greta Garbo and Bertrand Russell. Dripping with period character and surrounded by a seven-tiered garden with views out to the Ionian Sea and Mt Etna, it was recently opened as a B&B. It's only five minutes from Porta Catania but feels a world apart.

Casa Turchetti
B&B €€€

(☑094 262 50 13; www.casaturchetti.com; Salita dei Gracchi 18/20; d €220-260, junior ste €370; ❋ 🛜) Every detail is perfect at this painstakingly restored former music school converted to a luxurious B&B, on a back alley only two minutes above Piazza IX Aprile. Vintage furniture and fixtures, handcrafted woodwork and fine homespun sheets all contribute to the elegant feel; above all, guests appreciate the panoramic rooftop terrace, and the warmth of Sicilian hosts Pino and Francesca.

✗ Eating

Eating out in Taormina is expensive, and goes hand in hand with posing. Overpriced, touristy places abound.

★ Tischi Toschi
SICILIAN €€

(☑339 3642088; Via Paladini 3; meals €30-45; ⊙1-3pm Tue-Sun, plus 7.30-11.30pm daily) With only eight tables and four people running the show, this family-run, Slow Food–acclaimed trattoria offers a level of creativity and attention to detail that's generally lacking in touristy Taormina. The limited menu of six *primi* and six *secondi* changes regularly based on what's in season, and is filled with regional specialities that you won't find elsewhere.

Add in a charming front patio on a sidestreet staircase and you'll understand why booking is advisable.

La Piazzetta
SICILIAN €€

(☑094 262 63 17; Via Paladini 5; meals €25; ⊙closed Mon winter) Tucked into the corner of picturesque Piazza Paladini, this is an agreeable place to enjoy Sicilian classics from *pasta alla Norma* (pasta with basil, aubergine, ricotta and tomato) to fresh fish, all accompanied by a good list of local reds and whites.

Trattoria Da Nino
TRATTORIA €€

(☑0942 2 12 65; www.trattoriadaninotaormina.com; Via Luigi Pirandello 37; meals €25-35; ⊙12.30-3pm & 7.30-11pm) Bright and bustling, this place has been in business under the same family ownership for 50 years. Locals and tourists alike flock here for straightforward, reasonably priced Sicilian home cooking, including an excellent *caponata* plus fresh local fish served grilled, steamed, fried, stewed or rolled up in *involtini*.

Andreas
MODERN SICILIAN €€€

(☑0942 2 40 11; Via Bagnoli Croce 88; meals €35-55; ⊙1-2.30pm Wed-Sun, plus 8-11pm Tue-Sun) Accomplished chef Andreas Zangerl, a longtime fixture on Taormina's fine-dining scene at venues such as Casa Grugno and Hotel Metropole, opened this classy new restaurant in spring 2015. Culinary delights emerging from his kitchen celebrate the region's seafood, such as the beautifully presented appetiser of tuna prepared seven ways, or the delicious soup of fish, shellfish and wild fennel.

 ## Drinking & Nightlife

Wunderbar Caffè　　　　　　　　CAFE
(☑ 0942 62 50 32; www.wunderbarcaffe.it; Piazza IX Aprile 7; ◷ 9am-11pm) A Taormina landmark since the *dolce vita* 1960s, this glamorous and achingly expensive cafe has served them all – Tennessee Williams, who liked to watch 'the squares go by', Greta Garbo, Richard Burton and Elizabeth Taylor. With tables spread over the vibrant piazza and white-jacketed waiters taking the orders, it is still very much the quintessential Taormina watering hole.

 ## Shopping

Taormina is a window-shopper's paradise, especially along Corso Umberto. The quality in most places is high but don't expect any bargains.

Carlo Mirella Panarello　　　　CERAMICS
(Corso Umberto 122; ◷ 9am-1pm & 4-8.30pm) This eclectic shop is a fun place to browse for citrus-themed ceramics and Sicilian-style *coppole* (caps) in bold, colourful designs.

La Torinese　　　　　　　　FOOD, WINE
(Corso Umberto 59; ◷ 9.30am-1pm & 4-8.30pm Mon-Sat, 10am-1pm & 5-8.30pm Sun) Stock up on local olive oil, capers, marmalade, honey and wine. Smash-proof bubble wrapping helps to bring everything home in one piece.

Pafumi　　　　　　　　　　JEWELLERY
(Corso Umberto 251; ◷ 10am-9pm) Made in Sicily and not sold anywhere off the island, the colourful earrings, bracelets and pendants of the Isola Bella jewellery line are reason enough to browse at this shop near Porta Catania. Other Italian lines are also well represented.

Kerameion　　　　　　　　　CERAMICS
(www.kerameion.com; Corso Umberto 198; ◷ 9am-1pm & 3-8pm Mon-Sat) Three local artists run this shop specialising in colourful Sicilian tiles and made-to-order ceramics.

ℹ Information

Ospedale San Vincenzo (☑ 094 257 92 97; Contrada Sirina) Downhill, 2km from the centre.
Police Station (☑ 094 261 02 01; Corso Umberto 219)

Tourist Office (☑ 0942 2 32 43; Palazzo Corvaja, Piazza Santa Caterina; ◷ 8.30am-2.15pm & 3.30-6.45pm Mon-Fri year-round, 9am-1pm & 4-6.30pm Sat Apr-Oct, 9am-1pm Sun Jun-Sep) Has plenty of practical information.

ℹ Getting There & Around

BUS

Bus is the easiest way to reach Taormina. **Interbus** (www.interbus.it; Via Luigi Pirandello) goes to Messina (€4.30, 55 minutes to 1¾ hours, six daily Monday to Saturday, one on Sunday) and Catania (€5.10, 1¼ hours, hourly), the latter continuing to Catania's Fontanarossa airport (€8.20, 1½ hours).

CAR & MOTORCYCLE

Taormina is on the A18 autostrada and the SS114 between Messina and Catania. Driving near the historic centre is a complete nightmare and Corso Umberto is closed to traffic. The most convenient places to leave your car are the **Porta Catania car park** (per 24hr €15), at the western end of Corso Umberto, or the **Lumbi car park** (per 24hr €13.50) north of the centre, connected to Porta Messina (at Corso Umberto's eastern end) by a five-minute walk or a free yellow shuttle bus. Both car parks charge the same rates.

TRAIN

There are frequent trains to and from Messina (€3.95, 45 minutes to 1¼ hours) and Catania (€3.95, 45 minutes to one hour), but the awkward location of Taormina's station (a steep 4km below town) is a strong disincentive. If you arrive this way, catch a taxi (€15) or an Interbus coach (€1.90, 20 minutes, half hourly) up to town.

Catania

POP 296,000

Sicily's second biggest metropolis, Catania is a city of grit and raw energy, a thriving, entrepreneurial centre with a large university and a cosmopolitan urban culture. Yes, it has its rough edges, but it's hard not to love a city with a smiling elephant gracing its central square and gorgeous snowcapped Mt Etna floating on the horizon. Catania is a true city of the volcano, much of it constructed from the lava that poured down the mountain and engulfed the city in Etna's massive 1669 eruption. It is also lava-black in colour, as if a fine dusting of soot permanently covers its elegant buildings, most of which are the work of baroque master Giovanni Vaccarini.

In recent years, Catania has made steady moves to pedestrianise its historic centre, which you'll appreciate as you stroll the streets between Via Crociferi, Via Etnea and Piazza del Duomo, where most of the city's attractions are concentrated.

◉ Sights

If you're visiting multiple attractions or travelling frequently by bus and metro, consider picking up a Catania Pass (www.cataniapass. it; 1-/3-/5-day pass individual €12.50/16.50/20, family €23/30.50/38), which offers free museum admissions and unlimited use of public transport.

Piazza del Duomo   SQUARE
A Unesco World Heritage Site, Catania's central piazza is a set piece of contrasting lava and limestone, surrounded by buildings in the unique local baroque style and crowned by the grand Cattedrale di Sant'Agata (p809). At its centre stands Fontana dell'Elefante (1736), a naive, smiling black-lava elephant dating from Roman times, surmounted by an improbable Egyptian obelisk. Another fountain at the piazza's southwest corner, Fontana dell'Amenano, marks the entrance to Catania's fish market.

★ La Pescheria   MARKET
(Via Pardo; ⊙7am-2pm Mon-Sat) Catania's raucous fish market, which takes over the streets behind Piazza del Duomo every workday morning, is street theatre at its most thrilling. Tables groan under the weight of decapitated swordfish, ruby-pink prawns and trays full of clams, mussels, sea urchins and all manner of mysterious sea life. Fishmongers gut silvery fish and high-heeled housewives step daintily over pools of blood-stained water. It's absolutely riveting. Surrounding the market are a number of good seafood restaurants.

★ Graeco-Roman Theatre & Odeon   RUIN
(Via Vittorio Emanuele II 262; adult/reduced incl Casa Liberti €6/3; ⊙9am-7pm Mon-Sat, to 1.30pm Sun) These twin theatres west of Piazza del Duomo are Catania's most impressive Graeco-Roman ruins. Both are picturesquely sited in the thick of a crumbling residential neighbourhood, with laundry occasionally flapping on the rooftops of vine-covered buildings that appear to have sprouted organically from the half-submerged stage. Adjacent to the main theatre is the Casa Liberti, an elegantly restored 19th-century

palazzo with tiled floors and red wallpaper. It now houses two millennia worth of artefacts discovered during excavation of the theatres.

★ Teatro Massimo Bellini   THEATRE
(⊘095 730 61 11; www.teatromassimobellini.it; Via Perrotta 12; guided tours adult/reduced €6/3; ⊙tours 9.30am-noon Tue-Sat) A few blocks northeast of the *duomo*, this gorgeous opera house forms the centrepiece of Piazza Bellini. Square and opera house alike were named after composer Vincenzo Bellini, the father of Catania's vibrant modern musical scene.

Cattedrale di Sant'Agata   CATHEDRAL
(⊘095 32 00 44; Piazza del Duomo; ⊙8am-noon & 4-7pm) Inside the vaulted interior of this cathedral, beyond its impressive marble facade sporting two orders of columns taken from the Roman amphitheatre, lie the relics of the city's patron saint. Consider visiting the Museo Diocesano (www.museodiocesano catania.com; Piazza del Duomo; adult/reduced museum only €7/4, museum & baths €10/6; ⊙9am-2pm Mon, Wed & Fri, 9am-2pm & 3-6pm Tue & Thu, 9am-1pm Sat) next door for access to the Roman baths directly underneath the church and fine views from the roof terrace beneath the cathedral's dome.

Museo Belliniano   MUSEUM
(⊘095 715 05 35; Piazza San Francesco 3; adult/reduced €5/2; ⊙9am-7pm Mon-Sat, to 1pm Sun) One of Italy's great opera composers, Vincenzo Bellini was born in Catania in 1801. The house he grew up in has since been converted into this museum, which boasts an interesting collection of memorabilia, including original scores, photographs, pianos once played by Bellini, and the maestro's death mask.

Castello Ursino   CASTLE
Catania's forbidding 13th-century castle once guarded the city from atop a seafront cliff. However, the 1669 eruption of Mt Etna changed the landscape and the whole area to the south was reclaimed by the lava, leaving the castle completely landlocked. The castle now houses the Museo Civico (⊘095 34 58 30; Piazza Federico II di Svevia; adult/reduced €6/3; ⊙9am-6pm Mon-Sat, to 1pm Sun), home to the valuable archaeological collection of the Biscaris, Catania's most important aristocratic family. Exhibits include colossal classical sculpture, Greek vases and some fine mosaics.

Catania

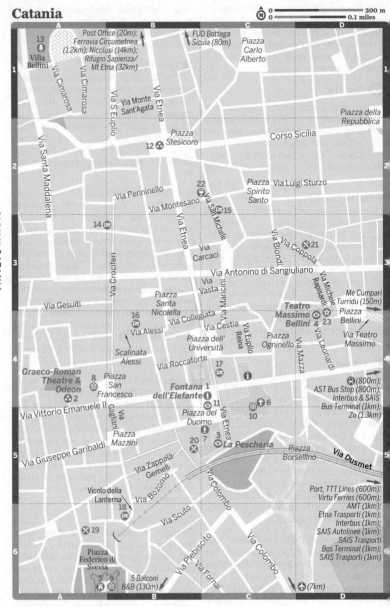

Villa Bellini PARK
(⊙8am-8pm) Escape the madding crowd and enjoy the fine views of Mt Etna from these lovely gardens along Via Etnea.

Roman Amphitheatre RUIN
The modest ruins of this Roman theatre, below street level in Piazza Stesicoro, are worth a quick look.

Catania

⦿ Top Sights

⦿ Sights

⊜ Sleeping

⊗ Eating

⊝ Drinking & Nightlife

⊛ Entertainment

SICILY CATANIA

⋆⋆ Festivals & Events

If visiting Catania in February or early March, don't miss **Carnevale** (www.carnevale acireale.com; ⊙ Feb) in nearby Acireale, one of Sicily's most colourful festivals.

Festa di Sant'Agata   RELIGIOUS
(www.festadisantagata.it; ⊙ 3-5 Feb) In Catania's biggest religious festival (3-5 February), one million Catanians follow the Fercolo (a silver reliquary bust of St Agata) along the main street of the city accompanied by spectacular fireworks.

⊨ Sleeping

Catania is served by a good range of reasonably priced accommodation, making it an excellent base for exploring the Ionian coast and Etna.

★ B&B Crociferi   B&B €
(☑ 095 715 22 66; www.bbcrociferi.it; Via Crociferi 81; d €75-85, tr €100-110, apt €135; ❋ 🛜) Perfectly positioned on pedestrianised Via Crociferi, this B&B in a beautifully decorated family home affords easy access to all the attractions of Catania's historic centre. Three palatial rooms (each with private bathroom across the hall) feature high ceilings, antique tiles, frescoes and artistic accoutrements from the owners' travels. There's also a glorious four-bed upstairs apartment with panoramic terrace. Book ahead.

★ Palazzu Stidda   APARTMENT €
(☑ 095 34 88 26; www.palazzu-stidda.com; Vicolo della Lanterna 5; s €40-60, d €70-100, q €130-150; 🛜 ♿) Creative, multilingual young hosts Giovanni and Patricia have poured their

hearts into creating these three family friendly apartments on a peaceful dead-end alley, with all the comforts of home plus a host of whimsical touches. Each has a flowery mini-balcony, and all are decorated with the owners' artwork, handmade furniture, family heirlooms and vintage finds.

Apartments 2 and 3 each come with a washing machine, kitchen, high chair and stroller, and ample space for a family of four. Apartment 1 is smaller and costs €10 to €20 less. Check the website for seasonal variations in price.

5 Balconi B&B   B&B €
(☑ 095 723 45 34; www.5balconi.it; Via Plebiscito 133; s/d without bathroom €35/50, with air-con €45/60; ❋ 🛜) The warm and generous hospitality of British-Sicilian hosts Rob and Cristina more than compensates for the slightly out-of-centre location at this lovingly remodelled antique *palazzo* in a workaday neighbourhood near Castello Ursino. Three high-ceilinged rooms share a pair of bathrooms; breakfast features fresh-baked croissants and organic fruit. Be advised that the street out front gets lots of traffic.

Ostello degli Elefanti   HOSTEL €
(☑ 095 226 56 91; www.ostellodeglielefanti.it; Via Etnea 28; dm €18-24, s €38-40, d €58-70; ❋ 🛜) Housed in a 17th-century *palazzo* a stone's throw from the Duomo, this brand-new hostel offers incredible location and value. Three dorms and one private room have frescoed high ceilings and panoramic balconies, with reading lights, USB ports and curtains for every bed. The marble-floored former ballroom doubles as a restaurant-lounge, while

the rooftop terrace-bar offers incomparable Etna vistas.

B&B Faro
B&B €

(☎ 349 4578856; www.bebfaro.it; Via San Michele 26; s/d/tr €50/80/100; ❋ @) Polished wood floors, double-glazed windows, modern bathroom fixtures, antique tiles and bold colours characterise this stylish, artist-owned B&B. Suites can sometimes be booked for the price of a double during slower periods, free bikes are provided for guests' use, and there's a studio downstairs where visiting artists are invited to come and paint.

Il Principe
HOTEL €€

(☎ 095 250 03 45; www.ilprincipehotel.com; Via Alessi 20/26; d €94-174, ste €254-314; ❋ @ 🛜) This boutique-style hotel in an 18th-century building features luxurious rooms and two-level suites on one of the liveliest nightlife streets in town (thank goodness for double glazing!). Perks include international cable TV, free wi-fi and fluffy bathrobes to wear on your way to the Turkish steam bath. Check online for special rates.

Eating

Popular street snacks in Catania include *arancini* (fried rice balls filled with meat, cheese, tomatoes and/or peas) and *seltz* (fizzy water with fresh-squeezed lemon juice and natural fruit syrup). Don't leave town without trying *pasta alla Norma* (pasta with basil, aubergine and ricotta), a Catania original named after Bellini's opera *Norma*.

Da Antonio
TRATTORIA €

(☎ 347 8330636; www.facebook.com/Trattoria DaAntonio; Via Castello Ursino 59; meals €19-25; ⊘ 12.30-2.30pm & 7.30-10pm Tue-Sun) This humble hideaway offers the quintessential trattoria experience: reasonably priced, delicious food served by unpretentious waitstaff. Despite having made inroads onto the tourist radar, it's still the kind of place where well-dressed local families come for Sunday lunch. The menu revolves around local fish, homemade pasta and classic Sicilian desserts featuring ricotta, pistachios, almonds and wild strawberries.

Trattoria di De Fiore
TRATTORIA €

(☎ 095 31 62 83; Via Coppola 24/26; meals €15-25; ⊘ 1-3pm & 7-11pm Tue-Sun) For over 50 years, septuagenarian chef Rosanna has been recreating her great-grandmother's recipes, including the best *pasta alla Norma* you'll taste anywhere in Sicily.

Service is excruciatingly slow, but for patient souls this is a rare chance to experience classic Catanian cooking from a bygone era. Don't miss Rosanna's trademark *zeppoline* (sugar-sprinkled ricotta-lemon fritters) at dessert time.

FUD Bottega Sicula
BURGERS €

(☎ 095 715 35 18; www.fud.it; Via Santa Filomena 35; burgers, panini & pizzas €6-10; ⊘ noon-3pm & 7pm-1am) Sporting pavement seating on trendy Via Santa Filomena, this back-alley eatery epitomises youthful Catania's embrace of 'Sicilian fast food', made with high-quality, locally sourced ingredients (think extra-virgin olive oil, Sicilian cheeses, Nebrodi black pork). With wry humour, every burger, *panino* and pizza on the menu is spelled using Italian phonetics ('cis burgh-er' for cheeseburger, 'cicchen burgher' for chicken burger etc).

★ Osteria Antica Marina
SEAFOOD €€

(☎ 095 34 81 97; www.anticamarina.it; Via Pardo 29; meals €30-50; ⊘ 1-3pm & 8-11pm Thu-Tue) With a front terrace directly overlooking the fishmongers' stalls in the piazza below, this classy trattoria is *the* place to come for seafood. A variety of tasting menus ranging from €25 to €45 showcase everything from swordfish to scampi, cuttlefish to calamari. All menus start with a dazzling array of fishy appetisers and end with divine lemon sorbet. Reservations are essential.

Me Cumpari Turridu
SICILIAN €€

(☎ 095 715 01 42; Via Ventimiglia 15; meals €27-40; ⊘ 1-2.30pm daily, plus 8-11.30pm Mon-Sat) A quirky little spot that mixes tradition and modernity both in food and decor, this place is a real discovery. Try the ricotta and marjoram ravioli in a pork sauce, or the cannellini with donkey-meat *ragù* (meat and tomato sauce). Vegetarians can opt for the Ustica lentil stew, with broad beans and fennel. Slow Food–recommended.

🍷 Drinking & Nightlife

Not surprisingly for a busy university town, Catania has a reputation for its effervescent nightlife. Areas that bustle with activity after dark include Via Montesano, Via Teatro Massimo, the steps at the western end of Via Alessi, and recent local favourite Via Santa Filomena.

★ Razmataz
BAR

(☎ 095 31 18 93; Via Montesano 17; ⊘ 8.30am-late) Wines by the glass, draught and bottled beer and an ample cocktail list are offered at this delightful wine bar with tables invitingly spread out across the tree-shaded flagstones of a sweet backstreet square. It doubles as a cafe in the morning, but really gets packed with locals from *aperitivo* time onward.

☆ Entertainment

For a current calendar of music, theatre and arts events around Catania, check the website www.lapisnet.it/catania.

Teatro Massimo Bellini   THEATRE
(☑ 095 730 61 11; www.teatromassimobellini. it; Via Perrotta 12) Catania's premier theatre is named after the city's most famous son, composer Vincenzo Bellini. Sporting the full red-and-gilt look, it stages a year-round season of opera and an eight-month program of classical music from November to June. Tickets, which are available online, start at around €13 and rise to €84 for a first-night front-row seat.

Zo   PERFORMING ARTS
(☑ 095 816 89 12; www.zoculture.it; Piazzale Asia 6) Part of the very cool Le Ciminiere complex (housed in Catania's former sulphur works), Zo is dedicated to promoting contemporary art and performance. It hosts an eclectic program of events ranging from club nights, concerts and film screenings to art exhibitions, dance performances, installations and theatre workshops. Check the website for upcoming events, many of which are free of charge.

❶ Information

Ospedale Vittorio Emanuele (☑ 091 743 54 52; www.policlinicovittorioemanuele.it; Via Plebiscito 628) Has a 24-hour emergency doctor.

Questura (☑ 095 736 71 11; Piazza Santa Nicolella 8) Police station.

Tourist Office (☑ 095 742 55 73; www.co mune.catania.it; Via Vittorio Emanuele 172; ⊙ 8am-7.15pm Mon-Sat) Very helpful city-run tourist office.

❶ Getting There & Away

AIR

Catania's airport, **Fontanarossa** (☑ 095 723 91 11; www.aeroporto.catania.it), is 7km southwest of the city centre. Alibus 457, operated by **AMT** (☑ 095 751 91 11; www.amt.ct.it), runs half hourly between 5.30am and midnight from the airport to Catania's central train station (€4, 30 minutes). **Etna Transporti/Interbus** (☑ 095 53 03 96; www.interbus.it; Via d'Amico 187) also runs a regular shuttle from the airport to Taormina (€8.20, 1½ hours, hourly 7.45am to 8.45pm). Stops for both buses are to the right as you exit the arrivals hall. All the main car-hire companies are represented at the airport.

BOAT

The ferry terminal is located southwest of the train station along Via VI Aprile.

TTT Lines (☑ 800 627414, 095 34 85 86; www. tttlines.info) TTT Lines runs nightly ferries from Catania to Naples (from €42, 11 hours).

Virtu Ferries (☑ 095 703 12 11; www.virtu ferries.com) From May through September, Virtu Ferries runs daily ferries from Pozzallo (south of Catania) to Malta (1¾ hours). Fares vary depending on length of stay in Malta (same-day return €85 to €136, open return €113 to €161 depending on the season). Coach transfer between Catania and Pozzallo (€10 each way) adds 2½ hours to the journey.

BUS

All long-distance buses leave from a terminal 250m north of the train station, with ticket offices across the street on Via d'Amico.

Interbus (☑ 095 53 03 96; www.interbus.it; Via d'Amico 187) runs buses to:
➡ **Piazza Armerina** (€9.20, 1¾ hours, two to four daily)
➡ **Ragusa** (€8.60, two hours, five to 12 daily)
➡ **Syracuse** (€6.20, 1½ hours, hourly Monday to Friday, fewer on weekends)
➡ **Taormina** (€5.10, 1¼ hours, hourly)

SAIS Trasporti (☑ 090 601 21 36; http://sais trasporti.it; Via d'Amico 181) goes to:
➡ **Agrigento** (€13.40, three hours, nine to 14 daily)
➡ **Rome** (€49, 10½ hours) Overnight service.

Its sister company **SAIS Autolinee** (☑ 095 53 61 68; www.saisautolinee.it; Via d'Amico 183) runs services to:
➡ **Messina** (€8.40, 1½ hours, hourly)
➡ **Palermo** (€12, 2¾ hours, eight to 10 daily)

CAR & MOTORCYCLE

Catania is easily reached from Messina on the A18 autostrada and from Palermo on the A19 – although travel on the latter was recently disrupted by an April 2015 viaduct collapse (see box p790). From either autostrada, signs for the centre of Catania will bring you to Via Etnea.

TRAIN

From Catania Centrale station on Piazza Papa Giovanni XXIII there are frequent trains.
Messina (€7, 1½ to two hours, hourly)
Palermo (€12.50, three hours, seven daily, three on Sunday)

Syracuse (€6.35 to €10, 1¼ hours, 10 daily, four on Sunday)

The private Ferrovia Circumetnea (p815) train circles Mt Etna, stopping at towns and villages on the volcano's slopes.

ℹ Getting Around

Several useful AMT city buses (p813) terminate in front of the train station, including buses 1-4 and 4-7 (both running hourly from the station to Via Etnea) and Alibus 457 (station to airport every 25 minutes from 4.40am to midnight). Also useful is bus D, which runs from Piazza Borsellino (just south of the *duomo*) to the local beaches.

Catania's one-line metro currently has only six stops, all on the periphery of town. For tourists, it's mainly useful as a way to get from the central train station to the Circumetnea train that goes around Mt Etna.

A 90-minute ticket for either bus or metro costs €1. A two-hour combined ticket for both costs €1.20.

For drivers, some words of warning: there are complicated one-way systems around the city and the centre is increasingly pedestrianised, which means parking is scarce. Furthermore, there's been a recent increase in organised petty theft from tourists driving through town; if you do drive, keep your doors and windows locked.

For a taxi, call **Radio Taxi Catania** (☑ 095 33 09 66; www.radiotaxicatania.org).

Mt Etna

ELEV 3329M

Dominating the landscape of eastern Sicily and visible from the moon (if you happen to be there), Mt Etna is Europe's largest volcano and one of the world's most active. Eruptions occur frequently, both from the volcano's four summit craters and from its slopes, which are littered with fissures and old craters. The volcano's most devastating eruptions occurred in 1669 and lasted 122 days. Lava poured down Etna's southern slope, engulfing much of Catania and dramatically altering the landscape. The volcano's most destructive recent eruption came in 2002, when lava flows caused an explosion in Sapienza, destroying two buildings and temporarily halting the cable-car service. Less destructive eruptions continue to occur regularly, and locals understandably keep a close eye on the smouldering peak.

Enshrined as a Unesco World Heritage Site in 2013, the volcano is surrounded by the huge **Parco dell'Etna**, the largest unspoilt wilderness remaining in Sicily. The park encompasses a remarkable variety of environments, from the severe, almost surreal, summit to deserts of lava and alpine forests.

◉ Sights & Activities

The southern approach to Mt Etna presents the easier ascent to the **craters**. The AST bus from Catania drops you off at **Rifugio Sapienza** (1923m) from where the **Funivia dell'Etna** (☑ 095 91 41 41; www.funiviaetna.com; return €35, incl bus & guide €65; ⊙ 9am-5.45pm Apr-Nov, to 3.45pm Dec-Mar) cable car runs up the mountain to 2500m. From the upper cable-car station it's a 3½- to four-hour return trip up the winding track to the authorised crater zone (2920m). Make sure you leave enough time to get up *and* down before the last cable car leaves at 4.45pm. You can pay an extra €30 for a guided 4WD tour to take you up from the cable car to the crater zone, but the guides provided by the Funivia tend to be perfunctory at best, and you'll have more freedom to explore if you go it alone.

An alternative ascent is from **Piano Provenzano** (1800m) on Etna's northern flank. This area was severely damaged during the 2002 eruptions, as still evidenced by the bleached skeletons of the surrounding pine trees. To reach Piano Provenzano you'll need a car, as there's no public transport beyond Linguaglossa, 16km away.

☞ Tours

Several Catania-based companies offer private excursions up the mountain.

Gruppo Guide Alpine Etna Sud　　WALKING
(☑ 095 791 47 55; www.etnaguide.com) The official guide service on Etna's southern flank, with an office just below Rifugio Sapienza.

Gruppo Guide Alpine Etna Nord　　WALKING
(☑ 095 777 45 02; www.guidetnanord.com) Offers volcano guide service from Linguaglossa on Etna's northern flank.

🛏 Sleeping & Eating

There's plenty of B&B accommodation around Mt Etna, particularly in the small, pretty town of Nicolosi. Contact Nicolosi's tourist information office for a full list.

Agriturismo San Marco　　AGRITURISMO €
(☑ 389 4237294; www.agriturismosanmarco.com; Rovitello; per person B&B/half-board/full board €35/53/68; 🛜 ⊠ ♿) Get back to basics at this

delightful *agriturismo* near Rovittello, on Etna's northern flank. The bucolic setting, rustic rooms, swimming pool, kids' play area and superb country cooking make it a relaxed place to kick back for a couple of days. Call ahead for directions.

Rifugio Sapienza   CHALET €
(☑ 095 91 53 21; www.rifugiosapienza.com; Piazzale Funivia; s/d €46/92; ☎) Offering comfortable accommodation with a good restaurant, this place adjacent to the cable car is the closest lodging to Etna's summit.

❶ Information

Catania's downtown tourist office provides information about Etna, as does the Parco dell'Etna office on the mountain's southern flank.

Parco dell'Etna (☑ 095 82 11 11; www.parco etna.ct.it; Via del Convento 45, Nicolosi; ☺9am-2pm & 4-7.30pm) About 1km from the centre of Nicolosi.

❶ Getting There & Away

BUS

AST (☑ 095 723 05 35; www.aziendasiciliana trasporti.it) runs one bus daily from Catania to Rifugio Sapienza (one way/return €4/6.60, two hours), leaving the car park opposite Catania's train station at 8.15am and arriving at Rifugio Sapienza at 10.15am. The return journey leaves Rifugio Sapienza at 4.30pm, arriving at Catania at 6.30pm.

TRAIN

You can circle Etna on the private **Ferrovia Circumetnea** (FCE; ☑ 095 54 11 11; www.circum etnea.it; Via Caronda 352a, Catania) train line. Catch the metro from Catania's main train station to the FCE station at Via Caronda (metro stop Borgo) or take bus 429 or 432 going up Via Etnea and ask to be let off at the Borgo metro stop.

The train follows a 114km trail around the base of the volcano, providing lovely views. It also passes through many of Etna's unique towns such as Adrano, Bronte and Randazzo. See the website for fares and timetables.

SYRACUSE & THE SOUTHEAST

Home to Sicily's most beautiful baroque towns and Magna Graecia's most magnificent ancient city, the southeast is one of Sicily's most compelling destinations. The classical charms of Syracuse are reason enough to visit, but once you leave the city behind you'll find an evocative checkerboard of river valleys and stone-walled citrus groves dotted with handsome towns.

Shattered by a devastating earthquake in 1693, the towns of Noto, Ragusa and Modica are the superstars here, rebuilt in the ornate and much-lauded Sicilian baroque style that lends the region a cohesive aesthetic appeal. Writer Gesualdo Bufalino described the southeast as an 'island within an island'; indeed, this pocket of Sicily has a remote, genteel air – a legacy of its glorious Greek heritage.

Syracuse

POP 124,000

A dense tapestry of overlapping cultures and civilisations, Syracuse is one of Sicily's most appealing cities. Settled by colonists from Corinth in 734 BC, this was considered to be the most beautiful city of the ancient world, rivalling Athens in power and prestige. Under the demagogue Dionysius the Elder, the city reached its zenith, attracting luminaries such as Livy, Plato, Aeschylus and Archimedes, and cultivating the sophisticated urban culture that was to see the birth of comic Greek theatre.

Arriving in today's drab modern downtown by train or bus, you could be excused for wondering what all the fuss is about. But cross the bridge to the ancient island neighbourhood of Ortygia, and Syracuse's irresistible appeal quickly becomes manifest: in the ancient Greek temple columns peeking out from the baroque walls of Ortygia's cathedral; the throngs of locals and tourists mingling in the reflected evening glow of Piazza del Duomo's vast marble pavements; the flash of fish swimming amidst the papyrus plants in the Fontana Aretusa; and the splash of sunbathers plunging off rocks into the blue Ionian Sea. Adding to the city's magic is Syracuse's annual theatre festival, where classical Greek dramas are staged in one of the Mediterranean's greatest surviving ancient theatres.

Add to this the city's ambitious and enlightened moves towards pedestrian-friendly measures and environmental sustainability (including the 2014 launch of a new fleet of electric minibuses), and you'll begin to understand why this has become Sicily's number one tourist destination. Syracuse is truly a city to savour.

Syracuse

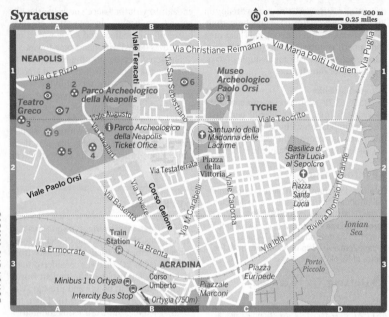

Syracuse

⦿ Top Sights

⦿ Sights

⦿ Ortygia

★ Duomo CATHEDRAL

(Map p818; Piazza del Duomo; adult/reduced €2/1; ⊙9am-6.30pm Mon-Sat Apr-Oct, to 5.30pm Nov-Mar) Built on the skeleton of a 5th-century BC Greek temple to Athena (note the Doric columns still visible inside and out), Syracuse's cathedral became a church when the island was evangelised by St Paul. Its most striking feature is the columned baroque facade (1728–53) added by Andrea Palma after the 1693 earthquake. A statue of the Virgin Mary crowns the rooftop, in the same spot where a golden statue of Athena once served as a beacon to homecoming Greek sailors.

★ Fontana Aretusa FOUNTAIN

(Map p818) Down the winding main street from the cathedral is this ancient spring, where fresh water still bubbles up just as it did in ancient times when it was the city's main water supply. Legend has it that the goddess Artemis transformed her beautiful handmaiden Aretusa into the spring to protect her from the unwelcome attention of the river god Alpheus.

La Giudecca AREA

Simply walking through Ortygia's tangled maze of alleys is an atmospheric experience, especially down the narrow lanes of **Via Maestranza**, the heart of the old guild quarter, and the crumbling Jewish ghetto of **Via della Giudecca**. At the Alla Giudecca hotel you can visit an ancient Jewish miqwe (Ritual Bath; Map p818; ☎0931 2 22 55; Via Alagona 52; tours in English & Italian €5; ⊙hourly

9am-7pm mid-May–Sep, 11am, noon, 4pm, 5pm & 6pm Oct–mid-May) some 20m below ground level. Blocked up in 1492 when the Jewish community was expelled from Ortygia, the baths were rediscovered during renovation work at the hotel.

Galleria Regionale di Palazzo Bellomo

GALLERY

(Map p818; ☑ 0931 6 95 11; www.regione.sicilia. it/beniculturali/palazzobellomo; Via Capodieci 16; adult/reduced €8/4; ☺ 9am-7pm Tue-Sat, 9am-1pm Sun) Housed in a 13th-century Catalan-Gothic palace, this art museum's eclectic collection ranges from early Byzantine and Norman stonework to 19th-century Calta-girone ceramics; in between, there's a good range of medieval religious paintings and sculpture.

Museo del Papiro

MUSEUM

(Map p818; ☑ 0931 2 21 00; www.museodelpapiro. it; Via Nizza 14; adult/reduced €5/2; ☺ 9.15am-2pm Tue-Sun Oct-Apr, 10am-7pm Tue-Sat, 10am-2pm Sun May-Sep) Moved to Ortygia and newly expanded in 2014, this museum exhibits a nice collection of papyrus documents and products, boats and an English-language film about the history of papyrus. The plant grows in abundance around the Ciane River, near Syracuse, and was used to make paper here in the 18th century.

Castello Maniace

CASTLE

(Map p818; admission €2; ☺ 9am-1.15pm Mon-Sat) Guarding the island's southern tip, Or-tygia's 13th-century castle is a lovely place to wander, gaze out over the water and contemplate Syracuse's past glories. It also houses occasional rotating exhibitions.

⊙ Mainland Syracuse

★ Parco Archeologico della Neapolis

ARCHAEOLOGICAL SITE

(Map p816; ☑ 0931 6 62 06; Viale Paradiso 14; adult/reduced €10/5, incl Museo Archeologico €13.50/7; ☺ 9am-6.30pm) For the classicist, Syracuse's real attraction is this archae-ological park, with its pearly white 5th-century-BC Teatro Greco (Map p816; Parco Archeologico della Neapolis). Hewn out of the rocky hillside, this 16,000-capacity amphi-theatre staged the last tragedies of Aeschy-lus (including *The Persians*), which were first performed here in his presence. In late spring it's brought to life with an annual sea-son of classical theatre.

Beside the theatre is the mysterious **La-tomia del Paradiso** (Garden of Paradise; Map p816; Parco Archeologico della Neapolis), a deep, precipitous limestone quarry out of which stone for the ancient city was extracted. Riddled with catacombs and filled with cit-rus and magnolia trees, it's also where the 7000 survivors of the war between Syracuse and Athens in 413 BC were imprisoned. The **Orecchio di Dionisio** (Ear of Dionysius; Map p816; Latomia del Paradiso, Parco Archeologico della Neapolis), a 23m-high grotto extending 65m back into the cliffside, was named by Caravaggio after the tyrant Dionysius, who is said to have used the almost perfect acoustics of the quarry to eavesdrop on his prisoners.

Back outside this area you'll find the entrance to the 2nd-century **Anfiteatro Romano** (Map p816; Parco Archeologico del-la Neapolis), originally used for gladiatorial combats and horse races. The Spaniards, little interested in archaeology, largely de-stroyed the site in the 16th century, using it as a quarry to build Ortygia's city walls. West of the amphitheatre is the 3rd-century-BC **Ara di Gerone II** (Altar of Hieron II; Map p816; Parco Archeologico della Neapolis), a monolithic sacrificial altar to Heron II where up to 450 oxen could be killed at one time.

To reach the park, take Sd'A Trasporti minibus 2 (€0.50, 15 minutes) from Molo Sant'Antonio, on the west side of the main bridge into Ortygia. Alternatively, walking from Ortygia will take about 30 minutes. If driving, park on Viale Augusto (tickets are available at the nearby souvenir kiosks).

★ Museo Archeologico Paolo Orsi

MUSEUM

(Map p816; ☑ 0931 48 95 11; www.regione.sicil-ia.it/beniculturali/museopaoloorsi; Viale Teocrito 66; adult/reduced €8/4, incl Parco Archeologico €13.50/7; ☺ 9am-6pm Tue-Sat, to 1pm Sun) About 500m east of the archaeological park, this modern museum contains one of Sicily's largest and most interesting archaeological collections. Allow plenty of time to inves-tigate the four sectors charting the area's pre-history, as well as Syracuse's develop-ment from foundation to the late Roman period.

Catacombe di San Giovanni

CATACOMB

(Map p816; Largo San Marciano; adult/reduced €8/5; ☺ 9.30am-12.30pm & 2.30-5.30pm Tue-Sun) A block north of the archaeological mu-seum, this vast labyrinth of 10,000 under-ground tombs dates back to Roman times.

Ortygia

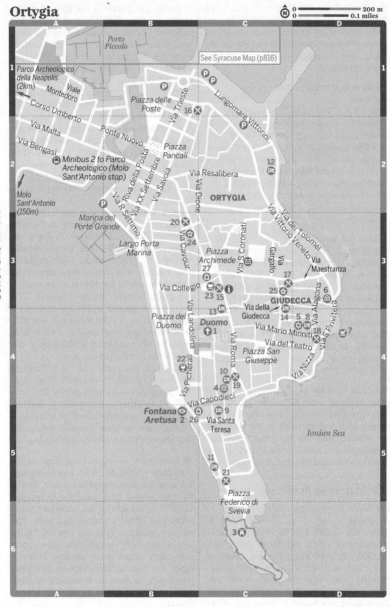

See Syracuse Map (p816)

A 30-minute guided tour ushers visitors through the catacombs as well as the atmospheric ruins of the **Basilica di San Giovanni**, Syracuse's earliest cathedral.

Activities

In midsummer, when Ortygia steams like a cauldron, people flock to the beaches south of town at **Arenella** (take bus 23 from Piazza della Posta) and **Fontane Bianche** (bus 21 or 22).

Ortygia

★**Solarium Forte Vigliena**   SWIMMING
(Map p818) FREE Flanked by the crenellated walls of Forte Vigliena along Ortygia's eastern waterfront, this platform surrounded by flat rocks is a favourite local hang-out for swimming and sunbathing in the summer months.

☆ Festivals & Events

★**Ciclo di Rappresentazioni Classiche**   THEATRE
(Festival of Greek Theatre; www.indafondazione. org; ⊙mid-May–Jun) Syracuse boasts the only school of classical Greek drama outside Athens, and in May and June it hosts live performances of Greek plays (in Italian) at the Teatro Greco, attracting Italy's finest performers. Tickets (€26 to €60) are available online, from the **Fondazione Inda ticket office** (Map p818; ☑0931 48 72 00; Corso Matteotti 29; ⊙10am-1pm Mon-Sat) in Ortygia or at the **ticket booth** (Map p816; ⊙10am-7pm) outside the theatre.

Festa di Santa Lucia   RELIGIOUS
(⊙13 Dec) On 13 December, the enormous silver statue of the city's patron saint wends its way from the cathedral to Piazza Santa Lucia accompanied by fireworks.

🛏 Sleeping

Stay on Ortygia for atmosphere. Cheaper accommodation is located around the train station.

B&B dei Viaggiatori, Viandanti e Sognatori   B&B €
(Map p818; ☑0931 2 47 81; www.bedandbreak fastsicily.it; Via Roma 156; s €35-50, d €55-70, tr €75-85, q €100; ❀🛜) Decorated with verve and boasting a prime Ortygia location, this relaxed B&B exudes a homey boho feel, with books and antique furniture juxtaposed against bright walls. Rooms are colourful and imaginatively decorated, while up top, the sunny roof terrace offers sweeping sea views.

Aretusa Vacanze   APARTMENT €
(Map p818; ☑0931 48 34 84; www.aretusava-canze.com; Vicolo Zuccalà 1; d €59-90, tr €70-120, q €105-147; ℗❀@🛜) This great budget option, elbowed into a tiny pedestrian street in a 17th-century building, has large rooms and apartments with kitchenettes, computers, wi-fi, satellite TV and small balconies from where you can shake hands with your neighbour across the way.

★**Hotel Gutkowski**   HOTEL €€
(Map p818; ☑0931 46 58 61; www.guthotel. it; Lungomare Vittorini 26; s €60-80, d €75-140; ❀@🛜) Book well in advance for one of the sea-view rooms at this calmly stylish hotel on the Ortygia waterfront, at the edge of La Giudecca neighbourhood. Rooms are divided between two buildings, both with pretty tiled floors, walls in teals, greys, blues and

browns, and with a minimal style and a mix of vintage and industrial details.

La Via della Giudecca
B&B €€

(Map p818; ☑389 6429934, 0931 6 84 46; www.laviadellagiudecca.it; Vicolo III alla Giudecca 4; d €70-120, with sea view €110-140, q €120-150; ✳@🖤) Founded in 2010, this charming, immaculate B&B rose phoenix-like from the ashes of a ruined older structure. Winning amenities include crisp white decor, wood floors, spacious rooms (three with sea-view balconies and several accommodating families), a prime location on a picturesque Giudecca piazza, and the warm reception of the Bellomo family (mother and daughters) who run the place.

Alla Giudecca
HOTEL €€

(Map p818; ☑0931 2 22 55; www.allagiudecca.it; Via Alagona 52; d €100-170; ✳@🖤) Located in the old Jewish quarter, this charming hotel boasts 23 suites with warm terracotta-tiled floors, exposed wood beams and lashings of heavy white linen. The communal areas are a warren of vaulted rooms full of museum-quality antiques and enormous tapestries, and feature cosy sofas gathered around huge fireplaces. A few more expensive rooms have sea views.

Hotel Roma
HOTEL €€

(Map p818; ☑0931 46 56 30; www.hotelroma siracusa.it; Via Roma 66; d €130-190; 🅿✳@🖤) Within steps of Piazza del Duomo, this *palazzo* has rooms with parquet floors, oriental rugs, wood-beam ceilings and tasteful artwork, plus free bike use, a gym and a sauna.

★ Henry's House
HOTEL €€€

(Map p818; ☑0931 2 13 61; http://hotelhenrys house.com; Via del Castello Maniace 68; s €120-160, d €150-230, ste €250-330; ✳🖤) Spy this place from outside and you might mistake it for a private home hosting a party you wish you'd been invited to. Directly overlooking Ortygia's waterfront, with three communal sun terraces perfect for lounging and soaking up the views, this gorgeous 17th-century *palazzo* was lovingly restored by antique collector Signor Corsaro before opening as a hotel in 2014.

The result is by far the nicest new lodging to have sprouted on Ortygia in recent years, with superb customer service provided by gregarious English-speaking brothers Francesco and Alberto, newly returned from London to help their father run the place. If you're in a mood to splurge, spring for one of the two upstairs suites (one has a terrace, both enjoy full-on views of the water).

Eating

Ortygia is the best place to eat. Its narrow lanes are chock-full of trattorias, restaurants, cafes and bars, and while some are obvious tourist traps, there are plenty of quality options in the mix. Most places specialise in seafood.

Sicilia in Tavola
SICILIAN €

(Map p818; ☑392 4610889; Via Cavour 28; meals €20-30; ⊙12.30-2.30pm & 7.30-10.30pm Tue-Sun) One of the longest established and most popular eateries on Via Cavour, this tiny trattoria has built its reputation on delicious homemade pasta and seafood. To taste both at once, try the *fettuccine allo scoglio* (pasta ribbons with mixed seafood). Adding to the fun is a bustling atmosphere and the cheerful clutter that adorns the wooden walls. Reservations recommended.

Caseificio Borderi
SANDWICHES €

(Map p818; Via Emanuele de Benedictis 6; sandwiches €5; ⊙6am-5.30pm Mon-Sat) No visit to Syracuse's market is complete without a stop at this colourful cheese shop near Ortygia's far northern tip. Veteran sandwich-master Andrea Borderi stands out front with a table full of cheeses, olives, greens, herbs, tomatoes and other fixings and engages in non-stop banter with customers while creating free-form sandwiches big enough to keep you fed all day.

★ A Putia delle Cose Buone
SICILIAN €€

(Map p818; ☑0931 44 92 79; www.aputiadelle cosebuone.it; Via Roma 8; meals €21-33; ⊙1-3pm & 7-11pm) From the garden gnomes greeting you at the door to the benches draped in colourful pillows, this lovely place feels welcoming from the word go. Then there's the food: creative, reasonably priced Sicilian dishes that make ample use of local seafood, veggies and extra-virgin olive oil (labelled EVO on the menu). Salads, vegan and vegetarian options also abound.

★ Le Vin De L'Assassin Bistrot
MEDITERRANEAN €€

(Map p818; ☑0931 6 61 59; Via Roma 115; meals €30-45; ⊙7.30-11pm Tue-Sun year-round, plus 12.30-2.30pm Sun Oct-May) Bringing a sophisticated touch to Ortygia's dining scene, this stylish restaurant takes an original French twist on Sicilian ingredients. The friendly Sicilian owner, Saro, spent years in Paris and is generous with advice on the plethora of offerings scrawled on the chalkboard nightly, including Breton oysters, impeccably dressed salads, a host of meat and fish mains, and creamy, chocolatey desserts.

Il Blu
SICILIAN €€

(Map p818; www.ristoranteilblu.it; Via Nizza 50; meals €25-30; ⊙noon-4pm & 6pm-3am Apr-Oct, shorter hours Nov-Mar) With its cosy front porch opposite Ortygia's waterfront, this is a great place for *aperitivi* after a dip in the sea. But it really shines at mealtimes, when owner Sebastian whips up two *primi* and two fresh-from-the-water seafood dishes daily according to his whim; think pasta with pistachios, capers, garlic and cherry tomatoes, or tuna steak with wild strawberries.

Taberna Sveva
SICILIAN €€

(Map p818; ☑0931 2 46 63; Piazza Federico di Svevia; meals €28-36; ⊙7-10.30pm nightly Jun-Sep, noon-3pm & 7-10.30pm Thu-Tue Oct-May) Away from the main tourist maelstrom, the charming Taberna Sveva is tucked in a quiet corner of Ortygia. On warm summer evenings the outdoor terrace is the place to sit, with alfresco tables set out on a tranquil cobbled square in front of Syracuse's 13th-century castle. The food is traditional Sicilian, so expect plenty of tuna and swordfish and some wonderful pasta.

Don Camillo
MODERN SICILIAN €€€

(Map p818; ☑0931 6 71 33; www.ristorantedoncamillosiracusa.it; Via Maestranza 96; meals €35-50; ⊙12.30-2.30pm & 7.30-10.30pm Mon-Sat) One of Ortygia's most elegant restaurants, Don Camillo specialises in top service, a classy atmosphere and innovative Sicilian cuisine. Try the starter of mixed shellfish in a thick soup of Noto almonds, lick your lips over the swordfish with orange blossom honey and sweet-and-sour vegetables, or savour the divine *tagliata di tonno* (tuna steak) with red pepper 'marmalade'.

🍷 Drinking & Nightlife

Syracuse is a vibrant university town, which means plenty of life on the streets after nightfall. Many places are clustered near Piazza del Duomo.

Barcollo
BAR

(Map p818; Via Pompeo Picherali 10; ⊙7pm-3am) Hidden away in a historic courtyard, this seductive bar has outdoor deck seating and serves *aperitivi* from 7pm to 10pm.

Biblios Cafè
CAFE

(Map p818; www.biblioscafe.it; Via del Consiglio Reginale 11; ⊙11am-3pm & 6pm-midnight Wed-Mon) This beloved bookshop-cafe organises a whole range of cultural activities, including wine-tasting, literary readings, art classes and language courses. It's a great place to drop in any time of day, for coffee, *aperitivi* or just to mingle.

☆ Entertainment

Piccolo Teatro dei Pupi
THEATRE

(Map p818; ☑328 5326600, 0931 46 55 40; www.pupari.com; Via della Giudecca 17; ⊙shows 4.30pm, 6 times weekly Apr-Oct, fewer Nov-Mar) Syracuse's beloved puppet theatre hosts regular performances; see its website for a calendar. You can also buy puppets at its workshop next door and visit the affiliated puppet museum.

🛍 Shopping

Massimo Izzo
JEWELLERY

(Map p818; www.massimoizzo.com; Piazza Archimede 25; ⊙4-8pm Mon, 9am-1pm & 4-8pm Tue-Sat) The flamboyant jewellery of Messina-born Massimo Izzo is not for the faint-hearted. Featuring bold idiosyncratic designs and made with Sciacca coral, gold and precious stones, his handmade pieces are often inspired by themes close to the Sicilian heart: the sea, theatre and classical antiquity.

Galleria Bellomo
CRAFTS

(Map p818; www.bellomogallery.com; Via Capodieci 15; ⊙10.30am-8pm Mon-Sat, 10.30am-5pm Sun Mar-Oct, closed Sun & lunchtime Nov-Feb) Papyrus paper is the reason to come to this Ortygia gallery near Fontana Aretusa. Here you'll find a range of papery products, including greeting cards, bookmarks and writing paper, as well as a series of watercolour landscapes. Prices start at around €3 for a postcard, rising to hundreds of euros for original works of art.

ℹ Information

Ospedale Umberto I (☑0931 72 40 33; Via Testaferrata 1) Hospital between the centre and Parco Archeologico.

Police Station (☑093 16 51 76; Piazza San Giuseppe) Ortygia's police station.

Tourist Office (Map p818; ☑800 055500, 0931 46 29 46; infoturismo@provsr.it; Via Roma 31; ⊙9am-6.30pm) City maps and lots of good information.

❶ Getting There & Away

Syracuse's train and bus stations are a block apart from each other, halfway between Ortygia and the archaeological park.

BUS

Long-distance buses operate from the bus stop along Corso Umberto, just east of Syracuse's train station.

Interbus (✆ 093 16 67 10; www.interbus.it) runs buses hourly on weekdays (less frequently on weekends) to Catania (€6.20, 1½ hours) and Fontanarossa airport (€6.20, 1¼ hours). Other Interbus destinations include Noto (€3.60, 55 minutes, two to five daily) and Palermo (€13.50, 3¾ hours, two to three daily).

AST (✆ 840 000323; www.aziendasiciliana trasporti.it) offers services to Ragusa (€7.20, 3¼ hours, five daily except Sunday), with intermediate stops in Noto (€4, 55 minutes) and Modica (€6.40, 2¾ hours).

CAR & MOTORCYCLE

The modern A18 and SS114 highways connect Syracuse with Catania and points north, while the SS115 runs south to Noto and Modica. Arriving by car, exit onto the eastbound SS124 and follow signs to Syracuse and Ortygia.

Traffic on Ortygia is restricted; you're better off parking and walking once you arrive on the island. Most convenient is the **Talete parking garage** at Ortygia's northern tip, which charges a 24-hour maximum of €10 (payable by cash or credit card at the machine when you leave). **Molo Sant'Antonio** on the mainland, just across the bridge from Ortygia, is another option.

TRAIN

From Syracuse's **train station** (Via Francesco Crispi), several trains depart daily for Messina (regional/InterCity train €9.70/19.50, 2½ to 3¼ hours) via Catania (€6.35/10, 1¼ hours). Some go on to Rome, Turin and Milan as well as other long-distance destinations. For Palermo, the bus is a better option. There are also local trains from Syracuse to Noto (€3.45, 30 minutes, eight daily except Sunday) and Ragusa (€7.65, two to 2½ hours, two daily except Sunday).

❶ Getting Around

BICYCLE

Syracuse's bike sharing program, **GoBike** (✆ 366 6917046; per day €10, or annual subscription €10, first 30min free, additional hr €1), allows visitors to pick up and return bikes at 12 locations around town. Register and pay fees at any location, including the train station.

BUS

In late 2014, Syracuse's new city government launched an innovative system of gray electric minibuses operated by **Sd'A Trasporti** (www.siracusadamare.it; single ticket/day pass/week pass €0.50/2/7). To reach Ortygia from the bus and train stations, hop aboard bus 1, which loops around the island every half hour or so, making stops at over a dozen convenient locations. To reach Parco Archeologico della Neapolis, take minibus 2 from Molo Sant'Antonio (just west of the bridge to Ortygia). For route maps, see Sd'A Trasporti's website.

Noto

POP 23,800 / ELEV 160M

Flattened by the devastating earthquake of 1693, Noto was grandly rebuilt by its nobles into the finest baroque town in Sicily. Now a Unesco World Heritage Site, the town is especially impressive in the early evening, when its golden-hued sandstone buildings seem to glow with a soft inner light, and at night when illuminations accentuate the beauty of its intricately carved facades. The baroque masterpiece is the work of Rosario Gagliardi and his assistant, Vincenzo Sinatra, local architects who also worked in Ragusa and Modica.

◉ Sights

Two piazzas break up the long Corso Vittorio Emanuele: Piazza dell'Immacolata to the east and Piazza XVI Maggio to the west. The latter is overlooked by the beautiful **Chiesa di San Domenico** and the adjacent **Dominican monastery**, both designed by Rosario Gagliardi. On the same square, Noto's elegant 19th-century **Teatro Comunale** is worth a look. For sweeping views of Noto's baroque splendour, climb to the rooftop terrace at **Chiesa di Santa Chiara** (Corso Vittorio Emanuele; admission €2; ⊙ 9.30am-1pm & 3-7pm) or the *campanile* (bell tower) of **Chiesa di San Carlo al Corso** (Corso Vittorio Emanuele; admission €2; ⊙ 10am-7pm Apr-Oct, 10am-1pm & 3-5pm Nov-Mar).

★**Cattedrale di San Nicolò**   CATHEDRAL (Piazza Municipio; ⊙ 9am-1pm & 3-8pm) Pride of place in Noto goes to San Nicolò Cathedral, a baroque beauty that had to undergo extensive renovation after its dome collapsed during a 1996 thunderstorm. The ensuing decade saw the cathedral scrubbed of centuries of dust and dirt before reopening in 2007. Today the dome, with its peachy glow, is once again the focal point of Noto's skyline.

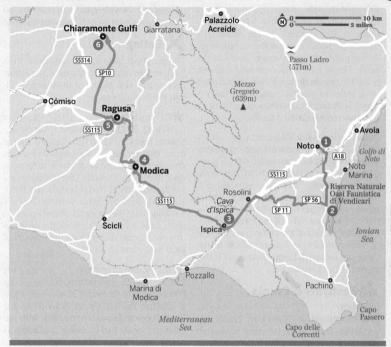

Driving Tour
Baroque Towns

START NOTO
END CHIARAMONTE GULFI
LENGTH 71KM; TWO DAYS

A land of remote rocky gorges, sweeping views and silent valleys, Sicily's southeastern corner is home to the 'baroque triangle', an area of Unesco-listed hilltop towns famous for their lavish baroque architecture. This tour takes in some of the finest baroque towns in Sicily, all within easy driving distance of each other.

Just over 35km south of Syracuse, ❶ **Noto** is home to what is arguably Sicily's most beautiful street – Corso Vittorio Emanuele, a pedestrianised boulevard lined with golden baroque *palazzi*. From Noto, head 12km south along the SP19 to the ❷ **Riserva Naturale Oasi Faunistica di Vendicari**, a coastal preserve whose trails, wetlands and beaches are prime territory for walking, bird-watching and swimming. Next, head 23km southwest along the SP56, SP11 and SS115 to ❸ **Ispica**, a hilltop town overlooking a huge canyon, the Cava d'Ispica, riddled with prehistoric tombs. Continuing up the SS115 for a further 18km brings you to ❹ **Modica**, a bustling town set in a deep rocky gorge. There's excellent accommodation here and a wealth of great restaurants, so this makes a good place to overnight. The best of the baroque sights are up in Modica Alta, the high part of town, but save some energy for the *passeggiata* (evening stroll) on Corso Umberto I in the lower town.

Next morning, a short, winding, up-and-down drive through rock-littered hilltops leads to ❺ **Ragusa**, one of Sicily's nine provincial capitals. The town is divided in two – it's the lower town, Ragusa Ibla, that you want, a claustrophobic warren of grey stone houses and elegant *palazzi* that opens up onto Piazza Duomo, a superb example of 18th-century town planning. Although you can eat well in Ragusa, consider lunching in ❻ **Chiaramonte Gulfi**, a tranquil hilltop town some 20km to the north along the SP10, famous for its olive oil and delicious pork.

Piazza Municipio
PIAZZA

About halfway along Corso Vittorio Emanuele is the graceful Piazza Municipio, flanked by Noto's most dramatic buildings. To the north, sitting in stately pomp at the head of Paolo Labisi's monumental staircase is the Cattedrale di San Nicolò, surrounded by a series of elegant palaces. To the left (west) is **Palazzo Landolina**, once home to the powerful Sant'Alfano family.

Palazzo Nicolaci di Villadorata
PALACE

(☑ 338 7427022; www.comune.noto.sr.it/palazzonicolaci; Via Nicolaci; admission €4; ☺ 10am-6.30pm) The striking facade of this 18th-century palace features wrought-iron balconies supported by a swirling pantomime of grotesque figures. Inside, the *palazzo's* richly brocaded walls and frescoed ceilings offer an idea of the sumptuous lifestyle of Sicilian nobles, as brought to life in the Giuseppe Tomasi di Lampedusa novel *Il gattopardo* (The Leopard).

Festivals & Events

Infiorata
CARNIVAL

(www.infioratadinoto.it; ☺ mid-May) Noto's big annual jamboree is the Infiorata, celebrated over three days around the third Sunday in May with parades, historical re-enactments and the decoration of Via Corrado Nicolaci with designs made entirely of flower petals.

Sleeping

Ostello Il Castello
HOSTEL €

(☑ 320 8388869; www.ostellodinoto.it; Via Fratelli Bandiera 1; dm €18, d €50-70; ☺) This hostel directly uphill from the centre offers excellent value for money. Many of the eight- to 16-bed dorms and private rooms (including some with terraces) command fabulous views over the *duomo* and the city's rooftops. Note that reception is closed in the middle of the day.

La Corte del Sole
INN €€

(☑ 0931 82 02 10; www.lacortedelsole.it; Contrada Bucachemi, Eloro, Lido di Noto; s €93-114, d €122-196; P✳@☺☺) Overlooking the green fields of Eloro is this stylish hotel housed in a traditional Sicilian *masseria* (fortified farmhouse). A delightful place to stay, it also offers a range of activities including **cooking lessons** (☑ 0931 82 02 10; www.lacortedel sole.it; Contrada Bucachemi; 3hr lesson per person €70; ☺ 9.30am-12.30pm Tue-Sat) run by the ho-

tel chef and, in winter, tours to study the 80 or so types of wild orchids found in the area.

Eating

The people of Noto are serious about their food, so take time to enjoy a meal and follow it up with a visit to one of the town's excellent ice-cream shops.

★ Caffè Sicilia
GELATERIA €

(☑ 0931 83 50 13; Corso Vittorio Emanuele 125; desserts from €2; ☺ 8am-11pm Tue-Sun) Dating from 1892 and especially renowned for its *granite*, this beloved place vies with its next-door neighbour, Dolceria Corrado Costanzo, for the honours of Noto's best dessert shop. Frozen desserts are made with the freshest seasonal ingredients (wild strawberries in springtime, for example), while the delicious *torrone* (nougat) bursts with the flavours of local honey and almonds.

★ Ristorante Crocifisso
SICILIAN €€

(☑ 0931 57 11 51; www.ristorantecrocifisso.it; Via Principe Umberto 48; meals €30-40; ☺ noon-3pm & 7.30-11pm Thu-Tue) Up in Noto Alta, this Slow Food–acclaimed restaurant with an extensive wine list is widely regarded as Noto's best. Sicilian classics such as *macco di fave* (broad bean purée with ricotta and toasted breadcrumbs) and *casarecce alla palermitana* (short handmade pasta with sardines and wild fennel) are complemented by juicy roast lamb, Marsala-glazed pork and pistachio- and sesame-crusted tuna.

Il Liberty
MODERN SICILIAN €€

(☑ 0931 57 32 26; www.illiberty.com; Via Cavour 40; meals €33-38; ☺ noon-3pm & 7.30-11pm Tue-Sun) Chef Giuseppe Angelino's contemporary spin on Sicilian cuisine is complemented by an excellent local wine list at this attractive eatery with a stone-vaulted dining room and small front terrace. The menu moves from superb appetisers like *millefoglie* – wafer-thin layers of crusty cheese and ground pistachios with minty sweet-and-sour vegetables – to desserts like blood orange *granita*.

ℹ Information

Tourist Office (☑ 0931 57 37 79; www.comune.noto.sr.it; Piazza XVI Maggio; ☺ 8am-2pm & 3-8pm Apr-Oct, to 7pm Nov-Mar) Helpful tourist office near the west end of Noto's main thoroughfare.

ⓘ Getting There & Around

BUS

From Largo Pantheon on the eastern edge of Noto's historic centre, AST and Interbus serve Catania (€8.40, 1¾ hours) and Syracuse (€3.60 to €4, 55 minutes). Service is less frequent on Sundays.

TRAIN

Trains run to Syracuse (€3.45, 30 minutes, eight daily except Sunday), but Noto's station is inconveniently located 1km downhill from the centre.

Modica

POP 54,700 / ELEV 296M

A powerhouse in Grecian times, Modica remains a superbly atmospheric town with its medieval and baroque buildings climbing steeply up either side of a deep gorge. The multilayered town is divided into Modica Alta (Upper Modica) and Modica Bassa (Lower Modica). A devastating flood in 1902 resulted in the wide avenues of Corso Umberto and Via Giarrantana (the river was dammed and diverted), which remain the main axes of the town, lined by *palazzi* and tiled stone houses.

⊙ Sights

Aside from simply wandering the streets and absorbing the atmosphere, a visit to the extraordinary Chiesa di San Giorgio (Corso San Giorgio; ⊙ 8am-1pm & 3.30-7.30pm) is a highlight. This church, Gagliardi's masterpiece, is a vision of pure rococo splendour, a butter-coloured confection perched on a majestic 250-step staircase. Its counterpoint in Modica Bassa is the Cattedrale di San Pietro (Corso Umberto I), another impressive church atop a rippling staircase lined with life-sized statues of the Apostles.

⊨ Sleeping

★ Villa Quartarella   AGRITURISMO €
(✆ 360 654829; www.quartarella.com; Contrada Quartarella; s €40, d €75-80) Spacious rooms, welcoming hosts and ample breakfasts make this converted villa in the countryside south of Modica an appealing choice for anyone travelling by car. Owners Francesco and Francesca are generous in sharing their love and encyclopaedic knowledge of local history, flora and fauna and can suggest a multitude of driving itineraries in the surrounding area.

B&B Il Cavaliere   B&B €
(✆ 0932 94 72 19; www.palazzoilcavaliere.it; Corso Umberto I 259; d €59-99, ste €89-135; ▣ 🛜) Angle for the beautiful front suite with original tiled floors and frescoed ceilings at this classy B&B in a 19th-century *palazzo*, just down from the bus stop on Modica's main strip. Equally charming are the large, high-ceilinged common rooms, including an elegant breakfast room with lovely views of Chiesa di San Giorgio. Standard rooms are less exciting.

✕ Eating & Drinking

Taverna Nicastro   SICILIAN €
(✆ 0932 94 58 84; www.tavernanicastro.it; Via S Antonino 30; meals €18-25; ⊙ 7.30-10pm Tue-Sat) With nearly 70 years of history and a long-standing Slow Food recommendation, this is one of the upper town's most authentic and atmospheric restaurants, and a bargain to boot. The carnivore-friendly menu includes grilled meat, lamb stew, rabbit with mint leaves, capers and olives, and pasta specialities such as ricotta ravioli with pork *ragù*.

ConTrade   MODERN SICILIAN €€
(✆ 0932 94 86 86; Via Clemente Grimaldi 74; meals €27-33; ⊙ noon-3pm & 6.30-11pm, closed Mon or Tue) Run by a husband-wife duo, and decorated with well-stocked wine racks under old stone arches, this recent arrival whips up beautifully presented classics from *caponata* to *cannoli*, interspersed with delicious personal creations such as Nebrodi black pork with mashed potatoes and walnuts. Service can be slow. Closing day varies seasonally.

Rappa Enoteca   WINE BAR
(Corso Santa Teresa 97-99; ⊙ 4.30pm-late Mon-Sat) High ceilings, antique mouldings, tiled floors and chandeliers create a delightful backdrop at this atmospheric *enoteca* in the upper town. Sample a wide range of Sicilian wines, along with cheese and meat platters.

🛍 Shopping

Dolceria Bonajuto   FOOD
(✆ 0932 94 12 25; www.bonajuto.it; Corso Umberto I 159; ⊙ 9am-8.30pm) Sicily's oldest chocolate factory is the perfect place to taste Modica's famous chocolate. Flavoured with cinnamon, vanilla, orange peel and even hot peppers, it's a legacy of the town's Spanish overlords who imported cocoa from their South American colonies.

❶ Information

Tourist Office (✆346 6558227; www.
comune.modica.rg.it; Corso Umberto I 141;
☺9am-1pm & 3.30-7pm Mon-Sat) City-run
tourist office in Modica Bassa.

❶ Getting There & Away

BUS

AST (✆0932 76 73 01; www.aziendasiciliana
trasporti.it) runs frequent buses Monday to
Saturday from Piazzale Falcone-Borsellino at
the top of Corso Umberto I to Syracuse (€6.40,
2¾ hours), Noto (€4, 1¾ hours) and Ragusa
(€2.70, 30 minutes); on Sunday, service is
limited (two buses each to Noto and Ragusa, no
service to Syracuse).

TRAIN

From Modica's station, 600m southwest of
the centre, there are four trains daily (except
Sunday) to Syracuse (€7, 1½ hours) and three
to Ragusa (€2.25, 25 minutes).

Ragusa

POP 72,800 / ELEV 502M

Like a grand old dame, Ragusa is a dignified and well-aged provincial town. Like
every other town in the region, Ragusa
collapsed after the 1693 earthquake; a
new town called Ragusa Superiore was
built on a high plateau above the original
settlement. But the old aristocracy were
loath to leave their tottering *palazzi* and
rebuilt Ragusa Ibla on the original site.
The two towns were only merged in 1927.

Ragusa Ibla remains the heart and soul
of the town, and has all the best restaurants and the majority of sights. A sinuous bus ride or some very steep and scenic
steps connect the lower town to its modern sister up the hill.

◉ Sights

Grand churches and *palazzi* line the
twisting, narrow streets of Ragusa Ibla,
interspersed with gelaterie and delightful piazzas where the local youth
stroll and the elderly gather on benches.
Palm-planted Piazza del Duomo, the centre of town, is dominated by the 18th-
century **Cattedrale di San Giorgio** (Piazza Duomo; ☺10am-12.30pm & 4-6.30pm), with
its magnificent neoclassical dome and
stained-glass windows.

At the eastern end of the old town is the
Giardino Ibleo (☺8am-8pm), a pleasant
public garden laid out in the 19th century and currently undergoing an extensive
renovation. It's the perfect spot for a picnic lunch.

⌯ Sleeping

L'Orto Sul Tetto   B&B €
(✆0932 24 77 85; www.lortosultetto.it; Via
Tenente di Stefano 56; s €45-60, d €70-110;
❄⦿) This sweet little B&B behind Ragusa's *duomo* offers an intimate experience,
with just three rooms and a lovely roof
terrace where breakfast is served.

Tenuta Zannafondo   B&B €
(✆0932 183 89 19; www.tenutazannafondo.
it; Contrada di Zannafondo; d €79; ❄⦿) Set
amidst olive-sprinkled hillsides lined
with stone walls, this recently converted
19th-century farmstead sits halfway between Ragusa and the coast (a 15-minute
drive from each). Its charm lies in the
tranquil cluster of independent stone-
walled cottages, each with its own little
terrace; two rooms in the main house are
less appealing. Breakfast is included, and
dinner is available on request.

✕ Eating

★**Quattro Gatti**   SICILIAN, SLOVAK €
(✆0932 24 56 12; Via Valverde 95; meals €20-
25; ☺8-11.30pm Tue-Sun) This cosy Sicilian-
Slovak–run eatery near the Giardino Ibleo
serves an amazing four-course fixed-price
menu bursting with fresh, local flavours.
The antipasti spread is especially memorable, as are the seasonally changing specials scribbled on the blackboard up front.
Slovak-inspired offerings such as goulash
and apple strudel round out a menu of Sicilian classics.

Gelati DiVini   GELATERIA €
(✆0932 22 89 89; www.gelatidivini.it; Piazza Duomo 20; ice cream from €2; ☺10am-midnight)
This exceptional gelateria makes wine-
flavoured ice creams like Marsala, passito
and muscat, plus other unconventional
offerings such as pine nut, watermelon,
ricotta, and chocolate with spicy peppers.

A Rusticana   TRATTORIA €€
(✆0932 22 79 81; Via Domenico Morelli 4; meals
€20-32; ☺12.30-3pm & 7.30-10pm Wed-Mon)
Fans of the *Montalbano* TV series will
want to eat here, as it's where scenes
set in the fictional Trattoria San Calogero were filmed. In reality, it's a cheerful,

SICILY'S BEST-PRESERVED ROMAN MOSAICS

Near the town of Piazza Armerina in central Sicily is the stunning 3rd-century Roman **Villa Romana del Casale**, a Unesco World Heritage Site and one of the few remaining sites of Roman Sicily. This sumptuous hunting lodge is thought to have belonged to Diocletian's co-emperor Marcus Aurelius Maximianus. Buried under mud in a 12th-century flood, it remained hidden for 700 years before its magnificent floor mosaics were discovered in the 1950s. Visit out of season or early in the day to avoid the hordes of tourists.

The mosaics cover almost the entire floor (3500 sq metres) of the villa and are considered unique for their narrative style, the range of subject matter and variety of colour – many are clearly influenced by African themes. Along the eastern end of the internal courtyard is the wonderful **Corridor of the Great Hunt**, vividly depicting chariots, rhinos, cheetahs, lions and the voluptuously beautiful Queen of Sheba. Across the corridor is a series of apartments, where floor illustrations reproduce scenes from Homer's *Odyssey*. But perhaps the most captivating of the mosaics is the so-called **Room of the Ten Girls in Bikinis**, with depictions of sporty girls in scanty bikinis throwing a discus, using weights and throwing a ball; they would blend in well on a Malibu beach. These most famous of Piazza Armerina's mosaics were fully reopened to the public in 2013 after years of painstaking restoration and are among Sicily's greatest classical treasures.

Travelling by car from Piazza Armerina, follow signs south of town to the SP15, then continue 5km to reach the villa.

Getting here without a car is more challenging. Buses operated by **Interbus** (p813) from Catania (€9.20, 1¾ hours) or **SAIS** (☑093 568 01 19; www.saisautolinee.it) from Enna (€3.60, 40 minutes) run to Piazza Armerina; from here catch a local bus (€1, 30 minutes, May to September only) or a taxi (€20) the remaining 5km.

boisterous trattoria whose generous portions and relaxed vine-covered terrace ensure a loyal clientele. The food is defiantly *casareccia* (home-style), so expect no-frills pasta and uncomplicated cuts of grilled meat.

Ristorante Duomo　　MODERN SICILIAN €€€
(☑0932 65 12 65; www.cicciosultano.it; Via Capitano Bocchieri 31; lunch menus €45-59, dinner tasting menus €120-190; ☺noon-3pm Tue-Sat, plus 7.30-11pm Mon-Sat) Widely regarded as one of Sicily's finest restaurants, Duomo comprises a cluster of small rooms outfitted like private parlours behind its stained-glass door, ensuring a suitably romantic ambience for chef Ciccio Sultano's refined creations. The menu abounds in classic Sicilian ingredients such as pistachios, fennel, almonds and Nero d'Avola wine, combined in imaginative and unconventional ways. Booking is essential.

ℹ Information

Tourist Office (☑366 8742621; infotourist. ibla@comune.ragusa.gov.it; Piazza della Repubblica; ☺9am-7pm Mon-Fri, to 2pm Sat

& Sun) Ragusa Ibla branch of the municipal tourist office.

ℹ Getting There & Around

BUS

Long-distance and municipal buses share a terminal on Via Zama in the upper town. Buy tickets at the Interbus/Etna kiosk in the main lot or at cafes around the corner. **Interbus** (www.interbus.it) runs to Catania (€8.60, two hours, five to 12 daily). **AST** (☑0932 68 18 18; www.aziendasicilianatrasporti.it) serves Syracuse (€7.20, 2¾ to 3¼ hours, three daily except Sunday) with intermediate stops in Modica (€2.70, 30 minutes) and Noto (€6, 2¼ hours).

Monday through Saturday, AST's city buses 11 and 33 (€1.10) run hourly between the Via Zama bus terminal and Giardino Ibleo in Ragusa Ibla. On Sundays, bus 1 makes a similar circuit.

TRAIN

From the station in the upper town, there's one direct train daily except Sunday to Syracuse (€7.65, two hours) via Noto (€5.75, 1½ hours).

FIONLINE/GETTY IMAGES ©

1. Teatro Greco, Taormina 2. Selinunte ruins 3. Doric Temple, Segesta 4. Mosaic, Villa Romana del Casale

OLIVIER CIRENDINI/GETTY IMAGES ©

A Graeco-Roman Legacy

As the crossroads of the Mediterranean since the dawn of time, Sicily has seen countless civilisations come and go. The island's classical treasure trove includes Greek temples and amphitheatres, Roman mosaics and a host of fine archaeological museums.

Valle dei Templi

Crowning the craggy heights of Agrigento's Valle dei Templi (p830) are five Doric temples – including stunning Tempio della Concordia, one of the best preserved in all of Magna Graecia. Throw in the superb archaeological museum and you've got Sicily's most cohesive and impressive collection of Greek treasures.

Villa Romana del Casale

Bikini-clad gymnasts and wild African beasts prance side by side in remarkable floor decorations in this ancient Roman hunting lodge (p827). Buried under mud for centuries and now gleaming from restoration work completed in 2013, they're the most extensive mosaics in Sicily and a Unesco World Heritage Site.

Segesta

Segesta's perfect Doric temple (p839) perches on a windswept hilltop above a rugged river gorge.

Taormina

With spectacular views of snowcapped Mt Etna and the Ionian Sea, Taormina's Teatro Greco (p804) makes the perfect venue for the town's summer film and arts festivals.

Selinunte

Selinunte's vast ruins (p835) poke out of wildflower-strewn fields beside the sparkling Mediterranean.

Syracuse

Once the most powerful city in the Mediterranean, Syracuse (p815) brims with reminders of its ancient past, from the Greek columns supporting Ortygia's cathedral to the annual festival of classical Greek drama, staged in a 2500-year-old amphitheatre.

CENTRAL SICILY & THE MEDITERRANEAN COAST

Central Sicily is a land of vast panoramas, undulating fields, severe mountain ridges and hilltop towns. Moving towards the Mediterranean, the perspective changes, as ancient temples jostle for position with modern high-rise apartments outside Agrigento, Sicily's most lauded classical site and also one of its busier modern cities.

Agrigento

POP 59,100 / ELEV 230M

Agrigento does not make a good first impression. Seen from a distance, the modern city's rows of unsightly apartment blocks loom incongruously on the hillside, distracting attention from the splendid Valley of the Temples below, where the ancient Greeks once built their great city of Akragas. Never fear: once you get down among the ruins, their monumental grace becomes apparent, and it's easy to understand how this remarkable complex of temples became Sicily's pre-eminent travel destination, first put on the tourist map by Goethe in the 18th century.

Three kilometres uphill from the temples, Agrigento's medieval core is a pleasant place to pass the evening after a day exploring the ruins. The intercity bus and train stations are both in the upper town, within a few blocks of Via Atenea, the main street of the medieval city.

◉ Sights

◉ Valle dei Templi

★ **Valley of the Temples** ARCHAEOLOGICAL SITE
(Valle dei Templi; www.parcovalledeitempli.it; adult/reduced €10/5, incl Museo Archeologico €13.50/7; ☺8.30am-7pm year-round, plus 8-10pm Mon-Fri, 8-11pm Sat & Sun mid-Jul–mid-Sep) Sicily's most enthralling archaeological site encompasses the ruined ancient city of Akragas, highlighted by the stunningly well-preserved **Tempio della Concordia** (Temple of Concord), one of several ridge-top temples that once served as beacons for homecoming sailors. The 1300-hectare park, 3km south of Agrigento, is split into eastern and western zones. Ticket offices with car parks are at the park's eastern edge and along the main road dividing the eastern and western zones.

★ **Museo Archeologico** MUSEUM
(☑0922 40 15 65; Contrada San Nicola 12; adult/reduced €8/4, incl Valley of the Temples €13.50/7; ☺9am-7pm Tue-Sat, 9am-1pm Sun & Mon) North of the temples, this wheelchair-accessible museum is one of Sicily's finest, with a huge collection of clearly labelled artefacts from the excavated site. Noteworthy are the dazzling displays of Greek painted ceramics and the awe-inspiring reconstructed telamon, a colossal statue recovered from the nearby Tempio di Giove.

◉ Medieval Agrigento

Chiesa di Santa Maria dei Greci CHURCH
(www.cattedraleagrigento.com; Salita Santa Maria dei Greci; ☺10am-1pm Mon-Sat) This small church stands on the site of a 5th-century Doric temple dedicated to Athena. Inside are some badly damaged Byzantine frescoes, the remains of a Norman ceiling and traces of the original Greek columns.

Monastero di Santo Spirito CONVENT
(☑0922 2 06 64; www.monasterosantospirito
ag.org; Calle Santo Spirito 9) At the top of a set of steps off Via Atenea, this convent was founded by Cistercian nuns around 1290. A handsome Gothic portal leads inside, where the nuns are still in residence, praying, meditating and baking heavenly sweets, including *cuscusu* (sweet couscous made with local pistachios), *dolci di mandorla* (almond pastries) and *conchiglie* (shell-shaped sweets filled with pistachio paste). Press the doorbell and say *'Vorrei comprare qualche dolce'* ('I'd like to buy a few sweets').

Tours

Associazione Guide Turistiche Agrigento WALKING TOUR
(☑345 8815992; www.agrigentoguide.org) Agrigento's official tour guide association offers guided visits of the Valley of the Temples, Agrigento and the surrounding area in English and eight other languages.

🎊 Festivals & Events

Sagra del Mandorlo in Fiore CULTURAL
(☺Feb) This 11-day folk festival spans two weekends in February, when the Valley of the Temples is cloaked in almond blossoms.

🛌 Sleeping

Fattoria Mosè AGRITURISMO €
(☑0922 60 61 15; www.fattoriamose.com; Via Mattia Pascal 4a; r per person €48, incl breakfast/half-board €58/81; ☒) If Agrigento's urban jungle's got you down, head for this authentic

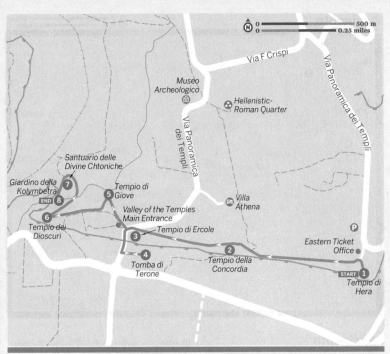

🏃 Archaeological Walking Tour
Valley of the Temples

START TEMPIO DI HERA
END GIARDINO DELLA KOLYMBETRA
LENGTH 3KM; THREE HOURS

Begin your exploration in the so-called Eastern Zone, home to Agrigento's best-preserved temples. From the eastern ticket office, a short walk leads to the 5th-century BC **1 Tempio di Hera**, perched on the ridgetop. Though partly destroyed by an earthquake, the colonnade remains largely intact, as does a long sacrificial altar. Traces of red are the result of fire damage likely dating to the Carthaginian invasion of 406 BC.

Next descend past a gnarled 500-year-old olive tree and a series of Byzantine tombs to the **2 Tempio della Concordia** (p830). This remarkable edifice, the model for Unesco's logo, has survived almost entirely intact since its construction in 430 BC, partly due to its conversion into a Christian basilica in the 6th century, and partly thanks to the shock-absorbing, earthquake-dampening qualities of the soft clay underlying its hard rock foundation.

Further downhill, the **3 Tempio di Ercole** is Agrigento's oldest, dating from the end of the 6th century BC. Down from the main temples, the miniature **4 Tomba di Terone** dates to 75 BC. Cross the pedestrian bridge into the Western Zone, stopping first at the **5 Tempio di Giove**. This would have been the world's largest Doric temple had its construction not been interrupted by the Carthaginian sacking of Akragas. A later earthquake reduced it to the crumbled ruin you see today. Lying flat on his back amid the rubble is an 8m-tall telamon (a sculpted figure of a man with arms raised), originally intended to support the temple's weight. It's actually a copy; the original is in Agrigento's archaeological museum.

Take a brief look at the ruined 5th-century BC **6 Tempio dei Dioscuri** and the 6th-century BC complex of altars and small buildings known as the **7 Santuario delle Divine Chtoniche**, before ending your visit in the **8 Giardino della Kolymbetra**, a lush garden in a natural cleft near the sanctuary.

Agrigento

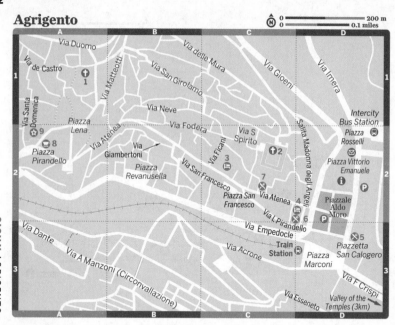

Agrigento

organic *agriturismo* 6km east of the Valley of the Temples. Four suites, six self-catering apartments and a pool offer ample space to relax. Guests can opt for reasonably priced dinners (including wine) built around the farm's organic produce, cook for themselves or even enjoy cooking courses on site.

PortAtenea B&B €
(☏ 349 0937492; www.portatenea.com; Via Atenea, cnr Via C Battisti; s €39-50, d €59-75, tr €79-95; ❋🛜) This five-room B&B wins plaudits for

its spacious, well-appointed rooms, its panoramic roof terrace overlooking the Valley of the Temples, and its convenient location at the entrance to the Old Town, just a stone's throw from the train and bus stations.

Camere a Sud B&B €
(☏ 349 6384424; www.camereasud.it; Via Ficani 6; r €60-70; ❋@🛜) This lovely B&B in the medieval centre has three guest rooms decorated with style and taste – traditional decor and contemporary textiles are matched with bright colours and modern art. Breakfast is served on the terrace in the warmer months.

Villa Athena HISTORIC HOTEL €€€
(☏ 092 259 62 88; www.hotelvillaathena.it; Via Passeggiata Archeologica 33; r €281-432, ste €408-842; 🅿❋@🛜🏊) With the Tempio della Concordia lit up in the near distance and palm trees lending an exotic *Arabian Nights* feel, this historic five-star hotel in an aristocratic 18th-century villa offers the ultimate luxury experience. The cavernous Villa Suite, floored in antique tiles with a free-standing jacuzzi and a vast terrace overlooking the temples, might well be Sicily's coolest hotel room.

🍴 Eating & Drinking

On a hot day, nothing refreshes like a chilled glass of almond milk, made from Agrigento's famous almonds mixed with sugar, water and a hint of lemon rind; the classic place to try it is at **Caffè Concordia** (Piazza Pirandello 36; ☉6am-9.30pm Tue-Sat) near Teatro Pirandello.

Trattoria Concordia　　　　　TRATTORIA €
(☑0922 2 26 68; Via Porcello 8; meals €18-30; ☉noon-3pm & 7-10.30pm Mon-Fri, 7-11pm Sat) Rough stone walls and wood-beamed ceilings lend a cosy atmosphere to this quintessential family run trattoria, tucked up a side alley in the Old Town. Traditional Sicilian starters (frittata, sweet-and-sour aubergine, ricotta and olives) are complemented by tasty grilled fish and meats.

Sal8　　　　　INTERNATIONAL €
(☑0922 66 19 90; Via Cesare Battisti 8; meals €15-25; ☉noon-11pm) Creative and reasonably priced light meals complement a good drinks list at this newly opened wine bar near the entrance to Via Atenea. Depending on the chef's whim, expect anything from sushi to seafood *tagliatelle* to tapas with a Sicilian twist – think shrimp and broad bean cakes or *panelle* (chickpea fritters) served with sparkling wine.

★**Kalòs**　　　　　MODERN SICILIAN €€
(☑092 22 63 89; www.ristorantekalos.it; Piazzetta San Calogero; meals €28-45; ☉12.30-3pm & 7-11pm Tue-Sun) For fine dining, head to this 'smart' restaurant just outside the historic centre. Five cute tables on little balconies offer a delightful setting to enjoy homemade pasta *all'agrigentina* (with fresh tomatoes, basil and almonds), grilled lamb chops, citrus shrimp or *spada gratinata* (baked swordfish covered in breadcrumbs). Superb desserts, including homemade *cannoli* and almond *semifreddi*, round out the menu.

☆ Entertainment

Teatro Pirandello　　　　　THEATRE
(☑0922 59 02 20; www.teatroluigipirandello.it; Piazza Pirandello; tickets €18-23) This city-run theatre is Sicily's third largest, after Palermo's Teatro Massimo and Catania's Teatro Massimo Bellini. Works by local hero Luigi Pirandello figure prominently. The program runs from November to early May.

ⓘ Information

Ospedale San Giovanni di Dio (☑0922 44 21 11; Contrada Consolida) North of the centre.

Police Station (☑0922 48 31 11; Piazza Vittorio Emanuele 2)

Tourist Office (☑800 236837; www.provincia. agrigento.it; Piazzale Aldo Moro 1; ☉8.30am-1pm & 2.30-7pm Mon-Fri, 8.30am-1pm Sat) In the provincial government building.

ⓘ Getting There & Away

BUS
The intercity bus station and ticket booths are located on Piazza Rosselli. **Cuffaro** (☑091 616 15 10; www.cuffaro.info) operates eight buses to Palermo (€9, two hours) Monday to Friday, six on Saturday and three on Sunday. **Autoservizi Camilleri** (☑0922 47 18 86; www.camilleri argentoelattuca.it) also runs to Palermo one to five times daily. **SAL** (Società Autolinee Licata; ☑0922 40 13 60; www.autolineesal.it) offers direct service to Palermo's Falcone-Borsellino airport (€12.60, 2¾ hours, three to four departures Monday to Saturday). **Lumia** (☑0922 2 04 14; www.autolineelumia.it) has departures to Trapani and its Birgi airport (€11.90, three to four hours, three daily Monday to Saturday, one on Sunday), while **SAIS Trasporti** (☑092 22 93 24; www.saistrasporti.it) runs buses to Catania (€13.40, three hours, 10 to 14 daily).

CAR & MOTORCYCLE
The SS189 links Agrigento with Palermo, while the SS115 runs along the coast, northwest towards Trapani and southeast to Syracuse.

Driving in the medieval town is near impossible due to all the pedestrianised streets. There's metered parking at the train station and free parking along Via Esseneto just below.

TRAIN
From Agrigento Centrale station (Piazza Marconi), direct trains run regularly to Palermo (€8.30, two hours, seven to 10 daily). Service to Catania (€10.40 to €17.60, 3¼ to 5¼ hours) is less frequent and requires a change of trains. For other destinations, you're better off taking the bus.

ⓘ Getting Around

TUA (Trasporti Urbani Agrigento; ☑0922 41 20 24; www.trasportiurbaniagrigento.it) runs buses down to the Valley of the Temples from the Intercity Bus Station, stopping in front of the train station en route. Take bus 1, 2 or 3 (tickets €1.20 from tobacconists, €1.70 on board) and get off at either the museum or the main entrance to the temples (between the Tempio di Giove and the Tempio di Ercole). The Linea Verde (Green Line) departs every 50 minutes from the train station, running the length of Via Atenea and looping through the medieval town centre.

WESTERN SICILY

Directly across the water from North Africa and still retaining vestiges of the Arab, Phoenician and Greek cultures that once prevailed here, western Sicily has a bit of the Wild West about it. There's plenty to stir the senses, from Trapani's savoury fish couscous, to the dazzling views from hilltop Erice, to the wild coastal beauty of Riserva Naturale dello Zingaro.

Marsala

POP 82,300

Best known for its sweet dessert wines, Marsala revolves around its lovely, elegant core of stately baroque buildings within a perfect square of walls. To the east and north lie less attractive modern outskirts that gradually peter out into the surrounding vineyards.

The city was originally founded by Phoenician escapees from the Roman onslaught at nearby Mozia. Not wanting to risk a second attack, they fortified their new home with 7m-thick walls, ensuring that it was the last Punic settlement to fall to the Romans. In AD 830 it was conquered by the Arabs, who gave it its current name, Marsa Allah (Port of God).

It was here in 1860 that Giuseppe Garibaldi, leader of the movement for Italian unification, landed in his rickety old boats with his 1000-strong army – a claim to fame that finds its way into every tourist brochure.

◉ Sights & Activities

For a taste of local life, take a stroll at sunset around pretty Piazza della Repubblica, heart of the historic centre.

Museo Archeologico Baglio Anselmi   MUSEUM
(☑0923 95 25 35; Lungomare Boeo; adult/reduced €4/2; ☉9am-8pm Tue-Sat, 9am-1.30pm Mon) Marsala's finest treasure is the partially reconstructed remains of a Carthaginian *liburna* (warship) sunk off the Egadi Islands during the First Punic War. Displayed alongside objects from its cargo, the ship's bare bones provide the only remaining physical evidence of the Phoenicians' seafaring superiority in the 3rd century BC, offering a glimpse of a civilisation extinguished by the Romans.

Whitaker Museum   MUSEUM
(☑0923 71 25 98; www.fondazionewhitaker.it; adult/child €9/5; ☉9.30am-1.30pm & 2.30-6.30pm Apr-Oct, 9am-3pm Nov-Mar) This museum on San Pantaleo island, 10km north of Marsala, houses a unique collection of Phoenician artefacts assembled over decades by amateur archaeologist Joseph Whitaker. Its greatest treasure (recently returned to Sicily after two years at London's British Museum and Los Angeles' Getty) is *Il giovinetto di Mozia,* a 5th-century-BC Carthaginian-influenced marble statue of a young man.

To get here, drive or bike to the Mozia dock 10km north of Marsala and catch one of the half-hourly, 10-minute ferries operated by Mozia Line (☑338 7860474, 0923 98 92 49; www.mozialine.com; adult/reduced €5/2.50; ☉9.15am-6.30pm).

Cantine Florio   WINERY
(☑0923 78 11 11; www.duca.it/cantineflorio; Via Vincenzo Florio 1; tours €10; ☉wine shop 9am-1pm & 3.30-6pm Mon-Fri, 9.30am-1pm Sat, English-language tours 3.30pm Mon-Fri, 10.30am Sat year-round, plus 11am Mon-Fri Apr-Oct) These venerable wine cellars just east of town open their doors to visitors to explain the Marsala-making process and the fascinating history of local viticulture. Afterwards visitors can sample the goods in Florio's spiffy tasting room (tastes of two Marsalas and a moscato, accompanied by hors d'oeuvres, are included in the tour price). Take bus 16 from Piazza del Popolo. Other producers in the same area include Pellegrino, Donnafugata, Rallo, Mavis and Intorcia.

🛏 Sleeping & Eating

★Il Profumo del Sale   B&B €
(☑0923 189 04 72; www.ilprofumodelsale.it; Via Vaccari 8; s €35-40, d €50-60; ☎) Perfectly positioned in Marsala's historic city centre, this lovely B&B offers three attractive rooms – including a palatial front unit with cathedral views from its small balcony – enhanced by welcoming touches like almond cookies, fine soaps and ample breakfasts featuring homemade bread and jams. Sophisticated owner Celsa is full of helpful tips about Marsala and the surrounding area.

Hotel Carmine   HOTEL €€
(☑0923 71 19 07; www.hotelcarmine.it; Piazza Carmine 16; s €75-105, d €105-130; ▣❄@☎) This lovely hotel in a converted 16th-century monastery has elegant rooms (especially numbers 7 and 30), with original blue-and-gold majolica tiles, stone walls, antique furniture and lofty beamed ceilings. Enjoy your cornflakes in the baronial-style breakfast room with its historic frescoes and over-the-top chandelier, or sip your drink by the roaring fireplace in winter. Modern perks include a rooftop solarium.

★San Lorenzo Osteria   SICILIAN €€
(SLO; ☑0923 71 25 93; Via Garraffa 60; meals €25-35; ☉7.30-10.30pm Wed-Mon; ☎) With roots as a wedding-catering business, this stylish eatery is a class act all round – from the ever-changing menu of fresh seafood scrawled

daily on the blackboard to the interior's sleek modern lines to the gorgeous presentation of the food. The stellar wine list features some local choices you won't find elsewhere.

Assud   MODERN SICILIAN €€
(☑ 0923 71 66 52; www.assud.eu; Via Armando Diaz 66; meals €25-35; ⊗ noon-3pm & 6.30-11pm Tue-Sun) Good wines accompany the short but sweet menu at this newcomer straddling Marsala's historic walls. The nightly evolving mix of inventive antipasti, *primi* and *secondi* (three to four in each category) might include anything from seafood couscous to a *tris di arancine* (three re-imagined versions of Sicily's classic rice balls, filled respectively with meat, aubergine and ricotta, and squid ink).

❶ Information

Tourist Office (☑ 0923 71 40 97, 0923 99 33 38; ufficioturistico.proloco@comune.marsala. tp.it; Via XI Maggio 100; ⊗ 8.30am-1.30pm & 3-8pm Mon-Fri, 8.30am-1.30pm Sat) Spacious office with comfy couches right off the main square; provides a wide range of maps and brochures.

❶ Getting There & Away

From Marsala, bus operators include **Lumia** (www.autolineelumia.it), which goes to Agrigento (€10.10, 2¾ hours, one to three daily), and **Salemi** (☑ 0923 98 11 20; www.autoservizisalemi. it) to Palermo (€11, 2½ hours, at least 11 daily).

Train is the best way to get to Trapani (€3.45, 30 minutes, 10 Monday through Saturday, four on Sunday).

Selinunte

The **ruins of Selinunte** (☑ 0924 4 62 77; adult/reduced €6/3; ⊗ 9am-6pm Apr-Oct, 9am-4pm Nov-Mar) are the most impressively sited in Sicily. The huge city was built in 628 BC on a promontory overlooking the sea, and over two and a half centuries became one of the richest and most powerful in the world. It was destroyed by the Carthaginians in 409 BC and finally fell to the Romans in about 350 BC, at which time it went into rapid decline and disappeared from history. The city's past is so remote that the names of the various temples have been forgotten and they are now identified by the letters A to G, M and O. The most impressive, **Temple E**, has been partially rebuilt, its columns pieced together from their fragments with part of its tympanum. Many of the carvings, particularly from **Temple C**, are now in the archaeological museum in Palermo. They

are on a par with the Parthenon marbles and clearly demonstrate the high cultural levels reached by Greek colonies in Sicily.

The ticket office and entrance to the ruins is located near the eastern temples. Try to visit in spring when the surroundings are ablaze with wildflowers.

For overnight stays, **Sicilia Cuore Mio** (☑ 0924 4 60 77; www.siciliacuoremio.it; Via della Cittadella 44; d €68-95; 🛜 🛖) is a lovely B&B with an upstairs terrace overlooking both the ruins and the sea. Guests enjoy breakfast (including homemade jams, *cannoli* and more) on a shady patio bordered by olive trees. Escape the touristy and mediocre restaurants near the ruins by heading for **Lido Zabbara** (☑ 0924 4 61 94; Via Pigafetta; buffet per person €12), a beachfront place in nearby Marinella di Selinunte with good grilled fish and a varied buffet. You could also drive 15km east to **Da Vittorio** (☑ 0925 7 83 81; www.ristorantevittorio.it; Porto Palo; meals €30-45) in Porto Palo, another great place to enjoy seafood, sunset and the sound of lapping waves.

Selinunte is midway between Agrigento and Trapani, about 10km south of the junction of the A29 and SS115 near Castelvetrano. **Autoservizi Salemi** (☑ 0924 8 18 26; http://autoservizisalemi.it/tratte/selinunte) runs five to seven buses daily from Selinunte to Castelvetrano (€2, 25 to 35 minutes), where you can make onward bus connections with **Lumia** (www.autolineelumia.it) to Agrigento (€8.60, two hours), or train connections to Marsala (€3.95, 35 to 45 minutes), Trapani (€5.75, 1¼ hours) and Palermo (€7.65, 2½ hours).

Trapani

POP 70,600

The lively port city of Trapani makes a convenient base for exploring Sicily's western tip. Its historic centre is filled with atmospheric pedestrian streets and some lovely churches and baroque buildings, although the heavily developed outskirts are rather bleak. The surrounding countryside is beautiful, ranging from the watery vastness of the **Saline di Trapani**, coastal salt ponds interspersed with windmills south of town, to the rugged mountainous shoreline to the north. Once situated at the heart of a powerful trading network that stretched from Carthage to Venice, Trapani's sickle-shaped spit of land hugs the precious harbour, nowadays busy with a steady stream of tourists and traffic to and from Pantelleria and the Egadi Islands.

SICILY SELINUNTE

◉ Sights

The narrow network of streets in Trapani's historic centre remains a Moorish labyrinth, although it takes much of its character from the fabulous 18th-century baroque of the Spanish period. Especially appealing is pedestrianised Corso Vittorio Emanuele, punctuated by the huge **Cattedrale di San Lorenzo** (Corso Vittorio Emanuele; ⊙ 8am-4pm), with its baroque facade and stuccoed interior, and flanked at its eastern end by another baroque confection, the **Palazzo Senatorio** (cnr Corso Vittorio Emanuele & Via Torrearsa). The best time to stroll here is in the early evening (around 7pm) when the *passeggiata* is in full swing. Several other fine examples of baroque architecture can be found along Via Garibaldi.

Chiesa del Purgatorio CHURCH
(🖉 0923 56 28 82; Via San Francesco d'Assisi; voluntary donation requested; ⊙ 7.30am-noon & 4-7pm Mon-Sat, 10am-noon & 4-7pm Sun) Just off the *corso* in the heart of the city, this church houses the impressive 18th-century *Misteri*, 20 life-sized wooden effigies depicting the story of Christ's Passion, which take centre stage during the city's dramatic Easter Week processions every year. Panels in English, Italian, French and German explain the story behind each figure.

Museo Nazionale Pepoli MUSEUM
(🖉 0923 55 32 69; www.comune.trapani.it/turismo/pepoli.htm; Via Conte Pepoli 180; adult/reduced €6/3; ⊙ 9am-5.30pm Mon-Sat, 9am-12.30pm Sun) In a former Carmelite monastery, this museum houses the collection of Conte Pepoli, who devoted his life to salvaging Trapani's local arts and crafts, most notably the garish coral carvings – once all the rage in Europe before Trapani's offshore coral banks were decimated. The museum also has a good collection of Gagini sculptures, silverwork, archaeological artefacts and religious art.

Egadi Islands ISLANDS
The islands of **Levanzo**, **Favignana** and **Marettimo** make a pleasant day trip from Trapani. For centuries the lucrative tuna industry fuelled the islands' economy, but overfishing of the surrounding waters means that the Egadi survive primarily on income from tourists who come to cycle, walk, dive or simply enjoy the relaxed pace of life. Siremar and Ustica Lines both run year-round hydrofoil service to the islands. The best range of meals and accommodation can be found on Favignana.

The islands' single greatest tourist attraction is Levanzo's **Grotta del Genovese**, a cave decorated with Mesolithic and Neolithic artwork, including a famous image of a prehistoric tuna. Marettimo offers off-the-beaten-track seclusion and excellent walking trails.

⚜ Festivals & Events

I Misteri RELIGIOUS
(www.processionemisteritp.it) Sicily's most venerated Easter procession is a four-day festival of extraordinary religious fervour. Nightly processions, bearing life-sized wooden effigies, make their way through the old quarter to a specially erected chapel in Piazza Lucatelli. The high point is on Good Friday when the celebrations reach fever pitch.

🛏 Sleeping

The most convenient – and nicest – place to stay is in Trapani's pedestrianised historic centre, just north of the port.

Ai Lumi B&B B&B €
(🖉 0923 54 09 22; www.ailumi.it; Corso Vittorio Emanuele 71; s €40-70, d €70-100, tr €90-125, q €100-150; ❋ 🕸 🎅) Housed in an 18th-century *palazzo*, this centrally located B&B offers 13 rooms of varying size. Best are the spacious apartments (numbers 32, 34 and 35), with kitchenettes and balconies overlooking Trapani's most elegant pedestrian street. Upstairs apartment 23 is also lovely, with a private balcony reached by a spiral staircase. Guests get discounts at the hotel's atmospheric restaurant next door.

Albergo Maccotta HOTEL €
(🖉 0923 2 84 18; www.albergomaccotta.it; Via degli Argentieri 4; s €30-40, d €55-75, breakfast per person €3; ❋ 🕸 @ 🎅) This unassuming hotel in the centre of the Old Town offers clean and neat rooms. There's no atmosphere to speak of, but prices are reasonable, the location is quiet and there's satellite TV in every room.

🍴 Eating

Sicily's Arab heritage and Trapani's unique position on the sea route to Tunisia have made couscous (or '*cuscusu*' as they sometimes spell it around here) a local speciality. It's also the centrepiece of annual festivals including nearby San Vito Lo Capo's well-established **Cous Cous Fest** (www.couscousfest.it; ⊙ mid-late Sep) and Trapani's recently launched **Cuscusu** (⊙ late May).

La Rinascente PASTICCERIA €
(🖉 0923 2 37 67; Via Gatti 3; cannoli €2; ⊙ 9am-1.30pm & 3-7pm Mon, Tue, Thu & Fri, 7.30am-2pm Sat & Sun) When you enter this bakery through the side door, you'll feel like you've

CANNOLI 101

Sugary treats can quickly become an obsession in Sicily. Among them, nothing compares to *cannoli*, the crown jewel of Sicilian sweets. Here's what you need to know:

➡ *Cannoli* are meant to be eaten with your fingers, even in a fancy restaurant. Leave the knife and fork behind, grasp that little sugary beauty between thumb and forefinger, and crunch away to your heart's content!

➡ *Cannoli* is actually the plural form, so if you just want one, ask for '*un cannolo*'. Of course, you could be excused for wanting two or more, in which case '*cannoli*' works just fine!

➡ A truly good *cannolo* will be filled on the spot with fresh ricotta. Don't go for the prefilled shells piled high in airport cafes and other tourist hang-outs. Left to sit for too long, the shell gets soggy, which defeats the whole crunchy beauty of the *cannoli* experience.

A few great places to try *cannoli*: Ti Vitti (p791), Me Cumpari Turridu (p812), Kalòs (p833), Pasticceria Cappello (p786), La Rinascente (p836).

barged into someone's kitchen – and you have! Thankfully, owner Giovanni Costadura's broad smile will quickly put you at ease, as will a taste of his homemade *cannoli*, which he'll create for you on the spot.

★ **Osteria La Bettolaccia**   SICILIAN €€
(☑ 0923 2 16 95; www.labettolaccia.it; Via Enrico Fardella 25; meals €30-45; ☺12.45-3pm Mon-Fri, plus 7.45-11pm Mon-Sat) Unwaveringly authentic, this perennial Slow Food favourite just two blocks from the ferry terminal is the perfect place to try *cous cous con zuppa di mare* (couscous with mixed seafood in a spicy fish sauce, with tomatoes, garlic and parsley). In response to its great popularity, the dining room was recently expanded, but it's still wise to book ahead.

Al Solito Posto   SICILIAN €€
(☑ 0923 2 45 45; www.trattoria-alsolitoposto.com; Via Orlandini 30; meals €25-35; ☺1-3pm & 8-11pm Mon-Sat) A 15-minute walk east of the centre, this local favourite is a well-deserved wearer of the Slow Food badge. Service can be a bit surly, but the food is superb, from *primi* such as *busiate con pesto alla trapanese* (corkscrew-shaped pasta with a sauce of almonds, garlic and tomatoes) to super-fresh seafood *secondi* (don't miss the local tuna in May and June) to the creamy-crunchy homemade *cannoli*. Book ahead.

ⓘ Orientation

Trapani's city centre sits on a sickle-shaped peninsula jutting west into the Mediterranean from the Sicilian mainland. The ferry and hydrofoil ports straggle along Via Ammiraglio Staiti at the peninsula's southern edge. Just a couple of blocks inland (to the north), Corso Vittorio

Emanuele marks the heart of the pedestrianised centre, with its handsome baroque churches and *palazzi*. The bus and train stations lie about 1km east of the centre.

ⓘ Information

Ospedale Sant'Antonio Abate (☑ 0923 80 91 11; www.asptrapani.it; Via Cosenza 82) Five kilometres east of the centre.

Questura (☑ 0923 59 81 11; Piazza Vittoria Veneto 1) Trapani's main police station.

Tourist Office (☑ 0923 54 45 33; www.trapaniwelcome.it; Piazzetta Saturno; ☺9am-4.30pm Mon & Thu, 9am-1pm Tue, Wed & Fri) Just north of the port, Trapani's tourist office offers city maps and information.

ⓘ Getting There & Around

Egatours (☑ 0923 2 17 54; www.egatourviaggi.it; Via Ammiraglio Staiti 13), a travel agency opposite the port, offers one-stop shopping for bus, plane and ferry tickets.

AIR

Trapani's small **Vincenzo Florio Airport** (TPS; Birgi Airport; ☑ 0923 61 01 11; www.airgest.it) is 17km south of town at Birgi. **Ryanair** (www.ryanair.com) offers direct flights to two dozen Italian and European cities, while Alitalia flies to the Mediterranean island of Pantelleria. **AST** (Azienda Siciliana Trasporti; ☑ 0923 2 10 21; www.astsicilia.it; Via Virgilio 20) operates hourly buses from 5.30am to 11.30pm connecting the airport with downtown Trapani (€4.90, 45 minutes).

BOAT

Ferry ticket offices are inside Trapani's ferry terminal, opposite Piazza Garibaldi. Hydrofoil ticket offices are 350m further east along Via Ammiraglio Staiti.

Ustica Lines (☑ 0923 87 38 13; www.ustica lines.it; Via Ammiraglio Staiti) and **Siremar** (☑ 0923 2 49 68; www.siremar.it; Via Ammiraglio Staiti) both operate hydrofoils year-round to the Egadi Island ports of Favignana (€12, 25 to 40 minutes), Levanzo (€12, 25 to 40 minutes) and Marettimo (€19, 1¼ hours). Ustica Lines also offers summer-only Saturday morning hydrofoil services to Ustica (€33, 2½ hours) and Naples (€99, seven hours).

Siremar offers year-round ferry service to Pantelleria (from €30, six to seven hours) and the Egadi Islands (Favignana €8.20, one to 1½ hours; Levanzo €8.20, one to 1½ hours; Marettimo €13.10, three hours). **Traghetti delle Isole** (☑ 0923 2 17 54; www.traghettidelleisole.it) also sails to Pantelleria five times weekly from June through September.

BUS

Intercity buses arrive and depart from the terminal 1km east of the centre (just southeast of the train station).

Segesta (☑ 0923 2 84 04; www.buscenter. it) runs express buses to Palermo (€9.60, two hours, hourly). Board at the bus stop across the street from Egatours or at the bus station.

Lumia (☑ 0923 2 17 54; www.autolineelumia. it) buses serve Agrigento (€11.90, 2¾ to 3¾ hours, one to three daily).

ATM (☑ 0923 55 95 75; www.atmtrapani.it) operates two free city buses (No 1 and 2), which make circular trips through Trapani, connecting the bus station, the train station and the port.

CAR & MOTORCYCLE

To bypass Trapani's vast suburbs and avoid the narrow streets of the city centre, follow signs from the A29 autostrada directly to the port, where you'll find abundant paid parking along the broad waterside avenue Via Ammiraglio Staiti, within walking distance of most attractions.

TRAIN

From Trapani's station on Piazza Umberto I, Trenitalia offers efficient connections to Marsala (€3.45, 30 minutes, 10 Monday to Saturday, five on Sunday). There are also three direct but slow daily trains to Palermo (€10.40, 3¾ hours).

Erice

POP 28,800 / ELEV 751M

One of Italy's most spectacular hill towns, Erice combines medieval charm with astounding 360-degree views. Erice sits on the legendary Mt Eryx (750m); on a clear day, you can see Cape Bon in Tunisia. Wander the medieval tangle of streets interspersed with churches, forts and tiny cobbled piazzas. The town has a seductive history as a centre for the cult of Venus. Settled by the mysterious Elymians, Erice was an obvious abode for the goddess of love, and the town followed the peculiar ritual of sacred prostitution, with the prostitutes themselves accommodated in the Temple of Venus. Despite countless invasions, the temple remained intact – no guesses why. Erice's tourist infrastructure is excellent. Posted throughout town, you'll find bilingual (Italian–English) informational displays along with town maps providing suggested walking routes.

⊙ Sights

The best views can be had from **Giardino del Balio**, which overlooks the turrets and wooded hillsides south to Trapani's saltpans, the Egadi Islands and the sea. Looking north, there are equally staggering views of San Vito Lo Capo's rugged headlands.

Castello di Venere   CASTLE
(☑ 339 8974843; www.fondazioneericearte.org/ castellodivenere.php; Via Castello di Venere; adult/ reduced €5/2.50; ⊙ 10am-1hr before sunset daily Apr-Oct, 10am-4pm Sat & holidays Nov-Mar) The Norman Castello di Venere was built in the 12th and 13th centuries over the Temple of Venus, long a site of worship for the ancient Elymians, Phoenicians, Greeks and Romans. The views from up top, extending to San Vito Lo Capo on one side and the Saline di Trapani on the other, are spectacular. To arrange midweek visits in winter, phone at least 24 hours in advance.

🛏 Sleeping & Eating

Hotels, many with their own restaurants, are scattered along Via Vittorio Emanuele, Erice's main street. After the tourists have left, the town has a beguiling medieval air.

Erice has a tradition of *dolci ericini* (Erice sweets) made by the local nuns. There are numerous pastry shops in town, the most famous being **Maria Grammatico** (☑ 0923 86 93 90; www.mariagrammatico.it; Via Vittorio Emanuele 14; pastries from €2; ⊙ 9am-10pm May, Jun & Sep, to 1am Jul & Aug, to 7pm Oct-Apr), revered for its *frutta martorana* (marzipan fruit) and almond pastries. If you like what you taste, you can even stick around and take cooking classes from Signora Grammatico herself!

Hotel Elimo   HOTEL €€
(☑ 0923 86 93 77; www.hotelelimo.it; Via Vittorio Emanuele 75; s €80-110, d €90-130, ste €150-170; ❋ 🕏) Communal spaces at this atmospheric historic house are filled with tiled beams,

SICILY'S OLDEST NATURE RESERVE

Saved from development and road projects by local protests, the tranquil **Riserva Naturale dello Zingaro** is the star attraction on the Golfo di Castellammare, halfway between Palermo and Trapani. Founded in 1981, this was Sicily's first nature reserve. Zingaro's wild coastline is a haven for the rare Bonelli's eagle along with 40 other species of bird. Mediterranean flora dusts the hillsides with wild carob and bright yellow euphorbia, and hidden coves, such as Capreria and Marinella Bays, provide tranquil swimming spots. The main entrance to the park is 2km north of the village of Scopello. Several walking trails are detailed on maps available free at the entrance or downloadable from the park website. The main 7km trail along the coast passes by the visitor centre and five museums documenting everything from local flora and fauna to traditional fishing methods.

Once home to tuna fishers, tiny **Scopello** now mainly hosts tourists. Its port, 1km below town and reachable by a walking path, has a picturesque **beach** (www.tonnaradiscopello.com; admission €3; ⊙ 9am-7pm) backed by a rust-red *tonnara* (tuna-processing plant) and dramatic *faraglioni* (rock towers) rising from the water.

Pensione Tranchina (☑ 0924 54 10 99; www.pensionetranchina.com; Via Diaz 7, Scopello; B&B per person €36-48, half-board per person €55-75; ✸ 🖥) is the nicest of several places to stay and eat clustered around the cobblestoned courtyard at Scopello's village centre. Friendly hosts Marisin and Salvatore offer comfortable rooms, a roaring fire on chilly evenings and superb home-cooked meals featuring local fish and home-grown fruit and olive oil. For drinks at sunset, head for the scenic back terrace at nearby **Bar Nettuno** (Baglio Scopello 1; ⊙ 9am-late).

SICILY SEGESTA

marble fireplaces, intriguing art, knick-knacks and antiques. The bedrooms are more mainstream, although many (along with the hotel terrace and restaurant) have breathtaking vistas south and west towards the Saline di Trapani, the Egadi Islands and the shimmering sea.

ℹ Information

The main **tourist office** (☑ 348 6912335; www.facebook.com/EriceTourism; Porta Trapani; ⊙ 2-6pm Mon, 10am-2pm & 3-6pm Tue-Sat, 10am-2pm Sun) is adjacent to Porta Trapani (Erice's old town gate); there's another branch 100m up the street at the **Enoteca Comunale** (☑ 0923 86 93 88; Via Conte Agostino Pepoli 11).

ℹ Getting There & Away

AST (p837) runs five buses daily (three on Sunday) between Erice and Trapani's bus terminal (€2.90, 45 minutes). Alternatively, catch the **funicular** (Funivia; ☑ 0923 86 97 20, 0923 56 93 06; www.funiviaerice.it; one way/return €5.50/9; ⊙ 1-8pm Mon, 8.10am-8pm Tue-Fri, 10am-10pm Sat, 10am-8pm Sun) opposite the car park at the foot of Erice's Via Vittorio Emanuele; the 10-minute descent drops you in Trapani near Ospedale Sant'Antonio Abate, where you can catch local bus 21 or 23 (€1.40) into the centre of Trapani.

Segesta

ELEV 304M

Set on the edge of a deep canyon in the midst of wild, desolate mountains, the 5th-century BC **ruins of Segesta** (☑ 0924 95 23 56; adult/reduced €6/3; ⊙ 9am-4pm Oct-Mar, 8.30am-1hr before sunset Apr-Sep) are a magical site. On windy days the 36 giant columns of its magnificent temple are said to act like an organ, producing mysterious notes.

The city, founded by the ancient Elymians, was in constant conflict with Selinunte in the south, whose destruction it sought with dogged determination and singular success. Time, however, has done to Segesta what violence inflicted on Selinunte; little remains now, save the **theatre** and the never-completed **Doric temple**, the latter dating from around 430 BC and remarkably well preserved. A shuttle bus (€1.50) runs every 30 minutes from the temple entrance 1.5km uphill to the theatre.

Tarantola (☑ 0924 3 10 20) runs four daily buses to Segesta from Trapani (one way/return €4/6.60, 45 minutes), plus three daily buses from Via Balsamo near Palermo's train station (one way/return €7/11.20, 1¼ hours); all buses stop just outside the entrance to the archaeological site. If driving, exit the A29dir at Segesta and follow signs 1.5km uphill to the site.

Sardinia

Best Places to Eat

➡ Martinelli's (p848)

➡ Josto al Duomo (p857)

➡ Trattoria Lo Romani (p864)

➡ Agriturismo Agrisole (p870)

➡ Jaddhu (p872)

Best Places to Stay

➡ Lemon House (p882)

➡ Il Cagliarese (p847)

➡ Agriturismo L'Oasi del Cervo (p854)

➡ B&B Costa Smeralda (p872)

➡ Casa Solotti (p877)

Why Go?

As DH Lawrence so succinctly put it: 'Sardinia is different.' Indeed, where else but on this 365-village, four-million-sheep island could you travel from shimmering bays to alpine forests, granite peaks to cathedral-like grottoes, rolling vineyards to one-time bandit towns – all in the space of a day? Sardinia baffles with prehistory at 7000 nuraghic sites, dazzles with its kaleidoscopic blue waters and whets appetites with island treats like spit-roasted suckling pig, sea urchins and crumbly *pecorino* cheese.

Over millennia islanders have carved out a unique identity, cuisine, culture and language. And whether you're swooning over the mega-yachts in the Costa Smeralda's fjord-like bays or kicking back at a rustic *agriturismo* (farm stay accommodation), you can't help but appreciate this island's love of the good life. Earthy and glamorous, adventurous and blissfully relaxed, Sardinia delights in being that little bit different.

When to Go
Cagliari

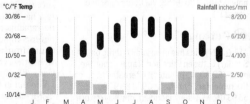

Feb Pre-Lenten shenanigans, from carnival madness to medieval jousting at Sa Sartiglia.

Mar–May Spring wildflowers, Easter parades, and hiking without the heat and crowds.

Jun–Aug Sun-kissed beaches, open-air festivals and folksy fun at Nuoro's Sagra del Redentore.

History

Little is known about Sardinia's prehistory, but the first islanders probably arrived from mainland Italy around 350,000 BC. By the Neolithic period (8000 to 3000 BC) tribal communities were thriving in north-central Sardinia. Their Bronze Age descendants, known as the nuraghic people, dominated the island until the Phoenicians arrived around 850 BC. The Carthaginians came next, followed by the Romans, who took over in the 3rd century BC.

In the Middle Ages, the island was divided into four independent *giudicati* (kingdoms), but by the 13th century the Pisans and Genoese were battling for control. They in turn were toppled by the Catalan-Aragonese from northern Spain, who also had to subdue bitter Sard resistance led by Eleonora d'Arborea (1340–1404), Sardinia's very own Joan of Arc.

Sardinia became Spanish territory after the unification of the Spanish kingdoms in 1479, and today there remains a tangible Hispanic feel to towns such as Alghero and Iglesias. In the ensuing centuries, Sardinia suffered as Spain's power crumbled; in 1720 the Italian Savoys took possession of the island. After Italian unity in 1861, Sardinia found itself under the boot of Rome.

In the aftermath of WWII, efforts were made to drag the island into the modern era. In 1946 a huge project was launched to rid the island of malaria and in 1948 Sardinia was granted its own autonomous regional parliament.

Coastal tourism arrived in the 1960s and has since become a mainstay of the Sardinian economy. Environmentalists breathed a sigh of relief in 2008 when NATO withdrew from the Maddalena islands after a 35-year sojourn.

ⓘ Getting There & Away

AIR

Flights from Italian and European cities serve **Elmas airport** (☏070 21 12 11; www.cagliariairport.it) in Cagliari; Alghero's Fertilia (p865); and the **Aeroporto Olbia Costa Smeralda** (☏0789 56 34 44; www.geasar.it) in Olbia. As well as major international carriers, several no-frills airlines operate direct flights, including **Ryanair** (www.ryanair.com), **easyJet** (www.easyjet.com), **TUIfly** (www.tuifly.com) and **Meridiana** (www.meridiana.it). Note that there is a marked increase in flights in summer, with many seasonal flights operating between June and September.

BOAT

Sardinia is accessible by ferry from Genoa, Livorno, Piombino, Civitavecchia and Naples, and from Palermo in Sicily. Ferries also run from Bonifacio and Porto Vecchio in Corsica, and from Marseilles via the Corsican ports of Ajaccio and Propriano. The arrival points in Sardinia are Olbia, Golfo Aranci, Santa Teresa di Gallura and Porto Torres in the north; Arbatax on the east coast; and Cagliari in the south. Services are most frequent from mid-June to mid-September. See www.traghettiweb.it and book ahead.

Ferry Operators

Corsica Ferries, Sardinia Ferries (☏0825 09 50 95; www.corsica-ferries.co.uk) To Golfo Aranci from Civitavecchia and Livorno. Also Sardinia to Corsica (April to September).

Grandi Navi Veloci (☏010 209 45 91; www.gnv.it) To Olbia and Porto Torres from Genoa.

La Méridionale (☏in France 491 994 509; www.lameridionale.fr) To Porto Torres from Marseille via Corsica.

Moby Lines (☏199 30 30 40; www.mobylines.it) Operates four daily crossings from Bonifacio to Santa Teresa di Gallura between mid-April and late September. High-season tickets cost from about €22 per person or €30 with a small car.

Saremar (☏199 11 88 77; www.saremar.it) Runs seasonal ferry services between Santa Teresa di Gallura and Bonifacio.

SNCM (☏in France 3260; www.sncm.fr) Ferries to Porto Torres from Marseille via Propriano or, less frequently, Ajaccio. From Propriano to Porto Torres, bank on about €26 per person or €38 with a car.

Tirrenia (☏892 123; www.tirrenia.it) To Cagliari from Civitavecchia, Naples, Palermo and Trapani; to Olbia from Civitavecchia and Genoa; to Arbatax from Civitavecchia and Genoa; to Porto Torres from Genoa.

ⓘ Getting Around

BUS

Sardinia's main bus company, **ARST** (ARST; ☏800 865042; www.arst.sardegna.it), runs most local and long-distance services.

CAR & MOTORCYCLE

Sardinia is best explored by road. There are rental agencies in Cagliari as well as in airports and major towns.

TRAIN

Trenitalia (☏892021; www.trenitalia.com) services link Cagliari with Oristano, Sassari, Porto Torres, Olbia and Golfo Aranci. Services are slow but generally reliable. Slow ARST trains serve Sassari, Alghero and Nuoro. Between mid-June and early September, ARST also operates a tourist train service, the Trenino Verde (p850).

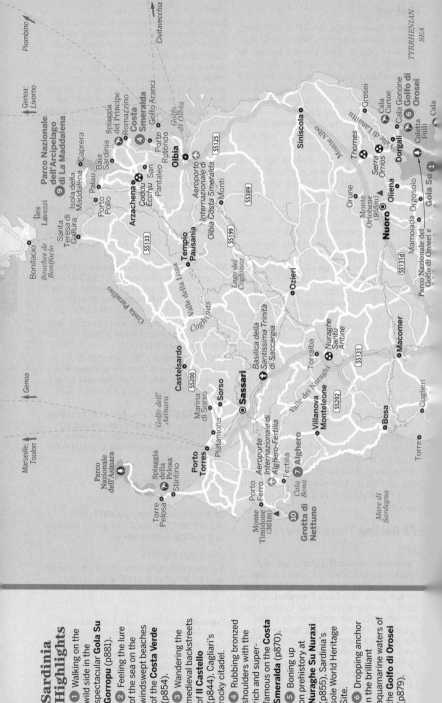

Sardinia Highlights

1 Walking on the wild side in the spectacular **Gola Su Gorropu** (p881).

2 Feeling the lure of the sea on the windswept beaches of the **Costa Verde** (p854).

3 Wandering the medieval backstreets of **Il Castello** (p844). Cagliari's rocky citadel.

4 Rubbing bronzed shoulders with the rich and super-famous on the **Costa Smeralda** (p870).

5 Boning up on prehistory at **Nuraghe Su Nuraxi** (p855). Sardinia's sole World Heritage Site.

6 Dropping anchor in the brilliant aquamarine waters of the **Golfo di Orosei** (p879).

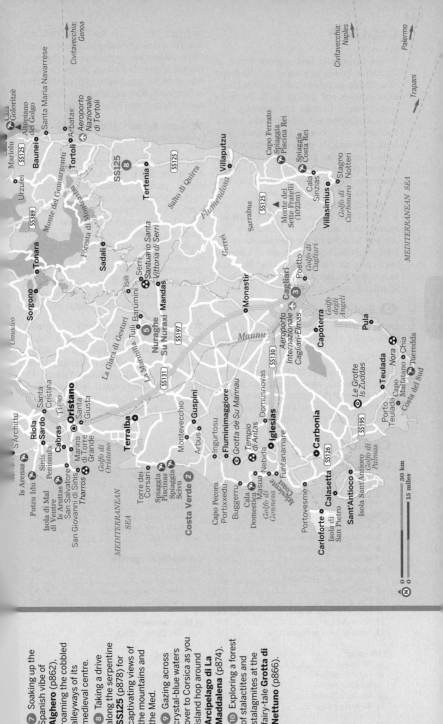

7 Soaking up the Spanish vibe of **Alghero** (p862), roaming the cobbled alleyways of its medieval centre.

8 Taking a drive along the serpentine **SS125** (p878) for captivating views of the mountains and the Med.

9 Gazing across crystal-blue waters over to Corsica as you island hop around **Arcipelago di La Maddalena** (p874).

10 Exploring a forest of stalactites and stalagmites at the fairy-tale **Grotta di Nettuno** (p866).

CAGLIARI

POP 149,343

Forget flying: the best way to arrive in Cagliari is by sea to witness the city rising in a jumble of golden-hued *palazzi* (mansions), domes and facades up to the rocky centrepiece, Il Castello. Cosmopolitan and cultured, Cagliari is Sardinia's most Italian-flavoured city. Vespas buzz down tree-fringed boulevards and locals relax at cafes tucked under the graceful arcades by the seafront. Swing east and you reach Poetto beach, the hub of summer life with its limpid waters and upbeat party scene.

At every turn, Cagliari's gripping history is spelled out, especially through archaeological sites, museums and churches. The city was founded by the Phoenicians in the 8th century BC, but came of age as a Roman port. Later, the Pisans arrived and treated it to a major medieval facelift, the results of which impress to this day.

◉ Sights

Cagliari's trophy sights cluster in the Castello, Stampace, Marina and Villanova districts.

★ Il Castello   HISTORIC SITE

This hilltop citadel is Cagliari's most iconic image, its domes, towers and *palazzi*, once home to the city's aristocracy, rising above the sturdy ramparts built by the Pisans and Aragonese. Inside the battlements, the old medieval city reveals itself like Pandora's box. The university, cathedral, museums and Pisan palaces are wedged into a jigsaw of narrow high-walled alleys. Sleepy though it may seem, the area harbours a growing crop of boutiques, bars and cafes that attract students, hipsters and bohemian types.

★ Museo Archeologico Nazionale   MUSEUM

(www.archeocaor.beniculturali.it; Piazza dell'Arsenale; adult/reduced €5/2.50; ⊙9am-8pm Tue-Sun) Of the four museums at the Citadella dei Musei, this is the undoubted star. Sardinia's premier archaeological museum displays artefacts spanning millennia of ancient history, including a superb collection of pint-sized nuraghic *bronzetti* (bronze figurines), which, in the absence of any written records, are a vital source of information on Sardinia's mysterious nuraghic culture (approximately 1800–500 BC). The museum takes a chronological spin, deftly moving from pre-nuraghic times to the Bronze and Iron Ages, the Phoenicians and Romans.

★ Cattedrale di Santa Maria   CATHEDRAL

(www.duomodicagliari.it; Piazza Palazzo 4; ⊙8am-noon & 4-8pm Mon-Sat, 8am-1pm & 4.30-8.30pm Sun) Cagliari's graceful 13th-century cathedral stands proud on Piazza Palazzo. Except for the square-based bell tower, little remains of the original Gothic structure: the clean Pisan-Romanesque facade is a

Cagliari

20th-century imitation, added between 1933 and 1938. Inside, the once-Gothic church disappears beneath a rich icing of baroque decor, the result of a radical late-17th-century makeover. Bright frescoes adorn the ceilings, and the three chapels on either side of the aisles spill over exuberantly with sculptural whirls.

Torre dell'Elefante TOWER
(Via Università; adult/reduced €3/2; ☉10am-7pm summer, 9am-5pm winter) One of only two Pisan towers still standing, the Torre

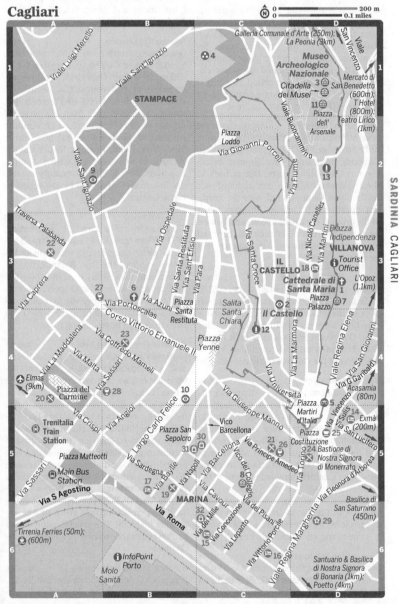

dell'Elefante was built in 1307 as a defence against the threatening Aragonese. Named after the sculpted elephant by the vicious-looking portcullis, the 42m-high tower became something of a horror show, thanks to its foul decor. The crenellated storey was added in 1852 and used as a prison for political detainees. Climb to the top for far-reaching views over the city's rooftops to the sea.

Anfiteatro Romano ARCHAEOLOGICAL SITE
(www.anfiteatroromano.it; Viale Sant'Ignazio; guided visit adult/reduced €5/3.50; ☺9am-6pm Fri-Sun) Cagliari's most impressive Roman monument is this amphitheatre. Dating back to the 2nd century AD, it is carved out of rock on the Buon Cammino hill, near the northern entrance to Il Castello. Although much of the original theatre has been cannibalised for building material, enough has survived to pique the imagination. You can explore it on a guided visit.

Torre di San Pancrazio TOWER
(Piazza Indipendenza; adult/reduced €3/2; ☺10am-7pm Tue-Sun summer, 9am-5pm winter) Over by the citadel's northeastern gate, this 36m-high tower is the Torre dell'Elefante's twin. Completed in 1305, it is built on the city's highest point and commands expansive views over the Golfo di Cagliari.

Bastione San Remy VIEWPOINT
The monumental stairway that ascends from busy Piazza Costituzione to Bastione San Remy is the most impressive way to reach Il Castello; save your legs by taking the panoramic elevator. Built between 1899 and 1902, the lookout is a mix of neoclassical and Liberty styles and affords sweeping views over Cagliari's jumbled rooftops to the Mediterranean.

At the time of research, the *bastione* (along with the piazza and ramparts above it) was closed for extensive restoration work; it is due to reopen in late 2015 or early 2016.

Pinacoteca Nazionale GALLERY
(www.pinacoteca.cagliari.beniculturali.it; Piazza dell'Arsenale; adult/reduced €5/2.50; ☺9am-8pm Tue-Sun) This gallery showcases a prized collection of 15th- to 17th-century art. Many of the best works are *retablos* (grand altarpieces), painted by Catalan and Genoese artists. Of those by known Sardinian painters, the four works by Pietro Cavaro, father of the so-called Stampace school and arguably Sardinia's most important artist, are outstanding. They include a moving *Deposizione* (Deposition) and portraits of St Peter, St Paul and St Augustine.

Museo del Duomo MUSEUM
(www.museoduomodicagliari.it; Via del Fossario 5; adult/reduced €4/2.50; ☺10am-1pm & 4.30-7.30pm Sat & Sun) Cathedral treasures are displayed at this compact museum. One standout is the *Trittico di Clemente VII,* which was moved here from the cathedral for safe keeping. This precious 15th-century painting in oil on timber has been attributed to the Flemish painter Rogier van der Weyden, or to one of his disciples. Another important work is the 16th-century *Retablo dei Beneficiati,* produced by the school of Pietro Cavaro.

Orto Botanico GARDENS
(Viale Sant'Ignazio da Laconi 11; adult/reduced €4/2; ☺9am-6pm Mon-Fri summer, 9am-1.30pm Mon-Fri winter) One of Italy's most famous botanical gardens, the Orto Botanico was established in 1858. Today it extends over five hectares and nurtures 3000 species of flora. Leafy arches lead to trickling fountains and gardens bristling with palm trees, cacti and ficus trees with huge snaking roots.

Galleria Comunale d'Arte GALLERY
(www.galleriacomunalecagliari.it; Viale San Vincenzo 2; adult/reduced €6/2.60; ☺10am-9pm Wed-Mon summer, 10am-6pm daily winter) Housed in a neoclassical villa north of Il Castello, this gallery zooms in on modern Sardinian art, including works by island artists like Tarquinio Sini (1891–1943). His humorous *contrasti* (contrasts) showing frumpily dressed Sardinian girls standing beside glamorous, coiffed flappers, explore the social tension between traditional Sardinian ways and a rapidly modernising world. Works by Giuseppe Biasi (1885–1945), depicting Sardinian life in rich oils and bold brush strokes, are another highlight. The gallery's palm-dotted garden commands terrific views of Cagliari's skyline.

Basilica di San Saturnino BASILICA
(Piazza San Cosimo; ☺officially 9am-1pm Tue-Sat, but variable) One of the oldest churches in

Sardinia, the Basilica di San Saturnino is a striking example of Paleo-Christian architecture. Based on a Greek-cross pattern, the domed basilica was built over a Roman necropolis in the 5th century, on the site where Saturninus, a much revered local martyr, was buried. According to legend, Saturninus was beheaded in 304 AD during emperor Diocletian's anti-Christian pogroms.

Chiesa di San Michele CHURCH
(Via Ospedale 2; ⊙8-11am & 6-9pm Mon-Sat, 8am-noon & 7-9pm Sun) Although consecrated in 1538, this church is best known for its lavish 18th-century decor, considered the finest example of rococo in Sardinia. The spectacle starts outside with the ebullient triple-arched baroque facade and continues through the vast colonnaded atrium and on into the magnificent octagonal interior, with six heavily decorated chapels radiating out from the centre, topped by a grand, brightly frescoed dome. Of particular note is the sacristy, with its vivid frescoes and intricate inlaid wood.

★ Santuario & Basilica di Nostra Signora di Bonaria CHURCH, VIEWPOINT
(www.bonaria.eu; Piazza Bonaria 2; donations welcome; ⊙6.30am-noon & 4.30-7.30pm) Crowning the Bonaria hill, around 1km southeast of Via Roma, is this hugely popular pilgrimage site. Devotees come from all over the world to pray to *Nostra Signora di Bonaria*, a wooden statue of the Virgin Mary and Christ, kept in a niche behind the altar, which is said to have saved a 14th-century Spanish ship during a storm. To the right of the sanctuary is the much larger basilica, which still acts as a landmark to returning sailors.

Piazza Yenne PIAZZA
The focal point of the Marina district, and indeed of central Cagliari, is Piazza Yenne. The small square is adorned with a statue of King Carlo Felice to mark the beginnings of the Carlo Felice Hwy (SS131), the project for which the monarch is best remembered. On summer nights, Piazza Yenne heaves as a young crowd flocks to its bars, gelaterie and pavement cafes.

Museo del Tesoro e Area Archeologica di Sant'Eulalia MUSEUM
(Vico del Collegio 2; adult/reduced €5/2.50; ⊙10am-1pm & 4-7pm Tue-Sun) In the heart of the Marina district, this museum contains a rich collection of religious art, as well as an

archaeological area, which extends for up to 200 sq metres beneath the adjacent **Chiesa di Sant' Eulalia**. The main drawcard here is a 13m section of excavated Roman road (constructed between the 1st and 2nd centuries AD), which archaeologists think would have connected with the nearby port.

★ Festivals & Events

Cagliari puts on a good show for Carnevale in February and Easter Holy Week, when a procession of hooded participants climbs up to the cathedral in Il Castello.

Festa di Sant'Efisio RELIGIOUS
Pilgrims descend in droves for this saintly celebration, held from 1 to 4 May. On opening day, Cagliaritani pour into the streets to greet the effigy of St Ephisius, Cagliari's patron saint, as it's paraded around the streets on a bullock-drawn carriage. Tickets for the stands (€15 to €25) are sold at **Box Office Tickets** (☑070 65 74 28; www.boxofficesardegna. it; Viale Regina Margherita 43).

🛏 Sleeping

★ Il Cagliarese B&B €
(☑339 6544083; www.ilcagliarese.it; Via Vittorio Porcile 19; s €45-70, d €60-90; ❄🛜) Bang in the heart of the Marina district, this snug B&B is a find. Mauro bends over backwards to please, and his sister, Titziana, plays the cake fairy at breakfast with her scrumptious pastries and tiramisu. The immaculate rooms sport homey touches such as embroidered fabrics and carved wooden furnishings.

Acasamia APARTMENT €
(☑347 5413872; Via Giuseppe Garibaldi 62; apt €65-70; ❄🛜) Just a few minutes' walk from Il Castello and the Marina neighbourhoods, you'll find this trio of lovingly kept

apartments, where dark parquet, stone walls and vintage-style furnishings create a snug, country feel. Your welcoming host, Loredana, has plenty of tips on exploring Cagliari and its surrounds.

Residenza Kastrum
B&B €

(☑348 0012280; www.kastrum.eu; Via Canelles 78; s €50-65, d €70-90, q €120-150; ❉ 🤖 ⛎) This cosy, characterful B&B has marvellous views over the city rooftops to the gulf from its hilltop Castello perch. The simple, spotless rooms are geared towards families (cots are available). Linger over breakfast and memorable sunsets on the terrace.

La Peonia
B&B €

(☑070 51 31 64; www.lapeonia.com; Via Riva Villasanta 77; s €50-65, d €70-86; ❉ 🤖 ⛎) Antonello and Vanna are your kindly hosts at this romantic neo-Gothic abode. Turn-of-the-century interiors with polished wood furnishings are a striking contrast to the sleek, monochrome bathrooms. Bus M from Piazza Matteotti pulls up in front of the B&B, 2.5km northeast of town.

Marina di Castello
B&B €

(☑070 289 04 77; www.bedandbreakfastcagliari city.it; Via Roma 75a; d €85-110; ❉ 🤖) Sabrina makes you feel instantly at ease at this cheery B&B, housed in a *palazzo* on Cagliari's main boulevard. The rooms are tastefully done out in silvers, bronzes and golds, with exposed brickwork, art and detailed fabrics lending a boutiquey touch. The roof terrace overlooking the marina is a relaxed spot for an afternoon coffee or sundowner.

T Hotel
DESIGN HOTEL €€

(☑070 4 74 00; www.thotel.it; Via dei Giudicati 66; s €99-132, d €116-178, ste €208-376; 🅿 ❉ 🤖 ⛎ ⛎) This hard-to-miss steel-and-glass tower adds a dash of contemporary design to the cityscape. The rooms reveal a linear, modish look, and the spa invites relaxation with its hydrotherapy pool and treatments. From Piazza Matteotti, take bus M to Via Bacaredda and walk 200m.

Hotel Miramare
BOUTIQUE HOTEL €€

(☑070 66 40 21; www.hotelmiramarecagliari.it; Via Roma 59; s €76-122, d €98-146, ste €145-235; 🤖 ⛎) This boutique four-star sits right on the sea-facing Via Roma. Rooms are individually styled and reach from pared-down contemporary cool to full-on belle époque glamour, with crimson walls, spangly chandeliers and high wooden beds. Wi-fi is available and kids under 12 stay free.

Eating

Dining hot spots include the Marina area, Via Sassari and Corso Vittorio Emanuele II. From November to March (mollusc season), *chioschi* (kiosks) serve sea-fresh sea urchins and mussels on Poetto beach.

Pizzeria Nansen
PIZZA €

(☑070 667 03 35; Corso Vittorio Emanuele II 269; pizzas €5-10; ⏱11.30am-2.30pm & 6.30-11.30pm Tue-Sun) The pizzas fly out of the oven quicker than you can say *delizioso* at this family run pizzeria. And they're terrific, too – thin, crisp and flavoursome.

Gocce di Gelato e Cioccolato
GELATERIA €

(Piazza del Carmine 21; ice creams & desserts €1.40-5; ⏱noon-10pm winter, to 1am summer) Stop by here for totally divine handmade gelati, desserts (try the millefeuille), spice-infused pralines and truffles.

L'Opoz
ITALIAN €

(☑070 858 48 94; Via Giardini 145; meals €11-18; ⏱7pm-2am Wed-Mon) Snuggled away just north of the centre, this artsy, red-walled bistro is a nicely chilled pick for an *aperitivo* (from €3) and bite to eat – the *tagliata* (sliced steak) particularly stands out, but chefs also knock up other dishes like mixed fish grill, pasta and veggie options.

★ Martinelli's
ITALIAN €€

(☑070 65 42 20; www.martinellis.it; Via Principe Amedeo 18; meals from €35; ⏱8.30pm-11.30pm Mon-Sat) Simplicity is the ethos underpinning this intimate, subtly lit bistro in the heart of the Marina district. Service is friendly without being overbearing, and the menu plays up seasonal, winningly fresh seafood along the lines of *fregola* (semolina pasta) with clams and sea bass cooked in vernaccia wine and olives.

St Remy
SARDINIAN €€

(☑070 65 73 77; www.stremy.it; Via Torino 16; meals €30-35; ⏱12.30-3pm & 7.30-10pm Mon-Fri, 7.30-10.30pm Sat) Tucked away on a side street, St Remy keeps the mood intimate in a vaulted, limewashed space with stone arches. The menu puts a creative spin on Sardinian flavours, with homemade pasta preluding mains like John Dory cooked in a white-wine and black-olive sauce – all cooked to a T and presented with panache.

Antica Cagliari
SARDINIAN €€

(📋070 734 01 98; www.anticacagliari.it; Via Sardegna 49; meals €25-40; ⊙12.30-3pm & 8-11.30pm) A cut above most restaurants in the Marina district, this beamed restaurant always has a good buzz. Go for Sardinian dishes like *fregola* with shellfish or whatever fish is fresh that day. Reserve ahead to snag one of the few tables on the pavement terrace.

Ristorante Ammentos
SARDINIAN €€

(📋070 65 10 75; Via Sassari 120; meals €20-30; ⊙1-2.30pm & 8-11pm Thu-Tue) Dine on authentic Sardinian fare in rustic surrounds at this popular trattoria. *Culurgiones* (ravioli) in a herby tomato sauce are a delicious lead to succulent meat dishes such as wild boar or goat stew.

Drinking & Nightlife

On warm nights, Piazza Yenne becomes one huge beer garden. It's a lively gathering spot to kick-start an evening.

Inu
WINE BAR

(www.inusardinianwinebar.it; Via Sassari 50; ⊙7pm-1am) Get versed in Sardinian wine at this contemporary, high-ceilinged *enoteca* (wine bar), which pairs throaty Cannonau reds and tangy Vermentino whites with top-quality tasting plates of local *salumi* (cured meats) and cheese.

Hop Corner
PUB

(Via Principe Amedeo 14; ⊙6.30pm-3am) This stone-vaulted pub is an atmospheric spot for speciality beers and ales, including some Italian ones, which pair nicely with homemade grub using Sardinian produce (the burgers are spot-on). It also hosts occasional live music evenings with a retro vibe.

Antico Caffè
CAFE

(www.anticocaffe1855.it; Piazza Costituzione 10; ⊙7am-2am) DH Lawrence and Grazia Deledda once frequented this grand old cafe, which opened its doors in 1855. Locals come to chat over leisurely coffees, frilly crêpes and salads. There's a pavement terrace, or you can settle inside amid the polished wood, marble and brass.

Il Merlo Parlante
PUB

(Via Portoscalas 69; ⊙5pm-midnight Tue-Sun) Cagliari's nearest thing to a student pub, this is a boisterous place with lager on tap, rock on the stereo and a young up-for-it international crowd.

Emerson
LOUNGE

(www.emersoncafe.it; Viale Poetto 4; ⊙9am-1am summer, 11am-5pm winter) Near the fourth bus stop, and one of the most popular of the seafront *chioschi,* this swank place is a bit of everything. Part cocktail lounge, part restaurant and part beach club, it dishes up everything from pasta to *aperitivi,* live music and sun loungers.

Entertainment

Cagliari's nightlife revolves around the city's bars and cafes, which in summer means the beach at Poetto. For the low-down, ask at the tourist office or pick up a copy of the local newspaper *L'Unione Sarda.* Online, you'll find listings at www.sardegnaconcerti.com (in Italian).

Teatro Lirico
THEATRE

(📋070 408 22 30; www.teatroliricodicagliari.it; Via Sant'Alenixedda) This is Cagliari's premier venue for classical music, opera and ballet. The line-up is fairly traditional but quality is high and concerts are well attended.

Shopping

For boutiques and designer labels, head to Via Roma and boutique-studded Via Giuseppe Garibaldi. The Marina district harbours some enticing craft and speciality shops.

★ Durke
FOOD

(Via Napoli 66; ⊙10.30am-1.30pm & 4.30-8pm Mon-Sat) In Sardinian, *durke* means 'sweet' and they don't come sweeter than this delightful old-fashioned store. Made according to age-old recipes, the sweets here are quite special and some of the best are made with nothing more than sugar, egg whites and almonds. Indulge on fruit-and-nut *papassinos,* moist *amaretti di sardegna* biscuits and *pardulas,* delicate ricotta cheesecakes flavoured with saffron.

Sapori di Sardegna
FOOD

(Via dei Mille 1; ⊙9.30am-9pm) Roberto, his brother and their enthusiastic team do a brisk trade in glorious Sardinian food at this breezy Marina emporium. Stop by for the finest *pecorino,* salami, *bottarga* (mullet roe), bread, wine and pretty-packed *dolci* (sweets). If you've got no room in your luggage, staff can arrange to ship orders worldwide.

WORTH A TRIP

SARDINIA'S BACKCOUNTRY BY TRAIN

If you're not in a rush, one of the best ways of exploring Sardinia's rugged interior is on the narrow-gauge **Trenino Verde** (070 265 76 12; www.trenino verde.com) train. There are four routes: Mandas–Arbatax (one way/return €20/28, 5¼ hours), Mandas–Isili–Sorgono (one way/return €15.50/21.50, 3½ hours), Macomer–Bosa (one way/return €11.50/16.50, two hours) and Sassari–Tempo–Palau (one way/return €20/28, 4¼ hours). Of these, the twisting Mandas–Arbatax line is particularly spectacular, crossing the remote highlands of the Parco Nazionale del Golfo di Orosei e del Gennargentu.

From the metro station on Piazza Repubblica in Cagliari, a metro runs to Monserrato, from where you can connect with trains for Mandas.

Loredana Mandas   JEWELLERY

(Via Sicilia 31; 9.30am-1pm & 4.30-8pm Mon-Sat) For something very special, seek out this jewellery workshop. You can watch Loredana create the exquisite gold filigree for which Sardinia is so famous, and then maybe buy a piece. A pair of gold earrings will set you back anything from €220 to €2100.

Mercato di San Benedetto   MARKET

(www.mercatosanbenedetto.com; Via San Francesco Cocco Ortu; 7am-2pm Mon-Sat) You can pick up all sorts of Sardinian goodies – seafood, tangy salami, *pecorino* the size of wagon wheels, horse steaks, you name it – at this historic food market.

ℹ Information

Cagliari is dotted with free wi-fi zones, but annoyingly you can only log on if you have an Italian SIM card (the password is sent to your mobile phone).

Banks and ATMs are widely available, particularly around the port and station, and on Piazza del Carmine and Corso Vittorio Emanuele II.

Guardia Medica (070 52 24 58; Via Talete) For an emergency call-out doctor.

InfoPoint Porto (338 6498498, 070 677 71 87; www.cagliariturismo.it; Stazione Marittima, Molo Sanità; 9am-8pm) At the port, this kiosk is handy for city info and maps.

Post Office (Via Logudoro 9; 8.20am-7.05pm Mon-Fri, 8.20am-12.35pm Sat)

Tourist Office (070 409 23 06; Palazzo Viceregio, Piazza Palazzo; 10am-7pm summer, 10.30am-4pm winter) This friendly tourist office in the Castello district is well stocked with city information and maps.

ℹ Getting There & Away

AIR

Cagliari's Elmas airport (p841) is 9km northwest of the centre. Flights connect with mainland Italy and European destinations, including Barcelona, London, Paris and Stuttgart. In summer, there are additional charter flights.

BOAT

Cagliari's ferry port is just off Via Roma. **Tirrenia** (892 123; www.tirrenia.it; Via Riva di Ponente 1) is the main operator, with year-round services to Civitavecchia, Naples, Palermo and Trapani. Book tickets at the port or at travel agencies.

BUS

From the main bus station on Piazza Matteotti, **Turmo Travel** (0789 2 14 87; www.gruppotur motravel.com) runs a twice-daily service to Olbia (€19, 4¼ hours) and a daily bus to Santa Teresa di Gallura (€22.50, 5½ hours). **ARST** (Azienda Regionale Sarda Trasporti; 800 865042; www.arst.sardegna.it) buses serve nearby Pula (€3, 50 minutes, hourly) and Villasimius (€4.50, 1½ hours, six to eight daily), as well as Oristano (€7, 1½ hours, two daily), Nuoro (€15.50, 2½ to five hours, two daily), Iglesias (€4.50, one to 1½ hours, two daily), Chia (€4.50, 1¼ hours, 10 daily) and Sassari (€14.50, 3¼ hours, three daily).

CAR & MOTORCYCLE

The island's main dual-carriage road, the SS131 Carlo Felice Hwy, links the capital with Porto Torres via Oristano and Sassari, and Olbia via Nuoro. The SS130 leads west to Iglesias.

TRAIN

The main Trenitalia station is on Piazza Matteotti. Trains from here serve Iglesias (€3.85, one hour, 16 daily), Sassari (€15.75, 3½ hours, five daily) and Porto Torres (€16.90, 3½ hours, one daily) via Oristano (€5.95, one to 1¼ hours, hourly). Trains to Olbia (€16.90, 3½ to four hours, five daily) and Golfo Aranci (€18.30, 4½ to seven hours, three daily) – the handiest station for the Costa Smeralda – involve a change at Oristano, Ozieri-Chilivani or Macomer.

ℹ Getting Around

TO/FROM THE AIRPORT

Buses run from Piazza Matteotti to Elmas airport (€4, 10 minutes, 32 daily) from 5.20am to 10.30pm. Between 9am and 10.30pm, departures are every hour and half past the hour. A taxi costs about €25.

BUS

CTM (Consorzio Trasporti e Mobilità; ☑ 070 209 12 10; www.ctmcagliari.it) bus routes cover the city and surrounding area. A standard ticket costs €1.20 from vending machines or €1.70 on board and is valid for 90 minutes; a daily ticket is €3.

CAR & MOTORCYCLE

On-street parking within the blue lines costs €1 per hour. Alternatively, there's a useful car park next to the train station, which costs €10 for 24 hours.

Driving in the centre of Cagliari, with its maze of one-way streets, is a pain; in any case, almost everywhere is accessible on foot. If you want to rent a car to explore further afield, there's a **Hertz** (☑ 070 65 10 78; www.hertz.it; Piazza Matteotti 8) on Piazza Matteotti and several car-rental agencies at the airport. Or if you just want to zip about town and over to Poetto, you can rent a Vespa from **Sardegna in Vespa** (☑ 070 24 01 01; www.sardegnainvespa.com; Isola Rent, Elmas airport; per day €56.80).

TAXI

There are taxi ranks at Piazza Matteotti, Piazza della Repubblica and on Largo Carlo Felice. Or call **Quattro Mori** (☑ 070 40 01 01; www.cagliaritaxi.com) or **Rossoblù** (☑ 070 66 55; www.radiotaxirossoblu.com).

AROUND CAGLIARI

Stretching east and north of Cagliari, the lonely Sarrabus is one of Sardinia's least-populated and least-developed areas. In its centre rise the bushy green peaks of the Monte dei Sette Fratelli, a remarkably wild hinterland where some of the island's last remaining deer wander undisturbed.

East of Poetto the SP17 hugs the coast prettily (if precariously) all the way round to Villasimius and then north along the Costa Rei, providing arresting views of azure sea and crescent-shaped coves.

Villasimius

Once a quiet fishing village surrounded by pines and *macchia* (Mediterranean scrub), Villasimius has grown into a cheerful summer resort and makes a handy base for exploring the sandy bays and transparent waters on this stretch of the coast.

THE ANCIENT CITY OF NORA

About 30km southwest of Cagliari, the archaeological zone of **Nora** (☑ 070 920 91 38 070 920 91 38; adult/reduced €7.50/4.50; ☙ 9am-sunset) is what's left of a once-powerful ancient city. Founded by Phoenicians in the 11th century BC, it passed into Carthaginian hands before being taken over by the Romans and becoming one of the most important cities on the island. Upon entry, you pass a single melancholy column from a former temple and then a small but beautifully preserved Roman theatre. To the west are the substantial remains of the **Terme al Mare** (Baths by the Sea). Four columns stand at the heart of what was a patrician villa; the surrounding rooms retain their mosaic floor decoration.

Regular buses connect Pula and Cagliari (€3, 45 minutes). From Pula there are frequent shuttle buses down to Nora (€1.20), 4km away.

⊙ Sights & Activities

★**Capo Carbonara** NATURE RESERVE
If you do just one day trip from Villasimius, make it the 15-minute drive south to Capo Carbonara, a protected marine park. The promontory dips spectacularly into the crystal-clear water of the Med. Besides perfect conditions for scuba divers, the area has some gorgeously secluded bays with white quartz sand, backed by cliffs cloaked in *macchia* and wildflowers. Walking trails teeter off in all directions. The drive takes you past the **Notteri salt lake**, where flamingos and shearwaters flock in winter.

Spiaggia del Riso BEACH
Just south of town lies Spiaggia del Riso, one of Villasimius' most striking beaches. This beautiful arc of pale golden sand is lapped by azure waters and scattered with granite boulders that have been polished smooth by the sea.

Stagno Notteri LAKE
Running all the way to Villasimius, this lagoon often hosts flamingos in winter. On its seaward side is the stunning **Spiaggia del Simius** beach with its Polynesian-blue waters.

SARDINIA VILLASIMIUS

DON'T MISS

TOP FIVE BEACHES IN SARDINIA

Chia (p853)

Spiaggia del Principe (p871)

Spiaggia Rena Bianca (p873)

Is Aruttas (p858)

Cala Goloritzè (p882)

Fiore di Maggio   BOAT TOUR

(☑345 6032042; www.fioredimaggio.eu; Località Campulongu; per adult/child incl lunch €45/30) These daily boat tours, departing at 10.30am and returning at 5pm, are a superb way to see the hidden bays and islands of the Capo Carbonara marine reserve. Take your bathers if you fancy a dip.

🍴 Sleeping & Eating

Hotel Mariposas   HOTEL €€

(☑070 79 00 84; www.hotelmariposas.it; Via Mar Nero 1; s €74-188, d €96-238; [P❋🅿🛜🏊🐕]) A short hop from the beach, this low-slung hotel is set in glorious flower-strewn gardens. The spacious rooms all have their own terrace or balcony, and there's an attractive pool that's perfect for whiling away an afternoon.

Ristorante Le Anforè   MEDITERRANEAN €€

(☑070 79 20 32; www.hotelleanfore.com; Via Pallaresus 16; meals €30; ⏱noon-2.30pm & 7.30-10.30pm Tue-Sun, 7.30-10.30pm Mon) The chef's love of fresh local produce shines through in Sardinian dishes such as *burrida* (marinated dogfish) and spaghetti with *ricci* (sea urchins) at this highly regarded restaurant. There's alfresco dining on the verandah overlooking gardens.

ℹ Getting There & Away

Buses run to and from Cagliari (€4.50, 1½ hours, six to eight daily).

Costa Rei

Stretching along Sardinia's southeastern coast, the Costa Rei's resorts are fairly nondescript, but the beaches are out of this world. The long sweep of coastline is frosted with pearly white strands of beach, lapped by azure water that beggars belief.

From Villasimius, take the SP17 as it hugs the coast north. The road actually runs inland, but you can access the sign-posted beaches via the dirt tracks that branch off the main road. Crystal-clear waters and the occasional snack-cum-cocktail bar await.

👁 Sights

Spiaggia Costa Rei   BEACH

Like the beaches to its south and north, Spiaggia Costa Rei is a dazzling white strand lapped by astonishingly clear blue-green water.

Spiaggia Piscina Rei   BEACH

North of the resort of Costa Rei, Spiaggia Piscina Rei continues the theme of blinding-white sand and turquoise water. A couple more beaches fill the remaining length of coast up to Capo Ferrato, beyond which drivable dirt trails lead north.

🍴 Sleeping

Villaggio Camping Capo Ferrato   CAMPGROUND €

(☑070 99 10 12; www.campingcapoferrato.it; Via Cilea 98; camping 2 people, car & tent €27.50-38; ⏱Apr-Oct; 🐕) Pitch a tent under the eucalyptus and mimosa trees at this beachfront campground by the southern entrance to the resort. There's a mini club (summer only) and a playground for kids.

ℹ Getting There & Away

The same ARST buses from Cagliari to Villasimius continue around to Costa Rei, taking about half an hour.

Costa del Sud & Chia

One of the most beautiful stretches of coast in southern Sardinia, the Costa del Sud runs 25km from Chia to Porto di Teulada. Popular with windsurfers and kite-surfers, Chia's two ravishing beaches are golden strips of sand divided by a Pisan watchtower.

👁 Sights & Activities

Running the 25km length of the Costa del Sud, the Strada Panoramica della Costa del Sud (known more prosaically as the SP71) is a panoramic road that snakes along the spectacular coastline between Porto di Teulada and Chia. It's a stunning drive whichever way you do it, with wonderful views at every turn and a succession of bays capped by Spanish-era watchtowers.

Starting in Porto di Teulada, the first stretch twists past several coves as it rises to the highpoint of Capo Malfatano. Along the way, Spiaggia Piscinni is a great place for a dip in incredible azure waters.

Beyond the cape, the popular Cala Teuradda beach boasts vivid emerald-green waters, summer snack bars and a conveniently situated bus stop.

From here the road climbs inland away from the water. For great coastal views, turn off along the narrow side road at Porto Campana and follow the dirt track to the lighthouse at Capo Spartivento. From here a series of beaches stretch north – watch out for signposts off the main coastal road to Cala Cipolla, a gorgeous spot backed by pine and juniper trees, Spiaggia Su Giudeu and Porto Campana.

Chia VILLAGE

More a collection of hotels, holiday homes and campsites than a traditional village, Chia is a hugely popular summer hangout. To see what all the fuss is about, head up to the Spanish watchtower and look down on its two ravishing beaches – to the west, the Spiaggia Sa Colonia, to the east, the smaller Spiaggia Su Portu.

A paradise for windsurfers and sports fans, these sandy beaches play host to the annual Chia Classic, a surf, windsurf and kitesurf event held between April and June.

🛏 Sleeping

Campeggio Torre Chia CAMPGROUND €

(✆070 923 00 54; www.campeggiotorrechia.it; Via del Porto 21, Chia; camping 2 people, car & tent €27-31, 4-person cottages €87-128; ⊗May-Oct) At the popular summer resort of Chia, this busy camping ground has shady pitches and a series of cottages a few hundred metres from the beach. The cottages, which sleep up to four, come with a double bedroom, a bathroom, kitchen facilities and a living room with sofa bed.

❶ Getting There & Away

From Cagliari, there are up to 10 daily buses to/from Chia (€4.50, 1¼ hours). Between mid-June and mid-September, two daily buses ply the Costa del Sud, linking Chia with Spiaggia Teulada (€3, 35 minutes).

IGLESIAS & THE SOUTHWEST

Iglesias

Surrounded by the skeletons of Sardinia's once-thriving mining industry, Iglesias is a historic town that hums with life in summer and slumbers in the colder months. Its historic centre, an appealing ensemble of lived-in piazzas, sun-bleached buildings and Aragonese-style wrought-iron balconies, creates an atmosphere that's as much Iberian as Sardinian – a vestige of its time as a Spanish colony. Its focal square, Piazza Quintino Sella, throngs with people during the evening *passeggiata* (stroll).

◉ Sights

★ **Cattedrale di Santa Chiara** CATHEDRAL

(Duomo; Piazza del Municipio; ⊗8am-6pm) Dominating the eastern flank of Piazza del Municipio, the Cattedrale di Santa Chiara boasts a lovely Pisan-flavoured facade and a chequerboard stone bell tower. The church was originally built in the late 13th century, but it was given a comprehensive makeover in the 16th century, which accounts for its current Catalan Gothic look. Inside, the highlight is a gilded altarpiece that once held the relics of St Antiochus.

Museo dell'Arte Mineraria MUSEUM

(✆328 8094091; www.museoartemineraria.it; Via Roma 47; adult/reduced €4/2; ⊗6.30-8.30pm Sat & Sun summer, by appointment rest of year) Just outside the historic centre, Iglesias' main museum is dedicated to the town's mining heritage. It displays up to 70 extraction machines, alongside tools and a series of thought-provoking black-and-white photos. But to get a real taste of the claustrophobic conditions in which the miners worked, duck down into the recreated tunnels. These were dug by mining students and were used to train senior workers until WWII, when they were used as air-raid shelters.

🛏 Sleeping & Eating

B&B Mare Monti Miniere B&B €

(✆348 3310585, 0781 4 17 65; www.maremonti miniere-bb.it; Via Trento 10; s €30, d €42-60, tr €65; ❄🤶) A warm welcome awaits at this cracking B&B. Situated in a quiet side street near the historic centre, it has three cheery and immaculately kept rooms with above-par

SARDINIA IGLESIAS

WORTH A TRIP

ISOLE DI SANT'ANTIOCO & SAN PIETRO

The southwest's two islands, Isola di Sant'Antioco and Isola di San Pietro, display very different characters. The larger and more developed of the two, Isola di Sant'Antioco boasts little of the obvious beauty you'd ordinarily associate with small Mediterranean islands, but it hides a rich history – it was founded by the Phoenicians in the 8th century BC and its historic hilltop centre is littered with necropolises.

Barely half an hour across the water, Isola di San Pietro presents a prettier picture with its pastel houses and bobbing fishing boats. A mountainous trachyte island measuring about 15km long and 11km wide, it's named after St Peter, who, legend has it, was marooned here during a storm on the way to Karalis (now Cagliari). Its main town, **Carloforte**, is the very image of Mediterranean chic, with graceful *palazzi*, crowded cafes and palm trees along the waterfront, and quaint cobbled streets. The island's restaurants dish up the local world-famous tuna.

Regular **Saremar** (📞 0781 85 40 050781 85 40 05; www.saremar.it; Corso Tagliafico 13) ferries sail to/from Carloforte (per person/person plus car €5.50/17.20, 30 minutes, 15 daily) and Calasetta (on Sant'Antioco; per person/person plus car €5.50/15.20, seven daily) from Portovesme on Sardinia. Alternatively, you can head south on the SS126 from Carbonia and cross the bridge to Sant'Antioco.

touches such as DVD players and bathrobes. It's independent of the main house, and there's also a smart studio flat with its own kitchen facilities. Thoughtful extras include beach towels and free bike hire.

★ **Trattoria Pintadera**   TRATTORIA **€€**
(📞 346 6770183; Via Manno 22; meals €30; ⏱ 12.30-2pm & 7.30-11pm) A welcoming family-run eatery in the *centro storico* (historic centre), Pintadera is the sort of place that gives Italian trattorias a good name. In a rustic stone *palazzo*, you sit down to hearty local pastas – try the ravioli stuffed with potato and mint – and buttery chargrilled steaks. Great food, a warm atmosphere and excellent value for money; it's a top choice.

ℹ Getting There & Away

There is a twice-daily bus service to/from Cagliari (€4.50, one to 1½ hours).

Costa Verde

One of Sardinia's great untamed coastal stretches, the Costa Verde (Green Coast) extends northwards from Capo Pecora to the small resort of Torre dei Corsari. Named after the green *macchia* that covers much of its mountainous hinterland, it's an area of wild, exhilarating beauty and spectacular, unspoilt beaches.

There's no road that follows the entire length of the Costa, so if you're driving northwards from Portixeddu (and you really do need to drive to get the best out of

this area), you have to head inland along the SS126 towards Arbus and Guspini.

◉ Sights

★ **Spiaggia di Piscinas**   BEACH
This magnificent beach is a picture of unspoilt beauty. A broad band of golden sand, it's sandwiched between a windswept sea and a vast expanse of dunes flecked by hardy green *macchia*. These towering dunes, known as Sardinia's desert, rise to heights of up to 60m.

The beach is signposted off the SS126 and accessible via Ingurtosu and a 9km dirt track.

Spiaggia di Scivu   BEACH
A 3km lick of fine sand backed by towering dunes and walls of sandstone, Spiaggia di Scivu is the most southerly of the Costa Verde's beaches. To get there take the SS126 and head towards Arbus (if heading north) or Fluminimaggiore (if heading south) and follow the signs about 12km south of Arbus.

🛏 Sleeping

★ **Agriturismo L'Oasi del Cervo**   AGRITURISMO **€**
(📞 347 3011318; www.oasidelcervo.com; Località Is Gennas, Montevecchio; s €40, d €60-70, half-board per person €46-60; 🅿 🐾) With 15 modest rooms and a remote location in the midst of *macchia*-cloaked hills, this working farm is a genuine country hideaway. It's all very down to earth, but the rooms are comfortable enough, the views are uplifting and the

WORTH A TRIP

SARDINIA'S WORLD HERITAGE SITE

Nuraghe Su Nuraxi (☑ 070 936 81 28; www.fondazionebarumini.it; adult/reduced €10/8; ☺ 9am-7pm summer, to 4pm winter) Sardinia's star archaeological site, most visited *nuraghe* (stone tower) and sole Unesco World Heritage Site, Nuraghe Su Nuraxi sits in the heart of the voluptuous green countryside near Barumini. The focal point is the 1500 BC tower, which originally stood on its own but was later incorporated into a fortified compound. Many of the settlement's buildings were erected in the Iron Age, and it's these that constitute the beehive of circular interlocking buildings that tumble down the hillside.

Note that visits are by guided tour only, usually in Italian, and that explanatory print-outs are available in English. It's also worth noting that queues are the norm in summer when it can get extremely hot on the exposed site.

homemade food is delicious. You'll see a sign for the *agriturismo* off the SP65 between Montevecchio and Torre dei Corsari.

ORISTANO & THE WEST

Oristano

POP 32,156

With its elegant shopping streets, ornate piazzas and popular cafes, Oristano's refined and animated centre is a lovely place to hang out. Though there's not a huge amount to see beyond some churches and an interesting archaeological museum, the city makes a good base for the surrounding area. Oristano was founded in the 11th century and became capital of the Giudicato d'Arborea, one of Sardinia's four independent provinces.

⊙ Sights

Torre di Mariano II   TOWER
(Piazza Roma) Little survives of the medieval walled town except for this 13th-century tower. Known also as the Torre di Cristoforo, it was the town's northern gate and an important part of the city's defences. The bell was added in the 15th century.

Statue of Eleonora   STATUE
(Piazza Eleonora d'Arborea) Piazza Eleonora d'Arborea became the city's central square through 19th-century urban reforms. Today it is a quiet spot where you can sit beneath the benign gaze of Queen Eleonora's statue. She holds the ground-breaking *Carta di Logu* (Code of Laws), an extraordinary law code she created that tackled land and prop-

erty legislation, as well as introducing a raft of women's rights.

Chiesa di San Francesco   CHURCH
(Via Sant'Antonio; ☺ open for mass only) The 14th-century *Crocifisso di Nicodemo*, considered one of Sardinia's most precious carvings, is the highlight of this 19th-century neoclassical church designed by Cagliari architect Gaetano Cima. Also take a look at the sacristy's 16th-century altarpiece by Pietro Cavaro.

★**Cattedrale di Santa Maria Assunta**   CATHEDRAL
(Duomo; Piazza del Duomo; ☺ 9am-7pm summer, to 6pm winter) Lording it over Oristano's skyline, the Duomo's onion-domed bell tower is one of the few remaining elements of the original 14th-century cathedral, itself a reworking of an earlier church damaged by fire in the late 12th century. The free-standing *campanile* (bell tower), topped by its conspicuous majolica-tiled dome, adds an exotic Byzantine feel to what is otherwise a typical 18th-century baroque complex.

Museo Antiquarium Arborense   MUSEUM
(☑ 0783 79 12 62; www.antiquariumarborense.it; Piazza Corrias; adult/reduced €5/2.50; ☺ 9am-8pm Mon-Fri, 9am-2pm & 3-8pm Sat & Sun) Oristano's principal museum boasts one of the island's major archaeological collections, with prehistoric artefacts from the Sinis Peninsula and finds from Carthaginian and Roman Tharros. There's also a small collection of *retabli* (painted altarpieces), including the 16th-century *Retablo del Santo Cristo*, by the workshop of Pietro Cavaro, which depicts a group of apparently beatific saints. But look closer and you'll see they all sport the instruments of their tortures slicing through their heads, necks and hearts.

Oristano

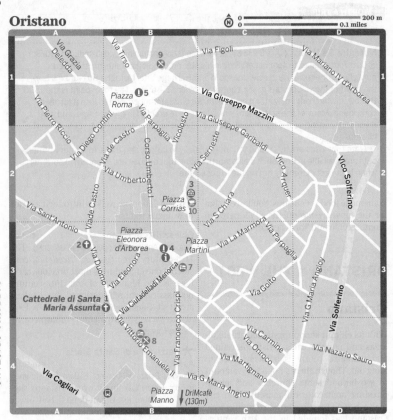

Oristano

◎ Top Sights

◎ Sights

🛏 Sleeping

✗ Eating

◎ Drinking & Nightlife

🎇 Festivals & Events

★ Sa Sartiglia   CARNIVAL
(⊙ Feb) Oristano's carnival is the most colourful on the island. It is attended in February by hundreds of costumed participants
and involves a medieval joust, horse racing
and incredible, acrobatic riding.

🛏 Sleeping

★ Eleonora B&B   B&B €
(📞 0783 7 04 35, 347 4817976; www.eleonora-
bed-and-breakfast.com; Piazza Eleonora d'Arborea 12; s €35-60, d €60-75, tr €75-95; ✳ 🛜)
This charming B&B scores on all counts:
location – it's in a medieval *palazzo* on
Oristano's central piazza; decor – rooms are
tastefully decorated with a mix of antique

furniture, exposed brick walls and gorgeous old tiles; and hospitality – owners Andrea and Paola are helpful and hospitable hosts. All this, and it's excellent value for money.

Duomo Albergo
HOTEL €€

(📞 0783 77 80 61; www.hotelduomo.net; Via Vittorio Emanuele II 34; s €65-80, d €108-135; ※ @) Oristano's top hotel is refined and elegantly understated. Behind its discreet facade, guest rooms reveal a low-key look with traditional fabrics and cooling white tones. In summer, breakfast is served in an internal courtyard, while gourmets can dine on creative Sardinian cuisine at the hotel's highly rated restaurant, Josto al Duomo.

✖ Eating & Drinking

La Torre
PIZZA €

(📞 0783 30 14 94; Piazza Roma 52; pizzas €4.50-10, meals €20-25; ⊙ noon-3pm & 6-10pm Tue-Sun) This place doesn't look like much from the outside; in fact, it's not so amazing inside either. No matter, it serves the best pizza in town. If you're off pizza but just want to enjoy the hectic atmosphere, there's a full menu of pastas and grilled main courses too.

DriMcafè
CAFE €

(📞 078 330 37 50; Via Cagliari 316; light snacks & meals €4-10; ⊙ 8am-8pm Sun-Fri, 8am-11pm Sat; ☞) This delightful laid-back hang-out brings a slice of boho warmth to Oristano, with its rust-red walls, mishmash of vintage furnishings, book shelves and chipper service. Besides speciality teas (including Moroccan mint) and homemade cakes, it rustles up daily specials, from risotto with radicchio to rosemary-rubbed lamb with seasonal vegetables.

★ Josto al Duomo
SARDINIAN €€

(📞 0783 77 80 61; www.jostoalduomo.net; Via Vittorio Emanuele 34; meals €35-45, 2-/3-/4-course tasting menus €16/25/43; ⊙ 1-3pm & 8-11pm Mon-Sat) Refined and intimate, this hotel restaurant is gathered around an inner courtyard perfect for alfresco dining. The menu is seasonal, but the onus is on creative dishes inspired by traditional Sardinian flavours and served with an artistic eye for detail. For wine aficionados, there's also a strong wine list featuring many interesting island labels.

Lola Mundo
CAFE

(Piazza Corrias 14; ⊙ 7am-midnight Mon-Sat) With its piazza seating and relaxing music, this popular *centro storico* cafe is a great spot to hang out over a coffee or aperitif.

❶ Information

Tourist Office (📞 0783 368 32 10; www.gooristano.com; Piazza Eleonora d'Arborea 18; ⊙ 8am-1pm & 3-6pm Mon-Thu, 8.30am-1pm Fri) Ask for the useful booklet *Oristano in Your Pocket*.

❶ Getting There & Around

From the **bus station** (Via Cagliari) direct buses run to/from Cagliari (€7, two hours, two daily), Bosa (€6, two hours, five daily) and Sassari (€8, two hours, three daily).

The main train station is in Piazza Ungheria, east of the town centre. Up to 15 daily trains, some of which involve a change, run between Oristano and Cagliari (€5.95, one to 1½ hours, hourly). Trains also serve Sassari (€10.15, two to 2½ hours, four daily) and Olbia (€11.50, 2¾ hours, five daily).

Tharros & the Sinis Peninsula

Spearing into the Golfo di Oristano, the Sinis Peninsula feels like a world apart with its glassy lagoons, low-lying countryside and snow-white beaches – among the best on the island. The peninsula has been inhabited since the 5th century BC. *Nuraghi* (stone towers) litter the landscape and the compelling Punic-Roman site of Tharros stands as testament to the area's former importance. Sports fans will enjoy great surfing, windsurfing and some fine diving.

◉ Sights & Activities

★ Area Archeologica di Tharros
ARCHAEOLOGICAL SITE

(📞 0783 37 00 19; adult/reduced €5/4, incl tower €6/5; ⊙ 9am-8pm summer, to 5pm winter) The choppy blue waters of the Golfo di Oristano provide a magnificent backdrop to the ruins of ancient Tharros. Founded by the Phoenicians in the 8th century BC, the city thrived as a Carthaginian naval base and was later taken over by the Romans. Much of what you see today dates to the 2nd and 3rd centuries AD, when the basalt streets were laid, and the aqueduct, baths and other major monuments were built.

Torre di San Giovanni Watchtower
TOWER

(adult/reduced €3/2, incl Tharros €6/5; ⊙ 9am-8pm summer, to 5pm winter) For a bird's-eye view of Tharros, head up to the late-16th-century Torre di San Giovanni watchtowers. Here you can look down on the ruins, as well as

WORTH A TRIP

EXPLORING THE SINIS PENINSULA

Is Aruttas One of the peninsula's most famous beaches, Is Aruttas is a pristine arc of white sand fronted by translucent aquamarine waters. For years its quartz sand was carted off to be used in aquariums and on beaches on the Costa Smeralda, but it's now illegal to take any. The beach is signposted and 5km west of the road north from San Salvatore.

Putzu Idu Backed by a motley set of holiday homes and beach bars, Putzu Idu's beach sits at the north of the peninsula. It's a picturesque strip of sand that's something of a watersport hot spot, with excellent surfing, windsurfing and kitesurfing. To the north, the **Capo Mannu** promontory is battered by some of the biggest waves in the Mediterranean.

Isola di Mal di Ventre This bare, rocky island 10km off the coast owes its strange name (Stomach-ache Island) to the sea-sickness that sailors often suffered while navigating its windy waters. Now uninhabited, it was home to a primitive nuraghic settlement and was later used by Saracen pirates. These days, the only people to visit are holidaymakers keen to search out the beaches on its eastern shores. To get to the island, **Maremania** (☑ 348 0084161; www.maluentu.it; tours adult/reduced €25/15; ☺ 8am-1pm & 3-7pm summer only) is one of several operators running boat tours from Putzu Idu between June and September.

Capo Mannu Windsurf School (☑ 347 6881793; www.capomannuwindsurf.it; Lungomare Putzu Idu) Runs windsurfing lessons and courses for all levels; also hires out boards and sail rigs. One-hour individual lessons start at €35, rig hire at €15 per hour.

the **Spiaggia di San Giovanni di Sinis**, a popular beach, which extends on both sides of the tower.

Chiesa di San Giovanni di Sinis CHURCH (☺ 9am-5pm) Just beyond the car park at the foot of the Tharros access road, you'll see the sandstone Chiesa di San Giovanni di Sinis, one of the two oldest churches in Sardinia (Cagliari's Basilica di San Saturnino is older). It owes its current form to an 11th-century makeover, although elements of the 6th-century Byzantine original remain, including the characteristic red dome. Inside, the bare walls lend a sombre and surprisingly spiritual atmosphere.

🛏 Sleeping & Eating

Agriturismo Sinis AGRITURISMO € (☑ 328 9312508, 0783 39 26 53; www.agriturismoilsinis.it; Località San Salvatore; half-board per person €52-65; ❈🄹) Near the dusty hamlet of San Salvatore, this working farm offers six guest rooms and wonderful earthy food. Rooms are frill-free but clean and airy, and views of the lush garden can be enjoyed from chairs on the patio.

Camping Is Aruttas CAMPGROUND € (☑ 0783 192 54 61; www.campingisaruttas.it; Località Marina Is Aruttas; camping 2 people, car & tent €25-42; ☺ Apr-Sep; 🛜) Within walking distance of the beach, Camping Is Aruttas provides modest camping facilities set amid olive trees and Mediterranean shrubbery.

Sa Peschiera 'e Mar 'e Pontis SEAFOOD €€ (☑ 0783 39 17 74; Strada Provinciale 6; menus €25-35; ☺ 1-2.30pm & 8-10.30pm, closed Wed & Sun dinner) Fronting the Pontis fishing cooperative on the road between Cabras and Tharros, this is a fantastic place to sample fresh seafood. The menu changes according to the daily catch, but pride of place goes to the local *muggine* (mullet) and prized *bottarga*. Bookings are recommended for weekday meals and are essential at weekends.

❶ Getting There & Around

In July and August, there are five daily buses for San Giovanni in Sinis from Oristano (€2, 35 minutes). Two weekday buses run to Putzu Idu from Oristano (€2.50, 55 minutes). In July and August, there are four additional services.

North Oristano Coast

Bosa

POP 8026

Bosa is one of Sardinia's most attractive towns. Seen from a distance, its rainbow townscape resembles a vibrant Paul Klee canvas, with pastel houses stacked on a steep hillside, tapering up to a stark, grey castle. In front, moored fishing boats bob on the glassy Temo river and palm trees line an elegant riverfront. Three kilometres west, Bosa Marina, the town's satellite beach resort, is less obviously attractive, with modern low-rise hotels, restaurants and holiday homes.

◉ Sights & Activities

★ **Castello Malaspina** CASTLE
(②0785 37 70 43; adult/reduced €5/3; ◎10am-1hr before sunset spring-autumn, 10am-1pm Sat & Sun winter) Commanding huge panoramic views, the hilltop castle was built in 1112 by the Tuscan Malaspina family. Little remains of the original structure except for the skeleton – imposing walls and a series of tough brick towers – and, inside, a humble 4th-century chapel, the **Chiesa di Nostra Signora di Regnos Altos**. This houses an extraordinary 14th-century fresco cycle depicting saints, ranging from a giant St Christopher to St Lawrence in the middle of his martyrdom.

★ **Museo Casa Deriu** MUSEUM
(②0785 37 70 43; Corso Vittorio Emanuele 59; adult/reduced €4.50/3; ◎10am-1pm & 3-5pm Tue-Sun, longer hours summer) Housed in an elegant 19th-century townhouse, Bosa's main museum showcases local arts and artisanal crafts. Each of the three floors has a different theme relating to the city and its past: the 1st floor hosts temporary exhibitions and displays of traditional hand embroidery; the 2nd floor displays the *palazzo*'s original 19th-century decor and furnishings; and the top floor is dedicated to Melkiorre Melis (1889–1982), a local painter and one of Sardinia's most important modern artists.

Cuccu BICYCLE RENTAL
(②0785 37 32 98; Via Roma 5; ◎9am-1pm & 4-8pm) To explore out of town, you can hire scooters (€40 per day) and bikes (€10 per day) at this mechanics' workshop on the southern side of the river.

🛏 Sleeping & Eating

La Torre di Alice B&B €
(②329 8570064, 347 6671785; www.latorredi alice.it; Via del Carmine 7; s €40-45, d €65-75, tr €85-95; ※ 🕸) This is a great budget choice in Bosa's medieval centre. Set in a wonderful old tower house near Piazza Episcopio, its five rooms are neat and comfortable, with low brick-vaulted ceilings, wrought-iron beds and relaxing decor. Breakfast is served at the rustic communal table in the colourful downstairs kitchen.

Corte Fiorita HOTEL €€
(②0785 37 70 58; www.albergo-diffuso.it; Via Lungo Temo de Gasperi 45; s €50-120, d €65-180; ※ @) A so-called *albergo diffuso*, Corte Fiorita has beautiful, spacious rooms in four *palazzi* across town: one on the riverfront and three in the historic centre. No two rooms are exactly the same, but the overall look is rustic-chic with plenty of exposed stonework, wooden beams and vaulted ceilings.

Pizzeria da Giovanni PIZZA €
(Via Ginnasio 6; pizza slices from €1.30; ◎daily) For a quick bite on the hoof, head to this humble, no-frills takeaway and join the locals for a taste of Giovanni's fabulous sliced pizza.

Al Gambero Rosso SARDINIAN €€
(②0785 37 41 50; Via Nazionale 12; meals €25-30; ◎12.30-3pm & 7-11pm Thu-Tue) Brimming with regulars, this unpretentious restaurant stands head and shoulders above most of Bosa's eateries with its friendly service and winningly fresh pasta and seafood. Menu stalwarts include pasta with prawns and artichokes and crispy fried calamari. Pizzas are delivered bubbling hot from a wood oven.

ⓘ Getting There & Away

All buses terminate at Piazza Zanetti. There are services to and from Alghero (€3.50, 55 minutes, two daily), Sassari (€6, 2¼ hours, three daily) and Oristano (€6, two hours, five daily). Get tickets at drinking hole **Gold Bar** (Via Azuni; ◎5am-midnight).

IMAGE SOURCE/GETTY IMAGES ©

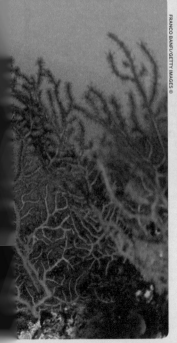

FRANCO BANFI/GETTY IMAGES ©

ANDY CHRISTIANI/GETTY IMAGES ©

1. Climbing, Santa Teresa di Gallura (p873)
Sardinia's rock formations make for breathtaking climbing.

2. Windsurfing (p53)
Porto Pollo and Chia (p852) are top spots for windsurfing in Sardinia.

3. Hiking, Gola Su Gorropu (p881)
This spectacular gorge, flanked by vertical 400m rock walls, has been dubbed the 'Grand Canyon of Europe'.

4. Diving (p52)
The gin-clear waters in Sardinia are a dream for divers.

ALGHERO & THE NORTHWEST

Alghero

POP 40,641

Pretty and petite, Alghero is one of Sardinia's most beautiful medieval towns, and even though crowds swell in July and August, the town has kept a tight clutch on its authentic character. Its *centro storico* is the island's best preserved; enclosed by robust, honey-coloured sea walls, this is a tight-knit enclave of shady cobbled lanes, Gothic *palazzi* and cafe-rimmed piazzas.

Below, yachts fill the marina and long, sandy beaches curve away to the north. Presiding over everything is a palpable Spanish atmosphere, a hangover from the city's past as a Catalan colony. Even today, more than three centuries after the Iberians left, a form of medieval Catalan is still spoken.

⊙ Sights

Torre Porta a Terra TOWER

(Piazza Porta Terra; ⊙ 9am-1pm & 4.30-9.30pm daily summer, 9am-1pm & 4.30-7.30pm Mon-Sat winter) FREE Near the Giardini Pubblici, the 14th-century Torre Porta a Terra is all that remains of Porta a Terra, one of the two main gates into the medieval city. A stumpy 23m-high tower known originally as Porta Reial, it now houses a small multimedia **museum** dedicated to the city's past and, on the 2nd floor, a terrace with sweeping, 360-degree views.

★ Sea Walls HISTORIC SITE

Alghero's golden sea walls, built around the *centro storico* by the Aragonese in the 16th century, are a highlight of the town's historic cityscape. Running from Piazza Sulis in the south to Porta a Mare and the marina in the north, they are crowned by a pedestrianised path that commands superb views over to Capo Caccia on the blue horizon. Restau-

SARDINIA ALGHERO

Alghero

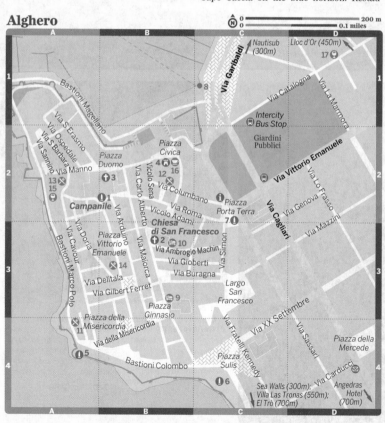

rants and bars line the walkway, providing the perfect perch to sit back and lap up the holiday atmosphere.

To walk the walls, also known as the *bastioni,* start at **Torre di Sulis** on the piazza of the same name. This tower originally closed off the defensive line of towers to the south of the old town. Continuing northwards along the **Bastioni Cristoforo Colombo**, you'll pass the **Torre di San Giacomo** before arriving on the main stretch, the **Bastioni Marco Polo** where most of the restaurants are lined up.

Cattedrale di Santa Maria　　CATHEDRAL
(Piazza Duomo; ⊙7am-1pm & 4-7.30pm) Overlooking Piazza Duomo, Alghero's oversized Cattedrale di Santa Maria appears out of place with its pompous neoclassical facade and fat Doric columns. An unfortunate 19th-century addition, the facade was the last in a long line of modifications that the hybrid cathedral has endured since it was built, originally on Catalan Gothic lines in the 16th century. Inside it's largely Renaissance, with some late-baroque baubles added in the 18th century.

Free guided tours of the cathedral are available between 10am and 1pm and then from 4pm to 6pm Monday to Friday between February and October.

★**Campanile**　　TOWER
(☑079 973 30 41; Via Principe Umberto; adult/reduced €2/free; ⊙10.30am-12.30pm Mon-Fri & 7-9pm Mon & Fri summer, 10.30am-12.30pm Mon, Tue, Thu & Fri & 4-6pm Mon & Fri autumn, by request Nov-May) Of more interest than the interior of the Cattedrale di Santa Maria is its striking *campanile*. Accessible through a Gothic doorway on Via Principe Umberto, this tall octagonal tower – the one you see rising

above Alghero's rooftops – is a fine example of Catalan Gothic architecture.

Piazza Civica　　PIAZZA
Just inside Porta a Mare, Piazza Civica is Alghero's showcase square. In a former life it was the administrative heart of the medieval city, but where Spanish aristocrats once met to debate affairs of empire, tourists now converge to browse jewellery displays in elegant shop windows, eat ice cream and drink at the city's grandest cafe. Caffè Costantino occupies the ground floor of the Gothic **Palazzo d'Albis**, where the Spanish emperor Charles V stayed in 1541.

★**Chiesa di San Francesco**　　CHURCH
(Via Carlo Alberto; ⊙approximately 8.30am-8pm) Alghero's finest church is a model of architectural harmony. Originally built to a Catalan Gothic design in the 14th century, it was later given a Renaissance facelift after it partially collapsed in 1593. Inside, interest is focused on the 18th-century polychrome marble altar and a strange 17th-century wooden sculpture of a haggard Christ tied to a column. Through the sacristy you can enter a beautiful 14th-century cloister, whose 22 columns connect a series of round arches.

🏃 **Activities**

North of Alghero's yacht-jammed port, Via Garibaldi sweeps up to the town's beaches, **Spiaggia di San Giovanni** and the adjacent **Spiaggia di Maria Pia**. Nicer by far, though, are the beaches near Fertilia.

Traghetti Navisarda　　BOAT TOUR
(☑079 95 06 03; www.navisarda.it; Banchina Dogana; adult/child return €15/8, cave entrance not included; ⊙tours hourly 9am-5pm Jun-Sep, 11am & 3pm March-May & Oct) From the port you can

SARDINIA ALGHERO

take a boat trip along the impressive northern coast to Capo Caccia and the grandiose Grotta di Nettuno cave complex. Traghetti Navisarda is one of a number of operators offering day cruises with lunch and swimming stops, and ferries up to the caves. The round trip, including cave visit, lasts approximately 2½ hours.

Nautisub
DIVING

(✆079 95 24 33; www.nautisub.com; Via Garibaldi 45; ⏰8.30am-1pm & 4.30-9pm Mon-Sat, 8.30am-12.30pm Sun summer, shorter hours winter) Operating out of a dive shop, this year-round outfit organises dives (from €45 or €60, including kit hire) and boat tours (from €45), and also offers kit hire.

🛏 Sleeping

Booking ahead is essential in July and August, when many hotels have a three- to four-night minimum-stay policy; it's also a good idea during the rest of the year.

★ B&B Benebenniu
B&B €

(✆380 1746726; www.benebenniu.com; Via Carlo Alberto 70; s €40-75, d €60-90, tr €75-105; ❄🛜🅿) A home away from home, this laid-back B&B exudes warmth and familiarity. Wonderfully located on a lively *centro storico* piazza, it has generously sized rooms with simple furnishings and plenty of natural light. The owner, Marija, is a delightful host and is more than happy to share her local tips and recommendations.

Lloc d'Or
B&B €

(✆391 1726083; www.llocdor.com; Via Logudoro 26; s €45-55, d €60-80; ❄🅿) Giovanni and Gemma are perfect hosts at this cute B&B with bright, nicely kept rooms. They go the extra mile to make you feel welcome – be it with beach towels, delicious breakfasts or tips on getting about town. It's just a couple of minutes' walk from the *lungomare* (seafront promenade) and harbour.

Hotel San Francesco
HOTEL €

(✆079 98 03 30; www.sanfrancescohotel.com; Via Ambrogio Machin 2; s €48-63, d €78-101, tr €100-135; ❄@🛜) This is one of the few hotels in Alghero's historic centre. Housed in an ex-convent – the monks still live on the 3rd floor – it has plain, comfortable rooms set around a 14th-century cloister where classical-music concerts are staged in summer.

★ Angedras Hotel
HOTEL €€

(✆079 973 50 34; www.angedras.it; Via Frank 2; s €60-95, d €65-139; 🅿❄🛜) A model of whitewashed Mediterranean elegance, the Angedras (which spells Sardegna backwards) offers cool, white rooms decorated in an understated Sardinian style. There's also an airy terrace good for iced drinks on hot summer evenings. Note that the hotel is a 15-minute walk from the historic centre.

Villa Las Tronas
HERITAGE HOTEL €€€

(✆079 98 18 18; www.hotelvillalastronas.it; Via Lungomare Valencia 1; s €154-297, d €220-407; ❄) Live like royalty at this palatial seafront hotel. Housed in a 19th-century palace once used by holidaying royals, it's set in its own lush gardens on a private headland. The rooms are pure fin de siècle with acres of brocade, elegant antiques and moody oil paintings. A spa with an indoor pool, sauna, hydro-massage and gym invites lingering.

🍴 Eating

Seafood rules in Alghero, a fishing town famous for its lobster, which is often served as *aragosta alla catalana* – Catalan-style with tomato and onion. From February to April, *riccio di mare* (sea urchins) pop up on menus. If you're eating along the sea walls, time dinner to catch sunset.

Lu Furat
PIZZA €

(✆079 973 60 52; Via Columbano 8; snacks €2-6; ⏰noon-3pm & 6.30-11.30pm Tue-Sun) Squeeze into this vaulted, hole-in-the-wall pizzeria and for a few euro you can snack on perfectly thin, crisp pizza or *fainè* (chickpea pancakes with pizza-style toppings). If you can't bag one of the few tables, get takeaway.

★ Trattoria Lo Romanì
TRATTORIA €€

(✆079 973 84 79; Via Principe Umberto 29; meals €30; ⏰7.30-11.30pm) Many Alghero restaurants serve *porcetto*, Sardinia's classic spit-roasted pork, but few places cook it to such buttery perfection. The crackling is spot on and the meat sweet and full of flavour. *Porcetto* apart, this is a delightful trattoria. Exposed sandstone walls and soft lighting create a warm, elegant atmosphere, service is attentive, and the fresh island food is excellent.

Mabrouk
SEAFOOD €€

(✆079 97 00 00; Via Santa Barbara 4; set menus €40; ⏰8pm-midnight Tue-Sun) A cosy seafood restaurant near the cathedral, Mabrouk is a wonderful place to feast on locally caught fish. What exactly is on the set menu depends on the day's catch, but with several antipasti, three pasta dishes and three main courses included, you won't go hungry.

Kings   SARDINIAN €€
(☑079 97 96 50; www.thekingsrestaurant.it; Via Cavour 123; meals €30-40; ⊘7-11.30pm; ☑🚇) With a sea-facing terrace on Alghero's honey-coloured ramparts, this restaurant cranks up the romance as day softens into dusk. Clean, bright Mediterranean flavours shine through in dishes like *tagliatelle* with clams and *bottarga* and grilled swordfish cooked with aubergines and tomatoes. There are dedicated menus for kids and vegetarians.

🍷 **Drinking & Entertainment**

Buena Vista   BAR
(Bastioni Marco Polo 47; cocktails €7; ⊘3.30pm-late) Fabulous mojitos go hand in hand with stunning sunset views at this buzzing little bar on the western walls. Upbeat tunes and a cavernous interior add to the friendly, laid-back vibe.

Il Blau Skybar   BAR
(www.hotelcatalunya.it; Via Catalogna 24; ⊘10am-3pm & 5-11pm) This chic little glass-walled number sits on the top floor of the Hotel Catalunya, taking in the full sweep of the marina, *centro storico* and bay. It's a stylish spot to watch the sun go down over an *aperitivo*.

Caffè Costantino   CAFE
(Piazza Civica 31; ⊘7.30am-1.30am, closed Mon winter) On Alghero's showpiece piazza, Caffè Costantino is the most famous cafe in town.

It's also one of the busiest, attracting a constant stream of tourists to its square-side tables. Join them for drinks and people-watching, but skip the mediocre, overpriced food.

El Trò   CLUB
(☑079 97 99 38; Via Lungomare Valencia 3; ⊘10.30am-6am) A restaurant, bar and disco on the rocks, El Trò is one of Alghero's historic nightlife addresses. It serves pizza by the metre and a regular dose of late-night dance music.

ℹ️ **Information**

Airport Tourist Office (☑079 97 71 28; ⊘9am-1pm & 3-7pm Mon-Sat) In the arrivals hall.

Farmacia Cabras (☑079 97 92 60; Via Fratelli Kennedy 12; ⊘9am-1pm & 4-8pm Mon-Sat) English-speaking service.

Ospedale Civile (☑079 995 51 11; Via Don Minzoni) The main hospital.

Police Station (☑079 972 00 00; Via Fratelli Kennedy 1)

Post Office (Via Carducci 35; ⊘8.20am-7.05pm Mon-Fri, 8.20am-12.35pm Sat)

Tourist Office (☑079 97 90 54; www.alghero-turismo.it; Piazza Porta Terra 9; ⊘8am-8pm Mon-Sat, 10am-1pm & 5-8pm Sun) English-speaking staff and tons of practical information.

ℹ️ **Getting There & Away**

AIR

Fertilia Airport (☑079 93 50 11; www.aero portodialghero.it) Located 10km north of town; serves domestic flights to and from Italy, and **Ryanair** (www.ryanair.com) flights to and from London, Frankfurt, Madrid, Paris and a number of other European cities.

PREHISTORIC WONDERS

To the untrained eye, the strange stone circles that litter Sardinia's interior are mysterious and incomprehensible. But to archaeologists they provide one of the few windows into the dark world of the Bronze Age *nuraghe* people. There are said to be up to 7000 *nuraghi* across the island, most built between 1800 and 500 BC. No one is absolutely certain what they were used for, although most experts think they were defensive watchtowers.

Even before they started building *nuraghi,* the Sardinians were busy digging tombs into the rock, known as **domus de janas** (fairy houses). More elaborate were the common graves fronted by stele called **tombe dei giganti** (giants' tombs).

Evidence of pagan religious practices is provided by **pozzi sacri** (well temples). Built from around 1000 BC, these were often constructed to capture light at the yearly equinoxes, hinting at a naturalistic religion as well as sophisticated building techniques. The well temple at Santa Cristina is a prime example.

WORTH A TRIP

TOP DROP

Sella e Mosca (☎ 079 99 77 00; www.
sellaemosca.com; ☺ guided tour 5.30pm
Mon-Sat summer, by request rest of year)
Sardinia's top wine producer has been
based at this 550-hectare estate since
1899. To learn more about its history
and production methods, join the free
afternoon tour of the estate's historic
cellars and lovingly tended museum.
Afterwards, stock up at the beautiful
enoteca (☺ 8.30am-8pm Mon-Sat summer, to 6.30pm winter). Private tastings
can also be organised.

From Alghero, three daily buses
(weekdays only) pass by the turn-off for
Sella e Mosca (€2, 25 minutes).

BUS

InterCity buses stop at and leave from Via Catalogna, by the Giardini Pubblici. Buy tickets at the ticket office in the gardens. Up to 10 daily buses run to Sassari (€3, one hour). There are also services to Porto Torres (€3.50, one hour, five daily) and Bosa (€3.50, 1½ hours, two daily with extra services in summer).

TRAIN

The train station is 1.5km north of the old town on Via Don Minzoni. Up to 12 trains run daily to/from Sassari (€2.20, 35 minutes).

❶ Getting Around

From the bus stops on Via Cagliari, bus line AF runs along the seafront and up to Fertilia airport (25 minutes, hourly between 5am and 11pm). Tickets, available at newsagents and *tabacchi* (tobacconists), cost €1, although you can also buy them on board for €1.50.

A taxi to/from the airport will cost between €20 and €25.

Cicloexpress (☎ 079 98 69 50; www.ciclo express.com; Via Garibaldi; ☺ 9am-1pm & 4-8pm Mon-Sat) hires out cars (from €60 per day), scooters (from €30) and bikes (from €8).

Around Alghero

Riviera del Corallo

Heading northwards from Alghero, the Riviera del Corallo (Coral Coast) road sweeps scenically around to the west, passing through the low-key resort of Fertilia and Porto Conte, a broad bay sprinkled with hotels and discreet villas. The end of the road, quite literally, is Capo Caccia, a rocky headland famous for its thrilling cave complex, the Grotta di Nettuno. Along the way are a couple of great beaches and some interesting archaeological sites.

◉ Sights & Activities

★ **Grotta di Nettuno** CAVE
(☎ 079 94 65 40; adult/reduced €13/9; ☺ 9am-7pm summer, to 3pm winter) Capo Caccia's principle crowd-puller is the Grotta di Nettuno, a haunting, underground fairyland of stalactites and stalagmites. The easiest way to get to the caves is to take the Navisarda (p863) ferry from Alghero, but for those with a head for heights, there's a vertiginous 654-step staircase, the **Escala del Cabirol**, that descends 110m of sheer cliff from the car park at the end of the Capo Caccia road.

To get to the caves by public transport, a daily bus departs from Via Catalogna (€2, 50 minutes) in Alghero at 9.15am and returns at midday. From June to September, there are two extra runs at 3.10pm and 5.10pm, returning at 4.05pm and 6.05pm.

Le Prigionette Nature Reserve NATURE RESERVE
(☎ 079 94 90 60; admission free but ID required; ☺ 8am-4pm Mon-Sat, 9am-5pm Sun) This reserve, just west of Porto Conte at the base of Monte Timidone (361m), is a beautiful pocket of uncontaminated nature. Encompassing 12 sq km of woodland, aromatic *macchia* and rocky coastline, it offers wonderful scenery and excellent walking with a network of well-marked tracks, suitable for hikers and cyclists. All around wildlife flourishes – deer, albino donkeys, Giara horses and wild boar roam the woods, while overhead, griffon vultures and falcons fly the skies.

Nuraghe di Palmavera ARCHAEOLOGICAL SITE
(admission €3; ☺ 9am-7pm summer, 10am-2pm winter) A few kilometres west of Fertilia on the road to Porto Conte, the Nuraghe di Palmavera is a 3500-year-old nuraghic village. At its centre stands a limestone tower and an elliptical building with a secondary sandstone tower that was added later. The ruins of smaller towers and bastion walls surround the central edifice, and beyond the walls are the packed remnants of circular dwellings, of which there may originally have been about 50.

Between April and September, a single weekday bus runs to the site from Alghero (€1.50), otherwise you'll need your own transport.

Spiaggia Mugoni
BEACH

The main focus of Porto Conte is Spiaggia Mugoni, a hugely popular beach that arcs round the bay's northeastern flank. With its fine white sand and protected waters, it makes an excellent venue for beginners to try their hand at water sports. The **Club della Vela** (📞 338 1489583; www.clubdellavela alghero.com; Località Mugoni) offers windsurfing, canoeing, kayaking and sailing courses, and also rents out boats.

ℹ️ Getting There & Away

Frequent buses run from Alghero to Fertilia (€1.20, 15 minutes) and Porto Conte (€1.50, 30 minutes).

Stintino & Parco Nazionale dell'Asinara

Once a forgotten tuna-fishing village, Stintino is now a sunny little resort, wedged tidily between two ports – one full of bobbing blue fishing boats (Porto Mannu), the other occupied by gleaming white yachts (Porto Minori). Its pastel-painted houses add charm, while its location near the fabulous Spiaggia della Pelosa and the Isola dell'Asinara makes it an excellent base.

◉ Sights & Activities

★ Spiaggia della Pelosa
BEACH

About 2.5km north of Stintino, the Spiaggia della Pelosa is a dreamy image of beach perfection: a salt-white strip of sand lapped by shallow, turquoise seas and fronted by strange, almost lunar, licks of land. Completing the picture is a Catalan-Aragonese watchtower over the water on the craggy Isola Piana.

Parco Nazionale dell'Asinara
NATIONAL PARK

(www.parcoasinara.org) Named after its resident *asini bianchi* (albino donkeys), the Isola dell'Asinara encompasses 51 sq km of *macchia,* rocky coastline and remote sandy beaches. The island, Sardinia's second largest, is now a national park, but for years it was off-limits as home to one of Italy's toughest maximum-security prisons.

The only way to reach it is with a licensed boat operator from Stintino or Porto Torres. Once there, you can explore independently, although access is restricted to certain areas.

Windsurfing Center Stintino
WINDSURFING

(📞 079 52 70 06; www.windsurfingcenter.it) On the beach at Pelosa, this outfit rents out windsurf rigs (from €17 per hour) and canoes (from €10 per hour), and also offers windsurfing and sailing courses. If that all sounds far too energetic, it can also sort you out with an umbrella and sun-loungers (from €20 per day).

Asinara Scuba Diving
DIVING

(📞 079 52 71 75; www.asinarascubadiving.com; Viale la Pelosa, Località Porto dell'Ancora) Just before Pelosa beach at the Club Hotel Ancora, this diving centre offers a range of dives around Capo del Falcone and the protected waters of the Parco Nazionale dell'Asinara.

Agenzia La Nassa
TOUR

(📞 079 52 00 60; www.escursioniasinara.it; Via Sassari 39, Stintino; ⊙ 9am-12.30pm & 4-7pm) This agency runs a number of tours around Parco Nazionale dell'Asinara. The cheapest option, available between June and September, covers your ferry passage only, leaving you free to walk or cycle within designated areas on the island. More expensive packages include 4WD or bus transport. Prices range from €18 to €65 per person.

🛏️ Sleeping & Eating

Albergo Silvestrino
HOTEL €

(📞 079 52 30 07; www.hotelsilvestrino.it; Via Sassari 14, Stintino; s €45-70, d €60-110; ⊙ closed Dec & Jan; ✴️ 🐾) Stintino's oldest hotel is still one of its best. Occupying a hard-to-miss red villa at the sea end of the main street, it offers summery rooms with cool tiled floors and unfussy furniture. Downstairs, the excellent in-house restaurant specialises in local seafood.

Skipper
ITALIAN €€

(📞 079 52 34 60; Lungomare Cristoforo Colombo 57; meals €25; ⊙ noon-midnight) A longstanding favourite, this casual waterfront bar-cum-restaurant is a jack of all trades. Sit on the sea-facing terrace and order anything from coffee and cocktails to seafood pastas, *zuppa gallurese* (a traditional casserole of bread, *ragù,* cheese and meat stock), hamburgers, salads and *panini.*

ℹ️ Getting There & Away

There are five daily buses on weekdays to Stintino from Porto Torres (€2.50, 30 minutes) and Sassari (€4, 70 minutes). Services increase between June and September.

Sassari

POP 130,658

Sardinia's sprawling second city requires a bit of work. On first sight, it's not an immediately appealing place, but persevere and you'll discover that beneath its rather scruffy veneer lies a proud and cultured university town with an unpretentious atmosphere and a bustling, workaday vibe. Once you are through to the inner sanctum it opens up, revealing a grand centre of wide boulevards, impressive piazzas and stately *palazzi*. In the evocative yet rundown *centro storico*, medieval alleys hum with activity as residents go about their business amid grimy facades and hidden churches.

◉ Sights

★ Museo Nazionale Sanna   MUSEUM

(☏079 27 22 03; www.museosannasassari.beni culturali.it; Via Roma 64; adult/reduced €4/2, 1st Sun of month free; ⊙9am-8pm Tue-Sun) Sassari's premier museum, housed in a grand Palladian villa, boasts a comprehensive archaeological collection and an ethnographical section dedicated to Sardinian folk art. The highlight is the nuraghic bronzeware, including weapons, bracelets, votive boats and figurines depicting humans and animals.

Piazza Italia   PIAZZA

Sassari's largest piazza, Piazza Italia, is one of Sardinia's most impressive public spaces. Covering about a hectare, it is surrounded by imposing 19th-century buildings, including the neoclassical **Palazzo della Provincia** (Piazza Italia), seat of the provincial government and, opposite, the neo-Gothic **Palazzo Giordano** (Piazza Italia), now home to the Banca di Credito Sardo. Presiding over everything is a statue of King Vittorio Emanuele II.

SADDLE UP FOR FESTIVAL FUN

Cavalcata Sarda (⊙May) One of Sardinia's most high-profile festivals is held in Sassari on the second-last Sunday of May. Thousands of people converge on the city to participate in costumed processions, to sing and dance, and to watch fearless horse-riders exhibit their acrobatic skills.

Duomo   CATHEDRAL

(Piazza Duomo; ⊙8.30am-noon & 4-7pm Mon-Sat, 8.30-11.30am & 5-6.45pm Sun) Sassari's Duomo, also known as the Cattedrale di San Nicola, dazzles with its 18th-century baroque facade, a giddy free-for-all of statues, reliefs, friezes and busts. It's all a front, though, because inside the cathedral reverts to its true Gothic character. The facade masks a late 15th-century Catalan Gothic body, which was itself built over an earlier Romanesque church. Little remains of this except for the 13th-century bell tower.

🛏 Sleeping

I Tetti di Sassari   B&B €

(☏340 8477926; www.bebsassari.it; Corso Trinità 193; s/d/tr €40/70/100; ✳🞱) Digs in Sassari can be uninspiring, but this cute little B&B bucks the trend, with gracious hosts (Patrizio and Daniella), comfy rooms, a friendly resident cat, decent breakfasts and a terrace with cracking views out across the city.

Hotel Vittorio Emanuele   HOTEL €€

(☏079 23 55 38; www.hotelvittorioemanuele.ss.it; Corso Vittorio Emanuele II 100-102; s €50-105, d €65-150; ✳@🞱) Occupying a renovated medieval *palazzo*, this slick three-star provides corporate comfort at reasonable rates. Rooms are comfortable, if anonymous, and the location, on the main drag in the historic centre, is convenient for pretty much everywhere.

🍴 Eating

Fainè alla Genovese Sassu   SARDINIAN €

(Via Usai 17; fainè from €4; ⊙7-11pm Mon-Sat) This bare, white-tiled eatery is Sassari's original purveyor of *fainè*. There's nothing else on the menu but with various types to choose from – sausage, onions, mushrooms, anchovies – the soft chickpea pancakes are ideal for a cheap, tasty fill-up.

L'Antica Hostaria   RISTORANTE €€

(☏079 20 00 60; Via Cavour 55; meals €40; ⊙1-3pm & 8-11pm Mon-Sat) Hidden behind a discreet exterior, L'Antica Hostaria is one of Sassari's top restaurants. In intimate surroundings you're treated to inventive dishes rooted in Sicilian and Sardinian culinary traditions. Desserts are also impressive, and there's an excellent list of island and Italian wines.

Information

Ospedale Civile SS Annunziata (☎079 206 10 00; Via De Nicola 14) Hospital south of the city centre.

Post Office (Via Brigata di Sassari 13; ⌚8.20am-7.05pm Mon-Fri, to 12.35pm Sat)

Tourist Office (☎079 200 80 72; Via Sebastiano Satta 13; ⌚9am-1.30pm & 3-6pm Tue-Fri, 9am-1.30pm Sat) Has information on Sassari and the surrounding area.

Getting There & Away

Sassari shares Alghero's Fertilia airport, about 28km west of the centre. Up to nine daily buses run from the stops on Via Padre Zirano to the aiport (€2.50, 30 minutes).

Intercity buses depart from and arrive at Via Padre Zirano. Services run to/from Alghero (€2.50 to €3, one hour, 10 daily), Oristano (€8, two hours, three daily), Porto Torres (€2, 30 minutes, hourly) and Castelsardo (€3, one hour, 11 weekdays and Saturdays, four Sundays). Further afield, there are buses to Nuoro (€8, 1¾ hours, six daily). For Cagliari (€15.75, 3½ hours, five daily) and Olbia (€7.35, 1¾ hours, seven daily), you're better off getting the train.

OLBIA, THE COSTA SMERALDA & THE GALLURA

Costa Smeralda evokes Sardinia's classic images: pearly white beaches, wind-whipped licks of rock tapering into azure seas, and ageing oligarchs cavorting with bikini-clad beauties on zillion-dollar yachts. In inland Gallura, you could be on another island entirely, with vine-striped hills rolling to quaint villages, granite mountains and mysterious *nuraghi*. Gallura's northern coast is wild, the preserve of the dolphins, divers and windsurfers who splash around in the crystal waters of La Maddalena marine reserve.

Olbia

POP 54,833

Often ignored in the mad summer dash to the Costa Smeralda, Olbia has more to offer than first meets the eye. Look beyond its industrial outskirts and you'll find a fetching city with a *centro storico* full of boutiques, wine bars and cafe-rimmed piazzas. Above all, Olbia is a refreshingly authentic and affordable alternative to the purpose-built resorts to the north and south.

Sights

★Museo Archeologico MUSEUM

(Isolotto di Peddone; ⌚10am-1pm & 5-8pm Wed-Sun) FREE Architect Vanni Maciocco designed Olbia's strikingly contemporary museum near the port. The museum spells out local history in artefacts, from Roman amulets and pottery to nuraghic finds. The highlight is the relic of a Roman vessel discovered in the old port. A multimedia display recreates the scene of the Vandals burning and sinking such ships in AD 450.

Chiesa di San Simplicio CHURCH

(Via San Simplicio; ⌚7.30am-1pm & 3.30-8pm) Considered to be Gallura's most important medieval monument, this Romanesque granite church was built in the late 11th and early 12th centuries on what was then the edge of town. It is a curious mix of Tuscan and Lombard styles with little overt decoration other than a couple of 13th-century frescoes depicting medieval bishops.

Chiesa di San Paolo CHURCH

(Via Cagliari; ⌚hours vary) Another granite church worth a look is the 18th-century Chiesa di San Paolo, spectacularly topped by a Valencian-style multicoloured tiled dome (added after WWII).

Sleeping

Porto Romano B&B €

(☎349 1927996; www.bedandbreakfastportoromano.it; Via A Nanni 2; d €60-80; ❄📶👪) We love the totally chilled vibe and the heartfelt *benvenuto* at this homey B&B, which is very close to the train station. Light, spacious and well-kept, the rooms have tiled floors and wood furnishings, and some come with balconies. You're welcome to use the shared kitchen and barbecue area.

★Hotel Panorama HOTEL €€

(☎0789 2 66 56; www.hotelpanoramaolbia.it; Via Giuseppe Mazzini 7; s €99-149, d €109-199, tr €168-232; P❄📶👪) The name says it all: the roof terrace at this friendly, central hotel has peerless views over the rooftops of Olbia to the sea and Monte Limbara. The rooms are fresh and elegant, with gleaming wooden floors and marble bathrooms, and there's a whirlpool and sauna for quiet moments.

La Locanda del Conte Mameli BOUTIQUE HOTEL €€

(☎0789 2 30 08; www.lalocandadelcontemameli.com; Via delle Terme 8; d €115-174, ste €144-329;

P✱🛜) Raising the style stakes is this boutique hotel, housed in an 18th-century *locanda* (inn) built for Count Mameli. A wrought-iron balustrade twists up to chic caramel-cream rooms with Orosei marble bathrooms. An original Roman well is the centrepiece of the vaulted breakfast room.

✖ Eating & Drinking

Pizzeria Dadino
PIZZA €

(☑340 3830176; Via Norvega 47; pizzas €5-10; ⊖6.30pm-late) What a delight! This pizzeria has everything going for it – superb pizzas, a cheery family vibe and wallet-friendly prices. It's worth the short trek from the centre.

★Agriturismo Agrisole
SARDINIAN €€

(☑349 0848163; www.agriturismo-agrisole. com; Via Sole Ruiu, Località Casagliana; menu incl drinks €30; ⊖mid-Jun–mid-Sep) Tucked serenely away in the countryside around 10km north of Olbia, this Gallurese *stazzo* (farmhouse) dishes up a feast of home cooking. Monica, your charming host, brings dish after marvellous dish to the table – antipasti, *fregola* (granular pasta), *porcetto* (roast suckling pig) and ricotta sweets. From Olbia, take the SS125 towards Arzachena/Palau, turning left at the signs at Km327.800.

La Lanterna
TRADITIONAL ITALIAN €€

(☑0789 2 30 82; Via Olbia 13; pizzas €6-16, meals €25-35; ⊖6pm-midnight Thu-Tue) The Lanterna distinguishes itself with its cosy subterranean setting of exposed stone and beams. The food is winningly fresh, with Sardinian dishes like handmade *gnocchetti sardi* (saffron-flavoured pasta) and saffron-infused *fregola* with scorpion fish *ragù* on the menu. The pizza is pretty good, too.

KKult
BAR

(www.kkult.com; Corso Umberto 39; ⊖8am-3am Tue-Sun) This contemporary split-level lounge-bar-cafe hybrid has a terrace on Olbia's main drag for watching the world go by over a coffee or cocktail. The pace picks up at the weekend with live music and DJ nights.

In Vino Veritas
WINE BAR

(Corso Umberto 4; ⊖8am-midnight) Bottles line the walls at this inviting wine bar. Snag a table to taste Sardinian wines from Vermentinos to Cannonaus, and artisanal beers, together with a tasting plate of local *salumi* and *formaggi*.

ℹ Information

Main Tourist Office (☑0789 5 22 06; www. olbiaturismo.it; Municipio, Corso Umberto; ⊖9am-9pm summer, 9am-7pm winter) This helpful tourist office should be your first port of call for info on Olbia.

ℹ Getting There & Around

AIR

Olbia's Aeroporto Internazionale di Olbia Costa Smeralda (p841) is about 5km southeast of the centre and handles flights from mainland Italian and major European cities. Low-cost operators include Air Berlin, easyJet, Jet2.com and Niki.

BOAT

Regular ferries arrive in Olbia from Genoa, Civitavecchia and Livorno. Book tickets at travel agents in town, or directly at the port.

BUS

Buses run from Olbia to destinations across the island. Get tickets from **Bar della Caccia** (Via Fiume D' Italia 1; ⊖6am-9pm Mon-Sat), just over the road from the main bus stops on Corso Vittorio Veneto; the timetable is posted in the window. Destinations include Arzachena (€2.50, 45 minutes, 12 daily) and Porto Cervo (€3.50, 1½ hours, five daily). Further afield you can get to Nuoro (€9, 2½ hours, eight daily), Santa Teresa di Gallura (€5, 1½ hours, seven daily) and Sassari (€7, 1½ hours, two daily) via Tempio Pausania (€3.50, 1¼ hours, seven daily). There are fewer connections on Sunday.

TRAIN

The train station is just off Corso Umberto. There are trains to Cagliari (€17, four hours, five daily), Sassari (€7.35, two hours, seven daily) and Golfo Aranci (€2.35, 25 minutes, five daily).

Costa Smeralda & Around

Stretching 55km from Porto Rotondo to the Golfo di Arzachena, the Costa Smeralda (Emerald Coast) is Sardinia's most feted summer destination, a gilded enclave of luxury hotels, secluded beaches and exclusive marinas. Ever since the Aga Khan bought the coast for a pittance in the 1960s, it has attracted A-listers and paparazzi hoping to snap celebs in compromising clinches. But despite all the superficial fluff, it remains stunning, with granite mountains plunging into emerald

COSTA SMERALDA BEACH CRAWL

You'll need your own set of wheels to hop between the most sublime beaches on the Costa Smeralda, but it's worth the effort. They're super-busy in July and August, so shun these months if you want these bays to yourself. The following are listed from north to south.

Spiaggia del Grande & Piccolo Pevero This twin set of stunning bays, 3km south of Porto Cervo, fulfills the Sardinian paradise dream with its floury sands and dazzlingly blue, shallow water. There's a small beach bar, too.

Spiaggia Romazzino Less busy than some, this curving sandy bay has remarkably clear water and is named after the rosemary bushes that grow in such abundance here. Look beyond the main bay to smaller coves for more seclusion.

Spiaggia del Principe Also known as Portu Li Coggi, this magnificent crescent of white sand is bound by unspoilt *macchia* and startlingly clear blue waters. Apparently it's the Aga Khan's favourite. It's around 2.5km east of Capriccioli.

Spiaggia Capriccioli Dotted with granite boulders and backed by fragrant *macchia*, this gorgeous half-moon bay has water that goes through the entire spectrum of blues and is shallow enough for tots. Umbrellas and sun beds are available to rent. It's near the little settlement of Capriccioli, just off the SP160.

Spiaggia Liscia Ruia Though busy in peak season, this beach is a beauty – a long arc of pale, fine sand and crystal-clear water. It's close to the neo-Moorish fantasy that is Hotel Cala di Volpe and signposted off the SP59.

waters in a series of dramatic fjord-like inlets.

The Costa's capital is **Porto Cervo**, a weird, artificial town whose pseudo-Moroccan architecture and perfectly manicured streets give it a strangely sterile atmosphere. It's dead out of season, but between June and September this is party central, with tanned beauties posing on the **Piazzetta** and cashed-up shoppers perusing the designer boutiques.

Inland, the rustic village of **San Pantaleo** merits a quick look, particularly on summer evenings when its picturesque piazza hosts a bustling market. Further north, the workaday town of **Arzachena** offers a number of interesting archaeological sites.

⊙ Sights & Activities

Coddu Ecchju   ARCHAEOLOGICAL SITE
(admission €3; ⊙9am-7pm) If you take the Arzachena–Luogosanto road south, you can follow signs to one of the most important *tombe dei giganti* in Sardinia. The most visible part of it is the oval-shaped central stele (standing stone). Both slabs of granite, one balanced on top of the other, show an engraved frame that apparently symbolises a door to the hereafter, closed to the living. On either side of the stele stand further tall slabs of granite that form a kind of semicircular guard of honour around the tomb.

Nuraghe di Albucciu   ARCHAEOLOGICAL SITE
(admission €3; ⊙9am-7pm) This is the nearest *nuraghe* to Arzachena, and certainly the easiest to find, on the main Olbia road, about 3km south of Arzachena. It's one of Gallura's finest prehistoric relics and unusual for several reasons, not least for its flat granite roof instead of the usual *tholos* (conical shape) and its warren of what appear to be emergency escape routes.

★**Cantine Surrau**   WINERY
(☑0789 8 29 33; www.vignesurrau.it; Località Chilvagghja; ⊙10am-10pm) Cantine Surrau takes a holistic approach to winemaking. Take a spin of the cellar and the gallery showcasing Sardinian art before tasting some of the region's crispest Vermentino white and beefiest Cannonau red wines. The standard tasting (€20) gets you three different wines served with *pane carasau* (Sardinian flatbread), cheese, *salumi* and olives, while the €35 tasting consists of five wines, local cheese, salami, *bottarga* and Sardinian sweets. Find the winery on the road between Arzachena and Porto Cervo.

DON'T MISS

SARDINIA'S TOP FIVE CLIMBS & HIKES

Gola Su Gorropu (p881) The trail to Gorropu from Genna 'e Silana pass is spectacular, taking in holm oak woods, boulder-strewn slopes and cave-riddled cliffs. It takes about two hours to go up, 1½ hours to come down.

Selvaggio Blu This is the big one: an epic four- to seven-day, 45km trek along the Golfo di Orosei's dramatic coastline, traversing wooded ravines, cliffs and caves. A guide is recommended as the trail is not well signposted and there's no water en route. If you are going it alone, be aware that it involves scrambling, fixed-rope routes and abseiling, so some alpine mountaineering experience is necessary. Visit the website www.selvaggioblu.it or get a copy of Enrico Spanu's *Book of Selvaggio Blu*.

Cala Luna (p879) There's fabulous climbing above a beautiful bay, which is a scenic two-hour clifftop walk from Cala Fuili or a speedy boat ride from Cala Gonone. The 56 routes range from 5c to 8b and include some tricky single pitches in caves with over-hangs.

La Poltrona This massive limestone amphitheatre close to Cala Gonone has compact rock and 75 bolted routes from grades 4 to 8a. Mornings get too hot here in summer, so wait until late afternoon.

Golgo–Cala Goloritzè (p882) It's an easy half-day hike along old mule trails from the plateau of Golgo to Cala Goloritzè, a perfect half-moon of white sand pummelled by astonishingly blue waters. Climbers can tackle its bizarre limestone pinnacles, including the Aguglia, a tough multipitch climb.

🛏 Sleeping

Villaggio Camping La Cugnana   CAMPGROUND €

(☏ 0789 3 31 84; www.campingcugnana.it; Località Cugnana; camping 2 people, car & tent €21-30; 🛜🍴📶) This seaside campground is located on the main road just north of Porto Rotondo. There's plenty to keep the kids amused with a swimming pool, a playground and organised activities. A free shuttle bus can whisk you to some of the better Costa Smeralda beaches.

★ B&B Costa Smeralda   B&B €€

(☏ 0789 9 98 11; www.bbcostasmeralda.com; Lu Cumitoni, Poltu Quatu; d €80-130; 🌀@🛜) Tucked in the hills above the fjordlike harbour of Poltu Quatu, 3km north of Porto Cervo, this is an especially charming B&B. Sunlight streams into rooms, which are a blaze of blue and white. There are tantalising sea views from the verandah, where you can enjoy some of Luciana's freshly made breads and pastries at breakfast.

B&B Lu Pastruccialeddu   B&B €€

(☏ 0789 8 17 77; www.pastruccialeddu.com; Località Lu Pastruccialeddu, Arzachena; s €70-100, d €90-120, ste €120-150; 🅿🌀📶) This is the real McCoy, a smashing B&B housed in a typical stone farmstead, with pristine rooms, a beautiful pool and two resident donkeys. It's

run by the ultra-hospitable Caterina Ruzittu, who prepares the sumptuous breakfasts – a vast spread of biscuits, yoghurt, freshly baked cakes, salami, cheese and cereals.

🍴 Eating

★ Jaddhu   SARDINIAN €€

(☏ 0789 8 06 36; www.jaddhu.com; Località Capichera; meals €35-45; ⏱ 12.30-3pm & 7.30-10.30pm May-Sep) Hidden in granite mountains brushed with olive, myrtle and mastic trees, this *stazzu* (Gallurese stone-built country house) has one of the finest restaurants in the region. Sit on the garden terrace for a fully blown Sardinian feast, from *zuppa cuata* (bread and cheese soup) to swordfish with almonds and candied lime, and spot-on *porcetto* with rosemary potatoes.

The restaurant is part of the Jaddhu Country Resort, situated 5.5km off the SS427 south of Arzachena.

Hivaoa   MEDITERRANEAN €€

(☏ 0789 9 14 51; www.ristorantehivaoa.com; Via Della Marina Nuova; pizzas €5-12, lunch menus €15, meals €30; ⏱ noon-midnight; 📶) Fine dining it is not, but if what you are seeking is a cheerful, affordable, family friendly place with decent food, Hivaoa hits the mark every time. Go for wood-oven pizza, filling steaks, seafood and pasta dishes.

Spinnaker
MODERN ITALIAN €€

(☎0789 9 12 26; www.ristorantespinnaker.com; Liscia di Vacca; meals around €40; ⊙12.30-2.30pm & 7.30-11.30pm daily Jun-Sep, Thu-Tue Mar-May & Oct) This fashionable restaurant buzzes with good-looking people, who come for the stylish ambience and fabulous seafood. Pair dishes like calamari with fresh artichokes or rock lobster with a local Vermentino white. The restaurant is on the road between Porto Cervo and Baia Sardinia.

ℹ Getting There & Away

Between June and September, **Sun Lines** (☎348 2609881; http://sunlineseliteservice.com) operates buses from Olbia airport to the Costa Smeralda, stopping at Porto Cervo and various other points along the coast. During the rest of the year, there's one daily bus between Porto Cervo and Olbia (€3.50, 1½ hours).

For Arzachena there are regular year-round services to and from Olbia (€2.50, 45 minutes, 12 daily).

Santa Teresa di Gallura
POP 5225

Bright and breezy Santa Teresa bags a prime seafront position on Gallura's arrestingly beautiful north coast, with some of the loveliest beaches and clearest seas on the island. The resort gets extremely busy in high season yet somehow retains a distinct local character. Nearby, Capo Testa is famous for its surreal wind-sculpted granite formations, while Corsica is a short ferry-hop away.

◎ Sights & Activities

Spiaggia Rena Bianca
BEACH

The 'just like the Caribbean' comments come thick and fast when it comes to this bay – a glorious sweep of pale sand lapped by shallow, crystal-clear aquamarine water. From the eastern tip, a trail threads along the coastline past granite boulders and formations that fire the imagination with their incredible shapes.

Torre di Longonsardo
TOWER

(admission €2; ⊙10am-1pm & 4-8pm Jun-Sep) The 16th-century Torre di Longonsardo is in a magnificent position, overlooking the natural deep port on one side and the entrance to the town's idyllic (but crowded) Spiaggia Rena Bianca on the other.

★ Capo Testa
WALKING

Four kilometres west of Santa Teresa, lighthouse-topped Capo Testa resembles a bizarre sculptural garden. Giant boulders lay strewn about the grassy slopes, their weird and wonderful forms the result of centuries of wind erosion.

Follow Via Capo Testa west of town and it's around an hour's hike to the cape. The walk itself is stunning, passing through boulder-strewn scrub and affording magnificent views of rock formations, rocky coves and the cobalt Mediterranean. You can stop en route for a swim and to admire the views of not-so-distant Corsica.

Consorzio delle Bocche
BOAT TOUR

(☎0789 75 51 12; www.consorziobocche.com; Piazza Vittorio Emanuele; ⊙9am-1pm & 5pm-12.30am May-Sep) This outfit runs various excursions, including trips to the Maddalena islands and down the Costa Smeralda (summer only). These cost around €42/22 per adult/child and include lunch (excluding drinks).

🛏 Sleeping

Most hotels are only open from Easter to October.

★ La Finestra Vista Corsica
B&B €

(☎340 4959276, 335 5884814; www.lafinestra vistacorsica.it; Via Lombardia 13; s €30-60, d €50-100; ❋ ≋) Rita is the good soul that bends over backwards to make you feel at home at her charming B&B, just above Rena Bianca beach. It's worth paying extra for a front-facing room, where (as the name suggests) the windows perfectly frame the view of Corsica across the Strait of Bonifacio. Rita's chocolate cake at breakfast is divine.

Camping La Liccia
CAMPGROUND €

(☎0789 75 51 90; www.campinglaliccia.com; SP90 Km59; camping 2 people, car & tent €26-33, 2-person bungalows €52-110; ≋ ⛱ ❋) ⊘ This eco-friendly campground, 5km west of town on the road towards Castelsardo, has fab facilities including a playground, pool and sports area.

B&B Domus de Janas
B&B €€

(☎338 499 02 21; www.bbdomusdejanas.it; Via Carlo Felice 20a; s €50-100, d €70-130, tr €80-140, q €100-160; ❋ ≋ ⛾) Daria and Simon are your affable hosts at this sweet B&B in the centre of town. There are cracking sea views from the terrace and the rooms are cheery, scattered with art and knick-knacks.

Hotel Moderno HOTEL €€
(☑ 393 9177814, 0789 75 42 33; www.moderno
hotel.eu; Via Umberto 39; s €65-80, d €75-140, tr
€105-180; ❄ 🛜) This is a homey, family run
pick near Piazza Vittorio Emanuele. Rooms
are bright and airy with little overt decor,
but traditional blue-and-white Gallurese
bedspreads and tiny balconies.

🍴 Eating & Drinking

Head to Piazza Vittorio Emanuele for alfresco drinks and people-watching.

★ **Agriturismo Saltara** SARDINIAN €€
(☑ 0789 75 55 97; www.agriturismosaltara.it; Località Saltara; meals €35-44; ⊙ 7.30-10.30pm;
🛜) Natalia and Gian Mario welcome you
warmly at this *agriturismo*, 10km south of
town off the SP90 (follow the signs up a dirt
track). Tables are scenically positioned under the trees for a home-cooked feast. Wood-
fired bread and garden vegetable antipasti
are a delicious lead to dishes like *pulilgioni*
(ricotta-filled ravioli with orange zest) and
roast suckling pig or wild boar.

Marlin PIZZA €€
(☑ 0789 75 45 57; www.ristorante-pizzeriamarlin.
com; Via Garibaldi 4; pizzas €4-12, meals €30;
⊙ noon-3pm & 7pm-midnight) Simple, friendly and reasonably priced, Marlin whips up
a decent pizza – try the house special with
tomato, mozzarella, salmon, prawns and
bottarga – and does basics like *spaghetti
vongole* (with clams) and grilled fish well.

❶ Information

Tourist Office (☑ 0789 75 41 27; www.comune
santateresagallura.it; Piazza Vittorio Emanuele
24; ⊙ 9am-1pm & 4.30-8pm) Very helpful, with
loads of information.

❶ Getting There & Around

From the bus terminus on Via Eleonora d'Arborea, buses run to and from Olbia (€5, 1½ hours,
seven daily) and Sassari (€7, 2½ hours, three
daily).

There are ferry services that run to Bonifacio
in Corsica.

Palau & Arcipelago di La Maddalena

On Sardinia's northeastern tip, Palau is a
well-to-do summer resort crowded with
surf shops, boutiques, bars and restaurants.
It's also the main gateway to Arcipelago di

La Maddalena's granite islands and jewel-
coloured waters.

An area of spectacular, windswept seascapes, La Maddalena is best explored by
boat, although the two main islands have
plenty of charm with their sunbaked ochre
buildings, cobbled piazzas and infectious
holiday atmosphere. A good place to base
yourself is the main town, La Maddalena,
on the south coast of the island of the same
name, which has a handful of guesthouses,
restaurants and cafes.

◉ Sights & Activities

The main activity around these parts is
beach-bumming or boating around the
islands.

★ **Parco Nazionale dell'Arcipelago
di La Maddalena** NATIONAL PARK
(www.lamaddalenapark.it) A national park since
1996, Parco Nazionale dell'Arcipelago di La
Maddalena consists of seven main islands
and 40 granite islets, as well as several small
islands to the south. The seven principal
islands are the high points of a valley, now
underwater, that once joined Sardinia and
Corsica. When the two split into separate islands, waters filled the strait now called the
Bocche di Bonifacio.

Over the centuries the prevailing wind,
the maestrale (northwesterly wind), has
helped to mould the granite into the bizarre natural sculptures that festoon the
archipelago.

Roccia dell'Orso VIEWPOINT
(adult/reduced €2/1; ⊙ 9am-7.30pm daily, to 9pm
summer; 🛜) This weather-beaten granite
sculpture sits on a high point 6km east of
Palau. The Roccia dell'Orso (Bear Rock)
looks considerably less bearlike up close, resembling more – dare we say it? – a dragon.
Analogies aside, the granite formations are
extraordinary, as are the far-reaching views
of the coast from up here.

Fortezza di Monte Altura FORT
(adult/reduced €3/2; ⊙ guided tours hourly
10.15am-12.15pm & 3.15-7.15pm summer, closed
winter) Standing sentinel on a rocky crag,
this sturdy 19th-century bastion was built
to help defend the north coast and Arcipelago di La Maddalena from invasion – something it was never called on to do. A guided
45-minute tour leads you to watchtowers
and battlements with panoramic views out

to sea. The fortress is signposted off the SS125, 3km west of Palau.

Dea del Mare   BOAT TOUR

(☎338 5079298, 334 7882993; www.deadelmare.com; Via Fonte Vecchia 76; day trips €80-110; ☉office 9am-4pm) Down at Palau's port, this highly regarded outfit offers boat excursions around the Maddalena islands, with a chipper crew and passenger numbers limited to 12. Trips include lunch with wine and time to swim on well-known beaches.

Nautilus   DIVING

(☎0789 70 90 58, 340 6339006; www.divesardegna.com; Piazza Fresi 8, Palau) There's excellent diving in the marine park. This PADI-accredited centre runs dives to 40 sites, with single dives starting at around €50. Kids' Bubblemaker courses are available.

🛏 Sleeping & Eating

It's strictly summer only in Palau and La Maddalena, where nearly everything closes from mid-October to Easter.

★B&B Petite Maison   B&B €

(☎0789 73 84 32, 340 6463722; www.lapetitmaison.net; Via Livenza 7, La Maddalena; d €85-130; 🛜) Liberally sprinkled with paintings and art deco furnishings, this B&B is a five-minute amble from the main square. Miriam's artistically presented breakfasts, with fresh homemade goodies, are served in a bougainvillea-draped garden. Credit cards (and kids) are not accepted.

L'Orso e Il Mare   B&B €

(☎331 2222000; www.orsoeilmare.com; Vicolo Diaz 1, Palau; d €70-115, tr €90-140; 🌀) Pietro gives his guests a genuinely warm welcome at this B&B, just steps from Piazza Fresi. The spacious rooms sport cool blue-and-white colour schemes. Breakfast is a fine spread of cakes, biscuits and fresh fruit salad.

Camping Baia Saraceno   CAMPGROUND €

(☎0789 70 94 03; www.baiasaraceno.com; Punta Nera, Palau; camping 2 people, car & tent €30-36, 2-person bungalows €60-110; 🛜🏊) Beautifully located on Palau's beach and shaded by pine trees, this campground has an on-site pizzeria, playground and dive centre.

ⓘ Information

Tourist Office (☎0789 70 70 25; www.palauturismo.com; Palazzo Fresi, Piazza Fresi; ☉9am-1pm & 3-7pm) The multilingual staff at the tourist office can provide information about the surrounding area, including the Arcipelago di La Maddalena.

ⓘ Getting There & Around

BOAT

Frequent car ferries to Isola Maddalena are operated by **Saremar** (☎199 118877; www.saremar.it) and **Delcomar** (☎0781 85 71 23; www.delcomar.it). The 15-minute crossing costs €6 per passenger and €13 for a small car (€1 less if you return the same day).

BUS

Services connect Palau with Olbia (€3.50, 1¼ hours, 10 daily), Santa Teresa di Gallura (€2, 40 minutes, five daily) and Arzachena (€1.50, 20 minutes, eight daily).

NUORO & THE EAST

If the Sardinians were to nominate one place as their geographical, cultural and spiritual heartland, this would surely be it. Nowhere is the force of nature more overpowering than here, where the Supramonte's limestone mountains give way to the Golfo di Orosei's plunging cliffs, grottoes and startling aquamarine waters.

Although larger towns are accessible by bus, you'll see more with your own set of wheels. A roller coaster of country roads leads to deep valleys concealing prehistoric *nuraghe,* the lonesome villages of the Barbagia steeped in bandit legends, and holm oak forests where wild pigs roam.

DON'T MISS

NUORO FROM ABOVE

Nuoro's spectacular backdrop is the granite peak of **Monte Ortobene** (955m), capped by a 7m-high bronze statue of the *Redentore* (Christ the Redeemer). The thickly wooded summit commands dress-circle views of the valley and the limestone mountains surrounding Oliena, which are at their most spectacular at dusk when the fading light makes their peaks blush pink. To reach it, follow the signs out of town on the SP42; it's about 7km east of the centre.

Nuoro

POP 36,635

Once an isolated hilltop village and a by-word for banditry, Nuoro had its cultural renaissance in the 19th and early 20th centuries when it became a hotbed of artistic talent. Today museums in the historic centre pay homage to local legends like Nobel Prize–winning author Grazia Deledda, acclaimed poet Sebastiano Satta, novelist Salvatore Satta and sculptor Francesco Ciusa.

⊙ Sights

Museo Etnografico Sardo   MUSEUM
(www.isresardegna.it; Via Antonio Mereu 56; adult/reduced €3/1; ⊙9am-1pm & 3-6pm Tue-Sun) Zooming in on Sardinian folklore, this museum harbours a peerless collection of filigree jewellery, carpets, tapestries, rich embroidery, musical instruments, weapons and masks. The highlight is the traditional costume display – the styles, colours and patterns speak volumes about the people and their villages. Look out for fiery red skirts from the fiercely independent mountain villages, the Armenian-influenced dresses of Orgosolo and Desulo finished with a blue-and-yellow silk border, and the hijab-like headdresses of the women of Ittiri and Osilo.

Museo d'Arte   GALLERY
(MAN; www.museoman.it; Via S Satta 15; adult/reduced €3/2; ⊙10am-1pm & 3-8pm Tue-Sun) Housed in a restored 19th-century townhouse, this is the only serious contemporary art gallery in Sardinia. Its permanent collection boasts more than 400 works by the island's top 20th-century painters, including Antonio Ballero, Giovanni Ciusa-Romagna, Mario Delitalia and abstract artist Mauro Manca. Local sculptors Francesco Ciusa and Costantino Nivola are also represented. The gallery also hosts more wide-ranging temporary exhibits, usually held on the ground and top floors.

Museo Deleddiano   MUSEUM
(www.isresardegna.it; Via Grazia Deledda 42; ⊙9am-1pm & 3-6pm Tue-Sun) FREE Up in the oldest part of town, the birthplace of Grazia Deledda (1871–1936) has been converted into this lovely little museum. The rooms, full of Deledda memorabilia, have been carefully restored to show what a well-to-do 19th-century Nuorese house actually looked like. Best of all is the material relating to her Nobel prize – a congratulatory telegram from the king of Italy and prize-giving ceremony photos that show her, proud and tiny, surrounded by a group of stiffly suited men.

🎊 Festivals & Events

Sagra del Redentore   RELIGIOUS
The *Sagra del Redentore* (Feast of Christ the Redeemer) in the last week of August is the main event in Nuoro. It's one of Sardinia's most exuberant folkloric festivals, attracting costumed participants from across the island and involving much parading, music-making and dancing. On the evening of 28 August a torchlit procession, starting at the Chiesa della Solitudine, winds its way through the city.

ⓘ GET A GUIDE

If you fancy striking out into the Supramonte, here's our pick of the best guides:

Cooperativa Gorropu (☑333 8507157, 347 4233650; www.gorropu.com; Passo Silana SS125, Km183, Urzulei) Sandra and Franco arrange all sorts of excursions, from trekking (€30 to €35) to canyoning and caving (€40 to €60).

Corrado Conca (☑347 2903101; www.corradoconca.it; Via Barzini 15, Sassari) Sardinia's hiking and climbing guru is a brilliant companion for the island's extreme seven-day Selvaggio Blu (Wild Blue) trek. Bank on paying around €550 per person.

Cooperativa Ghivine (☑0784 9 67 21, 338 8341618; www.ghivine.com; Via Lamarmora 69/e, Dorgali) A one-stop action shop, arranging treks to places like Gola Su Gorropu and Tiscali (both €40).

Dolmen (☑347 6698192; www.sardegnadascoprire.it; Via Vasco da Gama 18, Cala Gonone) This reliable operator runs 4WD tours into the Supramonte, canyoning excursions to the Gorropu and boat trips to the Grotta del Bue Marino. Bikes, scooters and dinghies are also available for hire. Call ahead for times and prices.

🛏 Sleeping & Eating

★ Casa Solotti
B&B €

(☏328 6028975, 0784 3 39 54; www.casasolotti.
it; Località Monte Ortobene; r per person €26-35;
🅿❄️🛜) This B&B reclines in a rambling
garden amid woods and walking trails
near the top of Monte Ortobene, 5km from
central Nuoro. Decorated with stone and
beams, the elegantly rustic rooms have tremendous views of the surrounding valley
and the Golfo di Orosei in the distance.
Staying here is a delight.

Silvia e Paolo
B&B €

(☏0784 3 12 80; www.silviaepaolo.it; Corso Garibaldi 58; s €33-40, d €55-65, tr €75; ❄️🛜🚗) Silvia and Paolo run this sweet B&B. Family
treasures from dolls to old leather trunks
make you feel right at home in the bright,
spacious rooms. There's a roof terrace for
observing the action on Corso Garibaldi by
day and stargazing by night, as well as a
tasteful living room with films, books and
maps of Sardinia.

Il Portico
SARDINIAN €€

(☏0784 23 29 09; www.ilporticonuoro.it; Via
Monsignor Bua 13; meals €40; ⊗12.30-2.30pm &
8-10.30pm Thu-Tue) You'll receive a heartfelt
welcome at this restaurant, where abstract
paintings grace the walls and jazzy music
plays. Behind the scenes, a talented hus-
band-and-wife team rustles up a feast of
local fare like *spaghetti ai ricci* (spaghetti
with sea urchins) and fresh gnocchi with
lamb *ragù*. Save room for the delectable
caramel-nougat *semifreddo*.

ℹ Information

Tourist Office (☏0784 44 18 23; www.pro
vincia.nuoro.it; Piazza Italia 7; ⊗8.30am-2pm
Mon-Fri, plus 3.30-7pm Tue) Has plenty of useful information on Nuoro and environs.

ℹ Getting There & Away

From the main bus station on Viale Sardegna
there are services to destinations throughout
the province and beyond. These include Dorgali
(€3.50, 45 minutes, six daily), Orosei (€3.50,
one hour, 10 daily), San Teodoro (€8, one hour
50 minutes, five daily), Baunei (€7, two hours,
four daily) and Tortolì (€6, two hours 40 minutes, five daily). There are also regular buses to
Oliena (€1.50, 20 minutes) and Orogosolo (€2,
35 minutes).

WORTH A TRIP

ORGOSOLO'S MURALS

For centuries Orgosolo was feared as a
centre of banditry and kidnapping. Nowadays, it's better known for the vibrant
graffiti-style murals that adorn its town
centre. Like satirical caricatures, they
depict all the big political events of the
20th century and are often very moving.
An outstanding example is a series
illustrating the death of 12-year-old Palestinian Mohammed el Dura as he hid
behind his father during a Gaza shoot-
out in 2000. Buses run to Orgosolo (€2,
35 minutes) from Nuoro.

Supramonte

Southeast of Nuoro rises the forbidding
limestone massif of the Supramonte, its
sheer walls like an iron curtain. This thrilling landscape forms the landward section of
the **Parco Nazionale del Golfo di Orosei e
del Gennargentu** (www.parcogennargentu.it),
Sardinia's largest national park. It tops out
at its impressively wild peak, 1463m Monte
Corrasi.

Oliena
POP 7355

From Nuoro you can see the multicoloured
rooftops and medieval churches of Oliena cupped in the palm of Monte Corrasi
(1463m). An atmospheric place with a greystone centre and a magnificent setting, it
was founded in Roman times and is today
famous for its blood-red Cannonau wine
and traditional Easter celebrations.

🏃 Activities

The countryside surrounding Oliena begs
outdoor escapades.

Sardegna Nascosta
HIKING

(☏349 4434665, 0784 28 85 50; www.sardegnana
scosta.it; Via Masiloghi 35) Arranges trips and
treks (€35 to €55 including lunch) with a
cultural focus, from hikes to Monte Corrasi,
Gola Su Gorropu and the Valle di Lanaittu to
canoeing, climbing and caving excursions.

Barbagia Insolita
ADVENTURE SPORTS

(☏0784 28 60 05; www.barbagiainsolita.it; Corso
Vittorio Emanuele 48) Takes you trekking to

SARDINIA SUPRAMONTE

WORTH A TRIP

ROAD TRIPPING

It's well worth getting behind the wheel to drive the 60km stretch of road from Dorgali to Santa Maria Navarrese. Serpentine and at times hair-raising, the SS125 threads through the mountain tops where the scenery is distractingly lovely: to the right the ragged limestone peaks of the Supramonte rear above wooded valleys and deep gorges; to the left mountains tumble down to the bright-blue sea. The first 20km to the Genna 'e Silana pass (1017m) are the most breathtaking.

Aside from the odd hell-for-leather Fiat, traffic is sparse, but you should take care at dusk, when wild pigs, goats, sheep and cows rule the road and bring down rocks.

Gola Su Gorropu (€40) and Tiscali (€35), canoeing on the Rio Cedrino (€40), quad biking (€60) and on 4WD escapades through the countryside (€40).

Cooperativa Enis　　ADVENTURE SPORTS
(☑0784 28 83 63; www.coopenis.it; Località Monte Maccione) This highly regarded adventure sports company offers superb guided treks and 4WD excursions into the Supramonte and along the Golfo di Orosei. These include Tiscali (€33), Gola Su Gorropu (€45), Cala Luna (€45) and the Supramonte di Orgosolo and Murales (€45). A packed lunch bumps up the cost by an extra €5.

🎊 Festivals & Events

Settimana Santa　　CULTURAL
The village is a hive of festive activity during Easter week. The culmination of the week-long celebrations is the S'Incontru (The Meeting), a boisterous Easter Sunday procession during which bearers carry a statue of Christ to meet a statue of the Virgin Mary in Piazza Santa Maria.

🛏 Sleeping & Eating

⭐ Agriturismo Guthiddai　　AGRITURISMO €
(☑0784 28 60 17; www.agriturismoguthiddai. com; Nuoro-Dorgali bivio Su Gologone; d €76-110, half-board per person €64-80; 🅿🛜🍴) On the road to Su Gologone, this bucolic, white-washed farmstead sits at the foot of rugged mountains, surrounded by fig, olive

and fruit trees. Olive oil, Cannonau wine and fruit and veg are all home produced. Rooms are exquisitely tiled in pale greens and cobalt blues. From Oliena, head to Dorgali, taking the turn-off right towards Valle di Lanaittu.

Hotel Monte Maccione　　HOTEL, CAMPGROUND €
(☑0784 28 83 63; www.coopenis.it; Località Monte Maccione; s/d/tr/q €49.50/80/114/144, camping 2 people & tent €18; 🅿🛜🍴) Run by the Cooperativa Enis, this place offers simple, rustic rooms and astonishingly lovely views from its hilltop location, 4km south of Oliena on the SP22. This back-to-nature retreat is a great choice if you want to strike out into the mountains on foot.

Su Gologone　　HOTEL €€€
(☑0784 28 75 12; www.sugologone.it; Località Su Gologone; s €145-220, d €255-350, ste €420-976; 🅿🌀🛜🌊🍴) Treat yourself to a spot of rural luxury at Su Gologone, nestled in glorious countryside 7km east of Oliena. Rooms are decorated with original artworks and handicrafts, and the facilities are top notch – there's a pool, a spa, a wine cellar and a restaurant (meals around €55), which is considered one of Sardinia's best.

ℹ Getting There & Away

ARST runs frequent buses from Via Roma to Nuoro (€1.50, 20 minutes, up to 12 Monday to Saturday, six Sunday).

Dorgali
POP 8524

Dorgali is a down-to-earth town with a grandiose backdrop, nestled at the foot of Monte Bardia and framed by vineyards and olive groves. Limestone peaks rear above the centre's pastel-coloured houses and steep, narrow streets, luring hikers and climbers to their summits.

◉ Sights

⭐ Grotta di Ispinigoli　　CAVE
(adult/reduced €7.50/3.50; ⏱tours on the hour 10am-6pm summer, 10am-noon & 3-5pm winter) A short drive north of Dorgali, the fairy-tale-like Grotta di Ispinigoli is a veritable forest of glittering stalagmites, including the world's second-tallest (the highest is in Mexico and stands at 40m). Unlike most caves of this type, which you enter from the side, here you descend 60m inside a giant 'well', at the centre of which stands the

magnificent 38m-high stalagmite. You can admire the tremendous rock formations, many of them sprouting from the walls like giant mushrooms and broccoli.

Serra Orrios   ARCHAEOLOGICAL SITE
(adult/reduced €5/2.50; ⊙hourly tours 9am-1pm & 3-6pm daily, shorter hours winter) Eleven kilometres northwest of Dorgali, at Km25 on the SP38, is Serra Orrios, a ruined nuraghic village inhabited between 1500 and 250 BC. Nestled among olive groves, the remains comprise a cluster of 70 or so horseshoe-shaped huts grouped around two basalt-hewn temples: Tempietto A, thought to be used by visiting pilgrims; and Tempietto B, for the villagers. There's a diagram near the entrance, which helps visitors understand the site, as the guided tours are in Italian only.

🛏 Sleeping & Eating

Sa Corte Antica   B&B €
(☑347 647 37 73; www.sacorteantica.it; Via Mannu 17; d €50-60, tr €65-75; ❄🔊) Gathered around an old stone courtyard, this B&B housed in an 18th-century townhouse oozes charm from every brick and beam. The rooms are traditional and peaceful, with reed ceilings and wrought-iron bedsteads. Enjoy homemade bread and *biscotti* at breakfast.

Ristorante Colibrì   SARDINIAN €€
(☑0784 9 60 54; Via Gramsci 14; meals €30; ⊙12.30-2.30pm & 7-10.30pm) Squirrelled away in an incongruous residential area (follow the numerous signs), this lemon-walled restaurant is the real McCoy for meat eaters. Stars of the menu include *cinghiale al rosmarino* (wild boar with rosemary), *capra alla selvatiza* (goat with thyme) and *porcetto*.

ⓘ Information

Proloco Dorgali (☑0784 9 62 43; www.dorgali.it; Via Lamarmora 108b; ⊙10am-1pm & 4-8pm Mon-Fri) Can provide information on Dorgali and Cala Gonone, including contact details for local trekking outfits and accommodation lists.

ⓘ Getting There & Away

Buses serve Nuoro (€3, 45 minutes, six daily) and Olbia (€7.50, 2¾ hours, two daily). Up to six daily services shuttle back and forth between Dorgali and Cala Gonone (€1.20, 25 minutes).

DON'T MISS

HIKING TO CALA LUNA

A favourite with rock climbers, crescent-shaped bay **Cala Luna** is wildly beautiful, backed by a lush ravine, framed by cave-pitted cliffs and pummelled by exquisite turquoise waters. It takes two to 2½ hours to reach it on foot from Cala Gonone, some 7km distant – follow the coastal trail from Cala Fuili. If you linger here after the boats have gone, you'll pretty much have the bay to yourself.

If your navigation skills are good, you could continue along a tough, unmarked trail to the striking **Arco Lupiru** rock arch (4km, around 1½ hours) or **Cala Sisine** (11km, four hours). Wild camping on the beaches is not permitted, but the authorities have been known to turn a blind eye to discreet campers.

Golfo di Orosei

For sheer stop-dead-in-your-tracks beauty, there's no place like this gulf, forming the seaward section of the Parco Nazionale del Golfo di Orosei e del Gennargentu. Here high mountains abruptly meet the sea, forming a crescent of dramatic cliffs riven by false inlets, scattered with horseshoe-shaped bays and lapped by exquisitely aquamarine waters.

Cala Gonone

Climbers, divers, sea kayakers, hikers and beach bums all rave about Cala Gonone. Backed by imperious tree-specked cliffs, the resort has kept the low-key, family friendly vibe of the small fishing village it once was. With an appealing line-up of hotels, bars and restaurants on its pine-fringed *lungomare,* Gonone makes a great base for outdoor adventures along this magnificent stretch of coast.

◉ Sights & Activities

Grotta del Bue Marino   CAVE
(adult/reduced €8/5; ⊙guided tours hourly 10am-noon & 3-5pm summer, 11am-3pm winter, groups only Oct-Mar) It's a scenic 40-minute hike from Cala Fuili, or a speedy boat ride from Cala Gonone, to this enchanting grotto. It was the last island refuge of the now-extinct monk seal – the *bue marino* or 'sea ox' as it

SARDINIA GOLFO DI OROSEI

KAYAKING THE COAST

Kayak Cardedu (☑ 348 9369401, 0782 7 51 85; www.cardedu-kayak.com; Località Perda Rubia, Cardedu) With the help of Kayak Cardedu, you can spend the day with your paddle slicing rhythmically through turquoise waters in the Tyrrhenian Sea. Owner Francesco caters to kayakers of all levels. His courses cost €150 for five two-hour lessons or, if you would prefer to go it alone, daily kayak rental starts at €25 per person. Be sure to bring your swimming gear in summer. Francesco can help organise longer tours and 'nautical camping' if you fancy fishing from the kayak and sleeping on secluded beaches.

On request, he can also arrange mountain-biking tours into the fertile valleys surrounding Cardedu (reckon on €30 to €40 for a half-day excursion), hikes along the striking red granite coastline, and walks up into the surrounding hills, which are littered with fine examples of *domus de janas* (prehistoric chamber tombs).

Cardedu is off the SS125, 30km south of Baunei.

was known by local fishermen). The watery gallery is impressive, with shimmering light playing on the strange shapes and Neolithic petroglyphs within the cave. Guided visits take place up to seven times a day. In peak season you may need to book.

Nuovo Consorzio Trasporti Marittimi BOAT TOUR
(☑ 0784 9 33 05; www.calagononecrociere.it; Porto Cala Gonone) This outfit offers tours including return trips to Cala Luna (€15), Cala Sisine (€22), Cala Mariolu (€30) and Cala Gabbiani (€30). A trip to the Grotta del Bue Marino costs €20, including entry to the cave. All tours are around €5 more in July and August. See the website for timetables.

Prima Sardegna ADVENTURE SPORTS
(☑ 0784 9 33 67; www.primasardegna.com; Via Lungomare Palmasera 32; ⊙ 9am-1pm & 4-8pm summer) Prima Sardegna arranges guided excursions to Tiscali and Gorropu (€40), as well as hikes and 4WD tours in the Supramonte. Daily bike/scooter/single-kayak/double-kayak rental costs €24/48/30/55. Mini cruises along the Golfo di Orosei cost between €35 and €45.

🛏 Sleeping

The resort goes into hibernation from October until Easter; bookings are essential in summer. Besides the following options, there's also a campground.

★ **Hotel L'Oasi** B&B €
(☑ 0784 9 31 11; www.loasihotel.it; Via Garcia Lorca 13; s €69-83, d €87-139; P ❄ 🖤) Perched on the cliffs above Cala Gonone and nestling in flowery gardens, this B&B offers en-

ticing sea views from many of its breezy rooms. It's worth paying an extra €15 or so for half-board, as the three-course dinners are prepared with fresh local produce. The friendly owners, the Carlesso family, can advise on activities from climbing to diving. L'Oasi is a 700m uphill walk from the harbour.

Agriturismo Nuraghe Mannu AGRITURISMO €
(☑ 0784 9 32 64, 393 288685824; www.agriturismonuraghemannu.com; Località Pranos; d €64-68, half-board per person €50-52, camping 2 people, car & tent €18-24; 🖤) 🌿 Immersed in greenery and with blissful sea views, this is an authentic, ecofriendly working farm with four simple rooms, a restaurant open to all, and home-produced bread, milk, ricotta and sweets at breakfast. For campers, there are also five tent pitches available.

Hotel Villa Gustui Maris HOTEL €€
(☑ 0784 92 00 76; www.villagustuimaris.it; Via Marco Polo 57; d €160-218, tr €220-276; ❄ @ ❄ 🖤) Wake up to sweeping views of the Golfo di Orosei at this Mediterranean villa-style hotel, a stiff 800m uphill walk from the resort centre. Rooms are bright and spacious, with tiled floors, lashings of cream and terracotta, and balconies or terraces. The pool is great for a scenic swim.

Hotel Nettuno B&B €€
(☑ 0784 9 33 10; www.nettuno-hotel.it; Via Vasco de Gama 26; d €80-135, tr €110-160, q €120-185; ❄ ❄ 🖤) Located a minute's walk from the beach, this family-run B&B is a supercentral choice. The simple tiled rooms are kept spick and span; a balcony will set you back an extra €10 per night. There's a shady garden for relaxing over a cool drink.

GORGE EXPLORATIONS

Gola Su Gorropu (☑ 328 8976563; www.gorropu.info; adult/reduced €5/3.50; ☺ 10.30am-5pm) Sardinia's most spectacular gorge is flanked by limestone walls towering up to 400m in height. The endemic *Aquilegia nuragica* plant grows here, and at quieter times it's possible to spot mouflon and golden eagles. From the Rio Flumineddu riverbed you can wander about 1km into the boulder-strewn ravine without climbing gear; follow the markers. After 500m you reach the narrowest point, just 4m wide, and the formidable **Hotel Supramonte**, a tough 8b multipitch climb up a vertical 400m rock face.

To hike into the gorge you'll need sturdy shoes and sufficient water. The most dramatic route begins from the car park opposite Hotel Silana at the **Genna 'e Silana** pass on the SS125 at kilometre 183. The 8km trail takes 1½ to two hours one way, so allow at least four hours for the return trek, longer if you plan to spend time exploring the gorge itself. While the descent is mostly easygoing, the climb back up is considerably tougher. The hike weaves through holm oak woods, boulder-strewn slopes and cave-riddled cliffs.

For a bird's-eye perspective of the gorge, you could take the 6km ridge trail from the car park to 888m **Punta Cucuttos**. It takes around 1½ hours one way.

Eating

Snack bars, cafes and gelaterie line the *lungomare*.

Gelateria Fancello GELATERIA €
(Viale Palmasera 26; ice-cream scoop €1.30; ☺ 2-10.30pm) Hazelnut, fig, yoghurt and lemon – the gelati and *sorbetti* (sorbet) here are the real deal. Stop by for a cone to lick as you stroll the promenade.

La Favorita ITALIAN, PIZZA €€
(☑ 0784 9 31 69; Viale Palmasera 30; pizzas €5-10, meals €30; ☺ 12.15-3pm & 7-11pm) There's always a good buzz at this incredibly popular restaurant and pizzeria with a lovely sea-facing terrace. Snag a table to dig into excellent wood-fired-oven pizzas, or go for fish dishes like ceviche with lemon, chilli and sweet potato and whatever is the catch that day.

Il Pescatore SEAFOOD €€
(☑ 0784 9 31 74; Via Acqua Dolce 7; meals €20-35; ☺ noon-2.30pm & 7-10.30pm; ꙮ) Fresh seafood is what this authentic place is about. Sit on the terrace for sea breezes and fishy delights, such as pasta with *ricci* and spaghetti with clams and *bottarga*, all washed down with half a litre of the crisp house white (€5).

❶ Information

Tourist Office (☑ 0784 9 36 96; www.dorgali. it; Viale Bue Marino 1a; ☺ 9am-1pm & 3-7pm May-Sep, 9am-1pm Oct-Apr) A very helpful office in the small park off to the right as you enter town.

❶ Getting There & Away

Up to seven daily buses run to Cala Gonone from Dorgali (€1.20, 20 minutes, seven daily) and up to six from Nuoro (€3.50, 70 minutes).

Ogliastra

Wedged in between the provinces of Nuoro and Cagliari, Ogliastra is a dramatic land of vast, unspoiled valleys, silent woods and windswept rock faces. The coastal stretches become increasingly dramatic the nearer you get to the Golfo di Orosei.

Santa Maria Navarrese

At the southern end of the Golfo di Orosei sits the low-key beach resort of Santa Maria Navarrese. Shipwrecked Basque sailors built a small church here in 1052, dedicated to Santa Maria di Navarra on the orders of the Princess of Navarre, who happened to be one of the survivors. The church was set in the shade of a grand olive tree that is still standing – some say it's nearly 2000 years old.

Lofty pines and eucalyptus trees back the beach lapped by transparent water. Offshore are several islets, including the **Isolotto di Ogliastra**, a giant hunk of pink porphyritic rock. The leafy northern end of the beach is topped by a watchtower built to look for raiding Saracens.

A handful of buses link Santa Maria Navarrese with Dorgali (€5, 1½ hours, two daily) and Nuoro (€7, 2½ hours, five daily).

Baunei

There is little reason to stop off in the shepherd's town of Baunei, but what is seriously worth your while is the 10km detour up to the Altopiano del Golgo, a strange, otherworldly plateau where goats, pigs and donkeys graze in *macchia* and woodland. From here a road snakes down to the rock spike of Pedra Longa, a natural monument and the starting point for Sardinia's star coastal trek, the Selvaggio Blu. You'll need your own wheels to get here.

◉ Sights & Activities

★Cala Goloritzè   BEACH

The last beachette of the gulf, Cala Goloritzè rivals the best. At the southern end, bizarre limestone figures soar away from the cliffside. Among them is jaw-dropping Monte Caroddi, aka Aguglia, a 148m-high needle of rock loved by climbers. Follow the signs from the Cooperativa Goloritzè at the Golgo plateau and it's a gentle 4.5km (about an hour) walk down (and a slightly tougher 1½ hours back) to Cala Goloritzè.

Il Golgo   LANDMARK

Follow the signs from Baunei up a 2km climb of impossibly steep switchbacks to the plateau. Head north following the Su Sterru (Il Golgo) signs for less than 1km, then leave your vehicle and walk over to this remarkable feat of nature – a 270m abyss just 40m wide at its base. Its funnel-like opening is now fenced off but, knowing the size of the drop, just peering into the dark opening is enough to bring on vertigo.

Chiesa di San Pietro   CHURCH

Standing lonesome on the Golgo plateau is this late-16th-century church, a humble construction flanked to one side by *cumbessias* – rough, largely open stone affairs that are not at all comfortable for the passing pilgrims who traditionally sleep here to celebrate the saint's day (Santi Pietro e Paolo, 29 June).

Cooperativa Goloritzè   HIKING

(☑368 7028980; www.coopgoloritze.com; Località Golgo) This highly regarded cooperative arranges excursions ranging from trekking to 4WD jeep trips. Many treks involve a descent through canyons to the Golfo di Orosei's dreamy beaches. Staff at the refuge also organise guides and logistical support for walkers attempting Sardinia's once-in-a-lifetime Selvaggio Blu trek.

⊨ Sleeping & Eating

★Lemon House   B&B €

(☑0782 66 95 07; www.peteranne.it; Via Dante 10, Lotzorai; r per person €30-42; ☎) Peter and Anne run this lime-hued B&B, a terrific base for outdoor escapades, with a bouldering wall for limbering up and a relaxing roof terrace for winding down. The sports-loving duo can arrange bike hire and pick-ups, lend you a GPS and give you invaluable tips on hiking, climbing, mountain biking and kayaking. Be sure to try the homemade lemon marmalade at breakfast. It's 10km south of Baunei, off the SS125.

Hotel Bia Maore   B&B €

(☑0782 61 10 33; www.biamaore.it; Via San Pietro 19; s €55-85, d €80-110, tr €100-140; P❉☎⊞) Perched like an eyrie above Baunei, this B&B has compelling views of the mountains and coast. The warm-hued rooms are decked out with handmade furnishings and Sardinian fabrics – the pick of them has a balcony overlooking the mountains and the Gulf of Ogliastra.

Locanda Il Rifugio   SARDINIAN €€

(☑368 7028980; www.coopgoloritze.com; Località Golgo; meals €25-35; ☉1-3pm & 8-11pm summer) Managed by the Cooperativa Goloritzè, this beautifully converted farmstead puts on a generous spread of regional fare such as *ladeddos* (potato gnocchi) and spit-roasted kid and suckling pig, washed down with local Cannonau red.

Understand Italy

Italy Today

This is the 'beautiful country', where even a cup of coffee is an exercise in perfection. Yet under the exquisite surface are some serious problems, in which corruption, nepotism and unstable governments have all played a part. But it isn't all doom and gloom. Italy's youngest-ever leader, Matteo Renzi, is effecting dramatic political changes, Pope Francis continues to reinvigorate the Vatican and Italians are using their ingenuity to address such issues as the cost of maintaining their illustrious heritage.

Best Blogs

Becoming Italian Word by Word (http://becomingitalianwordbyword. typepad.com) Italian language explored.
Parla Food (www.parlafood.com) By savvy food blogger Katie Parla.
Italian Food Forever (www.italian foodforever.com) Umbria-based, delicious recipes.

Best on Film

La Grande Bellezza (Great Beauty) Paolo Sorrentino's Fellini-esque tribute to Italy.
La Dolce Vita (Sweet Life) Federico Fellini capturing Italy's 1950s zeitgeist.
The Leopard Luchino Visconti's portrayal of the decaying Sicilian nobility.
Ladri di biciclette (Bicycle Thieves) A moving portrait of post-WWII Italy.

Best in Print

The Italians (Luigi Barzini) Revealing portrait of the Italian character.
The Leopard (Giuseppe Tomasi di Lampedusa) Masterpiece about tumultuous 19th-century Sicily.
The Italians (John Hooper) Italy correspondent assesses modern Italy.
Gomorrah (Paolo Saviano) Unput-downable epic about the Neapolitan Camorra (Mafia).

The Economy

Over the last 15 years, the Italian economy has stagnated. In Europe, Italy's public debt ranks among the highest while its economic growth is among the lowest.

Things are especially difficult for the young. Youth unemployment rose to over 44% in early 2015. The same year, it was calculated that the cost to the Italian economy of graduates fleeing the country in search of better opportunities elsewhere was around €23bn.

Nepotism and corruption don't help. In 2014 alone, three major transgressions were exposed: alleged corruption in awarding contracts for the Milan Expo; the 'Mafia Capitale' scandal, in which politicians were discovered to have liaised with criminals to steal funds from the Roman municipality; and corruption relating to the construction of the MOSE flood defence system that led to the resignation of the mayor of Venice.

At the Helm

The downfall of former prime minister Silvio Berlusconi, who was convicted of tax fraud in 2013, ushered in a new era in Italian politics. The 39-year-old Matteo Renzi, previously mayor of Florence, took over as leader of a right-left coalition in 2014, making him the third unelected prime minister since Berlusconi's fall (following Mario Monti and Enrico Letta). Renzi's cabinet is the youngest in Italian history and the first with an even gender balance.

Even before taking the role of prime minister, Renzi was known as '*il rottamatore*' (the scrapper), a name he continues to embrace as he attempts to change Italy's political landscape with a package of employment and electoral reforms. Soon after taking over from Letta, Renzi led his party to success in the European elections, but their share of the vote was just 24% in the 2015 local elections, as his Eurosceptic, anti-austerity opponents experienced a surge in support.

Renzi's challengers include the Five Star Movement, headed by comedian Beppe Grillo. The five stars refer to their five key issues: water, transport, internet access, sustainable development and environmentalism. The anti-establishment, Eurosceptic party has repeatedly received the second-highest number of votes in elections, but refuses to enter into any coalitions, which limits its power. On the political right is Matteo Salvini's anti-European, anti-immigration Lega Nord (Northern League).

At the spiritual helm, Pope Francis, the popular Argentinian pontiff elected in 2013, goes from strength to strength. Noted for his humble, less formal approach and concern for the poor, he has done much to restore the Church's image, attracting over 7 million pilgrims to the Vatican in 2014. His declaration of a Jubilee Holy Year from December 2015 to November 2016 has guaranteed an influx of visitors, providing Rome and Italy with both material and spiritual rewards.

The Migration Frontline

Even as young people leave Italy (over 94,000 in 2013), many migrants are risking their lives to enter the country. The number of people attempting the dangerous journey from North Africa rose by a third in 2015, with 62,000 migrants arriving by sea in the first half of the year. In October 2014 Italy ended its Mare Nostrum search-and-rescue missions, which cost an unsustainable €9 million per month; it was subsequently replaced by the much smaller joint–EU Operation Triton. It took a disaster in April 2015 in which over 800 people drowned to prompt the EU to further action, tripling the mission's budget.

Most migrants arrive in Italy on the tiny island of Lampedusa, which is just 113km from the North African coast. Few stay in Italy, however; most travel onwards to northern Europe where opportunities are greater. Renzi has been key in negotiations for a quota system whereby the EU share responsibility for migrants.

Saving Italy's Heritage

Italy has 51 Unesco World Heritage Sites, more than any other country, and looking after such a wealth of heritage is expensive. In recent years, walls have collapsed at Pompeii and a Raphael painting at Rome's Borghese Gallery warped due to a broken air-conditioning system. In answer to such problems, municipalities have been working on attracting private investment, a controversial but successful process. Completed projects include luxury brand Tod's €25-million clean-up of the Colosseum and Renzo Rossi's OTB group €5-million restoration of Venice's Rialto Bridge. The government continues to encourage this trend via large tax breaks.

POPULATION: **59.83 MILLION (2015)**

AREA: **301,230 SQ KM**

UNEMPLOYMENT: **12.5%**

ANNUAL PASTA CONSUMPTION PER PERSON: **26KG**

ANNUAL TOURIST VISITORS: **47.7 MILLION**

if Italy were 100 people

93 would be Italian
4 would be Albanian & Eastern European
1 would be North African
2 would be Others

belief systems
(% of population)

91 — Roman Catholics
3.5 — Other Religions
1.5 — Muslims
4 — Other Christians

population per sq km

ROME   ITALY   USA

♀ ≈ 30 people

History

Italy has only been a nation since 1861, prior to which it was last unified as part of the Roman Empire. It has wielded powerful influence as the headquarters of Catholicism, and Italy's dynamic city-states set the modern era in motion with the Renaissance. Italian unity was won in blood, fusing north and south in a dysfunctional yet enduring marriage. Even today, Italy still feels like a powerfully distinct collection of regions, a present that has deep roots in the past.

Etruscans, Greeks & Wolf-Raised Twins

Of the many tribes that emerged from the millennia of the Stone Age in ancient Italy, it was the Etruscans who dominated the peninsula by the 7th century BC. Etruria was based on city-states mostly concentrated between the Arno and Tiber rivers. Among them were Caere (modern-day Cerveteri), Tarquinii (Tarquinia), Veii (Veio), Perusia (Perugia), Volaterrae (Volterra) and Arretium (Arezzo). The name of their homeland is preserved in the name Tuscany, where the bulk of their settlements were (and still are) located.

Most of what we know of the Etruscan people has been deduced from artefacts and paintings unearthed at their burial sites, especially at Tarquinia, near Rome. Argument persists over whether the Etruscans had migrated from Asia Minor. They spoke a language that today has barely been deciphered. An energetic people, the Etruscans were redoubtable warriors and seamen, but lacked cohesion and discipline.

At home, the Etruscans farmed, and mined metals. Their gods were numerous and they were forever trying to second-guess them and predict future events through such rituals as examining the livers of sacrificed animals. They were also quick to learn from others. Much of their artistic tradition (which comes to us in the form of tomb frescoes, statuary and pottery) was influenced by the Greeks.

Indeed, while the Etruscans dominated the centre of the peninsula, Greek traders settled in the south in the 8th century BC, setting up a series of independent city-states along the coast and in Sicily that together were known as Magna Graecia. They flourished until the 3rd century BC

TIMELINE	c 700,000 BC	2000 BC	474 BC
	Primitive tribes lived in caves and hunted elephants, rhinoceroses, hippopotamuses and other hefty wild beasts on the Italian peninsula.	The Bronze Age reaches Italy. Hunter-gatherers have settled as farmers. The use of copper and bronze to fashion tools and arms marks a new sophistication.	The power of the Etruscans in Italy is eclipsed after Greek forces from Syracuse and Cumae join to crush an Etruscan armada off the southern Italian coast in the Battle of Cumae.

and the ruins of magnificent Doric temples in Italy's south (at Paestum) and on Sicily (at Agrigento, Selinunte and Segesta) stand as testimony to the splendour of Greek civilisation in Italy.

Attempts by the Etruscans to conquer the Greek settlements failed and accelerated the Etruscan decline. The death knell, however, would come from an unexpected source – the grubby but growing Latin town of Rome.

The origins of the town are shrouded in myth, which says it was founded by Romulus (who descended from Aeneas, a refugee from Troy whose mother was the goddess Venus) on 21 April 753 BC, on the site where he and his twin brother, Remus, had been suckled by a she-wolf as orphan infants. Romulus later killed Remus and the settlement was named Rome after him. At some point, legend merges with history. Seven kings are said to have followed Romulus and at least three were historical Etruscan rulers. In 509 BC, disgruntled Latin nobles turfed the last of the Etruscan kings, Tarquinius Superbus, out of Rome after his predecessor, Servius Tullius, had stacked the Senate with his allies and introduced citizenship reforms that undermined the power of the aristocracy. Sick of monarchy, the nobles set up the Roman Republic. Over the following centuries, this piffling Latin town would grow to become Italy's major power, sweeping aside the Etruscans, whose language and culture disappeared by the 2nd century AD.

The Roman Republic

Under the Republic, *imperium*, or regal power, was placed in the hands of two consuls who acted as political and military leaders and were elected for non-renewable one-year terms by an assembly of the people. The Senate, whose members were appointed for life, advised the consuls.

Although from the beginning monuments were emblazoned with the initials SPQR (Senatus Populusque Romanus, or the Senate and People of Rome), the 'people' initially had precious little say in affairs. (The initials are still used and many Romans would argue that little has changed.) Known as plebeians (literally 'the many'), the disenfranchised majority slowly wrested concessions from the patrician class in the more than two centuries that followed the founding of the Republic. Some plebeians were even appointed as consuls and, indeed, by about 280 BC most of the distinctions between patricians and plebeians had disappeared. That said, the apparently democratic system was largely oligarchic, with a fairly narrow political class (whether patrician or plebeian) vying for positions of power in government and the Senate.

The Romans were a rough-and-ready lot. Rome did not bother to mint coins until 269 BC, even though the neighbouring (and later conquered or allied) Etruscans and Greeks had long had their own currencies. The

The Romans devised a type of odometer that engaged with a vehicle's wheel to count every mile travelled.

396 BC	264–241 BC	218–146 BC	133 BC
Romans conquer the key Etruscan town of Veio, north of Rome, after an 11-year siege. Celebrations are short-lived, as invading Celtic tribes sweep across Italy and sack Rome in 390 BC.	War rages between Rome and the empire of Carthage, stretching across North Africa and into Spain, Sicily and Sardinia. By war's end Rome is the western Mediterranean's prime naval power.	Carthage sends Hannibal to invade Italy overland from the north in the Second Punic War. Rome invades Spain, Hannibal fails, and Carthage is destroyed in a third war from 149–146 BC.	Rome gains control of Sardinia, Sicily, Corsica, mainland Greece, Spain, most of North Africa and part of Asia Minor.

Etruscans and Greeks also brought writing to the attention of Romans, who found it useful for documents and technical affairs but hardly glowed in the literature department. Eventually, the Greek pantheon of gods formed the bedrock of Roman worship. Society was patriarchal and its prime building block the household *(familia)*. The head of the family *(pater familias)* had direct control over his wife, children and extended family. He was responsible for his children's education. Devotion to household gods (eg Panes, the spirits of the kitchen) was as strong as devotion to the pantheon of state gods, led at first by the Capitoline Triad of Jupiter (the sky god and chief protector of the state), Juno (the female equivalent of Jupiter and patron goddess of women) and Minerva (patron goddess of craftsmen). An earlier version of the triad included Mars (god of war) instead of Juno.

Slowly at first, then with gathering pace, Roman armies conquered the Italian peninsula. Defeated city-states were not taken over directly; they were instead obliged to become allies. They retained their government and lands but had to provide troops on demand to serve in the Roman army. This relatively light-handed touch was a key to success. Increasingly, the protection offered by Roman hegemony induced many cities to become allies voluntarily. Wars with Carthage and other rivals in the east led Rome to take control of Sardinia, Sicily, Corsica, mainland Greece, Spain, most of North Africa and part of Asia Minor by 133 BC.

As the empire grew, so did its ancient system of 'motorways'. With the roads came other bright concepts – postal services and wayside inns. Messages could be shot around the empire in a matter of days or weeks by sending dispatch riders. At ancient 'truck stops', the riders would change mounts, have a bite and continue on their way (more efficient than many modern European postal systems).

By the second half of the 2nd century BC, Rome was the most important city in the Mediterranean, with a population of 300,000. Most were lower-class freedmen or slaves living in often precarious conditions. Tenement housing blocks (mostly of brick and wood) were raised alongside vast monuments. One of the latter was the Circus Flaminius, the stage of some of the spectacular games held each year. These became increasingly important events for the people of Rome, who flocked to see gladiators and wild beasts in combat.

For Ancient Awe

Pantheon, Rome

Colosseum, Rome

Pompeii, Campania

Segesta, Sicily

Cerveteri, Lazio

Seizing the Day

Born in 100 BC, Gaius Julius Caesar would prove to be one of Rome's most masterful generals and capable administrators, but his hunger for power was probably his undoing.

He was a supporter of the consul Pompey (later known as Pompey the Great), who, since 78 BC, had become a leading figure in Rome after

46 BC	30 BC	AD 79	100–138
Julius Caesar assumes dictatorial powers.	Octavian (later Augustus) invades Egypt, Antony and Cleopatra commit suicide and Egypt becomes a province of Rome.	Mt Vesuvius showers molten rock and ash upon Pompeii and Herculaneum. Pliny the Younger later describes the eruption in letters and the towns are only rediscovered in the 18th century.	The Roman Empire reaches its most dominant extent, during the reign of Hadrian.

The Roman Empire

putting down rebellions in Spain and eliminating piracy. Caesar himself had been in Spain for several years dealing with border revolts; on his return to Rome in 60 BC, he formed an alliance with Pompey and another important commander and former consul, Crassus. They backed Caesar's candidacy as consul.

To consolidate his position in the Roman power game, Caesar needed a major military command. This he received with a mandate to govern the province of Gallia Narbonensis, a southern swath of modern France stretching from Italy to the Pyrenees, in 59 BC. Caesar raised troops and in the following year entered Gaul proper (modern France) to head off an invasion of Helvetic tribes from Switzerland and subsequently to bring other tribes to heel. What started as a defensive effort soon became a full-blown campaign of conquest. In the next five years, he subdued Gaul and made forays into Britain and across the Rhine. In 51 BC he stamped out the last great revolt in Gaul, led by Vercingetorix. Caesar was generous to

476	568	754–56	902
Germanic tribal leader Odovacar proclaims himself king in Rome. The peninsula sinks into chaos and only the eastern half of the empire survives intact.	Lombards invade and occupy northern Italy, leaving just Ravenna, Rome and southern Italy in the empire's hands. Other tribes invade Balkan territories and cut the eastern empire off from Italy.	Frankish king Pepin the Short enters Italy at the request of Pope Stephen II, defeats the Lombards and declares the creation of the Papal States.	Muslims from North Africa complete the occupation of Sicily, encouraging learning of the Greek classics, mathematics and other sciences. Agriculture flourishes and Sicily is relatively peaceful for two centuries.

his defeated enemies and consequently won over the Gauls. Indeed, they became his staunchest supporters in coming years.

By now, Caesar also had a devoted veteran army behind him. Jealous of the growing power of his one-time protégé, Pompey severed his political alliance and joined like-minded factions in the Senate to outlaw Caesar in 49 BC. On 7 January, Caesar crossed the Rubicon river into Italy and civil war began. His three-year campaign in Italy, Spain and the eastern Mediterranean proved a crushing victory. Upon his return to Rome in 46 BC, he assumed dictatorial powers.

He launched a series of reforms, overhauled the Senate and embarked on a building program (of which the Curia and Basilica Giulia remain). By 44 BC it was clear Caesar had no plans to restore the Republic, and dissent grew in the Senate, even among former supporters like Marcus Junius Brutus, who thought he had gone too far. A small band of conspirators led by Brutus finally stabbed him to death in a Senate meeting on the Ides of March (15 March), two years after he had been proclaimed dictator for life.

For Ancient Booty

Vatican Museums, Rome

Capitoline Museums, Rome

Museo Archeologico Nazionale, Naples

Museo Archeologico Paolo Orsi, Syracuse

Museo Nazionale Etrusco di Villa Giulia, Rome

In the years following Caesar's death, his lieutenant, Mark Antony (Marcus Antonius), and nominated heir, great-nephew Octavian, plunged into civil war against Caesar's assassins. Things calmed down as Octavian took control of the western half of the empire and Antony headed to the east, but when Antony fell head over heels for Cleopatra VII in 31 BC, Octavian went to war and finally claimed victory over Antony and Cleopatra at Actium, in Greece. The following year Octavian invaded Egypt, Antony and Cleopatra committed suicide and Egypt became a province of Rome.

Augustus & the Glories of Empire

Octavian was left as sole ruler of the Roman world and by 27 BC had been acclaimed Augustus (Your Eminence) and conceded virtually unlimited power by the Senate. In effect, he had become emperor.

Under Augustus, the arts flourished – his contemporaries included the poets Virgil, Horace and Ovid, as well as the historian Livy. He encouraged the visual arts, restored existing buildings and constructed many new ones. During his reign the Pantheon was raised, and he boasted that he had 'found Rome in brick and left it in marble'. The long period of comparatively enlightened rule that he initiated brought unprecedented prosperity and security to the Mediterranean.

By AD 100, the city of Rome was said to have had more than 1.5 million inhabitants and all the trappings of an imperial capital – its wealth and prosperity were obvious in the rich mosaics, marble temples, public baths, theatres, circuses and libraries. People of all races and conditions converged on the capital. Poverty was rife among an often disgruntled

962	1130	1202–03	1271
Otto I is crowned Holy Roman Emperor in Rome, the first in a long line of Germanic rulers. His meddling in Italian affairs leads to clashes between papacy and empire.	Norman invader Roger II is crowned King of Sicily, a century after the Normans landed in southern Italy, creating a united southern Italian kingdom.	Venice leads the Fourth Crusade to the Holy Land on a detour to Constantinople in revenge for attacks on Venetian interests there. The Crusaders topple the Byzantine emperor, installing a puppet ruler.	Venetian merchant Marco Polo embarks on a 24-year journey to Central Asia and China with his father and uncle. His written travel accounts help enlighten Europeans about Asia.

IMPERIAL INSANITY

Bribes? *Bunga bunga* parties? Think they're unsavoury? Spare a thought for the ancient Romans, who suffered their fair share of eccentric leaders. We salute some of the Empire's wackiest, weirdest and downright kinkiest rulers.

Tiberius (14–37) – A steady governing hand but prone to depression, Tiberius had a difficult relationship with the Senate and withdrew in his later years to Capri, where, they say, he devoted himself to drinking, orgies and fits of paranoia.

Gaius (Caligula) (37–41) – 'Little Shoes' made great-uncle Tiberius look tame. Sex (including with his sisters) and gratuitous, cruel violence were high on his agenda. He emptied the state's coffers and suggested making a horse consul, before being assassinated.

Claudius (41–54) – Apparently timid as a child, he proved ruthless with his enemies (among them 35 senators), whose executions he greatly enjoyed watching. According to English historian Edward Gibbon, he was the only one of the first 15 emperors not to take male lovers.

Nero (54–68) – Augustus' last descendant, Nero had his pushy stage mum murdered, his first wife's veins slashed, his second wife kicked to death and his third wife's ex-husband killed. The people accused him of playing the fiddle while Rome burned to the ground in 64. He blamed the disaster on the Christians, executed the evangelists Peter and Paul and had others thrown to wild beasts in a grisly public spectacle.

lower class. Augustus created Rome's first police force under a city prefect *(praefectus urbi)* to curb mob violence, which had long gone largely unchecked.

Augustus carried out other far-reaching reforms. He streamlined the army, which was kept at a standing total of around 300,000 men. Military service ranged from 16 to 25 years, but Augustus kept conscription to a minimum, making it a largely volunteer force. He consolidated Rome's three-tier class society. The richest and most influential class remained the Senators. Below them, the so-called Equestrians filled posts in public administration and supplied officers to the army (control of which was essential to keeping Augustus' position unchallenged). The bulk of the populace filled the ranks of the lower class. The system was by no means rigid and upward mobility was possible.

A century after Augustus' death in AD 14 (at age 75), the Roman Empire reached its greatest extent. Under Hadrian (76–138), it stretched from the Iberian peninsula, Gaul and Britain to a line that basically followed the Rhine and Danube rivers. All of the present-day Balkans and Greece, along with the areas known in those times as Dacia, Moesia and Thrace (considerable territories reaching to the Black Sea), were under

1282	1309	1321	1348
Charles of Anjou creates enemies in Sicily with heavy taxes on landowners, who rise in the Sicilian Vespers revolt. They hand control of Sicily to Peter III, King of Aragón.	Pope Clement V shifts the papacy to Avignon, France, for almost 70 years. Clement had been elected pope four years earlier but refused to rule in a hostile Rome.	Dante Alighieri completes his epic poem *La divina commedia* (The Divine Comedy). The Florentine poet, considered Italy's greatest literary figure, dies the same year.	The Black Death (bubonic plague) wreaks havoc across Italy and much of the rest of western Europe. Florence is said to have lost three-quarters of its populace.

SPAGHETTI

Roman control. Most of modern-day Turkey, Syria, Lebanon, Palestine and Israel were occupied by Rome's legions and linked up with Egypt. From there a deep strip of Roman territory stretched along the length of North Africa to the Atlantic coast of what is today northern Morocco. The Mediterranean was a Roman lake.

This situation lasted until the 3rd century. By the time Diocletian (245–305) became emperor, attacks on the empire from without and revolts within had become part and parcel of imperial existence. A new religious force, Christianity, was gaining popularity and persecution of Christians became common. This policy was reversed in 313 under Constantine I (c 272–337) in his Edict of Milan.

Inspired by a vision of the cross, Constantine defeated his own rival, Maxentius, on Rome's Ponte Milvio (Milvian Bridge) in 312, becoming the Roman Empire's first Christian leader and commissioning Rome's first Christian basilica, San Giovanni in Laterano.

The empire was later divided in two, with the second capital in Constantinople (founded by Constantine in 330), on the Bosporus (now Bosphorus) in Byzantium. It was this, the eastern empire, which survived as Italy and Rome were overrun. This rump empire stretched from parts of present-day Serbia and Montenegro across to Asia Minor, a coastal strip of what is now Syria, Lebanon, Jordan and Israel down to Egypt and a sliver of North Africa as far west as modern Libya. Attempts by Justinian I (482–565) to recover Rome and the shattered western half of the empire ultimately came to nothing.

Papal Power & Family Feuds

Ironically, the minority religion that Emperor Diocletian had tried so hard to stamp out saved the glory of the city of Rome. Through the chaos of invasion and counter-invasion that saw Italy succumb to Germanic tribes, the Byzantine reconquest and the Lombard occupation in the north, the papacy established itself in Rome as a spiritual and secular force. It invented the Donation of Constantine, a document in which Emperor Constantine I had supposedly granted the Church control of Rome and surrounding territory. What the popes needed was a guarantor with military clout. This they found in the Franks and a deal was done.

In return for formal recognition of the popes' control of Rome and surrounding Byzantine-held territories henceforth to be known as the Papal States, the popes granted the Carolingian Franks a leading (if ill-defined) role in Italy and their king, Charlemagne, the title of Holy Roman Emperor. He was crowned by Leo III on Christmas Day 800. The bond between the papacy and the Byzantine Empire was thus broken, and political power in what had been the Western Roman Empire shifted north of the Alps, where it would remain for more than 1000 years.

The Arabs introduced spaghetti to Sicily, where 'strings of pasta' were documented by the Arab geographer Al-Idrissi in Palermo in 1150.

1506	1508–12	1534	1582
Work starts on St Peter's Basilica, to a design by Donato Bramante, on the site of an earlier basilica in Rome. Work would continue on Christendom's showpiece church until 1626.	Pope Julius II commissions Michelangelo to paint the ceiling frescoes in the Sistine Chapel. Michelangelo decides the content, and the central nine panels recount stories from Genesis.	The accession of Pope Paul III marks the beginning of the Counter-Reformation.	Pope Gregory XIII replaces the Julian calendar (introduced by Julius Caesar) with the modern-day Gregorian calendar. The new calendar adds the leap year to keep in line with the earth's rotation.

The stage was set for a future of seemingly endless struggles. Similarly, Rome's aristocratic families engaged in battle for the papacy. For centuries, the imperial crown was fought over ruthlessly and Italy was frequently the prime battleground. Holy Roman emperors sought time and again to impose their control on increasingly independent-minded Italian cities, and even on Rome itself. In riposte, the popes continually sought to exploit their spiritual position to bring the emperors to heel and further their own secular ends.

The clash between Pope Gregory VII and Emperor Henry IV, in the last quarter of the 11th century, over who had the right to appoint bishops (who were powerful political players and hence important friends or dangerous foes) showed just how bitter these struggles could become. They became a focal point of Italian politics in the late Middle Ages and across the cities and regions of the peninsula two camps emerged: Guelphs (Guelfi, who backed the pope) and Ghibellines (Ghibellini, in support of the emperor).

For Medieval Mystique

Gubbio, Umbria

Bologna, Emilia-Romagna

Perugia, Umbria

Assisi, Umbria

Scanno, Abruzzo

The Wonder of the World

The Holy Roman Empire had barely touched southern Italy until Henry, son of the Holy Roman Emperor Frederick I (Barbarossa), married Constance de Hauteville, heir to the Norman throne in Sicily. The Normans had arrived in southern Italy in the 10th century, initially as pilgrims en route from Jerusalem, later as mercenaries attracted by the money to be made fighting for rival principalities and against the Arab Muslims in Sicily. Of Henry and Constance's match was born one of the most colourful figures of medieval Europe, Frederick II (1194–1250).

Crowned Holy Roman Emperor in 1220, Frederick was a German with a difference. Having grown up in southern Italy, he considered Sicily his natural base and left the German states largely to their own devices. A warrior and scholar, Frederick was an enlightened ruler with an absolutist vocation. A man who allowed freedom of worship to Muslims and Jews, he was not to everyone's liking, as his ambition was to finally bring all of Italy under the imperial yoke.

A poet, linguist, mathematician, and philosopher, Frederick founded a university in Naples and encouraged the spread of learning and the translation of Arab treatises. Having reluctantly carried out a crusade (marked more by negotiation than the clash of arms) in the Holy Land in 1228 and 1229 on pain of excommunication, Frederick returned to Italy to find Papal troops invading Neapolitan territory. Frederick soon had them on the run and turned his attention to gaining control of the complex web of city-states in central and northern Italy, where he found allies and many enemies, in particular the Lombard League. Years of inconclusive battles ensued, which even Frederick's death in 1250 did

Giuliano Procacci's *History of the Italian People* is one of the best general histories of the country in any language. It covers the period from the early Middle Ages until 1948.

HISTORY THE WONDER OF THE WORLD

1600	1714	1805	1814–15
Dominican monk and proud philosopher Giordano Bruno is burned alive at the stake in Rome for heresy after eight years of trial and torture at the hands of the Inquisition.	The end of the War of the Spanish Succession forces the withdrawal of Spanish forces from Lombardy. The Spanish Bourbon family establishes an independent Kingdom of the Two Sicilies.	Napoleon is proclaimed king of the newly constituted Kingdom of Italy, comprising most of the northern half of the country. A year later he takes the Kingdom of Naples.	After Napoleon's fall, the Congress of Vienna is held to re-establish the balance of power in Europe. The result for Italy is largely a return of the old occupying powers.

not end. Campaigning continued until 1268 under Frederick's successors, Manfredi (who fell in the bloody Battle of Benevento in 1266) and Corradino (captured and executed two years later by French noble Charles of Anjou, who had by then taken over Sicily and southern Italy).

Rise of the City-States

While the south of Italy tended to centralised rule, the north was heading the opposite way. Port cities such as Genoa, Pisa and especially Venice, along with internal centres such as Florence, Milan, Parma, Bologna, Padua, Verona and Modena, became increasingly hostile towards attempts by the Holy Roman Emperors to meddle in their affairs.

The cities' growing prosperity and independence also brought them into conflict with Rome. Indeed, at times Rome's control over some of its own Papal States was challenged. Caught between the papacy and the emperors, it was not surprising that these city-states were forever switching allegiances in an attempt to best serve their own interests.

Between the 12th and 14th centuries, they developed new forms of government. Venice adopted an oligarchic, 'parliamentary' system in an attempt at limited democracy. More commonly, the city-state created a *comune* (town council), a form of republican government dominated at first by aristocrats but then increasingly by the wealthy middle classes. The well-heeled families soon turned their attentions from business rivalry to political struggles, in which each aimed to gain control of the *signoria* (government).

In some cities, great dynasties, such as the Medici in Florence and the Visconti and Sforza in Milan, came to dominate their respective stages.

War between the city-states was constant and eventually a few – notably Florence, Milan and Venice – emerged as regional powers and absorbed their neighbours. Their power was based on a mix of trade, industry and conquest. Constellations of power and alliances were in constant flux, making changes in the city-states' fortunes the rule rather than the exception. Easily the most stable, and long the most successful of them, was Venice.

In Florence, prosperity was based on the wool trade, finance and general commerce. Abroad, its coinage, the *firenze* (florin), was king.

In Milan, the noble Visconti family destroyed its rivals and extended Milanese control over Pavia and Cremona, and later Genoa. Giangaleazzo Visconti (1351–1402) turned Milan from a city-state into a strong European power. The policies of the Visconti (up to 1450), followed by those of the Sforza family, allowed Milan to spread its power to the Ticino area of Switzerland and east to the Lago di Garda.

The Milanese sphere of influence butted up against that of Venice. By 1450 the lagoon city had reached the height of its territorial greatness. In

BANKING

Europe's first modern banks appeared in Genoa in the 12th century. The city claims the first recorded public bond (1150) and the earliest known exchange contract (1156). Italy's Banca Monte dei Paschi di Siena is the world's oldest surviving bank, counting coins since 1472.

1848	1860	1861	1889
European revolts spark rebellion in Italy, especially in Austrian-occupied Milan and Venice. Piedmont's King Carlo Alberto joins the fray against Austria, but within a year Austria recovers Lombardy and Veneto.	In the name of Italian unity, Giuseppe Garibaldi lands with 1000 men, the Red Shirts, in Sicily. He takes the island and lands in southern Italy.	By the end of the Franco-Austrian War (1859–61), Vittorio Emanuele II controls Lombardy, Sardinia, Sicily, southern and parts of central Italy and is proclaimed king of a newly united Italy.	Raffaele Esposito invents *pizza margherita* in honour of Queen Margherita, who takes her first bite of the Neapolitan staple on a royal visit to the city.

Politics in Italy's mercurial city-states could take a radical turn. When Florence's Medici clan rulers fell into disgrace (not for the last time) in 1494, the city's fathers decided to restore an earlier republican model of government.

Since 1481, the Dominican friar Girolamo Savonarola had been in Florence preaching repentance. His blood-curdling warnings of horrors to come if Florentines did not renounce their evil ways somehow captured everyone's imagination and the city submitted to a fiery theocracy. He called on the government to act on the basis of his divine inspiration. Drinking, whoring, partying, gambling, flashy fashion and other signs of wrongdoing were pushed well underground. Books, clothes, jewellery, fancy furnishings and art were burned on 'Bonfires of the Vanities'.

Pleasure-loving Florentines soon began to tire of this fundamentalism, as did Pope Alexander VI (possibly the least religious pope of all time) and the rival Franciscan religious order. The local economy was stagnant and Savonarola seemed increasingly out to lunch. The city government, or *signoria,* finally had the fiery friar arrested. After weeks at the hands of the city rack-master, he was hanged and burned at the stake as a heretic, along with two supporters, on 22 May 1498.

addition to its possessions in Greece, Dalmatia and beyond, Venice had expanded inland. The banner of the Lion of St Mark flew across northeast Italy, from Gorizia to Bergamo.

These dynamic, independent-minded cities proved fertile ground for the intellectual and artistic explosion that would take place across northern Italy in the 14th and 15th centuries – an explosion that would come to be known as the Renaissance and the birth of the modern world. Of them all, Florence was the cradle and launch pad for this fevered activity, in no small measure due to the generous patronage of the long-ruling Medici family.

A Nation is Born

The French Revolution at the end of the 18th century and the rise of Napoleon awakened hopes in Italy of independent nationhood. Since the glory days of the Renaissance, Italy's divided mini-states had gradually lost power and status on the European stage. By the late 18th century, the peninsula was little more than a tired, backward playground for the big powers and a Grand Tour hot spot for the romantically inclined.

Napoleon marched into Italy on several occasions, finishing off the Venetian republic in 1797 (ending 1000 years of Venetian independence) and creating the so-called Kingdom of Italy in 1805. That kingdom was in no way independent but the Napoleonic earthquake spurred many

America was named after Amerigo Vespucci, a Florentine navigator who, from 1497 to 1504, made several voyages of discovery in what would one day be known as South America.

1908	1915	1919	1922
On the morning of 28 December, Messina and Reggio di Calabria are struck by a 7.5-magnitude earthquake and a 13-metre-high tsunami. More than 80,000 lives are lost.	Italy enters WWI on the side of the Allies to win Italian territories still in Austrian hands, after Austria's offer to cede some of the territories is deemed insufficient.	Former socialist journalist Benito Mussolini forms a right-wing militant group, the Fasci Italiani di Combattimento (Italian Combat Fasces), precursor to his Fascist Party.	Mussolini and his Fascists stage a march on Rome in October. Doubting the army's loyalty, a fearful King Vittorio Emanuele III entrusts Mussolini with the formation of a government.

Italians to believe that a single Italian state could be created after the emperor's demise. But it was not to be so easy. The reactionary Congress of Vienna restored all the foreign rulers to their places in Italy.

Count Camillo Benso di Cavour (1810–61) of Turin, the prime minister of the Savoy monarchy, became the diplomatic brains behind the Italian unity movement. Through the pro-unity newspaper, *Il Risorgimento* (founded in 1847) and the publication of a parliamentary *Statuto* (Statute), Cavour and his colleagues laid the groundwork for unity.

Cavour conspired with the French and won British support for the creation of an independent Italian state. His 1858 treaty with France's Napoleon III foresaw French aid in the event of a war with Austria and the creation of a northern Italian kingdom, in exchange for parts of Savoy and Nice.

The bloody Franco-Austrian War (also known as the Second Italian War of Independence; 1859–61), unleashed in northern Italy, led to the occupation of Lombardy and the retreat of the Austrians to their eastern possessions in the Veneto. In the meantime, a wild card in the form of professional revolutionary Giuseppe Garibaldi had created the real chance of full Italian unity. Garibaldi took Sicily and southern Italy in a military blitz in the name of Savoy king Vittorio Emanuele II in 1860. Southern Italy was thus conquered, rather than willingly forming a union with the north.

Spotting the chance, Cavour and the king moved to take parts of central Italy (including Umbria and Le Marche) and so were able to proclaim the creation of a single Italian state in 1861. In the following nine years, Tuscany, the Veneto and Rome were all incorporated into the fledgling kingdom. Unity was complete and parliament was established in Rome in 1871. However, Italy is a collection of discrete regions rather than a nation, and this is perhaps where many of its contemporary problems lie. As one of the architects of unification, Massimo d'Azeglio, said in his memoirs, 'we made a nation, now we have to make the Italians.'

The turbulent new state saw violent swings between socialists and the right. Giovanni Giolitti, one of Italy's longest-serving prime ministers (heading five governments between 1892 and 1921), managed to bridge the political extremes and institute male suffrage. Women, however, were denied the right to vote until after WWII.

John Julius Norwich's *A History of Venice* is one of the all-time great works on the lagoon city in English and is highly readable. He has also published *Venice: Paradise of Cities*.

From the Trenches to Fascism

When war broke out in Europe in July 1914, Italy chose to remain neutral despite being a member of the Triple Alliance with Austria and Germany. Italy had territorial claims on Austrian-controlled Trento (Trentino), southern Tyrol, Trieste and even in Dalmatia (some of which it had tried and failed to take during the Austro-Prussian War of 1866). Under the

1929	1935	1940	1943
Mussolini and Pope Pius XI sign the Lateran Pact, which declares Catholicism as Italy's sole religion and the Vatican an independent state. Satisfied, the papacy acknowledges the Kingdom of Italy.	Italy seeks a new colonial conquest through the invasion of Abyssinia (Ethiopia) from Eritrea. The League of Nations condemns the invasion and imposes limited sanctions on Italy.	Italy enters WWII on Nazi Germany's side and invades Greece, which quickly proves to be a mistake. Greek forces counter-attack and enter southern Albania. Germany saves Italy in 1941.	Allies land in Sicily. King Vittorio Emanuele III sacks Mussolini. He is replaced by Marshall Badoglio, who surrenders after Allied landings in southern Italy. German forces free Mussolini from royal arrest.

terms of the Triple Alliance, Austria was due to hand over much of this territory in the event of occupying other land in the Balkans, but Austria refused to contemplate fulfilling this part of the bargain.

The Italian government was divided between non-interventionists and a war party. The latter, in view of Austria's intransigence, decided to deal with the Allies. In the London pact of April 1915, Italy was promised the territories it sought after victory. In May, Italy declared war on Austria and thus plunged into a 3½-year nightmare.

Italy and Austria engaged in a weary war of attrition. The Austro-Hungarian forces collapsed in November 1918, after which the Austrian Empire ceded the South Tyrol, Trieste, Trentino, and Istria to Italy in the postwar Paris Peace Conference. However, Italy failed to obtain additional territorial claims upon Dalmatia and Albania in Versailles, which left many Italians bitterly disappointed.

These were slim pickings after such a bloody and exhausting conflict. Italy lost 600,000 men and the war economy had produced a small concentration of powerful industrial barons while leaving the bulk of the civilian populace in penury. This cocktail was made all the more explosive as hundreds of thousands of demobbed servicemen returned home or shifted around the country in search of work. The atmosphere was perfect for a demagogue, who was not long in coming forth.

Benito Mussolini (1883–1945) was a young war enthusiast who had once been a socialist newspaper editor and one-time draft dodger. This time he volunteered for the front and only returned, wounded, in 1917. The experience of war and the frustration shared with many at the disappointing outcome in Versailles led him to form a right-wing militant political group that by 1921 had become the Fascist Party, with its black-shirted street brawlers and Roman salute. These were to become symbols of violent oppression and aggressive nationalism for the next 23 years. After his march on Rome in 1922 and victory in the 1924 elections, Mussolini, who called himself Il Duce (the Leader), took full control of the country by 1926, banning other political parties, trade unions not affiliated to the party and the free press.

By the 1930s, all aspects of Italian society were regulated by the party. The economy, banking, a massive public works program, the conversion of coastal malarial swamps into arable land and an ambitious modernisation of the armed forces were all part of Mussolini's grand plan.

On the international front, Mussolini at first showed a cautious hand, signing international cooperation pacts (including the 1928 Kellogg Pact solemnly renouncing war) and until 1935 moving close to France and the UK to contain the growing menace of Adolf Hitler's rapidly re-arming Germany.

Roberto Rossellini's *Roma città aperta* (Rome: Open City), starring Anna Magnani, is a classic of Italian neorealist cinema and a masterful look at wartime Rome. The film is the first in his Trilogy of War, followed by *Paisà* and *Germania anno zero* (Germany: Year Zero).

1944	1946	1957	1966
Mount Vesuvius explodes back into action on 18 March. The eruption is captured on film by USAAF (United States Army Air Forces) personnel stationed nearby.	Italians vote in a national referendum to abolish the monarchy and create a republic. King Umberto II leaves Italy and refuses to recognise the result.	Italy joins France, West Germany and the Benelux countries to sign the Treaty of Rome, which creates the European Economic Community (EEC). The treaty takes effect on 1 January 1958.	A devastating flood inundates Florence in early November, leaving around 100 people dead, 5000 families homeless and 14,000 movable artworks damaged. The flood is the city's worst since 1557.

HISTORY FROM THE TRENCHES TO FASCISM

That all changed when Mussolini decided to invade Abyssinia (Ethiopia) as the first big step to creating a 'new Roman empire'. This aggressive side of Mussolini's policy had already led to skirmishes with Greece over the island of Corfu and to military expeditions against nationalist forces in the Italian colony of Libya.

The League of Nations condemned the Abyssinian adventure (King Vittorio Emanuele III was declared Emperor of Abyssinia in 1936) and from then on Mussolini changed course, drawing closer to Nazi Germany. They backed the rebel General Franco in the three-year Spanish Civil War and in 1939 signed an alliance pact.

WWII broke out in September 1939 with Hitler's invasion of Poland. Italy remained aloof until June 1940, by which time Germany had overrun Norway, Denmark, the Low Countries and much of France. It seemed too easy and so Mussolini entered on Germany's side in 1940, a move Hitler must have regretted later. Germany found itself pulling Italy's chestnuts out of the fire in campaigns in the Balkans and North Africa and could not prevent Allied landings in Sicily in 1943.

By then, the Italians had had enough of Mussolini and his war, so the king had the dictator arrested. In September, Italy surrendered and the Germans, who had rescued Mussolini, occupied the northern two-thirds of the country and reinstalled the dictator.

The painfully slow Allied campaign up the peninsula and German repression led to the formation of the Resistance, which played a growing role in harassing German forces. Northern Italy was finally liberated in April 1945. Resistance fighters caught Mussolini as he fled north in the hope of reaching Switzerland. They shot him and his lover, Clara Petacci, before stringing up their corpses (along with others) in Milan's Piazzale

Tobias Jones' *The Dark Heart of Italy* is an engaging, personal look at contemporary Italy, plagued by (real or imagined) conspiracies, corruption and terrorism.

GOING THE DISTANCE FOR THE RESISTANCE

In 1943 and 1944, the Assisi Underground hid hundreds of Jewish Italians in Umbrian convents and monasteries, while the Tuscan Resistance forged travel documents for them – but the refugees needed those documents fast, before they were deported to concentration camps by Fascist officials. Enter the fastest man in Italy: Gino Bartali, world-famous Tuscan cyclist, Tour de France winner and three-time champion of the Giro d'Italia. After his death in 2003, documents revealed that during his 'training rides' throughout the war years, Bartali had carried Resistance intelligence and falsified documents to transport Jewish refugees to safe locations. Bartali was interrogated at the dreaded Villa Triste in Florence, where suspected anti-Fascists were routinely tortured – but he revealed nothing. Until his death, the long-distance hero downplayed, even to his children, his efforts to rescue Jewish refugees, saying, 'One does these things, and then that's that.'

1970	1980	1980	1999
Parliament approves the country's first-ever divorce legislation. Unwilling to accept this 'defeat', the Christian Democrats call a referendum to annul the law in 1974. Italians vote against the referendum.	A bomb in Bologna kills 85 and injures hundreds more. The Red Brigades and a Fascist cell both claim responsibility. Analysis later points to possible para-state terrorism in Operation Gladio.	At 7.34pm on 25 November, a 6.8–Richter scale earthquake strikes Campania. The quake kills almost 3000 people and causes widespread damage, including in the city of Naples.	Italy becomes a primary base in NATO's air war on Yugoslavia. Air strikes are carried out from the Aviano airbase from 24 May until 8 June.

Lotto. This was a far cry from Il Duce's hopes for a glorious burial alongside his ancient imperial idol, Augustus, in Rome.

The Grey and Red Years

In the aftermath of war, the left-wing Resistance was disarmed and Italy's political forces scrambled to regroup. The USA, through the economic largesse of the Marshall Plan, wielded considerable political influence and used this to keep the left in check.

Immediately after the war, three coalition governments succeeded one another. The third, which came to power in December 1945, was dominated by the newly formed right-wing Democrazia Cristiana (DC; Christian Democrats), led by Alcide De Gasperi. Italy became a republic in 1946 and De Gasperi's DC won the first elections under the new constitution in 1948, and remained prime minister until 1953.

Until the 1980s, the Partito Comunista Italiano (PCI; Communist Party), at first under Palmiro Togliatti and later the charismatic Enrico Berlinguer, played a crucial role in Italy's social and political development, in spite of being systematically kept out of government.

The popularity of the party led to a grey period in the country's history, the *anni di piombo* (years of lead) in the 1970s. Just as the Italian economy was booming, Europe-wide paranoia about the power of the communists in Italy fuelled a secretive reaction, that, it is said, was largely directed by the CIA and NATO. Even today, little is known about Operation Gladio, an underground paramilitary organisation supposedly behind various unexplained terror attacks in the country, apparently designed to create an atmosphere of fear in which, should the communists come close to power, a right-wing coup could be quickly carried out.

The 1970s were thus dominated by the spectre of terrorism and considerable social unrest, especially in the universities. Neo-fascist terrorists struck with a bomb blast in Milan in 1969. In 1978, the Brigate Rosse (Red Brigades, a group of young left-wing militants responsible for several bomb blasts and assassinations), claimed their most important victim – former DC prime minister Aldo Moro. His kidnap and murder some 54 days later (the subject of the 2003 film *Buongiorno, notte*) shook the country.

Despite the disquiet, the 1970s was also a time of positive change. In 1970, regional governments with limited powers were formed in 15 of the country's 20 regions (the other five, Sicily, Sardinia, Valle d'Aosta, Trentino-Alto Adige and Friuli Venezia Giulia, already had strong autonomy statutes). In the same year, divorce became legal and eight years later abortion was also legalised.

Despite Italians' lack of faith in politicians, come election time turnout is usually around 75%.

Paul Ginsborg's *A History of Contemporary Italy: Society and Politics, 1943–1988* remains one of the most readable and insightful books on postwar Italy.

2001	2004–05	2005	2006
Silvio Berlusconi's right-wing Casa delle Libertà (Liberties House) coalition wins an absolute majority in national polls. The following five years are marked by economic stagnation.	Tension between rival Camorra clans explodes on the streets of suburban Naples. In only four months, almost 50 people are gunned down in retribution attacks.	Pope John Paul II dies at age 84, prompting a wave of sorrow and chants of *santo subito* (sainthood now). He is succeeded by Benedict XVI, the German Cardinal Ratzinger.	Juventus, AC Milan and three other top Serie A football teams receive hefty fines in a match-rigging scandal that also sees Juventus stripped of its 2005 and 2006 championship titles.

Clean Hands, Berlusconi & Renzi

A growth spurt in the aftermath of WWII saw Italy become one of the world's leading economies, but by the 1970s the economy had begun to falter, and by the mid-1990s a new and prolonged period of crisis had set in. High unemployment and inflation, combined with a huge national debt and mercurial currency (the lira), led the government to introduce Draconian measures to cut public spending, allowing Italy to join the single currency (euro) in 2001.

The 1990s saw the Italian political scene rocked by the Tangentopoli ('kickback city') scandal. Led by a pool of Milanese magistrates, including the tough Antonio di Pietro, investigations known as Mani Pulite (Clean Hands) implicated thousands of politicians, public officials and businesspeople in scandals ranging from bribery and receiving kickbacks to blatant theft.

The old centre-right political parties collapsed in the wake of these trials and from the ashes rose what many Italians hoped might be a breath of fresh political air. Media magnate Silvio Berlusconi's Forza Italia (Go Italy) party swept to power in 2001 and again in April 2008 (after an inconclusive two-year interlude of centre-left government under former European Commission head Romano Prodi from 2006). Berlusconi's carefully choreographed blend of charisma, confidence, irreverence and promises of tax cuts appealed to many Italian voters, and he enjoyed political success and longevity that was incomprehensible to many outsiders.

However, Berlusconi's tenure saw the economic situation go from bad to worse, while a series of laws were passed that protected his extensive business interests, for example, granting the prime minister immunity from prosecution while in office. In 2011 Berlusconi was finally forced to resign due to the deepening debt crisis. A government of technocrats, headed by economist Mario Monti, took over until the inconclusive elections of February 2013. After lengthy post-electoral negotiations, Enrico Letta, a member of the Partito Democratico (PD), was named prime minister, steering a precarious right-left coalition. In 2014, he was toppled by the former mayor of Florence, Matteo Renzi, from the same party. Italy's youngest-ever leader, Renzi became the third unelected PM since Berlusconi's fall.

Despite the change of leadership and Renzi's dynamic style, whoever steers this hard-to-govern country has a tough job on their hands. Italy's problems remain the same, including the Mafia, corruption, nepotism, the brain drain, lack of growth, unemployment (particularly among the young) and the low birth rate, coupled with an ageing population.

The 2009 fillm *Videocracy* is a disturbing take on the nature of celebrity and Silvio Berlusconi's TV empire.

Silvio Berlusconi: Television, Power and Patrimony by Paul Ginsberg supplies an understanding of Berlusconi's power and influence.

2007	2011	2011	2014
Former heir to the Italian throne, Vittorio Emanuele di Savoia, is cleared of corruption and fraud charges in connection with alleged illicit dealings involving, among others, a casino.	Berlusconi stands trial in Milan in April on charges of abuse of power and paying for sex with under-aged Moroccan prostitute Karima El Mahroug (aka Ruby Heartstealer).	Berlusconi is forced to quit, and economist Mario Monti is put in charge, heading a government of technocrats.	Matteo Renzi becomes the youngest prime minister in the history of the republic, the third PM in succession to take control without an election.

Italian Art & Architecture

The history of Italian art and architecture underpins the history of Western art and architecture, from the classical, Renaissance and baroque to the explosive doctrine of the futurists and the conceptual play of Arte Povera in the 20th century. A roll call of Italian artists – Giotto, Botticelli, da Vinci, Michelangelo, Raphael, Caravaggio and Bernini – forged their vision into some of the greatest bodies of work of the millennia and are, centuries after their deaths, still household names the world over.

Art

The Ancient & the Classical

Greek colonists settled many parts of Sicily and southern Italy as early as the 8th century BC, naming it Magna Graecia and building great cities such as Syracuse and Taranto. These cities were famous for their magnificent temples, many of which were decorated with sculptures modeled on, or inspired by, masterpieces by Praxiteles, Lysippus and Phidias. In art, as in so many other realms, the ancient Romans looked to the Greeks for inspiration.

Sculpture flourished in southern Italy into the Hellenistic period. It also gained popularity in central Italy, where the art of the Etruscans was greatly refined by the contribution of Greek artisans, who arrived to trade.

In Rome, sculpture, architecture and painting flourished first under the republic and then the empire. But the art that was produced here during this period differed in keys ways from the Greek art that influenced it. Essentially secular, it focused less on ideals of aesthetic harmony and more on accurate representation, taking sculptural portraiture to new heights of verisimilitude, as innumerable versions of Pompey, Titus and Augustus showing a similar visage attest.

The Roman ruling class understood art could be used as a political tool, one that could construct a unified identity and cement status and power. As well as portraiture, Roman narrative art often took the form of relief decoration recounting the story of great military victories – the Colonna di Traiano (Trajan's Column) and the Ara Pacis Augustae (Altar of Peace) in Rome exemplify this tradition. Both are magnificent, monumental examples of art as propaganda, exalting the emperor and Rome in a form that no Roman citizen could possibly ignore.

Wealthy Roman citizens also dabbled in the arts, building palatial villas and adorning them with statues looted from the Greek world or copied from Hellenic originals. Today, museums in Rome burst at the seams with such trophies, from the Capitoline Museums' 'Made in Italy' *Galata morente* (Dying Gaul, c 240–200 BC) to the Vatican Museums' original Greek *Laocoön and His Sons* (c 160–140 BC).

And while the Etruscans had used wall painting – most notably in their tombs at centres like Tarquinia and Cerveteri in modern-day Lazio, it was the Romans who refined the form, refocusing on landscape scenes

Italy's dedicated art police, the Comando Carabinieri Tutela Patrimonio Culturale, tackle the looting of priceless heritage. It's estimated that over 100,000 ancient tombs have been ransacked by *tombaroli* (tomb raiders) alone; contents are sold to private and public collectors around the world.

to adorn the walls of the living. A visit to Rome's Museo Nazionale Romano: Palazzo Massimo alle Terme or to Naples' Museo Archeologico Nazionale offers sublime examples of the form.

The Glitter of Byzantine

Emperor Constantine, a convert to Christianity, made the ancient city of Byzantium his capital in 330 and renamed it Constantinople. The city became the great cultural and artistic centre of early Christianity and it remained so up to the time of the Renaissance, though its influence was not as fundamental as the art of ancient Rome.

Masterful Mosaics

....

Basilica di Sant'Apollinare in Classe, Ravenna

....

Basilica di San Vitale, Ravenna

....

Basilica di San Marco, Venice

....

Cattedrale di Monreale, Monreale

The Byzantine period was notable for its sublime ecclesiastical architecture, its extraordinary mosaic work and – to a lesser extent – its ethereal painting. Drawing inspiration from the symbol-drenched decoration of the Roman catacombs and the early Christian churches, the Byzantine de-emphasised the naturalistic aspects of the classical tradition and exalted the spirit over the body, glorifying God rather than humanity or the state. This was infused with the Near East's decorative traditions and love of luminous colour.

In Italy, the Byzantine virtuosity with mosaics was showcased in Ravenna, the capital of the Byzantine Empire's western regions in the 6th century. The city's Basilica di Sant'Apollinare in Classe, Basilica di San Vitale and Basilica di Sant'Apollinare Nuovo house some of the world's finest Byzantine art, their hand-cut glazed tiles *(tesserae)* balancing extraordinary naturalness with an epic sense of grandeur and mystery.

The Byzantine aesthetic is also evident in Venice, in the exoticism of the Basilica di San Marco, and in the technicoloured interior of Rome's Chiesa di San Prassede. Byzantine, Norman and Arab influences in Sicily fused to create a distinct regional style showcased in the mosaic-encrusted splendour of Palermo's Cappella Palatina, as well as the cathedrals of Monreale and Cefalù.

The Not-so-Dark Ages

Italy, and Italian art, was born out of the so-called dark ages. The barbarian invasions of the 5th and 6th centuries began a process that turned a unified empire into a land of small independent city-states, and it was these states – or rather the merchants, princes, clergy, corporations and guilds who lived within them – that created a culture of artistic patronage that engendered the great innovations in art and architecture that would define the Renaissance.

Italy has more World Heritage–Listed Sites than any other country in the world; many of its 51 listings are repositories of great art.

Clarity of religious message continued to outweigh the notion of faithful representation and be the driving force of artistic life during the medieval period. To the modern eye, the simplicity and coded allegorical narrative of both the painting and sculpture of this period can look stiff, though a closer look usually reveals a sublimity and grace, as well as a shared human experience, that speaks across the centuries.

Gothic Refinement

The Gothic style was much slower to take off in Italy than in the rest of Europe. But it did, marking the transition from medieval restraint to the Renaissance, and seeing artists once again drawing inspiration from life itself rather than concentrating solely on religious themes. Occurring at the same time as the development of court society and the rise of civic culture in the city-states, Gothic art was both sophisticated and elegant, highlighting attention to detail, a luminous palette and an increasingly refined technique. The first innovations were made in Pisa by sculptor Nicola Pisano (c 1220–84), who emulated the example of the French Gothic masters and studied classical sculpture in order to repre-

CAPITAL SCANDALS: CONTROVERSIAL ART IN ROME

➡ **The Last Judgment (1537–41), Michelangelo** There were more than just arms and legs dangling from Michelangelo's Sistine Chapel fresco in Rome's Vatican Museums. The depiction of full-frontal nudity on the chapel's altar horrified Catholic Counter-Reformation critics. No doubt Michelangelo turned in his grave when the offending bits were covered up.

➡ **Madonna and Child with St Anne (1605–06), Caravaggio** St Anne looks more 'beggar-woman' than 'beatified grandmother', but it's Mary who made the faithful blush on Caravaggio's canvas, her propped-up cleavage a little too 'flesh-and-bone' for the mother of God. The sexed-up scene was too much for the artist's client, who offered a '*Grazie*, but no *grazie*'. The painting now hangs in Rome's Museo e Galleria Borghese.

➡ **St Matthew and the Angel (1602), Caravaggio** In the original version, personal space (or the sheer lack of it) was the main problem for Caravaggio's client Cardinal del Monte. Featuring a sensual, handsome angel snuggling up to St Matthew, exactly what kind of inspiration the winged visitor was offering the saint was anybody's guess. And so Caravaggio went back to his easel, producing the prime-time version now gracing the Chiesa di San Luigi dei Francesi in Rome.

➡ **Conquering Venus (1805–08), Antonio Canova** When asked whether she minded posing nude, Paolina Bonaparte Borghese provocatively replied 'Why should I?' Given her well-known infidelities, this marble depiction of Napoleon's wayward sister as the Roman goddess of love merely confirmed her salacious reputation. This fact was not lost on her husband, Italian prince Camillo Borghese, who forbade the sculpture from leaving their home. You'll find it at the Museo e Galleria Borghese.

sent nature more convincingly, but the major strides forward occurred in Florence and Siena.

Giotto & the 'Rebirth' of Italian Art

The Byzantine painters in Italy knew how to make use of light and shade and had an understanding of the principles of foreshortening (how to convey an effect of perspective). It only required a genius to break the spell of their conservatism and to venture into a new world of naturalism. Enter Florentine painter Giotto di Bondone (c 1266–1337), whose brushstrokes focused on dramatic narrative and the accurate representation of figures and landscape. The Italian poet Giovanni Boccaccio wrote in his *Decameron* (1350–53) that Giotto was 'a genius so sublime that there was nothing produced by nature...that he could not depict to the life; his depiction looked not like a copy, but the real thing.'

Boccaccio wasn't the only prominent critic of the time to consider Giotto revolutionary – the first historian of Italian art, Giorgio Vasari, said in his *Lives of the Artists* (1550) that Giotto initiated the 'rebirth' (*rinascità* or *renaissance)* in art. Giotto's most famous works are all in the medium of the fresco (where paint is applied on a wall while the plaster is still damp), and his supreme achievement is the cycle gracing the walls of Padua's Cappella degli Scrovegni. It's impossible to overestimate Giotto's achievement with these frescoes, which illustrate the stories of the lives of the Virgin and Christ. Abandoning popular conventions such as the three-quarter view of head and body, he presented his figures from behind, from the side or turning around, just as the story demanded. Giotto had no need for lashings of gold paint and elaborate ornamentation either, opting to convey the scene's dramatic tension through a naturalistic rendition of figures and a radical composition that created the illusion of depth.

GIOTTO

Many Renaissance painters included self-portraits in their major works. Giotto didn't, possibly due to the fact that friends such as Giovanni Boccaccio described him as the ugliest man in Florence. With friends like those...

CARAVAGGIO

Giotto's oeuvre isn't limited to the frescoes in the Cappella degli Scrovegni. His Life of St Francis cycle in the Upper Church of the Basilica di San Francesco in Assisi is almost as extraordinary and was to greatly influence his peers, many of whom worked in Assisi during the decoration of the church. One of the most prominent of these was the Dominican friar Fra' Angelico (c 1395–1455), a Florentine painter who was famed for his mastery of colour and light. The *Annunciation* (c 1450) in the convent of the Museo di San Marco in Florence is arguably Fra' Angelico's most accomplished work.

The Sienese School

Giotto wasn't the only painter of his time to experiment with form, colour and composition and create a radical new style. The great Sienese master Duccio di Buoninsegna (c 1255–1319) successfully breathed new life into the old Byzantine forms using light and shade. His preferred medium was panel painting and his major work is probably his *Maestà* (Virgin Mary in Majesty; 1311) in Siena's Museo dell'Opera Metropolitana.

It was in Siena, too, that two new trends took off: the introduction of court painters and the advent of purely secular art.

The first of many painters to be given ongoing commissions by one major patron or court, Simone Martini (c 1284–1344) was almost as famous as Giotto in his day. His best-known painting is the stylised *Maestà* (1315–16) in Siena's Museo Civico, in which he pioneered his famous iridescent palette (one colour transformed into another within the same plane).

Also working in Siena at this time were the Lorenzetti brothers, Pietro (c 1280–1348) and Ambrogio (c 1290–1348), who are considered the greatest exponents of what, for a better term, can be referred to as secular painting. Ambrogio's magnificent *Allegories of Good and Bad Government* (1337–40) in the Museo Civico lauds the fruits of good government and the gruesome results of bad. In the frescoes, he applies the rules of perspective with an accuracy previously unseen, as well as significantly developing the Italian landscape tradition. In *Life in the Country,* one of the allegories, Ambrogio successfully depicts the time of day, the season, colour reflections and shadows – a naturalistic depiction of landscape that was quite unique at this time.

The Venetians

While Byzantine influence lingered longer in Venice than in many other parts of Italy, its grip on the city loosened by the early to mid-15th century. In *Polyptych of St James* (c 1450) by Michele Giambono (c 1400–62) in Venice's Gallerie dell'Accademia, the luscious locks and fair complexion of the archangel Michael channel the style of early Renaissance master Pisanello (c 1395–1455). The winds of change blow even stronger in fellow Accademia resident *Madonna with Child* (c 1455) by Jacopo Bellini (c 1396–1470). Featuring a bright-eyed baby Jesus and a patient, seemingly sleep-deprived Mary, it's an image any parent might relate to. Relatable emotions are equally strong in the biblical scenes of Andrea Mantegna (1431–1506); one can almost hear the sobbing in his *Lamentation over the Dead Christ* (c 1480) in Milan's Pinacoteca di Brera.

Tuscan painter Gentile da Fabriano (c 1370–1427) worked in Venice during the early stages of his transition to Renaissance realism, and his evolving style reputedly influenced Venetian Antonio Vivarini (c 1415–80), the latter's *Passion* polyptych in Venice's Ca' d'Oro radiating tremendous pathos. Antonio's brother, Bartolomeo Vivarini (c 1432–99) created a delightful altarpiece in Venice's I Frari, in which a baby Jesus wriggles out of the arms of his mother, squarely seated on her marble Renaissance throne.

In *M: The Man Who Became Caravaggio,* Peter Robb gives a passionate personal assessment of the artist's paintings and a colourful account of Caravaggio's life, arguing he was murdered for having sex with the pageboy of a high-ranking Maltese aristocrat.

ART, ANGER & ARTEMESIA

Sex, fame and notoriety: the life of Artemesia Gentileschi (1593–1652) could spawn a top-rating soap opera. One of the early baroque's greatest artists, and one of the few females, Gentileschi was born in Rome to Tuscan painter Orazio Gentileschi. Orazio wasted little time introducing his young daughter to the city's working artists. Among her mentors was Michelangelo Merisi da Caravaggio, whose chiaroscuro technique would deeply influence her own style.

At the tender age of 17, Gentileschi produced her first masterpiece, *Susanna and the Elders* (1610), now in the Schönborn Collection in Pommersfelden, Germany. Her depiction of the sexually harassed Susanna proved eerily foreboding: two years later Artemesia would find herself at the centre of a seven-month trial, in which Florentine artist Agostino Tassi was charged with her rape.

Out of Gentileschi's fury came the gripping, technically brilliant *Judith Slaying Holofernes* (1612–13). While the original hangs in Naples' Museo di Capodimonte, you'll find a larger, later version in Florence's Uffizi. Vengeful Judith would make a further appearance in *Judith and her Maidservant* (c 1613–14), now in Florence's Palazzo Pitti. While living in Florence, Gentileschi completed a string of commissions for Cosimo II of the Medici dynasty, as well as becoming the first female member of the prestigious Accademia delle Arti del Disegno (Academy of the Arts of Drawing).

After separating from her husband, Tuscan painter Pietro Antonio di Vincenzo Stiattesi, Gentileschi headed south to Naples sometime between 1626 and 1630. Here her creations would include *The Annunciation* (1630), also in Naples' Museo di Capodimonte, and her *Self-Portrait as the Allegory of Painting* (1630), housed in London's Kensington Palace. The latter work received praise for its simultaneous depiction of art, artist and muse; an innovation at the time. Gentileschi's way with the brush was not lost on King Charles I of England, who honoured the Italian talent with a court residency from 1638 to 1641.

Despite her illustrious career, Gentileschi inhabited a man's world. Nothing would prove this more than the surviving epitaphs commemorating her death, focused not on her creative brilliance, but on the gossip depicting her as a cheating nymphomaniac.

In 1475, visiting Sicilian painter Antonello da Messina (c 1430–79) introduced the Venetians to oil paints, and their knack for layering and blending colours made for a luminosity that would ultimately define the city's art. Among early ground-breakers was Giovanni Bellini (c 1430–1516). The son of Jacopo Bellini, his Accademia *Annunciation* (1500) deployed glowing reds and ambers to focus attention on the solitary figure of the kneeling Madonna, the angel Gabriel arriving in a rush of geometrically rumpled drapery.

Bellini's prowess with the palette was not lost on his students, among them Giorgione (1477–1510) and Titian (c 1488–1576). Giorgione preferred to paint from inspiration without sketching out his subject first, as in his enigmatic *La Tempesta* (The Storm; 1500), also in the Accademia. The younger Titian set himself apart with brushstrokes that brought his subjects to life, from his early and measured *St Mark Enthroned* (1510) in Venice's Chiesa di Santa Maria della Salute to his thick, textured swansong *Pietà* (1576) in the Accademia.

Titian raised the bar for a new generation of northern Italian masters, including Jacopo Robusti, aka Tintoretto (1518–94). Occasionally enhancing his palette with finely crushed glass, Tintoretto's action-packed biblical scenes read like a modern graphic novel. His wall and ceiling paintings in Venice's Scuola Grande di San Rocco are nail-bitingly spectacular, laced with holy superheroes, swooping angels, and deep, ominous shadows. Paolo Caliari, aka Veronese (1528–88) was another 16th-century artstar, the remarkable radiance of his hues captured in the *Feast in the House of Levi* (1573), another Accademia must-see.

British art critic Andrew Graham-Dixon has written three authoritative books on Italian art: *Michelangelo and the Sistine Chapel*; *Caravaggio: A Life Sacred & Profane*; and *Renaissance*, the companion book to the BBC TV series.

The Renaissance

Of Italy's countless artistic highs, none surpass the Renaissance. The age of Botticelli, da Vinci and Michelangelo is defined by a rediscovery of classical learning and humanist philosophy, driven by the spirit of scientific investigation. It also marks a seismic shift of the artists' own role; once considered a mere craftsman, the Renaissance artist is reborn as intellectual and philosopher.

Florence, Classicism & the Quattrocento

Giotto and the painters of the Sienese school introduced many innovations in art: the exploration of proportion, a new interest in realistic portraiture and the beginnings of a new tradition of landscape painting. At the start of the 15th century (Quattrocento), most of these were explored and refined in one city – Florence.

Sculptors Lorenzo Ghiberti (1378–1455) and Donatello (c 1382–1466) replaced the demure robe-clad statues of the Middle Ages with anatomically accurate figures evoking ancient Greece and Rome. Donatello's bronze *David* (c 1440–50) and *St George* (c 1416–17), both in Florence's Museo del Bargello, capture this spirit of antiquity.

Ghiberti's greatest legacy would be his bronze east doors (1424–52) for the baptistry in Florence's Piazza del Duomo. The original 10 relief panels heralded a giant leap from the late-Gothic art of the time, not only in their use of perspective, but also in the individuality bestowed upon the figures portrayed.

When the neighbouring Duomo's dome was completed in 1436, author, architect and philosopher Leon Battista Alberti called it the first great achievement of the 'new' architecture, one that equalled or even surpassed the great buildings of antiquity. Designed by Filippo

Brunelleschi (1377–1446), the dome was as innovative in engineering terms as the Pantheon's dome had been 1300 years before.

A New Perspective

While Brunelleschi was heavily influenced by the classical masters, he was able to do something that they hadn't – discover the mathematical rules by which objects appear to diminish as they recede. In so doing, Brunelleschi gave artists a whole new visual perspective.

The result was a new style of masterpiece, including Masaccio's *Trinity* (c 1424–25) in Florence's Basilica di Santa Maria Novella and Leonardo da Vinci's fresco *The Last Supper* (1495–98) in the refectory of Milan's Chiesa di Santa Maria delle Grazie. Andrea Mantegna (1431–1506) was responsible for the painting that is the most virtuosic of all perspectival experiments that occurred during this period – his highly realistic *Dead Christ* (c 1480), now in Milan's Pinacoteca di Brera.

These innovations in perspective were not always slavishly followed, however. Sandro Botticelli (c 1444–1510) pursued a Neoplatonic concept of ideal beauty that, along with his penchant for luminous decoration, resulted in flat

....

1. La Rotonda (p391), Vicenza, designed by Andrea Palladio
2. Lorenzo Ghiberti's bronze panels, Battistero di San Giovanni (p488), Florence

linear compositions and often improbable poses. *The Birth of Venus* (c 1485), now in Florence's Uffizi, is a deft and daring synthesis of poetry and politics, eroticism and spirituality, contemporary Florentine fashion and classical mythology.

High Renaissance Masters

By the early 16th century (Cinquecento), the epicentre of artistic innovation shifted from Florence to Rome and Venice. This reflected the political and social realities of the period, namely the transfer of power in Florence from the Medicis to the moral-crusading, book-burning friar Girolamo Savonarola (1452–98), and the desire of the popes in Rome to counter the influence of Martin Luther's Reformation through turning the city into a humbling showpiece. While the age delivered a bounty of talent, some of its luminaries shone exceedingly bright.

Donato Bramante

Donato Bramante (1444–1514) knew the power of illusion. In Milan's Chiesa di Santa Maria presso San Satiro, he feigned a choir using the trompe l'œil technique. In Rome, his classical obsession would shine through in his perfectly proportioned Tempietto of the Chiesa di San Pietro in Montorio, arguably the pinnacle of High Renaissance architecture. The Urbino native would go on to design St Peter's Basilica, though his Greek-cross floor plan would never be realised.

Leonardo da Vinci

Leonardo da Vinci (1452–1519), the quintessential polymath Renaissance man, took what some critics have described as the decisive step in the history of Western art – abandoning the balance that had previously been maintained between colour and line in painting and choosing to modulate his contours using colour. This technique, called sfumato, is perfectly displayed

1. Botticelli's *Birth of Venus*, Galleria degli Uffizi (p492), Florence 2. Michelangelo's *David*, Galleria dell'Accademia (p497), Florence

in his *Mona Lisa* (now in the Louvre in Paris). In Milan's Chiesa di Santa Maria delle Grazie, his *The Last Supper* bestowed dramatic individuality to each depicted figure.

Raphael Santi

Raphael Santi (1483–1520) would rise to the aforementioned challenge faced by the Quattrocento painters – achieving harmonious and accurate (in terms of perspective) arrangement of figures – in works such as *Triumph of Galatea* (c 1514) in Rome's Villa Farnesina and *La Scuola d'Atene* (The School of Athens) in the Vatican Museums' Stanza della Segnatur. Other inspiring works include his enigmatic *La Fornarina* in Rome's Galleria Nazionale d'Arte Antica: Palazzo Barberini, and *Portrait of Alessandro Farnese* in Naples' Palazzo Reale di Capodimonte.

Michelangelo Buonarroti

Michelangelo Buonarroti (1475–1564) saw himself first and foremost as a sculptor, creating incomparable works like the *Pietà* in St Peter's Basilica and *David* (1504) in Florence's Galleria dell'Accademia. As a painter, he would adorn the ceiling of Rome's Sistine Chapel, creating figures that were not just realistic, but emotive visual representations of the human experience. A true Renaissance Man, Michelangelo's talents extended to architecture – the dome atop St Peter's Basilica is another Michelangelo creation.

Andrea Palladio

Bramante's Tempietto would influence Andrea Palladio (1508–80) when he was designing La Rotonda in Vicenza. Like Bramante, northern Italy's greatest Renaissance architect was enamoured of classicism. His Palladian villas, such as the Brenta Riviera's Villa Foscari, radiate an elegant mathematical logic, perfectly proportioned and effectively accentuated with pediments and loggias. Classical influences also inform his Chiesa di San Giorgio Maggiore in Venice.

ITALIAN ART & ARCHITECTURE ART

WHO'S WHO IN RENAISSANCE & BAROQUE ART

➡ **Giotto di Bondone (c 1266–1337)** Said to have ushered in the Renaissance; two masterworks: the Cappella degli Scrovegni (1304–06) in Padua and the upper church (1306–11) in Assisi.

➡ **Donatello (c 1382–1466)** Florentine born and bred; his *David* (c 1440–50) in the collection of the Museo del Bargello in Florence was the first free-standing nude sculpture produced since the classical era.

➡ **Fra' Angelico (1395–1455)** Made a saint in 1982; his best-loved work is the *Annunciation* (c 1450) in the convent of the Museo di San Marco in Florence.

➡ **Sandro Botticelli (c 1444–1510)** *Primavera* (c 1482) and *The Birth of Venus* (c 1485) are among the best-loved of all Italian paintings; both in the Uffizi in Florence.

➡ **Domenico Ghirlandaio (1449–94)** A top Tuscan master; his frescoes include those in the Tornabuoni Chapel in Florence's Basilica di Santa Maria Novella.

➡ **Michelangelo Buonarroti (1475–1564)** The big daddy of them all; everyone knows *David* (1504) in the Galleria dell'Accademia in Florence and the Sistine Chapel ceiling (1508–12) in Rome's Vatican Museums.

➡ **Raphael Santi (1483–1520)** Originally from Urbino; painted luminous Madonnas and fell in love with a baker's daughter, immortalised in his painting *La Fornarina,* in Rome's Galleria Nazionale d'Arte Antica: Palazzo Barberini.

➡ **Titian (c 1490–1576)** Real name Tiziano Vecelli; seek out his *Assumption* (1516–18) in the Chiesa di Santa Maria Gloriosa dei Frari (I Frari), Venice.

➡ **Tintoretto (1518–1594)** The last great painter of the Italian Renaissance, known as 'Il Furioso' for the energy he put into his work; look for his *Last Supper* in Venice's Chiesa di Santo Stefano.

➡ **Annibale Caracci (1560–1609)** Bologna-born and best known for his baroque frescoes in Rome's Palazzo Farnese.

➡ **Michelangelo Merisi da Caravaggio (1573–1610)** Baroque's bad boy; his most powerful work is the *St Matthew Cycle* in Rome's Chiesa di San Luigi dei Francesi.

➡ **Gian Lorenzo Bernini (1598–1680)** The sculptor protégé of Cardinal Scipione Borghese; best known for his *Rape of Persephone* (1621–22) and *Apollo and Daphne* (1622–25) in Rome's Museo e Galleria Borghese.

From Mannerism to Baroque

The Italian equivalent of French Impressionism was the Macchiaioli movement based in Florence. Its major artists were Telemaco Signorini (1835–1901) and Giovanni Fattori (1825–1908). See their socially engaged and light-infused work in the Palazzo Pitti's Galleria d'Arte Moderna in Florence.

By 1520, artists such as Michelangelo and Raphael had pretty well achieved everything that former generations had tried to do and, alongside other artists, began distorting natural images in favour of heightened expression. This movement, which reached its heights in Titian's luminous *Assunta* (Assumption, 1516–18), in Venice's I Frari, and in Raphael's *La trasfigurazione* (Transfiguration, 1517–20), in the Vatican Museums' Pinacoteca, was derided by later critics, who labelled it mannerism. Pejorative as the term once was, the stylish artificiality of Agnolo Bronzino's Florentine court portraits has an almost 21st-century seductiveness.

Milanese-born enfant terrible Michelangelo Merisi da Caravaggio (1573–1610) had no sentimental attachment to classical models and no respect for 'ideal beauty'. He shocked contemporaries in his relentless search for truth and his radical, often visceral, realism. But even his most ardent detractors could not fail to admire his skill with the technique of chiaroscuro (the bold contrast of light and dark) and his employment of tenebrism, where dramatic chiaroscuro becomes a dominant and highly effective stylistic device. One look at his *Conversion of St Paul* and the

Crucifixion of St Peter (1600–01), both in Rome's Chiesa di Santa Maria del Popolo, or his *Le sette opere di Misericordia* (The Seven Acts of Mercy) in Naples' Pio Monte della Misericordia, and the raw emotional intensity of his work becomes clear.

This creative intensity was reflected in the artist's life. Described by the writer Stendhal as a 'great painter [and] a wicked man', Caravaggio fled to Naples in 1606 after killing a man in a street fight in Rome. Although his sojourn in Naples lasted only a year, it had an electrifying effect on the city's younger artists. Among these artists was Giuseppe (or Jusepe) de Ribera (1591–1652), an aggressive, bullying Spaniard whose *capo lavoro* (masterpiece), the *Pietà*, hangs in the Museo Nazionale di San Martino in Naples. Along with the Greek artist Belisiano Crenzio and Naples-born painter Giovanni Battista Caracciolo (known as Battistello), Ribera formed a cabal to stamp out any potential competition. Merciless in the extreme, they shied from nothing in order to get their way. Ribera reputedly won a commission for the Cappella del Tesoro in the Duomo by poisoning his rival Domenichino (1581–1641) and wounding the assistant of a second competitor, Guido Reni (1575–1642). Much to the relief of other nerve-racked artists, the cabal eventually broke up when Caracciolo died in 1642.

North of Rome, Annibale Caracci (1560–1609) was the major artist of the baroque Bolognese school. With his painter brother Agostino he worked in Bologna, Parma and Venice before moving to Rome to work for Cardinal Odoardo Farnese. In works such as his magnificent frescoes of mythological subjects in Rome's Palazzo Farnese, he employed innovative illusionistic elements that would prove inspirational to later baroque painters such as Cortona, Pozzo and Gaulli. However, Caracci never let the illusionism and energy of his works dominate the subject matter, as these later painters did. Inspired by Michelangelo and Raphael, he continued the Renaissance penchant for idealising and 'beautifying' nature.

Arguably the best known of all baroque artists was the sculptor Gian Lorenzo Bernini (1598–1680), who used works of religious art such as his *Ecstasy of St Theresa* in Rome's Chiesa di Santa Maria della Vittoria to arouse feelings of exaltation and mystic transport. In this and many other works he achieved an extraordinary intensity of facial expression and a totally radical handling of draperies. Instead of letting these fall in dignified folds in the approved classical manner, he made them writhe and whirl to intensify the effect of excitement and energy.

While creative boundary pushing was obviously at play, the baroque was also driven by the Counter-Reformation, with much of the work commissioned in an attempt to keep hearts and minds from the clutches of the Protestant church. Baroque artists were earlier adopters of the 'sex sells' mantra, depicting Catholic spirituality, rather ironically, through worldly joy, exuberant decoration and uninhibited sensuality.

The New Italy

Discontent at years of foreign rule – first under Napoleon and then under the Austrians – may have been good for political and philosophical thinkers but there was little innovation in art. The most notable product of this time was, ironically, the painting and engraving of views, most notably in Venice, to meet the demand of European travellers wanting Grand Tour souvenirs. The best-known painters of this school are Francesco Guardi (1712–93) and Giovanni Antonio Canaletto (1697–1768).

Despite all the talk of unity, the 19th-century Italian cities remained as they had been for centuries – highly individual centres of culture with sharply contrasting ways of life. Music was the supreme art of this period and the overwhelming theme in the visual arts was one of chaste refinement.

ITALIAN ART & ARCHITECTURE ART

Top Renaissance Sculptures

....

David, Michelangelo, Galleria dell'Accademia, Florence

....

David, Donatello, Museo del Bargello, Florence

....

Gates of Paradise, Ghilberti, Museo dell'Opera di Santa Maria del Fiore, Florence

....

Pietà, Michaelangelo, St Peter's Basilica, Rome

....

Tomb of Pope Julius II, Michelangelo, Basilica di San Pietro in Vincoli, Rome

---

Michelangelo's *David* is no stranger to close calls. In 1527, the lower part of his arm was broken off in a riot. In 1843, a hydrochloric 'spruce-up' stripped away some of the original surface, while in 1991 a disturbed, hammer-wielding Italian painter smashed the statue's second left toe.

The major artistic movement of the day was neoclassicism and its greatest Italian exponent was the sculptor Antonio Canova (1757–1822). Canova renounced movement in favour of stillness, emotion in favour of restraint and illusion in favour of simplicity. His most famous work is a daring sculpture of Paolina Bonaparte Borghese as a reclining *Venere vincitrice* (Conquering Venus), in Rome's Museo e Galleria Borghese.

Canova was the last Italian artist to win overwhelming international fame. Italian architecture, sculpture and painting had played a dominant role in the cultural life of Europe for some 400 years, but with Canova's death in 1822, this supremacy came to an end.

Modern & Contemporary

Italy entered the turbulent days of the early 20th century still in the throes of constructing a cohesive national identity. Futurism, led by poet Filippo Tommaso Marinetti (1876–1944) and painter Umberto Boccioni (1882–1916), grew out of this sense of urgent nationalism, and, as Italy's north rapidly industrialised, sought new ways to express the dynamism of the machine age. Futurists demanded a new art for a new world and denounced every attachment to the art of the past. Marinetti's *Manifesto del futurismo* (Futurist Manifesto, 1909) was reinforced by the publication of a 1910 futurist painting manifesto by Boccioni, Giacomo Balla (1871–1958), Luigi Russolo (1885–1947) and Gino Severini (1883–1966). The manifesto declared that 'Everything is in movement, everything rushes forward, everything is in constant swift change.' Boccioni's *Rissa in galleria* (Brawl in the Arcade, 1910) in the collection of Milan's Pinacoteca di Brera, clearly demonstrates the movement's fascination with frantic movement and with modern technology. After WWI, a number of the futurist painters, including Mario Sironi (1885–1961) and Carlo Carrà (1881–1966) became aligned with fascism, sharing a common philosophy of nationalism and violence. Milan's Museo del Novecento along with Trentino's Museo d'Arte Moderna e Contemporanea di Trento e Rovereto (MART) have the world's best collection of futurist works.

Paralleling Futurism's bullying bluster, the metaphysical movement of Giorgio de Chirico (1888–1978) produced paintings notable for their stillness and sense of foreboding. He and Carlo Carrà depicted disconnected images from the world of dreams, often in settings of classical Italian architecture, as in the *The Red Tower* (1913), now in Venice's Peggy Guggenheim Collection. Like futurism, the movement was short lived, but held powerful attraction for the French surrealist movement in the 1920s.

As Italy's north flourished in the 1950s, so did the local art scene. Artists such as Alberto Burri (1915–95) and the Argentine-Italian Lucio Fontana (1899–1968) experimented with abstraction. Fontana's punctured canvases were characterised by *spazialismo* (spatialism) and he also experimented with 'slash paintings', perforating his canvases with actual holes or slashes and dubbing them 'art for the space age'. Burri's assemblages were made of burlap, wood, iron and plastic and were avowedly anti-traditional. *Grande sacco* (Large Sack) of 1952, housed in Rome's Galleria Nazionale d'Arte Moderna e Contemporanea, caused a major controversy when it was first exhibited.

Piero Manzoni (1933–63) created highly ironic work that questioned the nature of the art object itself, such as his canned 'Artist's Shit' (1961) directly prefiguring conceptual art and earning him posthumous membership of the radical new movement of the 1960s, *Arte Povera* (Poor Art). Often using simple, often everyday materials in installation or performance work, artists such as Mario Merz (1925–2003), Michelangelo Pistoletto (b 1933), Giovanni Anselmo (b 1934), Luciano Fabro (b 1936–2007), Giulio Paolini (b 1940) and Greek-born Jannis Kounellis (b 1936)

Click onto www.exibart.com (mostly in Italian) for up-to-date listings of art exhibitions throughout Italy, as well as exhibition reviews, articles and interviews.

Italy's major contemporary art event is the Venice Biennale, held every odd-numbered year. It's the most important survey show on the international art circuit, welcoming over 300,000 visitors.

sought to make the art experience more 'real', and to attack institutional power.

The 1980s saw a return to painting and sculpture in a traditional (primarily figurative) sense. Dubbed 'Transavanguardia', this movement broke with the prevailing international focus on conceptual art and was thought by some critics to signal the death of avant-garde. The artists who were part of this movement include Sandro Chia (b 1946), Mimmo Paladino (b 1948), Enzo Cucchi (b 1949) and Francesco Clemente (b 1952).

While global interest in contemporary art and the art market has shown exponential growth over the last two decades, Italian art world insiders bemoan the country's art scene, citing a dearth of institutional support, no real market to speak of and a backward-gazing population. That said, Italy does have a number of innovative, engaged contemporary art champions, from museums such as Rome's MAXXI, Turin's Castello di Rivoli, Bologna's MAMbo and Museion in Bolzano. They are joined by a growing number of *fondazione* – private foundation collections, from the sprawling Fondazione Prada and edgy Hangar Bicocca in Milan to the magnificent Palazzo Grassi in Venice and the small but astutely curated Fondazione Sandretto Re Rebaudengo in Turin. Gagosian has set up a Roman gallery and Milan's dealers continue to flourish. Naples and Turin also have a small but significant number of contemporary galleries.

Due to the influence of superstar Italian curators such as Francesco Bonami and Massimiliano Gioni, Italian contemporary artists are often celebrated as much, if not more, on the international stage as at home. Italian artists to watch both at home and abroad include Rudolf Stingel (b 1956), Paolo Canevari (b 1963), Maurizio Cattelan (b 1960), Vanessa Beecroft (b 1969), Rä di Martino (b 1975), Paola Pivi (b 1971), Pietro Roccasalva (b 1970) and Francesco Vezzoli (b 1971) – variously working in painting, sculpture, photography, installation, video and performance.

Architecture

Italian architecture has an enduring obsession with the 'classical', a formula that pleases the eye and makes the soul soar. The Greeks, who established the style, employed it in the southern cities they colonised; the Romans refined and embellished it; Italian Renaissance architects rediscovered and tweaked it; and the Fascist architects of the 1930s returned to it in their powerful modernist buildings. Even today, architects such as Richard Meier are designing buildings in Italy that clearly reference classical prototypes.

Classical

Only one word describes the buildings of ancient Italy: monumental. From Verona's Roman Arena to Pozzuoli's Anfiteatro Flavio, giant stadiums rose above skylines. Aqueducts like those below Naples provided fresh water

8th–3rd Century BC Magna Graecia

Greek colonisers grace southern Italy with stoic temples, sweeping amphitheatres and elegant sculptures that later influence their Roman successors.

6th Century BC–4th Century AD Roman

Epic roads and aqueducts spread from Rome, alongside proud basilicas, colonnaded markets, sprawling thermal baths and frescoed villas.

4th–6th Century Byzantine

Newly Christian and based in Constantinople, the Roman Empire turns its attention to the construction of churches with exotic, Eastern mosaics and domes.

8th–12th Century Romanesque

Attention turns from height to the horizontal lines of a building. Churches are designed with a stand-alone *campanile* (bell tower) and baptistry.

13th & 14th Century Gothic

Northern European Gothic gets an Italian makeover, from the Arabesque spice of Venice's Cá d'Oro to the Romanesque flavour of Siena's cathedral.

Late 14th–15th Century Early Renaissance

Filippo Brunelleschi's elegant dome graces the Duomo in Florence, heralding a return to classicism and a bold new era of humanist thinking and rational, elegant design.

PALLADIO

Andrea Palladio did more than produce great architecture, he wrote about it too. His treatise *I quattro libri dell'architettura* (The Four Books On Architecture, 1570) provides a set of rules and principles based on the buildings of Roman antiquity. It remains a sacred text in the architectural canon.

to thousands, while temples such as Pompeii's Tempio di Apollo provided the faithful with awe-inspiring centres of worship.

Having learned a few valuable lessons from the Greeks, the Romans refined architecture to such a degree that their building techniques, designs and mastery of harmonious proportion underpin most of the world's architecture and urban design to this day.

And though the Greeks invented the architectural orders (Doric, Ionic and Corinthian), it was the Romans who employed them in bravura performances. Consider Rome's Colosseum, with its ground tier of Doric, middle tier of Ionic and penultimate tier of Corinthian columns. The Romans were dab hands at temple architecture too. Just witness Rome's exquisitely proportioned Pantheon, a temple whose huge but seemingly unsupported dome showcases the Roman invention of concrete.

Byzantine

After Constantine became Christianity's star convert, the empire's architects and builders turned their talents to the design and construction of churches. In Constantinople, churches were built in the style that became known as Byzantine. Brick buildings built on the Roman basilican plan but with domes, they had sober exteriors that formed a stark contrast to their magnificent, mosaic-encrusted interiors. Finding its way back to Italy in the mid-6th century, the style expressed itself on a grand scale in Venice's Basilica di San Marco, as well as more modestly in buildings like the Chiesa di San Pietro in Otranto, Puglia. The true stars of Italy's Byzantine scene, however, are Ravenna's Basilica di San Vitale and Basilica di Sant'Apollinare in Classe, both built on a cruciform plan.

Romanesque

The next development in ecclesiastical architecture in Italy came from Europe. The European Romanesque style became momentarily popular in four regional forms – the Lombard, Pisan, Florentine and Sicilian Norman. All displayed an emphasis on width and the horizontal lines of a building rather than height, and featured churches where the *campanile* (bell tower) and baptistry were separate to the church.

The use of alternating white and green marble defined the facades of the Florentine and Pisan styles, as seen in iconic buildings like Florence's Basilica di Santa Maria Novella and Duomo baptistry, as well as in Pisa's cathedral and baptistry.

The Lombard style featured elaborately carved facades and exterior decoration featuring bands and arches. Among its finest examples are the Lombard cathedral in Modena, Pavia's Basilica di San Michele and Brescia's unusually shaped Duomo Vecchio.

Down south, the Sicilian Norman style blended Norman, Saracen and Byzantine influences, from marble columns to Islamic-inspired pointed arches to glass tesserae detailing. One of the greatest examples of the form is the Cattedrale di Monreale, located just outside Palermo.

A Blast of Baroque

....
Lecce, Puglia
....
Noto, Sicily
....
Rome, Lazio
....
Naples, Campania
....
Catania, Sicily

Gothic

The Italians didn't wholeheartedly embrace the Gothic: its verticality, flying buttresses, grotesque gargoyles and over-the-top decoration were just too far from the classical ideal that seems to be embedded in the Italian psyche. The local version was generally much more restrained, a style beautifully exemplified by Naples' simple, elegant Basilica di San Lorenzo Maggiore. There were, of course, exceptions. The Venetians used the style in grand *palazzi* (mansions) such as the Ca' d'Oro and on the facades of high-profile public buildings like the Palazzo Ducale. The Milanese employed it in their flamboyant Duomo, and the Sienese came up with a distinctive melange in Siena's beautiful cathedral.

The Renaissance to the Baroque

Unlike the gradual, organic spread of the styles that preceded it, Renaissance architecture's adoption was a highly conscious and academic affair, helped along by the invention of the printing press. The Florentine Filippo Brunelleschi and the Venetian Andrea Palladio spread a doctrine of harmonic geometry and proportion, drawing on classical Roman principles.

This insistence on restraint and purity was sure to lead to a backlash, and it's no surprise that the next major architectural movement in Italy was noteworthy for its exuberant – some would say decadent – form. The baroque took its name from the Portuguese word *barroco*, used by fishermen to denote a misshapen pearl. Andrea Palma's facade of Syracuse's cathedral, Guarino Guarini's Palazzo Carignano in Turin, and Gian Lorenzo Bernini's baldachin in St Peter's in Rome are dramatic, curvaceous and downright sexy structures that bear little similarity to the classical ideal.

The baroque's show-stopping qualities were not lost on the Catholic Church. Threatened by the burgeoning Reformation to the north of the Alps, the Church commissioned a battalion of grandiose churches, palaces and art to dazzle the masses and reaffirm its authority. Rome soon became a showcase of this baroque exuberance, its impressive new statements including Giacomo della Porta's Chiesa del Gesù. Commissioned to celebrate the newly founded Jesuit order, the church's hallucinatory swirl of frescoes and gilded interiors were produced by baroque greats such as Battista Gaulli (aka Il Baciccio), Andrea Pozzo and Pietro da Cortona.

Even more prolific was Gian Lorenzo Bernini, who expressed the popes' claim to power with his sweeping new design of St Peter's Square, its colonnaded arms 'embracing' the faithful with a majesty that still moves visitors today. Yet not everyone was singing Bernini's praise, especially the artist's bitter rival, Francesco Borromini (1599–1667). Reclusive and tortured, Borromini looked down on his ebullient contemporary's lack of architectural training and formal stone-carving technique.

Glowing in the wealth of its Spanish rulers, 16th-century Naples also drew driven, talented architects and artists in search of commissions and fame. Due in part to the city's notoriously high density and lack of show-off piazzas, many invested less time on adorning hard-to-see facades and more on lavishing interiors. The exterior of churches like the Chiesa e Chiostro di San Gregorio Armeno gives little indication of the opulence inside, from cheeky cherubs and gilded ceilings to polychromatic marble walls and floors. The undisputed master of this marble work form was Cosimo Fanzago, whose pièce de résistance is the church inside the Museo Nazionale di San Martino in Naples – a mesmerising kaleidoscope of inlaid colours and patterns.

Considering the Neapolitans' weakness for all things baroque, it's not surprising that the Italian baroque's

---

15th & 16th Century High Renaissance

Rome ousts Florence from its position at the centre of the Renaissance, its newly created wonders including Il Tempietto and St Peter's Basilica.

Late 16th–Early 18th Century Baroque

Renaissance restraint gives way to theatrical flourishes as the Catholic Church uses spectacle to upstage the Protestant movement.

Mid-18th–Late 19th Century Neoclassical

Archaeologists rediscover the glories of Pompeii and Herculaneum and architects pay tribute in creations like Vicenza's La Rotonda and Naples' Villa Pignatelli.

19th Century Industrial

A newly unified Italy fuses industrial technology, consumer culture and ecclesiastical traditions in Milan's cathedral-like Galleria Vittorio Emanuele II.

Late 19th–Early 20th Century Liberty

Italy's art nouveau ditches classical linearity for whimsical curves and organic motifs.

Early–Mid-20th Century Modernism

Italian modernism takes the form of futurism (technology-obsessed and anti-historical) and rationalism (seeking a middle ground between a machine-driven utopia and Fascism's fetish for classicism).

Architectural Wonders

Italy is Europe's architectural overachiever, bursting at its elegant seams with triumphant temples, brooding castles and dazzling basilicas. If you can't see it all in one mere lifetime, why not start with five of the best?

Duomo, Milan

A forest of petrified pinnacles and fantastical beasts, Italy's ethereal Gothic glory (p239) is pure Milan: a product of centuries of pillaging, trend spotting, one-upmanship and mercantile ambition. Head to the top for a peek at the Alps.

Duomo, Florence

Florence's most famous landmark (p483) is more than a monumental spiritual masterpiece. It's a living, breathing testament to the explosion of creativity, artistry, ambition and wealth that would define Renaissance Florence.

Piazza dei Miracoli, Pisa

Pisa (p558) promises a threesome you won't forget: the Duomo, the Battistero and the infamous Leaning Tower. Together they make up a perfect Romanesque trio, artfully arranged like objets d'art on a giant green coffee table.

Colosseum, Rome

Almost 2000 years on, Rome's mighty ancient stadium (p66) still has the X factor. Once the domain of gladiatorial battles and ravenous wild beasts, its 50,000-seat magnitude radiates all the vanity and ingenuity of a once-glorious, intercontinental empire.

Basilica di San Marco, Venice

It's a case of East–West fusion at this Byzantine beauty (p339), founded in AD 829 and rebuilt twice since. Awash with glittering mosaics and home to the remains of Venice's patron saint, its layering of eras reflects the city's own worldly pedigree.

1. Duomo, Milan 2. Duomo, Florence 3. Colosseum, Rome
4. Battistero and Leaning Tower, Pisa

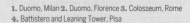

KNOW YOUR ARCHITECT

→ **Filippo Brunelleschi (1377–1446)** Brunelleschi blazed the neoclassical trail; his dome for Florence's Duomo announced the Renaissance's arrival.

→ **Donato Bramante (1444–1514)** After a stint as court architect in Milan, Bramante went on to design the tiny Tempietto and huge St Peter's Basilica in Rome.

→ **Michelangelo (1475–1564)** Architecture was but one of the many strings in this great man's bow; his masterworks are the dome of St Peter's Basilica and the Piazza del Campidoglio in Rome.

→ **Andrea Palladio (1508–80)** Western architecture's single most influential figure, Palladio turned classical Roman principles into elegant northern Italian villas.

→ **Gian Lorenzo Bernini (1598–1680)** The king of the Italian baroque is best known for his work in Rome, including the magnificent baldachin, piazza and colonnades at St Peter's.

grand finale would come in the form of the Palazzo Reale in Caserta, a 1200-room royal palace designed by Neapolitan architect Luigi Vanvitelli to upstage France's Palace of Versailles.

The Industrial & The Rational

Upstaged by political and social upheaval, architecture took a back seat in 19th-century Italy. One of the few movements of note stemmed directly from the Industrial Revolution and saw the application of industrial innovations in glass and metal to building design. Two monumental examples of the form are Galleria Vittorio Emanuele II in Milan and its southern sibling Galleria Umberto I in Naples.

By century's end, the art nouveau craze sweeping Europe inspired an Italian version, called 'Lo Stile Floreale' or 'Liberty'. It was notable for being more extravagant than most, evidenced in Giuseppe Sommaruga's Casa Castiglione (1903), a large block of flats at Corso Venezia 47 in Milan.

Italy's take on European modernism was rationalism, which strove to create an indigenous style that would fuse classical ideals with the charged industrial-age fantasies of the futurists. Its founding group was Gruppo 7, seven architects inspired by the Bauhaus; their most significant member, Giuseppe Terragni, designed the 1936 Casa del Fascio (now called Casa del Popolo) in Como. MIAR (Movimento Italiano per l'Architettura Razionale, the Italian Movement for Rational Architecture), a broader umbrella organisation, was led by Adalberto Libera, the influential architect best known for his Palazzo dei Congressi in EUR, a 20th-century suburb of Rome. EUR's most iconic building is the Palazzo della Civiltà del Lavoro (Palace of the Workers), designed by Giovanni Guerrini, Ernesto Bruno La Padula and Mario Romano, its arches and gleaming travertine skin referencing the Colosseum and ancient Rome's glory. With most of these commissions at the behest of Mussolini's government, rationalism is often known simply as 'Fascist Architecture', although the architects' uncompromising modernism eventually fell out of favour as the regime turned to a theatrical pastiche of classical styles. A rare example of rationalism on a domestic scale (and, rarer still, one that is open to the public) is Piero Portaluppi's Villa Necchi in Milan.

Into the Future

Italy's post-war boom may have driven an internationally acclaimed and deliciously cutting-edge design industry, but this was not reflected in its built environment. One of the few high points came in 1956, when architect Giò Ponti and engineer Pier Luigi Nervi designed Milan's slender Pirelli Tower.

Architects such as Carlo Scarpa, Aldo Rossi and Paolo Portoghesi then took Italian architecture in different directions. Veneto-based Scarpa was well known for his organic forms, most particularly the Brion Tomb and Sanctuary at San Vito d'Altivole. Writer and architect Rossi was awarded the Pritzker Prize in 1990, and was known for both his writing (eg *The Architecture of the City* in 1966) and design work. Rome-based Paolo Portoghesi is an architect, academic and writer with a deep interest in classical architecture. His best-known Italian building is the Central Mosque (1974) in Rome, famed for its luminously beautiful interior.

After a long period of decline, Italian architecture is back on the world stage, with architects and firms such as Massimiliano Fuksas; Mario Bellini; Matteo Thun; King, Roselli & Ricci; Cino Zucchi; Ian+; ABDR Architetti Associati; 5+1; Garofalo Miura; and Beniamino Servino designing innovative buildings both in Italy and internationally.

Italy's most brilliant starchitect is, however, Renzo Piano, whose international projects include London's scene-stealing Shard skyscraper and the Centre Culturel Tjibaou in Nouméa, New Caledonia. At home, recent projects include his bold Museo delle Scienze (MUSE) in Trento. Composed of a series of voids and volumes that seemingly float on water, its striking design echoes its dramatic mountain landscape. Further south in Rome, Piano's 2002 Auditorium Parco della Musica is considered one of his greatest achievements to date. Piano's status is so great, he was appointed as 'senator for life' in 2013.

Piano's heir apparent is Massimiliano Fuksas, whose projects are as whimsical as they are visually arresting. Take, for instance, his brand new Nuovo Centro Congressi (New Congress Center) in Rome's EUR, dubbed the *'Nuvola'* (Cloud) for its 'floating', glass-encased auditorium. Other Fuksas highlights include the futuristic Milan Trade Fair Building and the San Paolo Parish Church in Foligno.

High-profile foreign architects have also shaken things up. In Venice, David Chipperfield extended the Isola di San Michele's cemetery, while Tadao Ando oversaw the city's acclaimed Punta della Dogana and Palazzo Grassi renovation. In Rome, Richard Meier divided opinion with his 2006 Ara Pacis pavilion. The first major civic building in Rome's historic centre in more than half a century, the travertine, glass and steel structure was compared to a petrol station by art critic Vittorio Sgarbi. A little more love was given to Zaha Hadid's bold, sinuous MAXXI art gallery in northern Rome, which earned the Iraqi-British architect the prestigious RIBA (Royal Institute of British Architects) Sterling prize in 2010.

Not to be outdone, Milan's skyline is getting a 21st-century makeover, with the ambitious redevelopment of its Porta Nuova district. Home to Italy's tallest building (the 231m, César Pelli–designed UniCredit tower), the project also features Stefano Boeri's Bosco Verticale (Vertical Forest), a pair of eco-conscious apartment towers covered in the equivalent of a hectare of woodland. The city's ambitious CityLife project, a commercial, residential and parkland development centered around three experimental skyscrapers by Zaha Hadid, Arata Isozaki and Daniel Liebeskind, seems perpetually 'under construction', although Hadid's low-rise housing project welcomed its first residents in 2015 and at least one tower is due to open before 2017.

Mid–Late 20th Century Modern

Industrialised and economically booming, mid-century Italy shows off its wealth in commercial projects like Giò Ponti's slim-lined Pirelli skyscraper.

21st Century Contemporary

Italian architecture gets its groove back with the international success of starchitects like Renzo Piano, Massimiliano Fuksas and Gae Aulenti.

ITALIAN ART & ARCHITECTURE ARCHITECTURE

Modern Musts

Galleria Nazionale d'Arte Moderna e Contemporanea, Rome

....

Peggy Guggenheim Collection, Venice

....

Museo del Novecento, Milan

....

Fondazione Prada, Milan

....

Castello di Rivoli, Turin

....

MADRE, Naples

....

MAMbo, Bologna

....

Museion, Bolzano

The Italian Way of Life

Imagine you wake up tomorrow and discover you're an Italian. How would life be different, and what could you discover about Italy in just one day as a local? Read on...

A Day in the Life of an Italian

There are 12 minority languages officially recognised in Italy, consisting of native languages Friulian, Ladin and Sardinian, and the languages spoken in neighbouring countries, including French, Franco-Provençal, German, Catalan, Occitan, Slovene, Croatian, Albanian and Greek.

Sveglia! You're woken not by an alarm but by the burble and clatter of the *caffettiera,* the ubiquitous stovetop espresso-maker. You're running late, so you bolt down your coffee scalding hot (an acquired Italian talent) and pause briefly to ensure your socks match before dashing out the door. Yet still you walk blocks out of your way to buy your morning paper from Bucharest-born Nicolae, your favourite news vendor and (as a Romanian) part of Italy's largest migrant community. You chat briefly about his new baby – you may be late, but at least you're not rude.

On your way to work you scan the headlines: another boat of asylum seekers land on Sicilian shores, more coalition-government infighting and an announcement of new EU regulations on cheese. Outrageous! The cheese regulations, that is; the rest is to be expected. At work, you're buried in paperwork until noon, when it's a relief to join friends for lunch and a glass of wine. Afterwards you toss back another scorching espresso at your favourite bar and find out how your barista's latest audition went – it turns out you went to school with the sister of the director of the play, so you promise to put in a good word.

Back at work by 2pm, you multitask Italian-style, chatting with co-workers as you dash off work emails, text your schoolmate about the barista on your *telefonino* (mobile phone) and surreptitiously check *l'Internet* for employment listings – your work contract is due to expire soon. After a busy day like this, *aperitivi* are definitely in order, so at 6.30pm you head directly to the latest happy-hour hot spot. Your friends arrive, the decor is *molto design,* the vibe *molto cool* and the DJ *abbastanza hot,* until suddenly it's time for your English class – everyone's learning it these days, if only for the slang.

By the time you finally get home, it's already 9.30pm and dinner will have to be reheated. *Peccato!* (Shame!) You eat, absent-mindedly watching the latest episode of *MasterChef Italia* while recounting your day and complaining about cheese regulations to whoever's home – no sense giving reheated pasta your undivided attention. While brushing your teeth, you dream of a holiday in Anguilla, though without a raise, it'll probably be Abruzzo again this year.

Finally you make your way to bed and check Facebook one last time; your colleague Marco seems to be acclimatising to life in Sydney. He's the third person you know who has moved to Australia in recent years. You wonder what it would be like to live in a nation so young and booming. They say hard work pays over there. Marco has already been promoted, without the need of favours or influential contacts. Once again you entertain the thought of following in his footsteps, but then ponder the distance and start to pine for your *famiglia e amici* (family and friends). As you drift off, you console yourself in the knowledge that while it mightn't be perfect, they don't call Italy the *bel paese* (beautiful country) for nothing.

Being Italian

The People

Who are the people you'd encounter every day as an Italian? Just over 19% of your fellow citizens are smokers and 60.8% drive (or are driven) to work, compared to only 3.3% who cycle. A growing proportion of Italians are already retired. Indeed, one out of five is over 65, which explains the septuagenarians you'll notice on parade with dogs and grandchildren in parks, affably arguing about politics in cafes, and ruthlessly dominating bocce tournaments.

You might also notice a striking absence of children. Italy's birth rate is one of the lowest in Europe, at 8.4 per 1000 people in 2015, compared to 15.7 in Ireland, 12.8 in Britain and 12.6 in France.

North versus South

In his film *Ricomincio da tre* (I'm Starting from Three; 1980), acting great Massimo Troisi comically tackles the problems faced by Neapolitans forced to head north for work. Punchlines aside, the film reveals Italy's very real north–south divide; a divide still present more than 30 years on. While the north is celebrated for its fashion empires and moneyed metropolises, Italy's south (dubbed the 'Mezzogiorno') is often spotlit for its higher unemployment, crumbling infrastructure and Mafia-related police raids. At a deep semantic level, *settentrionale* (northern Italian) implies reservation, productivity and success, while *meridionale* (southern Italian) alludes to conservatism and laziness. From the Industrial Revolution in the 1960s, millions of southern Italians fled to the industrialised northern cities for factory jobs. Disparagingly nicknamed *terroni* (literally meaning 'of the soil'), these in-house 'immigrants' were often exposed to racist attitudes from their northern cousins. Decades on, the overt racism may have dissipated but the prejudices remain. Many northerners resent their taxes being used to 'subsidise' the south – a sentiment well exploited by the Lega Nord (Northern League) political party.

From Emigrants to Immigrants

From 1876 to 1976, Italy was a country of net emigration. With some 30 million Italian emigrants dispersed throughout Europe, the Americas and Australia, remittances from Italians abroad helped keep Italy's economy afloat during economic crises after Independence and WWII.

The tables have since turned. Political and economic upheavals in the 1980s brought new arrivals from Central Europe, Latin America and North Africa, including Italy's former colonies in Tunisia, Somalia and Ethiopia. More recently, waves of Chinese and Filipino immigrants have given Italian streetscapes a Far Eastern twist. While immigrants account for just over 8% of Italy's population today, the number is growing. In 2001, the country's foreign population (a number that excludes foreign-born people who take Italian citizenship) was 1.3 million. By 2015, that number had almost quadrupled to 5 million.

From a purely economic angle, these new arrivals are vital for the country's economic health. While most Italians today choose to live and work within Italy, fewer are entering blue-collar agricultural and industrial fields. Without immigrant workers to fill the gaps, Italy would be sorely lacking in tomato sauce and shoes. From kitchen hands to hotel

According to the OECD's 2015 Better Life Index, 90% of Italians surveyed knew of someone they could rely on in time of need, more than the OECD average of 88%. On the political front, voter turnout in Italy was 75% during recent elections; higher than the OECD average of 68%.

Today, people of Italian origin account for more than 40% of the population in Argentina and Uruguay, more than 10% in Brazil, more than 5% in Switzerland, the US and Venezuela, and more than 4% in Australia and Canada.

maids, it is often immigrants who take the low-paid service jobs that keep Italy's tourism economy afloat.

Despite this, not everyone is dusting off the welcome mat. In 2010, the shooting of an immigrant worker in the town of Rosarno, Calabria, sparked Italy's worst race riots in years. In 2013, a top-level football match between AC Milan and Roma was suspended after fans chanted racist abuse at Mario Balotelli, AC Milan's black, Italian-born striker. In October the following year, reports of an attempted rape by a group of immigrants sparked three days of protests outside an immigration centre in suburban Rome. The ferocity of the protests saw a number of Africans housed at the complex moved to another area. In March 2015, the troubled neighbourhood hit the headlines once more as protestors set fire to dumpsters near the complex. Not that such incidents are limited to Rome, with similar protests having taken place in Turin, Milan and Naples.

High unemployment, economic sluggishness and inadequate infrastructure continue to play significant roles in the rise of anti-immigration sentiment, with many Italians feeling that the country's economic woes are being merely exasperated by the growing number of new arrivals. Yet others argue that Italy's economic woes are to blame for inaccurate perceptions of immigrants in the country. A 2014 study conducted by British market researchers Ipsos MORI found that the average Italian believes that foreigners constitute 30% of the total population; a far cry from the actual figure of around 8%.

Figures released by the International Fund for Agricultural Development (IFAD) in 2015 show that immigrants in Italy had sent €9.2 billion to family and friends back home in 2014, including €2.93 billion to Africa, €2.75 billion to Asia Pacific and €2.66 billion to other European countries, including Romania and Albania.

Religion, Loosely Speaking

While almost 80% of Italians identify as Catholics, only around 15% of Italy's population regularly attends Sunday Mass. That said, the Church continues to exert considerable influence on public policy and political parties, especially those of the center- and far-right.

But in the land of the double park, even God's rules are up for interpretation. Sure, *mamma* still serves fish on Good Friday, but while she might consult *la Madonna* for guidance, chances are she'll get a second opinion from the *maga* (fortune-teller) on channel 32. It's estimated that around 13 million Italians use the services of psychics, astrologers and fortune-tellers. While the uncertainties stirred up by Italy's still-stagnant economy help drive these numbers, Italians have long been a highly superstitious bunch. From not toasting with water to not opening umbrellas inside the home, the country offers a long list of tips to keep bad luck at bay.

Superstitious beliefs are especially strong in Italy's south. Here *corni* (horn-shaped charms) adorn everything from necklines to rear-view mirrors to ward off the *malocchio* (evil eye), and devotion to local saints takes on an almost cultish edge. Every year in Naples, thousands cram into the Duomo to witness the blood of San Gennaro miraculously liquefy in the phial that contains it. When the blood liquefies, the city breathes a sigh of relief – it symbolises another year safe from disaster. When it failed in 1944, Mt Vesuvius erupted, and when it failed again in 1980 an earthquake struck the city that year. Coincidence? Perhaps. But even the most cynical Neapolitan would rather San Gennaro perform his magic trick...just in case.

John Turturro's film *Passione* (2010) is a *Buena Vista Social Club*-style exploration of Naples' rich and eclectic musical traditions. Spanning folk songs to contemporary tunes, it offers a fascinating insight into the city's complex soul.

It's Not What You Know...

From your day as an Italian, this much you know already: conversation is far too important to be cut short by tardiness or a mouthful of toothpaste. All that chatter isn't entirely idle, either: in Europe's most ancient, entrenched bureaucracy, social networks are essential to get things done. Putting in a good word for your barista isn't just a nice gesture, but an

FASHION FAMILY SAGAS

Tight as they may be, Italian families are not always examples of heart-warming domesticity. Indeed, some of Italy's most fashionable *famiglie* (families) prove that every clan has its problems, some small, some extra, extra large.

Consider the Versace bunch, fashion's favourite catwalking Calabrians. One of Italy's greatest exports, the familial dynasty was founded by Gianni, celebrity BFF and the man who single-handedly made bling chic. But not even the fashion gods could save the bearded genius, inexplicably shot dead outside his Miami mansion by serial killer Andrew Cunanan in 1997. With Gianni gone, creative control was passed to Donatella, Gianni's larger-than-life little sister. The subject of Anna Wintour's most unusual fashion memory – full-body spandex on horseback – the former coke-addled party queen flew herself to rehab on her daughter Allegra's 18th birthday.

Then there are the Florentine fashion rivals, the Gucci clan. Established by Guccio Gucci in 1904, the family firm reads like a bad Brazilian soap – power struggles between Rodolfo and Aldo (Guccio's sons) in the 1950s; assault charges by Paolo (Aldo's son) against siblings Roberto and Giorgio, and cousin Maurizio Gucci, in 1982; and a major fallout between Paolo and father Aldo over the offshore siphoning off of profits.

The last Gucci to run the company was Maurizio, who finally sold his share to Bahrain investment bank Investcorp in 1993 for a healthy US$170 million. Two years later, Maurizio was dead, gunned down outside his Milan office on the order of ex-wife, Patrizia Reggiani. Not only had Reggiani failed to forgive her husband's infidelity, she was far from impressed with her US$500,000 annual allowance. After all, this was the woman who famously quipped that she'd rather cry in a Rolls Royce than be happy on a bicycle. Offered parole in 2011 on condition of finding employment, Reggiani stayed true to form, stating: 'I've never worked a day in my life; I'm certainly not going to start now'. Despite the now-infamous quip, fashion's 'black widow', currently on day release, has found herself a gig, working part-time in a Milanese jewellery store…with a live macaw perched on her shoulder.

essential career boost. According to Italy's Ministry of Labour, over 60% of Italian firms rely on personal introductions for recruitment. Indeed, *clientelismo* (nepotism) is as much a part of the Italian lexicon as *caffè* (coffee) and *tasse* (taxes); a fact satirised in Massimiliano Bruno's film *Viva l'Italia* (2012), about a crooked, well-connected senator who secures jobs for his three children, among them a talentless TV actress with a speech impediment. The Italian film industry itself came under attack in 2012 when newspaper *Il Fatto Quotidiano* accused several members of the Italian Academy (which votes for the prestigious David di Donatello film awards) of having conflicts of interest. As the satirist Beppe Severgnini wryly comments in his book *La Bella Figura: A Field Guide to the Italian Mind,* 'If you want to lose an Italian friend or kill off a conversation, all you have to say is "On the subject of conflicts of interest…" If your interlocutor hasn't disappeared, he or she will smile condescendingly.'

Hotel Mamma

If you're between the ages of 18 and 34, there's a 66% chance that's not a roommate in the kitchen making your morning coffee: it's mum or dad. This is not because Italy is a nation of pampered *bamboccioni* (big babies) – at least, not entirely. With a general unemployment rate of 12.4% and a youth unemployment rate hovering around 44% in early 2015, it's no wonder that so many refuse to cut those apron strings.

While Italy's family-based social fabric provides a protective buffer for many during these challenging economic times, inter-generational solidarity has always been the basis of the Italian family. According to the time-honoured Italian social contract, you'd probably live with your

According to a 2015 report by Istat, 41.8% of Italians considered themselves satisfied with their economic situation, 80% with their health, and 90.2% with their family relationships. Almost 64% were satisfied with the quantity and quality of their leisure time.

parents until you start a career and a family of your own. Then after a suitable grace period for success and romance – a couple of years should do the trick – your parents might move in with you to look after your kids, and be looked after in turn.

As for those who don't live with family members, chances are they're still a quick stroll away, with 54% living within a 30-minute walk from close relatives. All this considered, it's hardly surprising to hear that famous mobile phone chorus at evening rush hour: '*Mamma, butta la pasta!*' (Mum, put the pasta in the water!).

Gender Inequality

It might string straight As in fashion, food and design, but Italy's performance in the gender equality stakes leaves much room for improvement. Despite the fact that half of Italy's current cabinet ministers are women – a conscious effort on the part of prime minister Matteo Renzi to redress the country's male-dominated parliament – sexism remains deeply entrenched in Italian society.

According to the Organisation for Economic Co-operation and Development (OECD), only 47% of Italian women are in the workforce, compared to 72% in Sweden, 69% in Germany and 60% in France. Statistics released by Italy's national bureau of statistics (Istat) indicate that the potential earnings of Italian women is half that of their male counterparts, reflecting both lower employment rates and pay. Though successful Italian businesswomen do exist – among them Poste Italiane chairperson Luisa Todini and Eni president Emma Marcegaglia – almost 95% of public company board members in Italy remain male, and of these, approximately 80% of them are older than 55.

Italian women fare no better on the domestic front. OECD figures reveal that Italian men spend 103 minutes per day cooking, cleaning or caring, less than a third as long as Italian women, who spend an average of 326 minutes per day on what the OECD labels unpaid work.

Interestingly, the tables are turned in education. According to the OECD's 2014 Gender Gap Index, entry rates into higher education for women were 74%, compared to 52% for men.

Italian Passions

Co-ordinated wardrobes, strong espresso and general admiration are not the only things that make Italian hearts sing. And while Italian passions are wide and varied, few define Italy like football and opera.

Better Living by Design

As an Italian, you actually did your co-workers a favour by being late to the office to give yourself a final once-over in the mirror. Unless you want your fellow employees to avert their gaze in dumbstruck horror, your socks had better match. The tram can wait as you make *la bella figura* (cut a fine figure).

Italians have strong opinions about aesthetics and aren't afraid to share them. A common refrain is *Che brutta!* (How hideous!), which may strike visitors as tactless. But consider it from an Italian point of view – everyone is rooting for you to look good, so who are you to disappoint? The shop assistant who tells you with brutal honesty that yellow is *not* your colour is doing a public service, and will consider it a personal triumph to see you outfitted in orange instead.

If it's a gift, you must allow 10 minutes for the sales clerk to *fa un bel pacchetto,* wrapping your purchase with string and an artfully placed sticker. This is the epitome of *la bella figura* – the sales clerk wants you to look good by giving a good gift. When you do, everyone basks in the

The World Economic Forum's 2014 Global Gender Gap Report ranked Italy 69th worldwide in terms of overall gender equality, up from 71st position in 2013. It ranked 114th in female economic participation and opportunity, 62nd in educational attainment and 37th in political empowerment.

Italian Style Icons

Bialetti *coffee-maker*

Cinzano *vermouth*

Acqua di Parma *cologne*

Piaggio *Vespa*

Olivetti 'Valentine' *typewriter*

glow: you as the gracious gift-giver and the sales clerk as savvy gift consultant, not to mention the flushed and duly honoured recipient.

As a national obsession, *la bella figura* gives Italy its undeniable edge in design, cuisine, art and architecture. Though the country could get by on its striking good looks, Italy is ever mindful of delightful details. They are everywhere you look and many places you don't: the intricately carved cathedral spire only the bell-ringer could fully appreciate, the toy duck hidden inside your chocolate *uova di Pasqua* (Easter egg), the absinthe-green silk lining inside a sober grey suit sleeve. Attention to such details earns you instant admiration in Italy – and an admission that, sometimes, non-Italians do have style.

Calcio (Football): Italy's Other Religion

Catholicism may be your official faith, but as an Italian your true religion is likely to be *calcio* (football). On any given weekend from September to May, chances are that you and your fellow *tifosi* (football fans) are at the *stadio* (stadium), glued to the TV or checking the score on your mobile phone. Come Monday, you'll be dissecting the match by the office water cooler.

Like politics and fashion, football is in the very DNA of Italian culture. Indeed, they sometimes even converge. Silvio Berlusconi first found fame as the owner of AC Milan and cleverly named his political party after a well-worn football chant. Fashion royalty Dolce & Gabbana declared football players 'the new male icons', using five of Italy's hottest on-field stars to launch its 2010 underwear collection. Decades earlier, 1960s singer Rita Pavone topped the charts with *La partita di pallone* (The Football Match), in which the frustrated pop princess sings '*Perchè, perchè la domenica mi lasci sempre sola per andare a vedere la partita di pallone?*' (Why, why do you always leave me alone on Sunday so you can go and watch the football match?). It's no coincidence that in Italian *tifoso* means both 'football fan' and 'typhus patient'. When the ball ricochets off the post and slips fatefully through the goalie's hands, when half the stadium is swearing while the other half is euphorically shouting *Gooooooooooooooool!*, 'fever pitch' is the term that comes to mind.

Nothing quite stirs Italian blood like a good (or a bad) game. Nine months after Italy's 2006 World Cup victory against France, hospitals in northern Italy reported a baby boom. In February the following year, rioting at a Palermo–Catania match in Catania left one policeman dead and around 100 injured. Blamed on the Ultras – a minority group of hard-core football fans – the violence shocked both Italy and the world, leading to a temporary ban of all matches in Italy and increased stadium security. A year earlier, the match-fixing 'Calciopoli' scandals resulted in revoked championship titles and temporary demotion of Serie A (top-tier national) teams, including the mighty Juventus.

Yet, the same game that divides also unites. You might be a Lazio-loathing, AS Roma supporter on any given day, but when the national *Azzurri* (The Blues) swag the World Cup, you are nothing but a heart-on-your-sleeve *italiano* (Italian). In his book *The 100 Things Everyone Needs to Know About Italy*, Australian journalist David Dale writes that Italy's 1982 World Cup win 'finally united twenty regions which, until then, had barely acknowledged that they were part of the one country.'

Opera: Let the Fat Lady Sing

At the stadium, your beloved *squadra* (team) hits the field to the roar of Verdi. OK, so you might not be first in line to see *Rigoletto* at La Fenice, but Italy's opera legacy remains a source of pride. After all, not only did you invent the art form, you gave the world some of its greatest composers,

Italy's culture of corruption and *calcio* (football) is captured in *The Dark Heart of Italy*, in which English expat author Tobias Jones wryly observes, 'Footballers or referees are forgiven nothing; politicians are forgiven everything.'

Italy was introduced to modern *calcio* in the late 19th century when the English factory barons of Turin, Genoa and Milan established teams to keep their workers fit.

THE ITALIAN WAY OF LIFE ITALIAN PASSIONS

CALCIO

MUSIC FOR THE MASSES

Most of the music you'll hear booming out of Italian cafes to inspire sidewalk singalongs is Italian *musica leggera* (popular music); a term covering home-grown rock, jazz, folk, hip hop and pop ballads. The scene's annual highlight is the Sanremo Music Festival (televised on RAI1), a Eurovision-style song comp responsible for launching the careers of chart-topping contemporary acts like Eros Ramazzotti, Giorgia, Laura Pausini and, more recently, singer-songwriter Marco Mengoni. In 2013, Mengoni won Sanremo for his ballad *L'essenziale*, using the same song later that year to represent Italy at Eurovision. The trend was repeated in 2015, when operatic pop trio Il Volo took their winning hit *Grande amore* to Eurovision, the soaring anthem winning Italy third place.

In the early 1960s, Sanremo helped launch the career of living music legend, Mina Mazzini. Famed for her powerful, three-octave voice and a musical versatility spanning pop, soul, blues, R&B and swing, the songstress dominated the charts throughout the 1960s and 1970s, her emancipated image and frank tunes about love and sex ruffling a few bourgeois feathers. Equally controversial was the late Fabrizio de André, an Italian Bob Dylan celebrated for his poetic lyrics, musing monotone and cutting criticism of religious hypocrisy. Sharp social observation and bitter-sweet sentiments also underpin the work of late singer-songwriter Pino Daniele, whose style fused Neapolitan music with blues and world-music influences.

compositions. and performers. Gioachino Rossini (1792–1868) transformed Pierre Beaumarchais' *Le Barbier de Séville* (The Barber of Seville) into one of the greatest comedic operas, Giuseppe Verdi (1813–1901) produced the epic *Aida,* while Giacomo Puccini (1858–1924) delivered staples such as *Tosca, Madama Butterfly* and *Turandot.*

Lyrical, intense and dramatic – it's only natural that opera bears the 'Made in Italy' label. Track pants might be traded in for tuxedos, but Italy's opera crowds can be just as ruthless as their pitch-side counterparts. Centuries on, the dreaded *fischi* (mocking whistles) still possess a mysterious power to blast singers right off stage. In December 2006, a substitute in street clothes had to step in for Sicilian-French star tenor Roberto Alagna when his off-night aria met with vocal disapproval at Milan's legendary La Scala. Best not to get them started about musicals and 'rock opera', eh?

The word *diva* was invented for legendary sopranos such as Parma's Renata Tebaldi and Italy's adopted Greek icon Maria Callas, whose rivalry peaked when *Time* quoted Callas saying that comparing her voice to Tebaldi's was like comparing 'champagne and Coca-Cola'. Both were fixtures at La Scala, along with the wildly popular Italian tenor to whom others are still compared, Enrico Caruso. Tenor Luciano Pavarotti (1935–2007) remains beloved for attracting broader public attention to opera, while best-selling blind tenor Andrea Bocelli became a controversial crossover sensation with what critics claim are overproduced arias sung with a strained upper register. Newer generations of stars include soprano Fiorenze Cedolins, who performed a requiem for the late Pope John Paul II, recorded *Tosca* arias with Andrea Bocelli and scored encores in Puccini's iconic *La Bohème* at the Arena di Verona Festival. Younger still is celebrated tenor Francesco Meli, a regular fixture at many of the world's great opera houses. Much sadder, however, was the fate of promising tenor Salvatore Licitra. Famed for stepping in for Pavarotti in his final show at New York's Metropolitan Opera, the 43-year-old died tragically after a motorcycle accident in 2011.

According to Istat, Italy's bureau of statistics, 69.5% of employed Italians work in services, 26.9% work in industry and 3.6% work in the agricultural sector. On the health front, OECD figures reveal that 46% of Italians aged 15 and over are overweight or obese, compared to 63.5% of Americans.

Italy on Page & Screen

From ancient Virgil to modern-day Eco, Italy's literary canon is awash with world-renowned scribes. The nation's film stock is equally robust, packed with visionary directors, iconic stars and that trademark Italian pathos.

Literature

Latin Classics

Roman epic poet Virgil (aka Vergilius) spent 11 years and 12 books tracking the outbound adventures and inner turmoil of Trojan hero Aeneas, from the fall of Troy to the founding of Rome. Virgil died in 19 BC with just 60 lines to go in his *Aeneid*, a kind of sequel to Greek epic poet Homer's *Iliad* and *Odyssey*. As Virgil himself observed: 'Time flies'.

Legend has it that fellow Roman Ovid (Ovidius) was a failed lawyer who married his daughter, but there's no question he told a ripping good tale. His *Metamorphoses* chronicled civilisation from murky mythological beginnings to Julius Caesar, and his how-to seduction manual *Ars amatoria* (The Art of Love) inspired countless Casanovas.

Timeless Poets

Some literature scholars claim that Shakespeare stole his best lines and plot points from earlier Italian playwrights and poets. Debatable though this may be, the Bard certainly had stiff competition from 13th-century Dante Alighieri as the world's finest romancer. Dante broke with tradition in *La divina commedia* (The Divine Comedy; c 1307–21) by using the familiar Italian, not the formal Latin, to describe travelling through the circles of hell in search of his beloved Beatrice. Petrarch (aka Francesco Petrarca; 1304–74) added wow to Italian woo with his sonnets, applying a strict structure of rhythm and rhyme to romance the idealised Laura.

If sonnets aren't your thing, try 1975 Nobel laureate Eugenio Montale, who wrings poetry out of the creeping damp of everyday life, or Ungaretti, whose WWI poems hit home with a few searing syllables.

Cautionary Fables

The most universally beloved Italian fabulist is Italo Calvino, whose titular character in *Il barone rampante* (The Baron in the Trees; 1957) takes to the treetops in a seemingly capricious act of rebellion that makes others rethink their own earthbound conventions. In Dino Buzzati's *Il deserto dei Tartari* (The Tartar Steppe; 1940), an ambitious officer posted to a mythical Italian border is besieged by boredom, thwarted expectations and disappearing youth while waiting for enemy hordes to materialise – a parable drawn from Buzzati's own dead-end newspaper job.

Over the centuries, Niccolo Machiavelli's *Il principe* (The Prince; 1532) has been referenced as a handy manual for budding autocrats, but also as a cautionary tale against unchecked 'Machiavellian' authority.

Any self-respecting Italian bookshelf features one or more Roman rhetoricians. To *fare la bella figura* (cut a fine figure) among academics, trot out a phrase from Cicero or Horace (Horatio), such as 'Where there is life there is hope' or 'Whatever advice you give, be brief.'

For Dante with a pop-culture twist, check out Sandow Birk and Marcus Sanders' satirical, slangy translation of *The Divine Comedy*, which sets *Inferno* in hellish Los Angeles traffic, *Purgatorio* in foggy San Francisco and *Paradiso* in New York.

PREMIO STREGA

Italy's most coveted literary prize, the Premio Strega, is awarded annually to a work of Italian prose fiction. Its youngest recipient to date is physicist-cum-writer Paolo Giordano, who, at 26, won for his debut novel *La solitudine dei numeri primi* (The Solitude of Prime Numbers; 2008).

Crime Pays

Crime fiction and *gialli* (mysteries) dominate Italy's best-seller list, and one of its finest writers is Gianrico Carofiglio. The former head of Bari's anti-Mafia squad, Carofiglio's novels include the award-winning *Testimone inconsapevole* (Involuntary Witness; 2002), which introduces the shady underworld of Bari's hinterland. Art also imitates life for judge-cum-novelist Giancarlo de Cataldo, whose best-selling novel *Romanzo criminale* (Criminal Romance; 2002) spawned both a TV series and film. Another crime writer with page-to-screen success is Andrea Camilleri, his savvy Sicilian inspector Montalbano starring in capers like *Il ladro di merendine* (The Snack Thief; 1996). Umberto Eco gave the genre an intellectual edge with his medieval detective tale *Il nome della rosa* (The Name of the Rose; 1980) and *Il pendolo di Foucault* (Foucault's Pendulum; 1988). In Eco's *Il cimitero di Praga* (The Prague Cemetery; 2010), historical events merge with the tale of a master killer and forger.

Historical Epics

Set during the Black Death in Florence, Boccaccio's *Decameron* (c 1350–53) has a visceral gallows humour that foreshadows Chaucer and Shakespeare. Italy's 19th-century struggle for unification parallels the story of star-crossed lovers in Alessandro Manzoni's *I promessi sposi* (The Betrothed; 1827, definitive version released 1842), and causes an identity crisis among Sicilian nobility in Giuseppe Tomasi di Lampedusa's *Il gattopardo* (The Leopard; published posthumously in 1958). Wartime survival strategies are chronicled in Elsa Morante's *La storia* (History; 1974) and in Primo Levi's autobiographical account of Auschwitz in *Se questo è un uomo* (If This Is a Man; 1947). WWII is the uninvited guest in *Il giardino dei Finzi-Contini* (The Garden of the Finzi-Continis; 1962), Giorgio Bassani's tale of a crush on a girl whose aristocratic Jewish family attempts to disregard the rising tide of anti-Semitism. In Margaret Mazzantini's *Venuto al mondo* (Twice Born; 2008), it's the Bosnian War that forms the backdrop to a powerful tale of motherhood and loss.

Social Realism

Italy has always been its own sharpest critic and several 20th-century Italian authors captured their own troubling circumstances with unflinching accuracy. Grazia Deledda's *Cosima* (1937) is her fictionalised memoir of coming of age and into her own as a writer in rural Sardinia. Deledda became one of the first women to win the Nobel Prize for Literature (1926) and set the tone for such bittersweet recollections of rural life as Carlo Levi's *Cristo si è fermato a Eboli* (Christ Stopped at Eboli; 1945).

Jealousy, divorce and parental failings are grappled head-on by pseudonymous author Elena Ferrante in her brutally honest *I giorni dell'abbandono* (The Days of Abandonment; 2002). In 2014, Ferrante published *Storia della bambina perduta* (The Story of the Lost Child), the final installment in her so-called Neapolitan series, four novels exploring the life-long friendship of two women born into a world of poverty, chaos and violence in 1950s Naples. Confronting themes also underline Alessandro Pipero's *Persecuzione* (Persecution; 2010), which sees an esteemed oncologist accused of child molestation. Its sequel, *Inseparabili* (2012), won the 2012 Premio Strega literature prize.

Italy's north–south divide is the focus of Luca Miniero's comedy smash *Benvenuti al Sud* (Welcome to the South; 2010). An adaptation of the French film *Bienvenue chez les Ch'tis* (Welcome to the Sticks; 2008), it tells the tale of a northern postmaster posted to a small Campanian town, bullet-proof vest in tow.

Cinema

Neorealist Grit

Out of the smouldering ruins of WWII emerged unflinching tales of woe, including Roberto Rossellini's *Roma, città aperta* (Rome: Open City; 1945), a story of love, betrayal and resistance in Nazi-occupied Rome. In

Vittorio De Sica's Academy-awarded *Ladri di biciclette* (Bicycle Thieves; 1948), a doomed father attempts to provide for his son without resorting to crime in war-ravaged Rome, while Pier Paolo Pasolini's *Mamma Roma* (1962) revolves around an ageing prostitute trying to make an honest living for herself and her deadbeat son.

Crime & Punishment

Italy's acclaimed new dramas combine the truthfulness of classic neo-realism, the taut suspense of Italian thrillers and the psychological revelations of Fellini. Among the best is Matteo Garrone's brutal Camorra exposé *Gomorrah* (2008). Based on Roberto Saviano's award-winning novel, the film won the Grand Prix at the 2008 Cannes Film Festival. Another Cannes success story is Paolo Sorrentino's *Il divo* (2008), which explores the life of former prime minister Giulio Andreotti. Mafiosi are among the cast in the deeply poignant *Cesare deve morire* (Caesar Must Die; 2012), a documentary about maximum-security prisoners staging Shakespeare's *Julius Caesar*. Directed by octogenarian brothers Paolo and Vittorio Taviani, the film scooped the Golden Bear at the 2012 Berlin Film Festival.

Romance all'italiana

It's only natural that a nation of hopeless romantics should provide some of the world's most tender celluloid moments. In Michael Radford's *Il postino* (The Postman; 1994), exiled poet Pablo Neruda brings poetry and passion to a drowsy Italian isle and a misfit postman, played with heartbreaking subtlety by the late Massimo Troisi. Another classic is Giuseppe Tornatore's Oscar-winning *Nuovo cinema paradiso* (Cinema Paradiso; 1988), a bittersweet tale about a director who returns to Sicily and rediscovers his true loves: the girl next door and the movies. In Silvio Sordini's *Pane e tulipani* (Bread and Tulips; 2000), a housewife left behind at a tour-bus pit stop runs away to Venice, where she befriends an anarchist florist, an eccentric masseuse and a suicidal Icelandic waiter – and gets pursued by an amateur detective. Equally contemporary is Ferzan Özpetek's *Mine vaganti* (Loose Cannons; 2010), a situation comedy about two gay brothers and their conservative Pugliese family.

Spaghetti Westerns

Emerging in the mid-1960s, Italian-style Westerns had no shortage of high-noon showdowns featuring flinty characters and Ennio Morricone's terminally catchy whistled tunes (*doodle-oodle-ooh, wah wah wah...*).

ITALY ON PAGE & SCREEN CINEMA

ZOMBIES

Crueller and bloodier than their American counterparts, Italian zombie films enjoy international cult status. One of the best is director Lucio Fulci's *Zombi 2* (aka Zombie Flesh Eaters; 1979). Fulci's other gore classics include *City of the Living Dead* (1980), *The Beyond* (1981) and *The House by the Cemetery* (1981).

THE GREAT DIRECTORS

➡ **Vittorio De Sica** Actor-turned-neorealist director whose Honorary Oscar for *Sciuscià* (Shoeshine; 1946) spawned the Academy's 'Best Foreign Film' category. Must-see: *Two Women* (1960)

➡ **Roberto Rossellini** Film critic François Truffaut called the influential neorealist the 'father of the French New Wave'. Must-see: *Roma, città aperta* (Rome: Open City; 1945)

➡ **Luchino Visconti** Famed for the Oscar-nominated *The Damned* (1969) and the lavish aesthetics of his films. Must-see: *Death in Venice* (1971)

➡ **Federico Fellini** One of history's most influential and awarded filmmakers, best known for fusing dreams and reality. Must-see: *8½* (1963)

➡ **Pier Paolo Pasolini** Controversial neorealist who championed the damned of postwar Italy. Must-see: *Mamma Roma* (1962)

➡ **Sergio Leone** King of spaghetti westerns and inventor of the extreme close-up in Westerns. Must-see: *C'era una volta il West (*Once Upon a Time in the West; 1968)

LOCATION! LOCATION!

Italy's cities, hills and coastlines set the scene for countless celluloid classics. Top billing goes to Rome, where Bernardo Bertolucci uses the Terme di Caracalla in the oedipal *La luna* (1979), Gregory Peck gives Audrey Hepburn a fright at the Bocca della Verità in William Wyler's *Roman Holiday* (1953), and Anita Ekberg cools off in the Trevi Fountain in Federico Fellini's *La dolce vita* (1960). Fellini's love affair with the Eternal City culminated in his silver-screen tribute, *Roma* (1972). More recent tributes include Woody Allen's romantic comedy *To Rome with Love* (2012) and Italian director Paolo Sorrentino's sumptuous, decadent *La grande bellezza* (2013).

Florence's Piazza della Signoria recalls James Ivory's *Room With a View* (1985). Further south, Siena's Piazza del Palio and Piazza della Paglietta stir fantasies of actor Daniel Craig – both featured in the 22nd James Bond instalment, *Quantum of Solace* (2008).

Venice enjoys a cameo in *The Talented Mr Ripley* (1999), in which Matt Damon and Gwyneth Paltrow also tan and toast on the Campanian islands of Procida and Ischia. Fans of *Il postino* will recognise Procida's pastel-hued Corricella, while on the mainland, Naples' elegant *palazzi* (mansions), fin-de-siècle cafes and tailors are flaunted in Gianluca Migliarotti's fashion documentary film *E poi c'è Napoli* (And Then There is Naples; 2014). In stark contrast is the cavernous landscape of Basilicata's Matera, which moonlights as Palestine in Mel Gibson's *Passion of the Christ* (2004).

Top of the directorial heap was Sergio Leone, whose Western debut *Per un pugno di dollari* (A Fistful of Dollars; 1964) helped launch a young Clint Eastwood's movie career. After Leone and Clintwood teamed up again in *Il buono, il brutto, il cattivo* (The Good, the Bad, and the Ugly; 1966), it was Henry Fonda's turn in Leone's *C'era una volta il West* (Once Upon a Time in the West; 1968), a story about a revenge-seeking widow.

Tragicomedies

Italy's best comedians pinpoint the exact spot where pathos intersects with the funny bone. A group of ageing pranksters turn on one another in Mario Monicelli's *Amici miei* (My Friends; 1975), a satire reflecting Italy's own postwar midlife crisis. Recent woes feed Massimiliano Bruno's biting *Viva l'Italia* (2012), its cast of corrupt politicians and nepotists cutting close to the nation's bone. Italy is slapped equally hard by Matteo Garrone's *Reality* (2012). Winner of the Grand Prix at the 2012 Cannes Film Festival, the darkly comic film revolves around a Neapolitan fishmonger desperately seeking fame through reality TV. Darker still is actor-director Roberto Benigni's Oscar-winning *La vita è bella* (Life is Beautiful; 1997), in which a father tries to protect his son from the brutalities of a Jewish concentration camp by pretending it's all a game. A more recent Oscar recipient is Paolo Sorrentino's *La grande bellezza* (The Great Beauty; 2013). Set in a decadent, champagne-fuelled Rome reminiscent of Federico Fellini's *La dolce vita*, the film revolves around Jep Gambardella, a greying, hedonistic bachelor haunted by lost love and memories of the past.

Shock & Horror

Sunny Italy's darkest dramas deliver style, suspense and falling bodies. In Michelangelo Antonioni's *Blow-Up* (1966), a swinging-'60s fashion photographer spies dark deeds unfolding in a photo of an elusive Vanessa Redgrave. Gruesome deeds unfold at a ballet school in Dario Argento's *Suspiria* (1977), while in Mario Monicelli's *Un borghese piccolo piccolo* (An Average Little Man; 1977), an ordinary man goes to extraordinary lengths for revenge. The latter stars Roman acting great Alberto Soldi in a standout example of a comedian nailing a serious role.

TOTÒ

A one-man 'Abbott and Costello', Antonio de Curtis (1898–1967), aka Totò, famously depicted Neapolitan *furbizia* (cunning). Appearing in over 100 films, including *Miseria e nobilità* (Misery & Nobility; 1954), his roles as a hustler living on nothing but his quick wits have guaranteed him cult status in Naples.

The Italian Table

You came for the food, right? Wise choice. One of the world's most revered cuisines, 'Italian food' is a handy umbrella term for the country's collection of regional cuisines. Despite this diversity, there is almost always one constant – whether you're tucking into a hearty *farro* (spelt) soup in a Tuscan *osteria* (casual tavern) or devouring a *pizza margherita* (tomato, basil and mozzarella pizza) in its home town, Naples, you'll be struck with culinary amnesia. Has anything tasted this good, ever? Probably not.

Tutti a Tavola

'Everyone to the table!' Traffic lights are merely suggestions and queues are fine ideas in theory, but this is one command every Italian heeds without question. To disobey would be unthinkable – what, you're going to eat your pasta cold? And insult the cook? Even anarchists wouldn't dream of it.

You never really know Italians until you've broken a crusty *pagnotta* (loaf of bread) with them – and once you've arrived in Italy, jump at any opportunity to do just that.

Morning Essentials

In Italy, *colazione* (breakfast) is a minimalist affair. Eggs, pancakes, ham, sausage, toast and orange juice are only likely to appear at weekend *brrrunch* (pronounced with the rolled Italian *r*), an American import popular at many trendy urban eateries. Expect to pay upwards of €20 to graze a buffet of hot dishes, cold cuts, pastries and fresh fruit, usually including your choice of coffee, juice or cocktail.

Italy's breakfast staple is *caffè* (coffee). Scalding-hot espresso, cappuccino (espresso with a goodly dollop of foamed milk) or *caffè latte* – the hot, milky espresso beverage Starbucks mistakenly shortened to *latte,* which will only get you a glass of milk in Italy. An alternative beverage is *orzo,* a slightly nutty, noncaffeinated roasted-barley beverage that looks like cocoa.

With a *tazza* (cup) in one hand, use the other for that most Italian of breakfast foods – a pastry. Some especially promising options include the following:

➜ **Cornetto** The Italian take on the French croissant is usually smaller, lighter, less buttery and slightly sweet, with an orange-rind glaze brushed on top. Fillings might include *cioccolato* (chocolate), *cioccolato bianco* (white chocolate), *crema* (custard) or varying flavours of *marmelata* (jam).

➜ **Crostata** The Italian breakfast tart with a dense, buttery crust is filled with your choice of fruit jam, such as *amarena* (sour cherry), *albicocca* (apricot) or *frutti di bosco* (wild berry). You may have to buy an entire tart instead of a single slice, but you won't be sorry.

➜ **Doughnuts** Chow down a *ciambella* (also called by its German name, *krapfen*), the classic fried-dough treat rolled in granulated sugar and sometimes filled with jam or custard. Join the line at kiosks and street fairs for *fritole,* fried dough studded with golden raisins and sprinkled with confectioners' sugar, and *zeppole*

Top Food & Wine Regions

Piedmont

Emilia-Romagna

Tuscany

Campania

Sicily

Tomatoes were not introduced to Italy until the 16th century, brought from the Americas. The word *pomodoro* literally means 'golden apple'.

(also called *bignè di San Giuseppe*), chewy doughnuts filled with ricotta or *zucca* (pumpkin), rolled in confectioners' sugar, and handed over in a paper cone to be devoured dangerously hot.

➡ **Viennoiserie** Italy's colonisation by the Austro-Hungarian Empire in the 19th century had its upside: a vast selection of sweet buns and other rich baked goods. Standouts include cream-filled brioches and *strudel di mele,* an Italian adaptation of the traditional Viennese *apfelstrudel.*

Lunch & Dinner

Italian food culture directly contradicts what we think we know of Italy. A nation prone to perpetual motion with Vespas, Ferraris and Bianchis pauses for *pranzo* (lunch) – hence the term *la pausa* to describe the midday break. In the cities, power-lunchers settle in at their favourite *ristoranti* and trattorias, while in smaller towns and villages, workers often head home for a two- to three-hour midday break, devouring a hot lunch and resting up before returning to work fortified by espresso.

Where *la pausa* has been scaled back to a scandalous hour and a half – barely enough time to get through the lines at the bank to pay bills and bolt some *pizza al taglio* (pizza by the slice) – *rosticcerie* (rotisseries) or *tavole calde* (literally 'hot tables') keep the harried sated with steamy, on-the-go options like roast chicken and *supplì* (fried risotto balls with a molten mozzarella centre). Bakeries and bars are also on hand with focaccia, *panini* and *tramezzini* (triangular, stacked sandwiches made with squishy white bread) providing a satisfying bite.

Traditionally, *cena* (dinner) is lunch's lighter sibling and cries of 'Oh, I can hardly eat anything tonight' are still common after a marathon weekend lunch. 'Maybe just a bowl of pasta, a salad, some cheese and fruit...'. Don't be fooled: even if you've been invited to someone's house for a 'light dinner', wine and elastic-waisted pants are always advisable.

But while your Italian hosts may insist you devour one more cream-filled *cannolo* (surely you don't have them back home...and even if you do, surely they're not as good?!), your waiter will usually show more mercy. Despite the Italians' 'more is more' attitude to food consumption, restaurant diners are rarely obliged to order both a *primo* and *secondo,* and antipasti and dessert are strictly optional.

That said, a lavish dinner at one of Italy's fine-dining hot spots, such as Modena's Osteria Francescana or Rome's Open Colonna, is a highlight few will want to skip.

Many top-ranked restaurants open only for dinner, with a set-price *degustazione* meal that leaves the major menu decisions to your chef and frees you up to concentrate on the noble quest to conquer four to six tasting courses. *Forza e coraggio!* (Strength and courage to you!)

For a comprehensive yet easy-to-use guide to Italian cooking, hunt down Marcella Hazan's award-winning *Essentials of Classic Italian Cooking* (1992), which incorporates two of her cult-status cookbooks.

APERITIVI: BUDGET FEASTING

Aperitivi are often described as a 'before-meal drink and light snacks'. Don't be fooled. Italian happy hour is a recession-friendly dinner disguised as a casual drink, accompanied by a buffet of antipasti, pasta salads, cold cuts and some hot dishes (this may include your fellow diners: *aperitivi* is prime time for hungry singles). You can methodically pillage buffets in cities including Milan, Turin, Rome, Naples and Palermo from about 5pm or 6pm to 8pm or 9pm for the price of a single drink – which crafty diners nurse for the duration – while Venetians enjoy *ombre* (half-glasses of wine) and bargain seafood *cicheti* (Venetian tapas). *Aperitivi* are wildly popular among the many young Italians who can't afford to eat dinner out, but still want a place to enjoy food with friends – leave it to Italy to find a way to put the glam into budget.

THE BIG FORK MANIFESTO
∙∙∙

The year is 1987. McDonald's has just begun expansion into Italy and lunch outside the bun seems to be fading into fond memory. Enter Carlo Petrini and a handful of other journalists from small-town Bra, Piedmont. Determined to buck the trend, these *neo-forchettoni* ('big forks', or foodies) created a manifesto. Published in the like-minded culinary magazine *Gambero Rosso*, they declared that a meal should be judged not by its speed, but by its pure pleasure.

The organisation they founded would soon become known worldwide as Slow Food (www.slowfood.com), and its mission to reconnect artisanal producers with enthusiastic, educated consumers has taken root with around 100,000 members in over 150 countries – not to mention Slow Food *agriturismi* (farm stay accommodation), restaurants, farms, wineries, cheesemakers and revitalised farmers' markets across Italy.

Held on even-numbered years in a former Fiat factory in Turin, Italy's top Slow Food event is the biennial **Salone del Gusto & Terre Madre** (www.salonedelgusto.com). Slow Food's global symposium, it features Slow Food producers, chefs, activists, restaurateurs, farmers, scholars, environmentalists and epicureans from around the world...not to mention the world's best finger food. Thankfully, odd years don't miss out on the epicurean enlightened either, with special events such as **Slow Fish** (http://slowfish.slowfood.it) in Genoa and **Cheese** (www.cheese.slowfood.it) in Bra.

Italian Menu 101

The *cameriere* (waiter) leads you to your table and hands you the menu. The scent of slow-cooked *ragù* (meat-and-tomato sauce) lingers in the air and your stomach rumbles in anticipation. Unfurl that *tovagliolo* (napkin), lick those lips and read on...

Antipasti (Appetisers)

The culinary equivalent of foreplay, antipasti are a good way to pique the appetite and sample a number of different dishes. Tantalising offerings on the antipasti menu may include the house bruschetta (grilled bread with a variety of toppings, from chopped tomato and garlic to black-truffle spread) or regional treats like *mozzarella di bufula* (buffalo mozzarella) or *salatini con burro d'acciughe* (pastry sticks with anchovy butter). Even if it's not on the menu, it's always worth requesting an *antipasto misto* (mixed antipasto), a platter of morsels including anything from *olive fritte* (fried olives) and *prosciutto e melone* (cured ham and cantaloupe) to *friarielli con peperoncino* (Neapolitan broccoli with chilli). At this stage, bread (and sometimes *grissini* – Turin-style breadsticks) are also deposited on the table as part of your €1 to €3 *pane e coperto* ('bread and cover' or table service).

> Less is more: most of the recipes in Ada Boni's classic *The Talisman Italian Cookbook* have fewer than 10 ingredients, yet the robust flavours of her osso bucco, polenta and wild duck with lentils are anything but simple.

Primo (First Course)

Starch is the star in Italian first courses, from pasta and gnocchi, to risotto and polenta. You may be surprised how generous the portions are – a *mezzo piatto* (half-portion) might do the trick for kids.

Primi menus usually include ostensibly vegetarian or vegan options, such as pasta *con pesto* – the classic Ligurian basil paste with *parmigiano reggiano* (Parmesan) and pine nuts – or Sicilian *alla Norma* (with basil, aubergine, ricotta and tomato), *risotto ai porcini* (risotto with pungent, earthy porcini mushrooms) or the extravagant *risotto al Barolo* (risotto with high-end Barolo wine, though actually any good dry red will do). But even if a dish sounds vegetarian in theory, before you order you may want to ask about the stock used in that risotto or polenta, or the ingredients in that suspiciously rich tomato sauce – there may be beef, ham or ground anchovies involved.

Carnivores will rejoice in such legendary dishes as pasta *all'amatriciana* (Roman pasta with a spicy tomato sauce, *pecorino* cheese and *guanciale*, or bacon-like pigs' cheeks), osso bucco *con risotto alla milanese* (Milanese veal shank and marrow melting into saffron risotto), Tuscan speciality *pappardelle alle cinghiale* (ribbon pasta with wild boar sauce) and northern favourite *polenta col ragù* (polenta with meat sauce). Near the coasts, look for seafood variations like *risotto al nero* (risotto cooked with black squid ink), *spaghetti alle vongole* (spaghetti with clam sauce) or *pasta ai frutti di mare* (pasta with seafood).

Secondo (Second Course)

Light lunchers usually call it a day after the *primo,* but *buongustai* (gourmands) pace themselves for meat, fish or *contorni* (side dishes, such as cooked vegetables) in the second course. These options may range from the outrageous *bistecca alla fiorentina*, a 3-inch-thick steak served on the bone in a puddle of juice, to more modest yet equally impressive *fritto misto di mare* (mixed fried seafood), *carciofi alla romana* (Roman artichokes stuffed with mint and garlic) or *pollo in tegame con barbe* (chicken casserole with salsify). A less inspiring option is *insalata mista* (mixed green salad), typically unadorned greens with vinegar and oil on the side – croutons, crumbled cheeses, nuts, dried fruit and other froufrou ingredients have no business in a classic Italian salad.

FIVE ICONIC FORMAGGI

Cheese fiends can expect soaring spirits (and cholesterol levels) in Italy, home to some of the world's most esteemed *formaggi* (cheeses). While there are hundreds of regional creations to nibble on, start with these prized heavyweights:

➡ **Parmigiano Reggiano** A grainy, nutty DOP cheese high in calcium and relatively low in fat. Produced in the northern provinces of Parma, Reggio Emilia, Modena, Bologna and Mantua, it's made using milk from free-range cows on a prized grass or hay diet. Parmigiano Reggiano is available *fresco* (aged less than 18 months), *vecchio* (aged 18 to 24 months) and *stravecchio* (aged 24 to 36 months). Beautiful with a bubbly Franciacorta or lighter, fruit-forward red.

➡ **Gorgonzola** Gloriously pungent, this washed-rind, blue-veined DOC cheese is produced in Lombardy and Piedmont. Made using whole cow's milk, it's generally aged three to four months. Varieties include the younger, sweeter *gorgonzola dolce* and the sharper, spicier *gorgonzola piccante* (also known as *stagionato* or *montagna*). To crank up the decadence, pair it with a sticky dessert wine.

➡ **Mozzarella** A chewy, silky cheese synonymous with Campania and Puglia and best eaten the day it's made. Top of the range is luscious, porcelain-white DOC *mozzarella di bufala* (buffalo mozzarella), produced using the whole milk of black water buffaloes. Variations include *burrata*, buffalo-milk mozzarella filled with cream. Mozzarella made using cow's milk is called *fior di latte.* Match all types with a dry, crisp white.

➡ **Provolone** Its roots in Basilicata, this semi-hard, wax-rind staple is now commonly produced in Lombardy and the Veneto. Like mozzarella, it's made using the *pasta filata* method, which sees the curd heated until it becomes stringy (*filata*). Aged two to three months, *provolone dolce* is milder and sweeter than the more piquant *provolone piccante*, itself aged for over four months. Pair with Pinot Grigio or a medium-bodied red.

➡ **Asiago** Hailing from the northern provinces of Vicenza, Trento, Padua and Treviso, pungent, full-flavoured Asiago DOP uses unpasteurised cow's milk from the Asiago plateau. Choose between milder, fresh *pressato* and strong, crumbly, aged *d'allevo*. The latter can be enjoyed at various stages of maturation, from sweeter *mezzano* (aged four to six months) and more bitter *vecchio* (aged over 10 months), to spicy *stravecchio* (aged for over two years). Wash it down with an earthy, tannin-heavy red.

Frutti e dolci

'*Siamo arrivati alla frutta*' ('We've arrived at the fruit') is an idiom roughly meaning 'we've hit rock bottom' – but hey, not until you've had one last tasty morsel. Your best bets on the fruit menu are local and seasonal. *Formaggi* (cheeses) are another option, but only diabetics or the French would go that route when there's room for *dolci* (sweets). *Biscotti* (twice-baked biscuits) made to dip in wine make for a delicious closure to the meal, but other great desserts include *zabaglione* (egg and marsala custard), *torta di ricotta e pera* (pear and ricotta cake), cream-stuffed profiteroles or *cannoli siciliani*, the ricotta-stuffed shell pastry immortalised thus in *The Godfather*: 'Leave the gun. Take the *cannoli*.'

Caffè (Coffee)

Most Italian mornings start with a creamy, frothy cappuccino (named for the Capuchin monks, with their brown hoods) which are rarely taken after about 11am and usually served not too hot. Otherwise it's espresso all the way, though you could ask for a tiny stain of milk in a *caffè macchiato* or a cheeky *caffè corretto* (espresso 'corrected' with a splash of grappa or brandy). On the hottest days of summer, a *granita di caffè* (coffee with shaved ice and whipped cream) is ideal.

The Vino Lowdown

A sit-down meal without *vino* (wine) in Italy is as unpalatable as pasta without sauce. Italian wines are considered among the most versatile and 'food friendly' in the world, specifically cultivated over the centuries to elevate regional cuisine. Here, wine is a consideration as essential as your choice of dinner date. Indeed, while the country's perfectly quaffable pilsner beers and occasional red ale pair well with roast meats, pizza and other quick eats, *vino* is considered appropriate for a proper meal – and since many wines cost less than a pint in Italy, this is not a question of price, but a matter of flavour.

Some Italian wines will be as familiar to you as old flames, including pizza-and-a-movie chianti or reliable summertime fling pinot grigio. But you'll also find some captivating Italian varietals and blends for which there is no translation (eg Brunello, Vermentino, Sciacchetrá), and intriguing Italian wines that have little in common with European and New World cousins of the same name, from merlot and pinot nero (aka pinot noir) to chardonnay.

Many visitors default to carafes of house reds or whites, which in Italy usually means young, fruit-forward reds to complement tomato sauces and chilled dry whites as seafood palate-cleansers. But with a little daring, you can pursue a wider range of options by the glass or half-bottle.

➡ **Sparkling wines** Franciacorta (Lombardy), *prosecco* (Veneto), Asti (aka Asti Spumante; Piedmont), Lambrusco (Emilia-Romagna)

➡ **Light, citrusy whites with grassy or floral notes** Vermentino (Sardinia), Orvieto (Umbria), Soave (Veneto), Tocai (Friuli)

➡ **Dry whites with aromatic herbal or mineral aspect** Cinque Terre (Liguria), Gavi (Piedmont), Falanghina (Campania), Est! Est!! Est!!! (Lazio)

➡ **Versatile, food-friendly reds with pleasant acidity** Barbera d'Alba (Piedmont), Montepulciano d'Abruzzo (Abruzzo), Valpolicella (Veneto), Chianti Classico (Tuscany), Bardolino (Lombardy)

➡ **Well-rounded reds, balancing fruit with earthy notes** Brunello di Montalcino (Tuscany), Refosco dal Pedulunco Rosso (Friuli), Dolcetto (Piedmont), Morellino di Scansano (Tuscany)

Don't believe the hype about espresso: one diminutive cup packs less of a caffeine wallop than a large cup of French-pressed or American-brewed coffee, and leaves drinkers less jittery.

Italy's oldest known wine is Chianti Classico, with favourable reviews dating from the 14th century and a growing region clearly defined by 1716.

➡ **Big, structured reds with velvety tannins** Amarone (Veneto), Barolo (Piedmont), Sagrantino di Montefalco secco (Umbria), Sassicaia and other 'super-Tuscan' blends (Tuscany)

➡ **Fortified and dessert wine** Sciacchetrá (Liguria), Colli Orientali del Friuli Picolit (Friuli), Vin Santo (Tuscany), Moscato d'Asti (Piedmont)

The average Italian adult consumes around 42L of wine per annum – a sobering figure compared with the 100L consumed on average back in the 1950s. Somewhat surprisingly, the world's top consumers of wine live in the Vatican City (74L per person).

Liquori (Liqueurs)

Failure to order a postprandial espresso may shock your server but you may yet save face by ordering a *digestivo* (digestive), such as a grappa (a potent grape-derived alcohol), *amaro* (a dark liqueur prepared from herbs) or *limoncello* (lemon liqueur). Fair warning though: Italian digestives can be an acquired taste and they pack a punch that might leave you snoring before *il conto* (the bill) arrives.

Festive Favourites

In Italy, culinary indulgence is the epicentre of any celebration and major holidays are defined by their specialities. Lent is heralded by Carnevale (Carnival), a time for *migliaccio di polenta* (a casserole of polenta, sausages, *pecorino* and *parmigiano reggiano*), *sanguinaccio* ('blood pudding' made with dark chocolate and cinnamon), *chiacchiere* (fried biscuits sprinkled with icing sugar) and Sicily's *mpagnuccata* (deep-fried dough tossed in soft caramel).

If you're here around 19 March (St Joseph's Feast Day), expect to eat *bignè di San Giuseppe* (fried doughnuts filled with cream or chocolate) in Rome, *zeppole* (fritters topped with lemon-scented cream, sour cherry and dusting sugar) in Naples and Bari, and *crispelle di riso* (citrus-scented rice fritters dipped in honey) in Sicily.

Lent specialities like Sicilian *quaresimali* (hard, light almond biscuits) give way to Easter binging with the obligatory lamb, *colomba* (dove-shaped cake) and *uove di pasqua* (foil-wrapped chocolate eggs with toy surprises inside). The dominant ingredient at this time is egg, also used to make traditional regional specialities like Genoa's *torta pasqualina* (pastry tart filled with ricotta, *parmigiano*, artichokes and hard-boiled eggs), Florence's *brodetto* (egg, lemon and bread broth) and Naples' legendary *pastiera* (shortcrust pastry tart filled with ricotta, cream, candied fruits and cereals flavoured with orange water).

Although some producers find these official Italian classifications unduly costly and creatively constraining, the DOCG (Denominazione di origine controllata e garantita) and DOC (Denominazione di origine controllata) designations are awarded to wines that meet regional quality-control standards.

At the other end of the calendar, Christmas means stuffed pasta, seafood dishes and one of Milan's greatest inventions: *panettone* (a yeasty, golden cake studded with raisins and dried fruit). Equally famous are Verona's simpler, raisin-free *pandoro* (a yeasty, star-shaped cake dusted with vanilla-flavoured icing sugar) and Siena's *panforte* (a chewy, flat cake made with candied fruits, nuts, chocolate, honey and spices). Further south, Neapolitans throw caution (and scales) to the wind with *raffioli* (sponge and marzipan biscuits), *struffoli* (tiny fried pastry balls dipped in honey and sprinkled with colourful candied sugar) and *pasta di mandorla* (marzipan), while their Sicilian cousins toast to the season with *cucciddatu* (ring-shaped cake made with dried figs, nuts, honey, vanilla, cloves, cinnamon and citrus fruits).

Of course, it's not all about religion. Some Italian holidays dispense with the spiritual premise and are all about the food. During spring, summer and early autumn, towns across Italy celebrate *sagre,* the festivals of local foods in season. You'll find a *sagra del tartufo* (truffles) in Umbria, *del pomodoro* (tomatoes) in Sicily and *del cipolle* (onions) in Puglia (wouldn't want to be downwind of that one). For a list of *sagre,* check out www.prodottitipici.com/sagre (in Italian).

Survival Guide

Directory A–Z

Accommodation

Accommodation in Italy can range from the sublime to the ridiculous with prices to match. The options are incredibly varied, from family-run *pensioni* and designer hotels to characterful B&Bs, serviced apartments, *agriturismi* (farm stays) and even *rifugi* (mountain huts) for weary mountain trekkers. Capturing the imagination even more are options spanning luxurious country villas and castles, tranquil convents and monasteries. When considering where to slumber, note the following tips:

➡ It pays to book ahead in high season, especially in popular coastal areas in the summer and popular ski resorts in the winter. In the urban centres you can usually find something if you leave it to luck, though reserving a room is essential during key events (such as the furniture and fashion fairs in Milan) when demand is extremely high.

➡ Accommodation rates can fluctuate enormously depending on the season, with Easter, summer and the Christmas/New Year period being the typical peak tourist times. Seasonality also varies according to location. Expect to pay top prices in the mountains during the ski season (December to March) or along the coast in summer (July and August). Conversely, summer in the parched cities can equal low season; in August especially, many city hotels charge as little as half price.

➡ Price also depends greatly on location. A bottom-end budget choice in Venice or Milan will set you back the price of a decent midrange option in, say, rural Campania. Where possible, we present the high-season rates for each accommodation option. Half-board equals breakfast and either lunch or dinner; full board includes breakfast, lunch and dinner.

➡ Some hotels, in particular the lower-end places, barely alter their prices throughout

the year. In low season there's no harm in bargaining for a discount, especially if you intend to stay for several days. It's also always worth checking for last-minute online deals on websites like www.lastminute.com, www.booking.com and www.hotelsitalyonline.com.

➡ Most hotels offer breakfast, though this can vary from bountiful buffets to more modest offerings of pastries, packaged yoghurt and fruit. The same is true of B&Bs, where morning food options can sometimes be little more than pre-packaged *cornetti* (croissants), biscuits, jam, coffee and tea.

➡ Hotels usually require that reservations be confirmed with a credit-card number. No-shows will be docked a night's accommodation.

BOOK YOUR STAY ONLINE

For more accommodation reviews by Lonely Planet authors, check out http://lonelyplanet.com/hotels/. You'll find independent reviews, as well as recommendations on the best places to stay. Best of all, you can book online.

B&Bs

B&Bs are a burgeoning sector of the Italian accommodation market and can be found throughout the country in both urban and rural settings. Options include everything from restored farmhouses, city *palazzi* (mansions) and seaside bungalows to rooms in family houses. Tariffs for a double room cover a wide range, from around €60 to €140.

Lists of B&Bs across the country are available online at the following sites:

BBItalia.it (www.bbitalia.it)

Bed-and-Breakfast.it (www. bed-and-breakfast.it)

Camping

Most campgrounds in Italy are major complexes with swimming pools, restaurants and supermarkets. They are graded according to a star system. Charges usually vary according to the season, peaking in July and August. Note that some places offer an all-inclusive price, while others charge separately for each person, tent, vehicle and/or campsite. Typical high-season prices range from around €10 to €20 per adult, up to €12 for children under 12, and from €5 to €25 for a site.

Italian campgrounds are generally set up for people travelling with their own vehicle, although some are accessible by public transport. In the major cities, grounds are often a long way from the historic centres. Most but not all have space for RVs. Tent campers are expected to bring their own equipment, although a few grounds offer tents for hire. Many also offer the alternative of bungalows or even simple, self-contained (self-catering) flats. In high season, some only offer deals for a week at a time.

Lists of campgrounds are available from local tourist offices or online at the following sites:

Campeggi.com (www.campeggi. com)

Camping.it (www.camping.it)

Italcamping.it (www.italcamping.it)

Canvas Holidays (www.canvasholidays.co.uk)

Eurocamp (www.eurocamp.co.uk)

Select Sites (www.select-site.com)

Convents & Monasteries

Some Italian convents and monasteries let out cells or rooms as a modest revenue-making exercise and happily take in tourists, while others only take in pilgrims or people who are on a spiritual retreat. Many impose a fairly early curfew, but prices tend to be quite reasonable.

A useful if ageing publication is Eileen Barish's *The Guide to Lodging in Italy's Monasteries*. A more recent book on the same subject is Charles M Shelton's *Beds and Blessings in Italy: A Guide to Religious Hospitality*. Other resources can assist you in your search:

MonasteryStays.com (www.monasterystays.com) A well-organised online booking centre for monastery and convent stays.

In Italy Online (www.initaly.com/agri/convents.htm) Offers a list of monastery and convent accommodation across the country, as well as a general holiday itinerary-planning service.

Chiesa di Santa Susana (www.santasusanna.org/coming ToRome/convents.html) This American Catholic church in Rome has searched out convent and monastery accommodation options around the country and posted a list on its website. Note that some places are just residential accommodation run by religious orders and not necessarily big on monastic atmosphere. The church doesn't handle bookings; to request a spot, you'll need to contact each individual institution directly.

Hostels

Ostelli per la gioventù (youth hostels) are run by the **Associazione Italiana Alberghi per la Gioventù** (AIG; ☑06 487 11 52; www.aighostels.it; Via Nicotera 1, Rome), affiliated with Hostelling International (www.hihostels.com). A valid HI card is required in all associated youth hostels in Italy. You can get this in your home country or directly at many hostels.

A full list of Italian hostels, with details of prices and locations, is available online or from hostels throughout the country. Nightly rates in basic dorms vary from around €15 to €40, which usually includes a buffet breakfast. You can often get lunch or dinner for an extra €10 or so. Many hostels also

---

THE SLUMBER TAX

Italy's *tassa di soggiorno* (accommodation tax) sees visitors charged an extra €1 to €7 per night 'room occupancy tax'.

Exactly how much you're charged may depend on several factors, including the type of accommodation (campground, guesthouse, hotel), a hotel's star rating and the number of people under your booking. Depending on their age and on the location of the accommodation, children may pay a discounted rate or be completely exempt from the tax.

Most of our listings do not include the hotel tax, although it's always a good idea to confirm whether taxes are included when booking.

FARMHOUSE HOLIDAYS

Live out your bucolic fantasies at one of Italy's growing number of *agriturismi* (farm stays). A long-booming industry in Tuscany and Umbria, farm stays are spreading across the country like freshly churned butter. While all *agriturismi* are required to grow at least one of their own products, the farm stays themselves range from rustic country houses with a handful of olive trees to elegant country estates with sparkling pools or fully functioning farms where guests can pitch in.

To find lists of *agriturismi*, ask at any tourist office or check online at one of these sites:

➡ **Agriturist** (www.agriturist.com)

➡ **Agriturismo.it** (www.agriturismo.it)

➡ **Agriturismo.net** (www.agriturismo.net)

➡ **Agriturismo.com** (www.agriturismo.com)

➡ **Agriturismo-Italia.net** (www.agriturismo-italia.net)

➡ **Agriturismo Vero** (www.agriturismovero.com)

offer singles and doubles (around €30/50) and family rooms.

A few AIG hostels still have a midday lockout period as well as a curfew of 11pm or midnight, although these restrictions are less common than in years past.

A growing contingent of independent hostels offers alternatives to HI hostels. Many are barely distinguishable from budget hotels. One of many hostel websites is www.hostelworld.com.

Hotels & Pensioni

While the difference between an *albergo* (hotel) and a *pensione* is often minimal, a *pensione* will generally be of one- to three-star quality while an *albergo* can be awarded up to five stars. *Locande* (inns) long fell into much the same category as *pensioni*, but the term has become a trendy one in some parts and reveals little about the quality of a place. *Affittacamere* are rooms for rent in private houses. They are generally simple affairs.

Quality can vary enormously and the official star system gives limited clues. One-star hotels/*pensioni*

tend to be basic and usually do not offer private bathrooms. Two-star places are similar but rooms will generally have a private bathroom. Three-star options usually offer reasonable standards. Four- and five-star hotels offer facilities such as room service, laundry and dry-cleaning.

Prices are highest in major tourist destinations. They also tend to be higher in northern Italy. A *camera singola* (single room) costs from €30. A *camera doppia* (twin beds) or *camera matrimoniale* (double room with a double bed) will cost from around €50.

Tourist offices usually have booklets with local accommodation listings. Many hotels are also signing up with (steadily proliferating) online accommodation-booking services. You could start your search here:

All Hotels in Italy (www.hotelsitalyonline.com)

Hotels web.it (www.hotelsweb.it)

In Italia (www.initalia.it)

Mountain Huts

The network of *rifugi* in the Alps, Apennines and other mountains is usually only open from June to late September. While some are little more than rudimentary shelters, many *rifugi* are more like Alpine hostels. Accommodation is generally in dormitories but some of the larger refuges have doubles. Many *rifugi* also offer guests hot meals and/or communal cooking facilities. Though mattresses, blankets and duvets are usually provided, most *rifugi* will require you to bring your own sleeping bag or travel sheet. Some places offer travel sheets for hire or purchase.

The price per person (which typically includes breakfast) ranges from €20 to €30 depending on the quality of the *rifugio* (it's more for a double room). A hearty post-walk single-dish dinner will set you back another €10 to €15.

Rifugi are marked on good walking maps. Those close to chair lifts and cable-car stations are usually expensive and crowded. Others are at high altitude and involve hours of hard walking. It is important to book in advance. Additional information can be obtained from the local tourist offices.

The Club Alpino Italiano (www.cai.it) owns and runs many of the mountain huts. Members of organisations such as the New Zealand Alpine Club and British Mountaineering Council can enjoy discounted rates for accommodation and meals. See the International Mountaineering and Climbing Federation website (www.theuiaa.org) for details.

Rental Accommodation

Finding rental accommodation in the major cities can be difficult and time-consuming; rental agencies (local and foreign) can assist, for a fee. Rental rates are higher for

OFFBEAT ACCOMMODATION

Looking for something out of the ordinary? Italy offers a plethora of sleeping options that you won't find anywhere else in the world.

➡ Down near Italy's heel, rent a *trullo*, one of the characteristic whitewashed conical houses of southern Puglia.

➡ Ancient *sassi* (cave dwellings) have found new life as boutique hotels in otherworldly Matera, a Unesco World Heritage–listed town in the southern region of Basilicata.

➡ Cruise northern Italy on the *Avemaria*, a hotel barge that sails from Mantua to Venice over seven leisurely days, with cultural and foodie pit stops, and the chance to cycle between locations.

➡ In Friuli Venezia Giulia, experience village life in an *albergo diffuso*, an award-winning concept in which self-contained (self-catering) apartments in neighbouring houses are rented to guests through a centralised hotel-style reception.

➡ In Naples, spend a night or two slumbering in the aristocratic *palazzo* of a Bourbon bishop. Now the Decumani Hotel de Charme, the property comes complete with a sumptuous baroque salon.

short-term leases. A studio or one-bedroom apartment anywhere near the centre of Rome will cost around €900 per month and it is usually necessary to pay a deposit (generally one month in advance). Expect to spend similar amounts in cities such as Florence, Milan, Naples and Venice.

Apartments and villas for rent are listed in local publications such as Rome's twice-weekly Porta Portese (www.portaportese.it) and the fortnightly Wanted in Rome (www.wantedinrome.com). Another option is to share an apartment; check out university noticeboards for student flats with vacant rooms. Tourist offices in resort areas (coastal towns in summer, ski towns in winter) also maintain lists of apartments and villas for rent.

If you're looking for an apartment, studio or room to rent for a short stay (such as a week or two) check the

websites of the following agencies:

Homelidays (www.homelidays.com) A huge number of rental accommodations of every description throughout Italy.

Holiday Lettings (www.holiday lettings.co.uk) Apartments and villas all over the country.

Interhome (www.interhome.co.uk) Almost 4000 holiday houses and apartments available in weekly blocks throughout Italy.

Villas

Numerous agencies offer villa accommodation in southern Italy – often in splendid rural locations not far from enchanting medieval towns or Mediterranean beaches. Operators include the following.

Cuendet (www.cuendet.com) One of the old hands in this business; offers properties across the country.

Ilios Travel (www.iliostravel.com) UK-based company with villas

and apartments in Campania and Sicily.

Long Travel (www.long-travel.co.uk) Specialises in Puglia, Sicily, Sardinia and other southern areas.

Think Sicily (www.thethinking traveller.com/thinksicily) Strictly Sicilian properties.

Customs Regulations

Within the European Union you are entitled to tax-free prices on fragrances, cosmetics and skincare; photographic and electrical goods; fashion and accessories; and gifts, jewellery and souvenirs where they are available and if there are no longer any allowance restrictions on these tax free items.

On leaving the EU, non-EU residents can reclaim value-added tax (VAT) on expensive purchases.

Duty free alowances are:

spirits & liqueurs	1L
wine	4L (or 2L of fortified wine)
perfume	60mL
cigarettes	200
other goods	up to a value of €300/430 (travelling by land/sea)

Discount Cards

Free admission to many galleries and cultural sites is available to those under 18 and over 65 years old; and visitors aged between 18 and 25 often qualify for a discount. In some cases, these discounts only apply to EU citizens.

Some cities or regions offer their own discount passes, such as Roma Pass (3 days €36), which offers free use of public transport and free or reduced admission to Rome's museums.

In many places around Italy, you can also save money by purchasing a *biglietto cumulativo*, a ticket that allows admission to a number of associated sights for less than the combined cost of separate admission fees.

Electricity

Electricity in Italy conforms to the European standard of 220V to 230V, with a frequency of 50Hz. Wall outlets typically accommodate plugs with two or three round pins (the latter grounded, the former not).

230V/50Hz

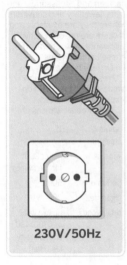

230V/50Hz

Embassies & Consulates

For foreign embassies and consulates in Italy not listed here, look under 'Ambasciate' or 'Consolati' in the telephone directory. Some countries also run honorary consulates in other cities.

Australian Embassy/Consulate Rome (☑emergencies 800 877790, info 06 85 27 21; www.italy.embassy.gov.au; Via Antonio Bosio 5, Rome; ⊙9am-5pm Mon-Fri); **Milan** (☑02 776 741; Via Borgogna 2, Milan; ⓂSan Babila)

Austrian Embassy/Consulate Rome (☑06 844 01 41; www.aussenministerium.at/rom; Via Pergolesi 3, Rome); **Milan**

(☑02 78 37 43; www.aussen ministerium.at/mailandgk; Piazza del Liberty 8/4, Milan)

Canadian Embassy/Consulate Rome (☑06 85 44 41; www.canadainternational.gc.ca/italy-italie; Via Zara 30, Rome); **Milan** (☑02 6269 4238; Piazza Cavour 3)

French Embassy/Consulate Rome (☑06 68 60 11; www.ambafrance-it.org; Piazza Farnese 67, Rome); **Milan** (☑02 655 91 41; www.amba-france-it.org/-Consulat-de-Milan-; Via della Moscova 12, Milan; ⓂTurati); **Naples** (☑081 598 07 11; www.am bafrance-it.org; Via Francesco Crispi 86, Naples; ⓂAmedeo)

German Embassy/Consulate Rome (☑06 49 21 31; www.rom.diplo.de; Via San Martino della Battaglia 4, Rome); **Milan** (☑02 623 11 01; www.mailand.diplo.de; Via Solferino 40, Milan; ⓂMoscova)

Irish Embassy Rome (☑06 585 23 81; www.ambasciata-irlanda.it; Villa Spada, Via Giacomo Medici 1, Rome)

Japanese Embassy/Consulate Rome (☑06 48 79 91; www.it.emb-japan.go.jp; Via Quintino Sella 60, Rome); **Milan** (☑02 624 11 41; www.milano.it.emb-japan.go.jp; Via Cesare Mangili 2/4, Milan; ⓂTurati)

Dutch Embassy/Consulate Rome (☑06 3228 6001; www.olanda.it; Via Michele Mercati 8, Rome); **Milan** (☑02 485 58 41; Via Gaetano Donizetti 20)

New Zealand Embassy/Consulate Rome (☑06 853 75 01; www.nzembassy.com/italy; Via Clitunno 44, Rome); **Milan**

YOUTH, STUDENT & TEACHER CARDS

CARD	WEBSITE	COST	ELIGIBILITY
European Youth Card (Carta Giovani)	www.eyca.org; www.cartagiovani.it	€10	under 30yr
International Student Identity Card (ISIC)	www.isic.org	US$25, UK£12, €13	full-time student
International Teacher Identity Card (ITIC)		US$25, UK£12, €10–18	full-time teacher
International Youth Travel Card (IYTC)		US$25, UK£12, €13	under 26yr

(☎02 7217 0001; www.nz embassy.com/italy; Via Terraggio 17, Milan; ⓂCadorna)

Slovenian Embassy Rome
(☎06 8091 4310; www.rim. veleposlanistvo.si; Via Leonardo Pisano 10, Rome)

Swiss Embassy/Consulate Rome (☎06 80 95 71; www. eda.admin.ch/roma; Via Barnaba Oriani 61, Rome); **Milan** (☎02 777 91 61; www.eda. admin.ch/milano; Via Palestro 2, Milan; ⓂTurati)

UK Embassy/Consulate Rome (☎06 4220 0001; ukinitaly. fco.gov.uk; Via XX Settembre 80a, Rome); **Milan** (☎06 4220 2431; Via San Paolo 7, Milan; ⓂSan Babila); **Naples** (☎081 423 89 11; ukinitaly.fco.gov.uk; Via dei Mille 40, Naples)

US Embassy/Consulate Rome (☎06 4 67 41; italy.usembassy. gov; Via Vittorio Veneto 121, Rome); **Florence** (☎055 26 69 51; italy.usembassy. gov; Lungarno Vespucci 38, Florence); **Milan** (☎02 29 03 51; milan.usconsulate.gov; Via Principe Amedeo 2/10; ⓂTurati); **Naples** (☎081 583 81 11; italy.usembassy. gov; Piazza della Repubblica 2, Naples; ⓂMergellina)

Food

For detailed information on eating in Italy see Eat & Drink Like a Local (p39) and The Italian Table (p931).

Gay & Lesbian Travellers

Homosexuality is legal (over the age of 16) and even widely accepted, but Italy is notably conservative in its attitudes, largely keeping in line with those of the Vatican. Overt displays of affection by homosexual couples can attract a negative response, especially in smaller towns.

There are gay venues in Rome, Milan and Bologna, and a handful in places such as Florence and Naples. Some coastal towns and

---

---

resorts (such as the Tuscan town of Viareggio or Taormina in Sicily) have much more action in summer.

Online resources include the following Italian-language websites:

Arcigay (www.arcigay.it) Bologna-based national organisation for the LGBTI community.

Circolo Mario Mieli (www.mario mieli.org) Rome-based cultural centre that organises debates, cultural events and social functions, including Gay Pride.

Coordinamento Lesbiche Italiano (CLR; www.clrbp.it) The national organisation for lesbians, holding regular conferences and literary evenings.

Gay.it (www.gay.it) Website featuring LGBT news, feature articles and gossip.

Pride (www.prideonline.it) National monthly magazine of art, music, politics and gay culture.

Health

Required Vaccinations

No jabs are required to travel to Italy, though the World Health Organization (WHO) recommends that all travellers should be covered for diphtheria, tetanus, the measles, mumps, rubella, polio and hepatitis B.

Health Insurance

Italy has a public health system that is legally bound to provide emergency care to everyone. EU nationals are entitled to reduced-cost, sometimes free, medical care with a European Health Insurance Card (EHIC), available from your home health authority; non-EU citizens should take out medical insurance.

If you do need health insurance, make sure you get a policy that covers you for the worst possible scenario, such as an accident requiring an emergency flight home. Find out in advance if your insurance plan will make payments directly to providers or reimburse you later for overseas health expenditures.

It's also worth finding out if there is a reciprocal arrangement between your country and Italy. If so, you may be covered for essential medical treatment and some subsidised medications while in Italy. Australia, for instance, has such an agreement: carry your Medicare card.

Availability of Health Care

Health care is readily available throughout Italy, but standards can

PRACTICALITIES

⇒ **Smoking** Banned in enclosed public spaces, which includes restaurants, bars, shops and public transport.

⇒ **Newspapers** The major national dailies are centre-left; try Rome-based *La Repubblica*, and the liberal-conservative, Milan-based *Corriere della Sera*.

⇒ **Radio** Tune in to Vatican Radio (www.radiovaticana.org; 93.3 FM and 105 FM in the Rome area; in Italian, English and other languages) for a rundown of what the pope is up to; or state-owned Italian RAI-1, RAI-2 and RAI-3 (www.rai.it), which broadcast all over the country and abroad. Commercial stations such as Rome's Radio Centro Suono (www.centrosuono.com) and Radio Città Futura (www.radiocittafutura.it), Milan-based left-wing Radio Popolare (www.radiopopolare.it) and Naples' Radio Kiss Kiss (www.kisskissnapoli.it) are all good for contemporary music.

⇒ **TV** Channels include state-run RAI-1, RAI-2 and RAI-3 (www.rai.it). The main commercial stations (mostly run by Silvio Berlusconi's Mediaset company) include Canale 5 (www.mediaset.it/canale5), Italia 1 (www.mediaset.it/italia1), Rete 4 (www.mediaset.it/rete4) and La 7 (www.la7.it).

⇒ **Weights & measurements** Metric

vary significantly. Public hospitals tend to be less impressive the further south you travel. Pharmacists can give you valuable advice and sell over-the-counter medication for minor illnesses. They can also advise you when more-specialised help is required and point you in the right direction. In major cities you are likely to find English-speaking doctors or a translator service available.

Pharmacies generally keep the same hours as other shops, closing at night and on Sundays. However, a handful remain open on a rotation basis *(farmacie di turno)* for emergency purposes. These are usually listed in newspapers. Closed pharmacies display a list of the nearest ones open.

If you need an ambulance anywhere in Italy, call ☑118. For emergency treatment, head straight to the *pronto soccorso* (casualty) section of a public hospital, where you can also get emergency dental treatment.

Insurance

A travel-insurance policy to cover theft, loss and medical problems is a very good

idea. It may also cover you for cancellation or delays to your travel arrangements. Paying for your ticket with a credit card can often provide limited travel accident insurance and you may be able to reclaim the payment if the operator doesn't deliver. Ask your credit-card company what it will cover.

Worldwide travel insurance is available at www.lonelyplanet.com/travel-insurance. You can buy, extend and claim online anytime – even if you're already on the road.

Internet Access

⇒ Numerous Italian cities and towns offer public wi-fi hotspots, including Rome, Bologna and Venice. To use them, you will generally need to register online using a credit card or an Italian mobile number. An easier option (no need for a local mobile number) is to head to a cafe or bar offering free wi-fi.

⇒ Most hotels, B&Bs, hostels and *agriturismi* offer free wi-fi to guests, though signals can vary in quality. There will usually be at least one fixed computer for guest use.

Language Courses

Italian language courses are run by private schools and universities throughout Italy. Rome and Florence are teeming with schools, while most other cities and major towns have at least one. For a list of language schools around the country, see Saena Iulia (www.saenaiulia.it); click on 'Italian resources' followed by 'Schools in Italy'.

Università per Stranieri di Perugia (www.unistrapg.it) The well-established and reasonably priced programs make this Italy's most famous language school for foreigners. Aside from standard language courses, the school also runs themed, practical courses ranging from art history and ceramics to Italian cuisine and opera.

Università per Stranieri di Siena (www.unistrasi.it) A similarly well-regarded program in one of Italy's most beautiful medieval cities.

Italian Foreign Ministry (www.esteri.it) Publishes a list on its website of the 83 worldwide branches of the Istituto Italiano di Cultura (IIC), a government-sponsored organisation promoting Italian culture and language. An excellent resource for studying Italian before you leave or finding out more about language learning opportunities in Italy. Locations include Australia (Melbourne and Sydney), the UK (London and Edinburgh), Ireland (Dublin), Canada (Toronto and Montreal), and the USA (Los Angeles, San Francisco, Chicago, New York and Washington, DC). Click on 'Foreign Policy', then 'Culture' and 'Italian Cultural Institutes'.

Legal Matters

Italy is generally a safe country to travel in. The average tourist will only have a brush with the law if robbed by a bag-snatcher or pickpocket.

Police

If you do run into trouble in Italy, you're likely to end up dealing with the *polizia statale* or the *carabinieri*. The former wear powder-blue trousers with a fuchsia stripe and a navy blue jacket, the latter wear black uniforms with a red stripe and drive dark-blue cars with a red stripe.

To contact the police in an emergency, dial ☑113.

Drugs & Alcohol

➡ If you're caught with what the police deem to be a dealable quantity of hard or soft drugs, you risk prison sentences of between six and 20 years.

➡ Possession for personal use may result in a fine, depending on the type of drug and quantity possessed.

➡ The legal limit for blood-alcohol when driving is 0.05% and random breath tests do occur.

Your Rights

➡ You should be given verbal and written notice of the charges laid against you within 24 hours by arresting officers.

➡ You have no right to a phone call upon arrest.

➡ The prosecutor must apply to a magistrate for you to be held in preventive custody awaiting trial (depending on the seriousness of the offence) within 48 hours of arrest.

➡ You have the right not to respond to questions without the presence of a lawyer.

➡ If the magistrate orders preventive custody, you have the right to then contest this within the following 10 days.

Maps

The city maps provided by Lonely Planet, combined with the good, free local maps available at most Italian tourist offices, will be sufficient for many travellers. For more-specialised maps, browse the good selection at national bookshop chain Feltrinelli (www.lafeltrinelli. it), or consult the websites listed here.

Touring Club Italiano (www. touringclub.com) Italy's largest map publisher operates shops around Italy and publishes decent 1:500,000 and 1:200,000 maps of Italy (€11.90 and €19.90 respectively), plus a series of 15 regional maps at 1:200,000 (€7.90 each) and an exhaustive series of walking guides with maps, co-published with the Club Alpino Italiano (CAI).

Tabacco (www.tabaccoeditrice. com) Publishes an excellent 1:25,000 scale series of walking maps, covering an area from Bormio in the west to the Slovenia border in the east.

Kompass (www.kompass-italia. it) Publishes 1:25,000 and 1:50,000 scale hiking maps of various parts of Italy, plus a nice series of 1:70,000 cycling maps.

Stanfords (www.stanfords. co.uk) Excellent UK-based shop that stocks many useful maps, including cycling maps.

Omni Resources (www.omni map.com) US-based online retailer with an impressive selection of Italian maps, including cycling and hiking maps.

Money

Italy's currency is the euro. The seven euro notes come in denominations of €500, €200, €100, €50, €20, €10 and €5. The eight euro coins are in denominations of €2 and €1, and 50, 20, 10, five, two and one cents.

ATMs & Credit Cards

➡ ATMs (known as 'Bancomat') are widely available throughout Italy and most will accept cards tied into the Visa, MasterCard, Cirrus and Maestro systems.

➡ Credit cards are good for payment in most hotels, restaurants, shops, supermarkets and tollbooths. Major cards such as Visa, MasterCard, Eurocard, Cirrus and Eurocheques are widely

ITALIAN POLICE ORGANISATIONS

Polizia statale (state police)	Thefts, visa extensions and permits
Carabinieri (military police)	General crime, public order and drug enforcement (often overlapping with the *polizia statale*)
Vigili urbani (local traffic police)	Parking tickets, towed cars
Guardia di finanza	Tax evasion, drug smuggling
Corpo forestale	Environmental protection

accepted. Amex is also recognised, though less common.

➡ Let your bank know when you are going abroad, in case they block your card when payments from unusual locations appear.

➡ Check any charges with your bank. Most banks charge a foreign exchange fee (usually around 1% to 3%) as well as a transaction charge of around 1%.
If your card is lost, stolen or swallowed by an ATM, you can telephone toll-free to have an immediate stop put on its use:

Amex ☑800 928391

Diners Club ☑800 393939

MasterCard ☑800 789525

Visa ☑800 819014

Changing Money
You can change money in banks, at post offices or in a *cambio* (exchange office). Post offices and banks tend to offer the best rates; exchange offices keep longer hours, but watch for high commissions and inferior rates.

Have your passport or some form of photo ID available when exchanging money.

Taxes & Refunds
A value-added tax of 22%, known as IVA (Imposta di Valore Aggiunto), is slapped onto just about everything in Italy. If you are a non-EU resident and spend more than €155 (€154.94 to be exact!) on a purchase, you can claim a refund when you leave. The refund only applies to purchases from affiliated retail outlets that display a 'Tax Free' sign. When you make your purchase, ask for a tax-refund voucher, to be filled in with the date of your purchase and its value. When you leave the EU, get this voucher stamped at customs and take it to the nearest tax-refund counter where you'll get an immediate refund, either in cash or charged your credit card. For more information, see www. taxrefund.it.

Tipping
Tipping is not generally expected nor demanded in Italy as it is in some other countries. This said, a discretionary tip for good service is appreciated in some circumstances. Use the following table as a guide.

Restaurant	10-15%, if service charge (*servizio*) not included
Bar	€0.10–0.20 if drinking at bar, 10% for table service
Top-end hotel	€4, for porter, maid, room service
Taxi	Round up to the nearest euro

Post
Le Poste (www.poste.it), Italy's postal system, is reasonably reliable, though parcels do occasionally go missing.

Francobolli (stamps) are available at post offices and authorised tobacconists (look for the big white-on-black 'T' sign). Since letters often need to be weighed, what you get at the tobacconist for international airmail will occasionally be an approximation of the proper rate. Tobacconists keep regular shop hours.

Most people use *posta prioritaria* (priority mail), Italy's

OPENING HOURS

BUSINESS TYPE	GENERAL HOURS	NOTES
Banks	8.30am-1.30pm & 3.30-4.30pm Mon-Fri	Exchange offices usually keep longer hours.
Cafes and Bars	7.30am-8pm	Some venues remain open until 1am or 2am.
Central post offices	8am-7pm Mon-Fri, 8.30am-noon Sat	Smaller branch post offices often close at 2pm on weekdays
Clubs	10pm-4am or 5am	May open earlier if they have eateries on the premises; things don't get seriously shaking until after midnight.
Restaurants	noon-2.30pm & 7.30-11pm or midnight	Sometimes even later in summer and in the south; kitchen often shuts an hour earlier than final closing time; most places close at least one day a week
Shops	9am-1pm & 3.30-7.30pm (or 4-8pm) Mon-Sat	In larger cities, department stores and supermarkets may stay open at lunchtime or on Sundays

most efficient mail service, guaranteed to deliver letters sent to Europe within three working days and to the rest of the world within four to nine working days. Letters up to 20g cost €0.95 within Europe, €2.30 to Africa, Asia and the Americas, and €3 to Australia and New Zealand. Letters weighing 21g to 50g cost €3 within Europe, €4 to Africa, Asia and the Americas, and €5 to Australia and New Zealand.

Public Holidays

Most Italians take their annual holiday in August, with the busiest period occurring around 15 August, known locally as Ferragosto. As a result, many businesses and shops close for at least part of that month. Settimana Santa (Easter Holy Week) is another busy holiday period for Italians.

National public holidays include the following:

Capodanno (New Year's Day) 1 January

Epifania (Epiphany) 6 January

Pasquetta (Easter Monday) March/April

Giorno della Liberazione (Liberation Day) 25 April

Festa del Lavoro (Labour Day) 1 May

Festa della Repubblica (Republic Day) 2 June

Ferragosto (Feast of the Assumption) 15 August

Festa di Ognisanti (All Saints' Day) 1 November

Festa dell'Immacolata Concezione (Feast of the Immaculate Conception) 8 December

Natale (Christmas Day) 25 December

Festa di Santo Stefano (Boxing Day) 26 December

Telephone
Directory Enquiries

National and international phone numbers can be requested at ☎1254 (or online at 1254.virgilio.it).

Domestic Calls

➡ Italian telephone area codes all begin with 0 and consist of up to four digits. The area code is followed by anything from four to eight digits. The area code is an integral part of the telephone number and must always be dialled, even when calling from next door.

➡ Mobile-phone numbers begin with a three-digit prefix such as 330.

➡ Toll-free (free-phone) numbers are known as *numeri verdi* and usually start with 800.

➡ Nongeographical numbers start with 840, 841, 848, 892, 899, 163, 166 or 199.

➡ Some six-digit national rate numbers are also in use (such as those for Alitalia, rail and postal information). As elsewhere in Europe, Italians choose from a host of providers of phone plans and rates, making it difficult to make generalisations about costs.

International Calls

➡ To call Italy from abroad, call your international access number, then Italy's country code (39) and then the area code of the location you want, including the leading 0.

➡ Avoid making international calls from a hotel, as rates are high.

➡ The cheapest options are free or low-cost computer programs/smartphone apps such as Skype and Viber.

➡ Another cheap option is to call from a private call centre, or from a payphone with an international calling card. These are commonly sold at newsstands and tobacconists.

➡ To call abroad from Italy dial 00, then the country and area codes, followed by the telephone number.

➡ To make a reverse-charge (collect) international call from a public telephone, dial ☎170. All phone operators speak English.

Mobile Phones

➡ Italian mobile phones operate on the GSM 900/1800 network, which is compatible with the rest of Europe and Australia but not always with the North American GSM or CDMA systems – check with your service provider.

➡ Most smartphones are multiband, meaning that they are compatible with a variety of international networks. Before bringing your own phone to Italy, check with your service provider to make sure it is compatible, and beware of calls being routed internationally (very expensive for a 'local' call).

➡ If you have a GSM dual-, tri- or quad-band phone that you can unlock (check with your service provider), it can cost as little as €10 to activate a prepaid (*prepagato*) SIM card in Italy. TIM (Telecom Italia Mobile; www.tim.it), Wind (www.wind.it) and Vodafone (www.vodafone.it) all offer SIM cards and have retail outlets across town. All SIM cards must be registered in Italy, so make sure you have a passport or ID card with you when you buy one.

➡ You can easily top up your Italian SIM with a recharge card (*ricarica*), available from most tobacconists, some bars, supermarkets and banks.

Payphones & Phonecards

You can still find public payphones around Italy. Most work and most take telephone cards (*schede telefoniche*), although you'll still find some that accept coins or credit cards. You can buy phonecards (€5, €10 or €20) at post offices, tobacconists and newsstands.

Time

➤ Italy is one hour ahead of GMT. When it is noon in London, it is 1pm in Italy.

➤ Daylight-saving time (when clocks are moved forward one hour) starts on the last Sunday in March and ends on the last Sunday in October.

➤ Italy uses a 24-hour clock.

Tourist Information

Four tiers of tourist office exist: local, provincial, regional and national.

Local & Provincial Tourist Offices

Despite their different names, provincial and local offices offer similar services. All deal directly with the public and most will respond to written and telephone requests for information. Staff can usually provide a city map, lists of hotels and information on the major sights. In larger towns and major tourist areas, English is generally spoken, along with other languages depending on the region (for example, German in Alto Adige, French in Valle d'Aosta).

Main offices are generally open Monday to Friday; some also open on weekends, especially in urban areas or during peak summer season. Affiliated information booths (at train stations and airports, for example) may keep slightly different hours.

Regional Tourist Authorities

Regional offices are generally more concerned with planning, budgeting, marketing and promotion than with offering a public information service. However, they still maintain some useful websites. In some cases you'll need to look for the Tourism or Turismo link within the regional site.

➤ **Abruzzo** (www.abruzzoturismo.it)

➤ **Basilicata** (www.aptbasilicata.it)

➤ **Calabria** (www.turiscalabria.it)

➤ **Campania** (www.incampania.com)

➤ **Emilia-Romagna** (www.emiliaromagnaturismo.it)

➤ **Friuli Venezia Giulia** (www.turismo.fvg.it)

➤ **Lazio** (www.visitlazio.com)

➤ **Le Marche** (www.le-marche.com)

➤ **Liguria** (www.turismoinliguria.it)

➤ **Lombardy** (www.turismo.regione.lombardia.it)

➤ **Molise** (www.regione.molise.it/turismo)

➤ **Piedmont** (www.piemonteitalia.eu)

➤ **Puglia** (www.viaggiareinpuglia.it)

➤ **Sardinia** (www.sardegnaturismo.it)

➤ **Sicily** (www.regione.sicilia.it/turismo)

➤ **Trentino-Alto Adige** (www.visittrentino.it)

➤ **Tuscany** (www.turismo.intoscana.it)

➤ **Umbria** (www.regione.umbria.it)

➤ **Valle d'Aosta** (www.lovevda.it)

➤ **Veneto** (www.veneto.eu)

Tourist Offices Abroad

The Italian National Tourist Office (www.enit.it) maintains offices in 23 cities on five continents. Contact information for all offices can be found on its website.

Travellers with Disabilities

Italy is not an easy country for travellers with disabilities and getting around can be a problem for wheelchair users. Even a short journey in a city or town can become a major expedition if cobblestone streets have to be negotiated. Although many buildings have lifts, they are not always wide enough for wheelchairs. Not an awful lot has been done to make life for the hearing or vision impaired easier.

The Italian National Tourist Office in your country may be able to provide advice on Italian associations for travellers with disabilities and information on what help is available.

If travelling by train, ring the national helpline (☎199 303060 to arrange assistance (6.45am to 9.30pm daily). Airline companies should be able to arrange

TOURIST OFFICES

OFFICE NAME	DESCRIPTION	MAIN FOCUS
Azienda di Promozione Turistica (APT)	Main provincial tourist office	Information on the town and its surrounding province
Azienda Autonoma di Soggiorno e Turismo (AAST) or Informazione e Assistenza ai Turisti (IAT)	Local tourist office in larger towns and cities	Town-specific information only (bus routes, museum opening times etc)
Pro Loco	Local tourist office in smaller towns and villages	Similar to AAST and IAT

assistance at airports if you notify them of your needs in advance. Alternatively, contact ADR Assistance (www.adrassistance.it) for assistance at Fiumicino or Ciampino airports. Some taxis are equipped to carry passengers in wheelchairs; ask for a taxi for a *sedia a rotelle* (wheelchair).

Italy's official tourism website (www.italia.it) offers a number of links for travellers with disabilities. Another online resource is Lonely Planet's Travel for All community on Google+, worth joining for information sharing and networking.

Accessible Italy (www.accessibleitaly.com) A San Marino–based company that specialises in holiday services for people with disabilities. This is the best first port of call.

Sage Traveling (www.sagetraveling.com) A US-based agency offering advice and tailor-made tours to assist mobility-impaired travellers in Europe.

Visas

➡ Italy is one of the 15 signatories of the Schengen Convention, an agreement whereby participating countries abolished customs checks at common borders. EU citizens do not need a Schengen tourist visa to enter Italy. Nationals of some other countries, including Australia, Canada, Israel, Japan, New Zealand, Switzerland and the USA, do not need a tourist visa for stays of up to 90 days. To check the visa requirements for your country, see www.schengenvisainfo.com/tourist-schengen-visa.

➡ All non-EU and non-Schengen nationals entering Italy for more than 90 days or for any reason other than tourism (such as study or work) may need a specific visa. See vistoperitalia.esteri.it or contact an Italian consulate for details.

GOVERNMENT TRAVEL ADVICE

The following government websites offer up-to-date travel advisories.

➡ **Australian Department of Foreign Affairs** (www.smartraveller.gov.au)

➡ **British Foreign & Commonwealth Office** (www.gov.uk/foreign-travel-advice)

➡ **Canadian Department of Foreign Affairs** (travel.gc.ca/travelling/health-safety)

➡ **New Zealand Ministry of Foreign Affairs & Trade** (www.safetravel.govt.nz)

➡ **US Department of State** (travel.state.gov)

Permesso di Soggiorno

➡ Non-EU citizens staying at the same address for more than one week are supposed to report to the police station to receive a *permesso di soggiorno* (a permit to remain in the country). Tourists staying in hotels are not required to do this.

➡ A *permesso di soggiorno* only really becomes a necessity if you plan to study, work (legally) or live in Italy. The exact requirements are always subject to change. Updated requirements can be found at www.poliziadistato.it.

➡ EU citizens do not require a *permesso di soggiorno*.

Volunteering

Concordia International Volunteer Projects (www.concordiavolunteers.org.uk) Short-term community-based projects covering the environment, archaeology, the arts and more. You might find yourself working as a volunteer on a restoration project or in a nature reserve.

European Youth Portal (europa.eu/youth) Has various links suggesting volunteering options across Europe.

World Wide Opportunities on Organic Farms (www.wwoof.it) For a membership fee of €35 this organisation provides a list of farmers and growers looking for volunteer workers.

Women Travellers

Italy is not a dangerous country for women to travel in. However, in some parts of the country women travelling alone may be subjected to a high level of unwanted attention. Eye-to-eye contact is the norm in Italy's daily flirtatious interplay. Eye contact can become outright staring the further south you travel.

Lone women may find it difficult to remain alone. In many places, local Lotharios will try it on with exasperating insistence. Foreign women in particular might be subjected to male attention in tourist towns like Florence and more generally in the south. If ignoring them doesn't work, politely tell your interlocutors you're waiting for your *marito* (husband) or *fidanzato* (boyfriend) and, if necessary, walk away. In most cases, passersby will assist you if you are in distress.

On crowded buses some men may attempt to grope female passengers. Either keep your back to the wall or make a loud fuss if someone tries to touch you. A loud '*Che schifo!*' (How disgusting!) will usually do the trick. You can report incidents to the police, who are required to press charges.

Transport

GETTING THERE & AWAY

A plethora of airlines link Italy with the rest of the world, and cut-rate carriers have significantly driven down the cost of flights from other European countries. Excellent rail and bus connections, especially with northern Italy, offer efficient overland transport, while car and passenger ferries operate to ports throughout the Mediterranean.

Entering the Country

➡ European Union and Swiss citizens can travel to Italy with their national identity card alone. All other nationalities must have a valid passport and may be required to fill out a landing card (at airports).

➡ By law you are supposed to have your passport or ID card with you at all times. You'll need one of these documents for police registration every time you check into a hotel.

➡ In theory there are no passport checks at land crossings from neighbouring countries, but random customs controls do occasionally still take place between Italy and Switzerland.

Air

Airports & Airlines

Italy's main intercontinental gateways are Rome's **Leonardo da Vinci airport** (www.adr.it/fiumicino) and Milan's **Malpensa airport** (www.milanomalpensa-airport.com). Both are served by non-stop flights from around the world. Venice's **Marco Polo airport** (www.veniceairport.it) is also served by a handful of intercontinental flights.

Dozens of international airlines compete with the country's revamped national carrier, Alitalia, rated a 3-star airline by UK aviation research company Skytrax. If you're flying from Africa or Oceania, you'll generally need to change planes at least once en route to Italy.

Intra-European flights serve plenty of other Italian cities; the leading mainstream carriers include Alitalia, Air France, British Airways, Lufthansa and KLM.

Cut-rate airlines, led by Ryanair and easyJet, fly from a growing number of European cities to more than two dozen Italian destinations, typically landing in smaller airports such as Rome's **Ciampino** (www.adr.it/ciampino).

Land

There are plenty of options for entering Italy by train, bus or private vehicle.

CLIMATE CHANGE & TRAVEL

Every form of transport that relies on carbon-based fuel generates CO_2, the main cause of human-induced climate change. Modern travel is dependent on planes, which may use less fuel per kilometre per person than most cars but travel much greater distances. The altitude at which aircraft emit gases (including CO_2) and particles also contributes to their climate change impact. Many websites offer 'carbon calculators' that allow people to estimate the carbon emissions generated by their journey and, for those who wish to do so, to offset the impact of the greenhouse gases emitted with contributions to portfolios of climate-friendly initiatives throughout the world. Lonely Planet offsets the carbon footprint of all staff and author travel.

Border Crossings

Aside from the coast roads linking Italy with France and Slovenia, border crossings into Italy mostly involve tunnels through the Alps (open year-round) or mountain passes (seasonally closed or requiring snow chains). The list below outlines the major points of entry.

Austria From Innsbruck to Bolzano via A22/E45 (Brenner Pass); Villach to Tarvisio via A23/E55

France From Nice to Ventimiglia via A10/E80; Modane to Turin via A32/E70 (Fréjus Tunnel); Chamonix to Courmayeur via A5/E25 (Mont Blanc Tunnel)

Slovenia From Sežana to Trieste via SR58/E70

Switzerland From Martigny to Aosta via SS27/E27 (Grand St Bernard Tunnel); Lugano to Como via A9/E35

Bus

Buses are the cheapest overland option to Italy, but services are less frequent, less comfortable and significantly slower than the train.

Eurolines (www.eurolines.com) is a consortium of coach companies with offices throughout Europe. Italy-bound buses head to Milan, Rome, Florence, Venice and other Italian cities. It offers a bus pass valid for 15/30 days

that costs €375/490 (reduced €315/405) in high season and €225/340 (reduced €195/265) in low season.

This pass allows unlimited travel between 53 European cities, including Milan, Venice, Florence and Rome.

Car & Motorcycle
FROM CONTINENTAL EUROPE

➡ Every vehicle travelling across an international border should display a nationality plate of its country of registration.

➡ Always carry proof of vehicle ownership and evidence of third-party insurance. If driving an EU-registered vehicle, your home country insurance is sufficient. Ask your insurer for a European Accident Statement (EAS) form, which can simplify matters in the event of an accident. The form can also be downloaded online at http://cartraveldocs.com/european-accident-statement.

➡ A European breakdown assistance policy is a good investment and can be obtained through the Automobile Club d'Italia.

➡ Italy's scenic roads are tailor-made for motorcycle touring, and motorcyclists

swarm into the country every summer. With a motorcycle you rarely have to book ahead for ferries and can enter restricted-traffic areas in cities. Crash helmets and a motorcycle licence are compulsory.

➡ The US-based **Beach's Motorcycle Adventures** (www.bmca.com) offers a number of two-week tours from April to October, with destinations including the Alps, Tuscany and Umbria, Sicily and Sardinia. For campervan and motorhome hire, check **IdeaMerge** (www.ideamerge.com).

FROM THE UK
You can take your car to Italy, via France, by ferry or via the Channel Tunnel (www.eurotunnel.com). The latter runs 49 daily crossings (35 minutes) between Folkestone and Calais in the high season.

For breakdown assistance, both the **AA** (www.theaa.com) and the **RAC** (www.rac.co.uk) offer comprehensive cover in Europe.

Train
Regular trains on two western lines connect Italy with France (one along the coast and the other from Turin into the French Alps). Trains from Milan head north into Swit-

---

DIRECT TRAINS TO ITALY FROM CONTINENTAL EUROPE

FROM	TO	FREQUENCY	DURATION (HR)	COST (€)
Geneva	Milan	four daily	4	79
	Venice	one daily	7	118
Munich	Florence	one nightly	9	113
	Rome	one nightly	12¼	145
	Venice	one to two daily/ one nightly	6¼/8¾	91/118
Paris	Milan	two to three daily/ one nightly	7½/10	113/95
	Turin	three daily	5½-6	98
	Venice	one nightly	13½	115
Vienna	Milan	one nightly	14	78
	Rome	one nightly	14	99
Zurich	Milan	seven daily	4	75

zerland and on towards the Benelux countries. Further east, two main lines head for the main cities in Central and Eastern Europe. Those crossing the Brenner Pass go to Innsbruck, Stuttgart and Munich. Those crossing at Tarvisio proceed to Vienna, Salzburg and Prague. The main international train line to Slovenia crosses near Trieste.

Depending on distances covered, rail can be highly competitive with air travel. Those travelling from neighbouring countries to northern Italy will find it is frequently more comfortable, less expensive and only marginally more time-consuming than flying.

Those travelling longer distances (say, from London, Spain, northern Germany or Eastern Europe) will doubtless find flying cheaper and quicker. Bear in mind, however, that the train is a much greener way to go – a trip by rail can contribute up to 10 times fewer carbon dioxide emissions per person than the same trip by air.

FROM CONTINENTAL EUROPE

➡ The comprehensive European Rail Timetable (UK£15.99), updated monthly, is available for purchase online at www.europeanrailtimetable.co.uk, as well as at a handful of bookshops in the UK and continental Europe (see the website for details).

➡ Reservations on international trains to/from Italy are always advisable, and sometimes compulsory.

INTERNATIONAL FERRY ROUTES FROM ITALY

DESTINATION COUNTRY	DESTINATION PORT(S)	ITALIAN PORT(S)	COMPANY
Albania	Durrës	Bari	Ventouris
	Durrës	Bari, Ancona, Trieste	Adria Ferries
Croatia	Dubrovnik	Bari	Jadrolinija
	Hvar	Pescara	SNAV
	Split	Ancona, Pescara	SNAV
	Split, Zadar	Ancona	Jadrolinija
	Vela Luka	Pescara	SNAV
	Umag, Poreč, Rovinj, Pula, Rabac, Mali Lošinj	Venice	Venezia Lines
France (Corsica)	Bastia	Livorno, Genoa	Moby Lines
	Bonifacio	Santa Teresa di Gallura	Moby Lines
Greece	Igoumenitsa, Patras	Brindisi	Grimaldi Lines
	Corfu, Igoumenitsa, Patras	Bari	Superfast, Anek Lines
	Igoumenitsa, Patras	Ancona	Superfast, Anek Lines
	Igoumenitsa, Patras	Venice	Superfast, Anek Lines
	Igoumenitsa, Patras	Trieste, Ancona	Minoan Lines
Malta	Valletta	Pozzallo, Catania	Virtu Ferries
Montenegro	Bar	Bari	Montenegro Lines
Morocco	Tangier	Genoa	GNV
	Tangier	Livorno	Grimaldi Lines
Spain	Barcelona	Genoa	GNV
	Barcelona	Civitavecchia, Livorno, Savona, Porto Torres	Grimaldi Lines
Tunisia	Tunis	Genoa, Civitaveccchia, Palermo	GNV
	Tunis	Genoa	Tirrenia
	Tunis	Civitavecchia, Palermo, Salerno	Grimaldi Lines

➡ Some international services include transport for private cars.

➡ Consider taking long journeys overnight, as the supplemental fare for a sleeper costs substantially less than Italian hotels.

FROM THE UK

➡ High-velocity passenger train Eurostar (www.eurostar.com) travels between London and Paris, or London and Brussels. Alternatively, you can get a train ticket that includes crossing the Channel by ferry.

➡ For the latest fare information on journeys to Italy, contact International Rail (www.internationalrail.com).

Sea

Multiple ferry companies connect Italy with countries throughout the Mediterranean. Many routes only operate in summer, when ticket prices also rise. Prices for vehicles vary according to their size.

The helpful website www.directferries.co.uk allows you to search routes and compare prices between the numerous international ferry companies servicing Italy. Another useful resource for ferries from Italy to Greece is www.ferries.gr.

International ferry companies that serve Italy:

Adria Ferries (www.adriaferries.com)

Anek Lines (www.anekitalia.com)

GNV (Grandi Navi Veloci; www.gnv.it)

Grimaldi Lines (www.grimaldi-lines.com)

Jadrolinija (www.jadrolinija.hr)

Moby Lines (ww.moby.it)

Montenegro Lines (www.montenegrolines.net)

SNAV (www.snav.it)

Superfast (www.superfast.com)

Tirrenia (www.tirrenia.it)

Venezia Lines (ww.venezialines.com)

Ventouris (www.ventouris.gr)

Virtu Ferries (www.virtuferries.com)

GETTING AROUND

Italy's network of train, bus, ferry and domestic air transport allows you to reach most destinations efficiently and relatively affordably.

With your own vehicle, you'll enjoy greater freedom, but *benzina* (petrol) and autostrada (motorway) tolls are expensive and Italian drivers have a style all their own. For many, the stress of driving and parking in urban areas may outweigh the delights of puttering about the countryside. One solution is to take public transport between large cities and rent a car only to reach more-remote rural destinations.

Air

Italy offers an extensive network of internal flights. The privatised national airline, Alitalia, is the main domestic carrier, with numerous low-cost airlines also operating across the country. Useful search engines for comparing multiple carriers' fares (including those of cut-price airlines) are www.skyscanner.com, www.kayak.com and www.azfly.it. Airport taxes are factored into the price of your ticket.

Alitalia (☎89 20 10; www.alitalia.com)

Blu-express (☎06 9895 6666; www.blu-express.com)

easyJet (www.easyjet.com)

Etihad Regional (☎06 8997 0422; www.etihadregional.com)

Meridiana (☎89 29 28; www.meridiana.it)

Ryanair (☎895 5895509; www.ryanair.com)

Volotea (☎895 8954404; www.volotea.com)

Bicycle

Cycling is very popular in Italy. The following tips will help ensure a pedal-happy trip:

➡ If bringing your own bike, you'll need to disassemble and pack it for the journey, and may need to pay an airline surcharge.

➡ Make sure to bring tools, spare parts, a helmet, lights and a secure bike lock.

➡ Bikes are prohibited on Italian autostradas (motorways).

➡ Bicycles can be wheeled onto regional trains displaying the bicycle logo. Simply purchase a separate bicycle ticket, valid for 24 hours (€3.50). Certain international trains, listed on Trenitalia's *'Bike on Board'* page, also allow transport of assembled bicycles for €12, paid on board. Bikes dismantled and stored in a bag can be taken for free, even on night trains.

➡ Most ferries also allow free bicycle passage.

➡ In the UK, **Cyclists' Touring Club** (CTC; www.ctc.org.uk) can help you plan your tour or organise a guided tour. Membership costs £41.50 for adults, £27 for seniors and £18 for under-18s.

➡ Bikes are available for hire in most Italian towns. City bikes start at €10/50 per day/week; mountain bikes a bit more. A growing number of Italian hotels offer free bikes for guests.

Boat

Craft *Navi* (large ferries) service Sicily and Sardinia, while *traghetti* (smaller ferries) and *aliscafi* (hydrofoils) service the smaller islands. Most ferries carry vehicles; hydrofoils do not.

ROAD DISTANCES (KM)

	Bari	Bologna	Florence	Genoa	Milan	Naples	Palermo	Perugia	Reggio di Calabria	Rome	Siena	Trento	Trieste	Turin	Venice
Bologna	681														
Florence	784	106													
Genoa	996	285	268												
Milan	899	218	324	156											
Naples	322	640	534	758	858										
Palermo	734	1415	1345	1569	1633	811									
Perugia	612	270	164	432	488	408	1219								
Reggio di Calabria	490	1171	1101	1325	1389	567	272	816							
Rome	482	408	302	526	626	232	1043	170	664						
Siena	714	176	70	296	394	464	1275	103	867	232					
Trento	892	233	339	341	218	874	1626	459	1222	641	375				
Trieste	995	308	414	336	420	948	1689	543	1445	715	484	279			
Turin	1019	338	442	174	139	932	1743	545	1307	702	460	349	551		
Venice	806	269	265	387	284	899	799	394	1296	567	335	167	165	415	
Verona	808	141	247	282	164	781	1534	377	1139	549	293	97	250	295	120

Note

Distances between Palermo and mainland towns do not take into account the ferry from Reggio di Calabria to Messina. Add an extra hour to your journey time to allow for this crossing

Routes Main embarkation points for Sicily and Sardinia are Genoa, Livorno, Civitavecchia and Naples. Ferries for Sicily also leave from Villa San Giovanni and Reggio Calabria. Main arrival points in Sardinia are Cagliari, Arbatax, Olbia and Porto Torres; in Sicily they're Palermo, Catania, Trapani and Messina.

Timetables and tickets Comprehensive website Direct Ferries (www.directferries.co.uk) allows you to search routes, compare prices and book tickets for ferry routes in Italy.

Overnight ferries Travellers can book a two- to four-person cabin or a *poltrona*, which is an airline-type armchair. Deck class (which allows you to sit/sleep in lounge areas or on deck) is available only on some ferries.

Bus

Routes Everything from meandering local routes to fast, reliable InterCity connections provided by numerous bus companies.

Timetables and tickets Available on bus company websites and from local tourist offices. Tickets are generally competitively priced with the train and often the only way to get to smaller towns. In larger cities most of the InterCity bus companies have ticket offices or sell tickets through agencies. In villages and even some good-sized towns, tickets are sold in bars or on the bus.

Advance booking Generally not required, but advisable for overnight or long-haul trips in high season.

Car & Motorcycle

Italy's extensive network of roads span numerous categories. The main ones include:

➡ **Autostradas** – An extensive, privatised network of motorways, represented on road signs by a white 'A' followed by a number on a green background. The main north–south link is the A1. Also known as the Autostrada del Sole ('Motorway of the Sun'), it extends from Milan to Naples. The main link from Naples south to Reggio di Calabria is the A3. There are tolls on most motorways, payable by cash or credit card as you exit.

➡ *Strade statali* (state highways) – Represented on maps by 'S' or 'SS'. Vary from toll-free, four-lane highways to two-lane main roads. The latter can be extremely slow, especially in mountainous regions.

➡ *Strade regionali* (regional highways connecting small villages) – Coded 'SR' or 'R'.

➡ *Strade provinciali* (provincial highways) – Coded 'SP' or 'P'.

➡ *Strade locali* – Often not even paved or mapped. For information in English about distances, driving times and fuel costs, see http://en.mappy.com. Additional information, including traffic conditions and toll costs, is available at www.autostrade.it.

Automobile Associations

The **Automobile Club d'Italia** (ACI; ☑803 116, from a foreign mobile 800 116800; www.aci.it) is a driver's best resource in Italy. Foreigners do not have to join to get 24-hour roadside emergency service but instead pay a per-incident fee.

Driving Licences

All EU driving licences are recognised in Italy. Travellers from other countries should obtain an International Driving Permit (IDP) through their national automobile association.

Fuel & Spare Parts

Italy's petrol prices vary from one service station (*benzinaio, stazione di servizio*) to another. At the time of writing, lead-free gasoline (*senza piombo;* 95 octane) was averaging €1.57 per litre, with diesel (*gasolio*) costing €1.37 per litre.

Spare parts are available at many garages or via the 24-hour ACI motorist assistance number ☑803 116 (or ☑800 116800 if calling with a non-Italian mobile phone account).

Hire

CAR

➡ Pre-booking via the internet often costs less than hiring a car in Italy. Online booking agency Rentalcars.com (www.rentalcars.com) compares the rates of numerous car-rental companies.

➡ Renters must generally be aged 21 or over, with a credit card and home-country driving licence or IDP.

➡ Consider hiring a small car, which will reduce your fuel expenses and help you negotiate narrow city lanes and tight parking spaces.

➡ Check with your credit-card company to see if it

offers a Collision Damage Waiver, which covers you for additional damage if you use that card to pay for the car.

The following companies have pick-up locations throughout Italy:

Auto Europe (www.autoeurope.com)

Avis (www.avis.com)

Budget (www.budget.com)

Europcar (www.europcar.com)

Hertz (www.hertz.it)

Italy by Car (www.italybycar.it)

Maggiore (www.maggiore.it)

Sixt (www.sixt.com)

MOTORCYCLE

Agencies throughout Italy rent motorbikes, ranging from small scooters to larger touring bikes. Prices start at around €35/150 per day/week for a 50cc scooter, or upwards of €80/400 per day/week for a 650cc motorcycle.

Road Rules

➡ Cars drive on the right side of the road and overtake on the left. Unless otherwise indicated, always give way to cars entering an intersection from a road on your right.

➡ Seatbelt use (front and rear) is required by law; violators are subject to an on-the-spot fine.

➡ Helmets are required on all two-wheeled vehicles.

➡ Day and night, it is compulsory to drive with

your headlights on outside built-up areas.

➡ It's obligatory to carry a warning triangle and fluorescent waistcoat in case of breakdown. Recommended accessories include a first-aid kit, spare-bulb kit and fire extinguisher.

➡ A licence is required to ride a scooter – a car licence will do for bikes up to 125cc; for anything over 125cc you'll need a motorcycle licence.

➡ Motorbikes can enter most restricted traffic areas in Italian cities, and traffic police generally turn a blind eye to motorcycles or scooters parked on footpaths.

➡ The blood alcohol limit is 0.05%; for drivers under 21 and those who have had their licence for less than three years, it's zero.

Unless otherwise indicated, speed limits are as follows:

➡ 130km/h on autostradas

➡ 110km/h on all main, non-urban roads

➡ 90km/h on secondary, non-urban roads

➡ 50km/h in built-up areas

Local Transport

Major cities all have good transport systems, including bus and underground-train networks. In Venice, the main public transport option is *vaporetti* (small passenger ferries).

TRAINS: HIGH-VELOCITY VS INTERCITY

FROM	TO	HIGH-VELOCITY DURATION (HR)	PRICE (€)	INTERCITY DURATION (HR)	PRICE (€)
Florence	Bologna	35min	24	1	12
Milan	Rome	3	79	7	38
Rome	Naples	1¼	39	2¼	26
Turin	Naples	5¾	99	9¾	74.50
Venice	Florence	2	45	2¾	28.50

INTERRAIL & EURAIL PASSES

Generally speaking, you'll need to cover a lot of ground to make a rail pass worthwhile. Before buying, consider where you intend to travel and compare the price of a rail pass to the cost of individual tickets on the Trenitalia website (www.trenitalia.com).

InterRail (www.interrail.eu) passes, available online and at most major stations and student-travel outlets, are for people who have been a resident in Europe for more than six months. A Global Pass encompassing 30 countries comes in five versions, ranging from five days' travel within a 10-day period to a full month's unlimited travel. There are four price categories: youth (12 to 25), adult (26 to 59), senior (60+) and family (one adult and up to two children), with different prices for 1st and 2nd class. The InterRail one-country pass for Italy can be used for three, four, six or eight days in one month and does not offer senior discounts. Cardholders get discounts on travel in the country where they purchase the ticket. See the website for full price details.

Eurail (www.eurail.com) passes, available for non-European residents, are good for travel in 28 European countries (not including the UK). They can be purchased online or from travel agencies outside of Europe.

The original Eurail pass, now known as the **Global Pass**, is valid for from five days' travel within a 10-day period to three months of unlimited travel.

Youth aged 12 to 25 are eligible for a 2nd-class pass; all others must buy the more expensive 1st-class pass (the family ticket allows up to two children aged 0 to 11 to travel free when accompanied by a paying adult).

Eurail offers several alternatives to the traditional Global Pass:

➡ The **Select Pass** allows five to 15 days of travel within a two-month period in four bordering countries of your choice.

➡ The two-country **Regional Pass** (France/Italy, Spain/Italy or Greece/Italy) allows four to 10 days of travel within a two-month period.

➡ The **One Country Pass** allows three to eight days of travel in Italy within a two-month period.

Bus & Metro

➡ Extensive *metropolitane* (metros) exist in Rome, Milan, Naples and Turin, with smaller metros in Genoa and Catania. The space-age *Minimetrò* in Perugia connects the train station with the city centre.

➡ Cities and towns of any size have an efficient *urbano* (urban) and *extraurbano* (suburban) bus system. Services are generally limited on Sundays and holidays.

➡ Purchase bus and metro tickets before boarding and validate them once on board. Passengers with unvalidated tickets are subject to a fine (between €50 and €110). Buy tickets from a *tabaccaio* (tobacconist's shop), newsstands, ticket booths or dispensing machines at bus and metro stations. Tickets usually cost around €1.20 to €2. Many cities offer good-value 24-hour or daily tourist tickets.

Taxi

➡ You can catch a taxi at the ranks outside most train and bus stations, or simply telephone for a radio taxi. Radio taxi meters start running from when you've called rather than when you're picked up.

➡ Charges vary somewhat from one region to another. Most short city journeys cost between €10 and €15. Generally, no more than four people are allowed in one taxi.

Train

Trains in Italy are convenient and relatively cheap compared with other European countries. The better train categories are fast and comfortable.

Trenitalia (☎892021; www.trenitalia.com) is the national train system that runs most services. Its privately owned competitor **Italo** (☎060708; www.italotreno.it) runs high-velocity trains on two lines, one between Turin and Salerno, and one between Venice and Salerno.

Train tickets must be stamped in the green machines (usually found at the head of rail platforms) just before boarding. Failure to do so usually results in fines.

Italy operates several types of trains:

Regionale/Interregionale Slow and cheap, stopping at all or most stations.

InterCity (IC) Faster services operating between major cities. Their international counterparts are called Eurocity (EC).

Alta Velocità (AV) State-of-the-art, high-velocity trains, including Frecciarossa, Frecciargento, Frecciabianca and Italo trains. with speeds of up to 300km/hr and connections to the major cities. More expensive than InterCity express trains, but journey times are cut by almost half.

Classes & Costs

Prices vary according to the class of service, time of travel and how far in advance you book. Most Italian trains have 1st- and 2nd-class seating; a 1st-class ticket typically costs from a third to half more than 2nd-class.

Travel on Trenitalia's InterCity and Alta Velocità (Frecciarossa, Frecciargento, Frecciabianca) trains means paying a supplement, included in the ticket price, determined by the distance you are travelling. If you have a standard ticket for a slower train and end up hopping on an IC train, you'll have to pay the difference on board. (You can only board an Alta Velocità train if you have a booking, so the problem does not arise in those cases.)

Reservations

➡ Reservations are obligatory on AV trains. On other services they're not and, outside of peak holiday periods, you should be fine without them.

➡ Reservations can be made on the Trenitalia and Italo websites, at railway station counters and self-service ticketing machines, or through travel agents.

➡ Both Trenitalia and Italo offer a variety of advance purchase discounts. Basically, the earlier you book, the greater the saving. Discounted tickets are limited, and refunds and changes are highly restricted. For all ticket options and prices, see the Trenitalia and Italo websites.

Train Passes

Trenitalia offers various discount passes, including the Carta Verde for youth and Carta d'Argento for seniors, but these are mainly useful for residents or long-term visitors, as they only pay for themselves with regular use over an extended period.

More interesting for short-term visitors are Eurail and InterRail passes.

Language

Standard Italian is taught and spoken throughout Italy. Regional dialects are an important part of identity in many parts of the country, but you'll have no trouble being understood anywhere if you stick to standard Italian, which we've also used in this chapter.

The sounds used in spoken Italian can all be found in English. If you read our coloured pronunciation guides as if they were English, you'll be understood. The stressed syllables are indicated with italics. Note that ai is pronounced as in 'aisle', ay as in 'say', ow as in 'how', dz as the 'ds' in 'lids', and that r is a strong and rolled sound. Keep in mind that Italian consonants can have a stronger, emphatic pronunciation – if the consonant is written as a double letter, it should be pronounced a little stronger, eg *sonno son*·no (sleep) versus *sono so*·no (I am).

BASICS

Hello.	Buongiorno.	bwon·jor·no
Goodbye.	Arrivederci.	a·ree·ve·der·chee
Yes./No.	Sì./No.	see/no
Excuse me.	Mi scusi. (pol)	mee skoo·zee
	Scusami. (inf)	skoo·za·mee
Sorry.	Mi dispiace.	mee dees·pya·che
Please.	Per favore.	per fa·vo·re
Thank you.	Grazie.	gra·tsye
You're welcome.	Prego.	pre·go

How are you?
Come sta/stai? (pol/inf)	ko·me sta/stai

Fine. And you?
Bene. E lei/tu? (pol/inf)	be·ne e lay/too

What's your name?
Come si chiama? (pol)	ko·me see kya·ma
Come ti chiami? (inf)	ko·me tee kya·mee

My name is ...
Mi chiamo ...	mee kya·mo ...

Do you speak English?
Parla/Parli inglese? (pol/inf)	par·la/par·lee een·gle·ze

I don't understand.
Non capisco.	non ka·pee·sko

ACCOMMODATION

campsite	campeggio	kam·pe·jo
guesthouse	pensione	pen·syo·ne
hotel	albergo	al·ber·go
youth hostel	ostello della gioventù	os·te·lo de·la jo·ven·too
Do you have a ... room?	Avete una camera ...?	a·ve·te oo·na ka·me·ra ...
double	doppia con letto matrimoniale	do·pya kon le·to ma·tree·mo·nya·le
single	singola	seen·go·la
How much is it per ...?	Quanto costa per ...?	kwan·to kos·ta per ...
night	una notte	oo·na no·te
person	persona	per·so·na
air-con	aria condizionata	a·rya kon·dee·tsyo·na·ta
bathroom	bagno	ba·nyo
window	finestra	fee·nes·tra

DIRECTIONS

Where's ...?
Dov'è ...?   do·ve ...

What's the address?
Qual'è l'indirizzo?   kwa·le leen·dee·ree·tso

Could you please write it down?
Può scriverlo,   pwo skree·ver·lo
per favore?   per fa·vo·re

Can you show me (on the map)?
Può mostrarmi   pwo mos·trar·mee
(sulla pianta)?   (soo·la pyan·ta)

EATING & DRINKING

What would you recommend?
Cosa mi consiglia?   ko·za mee kon·see·lya

What's the local speciality?
Qual'è la specialità   kwa·le la spe·cha·lee·ta
di questa regione?   dee kwe·sta re·jo·ne

Cheers!
Salute!   sa·loo·te

That was delicious!
Era squisito!   e·ra skwee·zee·to

Please bring the bill.
Mi porta il conto,   mee por·ta eel kon·to
per favore?   per fa·vo·re

I'd like to reserve a table for ...	*Vorrei prenotare un tavolo per ...*	vo·ray pre·no·ta·re oon ta·vo·lo per ...
(eight) o'clock	*le (otto)*	le (o·to)
(two) people	*(due) persone*	(doo·e) per·so·ne

I don't eat ...	*Non mangio ...*	non man·jo ...
eggs	*uova*	wo·va
fish	*pesce*	pe·she
nuts	*noci*	no·chee

Key Words

bar	*locale*	lo·ka·le
bottle	*bottiglia*	bo·tee·lya
breakfast	*prima colazione*	pree·ma ko·la·tsyo·ne
cafe	*bar*	bar
dinner	*cena*	che·na
drink list	*lista delle bevande*	lee·sta de·le be·van·de
fork	*forchetta*	for·ke·ta
glass	*bicchiere*	bee·kye·re
knife	*coltello*	kol·te·lo

KEY PATTERNS

To get by in Italian, mix and match these simple patterns with words of your choice:

When's (the next flight)?
A che ora è   a ke o·ra e
(il prossimo volo)?   (eel pro·see·mo vo·lo)

Where's (the station)?
Dov'è (la stazione)?   do·ve (la sta·tsyo·ne)

I'm looking for (a hotel).
Sto cercando   sto cher·kan·do
(un albergo).   (oon al·ber·go)

Do you have (a map)?
Ha (una pianta)?   a (oo·na pyan·ta)

Is there (a toilet)?
C'è (un gabinetto)?   che (oon ga·bee·ne·to)

I'd like (a coffee).
Vorrei (un caffè).   vo·ray (oon ka·fe)

I'd like to (hire a car).
Vorrei (noleggiare   vo·ray (no·le·ja·re
una macchina).   oo·na ma·kee·na)

Can I (enter)?
Posso (entrare)?   po·so (en·tra·re)

Could you please (help me)?
Può (aiutarmi),   pwo (a·yoo·tar·mee)
per favore?   per fa·vo·re

Do I have to (book a seat)?
Devo (prenotare   de·vo (pre·no·ta·re
un posto)?   oon po·sto)

lunch	*pranzo*	pran·dzo
market	*mercato*	mer·ka·to
menu	*menù*	me·noo
plate	*piatto*	pya·to
restaurant	*ristorante*	ree·sto·ran·te
spoon	*cucchiaio*	koo·kya·yo
vegetarian	*vegetariano*	ve·je·ta·rya·no

Meat & Fish

beef	*manzo*	man·dzo
chicken	*pollo*	po·lo
herring	*aringa*	a·reen·ga
lamb	*agnello*	a·nye·lo
lobster	*aragosta*	a·ra·gos·ta
mussels	*cozze*	ko·tse
oysters	*ostriche*	o·stree·ke
pork	*maiale*	ma·ya·le
prawn	*gambero*	gam·be·ro
salmon	*salmone*	sal·mo·ne
scallops	*capasante*	ka·pa·san·te

shrimp	gambero	gam·be·ro
squid	calamari	ka·la·ma·ree
trout	trota	tro·ta
tuna	tonno	to·no
turkey	tacchino	ta·kee·no
veal	vitello	vee·te·lo

Fruit & Vegetables

apple	mela	me·la
beans	fagioli	fa·jo·lee
cabbage	cavolo	ka·vo·lo
capsicum	peperone	pe·pe·ro·ne
carrot	carota	ka·ro·ta
cauliflower	cavolfiore	ka·vol·fyo·re
cucumber	cetriolo	che·tree·o·lo
grapes	uva	oo·va
lemon	limone	lee·mo·ne
lentils	lenticchie	len·tee·kye
mushroom	funghi	foon·gee
nuts	noci	no·chee
onions	cipolle	chee·po·le
orange	arancia	a·ran·cha
peach	pesca	pe·ska
peas	piselli	pee·ze·lee
pineapple	ananas	a·na·nas
plum	prugna	proo·nya
potatoes	patate	pa·ta·te
spinach	spinaci	spee·na·chee
tomatoes	pomodori	po·mo·do·ree

Other

bread	pane	pa·ne
butter	burro	boo·ro
cheese	formaggio	for·ma·jo
eggs	uova	wo·va
honey	miele	mye·le
jam	marmellata	mar·me·la·ta

Signs

Closed	Chiuso
Entrance	Entrata/Ingresso
Exit	Uscita
Men	Uomini
Open	Aperto
Prohibited	Proibito/Vietato
Toilets	Gabinetti/Servizi
Women	Donne

noodles	pasta	pas·ta
oil	olio	o·lyo
pepper	pepe	pe·pe
rice	riso	ree·zo
salt	sale	sa·le
soup	minestra	mee·nes·tra
soy sauce	salsa di soia	sal·sa dee so·ya
sugar	zucchero	tsoo·ke·ro
vinegar	aceto	a·che·to

Drinks

beer	birra	bee·ra
coffee	caffè	ka·fe
juice	succo	soo·ko
milk	latte	la·te
red wine	vino rosso	vee·no ro·so
tea	tè	te
water	acqua	a·kwa
white wine	vino bianco	vee·no byan·ko

EMERGENCIES

Help!
Aiuto! a·yoo·to

Leave me alone!
Lasciami in pace! la·sha·mee een pa·che

I'm lost.
Mi sono perso/a. (m/f) mee so·no per·so/a

Call the police!
Chiami la polizia! kya·mee la po·lee·tsee·a

Call a doctor!
Chiami un medico! kya·mee oon me·dee·ko

Where are the toilets?
Dove sono i do·ve so·no ee
gabinetti? ga·bee·ne·tee

I'm sick.
Mi sento male. mee sen·to ma·le

SHOPPING & SERVICES

I'd like to buy ...
Vorrei comprare ... vo·ray kom·pra·re ...

I'm just looking.
Sto solo guardando. sto so·lo gwar·dan·do

Can I look at it?
Posso dare un'occhiata? po·so da·re oo·no·kya·ta

How much is this?
Quanto costa questo? kwan·to kos·ta kwe·sto

It's too expensive.
È troppo caro. e tro·po ka·ro

There's a mistake in the bill.
C'è un errore nel conto. che oo·ne·ro·re nel kon·to

ATM	*Bancomat*	ban·ko·mat
post office	*ufficio postale*	oo·fee·cho pos·ta·le
tourist office	*ufficio del turismo*	oo·fee·cho del too·reez·mo

TIME & DATES

What time is it?
Che ora è? — ke o·ra e

It's (two) o'clock.
Sono le (due). — so·no le (doo·e)

Half past (one).
(L'una) e mezza. — (loo·na) e me·dza

in the morning	*di mattina*	dee ma·tee·na
in the afternoon	*di pomeriggio*	dee po·me·ree·jo
in the evening	*di sera*	dee se·ra
yesterday	*ieri*	ye·ree
today	*oggi*	o·jee
tomorrow	*domani*	do·ma·nee

Monday	*lunedì*	loo·ne·dee
Tuesday	*martedì*	mar·te·dee
Wednesday	*mercoledì*	mer·ko·le·dee
Thursday	*giovedì*	jo·ve·dee
Friday	*venerdì*	ve·ner·dee
Saturday	*sabato*	sa·ba·to
Sunday	*domenica*	do·me·nee·ka

TRANSPORT

boat	*nave*	na·ve
bus	*autobus*	ow·to·boos
ferry	*traghetto*	tra·ge·to
metro	*metropolitana*	me·tro·po·lee·ta·na
plane	*aereo*	a·e·re·o
train	*treno*	tre·no

bus stop	*fermata dell'autobus*	fer·ma·ta del ow·to·boos
ticket office	*biglietteria*	bee·lye·te·ree·a
timetable	*orario*	o·ra·ryo
train station	*stazione ferroviaria*	sta·tsyo·ne fe·ro·vyar·ya

... ticket	*un biglietto ...*	oon bee·lye·to
one way	*di sola andata*	dee so·la an·da·ta
return	*di andata e ritorno*	dee an·da·ta e ree·tor·no

Numbers

1	*uno*	oo·no
2	*due*	doo·e
3	*tre*	tre
4	*quattro*	kwa·tro
5	*cinque*	cheen·kwe
6	*sei*	say
7	*sette*	se·te
8	*otto*	o·to
9	*nove*	no·ve
10	*dieci*	dye·chee
20	*venti*	ven·tee
30	*trenta*	tren·ta
40	*quaranta*	kwa·ran·ta
50	*cinquanta*	cheen·kwan·ta
60	*sessanta*	se·san·ta
70	*settanta*	se·tan·ta
80	*ottanta*	o·tan·ta
90	*novanta*	no·van·ta
100	*cento*	chen·to
1000	*mille*	mee·lel

Does it stop at ...?
Si ferma a ...? — see fer·ma a ...

Please tell me when we get to ...
Mi dica per favore quando arriviamo a ... — mee dee·ka per fa·vo·re kwan·do a·ree·vya·mo a ...

I want to get off here.
Voglio scendere qui. — vo·lyo shen·de·re kwee

I'd like to hire a ...	*Vorrei noleggiare una ...*	vo·ray no·le·ja·re oo·na ...
bicycle	*bicicletta*	bee·chee·kle·ta
car	*macchina*	ma·kee·na
motorbike	*moto*	mo·to

bicycle pump	*pompa della bicicletta*	pom·pa de·la bee·chee·kle·ta
child seat	*seggiolino*	se·jo·lee·no
helmet	*casco*	kas·ko
mechanic	*meccanico*	me·ka·nee·ko
petrol	*benzina*	ben·dzee·na
service station	*stazione di servizio*	sta·tsyo·ne dee ser·vee·tsyo

Is this the road to ...?
Questa strada porta a ...? — kwe·sta stra·da por·ta a ...

Can I park here?
Posso parcheggiare qui? — po·so par·ke·ja·re kwee

GLOSSARY

abbazia – abbey

agriturismo – farm-stays

(pizza) al taglio – (pizza) by the slice

albergo – hotel

alimentari – grocery shop

anfiteatro – amphitheatre

aperitivo – pre-dinner drink and snack

APT – Azienda di Promozione Turistica; local town or city tourist office

autostrada – motorway; highway

battistero – baptistry

biblioteca – library

biglietto – ticket

borgo – archaic name for a small town, village or town sector

camera – room

campo – field; also a square in Venice

cappella – chapel

carabinieri – police with military and civil duties

Carnevale – carnival period between Epiphany and Lent

casa – house

castello – castle

cattedrale – cathedral

centro storico – historic centre

certosa – monastery belonging to or founded by Carthusian monks

chiesa – church

chiostro – cloister; covered walkway, usually enclosed by columns, around a quadrangle

cima – summit

città – town; city

città alta – upper town

città bassa – lower town

colonna – column

comune – equivalent to a municipality or county; a town or city council; historically, a self–governing town or city

contrada – district

corso – boulevard

duomo – cathedral

enoteca – wine bar

espresso – short black coffee

ferrovia – railway

festa – feast day; holiday

fontana – fountain

foro – forum

funivia – cable car

gelateria – ice-cream shop

giardino – garden

golfo – gulf

grotta – cave

isola – island

lago – lake

largo – small square

lido – beach

locanda – inn; small hotel

lungomare – seafront road/promenade

mar, mare – sea

masseria – working farm

mausoleo – mausoleum; stately and magnificent tomb

mercato – market

monte – mountain

necropoli – ancient name for cemetery or burial site

nord – north

nuraghe – megalithic stone fortress in Sardinia

osteria – casual tavern or eatery

palazzo – mansion; palace; large building of any type, including an apartment block

palio – contest

parco – park

passeggiata – traditional evening stroll

pasticceria – cake/pastry shop

pensione – guesthouse

piazza – square

piazzale – large open square

pietà – literally 'pity' or 'compassion'; sculpture, drawing or painting of the dead Christ supported by the Madonna

pinacoteca – art gallery

ponte – bridge

porta – gate; door

porto – port

reale – royal

rifugio – mountain hut; accommodation in the Alps

ristorante – restaurant

rocca – fortress

sala – room; hall

salumeria – delicatessen

santuario – sanctuary; 1. the part of a church above the altar; 2. an especially holy place in a temple (antiquity)

sassi – literally 'stones'; stone houses built in two ravines in Matera, Basilicata

scalinata – staircase

scavi – excavations

sestiere – city district in Venice

spiaggia – beach

stazione – station

stazione marittima – ferry terminal

strada – street; road

sud – south

superstrada – expressway; highway with divided lanes

tartufo – truffle

tavola calda – literally 'hot table'; pre-prepared meals, often self-service

teatro – theatre

tempietto – small temple

tempio – temple

terme – thermal baths

tesoro – treasury

torre – tower

trattoria – simple restaurant

Trenitalia – Italian State Railways; also known as Ferrovie dello Stato (FS)

trullo – conical house in Perugia

vaporetto – small passenger ferry in Venice

via – street; road

viale – avenue

vico – alley; alleyway

villa – town house; country house; also the park surrounding the house

Behind the Scenes

SEND US YOUR FEEDBACK

We love to hear from travellers – your comments keep us on our toes and help make our books better. Our well-travelled team reads every word on what you loved or loathed about this book. Although we cannot reply individually to your submissions, we always guarantee that your feedback goes straight to the appropriate authors, in time for the next edition. Each person who sends us information is thanked in the next edition – the most useful submissions are rewarded with a selection of digital PDF chapters.

Visit **lonelyplanet.com/contact** to submit your updates and suggestions or to ask for help. Our award-winning website also features inspirational travel stories, news and discussions.

Note: We may edit, reproduce and incorporate your comments in Lonely Planet products such as guidebooks, websites and digital products, so let us know if you don't want your comments reproduced or your name acknowledged. For a copy of our privacy policy visit lonelyplanet.com/privacy.

OUR READERS

Many thanks to the travellers who used the last edition and wrote to us with helpful hints, useful advice and interesting anecdotes: **A** Dale Andrews, Allan Arthur **B** Nikolas Becker **C** Stuart Cameron, Duncan Campbell, Elena Canales, Cécile Comblen, Nigel Cook **D** Quentin Davies, Kim Dorin, Niall Duddy **E** Jan van Egmond **F** Wan Fokkink **G** Jean-Baptiste Geraud, Colin Gratwick, Paul Guz **H** Donna Harshman, Gunther Hartog, Ian Haugh **K** James Kurtz **L** Mark Lusardi **M** Lorraine Macmillan, Kelsey McEwen, Jaime Monteiro **O** James Oakley **P** Lesley Parks, Michael Poesen **R** Carrie Ross **S** John Sharman, Colin Shelton, Jessica Smarsch, Sharon Spencer, Morten Steingrim **W** Cindy White, Peter Woods, Alexander & Caroline Wrigley **Z** Monika Zipperle

AUTHOR THANKS
Cristian Bonetto

A heartfelt thanks to my 'Re e Regina di Napoli', Stefano Baldan, Alfonso Sperandeo, Giovanna and Silvia Vendramin, Marco Guerra, Alessandro Durante, Sara Costenaro, Laura Durante Poloni, Gian Luigi Sartor, Francesca Zerbo, Lucia Sartor, Pietro Manno, Andrea Maglio, Susy Galeone and La Paranza, Diana Pedone, Lisa Crawshaw, Bonnie Alberts, Luca Coda, Harriet Driver, Alfredo Cefalo, Malgorzata Gajo, Giancarlo Di Maio, Gigi Crispino and Valentina Vellusi. At Lonely Planet, a big thanks to Anna Tyler and my talented co-writers.

Abigail Blasi

Molto grazie to Anna Tyler for all her help. Thanks to Luca, and thanks to Ai Ling and friends for all their insights for the Italy Today chapter.

Kerry Christiani

A huge *grazie* to all the wonderful locals and tourism pros who made my road to research incredibly smooth. I'd like to say a special thank you to Peter and Anne in Lotzorai, Corrado Conca for his arrampicata tips, Fabrizio Vella at Gola Su Gorropu and Francesco Mutoni of Kayak Cardedu. Last but not least, thanks to my husband, Andy Christiani, for being a brilliant travel companion.

Gregor Clark

Grazie mille to the many dozens of people who shared their love and knowledge of Sicily and Emilia-Romagna with me – from Angela, Francesco and Matilde in Palermo to Massimiliano and Massimo in Parma. Love and special thanks to my father, Henry Clark, who first showed me the wonders of Sicily and Ravenna. Back in Vermont, big hugs to Gaen, Meigan and Chloe, who always make coming home the best part of the trip.

Belinda Dixon

The kindness of strangers enriches travels – thank you to those who transformed my days. To Anna Tyler sincere thanks for the opportunity; to Lonely Planet's fellow Italy authors the same for virtual support. Jo & Liz: I still raise that glass of prosecco. JL: my thanks for still making me smile.

Duncan Garwood

A big thank you to fellow author Abi Blasi for all her generous suggestions, and to Anna Tyler at Lonely Planet for her unstinting support. For their tips and help with research, *grazie* to Silvia Prosperi, Barbara Lessona, Paolo Mazza, and the team at the Roman Guy. As always, a big, heartfelt hug to Lidia and the boys, Ben and Nick.

Paula Hardy

Grazie mille to all the fun and fashionable Venetians and Milanese who spilled the beans on their remarkable cities: Paola dalla Valentina, Melitta Rodini, Bruno Sacchi, Diego and Lucia Cattaneo, Monica Cesarato, Francesca Giubilei, Luca Berta, Marco Secchi, Nan McElroy, Eliana Argine and Julia Curtis. *Brava*, too, to coordinator Cristian Bonetto and to Lonely Planet destination editor, Anna Tyler, for steering a steady course. Last but not least, thanks to Rob for all the laughs along the way.

Brendan Sainsbury

Thanks to all the untold bus drivers, coffee baristas, pasta makers, museum curators and innocent bystanders who smoothed the path during my research. Special thanks to my wife, Liz, and nine-year-old son, Kieran, for their company on the road.

Donna Wheeler

Hospitality often entirely exceeds expectation in my regions – *grazie/dankeschön* to the Libardi family, Geoff Barkley, Martin Kirchlechner, Carolina Lantieri, Mark Spangaro, Gianna Vidoni, Daniela Boni, Dario Gai and my Ligurian-Piedmontese family, the Marolos. Special mention to Wayne Young, for the warm welcome and great tips. Much love and gratitude to Joe Guario for keeping both me and the Fiat 500 in fuel and tunes and a final big thanks to Cristian Bonetto for unflagging support and boundless bonhomie.

Nicola Williams

Grazie to those who shared their Tuscan love with me: in Florence, Betty Soldi & Matteo Perduca, Alessio & Assumi, Doreen & Carmello, Fabrizio Rangone, Judy Witts aka Divina Cucina, Roberto Romoli and gals about town Nardia Plumridge (@lostinflorence), Georgette Jupe (@girlinflorence), Flavia Cori (@Tuscanyicious) and Coral Sisk (@curious appetite). Heartfelt thanks to Pistoia experts Dr Paolo Bresci and Molly McIlwrath, Ilaria Leccarelli (Castiglion Fiorentino) and Elisabetta Pandolfini (Prato). My chunk of this book is dedicated to kid team supreme Niko, Mischa and Kaya Lüfkens, and super papa Matthias.

ACKNOWLEDGEMENTS

Climate map data adapted from Peel MC, Finlayson BL & McMahon TA (2007) 'Updated World Map of the Koppen-Geiger Climate Classification', *Hydrology and Earth System Sciences*, 11, 1633-44

Illustrations pp72-3, pp350-1, pp490-1, pp688-9 by Javier Martinez Zarracina

Cover photograph: San Quirico d'Orcia, Val d'Orcia, Tuscany; Maurizio Rellini/4C

THIS BOOK

This 12th edition of Lonely Planet's *Italy* guidebook was researched and written by Cristian Bonetto, Abigail Blasi, Kerry Christiani, Gregor Clark, Belinda Dixon, Duncan Garwood, Paula Hardy, Brendan Sainsbury, Helena Smith, Donna Wheeler and Nicola Williams. This guidebook was produced by the following:

Destination Editor
Anna Tyler
Product Editors
Briohny Hooper, Tracy Whitmey
Senior Cartographer
Anthony Phelan
Book Designer Wendy Wright
Assisting Editors Michelle Bennett, Melanie Dankel, Victoria Harrison, Jodie Martire, Susan Paterson, Chris Pitts, Kirsten Rawlings

Cartographers
Julie Dodkins, Michael Garrett, James Leversha
Cover Researcher
Naomi Parker
Thanks to Imogen Bannister, Andi Jones, Claire Murphy, Karyn Noble, Samantha Russell-Tulip, Dianne Schallmeiner, Luna Soo, Lauren Wellicome, Tony Wheeler

Index

Map Legend

Sights

- Beach
- Bird Sanctuary
- Buddhist
- Castle/Palace
- Christian
- Confucian
- Hindu
- Islamic
- Jain
- Jewish
- Monument
- Museum/Gallery/Historic Building
- Ruin
- Sento Hot Baths/Onsen
- Shinto
- Sikh
- Taoist
- Winery/Vineyard
- Zoo/Wildlife Sanctuary
- Other Sight

Activities, Courses & Tours

- Bodysurfing
- Diving
- Canoeing/Kayaking
- Course/Tour
- Skiing
- Snorkelling
- Surfing
- Swimming/Pool
- Walking
- Windsurfing
- Other Activity

Sleeping

- Sleeping
- Camping

Eating

- Eating

Drinking & Nightlife

- Drinking & Nightlife
- Cafe

Entertainment

- Entertainment

Shopping

- Shopping

Information

- Bank
- Embassy/Consulate
- Hospital/Medical
- Internet
- Police
- Post Office
- Telephone
- Toilet
- Tourist Information
- Other Information

Geographic

- Beach
- Hut/Shelter
- Lighthouse
- Lookout
- Mountain/Volcano
- Oasis
- Park
- Pass
- Picnic Area
- Waterfall

Population

- Capital (National)
- Capital (State/Province)
- City/Large Town
- Town/Village

Transport

- Airport
- Border crossing
- Bus
- Cable car/Funicular
- Cycling
- Ferry
- Metro station
- Monorail
- Parking
- Petrol station
- S-Bahn/Subway station
- Taxi
- T-bane/Tunnelbana station
- Train station/Railway
- Tram
- Tube station
- U-Bahn/Underground station
- Other Transport

Note: Not all symbols displayed above appear on the maps in this book

Routes

- Tollway
- Freeway
- Primary
- Secondary
- Tertiary
- Lane
- Unsealed road
- Road under construction
- Plaza/Mall
- Steps
- Tunnel
- Pedestrian overpass
- Walking Tour
- Walking Tour detour
- Path/Walking Trail

Boundaries

- International
- State/Province
- Disputed
- Regional/Suburb
- Marine Park
- Cliff
- Wall

Hydrography

- River, Creek
- Intermittent River
- Canal
- Water
- Dry/Salt/Intermittent Lake
- Reef

Areas

- Airport/Runway
- Beach/Desert
- Cemetery (Christian)
- Cemetery (Other)
- Glacier
- Mudflat
- Park/Forest
- Sight (Building)
- Sportsground
- Swamp/Mangrove

Belinda Dixon

Milan & the Italian Lakes Having cut her travel teeth on Italy's ferries and trains, rarely has a year passed when Belinda hasn't been back. Research highlights include gazing at mountains while ferry-hopping those gorgeous lakes, encountering Mantua's extraordinary art, tasting olive oil in Malcesine and Bardolino in, well, Bardolino – and always delighting in this, the *bel paese*.

Duncan Garwood

Rome & Lazio A Brit travel writer based in the Castelli Romani hills just outside Rome, Duncan has clocked up endless kilometres walking around the Italian capital and exploring the far-flung reaches of the surrounding Lazio region. He's co-author of the *Rome* city guide and has worked on the past six editions of this book as well as guides to Piedmont, Sicily, Sardinia, and Naples and the Amalfi Coast. He has also written on Italy for newspapers and magazines.

Paula Hardy

Milan & the Italian Lakes, Venice & the Veneto, Fashion, Design From Lido beaches to annual Biennales and spritz-fuelled aperitivo bars, Paula has contributed to Lonely Planet Italian guides for over 15 years, including previous editions of *Venice & the Veneto*, *Pocket Milan*, *The Italian Lakes*, *Sicily*, *Sardinia* and *Puglia & Basilicata*. When she's not scooting around the *bel paese*, she writes for a variety of travel publications and websites. Currently she divides her time between London, Italy and Morocco, and tweets her finds @paula6hardy.

Brendan Sainsbury

Abruzzo & Molise, Puglia, Basilicata & Calabria An expat Brit from Hampshire, England, now living near Vancouver, Canada, Brendan has covered Italy five times for Lonely Planet, reporting on 16 of its 20 regions. For this edition he braved world record snowfall in Abruzzo (in March!), suffered horizontal rain in Matera, and spent three minutes in a decontamination chamber in Reggio di Calabria. When not scribbling research notes for Lonely Planet in countries such as Cuba, Peru, Spain and Canada, Brendan likes to run up mountains, strum his flamenco guitar, and experience the pain and occasional pleasure of following Southampton Football Club.

Donna Wheeler

Turin, Piedmont & the Italian Riviera, Trento & the Dolomites, Venice & the Veneto, Friuli Venezia Giulia, Italian Art & Architecture Italy's border regions are Donna Wheeler's dream assignment: Alps, the sea, complex histories, plus spectacular wine and food. Donna has lived in Turin's Quadrilatero Romano and Genova's centro storico and been an Italian-by-marriage for almost two decades. A former commissioning editor and content strategist, she's written guidebooks to Italy, France, Tunisia, Algeria, Norway and Belgium and publishes on art, architecture, history and food for LonelyPlanet.com, BBC.com Travel, National Geographic *Traveler* and My Art Guides; she is also the creative director of travel magazine *She Came to Stay*.

Nicola Williams

Florence & Tuscany, Travel with Children British writer Nicola Williams lives on the southern shore of Lake Geneva. Thankfully for her Italianate soul, it is an easy hop through the Mont Blanc Tunnel to Italy where she has spent years eating her way around and revelling in its extraordinary art, architecture, cuisine and landscape. Hunting Tuscan white truffles in October is an annual family ritual. Nicola has worked on numerous titles for Lonely Planet, including *Italy*, *Milan, Turin & Genoa*, and *Piedmont*. She shares her travels on Twitter at @Tripalong.

Contributing Writer

Helena Smith wrote part of the Naples & Campania chapter.

OUR STORY

A beat-up old car, a few dollars in the pocket and a sense of adventure. In 1972 that's all Tony and Maureen Wheeler needed for the trip of a lifetime – across Europe and Asia overland to Australia. It took several months, and at the end – broke but inspired – they sat at their kitchen table writing and stapling together their first travel guide, *Across Asia on the Cheap*. Within a week they'd sold 1500 copies. Lonely Planet was born.

Today, Lonely Planet has offices in Franklin, London, Melbourne, Oakland, Beijing and Delhi, with more than 600 staff and writers. We share Tony's belief that 'a great guidebook should do three things: inform, educate and amuse'.

OUR WRITERS

Cristian Bonetto

Coordinating Author, Venice & the Veneto, Naples & Campania Thanks to his Italo-Australian heritage, Cristian gets to experience the *bel paese* (beautiful country) as both a local and an outsider. His musings on Italian cuisine, culture and style have appeared in media across the globe and his contributions for Lonely Planet include more than 30 travel guide editions, including *Naples & the Amalfi Coast*, *Venice & the Veneto, Denmark, New York City* and *Singapore*. For this guide, Cristian wrote the Plan Your Trip section, The Italian Way of Life, Italy on Page & Screen, The Italian Table and Survival Guide chapters. Follow Cristian on Twitter (@CristianBonetto) and Instagram (rexcat75).

Abigail Blasi

Italy Today, History Abigail moved to Rome in 2003 and lived there for three years, got married alongside Lago Bracciano and her first son was born in Rome. Nowadays she divides her time between Rome, Puglia and London. She has worked on four editions of Lonely Planet's *Italy* and *Rome* guides, written the *Best of Rome* guide, and written the 1st edition of *Puglia & Basilicata*. She also regularly writes about Italy for various publications, including the *Independent*, the *Guardian*, and Lonely Planet *Traveller*.

Kerry Christiani

Outdoor Experiences, Umbria & Le Marche, Sardinia Kerry has been drawn back to Italy again and again ever since she toured the country one hazy post-graduation summer in a 1960s bubble caravan. For this edition, she relished the chance to tour the hill towns of Umbria and Le Marche and explore the remoter parts of Sardinia's coast and mountains. An award-winning travel writer, Kerry authors a number of Lonely Planet guidebooks, including *Sardinia*, and contributes regularly to magazines, newspapers and blog sites. She tweets @kerrychristiani.

Gregor Clark

Emilia-Romagna & San Marino, Sicily Gregor caught the Italy bug at age 14 while living in Florence with his professor dad, who took him to see every fresco, mosaic and museum within a 1000km radius. He's lived in Florence and Le Marche, huffed and puffed across the Dolomites while researching LP's *Cycling Italy* and contributed to three previous editions of this guide. A lifelong polyglot with a Romance Languages degree, Gregor has written for Lonely Planet since 2000, with an emphasis on Mediterranean Europe and Latin America.

OVER PAGE | MORE WRITERS

Published by Lonely Planet Publications Pty Ltd
ABN 36 005 607 983
12th edition – Feb 2016
ISBN 978 1 74321 685 9
© Lonely Planet 2016   Photographs © as indicated 2016
10 9 8 7 6 5 4 3 2 1
Printed in China